Unlocking the BOOK of MORMON

MW00668278

UNLOCKING THE BOOK OF MORMON

A SIDE-BY-SIDE COMMENTARY

DANIEL H. LUDLOW • ED J. PINEGAR
RICHARD J. ALLEN • LEAUN G. OTTEN • C. MAX CALDWELL

Covenant Communications, Inc.

Covenant

Cover image: *One by One* © Walter Rane
Cover and book design © 2007 by Covenant Communications, Inc.

Published by Covenant Communications, Inc.
American Fork, Utah

Copyright © 2007 by Daniel H. Ludlow, Ed J. Pinegar, Richard J. Allen, Leaun G. Otten, and C. Max Caldwell

All rights reserved. No part of this work may be reproduced by any means without the express written permission of Covenant Communications, Inc., P.O. Box 416, American Fork, UT 84003. This work is not an official publication of The Church of Jesus Christ of Latter-day Saints. The views expressed within this work are the sole responsibility of the author and do not necessarily reflect the position of The Church of Jesus Christ of Latter-day Saints, Covenant Communications, Inc., or any other entity.

Printed in U.S.A.
First Printing: October 2007

15 14 13 12 11 10 09 08 07   10 9 8 7 6 5 4 3 2

ISBN 978-1-59811-463-8

INTRODUCTION

Take away the Book of Mormon and the revelations, and where is our religion? We have none (*HC*, 2:52). —Joseph Smith

In his title page, Moroni made very clear, as he surveyed the breadth and scope of the entire work for which he served as the final and consummate curator, what the Lord's purposes are for the Book of Mormon: "Which is to show unto the remnant of the House of Israel what great things the Lord hath done for their fathers; and that they may know the covenants of the Lord, that they are not cast off forever—And also to the convincing of the Jew and the Gentile that JESUS is the CHRIST, the ETERNAL GOD, manifesting himself unto all nations." Great merciful acts of God in the past, great covenant honor for the present, great hope for the future (i.e., that we are not cast off forever), all on the foundation of the atoning sacrifice of Jesus Christ—that is the four-fold message of the Book of Mormon. —Ed. J. Pinegar and Richard J. Allen

All of these purposes for writing the Book of Mormon [as stated by Moroni] embody principles that only have value when they find application in the lives of the readers. . . .

Gospel scholarship is not primarily having a knowledge of word meanings, or an explanation of languages or cultural practices. Rather, it is an understanding of gospel principles that have increased meaning to us as we abide by them in our personal lives. There is a marked difference between a feeling level and an academic level of gospel understanding. . . . The Savior's gospel principles are not complicated or difficult to understand. His gospel is simply beautiful and beautifully simple. —Leaun G. Otten and C. Max Caldwell

[T]he agenda of the whole work can be summarized in four points: (1) To preserve and present great stories from the past concerning the Lord's loving mercy to His children, (2) to teach great and sacred covenants for the present, (3) to engender great hope for the future (i.e., that we are not "cast off forever"), and (4) to build all of this upon the sure foundation of the Savior, the great Redeemer. This fourfold agenda is the key to the book's vitality. This scriptural mission of power captures the wonder of the Book of Mormon, as its influence is felt across the span of time and across its noble pages from first to last. —Ed J. Pinegar and Richard J. Allen

The boldness of my plans and measures can readily be tested by the touchstone of all schemes, systems, projects, and adventures—truth; for truth is a matter of fact; and the fact is, that by the power of God I translated the Book of Mormon from hieroglyphics, the knowledge of which was lost to the world, in which wonderful event I stood alone, an unlearned youth, to combat the worldly wisdom and multiplied ignorance of eighteen centuries, with a new revelation, which (if they would receive the everlasting Gospel) would open the eyes of more than eight hundred millions of people, and make "plain the old paths," wherein if a man walk in all the ordinances of God blameless, he shall inherit eternal life; and Jesus Christ, who was, and is, and is to come, has borne me safely over every snare and plan laid in secret or openly, through priestly hypocrisy, sectarian prejudice, popular philosophy, executive power, or law-defying mobocracy, to destroy me (*History of the Church*, 6:74). —Joseph Smith

The Lord sees all. He discerns our needs with perfect understanding. He is aware of our struggles: "For as the heavens are higher than the earth, so are my ways higher than your ways, and my thoughts than your thoughts" (Isa. 55:9). Accordingly, He prepared the Book of Mormon as a spiritual shield and bolster for His Saints in the latter days, and as a clarion call for all nations to feast at the banquet table of spiritual truth. Every word, every phrase, every story has meaning and significance for us as a means to increase our faith and courage to endure to the end. The Lord wants to elevate our perspective, to show us the merciful plan that will enable us, through the blessing of His Spirit, to traverse the landscape of mortal life successfully. As He told Joseph Smith: "Behold, there are many things engraven upon the plates of Nephi which do throw greater views upon my gospel; therefore, it is wisdom in me that you should translate this first part of the engravings of Nephi, and send forth in this work" (D&C 10:45). Is it not therefore beholden upon us all to apply these "greater views" diligently, with grateful hearts and minds for such a magnificent gift from God? —Ed J. Pinegar and Richard J. Allen

How to Use This Book

The left column on each page contains the actual text of the Book of Mormon without chapter headings or footnotes. The Book of Mormon text in this book appears on page numbers that correspond exactly to the page numbers in the Book of Mormon, making this book ideal for classroom use.

The right column on each page contains commentary that corresponds with the Book of Mormon text to its left.

In some places, there was too much commentary to fit in the right column adjacent to the Book of Mormon text. In each of these places, two pages follow, numbered A and B. These pages contain commentary in both columns that applies to the Book of Mormon text on the previous page.

Throughout the book, *Points of Interest* are indicated with an open-book icon. These include charts, illustrations, and text that might enrich your study of the Book of Mormon.

Finally, space has been provided throughout the book so you can take notes or write your impressions as you study the Book of Mormon.

Citations Used in This Book

Ludlow—Daniel H. Ludlow, *A Companion to Your Study of the Book of Mormon* (Salt Lake City: Deseret Book, 1976).

O/C—Leaun G. Otten and C. Max Caldwell, *Sacred Truths of the Book of Mormon*, 2 vols. (American Fork, Utah: Covenant Communications, 2007)

P/A—Ed J. Pinegar and Richard J. Allen, *Teachings and Commentaries on the Book of Mormon* (American Fork, Utah: Covenant Communications, 2003)

CR—*Conference Report*

HC—*History of The Church of Jesus Christ of Latter-day Saints*, 7 volumes

Text without a citation was written by the editor.

THE FIRST BOOK OF NEPHI

HIS REIGN AND MINISTRY

An account of Lehi and his wife Sariah, and his four sons, being called, (beginning at the eldest) Laman, Lemuel, Sam, and Nephi. The Lord warns Lehi to depart out of the land of Jerusalem, because he prophesieth unto the people concerning their iniquity and they seek to destroy his life. He taketh three days' journey into the wilderness with his family. Nephi taketh his brethren and returneth to the land of Jerusalem after the record of the Jews. The account of their sufferings. They take the daughters of Ishmael to wife. They take their families and depart into the wilderness. Their sufferings and afflictions in the wilderness. The course of their travels. They come to the large waters. Nephi's brethren rebel against him. He confoundeth them, and buildeth a ship. They call the place Bountiful. They cross the large waters into the promised land, &c. This is according to the account of Nephi; or in other words, I, Nephi, wrote this record.

CHAPTER 1

1. I, Nephi, having been born of goodly parents, therefore I was taught somewhat in all the learning of my father; and having seen many afflictions in the course of my days, nevertheless, having been highly favored of the Lord in all my days; yea, having had a great knowledge of the goodness and the mysteries of God, therefore I make a record of my proceedings in my days.
2. Yea, I make a record in the language of my father, which consists of the learning of the Jews and the language of the Egyptians.
3. And I know that the record which I make is true; and I make it with mine own hand; and I make it according to my knowledge.
4. For it came to pass in the commencement of the first year of the reign of Zedekiah, king of Judah, (my father, Lehi, having dwelt at Jerusalem in all his days); and in that same year there came many prophets, prophesying unto the people that they must repent, or the great city Jerusalem must be destroyed.
5. Wherefore it came to pass that my father, Lehi, as he went forth prayed unto the Lord, yea, even

POINT OF INTEREST

A contemporary of Lehi, Jeremiah prophesied over a period of 40 years, beginning during the 13th year of Josiah's reign in 626 B.C. After the fall of Jerusalem in 597 B.C., the Jews who escaped into Egypt took him with them and, according to tradition, stoned him to death a year later. Known as the "broken-hearted prophet" (as shown in this painting by Rembrandt), Jeremiah is credited with writing the Book of Jeremiah and Lamentations. His prophecies are included in the brass plates of Laban (1 Ne. 5:10–13).

1 Nephi 1:1

Wise are the Latter-day Saint parents who understand this divine principle of parenthood, who understand that the fulness of salvation is the exaltation of their families. Wise are the Latter-day Saint parents who have so ordered their lives that the teaching of the gospel of Jesus Christ to their children is the central function in their homes. They have eternal perspective. (O/C)

1 Nephi 1:2–3

In considering the problem of the language of the plates translated by Joseph Smith it is well to keep these facts in mind: (1) the word *language* has several different meanings and includes both spoken and written concepts, such as grammatical constructions, thought patterns, and exact phraseology; (2) Joseph Smith translated from two different records (the small plates of Nephi and the plates of Mormon); these plates were prepared and written nearly 1,000 years apart, and the language of one well might not be the language of the other. . . .

Moroni, writing approximately 1,000 years later than Nephi but having access to the small plates of Nephi, can see that their written characters have been altered during the 1,000-year period; thus the written characters on the plates of Mormon are called "reformed" Egyptian because they have been "altered" by the Nephites. (Ludlow)

1 Nephi 1:4

Several prophets are mentioned in the biblical account, which covers approximately the same time period as the beginning of the Book of Mormon (2 Kings 23–25; Jeremiah 1–52; and the Lamentations of Jeremiah 1–5). Among these prophets is Jeremiah. The Book of Mormon would indicate that another prophet in Jerusalem during this period was Lehi. Jeremiah was evidently a descendant of Judah, and his writings are found in the Bible—the "stick of Judah." Lehi was a descendant of Joseph who was sold into Egypt (see 1 Nephi 5:14), and the writings of Lehi are contained in the Book of Mormon—the "stick of Joseph." (Ludlow)

1 Nephi 1:4

Throughout the Book of Mormon, a number of verses begin with the phrase, "It came to pass." Hugh Nibley explained that in the Egyptian language, this expression is actually a grammatical requirement for tying pieces of text together—not simply an adorning phrase.

with all his heart, in behalf of his people.
6. And it came to pass as he prayed unto the Lord, there came a
pillar of fire and dwelt upon a rock before him; and he saw and
heard much; and because of the things which he saw and heard he
did quake and tremble exceedingly.
7. And it came to pass that he returned to his own house at
Jerusalem; and he cast himself upon his bed, being overcome with
the Spirit and the things which he had seen.
8. And being thus overcome with the Spirit, he was carried away
in a vision, even that he saw the heavens open, and he thought he
saw God sitting upon his throne, surrounded with numberless concourses of angels in the attitude of singing and praising their God.
9. And it came to pass that he saw One descending out of the
midst of heaven, and he beheld that his luster was above that of
the sun at noon-day.
10. And he also saw twelve others following him, and their brightness did exceed that of the stars in the firmament.
11. And they came down and went forth upon the face of the
earth; and the first came and stood before my father, and gave unto
him a book, and bade him that he should read.
12. And it came to pass that as he read, he was filled with the Spirit
of the Lord.
13. And he read, saying: Wo, wo, unto Jerusalem, for I have seen
thine abominations! Yea, and many things did my father read concerning Jerusalem — that it should be destroyed, and the inhabitants thereof; many should perish by the sword, and many should
be carried away captive into Babylon.
14. And it came to pass that when my father had read and seen
many great and marvelous things, he did exclaim many things unto
the Lord; such as: Great and marvelous are thy works, O Lord God
Almighty! Thy throne is high in the heavens, and thy power, and
goodness, and mercy are over all the inhabitants of the earth; and,
because thou art merciful, thou wilt not suffer those who come
unto thee that they shall perish!
15. And after this manner was the language of my father in the
praising of his God; for his soul did rejoice, and his whole heart was
filled, because of the things which he had seen, yea, which the
Lord had shown unto him.
16. And now I, Nephi, do not make a full account of the things
which my father hath written, for he hath written many things
which he saw in visions and in dreams; and he also hath written
many things which he prophesied and spake

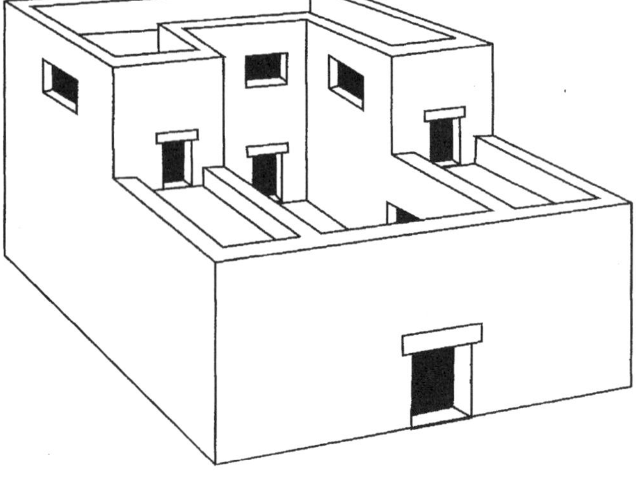

1 Nephi 1:4

Lehi and his family apparently fled from Jerusalem in "the first year of the reign of Zedekiah, king of Judah" (1 Nephi 1:4, 2:1–4). According to the Bible (2 Chronicles 36:11), Zedekiah was twenty-one years old when he was made king over the kingdom of Judah by Nebuchadnezzar, the leader of the Babylonian empire. However, the exact date of Zedekiah's ascension to the throne is not mentioned in the Bible, although nearly all of the scholars agree it must have been within a few years of 600 B.C. The Book of Mormon seems to indicate that the year 600 B.C. is correct for the departure of Lehi from Jerusalem. (See 1 Nephi 10:4 and 19:8.) (Ludlow)

1 Nephi 1:11

It would be well to learn from the experience of Lehi that scripture reading and pondering is important in the eyes of the Lord. He personally stood before Lehi and bade him to read. (O/C)

1 Nephi 1:16–17

In verse 17 Nephi states that he is going to make an abridgment of his father's record upon his own plates (apparently the small plates of Nephi), and "then will I make an account of mine own life." Chapters 1 through 8 of 1 Nephi seem to be a synopsis by Nephi of the record of Lehi; chapter 9 is an explanatory and transitional chapter; and finally at the beginning of chapter 10 Nephi states that he is now going "to give an account upon these plates of my proceedings" (1 Nephi 10:1). (Ludlow)

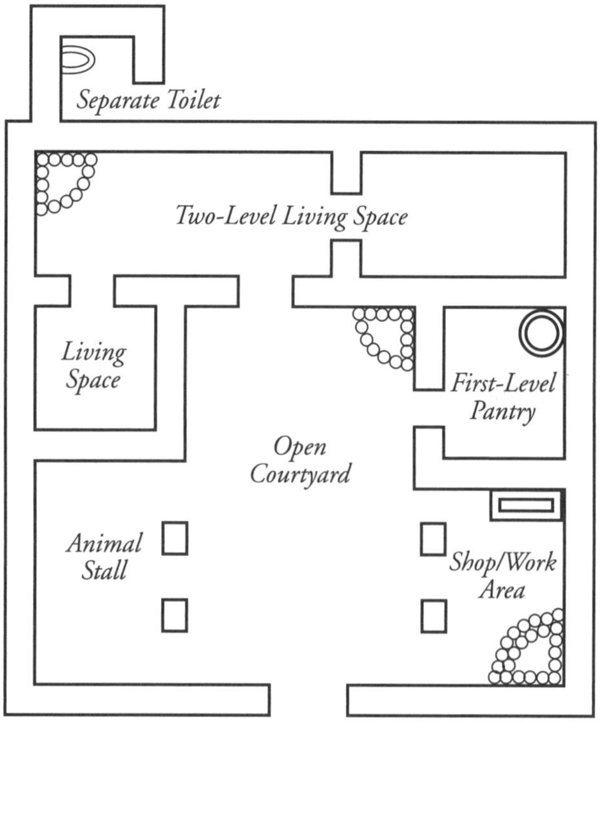

unto his children, of which I shall not make a full account.
17. But I shall make an account of my proceedings in my days. Behold, I make an abridgment of the record of my father, upon plates which I have made with mine own hands; wherefore, after I have abridged the record of my father then will I make an account of mine own life.
18. Therefore, I would that ye should know, that after the Lord had shown so many marvelous things unto my father, Lehi, yea, concerning the destruction of Jerusalem, behold he went forth among the people, and began to prophesy and to declare unto them concerning the things which he had both seen and heard.
19. And it came to pass that the Jews did mock him because of the things which he testified of them; for he truly testified of their wickedness and their abominations; and he testified that the things which he saw and heard, and also the things which he read in the book, manifested plainly of the coming of the Messiah, and also the redemption of the world.
20. And when the Jews heard these things they were angry with him; yea, even as with the prophets of old, whom they had cast out, and stoned, and slain; and they also sought his life, that they might take it away. But behold, I, Nephi, will show unto you that the tender mercies of the Lord are over all those whom he hath chosen, because of their faith, to make them mighty even unto the power of deliverance.

CHAPTER 2

1. FOR behold, it came to pass that the Lord spake unto my father, yea, even in a dream, and said unto him: Blessed art thou Lehi, because of the things which thou hast done; and because thou hast been faithful and declared unto this people the things which I commanded thee, behold, they seek to take away thy life.
2. And it came to pass that the Lord commanded my father, even in a dream, that he should take his family and depart into the wilderness.
3. And it came to pass that he was obedient unto the word of the Lord, wherefore he did as the Lord commanded him.
4. And it came to pass that he departed into the wilderness. And he left his house, and the land of his inheritance, and his gold, and his silver, and his precious things, and took nothing with him, save it

POINT OF INTEREST

Lehi and his family probably left behind a home similar to the four-room, two-level model at left. The drawings are based on the remains of what is referred to as the house of Ahiel, destroyed during the Babylonian seige. Whoever Ahiel was, a pillared Israelite home like this would have belonged to someone of prominence and includes an indoor toilet.

1 Nephi 2:1–3

What greater overseer of our travels could there be than the Lord? What greater road map than His divine decrees? A righteous branch of the house of Joseph had to be established in the promised land; therefore, it was imperative that Lehi and his family leave Jerusalem and settle in a new land according to the Lord's will. . . .

There were still wicked political leaders during these times, and many prophets, including Jeremiah (another of Lehi's contemporaries), were empowered of the Lord to warn the people with clarity and sharpness. The message of prophecy was clear: the people had to repent or the city of Jerusalem would be destroyed. Lehi, himself courageously active among the prophetic ranks, prayed earnestly on behalf of his people.

A vision was opened unto him concerning the coming of our beloved Savior Jesus Christ and of the imminent destruction of Jerusalem. Many would be carried away captive into Babylon. Lehi preached and prophesied to no avail. The people mocked him and sought to take away his life. Therefore, the Lord spoke to Lehi and commanded him to take his family into the wilderness.

We, like Lehi, have moments of truth in our lives when we must seek refuge in the Lord.

He will lead and guide us to safety, no matter what the outside circumstances. He will nurture us and bless us according to our needs (see Alma 7:11–12). We would be wise to remember that there is always safety in following the Lord and His commandments. (P/A)

1 Nephi 2:4

The word *wilderness* seems to be used in the Book of Mormon to refer to an uninhabited area or at least to an area only sparsely settled. Thus *wilderness* could either refer to a desert area (as it apparently does in 1 Nephi 2:4) or to a fertile area but one that is relatively uninhabited (as in 1 Nephi 18:6, 24–25; 2 Nephi 5:7). (Ludlow)

1 Nephi 2:2–6, 14; 9:1

The exact distance of the Valley of Lemuel from Jerusalem is not made clear in the Book of Mormon. The superscription to 1 Nephi (wherein Nephi states that Lehi "taketh three days' journey into the wilderness with his family" from the *land* of Jerusalem) seems to indicate a distance between the two locations that can be covered in a three-day journey. However, some students of the Book of Mormon interpret 1 Nephi 2:4–6 to mean that Lehi and his group traveled an indefinite number of days until they arrived "in the wilderness in the borders which are nearer the Red Sea"; then they traveled through that wilderness for three days to the Valley of Lemuel. (Ludlow)

were his family, and provisions, and tents, and departed into the
wilderness.
5. And he came down by the borders near the shore of the Red Sea;
and he traveled in the wilderness in the borders which are nearer
the Red Sea; and he did travel in the wilderness with his family,
which consisted of my mother, Sariah, and my elder brothers, who
were Laman, Lemuel, and Sam.
6. And it came to pass that when he had traveled three days in the
wilderness, he pitched his tent in a valley by the side of a river of
water.
7. And it came to pass that he built an altar of stones, and made an
offering unto the Lord, and gave thanks unto the Lord our God.
8. And it came to pass that he called the name of the river, Laman,
and it emptied into the Red Sea; and the valley was in the borders
near the mouth thereof.
9. And when my father saw that the waters of the river emptied into
the fountain of the Red Sea, he spake unto Laman, saying: O that
thou mightest be like unto this river, continually running into the
fountain of all righteousness!
10. And he also spake unto Lemuel: O that thou mightest be like
unto this valley, firm and steadfast, and immovable in keeping the
commandments of the Lord!
11. Now this he spake because of the stiffneckedness of Laman and
Lemuel; for behold they did murmur in many things against their
father, because he was a visionary man, and had led them out of
the land of Jerusalem, to leave the land of their inheritance, and
their gold, and their silver, and their precious things, to perish in
the wilderness. And this they said he had done because of the foolish imaginations of his heart.
12. And thus Laman and Lemuel, being the eldest, did murmur
against their father. And they did murmur because they knew not
the dealings of that God who had created them.
13. Neither did they believe that Jerusalem, that great city, could
be destroyed according to the words of the prophets. And they
were like unto the Jews who were at Jerusalem, who sought to take
away the life of my father.
14. And it came to pass that my father did speak unto them in the
valley of Lemuel, with power, being filled with the Spirit, until
their frames did shake before him. And he did confound them, that
they durst not utter against him; wherefore, they did as he commanded them.
15. And my father dwelt in a tent.
16. And it came to pass that I, Nephi, being exceedingly young,
nevertheless being large in stature, and also having great desires to
know of the mysteries of God,

1 Nephi 2:6

Although the term "river of water" probably seemed foreign to Joseph Smith (who was born in Vermont and reared in New York, where rivers are naturally composed of water), the use of the term in the Book of Mormon is consistent with both modern and ancient Hebrew and with other Semitic languages of the Middle East. Different words are used in these languages to differentiate between (1) a riverbed that has water flowing in it and (2) a dry riverbed. . . . This is one of many examples that prove the Book of Mormon is translation literature. It was not *written* by Joseph Smith; rather it was *translated* by him from ancient records. (Ludlow)

1 Nephi 2:7

The Book of Mormon uses the term "altar of stones" to refer to the sacrificial altar prepared by Lehi rather than the term "stone altar." There could be considerable difference between the two. An altar of stones could consist of a pile of uncut, separate, individual stones, whereas a stone altar could denote the use of cut rock, mortar, etc. In this connection it is of interest to note that in Exodus 20:25 the Lord said to Moses: "And if thou wilt make me an altar of stone, thou shalt not build it of hewn stone: for if thou lift up thy tool upon it, thou hast polluted it." (Ludlow)

1 Nephi 2:8, 10

In the background of Joseph Smith it was customary for the river and the valley through which the river flowed to carry the same name; hence, the Mississippi River and the Mississippi Valley, the Missouri River and the Missouri Valley. However, this is not necessarily the practice in the Middle East, and it evidently was not the practice there 600 years B.C., as is indicated by the fact that Lehi named the river after his son Laman and the valley through which the river flowed after his son Lemuel. (Ludlow)

wherefore, I did cry unto the Lord; and behold he did visit me, and
did soften my heart that I did believe all the words which had been
spoken by my father; wherefore, I did not rebel against him like
unto my brothers.
17. And I spake unto Sam, making known unto him the things
which the Lord had manifested unto me by his Holy Spirit. And it
came to pass that he believed in my words.
18. But, behold, Laman and Lemuel would not hearken unto my
words; and being grieved because of the hardness of their hearts I
cried unto the Lord for them.
19. And it came to pass that the Lord spake unto me, saying:
Blessed art thou, Nephi, because of thy faith, for thou hast sought
me diligently, with lowliness of heart.
20. And inasmuch as ye shall keep my commandments, ye shall
prosper, and shall be led to a land of promise; yea, even a land
which I have prepared for you; yea, a land which is choice above
all other lands.
21. And inasmuch as thy brethren shall rebel against thee, they
shall be cut off from the presence of the Lord.
22. And inasmuch as thou shalt keep my commandments, thou
shalt be made a ruler and a teacher over thy brethren.
23. For behold, in that day that they shall rebel against me, I will
curse them even with a sore curse, and they shall have no power
over thy seed except they shall rebel against me also.
24. And if it so be that they rebel against me, they shall be a
scourge unto thy seed, to stir them up in the ways of remembrance.

CHAPTER 3

1. AND it came to pass that I, Nephi, returned from speaking with the
Lord, to the tent of my father.
2. And it came to pass that he spake unto me, saying: Behold I
have dreamed a dream, in the which the Lord hath commanded
me that thou and thy brethren shall return to Jerusalem.
3. For behold, Laban hath the record of the Jews and also a genealogy of my forefathers, and they are engraven upon plates of brass.
4. Wherefore, the Lord hath commanded me that thou and thy
brothers should go unto the house of Laban, and seek the records,
and bring them down hither into the wilderness.
5. And now, behold thy brothers murmur, saying it is a hard thing
which I have required of them; but behold I have not required it of

POINT OF INTEREST

Lehi was probably a descendant of Manassite refugees who had fled south to Judah with others of the northern kingdom in 724–722 B.C. and would probably have lived in the Mishneh, which, in 600 B.C., was an upscale quarter of the city where wealthy types like Shallum the royal clothier and Lehi himself lived, as well as possibly Laban and Ishmael. Also, since the Middle Gate of Jerusalem was in use in Lehi's day, it could very well have been the portal through which Nephi entered Jerusalem on the night he "crept into the city and went forth towards the house of Laban."

1 Nephi 2:13

The term "Jew" is used in the Book of Mormon with two possible meanings: (1) a descendant of Judah, the son of Jacob (or, perhaps in a more general vein, a member of the house of Israel), and (2) a citizen of the kingdom of Judah of this particular period.

Lehi and his descendants are definitely not descendants of Judah (see 1 Nephi 5:14), but they might be considered Jews in the sense that they were citizens of the kingdom of Judah. Thus Nephi states, "I have charity for the Jew—I say Jew, because I mean them from whence I came" (2 Nephi 33:8). Also, the Lord refers to the Lamanites of our day as "a remnant" of the Jews (D&C 19:27). (Ludlow)

1 Nephi 3:3

In many of the Semitic languages (from which we get the thought patterns contained in the Book of Mormon) it is not customary to have the adjective precede the noun. Thus the Book of Mormon mentions the "plates of brass" of Laban but never refers to the "brass plates of Laban." (Ludlow)

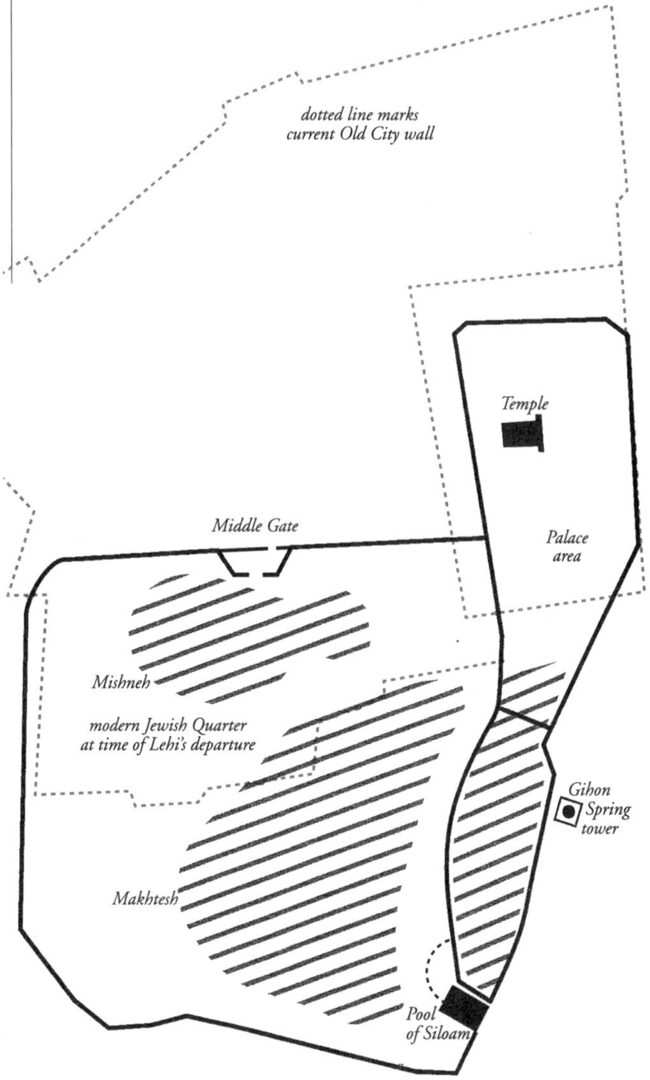

them, but it is a commandment of the Lord.
6. Therefore go, my son, and thou shalt be favored of the Lord, because thou hast not murmured.
7. And it came to pass that I, Nephi, said unto my father: I will go and do the things which the Lord hath commanded, for I know that the Lord giveth no commandments unto the children of men, save he shall prepare a way for them that they may accomplish the thing which he commandeth them.
8. And it came to pass that when my father had heard these words he was exceedingly glad, for he knew that I had been blessed of the Lord.
9. And I, Nephi, and my brethren took our journey in the wilderness, with our tents, to go up to the land of Jerusalem.
10. And it came to pass that when we had gone up to the land of Jerusalem, I and my brethren did consult one with another.
11. And we cast lots—who of us should go in unto the house of Laban. And it came to pass that the lot fell upon Laman; and Laman went in unto the house of Laban, and he talked with him as he sat in his house.
12. And he desired of Laban the records which were engraven upon the plates of brass, which contained the genealogy of my father.
13. And behold, it came to pass that Laban was angry, and thrust him out from his presence; and he would not that he should have the records. Wherefore, he said unto him: Behold thou art a robber, and I will slay thee.
14. But Laman fled out of his presence, and told the things which Laban had done, unto us. And we began to be exceedingly sorrowful, and my brethren were about to return unto my father in the wilderness.
15. But behold I said unto them that: As the Lord liveth, and as we live, we will not go down unto our father in the wilderness until we have accomplished the thing which the Lord hath commanded us.
16. Wherefore, let us be faithful in keeping the commandments of the Lord; therefore let us go down to the land of our father's inheritance, for behold he left gold and silver, and all manner of riches. And all this he hath done because of the commandments of the Lord.
17. For he knew that Jerusalem must be destroyed, because of the wickedness of the people.
18. For behold, they have rejected the words of the prophets. Wherefore, if my father should dwell in the land after he hath been commanded to flee out of the land, behold, he would also perish. Wherefore, it must needs be that he flee out of the land.
19. And behold, it is wisdom in God that we should obtain these records, that we may preserve unto our children the language of our fathers;
20. And also that we may preserve unto them the words which have been spoken by the mouth of all the holy prophets, which have been delivered unto them by the Spirit and power of God, since the world began, even down unto this present time.

1 Nephi 3:11

The "casting of lots" was practiced extensively by the Hebrews of Old Testament times. This authentic and typical use of the custom in the Book of Mormon would indicate again that this part of the story in the Book of Mormon is concerned with a group of people with a Hebrew background and that the Book of Mormon is a translation of an ancient record. (If you want to review some of the examples in the Bible where the casting of lots was used, see Leviticus 16:8; 1 Samuel 14:42; 1 Chronicles 26:13; Psalms 22:18; Isaiah 34:17; Joel 3:3; Obadiah 11; Jonah 1:7; Nahum 3:10; Matthew 27:35; Mark 15:24; John 19:24; Acts 1:26.) (Ludlow)

POINT OF INTEREST

The practice of casting lots is mentioned frequently in the Old and New Testaments and in the Book of Mormon; however, nothing is known about the lots themselves. They could have been sticks of various lengths, flat stones like coins, or some kind of dice. The closest modern practice to casting lots is likely flipping a coin or drawing straws.

21. And it came to pass that after this manner of language did I persuade my brethren, that they might be faithful in keeping the commandments of God.

22. And it came to pass that we went down to the land of our inheritance, and we did gather together our gold, and our silver, and our precious things.

23. And after we had gathered these things together, we went up again unto the house of Laban.

24. And it came to pass that we went in unto Laban, and desired him that he would give unto us the records which were engraven upon the plates of brass, for which we would give unto him our gold, and our silver, and all our precious things.

25. And it came to pass that when Laban saw our property, and that it was exceedingly great, he did lust after it, insomuch that he thrust us out, and sent his servants to slay us, that he might obtain our property.

26. And it came to pass that we did flee before the servants of Laban, and we were obliged to leave behind our property, and it fell into the hands of Laban.

27. And it came to pass that we fled into the wilderness, and the servants of Laban did not overtake us, and we hid ourselves in the cavity of a rock.

28. And it came to pass that Laman was angry with me, and also with my father; and also was Lemuel, for he hearkened unto the words of Laman. Wherefore Laman and Lemuel did speak many hard words unto us, their younger brothers, and they did smite us even with a rod.

29. And it came to pass as they smote us with a rod, behold, an angel of the Lord came and stood before them, and he spake unto them, saying: Why do ye smite your younger brother with a rod? Know ye not that the Lord hath chosen him to be a ruler over you, and this because of your iniquities? Behold ye shall go up to Jerusalem again, and the Lord will deliver Laban into your hands.

30. And after the angel had spoken unto us, he departed.

31. And after the angel had departed, Laman and Lemuel again began to murmur, saying: How is it possible that the Lord will deliver Laban into our hands? Behold, he is a mighty man, and he can command fifty, yea, even he can slay fifty; then why not us?

CHAPTER 4

1. AND it came to pass that I spake unto my brethren, saying: Let us go up again unto Jerusalem, and let us be faithful in keeping the commandments of the Lord; for behold he is mightier than all the earth, then why not mightier than Laban and his fifty, yea, or even than his tens of thousands?

2. Therefore let us go up; let us be strong like unto Moses; for he truly spake unto the waters of the Red Sea and they divided hither and thither, and our fathers came through, out of captivity, on dry ground, and the armies of Pharaoh

1 Nephi 4:1

During Lehi's time, the custodian of the priceless chronicles of God's dealings with His people, preserved on plates of brass, was an unscrupulous official in Jerusalem named Laban. Following Lehi's instructions to his sons to go to Laban's house and get the plates, Laman and Lemuel began to murmur. The younger Nephi became favored of the Lord because he didn't murmur. Out of this recorded event comes the oft-quoted statement of Nephi: "I will go and do the things which the Lord hath commanded, for I know that the Lord giveth no commandments unto the children of men, save he shall prepare a way for them that they may accomplish the thing which he commandeth them" (1 Ne. 3:7).

The Lord is our strength. He will provide a way if we will but do our part. We must persevere even as Nephi did following the failure of both attempts to get the plates, being threatened even unto death, and being beaten by his brothers. An angel appeared and chastised Laman and Lemuel, informing them that the Lord would deliver Laban into their hands, and still Laman and Lemuel murmured because they had doubt. Nephi's faith was evident as he explained that the Lord could do all things, of which the preservation of the Israelites at the Red Sea was one example. A great truth then comes forth to those who believe and trust in the Lord: "And I was led by the Spirit, not knowing beforehand the things which I should do" (1 Ne. 4:6).

President Heber J. Grant said, "Laban stole their wealth and trie ... troy them. Nephi's brethren commenced to m ... they took a rod and beat him with it. ... f the Lord stood before then ... p again, promising ... nto their hands.

"... ... uld only see an ange ... ful.' The seeing of ... you are keeping th

did follow and were drowned in the waters of the Red Sea.
3. Now behold ye know that this is true; and ye also know that an angel hath spoken unto you; wherefore can ye doubt? Let us go up; the Lord is able to deliver us, even as our fathers, and to destroy Laban, even as the Egyptians.
4. Now when I had spoken these words, they were yet wroth, and did still continue to murmur; nevertheless they did follow me up until we came without the walls of Jerusalem.
5. And it was by night; and I caused that they should hide themselves without the walls. And after they had hid themselves, I, Nephi, crept into the city and went forth towards the house of Laban.
6. And I was led by the Spirit, not knowing beforehand the things which I should do.
7. Nevertheless I went forth, and as I came near unto the house of Laban I beheld a man, and he had fallen to the earth before me, for he was drunken with wine.
8. And when I came to him I found that it was Laban.
9. And I beheld his sword, and I drew it forth from the sheath thereof; and the hilt thereof was of pure gold, and the workmanship thereof was exceedingly fine, and I saw that the blade thereof was of the most precious steel.
10. And it came to pass that I was constrained by the Spirit that I should kill Laban; but I said in my heart: Never at any time have I shed the blood of man. And I shrunk and would that I might not slay him.
11. And the Spirit said unto me again: Behold the Lord hath delivered him into thy hands. Yea, and I also knew that he had sought to take away mine own life; yea, and he would not hearken unto the commandments of the Lord; and he also had taken away our property.
12. And it came to pass that the Spirit said unto me again: Slay him, for the Lord hath delivered him into thy hands;
13. Behold the Lord slayeth the wicked to bring forth his righteous purposes. It is better that one man should perish than that a nation should dwindle and perish in unbelief.
14. And now, when I, Nephi, had heard these words, I remembered the words of the Lord which he spake unto me in the wilderness, saying that: Inasmuch as thy seed shall keep my commandments, they shall prosper in the land of promise.
15. Yea, and I also thought that they could not keep the commandments of the Lord according to the law of Moses, save they should have the law.
16. And I also knew that the law was engraven upon the plates of brass.
17. And again, I knew that the Lord had delivered Laban into my hands for this cause—that I might obtain the records according to his commandments.
18. Therefore I did obey the voice of the Spirit, and took Laban by the hair of the head, and I smote off his head with his own sword.
19. And after I had smitten off his

1 Nephi 4:6–18

The Lord protects the free agency of his children and the rights of the righteous. Thus, when the wicked (either an individual or a nation) become so "steeped in iniquity" that they obstruct the righteous purposes of God, he removes them from the earth. Such was apparently the case at the time of the flood, and several times since then the Lord has commanded that the wicked should be destroyed. (See Deuteronomy 7:2; 9:4; Joshua 6:21.)

Laban had already attempted murder for his private gain (1 Nephi 3:13, 24–26) and was evidently a very wicked person; thus he apparently fully deserved the fate that befell him. Also, as we shall discover later in the Book of Mormon (Omni, verses 15–19), the brass plates did keep part of the Lehite nation from dwindling and perishing "in unbelief" for many hundreds of years, just as the Spirit had prophesied. (Ludlow)

1 Nephi 4:10, 12–18

As Nephi faced the awesome challenge of taking a human life by divine commandment, he must have reflected on sentiments similar to those found in Hosea. "Who is wise, and he shall understand these things? Prudent, and he shall know them? For the ways of the Lord are right, and the just shall walk in them: but the transgressors shall fall therein" (Hosea 14:9). His former obedience and teachable humility helped him recognize the Spirit's voice of superior wisdom.

When we understand and appreciate a doctrine, principle, or commandment by the Spirit, it is easier to accept and live such things. We witness this all the time in teaching, whether in the mission field, in our quorums and classes, or in our homes.

The Prophet Joseph Smith said: "We cannot keep all the commandments without first knowing them, and we cannot know them all, or more than we now know unless we comply with or keep those we have already received. That which is wrong under one circumstance, may be, and often is, right under another.

"God said, 'Thou shalt not kill'; at another time He said 'Thou shalt utterly destroy.' This is the principle on which the government of heaven is conducted—by revelation adapted to the circumstances in which the children of the kingdom are placed. Whatever God requires is right, no matter what it is, although we may not see the reason thereof till long after the events transpire. . . .

"Everything that God gives us is lawful and right." (P/A)

head with his own sword, I took the garments of Laban and put them upon mine own body; yea, even every whit; and I did gird on his armor about my loins.
20. And after I had done this, I went forth unto the treasury of Laban. And as I went forth towards the treasury of Laban, behold, I saw the servant of Laban who had the keys of the treasury. And I commanded him in the voice of Laban, that he should go with me into the treasury.
21. And he supposed me to be his master, Laban, for he beheld the garments and also the sword girded about my loins.
22. And he spake unto me concerning the elders of the Jews, he knowing that his master, Laban, had been out by night among them.
23. And I spake unto him as if it had been Laban.
24. And I also spake unto him that I should carry the engravings, which were upon the plates of brass, to my elder brethren, who were without the walls.
25. And I also bade him that he should follow me.
26. And he, supposing that I spake of the brethren of the church, and that I was truly that Laban whom I had slain, wherefore he did follow me.
27. And he spake unto me many times concerning the elders of the Jews, as I went forth unto my brethren, who were without the walls.
28. And it came to pass that when Laman saw me he was exceedingly frightened, and also Lemuel and Sam. And they fled from before my presence; for they supposed it was Laban, and that he had slain me and had sought to take away their lives also.
29. And it came to pass that I called after them, and they did hear me; wherefore they did cease to flee from my presence.
30. And it came to pass that when the servant of Laban beheld my brethren he began to tremble, and was about to flee from before me and return to the city of Jerusalem.
31. And now I, Nephi, being a man large in stature, and also having received much strength of the Lord, therefore I did seize upon the servant of Laban, and held him, that he should not flee.
32. And it came to pass that I spake with him, that if he would hearken unto my words, as the Lord liveth, and as I live, even so that if he would hearken unto our words, we would spare his life.
33. And I spake unto him, even with an oath, that he need not fear; that he should be a free man like unto us if he would go down in the wilderness with us.
34. And I also spake unto him, saying: Surely the Lord hath commanded us to do this thing; and shall we not be diligent in keeping the commandments of the Lord? Therefore, if thou wilt go down into the wilderness to my father thou shalt have place with us.
35. And it came to pass that Zoram did take courage at the words which I spake. Now Zoram was the name of the servant; and he promised that he would go down into the wilderness unto our father. Yea, and he also made an oath unto us that he would tarry with us from that time forth.
36. Now we were desirous that he should tarry with us for this cause, that the Jews might not know concerning our flight into the wilderness, lest they should pursue us and destroy us.
37. And it came to pass that when

1 Nephi 4:22, 26

Scholars believe that the "elders of the Jews" referred to in these verses were likely the wise men of the local church or synagogue or leading community members. Some have suggested that these leaders—as well as representatives from well-respected families—may have formed a type of advisory council that worked with the king.

1 Nephi 4:32–37

Notice again the importance of an oath among these people; when they give their word to do something, they do it! Concerning the binding effect of an oath upon the desert people and their descendants, Dr. Hugh Nibley has written:

". . . when he [Zoram] saw the brethren and heard Nephi's real voice he got the shock of his life and in a panic made a break for the city. In such a situation there was only one thing Nephi could possibly have done, both to spare Zoram and to avoid giving alarm—and no westerner could have guessed what it was. Nephi, a powerful fellow, held the terrified Zoram in a vice-like grip long enough to swear a solemn oath in his ear, 'as the Lord liveth, and as I live,' that he would not harm him if he would listen. Zoram immediately relaxed, and Nephi swore another oath to him that he would be a free man if he would join the party: "Therefore, if thou wilt go down into the wilderness to my father thou shalt have place with us.' . . .

"But not every oath will do. To be most binding and solemn an oath should be by the life of something, even if it be but a blade of grass. The only oath more awful than that 'by my life' or (less commonly) 'by the life of my head,' is the *wa hayat Allah* 'by the life of God,' or 'as the Lord Liveth,' the exact Arabic equivalent of the ancient Hebrew *hai Elohim* . . .

"So we see that the only way that Nephi could possibly have pacified the struggling Zoram in an instant was to utter the one oath that no man would dream of breaking, the most solemn of all oaths to the Semite: "As the Lord liveth, and as I live!" (Ludlow)

POINT OF INTEREST

Kings of the Divided Kingdoms of Israel

Israel (Northern Kingdom)

975–954 B.C. *Jeroboam*
The Lord had promised Jeroboam the kingdom of Judah, but the king doubted, fearing that his people would want to return to the temple in Jerusalem. In time, he led Israel into idolatry.

Judah (Southern Kingdom)

975–957 B.C. *Rehoboam*
This wicked king rejected the prophet Ahijah's counsel, increased taxes, and led Judah into idolatry. At this time the pharaoh Shoshenq I pillaged the temple and royal palace in Jerusalem.

Zoram had made an oath unto us, our fears did cease concerning him.

38. And it came to pass that we took the plates of brass and the servant of Laban, and departed into the wilderness, and journeyed unto the tent of our father.

CHAPTER 5

1. AND it came to pass that after we had come down into the wilderness unto our father, behold, he was filled with joy, and also my mother, Sariah, was exceedingly glad, for she truly had mourned because of us.

2. For she had supposed that we had perished in the wilderness; and she also had complained against my father, telling him that he was a visionary man; saying: Behold thou hast led us forth from the land of our inheritance, and my sons are no more, and we perish in the wilderness.

3. And after this manner of language had my mother complained against my father.

4. And it had come to pass that my father spake unto her, saying: I know that I am a visionary man; for if I had not seen the things of God in a vision I should not have known the goodness of God, but had tarried at Jerusalem, and had perished with my brethren.

5. But behold, I have obtained a land of promise, in the which things I do rejoice; yea, and I know that the Lord will deliver my sons out of the hands of Laban, and bring them down again unto us in the wilderness.

6. And after this manner of language did my father, Lehi, comfort my mother, Sariah, concerning us, while we journeyed in the wilderness up to the land of Jerusalem, to obtain the record of the Jews.

7. And when we had returned to the tent of my father, behold their joy was full, and my mother was comforted.

8. And she spake, saying: Now I know of a surety that the Lord hath commanded my husband to flee into the wilderness; yea, and I also know of a surety that the Lord hath protected my sons, and delivered them out of the hands of Laban, and given them power whereby they could accomplish the thing which the Lord hath commanded them. And after this manner of language did she speak.

9. And it came to pass that they did rejoice exceedingly, and did offer sacrifice and burnt offerings unto the Lord; and they gave thanks unto the God of Israel.

10. And after they had given thanks unto the God of Israel, my father, Lehi, took the records which were engraven upon the plates of brass, and he did search them from the beginning.

11. And he beheld that they did contain the five books of Moses, which gave an account of the creation of the world, and also of Adam and Eve, who were our first parents;

1 Nephi 5:9

There is a law or principle of sacrifice. When the law is observed correctly, blessings are received from heaven. This concept is manifested by the spiritual unity of Lehi's family. After fulfilling the commandment of the Lord and obtaining the brass plates, ". . . they did rejoice exceedingly, and did offer sacrifice and burnt offerings unto the Lord; and they gave thanks unto the God of Israel" (1 Ne. 5:9). This principle is also expressed in the words of Moroni: ". . . for ye receive no witness until after the trial of your faith" (Ether 12:6). (O/C)

1 Nephi 5:10–11

The Bible is commonly understood to be the "stick of Judah" referred to by the Lord in his promise to Ezekiel. Latter-day Saints believe the Book of Mormon is part of the "stick of Joseph" mentioned by the Lord. It is possible that a portion of the original stick of Joseph was the brass plates of Laban, and still other portions might be the records of the Nephites as contained on the large and the small plates of Nephi. In this sense, then, our present Book of Mormon would be only an abridgment or condensation of the parts making up the original "stick of Joseph."

Lehi and Laban were both descendants of Joseph who was sold into Egypt. Thus, they had the right to include their writings on the "stick of Joseph." (Ludlow)

POINT OF INTEREST

This reproduction of a Roman wax tablet is made of wood and covered with a layer of wax. In Ezek. 37:16–19, when Ezekiel referred to the "sticks" of Judah (Bible) and Joseph (Book of Mormon), he probably borrowed the imagery from the ancient use of boards like these. Boards could also be made of ivory, and a stylus was used to write on them. They could then be bound together to protect the writing surface.

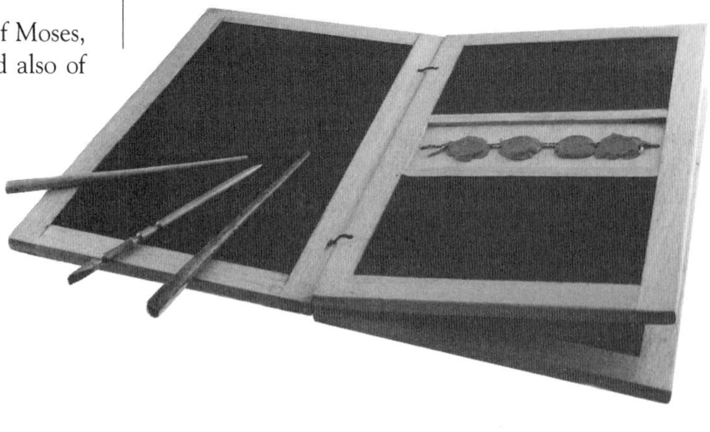

12. And also a record of the Jews from the beginning, even down
to the commencement of the reign of Zedekiah, king of Judah;
13. And also the prophecies of the holy prophets, from the beginning, even down to the commencement of the reign of Zedekiah;
and also many prophecies which have been spoken by the mouth
of Jeremiah.
14. And it came to pass that my father, Lehi, also found upon the
plates of brass a genealogy of his fathers; wherefore he knew that
he was a descendant of Joseph; yea, even that Joseph who was the
son of Jacob, who was sold into Egypt, and who was preserved by
the hand of the Lord, that he might preserve his father, Jacob, and
all his household from perishing with famine.
15. And they were also led out of captivity and out of the land of
Egypt, by that same God who had preserved them.
16. And thus my father, Lehi, did discover the genealogy of his
fathers. And Laban also was a descendant of Joseph, wherefore he
and his fathers had kept the records.
17. And now when my father saw all these things, he was filled
with the Spirit, and began to prophesy concerning his seed—
18. That these plates of brass should go forth unto all nations, kindreds, tongues, and people who were of his seed.
19. Wherefore, he said that these plates of brass should never perish; neither should they be dimmed any more by time. And he
prophesied many things concerning his seed.
20. And it came to pass that thus far I and my father had kept the
commandments wherewith the Lord had commanded us.
21. And we had obtained the records which the Lord had commanded us, and searched them and found that they were desirable;
yea, even of great worth unto us, insomuch that we could preserve
the commandments of the Lord unto our children.
22. Wherefore, it was wisdom in the Lord that we should carry
them with us, as we journeyed in the wilderness towards the land
of promise.

1 Nephi 5:11–13

The brass plates obtained from Laban contained the five books of Moses (apparently similar to the first five books of the Bible—the Pentateuch: Genesis, Exodus, Leviticus, Numbers, and Deuteronomy), a record of the Jews from the beginning down to Zedekiah, and the prophecies of the prophets from the beginning down to Jeremiah. (1 Nephi 3:3–20; 5:11–13.) This would explain how the biblical stories were known by the American Indian groups even before the arrival of the Catholic fathers and their Bibles after the time of Columbus. Historians have concluded the American Indians knew of the story of the creation, the flood, etc., before the time of Columbus, although they have not been able to explain how the Indians came into possession of this knowledge.

In volume 4 of his *Antiquities of Mexico*, Lord Kingsborough found so many evidences of biblical stories among the Indians that he concluded:

"It is unnecessary to attempt in this place to trace out any further scriptural analogies in the traditions and mythology of the New World, since the coincidences which have already been mentioned are sufficiently strong to warrant the conclusion that the Indians, at a period long antecedent to the arrival of the Spaniards in America, were acquainted with a portion at least of the Old Testament." (Ludlow)

CHAPTER 6

1. AND now I, Nephi, do not give the genealogy of my fathers in
this part of my record; neither at any time shall I give it after upon
these plates which I am writing; for it is given in the record which
has been kept by my father; wherefore, I do not write it in this
work.
2. For it sufficeth me to say that we are descendants of Joseph.
3. And it mattereth not to me that I am particular to give a full
account of all the things of my father, for they cannot be written
upon these

1 Nephi 6:3–6

Nephi was commanded of the Lord to make plates and to engrave thereon the record of his people and the record of his father—including his and Lehi's prophecies—that he might persuade men to come unto Christ and "for other wise purposes, which purposes are known unto the Lord" (1 Ne. 19:3). The scriptures are the words of our Savior Jesus Christ, and all scriptures testify of Christ. They are testaments or witnesses of our Savior. We are to live by every word that proceeds from the mouth of God (see D&C 84:43–46); they were written to invite all to come unto Christ and be perfected in Him (see Moro. 10:32). . . .

The purpose of this dispensation is to invite all to come unto Christ. Elder Bruce R. McConkie taught, "John, who bore testimony of Jesus, did so for one reason and one reason only: he was seeking to persuade men to believe in Christ, to come unto him, to accept him as the Son of God, and to be saved by obedience to the laws and ordinances of his gospel." (P/A)

plates, for I desire the room that I may write of the things of God.
4. For the fulness of mine intent is that I may persuade men to come unto the God of Abraham, and the God of Isaac, and the God of Jacob, and be saved.
5. Wherefore, the things which are pleasing unto the world I do not write, but the things which are pleasing unto God and unto those who are not of the world.
6. Wherefore, I shall give commandment unto my seed, that they shall not occupy these plates with things which are not of worth unto the children of men.

CHAPTER 7

1. AND now I would that ye might know, that after my father, Lehi, had made an end of prophesying concerning his seed, it came to pass that the Lord spake unto him again, saying that it was not meet for him, Lehi, that he should take his family into the wilderness alone; but that his sons should take daughters to wife, that they might raise up seed unto the Lord in the land of promise.
2. And it came to pass that the Lord commanded him that I, Nephi, and my brethren, should again return unto the land of Jerusalem, and bring down Ishmael and his family into the wilderness.
3. And it came to pass that I, Nephi, did again, with my brethren, go forth into the wilderness to go up to Jerusalem.
4. And it came to pass that we went up unto the house of Ishmael, and we did gain favor in the sight of Ishmael, insomuch that we did speak unto him the words of the Lord.
5. And it came to pass that the Lord did soften the heart of Ishmael, and also his household, insomuch that they took their journey with us down into the wilderness to the tent of our father.
6. And it came to pass that as we journeyed in the wilderness, behold Laman and Lemuel, and two of the daughters of Ishmael, and the two sons of Ishmael and their families, did rebel against us; yea, against me, Nephi, and Sam, and their father, Ishmael, and his wife, and his three other daughters.
7. And it came to pass in the which rebellion, they were desirous to return unto the land of Jerusalem.
8. And now I, Nephi, being grieved for the hardness of their hearts, therefore I spake unto them, saying, yea, even unto Laman and unto Lemuel: Behold ye are mine elder brethren, and how is it that ye are so hard in your hearts, and so blind in your minds, that ye have need that I, your younger brother, should speak unto you, yea, and set an example for you?
9. How is it that ye have not hearkened unto the word of the Lord?
10. How is it that ye have forgotten that ye have seen an angel of the Lord?

POINT OF INTEREST

The Western or Wailing Wall in Jerusalem (right, in a picture taken in A.D. 1870) is probably the most famous wall in history and was built in 516 B.C. as a retaining wall for the rebuilt temple. At the time of Lehi, the walls around the city were nowhere near this height. Hezekiah's wall, which surrounded the area where Lehi and his family probably lived, was only about 15 feet high.

1 Nephi 7:2

When Lehi's and Ishmael's families married, it fulfilled the prophecy in Genesis 48 (the descendants of Abraham and those by Isaac grew together on the American continent). Lehi was of the lineage of Manasseh, and Ishmael was of the lineage of Ephraim.

1 Nephi 7:2–5

The Lord commanded Lehi to send his sons back to Jerusalem once again to seek a partnership with Ishmael's family for the journey to the promised land. Once again, obedience was the opportunity to enter the pathway of vitality, for this action would allow Lehi's sons to take Ishmael's daughters to wife, that they might have posterity.

Laman and Lemuel did not murmur on the long trek back to Jerusalem. . . .

As Elder Russell M. Nelson said, "Perhaps each young man felt a bit better about it this time, knowing that there was the possibility he might be rewarded with one of the daughters of Ishmael to become his wife. This rugged discipline was but a prologue to Lehi's family's going subsequently all the way across what we now know as the Saudi Arabian Peninsula to its southeastern shore, where ships were to be built. And this challenge was but prelude to their ultimate destiny—to go across ocean waters to the promised land."

[Laman and Lemuel] again took up murmuring upon their return. Nephi admonished them to remember that they had seen an angel, that they had been delivered out of the hands of Laban, and that if they were faithful they could obtain a land of promise. Alternately, they could remain in Jerusalem and perish. (P/A)

11. Yea, and how is it that ye have forgotten what great things the Lord hath done for us, in delivering us out of the hands of Laban, and also that we should obtain the record?
12. Yea, and how is it that ye have forgotten that the Lord is able to do all things according to his will, for the children of men, if it so be that they exercise faith in him? Wherefore, let us be faithful to him.
13. And if it so be that we are faithful to him, we shall obtain the land of promise; and ye shall know at some future period that the word of the Lord shall be fulfilled concerning the destruction of Jerusalem; for all things which the Lord hath spoken concerning the destruction of Jerusalem must be fulfilled.
14. For behold, the Spirit of the Lord ceaseth soon to strive with them; for behold, they have rejected the prophets, and Jeremiah have they cast into prison. And they have sought to take away the life of my father, insomuch that they have driven him out of the land.
15. Now behold, I say unto you that if ye will return unto Jerusalem ye shall also perish with them. And now, if ye have choice, go up to the land, and remember the words which I speak unto you, that if ye go ye will also perish; for thus the Spirit of the Lord constraineth me that I should speak.
16. And it came to pass that when I, Nephi, had spoken these words unto my brethren, they were angry with me. And it came to pass that they did lay their hands upon me, for behold, they were exceedingly wroth, and they did bind me with cords, for they sought to take away my life, that they might leave me in the wilderness to be devoured by wild beasts.
17. But it came to pass that I prayed unto the Lord, saying: O Lord, according to my faith which is in thee, wilt thou deliver me from the hands of my brethren; yea, even give me strength that I may burst these bands with which I am bound.
18. And it came to pass that when I had said these words, behold, the bands were loosed from off my hands and feet, and I stood before my brethren, and I spake unto them again.
19. And it came to pass that they were angry with me again, and sought to lay hands upon me; but behold, one of the daughters of Ishmael, yea, and also her mother, and one of the sons of Ishmael, did plead with my brethren, insomuch that they did soften their hearts; and they did cease striving to take away my life.
20. And it came to pass that they were sorrowful, because of their wickedness, insomuch that they did bow down before me, and did plead with me that I would forgive them of the thing that they had done against me.
21. And it came to pass that I did frankly forgive them all that they had done, and I did exhort them that they would pray unto the Lord their God for forgiveness. And it came to pass that they did so. And after they had done praying unto the Lord we did again travel on our journey towards the tent of our father.
22. And it came to pass that we did

come down unto the tent of our father. And after I and my brethren and all the house of Ishmael had come down unto the tent of my father, they did give thanks unto the Lord their God; and they did offer sacrifice and burnt offerings unto him.

CHAPTER 8

1. AND it came to pass that we had gathered together all manner of seeds of every kind, both of grain of every kind, and also of the seeds of fruit of every kind.
2. And it came to pass that while my father tarried in the wilderness he spake unto us, saying: Behold, I have dreamed a dream; or, in other words, I have seen a vision.
3. And behold, because of the thing which I have seen, I have reason to rejoice in the Lord because of Nephi and also of Sam; for I have reason to suppose that they, and also many of their seed, will be saved.
4. But behold, Laman and Lemuel, I fear exceedingly because of you; for behold,methought I saw in my dream, a dark and dreary wilderness.
5. And it came to pass that I saw a man, and he was dressed in a white robe; and he came and stood before me.
6. And it came to pass that he spake unto me, and bade me follow him.
7. And it came to pass that as I followed him I beheld myself that I was in a dark and dreary waste.
8. And after I had traveled for the space of many hours in darkness, I began to pray unto the Lord that he would have mercy on me, according to the multitude of his tender mercies.
9. And it came to pass after I had prayed unto the Lord I beheld a large and spacious field.
10. And it came to pass that I beheld a tree, whose fruit was desirable to make one happy.
11. And it came to pass that I did go forth and partake of the fruit thereof; and I beheld that it was most sweet, above all that I ever before tasted. Yea, and I beheld that the fruit thereof was white, to exceed all the whiteness that I had ever seen.
12. And as I partook of the fruit thereof it filled my soul with exceedingly great joy; wherefore, I began to be desirous that my family should partake of it also; for I knew that it was desirable above all other fruit.
13. And as I cast my eyes round about, that perhaps I might discover my family also, I beheld a river of water; and it ran along, and it was near the tree of which I was partaking the fruit.
14. And I looked to behold from whence it came; and I saw the head thereof a little way off; and at the head thereof I beheld your mother Sariah, and Sam, and Nephi; and they stood as if they knew not whither they should go.
15. And it came to pass that I

1 Nephi 8

As the prophet Lehi, spokesperson of the Lord's will, tarried in the wilderness with his family, he reported experiencing a remarkable spiritual event: "Behold, I have dreamed a dream; or, in other words, I have seen a vision" (1 Ne. 8:2). What he saw with prophetic insight was a dynamic scene that instilled in him two diametrically opposite emotions—one of joy on behalf of his righteous sons, Sam and Nephi, and one of fear on behalf of Laman and Lemuel, whose attitude and behavior were scarcely in keeping with divine mandate (see 1 Ne. 8:3–4). Lehi unfolded for his family the details of the memorable tree of life vision that has become one of the most celebrated and compelling statements of the gospel plan, and the consequences of mortal choice, in all of holy writ.

The tree of life vision encompasses a multiplicity of symbols that invite informed interpretation and greater understanding based on the keys given in the scriptures themselves. This greater understanding leads in turn to daily applications, based on faith, that promote increased goodness and righteousness in life.

Elder Jeffrey R. Holland said, "The reader finds the first manifestation of the symbolic Christ in the vision of the Tree of Life. . . . Thus, at the very outset of the Book of Mormon, in its first fully developed allegory, Christ is portrayed as the source of eternal life and joy, the living evidence of divine love, and the means whereby God will fulfill his covenant with the house of Israel and indeed the entire family of man, returning them to all their eternal promises." (P/A)

1 Nephi 8

The tree of life is not an abstract model to be admired like a tapestry, but a road map that becomes a stunning self-revelation when we hold it up as a mirror in which to see ourselves and determine our position before God. (P/A)

1 Nephi 8:8

In several places in the scriptures the Lord has indicated that if we want an answer to our prayers we should first of all ask him. In 3 Nephi 18:20, the Lord has said: "And whatsoever ye shall ask the Father in my name, which is right, believing that ye shall receive, behold it shall be given unto you." The Lord evidently wanted to reveal some great spiritual truths to Lehi in this dream, but first of all he wanted Lehi to get into an inquiring (and thus a learning) attitude. Finally, after traveling "for the space of many hours in darkness," Lehi began to pray unto the Lord; then the remainder of the dream or vision was unfolded unto him. (Ludlow)

beckoned unto them; and I also did say unto them with a loud voice
that they should come unto me, and partake of the fruit, which was
desirable above all other fruit.
16. And it came to pass that they did come unto me and partake
of the fruit also.
17. And it came to pass that I was desirous that Laman and Lemuel
should come and partake of the fruit also; wherefore, I cast mine eyes
towards the head of the river, that perhaps I might see them.
18. And it came to pass that I saw them, but they would not come
unto me and partake of the fruit.
19. And I beheld a rod of iron, and it extended along the bank of
the river, and led to the tree by which I stood.
20. And I also beheld a strait and narrow path, which came along
by the rod of iron, even to the tree by which I stood; and it also led
by the head of the fountain, unto a large and spacious field, as if it
had been a world.
21. And I saw numberless concourses of people, many of whom
were pressing forward, that they might obtain the path which led
unto the tree by which I stood.
22. And it came to pass that they did come forth, and commence
in the path which led to the tree.
23. And it came to pass that there arose a mist of darkness; yea,
even an exceedingly great mist of darkness, insomuch that they
who had commenced in the path did lose their way, that they wandered off and were lost.
24. And it came to pass that I beheld others pressing forward, and
they came forth and caught hold of the end of the rod of iron;
and they did press forward through the mist of darkness, clinging
to the rod of iron, even until they did come forth and partake of
the fruit of the tree.
25. And after they had partaken of the fruit of the tree they did
cast their eyes about as if they were ashamed.
26. And I also cast my eyes round about, and beheld, on the other
side of the river of water, a great and spacious building; and it stood
as it were in the air, high above the earth.
27. And it was filled with people, both old and young, both male
and female; and their manner of dress was exceedingly fine; and
they were in the attitude of mocking and pointing their fingers
towards those who had come at and were partaking of the fruit.
28. And after they had tasted of the fruit they were ashamed,
because of those that were scoffing at them; and they fell away
into forbidden paths and were lost.
29. And now I, Nephi, do not speak all the words of my father.
30. But, to be short in writing, behold, he saw other multitudes
pressing forward; and they came and caught hold of the end of
the rod of iron; and they did press their way forward, continually holding

POINT OF INTEREST

Izapa Stela 5, represented at right, is one of many large, carved stones discovered in southern Mexico in 1941 by Smithsonian archaeologist Matthew W. Stirling. Originally known as the Tree of Life stone, it has been noted by many LDS scholars to have a variety of parallels with Lehi's dream.

fast to the rod of iron, until they came forth and fell down and partook of the fruit of the tree.

31. And he also saw other multitudes feeling their way towards that great and spacious building.

32. And it came to pass that many were drowned in the depths of the fountain; and many were lost from his view, wandering in strange roads.

33. And great was the multitude that did enter into that strange building. And after they did enter into that building they did point the finger of scorn at me and those that were partaking of the fruit also; but we heeded them not.

34. These are the words of my father: For as many as heeded them, had fallen away.

35. And Laman and Lemuel partook not of the fruit, said my father.

36. And it came to pass after my father had spoken all the words of his dream or vision, which were many, he said unto us, because of these things which he saw in a vision, he exceedingly feared for Laman and Lemuel; yea, he feared lest they should be cast off from the presence of the Lord.

37. And he did exhort them then with all the feeling of a tender parent, that they would hearken to his words, that perhaps the Lord would be merciful to them, and not cast them off; yea, my father did preach unto them.

38. And after he had preached unto them, and also prophesied unto them of many things, he bade them to keep the commandments of the Lord; and he did cease speaking unto them.

CHAPTER 9

1. AND all these things did my father see, and hear, and speak, as he dwelt in a tent, in the valley of Lemuel, and also a great many more things, which cannot be written upon these plates.

2. And now, as I have spoken concerning these plates, behold they are not the plates upon which I make a full account of the history of my people; for the plates upon which I make a full account of my people I have given the name of Nephi; wherefore, they are called the plates of Nephi, after mine own name; and these plates also are called the plates of Nephi.

3. Nevertheless, I have received a commandment of the Lord that I should make these plates, for the special purpose that there should be an account engraven of the ministry of my people.

4. Upon the other plates should be engraven an account of the reign of the kings, and the wars and contentions of my people; wherefore these plates are for the more part of the ministry; and the other plates are for the more part of the reign of the kings and the wars and contentions of my people.

1 Nephi 9:2

The "full account" is the historical record; the smaller plates of Nephi, or the special account of his ministry, is the ecclesiastical account.

POINT OF INTEREST

Kings of the Divided Kingdoms of Israel

Judah (Southern Kingdom)

957–955 B.C.	*Abijam* *This king found great success in battle against Jeroboam but "walked in all the sins of his father" (1 Kgs. 15:3).*
955–914 B.C.	*Asa* *Asa purged the land of all pagan cults and their sites of worship. He also kept his kingdom free of Egyptian influences for centuries after. At the end of his life, however, he threw the seer Hanani into jail for admonishing him to rely on divine help against Israel's King Baasha.*

5. Wherefore, the Lord hath commanded me to make these plates for a wise purpose in him, which purpose I know not.

6. But the Lord knoweth all things from the beginning; wherefore, he prepareth a way to accomplish all his works among the children of men; for behold, he hath all power unto the fulfilling of all his words. And thus it is. Amen.

CHAPTER 10

1. AND now I, Nephi, proceed to give an account upon these plates of my proceedings, and my reign and ministry; wherefore, to proceed with mine account, I must speak somewhat of the things of my father, and also of my brethren.

2. For behold, it came to pass after my father had made an end of speaking the words of his dream, and also of exhorting them to all diligence, he spake unto them concerning the Jews—

3. That after they should be destroyed, even that great city Jerusalem, and many be carried away captive into Babylon, according to the own due time of the Lord, they should return again, yea, even be brought back out of captivity; and after they should be brought back out of captivity they should possess again the land of their inheritance.

4. Yea, even six hundred years from the time that my father left Jerusalem, a prophet would the Lord God raise up among the Jews—even a Messiah, or, in other words, a Savior of the world.

5. And he also spake concerning the prophets, how great a number had testified of these things, concerning this Messiah, of whom he had spoken, or this Redeemer of the world.

6. Wherefore, all mankind were in a lost and in a fallen state, and ever would be save they should rely on this Redeemer.

7. And he spake also concerning a prophet who should come before the Messiah, to prepare the way of the Lord—

8. Yea, even he should go forth and cry in the wilderness: Prepare ye the way of the Lord, and make his paths straight; for there standeth one among you whom ye know not; and he is mightier than I, whose shoe's latchet I am not worthy to unloose. And much spake my father concerning this thing.

9. And my father said he should baptize in Bethabara, beyond Jordan; and he also said he should

Israel (Northern Kingdom)

954–953 B.C.	*Nadab*
953–930 B.C.	*Baasha*
930–929 B.C.	*Elah*
929 B.C.	*Zimri*
929–918 B.C.	*Omri*
	Each wicked king succeeded the other by murder or, in the case of Omri, by conquest. Omri built the capital city of Samaria and "did worse than all that were before him" (1 Kgs. 16:25).

1 Nephi 9:5–6

Within the scope of the Lord's foreknowledge was a view of an eventual theft of a translated manuscript, which necessitated an alternate plan in order that the world might have the more valuable record of ". . . the ministry and the prophecies, the more plain and precious parts of them, [that] should be written upon these [small] plates. . . ." (1 Ne.19:3). The Lord would not violate the divine principle of the agency of man. He would allow men to exercise their agency, even when it would be contrary to His divine will. Thus, the Lord's alternate plan left intact man's privilege to act with agency. (O/C)

1 Nephi 10–15

The teachings in the chapters listed above clearly mark the Book of Mormon first and foremost as a book concerned with the "foretelling" aspect of prophecy. Several hundred years before the events actually occurred, Lehi and Nephi knew (and saw in vision) major events that were going to happen to their descendants. This foretelling aspect of prophecy is, of course, impossible without the foreknowledge of God—that is, God must know essentially what is going to happen before it happens; otherwise he cannot tell his servants of these things. The crucial question is: Does the fact that God knows something is going to happen *cause* it to happen? If God's foreknowledge *causes* something to happen, this is essentially predestination inasmuch as the free agency of man is destroyed.

Concerning this question, James E. Talmage has written the following:

"Our Heavenly Father has a full knowledge of the nature and disposition of each of His children, a knowledge gained by long observation and experience in the past eternity of our primeval childhood; a knowledge compared with which that gained by earthly parents through mortal experience with their children is infinitesimally small. By reason of that surpassing knowledge, God reads the future of child and children, of men individually and of men collectively as communities and nations; He knows what each will do under given conditions, and sees the end from the beginning. His foreknowledge is based on intelligence and reason. He foresees the future as a state which naturally and surely will be; not as one which must be because He has arbitrarily willed that it shall be. . . .

"The Father of souls has endowed His children with the divine birthright of free agency; He does not and will not control them by arbitrary force; He impels no man toward sin; He compels none to righteousness. Unto man has been given freedom to act for himself; and, associated with this independence, is the fact of strict responsibility and the assurance of individual accountability." (Ludlow)

1 Nephi 10:4

It had been revealed to Nephi in a vision that the Savior or Messiah was to be born among the Jewish people, and 1 Nephi 10:4 indicates that even the exact year in which the Savior was to be born was revealed to him.

baptize with water; even that he should baptize the Messiah with water.
10. And after he had baptized the Messiah with water, he should behold and bear record that he had baptized the Lamb of God, who should take away the sins of the world.
11. And it came to pass after my father had spoken these words he spake unto my brethren concerning the gospel which should bepreached among the Jews, and also concerning the dwindling of the Jews in unbelief. And after they had slain the Messiah, who should come, and after he had been slain he should rise from the dead, and should make himself manifest, by the Holy Ghost, unto the Gentiles.
12. Yea, even my father spake much concerning the Gentiles, and also concerning the house of Israel, that they should be compared like unto an olive-tree, whose branches should be broken off and should be scattered upon all the face of the earth.
13. Wherefore, he said it must needs be that we should be led with one accord into the land of promise, unto the fulfilling of the word of the Lord, that we should be scattered upon all the face of the earth.
14. And after the house of Israel should be scattered they should be gathered together again; or, in fine, after the Gentiles had received the fulness of the Gospel, the natural branches of the olive-tree, or the remnants of the house of Israel, should be grafted in, or come to the knowledge of the true Messiah, their Lord and their Redeemer.
15. And after this manner of language did my father prophesy and speak unto my brethren, and also many more things which I do not write in this book; for I have written as many of them as were expedient for me in mine other book.
16. And all these things, of which I have spoken, were done as my father dwelt in a tent, in the valley of Lemuel.
17. And it came to pass after I, Nephi, having heard all the words of my father, concerning the things which he saw in a vision, and also the things which he spake by the power of the Holy Ghost, which power he received by faith on the Son of God—and the Son of God was the Messiah who should come—I, Nephi, was desirous also that I might see, and hear, and know of these things, by the power of the Holy Ghost, which is the gift of God unto all those who diligently seek him, as well in times of old

POINT OF INTEREST

A primary focus of Stela 5 is a fruit-laden tree resembling the ceiba tree, right, that is so common to the area where the stela was discovered. It is interesting to note that there are twelve distinct roots, which could represent each of the twelve tribes of Israel.

If Nephi is talking in specific rather than general terms, then Lehi left Jerusalem in 600 B.C. on the Christian calendar. That Nephi intends his time reference to be taken literally is indicated by the information contained in the following references: (1) 1 Nephi 19:8: "according to the words of the angel" the Messiah cometh "in six hundred years from the time my father left Jerusalem"; (2) 2 Nephi 25:19: "according to the words of the prophets, the Messiah cometh in six hundred years from the time that my father left Jerusalem"; and (3) 3 Nephi 1:1, 13: "it was six hundred years from the time that Lehi left Jerusalem" and the Savior said "on the morrow come I into the world." (Ludlow)

1 Nephi 10:12

Lehi's comparison of the house of Israel to an olive tree could have come from his reading of the brass plates, which contained the prophet Zenos's allegory of the olive tree quoted by Jacob in Jacob 5.

as in the time that he should manifest himself unto the children of
men.
18. For he is the same yesterday, to-day, and forever; and the way
is prepared for all men from the foundation of the world, if it so be
that they repent and come unto him.
19. For he that diligently seeketh shall find; and the mysteries of
God shall be unfolded unto them, by the power of the Holy Ghost,
as well in these times as in times of old, and as well in times of old
as in times to come; wherefore, the course of the Lord is one eternal round.
20. Therefore remember, O man, for all thy doings thou shalt be
brought into judgment.
21. Wherefore, if ye have sought to do wickedly in the days of your
probation, then ye are found unclean before the judgment-seat of
God; and no unclean thing can dwell with God; wherefore, ye
must be cast off forever.
22. And the Holy Ghost giveth authority that I should speak these
things, and deny them not.

CHAPTER 11

1. FOR it came to pass after I had desired to know the things that my
father had seen, and believing that the Lord was able to make them
known unto me, as I sat pondering in mine heart I was caught away in
the Spirit of the Lord, yea, into an exceedingly high mountain, which
I never had before seen, and upon which I never had before set my
foot.
2. And the Spirit said unto me: Behold, what desirest thou?
3. And I said: I desire to behold the things which my father saw.
4. And the Spirit said unto me: Believest thou that thy father saw
the tree of which he hath spoken?
5. And I said: Yea, thou knowest that I believe all the words of my
father.
6. And when I had spoken these words, the Spirit cried with a loud
voice, saying: Hosanna to the Lord, the most high God; for he is
God over all the earth, yea, even above all. And blessed art thou,
Nephi, because thou believest in the Son of the most high God;
wherefore, thou shalt behold the things which thou hast desired.
7. And behold this thing shall be given unto thee for a sign, that after
thou hast beheld the tree which bore the fruit which thy father tasted, thou shalt also behold a man descending out of heaven, and him
shall ye witness; and after ye have witnessed him ye shall bear record
that it is the Son of God.
8. And it came to pass that the Spirit said unto me: Look! And I

1 Nephi 11:1

Although it is not absolutely clear exactly what happened to Nephi when he was "caught away in the Spirit of the Lord, yea, into an exceeding high mountain" (1 Nephi 11:1), other prophets have referred to their visions and heavenly manifestations in a similar manner. Ezekiel states that the Spirit "lifted" him up "between the earth and the heaven, and brought me in the visions of God to Jerusalem." (Ezekiel 8:3; see also Ezekiel 3:12–27 and 37:1.) Also, Moses was "caught up into an exceedingly high mountain" (Moses 1:1); the Savior was shown the glory of the world from the heights of a mountain (Matthew 4:8); Paul was caught up "to the third heaven" (2 Corinthians 12:2–4); and the apostle John was "in the Spirit" when he saw and heard the great visions he recorded in Revelation (Revelation 1:10). (Ludlow)

1 Nephi 11:3–5

In not doubting his father, yet desiring to know for himself, Nephi provided a great example of honoring parents.

POINT OF INTEREST

Judah (Southern Kingdom)

914–893 B.C. — *Jehoshaphat*
This king spent the beginning of his reign destroying the pagan images and overseeing the instruction of his people in the Mosaic law. In a battle against Moab, Jehoshaphat prayed to the Lord for a deliverance that came when the opposing armies quarrelled and slew one another.

Israel (Northern Kingdom)

918–898 B.C. — *Ahab*
His wife Jezebel turned him to the worship of Baal, and the prophet Elijah demonstrated the Lord's power on Mt. Carmel. Ahab was succeeded by his equally wicked son.

898–897 B.C. — *Ahaziah*

looked and beheld a tree; and it was like unto the tree which my father had seen; and the beauty thereof was far beyond, yea, exceeding of all beauty; and the whiteness thereof did exceed the whiteness of the driven snow.
9. And it came to pass after I had seen the tree, I said unto the Spirit: I behold thou hast shown unto me the tree which is precious above all.
10. And he said unto me: What desirest thou?
11. And I said unto him: To know the interpretation thereof—for I spake unto him as a man speaketh; for I beheld that he was in the form of a man; yet nevertheless, I knew that it was the Spirit of the Lord; and he spake unto me as a man speaketh with another.
12. And it came to pass that he said unto me: Look! And I looked as if to look upon him, and I saw him not; for he had gone from before my presence.
13. And it came to pass that I looked and beheld the great city of Jerusalem, and also other cities. And I beheld the city of Nazareth; and in the city of Nazareth I beheld a virgin, and she was exceedingly fair and white.
14. And it came to pass that I saw the heavens open; and an angel came down and stood before me; and he said unto me: Nephi, what beholdest thou?
15. And I said unto him: A virgin, most beautiful and fair above all other virgins.
16. And he said unto me: Knowest thou the condescension of God?
17. And I said unto him: I know that he loveth his children; nevertheless, I do not know the meaning of all things.
18. And he said unto me: Behold, the virgin whom thou seest is the mother of the Son of God, after the manner of the flesh.
19. And it came to pass that I beheld that she was carried away in the Spirit; and after she had been carried away in the Spirit for the space of a time the angel spake unto me, saying: Look!
20. And I looked and beheld the virgin again, bearing a child in her arms.
21. And the angel said unto me: Behold the Lamb of God, yea, even the Son of the Eternal Father! Knowest thou the meaning of the tree which thy father saw?
22. And I answered him, saying: Yea, it is the love of God, which sheddeth itself abroad in the hearts of the children of men; wherefore, it is the most desirable above all things.
23. And he spake unto me, saying: Yea, and the most joyous to the soul.
24. And after he had said these words, he said unto me: Look! And I looked, and I beheld the Son of God going forth among the children of men; and I saw many fall down at his feet and worship him.
25. And it came to pass that I beheld that the rod of iron, which my father had seen, was the word of God, which led to the fountain of living waters, or to the tree of life;

1 Nephi 11:12–36

The vision recorded in these verses is the central message of the Book of Mormon—that only through the Savior Jesus Christ can we reach the tree of life.

1 Nephi 11:16

The . . . revealed word of God expresses the divine love the Father and the Son have for mortal man. They both descended from their exalted stations to be with and minister to mankind. In Nephi's vision, this divine love, or condescension, is revealed. Our Heavenly Father condescended to be the Father of His divine Son. (See 1 Ne. 11:12–25.) The Son condescended to redeem and save mankind. (See 1 Ne. 11:26–36.)

Pertaining to the condescension of God the Father, Elder Bruce R. McConkie taught, ". . . the condescension of God is that he is the Father literally of a Son born in mortality, in the language here, a Son born 'after the manner of the flesh.'" (O/C)

1 Nephi 11:20

The tree that Lehi and Nephi saw was a sign to them of the divine nature of Jesus Christ. After viewing the tree that his father saw, Nephi desired to know the interpretation thereof. The angel then showed him the birth of the Son of God, His mortal mother, and His divine Father, the Eternal God. (See 1 Ne. 11:9–21.) In the words of the angel: ". . . Behold the Lamb of God, yea, even the Son of the Eternal Father! Knowest thou the meaning of the tree which thy father saw?" (1 Ne. 11:21). Nephi responded by saying: ". . . it is the love of God. . ." (1 Ne. 11:22).

Commenting on the divine nature of Jesus Christ, President Ezra Taft Benson taught, "The Church of Jesus Christ of Latter-day Saints proclaims that Jesus Christ is the Son of God in the most literal sense. The body in which He performed His mission in the flesh was sired by that same Holy Being we worship as God, our Eternal Father. Jesus was not the son of Joseph, nor was He begotten by the Holy Ghost. He is the Son of the Eternal Father." (O/C)

which waters are a representation of the love of God; and I also
beheld that the tree of life was a representation of the love of God.
26. And the angel said unto me again: Look and behold the condescension of God!
27. And I looked and beheld the Redeemer of the world, of whom
my father had spoken; and I also beheld the prophet who should
prepare the way before him. And the Lamb of God went forth and
was baptized of him; and after he was baptized, I beheld the heavens open, and the Holy Ghost come down out of heaven and abide
upon him in the form of a dove.
28. And I beheld that he went forth ministering unto the people,
in power and great glory; and the multitudes were gathered together to hear him; and I beheld that they cast him out from among
them.
29. And I also beheld twelve others following him. And it came to
pass that they were carried away in the Spirit from before my face,
and I saw them not.
30. And it came to pass that the angel spake unto me again, saying: Look! And I looked, and I beheld the heavens open again, and
I saw angels descending upon the children of men; and they did
minister unto them.
31. And he spake unto me again, saying: Look! And I looked, and I
beheld the Lamb of God going forth among the children of men.
And I beheld multitudes of people who were sick, and who were
afflicted with all manner of diseases, and with devils and unclean
spirits; and the angel spake and showed all these things unto me.
And they were healed by the power of the Lamb of God; and the
devils and the unclean spirits were cast out.
32. And it came to pass that the angel spake unto me again, saying:
Look! And I looked and beheld the Lamb of God, that he was taken
by the people; yea, the Son of the everlasting God was judged of the
world; and I saw and bear record.
33. And I, Nephi, saw that he was lifted up upon the cross and
slain for the sins of the world.
34. And after he was slain I saw the multitudes of the earth, that
they were gathered together to fight against the apostles of the
Lamb; for thus were the twelve called by the angel of the Lord.
35. And the multitude of the earth was gathered together; and I
beheld that they were in a large and spacious building, like unto
the building which my father saw. And the angel of the Lord spake
unto me again, saying: Behold the world and the wisdom thereof;
yea, behold the house of Israel hath gathered together to fight
against the twelve apostles of the Lamb.
36. And it came to pass that I saw and bear record, that the great
and spacious building was the pride of the world; and it fell, and
the fall thereof was exceedingly great. And the angel of the Lord
spake unto me

1 Nephi 11:24–36

The "condescension of God" reminds us that the Savior of all manking left His divine throne to enter mortality as a completely helpless human infant, born in the meanest and most humble condition, and that He was willing to take on all the trials associated with mortality.

1 Nephi 11:27

Biblical scholars disagree as to whether or not the Holy Ghost really descended in the "form of a dove" at the time of the baptism of Jesus Christ. In the accounts in Matthew, Mark, and John, the translators have used the construction "like a dove," which could mean that the Holy Ghost descended in the manner of a dove or a bird; however, the account in Luke reads, "And the Holy Ghost descended in a bodily shape like a dove upon him." (Luke 3:22.)

The Prophet Joseph Smith has explained that these terms all mean that the Spirit descended "in the sign of the dove." His inspired statement is as follows:

"The sign of the dove was instituted before the creation of the world, a witness for the Holy Ghost, and the devil cannot come in the sign of a dove. The Holy Ghost is a personage, and is in the form of a personage. It does not confine itself to the *form* of a dove, but in *sign* of the dove. The Holy Ghost cannot be transformed into a dove; but the sign of a dove was given to John to signify the truth of the deed, as the dove is an emblem or token of truth and innocence." (Ludlow)

1 Nephi 11:29; 12:8–10

In fulfillment of this prophecy [3 Nephi 12:8–10], when the Savior came to the Nephites, he chose twelve men and gave them authority to minister in his name among the Nephites on this American continent in all the ordinances essential to their salvation. These twelve went forth healing the sick, performing many miracles, and administering the ordinances as they had been commanded to do. The fulness of the gospel, with the power and the authority of the Melchizedek Priesthood, was given to the Nephites the same as it was to the Church on the Eastern Hemisphere. . . .

While in every instance the Nephite Twelve are spoken of as disciples, the fact remains that they had been endowed with divine authority to be special witnesses for Christ among their own people. Therefore, they were virtually apostles to the Nephite race, although their jurisdiction was, as revealed to Nephi, eventually to be subject to the authority and jurisdiction of Peter and the Twelve chosen in Palestine.

According to the definition prevailing in the world, an apostle is a witness for Christ, or one who evangelizes a certain nation or people, "a zealous advocate of a doctrine or cause." Therefore, in this sense the Nephite Twelve became apostles, as special witnesses, just as did Joseph Smith and Oliver Cowdery in the dispensation of the fulness of times. (Ludlow)

again, saying: Thus shall be the destruction of all nations, kindreds, tongues, and people, that shall fight against the twelve apostles of the Lamb.

CHAPTER 12

1. AND it came to pass that the angel said unto me: Look, and
behold thy seed, and also the seed of thy brethren. And I looked
and beheld the land of promise; and I beheld multitudes of people,
yea, even as it were in number as many as the sand of the sea.
2. And it came to pass that I beheld multitudes gathered together
to battle, one against the other; and I beheld wars, and rumors of
wars, and great slaughters with the sword among my people.
3. And it came to pass that I beheld many generations pass away,
after the manner of wars and contentions in the land; and I beheld
many cities, yea, even that I did not number them.
4. And it came to pass that I saw a mist of darkness on the face of the
land of promise; and I saw lightnings, and I heard thunderings, and
earthquakes, and all manner of tumultuous noises; and I saw the earth
and the rocks, that they rent; and I saw mountains tumbling into
pieces; and I saw the plains of the earth, that they were broken up; and
I saw many cities that they were sunk; and I saw many that they were
burned with fire; and I saw many that did tumble to the earth, because
of the quaking thereof.
5. And it came to pass after I saw these things, I saw the vapor of
darkness, that it passed from off the face of the earth; and
behold, I saw multitudes who had not fallen because of the
great and terrible judgments of the Lord.
6. And I saw the heavens open, and the Lamb of God
descending out of heaven; and he came down and
showed himself unto them.
7. And I also saw and bear record that the Holy
Ghost fell upon twelve others; and they were
ordained of God, and chosen.
8. And the angel spake unto me, saying: Behold
the twelve disciples of the Lamb, who are chosen to minister unto thy seed.
9. And he said unto me: Thou rememberest
the twelve apostles of the Lamb? Behold they
are they who shall judge the twelve tribes of
Israel; wherefore, the twelve ministers of thy
seed shall be judged of them; for ye are of the
house of Israel.
10. And these twelve ministers whom thou
beholdest shall judge thy seed. And,
behold, they are righteous forever; for
because of their faith in the Lamb of God
their garments are made white in his
blood.
11. And the angel said unto me: Look!
And I looked, and beheld three generations
pass away in

POINT OF INTEREST

Stela 5 contains more than a hundred items, including gods, humans, animals, plants, and tools. Central to the image is the tree of life or world tree surrounded by twenty-two figures, including thirteen humans. Six humans on the ground around the tree likely represent the ancestral family of Izapan civilization as related in a sacred book of the Quiche Maya, the Popul Vuh. They have been compared to Lehi's family and are engaged in a form of worshipful instruction. Note how the following images compare to Lehi's account.

Stela 5 symbols:

1. *Tree of life/world tree with guardian spirits*
2. *River flows down from rain into water*
3. *Path goes from river head to the tree*
4. *Broad line next to path goes to the tree*

righteousness; and their garments were white even like unto the Lamb of God. And the angel said unto me: These are made white in the blood of the Lamb, because of their faith in him.
12. And I, Nephi, also saw many of the fourth generation who passed away in righteousness.
13. And it came to pass that I saw the multitudes of the earth gathered together.
14. And the angel said unto me: Behold thy seed, and also the seed of thy brethren.
15. And it came to pass that I looked and beheld the people of my seed gathered together in multitudes against the seed of my brethren; and they were gathered together to battle.
16. And the angel spake unto me, saying: Behold the fountain of filthy water which thy father saw; yea, even the river of which he spake; and the depths thereof are the depths of hell.
17. And the mists of darkness are the temptations of the devil, which blindeth the eyes, and hardeneth the hearts of the children of men, and leadeth them away into broad roads, that they perish and are lost.
18. And the large and spacious building, which thy father saw, is vain imaginations and the pride of the children of men. And a great and a terrible gulf divideth them; yea, even the word of the justice of the Eternal God, and the Messiah who is the Lamb of God, of whom the Holy Ghost beareth record, from the beginning of the world until this time, and from this time henceforth and forever.
19. And while the angel spake these words, I beheld and saw that the seed of my brethren did contend against my seed, according to the word of the angel; and because of the pride of my seed, and the temptations of the devil, I beheld that the seed of my brethren did overpower the people of my seed.
20. And it came to pass that I beheld, and saw the people of the seed of my brethren that they had overcome my seed; and they went forth in multitudes upon the face of the land.
21. And I saw them gathered together in multitudes; and I saw wars and rumors of wars among them; and in wars and rumors of wars I saw many generations pass away.
22. And the angel said unto me: Behold these shall dwindle in unbelief.
23. And it came to pass that I beheld, after they had dwindled in unbelief they became a dark, and loathsome, and a filthy people, full of idleness and all manner of abominations.

1 Nephi 12:17

Unless . . . [individuals] were exposed to temptation they never could know themselves, their own powers, their own weaknesses nor the power of God. If Satan had no power to tempt mankind, they would be in a state where they could neither know good nor evil; they could not know happiness nor misery. All their powers would lie dormant, for they would be destitute of that experience which prepares men to become like God, their Eternal Father (George Q. Cannon, *Gospel Truths*, 1:109).

5. Open field at the head of the river of dark mist (Fig. 8)
6. Generic figure from field
7. "Boxed man" symbol is the most elevated
8. Dark mist glyph includes bands to blind the eyes of Figure 6
9. Bird-serpent god leads to tree
10. Traveler led by Figure 9
11. Six figures represent parents, two younger brothers, and two older brothers subdued by the younger
12. Person at tree blinded by hood
13. Figure at tree receives fruit
14. High priest attends burnt sacrifice
15. Priest-king (Fig. 11c) directs worship

Each of the No. 11 figures could possibly represent a member of Lehi's family:
11a. Lehi attending a sacrificial altar or fire
11b. Sariah
11c. Nephi holds a stylus and is shaded by a parasol, an ancient symbol for royalty
11d. Sam is also shaded by the parasol and holds it in a supportive role
11e. Lemuel has his back to the tree
11f. Laman is also facing away from the tree

CHAPTER 13

1. AND it came to pass that the angel spake unto me, saying: Look! And I looked and beheld many nations and kingdoms.
2. And the angel said unto me: What beholdest thou? And I said: I behold many nations and kingdoms.
3. And he said unto me: These are the nations and kingdoms of the Gentiles.
4. And it came to pass that I saw among the nations of the Gentiles the formation of a great church.
5. And the angel said unto me: Behold the formation of a church which is most abominable above all other churches, which slayeth the saints of God, yea, and tortureth them and bindeth them down, and yoketh them with a yoke of iron, and bringeth them down into captivity.
6. And it came to pass that I beheld this great and abominable church; and I saw the devil that he was the founder of it.
7. And I also saw gold, and silver, and silks, and scarlets, and fine-twined linen, and all manner of precious clothing; and I saw many harlots.
8. And the angel spake unto me, saying: Behold the gold, and the silver, and the silks, and the scarlets, and the fine-twined linen, and the precious clothing, and the harlots, are the desires of this great and abominable church.
9. And also for the praise of the world do they destroy the saints of God, and bring them down into captivity.
10. And it came to pass that I looked and beheld many waters; and they divided the Gentiles from the seed of my brethren.
11. And it came to pass that the angel said unto me: Behold the wrath of God is upon the seed of thy brethren.
12. And I looked and beheld a man among the Gentiles, who was separated from the seed of my brethren by the many waters; and I beheld the Spirit of God, that it came down and wrought upon the man; and he went forth upon the many waters, even unto the seed of my brethren, who were in the promised land.
13. And it came to pass that I beheld the Spirit of God, that it wrought upon other Gentiles; and they went forth out of captivity, upon the many waters.
14. And it came to pass that I beheld many multitudes of the Gentiles upon the land of promise; and I beheld the wrath of God, that it was upon the seed of my brethren; and they were scattered before the Gentiles and were smitten.
15. And I beheld the Spirit of the Lord, that it was upon the Gentiles, and they did prosper and obtain the land for their inheritance; and I beheld that they were white, and exceedingly fair and beautiful, like unto my people before they were slain.
16. And it came to pass that I, Nephi, beheld that the Gentiles who had gone forth out of captivity did humble themselves before the Lord; and the power of the Lord was with them.
17. And I beheld that their mother Gentiles were gathered together

1 Nephi 13:3

The Nephites considered "Jews" to be people from the kingdom of Judah; the "Gentiles" were those from all other areas. The "nations and kingdoms of the Gentiles" referred to in this vision are the nations of Europe, to which many Latter-day Saints trace their ancestry.

1 Nephi 13:3

The scene is Europe and its inhabitants, who are called Gentiles. (See 1 Ne. 13:3.) The term *Gentile* is one that has variable usage. It can mean "non-Israelite" or "non-Jew," and among Latter-day Saints the term is sometimes used to mean "non-Mormon." But in the Book of Mormon, it commonly refers to the people of the world who are citizens of the great Christian nations. Elder Orson Whitney taught the following: "The word 'Gentile,' as used in 'Mormon' writings, is not a term of reproach. It comes from 'Gentilis,' meaning 'of a nation,' and is used in sacred history to designate the nations not of Israel. The Latter-day Saints are Gentiles in part; for while they claim literal descent from the Hebrew patriarchs, it is mostly through Ephraim, who 'mixed himself among the people,' (Hosea 7:8)—that is, among the peoples that have furnished proselytes to 'Mormonism' . . ." (O/C)

1 Nephi 13:4–6, 26, 28;14:10

These verses refer to the "great and abominable church" (which was established by Satan) and the gospel, or Church, of "the Lamb" (which was established by the Savior). The great determining factor is a question of loyalty: regardless of where your membership records are, to which lifestyle are you devoted?

1 Nephi 13:4–9, 28; 14:9–17

The terms "church of the devil" and "great and abominable church" are apparently used with two senses in the Book of Mormon.

1. All churches that are not the true church of Christ are false churches, and they thus represent the "church of the devil" to the extent that they contain error and lead people away from the true church and its saving principles and ordinances. As the Lord stated in the New Testament: "He that is not with me is against me." (Matthew 12:30.)

2. The "mother of abominations" (1 Nephi 14:9) that is "most abominable above all other churches" (1 Nephi 13:5) and is described in detail (1 Nephi 13:1–9, 26–29; 14:10–17; 22:13–14) as being the source of religious persecution and bigotry after the ministry of Christ (1 Nephi 13:26–28) might refer to the "mother" church from which other so-called Christian churches have protested or rebelled.

Elder Bruce R. McConkie has defined these terms:

"The titles *church of the devil* and *great and abominable church* are used to identify all churches or organizations of whatever name or nature—whether political, philosophical, educational, economic, social, fraternal, civic, or religious—which are designed to take men on a course that leads away from God and his laws and thus from salvation in the kingdom of God. . . .

"The resurrected Christ gave to the Nephites this test whereby they might distinguish the true Church from any other:

"1. It would be called in his name, for 'how be it my church save it be called in my name?' he said.

"2. It would be built upon his gospel, that is, the eternal plan of salvation with all its saving powers and graces would be had in it.

"3. The Father would show forth his works in it, meaning that miracles, righteousness, and every good fruit would abound in it.

"4. It would not be hewn down and cast into the fire as must surely come to pass with the great and abominable church. 'If it be not built upon my gospel, and is built upon the works of men, or upon the works of the devil, verily I say unto you they have joy in their works for a season, and by and by the end cometh, and they are hewn down and cast into the fire, from whence there is no return' (3 Ne. 27:4–12)." (Ludlow)

1 Nephi 13:6

The vision of Nephi is concluded. Nephi sees the blessings and cursings concerning the Gentiles, the conflict between the great and abominable church and the Church of the Lamb of God, and the revelations given to the Apostle John. The angel explains to Nephi that there are only two churches: the Church of the Lamb of God and the church of the devil. Due to the wickedness of mankind, the wrath of the Lord is poured out upon the great and abominable church, and there will also be wars and rumors of war.

Elder Bruce R. McConkie said, "The titles church of the devil and great and abominable church are used to identify all churches or organizations of whatever name or nature—whether political, philosophical, educational, economic, social, fraternal, civic, or religious—which are designed to take men on a course that leads away from God and his laws and thus from salvation in the kingdom of God. . . ." (P/A)

1 Nephi 13:12

[The Angel Moroni] was with Columbus, and gave him deep impressions, by dreams and by visions, respecting this New World. Tramelled by poverty and by an unpopular cause, yet his persevering and unyielding heart would not allow an obstacle in his way too great for him to overcome; and the angel of God helped him—was with him on the stormy deep, calmed the troubled elements, and guided his frail vessel to the desired haven (Orson Hyde, *Journal of Discourses*, 6:368).

1 Nephi 13:12

This prophecy apparently refers to the coming of Christopher Columbus to the continent that was later called the American continent. Abundant evidences exist that indicate Columbus was "wrought upon" by the Spirit of God as was shown unto Nephi. In his book *Columbus, Don Quixote of the Seas*, Jacob Wasserman quotes directly from the writings of Columbus as follows:

"From my first youth onward, I was a seaman, and have so continued until this day. . . . The Lord was well disposed to my desire, and he bestowed upon me courage and understanding. . . . Our Lord with provident hand unlocked my mind, sent me upon seas, and gave me fire for the deed. Those who heard of my emprise called it foolish, mocked me, and laughed. But who can doubt but that the Holy Ghost inspired me?"

Later in his book, Wasserman quotes from a letter written to King Ferdinand by Columbus wherein he said, "I came to your majesty as the emissary of the Holy Ghost." (Ludlow)

1 Nephi 13:12–19

The angel continued to show Nephi the future. Nephi saw the rise of the church of the devil, witnessed the discovery of America in modern times, saw that plain and precious things were taken out of the Bible, viewed events related to the Apostasy, and rejoiced over the Restoration of the gospel in latter days, including the coming forth of the Book of Mormon and other scriptures and the building up of Zion.

Among the gentile nations, Nephi saw the formation of the great and abominable church founded by the devil. The desires of this church were to have the things of the world and to bring the Saints down into captivity. It was this church that took the plain and precious things away from the Bible, causing so many to stumble, insomuch that Satan gained power over them. Nephi saw, however, that the Lord would remember the seed of his lineage and restore the plain and precious things, which shall come forth to all people.

The Spirit of God worked upon the Gentiles (Columbus and others) and brought them to the promised land, from which will flow the restored gospel. The Gentiles humbled themselves before the Lord and they were protected by the power of the Lord. We can surely see the importance of the coming forth of the Book of Mormon to restore the gospel (including the plain and precious things) that all might come to know and understand the true doctrine and the plan of redemption . . . that all might come unto Christ.

President Ezra Taft Benson taught that every priesthood member "should understand the divine plan designed by the Lord to raise up the first free people in modern times." (P/A)

Summarizing President Benson's list, this is how scripture says the "divine plan" was achieved:

1. God purposefully kept the American continent hidden until after the Roman Empire was divided and its various nations had established their independence (see 2 Ne. 1:6, 8).
2. At the proper time, God inspired Columbus to overcome tremendous odds and discover America (see 1 Ne. 13:12).
3. Europeans hoping to escape tyranny and oppression wanted to flee to America (see 1 Ne. 13:13–16).
4. European nations would try to dominate the people who had fled to America, but the American settlers would win their war for independence (see 1 Ne. 13:16–19).
5. The Gentiles who came to America would establish it as a land of liberty that would not have kings (see 2 Ne. 10:8–14).
6. God raised up a group of intelligent and inspired leaders to write the Constitution and establish the first truly free people in modern times (see D&C 101:80).
7. God declared that the United States Constitution was divinely inspired for the express purpose of eliminating bondage and preventing the violation of human rights and protection (see D&C 101:77–80).
8. God mandated that His people defend the Constitutional laws of the land (see D&C 98:5–10).

1 Nephi 13:16

The Lord, in His infinite wisdom, knew that the gospel of liberty and truth could be restored to the earth only in an environment where the principles of liberty and truth were honored and constitutionally secured unto each individual (see D&C 134; 98:5–6; 101:77, 80). He therefore prepared the seedbed of the Restoration by empowering an emerging segment of the gentile flock "who did humble themselves before the Lord" (1 Ne. 13:16, as Nephi saw it in vision) and caused that they should be "lifted up by the power of God above all nations, upon the face of the land which is choice above all other lands" (v. 30). It was this new gentile nation that would be blessed to facilitate the coming forth of the restored word of God in all of its purity and fulness so that the covenant promises to Israel could be fulfilled. (P/A)

1 Nephi 13:17–19

General George Washington repeatedly stated during the Revolutionary War—and most forcefully at its conclusion—that the independence the American troops won was a gift of God to the American colonies. WIthout that gift, he repeatedly maintained, the American armies by themselves were far too weak to win victory.

upon the waters, and upon the land also, to battle against them.
18. And I beheld that the power of God was with them, and also that the wrath of God was upon all those that were gathered together against them to battle.
19. And I, Nephi, beheld that the Gentiles that had gone out of captivity were delivered by the power of God out of the hands of all other nations.
20. And it came to pass that I, Nephi, beheld that they did prosper in the land; and I beheld a book, and it was carried forth among them.
21. And the angel said unto me: Knowest thou the meaning of the book?
22. And I said unto him: I know not.
23. And he said: Behold it proceedeth out of the mouth of a Jew. And I, Nephi, beheld it; and he said unto me: The book that thou beholdest is a record of the Jews, which contains the covenants of the Lord, which he hath made unto the house of Israel; and it also containeth many of the prophecies of the holy prophets; and it is a record like unto the engravings which are upon the plates of brass, save there are not so many; nevertheless, they contain the covenants of the Lord, which he hath made unto the house of Israel; wherefore, they are of great worth unto the Gentiles.
24. And the angel of the Lord said unto me: Thou hast beheld that the book proceeded forth from the mouth of a Jew; and when it proceeded forth from the mouth of a Jew it contained the fulness of the gospel of the Lord, of whom the twelve apostles bear record; and they bear record according to the truth which is in the Lamb of God.
25. Wherefore, these things go forth from the Jews in purity unto the Gentiles, according to the truth which is in God.
26. And after they go forth by the hand of the twelve apostles of the Lamb, from the Jews unto the Gentiles, thou seest the formation of a great and abominable church, which is most abominable above all other churches; for behold, they have taken away from the gospel of the Lamb many parts which are plain and most precious; and also many covenants of the Lord have they taken away.
27. And all this have they done that they might pervert the right ways of the Lord, that they might blind the eyes and harden the hearts of the children of men.
28. Wherefore, thou seest that after the book hath gone forth through the hands of the great and abominable church, that there are many plain and precious things taken away from the book, which is the book of the Lamb of God.
29. And after these plain and precious things were taken away it goeth forth unto all the nations of the Gentiles; and after it goeth forth unto all the nations of the Gentiles, yea, even across the many waters which thou hast seen with the Gentiles which have gone forth out of captivity, thou seest—because of the many plain and precious things which have been taken out of the

1 Nephi 13:20–23

The book that Nephi beheld in vision and which "proceedeth out of the mouth of a Jew" and contained "a record of the Jews" (1 Nephi 13:23) is evidently our present Old Testament. Reynolds and Sjodahl indicate in the following statement the appropriateness of these terms in referring to the Old Testament.

The prophet is here speaking of the Old Testament, as it was to appear through the labors of Ezra and his associates and successors.

When Lehi left Jerusalem, the so-called canon of the Old Testament, as we know it, was not yet completed. The five books of Moses, undoubtedly, had been collected and written on one roll, numerous copies of which must have been in existence. The writings of the prophets, such as Joshua, the Judges, Samuel, Kings down to the reign of Zedekiah, and the prophecies of Isaiah, Hosea, Amos, Micah, and parts of Jeremiah, and their contemporaries, Joel, Amos and Jonah, must have existed in separate volumes, and individual collectors may have owned more or less complete sets. The Book of Job, some of the Psalms, the Proverbs, the Song of Solomon, and Ecclesiastes were also known, even if not generally accepted as sacred scripture. There were also books by authors whose names are mentioned in the Bible, but whose writings have not come down to us. The collection of Laban, known in the Book of Mormon as the Brass Plates, must have been unusually complete, judging from the contents. It must have been a very valuable library. Such libraries must have been owned by prominent individuals.

Ezra undertook the work of collecting all the sacred writings that existed at his time. This work included not only the discovery of copies in various places, the rejection of those that were not authentic and the copying of manuscripts the contents of which could not otherwise be secured, but also the correction of the text, after careful examination of the variations that must have been found. It was this work that was shown to Nephi in his vision of the Old Testament, and therefore, he, very properly, says he beheld it coming "out of the mouth of a Jew."

This expression appears still more significant when we recall the fact that Ezra, after the completion of the Pentateuch, gathered the people and read it to them and expounded it for seven days, and submitted it to them for their acceptance (Nehemiah 8:1–18; 9:3). Then it, literally, proceeded out of the mouth of a Jew. This took place about 445 B.C., about 150 years after the exodus of Lehi.

The canon was gradually completed by the addition of the writings of Ezra, Nehemiah, and the prophets who lived during and after the exile, Ezekiel, Daniel, Obadiah, Habakkuk, Zephaniah, Haggai, Zechariah, and Malachi. The canon as thus completed was accepted by our Lord Himself, and it is, in this remarkable vision, called, on that account, "The Book of the Lamb of God" (1 Nephi 13:38). (Ludlow)

book, which were plain unto the understanding of the children of men, according to the plainness which is in the Lamb of God—because of these things which are taken away out of the gospel of the Lamb, an exceedingly great many do stumble, yea, insomuch that Satan hath great power over them.
30. Nevertheless, thou beholdest that the Gentiles who have gone forth out of captivity, and have been lifted up by the power of God above all other nations, upon the face of the land which is choice above all other lands, which is the land that the Lord God hath covenanted with thy father that his seed should have for the land of their inheritance; wherefore, thou seest that the Lord God will not suffer that the Gentiles will utterly destroy the mixture of thy seed, which are among thy brethren.
31. Neither will he suffer that the Gentiles shall destroy the seed of thy brethren.
32. Neither will the Lord God suffer that the Gentiles shall forever remain in that awful state of blindness, which thou beholdest they are in, because of the plain and most precious parts of the gospel of the Lamb which have been kept back by that abominable church, whose formation thou hast seen.
33. Wherefore saith the Lamb of God: I will be merciful unto the Gentiles, unto the visiting of the remnant of the house of Israel in great judgment.
34. And it came to pass that the angel of the Lord spake unto me, saying: Behold, saith the Lamb of God, after I have visited the remnant of the house of Israel—and this remnant of whom I speak is the seed of thy father—wherefore, after I have visited them in judgment, and smitten them by the hand of the Gentiles, and after the Gentiles do stumble exceedingly, because of the most plain and precious parts of the gospel of the Lamb which have been kept back by that abominable church, which is the mother of harlots, saith the Lamb—I will be merciful unto the Gentiles in that day, insomuch that I will bring forth unto them, in mine own power, much of my gospel, which shall be plain and precious, saith the Lamb.
35. For, behold, saith the Lamb: I will manifest myself unto thy seed, that they shall write many things which I shall minister unto them, which shall be plain and precious; and after thy seed shall be destroyed, and dwindle in unbelief, and also the seed of thy brethren, behold, these things shall be hid up, to come forth unto the Gentiles, by the gift and power of the Lamb.
36. And in them shall be written my gospel, saith the Lamb, and my rock and my salvation.
37. And blessed are they who shall seek to bring forth my Zion at that day, for they shall have the gift and the power of the Holy Ghost; and if they endure unto the end they

1 Ne 13:29

The church of the devil has successfully concealed its intent and designs of spiritual destruction of Father's children by openly endorsing and proclaiming the fragmented Bible as the fulness of the word of God. Multitudes of people have been enticed into thinking the current biblical text is adequate for the salvation of mankind. People who are unaware of the removal of precious parts are deceived into thinking they have the gospel in its fulness and need nothing more. So what exactly was taken out of the Bible that causes such stumbling blocks for the people? In an editorial published by The Church of Jesus Christ of Latter-day Saints, we read what the ancient biblical text was really like:

"The most striking thing about it was that, as originally written, the Old Testament WAS A TESTIMONY AND WITNESS FOR CHRIST! . . .

"If we had the Old Testament as it was originally written, mankind would have a most powerful—an infallible—witness that Jesus of Nazareth was indeed the Christ, that He gave the Law to Moses, that He was the God of Abraham, Isaac and Jacob, and that His coming into mortality was plainly foretold in a detailed manner, in holy writ. . . .

"The witness for Christ was the most important thing in that ancient record, and that is what was eliminated by enemies of Christ who sought to destroy all scriptural marks of identification which might have clearly identified Him as the Savior of the world. . . ." (O/C)

POINT OF INTEREST

After the conquest of the land of Canaan, the Twelve Tribes of Israel were given lands of inheritance by the prophet Joshua. They remained fairly independent throughout the period of the Judges until about 1095 B.C., when they formed a united monarchy under the newly anointed king, Saul. Israel remained a united kingdom during the reigns of Saul, David, and Solomon, after which the northern ten tribes rebelled against Solomon's son Rehoboam (975 B.C.), and formed a separate kingdom under Jeroboam. This northern kingdom, referred to as Israel (or Ephraim, after the dominant tribe), was eventually scattered by Assyria in 721 or 722 B.C., and has therefore become known as "the lost ten tribes." The southern kingdom, known as Judah, consisted of the tribes of Judah and Benjamin and was conquered by Babylon in 587 B.C. Thus began a period of captivity known as the Babylonian Exile, which ended fifty years later when King Cyrus of Persia allowed the Jews to return and rebuild Jerusalem. The name Canaan *is seen at left as found at the Merneptah Stele in the thirteenth century B.C.*

shall be lifted up at the last day, and shall be saved in the everlasting kingdom of the Lamb; and whoso shall publish peace, yea, tidings of great joy, how beautiful upon the mountains shall they be.
38. And it came to pass that I beheld the remnant of the seed of my
brethren, and also the book of the Lamb of God, which had proceeded forth from the mouth of the Jew, that it came forth from the
Gentiles unto the remnant of the seed of my brethren.
39. And after it had come forth unto them I beheld other books,
which came forth by the power of the Lamb, from the Gentiles
unto them, unto the convincing of the Gentiles and the remnant
of the seed of my brethren, and also the Jews who were scattered
upon all the face of the earth, that the records of the prophets and
of the twelve apostles of the Lamb are true.
40. And the angel spake unto me, saying: These last records, which
thou hast seen among the Gentiles, shall establish the truth of the
first, which are of the twelve apostles of the Lamb, and shall make
known the plain and precious things which have been taken away
from them; and shall make known to all kindreds, tongues, and people, that the Lamb of God is the Son of the Eternal Father, and the
Savior of the world; and that all men must come unto him, or they
cannot be saved.
41. And they must come according to the words which shall be
established by the mouth of the Lamb; and the words of the Lamb
shall be made known in the records of thy seed, as well as in the
records of the twelve apostles of the Lamb; wherefore they both shall
be established in one; for there is one God and one Shepherd over
all the earth.
42. And the time cometh that he shall manifest himself unto all
nations, both unto the Jews and also unto the Gentiles; and after he
has manifested himself unto the Jews and also unto the Gentiles,
then he shall manifest himself unto the Gentiles and also unto the
Jews, and the last shall be first, and the first shall be last.

CHAPTER 14

1. AND it shall come to pass, that if the Gentiles shall hearken
unto the Lamb of God in that day that he shall manifest himself
unto them in word, and also in power, in very deed, unto the taking away of their stumbling blocks—
2. And harden not their hearts

1 Nephi 13:39–40

Elder Joseph Fielding Smith taught that the other books which were to come forth in the last days ". . . are the Book of Mormon, the Doctrine and Covenants, and the revelations of the Lord to Joseph Smith. . . ." These books contain the fulness of the gospel, written to convince the world of the divinity of Jesus Christ, teaching people how they can come unto Him. They provide principles and precepts by which His kingdom is governed and His people are saved. These books contain plain and precious things. (O/C)

1 Nephi 13:40

The "last records" referred to in 1 Nephi 13:40 would include the Book of Mormon, the Doctrine and Covenants, the Pearl of Great Price, and any future scriptures that are yet to come forth from the true church of Jesus Christ. One purpose of the coming forth of these latter-day scriptures is to "establish the truth of the first" records referred to by the angel—our present Bible. This is one reason why Latter-day Saints refer to the Book of Mormon as a "second witness of the Bible" that helps to restore many of the essential doctrines and ordinances of the gospel. (Ludlow)

POINT OF INTEREST

After Nebuchadnezzar II (pictured in this engraving from a Marduk statue) captured Jerusalem in 597 B.C., he put Zedekiah on the throne. A weak and vacillating ruler, Zedekiah sometimes consulted with the prophet Jeremiah and sometimes threw Jeremiah in prison for revealing the Lord's will. When Zedekiah united with Egypt against Babylon, he brought about the siege and destruction of Jerusalem and its temple in 586 B.C.

against the Lamb of God, they shall be numbered among the seed of thy father; yea, they shall be numbered among the house of Israel; and they shall be a blessed people upon the promised land forever; they shall be no more brought down into captivity; and the house of Israel shall no more be confounded.

3. And that great pit, which hath been digged for them by that great and abominable church, which was founded by the devil and his children, that he might lead away the souls of men down to hell—yea, that great pit which hath been digged for the destruction of men shall be filled by those who digged it, unto their utter destruction, saith the Lamb of God; not the destruction of the soul, save it be the casting of it into that hell which hath no end.

4. For behold, this is according to the captivity of the devil, and also according to the justice of God, upon all those who will work wickedness and abomination before him.

5. And it came to pass that the angel spake unto me, Nephi, saying: Thou hast beheld that if the Gentiles repent it shall be well with them; and thou also knowest concerning the covenants of the Lord unto the house of Israel; and thou also hast heard that whoso repenteth not must perish.

6. Therefore, wo be unto the Gentiles if it so be that they harden their hearts against the Lamb of God.

7. For the time cometh, saith the Lamb of God, that I will work a great and a marvelous work among the children of men; a work which shall be everlasting, either on the one hand or on the other—either to the convincing of them unto peace and life eternal, or unto the deliverance of them to the hardness of their hearts and the blindness of their minds unto their being brought down into captivity, and also into destruction, both temporally and spiritually, according to the captivity of the devil, of which I have spoken.

8. And it came to pass that when the angel had spoken these words, he said unto me: Rememberest thou the covenants of the Father unto the house of Israel? I said unto him, Yea.

9. And it came to pass that he said unto me: Look, and behold that great and abominable church, which is the mother of abominations, whose founder is the devil.

10. And he said unto me: Behold there are save two churches only; the one is the church of the Lamb of God, and the other is the church of the devil; wherefore, whoso belongeth not to the church of the Lamb of God belongeth to that great church, which is the mother of abominations; and she is the whore of all the earth.

11. And it came to pass that I

1 Nephi 14:10

Elder B. H. Roberts discussed the far-reaching structure and influence of the devil's church as follows: "'The church of the devil' here alluded to, I understand to mean not any particular church among men, or any one sect of religion, but something larger than that—something that includes within its boundaries all evil wherever it may be found; as well in systems of ethics as in systems of religion—something that includes the whole empire of Satan—what I shall call 'The Kingdom of Evil'" (*Defense of the Faith and the Saints* [Salt Lake City: Deseret News, 1907], 1:30). (O/C)

POINT OF INTEREST

Judah (Southern Kingdom)

893–885 B.C.	*Joram* *This king formed a shaky alliance with the Northern Kingdom by marrying Ahab's daughter.*
885–884 B.C.	*Ahaziah* *Also called Jehoahaz, he united unsuccessfully with Israel against Aramea.*
884–878 B.C.	*Athaliah* *Joram's wife and Ahaziah's mother, Athaliah sought revenge for the murders of her son and brother and ordered the execution of all possible successors to David. One of her grandsons escaped the purge and was raised in secret by the priest Jehoiada.*
878–841 B.C.	*Joash* *Also known as Jehoash, he was seven years old when Jehoiada annointed him king and had Queen Athaliah put to death. Joash's reign was righteous as long as Jehoiada lived, but after the prophet's death, Joash turned to other gods and put the prophet Zechariah to death.*

Israel (Northern Kingdom)

897–884 B.C.	*Jehoram* *Another of Israel's wicked kings, he allied with Judah against Armea. He was wounded during the conflict and was then slain by his general, Jehu.*
884–856 B.C.	*Jehu* *The prophet Elisha instructed one of his students to annoint Jehu king, after which Jehu took his army to slay Jehoram. He put all the worshippers of Baal to death, although he left the idols at Dan and Bethel.*
856–842 B.C.	*Jehoahaz* *He was initially faithful, but soon he and his people returned to idol worship.*

looked and beheld the whore of all the earth, and she sat upon many waters; and she had dominion over all the earth, among all nations, kindreds, tongues, and people.

12. And it came to pass that I beheld the church of the Lamb of God, and its numbers were few, because of the wickedness and abominations of the whore who sat upon many waters; nevertheless, I beheld that the church of the Lamb, who were the saints of God, were also upon all the face of the earth; and their dominions upon the face of the earth were small, because of the wickedness of the great whore whom I saw.

13. And it came to pass that I beheld that the great mother of abominations did gather together multitudes upon the face of all the earth, among all the nations of the Gentiles, to fight against the Lamb of God.

14. And it came to pass that I, Nephi, beheld the power of the Lamb of God, that it descended upon the saints of the church of the Lamb, and upon the covenant people of the Lord, who were scattered upon all the face of the earth; and they were armed with righteousness and with the power of God in great glory.

15. And it came to pass that I beheld that the wrath of God was poured out upon that great and abominable church, insomuch that there were wars and rumors of wars among all the nations and kindreds of the earth.

16. And as there began to be wars and rumors of wars among all the nations which belonged to the mother of abominations, the angel spake unto me, saying: Behold, the wrath of God is upon the mother of harlots; and behold, thou seest all these things—

17. And when the day cometh that the wrath of God is poured out upon the mother of harlots, which is the great and abominable church of all the earth, whose founder is the devil, then, at that day, the work of the Father shall commence, in preparing the way for the fulfilling of his covenants, which he hath made to his people who are of the house of Israel.

18. And it came to pass that the angel spake unto me, saying: Look!

19. And I looked and beheld a man, and he was dressed in a white robe.

20. And the angel said unto me: Behold one of the twelve apostles of the Lamb.

21. Behold, he shall see and write the remainder of these things; yea, and also many things which have been.

22. And he shall also write concerning the end of the world.

23. Wherefore, the things which he shall write are just and true; and behold they are written in the book which thou beheld proceeding out of the mouth of the Jew; and at the time they proceeded out of the mouth of the Jew, or, at the time the book proceeded out of the mouth of the Jew, the things which were written were plain and pure, and most precious and easy to the understanding of all men.

1 Nephi 14:20–22, 27

The apostle John referred to here is the same apostle in the New Testament who is also known as John the Beloved (John 21:20) and John the Revelator. He is the author of the Gospel of John (John 21:24), the book of Revelation (Revelation 1:19), and the three epistles of John, which appear shortly before Revelation in the New Testament. (Ludlow)

POINT OF INTEREST

This defile or canyon is in Edom on the path from Israel to Egypt. Edom became independent from Israel in 914 B.C. during the reign of Jehoshaphat. The area's economy depended on the caravan trade between Israel and Egypt along the Incense Route. Edom probably exported salt from the Dead Sea region and balsam, which was used for perfume and temple incense in the ancient world.

24. And behold, the things which this apostle of the Lamb shall write are many things which thou hast seen; and behold, the remainder shalt thou see.
25. But the things which thou shalt see hereafter thou shalt not write; for the Lord God hath ordained the apostle of the Lamb of God that he should write them.
26. And also others who have been, to them hath he shown all things, and they have written them; and they are sealed up to come forth in their purity, according to the truth which is in the Lamb, in the own due time of the Lord, unto the house of Israel.
27. And I, Nephi, heard and bear record, that the name of the apostle of the Lamb was John, according to the word of the angel.
28. And behold, I, Nephi, am forbidden that I should write the remainder of the things which I saw and heard; wherefore the things which I have written sufficeth me; and I have written but a small part of the things which I saw.
29. And I bear record that I saw the things which my father saw, and the angel of the Lord did make them known unto me.
30. And now I make an end of speaking concerning the things which I saw while I was carried away in the spirit; and if all the things which I saw are not written, the things which I have written are true. And thus it is. Amen.

CHAPTER 15

1. AND it came to pass that after I, Nephi, had been carried away in the spirit, and seen all these things, I returned to the tent of my father.
2. And it came to pass that I beheld my brethren, and they were disputing one with another concerning the things which my father had spoken unto them.
3. For he truly spake many great things unto them, which were hard to be understood, save a man should inquire of the Lord; and they being hard in their hearts, therefore they did not look unto the Lord as they ought.
4. And now I, Nephi, was grieved because of the hardness of their hearts, and also, because of the things which I had seen, and knew they must unavoidably come to pass because of the great wickedness of the children of men.
5. And it came to pass that I was overcome because of my afflictions, for I considered that mine afflictions were great above all, because of the destruction of my people, for I had beheld their fall.
6. And it came to pass that after I had received strength I spake unto my brethren, desiring to know of them the cause of their disputations.
7. And they said: Behold, we cannot understand the words which our father hath spoken concerning the natural branches of the olive-tree, and also concerning the Gentiles.
8. And I said unto them: Have ye inquired of the Lord?

1 Nephi 15:8

Nephi gives a clue here as to how we can arrive at a knowledge of spiritual things. Lehi had told Nephi, Laman, and Lemuel of his dream. All three of them were evidently intrigued and interested in the possible interpretation of the symbols in their father's dream. Laman and Lemuel attempted to find their answers through the power of their own reasoning. Nephi, however, asked the Lord for the interpretation of these symbols, and as a result he received the great vision recorded in 1 Nephi 11–14. Nephi's question "Have ye inquired of the Lord?" teaches the same principle as that taught later by the resurrected Jesus Christ to the righteous Nephites of about A.D. 34: ". . . whatsoever ye shall ask the Father in my name, which is right, believing that ye shall receive, behold it shall be given unto you" (3 Nephi 18:20). (Ludlow)

POINT OF INTEREST

The dromedary camel is a large ungulate native to the area where Lehi and his family lived. This animal is well suited for desert travel and would have surely made up Lehi's and Ishmael's caravan. It is perhaps the best known of the camel family and is sometimes referred to as the Arabian camel. Some maintain that "dromedary" should be used only to refer to racing camels, since the name comes from the Greek word for "to run."

9. And they said unto me: We have not; for the Lord maketh no
such thing known unto us.
10. Behold, I said unto them: How is it that ye do not keep the
commandments of the Lord? How is it that ye will perish, because
of the hardness of your hearts?
11. Do ye not remember the things which the Lord hath said?—If
ye will not harden your hearts, and ask me in faith, believing that
ye shall receive, with diligence in keeping my commandments,
surely these things shall be made known unto you.
12. Behold, I say unto you, that the house of Israel was compared
unto an olive-tree, by the Spirit of the Lord which was in our father;
and behold are we not broken off from the house of Israel, and are
we not a branch of the house of Israel?
13. And now, the thing which our father meaneth concerning the
grafting in of the natural branches through the fulness of the
Gentiles, is, that in the latter days, when our seed shall have dwindled in unbelief, yea, for the space of many years, and many generations after the Messiah shall be manifested in body unto the children
of men, then shall the fulness of the gospel of the Messiah come unto
the Gentiles, and from the Gentiles unto the remnant of our seed—
14. And at that day shall the remnant of our seed know that they
are of the house of Israel, and that they are the covenant people
of the Lord; and then shall they know and come to the knowledge of their forefathers, and also to the knowledge of the gospel
of their Redeemer, which was ministered unto their fathers by
him; wherefore, they shall come to the knowledge of their
Redeemer and the very points of his doctrine, that they may
know how to come unto him and be saved.
15. And then at that day will they not rejoice and give praise unto
their everlasting God, their rock and their salvation? Yea, at that
day, will they not receive the strength and nourishment from the
true vine? Yea, will they not come unto the true fold of God?
16. Behold, I say unto you, Yea; they shall be remembered again
among the house of Israel; they shall be grafted in, being a natural
branch of the olive-tree, into the true olive-tree.
17. And this is what our father meaneth; and he meaneth that it
will not come to pass until after they are scattered by the Gentiles;
and he meaneth that it shall come by way of the Gentiles, that the
Lord may show his power unto the Gentiles, for the very cause that
he shall be rejected of the Jews, or of the house of Israel.
18. Wherefore, our father hath not spoken of our seed alone, but
also of all the house of Israel, pointing to the covenant which
should be fulfilled in the latter days; which covenant the Lord
made to our father Abraham, saying: In thy seed shall all the kindreds of the earth be blessed.

POINT OF INTEREST

Book of Mormon Translation Chronology

<u>1827</u>	
September 22	*Joseph obtains the plates*
December	*Joseph moves to Harmony, Penn.*
Winter 1827–1828	*Emma Smith serves as scribe*
<u>1828</u>	
Winter	*Emma Smith serves as scribe*
April–June	*Martin Harris serves as scribe*
June	*Harris loses the 116 pages*
September	*Translation resumes*
Winter 1828–1829	*Emma Smith, Reuben Hale, and Samuel H. Smith all serve as scribes*
<u>1829</u>	
Winter	*Emma Smith, Reuben Hale, and Samuel H. Smith all serve as scribes*
April–June	*Translation continues in the Peter Whitmer home*
Early June	*John Whitmer serves as scribe*
June 11	*Joseph obtains a copyright for the Book of Mormon*
June	*Joseph finishes translating the plates*

19. And it came to pass that I, Nephi, spake much unto them concerning these things; yea, I spake unto them concerning the
restoration of the Jews in the latter days.
20. And I did rehearse unto them the words of Isaiah, who spake
concerning the restoration of the Jews, or of the house of Israel; and
after they were restored they should no more be confounded, neither
should they be scattered again. And it came to pass that I did speak
many words unto my brethren, that they were pacified and did humble themselves before the Lord.
21. And it came to pass that they did speak unto me again, saying:
What meaneth this thing which our father saw in a dream? What
meaneth the tree which he saw?
22. And I said unto them: It was a representation of the tree of life.
23. And they said unto me: What meaneth the rod of iron which
our father saw, that led to the tree?
24. And I said unto them that it was the word of God; and whoso
would hearken unto the word of God, and would hold fast unto it,
they would never perish; neither could the temptations and the
fiery darts of the adversary overpower them unto blindness, to lead
them away to destruction.
25. Wherefore, I, Nephi, did exhort them to give heed unto the
word of the Lord; yea, I did exhort them with all the energies of my
soul, and with all the faculty which I possessed, that they would
give heed to the word of God and remember to keep his commandments always in all things.
26. And they said unto me: What meaneth the river of water
which our father saw?
27. And I said unto them that the water which my father saw was
filthiness; and so much was his mind swallowed up in other things
that he beheld not the filthiness of the water.
28. And I said unto them that it was an awful gulf, which separated the wicked from the tree of life, and also from the saints of God.
29. And I said unto them that it was a representation of that awful
hell, which the angel said unto me was prepared for the wicked.
30. And I said unto them that our father also saw that the justice
of God did also divide the wicked from the righteous; and the
brightness thereof was like unto the brightness of a flaming fire,
which ascendeth up unto God forever and ever, and hath no end.
31. And they said unto me: Doth this thing mean the torment of
the body in the days of probation, or doth it mean the final state of
the soul after the death of the temporal body, or doth it speak of
the things which are temporal?
32. And it came to pass that I said unto them that it was a representation of things both temporal and spiritual; for the day should
come that they must be judged of their works, yea, even the works
which were done by the temporal body in their days of probation.

1 Nephi 15:19

According to Elder Bruce R. McConkie, "restoration" means two things: (1) becoming converted to the true church, and (2) assembling in Zion or Jerusalem.

1 Nephi 15:23–24

Lehi's vision of the tree of life is both a supernal allegory of God's plan of loving redemption and a template for application in one's immediate life. What Lehi saw in prophetic vision had its source in the highest reaches of the spiritual firmament, yet it had enormous utility as a compass for the real experiences of the moment. Lehi was wise enough to see that his vision had meaning not just in concept and principle, but especially when applied to himself, his wife, and his family.

So it must be with us all. The tree of life is not an abstract model to be admired like a tapestry, but a road map that becomes a stunning self-revelation when we hold it up as a mirror in which to see ourselves and determine our position before God.

In the vision of the tree of life, we are granted a clear view of the types of people ever present on the mortal landscape and the different and distinct strategies that each of these groups might elect in their quest for their perception of a fulfilling lifestyle.

Referring to that vision and to its fulfillment in our day, President Ezra Taft Benson said, "When we read of the spreading curse of drugs, or read of the pernicious flood of pornography and immorality, do any of us doubt that these are the forbidden paths and rivers of filthiness Lehi described? . . .

"My dear brethren, this is an answer to the great challenge of our time. The word of God, as found in the scriptures, in the words of living prophets, and in personal revelation, has the power to fortify the Saints and arm them with the Spirit so they can resist evil, hold fast to the good, and find joy in this life." (P/A)

1 Nephi 15:25

As used in the Book of Mormon, the word *heed* implies permanent, steadfast obedience. It is the direct opposite of vacillating, transient obedience that is evident only during prosperity or ease. To heed implies a firm commitment to obey regardless of circumstances.

33. Wherefore, if they should die in their wickedness they must be
cast off also, as to the things which are spiritual, which are pertaining to righteousness; wherefore, they must be brought to stand
before God, to be judged of their works; and if their works have
been filthiness they must needs be filthy; and if they be filthy it must
needs be that they cannot dwell in the kingdom of God; if so, the
kingdom of God must be filthy also.
34. But behold, I say unto you, the kingdom of God is not filthy,
and there cannot any unclean thing enter into the kingdom of
God; wherefore there must needs be a place of filthiness prepared
for that which is filthy.
35. And there is a place prepared, yea, even that awful hell of
which I have spoken, and the devil is the preparator of it; wherefore the final state of the souls of men is to dwell in the kingdom
of God, or to be cast out because of that justice of which I have
spoken.
36. Wherefore, the wicked are rejected from the righteous, and
also from that tree of life, whose fruit is most precious and most
desirable above all other fruits; yea, and it is the greatest of all the
gifts of God. And thus I spake unto my brethren. Amen.

CHAPTER 16

1. AND now it came to pass that after I, Nephi, had made an end of
speaking to my brethren, behold they said unto me: Thou hast
declared unto us hard things, more than we are able to bear.
2. And it came to pass that I said unto them that I knew that I had
spoken hard things against the wicked, according to the truth; and
the righteous have I justified, and testified that they should be lifted up at the last day; wherefore, the guilty taketh the truth to be
hard, for it cutteth them to the very center.
3. And now my brethren, if ye were righteous and were willing to
hearken to the truth, and give heed unto it, that ye might walk
uprightly before God, then ye would not murmur because of the
truth, and say: Thou speakest hard things against us.
4. And it came to pass that I, Nephi, did exhort my brethren, with
all diligence, to keep the commandments of the Lord.
5. And it came to pass that they did humble themselves before the
Lord; insomuch that I had joy and great hopes of them, that they
would walk in the paths of righteousness.
6. Now, all these things were said

POINT OF INTEREST

This small kneeling statue likely represents Necho II and is located in the Brooklyn Museum. Necho, sometimes referred to as Nekau II, was a king of Egypt from 610–595 B.C. and played a part in the fall of Jerusalem. When Judah chose Jehoahaz to succeed Josiah, Necho deposed him and put Jehoiakim in his place. It was Necho with whom Zedekiah united against Babylon.

1 Nephi 15:36

The fruit—the greatest of all the gifts of God—represents the love of God, made manifest when He sent the Savior to atone for the sins of all mankind.

1 Nephi 16

Written by Nephi thirty years after the journey from Jerusalem, this chapter contains only highlights, with an emphasis on persuading us to come unto Christ.

1 Nephi 16:1

Those who are unrighteous find it more difficult to hear the words of the Lord.

1 Nephi 16:2–6

These brief verses are a summary or conclusion of the previous section.

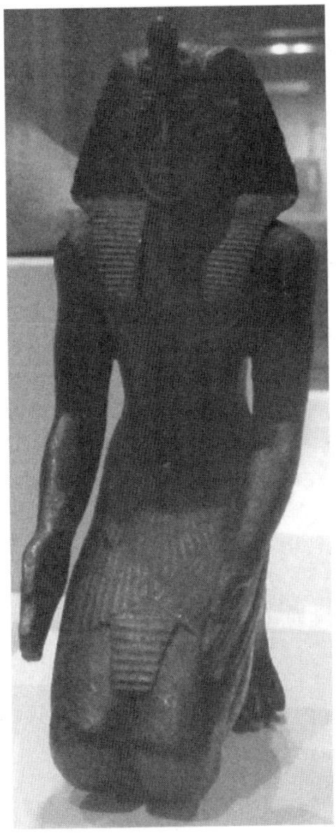

and done as my father dwelt in a tent in the valley which he called Lemuel.
7. And it came to pass that I, Nephi, took one of the daughters of Ishmael to wife; and also, my brethren took of the daughters of Ishmael to wife; and also Zoram took the eldest daughter of Ishmael to wife.
8. And thus my father had fulfilled all the commandments of the Lord which had been given unto him. And also, I, Nephi, had been blessed of the Lord exceedingly.
9. And it came to pass that the voice of the Lord spake unto my father by night, and commanded him that on the morrow he should take his journey into the wilderness.
10. And it came to pass that as my father arose in the morning, and went forth to the tent door, to his great astonishment he beheld upon the ground a round ball of curious workmanship; and it was of fine brass. And within the ball were two spindles; and the one pointed the way whither we should go into the wilderness.
11. And it came to pass that we did gather together whatsoever things we should carry into the wilderness, and all the remainder of ourprovisions which the Lord had given unto us; and we did take seed of every kind that we might carry into the wilderness.
12. And it came to pass that we did take our tents and depart into the wilderness, across the river Laman.
13. And it came to pass that we traveled for the space of four days, nearly a south-southeast direction, and we did pitch our tents again; and we did call the name of the place Shazer.
14. And it came to pass that we did take our bows and our arrows, and go forth into the wilderness to slay food for our families; and after we had slain food for our families we did return again to our families in the wilderness, to the place of Shazer. And we did go forth again in the wilderness, following the same direction, keeping in the most fertile parts of the wilderness, which were in the borders near the Red Sea.
15. And it came to pass that we did travel for the space of many days, slaying food by the way, with our bows and our arrows and our stones and our slings.
16. And we did follow the directions of the ball, which led us in the more fertile parts of the wilderness.
17. And after we had traveled for the space of many days, we did pitch our tents for the space of a time, that we might again rest ourselves and obtain food for our families.
18. And it came to pass that as I, Nephi, went forth to slay food, behold, I did break my bow, which was made of fine steel; and after I did break my bow, behold, my brethren were angry with me because of the loss of my bow, for we did obtain no food.
19. And it came to pass that we did return without food to our families, and being much fatigued, because of their journeying, they did suffer much for the want of food.
20. And it came to pass that Laman and Lemuel and the sons of Ishmael did begin to murmur exceedingly, because of their sufferings and afflictions in the wilderness; and also my father began to murmur against the Lord his God; yea, and they were all exceedingly sorrowful,

1 Nephi 16:10

The "round ball of curious workmanship" that was made of "fine brass" is later known in the Book of Mormon as the Liahona. (Alma 37:38.) This name is evidently a transliteration from the original language of Lehi, and Reynolds and Sjodahl have suggested the following meaning for it:

LIAHONA. This interesting word is Hebrew with an Egyptian ending. It is the name which Lehi gave to the ball or director he found outside his tent the very day he began his long journey through the "wilderness," after his little company had rested for some time in the Valley of Lemuel. (1 Nephi 16:10; Alma 37:38)

L is a Hebrew preposition meaning "to," and sometimes used to express the possessive case. *Iah* is a Hebrew abbreviated form of "Jehovah," common in Hebrew names. *On* is the Hebrew name of the Egyptian "City of the Sun." . . . *L-iah-on* means, therefore, literally, "To God is Light"; or, "of God is Light." That is to say, God gives light, as does the Sun. The final *a* reminds us that the Egyptian form of the Hebrew name *On* is *Annu*, and that seems to be the form Lehi used . .

Lehi gave the metal ball a name commemorative of one of the great experiences of his life . . . And, furthermore, he gave it a name that no one but a devout Hebrew influenced by Egyptian culture would have thought of. (Ludlow)

1 Nephi 16:13

The place name "Shazer," referring to the location where Lehi and his group rested for a while, is another possible transliteration of an original term used by Lehi and his group. Dr. Hugh Nibley has suggested the following possible meaning of this word:

"The first important stop after Lehi's party had left their base camp was at a place they called *Shazer*. The name is intriguing. The combination *shajer* is quite common in Palestinian place names; it is a collective meaning 'trees,' and many Arabs (especially in Egypt) pronounce it *shazher*. It appears in *Thoghret-as-Sajur* (the Pass of Trees), which is the ancient *Shaghur*, written *Segor* in the sixth century. It may be confused with *Shaghur* 'seepage,' which is held to be identical with *Shihor*, the 'black water' of Joshua 19:36. This last takes in western Palestine the form *Sozura*, suggesting the name of a famous water hole in South Arabia, called *Shisur* by Thomas and *Shisar* by Philby. . . . So we have *Shihor, Shaghur, Sajur, Saghir, Segor* (even *Zoar)*, *Shajar, Sozura, Shisur*, and *Shisar*, all connected somehow or other and denoting either seepage—a weak but reliable water supply—or a clump of trees. Whichever one prefers, Lehi's people could hardly have picked a better name for their first suitable stopping place than *Shazer*." (Ludlow)

even that they did murmur against the Lord.
21. Now it came to pass that I, Nephi, having been afflicted with
my brethren because of the loss of my bow, and their bows having
lost their springs, it began to be exceedingly difficult, yea, insomuch that we could obtain no food.
22. And it came to pass that I, Nephi, did speak much unto my
brethren, because they had hardened their hearts again, even unto
complaining against the Lord their God.
23. And it came to pass that I, Nephi, did make out of wood a bow,
and out of a straight stick, an arrow; wherefore, I did arm myself
with a bow and an arrow, with a sling and with stones. And I said
unto my father: Whither shall I go to obtain food?
24. And it came to pass that he did inquire of the Lord, for they
had humbled themselves because of my words; for I did say many
things unto them in the energy of my soul.
25. And it came to pass that the voice of the Lord came unto my
father; and he was truly chastened because of his murmuring
against the Lord, insomuch that he was brought down into the
depths of sorrow.
26. And it came to pass that the voice of the Lord said unto him:
Look upon the ball, and behold the things which are written.
27. And it came to pass that when my father beheld the things which
were written upon the ball, he did fear and tremble exceedingly, and
also my brethren and the sons of Ishmael and our wives.
28. And it came to pass that I, Nephi, beheld the pointers which
were in the ball, that they did work according to the faith and diligence and heed which we did give unto them.
29. And there was also written upon them a new writing, which was
plain to be read, which did give us understanding concerning the
ways of the Lord; and it was written and changed from time to time,
according to the faith and diligence which we gave unto it. And
thus we see that by small means the Lord can bring about great
things.
30. And it came to pass that I, Nephi, did go forth up into the top
of the mountain, according to the directions which were given
upon the ball.
31. And it came to pass that I did slay wild beasts, insomuch that
I did obtain food for our families.
32. And it came to pass that I did return to our tents, bearing the
beasts which I had slain; and now when they beheld that I had
obtained food, how great was their joy! And it came to pass that
they did humble themselves before the Lord, and did give thanks
unto him.
33. And it came to pass that we did again take our journey, traveling nearly the same course as in the beginning; and after we had
traveled for the space of many days we did pitch our tents again,
that we might tarry for the space of a time.
34. And it came to pass that Ishmael died, and was buried in the
place which was called Nahom.
35. And it came to pass that the daughters of Ishmael did mourn
exceedingly, because of the loss of

1 Nephi 16:23

The way in which Nephi solved the problem of obtaining food for his family gives us a powerful example of dignity and respect. Lehi had been wavering, yet Nephi took great care to recognize his authority as a prophet of God and as his father. Nephi made a new bow out of wood after his steel bow broke; he then gathered a sling and some stones and approached Lehi, asking where he should go to obtain food (see 1 Ne. 16:23). What a simple, yet profound, thing! Nephi could have gone directly to the Lord in prayer to be directed in his quest for food, yet he had enough humility and respect to go to his father and ask that he query the Lord for direction. Through this simple act at a difficult time for their family, Lehi's leadership in the family was restored and Nephi demonstrated his willingness to be taught and led.

their father, and because of their afflictions in the wilderness; and they did murmur against my father, because he had brought them out of the land of Jerusalem, saying: Our father is dead; yea, and we have wandered much in the wilderness, and we have suffered much affliction, hunger, thirst, and fatigue; and after all these sufferings we must perish in the wilderness with hunger.
36. And thus they did murmur against my father, and also against me; and they were desirous to return again to Jerusalem.
37. And Laman said unto Lemuel and also unto the sons of Ishmael: Behold, let us slay our father, and also our brother Nephi, who has taken it upon him to be our ruler and our teacher, who are his elder brethren.
38. Now, he says that the Lord has talked with him, and also that angels have ministered unto him. But behold, we know that he lies unto us; and he tells us these things, and he worketh many things by his cunning arts, that he may deceive our eyes, thinking, perhaps, that he may lead us away into some strange wilderness; and after he has led us away, he has thought to make himself a king and a ruler over us, that he may do with us according to his will and pleasure. And after this manner did my brother Laman stir up their hearts to anger.
39. And it came to pass that the Lord was with us, yea, even the voice of the Lord came and did speak many words unto them, and did chasten them exceedingly; and after they were chastened by the voice of the Lord they did turn away their anger, and did repent of their sins, insomuch that the Lord did bless us again with food, that we did not perish.

CHAPTER 17

1. AND it came to pass that we did again take our journey in the wilderness; and we did travel nearly eastward from that time forth. And we did travel and wade through much affliction in the wilderness; and our women did bear children in the wilderness.
2. And so great were the blessings of the Lord upon us, that while we did live upon raw meat in the wilderness, our women did give plenty of suck for their children, and were strong, yea, even like unto the men; and they began to bear their journeyings without murmurings.
3. And thus we see that the commandments of God must be fulfilled. And if it so be that the children of men keep the commandments of God he doth nourish them, and strengthen them, and provide means whereby they can accomplish the thing which he has commanded them; wherefore, he did provide means for us while we did sojourn in the wilderness.
4. And we did sojourn for the space of many years, yea, even eight years in the wilderness.
5. And we did come to the land which we called Bountiful, because

1 Nephi 16:34–35

The place names used by Lehi and his group provide readers of the Book of Mormon with some of the best means of testing the authenticity of the Book of Mormon from a linguistic viewpoint. Apparently most of these names were transliterated by Joseph Smith, and it should be remembered that the Prophet had not studied Semitic languages before his translation of the Book of Mormon. Yet, as Dr. Nibley indicates in the following quotation, the place names given by Lehi evidently came from a Semitic source:

"When Ishmael died on the journey, he 'was buried in the place which was called Nahom.' (1 Nephi 16:34.) Note that this is not '*a* place which *we* called Nahom,' but *the* place which *was* so called, a desert burial ground. Jaussen reports (*Rev. Biblique* X, 607) that though Bedouins sometimes bury the dead where they die, many carry the remains great distances to bury them. The Arabic root NHM has the basic meaning of 'to sigh or moan,' and occurs nearly always in the third form, 'to sigh or moan with another.' The Heb. *Nahum*, 'comfort,' is related, but that is not the form given in the Book of Mormon. At this place, we are told, 'the daughters of Ishmael did mourn exceedingly,' and are reminded that among the desert Arabs mourning rites are a monopoly of the women. (*Ibid.*, 90–91). (Ludlow)

1 Nephi 17

The so-called higher critics of the Bible have raised the question as to whether or not the miracles of the exodus of Israel under Moses actually happened as they are recorded in the Old Testament. (See Exodus 14:19–20, 26–31; 16:4, 15; 17:5–6; Numbers 21:6–9.) However, the Book of Mormon substantiates the actuality of these miraculous events. (1 Nephi 17:23, 26, 28, 29, 30, 41.) Inasmuch as Nephi's knowledge of these miracles came from the authentic account on the brass plates of Laban (1 Nephi 5:11), Latter-day Saints should have no question concerning the reliability of the biblical account. Once again the Book of Mormon serves as a witness to its companion scripture, the Bible. (Ludlow)

of its much fruit and also wild honey; and all these things were prepared of the Lord that we might not perish. And we beheld the sea, which we called Irreantum, which, being interpreted, is many waters.

6. And it came to pass that we did pitch our tents by the seashore; and notwithstanding we had suffered many afflictions and much difficulty, yea, even so much that we cannot write them all, we were exceedingly rejoiced when we came to the seashore; and we called the place Bountiful, because of its much fruit.

7. And it came to pass that after I, Nephi, had been in the land of Bountiful for the space of many days, the voice of the Lord came unto me, saying: Arise, and get thee into the mountain. And it came to pass that I arose and went up into the mountain, and cried unto the Lord.

8. And it came to pass that the Lord spake unto me, saying: Thou shalt construct a ship, after the manner which I shall show thee, that I may carry thy people across these waters.

9. And I said: Lord, whither shall I go that I may find ore to molten, that I may make tools to construct the ship after the manner which thou hast shown unto me?

10. And it came to pass that the Lord told me whither I should go to find ore, that I might make tools.

11. And it came to pass that I, Nephi, did make a bellows wherewith to blow the fire, of the skins of beasts; and after I had made a bellows, that I might have wherewith to blow the fire, I did smite two stones together that I might make fire.

12. For the Lord had not hitherto suffered that we should make much fire, as we journeyed in the wilderness; for he said: I will make thy food become sweet, that ye cook it not;

13. And I will also be your light in the wilderness; and I will prepare the way before you, if it so be that ye shall keep my commandments; wherefore, inasmuch as ye shall keep my commandments ye shall be led towards the promised land; and ye shall know that it is by me that ye are led.

14. Yea, and the Lord said also that: After ye have arrived in the promised land, ye shall know that I, the Lord, am God; and that I, the Lord, did deliver you from destruction; yea, that I did bring you out of the land of Jerusalem.

15. Wherefore, I, Nephi, did strive to keep the commandments of the Lord, and I did exhort my brethren to faithfulness and diligence.

16. And it came to pass that I did make tools of the ore which I did molten out of the rock.

17. And when my brethren saw that I was about to build a ship, they began to murmur against me, saying: Our brother is a fool, for he thinketh that he can build a ship; yea, and he also thinketh that he can cross these great waters.

18. And thus my brethren did complain against me, and were desirous that they might not labor, for they did not believe that I could build a ship; neither would they

1 Nephi 17:7–12

The voice of the Lord told Nephi to get into the mountain, where Nephi called upon the Lord. The Lord commanded Nephi to build a ship according to the directions that would be given him (see 1 Ne. 17). Laman and Lemuel doubted Nephi's ability and started to murmur. They complained about leaving Jerusalem, being unable to enjoy their wealth, and experiencing difficulties over the years in traveling. They doubted. They lacked faith. Throughout the Book of Mormon the prophets, and in this case Nephi, would attempt to show the doubting or wayward the goodness and mercy of God.

Nephi reminded his brothers about the following: The Lord had led the Israelites out of Egypt to safety, and the Egyptians had been drowned in the Red Sea; manna was provided for their food, water was given to them out of a rock, and the Lord led them day and night. The Israelites still hardened their hearts and reviled against Moses. The Israelites eventually became very wicked, and the Lord said that Jerusalem would be destroyed—this is when Lehi was commanded to leave Jerusalem.

The Lord favors the righteous but will destroy the wicked. Nephi exhorted Laman and Lemuel in regard to their iniquity and failing to remember the Lord, but their hearts "were past feeling" (1 Ne. 17:45). Nephi had great anguish for his brothers and was fearful that they might be cast off forever. Laman and Lemuel became very angry and attempted to seize Nephi, that they might throw him into the ocean. Nephi, being full of the Spirit, commanded them not to touch him. He bore a fervent testimony of his faith and willingness to do all things the Lord commanded him to do. Nephi confounded Laman and Lemuel and then, in response to the Lord's command, he shocked them as a testimony that the Lord surely is their God. They recognized the power of the Lord, and Nephi encouraged them to worship the Lord and to honor their parents. (P/A)

1 Nephi 17:12–13

Those who traveled through Arabia during Lehi's day ate most of their food raw; to build fires for cooking invited great danger by alerting prowling marauders to their location. At that time, there were tribes that supported themselves entirely by attacking and robbing unwary travelers, who generally carried with them goods and riches to establish themselves in their new location.

believe that I was instructed of the Lord.
19. And now it came to pass that I, Nephi, was exceedingly sorrowful because of the hardness of their hearts; and now when they saw
that I began to be sorrowful they were glad in their hearts, insomuch
that they did rejoice over me, saying: We knew that ye could not
construct a ship, for we knew that ye were lacking in judgment;
wherefore, thou canst not accomplish so great a work.
20. And thou art like unto our father, led away by the foolish imaginations of his heart; yea, he hath led us out of the land of
Jerusalem, and we have wandered in the wilderness for these many
years; and our women have toiled, being big with child; and they
have borne children in the wilderness and suffered all things, save
it were death; and it would have been better that they had died
before they came out of Jerusalem than to have suffered these
afflictions.
21. Behold, these many years we have suffered in the wilderness,
which time we might have enjoyed our possessions and the land of
our inheritance; yea, and we might have been happy.
22. And we know that the people who were in the land of Jerusalem
were a righteous people; for they kept the statutes and judgments of
the Lord, and all his commandments, according to the law of
Moses; wherefore, we know that they are a righteous people; and
our father hath judged them, and hath led us away because we
would hearken unto his words; yea, and our brother is like unto
him. And after this manner of language did my brethren murmur
and complain against us.
23. And it came to pass that I, Nephi, spake unto them, saying: Do
ye believe that our fathers, who were the children of Israel, would
have been led away out of the hands of the Egyptians if they had
not hearkened unto the words of the Lord?
24. Yea, do ye suppose that they would have been led out of
bondage, if the Lord had not commanded Moses that he should
lead them out of bondage?
25. Now ye know that the children of Israel were in bondage; and
ye know that they were laden with tasks, which were grievous to
be borne; wherefore, ye know that it must needs be a good thing
for them, that they should be brought out of bondage.
26. Now ye know that Moses was commanded of the Lord to do
that great work; and ye know that by his word the waters of the
Red Sea were divided hither and thither, and they passed through
on dry ground.
27. But ye know that the Egyptians were drowned in the Red Sea,
who were the armies of Pharaoh.
28. And ye also know that they were fed with manna in the wilderness.
29. Yea, and ye also know that Moses, by his word according to the
power of God which was in him, smote the rock, and there came

1 Nephi 17:22

Laman and Lemuel were wrong in their assessment of the people in the land of Jerusalem. They were *not* righteous—and had, in fact, been rebuked by Hosea, Isaiah, Amos, Jeremiah, and Micah in addition to Lehi.

1 Nephi 17:23

The Book of Mormon substantiates the Biblical account of Moses leading the exodus from Egypt. Nephi knew about the exodus because he had read the brass plates of Laban, which contained that account.

1 Nephi 17:25

The phrase "now ye know" indicates that Laman and Lemuel knew the story and had been taught these truths. The fact that Nephi stops using it indicates that Laman and Lemuel were too spiritually immature to apply the principles in their lives.

POINT OF INTEREST

Judah (Southern Kingdom)

841–811 B.C. — *Amaziah*
He was the first to employ a mercenary army of Israelite soldiers in an effort to bring Edom under Judah's yoke. When an unnamed prophet commanded him to send back the mercenaries, he did so and was rewarded with a decisive victory.

811–758 B.C. — *Uzziah*
His reign was one of the most prosperous since Solomon. Under the influence of the prophet Zechariah, he was faithful for a time to the Lord. However, he was struck with leprosy when he attempted to unworthily burn incense in the temple. Isaiah also served as prophet during his reign.

Israel (Northern Kingdom)

842–826 B.C. — *Jehoash*
He defeated Amaziah in battle and, advancing on Jerusalem, broke down a portion of the wall and carried away treasure from the temple and palace. He held Elisha in honor and wept at the prophet's deathbed.

826–773 B.C. — *Jeroboam II*
He expanded Israel's borders to its former limits, and he and the Israelite elite of the time were condemned in turn by the prophets Hosea, Joel, and Amos.

773–772 B.C. — *Zachariah*

772 B.C. — *Shallum (whose seal is above)*

772–761 B.C. — *Menahem*

761–759 B.C. — *Pekahiah*

forth water, that the children of Israel might quench their thirst.
30. And notwithstanding they being led, the Lord their God, their
Redeemer, going before them, leading them by day and giving light
unto them by night, and doing all things for them which were
expedient for man to receive, they hardened their hearts and
blinded their minds, and reviled against Moses and against the true
and living God.
31. And it came to pass that according to his word he did destroy
them; and according to his word he did lead them; and according
to his word he did do all things for them; and there was not any
thing done save it were by his word.
32. And after they had crossed the river Jordan he did make them
mighty unto the driving out of the children of the land, yea, unto
the scattering them to destruction.
33. And now, do ye suppose that the children of this land, who
were in the land of promise, who were driven out by our fathers,
do ye suppose that they were righteous? Behold, I say unto you,
Nay.
34. Do ye suppose that our fathers would have been more choice
than they if they had been righteous? I say unto you, Nay.
35. Behold, the Lord esteemeth all flesh in one; he that is righteous is favored of God. But behold, this people had rejected every
word of God, and they were ripe in iniquity; and the fulness of
the wrath of God was upon them; and the Lord did curse the land
against them, and bless it unto our fathers; yea, he did curse it
against them unto their destruction, and he did bless it unto our
fathers unto their obtaining power over it.
36. Behold, the Lord hath created the earth that it should be
inhabited; and he hath created his children that they should possess it.
37. And he raiseth up a righteous nation, and destroyeth the
nations of the wicked.
38. And he leadeth away the righteous into precious lands, and the
wicked he destroyeth, and curseth the land unto them for their
sakes.
39. He ruleth high in the heavens, for it is his throne, and this
earth is his footstool.
40. And he loveth those who will have him to be their God.
Behold, he loved our fathers, and he covenanted with them, yea,
even Abraham, Isaac, and Jacob; and he remembered the
covenants which he had made; wherefore, he did bring
them out of the land of Egypt.
41. And he did straiten them in the wilderness with his
rod; for they hardened their hearts, even as ye have; and
the Lord straitened them because of their iniquity. He
sent

1 Nephi 17:35

The Lord regards all as having equal value, though He favors those who are righteous.

1 Nephi 17:41

Laman and Lemuel were very much like the children of Israel under Moses—and Nephi was very much like Moses, leading the children of Israel.

POINT OF INTEREST

This dramatic painting by Milanese artist Francesco Hayaz depicts the destruction of the temple at Jerusalem.

fiery flying serpents among them; and after they were bitten he prepared a way that they might be healed; and the labor which they had to perform was to look; and because of the simpleness of the way, or the easiness of it, there were many who perished.
42. And they did harden their hearts from time to time, and they did revile against Moses, and also against God; nevertheless, ye know that they were led forth by his matchless power into the land of promise.
43. And now, after all these things, the time has come that they have become wicked, yea, nearly unto ripeness; and I know not but they are at this day about to be destroyed; for I know that the day must surely come that they must be destroyed, save a few only, who shall be led away into captivity.
44. Wherefore, the Lord commanded my father that he should depart into the wilderness; and the Jews also sought to take away his life; yea, and ye also have sought to take away his life; wherefore, ye are murderers in your hearts and ye are like unto them.
45. Ye are swift to do iniquity but slow to remember the Lord your God. Ye have seen an angel, and he spake unto you; yea, ye have heard his voice from time to time; and he hath spoken unto you in a still small voice, but ye were past feeling, that ye could not feel his words; wherefore, he has spoken unto you like unto the voice of thunder, which did cause the earth to shake as if it were to divide asunder.
46. And ye also know that by the power of his almighty word he can cause the earth that it shall pass away; yea, and ye know that by his word he can cause the rough places to be made smooth, and smooth places shall be broken up. O, then, why is it, that ye can be so hard in your hearts?
47. Behold, my soul is rent with anguish because of you, and my heart is pained; I fear lest ye shall be cast off forever. Behold, I am full of the Spirit of God, insomuch that my frame has no strength.
48. And now it came to pass that when I had spoken these words they were angry with me, and were desirous to throw me into the depths of the sea; and as they came forth to lay their hands upon me I spake unto them, saying: In the name of the Almighty God, I command you that ye touch me not, for I am filled with the power of God, even unto the consuming of my flesh; and whoso shall lay his hands upon me shall wither even as a dried reed; and he shall be as naught before the power of God, for God shall smite him.
49. And it came to pass that I, Nephi, said unto them that they should murmur no more against their father; neither should they withhold their labor from me, for God had commanded me that I should build a ship.
50. And I said unto them: If God had commanded me to do all things I could do them. If he should command me that I should say unto this water, be thou earth, it should be earth; and if I should say it, it would be done.
51. And now, if the Lord has such great power, and has wrought so

1 Nephi 17:44–45

These verses provide an interesting character sketch of Laman and Lemuel. They were men who had experienced direct divine visitation and who had received sure knowledge, but had refused to believe.

1 Nephi 17:48

Nephi's warning to his brothers is a powerful witness that the Lord was with him.

1 Nephi 17:50

This declaration is a powerful parallel to Moses parting the Red Sea.

many miracles among the children of men, how is it that he cannot instruct me, that I should build a ship?
52. And it came to pass that I, Nephi, said many things unto my
brethren, insomuch that they were confounded and could not contend against me; neither durst they lay their hands upon me nor
touch me with their fingers, even for the space of many days. Now
they durst not do this lest they should wither before me, so powerful was the Spirit of God; and thus it had wrought upon them.
53. And it came to pass that the Lord said unto me: Stretch forth
thine hand again unto thy brethren, and they shall not wither before
thee, but I will shock them, saith the Lord, and this will I do, that
they may know that I am the Lord their God.
54. And it came to pass that I stretched forth my hand unto my
brethren, and they did not wither before me; but the Lord did
shake them, even according to the word which he had spoken.
55. And now, they said: We know of a surety that the Lord is with
thee, for we know that it is the power of the Lord that has shaken us.
And they fell down before me, and were about to worship me, but I
would not suffer them, saying: I am thy brother, yea, even thy
younger brother; wherefore, worship the Lord thy God, and honor
thy father and thy mother, that thy days may be long in the land
which the Lord thy God shall give thee.

CHAPTER 18

1. AND it came to pass that they did worship the Lord, and did go
forth with me; and we did work timbers of curious workmanship.
And the Lord did show me from time to time after what manner I
should work the timbers of the ship.
2. Now I, Nephi, did not work the timbers after the manner which
was learned by men, neither did I build the ship after the manner
of men; but I did build it after the manner which the Lord had
shown unto me; wherefore, it was not after the manner of men.
3. And I, Nephi, did go into the mount oft, and I did pray oft unto
the Lord; wherefore the Lord showed unto me great things.
4. And it came to pass that after I had finished the ship, according to
the word of the Lord, my brethren beheld that it was good, and that
the workmanship thereof was exceedingly fine; wherefore, they did
humble themselves again before the Lord.
5. And it came to pass that the voice of the Lord came unto my
father, that we should arise and go down into the ship.
6. And it came to pass that on the morrow, after we had prepared all
things, much fruits and meat from the wilderness, and honey in
abundance, and provisions according to that which the Lord had
commanded us, we did go down into the ship, with all our loading
and our

1 Nephi 17:53

The word "shock" used here means to cause to shake or tremble. The Lord prompted Nephi to stretch forth his hand in this manner so he could demonstrate and establish his leadership over his older brothers.

1 Nephi 17:55

It is a common mistake to worship the man with the power instead of the *source* of the power. In this verse, Nephi reminds us that our worship should always be focused on the Lord.

1 Nephi 18:1

As used here, "curious workmanship" means an object of unusual design and superior craftsmanship.

1 Nephi 18:3

Throughout the history of mankind on this earth, mountains have been the preeminent meeting place between God and His children.

POINT OF INTEREST

"Nephi seems to have a really strong background in metallurgical activities. . . . Skills were taught by father to son, handed down—kept secret. . . . It is not uncommon for a child, . . . even in an upper class family, to be taught a trade. . . . You've got the metal plates of Laban—the brass plates. It may be that this particular clan was connected with metalwork, that they kept their records on metal plates for that reason." —Daniel Peterson in *Journey of Faith: From Jerusalem to the Promised Land* (American Fork, Utah: Covenant Communications, Inc., 2006.)

seeds, and whatsoever thing we had brought with us, every one according to his age; wherefore, we did all go down into the ship, with our wives and our children.
7. And now, my father had begat two sons in the wilderness; the elder was called Jacob and the younger Joseph.
8. And it came to pass after we had all gone down into the ship, and had taken with us our provisions and things which had been commanded us, we did put forth into the sea and were driven forth before the wind towards the promised land.
9. And after we had been driven forth before the wind for the space of many days, behold, my brethren and the sons of Ishmael and also their wives began to make themselves merry, insomuch that they began to dance, and to sing, and to speak with much rudeness, yea, even that they did forget by what power they had been brought thither; yea, they were lifted up unto exceeding rudeness.
10. And I, Nephi, began to fear exceedingly lest the Lord should be angry with us, and smite us because of our iniquity, that we should be swallowed up in the depths of the sea; wherefore, I, Nephi, began to speak to them with much soberness; but behold they were angry with me, saying: We will not that our younger brother shall be a ruler over us.
11. And it came to pass that Laman and Lemuel did take me and bind me with cords, and they did treat me with much harshness; nevertheless, the Lord did suffer it that he might show forth his power, unto the fulfilling of his word which he had spoken concerning the wicked.
12. And it came to pass that after they had bound me insomuch that I could not move, the compass, which had been prepared of the Lord, did cease to work.
13. Wherefore, they knew not whither they should steer the ship, insomuch that there arose a great storm, yea, a great and terrible tempest, and we were driven back upon the waters for the space of three days; and they began to be frightened exceedingly lest they should be drowned in the sea; nevertheless they did not loose me.
14. And on the fourth day, which we had been driven back, the tempest began to be exceedingly sore.
15. And it came to pass that we were about to be swallowed up in the depths of the sea. And after we had been driven back upon the waters for the space of four days, my brethren began to see that the judgments of God were upon them, and that they must perish save that they should repent of their iniquities; wherefore, they came unto me, and loosed the bands which were upon my wrists, and behold they had swollen exceedingly; and also mine ankles were much swollen, and great was the soreness thereof.
16. Nevertheless, I did look unto my God, and I did praise him all the day long; and I did not murmur against the Lord because of mine afflictions.
17. Now my father, Lehi, had said many things unto them, and also unto the sons of Ishmael; but, behold, they did breathe out much

1 Nephi 18:9

Brother Eldin Ricks has the following interesting statement in his *Book of Mormon Commentary*, vol. 1, pp. 218–19:

"There is a French translation by Brasseur de Bourbourg of a Mexican tradition that runs as follows: 'Here is the beginning of the accounts of the arrival of the Mexicans from the place named Aztlan. It was through the midst of the water that they made their way to this locality, being four tribes. And in coming they were *rowing* in their ships.' Bourbourg, who records this tradition in his *Ancient Monuments of Mexico*, explains that the word in the original language that he translated 'rowing' actually is the native word for 'dancing.' But because he could make no sense out of 'dancing' in reference to ships, he had translated it 'rowing'!"

Is it possible that the originators of this tradition knew more than the French scholar concerning the coming of the Mexicans to this continent? The Book of Mormon says absolutely nothing concerning the coming of the people *rowing* in their ships (apparently they were driven by the winds and currents—1 Nephi 18:8, 13, 21–23), but it does say something concerning their *dancing* in their ships. (Ludlow)

1 Nephi 18:10

Several experiences in the Book of Mormon indicate that the law of primogeniture (where the first-born son has special rights and privileges) was part of the belief and tradition of Lehi and his colony. Note particularly the following references in this regard: 1 Nephi 18:10; 2 Nephi 5:3; Mosiah 10:11–15. In only one chapter of 1 Nephi 18, we find at least three examples of the practice of this law.

1. Nephi's position of leadership was objected to by Laman and Lemuel, who were his elder brothers (1 Nephi 18:10; see also 16:37).

2. Despite the strong faith and numerous religious experiences of Nephi, most of the revelations from the Lord concerning the colony continued to come through his father, Lehi. (1 Nephi 18:5; see also 16:9, 23–26).

3. Lehi and his group entered the ship "every one according to his age." (1 Nephi 18:6). (Ludlow)

1 Nephi 18:11–16

As the Liahona ceased to operate in the environment of rebellion and wickedness, a violent tempest arose, threatening to engulf the little party in a watery death. It was only the awful threat of destruction—more so than the entreaties of the faithful and humble in the family circle—that induced the older brothers to desist. Nephi was released. Based on his faithfulness, the compass was reactivated, and the emigrants from old Jerusalem soon reached the land of promise. (P/A)

threatenings against anyone that should speak for me; and my parents being stricken in years, and having suffered much grief because of their children, they were brought down, yea, even upon their sick-beds.
18. Because of their grief and much sorrow, and the iniquity of my brethren, they were brought near even to be carried out of this time to meet their God; yea, their grey hairs were about to be brought down to lie low in the dust; yea, even they were near to be cast with sorrow into a watery grave.
19. And Jacob and Joseph also, being young, having need of much nourishment, were grieved because of the afflictions of their mother; and also my wife with her tears and prayers, and also my children, did not soften the hearts of my brethren that they would loose me.
20. And there was nothing save it were the power of God, which threatened them with destruction, could soften their hearts; wherefore, when they saw that they were about to be swallowed up in the depths of the sea they repented of the thing which they had done, insomuch that they loosed me.
21. And it came to pass after they had loosed me, behold, I took the compass, and it did work whither I desired it. And it came to pass that I prayed unto the Lord; and after I had prayed the winds did cease, and the storm did cease, and there was a great calm.
22. And it came to pass that I, Nephi, did guide the ship, that we sailed again towards the promised land.
23. And it came to pass that after we had sailed for the space of many days we did arrive at the promised land; and we went forth upon the land, and did pitch our tents; and we did call it the promised land.
24. And it came to pass that we did begin to till the earth, and we began to plant seeds; yea, we did put all our seeds into the earth, which we had brought from the land of Jerusalem. And it came to pass that they did grow exceedingly; wherefore, we were blessed in abundance.
25. And it came to pass that we did find upon the land of promise, as we journeyed in the wilderness, that there were beasts in the forests of every kind, both the cow and the ox, and the ass and the horse, and the goat and the wild goat, and all manner of wild animals, which were for the use of men. And we did find all manner of ore, both of gold, and of silver, and of copper.

CHAPTER 19

1. AND it came to pass that the Lord commanded me, wherefore I did make plates of ore that I might engraven upon them the record of my people. And upon the plates which I made I did engraven the record of my father, and also our journeyings in the wilderness, and the prophecies of my father; and also many of mine own prophecies have I engraven upon them.
2. And I knew not at the time when I made them that I should be commanded

1 Nephi 18:21

The word *compass* as used here does not refer to the magnetic instrument of the mariner (the magnetic compass was apparently not known in the western world until about the twelfth century A.D.), but refers to the Liahona or "director ball" given to Lehi by the Lord to show him the way whither they should travel. (1 Nephi 16:9–10; Alma 37:38.)

George Reynolds has explained the differences between these two "compasses":

"In the days of Moses, when he led the children of Israel out of Egypt a pillar of cloud by day and of fire by night moved in front of them. This the Hebrews followed. But to Lehi he gave this Liahona, or compass, as the ball was called and it pointed the way they should travel. It had one strange peculiarity, which was that it worked according to their faith and diligence. When they kept God's law it showed them much more clearly the way they should go than when they were careless or rebellious. Some people have confused this ball, because it is called a compass, with a mariner's compass, that sailors use at sea to direct the course of their ships. But there is a great difference between the two. The Liahona pointed the way that Lehi's company should travel while the needle in the mariner's compass points to the north. The one showed the way Lehi should go, the other informs the traveler which way he is going. The one was especially prepared by the Lord for Lehi and his companions and was used through faith only; the other can be used by all men, whether believers in the true God, pagans or infidels." (Ludlow)

1 Nephi 18:25

If Joseph Smith had been writing the Book of Mormon instead of translating it from ancient records, he would have been very foolish to have included references to horses on the American continent in Book of Mormon times. (1 Nephi 18:25; Enos 21.) In 1830, nearly all the historians and scholars were convinced there had been no horses on the American continent before the coming of Columbus. After the Book of Mormon was published, however, archaeological discoveries were made that clearly indicate that horses were in the Americas before Columbus arrived. In the asphalt deposits of Rancho LaBrea in southern California, numerous fossil remains of horses have been found that antedate Book of Mormon times. Although these discoveries do not absolutely prove horses were in the Americas in the time period covered by the Book of Mormon (about 2600 B.C. to A.D. 421), they do prove horses were there before the coming of Columbus.

Some scientists have now accepted the possibility that horses and men lived concurrently in the Americas before the coming of Columbus. Franklin S. Harris, Jr., quotes the zoologist Ivan T. Sanderson as saying: "There is a body of evidence both from the mainland of Central America and even from rock drawings in Haiti itself tending to show

of the Lord to make these plates; wherefore, the record of my father, and the genealogy of his fathers, and the more part of all our proceedings in the wilderness are engraven upon those first plates of which I have spoken; wherefore, the things which transpired before I made these plates are, of a truth, more particularly made mention upon the first plates.
3. And after I had made these plates by way of commandment, I,
Nephi, received a commandment that the ministry and the prophecies, the more plain and precious parts of them, should be written upon these plates; and that the things which were written should be kept for the instruction of my people, who should possess the land, and also for other wise purposes, which purposes are known unto the Lord.
4. Wherefore, I, Nephi, did make a record upon the other plates,
which gives an account, or which gives a greater account of the wars and contentions and destructions of my people. And this have I done, and commanded my people what they should do after I was gone; and that these plates should be handed down from one generation to another, or from one prophet to another, until further commandments of the Lord.
5. And an account of my making these plates shall be given here-
after; and then, behold, I proceed according to that which I have spoken; and this I do that the more sacred things may be kept for the knowledge of my people.
6. Nevertheless, I do not write anything upon plates save it be that
I think it be sacred. And now, if I do err, even did they err of old; not that I would excuse myself because of other men, but because of the weakness which is in me, according to the flesh, I would excuse myself.
7. For the things which some men esteem to be of great worth, both
to the body and soul, others set at naught and trample under their feet. Yea, even the very God of Israel do men trample under their feet; I say, trample under their feet but I would speak in other words—they set him at naught, and hearken not to the voice of his counsels.
8. And behold he cometh, according to the words of the angel, in
six hundred years from the time my father left Jerusalem.
9. And the world, because of their iniquity, shall judge him to be a
thing of naught; wherefore they scourge him, and he suffereth it; and they smite him, and he suffereth it. Yea, they spit upon him, and he suffereth it, because of his loving kindness and his long-suffering towards the children of men.
10. And the God of our fathers, who were led out of Egypt, out of
bondage, and also were preserved in the wilderness by him, yea, the

that the horse may have been known to man in the Americas before the coming of the Spaniards." (Ludlow)

1 Nephi 19:7–10

We claim scriptural authority for the assertion that Jesus Christ was and is God the Creator, the God who revealed Himself to Adam, Enoch, and all the antediluvial patriarchs and prophets down to Noah; the God of Abraham, Isaac and Jacob; the God of Israel as a united people, and the God of Ephraim and Judah after the disruption of the Hebrew nation; the God who made Himself known to the prophets from Moses to Malachi; the God of the Old Testament record; and the God of the Nephites. We affirm that Jesus Christ was and is Jehovah, the Eternal One (James E. Talmage, *Jesus the Christ*).

God of Abraham, and of Isaac, and the God of Jacob, yieldeth himself, according to the words of the angel, as a man, into the hands of wicked men, to be lifted up, according to the words of Zenock, and to be crucified, according to the words of Neum, and to be buried in a sepulchre, according to the words of Zenos, which he spake concerning the three days of darkness, which should be a sign given of his death unto those who should inhabit the isles of the sea, more especially given unto those who are of the house of Israel.

11. For thus spake the prophet: The Lord God surely shall visit all the house of Israel at that day, some with his voice, because of their righteousness, unto their great joy and salvation, and others with the thunderings and the lightnings of his power, by tempest, by fire, and by smoke, and vapor of darkness, and by the opening of the earth, and by mountains which shall be carried up.

12. And all these things must surely come, saith the prophet Zenos. And the rocks of the earth must rend; and because of the groanings of the earth, many of the kings of the isles of the sea shall be wrought upon by the Spirit of God, to exclaim: The God of nature suffers.

13. And as for those who are at Jerusalem, saith the prophet, they shall be scourged by all people, because they crucify the God of Israel, and turn their hearts aside, rejecting signs and wonders, and the power and glory of the God of Israel.

14. And because they turn their hearts aside, saith the prophet, and have despised the Holy One of Israel, they shall wander in the flesh, and perish, and become a hiss and a byword, and be hated among all nations.

15. Nevertheless, when that day cometh, saith the prophet, that they no more turn aside their hearts against the Holy One of Israel, then will he remember the covenants which he made to their fathers.

16. Yea, then will he remember the isles of the sea; yea, and all the people who are of the house of Israel, will I gather in, saith the Lord, according to the words of the prophet Zenos, from the four quarters of the earth.

17. Yea, and all the earth shall see the salvation of the Lord, saith the

1 Nephi 19:10

This is primarily pertinent to the descendants of Lehi. We note that people who were not on the Euro-Asian-African continents, which are all connected by land, were described as being on an isle of the sea. This description fits the inhabitants of the American continents as evidenced by a later statement of Nephi: "We are upon an isle of the sea" (2 Ne.10:20). Three signs are mentioned that would be manifested among these people (see 1 Ne. 19:10–12):

1. Three days of darkness would occur at the time of the death of the very God of Israel.

(Fulfillment—See 3 Ne. 8:20–23)

2. The voice of the very God of Israel would be heard by the righteous.

(Fulfillment—See 3 Ne. 11:3–10)

3. Great cataclysmic and destructive forces would alter the face of the earth in connection with His death.

(Fulfillment—See 3 Ne. 8:5–19) (O/C)

1 Nephi 19:10, 13

A careful reading of these words of Zenos seems to indicate that the "three days of darkness" that were to accompany the crucifixion of Christ were not to be a sign to those of the house of Israel around Jerusalem but only to those who lived away from Jerusalem or on "the isles of the sea." (1 Nephi 19:10.) The sign to be given to those at Jerusalem is listed later by Zenos wherein he states, "And as for those who are at Jerusalem . . . they shall be scourged by all people, because they crucify the God of Israel" (1 Nephi 19:13)" (Ludlow)

POINT OF INTEREST

The Nubian ibex is a desert-dwelling goat found in the mountainous areas of modern-day Israel, Saudi Arabia, Oman, Egypt, and Sudan. This type of ibex lives in herds composed solely of males or females. Nephi and his brothers probably hunted them for food. They are now endangered.

prophet; every nation, kindred, tongue and people shall be blessed.
18. And I, Nephi, have written these things unto my people, that perhaps I might persuade them that they would remember the Lord their Redeemer.
19. Wherefore, I speak unto all the house of Israel, if it so be that they should obtain these things.
20. For behold, I have workings in the spirit, which doth weary me even that all my joints are weak, for those who are at Jerusalem; for had not the Lord been merciful, to show unto me concerning them, even as he had prophets of old, I should have perished also.
21. And he surely did show unto the prophets of old all things concerning them; and also he did show unto many concerning us; wherefore, it must needs be that we know concerning them for they are written upon the plates of brass.
22. Now it came to pass that I, Nephi, did teach my brethren these things; and it came to pass that I did read many things to them, which were engraven upon the plates of brass, that they might know concerning the doings of the Lord in other lands, among people of old.
23. And I did read many things unto them which were written in the books of Moses; but that I might more fully persuade them to believe in the Lord their Redeemer I did read unto them that which was written by the prophet Isaiah; for I did liken all scriptures unto us, that it might be for our profit and learning.
24. Wherefore I spake unto them, saying: Hear ye the words of the prophet, ye who are a remnant of the house of Israel, a branch who have been broken off; hear ye the words of the prophet, which were written unto all the house of Israel, and liken them unto yourselves, that ye may have hope as well as your brethren from whom ye have been broken off; for after this manner has the prophet written.

CHAPTER 20

1. HEARKEN and hear this, O house of Jacob, who are called by the name of Israel, and are come forth out of the waters of Judah, or out of the waters of baptism, who swear by the name of the Lord, and make mention of the God of Israel, yet they swear not in truth nor in righteousness.
2. Nevertheless, they call themselves of the holy city, but they do not stay themselves upon the God of Israel, who is the Lord of Hosts; yea, the Lord of Hosts is his name.
3. Behold, I have declared the former things from the beginning; and they went forth out of my mouth, and I showed them. I did show them suddenly.
4. And I did it because I knew that thou art obstinate, and thy neck is an iron sinew, and thy brow brass;
5. And I have even from the beginning declared to thee; before it came

1 Nephi 19:21

Other revelations of our day were given to Adam (D&C 107:53–57), Enoch (Moses 7:41–67), the brother of Jared (Ether 3–4), Moses (Moses 1:8, 25–28), Isaiah (Isa. 2:1–5), Jeremiah (Jer. 3:14–18; 31:31–34), and Moroni (Mormon 8:34, 35; Ether 12:38–41).

POINT OF INTEREST

This sample, originally belonging to David Whitmer, may be a copy of the reformed Egyptian characters Joseph Smith made from the gold plates for Martin Harris to take to Charles Anthon, a linguist at Columbia College in New York.

to pass I showed them thee; and I showed them for fear lest thou
shouldst say—Mine idol hath done them, and my graven image, and
my molten image hath commanded them.
6. Thou hast seen and heard all this; and will ye not declare them?
And that I have showed thee new things from this time, even hidden things, and thou didst not know them.
7. They are created now, and not from the beginning, even before
the day when thou heardest them not they were declared unto
thee, lest thou shouldst say—Behold I knew them.
8. Yea, and thou heardest not; yea, thou knewest not; yea, from that
time thine ear was not opened; for I knew that thou wouldst deal very
treacherously, and wast called a transgressor from the womb.
9. Nevertheless, for my name's sake will I defer mine anger, and for
my praise will I refrain from thee, that I cut thee not off.
10. For, behold, I have refined thee, I have chosen thee in the furnace of affliction.
11. For mine own sake, yea, for mine own sake will I do this, for I
will not suffer my name to be polluted, and I will not give my glory
unto another.
12. Hearken unto me, O Jacob, and Israel my called, for I am he; I am
the first, and I am also the last.
13. Mine hand hath also laid the foundation of the earth, and my
right hand hath spanned the heavens. I call unto them and they
stand up together.
14. All ye, assemble yourselves, and hear; who among them hath
declared these things unto them? The Lord hath loved him; yea,
and he will fulfill his word which he hath declared by them; and he
will do his pleasure on Babylon, and his arm shall come upon the
Chaldeans.
15. Also, saith the Lord; I the Lord, yea, I have spoken; yea, I
have called him to declare, I have brought him, and he shall
make his way prosperous.
16. Come ye near unto me; I have not spoken in secret; from the
beginning, from the time that it was declared have I spoken; and
the Lord God, and his Spirit, hath sent me.
17. And thus saith the Lord, thy Redeemer, the Holy One of Israel;
I have sent him, the Lord thy God who teacheth thee to profit,
who leadeth thee by the way thou shouldst go, hath done it.
18. O that thou hadst hearkened to my commandments—then had
thy peace been as a river, and thy righteousness as the waves of the
sea.
19. Thy seed also had been as the sand; the offspring of thy bowels
like the gravel thereof; his name should not have been cut off nor
destroyed from before me.
20. Go ye forth of Babylon, flee ye from the Chaldeans, with a
voice of singing declare ye, tell this, utter to the end of the earth;
say ye: The

1 Nephi 20:14

In this verse, Isaiah refers to the period after the Jews were held captive by Babylon and the Lord intervened in their behalf.

1 Nephi 20:18

This verse provides a powerful reminder that the righteous need not fear.

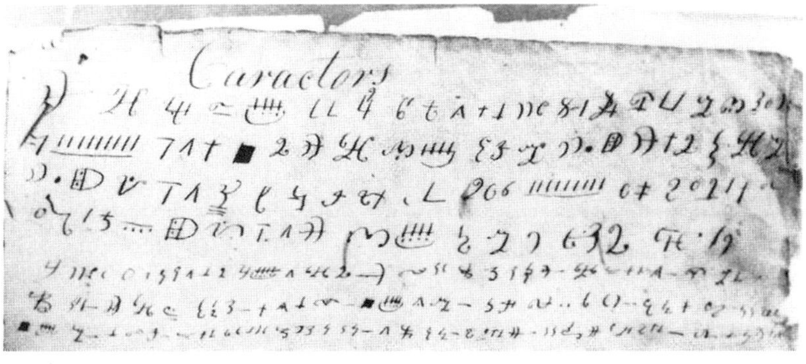

Lord hath redeemed his servant Jacob.
21. And they thirsted not; he led them through the deserts; he
caused the waters to flow out of the rock for them; he clave the
rock also and the waters gushed out.
22. And notwithstanding he hath done all this, and greater also,
there is no peace, saith the Lord, unto the wicked.

CHAPTER 21

1. AND again: Hearken, O ye house of Israel, all ye that are broken
off and are driven out because of the wickedness of the pastors of my
people; yea, all ye that are broken off, that are scattered abroad, who
are of my people, O house of Israel. Listen, O isles, unto me, and
hearken ye people from far; the Lord hath called me from the
womb; from the bowels of my mother hath he made mention of my
name.
2. And he hath made my mouth like a sharp sword; in the shadow
of his hand hath he hid me, and made me a polished shaft; in his
quiver hath he hid me;
3. And said unto me: Thou art my servant, O Israel, in whom I will
be glorified.
4. Then I said, I have labored in vain, I have spent my strength for
naught and in vain; surely my judgment is with the Lord, and my
work with my God.
5. And now, saith the Lord—that formed me from the womb that
I should be his servant, to bring Jacob again to him—though Israel
be not gathered, yet shall I be glorious in the eyes of the Lord, and
my God shall be my strength.
6. And he said: It is a light thing that thou shouldst be my servant
to raise up the tribes of Jacob, and to restore the preserved of Israel.
I will also give thee for a light to the Gentiles, that thou mayest be
my salvation unto the ends of the earth.
7. Thus saith the Lord, the Redeemer of Israel, his Holy One, to him
whom man despiseth, to him whom the nations abhorreth, to servant of rulers: Kings shall see and arise, princes also shall worship,
because of the Lord that is faithful.
8. Thus saith the Lord: In an acceptable time have I heard thee,
O isles of the sea, and in a day of salvation have I helped thee; and
I will preserve thee, and give thee my servant for a covenant of
the people, to establish the earth, to cause to inherit the desolate
heritages;
9. That thou mayest say to the prisoners: Go forth; to them that sit
in darkness: Show yourselves. They shall feed in the ways, and their
pastures shall be in all high places.
10. They shall not hunger nor thirst, neither shall the heat nor the
sun smite them; for he that hath mercy on them shall lead them,
even by the springs of water shall he guide them.
11. And I will make all my mountains a way, and my highways
shall be exalted.

1 Nephi 21:1

The following part of 1 Nephi 21:1 has been entirely left out of the Old Testament account: "And again: Hearken, O ye house of Israel, all ye that are broken off and are driven out, because of the wickedness of the pastors of my people; yea, all ye that are broken off, that are scattered abroad, who are of my people, O house of Israel." It is entirely possible that one of the "wicked pastors" of Israel objected to this statement and deleted it from the record of the scriptures that remained in Jerusalem. (Ludlow)

1 Nephi 21:1, 8; 22:4

According to a quotation by Reynolds and Sjodahl, "Sir Isaac Newton observes that to the Hebrews the continents of Asia and Africa were 'the earth,' because they had access to them by land, while the parts of the earth to which they sailed over the sea were 'the isles of the sea.'" (*Commentary on the Book of Mormon*, 1:214.)

Thus, Nephi not only refers to the isles of the sea as the location of other remnants of the house of Israel, but he also indicates that he and his people were then living upon an "isle of the sea" when he quite clearly is referring to the great land mass known as the American continent (2 Nephi 10:20–21). (Ludlow)

1 Nephi 21:6

In this verse, a "light thing" refers to something that is not enough. The Jews are warned here that it is not enough that they simply strengthen each other; they are expected to be an ensign to the nations and to carry the fulness of the gospel to the gentiles.

12. And then, O house of Israel, behold, these shall come from far; and lo, these from the north and from the west; and these from the land of Sinim.
13. Sing, O heavens; and be joyful, O earth; for the feet of those who are in the east shall be established; and break forth into singing, O mountains; for they shall be smitten no more; for the Lord hath comforted his people, and will have mercy upon his afflicted.
14. But, behold, Zion hath said: The Lord hath forsaken me, and my Lord hath forgotten me—but he will show that he hath not.
15. For can a woman forget her sucking child, that she should not have compassion on the son of her womb? Yea, they may forget, yet will I not forget thee, O house of Israel.
16. Behold, I have graven thee upon the palms of my hands; thy walls are continually before me.
17. Thy children shall make haste against thy destroyers; and they that made thee waste shall go forth of thee.
18. Lift up thine eyes round about and behold; all these gather themselves together, and they shall come to thee. And as I live, saith the Lord, thou shalt surely clothe thee with them all, as with an ornament, and bind them on even as a bride.
19. For thy waste and thy desolate places, and the land of thy destruction, shall even now be too narrow by reason of the inhabitants; and they that swallowed thee up shall be far away.
20. The children whom thou shalt have, after thou hast lost the first, shall again in thine ears say: The place is too strait for me; give place to me that I may dwell.
21. Then shalt thou say in thine heart: Who hath begotten me these, seeing I have lost my children, and am desolate, a captive, and removing to and fro? And who hath brought up these? Behold, I was left alone; these, where have they been?
22. Thus saith the Lord God: Behold, I will lift up mine hand to the Gentiles, and set up my standard to the people; and they shall bring thy sons in their arms, and thy daughters shall be carried upon their shoulders.
23. And kings shall be thy nursing fathers, and their queens thy nursing mothers; they shall bow down to thee with their face towards the earth, and lick up the dust of thy feet; and thou shalt know that I am the Lord; for they shall not be ashamed that wait for me.
24. For shall the prey be taken from the mighty, or the lawful captives delivered?
25. But thus saith the Lord, even the captives of the mighty shall be taken away, and the prey of the terrible shall be delivered; for I will contend with him that contendeth with thee, and I will save thy children.
26. And I will feed them that

1 Nephi 21:13–16

This poetic passage provides yet another reminder of Christ's saving role, that of protective, redeeming parent to Zion's children. He comforts his people and shows mercy when they are afflicted, as any loving father or mother would toward a child, but, as Nephi here reminds us through Isaiah, much more than any mortal father and mother could do. Although a mother may forget her sucking child (as unlikely as any parent might think that could be), Christ will not forget the children he has redeemed or the covenant he has made with them for salvation in Zion. The painful reminders of that watch care and covenant are the marks of the Roman nails graven upon the palms of his hands, a sign to his disciples in the Old World, his Nephite congregation in the New World, and to us in latter-day Zion that he is the Savior of the world. (Ludlow)

1 Nephi 21:15–16

In these two verses, the Lord helps us better understand His loving nature by reminding us of a woman's perspective. He promises us that He will never forget us, just as a woman can never forget a child to whom she gives birth and life-sustaining nurturing. That perspective can be drawn out to include other parallels as well. For example, a woman often carries with her permanent physical scars or other physical marks that remind her always of the profound sacrifices involved in giving birth to her child. Similarly, the resurrected Savior carries with Him the permanent physical marks of the nail prints in His hands and feet—marks that remind us of the profound and incomprehensible sacrifice He wrought for each of us.

oppress thee with their own flesh; they shall be drunken with their own blood as with sweet wine; and all flesh shall know that I, the Lord, am thy Savior and thy Redeemer, the Mighty One of Jacob.

CHAPTER 22

1. AND now it came to pass that after I, Nephi, had read these things which were engraven upon the plates of brass, my brethren came unto me and said unto me: What meaneth these things which ye have read? Behold, are they to be understood according to things which are spiritual, which shall come to pass according to the spirit and not the flesh?

2. And I, Nephi, said unto them: Behold they were manifest unto the prophet by the voice of the Spirit; for by the Spirit are all things made known unto the prophets, which shall come upon the children of men according to the flesh.

3. Wherefore, the things of which I have read are things pertaining to things both temporal and spiritual; for it appears that the house of Israel, sooner or later, will be scattered upon all the face of the earth, and also among all nations.

4. And behold, there are many who are already lost from the knowledge of those who are at Jerusalem. Yea, the more part of all the tribes have been led away; and they are scattered to and fro upon the isles of the sea; and whither they are none of us knoweth, save that we know that they have been led away.

5. And since they have been led away, these things have been prophesied concerning them, and also concerning all those who shall hereafter be scattered and be confounded, because of the Holy One of Israel; for against him will they harden their hearts; wherefore, they shall be scattered among all nations and shall be hated of all men.

6. Nevertheless, after they shall be nursed by the Gentiles, and the Lord has lifted up his hand upon the Gentiles and set them up for a standard, and their children have been carried in their arms, and their daughters have been carried upon their shoulders, behold these things of which are spoken are temporal; for thus are the covenants of the Lord with our fathers; and it meaneth us in the days to come, and also all our brethren who are of the house of Israel.

7. And it meaneth that the time cometh that after all the house of Israel have been scattered and confounded, that the Lord God will raise up a mighty nation among the Gentiles, yea, even upon the face of this land; and by them shall our seed be scattered.

8. And after our seed is scattered the

1 Nephi 22:3

"Scattering" can mean that (1) people lose their identity and are lost to history (as what happened with the ten tribes); (2) people leave the main group but maintain their identity (as what occurred with Lehi's colony); or (3) people are dispersed and scattered among other people (as what happened to the Jews). "Gathering" means gaining knowledge and truth.

1 Nephi 22:4

To the Hebrews, the world consisted of Asia and Africa. Anything they had to reach by sailing over water was considered an "isle of the sea."

1 Nephi 22:4–5

Saying that the tribes are "lost" does not mean that they have been removed to some mysterious location; as specified in the scriptures, they have been "scattered amond all nations." They are "lost," then, in the following ways:

- They do not have the gospel and the ordinances essential to exaltation
- They do not have the priesthood
- Their lineage can be established only by an ordained patriarch speaking by revelation
- They have been separated from the lands of their inheritance

As they recognize the truthfulness of the gospel and enter the waters of baptism, they will no longer be "lost" in the important spiritual sense of that word.

POINT OF INTEREST

These are images of different Assyrian officials and priests in their respective garments. It's interesting to note that while Assyria lasted more than two centuries, its successor, Babylon, left perhaps just as heavy a mark on civilization but in only seventy years. It was swept into oblivion by its successor, Persia.

Lord God will proceed to do a marvelous work among the
Gentiles, which shall be of great worth unto our seed; wherefore, it
is likened unto their being nourished by the Gentiles and being
carried in their arms and upon their shoulders.
9. And it shall also be of worth unto the Gentiles; and not only
unto the Gentiles but unto all the house of Israel, unto the making
known of the covenants of the Father of heaven unto Abraham,
saying: In thy seed shall all the kindreds of the earth be blessed.
10. And I would, my brethren, that ye should know that all the
kindreds of the earth cannot be blessed unless he shall make bare
his arm in the eyes of the nations.
11. Wherefore, the Lord God will proceed to make bare his arm in
the eyes of all the nations, in bringing about his covenants and his
gospel unto those who are of the house of Israel.
12. Wherefore, he will bring them again out of captivity, and they
shall be gathered together to the lands of their inheritance; and
they shall be brought out of obscurity and out of darkness; and they
shall know that the Lord is their Savior and their Redeemer, the
Mighty One of Israel.
13. And the blood of that great and abominable church, which is
the whore of all the earth, shall turn upon their own heads; for
they shall war among themselves, and the sword of their own
hands shall fall upon their own heads, and they shall be drunken
with their own blood.
14. And every nation which shall war against thee, O house of
Israel, shall be turned one against another, and they shall fall into
the pit which they digged to ensnare the people of the Lord. And all
that fight against Zion shall be destroyed, and that great whore, who
hath perverted the right ways of the Lord, yea, that great and abominable church, shall tumble to the dust and great shall be the fall of
it.
15. For behold, saith the prophet, the time cometh speedily that
Satan shall have no more power over the hearts of the children of
men; for the day soon cometh that all the proud and they who do
wickedly shall be as stubble; and the day cometh that they must be
burned.
16. For the time soon cometh that the fulness of the wrath of God
shall be poured out upon all the children

1 Nephi 22:12

This verse refers to three types of gathering: (1) the return of the Jews to Jerusalem, (2) the restoration of the Lost Tribes, and (3) all gaining knowledge of the truth regarding Jesus Christ.

1 Nephi 22:13

This verse prophesies that the great and abominable church—the church of the devil—will destroy itself.

1 Nephi 22:15

This prophecy is very similar to that made by Malachi (see Malachi 4:1), even though Malachi's record was written a hundred years later. According to Elder Bruce R. McConkie, both Nephi and Malachi were quoting the prophet Zenos.

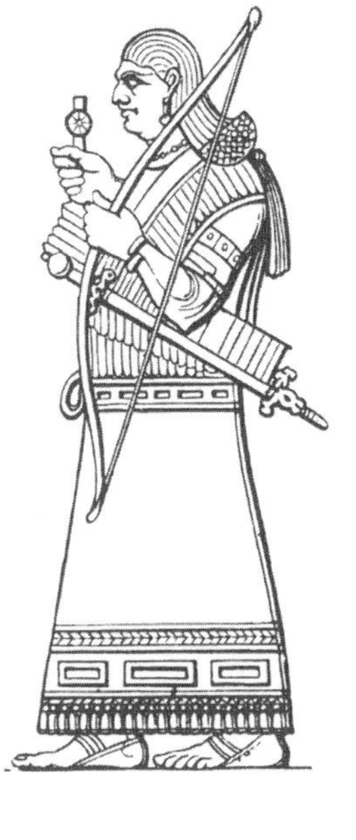

of men; for he will not suffer that the wicked shall destroy the
righteous.
17. Wherefore, he will preserve the righteous by his power, even if
it so be that the fulness of his wrath must come, and the righteous
be preserved, even unto the destruction of their enemies by fire.
Wherefore, the righteous need not fear; for thus saith the prophet,
they shall be saved, even if it so be as by fire.
18. Behold, my brethren, I say unto you, that these things must shortly come; yea, even blood, and fire, and vapor of smoke must come;
and it must needs be upon the face of this earth; and it cometh unto
men according to the flesh if it so be that they will harden their hearts
against the Holy One of Israel.
19. For behold, the righteous shall not perish; for the time surely
must come that all they who fight against Zion shall be cut off.
20. And the Lord will surely prepare a way for his people, unto the
fulfilling of the words of Moses, which he spake, saying: A prophet
shall the Lord your God raise up unto you, like unto me; him shall
ye hear in all things whatsoever he shall say unto you. And it shall
come to pass that all those who will not hear that prophet shall be
cut off from among the people.
21. And now I, Nephi, declare unto you, that this prophet of
whom Moses spake was the Holy One of Israel; wherefore, he shall
execute judgment in righteousness.
22. And the righteous need not fear, for they are those who shall
not be confounded. But it is the kingdom of the devil, which shall
be built up among the children of men, which kingdom is established among them which are in the flesh—
23. For the time speedily shall come that all churches which are
built up to get gain, and all those who are built up to get power
over the flesh, and those who are built up to become popular in the
eyes of the world, and those who seek the lusts of the flesh and the
things of the world, and to do all manner of iniquity; yea, in fine,
all those who belong to the kingdom of the devil are they who
need fear, and tremble, and quake; they are those who must be
brought low in the dust; they are those who must be consumed as
stubble; and this is according to the words of the prophet.
24. And the time cometh speedily that the righteous must be led
up as calves of the stall, and the Holy One of Israel must reign in
dominion, and might, and power, and great glory.
25. And he gathereth his children from the four quarters of the
earth; and he numbereth his sheep, and they know him; and there
shall be one fold and one shepherd; and he shall feed his sheep,
and in him they shall find pasture.
26. And because of the righteousness of his people, Satan has no
power; wherefore, he cannot be loosed for the space of many
years; for he hath no power over the hearts

1 Nephi 22:20

The prophet referred to in this verse is the Savior, Jesus Christ.

1 Nephi 22:26

Joseph Smith taught that the Savior and the resurrected Saints will reign over the earth during the thousand years of the Millennium. He further taught that they will not continuously dwell on the earth, but that they will visit it as necessary to carry out the duties of governing those who are here during that period.

1 Nephi 22:26

Our righteousness is what will destroy Satan.

of the people, for they dwell in righteousness, and the Holy One
of Israel reigneth.
27. And now behold, I, Nephi, say unto you that all these things
must come according to the flesh.
28. But, behold, all nations, kindreds, tongues, and people shall
dwell safely in the Holy One of Israel if it so be that they will
repent.
29. And now I, Nephi, make an end; for I durst not speak further
as yet concerning these things.
30. Wherefore, my brethren, I would that ye should consider that
the things which have been written upon the plates of brass are
true; and they testify that a man must be obedient to the commandments of God.
31. Wherefore, ye need not suppose that I and my father are the
only ones that have testified, and also taught them. Wherefore, if
ye shall be obedient to the commandments, and endure to the end,
ye shall be saved at the last day. And thus it is. Amen.

THE SECOND BOOK OF NEPHI

An account of the death of Lehi. Nephi's brethren rebel against him. The Lord warns Nephi to depart into the wilderness. His journeyings in the wilderness, and so forth.

CHAPTER 1

1. AND now it came to pass that after I, Nephi, had made an end
of teaching my brethren, our father, Lehi, also spake many things
unto them, and rehearsed unto them, how great things the Lord
had done for them in bringing them out of the land of Jerusalem.
2. And he spake unto them concerning their rebellions upon the
waters, and the mercies of God in sparing their lives, that they
were not swallowed up in the sea.
3. And he also spake unto them concerning the land of promise,
which they had obtained—how merciful the Lord had been in
warning us that we should flee out of the land of Jerusalem.
4. For, behold, said he, I have seen a vision, in which I know that
Jerusalem is destroyed; and had we remained in Jerusalem we
should also have perished.
5. But, said he, notwithstanding our afflictions, we have obtained
a land of promise, a land which is choice above all other lands; a
land which the Lord God hath covenanted

1 Nephi 22:31

It is quite evident that Nephi intended that the concluding verse of 1 Nephi should close a major part of his literary efforts. Thus, he concludes this section with the construction "And thus it is. Amen." Dr. Hugh Nibley has indicated that Nephi frequently closed the major sections of his writing with such a phrase; he also indicates that Nephi may have gotten this idea from the Egyptians: "Egyptian literary writings regularly close with the formula *iw-f-pw*, 'Thus it is,' 'and so it is.' Nephi ends the main sections of his book with the phrase, 'And thus it is. Amen.' (9:6; 14:30; 22:31.)" (Ludlow)

2 Nephi 1:1–6

Certainly Lehi's posterity are rightful heirs. They have a blood-line inheritance. Other groups have been inspired and guided to come to this land. They have been brought by the Lord. All of these are guests of the Lord, and should feel to rejoice, as Lehi did. They also may have avoided destruction in some other geographical place. Or they may have been led here to fulfill some purpose known only to the Lord. Whatever the reason, they should treasure their inheritance and privilege to live in this land of liberty.

But what about the people living here who do not trace their lineage to either group? Are they considered to be intruders? Should they feel they are only guests of those whose inheritance is the land? Elder James E. Talmage spoke of the covenant the Lord made with Lehi and taught the following:

"Mark you, I pray, the prophet [Lehi] knew that it was not to be a selfish inheritance, it was not to be kept forever solely for the habitation of his lineal descendants. It was to be for all those who were then to be led out from other countries by the hand of the Lord." . . . (CR, Oct. 1919, 97–98).

The message of the Lord's covenant with Lehi is clear. All who live in this designated promised land, regardless of their origin, have received a conditional inheritance based on faithful service to the Lord and obedience to His commandments. On the other hand, there shall be a loss of that inheritance if the people reject the Holy One of Israel. (See 2 Ne. 1:7–11.) (O/C)

2 Nephi 1:4

The destruction of Jerusalem referred to in 2 Nephi 1:4 is recorded in the Bible in 2 Kings 25. Lehi and his group had been warned by the Lord to flee from the land of Jerusalem so that they would escape this destruction. Most biblical scholars date the destruction of Jerusalem by the Babylonians somewhere between 586 B.C. and 590 B.C. Thus in his chronological footnotes in this section of the Book of Mormon, Brother Talmage suggests that the events following Lehi's vision of the destruction of Jerusalem took place sometime after about 588 B.C. (Ludlow)

with me should be a land for the inheritance of my seed. Yea, the
Lord hath covenanted this land unto me, and to my children forever, and also all those who should be led out of other countries by
the hand of the Lord.
6. Wherefore, I, Lehi, prophesy according to the workings of the
Spirit which is in me, that there shall none come into this land
save they shall be brought by the hand of the Lord.
7. Wherefore, this land is consecrated unto him whom he shall
bring. And if it so be that they shall serve him according to the
commandments which he hath given, it shall be a land of liberty
unto them; wherefore, they shall never be brought down into captivity; if so, it shall be because of iniquity; for if iniquity shall
abound cursed shall be the land for their sakes, but unto the righteous it shall be blessed forever.
8. And behold, it is wisdom that this land should be kept as yet
from the knowledge of other nations; for behold, many nations
would overrun the land, that there would be no place for an inheritance.
9. Wherefore, I, Lehi, have obtained a promise, that inasmuch as
those whom the Lord God shall bring out of the land of Jerusalem
shall keep his commandments, they shall prosper upon the face of
this land; and they shall be kept from all other nations, that they
may possess this land unto themselves. And if it so be that they
shall keep his commandments they shall be blessed upon the face
of this land, and there shall be none to molest them, nor to take
away the land of their inheritance; and they shall dwell safely forever.
10. But behold, when the time cometh that they shall dwindle in
unbelief, after they have received so great blessings from the hand
of the Lord—having a knowledge of the creation of the earth, and
all men, knowing the great and marvelous works of the Lord from
the creation of the world; having power given them to do all things
by faith; having all the commandments from the beginning, and
having been brought by his infinite goodness into this precious land
of promise—behold, I say, if the day shall come that they will reject
the Holy One of Israel, the true Messiah, their Redeemer and their
God, behold, the judgments of him that is just shall rest upon them.
11. Yea, he will bring other nations unto them, and he will give unto
them power, and he will take away from them the lands of their possessions, and he will cause them to be scattered and smitten.
12. Yea, as one generation passeth to another there shall be bloodsheds, and great visitations among them; wherefore, my sons, I
would that ye would remember; yea, I would that ye would heark-
en unto my words.
13. O that ye would awake; awake from a deep sleep, yea, even
from the sleep of hell, and shake off the awful chains by which ye
are bound, which are the chains which bind the children of men,
that they are carried away captive down to the eternal gulf of misery and woe.

2 Nephi 1:7–11

Elder James E. Talmage spoke of the covenant the Lord made with Lehi and taught the following:

"Mark you, I pray, the prophet [Lehi] knew that it was not to be a selfish inheritance, it was not to be kept forever solely for the habitation of his lineal descendants. It was to be for all those who were then to be led out from other countries by the hand of the Lord. . . . And so let us not fear that our nation is going to lose its identity, or is going to lose its sovereignty or is going to be overwhelmed or overpowered by other nations. It can not be so save through iniquity." (O/C)

2 Nephi 1:8

One of the great mysteries of history is how the existence of the great north and south American continents could be kept from the knowledge of the inhabitants of the Old World (Europe, Asia, and Africa). However, with the Lord all things are possible, and the Lord revealed to Lehi that it was wisdom in Him that the existence of this land should be kept from the knowledge of other nations; otherwise "many nations would overrun the land, that there would be no place for an inheritance" for Lehi and his descendants. (2 Nephi 1:8.) (Ludlow)

2 Nephi 1:12

Lehi offers up patriarchal exhortations to his family circle. He pleads with Laman and Lemuel to remember the goodness of God, repent and keep the commandments, put on the armor of righteousness, and rebel no more against their brother Nephi. He reminds them pointedly that only righteous behavior will preserve liberty in the land for those who occupy it. . . .

The Prophet Joseph Smith said that "if parents fail to do this and the children go astray and turn from the truth, then the Lord has said the sin shall be upon the heads of the parents. The loss of the children will be charged to the parents and they will be responsible for their apostasy and darkness. . . . I do not believe that it would be possible for me to be admitted into exaltation and glory in the Kingdom of God, if through my neglect of duty my children should become the children of darkness in this regard. . . . I will endeavor with all the power I possess to have them as true and faithful to this gospel as it is possible for me to be; because, without all of them in the Kingdom of God I would feel that my household was not perfect." (P/A)

14. Awake! and arise from the dust, and hear the words of a trembling parent, whose limbs ye must soon lay down in the cold and
silent grave, from whence no traveler can return; a few more days
and I go the way of all the earth.
15. But behold, the Lord hath redeemed my soul from hell; I have
beheld his glory, and I am encircled about eternally in the arms of
his love.
16. And I desire that ye should remember to observe the statutes
and the judgments of the Lord; behold, this hath been the anxiety
of my soul from the beginning.
17. My heart hath been weighed down with sorrow from time to
time, for I have feared, lest for the hardness of your hearts the Lord
your God should come out in the fulness of his wrath upon you, that
ye be cut off and destroyed forever;
18. Or, that a cursing should come upon you for the space of many
generations; and ye are visited by sword, and by famine, and are
hated, and are led according to the will and captivity of the devil.
19. O my sons, that these things might not come upon you, but
that ye might be a choice and a favored people of the Lord. But
behold, his will be done; for his ways are righteousness forever.
20. And he hath said that: Inasmuch as ye shall keep my commandments ye shall prosper in the land; but inasmuch as ye will
not keep my commandments ye shall be cut off from my presence.
21. And now that my soul might have joy in you, and that my heart
might leave this world with gladness because of you, that I might not
be brought down with grief and sorrow to the grave, arise from the
dust, my sons, and be men, and be determined in one mind and in
one heart, united in all things, that ye may not come down into captivity;
22. That ye may not be cursed with a sore cursing; and also, that ye
may not incur the displeasure of a just God upon you, unto the
destruction, yea, the eternal destruction of both soul and body.
23. Awake, my sons; put on the armor of righteousness. Shake off
the chains with which ye are bound, and come forth out of obscurity, and arise from the dust.
24. Rebel no more against your brother, whose views have been
glorious, and who hath kept the commandments from the time
that we left Jerusalem; and who hath been an instrument in the
hands of God, in bringing us forth into the land of promise; for
were it not for him, we must have perished with hunger in the
wilderness; nevertheless, ye sought to take away his

POINT OF INTEREST

Nabu (known as Nebo in the Bible) was the Babylonian god of wisdom and writing, represented by a clay writing tablet and stylus. He was introduced by the Amorites into Mesopotamia about the same time as was Marduk; but while Marduk became Babylon's main deity, Nabu was first called a scribe and minister to Marduk and was later assimilated as Marduk's son. He gradually took office as patron of the scribes, replacing the Sumerian goddess Nisaba. It is possibly in Nabu's name that Nebuchadnezzar II undertook the training and education of a select group of the conquered Israelites, including Daniel, Meshach, Shadrach, and Abed-nego.

life; yea, and he hath suffered much sorrow because of you.
25. And I exceedingly fear and tremble because of you, lest he shall
suffer again; for behold, ye have accused him that he sought power
and authority over you; but I know that he hath not sought for
power nor authority over you, but he hath sought the glory of God,
and your own eternal welfare.
26. And ye have murmured because he hath been plain unto you. Ye
say that he hath used sharpness; ye say that he hath been angry with
you; but behold, his sharpness was the sharpness of the power of the
word of God, which was in him; and that which ye call anger was the
truth, according to that which is in God, which he could not restrain,
manifesting boldly concerning your iniquities.
27. And it must needs be that the power of God must be with him,
even unto his commanding you that ye must obey. But behold, it
was not he, but it was the Spirit of the Lord which was in him,
which opened his mouth to utterance that he could not shut it.
28. And now my son, Laman, and also Lemuel and Sam, and also
my sons who are the sons of Ishmael, behold, if ye will hearken
unto the voice of Nephi ye shall not perish. And if ye will hearken unto him I leave unto you a blessing, yea, even my first blessing.
29. But if ye will not hearken unto him I take away my first blessing, yea, even my blessing, and it shall rest upon him.
30. And now Zoram, I speak unto you: Behold, thou art the servant
of Laban; nevertheless, thou hast been brought out of the land of
Jerusalem, and I know that thou art a true friend unto my son,
Nephi, forever.
31. Wherefore, because thou hast been faithful thy seed shall be
blessed with his seed, that they dwell in prosperity long upon the
face of this land; and nothing, save it shall be iniquity among
them, shall harm or disturb their prosperity upon the face of this
land forever.
32. Wherefore, if ye shall keep the commandments of the Lord, the
Lord hath consecrated this land for the security of thy seed with
the seed of my son.

2 Nephi 1:30–32

These verses illustrate how one can inherit covenant blessings through personal righteousness. Those blessings then continue to one's posterity, demonstrating the lasting effect of righteousness.

CHAPTER 2

1. AND now, Jacob, I speak unto you: Thou art my first-born in the
days of my tribulation in the wilderness. And behold, in thy childhood thou hast suffered afflictions and much sorrow, because of the
rudeness of thy brethren.
2. Nevertheless, Jacob, my first-born in the wilderness, thou knowest the greatness of God; and he shall consecrate thine afflictions
for thy gain.
3. Wherefore, thy soul shall be blessed, and thou shalt dwell safely
with thy brother, Nephi; and thy days shall be spent in the service
of thy God. Wherefore, I know that thou art redeemed, because of
the righteousness of thy Redeemer; for thou hast beheld that in the
fulness

2 Nephi 2:2

Our greatest growth occurs through affliction, which is why we should not ask our Heavenly Father to take it from us. As President Marion G. Romney stated, "If we can bear our afflictions with understanding, faith, and courage, we shall be strengthened and comforted in many ways. . . . I have seen people rise to great heights from what seemed to be unbearable burdens."

of time he cometh to bring salvation unto men.

4. And thou hast beheld in thy youth his glory; wherefore, thou art blessed even as they unto whom he shall minister in the flesh; for the Spirit is the same, yesterday, today, and forever. And the way is prepared from the fall of man, and salvation is free.

5. And men are instructed sufficiently that they know good from evil. And the law is given unto men. And by the law no flesh is justified; or, by the law men are cut off. Yea, by the temporal law they were cut off; and also, by the spiritual law they perish from that which is good, and become miserable forever.

6. Wherefore, redemption cometh in and through the Holy Messiah; for he is full of grace and truth.

7. Behold, he offereth himself a sacrifice for sin, to answer the ends of the law, unto all those who have a broken heart and a contrite spirit; and unto none else can the ends of the law be answered.

8. Wherefore, how great the importance to make these things known unto the inhabitants of the earth, that they may know that there is no flesh that can dwell in the presence of God, save it be through the merits, and mercy, and grace of the Holy Messiah, who layeth down his life according to the flesh, and taketh it again by the power of the Spirit, that he may bring to pass the resurrection of the dead, being the first that should rise.

9. Wherefore, he is the firstfruits unto God, inasmuch as he shall make intercession for all the children of men; and they that believe in him shall be saved.

10. And because of the intercession for all, all men come unto God; wherefore, they stand in the presence of him to be judged of him according to the truth and holiness which is in him. Wherefore, the ends of the law which the Holy One hath given, unto the inflicting of the punishment which is affixed, which punishment that is affixed is in opposition to that of the happiness which is affixed, to answer the ends of the atonement—

11. For it must needs be, that there is an opposition in all things. If not so, my first-born in the wilderness, righteousness could not be brought to pass, neither wickedness, neither holiness nor misery, neither good nor bad. Wherefore, all things must needs be acompound in one; wherefore,

POINT OF INTEREST

Genealogy of the Twelve Tribes of Israel

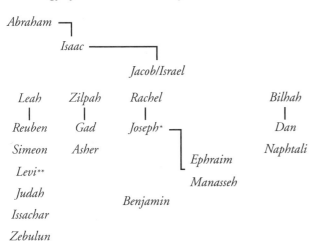

Abraham
- *Isaac*
  - *Jacob/Israel*

Leah: *Reuben*, *Simeon*, *Levi***, *Judah*, *Issachar*, *Zebulun*

Zilpah: *Gad*, *Asher*

Rachel: *Joseph** (*Ephraim*, *Manasseh*), *Benjamin*

Bilhah: *Dan*, *Naphtali*

* *Joseph, as the birthright son, received a double inheritance. Thus, rather than one tribe of Joseph, there are two tribes of Joseph—the tribes of his two sons, Ephraim and Manasseh.*

** *Levi is not counted among the twelve tribes of Israel. Rather than receiving a land inheritance with the other tribes, the tribe of Levi was given the priesthood as its inheritance (see Num. 8:14; 18:20; Joshua 18:7).*

2 Nephi 2:4

Lehi declared, ". . . there is a God, and he hath created all things, both the heavens and the earth, and all things that in them are" (2 Ne. 2:14). Life and material things did not come about by chance. They are all products of creative action by a creator who is a God. From the scriptures we learn of six periods of creation, during which time this creation process took place. At the conclusion of each period, God declared ". . . all things which I had made were good," except the last period during which mankind was placed on the earth, and He stated, ". . . all things which I had made were very good" (Moses 2:10, 12, 18, 21, 25, 31).

God is eternal and His creations are eternal. They did not need to be changed, improved, or evolve into something different. They would stay just as they were originally formed. (O/C)

2 Nephi 2:4

According to Orson Pratt, the Savior's atonement provided freedom for all from penalty for the original sin—without any condition on their part. In that way, salvation is free.

2 Nephi 2:8

No matter how righteous we are and what we achieve, we cannot return to God without Christ. Nonetheless, we must do our part, making every effort to achieve personal righteousness. As Elder James E. Talmage said, "All men are in need of the Savior's mediation, for all are transgressors. . . . Redemption from individual sin, while open for all to attain, is conditioned on individual effort."

2 Nephi 2:11

Lehi was no stranger to adversity and life-threatening challenges. He understood firsthand the goodness of God and the evils of Satan. . . . Within Lehi's own family, as within God's vast premortal realm, there were great differences in evidence: humility versus pride, spirituality versus selfishness, obedience versus rebellion. It is no wonder that the aging patriarch, in his parting discourse to his sons, sounded the eternal theme: "For it must needs be, that there is an opposition in all things" (2 Ne. 2:11). He could see clearly that Laman and Lemuel, and all who were with them, barring a change in their lifestyle, would harvest a miserable destiny of darkness and death. Conversely, Nephi and his circle would enjoy untold blessings of the Lord based on their faithfulness and obedience. (P/A)

if it should be one body it must needs remain as dead, having no life neither death, nor corruption nor incorruption, happiness nor misery, neither sense nor insensibility.
12. Wherefore, it must needs have been created for a thing of naught; wherefore there would have been no purpose in the end of its creation. Wherefore, this thing must needs destroy the wisdom of God and his eternal purposes, and also the power, and the mercy, and the justice of God.
13. And if ye shall say there is no law, ye shall also say there is no sin. If ye shall say there is no sin, ye shall also say there is no righteousness. And if there be no righteousness there be no happiness. And if there be no righteousness nor happiness there be no punishment nor misery. And if these things are not there is no God. And if there is no God we are not, neither the earth; for there could have been no creation of things, neither to act nor to be acted upon; wherefore, all things must have vanished away.
14. And now, my sons, I speak unto you these things for your profit and learning; for there is a God, and he hath created all things, both the heavens and the earth, and all things that in them are, both things to act and things to be acted upon.
15. And to bring about his eternal purposes in the end of man, after he had created our first parents, and the beasts of the field and the fowls of the air, and in fine, all things which are created, it must needs be that there was an opposition; even the forbidden fruit in opposition to the tree of life; the one being sweet and the other bitter.
16. Wherefore, the Lord God gave unto man that he should act for himself. Wherefore, man could not act for himself save it should be that he was enticed by the one or the other.
17. And I, Lehi, according to the things which I have read, must needs suppose that an angel of God, according to that which is written, had fallen from heaven; wherefore, he became a devil, having sought that which was evil before God.
18. And because he had fallen from heaven, and had become miserable forever, he sought also the misery of all mankind. Wherefore, he said unto Eve, yea, even that old serpent, who is the devil, who is the father of all lies, wherefore he said: Partake of the forbidden fruit, and ye shall not die, but ye shall be as God, knowing good and evil.
19. And after Adam and Eve had partaken of the forbidden fruit they were driven out of the garden of Eden, to till the earth.
20. And they have brought forth

POINT OF INTEREST

"Like most things in ancient Israel, the calendar is largely governed by religion. Each week has seven days, ending with a Sabbath. Days are determined from sundown to sundown, so . . . when we say "Thursday night," we mean the night before Thursday day. . . . The year is lunar and the months are called yerah *(which means "moon") or* hodesh *(which means "new moon"). These months determine religious festivals [and] alternate between twenty-nine and thirty days"* (John W. Welch and Robert D. Hunt, "Culturegram: Jerusalem 600 B.C.," *Glimpses of Lehi's Jerusalem* [Provo, Utah: FARMS, 2004]).

2 Nephi 2:11–27

Notice the major points in Lehi's argument as to why there must be opposition before a man can be truly free and before he can experience real joy: (1) Every law has both a punishment and a blessing attached to it. (2) Disobedience to law requires a punishment which results in misery. (3) Obedience to law provides a blessing which results in happiness (joy). (4) Without law there can be neither punishment nor blessing, neither misery nor happiness—only innocence. (5) Thus happiness (or joy) can exist only where the possibility of the opposite (unhappiness or misery) also exists. (6) In order to exercise free agency a person must have the possibility (and the freedom) of choice; in a world without law—and thus without choice—there could be no freedom of choice and thus no true exercise of free agency. (2 Nephi 2:15–16; see also Alma 12:31–32 and Alma 42:17–25.)

Lehi does not say it is necessary to choose evil in order to recognize good from evil, but he does make it quite clear that a choice of opposites is necessary for growth. (Ludlow)

2 Nephi 2:14

We will only mention here that the Lord created all things of spirit matter first, and then clothed the spirit creations with physical substance. (O/C)

2 Nephi 2:18–25

The Prophet Joseph Smith clarified that Adam did not commit sin by partaking of the forbidden fruit. The fact that Adam would eat and fall was an essential part of the plan that God had decreed from the beginning.

2 Nephi 2:18–25

Adam and Eve . . . were ordained of God to do what they did, and it was therefore expected that they would eat of the forbidden fruit in order that man might know both good and evil by passing through this school of experience which this life affords us (Wilford Woodruff, *Journal of Discourses*, 23:125).

children; yea, even the family of all the earth.
21. And the days of the children of men were prolonged, according to the will of God, that they might repent while in the flesh; wherefore, their state became a state of probation, and their time was lengthened, according to the commandments which the Lord God gave unto the children of men. For he gave commandment that all men must repent; for he showed unto all men that they were lost, because of the transgression of their parents.
22. And now, behold, if Adam had not transgressed he would not have fallen, but he would have remained in the garden of Eden. And all things which were created must have remained in the same state in which they were after they were created; and they must have remained forever, and had no end.
23. And they would have had no children; wherefore they would have remained in a state of innocence, having no joy, for they knew no misery; doing no good, for they knew no sin.
24. But behold, all things have been done in the wisdom of him who knoweth all things.
25. Adam fell that men might be; and men are, that they might have joy.
26. And the Messiah cometh in the fulness of time, that he may redeem the children of men from the fall. And because that they are redeemed from the fall they have become free forever, knowing good from evil; to act for themselves and not to be acted upon, save it be by the punishment of the law at the great and last day, according to the commandments which God hath given.
27. Wherefore, men are free according to the flesh; and all things are given them which are expedient unto man. And they are free to choose liberty and eternal life, through the great Mediator of all men, or to choose captivity and death, according to the captivity and power of the devil; for he seeketh that all men might be miserable like unto himself.
28. And now, my sons, I would that ye should look to the great Mediator, and hearken unto his great commandments; and be faithful unto his words, and choose eternal life, according to the will of his Holy Spirit;
29. And not choose eternal death, according to the will of the flesh and the evil which is therein, which giveth the spirit of the devil power to captivate, to bring you down to hell, that he may reign over you in his own kingdom.
30. I have spoken these few words unto you all, my sons, in the last days of my probation; and I have

2 Nephi 2:22–25

Lehi makes two major conclusions from these teachings: (1) the fall was necessary in order for "men to be"—that is, in order for Adam and Eve to have children. (2) A major purpose of man's existence is for him to have "joy." True joy was not possible for Adam and Eve before the fall. Lehi provides a wealth of information on this important subject in 2 Nephi 2:14–27. . . .

These truths are stated clearly by Lehi in 2 Nephi 2:22–23: "And now, behold, if Adam had not transgressed he would not have fallen . . . and they (Adam and Eve) *would have had no children*; wherefore they would have remained in a state of innocence, *having no joy*, for they knew no misery; doing no good, for they knew no sin." (Italics added.)

Once Adam and Eve knew the difference between good and evil and had been taught the gospel by an angel, they realized the necessity of the fall in order for them to have joy and to have increase (children). Adam then said: "Blessed be the name of God, for *because of my transgression* my eyes are opened, and in this life *I shall have joy*, and again in the flesh I shall see God. And Eve, his wife, heard all these things and was glad, saying: *Were it not for our transgression we never should have had seed*, and never should have known good and evil, and the joy of our redemption, and the eternal life which God giveth unto all the obedient." (Moses 5:10–11. Italics added.)

A careful examination of the status of Adam and Eve after the fall indicates there were two desirable effects of the fall (they knew good from evil and they had children), but also two undesirable effects so far as eternity is concerned (they suffered spiritual death because of their disobedience and they also became subject to physical death). The atonement of Jesus Christ, however, makes it possible to overcome both of the undesirable effects: spiritual death of an individual can be overcome through sincere repentance and obedience to God's commandments, and physical death has been overcome through the breaking of the bands of death by Jesus Christ through the resurrection. Thus, when the fall of Adam and the atonement of Jesus Christ are considered together, it is seen that both are part of God's plan of eternal progression for man. (Ludlow)

2 Nephi 2:23

Adam and Eve ate the fruit. One result was the replacement of the spirit matter that had previously flowed through their veins, providing their continuation of life. (This condition is the same in resurrected beings who live in the post-mortal life in a state of immortality, never again to experience death.) Blood replaced spirit matter following the partaking of the fruit, and the man and woman were then subject to disease, decay, and eventual death. It has been suggested that the fruit may have served a chemical purpose and acted as a catalyst, bringing about the emergence of blood for the first time in living things upon this earth. This change made possible the bearing of children with flesh and blood who would also live a mortal life, eventually die, and continue on to a later life of immortality. Elder Joseph Fielding Smith taught the following:

"When Adam and Eve were placed in the Garden of Eden, there was no blood in their bodies. Their lives were quickened by spirit; therefore they were in a state where they could have lived forever, and so likewise could every other mortal creature. When Adam fell, the change came upon all other living things and even the earth itself became mortal, and all things including the earth were redeemed from death through the atonement of Jesus Christ." (O/C)

2 Nephi 2:25

The Fall was an essential part of God's plan of salvation. Mankind needed an opportunity to exercise agency. How else could the spirit children of God have gained physical bodies through mortal parents? How else could they have struggled through the vicissitudes, temptations, and afflictions of mortality that are so essential to the acquisition and development of spiritual strength? Without a struggle, there is no strength. How else could they grow in their faith in Christ if they never experienced challenges and opposition to their faith? Elder Bruce R. McConkie observed, "All things were so created that they could fall or change, and thus was introduced the type and kind of existence needed to put into operation all of the terms and conditions of the Father's eternal plan of salvation. . . . Thus, just as surely as salvation comes because of the Atonement, so also salvation comes because of the Fall." (O/C)

2 Nephi 2:25

There was a dilemma. Adam and Eve were living without sufficient knowledge and understanding to obey their first commandment. The knowledge they lacked was locked up in the partaking of the fruit they were forbidden to eat, and they faced the consequence of death if they disobeyed the second commandment. Lehi described their circumstances while living in the garden: ". . . they would have had no children; wherefore they would have remained in a state of innocence, having no joy, for they knew no misery; doing no good, for they knew no sin" (2 Ne. 2:23; see also Moses 5:11). They would not be able to keep the first commandment unless they disobeyed the second one. Why would the Lord place them in such a situation? We learn from Lehi:

"For it must needs be, that there is an opposition in all things. If not so, . . . righteousness could not be brought to pass, neither wickedness, neither holiness nor misery, neither good nor bad.

POINT OF INTEREST

Judah (Southern Kingdom)

758–742 B.C. *Jotham*
When his father Uzziah was stricken with leprosy, scholars estimate that Jotham became the royal steward at age twenty-five and then ruled alone for sixteen years. He fought wars against Aramea and Israel and benefited from the counsel of the prophets Isaiah, Hosea, Amos, and Micah.

742–726 B.C. *Ahaz*
He became king at age twenty and introduced a number of pagan customs against the counsel and warnings of the prophets Isaiah, Hosea, and Micah. He sent silver and gold from the temple to Assyria's king together with a plea for help against Damascus and Israel.

726–697 B.C. *Hezekiah*
One of Judah's righteous kings, he made a number of preparations in anticipation of war, including a tunnel that provided underground access to the waters of Gihon Spring, which lay outside of the city. The Assyrian Sennacherib was defeated when "the angel of the Lord . . . smote . . . an hundred fourscore and five thousand" (2 Kgs. 19:35).

Israel (Northern Kingdom)

759–730 B.C. *Pekah*
With the aid of a band of Gileadites, he slew Pekahiah and took the throne. During his reign he entered an alliance with Aramea to beseige Jerusalem but was defeated by Tiglath-pileser II, an ally of Judah's King Ahaz.

730–721 B.C. *Hoshea*
His conspiracy to slay Pekah and take the throne was immediately followed by submission to Shalmaneser V. Hoshea eventually let his tribute to Assyria lapse, expecting support from Egypt, which never came. The kingdom of Israel fell, "and the king of Assyria brought men from Babylon, and from Cuthah, and from Ava, and from Hamath, and from Sepharvaim, and placed them in the cities of Samaria instead of the children of Israel: and they possessed Samaria, and dwelt in the cities thereof" (2 Kgs. 17: 24).

"And to bring about his [God's] eternal purposes in the end of man, after he had created our first parents. . . it must needs be that there was an opposition; even the forbidden fruit in opposition to the tree of life. . . .

"Wherefore, the Lord God gave unto man that he should act for himself. Wherefore, man could not act for himself save it should be that he was enticed by the one or the other" (2 Ne. 2:11, 15–16).

Adam and Eve ate the fruit. . . . Man needed to become mortal, but it had to be of his own choice through the exercise of his agency in the face of opposing options. He did what the Lord desired him to do. Adam transgressed a natural law, but he did not make a choice contrary to the will of the Lord. Therefore, his act is not categorized as a "sin" but rather a "transgression" of a natural law. (See A of F 2). . . .

Because some Bible texts are not clear or complete, many people have come to erroneous conclusions and misunderstandings. Elder Joseph Fielding Smith commented:

". . . Bible commentators [have been led] to speak of Adam and Eve as having frustrated and defeated the original plan of the Father, and they have spoken of the partaking of the fruit as 'Man's Shameful Fall.' Therefore there is a prevalent notion that if Adam and Eve had not partaken of this fruit, they and their posterity would have dwelt upon the earth in perfect peace and happiness without the trials and temptations that have become so prevalent through the generations of time, and there would have been no death.

"The simple fact is, as explained in the Book of Mormon and the revelations given to the Prophet Joseph Smith, the fall was a very essential part of the divine plan. Adam and Eve therefore did the very thing that the Lord intended them to do. . . . Adam made the wise decision." (O/C)

2 Nephi 2:27

Brigham Young said, "All rational beings have an agency of their own; and according to their own choice they will be saved or damned. The volition of the creature is free; this is a law of their existence and the Lord cannot violate his own law; were he to do that, he would cease to be God. He has placed life and death before his children, and it is for them to choose. If they choose life, they receive the blessing of life; if they choose death, they must abide the penalty. This is a law which has always existed from all eternity, and will continue to exist throughout all the eternities to come. Every intelligent being must have the power of choice, and God brings forth the results of the acts of his creatures to promote his Kingdom and subserve his purposes in the salvation and exaltation of his children." (P/A)

2 Nephi 2:30

As Lehi gathers his family members to his side during his final days of life, he directs a special message to his son Jacob, and, by extension, expressly to all his sons (2 Ne. 2:30), concerning the Atonement. It is instructive that he focuses on

POINT OF INTEREST

This map includes the current political boundaries in the Arabian Peninsula and is marked with areas relevant to Lehi and his family's journey in the wilderness. From Nihm (Nahom), a tribal burial ground, Nephi records that they traveled "nearly eastward from that time forth" (1 Ne. 17:1) until they arrived in Bountiful. LDS scholars differ as to where they think the Lehites ultimately pitched their tents, but most are divided between Khor Rori or Wadi Sayq (Khor Kharfot).

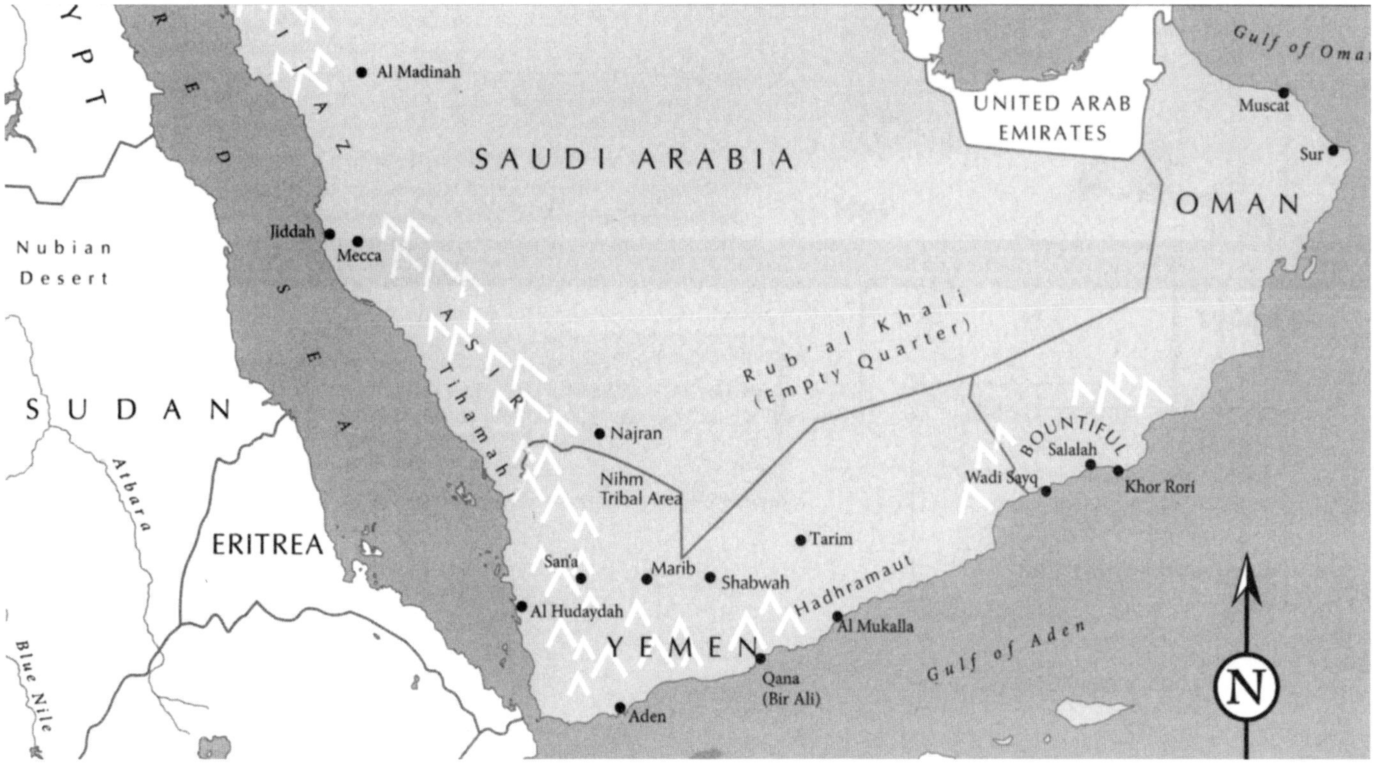

chosen the good part, according to the words of the prophet. And I have none other object save it be the everlasting welfare of your souls. Amen.

CHAPTER 3

1. AND now I speak unto you, Joseph, my last-born. Thou wast born in the wilderness of mine afflictions; yea, in the days of my greatest sorrow did thy mother bear thee.
2. And may the Lord consecrate also unto thee this land, which is a most precious land, for thine inheritance and the inheritance of thy seed with thy brethren, for thy security forever, if it so be that ye shall keep the commandments of the Holy One of Israel.
3. And now, Joseph, my last-born, whom I have brought out of the wilderness of mine afflictions, may the Lord bless thee forever, for thy seed shall not utterly be destroyed.
4. For behold, thou art the fruit of my loins; and I am a descendant of Joseph who was carried captive into Egypt. And great were the covenants of the Lord which he made unto Joseph.
5. Wherefore, Joseph truly saw our day. And he obtained a promise of the Lord, that out of the fruit of his loins the Lord God would raise up a righteous branch unto the house of Israel; not the Messiah, but a branch which was to be broken off, nevertheless, to be remembered in the covenants of the Lord that the Messiah should be made manifest unto them in the latter days, in the spirit of power, unto the bringing of them out of darkness unto light—yea, out of hidden darkness and out of captivity unto freedom.
6. For Joseph truly testified, saying: A seer shall the Lord my God raise up, who shall be a choice seer unto the fruit of my loins.
7. Yea, Joseph truly said: Thus saith the Lord unto me: A choice seer will I raise up out of the fruit of thy loins; and he shall be esteemed highly among the fruit of thy loins. And unto him will I give commandment that he shall do a work for the fruit of thy loins, his brethren, which shall be of great worth unto them, even to the bringing of them to the knowledge of the covenants which I have made with thy fathers.
8. And I will give unto him a commandment that he shall do none other work, save the work which I shall command him. And I will make him great in mine eyes; for he shall do my work.
9. And he shall be great like unto Moses, whom I have said I would raise up unto you, to deliver my people, O house of Israel.
10. And Moses will I raise up, to deliver thy people out of the land of Egypt.
11. But a seer will I raise up out of the fruit of thy loins; and unto him

this subject as his final discourse and exhortation to his posterity. Clearly the Atonement occupied a central place in his heart, as it should in the hearts of all followers of Christ.

In speaking of the Atonement, Elder Jeffrey R. Holland taught, "The literal meaning of the word atonement is self-evident: at-one-ment, the act of unifying or bringing together what has been separated or estranged. The atonement of Christ was indispensable because of the separating transgression, or fall, of Adam, which brought death into the world." (P/A)

2 Nephi 3:1–25

Four different men named Joseph are referred to in 2 Nephi 3 as follows: (1) Joseph who was sold into Egypt; he is also known as Joseph the son of Jacob (Israel)—verses 4–22; (2) Joseph the son of Lehi—verses 1–3, 22–25; (3) Joseph Smith, Sr., the father of the Prophet—verse 15, and (4) Joseph Smith, Jr., the Prophet—verses 7–9, 11, 14–15, 18–19. (Ludlow)

2 Nephi 3:3

The descendants of Joseph, the son of Lehi, were known as Nephites during much of the period covered by the Book of Mormon. However, when the Book of Mormon records the destruction of the Nephite nation (Mormon 6–8), this does not mean that all of the descendants of Joseph were destroyed. Joseph is specifically promised in this patriarchal blessing that his "seed shall not utterly be destroyed." (2 Nephi 3:3.) That this promise was literally fulfilled is indicated by the Lord when he said to Joseph Smith in 1828 that the Book of Mormon had to be translated and published so that it might go forth unto the "Josephites." (See D&C 3:17.) (Ludlow)

2 Nephi 3:9

The Prophet Joseph Smith is here compared to Moses; a thoughtful comparion shows that the two had a number of things in common. There are likely many other similarities, but as a beginning, both Moses and Joseph Smith:

- Were prophets, seers, and revelators
- Saw and spoke with the Savior
- Often stood alone in seeking the Lord's will and then communicating it to the people
- Performed miracles
- Relied heavily on a brother during their ministry (Moses on Aaron, Joseph on Hyrum)
- Established laws for their people through divine revelation
- Endured persecution and opposition from both friends and enemies
- Let their people in exodus to gain freedom from oppression.

will I give power to bring forth my word unto the seed of thy loins—and not to the bringing forth my word only, saith the Lord, but to the convincing them of my word, which shall have already gone forth among them.

12. Wherefore, the fruit of thy loins shall write; and the fruit of the loins of Judah shall write; and that which shall be written by the fruit of thy loins, and also that which shall be written by the fruit of the loins of Judah, shall grow together, unto the confounding of false doctrines and laying down of contentions, and establishing peace among the fruit of thy loins, and bringing them to the knowledge of their fathers in the latter days, and also to the knowledge of my covenants, saith the Lord.

13. And out of weakness he shall be made strong, in that day when my work shall commence among all my people, unto the restoring thee, O house of Israel, saith the Lord.

14. And thus prophesied Joseph, saying: Behold, that seer will the Lord bless; and they that seek to destroy him shall be confounded; for this promise, which I have obtained of the Lord, of the fruit of my loins, shall be fulfilled. Behold, I am sure of the fulfilling of this promise;

15. And his name shall be called after me; and it shall be after the name of his father. And he shall be like unto me; for the thing, which the Lord shall bring forth by his hand, by the power of the Lord shall bring my people unto salvation.

16. Yea, thus prophesied Joseph: I am sure of this thing, even as I am sure of the promise of Moses; for the Lord hath said unto me, I will preserve thy seed forever.

17. And the Lord hath said: I will raise up a Moses; and I will give power unto him in a rod; and I will give judgment unto him in writing. Yet I will not loose his tongue, that he shall speak much, for I will not make him mighty in speaking. But I will write unto him my law, by the finger of mine own hand; and I will make a spokesman for him.

18. And the Lord said unto me also: I will raise up unto the fruit of thy loins; and I will make for him a spokesman. And I, behold, I will give unto him that he shall write the writing of the fruit of thy loins, unto the fruit of thy loins; and the spokesman of thy loins shall declare it.

19. And the words which he shall write shall be the words which are expedient in my wisdom should go forth unto the fruit of thy loins. And it shall be as if the fruit of thy loins had cried unto them from the dust; for I know their faith.

20. And they shall cry from the dust; yea, even repentance unto their brethren, even after many generations have gone by them. And it shall come to pass that their cry shall go, even according to the simpleness of their words.

21. Because of their faith their words shall proceed forth out of

2 Nephi 3:12

The statement of the Lord to Joseph who was sold into Egypt concerning the writings of Judah and "the fruit of thy loins" (2 Nephi 3:12) is very similar to the statement of the Lord to Ezekiel concerning the "sticks" of Judah and Joseph (Ezekiel 37:15–22). When these two references are read together, it is clear that the "stick of Judah" is the Bible, whereas the "stick of Joseph" is the Book of Mormon.

In connection with the Book of Mormon's being the stick of Joseph, it is important to note that Lehi was a direct descendant of Joseph through Manasseh, Joseph's son. (Alma 10:3.) It is also reported by Erastus Snow that Joseph Smith said Ishmael was a descendant of Joseph through his other son, Ephraim. (*Journal of Discourses*, 23:184–85.) Thus the people of Lehi's colony were pure Josephites, and their record rightfully qualifies as part of the "stick of Joseph." (Ludlow)

2 Nephi 3:13

Emma Smith said, "Joseph Smith (as a young man) . . . could neither write nor dictate a coherent and well-worded letter, let alone dictate a book like the Book of Mormon, and though I was an active participant in the scenes that transpired, was present during the translation of the plates, and had cognizance of things as they transpired, it is marvelous to me—a marvel and a wonder—as much as to anyone else. . . . My belief is that the Book of Mormon is of divine authenticity—I have not the slightest doubt of it . . . when acting as his scribe, your father (she was being interrogated by her son) would dictate to me hour after hour; and when returning after meals, or interruptions, he would at once begin where he had left off, without either seeing the manuscript or having any portion of it read to him. This was an unusual thing for him to do. It would have been improbable that a learned man could do this and for one so ignorant and unlearned as he was, it was simply impossible."

my mouth unto their brethren who are the fruit of thy loins; and
the weakness of their words will I make strong in their faith, unto
the remembering of my covenant which I made unto thy fathers.
22. And now, behold, my son Joseph, after this manner did my
father of old prophesy.
23. Wherefore, because of this covenant thou art blessed; for thy
seed shall not be destroyed, for they shall hearken unto the words
of the book.
24. And there shall rise up one mighty among them, who shall do
much good, both in word and in deed, being an instrument in the
hands of God, with exceeding faith, to work mighty wonders, and
do that thing which is great in the sight of God, unto the bringing to pass much restoration unto the house of Israel, and unto the
seed of thy brethren.
25. And now, blessed art thou, Joseph. Behold, thou art little;
wherefore hearken unto the words of thy brother, Nephi, and it
shall be done unto thee even according to the words which I have
spoken. Remember the words of thy dying father. Amen.

CHAPTER 4

1. AND now, I, Nephi, speak concerning the prophecies of which
my father hath spoken, concerning Joseph, who was carried into
Egypt.
2. For behold, he truly prophesied concerning all his seed. And the
prophecies which he wrote, there are not many greater. And he
prophesied concerning us, and our future generations; and they are
written upon the plates of brass.
3. Wherefore, after my father had made an end of speaking concerning the prophecies of Joseph, he called the children of Laman,
his sons, and his daughters, and said unto them: Behold, my sons,
and my daughters, who are the sons and the daughters of my first-
born, I would that ye should give ear unto my words.
4. For the Lord God hath said that: Inasmuch as ye shall keep my commandments ye shall prosper in the land; and inasmuch as ye will not
keep my commandments ye shall be cut off from my presence.
5. But behold, my sons and my daughters, I cannot go down to my
grave save I should leave a blessing upon you; for behold, I know that
if ye are brought up in the way ye should go ye will not depart from
it.
6. Wherefore, if ye are cursed, behold, I leave my blessing upon
you, that the cursing may be taken from you and be answered upon
the heads of your parents.
7. Wherefore, because of my blessing the Lord God will not suffer
that ye shall perish; wherefore, he will be merciful unto you and
unto your seed forever.
8. And it came to pass that after my father had made an end of
speaking to the sons and daughters of Laman, he caused the sons and
daughters of Lemuel to be brought before him.
9. And he spake unto them, saying:

2 Nephi 4:2

Nephi mentions the prophecies of Joseph that were written on the brass plates of Laban, and, he concludes, "there are not many greater." (2 Nephi 4:2.) But where are these great prophecies of Joseph? Why do they not appear in the Old Testament? We do not know the answers to these questions, but the following observations might give some clues as to possible answers.

In the first place, Joseph's prophecies would logically be written most completely on the "stick" or record of Joseph; thus, they were probably included in detail on the brass plates of Laban. However, Joseph's prophecies are not found presently in the "stick" or record of Judah—the Bible. Again, this would indicate that the records on the brass plates of Laban were more comprehensive and complete than the records from which we get our Old Testament.

In the second place, evidently some of the writings of Joseph are still in existence but have not been published to the world. Joseph Smith said that he received some papyri scrolls that contained the record of Abraham and Joseph at the same time he obtained the Egyptian mummies from Michael Chandler. Concerning this record, Joseph Smith has written: "The record of Abraham and Joseph, found with the mummies, is beautifully written on papyrus, with black, and a small part red, ink or paint, in perfect preservation." (*History of the Church*, 2:348.) The Prophet next describes how the mummies and the record came into his possession and then concludes: "Thus I have given a brief history of the manner in which the writings of the fathers, Abraham and Joseph, have been preserved, and how I came in possession of the same—a correct translation of which I shall give in its proper place." (Ibid., 2:350–51.)

The record of Abraham translated by the Prophet was subsequently printed, and it is now known as the book of Abraham in the Pearl of Great Price. However, the translation of the book of Joseph has not yet been published. Evidently the record of Joseph was translated by the Prophet, but perhaps the reason it was not published was because the great prophecies therein were "too great" for the people of this day. (Ludlow)

Behold, my sons and my daughters, who are the sons and the
daughters of my second son; behold I leave unto you the same
blessing which I left unto the sons and daughters of Laman; wherefore, thou shalt not utterly be destroyed; but in the end thy seed
shall be blessed.
10. And it came to pass that when my father had made an end of
speaking unto them, behold, he spake unto the sons of Ishmael,
yea, and even all his household.
11. And after he had made an end of speaking unto them, he spake
unto Sam, saying: Blessed art thou, and thy seed; for thou shalt
inherit the land like unto thy brother Nephi. And thy seed shall be
numbered with his seed; and thou shalt be even like unto thy brother, and thy seed like unto his seed; and thou shalt be blessed in all
thy days.
12. And it came to pass after my father, Lehi, had spoken unto all
his household, according to the feelings of his heart and the Spirit
of the Lord which was in him, he waxed old. And it came to pass
that he died, and was buried.
13. And it came to pass that not many days after his death, Laman
and Lemuel and the sons of Ishmael were angry with me because of
the admonitions of the Lord.
14. For I, Nephi, was constrained to speak unto them, according to
his word; for I had spoken many things unto them, and also my
father, before his death; many of which sayings are written upon
mine other plates; for a more history part are written upon mine
other plates.
15. And upon these I write the things of my soul, and many of the
scriptures which are engraven upon the plates of brass. For my soul
delighteth in the scriptures, and my heart pondereth them, and
writeth them for the learning and the profit of my children.
16. Behold, my soul delighteth in the things of the Lord; and my
heart pondereth continually upon the things which I have seen
and heard.
17. Nevertheless, notwithstanding the great goodness of the Lord,
in showing me his great and marvelous works, my heart
exclaimeth: O wretched man that I am! Yea, my heart sorroweth
because of my flesh; my soul grieveth because of mine iniquities.
18. I am encompassed about, because of the temptations and the
sins which do so easily beset me.
19. And when I desire to rejoice, my heart groaneth because of my
sins; nevertheless, I know in whom I have trusted.
20. My God hath been my support; he hath led me through mine
afflictions in the wilderness; and he hath preserved me upon the
waters of the great deep.
21. He hath filled me with his love, even unto the consuming of
my flesh.
22. He hath confounded mine enemies, unto the causing of them
to quake before me.
23. Behold, he hath heard my cry by

2 Nephi 4:11

Although Nephi's brother Sam evidently had children (2 Nephi 4:11), there are no "Samites" mentioned in the Book of Mormon. Perhaps Lehi's promise to Sam that his seed would be numbered with the seed of Nephi (2 Nephi 4:11) helps to explain why the record does not refer to "Samites," whereas the descendants of the other sons of Lehi are referred to as Lamanites, Lemuelites, Nephites, Jacobites, and Josephites (Jacob 1:13). (Ludlow)

2 Nephi 4:18

Consider what Nephi has gone through: As a young man he was uprooted with little warning from his native environment to spend eight years in the desert, enduring adversity of all kinds, including life-threatening torment at the hands of his elder brothers. Then he completed a perilous sea journey halfway around the world to a strange new land. His father, the spiritual anchor of the family, has just passed away, and thus the elder brothers again take up their aggressive assault against him, forcing him and his immediate circle, upon divine warning, to flee into the wilderness and start anew.

Where does he now center his thoughts? On his love for the scriptures, on his own perceived weaknesses, on being grateful for divine guidance, and on his abiding and unshakable faith in the Lord. His heartfelt expression of love for the Lord—despite all the tribulation he has been called upon to endure—is the pinnacle of spiritual witness. Of him, Elder Neal A. Maxwell said, "The prophet Nephi, who had progressed and advanced spiritually to a remarkable degree, still lamented about 'sins which do easily beset me' (2 Nephi 4:18). Obviously, Nephi's sins were not major. But just as God cannot look upon sin with the lease degree of allowance (D&C 1:31), as we become more like Him, neither can we. The best people have a heightened awareness of what little of the worst is still in them!" (P/A)

day, and he hath given me knowledge by visions in the night-time.
24. And by day have I waxed bold in mighty prayer before him;
yea, my voice have I sent up on high; and angels came down and
ministered unto me.
25. And upon the wings of his Spirit hath my body been carried
away upon exceedingly high mountains. And mine eyes have
beheld great things, yea, even too great for man; therefore I was
bidden that I should not write them.
26. O then, if I have seen so great things, if the Lord in his condescension unto the children of men hath visited men in so much
mercy, why should my heart weep and my soul linger in the valley
of sorrow, and my flesh waste away, and my strength slacken,
because of mine afflictions?
27. And why should I yield to sin, because of my flesh? Yea, why
should I give way to temptations, that the evil one have place in
my heart to destroy my peace and afflict my soul? Why am I angry
because of mine enemy?
28. Awake, my soul! No longer droop in sin. Rejoice, O my heart,
and give place no more for the enemy of my soul.
29. Do not anger again because of mine enemies. Do not slacken
my strength because of mine afflictions.
30. Rejoice, O my heart, and cry unto the Lord, and say: O Lord, I
will praise thee forever; yea, my soul will rejoice in thee, my God,
and the rock of my salvation.
31. O Lord, wilt thou redeem my soul? Wilt thou deliver me out of
the hands of mine enemies? Wilt thou make me that I may shake
at the appearance of sin?
32. May the gates of hell be shut continually before me, because
that my heart is broken and my spirit is contrite! O Lord, wilt thou
not shut the gates of thy righteousness before me, that I may walk
in the path of the low valley, that I may be strict in the plain road!
33. O Lord, wilt thou encircle me around in the robe of thy righteousness! O Lord, wilt thou make a way for mine escape before
mine enemies! Wilt thou make my path straight before me! Wilt
thou not place a stumbling block in my way—but that thou
wouldst clear my way before me, and hedge not up my way, but
the ways of mine enemy.
34. O Lord, I have trusted in thee, and I will trust in thee forever.
I will not put my trust in the arm of flesh; for I know that cursed
is he that putteth his trust in the arm of flesh. Yea, cursed is he
that putteth his trust in man or maketh flesh his arm.
35. Yea, I know that God will give liberally to him that asketh. Yea,
my God will give me, if I ask not amiss; therefore I will lift up my
voice unto thee; yea, I will cry unto thee, my God, the rock of my
righteousness. Behold, my voice

2 Nephi 4:34

Some in the Church become eager to "steady the ark," getting distracted or preoccupied by some perceived problem involving a local leader. We are warned here against trusting "in the arm of flesh"—those very imperfect and very human people who are doing the best they can to fulfill callings they have been given. Instead, we are counseled here to focus on and put our trust in the perfect and immovable Savior, who leads us in absolute wisdom back to our eternal home.

POINT OF INTEREST

Where in Bountiful did the Lehites pitch their tents?

1 Nephi specifications	Khor Rori	Khor Kharfot
Surrounding area fertile (17:5–7)		X
Fruit and wild honey (17:5–6; 18:6)		X
Shipbuilding timber (18:1–2)		X
Nearby "mount" (17:7; 18:3)		X
Flint deposits (17:9–11, 16)	*none known*	X
Unpopulated area (17:5–6, 8–11; 18:1–2, 6)		X

shall forever ascend up unto thee, my rock and mine everlasting God. Amen.

CHAPTER 5

1. BEHOLD, it came to pass that I, Nephi, did cry much unto the Lord my God, because of the anger of my brethren.
2. But behold, their anger did increase against me, insomuch that they did seek to take away my life.
3. Yea, they did murmur against me, saying: Our younger brother thinks to rule over us; and we have had much trial because of him; wherefore, now let us slay him, that we may not be afflicted more because of his words. For behold, we will not have him to be our ruler; for it belongs unto us, who are the elder brethren, to rule over this people.
4. Now I do not write upon these plates all the words which they murmured against me. But it sufficeth me to say, that they did seek to take away my life.
5. And it came to pass that the Lord did warn me, that I, Nephi, should depart from them and flee into the wilderness, and all those who would go with me.
6. Wherefore, it came to pass that I, Nephi, did take my family, and also Zoram and his family, and Sam, mine elder brother and his family, and Jacob and Joseph, my younger brethren, and also my sisters, and all those who would go with me. And all those who would go with me were those who believed in the warnings and the revelations of God; wherefore, they did hearken unto my words.
7. And we did take our tents and whatsoever things were possible for us, and did journey in the wilderness for the space of many days. And after we had journeyed for the space of many days we did pitch our tents.
8. And my people would that we should call the name of the place Nephi; wherefore, we did call it Nephi.
9. And all those who were with me did take upon them to call themselves the people of Nephi.
10. And we did observe to keep the judgments, and the statutes, and the commandments of the Lord in all things according to the law of Moses.
11. And the Lord was with us; and we did prosper exceedingly; for we did sow seed, and we did reap again in abundance. And we began to raise flocks, and herds, and animals of every kind.
12. And I, Nephi, had also brought the records which were engraven upon the plates of brass; and also the ball, or compass, which was prepared for my father by the hand of the Lord, according to that which is written.
13. And it came to pass that we began to prosper exceedingly, and to multiply in the land.
14. And I, Nephi, did take the sword of Laban, and after the manner

2 Nephi 5:6

This is the only specific reference in the Book of Mormon that Nephi had sisters as well as brothers. How many sisters there were, whether they were older or younger than Nephi, or what their names may have been are questions not answered in our present Book of Mormon. However, the following statement by Erastus Snow may provide information on some of the sisters of Nephi:

> The Prophet Joseph informed us that the record of Lehi, was contained on the 116 pages that were first translated and subsequently stolen, and of which an abridgment is given us in the first Book of Nephi, which is the record of Nephi individually, he himself being of the lineage of Manasseh; but that Ishmael was of the lineage of Ephraim, and that his sons married into Lehi's family, and Lehi's sons married Ishmael's daughters . . . (*Journal of Discourses*, 23:184.)

The words that Ishmael's sons "married into Lehi's family" would seem to indicate that the two sons of Ishmael (see 1 Nephi 7:6) were married to Lehi's daughters (and thus to two of the sisters of Nephi). However, the sisters referred to in 2 Nephi 5:6 are evidently still other sisters, because the sisters mentioned here follow Nephi when the schism with Laman occurs, whereas the sisters of Nephi who were married to the sons of Ishmael evidently stayed with their husbands and joined with Laman. (See Alma 3:7 and 47:35.) (Ludlow)

of it did make many swords, lest by any means the people who were
now called Lamanites should come upon us and destroy us; for I
knew their hatred towards me and my children and those who were
called my people.
15. And I did teach my people to build buildings, and to work in
all manner of wood, and of iron, and of copper, and of brass, and of
steel, and of gold, and of silver, and of precious ores, which were in
great abundance.
16. And I, Nephi, did build a temple; and I did construct it after the
manner of the temple of Solomon save it were not built of so many
precious things; for they were not to be found upon the land, wherefore, it could not be built like unto Solomon's temple. But the manner of the construction was like unto the temple of Solomon; and the
workmanship thereof was exceedingly fine.
17. And it came to pass that I, Nephi, did cause my people to be
industrious, and to labor with their hands.
18. And it came to pass that they would that I should be their king.
But I, Nephi, was desirous that they should have no king; nevertheless, I did for them according to that which was in my power.
19. And behold, the words of the Lord had been fulfilled unto my
brethren, which he spake concerning them, that I should be their
ruler and their teacher. Wherefore, I had been their ruler and their
teacher, according to the commandments of the Lord, until the
time they sought to take away my life.
20. Wherefore, the word of the Lord was fulfilled which he spake
unto me, saying that: Inasmuch as they will not hearken unto thy
words they shall be cut off from the presence of the Lord. And
behold, they were cut off from his presence.
21. And he had caused the cursing to come upon them, yea, even a
sore cursing, because of their iniquity. For behold, they had hardened their hearts against him, that they had become like unto a
flint; wherefore, as they were white, and exceedingly fair and
delightsome, that they might not be enticing unto my people the
Lord God did cause a skin of blackness to come upon them.
22. And thus saith the Lord God: I will cause that they shall be
loathsome unto thy people, save they shall repent of their iniquities.
23. And cursed shall be the seed of him that mixeth with their
seed; for they shall be cursed even with the same cursing. And the
Lord spake it, and it was done.
24. And because of their cursing which was upon them they did
become an idle people, full of

Laman & Lemuel - are cut off just like 1 Ne: 2 said

2 Nephi 5:16

Whenever the Lord's Church has been upon the earth, He has commanded His saints to build temples unto Him. . . . Within His temples the Lord endows His faithful with power from on high. It is within this holy sanctuary that families are sealed together for time and all eternity. (O/C)

2 Nephi 5:21–23

The mark of the curse that came upon the Lamanites was that "a skin of blackness" came upon them. A major purpose of this mark was that the Lamanites "might not be enticing" unto the Nephites. (2 Nephi 5:21.) The Lord stated further that the "seed of him that mixeth" with the unrighteous Lamanites "shall be cursed even with the same cursing." (2 Nephi 5:23.)

This is the only reference in the entire Book of Mormon where a definite color adjective is used to refer to this mark. All other references call it, a "skin of darkness" or a "dark skin." It is of interest to note that the terms "blackness" and "darkness" are interchangeable in the Hebrew. Even in modern Hebrew it is not unusual for some skilled translator to render a word *black* whereas other equally skilled translators select *dark* as the best translation. (Ludlow)

POINT OF INTEREST

"In earlier centuries, a person's wealth was counted in terms of sheep and cattle. In Lehi's era, however, gold and silver have become indicators of wealth (1 Ne. 2:4) and are common media of exchange (1 Ne. 3:24). Different values are placed on those metals by weight. The most basic measure . . . is the sheqel [below]. This word in Hebrew simply means 'to weigh'" (John W. Welch and Robert D. Hunt, "Culturegram: Jerusalem 600 B.C.," *Glimpses of Lehi's Jerusalem* [Provo, Utah: FARMS, 2004]).

mischief and subtlety, and did seek in the wilderness for beasts of prey.
25. And the Lord God said unto me: They shall be a scourge unto thy seed, to stir them up in remembrance of me; and inasmuch as they will not remember me, and hearken unto my words, they shall scourge them even unto destruction.
26. And it came to pass that I, Nephi, did consecrate Jacob and Joseph, that they should be priests and teachers over the land of my people.
27. And it came to pass that we lived after the manner of happiness.
28. And thirty years had passed away from the time we left Jerusalem.
29. And I, Nephi, had kept the records upon my plates, which I had made, of my people thus far.
30. And it came to pass that the Lord God said unto me: Make other plates; and thou shalt engraven many things upon them which are good in my sight, for the profit of thy people.
31. Wherefore, I, Nephi, to be obedient to the commandments of the Lord, went and made these plates upon which I have engraven these things.
32. And I engraved that which is pleasing unto God. And if my people are pleased with the things of God they will be pleased with mine engravings which are upon these plates.
33. And if my people desire to know the more particular part of the history of my people they must search mine other plates.
34. And it sufficeth me to say that forty years had passed away, and we had already had wars and contentions with our brethren.

CHAPTER 6

1. THE words of Jacob, the brother of Nephi, which he spake unto the people of Nephi:
2. Behold, my beloved brethren, I, Jacob, having been called of God, and ordained after the manner of his holy order, and having been consecrated by my brother Nephi, unto whom ye look as a king or a protector, and on whom ye depend for safety, behold ye know that I have spoken unto you exceedingly many things.
3. Nevertheless, I speak unto you again; for I am desirous for the welfare of your souls. Yea, mine anxiety is great for you; and ye yourselves know that it ever has been. For I have exhorted you with all diligence; and I have taught you the words of my father; and I have spoken unto you concerning all things which are written, from the creation of the world.
4. And now, behold, I would speak unto you concerning things which are, and which are to come; wherefore, I will read you the words of Isaiah. And they are the words which my brother has desired that I should speak unto you. And I speak unto you for your sakes, that ye may learn and glorify the name of your God.
5. And now, the words which I shall read are they which Isaiah spake concerning all the house of Israel;

2 Nephi 5:25

Here we see a very positive aspect of the wicked and ferocious Lamanites, who were to become a "scourge" to the Nephites: they were to "stir them up in remembrance" of the Lord. The greatest problems for the Nephites didn't occur when the Lamanites were threatening or attacking them—they occurred when the Nephites forgot the Lord and failed to keep His commandments.

2 Nephi 5:26

Priests and *teachers* in this verse do not refer to offices in the Aaronic priesthood. In Lehi's day, the Aaronic priesthood was a hereditary priesthood, conferred only upon Levites, none of whom left Jerusalem with Lehi. Instead, the priests and teachers referred to here were Melchizedek priesthood holders who were consecrated to teach, preach, and baptize.

2 Nephi 5:26 The priesthood of the Nephites

Many references in the Book of Mormon indicate that the Nephites held the priesthood—that is, they had the power and authority to act in the name of God. However, the Book of Mormon does not refer specifically to the two major divisions in the priesthood, the Aaronic Priesthood and the Melchizedek Priesthood. Thus the question has frequently arisen as to exactly what priesthood was held by the Nephites. Joseph Fielding Smith gives his answer in the following comprehensive statement:

"The Nephites were descendants of Joseph. Lehi discovered this when reading the brass plates. He was a descendant of Manasseh, and Ishmael, who accompanied him with his family, was of the tribe of Ephraim. Therefore there were no Levites who accompanied Lehi to the Western Hemisphere. Under these conditions the Nephites officiated by virtue of the Melchizedek Priesthood from the days of Lehi to the days of the appearance of our Savior among them. It is true that Nephi 'consecrated Jacob and Joseph' that they should be priests and teachers over the land of the Nephites, but the fact that plural terms *priests* and *teachers* were used indicates that this was not a reference to the definite office in the priesthood in either case, but it was a general assignment to teach, direct, and admonish the people. Otherwise the terms *priest* and *teacher* would have been given, in the singular. Additional light is thrown on this appointment showing that these two brothers of Nephi held the Melchizedek Priesthood, in the sixth chapter, second verse of 2 Nephi, where Jacob makes this explanation regarding the priesthood which he and Joseph held: 'Behold, my beloved brethren, I, Jacob, having been called of God, and ordained *after the manner of his holy order*, and having been consecrated by my brother Nephi, unto whom ye look as a king or a protector, and on whom ye depend for safety, behold ye know that I have spoken unto you exceeding many things.'

"This seems to be a confirmation of the ordinations that he and his brother Joseph received in the Melchizedek Priesthood. All through the Book of Mormon we find references to the Nephites officiating by virtue of the Higher Priesthood after the holy order. Alma, discoursing on the subject before the people of the city of Ammonihah, said: 'And again, my brethren, I would cite your minds forward to the time when the Lord God gave these commandments unto his children; and I would that ye should remember that the Lord God ordained priests, after his holy order, which was after the order of his Son, to teach these things unto the people.' (Alma 13:1. See also D&C 107:1–4.)

"In the opening verses of Alma, Chapter 43, Mormon records the following: 'And now it came to pass that the sons of Alma did go forth among the people . . . and . . . they preached the word, and the truth, according to the spirit of prophecy and revelation; and they preached after the holy order of God by which they were called.'

"From these and numerous other passages we learn that it was by the authority of the Melchizedek Priesthood that the Nephites administered from the time they left Jerusalem until the time of the coming of Jesus Christ. By the power of this priesthood they baptized, confirmed, and ordained. During these years they also observed the law of Moses. They offered sacrifice and performed the duties which in Israel had been assigned to the priests and Levites. They observed in every detail the requirements of the law. When the Savior came to them, he fulfilled the carnal law and did away with the sacrifice by the shedding of blood of animals. He informed the Nephites that in him the law of Moses was fulfilled.

"When the Savior came to the Nephites, he established the Church in its fulness among them, and he informed them that former things had passed away, for they were all fulfilled in him. He gave the Nephites all the authority of the priesthood which we exercise today. Therefore we are justified in the belief that not only was the fulness of the Melchizedek Priesthood conferred, but also the Aaronic, just as we have it in the Church today; and this Aaronic Priesthood remained with them from this time until, through wickedness, all priesthood ceased. We may be assured that in the days of Moroni the Nephites did ordain teachers and priests in the Aaronic Priesthood; but before the visit of the Savior they officiated in the Melchizedek Priesthood." (Ludlow)

2 Nephi 5:27

The Prophet Joseph Smith said, "... God has designed our happiness—and the happiness of all His creatures, he never has—He never will institute an ordinance or give a commandment to His people that is not calculated in its nature to promote that happiness which He has designed."

2 Nephi 5:28–31

All of the material so far in the Book of Mormon has come from the small plates of Nephi. Although the account in First Nephi evidently begins around 600 B.C., it is quite clear from 2 Nephi 5:28–33 that the small plates were not prepared until thirty years after Lehi left Jerusalem, or approximately 570 B.C. Thus, when Nephi started to write on the small plates in 570 B.C., he evidently started listing events in his earlier life, dating from the time his father left Jerusalem. This might be somewhat analogous to your starting this year a life history but writing first in your history some of the events of your childhood. (Ludlow)

2 Nephi 6:6

The Lord prophesied through Isaiah that in the last days he would set up his standard to the people of the earth. This "standard" evidently refers to The Church of Jesus Christ of Latter-day Saints, as is indicated in this statement by President Marion G. Romney:

"This Church is the standard which Isaiah said the Lord would set up for the people in the latter days. This Church was given to be a light to the world and to be a standard for God's people and for the Gentiles to seek to. This Church is the ensign on the mountain spoken of by the Old Testament prophets. It is the way, the truth, and the life." (Ludlow)

2 Nephi 6:6

As described in Numbers 2, tribes of Israel were assigned ranks as they traveled from Egypt to Palestine. A representative of each tribe would hold up a "standard"—a flag or banner—so members of the tribe could quickly find their place in a march or a camp. Today, the "standard" is the gospel, which invites the lost and scattered tribes to gather and find refuge.

POINT OF INTEREST

This map represents Orson Pratt's view of Book of Mormon geography. Unfortunately, the geographical information in the Book of Mormon is too limited to correlate with any specific setting with certainty.

wherefore, they may be likened unto you, for ye are of the house of
Israel. And there are many things which have been spoken by
Isaiah which may be likened unto you, because ye are of the house
of Israel.
6. And now, these are the words: Thus saith the Lord God: Behold,
I will lift up mine hand to the Gentiles, and set up my standard to
the people; and they shall bring thy sons in their arms, and thy
daughters shall be carried upon their shoulders.
7. And kings shall be thy nursing fathers, and their queens thy
nursing mothers; they shall bow down to thee with their faces
towards the earth, and lick up the dust of thy feet; and thou shalt
know that I am the Lord; for they shall not be ashamed that wait
for me.
8. And now I, Jacob, would speak somewhat concerning these
words. For behold, the Lord has shown me that those who were at
Jerusalem, from whence we came, have been slain and carried away
captive.
9. Nevertheless, the Lord has shown unto me that they should
return again. And he also has shown unto me that the Lord God,
the Holy One of Israel, should manifest himself unto them in the
flesh; and after he should manifest himself they should scourge him
and crucify him, according to the words of the angel who spake it
unto me.
10. And after they have hardened their hearts and stiffened their
necks against the Holy One of Israel, behold the judgments of the
Holy One of Israel shall come upon them. And the day cometh
that they shall be smitten and afflicted.
11. Wherefore, after they are driven to and fro, for thus saith the
angel, many shall be afflicted in the flesh, and shall not be suffered
to perish, because of the prayers of the faithful; they shall be scattered, and smitten, and hated; nevertheless, the Lord will be merciful unto them, that when they shall come to the knowledge of their
Redeemer, they shall be gathered together again to the lands of
their inheritance.
12. And blessed are the Gentiles, they of whom the prophet has
written; for behold, if it so be that they shall repent and fight not
against Zion, and do not unite themselves to that great and abominable church, they shall be saved; for the Lord God will fulfil his
covenants which he has made unto his children; and for this cause
the prophet has written these things.
13. Wherefore, they that fight against Zion and the covenant people of the Lord shall lick up the dust of their feet; and the people
of the Lord shall not be ashamed. For the people of the Lord are
they who wait for him; for they still wait for the coming of the
Messiah.

POINT OF INTEREST

Judah (Southern Kingdom)

697–642 B.C. *Manasseh*
He began his reign at age twelve and in time reversed his father Hezekiah's reforms by reinstating pagan worship in the temple at Jerusalem. According to tradition he killed Isaiah by sawing him in half. Manasseh was taken captive by the king of Assyria and was probably treated cruelly. When his kingdom was restored, he abandoned his idolatrous ways but made no thorough reformation.

642–640 B.C. *Amon*
He became king at age twenty-two and restored idolatry, setting up the images his father had cast down. He was assassinated by his own servants.

640–609 B.C. *Josiah*
Some historians credit him with establishing Jewish scripture in a written form. He repaired the temple and destroyed all the idols, including slaughtering the pagan priests not only in Jerusalem but also in the cities of Manasseh, Ephraim, Simeon, and Naphtali (2 Kgs. 23:8; 2 Chr. 34:6). The priest Hilkiah discovered a scroll of the Book of Deuteronomy in the process, and Josiah had it read in a crowd in Jerusalem, as portrayed in an engraving by Julius Schnorr von Carolsfeld (above).

14. And behold, according to the words of the prophet, the Messiah
will set himself again the second time to recover them; wherefore,
he will manifest himself unto them in power and great glory, unto
the destruction of their enemies, when that day cometh when they
shall believe in him; and none will he destroy that believe in him.
15. And they that believe not in him shall be destroyed, both by fire,
and by tempest, and by earthquakes, and by bloodsheds, and by pestilence, and by famine. And they shall know that the Lord is God, the
Holy One of Israel.
16. For shall the prey be taken from the mighty, or the lawful captive delivered?
17. But thus saith the Lord: Even the captives of the mighty shall
be taken away, and the prey of the terrible shall be delivered; for
the Mighty God shall deliver his covenant people. For thus saith
the Lord: I will contend with them that contendeth with thee—
18. And I will feed them that oppress thee, with their own flesh;
and they shall be drunken with their own blood as with sweet
wine; and all flesh shall know that I the Lord am thy Savior and
thy Redeemer, the Mighty One of Jacob.

CHAPTER 7

1. YEA, for thus saith the Lord: Have I put thee away, or have I cast
thee off forever? For thus saith the Lord: Where is the bill of your
mother's divorcement? To whom have I put thee away, or to which
of my creditors have I sold you? Yea, to whom have I sold you?
Behold, for your iniquities have ye sold yourselves, and for your
transgressions is your mother put away.
2. Wherefore, when I came, there was no man; when I called, yea,
there was none to answer. O house of Israel, is my hand shortened
at all that it cannot redeem, or have I no power to deliver? Behold,
at my rebuke I dry up the sea, I make their rivers a wilderness and
their fish to stink because the waters are dried up, and they die
because of thirst.
3. I clothe the heavens with blackness, and I make sackcloth their
covering.
4. The Lord God hath given
me the tongue of the learned,
that I should know how to
speak a word in season unto
thee, O house of Israel. When

2 Nephi 6:14

Ancient Israel once had a close relationship with the Lord and were identified as His people. The Lord promised that he would ". . . recover them. . . [and] manifest himself unto them in power and great glory. . . when they shall believe in him. . . ." (2 Ne. 6:14). They are to be restored to that spiritual relationship and, once again, belong to Him when they accept the restored gospel and become members of The Church of Jesus Christ of Latter-day Saints. They will then carry His name as covenant children of Christ and be restored to their place in the eternal kingdom of our Heavenly Father. (O/C)

POINT OF INTEREST

In 2 Ne. 5:16, Nephi relates that he "did build a temple . . . after the manner of the temple of Solomon." Below is a basic layout of Solomon's temple, based on historical documents, minus the brazen sea and altar.

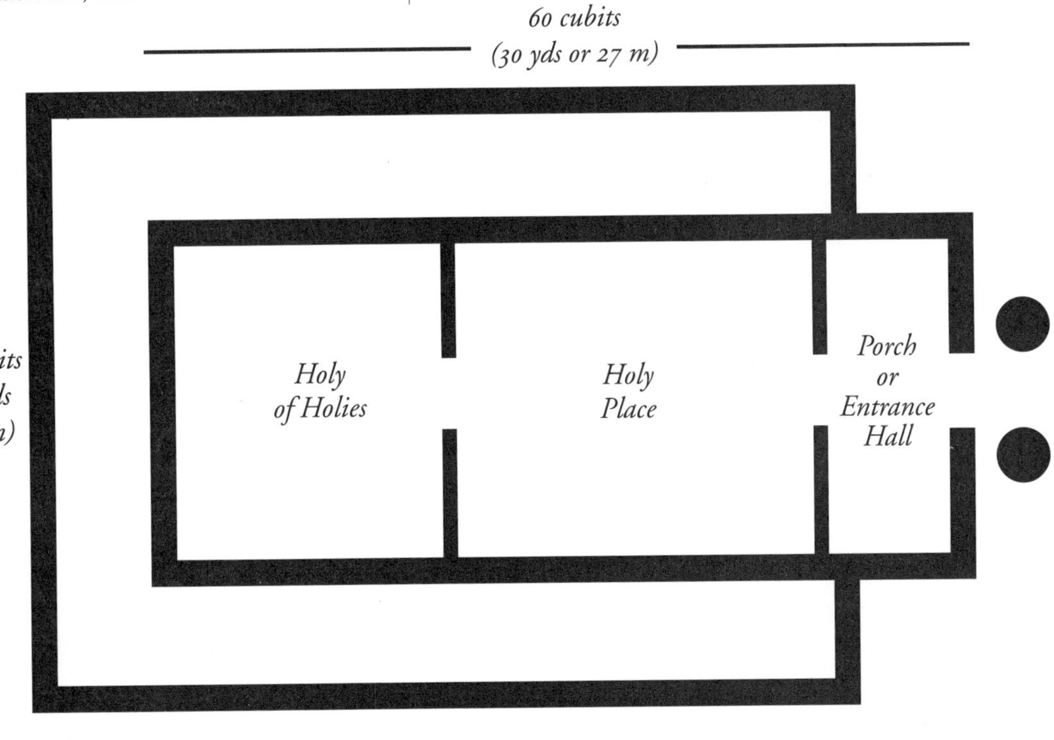

ye are weary he waketh morning by morning. He waketh mine ear to hear as the learned.

5. The Lord God hath opened mine ear, and I was not rebellious, neither turned away back.

6. I gave my back to the smiter, and my cheeks to them that plucked off the hair. I hid not my face from shame and spitting.

7. For the Lord God will help me, therefore shall I not be confounded. Therefore have I set my face like a flint, and I know that I shall not be ashamed.

8. And the Lord is near, and he justifieth me. Who will contend with me? Let us stand together. Who is mine adversary? Let him come near me, and I will smite him with the strength of my mouth.

9. For the Lord God will help me. And all they who shall condemn me, behold, all they shall wax old as a garment, and the moth shall eat them up.

10. Who is among you that feareth the Lord, that obeyeth the voice of his servant, that walketh in darkness and hath no light?

11. Behold all ye that kindle fire, that compass yourselves about with sparks, walk in the light of your fire and in the sparks which ye have kindled. This shall ye have of mine hand—ye shall lie down in sorrow.

CHAPTER 8

1. HEARKEN unto me, ye that follow after righteousness. Look unto the rock from whence ye are hewn, and to the hole of the pit from whence ye are digged.

2. Look unto Abraham, your father, and unto Sarah, she that bare you; for I called him alone, and blessed him.

3. For the Lord shall comfort Zion, he will comfort all her waste places; and he will make her wilderness like Eden, and her desert like the garden of the Lord. Joy and gladness shall be found therein, thanksgiving and the voice of melody.

4. Hearken unto me, my people; and give ear unto me, O my nation; for a law shall proceed from me, and I will make my judgment to rest for a light for the people.

5. My righteousness is near; my salvation is gone forth, and mine arm shall judge the people. The isles shall wait upon me, and on mine arm shall they trust.

6. Lift up your eyes to the heavens, and look upon the earth beneath; for the heavens shall vanish away like smoke, and the earth shall wax old like a garment; and they that dwell therein shall die in like manner. But my salvation shall be forever, and my righteousness shall not be abolished.

7. Hearken unto me, ye that know righteousness, the people in whose heart I have written my law, fear

2 Nephi 7:7–9

Elder Joseph Fielding Smith provided the following assurance: "If members of the Church would place more confidence in the word of the Lord and less confidence in the theories of men, they would be better off. I will give you a key for your guidance. Any doctrine, whether it comes in the name of religion, science, philosophy, or whatever it may be, that is in conflict with the revelations of the Lord that have been accepted by the Church as coming from the Lord, will fail. It may appear to be very plausible; it may be put before you in such a way that you cannot answer it, it may appear to be established by evidence that cannot be controverted, but all you need do is to bide your time. Time will level all things" (*The Utah Genealogical and Historical Magazine*, Oct. 1930, 155–56). (O/C)

ye not the reproach of men, neither be ye afraid of their revilings.
8. For the moth shall eat them up like a garment, and the worm
shall eat them like wool. But my righteousness shall be forever, and
my salvation from generation to generation.
9. Awake, awake! Put on strength, O arm of the Lord; awake as in
the ancient days. Art thou not he that hath cut Rahab, and wounded the dragon?
10. Art thou not he who hath dried the sea, the waters of the great
deep; that hath made the depths of the sea a way for the ransomed to
pass over?
11. Therefore, the redeemed of the Lord shall return, and come
with singing unto Zion; and everlasting joy and holiness shall be
upon their heads; and they shall obtain gladness and joy; sorrow
and mourning shall flee away.
12. I am he; yea, I am he that comforteth you. Behold, who art
thou, that thou shouldst be afraid of man, who shall die, and of the
son of man, who shall be made like unto grass?
13. And forgettest the Lord thy maker, that hath stretched forth
the heavens, and laid the foundations of the earth, and hast feared
continually every day, because of the fury of the oppressor, as if he
were ready to destroy? And where is the fury of the oppressor?
14. The captive exile hasteneth, that he may be loosed, and that
he should not die in the pit, nor that his bread should fail.
15. But I am the Lord thy God, whose waves roared; the Lord of
Hosts is my name.
16. And I have put my words in thy mouth, and have covered thee
in the shadow of mine hand, that I may plant the heavens and lay
the foundations of the earth, and say unto Zion: Behold, thou art
my people.
17. Awake, awake, stand up, O Jerusalem, which hast drunk at the
hand of the Lord the cup of his fury—thou hast drunken the dregs
of the cup of trembling wrung out—
18. And none to guide her among all the sons she hath brought
forth; neither that taketh her by the hand, of all the sons she hath
brought up.
19. These two sons are come unto thee, who shall be sorry for
thee—thy desolation and destruction, and the famine and the
sword—and by whom shall I comfort thee?
20. Thy sons have fainted, save these two; they lie at the head of
all the streets; as a wild bull in a net, they are full of the fury of the
Lord, the rebuke of thy God.
21. Therefore hear now this, thou afflicted, and drunken, and not
with wine:
22. Thus saith thy Lord, the Lord and thy God pleadeth the cause
of his people; behold, I have taken out of thine hand the cup of
trembling, the dregs of the cup of my fury; thou shalt no more
drink it again.
23. But I will put it into the hand

2 Nephi 8:19–20

Elder Bruce R. McConkie taught that these "two sons" would be members of the Council of the Twelve or the First Presidency who will labor among the rebellious Jews for roughly the same amount of time as the Savior labored among the Jews of His day.

POINT OF INTEREST

In pre-Islamic Arabia, there existed many nomadic tribes that spoke a variety of languages. Split between tribes from the northern and the southern parts of the peninsula occupying mostly the coastal regions, these tribes were in constant conflict and lacked unification through religion as most practiced a variety of polytheistic religions set up by the tribal families. The predominant languages of the region were Hebrew, Aramaic, and Syriac. Later, when the rise of Islam occurred around a.d. 630, the unification under the religion of Islam brought the primary use of Arabic as the language standard as Classic Arabic was and still is the language of the Islamic holy book, the Qur'an (Frederick Mathewson Denny, *An Introduction to Islam* [Upper Saddle River, N.J.: Pearson Prentice Hall, 2006]).

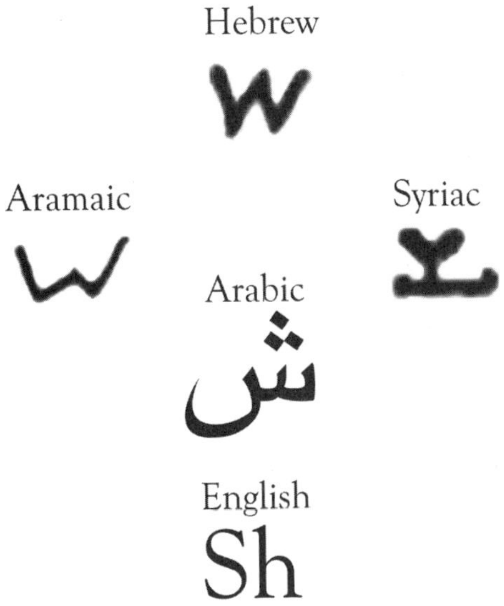

of them that afflict thee; who have said to thy soul: Bow down, that we may go over—and thou hast laid thy body as the ground and as the street to them that went over.

24. Awake, awake, put on thy strength, O Zion; put on thy beautiful garments, O Jerusalem, the holy city; for henceforth there shall no more come into thee the uncircumcised and the unclean.

25. Shake thyself from the dust; arise, sit down, O Jerusalem; loose thyself from the bands of thy neck, O captive daughter of Zion.

CHAPTER 9

1. AND now, my beloved brethren, I have read these things that ye might know concerning the covenants of the Lord that he has covenanted with all the house of Israel—

2. That he has spoken unto the Jews, by the mouth of his holy prophets, even from the beginning down, from generation to generation, until the time comes that they shall be restored to the true church and fold of God; when they shall be gathered home to the lands of their inheritance, and shall be established in all their lands of promise.

3. Behold, my beloved brethren, I speak unto you these things that ye may rejoice, and lift up your heads forever, because of the blessings which the Lord God shall bestow upon your children.

4. For I know that ye have searched much, many of you, to know of things to come; wherefore I know that ye know that our flesh must waste away and die; nevertheless, in our bodies we shall see God.

5. Yea, I know that ye know that in the body he shall show himself unto those at Jerusalem, from whence we came; for it is expedient that it should be among them; for it behooveth the great Creator that he suffereth himself to become subject unto man in the flesh, and die for all men, that all men might become subject unto him.

6. For as death hath passed upon all men, to fulfil the merciful plan of the great Creator, there must needs be a power of resurrection, and the resurrection must needs come unto man by reason of the fall; and the fall came by reason of transgression; and because man became fallen they were cut off from the presence of the Lord.

7. Wherefore, it must needs be an infinite atonement—save it should be an infinite atonement this corruption

2 Nephi 8:24–25

The Prophet Joseph Smith was asked what Isaiah meant when he wrote the words quoted in 2 Nephi 8:24–25. His response was as follows: "He had reference to those whom God should call in the last days, who should hold the power of priesthood to bring again Zion, and the redemption of Israel; and to put on her strength is to put on the authority of the priesthood, which she, Zion, has a right to by lineage; also to return to that power which she had lost" (D&C 113:8). (O/C)

2 Nephi 9:2

Speaking of Israel, the Lord promised that when the day comes that they ". . . come to the knowledge of their Redeemer, they shall be gathered together again to the lands of their inheritance" (2 Ne. 6:11). Jacob also said ". . . [when] the time comes that they shall be restored to the true church and fold of God. . . they shall be gathered home to the lands of their inheritance, and shall be established in all their lands of promise" (2 Ne. 9:2). After they join the Lord's Church, suggested Elder Bruce R. McConkie, they will be gathered ". . . to whatever places are appointed for the worship of the Lord and the receipt of the fulness of his blessings." Those places may be geographical lands, or they may be Church unit designations such as stakes and wards. (O/C)

could not put on incorruption. Wherefore, the first judgment which came upon man must needs have remained to an endless duration. And if so, this flesh must have laid down to rot and to crumble to its mother earth, to rise no more.
8. O the wisdom of God, his mercy and grace! For behold, if the flesh should rise no more our spirits must become subject to that angel who fell from before the presence of the Eternal God, and became the devil, to rise no more.
9. And our spirits must have become like unto him, and we become devils, angels to a devil, to be shut out from the presence of our God, and to remain with the father of lies, in misery, like unto himself; yea, to that being who beguiled our first parents, who transformeth himself nigh unto an angel of light, and stirreth up the children of men unto secret combinations of murder and all manner of secret works of darkness.
10. O how great the goodness of our God, who prepareth a way for our escape from the grasp of this awful monster; yea, that monster, death and hell, which I call the death of the body, and also the death of the spirit.
11. And because of the way of deliverance of our God, the Holy One of Israel, this death, of which I have spoken, which is the temporal, shall deliver up its dead; which death is the grave.
12. And this death of which I have spoken, which is the spiritual death, shall deliver up its dead; which spiritual death is hell; wherefore, death and hell must deliver up their dead, and hell must deliver up its captive spirits, and the grave must deliver up its captive bodies, and the bodies and the spirits of men will be restored one to the other; and it is by the power of the resurrection of the Holy One of Israel.
13. O how great the plan of our God! For on the other hand, the paradise of God must deliver up the spirits of the righteous, and the grave deliver up the body of the righteous; and the spirit and the body is restored to itself again, and all men become incorruptible, and immortal, and they are living souls, having a perfect knowledge like unto us in the flesh, save it be that our knowledge shall be perfect.
14. Wherefore, we shall have a perfect knowledge of all our guilt, and our uncleanness, and our nakedness; and the righteous shall

2 Nephi 9:6

Without death, we would have no relief from the hazards and challenges of mortality, which commonly cause sorrow and suffering. No one wants to indefinitely prolong life on earth. In the natural course of life, bodies wear out, and bodily functions deteriorate. Physical and mental limitations and ailments commonly increase in frequency and intensity as people grow older. The Lord wanted us to come to earth, but he didn't want us to stay on earth any longer than necessary for us to complete his purposes and designs. Therefore, separation of our spirit from our mortal body is a desirable conclusion to mortal life, though that separation is not permanent. (O/C)

2 Nephi 9:6–9

The atonement of Jesus Christ met fully the demands of justice in regard to the original transgression of Adam. Thus, the atonement is "infinite" because it applies to everyone in (1) removing the permanent effects of physical death for everyone by providing for the resurrection, and (2) giving every person the opportunity of having the effects of spiritual death (alienation from the Spirit of God through sin) removed through the repentance of individual sins.

The term "spiritual death" is used in the Book of Mormon to refer to a spiritual alienation from God; according to Alma, it occurs when one dies "as to things pertaining unto righteousness." (Alma 12:16.) One definition of the word *spiritual* is "of or pertaining to the spirit or things of the spirit"; the definition of *death* includes the idea of separation. Thus spiritual death rightfully refers to a state of spiritual separation from God; it may or may not have anything to do with a physical separation from God. . . .

The first spiritual death of Adam and Eve was fully atoned for by the Savior and Redeemer of mankind. Because of the atonement of Jesus Christ, a newborn child on this earth is not spiritually dead but is alive "in Christ, even from the foundation of the world." (Moroni 8:12.) However, when a person arrives at the age of accountability, learns the difference between good and evil, and then commits sin, he suffers his first individual spiritual death. He becomes spiritually dead because he alienates himself from the Spirit of God. This type of spiritual death is referred to in the scripture as the *first* spiritual death. If a person fully repents of his sins, accepts the atonement of the Savior, and is baptized of water and of the Spirit, he can be spiritually born again through the cleansing action of the Holy Ghost and thus can regain God's presence. If he does not meet the requirements of this rebirth, he cannot regain the presence of God. (John 3:5.) . . .

Another type of spiritual death mentioned in the scriptures is the "*second* spiritual death." This more serious spiritual death occurs when a person commits the sin against the Holy Ghost—"Having denied the Holy Spirit after having received it, and having denied the Only Begotten Son of the Father, having crucified him unto themselves and put him to an open shame. . . . And the only ones on whom the second death shall have any power." (D&C 76:35, 37.) The effects of this sin are eternal, for the sinner never can make full payment for the law he has broken. Indeed, by denying the atonement of Jesus Christ and the cleansing power of the Holy Ghost, the sinner has denied the very power upon which forgiveness and redemption are based. These sinners become sons of perdition, and they "shall be chained down to an everlasting destruction" (Alma 12:17) and become "the only ones who shall not be redeemed in the due time of the Lord" (D&C 76:38). (Ludlow)

2 Nephi 9:7–9

The Savior's Atonement was in very fact infinite, because it is without end. In its infinite nature, it:

- Involved infinite suffering for the sins, illnesses, and pains of all mankind
- Covers the infinite number of men and women created by Him
- Applies to the infinite number of worlds created by Him (see Moses 1:33), and all forms of life on all of those worlds
- Brings the gift of resurrection to all who have ever lived
- Affects the endless expanses of eternity, incomprehensible to our finite minds
- Forever put an end to animal sacrifice
- Was done only once, intended to permanently cover all (see Heb. 10:10)

Only the Savior—born to an immortal Father and a mortal mother—was the infinite Being qualified to make such an infinite Atonement.

POINT OF INTEREST

Mayan wall design

2 Nephi 9:10

One definition of the word spiritual is 'of or pertaining to the spirit or things of the spirit'; the definition of death includes the idea of separation. Thus spiritual death rightfully refers to a state of spiritual separation from God; it may or may not have anything to do with a physical separation from God. (Ludlow)

2 Nephi 9:13

Brigham Young said, "Where is the spirit world? It is right here. . . . Can you see it with your natural eyes? No. Can you see spirits in this room? No. Suppose the Lord should touch your eyes that you might see, could you then see the spirits? Yes, as plainly as you now see bodies. . . ."

2 Nephi 9:14, 33

As soon as we are resurrected, we will have a perfect knowledge of how we lived our lives—whether we lived in accordance to the commandments. Our knowledge of all things, on the other hand, will not be perfect at the time of resurrection; instead, we will engage in what Joseph Smith called the "great work" of continuing to learn beyond the grave.

have a perfect knowledge of their enjoyment, and their righteousness, being clothed with purity, yea, even with the robe of righteousness.
15. And it shall come to pass that when all men shall have passed
from this first death unto life, insomuch as they have become
immortal, they must appear before the judgment-seat of the Holy
One of Israel; and then cometh the judgment, and then must they
be judged according to the holy judgment of God.
16. And assuredly, as the Lord liveth, for the Lord God hath spoken it, and it is his eternal word, which cannot pass away, that
they who are righteous shall be righteous still, and they who are
filthy shall be filthy still; wherefore, they who are filthy are the
devil and his angels; and they shall go away into everlasting fire,
prepared for them; and their torment is as a lake of fire and brimstone, whose flame ascendeth up forever and ever and has no end.
17. O the greatness and the justice of our God! For he executeth all
his words, and they have gone forth out of his mouth, and his law must
be fulfilled.
18. But, behold, the righteous, the saints of the Holy One of Israel,
they who have believed in the Holy One of Israel, they who have
endured the crosses of the world, and despised the shame of it, they
shall inherit the kingdom of God, which was prepared for them
from the foundation of the world, and their joy shall be full forever.
19. O the greatness of the mercy of our God, the Holy One of
Israel! For he delivereth his saints from that awful monster the
devil, and death, and hell, and that lake of fire and brimstone,
which is endless torment.
20. O how great the holiness of our God! For he knoweth all
things, and there is not anything save he knows it.
21. And he cometh into the world that he may save all men if they
will hearken unto his voice; for behold, he suffereth the pains of all
men, yea, the pains of every living creature, both men, women, and
children, who belong to the family of Adam.
22. And he suffereth this that the resurrection might pass upon all
men, that all might stand before him at the great and judgment
day.
23. And he commandeth all men that they must repent, and be
baptized in his name, having perfect faith in the Holy One of
Israel, or they cannot be saved in the kingdom of God.

2 Nephi 9:20

Some who hear that God the Father enjoys "eternal progression" erroneously interpret that to mean that He is continually learning and gaining knowledge. Such is not the case, as this verse makes clear; God knows all things. As far as He is concerned, "eternal progression" means that His kingdoms are constantly increasing.

2 Nephi 9:20

. . . God is the only supreme governor and independent being in whom all fulness and perfection dwell; who *is* omnipotent [all powerful], omnipresent [everywhere present] and omniscient [all knowing]; without beginning of days or end of life; and that in him every good gift and every good principle dwell. . . .

. . . Without the knowledge of all things, God would not be able to save any portion of his creatures; for it is by reason of the knowledge which he has of all things, from the beginning to the end, that enables him to give the understanding to his creatures by which they are made partakers of eternal life; and if it were not for the idea existing in the minds of men that God had all knowledge it would be impossible for them to exercise faith in him. ("Lectures on Faith," Lecture 2, paragraph 2; Lecture 4, paragraph 11.)

Joseph Fielding Smith quotes his grandfather, Hyrum Smith, as having said: "I would not serve a God that had not all wisdom and all power." Then Joseph Fielding Smith continues, "Do we believe that God has all 'wisdom'? If so, in that, he is absolute. If there is something he does not know, then he is not absolute in 'wisdom,' and to think such a thing is absurd." (*Doctrines of Salvation*, 1:5.)

President Smith indicates possible areas in which God is progressing (glory, honor, etc.), and then concludes, "Do you not see that it is in this manner that our Eternal Father is progressing? Not by seeking knowledge which he does not have, for such a thought cannot be maintained in the light of scripture. It is not through ignorance and learning hidden truth that he progresses, for if there are truths which he does not know, then these things are greater than he, and this cannot be." (Ludlow)

POINT OF INTEREST

Huascar, pictured at right, was the thirteenth emperor of the Incas.

24. And if they will not repent and believe in his name, and be baptized in his name, and endure to the end, they must be damned; for the Lord God, the Holy One of Israel, has spoken it.
25. Wherefore, he has given a law; and where there is no law given there is no punishment; and where there is no punishment there is no condemnation; and where there is no condemnation the mercies of the Holy One of Israel have claim upon them, because of the atonement; for they are delivered by the power of him.
26. For the atonement satisfieth the demands of his justice upon all those who have not the law given to them, that they are delivered from that awful monster, death and hell, and the devil, and the lake of fire and brimstone, which is endless torment; and they are restored to that God who gave them breath, which is the Holy One of Israel.
27. But wo unto him that has the law given, yea, that has all the commandments of God, like unto us, and that transgresseth them, and that wasteth the days of his probation, for awful is his state!
28. O that cunning plan of the evil one! O the vainness, and the frailties, and the foolishness of men! When they are learned they think they are wise, and they hearken not unto the counsel of God, for they set it aside, supposing they know of themselves, wherefore, their wisdom is foolishness and it profiteth them not. And they shall perish.
29. But to be learned is good if they hearken unto the counsels of God.
30. But wo unto the rich, who are rich as to the things of the world. For because they are rich they despise the poor, and they persecute the meek, and their hearts are upon their treasures; wherefore, their treasure is their god. And behold, their treasure shall perish with them also.
31. And wo unto the deaf that will not hear; for they shall perish.
32. Wo unto the blind that will not see; for they shall perish also.
33. Wo unto the uncircumcised of heart, for a knowledge of their

2 Nephi 9:23–24

The teachings of Jacob clearly indicate that the early Nephites considered baptism an essential ordinance of the gospel. (2 Nephi 9:23–24.) Nephi also taught the necessity of baptism (2 Nephi 31:5–13), and then, referring to the baptism of the Savior, he counseled his followers to "do the things which I have told you I have seen that your Lord and your Redeemer should do; for, for this cause have they been shown unto me, that ye might know the gate by which ye should enter. For the gate by which ye should enter is repentance and baptism by water" (2 Nephi 31:17).

Concerning baptisms by the early Nephites, Joseph Fielding Smith has written:

The Book of Mormon teaches us that baptism for the remission of sins was a fundamental principle of the gospel among the Nephites from the time of Lehi all through their history. . . .

All through the Book of Mormon there are references to baptism as an ordinance for the remission of sins. What their word for baptism was is not revealed, but in the translation the Prophet Joseph Smith used the familiar expression of our time. (*Answers to Gospel Questions*, 2:66.)

The Lord indicates in the Pearl of Great Price that baptism has been practiced as an ordinance of the gospel since the fall of Adam (Moses 5:58; 6:52), with Adam himself being baptized (Moses 6:64–65). The purpose and necessity of baptism is clearly and beautifully explained by the Lord in this scripture. (Moses 6:52–63.)

The following statement provides additional information on the baptisms performed before the birth of Christ:

In the former ages of the world, before the Savior came in the flesh, "the saints" were baptized in the name of Jesus Christ to come, because there never was any other name whereby men could be saved; and after he came in the flesh and was crucified, then *the saints* were baptized in the name of Jesus Christ, crucified, risen from the dead and ascended into heaven, that they might be buried in baptism like him, and be raised in glory like him, that as there was but *one* Lord, *one* faith, *one* baptism, and *one* God and father of us all, even so there was but *one* door to the mansions of bliss. Amen. (*Times and Seasons*, 3:905.) (Ludlow)

iniquities shall smite them at the last day.

34. Wo unto the liar, for he shall be thrust down to hell.

35. Wo unto the murderer who deliberately killeth, for he shall die.

36. Wo unto them who commit whoredoms, for they shall be thrust down to hell.

37. Yea, wo unto those that worship idols, for the devil of all devils delighteth in them.

38. And, in fine, wo unto all those who die in their sins; for they shall return to God, and behold his face, and remain in their sins.

39. O, my beloved brethren, remember the awfulness in transgressing against that Holy God, and also the awfulness of yielding to the enticings of that cunning one. Remember, to be carnally-minded is death, and to be spiritually-minded is life eternal.

40. O, my beloved brethren, give ear to my words. Remember the greatness of the Holy One of Israel. Do not say that I have spoken hard things against you; for if ye do, ye will revile against the truth; for I have spoken the words of your Maker. I know that the words of truth are hard against all uncleanness; but the righteous fear them not, for they love the truth and are not shaken.

41. O then, my beloved brethren, come unto the Lord, the Holy One. Remember that his paths are righteous. Behold, the way for man is narrow, but it lieth in a straight course before him, and the keeper of the gate is the Holy One of Israel; and he employeth no servant there; and there is none other way save it be by the gate; for he cannot be deceived, for the Lord God is his name.

42. And whoso knocketh, to him will he open; and the wise, and the learned, and they that are rich, who are puffed up because of their learning, and their wisdom, and their riches—yea, they are they whom he despiseth; and save they shall cast these things away, and consider themselves fools before God, and come down in the depths of humility, he will not open unto them.

43. But the things of the wise and the prudent shall be hid from them forever—yea, that happiness which is prepared for the saints.

44. O, my beloved brethren, remember my words. Behold, I take off my garments, and I shake them before you; I pray the God of my salvation that he view me with his

2 Nephi 9:39–41

Jacob's remarkable sermon on the Atonement (2 Ne. 9–10) is more than a concept piece. It is an action piece, which calls for a pattern of behavior that will bring one closer to the Savior and generate an improved condition in one's life. The Book of Mormon contains some of the plainest statements about the Atonement—its doctrine and its application—in all of the scriptures. No wonder the Lord reserved this scriptural chronicle for our age, an age of complexity, sophistication, and rationalization. We needed clarity. We needed simplicity. We needed unfettered truth. What Jacob, Alma, Amulek, and others taught about the Atonement is crystal clear, as Nephi was to state shortly thereafter: "And now behold, my people, ye are a stiffnecked people; wherefore, I have spoken plainly unto you, that ye cannot misunderstand. And the words which I have spoken shall stand as a testimony against you; for they are sufficient to teach any man the right way; for the right way is to believe in Christ and deny him not; for by denying him ye also deny the prophets and the law" (2 Ne. 25:28).

Jacob offered counsel on things to be aware of that would impede our reception of the blessings of the Atonement. Though King Benjamin said there are many ways to sin (see Mosiah 4:29), here are a few examples of that which bars us from experiencing the full joy of Christ's embrace in our lives:

1. Transgressing the laws and failing to repent (see 2 Ne. 9:27). . . .

2. Wasting away our lives through idleness (see 2 Ne. 9:27). . . .

3. Relying on one's own learning and not taking the counsel of God (see 2 Ne. 9:28–29). . . . The so-called learning of man changes with the passage of time. God's knowledge concerns verities . . . eternal and absolute truth. . . .

4. Allowing riches to become our treasure (see 2 Ne. 9:30). . . .

5. Unwilling to hear the word of God . . . for they shall perish (see 2 Ne. 9:31). . . . In the vision of the tree of life, those who did not hold to the iron rod wandered off in strange paths and ended up in the spacious building or else perished in the depths of the river (hell).

6. Those who will not see . . . for they shall perish also (see 2 Ne. 9:32). (P/A)

2 Nephi 9:41

The inspired prophet Jacob maintains that the "keeper of the gate" of heaven is "the Holy One of Israel; and he employeth no servant there." (2 Nephi 9:41.) The "Holy One of Israel" is Jesus Christ; thus the tradition in Christianity that Peter is the keeper of the gate of heaven is apparently false and without scriptural foundation. (Ludlow)

all-searching eye; wherefore, ye shall know at the last day, when all
men shall be judged of their works, that the God of Israel did witness that I shook your iniquities from my soul, and that I stand
with brightness before him, and am rid of your blood.
45. O, my beloved brethren, turn away from your sins; shake off the
chains of him that would bind you fast; come unto that God who
is the rock of your salvation.
46. Prepare your souls for that glorious day when justice shall be
administered unto the righteous, even the day of judgment, that ye
may not shrink with awful fear; that ye may not remember your
awful guilt in perfectness, and be constrained to exclaim: Holy,
holy are thy judgments, O Lord God Almighty—but I know my
guilt; I transgressed thy law, and my transgressions are mine; and
the devil hath obtained me, that I am a prey to his awful misery.
47. But behold, my brethren, is it expedient that I should awake
you to an awful reality of these things? Would I harrow up your
souls if your minds were pure? Would I be plain unto you according to the plainness of the truth if ye were freed from sin?
48. Behold, if ye were holy I would speak unto you of holiness; but
as ye are not holy, and ye look upon me as a teacher, it must needs
be expedient that I teach you the consequences of sin.
49. Behold, my soul abhorreth sin, and my heart delighteth in
righteousness; and I will praise the holy name of my God.
50. Come, my brethren, every one that thirsteth, come ye to the
waters; and he that hath no money, come buy and eat; yea, come
buy wine and milk without money and without price.
51. Wherefore, do not spend money for that which is of no worth,
nor your labor for that which cannot satisfy. Hearken diligently
unto me, and remember the words which I have spoken; and come
unto the Holy One of Israel, and feast upon that which perisheth
not, neither can be corrupted, and let your soul delight in fatness.
52. Behold, my beloved brethren, remember the words of your
God; pray unto him continually by day, and give thanks unto his
holy name by night. Let your hearts rejoice.
53. And behold how great the covenants of the Lord, and how
great his condescensions unto the children of men; and because of
his greatness, and his grace and mercy, he has promised unto us
that our seed shall not utterly be destroyed, according to the flesh,
but that he would preserve them; and in future generations they
shall become a righteous branch unto the house of Israel.
54. And now, my brethren, I would speak unto you more; but on
the morrow I will declare unto you the remainder of my words.
Amen.

POINT OF INTEREST

Monument No. 12 at La Venta Museum in Villahermosa, Tabasco, Mexico.

CHAPTER 10

1. And now I, Jacob, speak unto you again, my beloved brethren, concerning this righteous branch of which I have spoken.

2. For behold, the promises which we have obtained are promises unto us according to the flesh; wherefore, as it has been shown unto me that many of our children shall perish in the flesh because of unbelief, nevertheless, God will be merciful unto many; and our children shall be restored, that they may come to that which will give them the true knowledge of their Redeemer.

3. Wherefore, as I said unto you, it must needs be expedient that Christ—for in the last night the angel spake unto me that this should be his name—should come among the Jews, among those who are the more wicked part of the world; and they shall crucify him—for thus it behooveth our God, and there is none other nation on earth that would crucify their God.

4. For should the mighty miracles be wrought among other nations they would repent, and know that he be their God.

5. But because of priestcrafts and iniquities, they at Jerusalem will stiffen their necks against him, that he be crucified.

6. Wherefore, because of their iniquities, destructions, famines, pestilences, and bloodshed shall come upon them; and they who shall not be destroyed shall be scattered among all nations.

7. But behold, thus saith the Lord God: When the day cometh that they shall believe in me, that I am Christ, then have I covenanted with their fathers that they shall be restored in the flesh, upon the earth, unto the lands of their inheritance.

8. And it shall come to pass that they shall be gathered in from their long dispersion, from the isles of the sea, and from the four parts of the earth; and the nations of the Gentiles shall be great in the eyes of me, saith God, in carrying them forth to the lands of their inheritance.

9. Yea, the kings of the Gentiles shall be nursing fathers unto them, and their queens shall become nursing mothers; wherefore, the promises of the Lord are great unto the Gentiles, for he hath spoken it, and who can dispute?

10. But behold, this land, said God, shall be a land of thine inheritance, and the Gentiles shall be blessed upon the land.

11. And this land shall be a land of

2 Nephi 10:3

This prophecy was undoubtedly a surprising one on several levels—especially in the sense that it named the Savior and told where He would be born. Perhaps most surprising, however, was the prophecy that He would be crucified. According to the Law of Moses, there were only four acceptable ways of executing someone: beheading, stoning, strangling, and burning. Crucifixion was not part of Jewish tradition and would not have been an expected way to impose the death penalty.

2 Nephi 10:3

In order for Jesus Christ fully to atone or pay for the transgression of Adam, it was evidently necessary for his life to be taken so that the demands of justice could be fully met. Thus it was necessary for him to live upon the earth at a time when the people would be wicked enough to take his life. Jacob mentions it was necessary that the Savior come "among those who are the more wicked part of the world" as "there is none other nation on earth that would crucify their God" (2 Nephi 10:3). (Ludlow)

liberty unto the Gentiles, and there shall be no kings upon the
land, who shall raise up unto the Gentiles.
12. And I will fortify this land against all other nations.
13. And he that fighteth against Zion shall perish, saith God.
14. For he that raiseth up a king against me shall perish, for I, the
Lord, the king of heaven, will be their king, and I will be a light unto
them forever, that hear my words.
15. Wherefore, for this cause, that my covenants may be fulfilled
which I have made unto the children of men, that I will do unto
them while they are in the flesh, I must needs destroy the secret
works of darkness, and of murders, and of abominations.
16. Wherefore, he that fighteth against Zion, both Jew and
Gentile, both bond and free, both male and female, shall perish;
for they are they who are the whore of all the earth; for they who
are not for me are against me, saith our God.
17. For I will fulfil my promises which I have made unto the children of men, that I will do unto them while they are in the flesh—
18. Wherefore, my beloved brethren, thus saith our God: I will
afflict thy seed by the hand of the Gentiles; nevertheless, I will
soften the hearts of the Gentiles, that they shall be like unto a
father to them; wherefore, the Gentiles shall be blessed and numbered among the house of Israel.
19. Wherefore, I will consecrate this land unto thy seed, and them
who shall be numbered among thy seed, forever, for the land of
their inheritance; for it is a choice land, saith God unto me, above
all other lands, wherefore I will have all men that dwell thereon
that they shall worship me, saith God.
20. And now, my beloved brethren, seeing that our merciful God has
given us so great knowledge concern-
ing these things, let us remember
him, and lay aside our sins, and not
hang down our heads, for we are not
cast off; nevertheless, we have been
driven out of the land of our inheritance; but we have been led to a better land, for the Lord has made the
sea our path, and we are upon an isle
of the sea.
21. But great are the promises of the
Lord unto them who are upon the
isles of the sea; wherefore as it says
isles, there must needs be more than
this, and they are inhabited also by
our brethren.
22. For behold, the Lord God has

POINT OF INTEREST

Several animals are mentioned in the Book of Mormon, some of which might have been unfamiliar to Joseph Smith as he translated. Here are some ideas:

Book of Mormon name	Candidate animal
Elephant	*Mastadon, Mammoth*
Curelom	*Sloth, Bison, Llama, Alpaca, Tapir, Mastadon, Mammoth*
Cumom	*See "Curelom"*
Cow	*Deer, Brocket, Bison*
Horse	*Deer, Tapir, Horse*
Ox	*Tapir, Bison*
Ass	*Tapir*
Sheep	*Paca or Agouti*
Goat	*Brocket, Deer*
Swine	*Peccary*
Dog	*Dog*

Alpacas are a domesticated species of South American camelid and are typical of the Andes of Ecuador, southern Peru, northern Bolivia, and northern Chile. They're smaller than llamas and are not typically used as beasts of burden but rather for their fiber.

led away from time to time from the house of Israel, according to his will and pleasure. And now behold, the Lord remembereth all them who have been broken off, wherefore he remembereth us also.
23. Therefore, cheer up your hearts, and remember that ye are free to act for yourselves—to choose the way of everlasting death or the way of eternal life.
24. Wherefore, my beloved brethren, reconcile yourselves to the will of God, and not to the will of the devil and the flesh; and remember, after ye are reconciled unto God, that it is only in and through the grace of God that ye are saved.
25. Wherefore, may God raise you from death by the power of the resurrection, and also from everlasting death by the power of the atonement, that ye may be received into the eternal kingdom of God, that ye may praise him through grace divine. Amen.

CHAPTER 11

1. AND now, Jacob spake many more things to my people at that time; nevertheless only these things have I caused to be written, for the things which I have written sufficeth me.
2. And now I, Nephi, write more of the words of Isaiah, for my soul delighteth in his words. For I will liken his words unto my people, and I will send them forth unto all my children, for he verily saw my Redeemer, even as I have seen him.
3. And my brother, Jacob, also has seen him as I have seen him; wherefore, I will send their words forth unto my children to prove unto them that my words are true. Wherefore, by the words of three, God hath said, I will establish my word. Nevertheless, God sendeth more witnesses, and he proveth all his words.
4. Behold, my soul delighteth in proving unto my people the truth of the coming of Christ; for, for this end hath the law of Moses been given; and all things which have been given of God from the beginning of the world, unto man, are the typifying of him.
5. And also my soul delighteth in the covenants of the Lord which he hath made to our fathers; yea, my soul delighteth in his grace, and in his justice, and power, and mercy in the great and eternal plan of deliverance from death.
6. And my soul delighteth in proving unto my people that save Christ should come all men must perish.
7. For if there be no Christ there be no God; and if there be no God we

2 Nephi 11:2–3

We know that there were three witnesses to the Book of Mormon at the time it was translated—Oliver Cowdery, David Whitmer, and Martin Harris all bore witness that they had seen the plates and the engravings on them. Their written testimony appears in the opening pages of the book. In a similar way, the first three to bear testimony of the divinity of the Savior within the text of the book were Nephi, Jacob, and Isaiah. In this way, Nephi, Jacob, and Isaiah, cited in these verses, become a type or shadow for the three witnesses of our day.

2 Nephi 11:2–3

God has said through his prophets, "In the mouth of two or three witnesses shall every word be established." (2 Corinthians 13:1.) Nephi was apparently aware of this system of witnesses when he introduced three great pre-Christian witnesses of the coming of Jesus Christ: Isaiah, Nephi himself, and Nephi's brother Jacob. Nephi then continues: "Wherefore, by the words of three, God hath said, I will establish my word" (2 Nephi 11:3). (Ludlow)

are not, for there could have been no creation. But there is a God,
and he is Christ, and he cometh in the fulness of his own time.
8. And now I write some of the words of Isaiah, that whoso of my
people shall see these words may lift up their hearts and rejoice for
all men. Now these are the words, and ye may liken them unto you
and unto all men.

CHAPTER 12

1. THE word that Isaiah, the son of Amoz, saw concerning Judah
and Jerusalem:
2. And it shall come to pass in the last days, when the mountain of the
Lord's house shall be established in the top of the mountains, and shall
be exalted above the hills, and all nations shall flow unto it.
3. And many people shall go and say, Come ye, and let us go up to
the mountain of the Lord, to the house of the God of Jacob; and
he will teach us of his ways, and we will walk in his paths; for out
of Zion shall go forth the law, and the word of the Lord from
Jerusalem.
4. And he shall judge among the nations, and shall rebuke many people: and they shall beat their swords into plow-shares, and their spears
into pruning-hooks—nation shall not lift up sword against nation,
neither shall they learn war any more.
5. O house of Jacob, come ye and let us walk in the light of the
Lord; yea, come, for ye have all gone astray, every one to his wicked
ways.
6. Therefore, O Lord, thou hast forsaken thy people, the house of
Jacob, because they be replenished from the east, and hearken
unto soothsayers like the Philistines, and they please themselves
in the children of strangers.
7. Their land also is full of silver and gold, neither is there any end
of their treasures; their land is also full of horses, neither is there
any end of their chariots.
8. Their land is also full of idols; they worship the work of their
own hands, that which their own fingers have made.
9. And the mean man boweth not down, and the great man humbleth himself not, therefore, forgive him not.
10. O ye wicked ones, enter into the rock, and hide thee in the
dust, for the fear of the Lord and the glory of his majesty shall smite
thee.
11. And it shall come to pass that the lofty looks of man shall be
humbled, and the haughtiness of men shall be bowed down, and
the Lord alone shall be exalted in that day.
12. For the day of the Lord of

POINT OF INTEREST

According to scripture, Isaiah saw the Lord "in the year that king Uzziah died" (Isa. 6:1), which was in about 758 B.C. He served and ministered as a prophet until sometime in Manasseh's reign. There is a tradition that he was killed by the king, who was said to have put Isaiah in a hollow log and then cut him in half. Isaiah is portrayed in this painting by Ugolino di Nerio.

2 Nephi 12:2–3

In these verses, the term *mountain of the Lord* refers to the temple of the Lord—the Salt Lake Temple, a place of great revelation—built in the top of the mountains.

2 Nephi 12:2–3

The gathering of Israel to any designated spot—as in these verses, to the mountains of Zion—is not the most important aspect of bringing these people together. The far more important aspect is the fulfillment of the covenant between the Lord and Abraham in which the Savior promised that through Abraham's direct lineage all the families of the earth would be blessed with the blessings of the gospel (see Abr. 2:8–11). One factor that will help facilitate that, of course, is the fact that the Americas were identified as the place of Joseph's inheritance and that in the latter days this "Zion" became the place where gospel blessings were initially available. Today it remains the headquarters from which those blessings flow.

Hosts soon cometh upon all nations, yea, upon every one; yea, upon the proud and lofty, and upon every one who is lifted up, and he shall be brought low.
13. Yea, and the day of the Lord shall come upon all the cedars of Lebanon, for they are high and lifted up; and upon all the oaks of Bashan;
14. And upon all the high mountains, and upon all the hills, and upon all the nations which are lifted up, and upon every people;
15. And upon every high tower, and upon every fenced wall;
16. And upon all the ships of the sea, and upon all the ships of Tarshish, and upon all pleasant pictures.
17. And the loftiness of man shall be bowed down, and the haughtiness of men shall be made low; and the Lord alone shall be exalted in that day.
18. And the idols he shall utterly abolish.
19. And they shall go into the holes of the rocks, and into the caves of the earth, for the fear of the Lord shall come upon them and the glory of his majesty shall smite them, when he ariseth to shake terribly the earth.
20. In that day a man shall cast his idols of silver, and his idols of gold, which he hath made for himself to worship, to the moles and to the bats;
21. To go into the clefts of the rocks, and into the tops of the ragged rocks, for the fear of the Lord shall come upon them and the majesty of his glory shall smite them, when he ariseth to shake terribly the earth.
22. Cease ye from man, whose breath is in his nostrils; for wherein is he to be accounted of?

CHAPTER 13

1. FOR behold, the Lord, the Lord of Hosts, doth take away from Jerusalem, and from Judah, the stay and the staff, the whole staff of bread, and the whole stay of water—
2. The mighty man, and the man of war, the judge, and the prophet, and the prudent, and the ancient;
3. The captain of fifty, and the honorable man, and the counselor, and the cunning artificer, and the eloquent orator.
4. And I will give children unto them to be their princes, and babes shall rule over them.
5. And the people shall be oppressed, every one by another, and every one by his neighbor; the child shall behave himself proudly against the ancient, and the base against the honorable.
6. When a man shall take hold of his brother of the house of his father, and shall say: Thou hast clothing, be thou our ruler, and let not this ruin come under thy hand—
7. In that day shall he swear, saying: I will not be a healer; for in my house there is neither bread nor clothing; make me not a ruler of the people.
8. For Jerusalem is ruined, and Judah is fallen, because their

2 Nephi 12–24

The early prophets of the Book of Mormon frequently quoted from the writings of Isaiah that appeared on the brass plates of Laban. (1 Nephi 5:11–13; 19:21–23.) Of the 433 verses of Isaiah quoted in the Book of Mormon, 199 verses are word-for-word the same as the corresponding verses in the King James Version of the Old Testament. The so-called Isaiah problem is this: How do Latter-day Saints account for this striking similarity in nearly half of the verses and the differences in the remainder of the verses?

In order to attempt an explanation of this problem, a person should consider the following points. Joseph Smith did not explain in great detail the process used in translating the Book of Mormon; he merely stated, "through the medium of the Urim and Thummim I translated the record by the gift and power of God." (*Millennial Star*, 18:118.) However, it is quite evident that the process of translation was not automatic; Joseph Smith not only had to exercise faith in the translation procedure, but he also had to put forth mental and spiritual effort. Oliver Cowdery's unsuccessful attempt to translate indicates clearly that the translation of the Book of Mormon was more than a mechanical process. (See D&C 8:1–3, 10–11; 9:7–9.)

Also, translation is frequently concerned with general ideas rather than specific words; even the best translators do not translate the same material from one language into another word-for-word the same. There appears to be only one answer to explain the word-for-word similarities between the verses of Isaiah in the Bible and the same verses in the Book of Mormon. When Joseph Smith translated the Isaiah references from the small plates of Nephi, he evidently opened his King James Version of the Bible and compared the impression he had received in translating with the words of the King James scholars. If his translation was essentially the same as that of the King James Version, he apparently quoted the verse from the Bible; then his scribe, Oliver Cowdery, copied it down. However, if Joseph Smith's translation did not agree precisely with that of the King James scholars, he would dictate his own translation to the scribe. This procedure in translation would account for both the 234 verses of Isaiah that were changed or modified by the Prophet Joseph and the 199 verses that were translated word-for-word the same. Although some critics might question this procedure of translation, scholars today frequently use this same procedure in translating the biblical manuscripts among the Dead Sea Scrolls. (Ludlow)

2 Nephi 12:20

Victor Ludlow pointed out the irony that people who so valued their temporal treasures would throw them to moles and bats—creatures who were unable to even *see* these treasures because, having lived so long in darkness, they are blind.

tongues and their doings have been against the Lord, to provoke
the eyes of his glory.
9. The show of their countenance doth witness against them, and
doth declare their sin to be even as Sodom, and they cannot hide
it. Wo unto their souls, for they have rewarded evil unto themselves!
10. Say unto the righteous that it is well with them; for they shall
eat the fruit of their doings.
11. Wo unto the wicked, for they shall perish; for the reward of
their hands shall be upon them!
12. And my people, children are their oppressors, and women rule
over them. O my people, they who lead thee cause thee to err and
destroy the way of thy paths.
13. The Lord standeth up to plead, and standeth to judge the people.
14. The Lord will enter into judgment with the ancients of his people and the princes thereof; for ye have eaten up the vineyard and
the spoil of the poor in your houses.
15. What mean ye? Ye beat my people to pieces, and grind the faces
of the poor, saith the Lord God of Hosts.
16. Moreover, the Lord saith: Because the daughters of Zion are
haughty, and walk with stretched-forth necks and wanton eyes,
walking and mincing as they go, and making a tinkling with their
feet—
17. Therefore the Lord will smite with a scab the crown of the head
of the daughters of Zion, and the Lord will discover their secret
parts.
18. In that day the Lord will take away the bravery of their tinkling
ornaments, and cauls, and round tires like the moon;
19. The chains and the bracelets, and the mufflers;
20. The bonnets, and the ornaments of the legs, and the head-
bands, and the tablets, and the ear-rings;
21. The rings, and nose jewels;
22. The changeable suits of apparel, and the mantles, and the wim-
ples, and the crisping-pins;
23. The glasses, and the fine linen, and hoods, and the veils.
24. And it shall come to pass, instead of sweet smell there shall be
stink; and instead of a girdle, a rent; and instead of well set hair,
baldness; and instead of a stomacher, a girding of sackcloth; burning instead of beauty.
25. Thy men shall fall by the sword and thy mighty in the war.
26. And her gates shall lament and mourn; and she shall be desolate, and shall sit upon the ground.

CHAPTER 14

1. AND in that day, seven women shall take hold of one man, saying: We will eat our own bread, and wear our own apparel; only let
us be called by thy name to take away our reproach.
2. In that day shall the branch of the Lord be beautiful and glorious;
the fruit of the earth excellent and

comely to them that are escaped of Israel.
3. And it shall come to pass, they that are left in Zion and remain in Jerusalem shall be called holy, every one that is written among the living in Jerusalem—
4. When the Lord shall have washed away the filth of the daughters of Zion, and shall have purged the blood of Jerusalem from the midst thereof by the spirit of judgment and by the spirit of burning.
5. And the Lord will create upon every dwelling-place of mount Zion, and upon her assemblies, a cloud and smoke by day and the shining of a flaming fire by night; for upon all the glory of Zion shall be a defence.
6. And there shall be a tabernacle for a shadow in the daytime from the heat, and for a place of refuge, and a covert from storm and from rain.

CHAPTER 15

1. AND then will I sing to my well-beloved a song of my beloved, touching his vineyard. My well-beloved hath a vineyard in a very fruitful hill.
2. And he fenced it, and gathered out the stones thereof, and planted it with the choicest vine, and built a tower in the midst of it, and also made a wine-press therein; and he looked that it should bring forth grapes, and it brought forth wild grapes.
3. And now, O inhabitants of Jerusalem, and men of Judah, judge, I pray you, betwixt me and my vineyard.
4. What could have been done more to my vineyard that I have not done in it? Wherefore, when I looked that it should bring forth grapes it brought forth wild grapes.
5. And now go to; I will tell you what I will do to my vineyard—I will take away the hedge thereof, and it shall be eaten up; and I will break down the wall thereof, and it shall be trodden down;
6. And I will lay it waste; it shall not be pruned nor digged; but there shall come up briers and thorns; I will also command the clouds that they rain no rain upon it.
7. For the vineyard of the Lord of Hosts is the house of Israel, and the men of Judah his pleasant plant; and he looked for judgment, and behold, oppression; for righteousness, but behold, a cry.
8. Wo unto them that join house to house, till there can be no place, that they may be placed alone in the midst of the earth!
9. In mine ears, said the Lord of Hosts, of a truth many houses shall be desolate, and great and fair cities without inhabitant.
10. Yea, ten acres of vineyard shall yield one bath, and the seed of a homer shall yield an ephah.
11. Wo unto them that rise up early in the morning, that they may follow strong drink, that continue until night, and wine inflame them!
12. And the harp, and the viol, the tabret, and pipe, and wine are in their feasts; but they regard not

2 Nephi 14:6

The Church of Jesus Christ of Latter-day Saints is this place of safety to all Saints who keep their covenants. They receive divine guidance through the Lord's holy spirit. They associate with clean and faithful people, who give heed to and follow the Lord's living prophets. They rejoice in the truth and bask in the light of the living Christ. (O/C)

2 Nephi 15:8

In ancient Israel, land was not to be sold; it was supposed to remain in the family's ownership forever as part of their heritage (see Micah 2:12). If a family became economically devastated and was forced into selling its land, tradition required that the land was to be returned to the family during the year of the jubilee—which, by Jewish law, was every fifty years. "Wo"—a condition of deep suffering, affliction, and grief—will come upon the wealthy landowners who took advantage of the poor, buying up their proprty and subsequently robbing them of their heritage.

the work of the Lord, neither consider the operation of his hands.
13. Therefore, my people are gone into captivity, because they have no knowledge; and their honorable men are famished, and their multitude dried up with thirst.
14. Therefore, hell hath enlarged herself, and opened her mouth without measure; and their glory, and their multitude, and their pomp, and he that rejoiceth, shall descend into it.
15. And the mean man shall be brought down, and the mighty man shall be humbled, and the eyes of the lofty shall be humbled.
16. But the Lord of Hosts shall be exalted in judgment, and God that is holy shall be sanctified in righteousness.
17. Then shall the lambs feed after their manner, and the waste places of the fat ones shall strangers eat.
18. Wo unto them that draw iniquity with cords of vanity, and sin as it were with a cart rope;
19. That say: Let him make speed, hasten his work, that we may see it; and let the counsel of the Holy One of Israel draw nigh and come, that we may know it.
20. Wo unto them that call evil good, and good evil, that put darkness for light, and light for darkness, that put bitter for sweet, and sweet for bitter!
21. Wo unto the wise in their own eyes and prudent in their own sight!
22. Wo unto the mighty to drink wine, and men of strength to mingle strong drink;
23. Who justify the wicked for reward, and take away the righteousness of the righteous from him!
24. Therefore, as the fire devoureth the stubble, and the flame consumeth the chaff, their root shall be rottenness, and their blossoms shall go up as dust; because they have cast away the law of the Lord of Hosts, and despised the word of the Holy One of Israel.
25. Therefore, is the anger of the Lord kindled against his people, and he hath stretched forth his hand against them, and hath smitten them; and the hills did tremble, and their carcasses were torn in the midst of the streets. For all this his anger is not turned away, but his hand is stretched out still.
26. And he will lift up an ensign to the nations from far, and will hiss unto them from the end of the earth; and behold, they shall come with speed swiftly; none shall be weary nor stumble among them.
27. None shall slumber nor sleep; neither shall the girdle of their loins be loosed, nor the latchet of their shoes be broken;
28. Whose arrows shall be sharp, and all their bows bent, and their horses' hoofs shall be counted like flint, and their wheels like a whirlwind, their roaring like a lion.
29. They shall roar like young lions; yea, they shall roar, and lay hold of the prey, and shall carry away safe, and none shall deliver.
30. And in that day they shall roar against them like the roaring of the

2 Nephi 15:26–29 Possible interpretation of Isaiah 5:26–29

In Isaiah 2:2 (also 2 Nephi 12:2) the prophet Isaiah indicates that he is going to talk about those things which are to "come to pass in the last days." The material Isaiah gives us in Isaiah 5 (2 Nephi 15) evidently pertains to this same time period; thus the events enumerated here are to take place primarily in the dispensation of the fulness of times. Concerning the possible fulfillment of this prophecy by Isaiah, Elder LeGrand Richards has written:

"In fixing the time of the great gathering, Isaiah seemed to indicate that it would take place in the day of the railroad train and the airplane:

"And he will lift up an ensign to the nations from far, and will hiss unto them from the end of the earth: and, behold, *they shall come with speed swiftly*:

"None shall be weary nor stumble among them; none shall slumber nor sleep; neither shall the girdle of their loins be loosed, nor the latchet of their shoes be broken:

"Whose arrows are sharp, and all their bows bent, their horses' hoofs shall be counted like flint, and their wheels like a whirlwind:

"Their roaring shall be like a lion, they shall roar like young lions: yea, they shall roar, and lay hold of the prey, and shall carry it away safe, and none shall deliver it" (Isaiah 5:26–29).

Since there were neither trains nor airplanes in that day, Isaiah could hardly have mentioned them by name. However, he seems to have described them in unmistakable words. How better could "their horses' hoofs be counted like flint, and their wheels like a whirlwind" than in the modern train? How better could "their roaring . . . be like a lion" than in the roar of the airplane? Trains and airplanes do not stop for night. Therefore, was not Isaiah justified in saying: "none shall slumber nor sleep; neither shall the girdle of their loins be loosed, nor the latchet of their shoes be broken"? With this manner of transportation the Lord can really "hiss unto them from the end of the earth," that "they shall come with speed swiftly." Indicating that Isaiah must have foreseen the airplane, he stated: "Who are these that fly as a cloud, and as the doves to their windows?" (Isaiah 60:8). (Ludlow)

2 Nephi 15:26–30

In the latter days, the term *ensign* refers to the entirety of the Lord's work among His children. As components of that work, *ensign* is also used to refer to the Book of Mormon, the gathering, missionary work, Zion, and other such things.

sea; and if they look unto the land, behold, darkness and sorrow, and the light is darkened in the heavens thereof.

CHAPTER 16

1. In the year that king Uzziah died, I saw also the Lord sitting upon a throne, high and lifted up, and his train filled the temple.
2. Above it stood the seraphim; each one had six wings; with twain he covered his face, and with twain he covered his feet, and with twain he did fly.
3. And one cried unto another, and said: Holy, holy, holy, is the Lord of Hosts; the whole earth is full of his glory.
4. And the posts of the door moved at the voice of him that cried, and the house was filled with smoke.
5. Then said I: Wo is unto me! for I am undone; because I am a man of unclean lips; and I dwell in the midst of a people of unclean lips; for mine eyes have seen the King, the Lord of Hosts.
6. Then flew one of the seraphim unto me, having a live coal in his hand, which he had taken with the tongs from off the altar;
7. And he laid it upon my mouth, and said: Lo, this has touched thy lips; and thine iniquity is taken away, and thy sin purged.
8. Also I heard the voice of the Lord, saying: Whom shall I send, and who will go for us? Then I said: Here am I; send me.
9. And he said: Go and tell this people—Hear ye indeed, but they understood not; and see ye indeed, but they perceived not.
10. Make the heart of this people fat, and make their ears heavy, and shut their eyes—lest they see with their eyes, and hear with their ears, and understand with their heart, and be converted and be healed.
11. Then said I: Lord, how long? And he said: Until the cities be wasted without inhabitant, and the houses without man, and the land be utterly desolate;
12. And the Lord have removed men far away, for there shall be a great forsaking in the midst of the land.
13. But yet there shall be a tenth, and they shall return, and shall be eaten, as a teil-tree, and as an oak whose substance is in them when they cast their leaves; so the holy seed shall be the substance thereof.

CHAPTER 17

1. And it came to pass in the days of Ahaz the son of Jotham, the son of Uzziah, king of Judah, that Rezin, king of Syria, and Pekah the son of Remaliah, king of Israel, went up toward Jerusalem to war against it, but could not prevail against it.
2. And it was told the house of David, saying: Syria is confederate with Ephraim. And his heart was moved, and the heart of his people, as the trees of the wood are moved with the wind.
3. Then said the Lord unto Isaiah: Go forth now to meet Ahaz, thou

2 Nephi 16:9–11

The prophet Isaiah was quoted extensively not only by the Book of Mormon prophets but also by the writers of the New Testament and by the Savior himself. In fact, in our present New Testament the Savior quoted Isaiah more than all the other Old Testament prophets combined. Concerning the essential idea expressed in Isaiah 6:9–11 (and also in 2 Nephi 16:9–11), the Savior said the following concerning the people of his day:

Therefore speak I to them in parables: because they seeing see not; and hearing they hear not, neither do they understand.

And in them is fulfilled the prophecy of Esaias, which saith, By hearing ye shall hear, and shall not understand; and seeing ye shall see, and shall not perceive:

For this people's heart is waxed gross, and their ears are dull of hearing, and their eyes they have closed; lest at any time they should see with their eyes, and hear with their ears, and should understand with their heart, and should be converted, and I should heal them. (Matthew 13:13–15.)

Also, the author of Acts quotes Paul as having said the following concerning Isaiah's words:

Well spake the Holy Ghost by Esaias the prophet unto our fathers, Saying, Go unto this people, and say, Hearing ye shall hear, and shall not understand; and seeing ye shall see, and not perceive:

For the heart of this people is waxed gross, and their ears are dull of hearing, and their eyes have they closed; lest they should see with their eyes, and hear with their ears, and understand with their heart, and should be converted, and I should heal them. (Acts 28:25–27.) (Ludlow)

and Shearjashub thy son, at the end of the conduit of the upper pool in the highway of the fuller's field;

4. And say unto him: Take heed, and be quiet; fear not, neither be faint-hearted for the two tails of these smoking firebrands, for the fierce anger of Rezin with Syria, and of the son of Remaliah.

5. Because Syria, Ephraim, and the son of Remaliah, have taken evil counsel against thee, saying:

6. Let us go up against Judah and vex it, and let us make a breach therein for us, and set a king in the midst of it, yea, the son of Tabeal.

7. Thus saith the Lord God: It shall not stand, neither shall it come to pass.

8. For the head of Syria is Damascus, and the head of Damascus, Rezin; and within threescore and five years shall Ephraim be broken that it be not a people.

9. And the head of Ephraim is Samaria, and the head of Samaria is Remaliah's son. If ye will not believe surely ye shall not be established.

10. Moreover, the Lord spake again unto Ahaz, saying:

11. Ask thee a sign of the Lord thy God; ask it either in the depths, or in the heights above.

12. But Ahaz said: I will not ask, neither will I tempt the Lord.

13. And he said: Hear ye now, O house of David; is it a small thing for you to weary men, but will ye weary my God also?

14. Therefore, the Lord himself shall give you a sign—Behold, a virgin shall conceive, and shall bear a son, and shall call his name Immanuel.

15. Butter and honey shall he eat, that he may know to refuse the evil and to choose the good.

16. For before the child shall know to refuse the evil and choose the good, the land that thou abhorrest shall be forsaken of both her kings.

17. The Lord shall bring upon thee, and upon thy people, and upon thy father's house, days that have not come from the day that Ephraim departed from Judah, the king of Assyria.

18. And it shall come to pass in that day that the Lord shall hiss for the fly that is in the uttermost part of Egypt, and for the bee that is in the land of Assyria.

19. And they shall come, and shall rest all of them in the desolate valleys, and in the holes of the rocks, and upon all thorns, and upon all bushes.

20. In the same day shall the Lord shave with a razor that is hired, by them beyond the river, by the king of Assyria, the head, and the hair of the feet; and it shall also consume the beard.

21. And it shall come to pass in that day, a man shall nourish a young cow and two sheep;

22. And it shall come to pass, for the abundance of milk they shall give he shall eat butter; for butter and honey shall every one eat that is left in the land.

23. And it shall come to pass in that day, every place shall be, where there were a thousand vines at a thousand silverlings, which shall be for briers and thorns.

24. With arrows and with bows shall men come thither, because all the land shall become briers and thorns.

25. And all hills that shall be digged with the mattock, there shall not come thither the fear of briers and thorns; but it shall be for the sending forth of oxen, and the treading of lesser cattle.

POINT OF INTEREST

According to traditions about Quetzalcoatl, the god's spilled blood causes the bones of the dead to come back to life.

CHAPTER 18

1. MOREOVER, the word of the Lord said unto me: Take thee a great roll, and write in it with a man's pen, concerning Maher-shalal-hash-baz.
2. And I took unto me faithful witnesses to record, Uriah the priest, and Zechariah the son of Jeberechiah.
3. And I went unto the prophetess; and she conceived and bare a son. Then said the Lord to me: Call his name, Maher-shalal-hash-baz.
4. For behold, the child shall not have knowledge to cry, My father, and my mother, before the riches of Damascus and the spoil of Samaria shall be taken away before the king of Assyria.
5. The Lord spake also unto me again, saying:
6. Forasmuch as this people refuseth the waters of Shiloah that go softly, and rejoice in Rezin and Remaliah's son;
7. Now therefore, behold, the Lord bringeth up upon them the waters of the river, strong and many, even the king of Assyria and all his glory; and he shall come up over all his channels, and go over all his banks.
8. And he shall pass through Judah; he shall overflow and go over, he shall reach even to the neck; and the stretching out of his wings shall fill the breadth of thy land, O Immanuel.
9. Associate yourselves, O ye people, and ye shall be broken in pieces; and give ear all ye of far countries; gird yourselves, and ye shall be broken in pieces; gird yourselves, and ye shall be broken in pieces.
10. Take counsel together, and it shall come to naught; speak the word, and it shall not stand; for God is with us.
11. For the Lord spake thus to me with a strong hand, and instructed me that I should not walk in the way of this people, saying:
12. Say ye not, A confederacy, to all to whom this people shall say, A confederacy; neither fear ye their fear, nor be afraid.
13. Sanctify the Lord of Hosts himself, and let him be your fear, and let him be your dread.
14. And he shall be for a sanctuary; but for a stone of stumbling, and for a rock of offense to both the houses of Israel, for a gin and a snare to the inhabitants of Jerusalem.
15. And many among them shall stumble and fall, and be broken, and be snared, and be taken.
16. Bind up the testimony, seal the law among my disciples.
17. And I will wait upon the Lord, that hideth his face from the house of Jacob, and I will look for him.
18. Behold, I and the children whom the Lord hath given me are for signs and for wonders in Israel from the Lord of Hosts, which dwelleth in Mount Zion.
19. And when they shall say unto you: Seek unto them that have familiar spirits, and unto wizards

2 Nephi 18:18

Isaiah had two sons: Maher-shalal-hash-baz (Hebrew for "in making speed to the spoil, he hasteneth the prey") and Shearjashub (Hebrew for "the remnant shall return"). Both names are symbolic of the Lord's intentions for Israel.

that peep and mutter—should not a people seek unto their God for the living to hear from the dead?
20. To the law and to the testimony; and if they speak not according to this word, it is because there is no light in them.
21. And they shall pass through it hardly bestead and hungry; and it shall come to pass that when they shall be hungry, they shall fret themselves, and curse their king and their God, and look upward.
22. And they shall look unto the earth and behold trouble, and darkness, dimness of anguish, and shall be driven to darkness.

CHAPTER 19

1. NEVERTHELESS, the dimness shall not be such as was in her vexation, when at first he lightly afflicted the land of Zebulun, and the land of Naphtali, and afterwards did more grievously afflict by the way of the Red Sea beyond Jordan in Galilee of the nations.
2. The people that walked in darkness have seen a great light; they that dwell in the land of the shadow of death, upon them hath the light shined.
3. Thou hast multiplied the nation, and increased the joy—they joy before thee according to the joy in harvest, and as men rejoice when they divide the spoil.
4. For thou hast broken the yoke of his burden, and the staff of his shoulder, the rod of his oppressor.
5. For every battle of the warrior is with confused noise, and garments rolled in blood; but this shall be with burning and fuel of fire.
6. For unto us a child is born, unto us a son is given; and the government shall be upon his shoulder; and his name shall be called, Wonderful, Counselor, The Mighty God, The Everlasting Father, The Prince of Peace.
7. Of the increase of government and peace there is no end, upon the throne of David, and upon his kingdom to order it, and to establish it with judgment and with justice from henceforth, even forever. The zeal of the Lord of Hosts will perform this.
8. The Lord sent his word unto Jacob and it hath lighted upon Israel.
9. And all the people shall know, even Ephraim and the inhabitants of Samaria, that say in the pride and stoutness of heart:
10. The bricks are fallen down, but we will build with hewn stones; the sycamores are cut down, but we will change them into cedars.
11. Therefore the Lord shall set up the adversaries of Rezin against him, and join his enemies together;
12. The Syrians before and the Philistines behind; and they shall devour Israel with open mouth. For all this his anger is not turned away, but his hand is stretched out still.
13. For the people turneth not unto him that smiteth them, neither do they seek the Lord of Hosts.
14. Therefore will the Lord cut off

2 Nephi 19:6

The names assigned to the Savior in this verse indicate service He will render: Christ is the wonder of the ages, a counselor in the ways of eternal life (see Jacob 4:10), and the everlasting father of those who covenant in baptism.

2 Nephi 19:13

This verse is Isaiah's prophecy that Israel will reject Jesus.

from Israel head and tail, branch and rush in one day.
15. The ancient, he is the head; and the prophet that teacheth lies, he is the tail.
16. For the leaders of this people cause them to err; and they that are led of them are destroyed.
17. Therefore the Lord shall have no joy in their young men, neither shall have mercy on their fatherless and widows; for every one of them is a hypocrite and an evildoer, and every mouth speaketh folly. For all this his anger is not turned away, but his hand is stretched out still.
18. For wickedness burneth as the fire; it shall devour the briers and thorns, and shall kindle in the thickets of the forests, and they shall mount up like the lifting up of smoke.
19. Through the wrath of the Lord of Hosts is the land darkened, and the people shall be as the fuel of the fire; no man shall spare his brother.
20. And he shall snatch on the right hand and be hungry; and he shall eat on the left hand and they shall not be satisfied; they shall eat every man the flesh of his own arm—
21. Manasseh, Ephraim; and Ephraim, Manasseh; they together shall be against Judah. For all this his anger is not turned away, but his hand is stretched out still.

2 Nephi 19:21

Through all the tribulation described in the previous verses, the coming of the Messiah is proof that "his arm is stretched out still."

CHAPTER 20

1. Wo unto them that decree unrighteous decrees, and that write grievousness which they have prescribed;
2. To turn away the needy from judgment, and to take away the right from the poor of my people, that widows may be their prey, and that they may rob the fatherless!
3. And what will ye do in the day of visitation, and in the desolation which shall come from far? to whom will ye flee for help? and where will ye leave your glory?
4. Without me they shall bow down under the prisoners, and they shall fall under the slain. For all this his anger is not turned away, but his hand is stretched out still.
5. O Assyrian, the rod of mine anger, and the staff in their hand is their indignation.
6. I will send him against a hypocritical nation, and against the people of my wrath will I give him a charge to take the spoil, and to take the prey, and to tread them down like the mire of the streets.
7. Howbeit he meaneth not so, neither doth his heart think so; but in his heart it is to destroy and cut off nations not a few.
8. For he saith: Are not my princes altogether kings?
9. Is not Calno as Carchemish? Is not Hamath as Arpad? Is not Samaria as Damascus?
10. As my hand hath founded the

2 Nephi 20:6

This prophecy was fulfilled when the king of Assyria captured the northern kingdom of Israel (the "hypocritical nation" referred to in this verse).

kingdoms of the idols, and whose graven images did excel them of Jerusalem and of Samaria;
11. Shall I not, as I have done unto Samaria and her idols, so do to Jerusalem and to her idols?
12. Wherefore it shall come to pass that when the Lord hath performed his whole work upon Mount Zion and upon Jerusalem, I will punish the fruit of the stout heart of the king of Assyria, and the glory of his high looks.
13. For he saith: By the strength of my hand and by my wisdom I have done these things; for I am prudent; and I have moved the borders of the people, and have robbed their treasures, and I have put down the inhabitants like a valiant man;
14. And my hand hath found as a nest the riches of the people; and as one gathereth eggs that are left have I gathered all the earth; and there was none that moved the wing, or opened the mouth, or peeped.
15. Shall the ax boast itself against him that heweth therewith? Shall the saw magnify itself against him that shaketh it? As if the rod should shake itself against them that lift it up, or as if the staff should lift up itself as if it were no wood!
16. Therefore shall the Lord, the Lord of Hosts, send among his fat ones, leanness; and under his glory he shall kindle a burning like the burning of a fire.
17. And the light of Israel shall be for a fire, and his Holy One for a flame, and shall burn and shall devour his thorns and his briers in one day;
18. And shall consume the glory of his forest, and of his fruitful field, both soul and body; and they shall be as when a standard-bearer fainteth.
19. And the rest of the trees of his forest shall be few, that a child may write them.
20. And it shall come to pass in that day, that the remnant of Israel, and such as are escaped of the house of Jacob, shall no more again stay upon him that smote them, but shall stay upon the Lord, the Holy One of Israel, in truth.
21. The remnant shall return, yea, even the remnant of Jacob, unto the mighty God.
22. For though thy people Israel be as the sand of the sea, yet a remnant of them shall return; the consumption decreed shall overflow with righteousness.
23. For the Lord God of Hosts shall make a consumption, even determined in all the land.
24. Therefore, thus saith the Lord God of Hosts: O my people that dwellest in Zion, be not afraid of the Assyrian; he shall smite thee with a rod, and shall lift up his staff against thee, after the manner of Egypt.
25. For yet a very little while, and the indignation shall cease, and mine anger in their destruction.
26. And the Lord of Hosts shall stir up a scourge for him according to the slaughter of Midian at the rock of Oreb; and as his rod was upon the sea so shall he lift it up after the manner of Egypt.

2 Nephi 20:22

We are the fulfillment of this prophecy—the remnant of Jacob who trust in the Lord and are overflowing with righteousness.

27. And it shall come to pass in that day that his burden shall be taken away from off thy shoulder, and his yoke from off thy neck, and the yoke shall be destroyed because of the anointing.
28. He is come to Aiath, he is passed to Migron; at Michmash he hath laid up his carriages.
29. They are gone over the passage; they have taken up their lodging at Geba; Ramath is afraid; Gibeah of Saul is fled.
30. Lift up the voice, O daughter of Gallim; cause it to be heard unto Laish, O poor Anathoth.
31. Madmenah is removed; the inhabitants of Gebim gather themselves to flee.
32. As yet shall he remain at Nob that day; he shall shake his hand against the mount of the daughter of Zion, the hill of Jerusalem.
33. Behold, the Lord, the Lord of Hosts shall lop the bough with terror; and the high ones of stature shall be hewn down; and the haughty shall be humbled.
34. And he shall cut down the thickets of the forests with iron, and Lebanon shall fall by a mighty one.

CHAPTER 21

1. AND there shall come forth a rod out of the stem of Jesse, and a branch shall grow out of his roots.
2. And the Spirit of the Lord shall rest upon him, the spirit of wisdom and understanding, the spirit of counsel and might, the spirit of knowledge and of the fear of the Lord;
3. And shall make him of quick understanding in the fear of the Lord; and he shall not judge after the sight of his eyes, neither reprove after the hearing of his ears.
4. But with righteousness shall he judge the poor, and reprove with equity for the meek of the earth; and he shall smite the earth with the rod of his mouth, and with the breath of his lips shall he slay the wicked.
5. And righteousness shall be the girdle of his loins, and faithfulness the girdle of his reins.
6. The wolf also shall dwell with the lamb, and the leopard shall lie down with the kid, and the calf and the young lion and fatling together; and a little child shall lead them.
7. And the cow and the bear shall feed; their young ones shall lie down together; and the lion shall eat straw like the ox.
8. And the sucking child shall play on the hole of the asp, and the weaned child shall put his hand on the cockatrice's den.
9. They shall not hurt nor destroy in all my holy mountain, for the earth shall be full of the knowledge

2 Nephi 21

The eleventh chapter of Isaiah (which is quoted in 2 Nephi 21) is evidently one of the most important chapters in all scripture. Not only does Jacob quote it here from the brass plates of Laban, but on September 21, 1823, the resurrected angel Moroni quoted this chapter to Joseph Smith and said it was about to be fulfilled. Also, a section of the Doctrine and Covenants (section 113) is devoted primarily to an explanation of this chapter. (Ludlow)

2 Nephi 21:1–16

The house of Israel has been scattered among all nations. Some of the tribes are lost, and their activities are not known to us today. The Lord has inspired His holy prophets to declare that Israel would be gathered again. This gathering will be both spiritual and physical. The restoration of the gospel of Jesus Christ through his prophet, Joseph Smith, signaled the beginning of this great process. Nephi, desiring that all men might rejoice in this great gathering, recorded this prophecy from Isaiah, so that all men might rejoice in Christ. . . .

The gathering of Israel in the latter days is the gathering of the elect of God. The Savior declared: ". . . even so will I gather mine elect from the four quarters of the earth, even as many as will believe in me, and hearken unto my voice" (D&C 33:6).

This gathering of Israel separates the righteous from the wicked. The destruction of Babylon was a shadow or type of the destruction of the wicked that will take place at the Savior's Second Coming. (See 2 Ne. 23.) The wickedness of Babylon is used by the Lord to symbolize worldliness or the wickedness of the world. The righteous will be gathered, triumph over wickedness (the world). and bask in millennial peace. (See 2 Ne. 24.) As this great day of rejoicing approaches, even the Second Coming of our Lord and Savior, the Saints are commanded to "Go ye out from among the nations, even from Babylon, from the midst of wickedness, which is spiritual Babylon" (D&C 133:14). (O/C)

of the Lord, as the waters cover the sea.
10. And in that day there shall be a root of Jesse, which shall stand for an ensign of the people; to it shall the Gentiles seek; and his rest shall be glorious.
11. And it shall come to pass in that day that the Lord shall set his hand again the second time to recover the remnant of his people which shall be left, from Assyria, and from Egypt, and from Pathros, and from Cush, and from Elam, and from Shinar, and from Hamath, and from the islands of the sea.
12. And he shall set up an ensign for the nations, and shall assemble the outcasts of Israel, and gather together the dispersed of Judah from the four corners of the earth.
13. The envy of Ephraim also shall depart, and the adversaries of Judah shall be cut off; Ephraim shall not envy Judah, and Judah shall not vex Ephraim.
14. But they shall fly upon the shoulders of the Philistines towards the west; they shall spoil them of the east together; they shall lay their hand upon Edom and Moab; and the children of Ammon shall obey them.
15. And the Lord shall utterly destroy the tongue of the Egyptian sea; and with his mighty wind he shall shake his hand over the river, and shall smite it in the seven streams, and make men go over dry shod.
16. And there shall be a highway for the remnant of his people which shall be left, from Assyria, like as it was to Israel in the day that he came up out of the land of Egypt.

CHAPTER 22

1. AND in that day thou shalt say: O Lord, I will praise thee; though thou wast angry with me thine anger is turned away, and thou comfortedst me.
2. Behold, God is my salvation; I will trust, and not be afraid; for the Lord JEHOVAH is my strength and my song; he also has become my salvation.
3. Therefore, with joy shall ye draw water out of the wells of salvation.
4. And in that day shall ye say: Praise the Lord, call upon his name, declare his doings among the people, make mention that his name is exalted.
5. Sing unto the Lord; for he hath done excellent things; this is known in all the earth.
6. Cry out and shout, thou inhabitant of Zion; for great is the Holy One of Israel in the midst of thee.

CHAPTER 23

2 Nephi 21:10–12

A careful reading of these verses would seem to indicate they pertain to a time in the distant future from the days of Isaiah when the remnants of Israel are to be gathered together again. Concerning a possible interpretation of these verses, Elder LeGrand Richards has written:

"From this scripture we learn that the events described were to be in the future: 'The Lord shall set his hand again the second time to recover the remnant of his people.' There could not be a 'second time' unless there had been a first. The first time was when the Lord led Israel out of Egyptian bondage and captivity. When did the Lord set his hand the 'second time' to recover the remnant of his people? This we will now consider. From the above scripture we learn that three important events were to transpire: (1) He shall set up an ensign for the nations; (2) he shall assemble the outcasts of Israel; (3) he shall gather together the dispersed of Judah from the four corners of the earth.

"It is clear there are to be two gathering places—one for Israel and one for Judah. . . .

"When speaking of Israel, most people have the Jews in mind; and when referring to the gathering of Israel, they have in mind the return of the Jews to the land of Jerusalem. It should be remembered that the Jews, the descendants of Judah, represent but one of the twelve branches, or tribes, of the house of Israel—the family of Jacob.

"The twelve tribes of Israel were divided under two great heads—Judah, comprising the smaller group, and Israel, the larger group." (Ludlow)

1. THE burden of Babylon, which Isaiah the son of Amoz did see.
2. Lift ye up a banner upon the high mountain, exalt the voice unto them, shake the hand, that they may go into the gates of the nobles.
3. I have commanded my sanctified ones, I have also called my mighty ones, for mine anger is not upon them that rejoice in my highness.
4. The noise of the multitude in the mountains like as of a great people, a tumultuous noise of the kingdoms of nations gathered together, the Lord of Hosts mustereth the hosts of the battle.
5. They come from a far country, from the end of heaven, yea, the Lord, and the weapons of his indignation, to destroy the whole land.
6. Howl ye, for the day of the Lord is at hand; it shall come as a destruction from the Almighty.
7. Therefore shall all hands be faint, every man's heart shall melt;
8. And they shall be afraid; pangs and sorrows shall take hold of them; they shall be amazed one at another; their faces shall be as flames.
9. Behold, the day of the Lord cometh, cruel both with wrath and fierce anger, to lay the land desolate; and he shall destroy the sinners thereof out of it.
10. For the stars of heaven and the constellations thereof shall not give their light; the sun shall be darkened in his going forth, and the moon shall not cause her light to shine.
11. And I will punish the world for evil, and the wicked for their iniquity; I will cause the arrogancy of the proud to cease, and will lay down the haughtiness of the terrible.
12. I will make a man more precious than fine gold; even a man than the golden wedge of Ophir.
13. Therefore, I will shake the heavens, and the earth shall remove out of her place, in the wrath of the Lord of Hosts, and in the day of his fierce anger.
14. And it shall be as the chased roe, and as a sheep that no man taketh up; and they shall every man turn to his own people, and flee every one into his own land.
15. Every one that is proud shall be thrust through; yea, and every one that is joined to the wicked shall fall by the sword.
16. Their children also shall be dashed to pieces before their eyes; their houses shall be spoiled and their wives ravished.
17. Behold, I will stir up the Medes against them, which shall not regard silver and gold, nor shall they delight in it.
18. Their bows shall also dash the young men to pieces; and they shall have no pity on the fruit of the womb; their eyes shall not spare children.
19. And Babylon, the glory of kingdoms, the beauty of the Chaldees' excellency, shall be as when God overthrew Sodom and Gomorrah.

2 Nephi 23:1

The "burden of Babylon" referred to in this verse is the prophecy of doom against Babylon. "Babylon" has both a literal and a figurative meaning. It was once a great city (600 B.C.) that fell, went through a long decline, was deserted, and was never again inhabited. Figuratively, it is the name of Satan's kingdom—the world or the church of the devil—which will come to utter destruction.

2 Nephi 23:6–13

These verses describe the destruction that will take place in the day of the Lord, or the period just preceding the Second Coming.

2 Nephi 23:14–22

The history of Babylon is both sad and interesting. It was easily conquered in 538 B.C. by the Medes, who came from Persia. In 518 B.C.., the walls were destroyed, and the city never again enjoyed its position as capital of a Mesopotamian power. Once Alexander the Great conquered the Persians a couple of centuries later, Babylon decline rapidly in cultural and commercial importance until, by the time the Savior was born, only a handful of mathematicians and astronomers continued to live in the city. Eventually, this small number of scientists wandered off to settle in more prosperous regions, and Babylon became completely deserted—nothing more than a mound covered by brush, used for grazing by nomadic flocks.

20. It shall never be inhabited, neither shall it be dwelt in from generation to generation: neither shall the Arabian pitch tent there; neither shall the shepherds make their fold there.
21. But wild beasts of the desert shall lie there; and their houses shall be full of doleful creatures; and owls shall dwell there, and satyrs shall dance there.
22. And the wild beasts of the islands shall cry in their desolate houses, and dragons in their pleasant palaces; and her time is near to come, and her day shall not be prolonged. For I will destroy her speedily; yea, for I will be merciful unto my people, but the wicked shall perish.

CHAPTER 24

1. FOR the Lord will have mercy on Jacob, and will yet choose Israel, and set them in their own land; and the strangers shall be joined with them, and they shall cleave to the house of Jacob.
2. And the people shall take them and bring them to their place; yea, from far unto the ends of the earth; and they shall return to their lands of promise. And the house of Israel shall possess them, and the land of the Lord shall be for servants and handmaids; and they shall take them captives unto whom they were captives; and they shall rule over their oppressors.
3. And it shall come to pass in that day that the Lord shall give thee rest, from thy sorrow, and from thy fear, and from the hard bondage wherein thou wast made to serve.
4. And it shall come to pass in that day, that thou shalt take up this proverb against the king of Babylon, and say: How hath the oppressor ceased, the golden city ceased!
5. The Lord hath broken the staff of the wicked, the scepters of the rulers.
6. He who smote the people in wrath with a continual stroke, he that ruled the nations in anger, is persecuted, and none hindereth.
7. The whole earth is at rest, and is quiet; they break forth into singing.
8. Yea, the fir-trees rejoice at thee, and also the cedars of Lebanon, saying: Since thou art laid down no feller is come up against us.
9. Hell from beneath is moved for thee to meet thee at thy coming; it stirreth up the dead for thee, even all the chief ones of the earth; it hath raised up from their thrones all the kings of the nations.
10. All they shall speak and say unto thee: Art thou also become weak as we? Art thou become like unto us?
11. Thy pomp is brought down to the grave; the noise of thy viols is not heard; the worm is spread under thee, and the worms cover thee.
12. How art thou fallen from heaven, O Lucifer, son of the morning! Art thou cut down to the ground, which did weaken the nations!
13. For thou hast said in thy heart: I will ascend into heaven, I will

2 Nephi 24:8

The word *feller* as it is used in Isaiah 14:8 (and in 2 Nephi 24:8) refers to a person who fells or cuts down trees. Thus, literally, a feller is "one who fells" or "one who cuts off.." (Ludlow)

2 Nephi 24:12–13

The term *Lucifer* is apparently the title or name of the personage in the pre-earthly existence who is now referred to as Satan or the devil. The fact that Isaiah refers to Lucifer and his role in the pre-earthly existence would seem to indicate that the Old Testament prophets were acquainted with the doctrine of a pre-earthly existence. It may be that Isaiah and others of the ancient prophets had access to the writings of Moses that are not in our present Old Testament but which were revealed anew to the Prophet Joseph Smith in December 1830. These writings of Moses include the following statement concerning Lucifer and his role in the pre-earthly councils:

> Wherefore, because that Satan rebelled against me, and sought to destroy the agency of man, which I, the Lord God, had given him, and also, that I should give unto him mine own power; by the power of mine Only Begotten, I caused that he should be cast down;
>
> And he became Satan, yea, even the devil, the father of all lies, to deceive and to blind men, and to lead them captive at his will, even as many as would not hearken unto my voice (Moses 4:3–4). (Ludlow)

exalt my throne above the stars of God; I will sit also upon the mount of the congregation, in the sides of the north;

14. I will ascend above the heights of the clouds; I will be like the Most High.

15. Yet thou shalt be brought down to hell, to the sides of the pit.

16. They that see thee shall narrowly look upon thee, and shall consider thee, and shall say: Is this the man that made the earth to tremble, that did shake kingdoms?

17. And made the world as a wilderness, and destroyed the cities thereof, and opened not the house of his prisoners?

18. All the kings of the nations, yea, all of them, lie in glory, every one of them in his own house.

19. But thou art cast out of thy grave like an abominable branch, and the remnant of those that are slain, thrust through with a sword, that go down to the stones of the pit; as a carcass trodden under feet.

20. Thou shalt not be joined with them in burial, because thou hast destroyed thy land and slain thy people; the seed of evil-doers shall never be renowned.

21. Prepare slaughter for his children for the iniquities of their fathers, that they do not rise, nor possess the land, nor fill the face of the world with cities.

22. For I will rise up against them, saith the Lord of Hosts, and cut off from Babylon the name, and remnant, and son, and nephew, saith the Lord.

23. I will also make it a possession for the bittern, and pools of water; and I will sweep it with the besom of destruction, saith the Lord of Hosts.

24. The Lord of Hosts hath sworn, saying: Surely as I have thought, so shall it come to pass; and as I have purposed, so shall it stand—

25. That I will bring the Assyrian in my land, and upon my mountains tread him under foot; then shall his yoke depart from off them, and his burden depart from off their shoulders.

26. This is the purpose that is purposed upon the whole earth; and this is the hand that is stretched out upon all nations.

27. For the Lord of Hosts hath purposed, and who shall disannul? And his hand is stretched out, and who shall turn it back?

28. In the year that king Ahaz died was this burden.

29. Rejoice not thou, whole Palestina, because the rod of him that smote thee is broken; for out of the serpent's root shall come forth a cockatrice, and his fruit shall be a fiery flying serpent.

30. And the first-born of the poor shall feed, and the needy shall lie down in safety; and I will kill thy root with famine, and he shall slay thy remnant.

31. Howl, O gate; cry, O city; thou, whole Palestina, art dissolved; for there shall come from the north a smoke, and none shall be alone in his appointed times.

32. What shall then answer the messengers of the nations? That the Lord hath founded Zion, and the poor of his people shall trust in it.

CHAPTER 25

2 Nephi 24:12–17

This verse is the only place in the entire Book of Mormon where the name "Lucifer" is used. (It is also mentioned only once in the Bible, in Isa.14:12.) From the Doctrine and Covenants, we learn that the name Lucifer—the name by which Satan was known in the pre-existence (see D&C 76:26)—means "light-bearer." We also learn that he at one time had "authority in the presence of God" (D&C 76:25), but lost that authority because of open rebellion. After that, he was called Perdition (see D&C 76:26), which means "destruction." The Sons of Perdition are those over whom Satan has complete power as a result of their most heinous sin, that of denying the Holy Ghost.

POINT OF INTEREST

Judah (Southern Kingdom)

609 B.C. — *Jehoahaz*
He disregarded the reforms of his father, Josiah. When Necho II marched on Jerusalem, he captured Jehoahaz and appointed Eliakim as king (who was two years older than his brother Jehoahaz), who took the throne name Jehoiakim. Jehoahaz was the first king of Judah to die in exile.

609–598 B.C. — *Jehoiakim*
After Egypt fell to the Chaldeans, Nebuchadnezzar II invaded and conquered Judah. Jehoiakim was allowed to rule, but as a vassal king. He repeated the idolatry and corruption of Manasseh's reign, and when he refused tribute and revolted against Babylon, Nebuchadnezzar sent bands of Chaldeans, Arameans, Moabites, and Ammonites to pillage the country. Jehoiakim was murdered and thrown over the wall of Jerusalem as proof to the besieging army of his death.

598 B.C. — *Jehoiachin*
Became king at age eighteen and ruled for three months, when the Babylonians removed him.

598–587 B.C. — *Zedekiah*
Despite Jeremiah's counsel, Zedekiah "did evil in the sight of the Lord" (2 Kgs. 24:19). When he tried to stand up to Babylon, Nebuchadnezzar sacked the city and temple to ruins, put Zedekiah's sons to death in front of him (minus Mulek), and then put out his eyes and carried him captive to Babylon.

1. NOW I, Nephi, do speak somewhat concerning the words which
I have written, which have been spoken by the mouth of Isaiah.
For behold, Isaiah spake many things which were hard for many of
my people to understand; for they know not concerning the manner of prophesying among the Jews.
2. For I, Nephi, have not taught them many things concerning the
manner of the Jews; for their works were works of darkness, and
their doings were doings of abominations.
3. Wherefore, I write unto my people, unto all those that shall
receive hereafter these things which I write, that they may know
the judgments of God, that they come upon all nations, according
to the word which he hath spoken.
4. Wherefore, hearken, O my people, which are of the house of
Israel, and give ear unto my words; for because the words of Isaiah
are not plain unto you, nevertheless they are plain unto all those
that are filled with the spirit of prophecy. But I give unto you a
prophecy, according to the spirit which is in me; wherefore I shall
prophesy according to the plainness which hath been with me
from the time that I came out from Jerusalem with my father; for
behold, my soul delighteth in plainness unto my people, that
they may learn.
5. Yea, and my soul delighteth in the words of Isaiah, for I came out
from Jerusalem, and mine eyes hath beheld the things of the Jews,
and I know that the Jews do understand the things of the prophets,
and there is none other people that understand the things which
were spoken unto the Jews like unto them, save it be that they are
taught after the manner of the things of the Jews.
6. But behold, I, Nephi, have not taught my children after the
manner of the Jews; but behold, I, of myself, have dwelt at
Jerusalem, wherefore I know concerning the regions round about;
and I have made mention unto my children concerning the judgments of God, which hath come to pass among the Jews, unto my
children, according to all that which Isaiah hath spoken, and I do
not write them.
7. But behold, I proceed with mine own prophecy, according to my
plainness; in the which I know that no man can err; nevertheless, in
the days that the prophecies of Isaiah shall be fulfilled men shall
know of a surety, at the times when they shall come to pass.
8. Wherefore, they are of worth unto the children of men, and he
that supposeth that they are not, unto them will I speak particularly, and confine the words unto mine own people; for I know that
they shall be of great worth unto them in the last days; for in that
day shall they understand them; wherefore, for their good have I
written them.
9. And as one generation hath been destroyed among the Jews
because of iniquity, even so have they been destroyed from generation to

2 Nephi 24:20

In telling us that "the seed of evil-doers shall never be renowned," Isaiah is prophesying that the evil nations of the world will fall and be destroyed, just as Satan will.

2 Nephi 25:4

According to Elder Bruce R. McConkie, there is no way to understand scripture unless we have the same spirit of prophecy that rested on the one who originally uttered that truth. To understand and properly interpret scripture, we must be enlightened by the Holy Ghost. We need a testimony of Jesus, which is the spirit of prophecy.

2 Nephi 25:8

Isaiah saw our day and wrote prophecies about it. In particular, he saw the work of the Prophet Joseph Smith, the Restoration of the gospel, and the coming forth of the Book of Mormon—all events that would result in marvelous blessings for all men.

generation according to their iniquities; and never hath any of
them been destroyed save it were foretold them by the prophets of
the Lord.
10. Wherefore, it hath been told them concerning the destruction
which should come upon them, immediately after my father left
Jerusalem; nevertheless, they hardened their hearts; and according
to my prophecy they have been destroyed, save it be those which
are carried away captive into Babylon.
11. And now this I speak because of the spirit which is in me. And
notwithstanding they have been carried away they shall return
again, and possess the land of Jerusalem; wherefore, they shall be
restored again to the land of their inheritance.
12. But, behold, they shall have wars, and rumors of wars; and
when the day cometh that the Only Begotten of the Father, yea,
even the Father of heaven and of earth, shall manifest himself unto
them in the flesh, behold, they will reject him, because of their
iniquities, and the hardness of their hearts, and the stiffness of
their necks.
13. Behold, they will crucify him; and after he is laid in a sepulchre
for the space of three days he shall rise from the dead, with healing
in his wings; and all those who shall believe on his name shall be
saved in the kingdom of God. Wherefore, my soul delighteth to
prophesy concerning him, for I have seen his day, and my heart
doth magnify his holy name.
14. And behold it shall come to pass that after the Messiah hath
risen from the dead, and hath manifested himself unto his people,
unto as many as will believe on his name, behold, Jerusalem shall
be destroyed again; for wo unto them that fight against God and
the people of his church.
15. Wherefore, the Jews shall be scattered among all nations; yea,
and also Babylon shall be destroyed; wherefore, the Jews shall be
scattered by other nations.
16. And after they have been scattered, and the Lord God hath
scourged them by other nations for the space of many generations,
yea, even down from generation to generation until they shall be
persuaded to believe in Christ, the Son of God, and the atonement, which is infinite for all mankind—and when that day shall
come that they shall believe in Christ, and worship the Father in
his name, with pure hearts and clean hands, and look not forward
any more for another Messiah, then, at that time, the day will
come that it must needs be expedient that they should believe
these things.
17. And the Lord will set his hand

2 Nephi 25:10–20

These words of Nephi reveal marvelous information. We learn that the Old Testament prophets knew the exact year the Savior would be born, and therefore could count back from that event to know the year in which they were living. Nephi learned the year of the birth of Christ from the writings of the prophets on the brass plates. He also stated that the writings contained the name of the Son of God. (See 2 Ne. 25:19.) If Nephi could discover that information from the scriptures, then the Jewish leaders who had access to those prophetic writings knew the same thing.

Because of Nephi's writings, we know that the Jewish leaders knew Jesus was the Messiah, simply because He had the correct name, He was born during the correct year, and He fulfilled all other prophecies that would identify Him as the Messiah. On one occasion in Jerusalem, Jesus reasoned with the Jews when they accused him of blasphemy because He had claimed to be the Son of God. Jesus challenged them to "Search the scriptures; for in them ye think ye have eternal life: and *they are they which testify of me*" (John 5:39, *emphasis added*). Jesus knew they knew who He was, because the Old Testament scriptural prophecies plainly identified him. (O/C)

2 Nephi 25:16–17

Before any physical gethering can take place, there must be a spiritual gathering. That gathering will occur as Israel accepts Jesus Christ as the Savior of all mankind.

again the second time to restore his people from their lost and fallen state. Wherefore, he will proceed to do a marvelous work and a wonder among the children of men.
18. Wherefore, he shall bring forth his words unto them, which words shall judge them at the last day, for they shall be given them for the purpose of convincing them of the true Messiah, who was rejected by them; and unto the convincing of them that they need not look forward any more for a Messiah to come, for there should not any come, save it should be a false Messiah which should deceive the people; for there is save one Messiah spoken of by the prophets, and that Messiah is he who should be rejected of the Jews.
19. For according to the words of the prophets, the Messiah cometh in six hundred years from the time that my father left Jerusalem; and according to the words of the prophets, and also the word of the angel of God, his name shall be Jesus Christ, the Son of God.
20. And now, my brethren, I have spoken plainly that ye cannot err. And as the Lord God liveth that brought Israel up out of the land of Egypt, and gave unto Moses power that he should heal the nations after they had been bitten by the poisonous serpents, if they would cast their eyes unto the serpent which he did raise up before them, and also gave him power that he should smite the rock and the water should come forth; yea, behold I say unto you, that as these things are true, and as the Lord God liveth, there is none other name given under heaven save it be this Jesus Christ, of which I have spoken, whereby man can be saved.
21. Wherefore, for this cause hath the Lord God promised unto me that these things which I write shall be kept and preserved, and handed down unto my seed, from generation to generation, that the promise may be fulfilled unto Joseph, that his seed should never perish as long as the earth should stand.
22. Wherefore, these things shall go from generation to generation as long as the earth shall stand; and they shall go according to the will and pleasure of God; and the nations who shall possess them shall be judged of them according to the words which are written.
23. For we labor diligently to write, to persuade our children, and also our brethren, to believe in Christ, and to be reconciled to God; for we

2 Nephi 25:20–30

The Book of Mormon prophets clearly understood that the law of Moses did not contain the fulness of the saving principles of the gospel of Jesus Christ. They realized the law of Moses was given to prepare the people for the greater truths which were to be revealed. In 2 Nephi 25:24, Nephi writes: "And, notwithstanding we believe in Christ, we keep the law of Moses, and look forward with steadfastness unto Christ, until the law shall be fulfilled." Unfortunately, some of the people subsequently misunderstood this prophecy of Nephi and assumed that the law of Moses was fulfilled when the Savior was born upon the earth. However, it was made clear to them that the law of Moses was not to be fulfilled until after the resurrection of the Savior. (See 3 Nephi 1:24–25.) (Ludlow)

2 Nephi 25:23

An important doctrine is clarified here that separates The Church of Jesus Christ of Latter-day Saints from other Christian faiths, which preach that we are saved by grace. Nephi here specifies that we are, indeed, saved by the grace of the Savior—as imperfect mortals, it is impossible for us to attain salvation or exaltation without His atoning sacrifice. He makes possible all things for us. But Nephi then adds the crucial and saving doctrine that the Savior's grace becomes efficacious for us only after we have done all that we can do in living a life of obedience, faith, trust, repentance, and good works. It is only after doing "all we can do" that we become beneficiaries of the Savior's amazing grace.

know that it is by grace that we are saved, after all we can do.
24. And, notwithstanding we believe in Christ, we keep the law of Moses, and look forward with steadfastness unto Christ, until the law shall be fulfilled.
25. For, for this end was the law given; wherefore the law hath become dead unto us, and we are made alive in Christ because of our faith; yet we keep the law because of the commandments.
26. And we talk of Christ, we rejoice in Christ, we preach of Christ, we prophesy of Christ, and we write according to our prophecies, that our children may know to what source they may look for a remission of their sins.
27. Wherefore, we speak concerning the law that our children may know the deadness of the law; and they, by knowing the deadness of the law, may look forward unto that life which is in Christ, and know for what end the law was given. And after the law is fulfilled in Christ, that they need not harden their hearts against him when the law ought to be done away.
28. And now behold, my people, ye are a stiffnecked people; wherefore, I have spoken plainly unto you, that ye cannot misunderstand. And the words which I have spoken shall stand as a testimony against you; for they are sufficient to teach any man the right way; for the right way is to believe in Christ and deny him not; for by denying him ye also deny the prophets and the law.
29. And now behold, I say unto you that the right way is to believe in Christ, and deny him not; and Christ is the Holy One of Israel; wherefore ye must bow down before him, and worship him with all your might, mind, and strength, and your whole soul; and if ye do this ye shall in nowise be cast out.
30. And, inasmuch as it shall be expedient, ye must keep the performances and ordinances of God until the law shall be fulfilled which was given unto Moses.

CHAPTER 26

1. AND after Christ shall have risen from the dead he shall show himself unto you, my children, and my beloved brethren; and the words which he shall speak unto you shall be the law which ye shall do.
2. For behold, I say unto you that I have beheld that many generations shall pass away, and there shall be great wars and contentions among my people.
3. And after the Messiah shall come there shall be signs given unto my people of his birth, and also of his death and resurrection; and great and terrible shall that day be unto the wicked, for they shall perish; and they perish because they cast

2 Nephi 25:23

Having through the grace of God escaped with his family from the predicted destruction of Jerusalem, Nephi knew firsthand the sureness of God's word with respect to the impending judgments that must in due course come upon the wicked should they reject the warnings of the prophets. . . . Thus Nephi issues his confirmation of God's design with respect to the geopolitical flow of history: no nation, no people, no generation can escape the judgments of God.

The scattering and gathering will proceed on the basis of God's purposes for mankind, according to their responsiveness to the word of truth as proclaimed by God's emissaries. Nephi had seen through prophetic vision the ultimate destiny of Israel's remnants throughout history, even down to the ushering in of the millennial reign. He yearned for the well-being of his people and their posterity. He agonized over their spiritual welfare. That is the context for his famous statement: "For we labor diligently to write, to persuade our children, and also our brethren, to believe in Christ, and to be reconciled to God; for we know that it is by grace that we are saved, after all we can do" (2 Ne. 25:23). And furthermore: "And we talk of Christ, we rejoice in Christ, we preach of Christ, we prophesy of Christ, and we write according to our prophecies, that our children may know to what source they may look for a remission of their sins" (2 Ne. 25:26).

All of these convictions were at work in Nephi's soul as he laid out his commentary on Isaiah and foresaw clearly the events of the latter days when these writings would be fulfilled—both unto the destruction of the wicked as well as the blessing of the faithful. President Joseph Fielding Smith said:

"As it was pointed out by Isaiah and others of the prophets many hundreds of years before his birth, Christ took upon himself the transgressions of all men and suffered for them, that they might escape, on conditions of their repentance, and acceptance of his gospel, and their faithfulness to the end (Isa. 53:1–12; 2 Ne. 9:17–27; 31:11–21). So we are saved by grace and that not of ourselves. It is the gift of God. (2 Ne. 10:24–25; 25:23; Moro. 10:32–33).

"If Jesus Christ had not died for us, there would have come to us no salvation, and we would have remained absolutely in our sins, without redemption, and would have become subject to Satan and his emissaries forever and ever (2 Ne. 9:6–9)." (P/A)

2 Nephi 25:23

In discussing works and grace, C. S. Lewis likened them to two edges of a pair of scissors: both are necessary to get the job done. In like manner, both grace and works are necessary to our salvation—one without the other can never accomplish the desired result.

out the prophets, and the saints, and stone them, and slay them; wherefore the cry of the blood of the saints shall ascend up to God from the ground against them.
4. Wherefore, all those who are proud, and that do wickedly, the day that cometh shall burn them up, saith the Lord of Hosts, for they shall be as stubble.
5. And they that kill the prophets, and the saints, the depths of the earth shall swallow them up, saith the Lord of Hosts; and mountains shall cover them, and whirlwinds shall carry them away, and buildings shall fall upon them and crush them to pieces and grind them to powder.
6. And they shall be visited with thunderings, and lightnings, and earthquakes, and all manner of destructions, for the fire of the anger of the Lord shall be kindled against them, and they shall be as stubble, and the day that cometh shall consume them, saith the Lord of Hosts.
7. O the pain, and the anguish of my soul for the loss of the slain of my people! For I, Nephi, have seen it, and it well nigh consumeth me before the presence of the Lord; but I must cry unto my God: Thy ways are just.
8. But behold, the righteous that hearken unto the words of the prophets, and destroy them not, but look forward unto Christ with steadfastness for the signs which are given, notwithstanding all persecution—behold, they are they which shall not perish.
9. But the Son of righteousness shall appear unto them; and he shall heal them, and they shall have peace with him, until three generations shall have passed away, and many of the fourth generation shall have passed away in righteousness.
10. And when these things have passed away a speedy destruction cometh unto my people; for, notwithstanding the pains of my soul, I have seen it; wherefore, I know that it shall come to pass; and they sell themselves for naught; for, for the reward of their pride and their foolishness they shall reap destruction; for because they yield unto the devil and choose works of darkness rather than light, therefore they must go down to hell.
11. For the Spirit of the Lord will not always strive with man. And when the Spirit ceaseth to strive with man then cometh speedy destruction, and this grieveth my soul.
12. And as I spake concerning the convincing of the Jews, that Jesus is the very Christ, it must needs be that the Gentiles be convinced also that Jesus is the Christ, the Eternal God;
13. And that he manifesteth himself unto all those who believe in

2 Nephi 26:5–6

Through his vision of the destruction of his people, Nephi sees and describes the punishments and calamities that will befall them. In this example, as in all others, the eventual victory of good over evil will be centered in Jesus Christ.

2 Nephi 26:10

Nephi refers here to the fifth generation of his people after the visit of Christ to the American continent; he knows their destruction will result from their own wickedness.

2 Nephi 26:12

"Jews" in this verse refers to Israel.

him, by the power of the Holy Ghost; yea, unto every nation, kindred, tongue, and people, working mighty miracles, signs, and
wonders, among the children of men according to their faith.
14. But behold, I prophesy unto you concerning the last days;
concerning the days when the Lord God shall bring these things
forth unto the children of men.
15. After my seed and the seed of my brethren shall have dwindled
in unbelief, and shall have been smitten by the Gentiles; yea, after
the Lord God shall have camped against them round about, and
shall have laid siege against them with a mount, and raised forts
against them; and after they shall have been brought down low in
the dust, even that they are not, yet the words of the righteous
shall be written, and the prayers of the faithful shall be heard, and
all those who have dwindled in unbelief shall not be forgotten.
16. For those who shall be destroyed shall speak unto them out of the
ground, and their speech shall be low out of the dust, and their voice
shall be as one that hath a familiar spirit; for the Lord God will give
unto him power, that he may whisper concerning them, even as it
were out of the ground; and their speech shall whisper out of the dust.
17. For thus saith the Lord God: They shall write the things which
shall be done among them, and they shall be written and sealed up in
a book, and those who have dwindled in unbelief shall not have them,
for they seek to destroy the things of God.
18. Wherefore, as those who have been destroyed have been
destroyed speedily; and the multitude of their terrible ones shall be
as chaff that passeth away—yea, thus saith the Lord God: It shall
be at an instant, suddenly—
19. And it shall come to pass, that those who have dwindled in
unbelief shall be smitten by the hand of the Gentiles.
20. And the Gentiles are lifted up in the pride of their eyes, and
have stumbled, because of the greatness of their stumbling block,
that they have built up many churches; nevertheless, they put
down the power and miracles of God, and preach up unto themselves their own wisdom and their own learning, that they may get
gain and grind upon the face of the poor.
21. And there are many churches built up which cause envyings,
and strifes, and malice.
22. And there are also secret combinations, even as in times of old,
according to the combinations of the devil, for he is the founder of

2 Nephi 26:14

Nephi has to look as far into the future as our day to see these prophecies fulfilled.

2 Nephi 26:16

Nephi is evidently quoting from a statement found in Isaiah 29:4 when he refers to a destroyed people whose record shall come "out of the ground, and their speech shall be low out of the dust, and their voice shall be as one that hath a familiar spirit." (2 Nephi 26:16.) Some biblical scholars have maintained that witchcraft is being referred to in that portion of Isaiah 29:4 which says that the voice shall be "as one that hath a familiar spirit." These scholars evidently arrived at this interpretation because of similar wording in other parts of the Bible. For example, in Leviticus we read: "Regard not them that have familiar spirits, neither seek after wizards, to be defiled by them" (Leviticus 19:31), and "A man also or woman that hath a familiar spirit, or that is a wizard, shall surely be put to death" (Leviticus 20:27). (For further biblical references indicating that the term "familiar spirits" might sometimes refer to witches, see 1 Samuel 28:7; 2 Kings 21:6; 1 Chronicles 10:13; Isaiah 8:19 and 19:3.)

However, a careful reading of this scripture, particularly when read together with Nephi's explanation, would indicate that the term it "hath a familiar spirit" means that this record (the Book of Mormon) would speak with a "familiar voice" to those who already have the Bible. In other words, Nephi is evidently saying here that the doctrinal teachings of the Book of Mormon would seem familiar to people who had already read and accepted the Bible. (Ludlow)

2 Nephi 26:17

The Book of Mormon will be the most important factor in bringing modern-day people to Jesus Christ.

2 Nephi 26:20

The "stumbling block" referred to in this verse is the lack of knowledge and spiritual understanding in the last days. The cause is an imperfect Bible, subject to omissions and inaccurate translation; the solution is the Book of Mormon. Those who were in apostasy in Joseph Smith's day stumbled because they did not recognize a prophet.

all these things; yea, the founder of murder, and works of darkness; yea, and he leadeth them by the neck with a flaxen cord, until he bindeth them with his strong cords forever.
23. For behold, my beloved brethren, I say unto you that the Lord God worketh not in darkness.
24. He doeth not anything save it be for thebenefit of the world; for he loveth the world, even that he layeth down his own life that he may draw all men unto him. Wherefore, he commandeth none that they shall not partake of his salvation.
25. Behold, doth he cry unto any, saying: Depart from me? Behold, I say unto you, Nay; but he saith: Come unto me all ye ends of the earth, buy milk and honey, without money and without price.
26. Behold, hath he commanded any that they should depart out of the synagogues, or out of the houses of worship? Behold, I say unto you, Nay.
27. Hath he commanded any that they should not partake of his salvation? Behold I say unto you, Nay; but he hath given it free for all men; and he hath commanded his people that they should persuade all men to repentance.
28. Behold, hath the Lord commanded any that they should not partake of his goodness? Behold I say unto you, Nay; but all men are privileged the one like unto the other, and none are forbidden.
29. He commandeth that there shall be no priestcrafts; for, behold priestcrafts are that men preach and set themselves up for a light unto the world, that they may get gain and praise of the world; but they seek not the welfare of Zion.
30. Behold, the Lord hath forbidden this thing; wherefore, the Lord God hath given a commandment that all men should have charity, which charity is love. And except they should have charity they were nothing. Wherefore, if they should have charity they would not suffer the laborer in Zion to perish.
31. But the laborer in Zion shall labor for Zion; for if they labor for money they shall perish.
32. And again, the Lord God hath commanded that men should not murder; that they should not lie; that they should not steal; that they should not take the name of the Lord their God in vain; that they should not envy; that they should not have malice; that they should not contend one with another; that they should not commit whoredoms; and that they should do none of these things; for whoso doeth them shall perish.
33. For none of these iniquities come of the Lord; for he doeth that which is good among the children of men; and he doeth nothing save it be plain unto the children of men; and he inviteth them all to come unto him and partake of his goodness; and he denieth none that come

2 Nephi 26:29

The word *priestcraft* is used in the Book of Mormon to refer to the teachings of those people who would make a craft (or business) out of being a priest (or religious leader) to the people. Nephi indicates one danger of priestcraft is that such professional religious leaders would be more concerned with teaching those things which were popular and acceptable unto the people than they would in preaching the word of God. Thus they seek to "get gain and praise of the world; but they seek not the welfare of Zion." (2 Nephi 26:29.)

Priestcraft should not be confused with priesthood. There is a great deal of difference between the two, as is indicated in the following statement by George Q. Cannon: "There is a difference between priestcraft and Priesthood. Priestcraft builds up itself, it is not authorized of God. Priestcraft oppresses the people; but the Priesthood of God emancipates men and women and makes them free." (*Journal of Discourses*, 13:55.)

In defining priestcraft and explaining why it must eventually be destroyed, Elder Bruce R. McConkie said, ". . . false priests, professing ministers, those claiming but not possessing priesthood, are engaged, to a greater or lesser degree, in the iniquitous practice of priestcraft. Priesthood and priestcraft are two opposites; one is of God, the other of the devil.

"Apostasy is born of priestcrafts (2 Ne. 10:5; 3 Ne. 16:10; D. & C. 33:4), for those who engage in them follow vain things, teach false doctrines, love riches, and aspire to personal honors. (Alma 1:12, 16.) Men are commanded to repent of their priestcrafts (3 Ne. 30:2), and eventually, in the millennial day, these great evils will be done away (3 Ne. 21:19)." (Ludlow)

unto him, black and white, bond and free, male and female; and he remembereth the heathen; and all are alike unto God, both Jew and Gentile.

CHAPTER 27

1. BUT, behold, in the last days, or in the days of the Gentiles—yea, behold all the nations of the Gentiles and also the Jews, both those who shall come upon this land and those who shall be upon other lands, yea, even upon all the lands of the earth, behold, they will be drunken with iniquity and all manner of abominations—
2. And when that day shall come they shall be visited of the Lord of Hosts, with thunder and with earthquake, and with a great noise, and with storm, and with tempest, and with the flame of devouring fire.
3. And all the nations that fight against Zion, and that distress her, shall be as a dream of a night vision; yea, it shall be unto them, even as unto a hungry man which dreameth, and behold he eateth but he awaketh and his soul is empty; or like unto a thirsty man which dreameth, and behold he drinketh but he awaketh and behold he is faint, and his soul hath appetite; yea, even so shall the multitude of all the nations be that fight against Mount Zion.
4. For behold, all ye that doeth iniquity, stay yourselves and wonder, for ye shall cry out, and cry; yea, ye shall be drunken but not with wine, ye shall stagger but not with strong drink.
5. For behold, the Lord hath poured out upon you the spirit of deep sleep. For behold, ye have closed your eyes, and ye have rejected the prophets; and your rulers, and the seers hath he covered because of your iniquity.
6. And it shall come to pass that the Lord God shall bring forth unto you the words of a book, and they shall be the words of them which have slumbered.
7. And behold the book shall be sealed; and in the book shall be a revelation from God, from the beginning of the world to the ending thereof.
8. Wherefore, because of the things which are sealed up, the things which are sealed shall not be delivered in the day of the wickedness and abominations of the people. Wherefore the book shall be kept from them.
9. But the book shall be delivered unto a man, and he shall deliver the words of the book, which are the words of those who have slumbered in the dust, and he shall deliver these words unto another;
10. But the words which are sealed he shall not deliver, neither shall he deliver the book. For the book shall

2 Nephi 27:6–7, 11

The sealed portion of the Book of Mormon contains, as stated here, a history of the world from beginning to end. Elder Bruce R. McConkie taught that it will be translated during the Millennium and will include, among other things, an account of life in the preexistence, the fulness of temple ordinances, and the ministry of translated beings.

2 Nephi 27:9, 15–18

Nephi's prophecy concerning the words of the book which the translator shall "deliver . . . to another, that he may show them unto the learned" (2 Nephi 27:15) apparently refers (1) to Joseph Smith's giving a copy of some of the characters to Martin Harris and (2) to the subsequent visit of Martin Harris with Professor Charles Anthon. Sometime between December 1827 and February 1828, Joseph Smith copied a number of the characters from the plates in his possession and translated some of them by means of the Urim and Thummim. In February 1828, Martin Harris visited the Prophet in Pennsylvania, obtained a transcript of the characters, and took it to Professor Charles Anthon of New York City. For an account of what occurred, we have the following statement made by Martin Harris to Joseph Smith:

"I went to the city of New York, and presented the characters which had been translated, with the translation thereof, to Professor Charles Anthon, a gentlemen celebrated for his literary attainments. Professor Anthon stated that the translation was correct, more so than any he had before seen translated from the Egyptian. I then showed him those which were not yet translated, and he said that they were Egyptian, Chaldaic, Assyriac, and Arabic; and he said they were true characters. He gave me a certificate, certifying to the people of Palmyra that they were true characters, and that the translation of such of them as had been translated was also correct. I took the certificate and put it into my pocket, and was just leaving the house, when Mr. Anthon called me back, and asked me how the young man found out that there were gold plates in the place where he found them. I answered that an angel of God had revealed it unto him.

"He then said to me, 'Let me see that certificate.' I accordingly took it out of my pocket and gave it to him, when he took it and tore it to pieces, saying that there was no such thing now as ministering of angels, and that if I would bring the plates to him he would translate them. I informed him that part of the plates were sealed, and that I was forbidden to bring them. He replied, 'I cannot read a sealed book.' I left him and went to Dr. Mitchell, who sanctioned what Professor Anthon had said respecting both the characters and the translation." (Ludlow)

be sealed by the power of God, and the revelation which was sealed shall be kept in the book until the own due time of the Lord, that they may come forth; for behold, they reveal all things from the foundation of the world unto the end thereof.

11. And the day cometh that the words of the book which were sealed shall be read upon the house tops; and they shall be read by the power of Christ; and all things shall be revealed unto the children of men which ever have been among the children of men, and which ever will be even unto the end of the earth.

12. Wherefore, at that day when the book shall be delivered unto the man of whom I have spoken, the book shall be hid from the eyes of the world, that the eyes of none shall behold it save it be that three witnesses shall behold it, by the power of God, besides him to whom the book shall be delivered; and they shall testify to the truth of the book and the things therein.

13. And there is none other which shall view it, save it be a few according to the will of God, to bear testimony of his word unto the children of men; for the Lord God hath said that the words of the faithful should speak as if it were fromthe dead.

14. Wherefore, the Lord God will proceed to bring forth the words of the book; and in the mouth of as many witnesses as seemeth him good will he establish his word; and wo be unto him that rejecteth the word of God!

15. But behold, it shall come to pass that the Lord God shall say unto him to whom he shall deliver the book: Take these words which are not sealed and deliver them to another, that he may show them unto the learned, saying: Read this, I pray thee. And the learned shall say: Bring hither the book, and I will read them.

16. And now, because of the glory of the world and to get gain will they say this, and not for the glory of God.

17. And the man shall say: I cannot bring the book, for it is sealed.

18. Then shall the learned say: I cannot read it.

19. Wherefore it shall come to pass, that the Lord God will deliver again the book and the words thereof to him that is not learned; and the man that is not learned shall say: I am not learned.

20. Then shall the Lord God say unto him: The learned shall not read them, for they have rejected them, and I am able to do mine own work; wherefore thou shalt read the words which I shall give unto thee.

21. Touch not the things which are sealed, for I will bring them forth in mine own due time; for I will show unto the children of men that I am able to do mine own work.

22. Wherefore, when thou hast read the words which I have commanded thee, and obtained the witnesses which I have promised unto thee, then shalt thou seal up the book again, and hide it up unto me, that I may preserve the words which thou hast not read, until I shall see fit in mine own wisdom to reveal all things unto the children of men.

23. For behold, I am God; and I am a God of miracles; and I will show

2 Nephi 27:12–13

The Lord allowed Joseph Smith to have two sets of special witnesses to the Book of Mormon: (1) the three witnesses—Oliver Cowdery, David Whitmer, and Martin Harris, and (2) the eight witnesses—Christian Whitmer, Jacob Whitmer, Peter Whitmer, Jr., John Whitmer, Hiram Page, Joseph Smith, Sen., Hyrum Smith, Samuel H. Smith.

In 2 Nephi 27:12 the three persons who should behold the record "by the power of God" evidently are the three special witnesses. In their testimony they declared they had seen an angel, had heard the voice of the Lord, and had been shown the plates "by the power of God, and not of man."

In 2 Nephi 27:13, the few other witnesses who should view the record "according to the will of God, to bear testimony of his word unto the children of men" evidently include the eight special witnesses. (Ludlow)

2 Nephi 27:20

Because the plural pronoun *they* is used to describe the learned who will reject the Book of Mormon, it must refer to more than just Professor Charles Anthon, who originally certified that the characters from which the Book of Mormon was translated were authentic but who then refused to accept the book. This verse refers to all the learned of the world who refuse to accept the book or the miraculous way in which it came forth.

POINT OF INTEREST

Peccaries, known in Spanish as javelina *or* pecari, *are even-toed ungulates, as are swine and hippopotami. They are native to the New World. The collared peccary, pictured here, is found in an areas that extends from the southwestern United States into South America. They cannot be domesticated.*

unto the world that I am the same yesterday, today, and forever; and I work not among the children of men save it be according to their faith.
24. And again it shall come to pass that the Lord shall say unto him that shall read the words that shall be delivered him:
25. Forasmuch as this people draw near unto me with their mouth, and with their lips do honor me, but have removed their hearts far from me, and their fear towards me is taught by the precepts of men—
26. Therefore, I will proceed to do a marvelous work among this people, yea, a marvelous work and a wonder, for the wisdom of their wise and learned shall perish, and the understanding of their prudent shall be hid.
27. And wo unto them that seek deep to hide their counsel from the Lord! And their works are in the dark; and they say: Who seeth us, and who knoweth us? And they also say: Surely, your turning of things upside down shall be esteemed as the potter's clay. But behold, I will show unto them, saith the Lord of Hosts, that I know all their works. For shall the work say of him that made it, he made me not? Or shall the thing framed say of him that framed it, he had no understanding?
28. But behold, saith the Lord of Hosts: I will show unto the children of men that it is yet a very little while and Lebanon shall be turned into a fruitful field; and the fruitful field shall be esteemed as a forest.
29. And in that day shall the deaf hear the words of the book, and the eyes of the blind shall see out of obscurity and out of darkness.
30. And the meek also shall increase, and their joy shall be in the Lord, and the poor among men shall rejoice in the Holy One of Israel.
31. For assuredly as the Lord liveth they shall see that the terrible one is brought to naught, and the scorner is consumed, and all that watch for iniquity are cut off;
32. And they that make a man an offender for a word, and lay a snare for him that reproveth in the gate, and turn aside the just for a thing of naught.
33. Therefore, thus saith the Lord, who redeemed Abraham, concerning the house of Jacob: Jacob shall not now be ashamed, neither shall his face now wax pale.
34. But when he seeth his children, the work of my hands, in the midst of him, they shall sanctify my name, and sanctify the Holy One of Jacob, and shall fear the God of Israel.
35. They also that erred in spirit shall come to understanding, and they that murmured shall learn doctrine.

CHAPTER 28

1. AND now, behold, my brethren, I have spoken unto you, according as

2 Nephi 27:26

"A marvelous work and a wonder" refers to the restitution of all things previously lost to the children of men.

2 Nephi 27:29

Nephi knew through prophetic insight that his record would be brought forth in the fulness of times as a light shining out of the darkness. He also discerned that the record would be received by many with disbelief because of the blindness of sectarian philosophy, whereby the canon of scripture was believed closed. . . .

Nephi had learned from his father's visions about the course of Israel's history and future destiny. Nephi himself, after much prayer and fasting, was privileged to partake of the heavenly vision firsthand (see 1 Ne. 12–14). . . .We are the beneficiaries of Nephi's inspired commentary (see 1 Ne. 15; 2 Ne. 26–27) and his own related prophetic utterances and counsel (2 Ne. 28–33). Nephi illuminates with clarity the presentation in Isaiah 29 concerning the mysterious sealed book, a reference that has seemed fairly cryptic to the world. Nephi makes clear that this sealed book is none other than the record that he himself had initiated at God's command. With prophetic eye he looks forward to a time when this very record, extended and completed by a series of inspired prophets and compilers over the ages, would be brought forth "by the power of God" (Morm. 8:16) to a latter-day world hungry for the fulness of the everlasting gospel of Jesus Christ.

In speaking about the importance of the Book of Mormon, President Ezra Taft Benson remarked, "The Saints were given the Book of Mormon to read before they were given the revelations outlining such great doctrines as the three degrees of glory, celestial marriage, or work for the dead. It came before priesthood quorums and Church organization. Doesn't this tell us something about how the Lord views this sacred work?" (P/A)

2 Nephi 28–30

2 Nephi 28–30 is directly for us in our day; these verses warn us of and tell us how to avoid the dangers of our day, such as false churches, widespread apostasy, deception, and those who teach false doctrine, excuse sin and wickedness, and persecute the meek.

the Spirit hath constrained me; wherefore, I know that they must surely come to pass.

2. And the things which shall be written out of the book shall be of great worth unto the children of men, and especially unto our seed, which is a remnant of the house of Israel.

3. For it shall come to pass in that day that the churches which are built up, and not unto the Lord, when the one shall say unto the other: Behold, I, I am the Lord's; and the others shall say: I, I am the Lord's; and thus shall every one say that hath built up churches, and not unto the Lord—

4. And they shall contend one with another; and their priests shall contend one with another, and they shall teach with their learning, and deny the Holy Ghost, which giveth utterance.

5. And they deny the power of God, the Holy One of Israel; and they say unto the people: Hearken unto us, and hear ye our precept; for behold there is no God today, for the Lord and the Redeemer hath done his work, and he hath given his power unto men;

6. Behold, hearken ye unto my precept; if they shall say there is a miracle wrought by the hand of the Lord, believe it not; for this day he is not a God of miracles; he hath done his work.

7. Yea, and there shall be many which shall say: Eat, drink, and be merry, for tomorrow we die; and it shall be well with us.

8. And there shall also be many which shall say: Eat, drink, and be merry; nevertheless, fear God—he will justify in committing a little sin; yea, lie a little, take the advantage of one because of his words, dig a pit for thy neighbor; there is no harm in this; and do all these things, for tomorrow we die; and if it so be that we are guilty, God will beat us with a few stripes, and at last we shall be saved in the kingdom of God.

9. Yea, and there shall be many which shall teach after this manner, false and vain and foolish doctrines, and shall be puffed up in their hearts, and shall seek deep to hide their counsels from the Lord; and their works shall be in the dark.

10. And the blood of the saints shall cry from the ground against them.

11. Yea, they have all gone out of the way; they have become corrupted.

12. Because of pride, and because of false teachers, and false doctrine, their churches have become corrupted, and their churches are lifted up; because of pride they are puffed up.

13. They rob the poor because of their fine sanctuaries; they rob the poor because of their fine clothing;

2 Nephi 28:7–8

These verses expose one of the greatest lies of the adversary: that it is better to sin and repent than to avoid sin altogether. While the ability to repent is a priceless gift from the Savior, we cannot ignore the catastrophic spiritual and sometimes physical effects of sin.

2 Nephi 28:7–8

Any person who has carefully studied the teachings of modern theologians recognizes that many of them now teach there is no such thing as "sin against God"; they claim sin is simply doing wrong against oneself. In such a philosophy, the person can rationalize whether or not he is committing sin. Nephi's prophecy concerning the false teachings of the last days seems to be literally fulfilled in this modern theology, which even questions the existence of God and of life after death. The philosophy that "God is dead" comprises a significant part of modern theology. Concerning the inherent weakness of a philosophy of "Eat, drink, and be merry, for tomorrow we die" (2 Nephi 28:7), President John Taylor has written:

"If I am a being that came into the world yesterday, and leaves it again tomorrow, I might as well have one religion as another, or none at all; 'let us eat and drink; for tomorrow we die.' If I am an eternal being, I want to know something about that eternity with which I am associated. I want to know something about God, the devil, heaven, and hell. If hell is a place of misery, and heaven a place of happiness, I want to know how to escape the one, and obtain the other. If I cannot know something about these things which are to come in the eternal world, I have no religion. . . . If there is a God, I want a religion that supplies some means of certain and tangible communication with Him. If there is a heaven, I want to know what sort of a place it is. If there are angels, I want to know their nature, and their occupation, and of what they are composed. If I am an eternal being, I want to know what I am to do when I get through with time. . . ." (Ludlow)

and they persecute the meek and the poor in heart, because in their
pride they are puffed up.
14. They wear stiff necks and high heads; yea, and because of
pride, and wickedness, and abominations, and whoredoms, they
have all gone astray save it be a few, who are the humble followers of Christ; nevertheless, they are led, that in many instances
they do err because they are taught by the precepts of men.
15. O the wise, and the learned, and the rich, that are puffed up in
the pride of their hearts, and all those who preach false doctrines,
and all those who commit whoredoms, and pervert the right way
of the Lord, wo, wo, wo be unto them, saith the Lord God
Almighty, for they shall be thrust down to hell!
16. Wo unto them that turn aside the just for a thing of naught and
revile against that which is good, and say that it is of no worth! For
the day shall come that the Lord God will speedily visit the inhabitants of the earth; and in that day that they are fully ripe in iniquity they shall perish.
17. But behold, if the inhabitants of the earth shall repent of their
wickedness and abominations they shall not be destroyed, saith the
Lord of Hosts.
18. But behold, that great and abominable church, the whore of all
the earth, must tumble to the earth, and great must be the fall
thereof.
19. For the kingdom of the devil must shake, and they which
belong to it must needs be stirred up unto repentance, or the devil
will grasp them with his everlasting chains, and they be stirred up
to anger, and perish;
20. For behold, at that day shall he rage in the hearts of the children of men, and stir them up to anger against that which is good.
21. And others will he pacify, and lull them away into carnal security, that they will say: All is well in Zion; yea, Zion prospereth, all
is well—and thus the devil cheateth their souls, and leadeth them
away carefully down to hell.
22. And behold, others he flattereth away, and telleth them there
is no hell; and he saith unto them: I am no devil, for there is
none—and thus he whispereth in their ears, until he grasps them
with his awful chains, from whence there is no deliverance.
23. Yea, they are grasped with death, and hell; and death, and hell,
and the devil, and all that have been seized therewith must stand
before the throne of God, and be judged according to their works,
from whence they must go into the place prepared for them, even
a lake of fire and brimstone, which is endless torment.
24. Therefore, wo be unto him that is at ease in Zion!

2 Nephi 28:20–21

One of the clever ways in which the adversary leads us "carefully down to hell" is by convincing us to commit a series of "minor" sins and then tricking us into thinking that what we're doing is not so bad. Against this backdrop, we note Lewis's firm (and insightful) belief that the devil will never tempt humans to commit a major sin when a minor one will do the job. As Screwtape instructs his nephew, "Murder is no better than cards if cards can do the trick. Indeed, the safest road to Hell is the gradual one—the gentle slope, soft underfoot, without sudden turnings, without milestones, without signposts" (C. S. Lewis, *The Screwtape Letters* [London: HarperCollins, 1988], 54).

2 Nephi 28:21

Nephi's warning against teaching that "all is well in Zion" evidently refers to a situation in which people say everything is well when actually it is not. Concerning such a condition, President Wilford Woodruff has warned:

"Can we fold our arms in peace and cry 'all is peace in Zion,' when, so far as we have the power of the priesthood resting upon us, we can see the condition of the world? Can we imagine that our garments will be clean without lifting our voice before our fellowmen and warning them of the things that are at their doors? No, we cannot. There never was a set of men since God made the world under a stronger responsibility to warn this generation, to lift up our voices long and loud, day and night so far as we have the opportunity and declare the words of God unto this generation. We are required to do this. This is our calling. It is our duty. It is our business" (*Journal of Discourses*, 21:122). (Ludlow)

25. Wo be unto him that crieth: All is well!
26. Yea, wo be unto him that hearkeneth unto the precepts of men, and denieth the power of God, and the gift of the Holy Ghost!
27. Yea, wo be unto him that saith: We have received, and we need no more!
28. And in fine, wo unto all those who tremble, and are angry because of the truth of God! For behold, he that is built upon the rock receiveth it with gladness; and he that is built upon a sandy foundation trembleth lest he shall fall.
29. Wo be unto him that shall say: We have received the word of God, and we need no more of the word of God, for we have enough!
30. For behold, thus saith the Lord God: I will give unto the children of men line upon line, precept upon precept, here a little and there a little; and blessed are those who hearken unto my precepts, and lend an ear unto my counsel, for they shall learn wisdom; for unto him that receiveth I will give more; and from them that shall say, We have enough, from them shall be taken away even that which they have.
31. Cursed is he that putteth his trust in man, or maketh flesh his arm, or shall hearken unto the precepts of men, save their precepts shall be given by the power of the Holy Ghost.
32. Wo be unto the Gentiles, saith the Lord God of Hosts! For notwithstanding I shall lengthen out mine arm unto them from day to day, they will deny me; nevertheless, I will be merciful unto them, saith the Lord God, if they will repent and come unto me; for mine arm is lengthened out all the day long, saith the Lord God of Hosts.

CHAPTER 29

1. BUT behold, there shall be many—at that day when I shall proceed to do a marvelous work among them, that I may remember my covenants which I have made unto the children of men, that I may set my hand again the second time to recover my people, which are of the house of Israel;
2. And also, that I may remember the promises which I have made unto thee, Nephi, and also unto thy father, that I would remember your seed; and that the words of your seed should proceed forth out of my mouth unto your seed; and my words shall hiss forth unto the ends of the earth, for a standard unto my people, which are of the house of Israel;
3. And because my words shall hiss forth—many of the Gentiles shall say: A Bible! A Bible! We have

2 Nephi 28:30

One of the principles upon which God operates is to give his children only as much of the law as they are able to live. Otherwise, if he gives laws to his children that they are not able to keep, then they would come under condemnation. God has said, "I will give unto the children of men line upon line, precept upon precept, here a little and there a little; and blessed are those who hearken unto my precepts, and lend an ear unto my counsel, for they shall learn wisdom; for unto him that receiveth I will give more; *and from them that shall say, We have enough, from them shall be taken away even that which they have.*" (2 Nephi 28:30. Italics added.)

In relationship to the coming forth of the Book of Mormon, this principle of the Lord works somewhat as follows:

1. "For unto him that receiveth, I will give more"—in other words, unto those who accept the Book of Mormon will be given additional scriptures (such as the Doctrine and Covenants and the Pearl of Great Price).

2. "And from them that shall say, We have enough, from them shall be taken away even that which they have"—those who believe the Bible is enough and who say they do not need the Book of Mormon, from them shall be taken away "even that which they have" (the Bible). Thus, readers of this prophecy should not be surprised to note that since 1830 the Bible has largely been "taken away" from the Christian world. When the Book of Mormon was published, most Christians and nearly all Christian ministers believed the Bible to be the true word of God. However, after these same people rejected the Book of Mormon, they largely lost their testimonies of the Bible until now only a comparatively few Christians (and very few Christian ministers) actually believe the Bible is the true word of God. (Ludlow)

got a Bible, and there cannot be any more Bible.
4. But thus saith the Lord God: O fools, they shall have a Bible; and it shall proceed forth from the Jews, mine ancient covenant people. And what thank they the Jews for the Bible which they receive from them? Yea, what do the Gentiles mean? Do they remember the travails, and the labors, and the pains of the Jews, and their diligence unto me, in bringing forth salvation unto the Gentiles?
5. O ye Gentiles, have ye remembered the Jews, mine ancient covenant people? Nay; but ye have cursed them, and have hated them, and have not sought to recover them. But behold, I will return all these things upon your own heads; for I the Lord have not forgotten my people.
6. Thou fool, that shall say: A Bible, we have got a Bible, and we need no more Bible. Have ye obtained a Bible save it were by the Jews?
7. Know ye not that there are more nations than one? Know ye not that I, the Lord your God, have created all men, and that I remember those who are upon the isles of the sea; and that I rule in the heavens above and in the earth beneath; and I bring forth my word unto the children of men, yea, even upon all the nations of the earth?
8. Wherefore murmur ye, because that ye shall receive more of my word? Know ye not that the testimony of two nations is a witness unto you that I am God, that I remember one nation like unto another? Wherefore, I speak the same words unto one nation like unto another. And when the two nations shall run together the testimony of the two nations shall run together also.
9. And I do this that I may prove unto many that I am the same yesterday, today, and forever; and that I speak forth my words according to mine own pleasure. And because that I have spoken one word ye need not suppose that I cannot speak another; for my work is not yet finished; neither shall it be until the end of man, neither from that time henceforth and forever.
10. Wherefore, because that ye have a Bible ye need not suppose that it contains all my words; neither need ye suppose that I have not caused more to be written.
11. For I command all men, both in the east and in the west, and in the north, and in the south, and in the islands of the sea, that they shall write the words which I speak unto them; for out of the books which shall be written I will judge the world, every man according to their works, according to that which is written.
12. For behold, I shall speak unto the Jews and they shall write it; and I shall also speak unto the

POINT OF INTEREST

Tapirs can be found in the jungle and forest regions of Central and South America. In general they are 3 feet high (1 meter) at the shoulder and 7 feet long (2 meters). All four species of tapir are classified as endangered or vulnerable. Their closest relatives are horses and rhinoceroses.

2 Nephi 29:11–14

"In the mouth of two or three witnesses shall every word be established." (2 Corinthians 13:1.) The Bible, which contains the preceding statement, is one of the scriptural witnesses in which the word of God is established. But where are the second or the third witnesses? Latter-day Saints believe that the Book of Mormon is a second witness for the gospel of Jesus Christ; and in 2 Nephi 29:11–14 the Lord mentions a third scriptural witness that is yet to come forth: the record of the lost tribes of Israel. Thus the great "triple combination" of the last days will evidently consist of three great scriptural witnesses that testify of each other and will also witness of the divinity of Jesus Christ and his gospel. (Ludlow)

Nephites and they shall write it; and I shall also speak unto the other tribes of the house of Israel, which I have led away, and they shall write it; and I shall also speak unto all nations of the earth and they shall write it.
13. And it shall come to pass that the Jews shall have the words of the Nephites, and the Nephites shall have the words of the Jews; and the Nephites and the Jews shall have the words of the lost tribes of Israel; and the lost tribes of Israel shall have the words of the Nephites and the Jews.
14. And it shall come to pass that my people, which are of the house of Israel, shall be gathered home unto the lands of their possessions; and my word also shall be gathered in one. And I will show unto them that fight against my word and against my people, who are of the house of Israel, that I am God, and that I covenanted with Abraham that I would remember his seed forever.

CHAPTER 30

1. AND now behold, my beloved brethren, I would speak unto you; for I, Nephi, would not suffer that ye should suppose that ye are more righteous than the Gentiles shall be. For behold, except ye shall keep the commandments of God ye shall all likewise perish; and because of the words which have been spoken ye need not suppose that the Gentiles are utterly destroyed.
2. For behold, I say unto you that as many of the Gentiles as will repent are the covenant people of the Lord; and as many of the Jews as will not repent shall be cast off; for the Lord covenanteth with none save it be with them that repent and believe in his Son, who is the Holy One of Israel.
3. And now, I would prophesy somewhat more concerning the Jews and the Gentiles. For after the book of which I have spoken shall come forth, and be written unto the Gentiles, and sealed up again unto the Lord, there shall be many which shall believe the words which are written; and they shall carry them forth unto the remnant of our seed.
4. And then shall the remnant of our seed know concerning us, how that we came out from Jerusalem, and that they are descendants of the Jews.
5. And the gospel of Jesus Christ shall be declared among them; wherefore, they shall be restored unto the knowledge of their fathers, and also to the knowledge of Jesus Christ, which was had among their fathers.

2 Nephi 29:13–14

From the earliest days of the Restoration, the Book of Mormon has drawn noble truth seekers into the fold. Take the story of Joseph Smith's younger brother, Samuel Harrison Smith, who as a 22-year-old returned from his mission somewhat discouraged with the results. Yet look at what came of his labors: on Saturday, 14 April 1832, Brigham Young, "the Lion of the Lord" (*HC*, 7:435), was baptized after two years of intensive study and prayer centered on the Book of Mormon, a copy of which his brother Phineas had given him. Phineas had purchased the copy from Samuel Harrison Smith in April 1830, during Samuel's early missionary labors. . . .

Is it any wonder that the Lord has commanded us to share the Book of Mormon with others so that they, too, can learn divine truth through spiritual confirmation (see Moro. 10:4)? As Nephi testified, the coming forth of the Book of Mormon is undeniable evidence that the Lord will fulfill His solemn promise set forth in 2 Nephi 29:14. (P/A)

2 Nephi 30:4–7

When read in context, these verses concerning the eventual blessings of the Lamanites quite clearly refer to the last days. Concerning the future destiny of the Lamanites as they come into the Church, President Spencer W. Kimball has written:

"The Lamanites must rise in majesty and power. We must took forward to the day when they will be 'white and delightsome,' [2 Nephi 30:6], sharing the freedoms and blessings which we enjoy; when they shall have economic security, culture, refinement, and education; when they shall be operating farms and businesses and industries and shall be occupied in the professions and in teaching; when they shall be organized into wards and stakes of Zion, furnishing much of their own leadership; when they shall build and occupy and fill the temples, and serve in them as the natives are now serving in the Hawaiian Temple where I found last year the entire service conducted by them and done perfectly. And in the day when their prophet shall come, one shall rise . . . mighty among them . . . being an instrument in the hands of God, with exceeding faith, to work mighty wonders. . . . (2 Nephi 3:24.)" (Ludlow)

6. And then shall they rejoice; for they shall know that it is a blessing unto them from the hand of God; and their scales of darkness shall begin to fall from their eyes; and many generations shall not pass away among them, save they shall be a pure and delightsome people.
7. And it shall come to pass that the Jews which are scattered also shall begin to believe in Christ; and they shall begin to gather in upon the face of the land; and as many as shall believe in Christ shall also become a delightsome people.
8. And it shall come to pass that the Lord God shall commence his work among all nations, kindreds, tongues, and people, to bring about the restoration of his people upon the earth.
9. And with righteousness shall the Lord God judge the poor, and reprove with equity for the meek of the earth. And he shall smite the earth with the rod of his mouth; and with the breath of his lips shall he slay the wicked.
10. For the time speedily cometh that the Lord God shall cause a great division among the people, and the wicked will he destroy; and he will spare his people, yea, even if it so be that he must destroy the wicked by fire.
11. And righteousness shall be the girdle of his loins, and faithfulness the girdle of his reins.
12. And then shall the wolf dwell with the lamb; and the leopard shall lie down with the kid, and the calf, and the young lion, and the fatling, together; and a little child shall lead them.
13. And the cow and the bear shall feed; their young ones shall lie down together; and the lion shall eat straw like the ox.
14. And the sucking child shall play on the hole of the asp, and the weaned child shall put his hand on the cockatrice's den.
15. They shall not hurt nor destroy in all my holy mountain; for the earth shall be full of the knowledge of the Lord as the waters cover the sea.
16. Wherefore, the things of all nations shall be made known; yea, all things shall be made known unto the children of men.
17. There is nothing which is secret save it shall be revealed; there is no work of darkness save it shall be made manifest in the light; and there is nothing which is sealed upon the earth save it shall be loosed.
18. Wherefore, all things which have been revealed unto the children of men shall at that day be revealed; and Satan shall have power over the hearts of the children of men no more, for a long time. And now, my beloved brethren, I make an end of my sayings.

CHAPTER 31

2 Nephi 30:6

Scholars have pointed out that anciently, people in the East used girdles to confine their long robes while they were working or traveling. To "gird up your loins" means to prepare yourself in all ways to exert great effort.

2 Nephi 30:11

The 1840 edition of the Book of Mormon—the only one personally revised by Joseph Smith—also read "pure and delightsome." This phrase was changed in subsequent editions of the book to "white and delightsome." In 1981 the phrase was changed to be consistent with the 1840 edition and to reflect the judgment by current prophets that it is purity, not skin color, that makes one delightsome to the Lord.

1. AND now I, Nephi, make an end of my prophesying unto you, my beloved brethren. And I cannot write but a few things, which I know must surely come to pass; neither can I write but a few of the words of my brother Jacob.
2. Wherefore, the things which I have written sufficeth me, save it be a few words which I must speak concerning the doctrine of Christ; wherefore, I shall speak unto you plainly, according to the plainness of my prophesying.
3. For my soul delighteth in plainness; for after this manner doth the Lord God work among the children of men. For the Lord God giveth light unto the understanding; for he speaketh unto men according to their language, unto their understanding.
4. Wherefore, I would that ye should remember that I have spoken unto you concerning that prophet which the Lord showed unto me, that should baptize the Lamb of God, which should take away the sins of the world.
5. And now, if the Lamb of God, he being holy, should have need to be baptized by water, to fulfil all righteousness, O then, how much more need have we, being unholy, to be baptized, yea, even by water!
6. And now, I would ask of you, my beloved brethren, wherein the Lamb of God did fulfil all righteousness in being baptized by water?
7. Know ye not that he was holy? But notwithstanding he being holy, he showeth unto the children of men that, according to the flesh he humbleth himself before the Father, and witnesseth unto the Father that he would be obedient unto him in keeping his commandments.
8. Wherefore, after he was baptized with water the Holy Ghost descended upon him in the form of a dove.
9. And again, it showeth unto the children of men the straightness of the path, and the narrowness of the gate, by which they should enter, he having set the example before them.
10. And he said unto the children of men: Follow thou me. Wherefore, my beloved brethren, can we follow Jesus save we shall be willing to keep the commandments of the Father?
11. And the Father said: Repent ye, repent ye, and be baptized in the name of my Beloved Son.
12. And also, the voice of the Son came unto me, saying: He that is baptized in my name, to him will the Father give the Holy Ghost, like unto me; wherefore, follow me, and do the things which ye have seen me do.
13. Wherefore, my beloved brethren, I know that if ye shall follow the Son, with full purpose of heart, acting no hypocrisy and no deception before God, but with real intent, repenting of your sins, witnessing unto the Father that ye are willing to take upon you the name

2 Nephi 31:5–21

Other evidence exists, in the scriptures and elsewhere, that baptism was also performed by other groups before the birth of Christ. The *Jewish Encyclopedia* indicates that baptism was a common practice in ancient Israel: "Baptism was practiced in ancient Judaism (Hasidic or Essene), first as a means of penitence . . . to receive the spirit of God, or to be permitted to stand in the presence of God, man must undergo baptism." (Vol. 2, p. 499.) Concerning the mode of baptism, the *Encyclopedia* says ". . . this [baptism] is only valid when performed by immersion in a natural fountain or stream or in a properly constructed [vessel]. This rule was, of course, also preserved in the temple at Jerusalem." (Vol. 1, pp. 68–69.)

The fact that baptism was practiced in ancient Israel might help explain why the Savior was not criticized by the orthodox Jewish people when he was baptized. The Pharisees were quick to criticize the Savior whenever he did anything contrary to their law. However, not a single word of criticism concerning the baptism of Jesus Christ is found in the entire New Testament! (Ludlow)

2 Nephi 31:11–12

Nephi now comes to the moment in his ministry where he must bring his sacred account on the small plates to a close. He has beheld many grand and extraordinary things pertaining to the design of heaven for humankind. He has viewed the generations of time, witnessed the coming and going of nations, perceived the flow of history from the beginning even until the end, and has watched the inevitable decline of the rebellious and the inexorable prosperity of the covenant faithful. Of all these grand episodes and supernal revelations, what does he, in his final remarks, choose to emphasize in his closing witness for future readers? It is the simple and pure doctrine of Christ. It is a solemn reminder of the efficacy of the principles of faith, repentance, baptism, and the gift of the Holy Ghost. It is an earnest plea to his readers to take upon themselves the name of Christ and endure to the end. All of this constitutes the key to joy and exaltation, and Nephi places his seal of testimony upon these final words of counsel as central to the gospel of Jesus Christ. (P/A)

of Christ, by baptism—yea, by following your Lord and your Savior
down into the water, according to his word, behold, then shall ye
receive the Holy Ghost; yea, then cometh the baptism of fire and
of the Holy Ghost; and then can ye speak with the tongue of
angels, and shout praises unto the Holy One of Israel.
14. But, behold, my beloved brethren, thus came the voice of the
Son unto me, saying: After ye have repented of your sins, and witnessed unto the Father that ye are willing to keep my commandments, by the baptism of water, and have received the baptism of
fire and of the Holy Ghost, and can speak with a new tongue, yea,
even with the tongue of angels, and after this should deny me, it
would have been better for you that ye had not known me.
15. And I heard a voice from the Father, saying: Yea, the words of
my Beloved are true and faithful. He that endureth to the end, the
same shall be saved.
16. And now, my beloved brethren, I know by this that unless a
man shall endure to the end, in following the example of the Son
of the living God, he cannot be saved.
17. Wherefore, do the things which I have told you I have seen
that your Lord and your Redeemer should do; for, for this cause
have they been shown unto me, that ye might know the gate by
which ye should enter. For the gate by which ye should enter is
repentance and baptism by water; and then cometh a remission of
your sins by fire and by the Holy Ghost.
18. And then are ye in this strait and narrow path which leads to
eternal life; yea, ye have entered in by the gate; ye have done
according to the commandments of the Father and the Son; and ye
have received the Holy Ghost, which witnesses of the Father and
the Son, unto the fulfilling of the promise which he hath made,
that if ye entered in by the way ye should receive.
19. And now, my beloved brethren, after ye have gotten into this
strait and narrow path, I would ask if all is done? Behold, I say unto
you, Nay; for ye have not come thus far save it were by the word of
Christ with unshaken faith in him, relying wholly upon the merits
of him who is mighty to save.
20. Wherefore, ye must press
forward with a steadfastness in
Christ, having a perfect brightness of hope, and a love of God
and of all men. Wherefore, if ye
shall press forward, feasting
upon the word of Christ, and
endure to the end, behold, thus
saith the Father: Ye shall have
eternal life.
21. And now, behold, my
beloved brethren, this is the
way; and there

2 Nephi 31:13, 17

The baptismal ordinance has two parts. First comes the baptism by water, in which sins are figuratively "washed away." The actual purging of those sins is done as though by fire, by the Holy Ghost. Both parts are necessary for the cleansing effect of baptism to take place.

2 Nephi 31:20

This eloquent verse inspires us to press forward with full effort, committing ourselves to go the full distance—just as the Savior followed through by going the full distance to complete His mission in mortality.

POINT OF INTEREST

Below is an example of how civilizations build over each other. The modern structure at the top is the Catholic Church of Nuestra Señora de los Remedios, built on the ruins of the Great Pyramid of Cholula. The pyramid, located in Puebla, Mexico, is the largest in volume in the world.

is none other way nor name given under heaven whereby man can be saved in the kingdom of God. And now, behold, this is the doctrine of Christ, and the only and true doctrine of the Father, and of the Son, and of the Holy Ghost, which is one God, without end. Amen.

CHAPTER 32

1. AND now, behold, my beloved brethren, I suppose that ye ponder somewhat in your hearts concerning that which ye should do after ye have entered in by the way. But, behold, why do ye ponder these things in your hearts?
2. Do ye not remember that I said unto you that after ye had received the Holy Ghost ye could speak with the tongue of angels? And now, how could ye speak with the tongue of angels save it were by the Holy Ghost?
3. Angels speak by the power of the Holy Ghost; wherefore, they speak the words of Christ. Wherefore, I said unto you, feast upon the words of Christ; for behold, the words of Christ will tell you all things what ye should do.
4. Wherefore, now after I have spoken these words, if ye cannot understand them it will be because ye ask not, neither do ye knock; wherefore, ye are not brought into the light, but must perish in the dark.
5. For behold, again I say unto you that if ye will enter in by the way, and receive the Holy Ghost, it will show unto you all things what ye should do.
6. Behold, this is the doctrine of Christ, and there will be no more doctrine given until after he shall manifest himself unto you in the flesh. And when he shall manifest himself unto you in the flesh, the things which he shall say unto you shall ye observe to do.
7. And now I, Nephi, cannot say more; the Spirit stoppeth mine utterance, and I am left to mourn because of the unbelief, and the wickedness, and the ignorance, and the stiffneckedness of men; for they will not search knowledge, nor understand great knowledge, when it is given unto them in plainness, even as plain as word can be.
8. And now, my beloved brethren, I perceive that ye ponder still in your hearts; and it grieveth me that I must speak concerning this thing. For if ye would hearken unto the Spirit which teacheth a man to pray ye would know that ye must pray; for the evil spirit teacheth not a man to pray, but teacheth him that he must not pray.
9. But behold, I say unto you that ye must pray always, and not faint; that ye must not perform any thing unto the Lord save in the first place ye shall pray unto the Father in

2 Nephi 32:3

Parley P. Pratt taught that the Holy Ghost quickens the intellect; enlarges, expands, and purifies all passions and affections; inspires, develops, cultivates, and matures; inspires virtue, kindness, goodness, tenderness, gentleness, and charity; develops beauty of person; and tends to health, vigor, and social feelings.

2 Nephi 32:3

Perhaps we should ponder in our hearts whether we really do feast upon the word. Do we consume and feast upon, or do we only occasionally taste the word of the Lord as delivered to us by the prophets? Perhaps it appears so rarely on our personal and family menus that we are not ". . . nourished by the good word of God . . ." (Moro. 6:4). (O/C)

2 Nephi 32:3

Nephi, being both a visionary servant of the Lord and a practical guide for his people, leaves a legacy of inspired advice. Follow divine counsel. Follow the Spirit. Pray always in the name of the Christ "that thy performance may be for the welfare of thy soul" (2 Ne. 32:9).

President Ezra Taft Benson counseled, "His gospel is the perfect prescription for all human problems and social ills. But His gospel is effective only as it is applied in our lives. Therefore, we must 'feast upon the words of Christ; for behold, the words of Christ will tell [us] all things what [we] should do' (2 Ne. 32:3)."

If ever there was a panacea for life, it is the word of God and the Holy Spirit. Feasting upon the word should be a daily happening. It will keep us on the strait and narrow path and help us overcome temptation (see 1 Ne. 15:24) as we continually nurture it through faith, diligence, and patience (see Alma 32:40–43). When we keep the commandments we will be blessed to have His Spirit to be with us always (see D&C 20:77). (P/A)

2 Nephi 32:8–9

Earnest, pleading, yearning, hungering prayer is key to regaining the Spirit if we have lost it. Such prayer can also yield revelation, which is promised us through our faithfulness; the Lord withholds much that He would otherwise reveal if we were only prepared to receive it.

the name of Christ, that he will consecrate thy performance unto thee, that thy performance may be for the welfare of thy soul.

CHAPTER 33

1. AND now I, Nephi, cannot write all the things which were taught among my people; neither am I mighty in writing, like unto speaking; for when a man speaketh by the power of the Holy Ghost the power of the Holy Ghost carrieth it unto the hearts of the children of men.

2. But behold, there are many that harden their hearts against the Holy Spirit, that it hath no place in them; wherefore, they cast many things away which are written and esteem them as things of naught.

3. But I, Nephi, have written what I have written, and I esteem it as of great worth, and especially unto my people. For I pray continually for them by day, and mine eyes water my pillow by night, because of them; and I cry unto my God in faith, and I know that he will hear my cry.

4. And I know that the Lord God will consecrate my prayers for the gain of my people. And the words which I have written in weakness will be made strong unto them; for it persuadeth them to do good; it maketh known unto them of their fathers; and it speaketh of Jesus, and persuadeth them to believe in him, and to endure to the end, which is life eternal.

5. And it speaketh harshly against sin, according to the plainness of the truth; wherefore, no man will be angry at the words which I have written save he shall be of the spirit of the devil.

6. I glory in plainness; I glory in truth; I glory in my Jesus, for he hath redeemed my soul from hell.

7. I have charity for my people, and great faith in Christ that I shall meet many souls spotless at his judgment-seat.

8. I have charity for the Jew—I say Jew, because I mean them from whence I came.

9. I also have charity for the Gentiles. But behold, for none of these can I hope except they shall be reconciled unto Christ, and enter into the narrow gate, and walk in the strait path which leads to life, and continue in the path until the end of the day of probation.

10. And now, my beloved brethren, and also Jew, and all ye ends of the earth, hearken unto these words and believe in Christ; and if ye believe not in these words believe in Christ.

2 Nephi 33:10–11

In his farewell address, Nephi warns us as future readers of his record that we have the responsibility to decide whether or not we believe the things he has written. He also informs us that if we truly believe in Christ we will believe in his words, "for they are the words of Christ." (2 Nephi 33:10.) In conclusion, he warns: "And if they are not the words of Christ, judge ye—for Christ will show unto you, with power and great glory, that they are his words, at the last day" (2 Nephi 33:11). (Ludlow)

And if ye shall believe in Christ ye will believe in these words, for they are the words of Christ, and he hath given them unto me; and they teach all men that they should do good.
11. And if they are not the words of Christ, judge ye—for Christ will show unto you, with power and great glory, that they are his words, at the last day; and you and I shall stand face to face before his bar; and ye shall know that I have been commanded of him to write these things, notwithstanding my weakness.
12. And I pray the Father in the name of Christ that many of us, if not all, may be saved in his kingdom at that great and last day.
13. And now, my beloved brethren, all those who are of the house of Israel, and all ye ends of the earth, I speak unto you as the voice of one crying from the dust: Farewell until that great day shall come.
14. And you that will not partake of the goodness of God, and respect the words of the Jews, and also my words, and the words which shall proceed forth out of the mouth of the Lamb of God, behold, I bid you an everlasting farewell, for these words shall condemn you at the last day.
15. For what I seal on earth, shall be brought against you at the judgment bar; for thus hath the Lord commanded me, and I must obey. Amen.

2 Nephi 33:11

There are others who express that we will meet authors of the Book of Mormon face-to-face at the day of judgment. Two of these are Ether (see Ether 12:38, 39) and Moroni (see Moroni 10:27–29).

THE BOOK OF JACOB

THE BROTHER OF NEPHI

The words of his preaching unto his brethren. He confoundeth a man who seeketh to overthrow the doctrine of Christ. A few words concerning the history of the people of Nephi.

CHAPTER 1

1. For behold, it came to pass that fifty and five years had passed away from the time that Lehi left Jerusalem; wherefore, Nephi gave me, Jacob, a commandment concerning the small plates, upon which these things are engraven.
2. And he gave me, Jacob, a commandment that I should write upon these plates a few of the things which I consider to be most precious; that I should not touch, save it were lightly, concerning the history of this people which are called the people of Nephi.
3. For he said that the history of his

Jacob

Jacob was between forty-four and fifty-four years of age when Nephi gave him the plates. The oldest of the two sons born to Lehi in the wilderness, he saw the Savior. Jacob bridged the gap between the old and new promised lands, making him sensitive to both the Jews and his own people.

Jacob 1:2

This verse provides evidence that Jacob had heeded the counsel of Lehi to follow Nephi and had remained righteous. It also sets forth excellent criteria for us in determining what to include in our own personal journals and histories.

people should be engraven upon his other plates, and that I should preserve these plates and hand them down unto my seed, from generation to generation.

4. And if there were preaching which was sacred, or revelation which was great, or prophesying, that I should engraven the heads of them upon these plates, and touch upon them as much as it were possible, for Christ's sake, and for the sake of our people.

5. For because of faith and great anxiety, it truly had been made manifest unto us concerning our people, what things should happen unto them.

6. And we also had many revelations, and the spirit of much prophecy; wherefore, we knew of Christ and his kingdom, which should come.

7. Wherefore we labored diligently among our people, that we might persuade them to come unto Christ, and partake of the goodness of God, that they might enter into his rest, lest by any means he should swear in his wrath they should not enter in, as in the provocation in the days of temptation while the children of Israel were in the wilderness.

8. Wherefore, we would to God that we could persuade all men not to rebel against God, to provoke him to anger, but that all men would believe in Christ, and view his death, and suffer his cross and bear the shame of the world; wherefore, I, Jacob, take it upon me to fulfil the commandment of my brother Nephi.

9. Now Nephi began to be old, and he saw that he must soon die; wherefore, he anointed a man to be a king and a ruler over his people now, according to the reigns of the kings.

10. The people having loved Nephi exceedingly, he having been a great protector for them, having wielded the sword of Laban in their defence, and having labored in all his days for their welfare—

11. Wherefore, the people were desirous to retain in remembrance his name. And whoso should reign in his stead were called by the people, second Nephi, third Nephi, and so forth, according to the reigns of the kings; and thus they were called by the people, let them be of whatever name they would.

12. And it came to pass that Nephi died.

13. Now the people which were not Lamanites were Nephites; nevertheless, they were called Nephites, Jacobites, Josephites, Zoramites, Lamanites, Lemuelites, and Ishmaelites.

14. But I, Jacob, shall not hereafter distinguish them by these names, but I shall call them Lamanites that seek to destroy the people of Nephi, and those who are friendly to Nephi I shall call Nephites, or the people of Nephi, according to the reigns of the kings.

Jacob 1:4

"Heads" in this context means the most important parts.

Jacob 1:8

According to Elder Bruce R. McConkie, suffering the Savior's cross involves not only experiencing and enduring our own trials and afflictions, but consistently rendering service, consecration, devotion, and obedience.

Jacob 1:10

Ask yourself; can this be said of me? Do I exhibit these traits toward those within my stewardship?

Jacob 1:11

It is not clear who succeeded Nephi as king over the Nephites. Some Book of Mormon scholars have surmised that Nephi's successor was probably Jacob; they say Jacob failed to mention this here because of his modesty. However, other scholars feel that Nephi was probably succeeded as king by one of his sons.

Jacob 1:13–14

The terms *Nephite* and *Lamanite* are not racial designations. Instead, these names identified groups that may have included diverse races, and the names were used to identify religious, cultural, and military groups.

Jacob 1:14

In general, the terms "Nephites" and "Lamanites" are used with the same meaning for the first 500 years of Nephite history. The term *Nephites* refers to all those who followed after Nephi and to their descendants. The term *Lamanites* refers to those who followed after Laman and to their descendants. However, it is mentioned later in the Book of Mormon that there were no "ites" of any kind during the 200-year Golden Age immediately after the appearance of the resurrected Jesus Christ. (See 4 Nephi 17.)

After this 200-year period of righteousness, the terms "Lamanites" and "Nephites" are used again, but with somewhat different meanings than those used earlier in the Book of Mormon. (Ludlow)

15. And now it came to pass that the people of Nephi, under the reign of the second king, began to grow hard in their hearts, and indulge themselves somewhat in wicked practices, such as like unto David of old desiring many wives and concubines, and also Solomon, his son.
16. Yea, and they also began to search much gold and silver, and began to be lifted up somewhat in pride.
17. Wherefore I, Jacob, gave unto them these words as I taught them in the temple, having first obtained mine errand from the Lord.
18. For I, Jacob, and my brother Joseph had been consecrated priests and teachers of this people, by the hand of Nephi.
19. And we did magnify our office unto the Lord, taking upon us the responsibility, answering the sins of the people upon our own heads if we did not teach them the word of God with all diligence; wherefore, by laboring with our might their blood might not come upon our garments; otherwise their blood would come upon our garments, and we would not be found spotless at the last day.

CHAPTER 2

1. THE words which Jacob, the brother of Nephi, spake unto the people of Nephi, after the death of Nephi:
2. Now, my beloved brethren, I, Jacob, according to the responsibility which I am under to God, to magnify mine office with soberness, and that I might rid my garments of your sins, I come up into the temple this day that I might declare unto you the word of God.
3. And ye yourselves know that I have hitherto been diligent in the office of my calling; but I this day am weighed down with much more desire and anxiety for the welfare of your souls than I have hitherto been.
4. For behold, as yet, ye have been obedient unto the word of the Lord, which I have given unto you.
5. But behold, hearken ye unto me, and know that by the help of the all-powerful Creator of heaven and earth I can tell you concerning your thoughts, how that ye are beginning to labor in sin, which sin appeareth very abominable unto me, yea, and abominable unto God.
6. Yea, it grieveth my soul and causeth me to shrink with shame before the presence of my Maker, that I must testify unto you concerning the wickedness of your hearts.
7. And also it grieveth me that I must use so much boldness of speech concerning you, before your wives and your children, many of whose feelings are exceedingly tender and chaste and delicate

Jacob 1:19

The righteous leaders of the Nephites on the American continent apparently had the same keen sense of responsibility as was held by the righteous Hebrew leaders on the eastern continent. Jacob mentions that he and his brother Joseph, in becoming the religious leaders of the people, had taken upon themselves "the responsibility, answering the sins of the people upon our own heads if we did not teach them the word of God with all diligence." (Jacob 1:19.)

Ezekiel was one of the leaders of Israel on the eastern continent at about this same period. Concerning the responsibility of the leader to the people, Ezekiel recorded the following instructions from the Lord:

"Again the word of the Lord came unto me, saying,

"Son of man, speak to the children of thy people, and say unto them, When I bring the sword upon a land, if the people of the land take a man of their coasts, and set him for their watchman:

"If when he seeth the sword come upon the land, he blow the trumpet, and warn the people;

"Then whosoever heareth the sound of the trumpet, and taketh not warning; if the sword come, and take him away, his blood shall be upon his own head.

"He heard the sound of the trumpet, and took not warning; his blood shall be upon him. But he that taketh warning shall deliver his soul.

"But if the watchman see the sword come, and blow not the trumpet, and the people be not warned; if the sword come, and take any person from among them, he is taken away in his iniquity; but his blood will I require at the watchman's hand.

"So thou, O son of man, I have set thee a watchman unto the house of Israel; therefore thou shalt hear the word at my mouth, and warn them from me" (Ezekiel 33:1–7). (Ludlow)

Jacob 1:19

To "magnify our office" is the same thing as magnifying a calling: learning what the calling entails and then devoting strength, energy, talent, and resources to enlarging that calling. It begins by attaching importance to the calling and committing ourselves to its performance. Magnifying each calling we accept actually carries eternal consequences. President John Taylor said, "If you do not magnify your calling, God will hold you responsible for those whom you might have saved had you done your duty."

before God, which thing is pleasing unto God;
8. And it supposeth me that they have come up hither to hear the pleasing word of God, yea, the word which healeth the wounded soul.
9. Wherefore, it burdeneth my soul that I should be constrained, because of the strict commandment which I have received from God, to admonish you according to your crimes, to enlarge the wounds of those who are already wounded, instead of consoling and healing their wounds; and those who have not been wounded, instead of feasting upon the pleasing word of God have daggers placed to pierce their souls and wound their delicate minds.
10. But, notwithstanding the greatness of the task, I must do according to the strict commands of God, and tell you concerning your wickedness and abominations, in the presence of the pure in heart, and the broken heart, and under the glance of the piercing eye of the Almighty God.
11. Wherefore, I must tell you the truth according to the plainness of the word of God. For behold, as I inquired of the Lord, thus came the word unto me, saying: Jacob, get thou up into the temple on the morrow, and declare the word which I shall give thee unto this people.
12. And now behold, my brethren, this is the word which I declare unto you, that many of you have begun to search for gold, and for silver, and for all manner of precious ores, in the which this land, which is a land of promise unto you and to your seed, doth abound most plentifully.
13. And the hand of providence hath smiled upon you most pleasingly, that you have obtained many riches; and because some of you have obtained more abundantly than that of your brethren ye are lifted up in the pride of your hearts, and wear stiff necks and high heads because of the costliness of your apparel, and persecute your brethren because ye suppose that ye are better than they.
14. And now, my brethren, do ye suppose that God justifieth you in this thing? Behold, I say unto you, Nay. But he condemneth you, and if ye persist in these things his judgments must speedily come unto you.
15. O that he would show you that he can pierce you, and with one glance of his eye he can smite you to the dust!
16. O that he would rid you from this iniquity and abomination. And, O that ye would listen unto the word of his commands, and let not this pride of your hearts destroy your souls!
17. Think of your brethren like unto yourselves, and be familiar with all and free with your substance, that they may be rich like unto you.
18. But before ye seek for riches, seek ye for the kingdom of God.
19. And after ye have obtained a hope in Christ ye shall obtain riches, if ye seek them; and ye will seek them for the intent to do good—

Jacob 2:12

Money is a medium of exchange, and is of itself neutral. Our attitude toward it is what removes it from its neutral position. When it comes to accumulating wealth, our first priority should be building the kingdom of God. Our most basic relationships—with God and with our fellow man—should determine our attitude toward material things.

Jacob 2:18–19

The Book of Mormon does not teach that riches *per se* are evil. It does, however, indicate that the love of riches is evil, because then the craving for wealth is motivated by the wrong reasons.

However, Jacob promises here that if a person truly seeks the kingdom of God first and then desires riches, he will seek wealth for the right reasons: to clothe the naked, to feed the hungry, etc. (Ludlow)

Jacob 2:18–19

The sin of pride is condemned by the Lord. (See Jacob 2:14.) This sin is manifested in all walks of life and is spiritually devastating to the soul. In the case of the Nephites, it was the result of seeking riches for the wrong reasons. Those who embrace this sin are not justified before God, yet suppose that they are better than their brethren. (See Jacob 2:14.)

The Lord's counsel to His children in their endeavors to obtain earthly riches is set out in verses 18 and 19, wherein they are told that if they seek riches, it will be "for the intent to do good—to clothe the naked, and to feed the hungry, and to liberate the captive, and administer relief to the sick and the afflicted" (Jacob 2:19).

As noted, the sin of pride is not justified before God. It is condemned by Him and is abominable in His sight. Elder Ezra Taft Benson enlightens our understanding as to the resultant consequences when yielding to the sin of pride. He said:

"One of Satan's greatest tools is pride: to cause a man or a woman to center so much attention on self that he or she becomes insensitive to his Creator or fellow beings. . . . Pride does not look up to God and care about what is right. It looks sideways to man and argues who is right. Pride is manifest in the spirit of contention. . . . To the proud, the applause of the world rings in their ears; to the humble, the applause of heaven warms their hearts." (O/C)

Jacob 2:19

As we lose sight of the brotherhood of man, we turn to coveting, dishonesty, selfishness, and neglect of the poor.

to clothe the naked, and to feed the hungry, and to liberate the captive, and administer relief to the sick and the afflicted.
20. And now, my brethren, I have spoken unto you concerning pride; and those of you which have afflicted your neighbor, and persecuted him because ye were proud in your hearts, of the things which God hath given you, what say ye of it?
21. Do ye not suppose that such things are abominable unto him who created all flesh? And the one being is as precious in his sight as the other. And all flesh is of the dust; and for the selfsame end hath he created them, that they should keep his commandments and glorify him forever.
22. And now I make an end of speaking unto you concerning this pride. And were it not that I must speak unto you concerning a grosser crime, my heart would rejoice exceedingly because of you.
23. But the word of God burdens me because of your grosser crimes. For behold, thus saith the Lord: This people begin to wax in iniquity; they understand not the scriptures, for they seek to excuse themselves in committing whoredoms, because of the things which were written concerning David, and Solomon his son.
24. Behold, David and Solomon truly had many wives and concubines, which thing was abominable before me, saith the Lord.
25. Wherefore, thus saith the Lord, I have led this people forth out of the land of Jerusalem, by the power of mine arm, that I might raise up unto me a righteous branch from the fruit of the loins of Joseph.
26. Wherefore, I the Lord God will not suffer that this people shall do like unto them of old.
27. Wherefore, my brethren, hear me, and hearken to the word of the Lord: For there shall not any man among you have save it be one wife; and concubines he shall have none;
28. For I, the Lord God, delight in the chastity of women. And whoredoms are an abomination before me; thus saith the Lord of Hosts.
29. Wherefore, this people shall keep my commandments, saith the Lord of Hosts, or cursed be the land for their sakes.
30. For if I will, saith the Lord of Hosts, raise up seed unto me, I will command my people; otherwise they shall hearken unto these things.
31. For behold, I, the Lord, have seen the sorrow, and heard the mourning of the daughters of my people in the land of Jerusalem, yea, and in all the lands of my people, because of the wickedness and abominations of their husbands.
32. And I will not suffer, saith the Lord of Hosts, that the cries of the fair daughters of this people, which I have led out of the land of Jerusalem, shall come up unto me against the men of my people, saith the Lord of Hosts.
33. For they shall not lead away captive the daughters of my people because of their tenderness, save I shall visit them with a sore curse, even unto destruction; for they shall not commit whoredoms, like unto

Jacob 2:23

Jacob clearly taught that whoredoms are an abomination before the Lord. (Jacob 2:23, 28.) The word *whoredom* as used here by Jacob could refer either to the sin of fornication or to the sin of adultery.

The leaders of the Church in this dispensation have been strong in condemning these types of sins. Following is an excerpt from an official statement published over the signatures of the First Presidency of the Church concerning this matter:

"By virtue of the authority in us vested as the First Presidency of the Church, we warn our people who are offending, of the degradation, the wickedness, the punishment that attend upon unchastity; we urge you to remember the blessings which flow from the living of the clean life; we call upon you to keep, day in and day out, the way of strictest chastity, through which only can God's choice gifts come to you and His Spirit abide with you." (Ludlow)

Jacob 2:24, 27; 3:5

A *concubine* often refers to a woman who is used for sexual purposes outside of marriage. The same term, however, is used to designate a wife who has lower social status than her husband's other wives. In this verse, Jacob is warning against men who either take wives without the consent of the Lord or who engage in sexual relationships outside the marriage covenant.

Jacob 2:24–30

Jacob indicates that if the Lord commands people to practice polygamy in order to "raise up seed" unto himself, then the people should practice polygamy. (Jacob 2:30.) However, if the Lord does not command the people to practice polygamy, then a man should not have more than one wife. (Verse 27.) Jacob makes it clear that the Nephites were not to practice polygamy (Jacob 2:25–27). (Ludlow)

them of old, saith the Lord of Hosts.
34. And now behold, my brethren, ye know that these commandments were given to our father, Lehi; wherefore, ye have known
them before; and ye have come unto great condemnation; for ye
have done these things which ye ought not to have done.
35. Behold, ye have done greater iniquities than the Lamanites,
our brethren. Ye have broken the hearts of your tender wives, and
lost the confidence of your children, because of your bad examples
before them; and the sobbings of their hearts ascend up to God
against you. And because of the strictness of the word of God,
which cometh down against you, many hearts died, pierced with
deep wounds.

CHAPTER 3

1. BUT behold, I, Jacob, would speak unto you that are pure in
heart. Look unto God with firmness of mind, and pray unto him
with exceeding faith, and he will console you in your afflictions,
and he will plead your cause, and send down justice upon those
who seek your destruction.
2. O all ye that are pure in heart, lift up your heads and receive the
pleasing word of God, and feast upon his love; for ye may, if your
minds are firm, forever.
3. But, wo, wo, unto you that are not pure in heart, that are filthy
this day before God; for except ye repent the land is cursed for your
sakes; and the Lamanites, which are not filthy like unto you, nevertheless they are cursed with a sore cursing, shall scourge you even
unto destruction.
4. And the time speedily cometh, that except ye repent they shall
possess the land of your inheritance, and the Lord God will lead
away the righteous out from among you.
5. Behold, the Lamanites your brethren, whom ye hate because of
their filthiness and the cursing which hath come upon their skins, are
more righteous than you; for they have not forgotten the commandment of the Lord, which was given unto our father—that they should
have save it were one wife, and concubines they should have none,
and there should not be whoredoms committed among them.
6. And now, this commandment they observe to keep; wherefore,
because of this observance, in keeping this commandment, the
Lord God will not destroy them, but will be merciful unto them;
and one day they shall become a blessed people.
7. Behold, their husbands love their wives, and their wives love
their husbands; and their husbands and their wives love their children; and their unbelief and their hatred towards you is because of
the iniquity of their fathers; wherefore,

POINT OF INTEREST

The Zapotec civilization flourished in southern Mesoamerica, in the vicinity of Oaxaca, Mexico. Archaeological evidence indicates that the culture goes back at least 2,500 years. At right is part of a Zapotec manuscript located in the Imperial Library in Vienna, Austria.

how much better are you than they, in the sight of your great Creator?
8. O my brethren, I fear that unless ye shall repent of your sins that their skins will be whiter than yours, when ye shall be brought with them before the throne of God.
9. Wherefore, a commandment I give unto you, which is the word of God, that ye revile no more against them because of the darkness of their skins; neither shall ye revile against them because of their filthiness; but ye shall remember your own filthiness, and remember that their filthiness came because of their fathers.
10. Wherefore, ye shall remember your children, how that ye have grieved their hearts because of the example that ye have set before them; and also, remember that ye may, because of your filthiness, bring your children unto destruction, and their sins be heaped upon your heads at the last day.
11. O my brethren, hearken unto my words; arouse the faculties of your souls; shake yourselves that ye may awake from the slumber of death; and loose yourselves from the pains of hell that ye may not become angels to the devil, to be cast into that lake of fire and brimstone which is the second death.
12. And now I, Jacob, spake many more things unto the people of Nephi, warning them against fornication and lasciviousness, and every kind of sin, telling them the awful consequences of them.
13. And a hundredth part of the proceedings of this people, which now began to be numerous, cannot be written upon these plates; but many of their proceedings are written upon the larger plates, and their wars, and their contentions, and the reigns of their kings.
14. These plates are called the plates of Jacob, and they were made by the hand of Nephi. And I make an end of speaking these words.

CHAPTER 4

1. NOW behold, it came to pass that I, Jacob, having ministered much unto my people in word, (and I cannot write but a little of my words, because of the difficulty of engraving our words upon plates) and we know that the things which we write upon plates must remain;
2. But whatsoever things we write upon anything save it be upon plates must perish and vanish away; but we can write a few words upon plates, which will give our children, and also our beloved brethren, a small degree of knowledge concerning us, or concerning their fathers—
3. Now in this thing we do rejoice; and we labor diligently to engraven these words upon plates, hoping that our beloved brethren and our children will receive them with thankful hearts, and look upon them that they may learn with joy and not with sorrow, neither with contempt, concerning their first parents.

Jacob 3:10

The doctrine that parents are at least partially responsible for the acts of their children is clearly taught in latter-day scriptures. In fact, as is indicated in the following scripture, parents are responsible for the sins of their children if the parents do not teach them the gospel:

And again, inasmuch as parents have children in Zion, or in any of her stakes which are organized, that teach them not to understand the doctrine of repentance, faith in Christ the Son of the living God, and of baptism and the gift of the Holy Ghost by the laying on of the hands, when eight years old, the sin be upon the heads of the parents. . . .

And they shall also teach their children to pray, and to walk uprightly before the Lord (D&C 68:25, 28). (Ludlow)

Jacob 3:14

Apparently the "plates of Jacob" referred to here are the same set of plates referred to elsewhere as the small plates of Nephi. Jacob admits these plates were "made by the hand of Nephi." (Jacob 3:14.) Evidently they are now called the plates of Jacob because the historian who is writing on the plates is now Jacob. (Ludlow)

As commanded by Nephi, Jacob wrote only the things of the soul.

Jacob 4:3

Jacob explains not only his purpose for writing on the plates, but lets us see a little of what the experience was like for him.

4. For, for this intent have we written these things, that they may know that we knew of Christ, and we had a hope of his glory many hundred years before his coming; and not only we ourselves had a hope of his glory, but also all the holy prophets which were before us.
5. Behold, they believed in Christ and worshiped the Father in his name, and also we worship the Father in his name. And for this intent we keep the law of Moses, it pointing our souls to him; and for this cause it is sanctified unto us for righteousness, even as it was accounted unto Abraham in the wilderness to be obedient unto the commands of God in offering up his son Isaac, which is a similitude of God and his Only Begotten Son.
6. Wherefore, we search the prophets, and we have many revelations and the spirit of prophecy; and having all these witnesses we obtain a hope, and our faith becometh unshaken, insomuch that we truly can command in the name of Jesus and the very trees obey us, or the mountains, or the waves of the sea.
7. Nevertheless, the Lord God showeth us our weakness that we may know that it is by his grace, and his great condescensions unto the children of men, that we have power to do these things.
8. Behold, great and marvelous are the works of the Lord. How unsearchable are the depths of the mysteries of him; and it is impossible that man should find out all his ways. And no man knoweth of his ways save it be revealed unto him; wherefore, brethren, despise not the revelations of God.
9. For behold, by the power of his word man came upon the face of the earth, which earth was created by the power of his word. Wherefore, if God being able to speak and the world was, and to speak and man was created, O then, why not able to command the earth, or the workmanship of his hands upon the face of it, according to his will and pleasure?
10. Wherefore, brethren, seek not to counsel the Lord, but to take counsel from his hand. For behold, ye yourselves know that he counseleth in wisdom, and in justice, and in great mercy, over all his works.
11. Wherefore, beloved brethren, be reconciled unto him through the atonement of Christ, his Only Begotten

Jacob 4:8–17

The prophets were guided by truth emanating from the Savior through these three infallible means of delivery: scriptures, living prophets, and the Holy Spirit. We should learn and be guided in the same manner. Any opinion, philosophy, suggestion, or temptation that is not in harmony with truth that comes through one or more of these sources should be ignored and discarded, that we might not be deceived. (See also D&C 52:9, 36.) Those who follow this pattern of the prophets have a hope in Christ's glory.

However, this hope, once obtained, can only be retained if we also subscribe our lives to the further counsel of Jacob (see Jacob 4):

a. Acknowledge revelations of God—verse 8
b. Respect sovereignty of God—verse 9
c. Take counsel from the Lord—verse 10
d. Be eligible for the blessings of the Atonement—verses 11–12
e. Avoid going beyond the mark—verse 14
f. Build on the only sure foundation—verses 15–17

Elder Dean L. Larsen provided some marvelous insights on the above teachings recorded in Jacob's writings:

"Jacob speaks of people who placed themselves in serious jeopardy in spiritual things because they were unwilling to accept simple, basic principles of truth. . . . They went beyond the mark of wisdom and prudence, and obviously failed to stay within the circle of fundamental gospel truths, which provide a basis for faith. . . . As they became infatuated by these 'things that they could not understand,' their comprehension of and faith in the redeeming role of a true Messiah was lost, and the purpose of life became confused. . . .

"In today's complicated world with its diversity of demands and sometimes distracting voices, it is so important for us to keep our eyes upon the basic things that matter most and that will have the greatest eternal consequence for us." (O/C)

Son, and ye may obtain a resurrection, according to the power of the resurrection which is in Christ, and be presented as the first-fruits of Christ unto God, having faith, and obtained a good hope of glory in him before he manifesteth himself in the flesh.
12. And now, beloved, marvel not that I tell you these things; for why not speak of the atonement of Christ, and attain to a perfect knowledge of him, as to attain to the knowledge of a resurrection and the world to come?
13. Behold, my brethren, he that prophesieth, let him prophesy to the understanding of men; for the Spirit speaketh the truth and lieth not. Wherefore, it speaketh of things as they really are, and of things as they really will be; wherefore, these things are manifested unto us plainly, for the salvation of our souls. But behold, we are not witnesses alone in these things; for God also spake them unto prophets of old.
14. But behold, the Jews were a stiffnecked people; and they despised the words of plainness, and killed the prophets, and sought for things that they could not understand. Wherefore, because of their blindness, which blindness came by looking beyond the mark, they must needs fall; for God hath taken away his plainness from them, and delivered unto them many things which they cannot understand, because they desired it. And because they desired it God hath done it, that they may stumble.
15. And now I, Jacob, am led on by the Spirit unto prophesying; for I perceive by the workings of the Spirit which is in me, that by the stumbling of the Jews they will reject the stone upon which they might build and have safe foundation.
16. But behold, according to the scriptures, this stone shall become the great, and the last, and the only sure foundation, upon which the Jews can build.
17. And now, my beloved, how is it possible that these, after having rejected the sure foundation, can ever build upon it, that it may become the head of their corner?
18. Behold, my beloved brethren, I will unfold this mystery unto you; if I do not, by any means, get shaken from my firmness in the Spirit, and stumble because of my over anxiety for you.

CHAPTER 5

Jacob 4:14–17

In trying to explain why the Jewish people did not accept the Savior when he came, Jacob said it was because of the blindness of the Jews "which blindness came by looking beyond the mark." (Jacob 4:14.) Although the meaning of this idiomatic expression is not absolutely clear, some Book of Mormon scholars have suggested that the Jewish people were "looking beyond the mark" insofar as they expected the Savior to do at his first coming those things which it was prophesied he should do at his second coming. Thus, when the Savior did not lead the Jewish people to victory over their enemies during his earthly existence, he was largely rejected by the Jews. Jacob, however, prophesies that in the last days the Jews will once again build upon the sure foundation of Jesus Christ. (Ludlow)

Jacob 5

The olive tree is an excellent symbol for the house of Israel for a number of reasons. First, the olive tree is a living thing that provides shelter from the harsh sun and produces good fruit if it is properly pruned and cared for. It requires constant nourishment to survive—though it prefers poor, rocky soil, it must be constantly fertilized—but is flexible enough to survive high winds and other forces. The olive tree is different from other fruit-bearing trees: if the green slip of an olive tree is planted and allowed to grow, it develops into a wild olive tree—a bush with branches that grow into a wild tangle of branches that produce only small quantities of a worthless fruit. In order to become a tame and productive tree, the wild tree has to be completely cut back and a branch from a tame olive tree has to be grafted into the main stem. With careful nourishment, pruning, and cultivation, the tree will begin to produce fruit in about seven years, but will not reach full production for fifteen years. If properly cared for, it will continue to produce fruit for centuries. As the olive tree finally begins to die, the top of the tree withers first; the roots send up new green shoots that, if cared for properly, mature into full-grown olive trees. Thus, the tree itself may produce fruit for centuries, but because of the shoots it sends up, it may keep producing new olive trees for thousands of years. Even if an olive tree is cut down, new sprouts are sent up from the root around the margins of the stump, creating a grove of as many as five trees where there was originally only one.

1. BEHOLD, my brethren, do ye not remember to have read the words of the prophet Zenos, which he spake unto the house of Israel, saying:
2. Hearken, O ye house of Israel, and hear the words of me, a prophet of the Lord.
3. For behold, thus saith the Lord, I will liken thee, O house of Israel, like unto a tame olive-tree, which a man took and nourished in his vineyard; and it grew, and waxed old, and began to decay.
4. And it came to pass that the master of the vineyard went forth, and he saw that his olive-tree began to decay; and he said: I will prune it, and dig about it, and nourish it, that perhaps it may shoot forth young and tender branches, and it perish not.
5. And it came to pass that he pruned it, and digged about it, and nourished it according to his word.
6. And it came to pass that after many days it began to put forth somewhat a little, young and tender branches; but behold, the main top thereof began to perish.
7. And it came to pass that the master of the vineyard saw it, and he said unto his servant: It grieveth me that I should lose this tree; wherefore, go and pluck the branches from a wild olive-tree, and bring them hither unto me; and we will pluck off those main branches which are beginning to wither away, and we will cast them into the fire that they may be burned.
8. And behold, saith the Lord of the vineyard, I take away many of these young and tender branches, and I will graft them whithersoever I will; and it mattereth not that if it so be that the root of this tree will perish, I may preserve the fruit thereof unto myself; wherefore, I will take these young and tender branches, and I will graft them whithersoever I will.
9. Take thou the branches of the wild olive-tree, and graft them in, in the stead thereof; and these which I have plucked off I will cast into the fire and burn them, that they may not cumber the ground of my vineyard.
10. And it came to pass that the servant of the Lord of the vineyard did according to the word of the Lord of the vineyard, and grafted in the branches of the wild olive-tree.
11. And the Lord of the vineyard caused that it should be digged about, and pruned, and nourished, saying unto his servant: It grieveth me that I should lose this tree; wherefore, that perhaps I might preserve the roots thereof that they perish not, that I might preserve them unto myself, I have done this thing.
12. Wherefore, go thy way; watch the tree, and nourish it, according to my words.
13. And these will I place in the nethermost part of my vineyard, whithersoever I will, it mattereth not unto thee; and I do it that I may preserve unto myself the natural branches of the tree; and also, that I may lay up fruit thereof against the season, unto myself; for it grieveth me that I should lose this tree and the fruit thereof.
14. And it came to pass that the Lord of the vineyard went his way, and hid the natural branches of the

Jacob 5

The remarkable allegory or parable of Zenos contained in the fifth chapter of Jacob makes up the longest single chapter in the Book of Mormon. One of the difficulties of the allegory—and of all allegories—is to know how literally it should be interpreted. The dictionary defines an allegory as "the veiled presentation, in a figurative story, of a meaning metaphorically implied but not expressly stated." In other words, an allegory is the description of one thing under the image of another. The images (or symbols) used by Zenos in his allegory together with their possible meanings are as follows:

1. A tame olive tree: this represents the house of Israel.
2. A wild olive tree: this refers to the gentiles—those who are not of the house of Israel by birth.
3. Natural branches of the tame olive tree that are grafted (planted) in the vineyard: these refer to various scatterings of portions of the house of Israel throughout the world.
4. The vineyard: this represents the world.
5. The grafting in of the branches of the wild olive tree into the tame olive tree: this refers to the conversion of the gentiles or the adoption by the gentiles of the covenants of the house of Israel.
6. The master or Lord of the vineyard: this evidently refers to the Lord of the earth—Jesus Christ.
7. The servant: this apparently refers to the prophet of the Lord; perhaps there was a different servant during each of these scatterings and gatherings.

These identical symbols were used by Paul in his letter to the Romans (see Romans 11:17–24), which might indicate Paul was acquainted with the allegory by Zenos. The ten "lost" tribes of Israel and the Lehite and Mulekite colonies could all be included among the various graftings (plantings) of the natural branches of the tame olive tree into the "nethermost part" of the vineyard. The last planting referred to (in Jacob 5:25, 40, 43–44) evidently refers to the Nephite-Lamanite groups that descended from the Lehite colony. (Ludlow)

Jacob 5

The allegory of the olive tree is rich with symbolism, and—as with many allegories—each symbol potentially has multiple meanings. For example, in this allegory, the vineyard may symbolize several different things: the house of Israel, the individual son or daughter of God, or the entire human family. The important factor is not exactly what the vineyard represents, but the repeated diligent efforts of the Lord of the vineyard—our Savior, Jesus Christ—to nourish, cultivate, and protect the trees of the vineyard.

tame olive-tree in the nethermost parts of the vineyard, some in
one and some in another, according to his will and pleasure.
15. And it came to pass that a long time passed away, and the Lord
of the vineyard said unto his servant: Come, let us go down into
the vineyard, that we may labor in the vineyard.
16. And it came to pass that the Lord of the vineyard, and also the
servant, went down into the vineyard to labor. And it came to pass
that the servant said unto his master: Behold, look here; behold
the tree.
17. And it came to pass that the Lord of the vineyard looked and
beheld the tree in the which the wild olive branches had been
grafted; and it had sprung forth and begun to bear fruit. And he
beheld that it was good; and the fruit thereof was like unto the natural fruit.
18. And he said unto the servant: Behold, the branches of the wild
tree have taken hold of the moisture of the root thereof, that the
root thereof hath brought forth much strength; and because of the
much strength of the root thereof the wild branches have brought
forth tame fruit. Now, if we had not grafted in these branches, the
tree thereof would have perished. And now, behold, I shall lay up
much fruit, which the tree thereof hath brought forth; and the fruit
thereof I shall lay up against the season, unto mine own self.
19. And it came to pass that the Lord of the vineyard said unto
the servant: Come, let us go to the nethermost part of the vineyard, and behold if the natural branches of the tree have not
brought forth much fruit also, that I may lay up of the fruit thereof against the season, unto mine own self.
20. And it came to pass that they went forth whither the master
had hid the natural branches of the tree, and he said unto the servant: Behold these; and he beheld the first that it had brought
forth much fruit; and he beheld also that it was good. And he said
unto the servant: Take of the fruit thereof, and lay it up against the
season, that I may preserve it unto mine own self; for behold, said
he, this long time have I nourished it, and it hath brought forth
much fruit.
21. And it came to pass that the servant said unto his master: How
comest thou hither to plant this tree, or this branch of the tree? For
behold, it was the poorest spot in all the land of thy vineyard.
22. And the Lord of the vineyard said unto him: Counsel me not;
I knew that it was a poor spot of ground; wherefore, I said unto
thee, I have nourished it this long time, and thou beholdest that it
hath brought forth much fruit.
23. And it came to pass that the Lord of the vineyard said unto his
servant: Look hither; behold I have planted another branch of the
tree also; and thou knowest that this spot of ground was poorer
than the first. But, behold the tree. I have nourished it this long
time, and it hath brought forth much fruit; therefore, gather it, and
lay it up against the season, that I may preserve it unto mine own
self.
24. And it came to pass that the Lord of the vineyard said again
unto his servant: Look hither, and behold another branch also,
which I have planted; behold that I have nourished it also, and it
hath brought forth fruit.
25. And he said unto the servant: Look hither and behold the last.
Behold, this have I planted in a good spot of ground; and I have

POINT OF INTEREST

Symbolism in Zenos's allegory

Metaphor	Meaning
vineyard	*this world*
master of the vineyard	*Christ*
servant	*prophets and others called to serve*
tame olive tree	*house of Israel*
wild olive tree	*non-Israel or apostate Israel*
top of tree	*Israel's leaders*
branches	*different parts of Israel*
roots	*word of God, including covenants and promises*
fruit	*works and lives*
pruning, digging, dunging	*nurturing Israel*
transplanting	*scattering around the world or restoring to original position*
grafting	*being joined to Israel*
decay	*apostasy*
casting into fire	*God's judgments*

nourished it this long time, and only a part of the tree hath brought forth tame fruit, and the other part of the tree hath brought forth wild fruit; behold, I have nourished this tree like unto the others.

26. And it came to pass that the Lord of the vineyard said unto the servant: Pluck off the branches that have not brought forth good fruit, and cast them into the fire.

27. But behold, the servant said unto him: Let us prune it, and dig about it, and nourish it a little longer, that perhaps it may bring forth good fruit unto thee, that thou canst lay it up against the season.

28. And it came to pass that the Lord of the vineyard and the servant of the Lord of the vineyard did nourish all the fruit of the vineyard.

29. And it came to pass that a long time had passed away, and the Lord of the vineyard said unto his servant: Come, let us go down into the vineyard, that we may labor again in the vineyard. For behold, the time draweth near, and the end soon cometh; wherefore, I must lay up fruit against the season, unto mine own self.

30. And it came to pass that the Lord of the vineyard and the servant went down into the vineyard; and they came to the tree whose natural branches had been broken off, and the wild branches had been grafted in; and behold all sorts of fruit did cumber the tree.

31. And it came to pass that the Lord of the vineyard did taste of the fruit, every sort according to its number. And the Lord of the vineyard said: Behold, this long time have we nourished this tree, and I have laid up unto myself against the season much fruit.

32. But behold, this time it hath brought forth much fruit, and there is none of it which is good. And behold, there are all kinds of bad fruit; and it profiteth me nothing, notwithstanding all our labor; and now it grieveth me that I should lose this tree.

33. And the Lord of the vineyard said unto the servant: What shall we do unto the tree, that I may preserve again good fruit thereof unto mine own self?

34. And the servant said unto his master: Behold, because thou didst graft in the branches of the wild olive-tree they have nourished the roots, that they are alive and they have not perished; wherefore thou beholdest that they are yet good.

35. And it came to pass that the Lord of the vineyard said unto his servant: The tree profiteth me nothing, and the roots thereof profit me nothing so long as it shall bring forth evil fruit.

36. Nevertheless, I know that the roots are good, and for mine own purpose I have preserved them; and because of their much strength they have hitherto brought forth, from the wild branches, good fruit.

37. But behold, the wild branches have grown and have overrun the roots thereof; and because that the wild branches have overcome the roots thereof it hath brought forth much evil fruit; and because that it hath brought forth so much evil fruit thou beholdest that it beginneth to perish; and it will soon become ripened, that it may be cast into the fire, except we should do something for it to preserve it.

38. And it came to pass that the Lord of the vineyard said unto his servant: Let us go down into the nethermost parts of the vineyard, and behold if the natural branches have also brought forth evil fruit.

39. And it came to pass that they

Jacob 5:27

This is an example of prophets pleading our case with the Lord, asking that they be allowed to try longer with us.

Jacob 5:31

The exercise of agency can result in iniquity and apostasy despite the care and attention of loved ones, Church leaders, and the Lord.

POINT OF INTEREST

To appreciate the true miracle and divinity attending the translation of the Book of Mormon, compare its translation to that of the King James Version of the Bible. Fifty British scholars completed their translation of the Bible in seven years, at an average rate of one page per day. In contrast, Joseph Smith—who, though he had scribes, worked alone as the sole translator—finished his translation in eighty-five days at an average rate of ten pages per day. Add to that scenario the fact that Biblical translators were working from Greek text, while Joseph Smith worked from reformed Egyptian hieroglyphics.

went down into the nethermost parts of the vineyard. And it came to pass that they beheld that the fruit of the natural branches had become corrupt also; yea, the first and the second and also the last; and they had all become corrupt.
40. And the wild fruit of the last had overcome that part of the tree which brought forth good fruit, even that the branch had withered away and died.
41. And it came to pass that the Lord of the vineyard wept, and said unto the servant: What could I have done more for my vineyard?
42. Behold, I knew that all the fruit of the vineyard, save it were these, had become corrupted. And now these which have once brought forth good fruit have also become corrupted; and now all the trees of my vineyard are good for nothing save it be to be hewn down and cast into the fire.
43. And behold this last, whose branch hath withered away, I did plant in a good spot of ground; yea, even that which was choice unto me above all other parts of the land of my vineyard.
44. And thou beheldest that I also cut down that which cumbered this spot of ground, that I might plant this tree in the stead thereof.
45. And thou beheldest that a part thereof brought forth good fruit, and a part thereof brought forth wild fruit; and because I plucked not the branches thereof and cast them into the fire, behold, they have overcome the good branch that it hath withered away.
46. And now, behold, notwithstanding all the care which we have taken of my vineyard, the trees thereof have become corrupted, that they bring forth no good fruit; and these I had hoped to preserve, to have laid up fruit thereof against the season, unto mine own self. But, behold, they have become like unto the wild olive-tree, and they are of no worth but to be hewn down and cast into the fire; and it grieveth me that I should lose them.
47. But what could I have done more in my vineyard? Have I slackened mine hand, that I have not nourished it? Nay, I have nourished it, and I have digged about it, and I have pruned it, and I have dunged it; and I have stretched forth mine hand almost all the day long, and the end draweth nigh. And it grieveth me that I should hew down all the trees of my vineyard, and cast them into the fire that they should be burned. Who is it that has corrupted my vineyard?
48. And it came to pass that the servant said unto his master: Is it not the loftiness of thy vineyard—have not the branches thereof overcome the roots which are good? And because the branches have overcome the roots thereof, behold they grew faster than the strength of the roots, taking strength unto themselves. Behold, I say, is not this the cause that the trees of thy vineyard have become corrupted?
49. And it came to pass that the Lord of the vineyard said unto the servant: Let us go to and hew down the trees of the vineyard and cast them into the fire, that they shall not cumber the ground of my vineyard, for I have done all. What could I have done more for my vineyard?
50. But, behold, the servant said unto the Lord of the vineyard: Spare it a little longer.

Jacob 5:47

The source of corruption is pride: We take upon ourselves credit for the good things that happen in our lives. We rely on our own strength and intelligence, forgetting the Lord and His hand in our lives.

51. And the Lord said: Yea, I will spare it a little longer, for it grieveth me that I should lose the trees of my vineyard.
52. Wherefore, let us take of the branches of these which I have
planted in the nethermost parts of my vineyard, and let us graft
them into the tree from whence they came; and let us pluck from
the tree those branches whose fruit is most bitter, and graft in the
natural branches of the tree in the stead thereof.
53. And this will I do that the tree may not perish, that, perhaps,
I may preserve unto myself the roots thereof for mine own purpose.
54. And, behold, the roots of the natural branches of the tree
which I planted whithersoever I would are yet alive; wherefore,
that I may preserve them also for mine own purpose, I will take of
the branches of this tree, and I will graft them in unto them. Yea,
I will graft in unto them the branches of their mother tree, that I
may preserve the roots also unto mine own self, that when they
shall be sufficiently strong perhaps they may bring forth good fruit
unto me, and I may yet have glory in the fruit of my vineyard.
55. And it came to pass that they took from the natural tree which
had become wild, and grafted in unto the natural trees, which also had
become wild.
56. And they also took of the natural trees which had become
wild, and grafted into their mother tree.
57. And the Lord of the vineyard said unto the servant: Pluck not
the wild branches from the trees, save it be those which are most
bitter; and in them ye shall graft according to that which I have
said.
58. And we will nourish again the trees of the vineyard, and we
will trim up the branches thereof; and we will pluck from the trees
those branches which are ripened, that must perish, and cast them
into the fire.
59. And this I do that, perhaps, the roots thereof may take strength
because of their goodness; and because of the change of the
branches, that the good may overcome the evil.
60. And because that I have preserved the natural branches and
the roots thereof, and that I have grafted in the natural branches
again into their mother tree, and have preserved the roots of
their mother tree, that, perhaps, the trees of my vineyard may
bring forth again good fruit; and that I may have joy again in the
fruit of my vineyard, and, perhaps, that I may rejoice exceedingly that I have preserved the roots and the branches of the first
fruit—
61. Wherefore, go to, and call servants, that we may labor diligently with our might in the vineyard, that we may prepare the
way, that I may bring forth again the natural fruit, which natural
fruit is good and the most precious above all other fruit.
62. Wherefore, let us go to and labor with our might this last time,
for behold the end draweth nigh, and this is for the last time that
I shall prune my vineyard.
63. Graft in the branches; begin at the last that they may be first,
and that the first may be last, and dig about the trees, both old and
young, the first and the last; and the last and the first, that all may
be nourished once again for the last time.
64. Wherefore, dig about them,

Jacob 5:52

The grafting described in this verse refers to the gathering of Israel and their being grafted back in to the main body of the Church.

Jacob 5:57

As prophesied in this verse, official Church discipline is now saved for only the most heinous offenses and offenders—those "which are the most bitter."

Jacob 5:62

This verse refers to the living prophets who have led the Church in this, the dispensation of the fulness of times.

and prune them, and dung them once more, for the last time, for
the end draweth nigh. And if it be so that these last grafts shall
grow, and bring forth the natural fruit, then shall ye prepare the
way for them, that they may grow.
65. And as they begin to grow ye shall clear away the branches
which bring forth bitter fruit, according to the strength of the good
and the size thereof; and ye shall not clear away the bad thereof all
at once, lest the roots thereof should be too strong for the graft,
and the graft thereof shall perish, and I lose the trees of my vineyard.
66. For it grieveth me that I should lose the trees of my vineyard;
wherefore ye shall clear away the bad according as the good shall
grow, that the root and the top may be equal in strength, until the
good shall overcome the bad, and the bad be hewn down and cast
into the fire, that they cumber not the ground of my vineyard; and
thus will I sweep away the bad out of my vineyard.
67. And the branches of the natural tree will I graft in again into
the natural tree;
68. And the branches of the natural tree will I graft into the natural branches of the tree; and thus will I bring them together again,
that they shall bring forth the natural fruit, and they shall be one.
69. And the bad shall be cast away, yea, even out of all the land of
my vineyard; for behold, only this once will I prune my vineyard.
70. And it came to pass that the Lord of the vineyard sent his servant; and the servant went and did as the Lord had commanded
him, and brought other servants; and they were few.
71. And the Lord of the vineyard said unto them: Go to, and labor
in the vineyard, with your might. For behold, this is the last time
that I shall nourish my vineyard; for the end is nigh at hand, and
the season speedily cometh; and if ye labor with your might with
me ye shall have joy in the fruit which I shall lay up unto myself
against the time which will soon come.
72. And it came to pass that the servants did go and labor with
their mights; and the Lord of the vineyard labored also with them;
and they did obey the commandments of the Lord of the vineyard
in all things.
73. And there began to be the natural fruit again in the vineyard;
and the natural branches began to grow and thrive exceedingly;
and the wild branches began to be plucked off and to be cast away;
and they did keep the root and the top thereof equal, according to
the strength thereof.
74. And thus they labored, with all diligence, according to the
commandments of the Lord of the vineyard, even until the bad
had been cast away out of the vineyard, and the Lord had preserved
unto himself that the trees had become again the natural fruit; and
they became like unto one body; and the fruits were equal; and the
Lord of the vineyard had preserved unto himself the natural fruit,
which was most precious unto him from the beginning.
75. And it came to pass that when the Lord of the vineyard saw
that his fruit was good, and that his vineyard was no more corrupt,
he called up his servants, and said unto them: Behold, for this last
time have we nourished my vineyard; and thou beholdest that I
have done according to my will; and I have preserved the natural
fruit, that it

Jacob 5:68

When the Savior says He will "bring them together again," He is referring to the gathering of the scattered Jews.

Jacob 5:70

The "servants" referred to in this verse—as well as in verse 61—are the missionaries who teach the gospel throughout the world.

Jacob 5:73

The process described in this verse prophesies about the growth of the righteous in these latter days.

is good, even like as it was in the beginning. And blessed art thou;
for because ye have been diligent in laboring with me in my vineyard, and have kept my commandments, and have brought unto
me again the natural fruit, that my vineyard is no more corrupted,
and the bad is cast away, behold ye shall have joy with me because
of the fruit of my vineyard.
76. For behold, for a long time will I lay up of the fruit of my vineyard unto mine own self against the season, which speedily cometh;
and for the last time have I nourished my vineyard, and pruned it,
and dug about it, and dunged it; wherefore I will lay up unto mine
own self of the fruit, for a long time, according to that which I have
spoken.
77. And when the time cometh that evil fruit shall again come
into my vineyard, then will I cause the good and the bad to be
gathered; and the good will I preserve unto myself, and the bad will
I cast away into its own place. And then cometh the season and
the end; and my vineyard will I cause to be burned with fire.

Jacob 5:76

The "season" referred to in this verse is the millennial reign of the Savior.

Jacob 5:77

This prophecy describes the destruction of evil and the final cleansing of the earth as it is burned in preparation for receiving its celestial glory.

CHAPTER 6

1. AND now, behold, my brethren, as I said unto you that I would
prophesy, behold, this is my prophecy—that the things which this
prophet Zenos spake, concerning the house of Israel, in the which
he likened them unto a tame olive-tree, must surely come to pass.
2. And the day that he shall set his hand again the second time to
recover his people, is the day, yea, even the last time, that the servants of the Lord shall go forth in his power, to nourish and prune
his vineyard; and after that the end soon cometh.
3. And how blessed are they who have labored diligently in his
vineyard; and how cursed are they who shall be cast out into their
own place! And the world shall be burned with fire.
4. And how merciful is our God unto us, for he remembereth the
house of Israel, both roots and branches; and he stretches forth his
hands unto them all the day long; and they are a stiffnecked and a
gainsaying people; but as many as will not harden their hearts shall
be saved in the kingdom of God.
5. Wherefore, my beloved brethren, I beseech of you in
words of soberness that ye would repent, and come with
full purpose of heart, and cleave unto God as he cleaveth
unto you. And while his arm of mercy is extended
towards you in

Jacob 6:4

Found in this verse is powerful and convincing testimony that the Lord loves us and wants to save us.

POINT OF INTEREST

The olive was an important plant in biblical times, and olive trees are frequently mentioned in scripture. Because of all its uses—from the wood to the oil to the fruit—some have considered it the ultimate "tree of life" symbol. Zenos relies on the imagery of olive culture for his famous allegory, related in Jacob 5.

the light of the day, harden not your hearts.
6. Yea, today, if ye will hear his voice, harden not your hearts; for why will ye die?
7. For behold, after ye have been nourished by the good word of God all the day long, will ye bring forth evil fruit, that ye must be hewn down and cast into the fire?
8. Behold, will ye reject these words? Will ye reject the words of the prophets; and will ye reject all the words which have been spoken concerning Christ, after so many have spoken concerning him; and deny the good word of Christ, and the power of God, and the gift of the Holy Ghost, and quench the Holy Spirit, and make a mock of the great plan of redemption, which hath been laid for you?
9. Know ye not that if ye will do these things, that the power of the redemption and the resurrection, which is in Christ, will bring you to stand with shame and awful guilt before the bar of God?
10. And according to the power of justice, for justice cannot be denied, ye must go away into that lake of fire and brimstone, whose flames are unquenchable, and whose smoke ascendeth up forever and ever, which lake of fire and brimstone is endless torment.
11. O then, my beloved brethren, repent ye, and enter in at the strait gate, and continue in the way which is narrow, until ye shall obtain eternal life.
12. O be wise; what can I say more?
13. Finally, I bid you farewell, until I shall meet you before the pleasing bar of God, which bar striketh the wicked with awful dread and fear. Amen.

CHAPTER 7

1. AND now it came to pass after some years had passed away, there came a man among the people of Nephi, whose name was Sherem.
2. And it came to pass that he began to preach among the people, and to declare unto them that there should be no Christ. And he preached many things which were flattering unto the people; and this he did that he might overthrow the doctrine of Christ.
3. And he labored diligently that he might lead away the hearts of the people, insomuch that he did lead away many hearts; and he knowing that I, Jacob, had faith in Christ who should come, he sought much opportunity that he might come unto me.
4. And he was learned, that he had a perfect knowledge of the language of the people; wherefore, he could use much flattery, and much power of speech, according to the power of the devil.
5. And he had hope to shake me from the faith, notwithstanding the many revelations and the many things which I had seen concerning

Jacob 6:7–10

Prophesied in these verses is the fate of those who do not repent and who fail to come unto Christ.

Jacob 7:1

Sherem was willing to believe the teachings of previous prophets, but not those of the living prophet (Jacob).

Jacob 7:1–7

Jacob's concise record ends with an account of his dealings with the anti-Christ Sherem, whose brief ascendancy and sudden defeat represent the first of several such episodes reported in the Book of Mormon concerning those who would flatter the people away into spiritual detours. Against every anti-Christ, there is the ultimate antidote: the indisputable testimony of Christ as evidenced in the scriptures and confirmed through the Holy Ghost (see Jacob 7:11–12). Through the power of God, Sherem's misguided campaign came to naught: "And it came to pass that peace and the love of God was restored again among the people; and they searched the scriptures, and hearkened no more to the words of this wicked man" (Jacob 7:23).

The Lord has a great work for us to do in this the dispensation of the fulness of times.

We are to take the gospel to every nation, kindred, tongue, and people. This is the last time He will set His hand to recover and gather His people. Let us watch and be ready and prepare ourselves against the power of Satan, for he seeks to bring us down to hell.

Let us not be deceived by the sophistries of men, the lusts of the flesh, or anything that takes us away from the gospel of Jesus Christ. These are anti-Christs. The gospel message sounds with clarion echoes: Hold to the iron rod, pray with faith, listen to the Spirit, and follow our living prophets.

We are not involved in a work of the hour, nor in a work of the month or year. We are involved in a work that stretches from the foundations of the earth even until the ushering in of Christ's imminent return and beyond. The scriptures impart to us the divine perspective of how God's plan spans the eternities for the good of mankind. We are the servants in the Lord's vineyard who have the charge to help cultivate, nurture, and harvest the covenant crop. Through faith and diligence we can be wise and honor covenant principles. We can prevail over the pernicious forces of evil that would undermine and discredit the Doctrine of Christ. We can rise valiant and victorious to hear one day the blessed words in the Savior's parable: "Well done, thou good and faithful servant: thou hast been faithful over a few things, I will make thee ruler over many things: enter thou into the joy of thy lord" (Matt. 25:21; cf. Jacob 5:75; D&C 18:16). (P/A)

these things; for I truly had seen angels, and they had ministered unto me. And also, I had heard the voice of the Lord speaking unto me in very word, from time to time; wherefore, I could not be shaken.
6. And it came to pass that he came unto me, and on this wise did he speak unto me, saying: Brother Jacob, I have sought much opportunity that I might speak unto you; for I have heard and also know that thou goest about much, preaching that which ye call the gospel, or the doctrine of Christ.
7. And ye have led away much of this people that they pervert the right way of God, and keep not the law of Moses which is the right way; and convert the law of Moses into the worship of a being which ye say shall come many hundred years hence. And now behold, I, Sherem, declare unto you that this is blasphemy; for no man knoweth of such things; for he cannot tell of things to come. And after this manner did Sherem contend against me.
8. But behold, the Lord God poured in his Spirit into my soul, insomuch that I did confound him in all his words.
9. And I said unto him: Deniest thou the Christ who shall come? And he said: If there should be a Christ, I would not deny him; but I know that there is no Christ, neither has been, nor ever will be.
10. And I said unto him: Believest thou the scriptures? And he said, Yea.
11. And I said unto him: Then ye do not understand them; for they truly testify of Christ. Behold, I say unto you that none of the prophets have written, nor prophesied, save they have spoken concerning this Christ.
12. And this is not all—it has been made manifest unto me, for I have heard and seen; and it also has been made manifest unto me by the power of the Holy Ghost; wherefore, I know if there should be no atonement made all mankind must be lost.
13. And it came to pass that he said unto me: Show me a sign by this power of the Holy Ghost, in the which ye know so much.
14. And I said unto him: What am I that I should tempt God to show unto thee a sign in the thing which thou knowest to be true? Yet thou wilt deny it, because thou art of the devil. Nevertheless, not my will be done; but if God shall smite thee, let that be a sign unto thee that he has power, both in heaven and in earth; and also, that Christ shall come. And thy will, O Lord, be done, and not mine.
15. And it came to pass that when I, Jacob, had spoken these words, the power of the Lord came upon him, insomuch that he fell to the earth. And it came to pass that he was nourished for the space of many days.
16. And it came to pass that he said unto the people: Gather together on the morrow, for I shall die; wherefore, I desire to speak unto the people before I shall die.
17. And it came to pass that on the morrow the multitude were gathered together; and he spake plainly unto them and denied the things which he had taught them, and confessed the Christ, and the power

Jacob 7:1–20

Sherem is one of the first avowed anti-Christs in the Book of Mormon. It might be profitable, therefore, to review his teachings, because later anti-Christs (Nehor, Korihor, etc.) teach essentially these same things. Sherem (1) preached those things which were flattering unto the people (Jacob 7:2); (2) claimed that no man can tell of things to come (Jacob 7:7); (3) claimed to believe in the scriptures, but clearly did not understand them (Jacob 7:10–11); (4) denied the existence of Christ (Jacob 7:9); (5) would not accept evidence unless it could be perceived through the physical senses, and thus asked for a sign he could feel (Jacob 7:13). (Ludlow)

Jacob 7:13

Signs always *follow* belief in the true gospel and are not provided to convince or convert; seeking of signs for this purpose is evidence of gross wickedness. It is important, though, that we not confuse signs and gifts of the Spirit. Elder Bruce R. McConkie encouraged us to seek the gifts of the Spirit through faith, humility, and devotion to righteousness—a process that it not to be confused with sign-seeking.

of the Holy Ghost, and the ministering of angels.
18. And he spake plainly unto them, that he had been deceived by the power of the devil. And he spake of hell, and of eternity, and of eternal punishment.
19. And he said: I fear lest I have committed the unpardonable sin, for I have lied unto God; for I denied the Christ, and said that I believed the scriptures; and they truly testify of him. And because I have thus lied unto God I greatly fear lest my case shall be awful; but I confess unto God.
20. And it came to pass that when he had said these words he could say no more, and he gave up the ghost.
21. And when the multitude had witnessed that he spake these things as he was about to give up the ghost, they were astonished exceedingly; insomuch that the power of God came down upon them, and they were overcome that they fell to the earth.
22. Now, this thing was pleasing unto me, Jacob, for I had requested it of my Father who was in heaven; for he had heard my cry and answered my prayer.
23. And it came to pass that peace and the love of God was restored again among the people; and they searched the scriptures, and hearkened no more to the words of this wicked man.
24. And it came to pass that many means were devised to reclaim and restore the Lamanites to the knowledge of the truth; but it all was vain, for they delighted in wars and bloodshed, and they had an eternal hatred against us, their brethren. And they sought by the power of their arms to destroy us continually.
25. Wherefore, the people of Nephi did fortify against them with their arms, and with all their might, trusting in the God and rock of their salvation; wherefore, they became as yet, conquerors of their enemies.
26. And it came to pass that I, Jacob, began to be old; and the record of this people being kept on the other plates of Nephi, wherefore, I conclude this record, declaring that I have written according to the best of my knowledge, by saying that the time passed away with us, and also our lives passed away like as it were unto us a dream, we being a lonesome and a solemn people, wanderers, cast out from Jerusalem, born in tribulation, in a wilderness, and hated of our brethren, which caused wars and contentions; wherefore, we did mourn out our days.
27. And I, Jacob, saw that I must soon go down to my grave; wherefore, I said unto my son Enos: Take these plates. And I told him the things which my brother Nephi had commanded me, and he promised obedience unto the commands. And I make an end of my writing upon these plates, which writing has been small; and to the reader I bid farewell, hoping that many of my brethren may read my words. Brethren, adieu.

Jacob 7:19

When Sherem admitted he had been deceived by the devil, he feared lest he had committed "the unpardonable sin," for he had lied unto God and had denied the Christ. Although it is not clear in the Book of Mormon whether or not Sherem was guilty of committing the unpardonable sin, the Lord has explained in other scriptures the characteristics of those who do commit this sin. [See D&C 76:31–37.] . . . Orson Pratt has explained the meaning of the term "second death," which is used in this scripture and which comes upon the sons of perdition:

> Second death, what is that? After you have been redeemed from the grave, and come into the presence of God, you will have to stand there to be judged; and if you have done evil, you will be banished everlastingly from His presence—body and spirit united together; this is what is called the second death. Why is it called the second death? Because the first is the dissolution of body and spirit, and the second is . . . a banishment—a becoming dead to the things of righteousness . . . (*Journal of Discourses*, 1:288). (Ludlow)

Jacob 7:27

Some anti-LDS critics of the Book of Mormon have raised the question as to how Jacob could possibly have used such a word as *adieu* when this word clearly comes from the French language, which was not developed until hundreds of years after the time of Jacob. Such critics evidently overlook the fact that the Book of Mormon is translation literature, and Joseph Smith felt free in his translation to use any words familiar to himself and his readers that would best convey the meaning of the original author. It is interesting to note that there is a Hebrew word *Lehitra 'ot*, which has essentially the same meaning in Hebrew as the word *adieu* has in French. Both of these words are much more than a simple farewell; they include the idea of a blessing. Would it be unreasonable to remind these critics that *none of the words* contained in the English translation of the book of Jacob were used by Jacob himself? These words all come from the English language, which did not come into existence until long after Jacob's time! (Ludlow)

THE BOOK OF ENOS

1. BEHOLD, it came to pass that I, Enos, knowing my father that he was a just man—for he taught me in his language, and also in the nurture and admonition of the Lord—and blessed be the name of my God for it—

2. And I will tell you of the wrestle which I had before God, before I received a remission of my sins.

3. Behold, I went to hunt beasts in the forests; and the words which I had often heard my father speak concerning eternal life, and the joy of the saints, sunk deep into my heart.

4. And my soul hungered; and I kneeled down before my Maker, and I cried unto him in mighty prayer and supplication for mine own soul; and all the day long did I cry unto him; yea, and when the night came I did still raise my voice high that it reached the heavens.

5. And there came a voice unto me, saying: Enos, thy sins are forgiven thee, and thou shalt be blessed.

6. And I, Enos, knew that God could not lie; wherefore, my guilt was swept away.

7. And I said: Lord, how is it done?

8. And he said unto me: Because of thy faith in Christ, whom thou hast never before heard nor seen. And many years pass away before he shall manifest himself in the flesh; wherefore, go to, thy faith hath made thee whole.

9. Now, it came to pass that when I had heard these words I began to feel a desire for the welfare of my brethren, the Nephites; wherefore, I did pour out my whole soul unto God for them.

10. And while I was thus struggling in the spirit, behold, the voice of the Lord came into my mind again, saying: I will visit thy brethren according to their diligence in keeping my commandments. I have given unto them this land, and it is a holy land; and I curse it not save it be for the cause of iniquity; wherefore, I will visit thy brethren according as I have said; and their transgressions will I bring down with sorrow upon their own heads.

11. And after I, Enos, had heard these words, my faith began to be unshaken in the Lord; and I prayed unto him with many long

Enos 1:1–10

Although small in number of verses, the book of Enos teaches some important concepts. For example, Enos tells us something concerning one way in which revelation can be received when he says "there came a voice unto me, saying" (verse 5) and "the voice of the Lord came into my mind again, saying" (verse 10). Concerning this type of revelation, President Harold B. Lee said:

Another way by which we receive revelation is the way that the Prophet Enos spoke of. After he'd gone up and received the great commission to carry on the work and to write the record, he pens this very significant statement in his record in the Book of Mormon. "And while I was thus struggling in the spirit, the voice of the Lord came into my mind saying—." In other words, sometimes we hear the voice of the Lord coming into our minds and when it comes the impressions are just as strong as though he were talking as with a trumpet into our ear. . . . (Ludlow)

strugglings for my brethren, the Lamanites.
12. And it came to pass that after I had prayed and labored with all diligence, the Lord said unto me: I will grant unto thee according to thy desires, because of thy faith.
13. And now behold, this was the desire which I desired of him—that if it should so be, that my people, the Nephites, should fall into transgression, and by any means be destroyed, and the Lamanites should not be destroyed, that the Lord God would preserve a record of my people, the Nephites; even if it so be by the power of his holy arm, that it might be brought forth at some future day unto the Lamanites, that, perhaps, they might be brought unto salvation—
14. For at the present our strugglings were vain in restoring them to the true faith. And they swore in their wrath that, if it were possible, they would destroy our records and us, and also all the traditions of our fathers.
15. Wherefore, I knowing that the Lord God was able to preserve our records, I cried unto him continually, for he had said unto me: Whatsoever thing ye shall ask in faith, believing that ye shall receive in the name of Christ, ye shall receive it.
16. And I had faith, and I did cry unto God that he would preserve the records; and he covenanted with me that he would bring them forth unto the Lamanites in his own due time.
17. And I, Enos, knew it would be according to the covenant which he had made; wherefore my soul did rest.
18. And the Lord said unto me: Thy fathers have also required of me this thing; and it shall be done unto them according to their faith; for their faith was like unto thine.
19. And now it came to pass that I, Enos, went about among the people of Nephi, prophesying of things to come, and testifying of the things which I had heard and seen.
20. And I bear record that the people of Nephi did seek diligently to restore the Lamanites unto the true faith in God. But our labors were vain; their hatred was fixed, and they were led by their evil nature that they became wild, and ferocious, and a blood-thirsty people, full of idolatry and filthiness; feeding upon beasts of prey; dwelling in tents, and wandering about in the wilderness with a short skin girdle about their loins and their heads shaven; and their skill was in the bow, and in the cimeter, and the ax. And many of them did eat nothing save it was raw meat; and they were continually seeking to destroy us.
21. And it came to pass that the people of Nephi did till the land, and raise all manner of grain, and of fruit, and flocks of herds, and flocks of all manner of cattle of every kind, and goats, and wild goats, and also many horses.
22. And there were exceedingly

Enos 1:5, 10

The type of spiritual communication experienced by Enos is difficult—if not impossible—to describe. These kinds of communications generally are not heard with our ears or seen with our eyes. More often than not, they are felt by the heart.

Enos 1:11–18

Another important principle taught in the book of Enos is that the Lord will keep all the covenants he has made with his people. In verse 16, Enos tells us that the Lord covenanted with him that the records of the Nephites would come forth unto the Lamanites in the Lord's own due time. . . .

And, if they (the saints) will exercise their faith aright, there is no good thing, which they can desire, that will be withheld from them. Because you do not get all your prayers answered and your desires granted immediately, you must not therefore be disheartened. Remember the instruction upon this point imparted by Jesus through the parable of the importunate widow, and remember, also, that though your prayers may not be answered immediately, if they are offered in the name of Jesus and in faith, nothing being left undone by you that is required, they will live on the records of heaven and in the remembrance of the Lord, and yet bear fruit. The ancient fathers asked for blessings in their prayers, which are even now being granted—thousands of years after the death of their mortal bodies. And many centuries ago the servants of the Lord among the Nephites made known to the Lord the desires of their hearts respecting their brethren in their prayers, and they yet await their fulfilment; but they know the promise of the Lord is sure and cannot fail. . . . Though heaven and earth pass away, not one word that the Lord has spoken, not one promise that he has made, can pass away or remain unfulfilled. If they have waited thus patiently for the fulfilment of their prayers, cannot we, if necessary, do so also? (*Millennial Star*, 25:74–75.) (Ludlow)

many prophets among us. And the people were a stiffnecked people, hard to understand.

23. And there was nothing save it was exceeding harshness, preaching and prophesying of wars, and contentions, and destructions, and continually reminding them of death, and the duration of eternity, and the judgments and the power of God, and all these things—stirring them up continually to keep them in the fear of the Lord. I say there was nothing short of these things, and exceedingly great plainness of speech, would keep them from going down speedily to destruction. And after this manner do I write concerning them.

24. And I saw wars between the Nephites and Lamanites in the course of my days.

25. And it came to pass that I began to be old, and an hundred and seventy and nine years had passed away from the time that our father Lehi left Jerusalem.

26. And I saw that I must soon go down to my grave, having been wrought upon by the power of God that I must preach and prophesy unto this people, and declare the word according to the truth which is in Christ. And I have declared it in all my days, and have rejoiced in it above that of the world.

27. And I soon go to the place of my rest, which is with my Redeemer; for I know that in him I shall rest. And I rejoice in the day when my mortal shall put on immortality, and shall stand before him; then shall I see his face with pleasure, and he will say unto me: Come unto me, ye blessed, there is a place prepared for you in the mansions of my Father. Amen.

THE BOOK OF JAROM

1. NOW behold, I, Jarom, write a few words according to the commandment of my father, Enos, that our genealogy may be kept.

2. And as these plates are small, and as these things are written for the intent of the benefit of our brethren the Lamanites, wherefore, it must needs be that I write a little; but I shall not write the things of my prophesying, nor of my revelations. For what could I write more than my fathers have written? For have not they revealed the plan of salvation? I say unto you, Yea; and this sufficeth me.

3. Behold, it is expedient that much

Enos 1:27

This verse describes the reward for Enos (and all of us) for a life of righteousness—he could look forward with joy to seeing Christ instead of feeling fear and dread over sins not repented of.

Jarom 1:2

The writers of the Book of Mormon clearly understood that their writings were going to benefit the Lamanites and their descendants more than their own descendants. (Enos 11–17; Jarom 2.) Yet many of the writers continued with their recording efforts even during periods when the Lamanites were their bitter enemies. (Enos 20; Jarom 6–7; Mormon 2:2–3, 17–18.) (Ludlow)

POINT OF INTEREST

The ruins of Monte Albán, below, represent the first major city in the western hemisphere and the center of a Zapotec state that dominated much of what is now Oaxaca, Mexico. Archaeological evidence includes buildings, ball courts, elaborate tombs, and grave goods.

should be done among this people, because of the hardness of their hearts, and the deafness of their ears, and the blindness of their minds, and the stiffness of their necks; nevertheless, God is exceedingly merciful unto them, and has not as yet swept them off from the face of the land.
4. And there are many among us who have many revelations, for they are not all stiffnecked. And as many as are not stiffnecked and have faith, have communion with the Holy Spirit, which maketh manifest unto the children of men, according to their faith.
5. And now, behold, two hundred years had passed away, and the people of Nephi had waxed strong in the land. They observed to keep the law of Moses and the sabbath day holy unto the Lord. And they profaned not; neither did they blaspheme. And the laws of the land were exceedingly strict.
6. And they were scattered upon much of the face of the land, and the Lamanites also. And they were exceedingly more numerous than were they of the Nephites; and they loved murder and would drink the blood of beasts.
7. And it came to pass that they came many times against us, the Nephites, to battle. But our kings and our leaders were mighty men in the faith of the Lord; and they taught the people the ways of the Lord; wherefore, we withstood the Lamanites and swept them away out of our lands, and began to fortify our cities, or whatsoever place of our inheritance.
8. And we multiplied exceedingly, and spread upon the face of the land, and became exceedingly rich in gold, and in silver, and in precious things, and in fine workmanship of wood, in buildings, and in machinery, and also in iron and copper, and brass and steel, making all manner of tools of every kind to till the ground, and weapons of war—yea, the sharp pointed arrow, and the quiver, and the dart, and the javelin, and all preparations for war.
9. And thus being prepared to meet the Lamanites, they did not prosper against us. But the word of the Lord was verified, which he spake unto our fathers, saying that: Inasmuch as ye will keep my commandments ye shall prosper in the land.
10. And it came to pass that the prophets of the Lord did threaten the people of Nephi, according to the word of God, that if they did not keep the commandments, but should fall into transgression, they should be destroyed from off the face of the land.
11. Wherefore, the prophets, and the priests, and the teachers, did labor diligently, exhorting with all long-suffering the people to diligence; teaching the law of Moses, and the intent for which it was given; persuading them to look forward unto the Messiah, and believe in him to come as though he already

Jarom 1:4

This verse describes the key qualities of spiritual people: they have faith and they are not proud. It also gives strong indication that there was a solid group of believers despite the many who had apostatized.

Jarom 1:8

Jarom's statement that in his days the Nephites had become skilled in "fine workmanship of wood, in buildings, and in machinery, and also in iron and copper, and brass and steel, making all manner of tools of every kind to till the ground, and weapons of war" would seem to indicate a very high state of civilization among these people of the fourth century B.C. Interestingly enough, archaeologists are now uncovering evidence from this time period that tends to verify this high state of civilization. Indeed, some archaeologists have now admitted that these people had some skills that we do not possess today. (Ludlow)

Jarom's description of this advanced civilization contrasts with the rural, pastoral society that existed in his father's day.

Jarom 1:11

Described here is the extremely effective teaching method used by the prophets. This verse also contains a challenge to the people of Jarom's day to believe in the Savior as if He had already come. In a similar challenge for us, how different would our lives be if we lived as though the Second Coming were already here?

was. And after this manner did they teach them.

12. And it came to pass that by so doing they kept them from being destroyed upon the face of the land; for they did prick their hearts with the word, continually stirring them up unto repentance.

13. And it came to pass that two hundred and thirty and eight years had passed away—after the manner of wars, and contentions, and dissensions, for the space of much of the time.

14. And I, Jarom, do not write more, for the plates are small. But behold, my brethren, ye can go to the other plates of Nephi; for behold, upon them the records of our wars are engraven, according to the writings of the kings, or those which they caused to be written.

15. And I deliver these plates into the hands of my son Omni, that they may be kept according to the commandments of my fathers.

THE BOOK OF OMNI

1. BEHOLD, it came to pass that I, Omni, being commanded by my father, Jarom, that I should write somewhat upon these plates, to preserve our genealogy—

2. Wherefore, in my days, I would that ye should know that I fought much with the sword to preserve my people, the Nephites, from falling into the hands of their enemies, the Lamanites. But behold, I of myself am a wicked man, and I have not kept the statutes and the commandments of the Lord as I ought to have done.

3. And it came to pass that two hundred and seventy and six years had passed away, and we had many seasons of peace; and we had many seasons of serious war and bloodshed. Yea, and in fine, two hundred and eighty and two years had passed away, and I had kept these plates according to the commandments of my fathers; and I conferred them upon my son Amaron. And I make an end.

4. And now I, Amaron, write the things whatsoever I write, which are few, in the book of my father.

5. Behold, it came to pass that three hundred and twenty years had passed away, and the more wicked part of the Nephites were destroyed.

6. For the Lord would not suffer, after he had led them out of the land of Jerusalem and kept and preserved them from falling into the hands of their enemies, yea, he would not suffer that the words should not be

Omni 1:1–3, 4–8, 9, 10–11, 12–30

The first five books in our present Book of Mormon (1 Nephi, 2 Nephi, Jacob, Enos, and Jarom) comprise 129 pages, cover a period of approximately 239 years, and are written by four men. The brief book of Omni comprises less than three pages, covers a possible time period of 231 years, and is written by five different writers.

Although some of the five writers in the book of Omni attempt to explain why their writings are not more extensive, perhaps we should examine again the purpose of the small plates of Nephi and then relate this purpose to the reasons given by these men. The small plates of Nephi were to contain the religious history of the Nephite people. Thus the record on these plates primarily consisted of the prophecies and religious teachings of the Nephite leaders. The fact that the writings of five men occupy such a small segment as the book of Omni would indicate this was a period of great apostasy—thus there were no new prophecies or religious teachings to be added to the record.

The first three verses in this book were written by Omni, and he admits he was a wicked man. Verses 4–8 were written by Amaron, who states that the "more wicked part of the Nephites were destroyed" because of the judgments of God; this statement also indicates a period of apostasy and wickedness. The next writer, Chemish, wrote only one verse. Abinadom, the son of Chemish, wrote twice as much as his father—two verses! In these verses Abinadom states that he knows of no revelation nor prophecy except those that were written (verse 11); again this would indicate a period of great apostasy and wickedness. The final 19 verses (verses 12–30) were written by Amaleki, the son of Abinadom. His writings also indicate that he lived in a time of apostasy; in fact, it was during his lifetime that the Lord warned Mosiah to lead a small righteous group of people away from the wicked Nephites. (Ludlow)

verified, which he spake unto our fathers, saying that: Inasmuch as ye will not keep my commandments ye shall not prosper in the land.
7. Wherefore, the Lord did visit them in great judgment; nevertheless, he did spare the righteous that they should not perish, but did deliver them out of the hands of their enemies.
8. And it came to pass that I did deliver the plates unto my brother Chemish.
9. Now I, Chemish, write what few things I write, in the same book with my brother; for behold, I saw the last which he wrote, that he wrote it with his own hand; and he wrote it in the day that he delivered them unto me. And after this manner we keep the records, for it is according to the commandments of our fathers. And I make an end.
10. Behold, I, Abinadom, am the son of Chemish. Behold, it came to pass that I saw much war and contention between my people, the Nephites, and the Lamanites; and I, with my own sword, have taken the lives of many of the Lamanites in the defence of my brethren.
11. And behold, the record of this people is engraven upon plates which is had by the kings, according to the generations; and I know of no revelation save that which has been written, neither prophecy; wherefore, that which is sufficient is written. And I make an end.
12. Behold, I am Amaleki, the son of Abinadom. Behold, I will speak unto you somewhat concerning Mosiah, who was made king over the land of Zarahemla; for behold, he being warned of the Lord that he should flee out of the land of Nephi, and as many as would hearken unto the voice of the Lord should also depart out of the land with him, into the wilderness—
13. And it came to pass that he did according as the Lord had commanded him. And they departed out of the land into the wilderness, as many as would hearken unto the voice of the Lord; and they were led by many preachings and prophesyings. And they were admonished continually by the word of God; and they were led by the power of his arm, through the wilderness until they came down into the land which is called the land of Zarahemla.
14. And they discovered a people, who were called the people of Zarahemla. Now, there was great rejoicing among the people of Zarahemla; and also Zarahemla did rejoice exceedingly, because the Lord had sent the people of Mosiah with the plates of brass which contained the record of the Jews.
15. Behold, it came to pass that Mosiah discovered that the people of Zarahemla came out from Jerusalem at the time that Zedekiah, king of Judah, was carried away captive into Babylon.
16. And they journeyed in the wilderness, and were brought by the hand of the Lord across the great waters, into the land where Mosiah discovered them; and they had dwelt there from that time forth.
17. And at the time that Mosiah discovered them, they had become exceedingly numerous. Nevertheless, they had had many wars and serious contentions, and had fallen by the sword from time to time; and

Omni 1:10–11

The men listed here did not add to the record, but they did bless us by keeping the records safe.

Omni 1:12–19

Most Latter-day Saints refer to the people of Zarahemla as the "Mulekites," although the word *Mulekite* does not appear a single time in the Book of Mormon. The people of Zarahemla were descendants of a colony of people who left Jerusalem about 589 B.C. at the time of the Babylonian captivity. (Omni 15.) Included in this colony was Mulek (the ancestor of Zarahemla and one of the sons of Zedekiah, the king of Judah—Mosiah 25:2 and Helaman 8:21). Inasmuch as only descendants of Judah could serve as the rulers of the kingdom of Judah, Mulek and his descendants were of the tribe of Judah. Of course, representatives of some of the other tribes of Israel might have been included among the people of Zarahemla.

It is interesting to note that although the progenitors of Mosiah's group and of the people of Zarahemla left Jerusalem within about twelve years of each other, and evidently spoke the same language then, yet about four hundred years later their descendants could not even understand each other. The reason for this is that the language of the people of Zarahemla "had become corrupted" because they "had brought no records with them; and they denied the being of their Creator." (Omni 17.) Thus the earlier counsel to Nephi seems to be substantiated that "it is better that one man should perish" in order to obtain records and scriptures than "that a nation should dwindle and perish in unbelief" (1 Nephi 4:13). (Ludlow)

Omni 1:13, 27, 28

The concept of going "up" when you go north and of going "down" when you go south is of relatively recent origin, and thus was not used by the Nephites. When the Nephites stated they went from Nephi down to Zarahemla, they were referring to elevation and not to direction. Zarahemla was definitely lower in elevation than Nephi because the river Sidon had its head in the land of Nephi but flowed down through the center of the land of Zarahemla (Alma 16:6–7; 22:27–29). (Ludlow)

their language had become corrupted; and they had brought no records with them; and they denied the being of their Creator; and Mosiah, nor the people of Mosiah, could understand them.
18. But it came to pass that Mosiah caused that they should be taught in his language. And it came to pass that after they were taught in the language of Mosiah, Zarahemla gave a genealogy of his fathers, according to his memory; and they are written, but not in these plates.
19. And it came to pass that the people of Zarahemla, and of Mosiah, did unite together; and Mosiah was appointed to be their king.
20. And it came to pass in the days of Mosiah, there was a large stone brought unto him with engravings on it; and he did interpret the engravings by the gift and power of God.
21. And they gave an account of one Coriantumr, and the slain of his people. And Coriantumr was discovered by the people of Zarahemla; and he dwelt with them for the space of nine moons.
22. It also spake a few words concerning his fathers. And his first parents came out from the tower, at the time the Lord confounded the language of the people; and the severity of the Lord fell upon them according to his judgments, which are just; and their bones lay scattered in the land northward.
23. Behold, I, Amaleki, was born in the days of Mosiah; and I have lived to see his death; and Benjamin, his son, reigneth in his stead.
24. And behold, I have seen, in the days of king Benjamin, a serious war and much bloodshed between the Nephites and the Lamanites. But behold, the Nephites did obtain much advantage over them; yea, insomuch that king Benjamin did drive them out of the land of Zarahemla.
25. And it came to pass that I began to be old; and, having no seed, and knowing king Benjamin to be a just man before the Lord, wherefore, I shall deliver up these plates unto him, exhorting all men to come unto God, the Holy One of Israel, and believe in prophesying, and in revelations, and in the ministering of angels, and in the gift of speaking with tongues, and in the gift of interpreting languages, and in all things which are good; for there is nothing which is good save it comes from the Lord: and that which is evil cometh from the devil.
26. And now, my beloved brethren, I would that ye should come unto Christ, who is the Holy One of Israel, and partake of his salvation, and the power of his redemption. Yea, come unto him, and offer your whole souls as an offering unto him, and continue in fasting and praying, and endure to the end; and as the Lord liveth ye will be saved.
27. And now I would speak somewhat concerning a certain number who went up into the wilderness to return to the land of Nephi; for there was a large number who were desirous to possess the land of their inheritance.
28. Wherefore, they went up into

Omni 1:20–22

The Coriantumr who lived with the people of Zarahemla for a short period was the last military leader of the Jaredite nation. (Ether 12:1; 13:20–22.) The Book of Mormon does not specifically state when Coriantumr lived with the people of Zarahemla, but it would have to be sometime after 589 B.C. (when the colony of Mulek first left Jerusalem) and before about 200 B.C. (when Mosiah and his group first came into the land of Zarahemla). The twentieth verse of Omni tells of a large stone that was brought to Mosiah and which contained an account of Coriantumr. However, this does not necessarily indicate that Coriantumr was still alive in the days of Mosiah; his stay of "nine moons" among the people of Zarahemla could have occurred decades or even centuries before the time of Mosiah (Ludlow)

Omni 1:25, 30

The first 132 pages in the current edition of the Book of Mormon came from the first-person account of the nine writers on the small plates of Nephi. These writers were Nephi, Jacob, Enos, Jarom, Omni, Amaron, Chemish, Abinadom, and Amaleki. Inasmuch as Amaleki did not have any children to whom he could give the plates, he delivered them to King Benjamin (Omni 25). Thus the same man, King Benjamin, came into control of both the small plates of Nephi and the large plates of Nephi, and apparently he decided to discontinue the small plates. Mormon did not abridge the writings on the small plates of Nephi; in fact, he had virtually nothing to do with these plates except that he put them "with the remainder" of his records (Words of Mormon 5–6). (Ludlow)

the wilderness. And their leader being a strong and mighty man, and a stiffnecked man, wherefore he caused a contention among them; and they were all slain, save fifty, in the wilderness, and they returned again to the land of Zarahemla.
29. And it came to pass that they also took others to a considerable number, and took their journey again into the wilderness.
30. And I, Amaleki, had a brother, who also went with them; and I have not since known concerning them. And I am about to lie down in my grave; and these plates are full. And I make an end of my speaking.

THE WORDS OF MORMON

1. AND now I, Mormon, being about to deliver up the record which I have been making into the hands of my son Moroni, behold I have witnessed almost all the destruction of my people, the Nephites.
2. And it is many hundred years after the coming of Christ that I deliver these records into the hands of my son; and it supposeth me that he will witness the entire destruction of my people. But may God grant that he may survive them, that he may write somewhat concerning them, and somewhat concerning Christ, that perhaps some day it may profit them.
3. And now, I speak somewhat concerning that which I have written; for after I had made an abridgment from the plates of Nephi, down to the reign of this king Benjamin, of whom Amaleki spake, I searched among the records which had been delivered into my hands, and I found these plates, which contained this small account of the prophets, from Jacob down to the reign of this king Benjamin, and also many of the words of Nephi.
4. And the things which are upon these plates pleasing me, because of the prophecies of the coming of Christ; and my fathers knowing that many of them have been fulfilled; yea, and I also know that as many things as have been prophesied concerning us down to this day have been fulfilled, and as many as go beyond this day must surely come to pass—
5. Wherefore, I chose these things, to finish my record upon them, which remainder of my record I shall take from the plates of Nephi; and I cannot write the hundredth part of the things of my people.
6. But behold, I shall take these

Words of Mormon

The writings on the small plates of Nephi did not give an account of the early reign of King Benjamin. In order for the writings on the small plates to coincide, time wise, with the writings on the large plates of Nephi, Mormon gave a small account of the early life of King Benjamin. The Words of Mormon is a connecting bridge of the two records. Why did Mormon choose to give two accounts of Nephite history down to the reign of King Benjamin? There are two reasons that we know. First: The Lord inspired Mormon to include the small plates of Nephi with his abridgement. (See Words of Mormon 1:7.) Second: Joseph Smith began his translation of the Book of Mormon from Mormon's abridgment of the large plates of Nephi. Martin Harris was given permission to take the first 116 pages of the translation to his home for his wife and a few others to read. They were stolen by conspiring men who altered the words in an attempt to destroy Joseph Smith's claim to divine revelation. The Lord's enemies intended to wait for Joseph Smith to retranslate and publish what they had stolen. Then they would bring forth their altered version of the original translation and claim Joseph was a false prophet. The Lord directed Joseph Smith to translate the small plates of Nephi, covering the same period of Nephite history, rather than retranslate Mormons' abridgement of the large plates of Nephi. (See D&C 10:8–23, 34–35.) (O/C)

Words of Mormon 1:5–6, 9–18

In verse 5, Mormon mentions that he is going to finish his record upon "these things" and that he will take the remainder of his record "from the plates of Nephi." Several questions have been raised concerning this brief verse by Mormon: (1) First of all, to what is he referring when he states he is going to finish *his record*? (2) To what plates is he referring when he says he will finish his record upon *these things*? (3) To what section of his writings is he referring when he talks of the *remainder* of his record?

Most Book of Mormon scholars have assumed that when Mormon refers to finishing "his record" he had in mind the rest of his writings in the small section entitled The Words of Mormon. Most scholars also assume that "these things" refer to the small plates of Nephi. If this interpretation is correct, then the section entitled The Words of Mormon was written at the end of the small plates of Nephi. According to these scholars, the fact that Amaleki says the small plates of Nephi are already full (Omni 30) does not necessarily rule out the possibility of adding the brief notes that make up The Words of Mormon.

Mormon's reference to the "remainder" of his record is a little more confusing. Some scholars believe that here Mormon is referring to the rest of his writings in The Words of Mormon, the ideas of which he obtained from the large plates of Nephi. Other scholars, however, believe that Mormon is referring to that portion of his abridgment from the large plates of Nephi which he has not yet written on his plates of Mormon. Unfortunately, the pronoun reference in verse 5 does not make it possible to determine Mormon's meaning exactly (Ludlow).

plates, which contain these prophesyings and revelations, and put
them with the remainder of my record, for they are choice unto
me; and I know they will be choice unto my brethren.
7. And I do this for a wise purpose; for thus it whispereth me,
according to the workings of the Spirit of the Lord which is in me.
And now, I do not know all things; but the Lord knoweth all things
which are to come; wherefore, he worketh in me to do according
to his will.
8. And my prayer to God is concerning my brethren, that they may
once again come to the knowledge of God, yea, the redemption of
Christ; that they may once again be a delightsome people.
9. And now I, Mormon, proceed to finish out my record, which I
take from the plates of Nephi; and I make it according to the
knowledge and the understanding which God has given me.
10. Wherefore, it came to pass that after Amaleki had delivered up
these plates into the hands of king Benjamin, he took them and
put them with the other plates, which contained records which
had been handed down by the kings, from generation to generation until the days of king Benjamin.
11. And they were handed down from king Benjamin, from generation to generation until they have fallen into my hands. And I,
Mormon, pray to God that they may be preserved from this time
henceforth. And I know that they will be preserved; for there are
great things written upon them, out of which my people and their
brethren shall be judged at the great and last day, according to the
word of God which is written.
12. And now, concerning this king Benjamin—he had somewhat
of contentions among his own people.
13. And it came to pass also that the armies of the Lamanites came
down out of the land of Nephi, to battle against his people. But
behold, king Benjamin gathered together his armies, and he did
stand against them; and he did fight with the strength of his own
arm, with the sword of Laban.
14. And in the strength of the Lord they did contend against their
enemies, until they had slain many thousands of the Lamanites.
And it came to pass that they did contend against the Lamanites
until they had driven them out of all the lands of their inheritance.
15. And it came to pass that after there had been false Christs, and
their mouths had been shut, and they punished according to their
crimes;
16. And after there had been false prophets, and false preachers
and teachers among the people, and all these having been punished according to their crimes; and after there having been much
contention and many dissensions away unto the Lamanites,
behold, it came to pass that king Benjamin, with the assistance of
the holy prophets who were among his people—
17. For behold, king Benjamin was

Words of Mormon 1:5–7

Several times throughout the Book of Mormon we are told that the small plates of Nephi were created "for a wise purpose." The first thing that comes to mind, of course, is the fact that 116 pages of manuscript taken from the large plates were lost, and the Lord knew ahead of time that such would be the case. But Elder Jeffrey R. Holland suggested that perhaps a greater purpose of the small plates was to provide a platform for three great witnesses—Nephi, Jacob, and Isaiah—to testify that Jesus is the Christ. Though we don't know what we lost from the 116 pages, we do know that we gained testimony that could very well constitute the "wise purpose" spoken of by the Lord.

POINT OF INTEREST

Kings in the Land of Zarahemla

Mosiah I	*Between 270–130 B.C. (Omni 1:19). Nephite king whom the Lord warned to flee the land of Nephi to the land of Zarahemla, where they discovered "the people of Zarahemla," another righteous group from Jerusalem. These two groups united, and Mosiah was appointed king over all.*
Benjamin	*Between 270–130 B.C. (Omni 1:23). Son of Mosiah I, who led the Nephites in a crucial time of war and fought with "his own arm" to protect his people from invading Lamanites (W of M 1:13). His farewell address had great impact on Nephites of the day and on generations to come.*
Mosiah II	*About 124 B.C. (Mosiah 6:4). Righteous son of King Benjamin who was appointed by his father. At the end of his reign, Mosiah II proposes there be an end to the monarchy and creates an alternative political system using elected judges, with a "chief judge" at the head. This political office is now separated from the head of the church, which is now referred to as the office of "high priest."*

a holy man, and he did reign over his people in righteousness; and there were many holy men in the land, and they did speak the word of God with power and with authority; and they did use much sharpness because of the stiffneckedness of the people—
18. Wherefore, with the help of these, king Benjamin, by laboring with all the might of his body and the faculty of his whole soul, and also the prophets, did once more establish peace in the land.

THE BOOK OF MOSIAH

CHAPTER 1

1. AND now there was no more contention in all the land of Zarahemla, among all the people who belonged to king Benjamin, so that king Benjamin had continual peace all the remainder of his days.
2. And it came to pass that he had three sons; and he called their names Mosiah, and Helorum, and Helaman. And he caused that they should be taught in all the language of his fathers, that thereby they might become men of understanding; and that they might know concerning the prophecies which had been spoken by the mouths of their fathers, which were delivered them by the hand of the Lord.
3. And he also taught them concerning the records which were engraven on the plates of brass, saying: My sons, I would that ye should remember that were it not for these plates, which contain these records and these commandments, we must have suffered in ignorance, even at this present time, not knowing the mysteries of God.
4. For it were not possible that our father, Lehi, could have remembered all these things, to have taught them to his children, except it were for the help of these plates; for he having been taught in the language of the Egyptians therefore he could read these engravings, and teach them to his children, that thereby they could teach them to their children, and so fulfilling the commandments of God, even down to this present time.
5. I say unto you, my sons, were it not for these things, which have been kept and preserved by the hand of God, that we might read and understand of his mysteries, and have his commandments always

Mosiah 1:1–2

Note that the main story in the book of Mosiah is told in the third person rather than in the first person as was the custom in the earlier books of the Book of Mormon. The reason for this is that someone else is now telling the story, and that "someone else" is Mormon. With the beginning of the book of Mosiah we start our study of Mormon's abridgment of various books that had been written on the large plates of Nephi. (3 Nephi 5:8–12.) The book of Mosiah and the five books that follow—Alma, Helaman, 3 Nephi, 4 Nephi, and Mormon—were all abridged or condensed by Mormon from the large plates of Nephi, and these abridged versions were written by Mormon on the plates that bear his name, the plates of Mormon. These are the same plates that were given to Joseph Smith by the angel Moroni on September 22, 1827. (Ludlow)

Mosiah 1:1–5

The statement that "Lehi . . . having been taught in the language of the Egyptians therefore he could read" the engravings on the brass plates of Laban quite clearly indicates these plates were written in the Egyptian language. Thus they were almost certainly not started until after the flood and the tower of Babel, as there was no Egyptian language before those events. The brass plates were probably not started until after the Israelites went down into Egypt in the days of Joseph, although the writers on these plates may have had access to records that had been written earlier.

Two other evidences supporting this thesis are: (1) Laban "was a descendant of Joseph, wherefore he and his fathers had kept the records" (1 Nephi 5:16), and (2) the great prophecies "of Joseph, who was carried into Egypt . . . are written upon the plates of brass" (2 Nephi 4:1–2), as these records contained "the five books of Moses" (1 Nephi 5:11). Other writers continued recording on these plates "even down to the commencement of the reign of Zedekiah, king of Judah" (1 Nephi 5:12)—the very year Lehi left Jerusalem (1 Nephi 1:4). (Ludlow)

before our eyes, that even our fathers would have dwindled in unbelief, and we should have been like unto our brethren, the Lamanites, who know nothing concerning these things, or even do not believe them when they are taught them, because of the traditions of their fathers, which are not correct.

6. O my sons, I would that ye should remember that these sayings are true, and also that these records are true. And behold, also the plates of Nephi, which contain the records and the sayings of our fathers from the time they left Jerusalem until now, and they are true; and we can know of their surety because we have them before our eyes.

7. And now, my sons, I would that ye should remember to search them diligently, that ye may profit thereby; and I would that ye should keep the commandments of God, that ye may prosper in the land according to the promises which the Lord made unto our fathers.

8. And many more things did king Benjamin teach his sons, which are not written in this book.

9. And it came to pass that after king Benjamin had made an end of teaching his sons, that he waxed old, and he saw that he must very soon go the way of all the earth; therefore, he thought it expedient that he should confer the kingdom upon one of his sons.

10. Therefore, he had Mosiah brought before him; and these are the words which he spake unto him, saying: My son, I would that ye should make a proclamation throughout all this land among all this people, or the people of Zarahemla, and the people of Mosiah who dwell in the land, that thereby they may be gathered together; for on the morrow I shall proclaim unto this my people out of mine own mouth that thou art a king and a ruler over this people, whom the Lord our God hath given us.

11. And moreover, I shall give this people a name, that thereby they may be distinguished above all the people which the Lord God hath brought out of the land of Jerusalem; and this I do because they have been a diligent people in keeping the commandments of the Lord.

12. And I give unto them a name that never shall be blotted out, except it be through transgression.

13. Yea, and moreover I say unto you, that if this highly favored people of the Lord should fall into transgression, and become a wicked and an adulterous people, that the Lord will deliver them up, that thereby they become weak like unto their brethren; and he will no more preserve them by his matchless and marvelous power, as he has hitherto preserved our fathers.

14. For I say unto you, that if he had not extended his arm in the preservation of our fathers they must have fallen into the hands of the Lamanites, and become victims to their hatred.

15. And it came to pass that after king Benjamin had made an end of these sayings to his son, that he gave him charge concerning all the affairs of the kingdom.

16. And moreover, he also gave him charge concerning the records which

Mosiah 1:10

In response to the king's request, the people came to the temple where he was to deliver his message to them. It is interesting they didn't just present themselves at a meeting. They prepared themselves for the experience in at least two important ways.

First, there was an attitude preparation. They went up to the temple ***to hear*** that which would be spoken. (See Mosiah 2:1.) As we attend meetings, we would all do well to listen carefully to the words that are spoken, think on their source, and determine how they can be of value to us as we give heed to them. For us to really hear, there must be a desire to learn, a worthiness to receive, and a spiritual responsiveness to the message. It is not uncommon for us to receive a message that is not spoken by the speakers. The Holy Spirit sometimes does His own speaking.

Secondly, they sacrificed and gave thanks. (See Mosiah 2:3–4.) . . . It would be a worthwhile practice for us to kneel in prayer as part of our preparation and prior to our going. [to our meetings]. We could thank the Lord that He has prepared a meeting, that we have been invited to attend, and then pray for those who are responsible for the content of the meeting. Think of the impressions and impact on children who hear such prayers from parents who provide these patterns in their homes (O/C)

were engraven on the plates of brass; and also the plates of Nephi;
and also, the sword of Laban, and the ball or director, which led our
fathers through the wilderness, which was prepared by the hand of
the Lord that thereby they might be led, every one according to the
heed and diligence which they gave unto him.
17. Therefore, as they were unfaithful they did not prosper nor
progress in their journey, but were driven back, and incurred the
displeasure of God upon them; and therefore they were smitten
with famine and sore afflictions, to stir them up in remembrance of
their duty.
18. And now, it came to pass that Mosiah went and did as his father
had commanded him, and proclaimed unto all the people who were
in the land of Zarahemla that thereby they might gather themselves
together, to go up to the temple to hear the words which his father
should speak unto them.

Mosiah 1:18

This is the first reference to a temple in the land of Zarahemla. The building of a temple mentioned earlier in the Book of Mormon (2 Nephi 5:16) refers to the temple in the land of Nephi. Our present Book of Mormon does not provide any additional information concerning when or by whom this temple in Zarahemla was constructed. (Ludlow)

CHAPTER 2

1. AND it came to pass that after Mosiah had done as his father had
commanded him, and had made a proclamation throughout all the
land, that the people gathered themselves together throughout all
the land, that they might go up to the temple to hear the words
which king Benjamin should speak unto them.
2. And there were a great number, even so many that they did not
number them; for they had multiplied exceedingly and waxed great
in the land.
3. And they also took of the firstlings of their flocks, that they
might offer sacrifice and burnt offerings according to the law of
Moses;
4. And also that they might give thanks to the Lord their God,
who had brought them out of the land of Jerusalem, and who
had delivered them out of the hands of their enemies, and had
appointed just men to be their teachers, and also a just man
to be their king, who had established peace in the land of
Zarahemla, and who had taught them to keep the commandments of God, that they might rejoice and be filled
with love towards God and all men.
5. And it came to pass that when they came up to the
temple, they pitched their tents round about, every man
according to his family, consisting of his wife, and his
sons, and his daughters, and their sons, and their daughters, from the eldest down to the youngest, every family
being separate one from another.
6. And they pitched their tents round about the temple,
every man having his tent with the door thereof towards
the temple, that thereby they might remain in their tents
and hear the words which king Benjamin should speak unto
them;

Mosiah 2:2

Since these people had only been given a day's notice, it is likely that the population at this time numbered in the thousands.

POINT OF INTEREST

Ball courts were a regular feature in Mesoamerican cities. At left is a ball court maker from Chin Kul Tic in Chiapas, Mexico.

7. For the multitude being so great that king Benjamin could not teach them all within the walls of the temple, therefore he caused a tower to be erected, that thereby his people might hear the words which he should speak unto them.
8. And it came to pass that he began to speak to his people from the tower; and they could not all hear his words because of the greatness of the multitude; therefore he caused that the words which he spake should be written and sent forth among those that were not under the sound of his voice, that they might also receive his words.
9. And these are the words which he spake and caused to be written, saying: My brethren, all ye that have assembled yourselves together, you that can hear my words which I shall speak unto you this day; for I have not commanded you to come up hither to trifle with the words which I shall speak, but that you should hearken unto me, and open your ears that ye may hear, and your hearts that ye may understand, and your minds that the mysteries of God may be unfolded to your view.
10. I have not commanded you to come up hither that ye should fear me, or that ye should think that I of myself am more than a mortal man.
11. But I am like as yourselves, subject to all manner of infirmities in body and mind; yet I have been chosen by this people, and consecrated by my father, and was suffered by the hand of the Lord that I should be a ruler and a king over this people; and have been kept and preserved by his matchless power, to serve you with all the might, mind and strength which the Lord hath granted unto me.
12. I say unto you that as I have been suffered to spend my days in your service, even up to this time, and have not sought gold nor silver nor any manner of riches of you;
13. Neither have I suffered that ye should be confined in dungeons, nor that ye should make slaves one of another, nor that ye should murder, or plunder, or steal, or commit adultery; nor even have I suffered that ye should commit any manner of wickedness, and have taught you that ye should keep the commandments of the Lord, in all things which he hath commanded you—
14. And even I, myself, have labored with mine own hands that I might serve you, and that ye should not be laden with taxes, and that there should nothing come upon you which was grievous to be borne—and of all these things which I have spoken, ye yourselves are witnesses this day.
15. Yet, my brethren, I have not done these things that I might boast, neither do I tell these things that thereby I might accuse you; but I tell you these things that ye may know that I can answer a clear conscience before God this day.
16. Behold, I say unto you that because I said unto you that I had spent my days in your service, I do not desire to boast, for I have only been in the service of God.
17. And behold, I tell you these things that ye may learn wisdom; that ye may learn that when ye are in the service of your fellow beings

Mosiah 2:11–16

King Benjamin followed established tradition (see Deut. 17:14–20) by beginning his address with an accounting of his stewardship. As he begins, he does not exalt himself over his people, but rather acknowledges the hand of the Lord in preserving him and keeping him—one of the greatest examples of humility in the scriptures.

Mosiah 2:15–16

One of the major factors in King Benjamin's clear conscience is the fact that he had ruled in righteousness by serving both his people and the Lord.

Mosiah 2:17

In this statement Benjamin includes the essence of the two great commandments that were later enunciated by the Savior: (1) that we should love God with all our heart, soul, and mind, and (2) that we should love our neighbors as ourselves. (Matthew 22:37–40.)

If we truly love God and keep his commandments, we will serve our brothers because he has commanded us to love them. Therefore, as King Benjamin indicates, when we are in the service of our fellow beings we are only in the service of our God. (Ludlow)

Mosiah 2:17

Elder Antoine R. Ivins of the First Council of Seventy emphasized the necessity of having a proper motive in our service opportunities: "The great value, I believe, that the Church has for us is the opportunity it gives us to serve, for, after all, the great benefits of life come from service. . . . I would that every man who accepts a responsibility in a priesthood quorum would accept it because of the opportunity for service which it offers him; not that he be a good deacon so he may be the president of his quorum. . . . Not to be a good bishop, that when the stake is reorganized he may become the president of the stake, because if he serves with that motive, there is very likely to be a day of disappointment for him, but if he serves because he loves to, if he serves because he loves his fellows, then whether the other things come or not, he is never disappointed."

King Benjamin, a great and powerful priesthood leader, could reflect upon his years of service with a clear conscience and without regrets because:

a. His primary objective in his personal life had been to keep the Lord's commandments.

b. He had served God and taught the people to keep the Lord's commandments.

c. He depended on and acknowledged the Lord as the source of his strength and accomplishments. (O/C)

ye are only in the service of your God.
18. Behold, ye have called me your king; and if I, whom ye call your king, do labor to serve you, then ought not ye to labor to serve one another?
19. And behold also, if I, whom ye call your king, who has spent his days in your service, and yet has been in the service of God, do merit any thanks from you, O how you ought to thank your heavenly King!
20. I say unto you, my brethren, that if you should render all the thanks and praise which your whole soul has power to possess, to that God who has created you, and has kept and preserved you, and has caused that ye should rejoice, and has granted that ye should live in peace one with another—
21. I say unto you that if ye should serve him who has created you from the beginning, and is preserving you from day to day, by lending you breath, that ye may live and move and do according to your own will, and even supporting you from one moment to another—I say, if ye should serve him with all your whole souls yet ye would be unprofitable servants.
22. And behold, all that he requires of you is to keep his commandments; and he has promised you that if ye would keep his commandments ye should prosper in the land; and he never doth vary from that which he hath said; therefore, if ye do keep his commandments he doth bless you and prosper you.
23. And now, in the first place, he hath created you, and granted unto you your lives, for which ye are indebted unto him.
24. And secondly, he doth require that ye should do as he hath commanded you; for which if ye do, he doth immediately bless you; and therefore he hath paid you. And ye are still indebted unto him, and are, and will be, forever and ever; therefore, of what have ye to boast?
25. And now I ask, can ye say aught of yourselves? I answer you, Nay. Ye cannot say that ye are even as much as the dust of the earth; yet ye were created of the dust of the earth; but behold, it belongeth to him who created you.
26. And I, even I, whom ye call your king, am no better than ye yourselves are; for I am also of the dust. And ye behold that I am old, and am about to yield up this mortal frame to its mother earth.
27. Therefore, as I said unto you that I had served you, walking with a clear conscience before God, even so I at this time have caused that ye should assemble yourselves together, that I might be found blameless, and that your blood should not come upon me, when I shall stand to be judged of God of the things whereof he hath commanded me concerning you.
28. I say unto you that I have caused that ye should assemble yourselves together that I might

Mosiah 2:20–21

Many precious testimonies in the Book of Mormon take the form of benedictory statements from revered leaders. Messages of this type include . . . King Benjamin's masterful sermon before the people of Zarahemla prior to his death. The King's son and heir apparent, Mosiah, had sent a proclamation throughout the realm for the people to gather themselves together at the temple to hear the speech. In a singularly significant manner, each family was united with the doorway to their tent positioned toward the temple. One can imagine row upon row of concentric family circles radiating outward from the temple grounds as far as the eye could see, with all hearts tuned to receive the sacred instruction—"that they might rejoice and be filled with love toward God and all men" (Mosiah 2:4).

Commenting on that sermon, President Joseph Fielding Smith said, "We are told that we are unprofitable servants, (Mosiah 2:21–25; Luke 17:5–10) and so we are, if we think of trying to pay our Savior back for what he has done for us, for that we never can do; and we cannot by any number of acts, or a full life of faithful service, place our Savior in our debt." (P/A)

Mosiah 2:25–26; 4:2, 5, 11

Many of us, having experienced the death of a loved one, have had the occasion to see what a body of flesh and bones is like when separated from the spirit. While all the essential physical organs are still there, the body is lifeless; though equipped with the elegant musculoskeletal structure of the human body, it cannot move even the smallest finger or toe. There is no facial expression, no hint at thought or personality, even though the human brain remains intact. Without the living spirit, the body becomes little more than a motionless lump of clay.

Such was the case when Adam, the first of all men on this earth, was created in God's own image. Adam's body was a masterpiece, but was void of all powers, thoughts, and abilities until endowed with a spirit.

President Spencer W. Kimball addressed the importance of the spirit when he said that "science tells us that without the spirit about all that is left is a quantity of water, fat enough to make about seven bars of soap, sulphur enough to rid one dog of fleas, iron enough for a large nail, magnesium for one dose, lime enough to whitewash a chicken coop, phosphorous sufficient to tip some 2200 matches, potassium enough to explode a toy cannon, sugar to fill a shaker, and little more. But with a spirit directing mental processes and physical maneuvers man is 'little lower than the angels' and is 'crowned . . . with glory and honour' (Psalm 8:5)."

Mosiah 2:28

King Benjamin was able to "rid my garments of your blood" because, having taught his people the truth, he would not be held accountable for any of their unrighteous acts.

rid my garments of your blood, at this period of time when I am
about to go down to my grave, that I might go down in peace, and
my immortal spirit may join the choirs above in singing the praises of a just God.
29. And moreover, I say unto you that I have caused that ye should
assemble yourselves together, that I might declare unto you that I
can no longer be your teacher, nor your king;
30. For even at this time, my whole frame doth tremble exceedingly while attempting to speak unto you; but the Lord God doth
support me, and hath suffered me that I should speak unto you, and
hath commanded me that I should declare unto you this day, that
my son Mosiah is a king and a ruler over you.
31. And now, my brethren, I would that ye should do as ye have
hitherto done. As ye have kept my commandments, and also the
commandments of my father, and have prospered, and have been
kept from falling into the hands of your enemies, even so if ye shall
keep the commandments of my son, or the commandments of God
which shall be delivered unto you by him, ye shall prosper in the
land, and your enemies shall have no power over you.
32. But, O my people, beware lest there shall arise contentions
among you, and ye list to obey the evil spirit, which was spoken of
by my father Mosiah.
33. For behold, there is a wo pronounced upon him who listeth to
obey that spirit; for if he listeth to obey him, and remaineth and
dieth in his sins, the same drinketh damnation to his own soul; for
he receiveth for his wages an everlasting punishment, having
transgressed the law of God contrary to his own knowledge.
34. I say unto you, that there are not any among you, except it be
your little children that have not been taught concerning these
things, but what knoweth that ye are eternally indebted to your
heavenly Father, to render to him all that you have and are; and
also have been taught concerning the records which contain the
prophecies which have been spoken by the holy prophets, even
down to the time our father, Lehi, left Jerusalem;
35. And also, all that has been spoken by our fathers until now.
And behold, also, they spake that which was commanded them of
the Lord; therefore, they are just and true.
36. And now, I say unto you, my brethren, that after ye have
known and have been taught all these things, if ye should
transgress and go contrary to that which has been spoken, that ye do withdraw yourselves from the Spirit
of the Lord, that it may have no place in you to
guide you in wisdom's paths that ye may be
blessed, prospered, and preserved—
37. I say unto you, that the man that doeth
this, the same cometh out in open rebellion against God; therefore he listeth to
obey the evil spirit, and becometh an
enemy to all righteousness; therefore, the
Lord

Mosiah 2:33

According to President Joseph Fielding Smith, eternal or everlasting punishment is not so named because it must be endured forever. It is called "eternal" or "everlasting" because, as God's punishment, it is fixed. The same punishment always follows the same offense. When the penalty is paid, the one who sinned is released.

has no place in him, for he dwelleth not in unholy temples.
38. Therefore if that man repenteth not, and remaineth and dieth
an enemy to God, the demands of divine justice do awaken his
immortal soul to a lively sense of his own guilt, which doth cause
him to shrink from the presence of the Lord, and doth fill his breast
with guilt, and pain, and anguish, which is like an unquenchable
fire, whose flame ascendeth up forever and ever.
39. And now I say unto you, that mercy hath no claim on that
man; therefore his final doom is to endure a never-ending torment.
40. O, all ye old men, and also ye young men, and you little children who can understand my words, for I have spoken plainly unto
you that ye might understand, I pray that ye should awake to a
remembrance of the awful situation of those that have fallen into
transgression.
41. And moreover, I would desire that ye should consider on the
blessed and happy state of those that keep the commandments of
God. For behold, they are blessed in all things, both temporal and
spiritual; and if they hold out faithful to the end they are received
into heaven, that thereby they may dwell with God in a state of
never-ending happiness. O remember, remember that these things
are true; for the Lord God hath spoken it.

CHAPTER 3

1. AND again my brethren, I would call your attention, for I have
somewhat more to speak unto you; for behold, I have things to tell
you concerning that which is to come.
2. And the things which I shall tell you are made known unto me
by an angel from God. And he said unto me: Awake; and I awoke,
and behold he stood before me.
3. And he said unto me: Awake, and hear the words which I shall tell
thee; for behold, I am come to declare unto you the glad tidings of
great joy.
4. For the Lord hath heard thy prayers, and hath judged of thy
righteousness, and hath sent me to declare unto thee that thou
mayest rejoice; and that thou mayest declare unto thy people, that
they may also be filled with joy.
5. For behold, the time cometh, and is not far distant, that with
power, the Lord Omnipotent who reigneth, who was, and is from
all eternity to all eternity, shall come down from heaven among
the

POINT OF INTEREST

A mammoth is an extinct relative of the elephant and is considered by some to be a candidate for the Book of Mormon elephant, curelom, or cumom. However, scientists believe mammoths became extinct around 4,500 years ago, which means only the Jaredites would have had a chance to use them in any capacity. The mastadon is similar in size and shape to the mammoth, but became extinct more than 5,000 years before the mammoth. Nothing is known about the likelihood of being able to domesticate either animal.

Mosiah 2:38; 3:27

The major Christian churches that believe in a place called hell refer to it as a place of endless burnings and punishment. The leaders of these churches evidently get this belief partially from their interpretation of such scriptures as Luke 16:28 (where hell is referred to as a "place of torment") and from Matthew 13:42 (where hell is referred to as a "furnace of fire," where there will be "wailing and gnashing of teeth"). However, the exact wording that hell is a place "where people are continually burning but are never consumed" is not found in the scriptures; largely this concept comes from false interpretations by men. In the Doctrine and Covenants the Lord has explained what is meant by the terms "endless torment" and "eternal damnation":

"Nevertheless, it is not written that there shall be no end to this torment, but it is written *endless torment.*

"Again, it is written *eternal damnation;* wherefore it is more express than other scriptures, that it might work upon the hearts of the children of men, altogether for my name's glory.

"Wherefore, I will explain unto you this mystery, for it is meet unto you to know even as mine apostles.

"I speak unto you that are chosen in this thing, even as one, that you may enter into my rest.

"For, behold, the mystery of godliness, how great is it! For, behold, I am endless, and the punishment which is given from my hand is endless punishment, for Endless is my name. Wherefore—Eternal punishment is God's punishment.

"Endless punishment is God's punishment." (D&C 19:6–12. Italics added.)

The Book of Mormon indicates that hell as a place is not a place of eternal fire. However, the feeling of guilt, pain, and anguish that the sinner feels is "like an unquenchable fire" (Mosiah 2:38), and his torment is "as a lake of fire and brimstone" (Mosiah 3:27). (Ludlow)

Mosiah 3

Mosiah 3 contains perhaps the greatest sermon ever delivered on the Atonement, which was recited to King Benjamin by an angel. Later in Mosiah we learn that as a result of the Atonement, all mankind will be redeemed, when otherwise all would have perished. The only ones who will not stand to take advantage of the Savior's infinite Atonement are those who rebel against God and die in their sins, as detailed in Mosiah 15.

children of men, and shall dwell in a tabernacle of clay, and shall
go forth amongst men, working mighty miracles, such as healing
the sick, raising the dead, causing the lame to walk, the blind to
receive their sight, and the deaf to hear, and curing all manner of
diseases.
6. And he shall cast out devils, or the evil spirits which dwell in
the hearts of the children of men.
7. And lo, he shall suffer temptations, and pain of body, hunger,
thirst, and fatigue, even more than man can suffer, except it be
unto death; for behold, blood cometh from every pore, so great
shall be his anguish for the wickedness and the abominations of his
people.
8. And he shall be called Jesus Christ, the Son of God, the Father
of heaven and earth, the Creator of all things from the beginning;
and his mother shall be called Mary.
9. And lo, he cometh unto his own, that salvation might come unto
the children of men even through faith on his name; and even after
all this they shall consider him a man, and say that he hath a devil,
and shall scourge him, and shall crucify him.
10. And he shall rise the third day from the dead; and behold, he
standeth to judge the world; and behold, all these things are done
that a righteous judgment might come upon the children of men.
11. For behold, and also his blood atoneth for the sins of those who
have fallen by the transgression of Adam, who have died not
knowing the will of God concerning them, or who have ignorantly sinned.
12. But wo, wo unto him who knoweth that he rebelleth against
God! For salvation cometh to none such except it be through
repentance and faith on the Lord Jesus Christ.
13. And the Lord God hath sent his holy prophets among all the
children of men, to declare these things to every kindred, nation,
and tongue, that thereby whosoever should believe that Christ
should come, the same might receive remission of their sins, and
rejoice with exceedingly great joy, even as though he had already
come among them.

POINT OF INTEREST

At right is a Peruvian design. Peru was home to the Norte Chico civilization, one of the oldest in the world, and to the Inca Empire, the largest state in pre-Columbian America.

Mosiah 3:7

We have read of the great struggle the Savior underwent in the Garden of Gethsemane, as the agony of suffering all the sins and pains of mankind was so great as to cause Him to sweat great drops of blood from every pore. Such suffering is incomprehensible to us, and could not have been borne by mortal man. It took one who was born of a mortal mother and an immortal Father to bear such agony. It is important to realize that the experience of Gethsemane was repeated at Calvary when, during the last three hours of His mortal life, the Savior again repeated the agony of the Garden.

Mosiah 3:11, 16–18

Most of the so-called Christian churches today teach the doctrine of original sin. Essentially, this doctrine is that all of us are born sinful onto this earth because of the original transgression of Adam and Eve. . . .

[T]he many churches that believe in the doctrine of original sin also usually teach that original sin can be removed only through baptism. Such teachings deny the right of unbaptized people, including unbaptized infants, to gain the presence of God (heaven). However, the Book of Mormon prophets clearly and definitely teach that the atonement of Jesus Christ fully atones: (1) for the original transgression of Adam and Eve, (2) for the sins of unbaptized infants who die before they are accountable, and (3) for the sins of all people who die without having an opportunity to receive the "will of God concerning them." In his famous discourse on the atonement, King Benjamin says concerning the Savior: ". . . his blood atoneth for the sins of those who have fallen by the transgression of Adam, who have died not knowing the will of God concerning them, or who have ignorantly sinned" (Mosiah 3:11). (Ludlow)

14. Yet the Lord God saw that his people were a stiffnecked people, and he appointed unto them a law, even the law of Moses.
15. And many signs, and wonders, and types, and shadows showed he unto them, concerning his coming; and also holy prophets spake unto them concerning his coming; and yet they hardened their hearts, and understood not that the law of Moses availeth nothing except it were through the atonement of his blood.
16. And even if it were possible that little children could sin they could not be saved; but I say unto you they are blessed; for behold, as in Adam, or by nature, they fall, even so the blood of Christ atoneth for their sins.
17. And moreover, I say unto you, that there shall be no other name given nor any other way nor means whereby salvation can come unto the children of men, only in and through the name of Christ, the Lord Omnipotent.
18. For behold he judgeth, and his judgment is just; and the infant perisheth not that dieth in his infancy; but men drink damnation to their own souls except they humble themselves and become as little children, and believe that salvation was, and is, and is to come, in and through the atoning blood of Christ, the Lord Omnipotent.
19. For the natural man is an enemy to God, and has been from the fall of Adam, and will be, forever and ever, unless he yields to the enticings of the Holy Spirit, and putteth off the natural man and becometh a saint through the atonement of Christ the Lord, and becometh as a child, submissive, meek, humble, patient, full of love, willing to submit to all things which the Lord seeth fit to inflict upon him, even as a child doth submit to his father.
20. And moreover, I say unto you, that the time shall come when the knowledge of a Savior shall spread throughout every nation, kindred, tongue, and people.
21. And behold, when that time cometh, none shall be found blameless before God, except it be little children, only through repentance and faith on the name of the Lord God Omnipotent.
22. And even at this time, when thou shalt have taught thy people the things which the Lord thy God hath commanded thee, even then

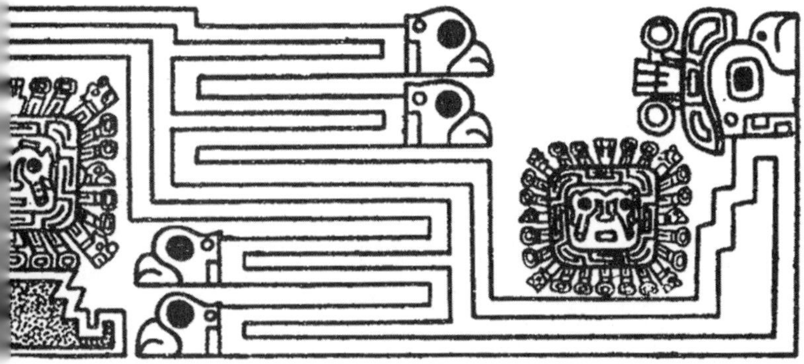

Mosiah 3:15–27

The law of justice works in relationship to the other laws of God in the moral realm. In essence, the law of justice might be explained as follows: (1) every law has both a punishment and a blessing attached to it; (2) whenever the law is transgressed (broken), a punishment (or suffering) must be inflicted; (3) whenever a law is kept (obeyed), a blessing (or reward) must be given.

The law of justice requires that God must be a God of order and that he must be just and impartial. Because of the law of justice, God can make such statements as these: "I the Lord, am bound when ye do what I say; but when ye do not what I say, ye have no promise" (Doctrine and Covenants 82:10); "There is a law, irrevocably decreed in heaven before the foundations of this world, upon which all blessings are predicated—And when we obtain any blessing from God, it is by obedience to that law upon which it is predicated" (Doctrine and Covenants 130:20–21).

The law of mercy agrees entirely with the law of justice. However, the law of mercy introduces the possibility of vicarious payment of the laws that have been transgressed. In essence, the law of mercy might be paraphrased as follows: Whenever a law is transgressed (or broken), a payment (or suffering or atonement) must be made; however, the person who transgressed the law does not need to make payment *if* he will repent and *if* he can find someone else who is both able and willing to make payment. Note that the law of mercy insists that the demands of the law of justice be met fully. As Alma stated, . . . "justice exerciseth all his demands, and also mercy claimeth all which is her own; and thus, none but the truly penitent are saved. What, do ye suppose that mercy can rob justice? I say unto you, Nay; not one whit. If so, God would cease to be God." (Alma 42:24–25.)

The law of justice made the atonement of Jesus Christ necessary. When Adam fell, he transgressed a law that had physical and spiritual death as its punishment. Thus the law of justice demanded payment (or atonement) for the broken (or transgressed) law. (Ludlow)

The law of mercy made the atonement of Jesus Christ possible. In order for Jesus Christ to pay fully for the law Adam had transgressed, it was necessary that the Savior be both able and willing to make atonement. He was willing to make payment because of his great love for mankind, and he was able to make payment because he lived a sinless life and because he was actually, literally, biologically the Son of God in the flesh. Thus he had the power to atone for the spiritual and physical deaths introduced by the fall of Adam and Eve. Because of this atonement (or payment), he is rightfully referred to as the Savior and Redeemer of all mankind.

Every person benefits unconditionally from two major aspects of the atonement: (1) the resurrection, and (2) the full payment for the original transgression of Adam and Eve. However, as Mosiah indicates, there are also some conditional aspects of the atonement, and in order to benefit from these a person must repent of his sins. Otherwise, "mercy . . . could have claim" upon the person "no more forever," for the law of mercy is made active in the life of a person only upon the conditions of repentance. (Mosiah 3:25–27). (Ludlow)

Mosiah 3:19

We might ask ourselves as members of The Church of Jesus Christ of Latter-day Saints if we fall into the category of "the natural man." We might be wise to inventory ourselves against a set of broad categories of the natural man, as identified by Robert Millet:

1. The natural man cannot or does not perceive spiritual realities (see *Journal of Discourses* 1:2).
2. The natural man allows into his life those things that are harsh, vulgar, and crude.
3. Instead of seeking to do the Lord's will, the natural man pits his own will against that of the Lord—wishing, ultimately, that the Lord would agree with him.
4. The natural man seeks to have more, do more, and be more than those around him; this competitive nature eventually saps the joy out of accomplishment and causes the natural man to focus on elevating himself at the cost of diminishing those around him.

Mosiah 3:19

The word *saint* comes from the Hebrew word "Kadosh," which means to separate, to be apart from, and to become sacred and holy (Wilhelm Gesenius, Edward Robinson, Francis Brown, S.R. Driver, and Charles A. Briggs, *A Hebrew and English Lexicon of the Old Testament, with an Appendix Containing the Biblical Aramaic* [Oxford: Clarendon Press, 1953], 872). As saints in these latter days, we are called on to separate ourselves from the things of the world, standing apart from those influences that would sully or soil us. As we separate ourselves and stand apart from the world, we will be better able to recognize the sacred in our lives and we will eventually become more holy through consistent obedience.

Mosiah 3:19

The following statements illustrate the principle:

Being a saint is not just praying; it is *being* a prayerful person.

It is not just keeping the Sabbath; it is *being* a Sabbath keeper.

It is not just in paying tithes; it is *being* a full tithe payer.

It is not just resisting immoral temptations; it is *being* morally clean.

It is not just in giving; it is *being* a giver.

It is not just serving; it is *being* a servant.

It is not just home teaching; it is *being* a home teacher.

It is not just rendering obedience; it is *being* an obedient person.

It is not just repenting; it is *being* repentant.

It is not just bearing witness; it is *being* a witness.

It is not just coming to Christ; it is *being* Christlike.

BEING a true child of God and disciple of Christ is the fulfillment of our premortal hopes and commitments, the purpose of our *doing* all things the Lord commands, and the result of our efforts to become a Saint through the Atonement of Christ. (O/C)

POINT OF INTEREST

The Aztec calendar at right was used by the Aztecs, as well as other pre-Columbians in central Mexico. The calendar has a 365-day calendar cycle called xiuhpohualli *(year count) and a 260-day ritual cycle called* tonalpohualli *(day count). These two cycles formed a 52-year "century," sometimes called the "calendar round." Each calendar year began with the first appearance of the Pleiades constellation in the east immediately before the dawn light.*

Mosiah 3:19 and 4:2

One of the most disputed issues among so-called Christian theologians has been the question of the basic nature of man. Some of these theologians have argued that man is born evil into this world as an infant; thus the only way this evil can be removed is by receiving the sacrament of baptism. Still other theologians have argued that man is born innocent and remains basically good; some of them thus conclude that inasmuch as man is basically good he has no need for a redeemer to atone for his sins.

It should be clear to students of the Book of Mormon that the prophets definitely reject both the doctrine of the natural depravity of man and the doctrine that man is so good by nature he has no need for a redeemer. Benjamin, the prophet and king of the Nephites, said that "an angel from God" taught him that although infants are born in a state of innocence, after they become accountable they can become enemies to God if they do not accept the saving principles and ordinances of the gospel.

In explaining how man can be born innocent but yet can become an enemy to God, David H. Yarn has written:

"It is important that the teaching of King Benjamin be distinguished from the apostate doctrine of depravity. Man is not born evil, but innocent. He is innocent until he reaches the age of accountability, but he grows up in a world of sin and as an agent makes choices from among a vast complex of enticements; and when he becomes accountable and refuses to make his will submissive to God by accepting Him and making covenants with Him, he is "carnal, sensual, and devilish. . . ."

Summarily put, the natural man (he who is carnal, sensual, and devilish, he who is an enemy to God) is the man who has not humbled himself before God and made covenants with God by receiving the revealed ordinances at the hands of God's authorized servants; or the man who, having done these things, has failed to live according to the covenants made in baptism and to the injunction given when he was confirmed a member of the Church—"Receive the Holy Ghost." (Ludlow)

are they found no more blameless in the sight of God, only according to the words which I have spoken unto thee.
23. And now I have spoken the words which the Lord God hath commanded me.
24. And thus saith the Lord: They shall stand as a bright testimony against this people, at the judgment day; whereof they shall be judged, every man according to his works, whether they be good, or whether they be evil.
25. And if they be evil they are consigned to an awful view of their own guilt and abominations, which doth cause them to shrink from the presence of the Lord into a state of misery and endless torment, from whence they can no more return; therefore they have drunk damnation to their own souls.
26. Therefore, they have drunk out of the cup of the wrath of God, which justice could no more deny unto them than it could deny that Adam should fall because of his partaking of the forbidden fruit; therefore, mercy could have claim on them no more forever.
27. And their torment is as a lake of fire and brimstone, whose flames are unquenchable, and whose smoke ascendeth up forever and ever. Thus hath the Lord commanded me. Amen.

CHAPTER 4

1. AND now, it came to pass that when king Benjamin had made an end of speaking the words which had been delivered unto him by the angel of the Lord, that he cast his eyes round about on the multitude, and behold they had fallen to the earth, for the fear of the Lord had come upon them.
2. And they had viewed themselves in their own carnal state, even less than the dust of the earth. And they all cried aloud with one voice, saying: O have mercy, and apply the atoning blood of Christ that we may receive forgiveness of our sins, and our hearts may be purified; for we believe in Jesus Christ, the Son of God, who created heaven and earth, and all things; who shall come down among the children of men.
3. And it came to pass that after they had spoken these words the Spirit of the Lord came upon them, and they were filled with joy, having received a remission of their sins, and having peace of conscience, because of the exceeding faith which they had in Jesus Christ who should come, according to the words which king Benjamin had spoken unto them.
4. And king Benjamin again opened his mouth and began to speak unto them, saying: My friends and my brethren, my kindred and my people, I would again call your attention, that ye may hear and

Mosiah 4:3

Sins are personal, belonging to sinners and no one else. Godly sorrow for sins is an admission by sinners that they accept responsibility for having offended their Lawgiver. Having a desire to be cleansed of sin and to be in harmony with the Lord's commandments motivates sinners to acknowledge and confess their sins. Self-conviction also motivates sinners to repair damages their actions may have inflicted upon another child of God. . . .

God is the author of salvation, not man. The Lord atoned for man's sins by freely sacrificing His sinless life. He is the Lawgiver and by His grace sinners are cleansed. Pleading to God for mercy, the sinner acknowledges that forgiveness of sin and healing of the soul is the prerogative of deity.

Faith is a gift from God to man. To say we have faith in the Lord Jesus Christ and not some other so-called God or important figure is to have a testimony of the mission of the Lord Jesus Christ. It is only through faith in the Savior that sins are remitted. Someone once said, "Receiving divine forgiveness of sins is like having our Father in Heaven put His arms around us and being drawn into His bosom."

King Benjamin's people knew their sins were forgiven when ". . . the Spirit of the Lord came upon them, and they were filled with joy, having received a remission of their sins, and having peace of conscience . . ." (Mosiah 4:3). Through the power of the Holy Ghost sins are remitted and the soul is healed.

Speaking of healing the soul, Marion G. Romney said, "Somebody recently asked how one could know when he is converted. The answer is simple. He may be assured of it when by the power of the Holy Spirit his soul is healed. When this occurs, he will recognize it by the way he feels, for he will feel as the people of Benjamin felt when they received remission of sins. The record says, '. . . the Spirit of the Lord came upon them, and they were filled with joy, having received a remission of their sins, and having peace of conscience. . . .'" (O/C)

understand the remainder of my words which I shall speak unto you.

5. For behold, if the knowledge of the goodness of God at this time has awakened you to a sense of your nothingness, and your worthless and fallen state—

6. I say unto you, if ye have come to a knowledge of the goodness of God, and his matchless power, and his wisdom, and his patience, and his long-suffering towards the children of men; and also, the atonement which has been prepared from the foundation of the world, that thereby salvation might come to him that should put his trust in the Lord, and should be diligent in keeping his commandments, and continue in the faith even unto the end of his life, I mean the life of the mortal body—

7. I say, that this is the man who receiveth salvation, through the atonement which was prepared from the foundation of the world for all mankind, which ever were since the fall of Adam, or who are, or who ever shall be, even unto the end of the world.

8. And this is the means whereby salvation cometh. And there is none other salvation save this which hath been spoken of; neither are there any conditions whereby man can be saved except the conditions which I have told you.

9. Believe in God; believe that he is, and that he created all things, both in heaven and in earth; believe that he has all wisdom, and all power, both in heaven and in earth; believe that man doth not comprehend all the things which the Lord can comprehend.

10. And again, believe that ye must repent of your sins and forsake them, and humble yourselves before God; and ask in sincerity of heart that he would forgive you; and now, if you believe all these things see that ye do them.

11. And again I say unto you as I have said before, that as ye have come to the knowledge of the glory of God, or if ye have known of his goodness and have tasted of his love, and have received a remission of your sins, which causeth such exceedingly great joy in your souls, even so I would that ye should remember, and always retain in remembrance, the greatness of God, and your own nothingness, and his goodness and long-suffering towards you, unworthy creatures, and humble yourselves even in the depths of humility, calling on the name of the Lord daily, and standing steadfastly in the faith of that which is to come, which was spoken by the mouth of the angel.

12. And behold, I say unto you that if ye do this ye shall always rejoice, and be filled with the love of God, and always retain a remission of your sins; and ye shall grow in the knowledge of the glory of him that created you, or in the knowledge of that which is just and true.

13. And ye will not have a mind to injure one another, but to live peaceably, and to render to every

Mosiah 4:6–11

When the people heard Benjamin's discourse and asked him how they could "apply the atoning blood of Christ that we may receive forgiveness of our sins, and our hearts may be purified" (Mosiah 4:2), Benjamin told them they (1) must believe in the goodness of God and in the atonement of Jesus Christ, (2) must repent of their sins and forsake them, and (3) must humble themselves before God and ask in sincerity of heart for forgiveness. (Mosiah 4:6–10.)

Although Benjamin did not specifically mention baptism by water and by the Holy Ghost, it seems reasonable to assume that the people whom Benjamin was addressing had already received these ordinances for the following reasons: (1) the Nephites had authority to baptize (2 Nephi 6:2); (2) they plainly understood that baptism was essential to salvation (2 Nephi 9:23–24); (3) apparently the righteous Nephites had practiced baptism from the beginning of the Book of Mormon (2 Nephi 31:17). (Ludlow)

Mosiah 4:12

King Benjamin brings his people to the point where they have repented in full faith. . . . He then continues his speech by guiding the people step by step toward a firm understanding of how they, having once tasted the love of God, might assure the continuation of this divine blessing in their lives forever, and "always retain a remission of your sins" (Mosiah 4:12). It is an inspiring exercise in transitions: from an inception to an unfolding, from a desirable moment of achievement to an enduring pattern of righteousness, from the sprouting of a seed (as Alma would later explain) to the maturing of "a tree springing up unto everlasting life" (Alma 32:41).

Commenting on these transitions, President Harold B. Lee said: "What must I do to be saved? As I pondered these words, I thought of three essentials that are necessary to inspire one to live a Christlike life—or, speaking more accurately in the language of the scriptures, to live more perfectly as the Master lived. . . . There must be awakened in the individual who would be taught or who would live perfectly an awareness of his needs. . . . A man must be "born again" if he would reach perfection. . . . And then finally the third essential: to help the learner to know the gospel by living the gospel. Spiritual certainty that is necessary to salvation must be preceded by a maximum of individual effort. Grace, or the free gift of the Lord's atoning power, must be preceded by personal striving." (P/A)

man according to that which is his due.
14. And ye will not suffer your children that they go hungry, or
naked; neither will ye suffer that they transgress the laws of God,
and fight and quarrel one with another, and serve the devil, who is
the master of sin, or who is the evil spirit which hath been spoken
of by our fathers, he being an enemy to all righteousness.
15. But ye will teach them to walk in the ways of truth and soberness; ye will teach them to love one another, and to serve one
another.
16. And also, ye yourselves will succor those that stand in need of
your succor; ye will administer of your substance unto him that
standeth in need; and ye will not suffer that the beggar putteth up
his petition to you in vain, and turn him out to perish.
17. Perhaps thou shalt say: The man has brought upon himself his
misery; therefore I will stay my hand, and will not give unto him of
my food, nor impart unto him of my substance that he may not suffer, for his punishments are just—
18. But I say unto you, O man, whosoever doeth this the same hath
great cause to repent; and except he repenteth of that which he
hath done he perisheth forever, and hath no interest in the kingdom of God.
19. For behold, are we not all beggars? Do we not all depend upon
the same Being, even God, for all the substance which we have, for
both food and raiment, and for gold, and for silver, and for all the
riches which we have of every kind?
20. And behold, even at this time, ye have been calling on his
name, and begging for a remission of your sins. And has he suffered
that ye have begged in vain? Nay; he has poured out his Spirit
upon you, and has caused that your hearts should be filled with joy,
and has caused that your mouths should be stopped that ye could
not find utterance, so exceedingly great was your joy.
21. And now, if God, who has created you, on whom you are
dependent for your lives and for all that ye have and are, doth
grant unto you whatsoever ye ask that is right, in faith, believing
that ye shall receive, O then, how ye ought to impart of the substance that ye have one to another.
22. And if ye judge the man who putteth up his petition to you for
your substance that he perish not, and condemn him, how much
more just will be your condemnation for withholding your substance, which doth not belong to you but to God, to whom also
your life belongeth; and yet ye put up no petition, nor repent of the
thing which thou hast done.
23. I say unto you, wo be unto that man, for his substance shall perish with him; and now, I say these things unto those who are rich
as pertaining to the things of this world.
24. And again, I say unto the poor, ye who have not and yet have
sufficient, that ye remain from day to day; I mean all you who deny

POINT OF INTEREST

Below at top is the Aztec glyph for a marketplace with footprints to indicate a bustling crowd. Directly below the glyph is a representation of the constellation Pleiades, which the Aztecs called "Marketplace" (see John L. Sorenson, *Images of Ancient America: Visualizing Book of Mormon Life* [Provo, Utah: FARMS, 1998]).

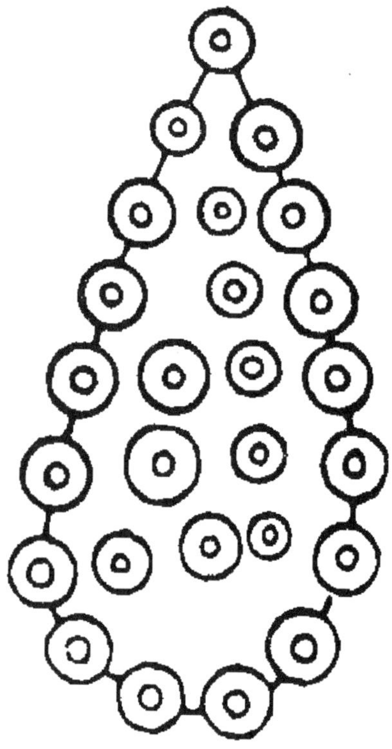

the beggar, because ye have not; I would that ye say in your hearts that: I give not because I have not, but if I had I would give.
25. And now, if ye say this in your hearts ye remain guiltless, otherwise ye are condemned; and your condemnation is just for ye covet that which ye have not received.
26. And now, for the sake of these things which I have spoken unto you—that is, for the sake of retaining a remission of your sins from day to day, that ye may walk guiltless before God—I would that ye should impart of your substance to the poor, every man according to that which he hath, such as feeding the hungry, clothing the naked, visiting the sick and administering to their relief, both spiritually and temporally, according to their wants.
27. And see that all these things are done in wisdom and order; for it is not requisite that a man should run faster than he has strength. And again, it is expedient that he should be diligent, that thereby he might win the prize; therefore, all things must be done in order.
28. And I would that ye should remember, that whosoever among you borroweth of his neighbor should return the thing that he borroweth, according as he doth agree, or else thou shalt commit sin; and perhaps thou shalt cause thy neighbor to commit sin also.
29. And finally, I cannot tell you all the things whereby ye may commit sin; for there are divers ways and means, even so many that I cannot number them.
30. But this much I can tell you, that if ye do not watch yourselves, and your thoughts, and your words, and your deeds, and observe the commandments of God, and continue in the faith of what ye have heard concerning the coming of our Lord, even unto the end of your lives, ye must perish. And now, O man, remember, and perish not.

CHAPTER 5

1. AND now, it came to pass that when king Benjamin had thus spoken to his people, he sent among them, desiring to know of his people if they believed the words which he had spoken unto them.
2. And they all cried with one voice, saying: Yea, we believe all the words which thou hast spoken unto us; and also, we know of their surety and truth, because of the Spirit of the Lord Omnipotent, which has wrought a mighty change in us, or in our hearts, that we have no more disposition to do evil, but to do good continually.
3. And we, ourselves, also, through the infinite goodness of God, and the manifestations of his Spirit, have great views of that which is to come; and were it expedient, we could prophesy of all things.
4. And it is the faith which we have had on the things which our king has spoken unto us that has brought

Mosiah 4:30

To live in a saved or sanctified condition before God is to retain a daily remission of sins. Speaking of present salvation, Brigham Young said:

"It is present salvation and the present influence of the Holy Ghost that we need every day to keep us on saving ground.

"I want present salvation. I preach, comparatively, but little about the eternities and Gods, and their wonderful works in eternity; and do not tell who first made them, nor how they were made; for I know nothing about that. Life is for us, and it is for us to receive it today, and not wait for the millennium. Let us take a course to be saved today, and, when evening comes, review the acts of the day, repent of our sins, if we have any to repent of, and say our prayers; then we can lie down and sleep in peace until the morning, arise with gratitude to God, commence the labors of another day, and strive to live the whole day to God and nobody else" (*Journal of Discourses*, 8:124–125). (O/C)

Mosiah 5:2

The "mighty change of heart" referred to by King Benjamin (and, later, by Alma) means, as described in this verse, that those experiencing this change had "no more disposition to do evil, but to do good continually." Elder Dallin H. Oaks taught that it is this kind of change that is required of us if we are to be saved and to dwell with God.

us to this great knowledge, whereby we do rejoice with such
exceedingly great joy.
5. And we are willing to enter into a covenant with our God to do
his will, and to be obedient to his commandments in all things that
he shall command us, all the remainder of our days, that we may
not bring upon ourselves a never-ending torment, as has been spoken by the angel, that we may not drink out of the cup of the wrath
of God.
6. And now, these are the words which king Benjamin desired of
them; and therefore he said unto them: Ye have spoken the words
that I desired; and the covenant which ye have made is a righteous
covenant.
7. And now, because of the covenant which ye have made ye shall
be called the children of Christ, his sons, and his daughters; for
behold, this day he hath spiritually begotten you; for ye say that
your hearts are changed through faith on his name; therefore, ye
are born of him and have become his sons and his daughters.
8. And under this head ye are made free, and there is no other head
whereby ye can be made free. There is no other name given whereby salvation cometh; therefore, I would that ye should take upon
you the name of Christ, all you that have entered into the
covenant with God that ye should be obedient unto the end of
your lives.
9. And it shall come to pass that whosoever doeth this shall be
found at the right hand of God, for he shall know the name by
which he is called; for he shall be called by the name of Christ.
10. And now it shall come to pass, that whosoever shall not take
upon him the name of Christ must be called by some other name;
therefore, he findeth himself on the left hand of God.
11. And I would that ye should remember also, that this is the
name that I said I should give unto you that never should be blotted out, except it be through transgression; therefore, take heed
that ye do not transgress, that the name be not blotted out of your
hearts.
12. I say unto you, I would that ye should remember to retain the
name written always in your hearts, that ye are not found on the
left hand of God, but that ye hear and know the voice by which ye
shall be called, and also, the name by which he shall call you.
13. For how knoweth a man the master whom he has not served, and
who is a stranger unto him, and is far from the thoughts and intents
of his heart?
14. And again, doth a man take an ass which belongeth to his
neighbor, and keep him? I say unto you, Nay; he will not even suffer that he shall feed among his flocks, but will drive him away, and
cast him out. I say unto you, that even so shall it be among you if
ye know not the name by which ye are called.
15. Therefore, I would that ye should be steadfast and immovable,
always abounding in good works, that Christ, the Lord God
Omnipotent,

Mosiah 5:5

According to President Ezra Taft Benson, the people had already been baptized, but had not been fully converted. They now needed to renew their covenants and become sanctified.

Mosiah 5:7

President Joseph Fielding Smith taught that a child is one who is begotten or is given life by another. Christ gave us life from death, becoming our father by giving us immortality. In taking His name upon us, we can also receive his nature—just as a child takes the name, and often the nature, of earthly parents. Will we each pay the price to become a son or daughter of Christ?

Mosiah 5:9, 10

The right hand of God represents mercy, righteousness, power, and salvation. The left hand of God symbolizes justice, uncleanness, and damnation.

Mosiah 5:13

President James E. Faust counsels that developing a relationship with Christ requires daily prayer, daily selfless service to others, daily striving for increased obedience and perfection, daily acknowledgment of Christ's divinity, and daily scripture study. Through these devoted efforts to come to know Christ, "he will unveil his face unto you" (D&C 88:67).

may seal you his, that you may be brought to heaven, that ye may have everlasting salvation and eternal life, through the wisdom, and power, and justice, and mercy of him who created all things, in heaven and in earth, who is God above all. Amen.

CHAPTER 6

1. AND now, king Benjamin thought it was expedient, after having finished speaking to the people, that he should take the names of all those who had entered into a covenant with God to keep his commandments.
2. And it came to pass that there was not one soul, except it were little children, but who had entered into the covenant and had taken upon them the name of Christ.
3. And again, it came to pass that when king Benjamin had made an end of all these things, and had consecrated his son Mosiah to be a ruler and a king over his people, and had given him all the charges concerning the kingdom, and also had appointed priests to teach the people, that thereby they might hear and know the commandments of God, and to stir them up in remembrance of the oath which they had made, he dismissed the multitude, and they returned, every one, according to their families, to their own houses.
4. And Mosiah began to reign in his father's stead. And he began to reign in the thirtieth year of his age, making in the whole, about four hundred and seventy-six years from the time that Lehi left Jerusalem.
5. And king Benjamin lived three years and he died.
6. And it came to pass that king Mosiah did walk in the ways of the Lord, and did observe his judgments and his statutes, and did keep his commandments in all things whatsoever he commanded him.
7. And king Mosiah did cause his people that they should till the earth. And he also, himself, did till the earth, that thereby he might not become burdensome to his people, that he might do according to that which his father had done in all things. And there was no contention among all his people for the space of three years.

Mosiah 6:2

A covenant is a solemn agreement between God and man. It lifts us, makes us free, and keeps open the channel between us and the Lord. This verse, indicating that all adults entered into the covenant to keep God's commandments, demonstrates how powerful King Benjamin's sermon was.

Mosiah 6:3

Benjamin named his son after his father, Mosiah. The son kept this record (the book of Mosiah); the father was commanded to flee into the wilderness because of the wickedness of the Nephites.

CHAPTER 7

1. AND now, it came to pass that after king Mosiah had had continual peace for the space of three years, he was desirous to know concerning the people who went up to dwell in the land of Lehi-Nephi, or in the city of Lehi-Nephi; for his people had heard nothing from them from the time they left the land of Zarahemla; therefore, they wearied him with their teasings.
2. And it came to pass that king Mosiah granted that sixteen of their strong men might go up to the land of Lehi-Nephi, to inquire concerning their brethren.

Mosiah 7

This begins the account of the colony of Nephites that has returned south (see Omni 1:27, 28). Verses 7 and 8 tell that the searchers found the colonists in bondage; verses 19–22 describe how the colonists were delivered from bondage; and verses 23–24 show how Alma's followers were delivered.

3. And it came to pass that on the morrow they started to go up,
having with them one Ammon, he being a strong and mighty man,
and a descendant of Zarahemla; and he was also their leader.
4. And now, they knew not the course they should travel in the
wilderness to go up to the land of Lehi-Nephi; therefore they wandered many days in the wilderness, even forty days did they wander.
5. And when they had wandered forty days they came to a hill,
which is north of the land of Shilom, and there they pitched their
tents.
6. And Ammon took three of his brethren, and their names were
Amaleki, Helem, and Hem, and they went down into the land of
Nephi.
7. And behold, they met the king of the people who were in the
land of Nephi, and in the land of Shilom; and they were surrounded by the king's guard, and were taken, and were bound, and were
committed to prison.
8. And it came to pass when they had been in prison two days they
were again brought before the king, and their bands were loosed;
and they stood before the king, and were permitted, or rather commanded, that they should answer the questions which he should
ask them.
9. And he said unto them: Behold, I am Limhi, the son of Noah,
who was the son of Zeniff, who came up out of the land of
Zarahemla to inherit this land, which was the land of their fathers,
who was made a king by the voice of the people.
10. And now, I desire to know the cause whereby ye were so bold
as to come near the walls of the city, when I, myself, was with my
guards without the gate?
11. And now, for this cause have I suffered that ye should be preserved, that I might inquire of you, or else I should have caused that
my guards should have put you to death. Ye are permitted to speak.
12. And now, when Ammon saw that he was permitted to speak,
he went forth and bowed himself before the king; and rising again
he said: O king, I am very thankful before God this day that I am
yet alive, and am permitted to speak; and I will endeavor to speak
with boldness;
13. For I am assured that if ye had known me ye would not have suffered that I should have worn these bands. For I am Ammon, and am
a descendant of Zarahemla, and have come up out of the land of
Zarahemla to inquire concerning our brethren, whom Zeniff brought
up out of that land.
14. And now, it came to pass that after Limhi had heard the words
of Ammon, he was exceedingly glad, and said: Now, I know of a
surety that my brethren who were in the land of Zarahemla are yet
alive. And now, I will rejoice; and on the morrow I will cause that
my people shall rejoice also.
15. For behold, we are in bondage to the Lamanites, and are taxed
with a tax which is grievous to be borne. And now, behold, our
brethren will deliver us out of our bondage, or out of the hands of the

POINT OF INTEREST

At right is an image of a priest figure from the Tablet of the Sun found at the Palace of Palenque in Chiapas, Mexico.

Lamanites, and we will be their slaves; for it is better that we be slaves
to the Nephites than to pay tribute to the king of the Lamanites.
16. And now, king Limhi commanded his guards that they should no
more bind Ammon nor his brethren, but caused that they should go
to the hill which was north of Shilom, and bring their brethren into
the city, that thereby they might eat, and drink, and rest themselves
from the labors of their journey; for they had suffered many things;
they had suffered hunger, thirst, and fatigue.
17. And now, it came to pass on the morrow that king Limhi sent
a proclamation among all his people, that thereby they might gather themselves together to the temple, to hear the words which he
should speak unto them.
18. And it came to pass that when they had gathered themselves
together that he spake unto them in this wise, saying: O ye, my
people, lift up your heads and be comforted; for behold, the time is
at hand, or is not far distant, when we shall no longer be in subjection to our enemies, notwithstanding our many strugglings,
which have been in vain; yet I trust there remaineth an effectual
struggle to be made.
19. Therefore, lift up your heads, and rejoice, and put your trust in
God, in that God who was the God of Abraham, and Isaac, and
Jacob; and also, that God who brought the children of Israel out of
the land of Egypt, and caused that they should walk through the
Red Sea on dry ground, and fed them with manna that they might
not perish in the wilderness; and many more things did he do for
them.
20. And again, that same God has brought our fathers out of the
land of Jerusalem, and has kept and preserved his people even until
now; and behold, it is because of our iniquities and abominations
that he has brought us into bondage.
21. And ye all are witnesses this day, that Zeniff, who was made
king over this people, he being over-zealous to inherit the land of
his fathers, therefore being deceived by the cunning and craftiness
of king Laman, who having entered into a treaty with king Zeniff,
and having yielded up into his hands the possessions of a part of
the land, or even the city of Lehi-Nephi, and the city of Shilom;
and the land round about—
22. And all this he did, for the sole purpose of bringing this people
into subjection or into bondage. And behold, we at this time do
pay tribute to the king of the Lamanites, to the amount of one half
of our corn, and our barley, and even all our grain of every kind,
and one half of the increase of our flocks and our herds; and even
one half of all we have or possess the king of the Lamanites doth
exact of us, or our lives.
23. And now, is not this grievous to be borne? And is not this, our
affliction, great? Now behold, how great reason we have to mourn.
24. Yea, I say unto you, great are the reasons which we have to
mourn; for behold how many of our brethren have been slain, and
their blood has been spilt in vain, and all because of iniquity.
25. For if this people had not fallen into transgression the Lord
would not have suffered that this great evil should come upon them.
But behold,

Mosiah 7:17

This is the first reference to a temple in the land of Lehi-Nephi. The two earlier temples mentioned in the Book of Mormon were located in the land of Nephi (2 Nephi 5:16) and in the land of Zarahemla (Mosiah 1:18). No further information is provided in our present Book of Mormon concerning when or by whom this temple in the land of Lehi-Nephi was first constructed. (Ludlow)

they would not hearken unto his words; but there arose contentions
among them, even so much that they did shed blood among themselves.
26. And a prophet of the Lord have they slain; yea, a chosen man
of God, who told them of their wickedness and abominations, and
prophesied of many things which are to come, yea, even the coming of Christ.
27. And because he said unto them that Christ was the God, the
Father of all things, and said that he should take upon him the
image of man, and it should be the image after which man was created in the beginning; or in other words, he said that man was created after the image of God, and that God should come down
among the children of men, and take upon him flesh and blood,
and go forth upon the face of the earth—
28. And now, because he said this, they did put him to death; and
many more things did they do which brought down the wrath of
God upon them. Therefore, who wondereth that they are in
bondage, and that they are smitten with sore afflictions?
29. For behold, the Lord hath said: I will not succor my people in
the day of their transgression; but I will hedge up their ways that
they prosper not; and their doings shall be as a stumbling block
before them.
30. And again, he saith: If my people shall sow filthiness they shall
reap the chaff thereof in the whirlwind; and the effect thereof is
poison.
31. And again he saith: If my people shall sow filthiness they shall
reap the east wind, which bringeth immediate destruction.
32. And now, behold, the promise of the Lord is fulfilled, and ye
are smitten and afflicted.
33. But if ye will turn to the Lord with full purpose of heart, and
put your trust in him, and serve him with all diligence of mind, if
ye do this, he will, according to his own will and pleasure, deliver
you out of bondage.

Mosiah 7:26

The prophet who is mentioned in this verse as having been killed because of the wickedness and abominations of the people is the prophet Abinadi. The teachings of Abinadi are found in Mosiah, chapters 11–17. (Ludlow)

Mosiah 7:29–30

This is similar to what happened to the Saints in Jackson County, Missouri, who were not faithful in keeping their covenants (see D&C 101:7–8).

Mosiah 7:33

Repeated prayers for deliverance uttered by Limhi's people had gone unanswered. The key to deliverance is found in this verse: turning to the Lord with full purpose of heart and serving Him with all diligence of mind.

CHAPTER 8

1. AND it came to pass that after king Limhi had made an end
of speaking to his people, for he spake many things unto them
and only a few of them have I written in this book, he told his
people all the things concerning their brethren who were in
the land of Zarahemla.
2. And he caused that Ammon should stand up before the
multitude, and rehearse unto them all that had happened
unto their brethren from the time that Zeniff went up out
of the land even until the time that he himself came up
out of the land.
3. And he also rehearsed unto them the last words
which king Benjamin had taught them, and
explained them to the people of king Limhi, so
that they might understand all the words which he
spake.

4. And it came to pass that after he had done all this, that king Limhi dismissed the multitude, and caused that they should return every one unto his own house.
5. And it came to pass that he caused that the plates which contained the record of his people from the time that they left the land of Zarahemla, should be brought before Ammon, that he might read them.
6. Now, as soon as Ammon had read the record, the king inquired of him to know if he could interpret languages, and Ammon told him that he could not.
7. And the king said unto him: Being grieved for the afflictions of my people, I caused that forty and three of my people should take a journey into the wilderness, that thereby they might find the land of Zarahemla, that we might appeal unto our brethren to deliver us out of bondage.
8. And they were lost in the wilderness for the space of many days, yet they were diligent, and found not the land of Zarahemla but returned to this land, having traveled in a land among many waters, having discovered a land which was covered with bones of men, and of beasts, and was also covered with ruins of buildings of every kind, having discovered a land which had been peopled with a people who were as numerous as the hosts of Israel.
9. And for a testimony that the things that they had said are true they have brought twenty-four plates which are filled with engravings, and they are of pure gold.
10. And behold, also, they have brought breastplates, which are large, and they are of brass and of copper, and are perfectly sound.
11. And again, they have brought swords, the hilts thereof have perished, and the blades thereof were cankered with rust; and there is no one in the land that is able to interpret the language or the engravings that are on the plates. Therefore I said unto thee: Canst thou translate?
12. And I say unto thee again: Knowest thou of any one that can translate? For I am desirous that these records should be translated into our language; for, perhaps, they will give us a knowledge of a remnant of the people who have been destroyed, from whence these records came; or, perhaps, they will give us a knowledge of this very people who have been destroyed; and I am desirous to know the cause of their destruction.
13. Now Ammon said unto him: I can assuredly tell thee, O king, of a man that can translate the records; for he has wherewith that he can look, and translate all records that are of ancient date; and it is a gift from God. And the things are called interpreters, and no man can look in them except he be commanded, lest he should look for that he ought not and he should perish. And whosoever is commanded to look in them, the same is called seer.
14. And behold, the king of the people who are in the land of Zarahemla is the man that is commanded to do these things, and who has this high gift from God.
15. And the king said that a seer is greater than a prophet.
16. And Ammon said that a seer is a revelator and a prophet also; and a gift which is greater can no man

Mosiah 8:7–12

The evidences of destruction that were discovered by the forty-three scouts sent out by King Limhi are the remains of the great Jaredite civilization of which we will read in the book of Ether. (Ludlow)

Mosiah 8:13

The records in the book of Ether contained visions given to the brother of Jared. He was commanded not to make them public in his lifetime, but to record them in the language that was used before the Tower of Babel (no longer known), then to seal them.

Mosiah 8:13–17

The word *seer* literally means one who sees: a see-er. Ammon says a seer is a person who has the right to use the "interpreters" or the Urim and Thummin. (Mosiah 8:13–17; see also Mosiah 28:10–16.) He states further: "a seer is a revelator and a prophet also; and a gift which is greater can no man have." (Mosiah 8:16.) Members of The Church of Jesus Christ of Latter-day Saints regularly sustain the members of the First Presidency, the Council of the Twelve Apostles, and the Patriarch to the Church as "Prophets, Seers, and Revelators." (Ludlow)

Mosiah 8:13–17

"Seer" and "Prophet" are interchangeable terms, supposed by many to signify one and the same thing. Strictly speaking, however, this is not correct. A seer is greater than a prophet. One may be a prophet without being a seer; but a seer is essentially a prophet—if by "prophet" is meant not only a spokesman, but likewise a foreteller. Joseph Smith was both prophet and seer (Orson F. Whitney, *Saturday Night Thoughts* [Salt Lake City: *Deseret News*, 1921], 39). (P/A)

Mosiah 8:14–17

The President of the Church, the First Presidency, and the Council of the Twelve are all sustained as prophets, seers, and revelators. A seer is a prophet who is chosen to possess and use the Urim and Thummim.

POINT OF INTEREST

The Temple of the Sun (left) at Palenque, Mexico, contains some of Mesoamerica's most elaborate hieroglyphics.

have, except he should possess the power of God, which no man can; yet a man may have great power given him from God.
17. But a seer can know of things which are past, and also of things which are to come, and by them shall all things be revealed, or, rather, shall secret things be made manifest, and hidden things shall come to light, and things which are not known shall be made known by them, and also things shall be made known by them which otherwise could not be known.
18. Thus God has provided a means that man, through faith, might work mighty miracles; therefore he becometh a great benefit to his fellow beings.
19. And now, when Ammon had made an end of speaking these words the king rejoiced exceedingly, and gave thanks to God, saying: Doubtless a great mystery is contained within these plates, and these interpreters were doubtless prepared for the purpose of unfolding all such mysteries to the children of men.
20. O how marvelous are the works of the Lord, and how long doth he suffer with his people; yea, and how blind and impenetrable are the understandings of the children of men; for they will not seek wisdom, neither do they desire that she should rule over them!
21. Yea, they are as a wild flock which fleeth from the shepherd, and scattereth, and are driven, and are devoured by the beasts of the forest.

THE RECORD OF ZENIFF—*An account of his people, from the time they left the land of Zarahemla until the time that they were delivered out of the hands of the Lamanites. Comprising chapters 9 through 22 inclusive.*

CHAPTER 9

1. I, Zeniff, having been taught in all the language of the Nephites, and having had a knowledge of the land of Nephi, or of the land of our fathers' first inheritance, and having been sent as a spy among the Lamanites that I might spy out their forces, that our army might come upon them and destroy them—but when I saw that which was good among them I was desirous that they should not be destroyed.
2. Therefore, I contended with my brethren in the wilderness, for I would that our ruler should make a treaty with them; but he being an austere and a bloodthirsty man commanded that I should be slain; but I was rescued by the shedding of much blood; for father fought against father, and brother against brother, until the greater number of our army was destroyed in the wilderness; and we returned, those of us that were spared, to the land of Zarahemla, to relate that tale to their wives and their children.
3. And yet, I being over-zealous to inherit the land of our fathers, collected as many as were desirous to go up to possess the land, and started again on our journey into the wilderness to go up to the land; but we were smitten with famine and sore afflictions; for we were slow to remember the Lord our God.
4. Nevertheless, after many days' wandering in the wilderness we pitched our tents in the place where our brethren were slain, which was near to the land of our fathers.
5. And it came to pass that I went again with four of my men into the

Mosiah 9

It is through the Limhi/Noah/Zeniff chronicle (Mosiah 9–22) that we experience an amazing resonance of the scattering/gathering theme, which is a leitmotif throughout the Book of Mormon. Limhi and his people, as it turns out, are in bondage to the Lamanites because of the festering iniquity that has crept in among them through the materialistic and lascivious living of the previous King Noah and his minions. We witness the joy of Limhi and his people upon the arrival of Ammon, in whom they see the answer to their prayers for deliverance and the opportunity to return to the safety of Zarahemla. It is a chronic pattern captured once again by the ancient prophet-historians for the benefit of modern readers: sin and depravity lead to bondage—because they "were slow to remember the Lord our God"—(Mosiah 9:3); repentance and righteousness lead to liberty. God's people are scattered and gathered according to His design for the immortality and eternal life of man. (P/A)

Mosiah 9:1

Chapters 9 and 10 of Mosiah are evidently taken verbatim from a record originally prepared by Zeniff. Note that these two chapters are written in the first person: "I, Zeniff," etc. Beginning with chapter 11, the account is written in the third person, although these materials also evidently come from the record of Zeniff. (Ludlow)

city, in unto the king, that I might know of the disposition of the
king, and that I might know if I might go in with my people and
possess the land in peace.
6. And I went in unto the king, and he covenanted with me that
I might possess the land of Lehi- Nephi, and the land of Shilom.
7. And he also commanded that his people should depart out of the
land, and I and my people went into the land that we might possess it.
8. And we began to build buildings, and to repair the walls of the
city, yea, even the walls of the city of Lehi-Nephi, and the city of
Shilom.
9. And we began to till the ground, yea, even with all manner of
seeds, with seeds of corn, and of wheat, and of barley, and with
neas, and with sheum, and with seeds of all manner of fruits; and
we did begin to multiply and prosper in the land.
10. Now it was the cunning and the craftiness of king Laman, to
bring my people into bondage, that he yielded up the land that we
might possess it.
11. Therefore it came to pass, that after we had dwelt in the land
for the space of twelve years that king Laman began to grow
uneasy, lest by any means my people should wax strong in the land,
and that they could not overpower them and bring them into
bondage.
12. Now they were a lazy and an idolatrous people; therefore they
were desirous to bring us into bondage, that they might glut themselves with the labors of our hands; yea, that they might feast
themselves upon the flocks of our fields.
13. Therefore it came to pass that king Laman began to stir up his
people that they should contend with my people; therefore there
began to be wars and contentions in the land.
14. For, in the thirteenth year of my reign in the land of Nephi,
away on the south of the land of Shilom, when my people were
watering and feeding their flocks, and tilling their lands, a numerous host of Lamanites came upon them and began to slay them,
and to take off their flocks, and the corn of their fields.
15. Yea, and it came to pass that they fled, all that were not overtaken, even into the city of Nephi, and did call upon me for protection.
16. And it came to pass that I did arm them with bows, and with
arrows, with swords, and with cimeters, and with clubs, and with
slings, and with all manner of weapons which we could invent, and
I and my people did go forth against the Lamanites to battle.
17. Yea, in the strength of the Lord did we go forth to battle against
the Lamanites; for I and my people did cry mightily to the Lord
that he would deliver us out of the hands of our enemies, for we
were awakened to a remembrance of the deliverance of our fathers.
18. And God did hear our cries and did answer our prayers; and we
did go forth in his might; yea, we did go forth against the
Lamanites, and in one day and a night we did slay three thousand
and forty-three; we did slay them even until we had driven them
out of our land.
19. And I, myself, with mine own hands, did help to bury their dead.
And behold, to our great sorrow and lamentation, two hundred and
seventy-nine of our brethren were slain.

Mosiah 9:9

Although the equivalent of the word *corn* is used in some Semitic languages to refer to various types of cereals, including wheat, Joseph Smith would probably translate it here so it would be clear to the understanding of his readers in the United States. Thus, the "corn" here is probably maize, which is frequently called corn in the Americas. It is not clear what crops are referred to by the titles of "neas" and "sheum." (Ludlow)

POINT OF INTEREST

In the current English-language edition of the Book of Mormon, 433 verses of Isaiah appear. (Those verses represent approximately a third of the book of Isaiah as it appears in the King James Version of the Bible.) Of those 433 verses, 233 verses (roughly half) are different in the Book of Mormon than in the King James Version of the Bible, while 200 of the verses have the same wording as in the Bible. Of the 433 verses that appear in the Book of Mormon, 391 describe the mission or attributes of the Savior, making Isaiah not only a significant contributor to the Book of Mormon, but one of its significant witnesses of Jesus Christ.

CHAPTER 10

1. AND it came to pass that we again began to establish the kingdom and we again began to possess the land in peace. And I caused that there should be weapons of war made of every kind, that thereby I might have weapons for my people against the time the Lamanites should come up again to war against my people.
2. And I set guards round about the land, that the Lamanites might not come upon us again unawares and destroy us; and thus I did guard my people and my flocks, and keep them from falling into the hands of our enemies.
3. And it came to pass that we did inherit the land of our fathers for many years, yea, for the space of twenty and two years.
4. And I did cause that the men should till the ground, and raise all manner of grain and all manner of fruit of every kind.
5. And I did cause that the women should spin, and toil, and work, and work all manner of fine linen, yea, and cloth of every kind, that we might clothe our nakedness; and thus we did prosper in the land—thus we did have continual peace in the land for the space of twenty and two years.
6. And it came to pass that king Laman died, and his son began to reign in his stead. And he began to stir his people up in rebellion against my people; therefore they began to prepare for war, and to come up to battle against my people.
7. But I had sent my spies out round about the land of Shemlon, that I might discover their preparations, that I might guard against them, that they might not come upon my people and destroy them.
8. And it came to pass that they came up upon the north of the land of Shilom, with their numerous hosts, men armed with bows, and with arrows, and with swords, and with cimeters, and with stones, and with slings; and they had their heads shaved that they were naked; and they were girded with a leathern girdle about their loins.
9. And it came to pass that I caused that the women and children of my people should be hid in the wilderness; and I also caused that all my old men that could bear arms, and also all my young men that were able to bear arms, should gather themselves together to go to battle against the Lamanites; and I did place them in their ranks, every man according to his age.
10. And it came to pass that we did go up to battle against the Lamanites; and I, even I, in my old age, did go up to battle against the Lamanites. And it came to pass that we did go up in the strength of the Lord to battle.
11. Now, the Lamanites knew nothing concerning the Lord, nor the strength of the Lord, therefore they depended upon their own strength. Yet they were a strong people, as to the strength of men.
12. They were a wild, and ferocious, and a blood-thirsty people, believing in the tradition of their fathers, which is this—Believing that they were driven out of the land of Jerusalem because of the iniquities of their fathers, and that they were wronged in the wilderness by their brethren, and they were also wronged while crossing the sea;
13. And again, that they were

Mosiah 10:6

Evidently the Lamanites have used the same procedure as the Nephites did in their early history of naming their kings after their earliest leader. Jacob 1:11 mentions that the kings who succeeded Nephi were known as "second Nephi, third Nephi, and so forth, according to the reigns of the kings." Thus it should not be too surprising to discover that the king of the Lamanites in approximately 178 B.C. was still known as "King Laman" (Mosiah 10:6), although the original leader after whom the king was named had lived some four hundred years before. Also, later in the Book of Mormon we discover that the son who succeeded this king is also known as Laman. (See Mosiah 24:3.) (Ludlow)

Mosiah 10:12–17

False traditions had been handed down by the Lamanites from generation to generation, and, with the passage of time, some of these false teachings were apparently accepted by many of the Lamanites as being true. Some of these false teachings were:

1. That Laman and Lemuel were driven out of the land of Jerusalem "because of the iniquities of their father." (Actually Lehi and his group were led away from Jerusalem and impending destruction because of the righteousness of Lehi.)
2. That Laman and Lemuel were "wronged" by their brethren "in the wilderness" . . . "while crossing the sea" . . . "while in the land of their first inheritance." (The Lord was directing the righteous leaders, Lehi and Nephi, as to what should be done.)
3. That Nephi had wrongfully "taken the ruling of the people" out of the hands of Laman and Lemuel. (The Lord designated Nephi as the new leader because of his faithfulness in keeping the commandments.)
4. That Nephi robbed Laman and Lemuel by taking "the records which were engraven on the plates of brass." (Nephi was rightfully entitled to these records because he was God's chosen religious leader of the group.)

Because of these false traditions the Lamanites had taught their children that they should hate, rob, and murder the Nephites; therefore, the Lamanites had "an eternal hatred towards the children of Nephi" (Mosiah 10:17). (Ludlow)

wronged while in the land of their first inheritance, after they had crossed the sea, and all this because that Nephi was more faithful in keeping the commandments of the Lord—therefore he was favored of the Lord, for the Lord heard his prayers and answered them, and he took the lead of their journey in the wilderness.

14. And his brethren were wroth with him because they understood not the dealings of the Lord; they were also wroth with him upon the waters because they hardened their hearts against the Lord.

15. And again, they were wroth with him when they had arrived in the promised land, because they said that he had taken the ruling of the people out of their hands; and they sought to kill him.

16. And again, they were wroth with him because he departed into the wilderness as the Lord had commanded him, and took the records which were engraven on the plates of brass, for they said that he robbed them.

17. And thus they have taught their children that they should hate them, and that they should murder them, and that they should rob and plunder them, and do all they could to destroy them; therefore they have an eternal hatred towards the children of Nephi.

18. For this very cause has king Laman, by his cunning, and lying craftiness, and his fair promises, deceived me, that I have brought this my people up into this land, that they may destroy them; yea, and we have suffered these many years in the land.

19. And now I, Zeniff, after having told all these things unto my people concerning the Lamanites, I did stimulate them to go to battle with their might, putting their trust in the Lord; therefore, we did contend with them, face to face.

20. And it came to pass that we did drive them again out of our land; and we slew them with a great slaughter, even so many that we did not number them.

21. And it came to pass that we returned again to our own land, and my people again began to tend their flocks, and to till their ground.

22. And now I, being old, did confer the kingdom upon one of my sons; therefore, I say no more. And may the Lord bless my people. Amen.

CHAPTER 11

1. AND now it came to pass that Zeniff conferred the kingdom upon Noah, one of his sons; therefore Noah began to reign in his stead; and he did not walk in the ways of his father.

2. For behold, he did not keep the commandments of God, but he did walk after the desires of his own heart. And he had many wives and concubines. And he did cause his people to commit sin, and do that which was abominable in the sight of the Lord. Yea, and they did commit whoredoms and all manner of wickedness.

3. And he laid a tax of one fifth part of all they possessed, a fifth part of their gold and of their silver,

Mosiah 10:16

As the designaed religious leader, Nephi was entitled to the plates. The Lord had designated him the leader because of his faithfulness.

Mosiah 11:1

Mormon evidently now begins abridging the original record of Zeniff. Note that chapter 11 is primarily written in the third person, whereas chapters 9 and 10 were written in the first person. Note also how Mormon tells us in one brief statement of the wicked character of King Noah: "he did not walk in the ways of his father." (Ludlow)

Noah walked in darkness and sin, lured people away from God, and reigned in cruelty. He is the prime example of unrighteous leadership.

Mosiah 11:2

According to Elder Bruce R. McConkie, concubines were secondary wives who were not equal in the caste system. In Old Testament times, the Lord approved having concubines, and those who had concubines did not violate the law of chastity. In the time of King Noah, however, it refers to the practice of living with more than one woman in or out of marriage without God's approval. "Whoredoms" are any perversion of the laws of chastity and virtue.

and a fifth part of their ziff, and of their copper, and of their brass and their iron; and a fifth part of their fatlings; and also a fifth part of all their grain.
4. And all this did he take to support himself, and his wives and his concubines; and also his priests, and their wives and their concubines; thus he had changed the affairs of the kingdom.
5. For he put down all the priests that had been consecrated by his father, and consecrated new ones in their stead, such as were lifted up in the pride of their hearts.
6. Yea, and thus they were supported in their laziness, and in their idolatry, and in their whoredoms, by the taxes which king Noah had put upon his people; thus did the people labor exceedingly to support iniquity.
7. Yea, and they also became idolatrous, because they were deceived by the vain and flattering words of the king and priests; for they did speak flattering things unto them.
8. And it came to pass that king Noah built many elegant and spacious buildings; and he ornamented them with fine work of wood, and of all manner of precious things, of gold, and of silver, and of iron, and of brass, and of ziff, and of copper;
9. And he also built him a spacious palace, and a throne in the midst thereof, all of which was of fine wood and was ornamented with gold and silver and with precious things.
10. And he also caused that his workmen should work all manner of fine work within the walls of the temple, of fine wood, and of copper, and of brass.
11. And the seats which were set apart for the high priests, which were above all the other seats, he did ornament with pure gold; and he caused a breastwork to be built before them, that they might rest their bodies and their arms upon while they should speak lying and vain words to his people.
12. And it came to pass that he built a tower near the temple; yea, a very high tower, even so high that he could stand upon the top thereof and overlook the land of Shilom, and also the land of Shemlon, which was possessed by the Lamanites; and he could even look over all the land round about.
13. And it came to pass that he caused many buildings to be built in the land Shilom; and he caused a great tower to be built on the hill north of the land Shilom, which had been a resort for the children of Nephi at the time they fled out of the land; and thus he did do with the riches which he obtained by the taxation of his people.
14. And it came to pass that he placed his heart upon his riches, and he spent his time in riotous living with his wives and his concubines; and so did also his priests spend their time with harlots.
15. And it came to pass that he planted vineyards round about in the land; and he built wine-presses, and made wine in abundance; and therefore he became a wine-bibber, and also his people.
16. And it came to pass that the Lamanites began to come in upon his people, upon small numbers, and to slay them in their fields, and while they were tending their flocks.
17. And king Noah sent guards round about the land to keep them

Mosiah 11:3–15

These verses show the stunning contrast between Noah and Zeniff.

Mosiah 11:3

Ziff is a metal that is now unknown. In Hebrew, the word means "brightness."

Mosiah 11:6–9

These verses describe how a wicked government can lead the people to become wicked.

Mosiah 11:7

Vain people often allow themselves to be seduced more easily. Unrighteous governments of all ages have maintained power by appealing to the vanity of the people over whom they rule—usually by constructing huge buildings and by achieving victory in war.

Mosiah 11:16

This verse describes the literal fulfillment of prophecy (see 1 Nephi 2:21–24).

off; but he did not send asufficient number, and the Lamanites came upon them and killed them, and drove many of their flocks out of the land; thus the Lamanites began to destroy them, and to exercise their hatred upon them.
18. And it came to pass that king Noah sent his armies against them, and they were driven back, or they drove them back for a time; therefore, they returned rejoicing in their spoil.
19. And now, because of this great victory they were lifted up in the pride of their hearts; they did boast in their own strength, saying that their fifty could stand against thousands of the Lamanites; and thus they did boast, and did delight in blood, and the shedding of the blood of their brethren, and this because of the wickedness of their king and priests.
20. And it came to pass that there was a man among them whose name was Abinadi; and he went forth among them, and began to prophesy, saying: Behold, thus saith the Lord, and thus hath he commanded me, saying, Go forth, and say unto this people, thus saith the Lord—Wo be unto this people, for I have seen their abominations, and their wickedness, and their whoredoms; and except they repent I will visit them in mine anger.
21. And except they repent and turn to the Lord their God, behold, I will deliver them into the hands of their enemies; yea, and they shall be brought into bondage; and they shall be afflicted by the hand of their enemies.
22. And it shall come to pass that they shall know that I am the Lord their God, and am a jealous God, visiting the iniquities of my people.
23. And it shall come to pass that except this people repent and turn unto the Lord their God, they shall be brought into bondage; and none shall deliver them, except it be the Lord the Almighty God.
24. Yea, and it shall come to pass that when they shall cry unto me I will be slow to hear their cries; yea, and I will suffer them that they be smitten by their enemies.
25. And except they repent in sackcloth and ashes, and cry mightily to the Lord their God, I will not hear their prayers, neither will I deliver them out of their afflictions; and thus saith the Lord, and thus hath he commanded me.
26. Now it came to pass that when Abinadi had spoken these words unto them they were wroth with him, and sought to take away his life; but the Lord delivered him out of their hands.
27. Now when king Noah had heard of the words which Abinadi had spoken unto the people, he was also wroth; and he said: Who is Abinadi, that I and my people should be judged of him, or who is the Lord, that shall bring upon my people such great affliction?
28. I command you to bring Abinadi hither, that I may slay him, for he has said these things that he might stir up my people to anger one with another, and to raise contentions among my people; therefore I will slay him.
29. Now the eyes of the people were blinded; therefore they hardened their hearts against the words of

Mosiah 11:19

Victory at war is one of the most common ways in which unrighteous leaders appeal to the vanity of the people. President Spencer W. Kimball lamented that, on the whole, we are a war-like and idolatrous people, which is repugnant to the Lord. These qualities too easily distract us from our assignment to prepare for the Lord's Second Coming.

Mosiah 11:20–25

Abinadi offered two clear choices, which are still valid today: the people could either repent or be taken into bondage.

Mosiah 11:26–29

What is recorded in these verses is a typical reaction of wicked people to a prophet of God—truth hurts. In contrast, false prophets and corrupt priests flourish because they salve the wicked and tell them that their wicked acts are acceptable to God.

Mosiah 11:29

Each of us is responsible for seeking and listening to the gentle whisperings of the Spirit in our lives, and acting in compliance with what we are directed by the Spirit. There is for us an extra measure of direction from the living prophets who are set in place to guide and direct us. Hardening our hearts against the words of those prophets can in fact limit our ability to receive direction from the Spirit as well, leaving us in a void in which we have no direction.

Mosiah 11:29

We are blessed to have living prophets, seers, and revelators to guide the Church and teach us how to conduct our lives. As we live by every word that proceeds forth from the mouth of God, we will live by the words of our living prophet, who is in fact His mouthpiece. This shows our love and commitment, while keeping us on the straight and narrow path that leads to eternal life. Speaking of the blessing of a living prophet, President Howard W. Hunter said, "As the prophets from the beginning to the present day pass in review before our memory, we become aware of the great blessing which comes to us from the influence of a living prophet. History should teach us that unless we are willing to heed the warnings and follow the teachings of a prophet of the Lord, we will be subject to the judgments of God." (P/A)

Abinadi, and they sought from that time forward to take him. And king Noah hardened his heart against the word of the Lord, and he did not repent of his evil doings.

CHAPTER 12

1. AND it came to pass that after the space of two years that Abinadi came among them in disguise, that they knew him not, and began to prophesy among them, saying: Thus has the Lord commanded me, saying—Abinadi, go and prophesy unto this my people, for they have hardened their hearts against my words; they have repented not of their evil doings; therefore, I will visit them in my anger, yea, in my fierce anger will I visit them in their iniquities and abominations.

2. Yea, wo be unto this generation! And the Lord said unto me: Stretch forth thy hand and prophesy saying: Thus saith the Lord, it shall come to pass that this generation, because of their iniquities, shall be brought into bondage, and shall be smitten on the cheek; yea, and shall be driven by men, and shall be slain; and the vultures of the air, and the dogs, yea, and the wild beasts, shall devour their flesh.

3. And it shall come to pass that the life of king Noah shall be valued even as a garment in a hot furnace; for he shall know that I am the Lord.

4. And it shall come to pass that I will smite this my people with sore afflictions, yea, with famine and with pestilence; and I will cause that they shall howl all the day long.

5. Yea, and I will cause that they shall have burdens lashed upon their backs; and they shall be driven before like a dumb ass.

6. And it shall come to pass that I will send forth hail among them, and it shall smite them; and they shall also be smitten with the east wind; and insects shall pester their land also, and devour their grain.

7. And they shall be smitten with a great pestilence—and all this will I do because of their iniquities and abominations.

8. And it shall come to pass that except they repent I will utterly destroy them from off the face of the earth; yet they shall leave a record behind them, and I will preserve them for other nations which shall possess the land; yea, even this will I do that I may discover the abominations of this people to other nations. And many things did Abinadi prophesy against this people.

9. And it came to pass that they were angry with him; and they took him and carried him bound before the king, and said unto the king: Behold, we have brought a man before thee who has prophesied evil concerning thy people, and saith that God will destroy them.

10. And he also prophesieth evil concerning thy life, and saith that thy life shall be as a garment in a furnace of fire.

11. And again, he saith that thou

Mosiah 12:2, 4–7

For the literal fulfillment of these prophecies, see Mosiah 21.

Mosiah 12:3–8

Abinadi's message was much more harsh this time. For the fulfillment of the prophecy in verse 3, see Mosiah 19.

POINT OF INTEREST

Kings in the Land of Nephi

Zeniff	*Around 200 B.C. (Mosiah 9:3–6). Nephite spy sent to land of Nephi, who then desired to reclaim this land of his fathers and led away a group of Nephites to begin a new colony. The Lamanite king Laman gave Zeniff's group the land of Nephi-Lehi and the land Shilom.*
Noah	*Around 160 B.C. (Mosiah 10:22). Zeniff's wicked son who was king at the time of Abinadi's ministry. He put Abinadi to death by fire but, as prophesied, was then put to death in the same manner by his own wicked priests. At the time of Noah's death, his people fell into Lamanite bondage with most of its inhabitants taken captive.*
Limhi	*Between 145–122 B.C. (Mosiah 19:26). One of King Noah's "just" sons, Limhi was taken captive by Lamanites during his father's rule. King Noah died while his son Limhi was in captivity. After Noah's former subjects covenant to give half the Lamanites half of their increase, Limhi and his people are freed and he is then appointed to rule.*

shalt be as a stalk, even as a dry stalk of the field, which is run over by the beasts and trodden under foot.
12. And again, he saith thou shalt be as the blossoms of a thistle, which, when it is fully ripe, if the wind bloweth, it is driven forth upon the face of the land. And he pretendeth the Lord hath spoken it. And he saith all this shall come upon thee except thou repent, and this because of thine iniquities.
13. And now, O king, what great evil hast thou done, or what great sins have thy people committed, that we should be condemned of God or judged of this man?
14. And now, O king, behold, we are guiltless, and thou, O king, hast not sinned; therefore, this man has lied concerning you, and he has prophesied in vain.
15. And behold, we are strong, we shall not come into bondage, or be taken captive by our enemies; yea, and thou hast prospered in the land, and thou shalt also prosper.
16. Behold, here is the man, we deliver him into thy hands; thou mayest do with him as seemeth thee good.
17. And it came to pass that king Noah caused that Abinadi should be cast into prison; and he commanded that the priests should gather themselves together that he might hold a council with them what he should do with him.
18. And it came to pass that they said unto the king: Bring him hither that we may question him; and the king commanded that he should be brought before them.
19. And they began to question him, that they might cross him, that thereby they might have wherewith to accuse him; but he answered them boldly, and withstood all their questions, yea, to their astonishment; for he did withstand them in all their questions, and did confound them in all their words.
20. And it came to pass that one of them said unto him: What meaneth the words which are written, and which have been taught by our fathers, saying:
21. How beautiful upon the mountains are the feet of him that bringeth good tidings; that publisheth peace; that bringeth good tidings of good; that publisheth salvation; that saith unto Zion, Thy God reigneth;
22. Thy watchmen shall lift up the voice; with the voice together shall they sing; for they shall see eye to eye when the Lord shall bring again Zion;
23. Break forth into joy; sing together ye waste places of Jerusalem; for the Lord hath comforted his people, he hath redeemed Jerusalem;
24. The Lord hath made bare his holy arm in the eyes of all the nations, and all the ends of the earth shall see the salvation of our God?
25. And now Abinadi said unto them: Are you priests, and pretend to teach this people, and to understand the spirit of prophesying, and yet desire to know of me what these things mean?
26. I say unto you, wo be unto you for perverting the ways of the Lord! For if ye understand these things ye have not taught them; therefore, ye have perverted the ways of the Lord.
27. Ye have not applied your hearts to understanding; therefore, ye have not been wise. Therefore, what teach ye this people?
28. And they said: We teach the law of Moses.
29. And again he said unto them:

Mosiah 12:19

The process Abinadi went through with the priests demonstrates the same tactics used by the Sanhedrin against the Savior (see Mark 14:55–64).

Mosiah 12:20–24

The "words" referred to here are the words of Isaiah. When challenged with the words of Isaiah, Abinadi told the priests that their lack of understanding was a result of their own wickedness.

Mosiah 12:25

Abinadi chastised the priests for failing to live what they should have been teaching—the Law of Moses and the Ten Commandments.

If ye teach the law of Moses why do ye not keep it? Why do ye set your hearts upon riches? Why do ye commit whoredoms and spend your strength with harlots, yea, and cause this people to commit sin, that the Lord has cause to send me to prophesy against this people, yea, even a great evil against this people?
30. Know ye not that I speak the truth? Yea, ye know that I speak the truth; and you ought to tremble before God.
31. And it shall come to pass that ye shall be smitten for your iniquities, for ye have said that ye teach the law of Moses. And what know ye concerning the law of Moses? Doth salvation come by the law of Moses? What say ye?
32. And they answered and said that salvation did come by the law of Moses.
33. But now Abinadi said unto them: I know if ye keep the commandments of God ye shall be saved; yea, if ye keep the commandments which the Lord delivered unto Moses in the mount of Sinai, saying:
34. I am the Lord thy God, who hath brought thee out of the land of Egypt, out of the house of bondage.
35. Thou shalt have no other God before me.
36. Thou shalt not make unto thee any graven image, or any likeness of any thing in heaven above, or things which are in the earth beneath.
37. Now Abinadi said unto them, Have ye done all this? I say unto you, Nay, ye have not. And have ye taught this people that they should do all these things? I say unto you, Nay, ye have not.

Mosiah 12:33

Abinadi knew the Ten Commandments because the brass plates Nephi got from Laban contained the five books of Moses.

CHAPTER 13

1. AND now when the king had heard these words, he said unto his priests: Away with this fellow, and slay him; for what have we to do with him, for he is mad.
2. And they stood forth and attempted to lay their hands on him; but he withstood them, and said unto them:
3. Touch me not, for God shall smite you if ye lay your hands upon me, for I have not delivered the message which the Lord sent me to deliver; neither have I told you that which ye requested that I should tell; therefore, God will not suffer that I shall be destroyed at this time.
4. But I must fulfil the commandments wherewith God has commanded me; and because I have told you the truth ye are angry with me. And again, because I have spoken the word of God ye have judged me that I am mad.
5. Now it came to pass after Abinadi had spoken these words that the people of king Noah durst not lay their hands on him, for the Spirit of the Lord was upon him; and his face shone with exceeding luster, even as Moses' did while in the mount of Sinai, while speaking with the Lord.
6. And he spake with power and authority from God; and he continued his words, saying:
7. Ye see that ye have not power to

Mosiah 13:5

Notice the following interesting reference concerning Abinadi as he made his defense before Noah and the wicked priests: "the Spirit of the Lord was upon him; and his face shone with exceeding luster, *even as Moses' did while in the mount of Sinai*, while speaking with the Lord." (Italics added.) This statement is of particular interest because of the controversy among biblical scholars and translators concerning the facial appearance of Moses after he had talked with the Lord on the mount of Sinai. The King James Version renders Exodus 34:30 as follows: "And when Aaron and all the children of Israel saw Moses, behold, the skin of his face shone; and they were afraid to come nigh him." However, the Catholic translators of the Douay Version followed the pattern of the Septuagint Bible by translating the same verse as follows: "And he knew not that his face was horned from the conversation with the Lord. And Aaron and the children of Israel seeing the face of Moses horned, were afraid to come near." Because of this faulty interpretation, the great sculptor Michelangelo put horns on his famous statue of Moses! The Book of Mormon again comes to the support of its companion scripture, the Bible, and clarifies an area of controversy; the face of Moses "shone" when he came off the mount. (Ludlow)

slay me, therefore I finish my message. Yea, and I perceive that it cuts you to your hearts because I tell you the truth concerning your iniquities.
8. Yea, and my words fill you with wonder and amazement, and with anger.
9. But I finish my message; and then it matters not whither I go, if it so be that I am saved.
10. But this much I tell you, what you do with me, after this, shall be as a type and a shadow of things which are to come.
11. And now I read unto you the remainder of the commandments of God, for I perceive that they are not written in your hearts; I perceive that ye have studied and taught iniquity the most part of your lives.
12. And now, ye remember that I said unto you: Thou shalt not make unto thee any graven image, or any likeness of things which are in heaven above, or which are in the earth beneath, or which are in the water under the earth.
13. And again: Thou shalt not bow down thyself unto them, nor serve them; for I the Lord thy God am a jealous God, visiting the iniquities of the fathers upon the children, unto the third and fourth generations of them that hate me;
14. And showing mercy unto thousands of them that love me and keep my commandments.
15. Thou shalt not take the name of the Lord thy God in vain; for the Lord will not hold him guiltless that taketh his name in vain.
16. Remember the sabbath day, to keep it holy.
17. Six days shalt thou labor, and do all thy work;
18. But the seventh day, the sabbath of the Lord thy God, thou shalt not do any work, thou, nor thy son, nor thy daughter, thy man-servant, nor thy maid-servant, nor thy cattle, nor thy stranger that is within thy gates;
19. For in six days the Lord made heaven and earth, and the sea, and all that in them is; wherefore the Lord blessed the sabbath day, and hallowed it.
20. Honor thy father and thy mother, that thy days may be long upon the land which the Lord thy God giveth thee.
21. Thou shalt not kill.
22. Thou shalt not commit adultery. Thou shalt not steal.
23. Thou shalt not bear false witness against thy neighbor.
24. Thou shalt not covet thy neighbor's house, thou shalt not covet thy neighbor's wife, nor his man-servant, nor his maid-servant, nor his ox, nor his ass, nor anything that is thy neighbor's.
25. And it came to pass that after Abinadi had made an end of these sayings that he said unto them: Have ye taught this people that they should observe to do all these things for to keep these commandments?
26. I say unto you, Nay; for if ye had, the Lord would not have caused me to come forth and to prophesy evil concerning this people.
27. And now ye have said that salvation cometh by the law of Moses. I say unto you that it is expedient that ye should keep the law of Moses as yet; but I say unto you,

Mosiah 13:11–26

Because the Ten Commandments were given to Moses on Sinai, some have wrongly assumed that they are part of the Law of Moses. When Moses came down from Sinai, the higher priesthood that he had been given, along with its ordinances, was taken from the people because of their transgressions. But the laws we know as the Ten Commandments were retained and were given to the people by Moses. Instead of being part of the Law of Moses, they are part of the higher law that was restored as part of the fullness of the gospel, which is demonstrated by the fact that they are reiterated not only here, but in the Doctrine and Covenants (see D&C 59:5–12).

Mosiah 13:27

While Abinadi attempted to teach the true meaning of the law of sacrifice, he emphasized that the Law of Moses was a preparatory law only that paved the way for the higher law to be brought by the Savior.

that the time shall come when it shall no more be expedient to keep
the law of Moses.
28. And moreover, I say unto you, that salvation doth not come by
the law alone; and were it not for the atonement, which God himself shall make for the sins and iniquities of his people, that they
must unavoidably perish, notwithstanding the law of Moses.
29. And now I say unto you that it was expedient that there should
be a law given to the children of Israel, yea, even a very strict law;
for they were a stiffnecked people, quick to do iniquity, and slow to
remember the Lord their God;
30. Therefore there was a law given them, yea, a law of performances and of ordinances, a law which they were to observe strictly
from day to day, to keep them in remembrance of God and their
duty towards him.
31. But behold, I say unto you, that all these things were types of
things to come.
32. And now, did they understand the law? I say unto you, Nay,
they did not all understand the law; and this because of the hardness of their hearts; for they understood not that there could not
any man be saved except it were through the redemption of God.
33. For behold, did not Moses prophesy unto them concerning the
coming of the Messiah, and that God should redeem his people?
Yea, and even all the prophets who have prophesied ever since the
world began—have they not spoken more or less concerning these
things?
34. Have they not said that God himself should come down among
the children of men, and take upon him the form of man, and go
forth in mighty power upon the face of the earth?
35. Yea, and have they not said also that he should bring to pass
the resurrection of the dead, and that he, himself, should be
oppressed and afflicted?

CHAPTER 14

1. YEA, even doth not Isaiah say: Who hath believed our report,
and to whom is the arm of the Lord revealed?
2. For he shall grow up before him as a tender plant, and as a root
out of dry ground; he hath no form nor comeliness; and when we
shall see him there is no beauty that we should desire him.
3. He is despised and rejected of men; a man of sorrows, and
acquainted with grief; and we hid as it were our faces from him; he
was despised, and we esteemed him not.
4. Surely he has borne our griefs, and carried our sorrows; yet we
did esteem him stricken, smitten of God, and afflicted.

Mosiah 13:28

The words "repent or perish" make up possibly the most important message we can gain from the scriptures. In this phrase, there are no excuses—as President Marion G. Romney taught, this phrase represents the natural and logical consequence of disobedience to the laws of God, laws that were declared before the foundations of this world (see D&C 130:20).

Mosiah 13:29–31

Robert Millet aptly described the Law of Moses as a type of "spiritual busywork," designed to keep people constantly involved. In reality, he points out, all of the aspects of the Law of Moses point toward the anticipated coming of the Savior, Jesus Christ.

Mosiah 13:33–35

God our Father, Elohim, is the author of the plan of salvation. He taught His plan to His children; chose Jehovah, one of His spirit children, to be the Redeemer; and ordered all things for the salvation of His children. Speaking of God the Father's plan of salvation, Bruce R. McConkie said, "God ordained the plan. He established it. It is his plan. It was not adopted by the Father following one suggestion coming from Christ and another originating with Lucifer. The Father is the author of the plan of salvation. . . ." (O/C)

Mosiah 14:1–12

Biblical scholars have long disputed whether or not chapter 53 of Isaiah really pertained to the life and mission of Jesus Christ. The fact that Abinadi quotes this chapter (Mosiah 14) in an attempt to convince the people of the coming of the Messiah would indicate that these particular writings of Isaiah definitely do pertain to Jesus Christ. (Ludlow)

5. But he was wounded for our transgressions, he was bruised for our iniquities; the chastisement of our peace was upon him; and with his stripes we are healed.
6. All we, like sheep, have gone astray; we have turned every one to his own way; and the Lord hath laid on him the iniquities of us all.
7. He was oppressed, and he was afflicted, yet he opened not his mouth; he is brought as a lamb to the slaughter, and as a sheep before her shearers is dumb so he opened not his mouth.
8. He was taken from prison and from judgment; and who shall declare his generation? For he was cut off out of the land of the living; for the transgressions of my people was he stricken.
9. And he made his grave with the wicked, and with the rich in his death; because he had done no evil, neither was any deceit in his mouth.
10. Yet it pleased the Lord to bruise him; he hath put him to grief; when thou shalt make his soul an offering for sin he shall see his seed, he shall prolong his days, and the pleasure of the Lord shall prosper in his hand.
11. He shall see the travail of his soul, and shall be satisfied; by his knowledge shall my righteous servant justify many; for he shall bear their iniquities.
12. Therefore will I divide him a portion with the great, and he shall divide the spoil with the strong; because he hath poured out his soul unto death; and he was numbered with the transgressors; and he bore the sins of many, and made intercession for the transgressors.

CHAPTER 15

1. AND now Abinadi said unto them: I would that ye should understand that God himself shall come down among the children of men, and shall redeem his people.
2. And because he dwelleth in flesh he shall be called the Son of God, and having subjected the flesh to the will of the Father, being the Father and the Son—
3. The Father, because he was conceived by the power of God; and the Son, because of the flesh; thus becoming the Father and Son—

Mosiah 15:1–4

Jesus Christ is referred to several times in the Book of Mormon as both the Father and the Son. (Mosiah 15:1–4; Ether 3:14.) The question might well be asked: In what way (or in what sense) is Jesus Christ both the "Father" and the "Son"? The words *Father* and *Son* are titles rather than names; thus they may be used to refer to more than one person. The term *Father* may rightfully be used to refer to Jesus Christ in the following areas:

(1) Jesus Christ is the Father of those who accept the gospel because it is through his atonement that the gospel is made active on this earth. (Mosiah 5:7; 15:10–13; see also D&C 25:1; 39:1–4; and Ether 3.)

(2) Jesus Christ is the Father of this earth in the sense that he created this earth under the direction of his Father. (Mosiah 15:4; 16:15; see also Alma 11:38–39; 3 Nephi 9:15; Ether 4:7; D&C 45:1.)

(3) Jesus Christ is the Father because of divine investiture of power—that is, Jesus Christ has been given the power to act for and represent his Father on this earth. (Read particularly D&C 93:2–4, 17.)

(4) Other dictionary definitions of *Father* that might be used to refer to Jesus Christ are as follows: "one to whom respect is due"; "one who cares as a father might"; "an originator, source, or prototype"; "one who claims or accepts responsibility."

The term *Son* also has varied meanings. Jesus Christ is rightfully referred to as the Son in the following senses: (1) Jesus Christ is the firstborn of God in the spirit (Colossians 1:15–19; D&C 93:21); (2) Jesus Christ is the Only Begotten Son of God in the flesh (Jacob 4:5, 11; Alma 12:33–34; 13:5; John 1:18, 3:16); (3) Jesus Christ submitted his will to the will of his Father (Mosiah 15:2–7). (Ludlow)

4. And they are one God, yea, the very Eternal Father of heaven and of earth.

5. And thus the flesh becoming subject to the Spirit, or the Son to the Father, being one God, suffereth temptation, and yieldeth not to the temptation, but suffereth himself to be mocked, and scourged, and cast out, and disowned by his people.

6. And after all this, after working many mighty miracles among the children of men, he shall be led, yea, even as Isaiah said, as a sheep before the shearer is dumb, so he opened not his mouth.

7. Yea, even so he shall be led, crucified, and slain, the flesh becoming subject even unto death, the will of the Son being swallowed up in the will of the Father.

8. And thus God breaketh the bands of death, having gained the victory over death; giving the Son power to make intercession for the children of men—

9. Having ascended into heaven, having the bowels of mercy; being filled with compassion towards the children of men; standing betwixt them and justice; having broken the bands of death, taken upon himself their iniquity and their transgressions, having redeemed them, and satisfied the demands of justice.

10. And now I say unto you, who shall declare his generation? Behold, I say unto you, that when his soul has been made an offering for sin he shall see his seed. And now what say ye? And who shall be his seed?

11. Behold I say unto you, that whosoever has heard the words of the prophets, yea, all the holy prophets who have prophesied concerning the coming of the Lord—I say unto you, that all those who have hearkened unto their words, and believed that the Lord would redeem his people, and have looked forward to that day for a remission of their sins, I say unto you, that these are his seed, or they are the heirs of the kingdom of God.

12. For these are they whose sins he has borne; these are they for whom he has died, to redeem them from their transgressions. And now, are they not his seed?

13. Yea, and are not the prophets, every one that has opened his mouth to prophesy, that has not fallen into transgression, I mean all the holy prophets ever since the world began? I say unto you that they are his seed.

14. And these are they who have published peace, who have brought good tidings of good, who have published salvation; and said unto Zion: Thy God reigneth!

Mosiah 15:11–19

When the wicked priests of King Noah started to question Abinadi, they asked him to interpret the following words of Isaiah: "How beautiful upon the mountains are the feet of him that bringeth good tidings; that publisheth peace; that bringeth good tidings of good; that publisheth salvation; that saith unto Zion, Thy God reigneth." (Mosiah 12:21; Isaiah 52:7.) . . . Abinadi gives the answer in Mosiah 15:11–19: those who are heirs of the kingdom of God including "all the holy prophets ever since the world began." (Mosiah 15:12–13.) Abinadi mentions specifically "the founder of peace, yea, even the Lord" (Mosiah 15:18). (Ludlow)

POINT OF INTEREST

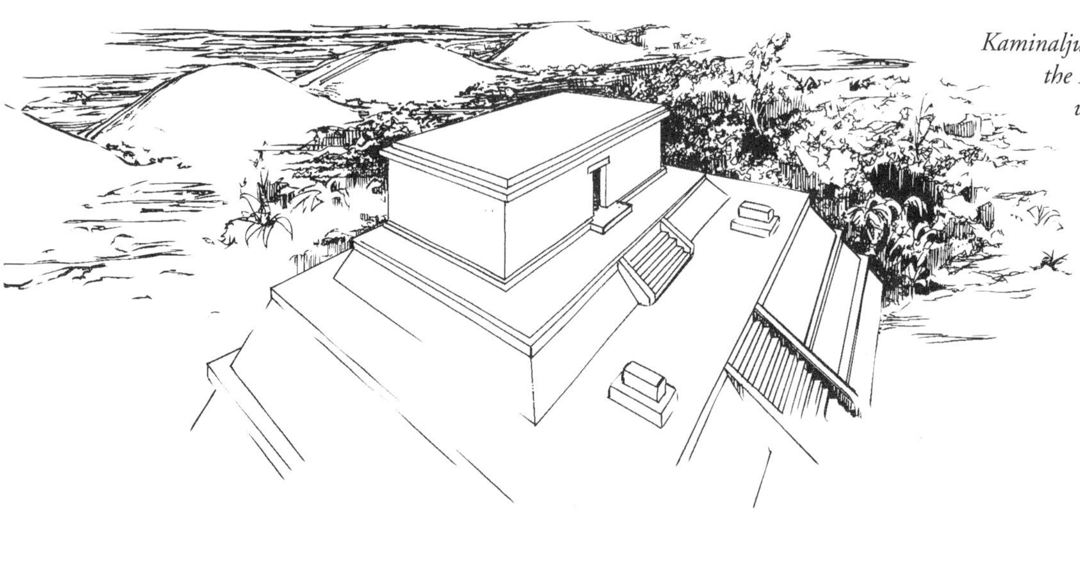

Kaminaljuyu, a pre-Columbian site of the Mayan civilization, lies in a valley in the outskirts of Guatemala City and contains a total of more than 100 platforms and mounds. Some LDS scholars propose it as the site of the the city and/or land of Nephi.

15. And O how beautiful upon the mountains were their feet!
16. And again, how beautiful upon the mountains are the feet of those that are still publishing peace!
17. And again, how beautiful upon the mountains are the feet of those who shall hereafter publish peace, yea, from this time henceforth and forever!
18. And behold, I say unto you, this is not all. For O how beautiful upon the mountains are the feet of him that bringeth good tidings, that is the founder of peace, yea, even the Lord, who has redeemed his people; yea, him who has granted salvation unto his people;
19. For were it not for the redemption which he hath made for his people, which was prepared from the foundation of the world, I say unto you, were it not for this, all mankind must have perished.
20. But behold, the bands of death shall be broken, and the Son reigneth, and hath power over the dead; therefore, he bringeth to pass the resurrection of the dead.
21. And there cometh a resurrection, even a first resurrection; yea, even a resurrection of those that have been, and who are, and who shall be, even until the resurrection of Christ—for so shall he be called.
22. And now, the resurrection of all the prophets, and all those that have believed in their words, or all those that have kept the commandments of God, shall come forth in the first resurrection; therefore, they are the first resurrection.
23. They are raised to dwell with God who has redeemed them; thus they have eternal life through Christ, who has broken the bands of death.
24. And these are those who have part in the first resurrection; and these are they that have died before Christ came, in their ignorance, not having salvation declared unto them. And thus the Lord bringeth about the restoration of these; and they have a part in the first resurrection, or have eternal life, being redeemed by the Lord.
25. And little children also have eternal life.
26. But behold, and fear, and tremble before God, for ye ought to tremble; for the Lord redeemeth none such that rebel against him and die in their sins; yea, even all those that have perished in their sins ever since the world began, that have wilfully rebelled against God, that have known the commandments of God, and would not keep them; these are they that have no part in the first resurrection.
27. Therefore ought ye not to tremble? For salvation cometh to none such; for the Lord hath redeemed none such; yea, neither can the Lord redeem such; for he cannot deny himself; for he cannot deny justice when it has its claim.
28. And now I say unto you that the time shall come that the salvation of the Lord shall be declared to every nation, kindred, tongue, and people.
29. Yea, Lord, thy watchmen shall lift up their voice; with the voice together shall they sing; for

Mosiah 15:21–26

To those who lived before the Savior was resurrected, His resurrection was known as the "first resurrection." To those who lived after that pivotal point in mankind's history, the "first resurrection" will take place at the Second Coming. Some who have inherited celestial glory were resurrected with the Savior and others of that group have been resurrected since that time (see D&C 88:96–102). All those who have not yet been resurrected at the Savior's Second Coming will be resurrected either at that time or as the Millennium draws to a close.

Mosiah 15:24

Millions of people who have lived on the earth were not taught the plan of salvation, but were true, faithful, and devout to the principles they were taught as tenets of their various religions. These people, according to President Joseph Fielding Smith, will not be held responsible for doctrines they were not taught and about which they had no knowledge. Those of us who have been taught these truths, however, will be held accountable for our deeds in the flesh as judged against the doctrines of those truths.

Mosiah 15:25

Joseph Smith said, "I have meditated upon the subject, and asked the question, why it is that infants, innocent children, are taken away from us. . . . The Lord takes many away even in infancy, that they may escape the envy of man, and the sorrows and evils of this present world; they were too pure, too lovely, to live on earth; therefore, if rightly considered, instead of mourning we have reason to rejoice as they are delivered from evil, and we shall soon have them again."

they shall see eye to eye, when the Lord shall bring again Zion.
30. Break forth into joy, sing together, ye waste places of Jerusalem; for the Lord hath comforted his people, he hath redeemed Jerusalem.
31. The Lord hath made bare his holy arm in the eyes of all the nations; and all the ends of the earth shall see the salvation of our God.

CHAPTER 16

1. AND now, it came to pass that after Abinadi had spoken these words he stretched forth his hand and said: The time shall come when all shall see the salvation of the Lord; when every nation, kindred, tongue, and people shall see eye to eye and shall confess before God that his judgments are just.
2. And then shall the wicked be cast out, and they shall have cause to howl, and weep, and wail, and gnash their teeth; and this because they would not hearken unto the voice of the Lord; therefore the Lord redeemeth them not.
3. For they are carnal and devilish, and the devil has power over them; yea, even that old serpent that did beguile our first parents, which was the cause of their fall; which was the cause of all mankind becoming carnal, sensual, devilish, knowing evil from good, subjecting themselves to the devil.
4. Thus all mankind were lost; and behold, they would have been endlessly lost were it not that God redeemed his people from their lost and fallen state.
5. But remember that he that persists in his own carnal nature, and goes on in the ways of sin and rebellion against God, remaineth in his fallen state and the devil hath all power over him. Therefore he is as though there was no redemption made, being an enemy to God; and also is the devil an enemy to God.
6. And now if Christ had not come into the world, speaking of things to come as though they had already come, there could have been no redemption.
7. And if Christ had not risen from the dead, or have broken the bands of death that the grave should have no victory, and that death should have no sting, there could have been no resurrection.
8. But there is a resurrection, therefore the grave hath no victory, and the sting of death is swallowed up in Christ.
9. He is the light and the life of the world; yea, a light that is endless,

Mosiah 16:6

Although he lived nearly 150 years before the birth of Christ, Abinadi was so certain Jesus Christ was going to be born on the earth that he sometimes referred to the life of the Savior in the past tense. He was aware, of course, that he was doing this. In Mosiah 16:6 he states: ". . . and now if Christ *had not* come into the world, *speaking of things to come as though they had already come*, there could have been no redemption" (Italics added). (Ludlow)

that can never be darkened; yea, and also a life which is endless, that there can be no more death.
10. Even this mortal shall put on immortality, and this corruption shall put on incorruption, and shall be brought to stand before the bar of God, to be judged of him according to their works whether they be good or whether they be evil—
11. If they be good, to the resurrection of endless life and happiness; and if they be evil, to the resurrection of endless damnation, being delivered up to the devil, who hath subjected them, which is damnation—
12. Having gone according to their own carnal wills and desires; having never called upon the Lord while the arms of mercy were extended towards them; for the arms of mercy were extended towards them, and they would not; they being warned of their iniquities and yet they would not depart from them; and they were commanded to repent and yet they would not repent.
13. And now, ought ye not to tremble and repent of your sins, and remember that only in and through Christ ye can be saved?
14. Therefore, if ye teach the law of Moses, also teach that it is a shadow of those things which are to come—
15. Teach them that redemption cometh through Christ the Lord, who is the very Eternal Father. Amen.

CHAPTER 17

1. AND now it came to pass that when Abinadi had finished these sayings, that the king commanded that the priests should take him and cause that he should be put to death.
2. But there was one among them whose name was Alma, he also being a descendant of Nephi. And he was a young man, and he believed the words which Abinadi had spoken, for he knew concerning the iniquity which Abinadi has testified against them; therefore he began to plead with the king that he would not be angry with Abinadi, but suffer that he might depart in peace.
3. But the king was more wroth, and caused that Alma should be cast out from among them, and sent his servants after him that they might slay him.
4. But he fled from before them and hid himself that they found him not. And he being concealed for many days did write all the words which Abinadi had spoken.
5. And it came to pass that the king caused that his guards should surround Abinadi and take him; and they bound him and cast him into prison.
6. And after three days, having counseled with his priests, he caused that he should again be brought before him.
7. And he said unto him: Abinadi, we have found an accusation against thee, and thou art worthy of death.
8. For thou hast said that God himself should come down among

Mosiah 16:11

"Endless damnation" does not mean the damnation lasts forever; it is referred to as *endless* because it is of God, who is endless and everlasting.

Mosiah 16:13–15

Abinadi's final testimony to the wicked priests ends with his conviction that obedience to the Law of Moses is empty without the Savior.

Mosiah 17:2

After refuting the evil position of King Noah and his priests through the exquisite word of God, Abinadi dies as a martyr, "having sealed the truth of his words by his death" (Mosiah 17:20). He had but one purpose—to do the will of the Father, and through his extraordinary display of courage, he left a legacy of what it means to be spiritually committed to the sacrifice of all things while on the Lord's errand. Alma, a priest in Noah's court, was converted by Abinadi's teachings and conveyed the gospel message thereafter to a flourishing new branch of Israel.

Speaking of Abinadi, Elder Joseph B. Wirthlin said, "Abinadi may have felt that he failed as a missionary because he had only one convert, so far as the record shows. However, that one convert, Alma, and his descendants were spiritual leaders among the Nephites and Lamanites for about three hundred years. His son Alma became the first chief judge of the Nephite people and the high priest over the Church. Alma's other descendants who became prominent religious leaders include his grandson Helaman; his great-grandson Nephi; and his great-great-great-grandson Nephi, who was the chief disciple of the resurrected Jesus Christ. All of this resulted from Abinadi's lone convert." (P/A)

Mosiah 17:2–4

One of the wicked priests of King Noah is a man named Alma, who is a descendant of Nephi. When first introduced in the Book of Mormon, Alma is a young man in the process of being converted by Abinadi. (Mosiah 17:2.) Much of the religious history of the Nephite nation for the next three hundred years is concerned with this man and his descendants. Alma not only begins a religious revival among his own people, but later he is given power by King Mosiah to establish churches throughout all the land of Zarahemla. (See Mosiah 25:19.) . . .

Abinadi may have felt that he had failed as a missionary; so far as the record indicates, his only convert was Alma. However, as mentioned above, the missionary efforts of Abinadi affected the religious life of the Nephites for hundreds of years. (Ludlow)

the children of men; and now, for this cause thou shalt be put to death unless thou wilt recall all the words which thou hast spoken evil concerning me and my people.
9. Now Abinadi said unto him: I say unto you, I will not recall the words which I have spoken unto you concerning this people, for they are true; and that ye may know of their surety I have suffered myself that I have fallen into your hands.
10. Yea, and I will suffer even until death, and I will not recall my words, and they shall stand as a testimony against you. And if ye slay me ye will shed innocent blood, and this shall also stand as a testimony against you at the last day.
11. And now king Noah was about to release him, for he feared his word; for he feared that the judgments of God would come upon him.
12. But the priests lifted up their voices against him, and began to accuse him, saying: He has reviled the king. Therefore the king was stirred up in anger against him, and he delivered him up that he might be slain.
13. And it came to pass that they took him and bound him, and scourged his skin with faggots, yea, even unto death.
14. And now when the flames began to scorch him, he cried unto them, saying:
15. Behold, even as ye have done unto me, so shall it come to pass that thy seed shall cause that many shall suffer the pains that I do suffer, even the pains of death by fire; and this because they believe in the salvation of the Lord their God.
16. And it will come to pass that ye shall be afflicted with all manner of diseases because of your iniquities.
17. Yea, and ye shall be smitten on every hand, and shall be driven and scattered to and fro, even as a wild flock is driven by wild and ferocious beasts.
18. And in that day ye shall be hunted, and ye shall be taken by the hand of your enemies, and then ye shall suffer, as I suffer, the pains of death by fire.
19. Thus God executeth vengeance upon those that destroy his people. O God, receive my soul.
20. And now, when Abinadi had said these words, he fell, having suffered death by fire; yea, having been put to death because he would not deny the commandments of God, having sealed the truth of his words by his death.

CHAPTER 18

1. AND now, it came to pass that Alma, who had fled from the servants of king Noah, repented of his sins and iniquities, and went about privately among the people, and began to teach the words of Abinadi—
2. Yea, concerning that which was to come, and also concerning the resurrection of the dead, and the redemption of the people, which was to be brought to pass through

Mosiah 17:10

Sacrifice is at the heart of the gospel of Jesus Christ. In comparison with the infinite atoning sacrifice of the Savior, there is nothing that man can do by way of a quid pro quo. Thus the sacrifice of all things in devotion to the cause of immortality and eternal life is never too high a price to pay, and even the sacrifice of all things leaves man a debtor before God (see Mosiah 2:21). (P/A)

Mosiah 17:20

[Abinadi] had but one purpose—to do the will of the Father, and through his extraordinary display of courage, he left a legacy of what it means to be spiritually committed to the sacrifice of all things while on the Lord's errand. (P/A)

Mosiah 17:20

In Abinadi's teachings we come to know the goodness of God and His plan of redemption that comes only through His beloved Son, Jesus Christ. To take full advantage of His atoning sacrifice, it is incumbent upon us to repent and come unto Him. The plea of Abinadi, like that of all the holy prophets, past and present, resonates through the generations of time: Repent and come unto Christ. That is the universal message of the prophets. By sincere repentance and adherence to gospel covenants, we can become the sons and daughters of God. . . . If repentant, we will submit to the will of the Father in all things, as did Abinadi. . . . Abinadi would not retract his testimony against his unrighteous detractors. He suffered death by fire because he would not deny the commandments of God—thus becoming a martyr by sealing his testimony of truth by his death. As was said of the Carthage massacre, "The testators are now dead, and their testament is in force" (D&C 135:5). We may not be asked to die for our beliefs, but we have certainly been asked to live for our beliefs. Let us realize that standing, living, and testifying for the truth is our duty. (P/A)

the power, and sufferings, and death of Christ, and his resurrection and ascension into heaven.
3. And as many as would hear his word he did teach. And he taught them privately, that it might not come to the knowledge of the king. And many did believe his words.
4. And it came to pass that as many as did believe him did go forth to a place which was called Mormon, having received its name from the king, being in the borders of the land having been infested, by times or at seasons, by wild beasts.
5. Now, there was in Mormon a fountain of pure water, and Alma resorted thither, there being near the water a thicket of small trees, where he did hide himself in the daytime from the searches of the king.
6. And it came to pass that as many as believed him went thither to hear his words.
7. And it came to pass after many days there were a goodly number gathered together at the place of Mormon, to hear the words of Alma. Yea, all were gathered together that believed on his word, to hear him. And he did teach them, and did preach unto them repentance, and redemption, and faith on the Lord.
8. And it came to pass that he said unto them: Behold, here are the waters of Mormon (for thus were they called) and now, as ye are desirous to come into the fold of God, and to be called his people, and are willing to bear one another's burdens, that they may be light;
9. Yea, and are willing to mourn with those that mourn; yea, and comfort those that stand in need of comfort, and to stand as witnesses of God at all times and in all things, and in all places that ye may be in, even until death, that ye may be redeemed of God, and be numbered with those of the first resurrection, that ye may have eternal life—
10. Now I say unto you, if this be the desire of your hearts, what have you against being baptized in the name of the Lord, as a witness before him that ye have entered into a covenant with him, that ye will serve him and keep his commandments, that he may pour out his Spirit more abundantly upon you?
11. And now when the people had heard these words, they clapped their hands for joy, and exclaimed: This is the desire of our hearts.
12. And now it came to pass that Alma took Helam, he being one of the first, and went and stood forth in the water, and cried, saying: O Lord, pour out thy Spirit upon thy servant, that he may do this work with holiness of heart.
13. And when he had said these words, the Spirit of the Lord was upon him, and he said: Helam, I baptize thee, having authority from the Almighty God, as a testimony that ye have entered into a covenant to serve him until you are dead as to the mortal body; and may the Spirit of the Lord be poured out upon you; and may he grant unto you eternal life, through the redemption of Christ, whom he has prepared from the foundation of the world.
14. And after Alma had said these words, both Alma and Helam were

Mosiah 18:4

The word *Mormon* is used chronologically for the first time in Mosiah 18:4. Although the word appears earlier than this in the Book of Mormon it has always referred to the name of the great prophet, historian, and military leader who lived several hundred years after the time of Christ. The place called "Mormon" referred to in Mosiah 18:4 received its name "from the king." No further information is given concerning this king. (Ludlow)

Mosiah 18:8–10

Sometimes we use the terms "commitment" or "promise" as though they were synonymous with the word "covenant." For many people of the world that may be true. They are meaningful and motivating words of behavior. But a covenant is much more. Covenants come from God by revelation, and the authority to bind man and God in a covenant relationship can only be bestowed by those authorized to represent Him in the performing of covenant ordinances. No one outside the Lord's Church is involved in covenants, though others may make various kinds of commitments or promises. But a covenant with the Lord is of far greater significance. We all need to give serious thought to the Lord's expectations of us and His promises to us as we fulfill our responsibilities. (O/C)

Mosiah 18:11

The ordinance of baptism is the sacred ceremonial declaration that one is willing to take upon himself or herself the name of Christ and live by solemn covenant in accordance with His laws. Such an ordinance, bestowing renewal, rebirth, cleansing, liberation, and spiritual adoption into the family of Christ, is a thing of transcendent beauty and joy. (P/A)

Mosiah 18:12–18

Some have wondered why Alma went down into the water with Helam—a practice that is not associated with traditional baptism. Alma wanted to be buried in the water with Helam in order to cleanse himself and in order to indicate his full repentance after becoming involved with the priests of wicked King Noah.

buried in the water; and they arose and came forth out of the water rejoicing, being filled with the Spirit.
15. And again, Alma took another, and went forth a second time into the water, and baptized him according to the first, only he did not bury himself again in the water.
16. And after this manner he did baptize every one that went forth to the place of Mormon; and they were in number about two hundred and four souls; yea, and they were baptized in the waters of Mormon, and were filled with the grace of God.
17. And they were called the church of God, or the church of Christ, from that time forward. And it came to pass that whosoever was baptized by the power and authority of God was added to his church.
18. And it came to pass that Alma, having authority from God, ordained priests; even one priest to every fifty of their number did he ordain to preach unto them, and to teach them concerning the things pertaining to the kingdom of God.
19. And he commanded them that they should teach nothing save it were the things which he had taught, and which had been spoken by the mouth of the holy prophets.
20. Yea, even he commanded them that they should preach nothing save it were repentance and faith on the Lord, who had redeemed his people.
21. And he commanded them that there should be no contention one with another, but that they should look forward with one eye, having one faith and one baptism, having their hearts knit together in unity and in love one towards another.
22. And thus he commanded them to preach. And thus they became the children of God.
23. And he commanded them that they should observe the sabbath day, and keep it holy, and also every day they should give thanks to the Lord their God.
24. And he also commanded them that the priests whom he had ordained should labor with their own hands for their support.
25. And there was one day in every week that was set apart that they should gather themselves together to teach the people, and to worship the Lord their God, and also, as often as it was in their power, to assemble themselves together.
26. And the priests were not to depend upon the people for their support; but for their labor they were to receive the grace of God, that they might wax strong in the Spirit, having the knowledge of God, that they might teach with power and authority from God.
27. And again Alma commanded that the people of the church should impart of their substance, every one according to that which he had; if he have more abundantly he should impart more abundantly; and of him that had but little, but

Mosiah 18:12–18

The Book of Mormon does not specifically state whether or not Alma had been baptized before or how he got his authority to baptize. The record merely says that Alma immersed himself in the water when he baptized Helam (Mosiah 18:14–15) and that "Alma, having authority from God, ordained priests." (Mosiah 18:18.) Alma may have been ordained by Abinadi, but the record is not clear on this point. Joseph Fielding Smith feels that Alma held the priesthood before he became involved with King Noah. (Ludlow)

Mosiah 18:21

As members of the Church we have solemn responsibilities toward our fellowmen. These are not merely suggestions, but commandments. Let us remember our covenants at baptism as taught in D&C 20:37 and Moro. 6:1–4. (P/A)

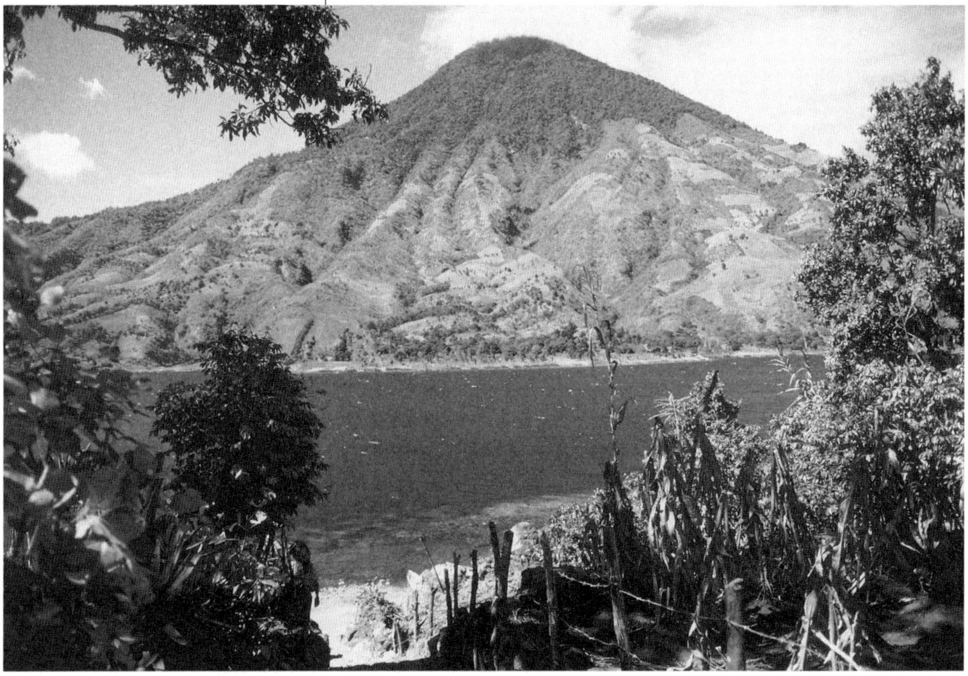

little should be required; and to him that had not should be given.
28. And thus they should impart of their substance of their own
free will and good desires towards God, and to those priests that
stood in need, yea, and to every needy, naked soul.
29. And this he said unto them, having been commanded of God;
and they did walk uprightly before God, imparting to one another both temporally and spiritually according to their needs and
their wants.
30. And now it came to pass that all this was done in Mormon, yea,
by the waters of Mormon, in the forest that was near the waters of
Mormon; yea, the place of Mormon, the waters of Mormon, the
forest of Mormon, how beautiful are they to the eyes of them who
there came to the knowledge of their Redeemer; yea, and how
blessed are they, for they shall sing to his praise forever.
31. And these things were done in the borders of the land, that
they might not come to the knowledge of the king.
32. But behold, it came to pass that the king, having discovered a
movement among the people, sent his servants to watch them.
Therefore on the day that they were assembling themselves together to
hear the word of the Lord they were discovered unto the king.
33. And now the king said that Alma was stirring up the people to
rebellion against him; therefore he sent his army to destroy them.
34. And it came to pass that Alma and the people of the Lord were
apprised of the coming of the king's army; therefore they took their
tents and their families and departed into the wilderness.
35. And they were in number about four hundred and fifty souls.

CHAPTER 19

1. AND it came to pass that the army of the king returned, having
searched in vain for the people of the Lord.
2. And now behold, the forces of the king were small, having been
reduced, and there began to be a division among the remainder of
the people.
3. And the lesser part began to breathe out threatenings against
the king, and there began to be a great contention among them.
4. And now there was a man among them whose name was Gideon,
and he being a strong man and an enemy to the king, therefore he
drew his sword, and swore in his wrath that he would slay the king.
5. And it came to pass that he fought with the king; and when the
king saw that he was about to overpower him, he fled and ran and
got upon the tower which was near the temple.
6. And Gideon pursued after him and was about to get upon the
tower to slay the king, and the king cast his eyes round about
towards the land of Shemlon, and behold, the army of the
Lamanites were within the borders of the land.
7. And now the king cried out in the anguish of his soul, saying:
Gideon, spare me, for the Lamanites are upon us, and they will
destroy us; yea, they will destroy my people.
8. And now the king was not so much concerned about his people
as

Mosiah 19–22

Chapters 19–22 are taken from the record of Zeniff's colony. They describe how Limhi's people were led into bondage, then point out the conditoins that brought about their deliverance.

POINT OF INTEREST

Lake Atitlán, in the Guatemalan Highlands, is the deepest lake in Central America. Estimates of its maximum depth are about a quarter of a mile (340 m), but its bottom has not been completely sounded. The lake is considered by some scholars as a viable candidate for the waters of Mormon.

he was about his own life; nevertheless, Gideon did spare his life.
9. And the king commanded the people that they should flee before the Lamanites, and he himself did go before them, and they did flee into the wilderness, with their women and their children.
10. And it came to pass that the Lamanites did pursue them, and did overtake them, and began to slay them.
11. Now it came to pass that the king commanded them that all the men should leave their wives and their children, and flee before the Lamanites.
12. Now there were many that would not leave them, but had rather stay and perish with them. And the rest left their wives and their children and fled.
13. And it came to pass that those who tarried with their wives and their children caused that their fair daughters should stand forth and plead with the Lamanites that they would not slay them.
14. And it came to pass that the Lamanites had compassion on them, for they were charmed with the beauty of their women.
15. Therefore the Lamanites did spare their lives, and took them captives and carried them back to the land of Nephi, and granted unto them that they might possess the land, under the conditions that they would deliver up king Noah into the hands of the Lamanites, and deliver up their property, even one half of all they possessed, one half of their gold, and their silver, and all their precious things, and thus they should pay tribute to the king of the Lamanites from year to year.
16. And now there was one of the sons of the king among those that were taken captive, whose name was Limhi.
17. And now Limhi was desirous that his father should not be destroyed; nevertheless, Limhi was not ignorant of the iniquities of his father, he himself being a just man.
18. And it came to pass that Gideon sent men into the wilderness secretly, to search for the king and those that were with him. And it came to pass that they met the people in the wilderness, all save the king and his priests.
19. Now they had sworn in their hearts that they would return to the land of Nephi, and if their wives and their children were slain, and also those that had tarried with them, that they would seek revenge, and also perish with them.
20. And the king commanded them that they should not return; and they were angry with the king, and caused that he should suffer, even unto death by fire.
21. And they were about to take the priests also and put them to death, and they fled before them.
22. And it came to pass that they were about to return to the land of Nephi, and they met the men of Gideon. And the men of Gideon told them of all that had happened to their wives and their children; and that the Lamanites had granted unto them that they might possess the land by paying a tribute to the Lamanites of one half of all they possessed.
23. And the people told the men of Gideon that they had slain the king, and his priests had fled from them farther into the wilderness.
24. And it came to pass that after they had ended the ceremony, that they returned to the land of Nephi, rejoicing, because their wives and their children were not slain; and they told Gideon what they had done to the king.
25. And it came to pass that the

Mosiah 19:20

This verse fulfilled Abinadi's prophecy, detailed in Mosiah 12:3.

"Let us realize that when the prophets speak it is the same as the Lord speaking. When we come to understand and appreciate this eternal verity we will be more obedient to our prophets both living and dead. The words of our prophets will be fulfilled." (P/A)

king of the Lamanites made an oath unto them, that his people should not slay them.
26. And also Limhi, being the son of the king, having the kingdom conferred upon him by the people, made oath unto the king of the Lamanites that his people should pay tribute unto him, even one half of all they possessed.
27. And it came to pass that Limhi began to establish the kingdom and to establish peace among his people.
28. And the king of the Lamanites set guards round about the land, that he might keep the people of Limhi in the land, that they might not depart into the wilderness; and he did support his guards out of the tribute which he did receive from the Nephites.
29. And now king Limhi did have continual peace in his kingdom for the space of two years, that the Lamanites did not molest them nor seek to destroy them.

CHAPTER 20

1. NOW there was a place in Shemlon where the daughters of the Lamanites did gather themselves together to sing, and to dance, and to make themselves merry.
2. And it came to pass that there was one day a small number of them gathered together to sing and to dance.
3. And now the priests of king Noah, being ashamed to return to the city of Nephi, yea, and also fearing that the people would slay them, therefore they durst not return to their wives and their children.
4. And having tarried in the wilderness, and having discovered the daughters of the Lamanites, they laid and watched them;
5. And when there were but few of them gathered together to dance, they came forth out of their secret places and took them and carried them into the wilderness; yea, twenty and four of the daughters of the Lamanites they carried into the wilderness.
6. And it came to pass that when the Lamanites found that their daughters had been missing, they were angry with the people of Limhi, for they thought it was the people of Limhi.
7. Therefore they sent their armies forth; yea, even the king himself went before his people; and they went up to the land of Nephi to destroy the people of Limhi.
8. And now Limhi had discovered them from the tower, even all their preparations for war did he discover; therefore he gathered his people together, and laid wait for them in the fields and in the forests.
9. And it came to pass that when the Lamanites had come up, that the people of Limhi began to fall upon them from their waiting places, and began to slay them.
10. And it came to pass that the battle became exceedingly sore, for they fought like lions for their prey.
11. And it came to pass that the people of Limhi began to drive the Lamanites before them; yet they were not half so numerous as the Lamanites. But they fought for their lives, and for their wives, and for their children; therefore they exerted themselves and like dragons did they fight.
12. And it came to pass that they found the king of the Lamanites

POINT OF INTEREST

Below are columns in the shape of warriors at the ruins of Tula in Hidalgo, Mexico. The site has a number of similarities to Chichén Itzá, including these columns.

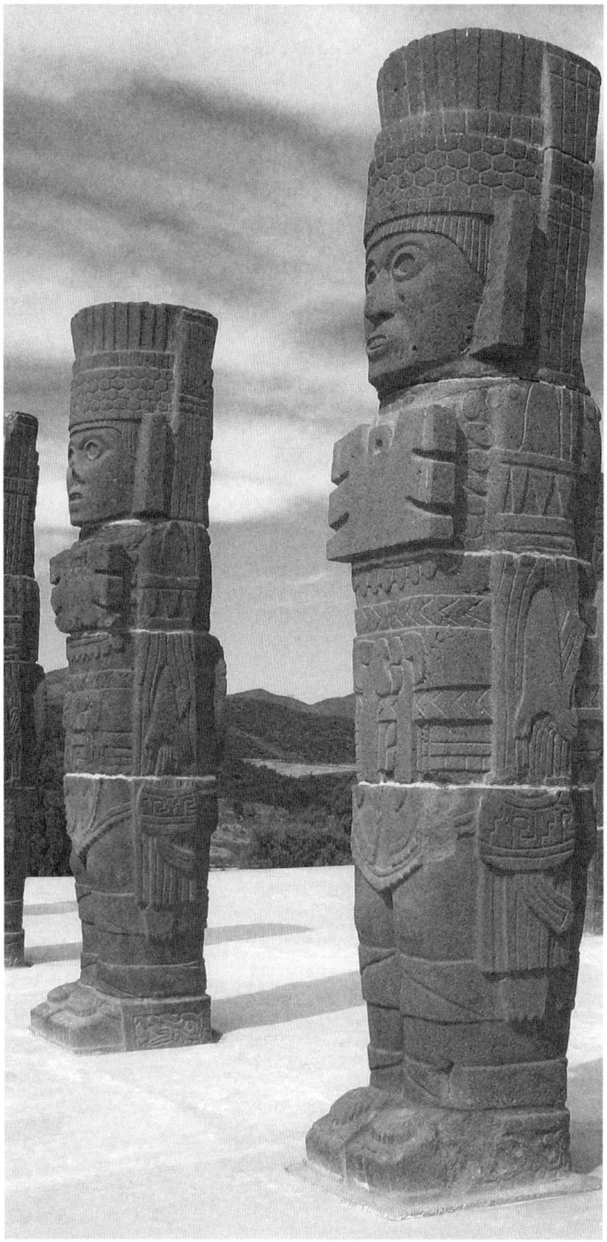

among the number of their dead; yet he was not dead, having been wounded and left upon the ground, so speedy was the flight of his people.

13. And they took him and bound up his wounds, and brought him before Limhi, and said: Behold, here is the king of the Lamanites; he having received a wound has fallen among their dead, and they have left him; and behold, we have brought him before you; and now let us slay him.

14. But Limhi said unto them: Ye shall not slay him, but bring him hither that I may see him. And they brought him. And Limhi said unto him: What cause have ye to come up to war against my people? Behold, my people have not broken the oath that I made unto you; therefore, why should ye break the oath which ye made unto my people?

15. And now the king said: I have broken the oath because thy people did carry away the daughters of my people; therefore, in my anger I did cause my people to come up to war against thy people.

16. And now Limhi had heard nothing concerning this matter; therefore he said: I will search among my people and whosoever has done this thing shall perish. Therefore he caused a search to be made among his people.

17. Now when Gideon had heard these things, he being the king's captain, he went forth and said unto the king: I pray thee forbear, and do not search this people, and lay not this thing to their charge.

18. For do ye not remember the priests of thy father, whom this people sought to destroy? And are they not in the wilderness? And are not they the ones who have stolen the daughters of the Lamanites?

19. And now, behold, and tell the king of these things, that he may tell his people that they may be pacified towards us; for behold they are already preparing to come against us; and behold also there are but few of us.

20. And behold, they come with their numerous hosts; and except the king doth pacify them towards us we must perish.

21. For are not the words of Abinadi fulfilled, which he prophesied against us—and all this because we would not hearken unto the words of the Lord, and turn from our iniquities?

22. And now let us pacify the king, and we fulfil the oath which we have made unto him; for it is better that we should be in bondage than that we should lose our lives; therefore, let us put a stop to the shedding of so much blood.

23. And now Limhi told the king all the things concerning his father, and the priests that had fled into the wilderness, and attributed the carrying away of their daughters to them.

24. And it came to pass that the king was pacified towards his people; and he said unto them: Let us go forth to meet my people, without arms; and I swear unto you with an oath that my people shall not slay thy people.

25. And it came to pass that they followed the king, and went forth without arms to meet the Lamanites. And it came to pass that they did meet the Lamanites; and the king of the Lamanites did bow himself down before them, and did plead in behalf of the people of Limhi.

26. And when the Lamanites saw the people of Limhi, that they were without arms, they had compassion on them and were pacified towards them, and returned with their king in peace to their own land.

Mosiah 20:21

There is a principle in the heavens according to which blessings are predicated upon obedience to divine law (see D&C 130:20). The scriptures provide ample evidence that the degree of liberty enjoyed by the Saints of God is a function of their humility, valor, and willingness to be instructed of the Spirit:

"And they did humble themselves even in the depths of humility; and they did cry mightily to God; yea, even all the day long did they cry unto their God that he would deliver them out of their afflictions.

"And now the Lord was slow to hear their cry because of their iniquities; nevertheless the Lord did hear their cries, and began to soften the hearts of the Lamanites that they began to ease their burdens; yet the Lord did not see fit to deliver them out of bondage" (Mosiah 21:14–15).

Limhi's people were in bondage to the Lamanites, which fulfilled Abinadi's prophetic warning. Thus Limhi's people were chastened of the Lord that they might learn obedience and humility. They finally humbled themselves and were delivered by the Lord out of the hands of their enemies so that they could return with their records to Zarahemla (see Mosiah 7:33; 20:21; 21:4; 22:13).

President Marion G. Romney commented that "the free agency possessed by any one person is increased or diminished by the use to which he puts it. Every wrong decision one makes restricts the area in which he can thereafter exercise his agency. The further one goes in the making of wrong decisions in the exercise of free agency, the more difficult it is for him to recover the lost ground. One can, by persisting long enough, reach the point of no return. He then becomes an abject slave." (P/A)

CHAPTER 21

1. AND it came to pass that Limhi and his people returned to the city of Nephi, and began to dwell in the land again in peace.
2. And it came to pass that after many days the Lamanites began again to be stirred up in anger against the Nephites, and they began to come into the borders of the land round about.
3. Now they durst not slay them, because of the oath which their king had made unto Limhi; but they would smite them on their cheeks, and exercise authority over them; and began to put heavy burdens upon their backs, and drive them as they would a dumb ass—
4. Yea, all this was done that the word of the Lord might be fulfilled.
5. And now the afflictions of the Nephites were great, and there was no way that they could deliver themselves out of their hands, for the Lamanites had surrounded them on every side.
6. And it came to pass that the people began to murmur with the king because of their afflictions; and they began to be desirous to go against them to battle. And they did afflict the king sorely with their complaints; therefore he granted unto them that they should do according to their desires.
7. And they gathered themselves together again, and put on their armor, and went forth against the Lamanites to drive them out of their land.
8. And it came to pass that the Lamanites did beat them, and drove them back, and slew many of them.
9. And now there was a great mourning and lamentation among the people of Limhi, the widow mourning for her husband, the son and the daughter mourning for their father, and the brothers for their brethren.
10. Now there were a great many widows in the land, and they did cry mightily from day to day, for a great fear of the Lamanites had come upon them.
11. And it came to pass that their continual cries did stir up the remainder of the people of Limhi to anger against the Lamanites; and they went again to battle, but they were driven back again, suffering much loss.
12. Yea, they went again even the third time, and suffered in the like manner; and those that were not slain returned again to the city of Nephi.
13. And they did humble themselves even to the dust, subjecting themselves to the yoke of bondage, submitting themselves to be smitten, and to be driven to and fro, and burdened, according to the desires of their enemies.
14. And they did humble themselves even in the depths of humility; and they did cry mightily to God; yea, even all the day long did they cry unto their God that he would deliver them out of their afflictions.
15. And now the Lord was slow to hear their cry because of their iniquities; nevertheless the Lord

Mosiah 21:7, 11–12, 14–16

In summarizing the fall of the Roman Empire, historian Will Durant wrote, "A great civilization is not conquered from without until it has destroyed itself within. The essential causes of Rome's decline lay in her people, her morals, her class struggle, her failing trade, her bureaucratic despotism, her stifling taxes, her consuming wars . . . ." (Will Durant, *Caesar and Christ: The Story of Civilization III* [New York: Simon and Schuster, 1980]).

Mosiah 21:14–15

It is also of equal importance that men should have the idea of the existence of the attribute of judgment in God, in order that they may exercise faith in him for life and salvation; for without the idea of the existence of this attribute in the Deity, it would be impossible for men to exercise faith in him for life and salvation, seeing that it is through the exercise of this attribute that the faithful in Christ Jesus are delivered out of the hands of those who seek their destruction; for if God were not to come out in swift judgment against the workers of iniquity and the powers of darkness, his saints could not be saved; for it is by judgment that the Lord delivers his saints out of the hands of all their enemies, and those who reject the gospel of our Lord Jesus Christ. But no sooner is the idea of the existence of this attribute planted in the minds of men, than it gives power to the mind for the exercise of faith and confidence in God, and they are enabled by faith to lay hold on the promises which are set before them, and wade through all the tribulations and afflictions to which they are subjected by reason of the persecution from those who know not God, and obey not the gospel of our Lord Jesus Christ, believing that in due time the Lord will come out in swift judgment against their enemies, and they shall be cut off from before him, and that in his own due time he will bear them off conquerors, and more than conquerors, in all things (Joseph Smith, *Lectures on Faith*).

did hear their cries, and began to soften the hearts of the
Lamanites that they began to ease their burdens; yet the Lord did
not see fit to deliver them out of bondage.
16. And it came to pass that they began to prosper by degrees in
the land, and began to raise grain more abundantly, and flocks, and
herds, that they did not suffer with hunger.
17. Now there was a great number of women, more than there was
of men; therefore king Limhi commanded that every man should
impart to the support of the widows and their children, that they
might not perish with hunger; and this they did because of the
greatness of their number that had been slain.
18. Now the people of Limhi kept together in a body as much as it
was possible, and secured their grain and their flocks;
19. And the king himself did not trust his person without the walls
of the city, unless he took his guards with him, fearing that he
might by some means fall into the hands of the Lamanites.
20. And he caused that his people should watch the land round
about, that by some means they might take those priests that fled
into the wilderness, who had stolen the daughters of the
Lamanites, and that had caused such a great destruction to come
upon them.
21. For they were desirous to take them that they might punish
them; for they had come into the land of Nephi by night, and carried off their grain and many of their precious things; therefore
they laid wait for them.
22. And it came to pass that there was no more disturbance
between the Lamanites and the people of Limhi, even until the
time that Ammon and his brethren came into the land.
23. And the king having been without the gates of the city with
his guard, discovered Ammon and his brethren; and supposing
them to be priests of Noah therefore he caused that they should
be taken, and bound, and cast into prison. And had they been the
priests of Noah he would have caused that they should be put to
death.
24. But when he found that they were not, but that they were his
brethren, and had come from the land of Zarahemla, he was filled
with exceedingly great joy.
25. Now king Limhi had sent, previous to the coming of Ammon,
a small number of men to search for the land of Zarahemla; but
they could not find it, and they were lost in the wilderness.
26. Nevertheless, they did find a land which had been peopled;
yea, a land which was covered with dry bones; yea, a land which
had been peopled and which had been destroyed; and they, having supposed it to be the land of Zarahemla, returned to the land
of Nephi, having arrived in the borders of the land not many days
before the coming of Ammon.
27. And they brought a record with them, even a record of the
people whose bones they had found; and it was engraven on plates
of ore.
28. And now Limhi was again filled with joy in learning from the
mouth of Ammon that king Mosiah had a gift from God, whereby
he could interpret such engravings; yea, and Ammon also did
rejoice.
29. Yet Ammon and his brethren were filled with sorrow because
so

Mosiah 21:26

The forty-three men dispatched by King Limhi found the land of the Jaredites. The record referred to in verse 27 is the book of Ether.

many of their brethren had been slain;

30. And also that king Noah and his priests had caused the people to commit so many sins and iniquities against God; and they also did mourn for the death of Abinadi; and also for the departure of Alma and the people that went with him, who had formed a church of God through the strength and power of God, and faith on the words which had been spoken by Abinadi.

31. Yea, they did mourn for their departure, for they knew not whither they had fled. Now they would have gladly joined with them, for they themselves had entered into a covenant with God to serve him and keep his commandments.

32. And now since the coming of Ammon, king Limhi had also entered into a covenant with God, and also many of his people, to serve him and keep his commandments.

33. And it came to pass that king Limhi and many of his people were desirous to be baptized; but there was none in the land that had authority from God. And Ammon declined doing this thing, considering himself an unworthy servant.

34. Therefore they did not at that time form themselves into a church, waiting upon the Spirit of the Lord. Now they were desirous to become even as Alma and his brethren, who had fled into the wilderness.

35. They were desirous to be baptized as a witness and a testimony that they were willing to serve God with all their hearts; nevertheless they did prolong the time; and an account of their baptism shall be given hereafter.

36. And now all the study of Ammon and his people, and king Limhi and his people, was to deliver themselves out of the hands of the Lamanites and from bondage.

CHAPTER 22

1. AND now it came to pass that Ammon and king Limhi began to consult with the people how they should deliver themselves out of bondage; and even they did cause that all the people should gather themselves together; and this they did that they might have the voice of the people concerning the matter.

2. And it came to pass that they could find no way to deliver themselves out of bondage, except it were to take their women and children, and their flocks, and their herds, and their tents, and depart into the wilderness; for the Lamanites being so numerous, it was impossible for the people of Limhi to contend with them, thinking to deliver themselves out of bondage by the sword.

3. Now it came to pass that Gideon went forth and stood before the king, and said unto him: Now O king, thou hast hitherto hearkened unto my words many times when we have been contending with our brethren, the Lamanites.

4. And now O king, if thou hast not found me to be an unprofitable servant, or if thou hast hitherto listened to my words in any degree, and they have been of service to thee, even so I desire that thou wouldst listen to my words at this time, and I will be thy servant and deliver this people out of bondage.

5. And the king granted unto him that he might speak. And Gideon said unto him:

6. Behold the back pass, through the back wall, on the back side of the city. The Lamanites, or the

Mosiah 21:35

Though their desire to be baptized was strong, they waited to be baptized because no one there had the proper authority to perform the ordinance.

POINT OF INTEREST

This kneeling figure is part of a wall carving in the Temple of the Sun at Palenque, Mexico.

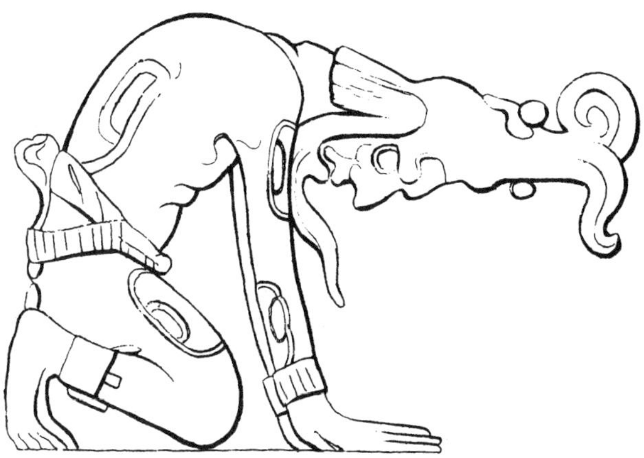

guards of the Lamanites, by night are drunken; therefore let us send a proclamation among all this people that they gather together their flocks and herds, that they may drive them into the wilderness by night.
7. And I will go according to thy command and pay the last tribute of wine to the Lamanites, and they will be drunken; and we will pass through the secret pass on the left of their camp when they are drunken and asleep.
8. Thus we will depart with our women and our children, our flocks, and our herds into the wilderness; and we will travel around the land of Shilom.
9. And it came to pass that the king hearkened unto the words of Gideon.
10. And king Limhi caused that his people should gather their flocks together; and he sent the tribute of wine to the Lamanites; and he also sent more wine, as a present unto them; and they did drink freely of the wine which king Limhi did send unto them.
11. And it came to pass that the people of king Limhi did depart by night into the wilderness with their flocks and their herds, and they went round about the land of Shilom in the wilderness, and bent their course towards the land of Zarahemla, being led by Ammon and his brethren.
12. And they had taken all their gold, and silver, and their precious things, which they could carry, and also their provisions with them, into the wilderness; and they pursued their journey.
13. And after being many days in the wilderness they arrived in the land of Zarahemla, and joined Mosiah's people, and became his subjects.
14. And it came to pass that Mosiah received them with joy; and he also received their records, and also the records which had been found by the people of Limhi.
15. And now it came to pass when the Lamanites had found that the people of Limhi had departed out of the land by night, that they sent an army into the wilderness to pursue them;
16. And after they had pursued them two days, they could no longer follow their tracks; therefore they were lost in the wilderness.

An account of Alma and the people of the Lord, who were driven into the wilderness by the people of king Noah. Comprising chapters 23 and 24.

CHAPTER 23

1. NOW Alma, having been warned of the Lord that the armies of king Noah would come upon them, and having made it known to his people, therefore they gathered together their flocks, and took of their grain, and departed into the wilderness before the armies of king Noah.
2. And the Lord did strengthen them, that the people of king Noah could not overtake them to destroy them.
3. And they fled eight days' journey into the wilderness.
4. And they came to a land, yea, even a very beautiful and pleasant land, a land of pure water.
5. And they pitched their tents, and began to till the ground, and began

Mosiah 22:14

The early history contained in the Book of Mormon is obtained from three sets of plates: the brass plates of Laban, the small plates of Nephi, and the large plates of Nephi. However, when Limhi's people join with the people of King Mosiah in the land of Zarahemla they bring with them two additional sets of plates: (1) their own records, which are known as the record of Zeniff, and (2) the "records which had been found by the people of Limhi," which are later identified as the records of Ether. (See Ether 1:1–2.) When Alma and his people come into the land of Zarahemla, they also evidently bring their own records with them. (See Mosiah 25:6 and also the superscription before Alma, chapter 23.) (Ludlow)

Mosiah 23:3; 24:25

The story of the flight of Alma and his people gives us the best clue in the Book of Mormon to the distance between the lands of Nephi and Zarahemla. It takes Alma and his group eight days to go from the waters of Mormon (in the borders of the land of Nephi—Mosiah 18:4) to the land of Helam (Mosiah 23:3). Then when they finally leave Helam, it takes them an additional twelve days of travel to go to the land of Zarahemla. (Mosiah 24:25.) Thus approximately twenty days are spent *in travel* by Alma and his group in going from the borders of the land of Nephi to the land of Zarahemla. (Ludlow)

to build buildings; yea, they were industrious, and did labor exceedingly.
6. And the people were desirous that Alma should be their king, for he was beloved by his people.
7. But he said unto them: Behold, it is not expedient that we should have a king; for thus saith the Lord: Ye shall not esteem one flesh above another, or one man shall not think himself above another; therefore I say unto you it is not expedient that ye should have a king.
8. Nevertheless, if it were possible that ye could always have just men to be your kings it would be well for you to have a king.
9. But remember the iniquity of king Noah and his priests; and I myself was caught in a snare, and did many things which were abominable in the sight of the Lord, which caused me sore repentance;
10. Nevertheless, after much tribulation, the Lord did hear my cries, and did answer my prayers, and has made me an instrument in his hands in bringing so many of you to a knowledge of his truth.
11. Nevertheless, in this I do not glory, for I am unworthy to glory of myself.
12. And now I say unto you, ye have been oppressed by king Noah, and have been in bondage to him and his priests, and have been brought into iniquity by them; therefore ye were bound with the bands of iniquity.
13. And now as ye have been delivered by the power of God out of these bonds; yea, even out of the hands of king Noah and his people, and also from the bonds of iniquity, even so I desire that ye should stand fast in this liberty wherewith ye have been made free, and that ye trust no man to be a king over you.
14. And also trust no one to be your teacher nor your minister, except he be a man of God, walking in his ways and keeping his commandments.
15. Thus did Alma teach his people, that every man should love his neighbor as himself, that there should be no contention among them.
16. And now, Alma was their high priest, he being the founder of their church.
17. And it came to pass that none received authority to preach or to teach except it were by him from God. Therefore he consecrated all their priests and all their teachers; and none were consecrated except they were just men.
18. Therefore they did watch over their people, and did nourish them with things pertaining to righteousness.
19. And it came to pass that they began to prosper exceedingly in the land; and they called the land Helam.
20. And it came to pass that they did multiply and prosper exceedingly in the land of Helam; and they built a city, which they called the city of Helam.
21. Nevertheless the Lord seeth fit

Mosiah 23:8

The Book of Mormon gives several valuable principles concerning different types of government. Mosiah 23:8 indicates that a monarchy would be a good system of government "if it were possible that ye could always have just men to be your kings." Thus, apparently nothing is inherently wrong with a monarchal system of government. In fact, the scriptures indicate that when Jesus Christ comes on the earth during the Millennium he will rule as King of kings; this evidently means we will then have a monarchal system of government. (Ludlow)

Mosiah 23:16–17

In the part of the Book of Mormon where we first read that Alma was the "founder of their church," the pronoun *their* refers only to the people who were with Alma in the wilderness; it does not refer to the entire Nephite nation. Thus when the statement is read in context, the true meaning is clear; this meaning is also clarified later in the record when it states that King Mosiah gave authority to Alma over the churches in Zarahemla. (Mosiah 26:8.) A brief historical setting of this period is provided by Joseph Fielding Smith in his answer to the question "Did the Nephites Have a Church Organization before the Days of Alma?"

The main body of the Nephites, under the second King Mosiah, was still intact in the land of Zarahemla. The reference stating that Alma was the founder of their church has reference only to the refugees who were fleeing from the land of the Nephites' first inheritance. In course of time they found their way back to the main body of the Church and Alma was consecrated as the high priest over the Church in all of the lands occupied by the Nephites. (Ludlow)

Mosiah 23:21

So very often, we have difficulty developing faith because we don't see a reason to comply at the time we receive counsel and direction. That is why we need patience. We must not wait until we see the purpose before we place our faith in the Lord's counsel and promises. If we wait to see the reason, it may be too late to use our faith. Our lack of trust may cause us to lose valuable opportunities for personal growth. (O/C)

to chasten his people; yea, he trieth their patience and their faith.
22. Nevertheless—whosoever putteth his trust in him the same
shall be lifted up at the last day. Yea, and thus it was with this people.
23. For behold, I will show unto you that they were brought into
bondage, and none could deliver them but the Lord their God, yea,
even the God of Abraham and Isaac and of Jacob.
24. And it came to pass that he did deliver them, and he did show
forth his mighty power unto them, and great were their rejoicings.
25. For behold, it came to pass that while they were in the land of
Helam, yea, in the city of Helam, while tilling the land round about,
behold an army of the Lamanites was in the borders of the land.
26. Now it came to pass that the brethren of Alma fled from their
fields, and gathered themselves together in the city of Helam; and
they were much frightened because of the appearance of the
Lamanites.
27. But Alma went forth and stood among them, and exhorted
them that they should not be frightened, but that they should
remember the Lord their God and he would deliver them.
28. Therefore they hushed their fears, and began to cry unto the
Lord that he would soften the hearts of the Lamanites, that they
would spare them, and their wives, and their children.
29. And it came to pass the the Lord did soften the hearts of the
Lamanites. And Alma and his brethren went forth and delivered
themselves up into their hands; and the Lamanites took possession
of the land of Helam.
30. Now the armies of the Lamanites, which had followed after the
people of king Limhi, had been lost in the wilderness for many
days.
31. And behold, they had found those priests of king Noah, in a
place which they called Amulon; and they had begun to possess
the land of Amulon and had begun to till the ground.
32. Now the name of the leader of those priests was Amulon.
33. And it came to pass that Amulon did plead with the
Lamanites; and he also sent forth their wives, who were the daughters of the Lamanites, to plead with their brethren, that they
should not destroy their husbands.
34. And the Lamanites had compassion on Amulon and his
brethren, and did not destroy them, because of their wives.
35. And Amulon and his brethren did join the Lamanites, and
they were traveling in the wilderness in search of the land of
Nephi when they discovered the land of Helam, which was possessed by Alma and his brethren.
36. And it came to pass that the Lamanites promised unto Alma
and his brethren, that if they would show them the way which led
to the land of Nephi that they would grant unto them their lives
and their liberty.
37. But after Alma had shown them the way that led to the land of
Nephi the Lamanites would not keep their promise; but they set
guards round about the land of Helam, over Alma and his brethren.
38. And the remainder of them went to the land of Nephi; and a
part of them returned to the land of Helam, and also brought with
them the wives and the children of the guards who had been left
in the land.

Mosiah 23:22

Even when we are sorely tried, the Lord will deliver us in His own time if we have faith.

39. And the king of the Lamanites had granted unto Amulon that he should be a king and a ruler over his people, who were in the land of Helam; nevertheless he should have no power to do anything contrary to the will of the king of the Lamanites.

CHAPTER 24

1. AND it came to pass that Amulon did gain favor in the eyes of the king of the Lamanites; therefore, the king of the Lamanites granted unto him and his brethren that they should be appointed teachers over his people, yea, even over the people who were in the land of Shemlon, and in the land of Shilom, and in the land of Amulon.
2. For the Lamanites had taken possession of all these lands; therefore, the king of the Lamanites had appointed kings over all these lands.
3. And now the name of the king of the Lamanites was Laman, being called after the name of his father; and therefore he was called king Laman. And he was king over a numerous people.
4. And he appointed teachers of the brethren of Amulon in every land which was possessed by his people; and thus the language of Nephi began to be taught among all the people of the Lamanites.
5. And they were a people friendly one with another; nevertheless they knew not God; neither did the brethren of Amulon teach them anything concerning the Lord their God, neither the law of Moses; nor did they teach them the words of Abinadi;
6. But they taught them that they should keep their record, and that they might write one to another.
7. And thus the Lamanites began to increase in riches, and began to trade one with another and wax great, and began to be a cunning and a wise people, as to the wisdom of the world, yea, a very cunning people, delighting in all manner of wickedness and plunder, except it were among their own brethren.
8. And now it came to pass that Amulon began to exercise authority over Alma and his brethren, and began to persecute him, and cause that his children should persecute their children.
9. For Amulon knew Alma, that he had been one of the king's priests, and that it was he that believed the words of Abinadi and was driven out before the king, and therefore he was wroth with him; for he was subject to king Laman, yet he exercised authority over them, and put tasks upon them, and put task-masters over them.
10. And it came to pass that so great were their afflictions that they began to cry mightily to God.
11. And Amulon commanded them that they should stop their cries; and he put guards over them to watch them, that whosoever should be found calling upon God should be put to death.
12. And Alma and his people did not raise their voices to the Lord their God, but did pour out their hearts to him; and he did know the thoughts of their hearts.
13. And it came to pass that the voice of the Lord came to them in their afflictions, saying: Lift up

Mosiah 24

Chapter 24 is the final account of Alma's deliverance. Mormon inserted the entire portion because of the lessons we can learn from it and apply today.

Mosiah 24:3–4

During the hundreds of years when the Nephites and Lamanites had lived apart, their languages had changed to such an extent that it was difficult for them to communicate with each other. During the period of history between 145 and 123 B.C., however, the king of the Lamanites "appointed teachers of the brethren of Amulon" (the wicked priests of King Noah who were Nephites by birth) to teach the Nephite language "among all the people of the Lamanites." (Mosiah 24:4.) Thus the two groups evidently start speaking the same language again. This fact takes on added significance later in the Book of Mormon when we read about the missionary efforts between these two groups. (Ludlow)

POINT OF INTEREST

The city of Copán is in western Honduras near the Guatemalan border and is the site of a major Mayan kingdom. At left are drawings of the four sides of an altar at the site that represent the transfer of power between kings.

your heads and be of good comfort, for I know of the covenant which ye have made unto me; and I will covenant with my people and deliver them out of bondage.
14. And I will also ease the burdens which are put upon your shoulders, that even you cannot feel them upon your backs, even while you are in bondage; and this will I do that ye may stand as witnesses for me hereafter, and that ye may know of a surety that I, the Lord God, do visit my people in their afflictions.
15. And now it came to pass that the burdens which were laid upon Alma and his brethren were made light; yea, the Lord did strengthen them that they could bear up their burdens with ease, and they did submit cheerfully and with patience to all the will of the Lord.
16. And it came to pass that so great was their faith and their patience that the voice of the Lord came unto them again, saying: Be of good comfort, for on the morrow I will deliver you out of bondage.
17. And he said unto Alma: Thou shalt go before this people, and I will go with thee and deliver this people out of bondage.
18. Now it came to pass that Alma and his people in the night-time gathered their flocks together, and also of their grain; yea, even all the night-time were they gathering the flocks together.
19. And in the morning the Lord caused a deep sleep to come upon the Lamanites, yea, and all their task-masters were in a profound sleep.
20. And Alma and his people departed into the wilderness; and when they had traveled all day they pitched their tents in a valley, and they called the valley Alma, because he led their way in the wilderness.
21. Yea, and in the valley of Alma they poured out their thanks to God because he had been merciful unto them, and eased their burdens, and had delivered them out of bondage; for they were in bondage, and none could deliver them except it were the Lord their God.
22. And they gave thanks to God, yea, all their men and all their women and all their children that could speak lifted their voices in the praises of their God.
23. And now the Lord said unto Alma: Haste thee and get thou and this people out of this land, for the Lamanites have awakened and do pursue thee; therefore get thee out of this land, and I will stop the Lamanites in this valley that they come no further in pursuit of this people.
24. And it came to pass that they departed out of the valley, and took their journey into the wilderness.
25. And after they had been in the wilderness twelve days they arrived in the land of Zarahemla; and king Mosiah did also receive them with joy.

CHAPTER 25

1. AND now king Mosiah caused that all the people should be gathered together.
2. Now there were not so many of the children of Nephi, or so many of those who were descendants of

Mosiah 24:14–15

I rejoice in afflictions, for they are necessary to humble and prove us, that we may comprehend ourselves, become acquainted with our weaknesses and infirmities; and I rejoice when I triumph over them, because God answers my prayers, therefore I feel to rejoice all the day long (Brigham Young, *Journal of Discourses* 1:17).

Mosiah 24:14–15

In a devotional to students at Brigham Young University, Elder Neal A. Maxwell counseled that we must not only have faith in the Lord, but in His timing—and pointed out that such is one of the most difficult things in which we must have faith.

Nephi, as there were of the people of Zarahemla, who was a descendant of Mulek, and those who came with him into the wilderness.
3. And there were not so many of the people of Nephi and of the people of Zarahemla as there were of the Lamanites; yea, they were not half so numerous.
4. And now all the people of Nephi were assembled together, and also all the people of Zarahemla, and they were gathered together in two bodies.
5. And it came to pass that Mosiah did read, and caused to be read, the records of Zeniff to his people; yea, he read the records of the people of Zeniff, from the time they left the land of Zarahemla until they returned again.
6. And he also read the account of Alma and his brethren, and all their afflictions, from the time they left the land of Zarahemla until the time they returned again.
7. And now, when Mosiah had made an end of reading the records, his people who tarried in the land were struck with wonder and amazement.
8. For they knew not what to think; for when they beheld those that had been delivered out of bondage they were filled with exceedingly great joy.
9. And again, when they thought of their brethren who had been slain by the Lamanites they were filled with sorrow, and even shed many tears of sorrow.
10. And again, when they thought of the immediate goodness of God, and his power in delivering Alma and his brethren out of the hands of the Lamanites and of bondage, they did raise their voices and give thanks to God.
11. And again, when they thought upon the Lamanites, who were their brethren, of their sinful and polluted state, they were filled with pain and anguish for the welfare of their souls.
12. And it came to pass that those who were the children of Amulon and his brethren, who had taken to wife the daughters of the Lamanites, were displeased with the conduct of their fathers, and they would no longer be called by the names of their fathers, therefore they took upon themselves the name of Nephi, that they might be called the children of Nephi and be numbered among those who were called Nephites.
13. And now all the people of Zarahemla were numbered with the Nephites, and this because the kingdom had been conferred upon none but those who were descendants of Nephi.
14. And now it came to pass that when Mosiah had made an end of speaking and reading to the people, he desired that Alma should also speak to the people.
15. And Alma did speak unto them, when they were assembled together in large bodies, and he went from one body to another, preaching unto the people repentance and faith on the Lord.
16. And he did exhort the people of Limhi and his brethren, all those that had been delivered out of bondage, that they should remember that it was the Lord that did deliver them.
17. And it came to pass that after Alma had taught the people many things, and had made an end of speaking to them, that king Limhi was desirous that he might be baptized; and all his people were

Mosiah 25:15

Alma and the sons of Mosiah, following their conversion, had a great desire to share the gospel with all people—especially the Lamanites. As a result, they dedicated their lives to preaching the gospel, and their example continues, even today, to radiate an influence for good in the ongoing process of building up the kingdom of God.

The sons of Mosiah were converted to the Lord. They were filled with charity. They could not bear that any human soul should perish and endure endless torment. The very thought caused them to quake and tremble.

Speaking of the desire to share the gospel, President Ezra Taft Benson said, "As a member of the Church, do you realize that, as a member-missionary, you have a sacred responsibility to share the gospel with friends and family? The Lord needs every member of the Church having the faith and courage to set a date to have someone prepared to be taught by the missionaries."

When we are truly converted, we will feel like the sons of Mosiah. We will have an overwhelming concern for the welfare of others. We will seek to serve and bless their lives (see Mosiah 18:8–9; D&C 108:7; Matt. 25:40). The question we need to answer is how much do we love God and our fellow brothers and sisters . . . for on this commandment—love—hangs all the law and the prophets. (P/A)

desirous that they might be baptized also.
18. Therefore, Alma did go forth into the water and did baptize
them; yea, he did baptize them after the manner he did his
brethren in the waters of Mormon; yea, and as many as he did baptize did belong to the church of God; and this because of their
belief on the words of Alma.
19. And it came to pass that king Mosiah granted unto Alma that
he might establish churches throughout all the land of Zarahemla;
and gave him power to ordain priests and teachers over every
church.
20. Now this was done because there were so many people that
they could not all be governed by one teacher; neither could they
all hear the word of God in one assembly;
21. Therefore they did assemble themselves together in different
bodies, being called churches; every church having their priests
and their teachers, and every priest preaching the word according
as it was delivered to him by the mouth of Alma.
22. And thus, notwithstanding there being many churches they
were all one church, yea, even the church of God; for there was
nothing preached in all the churches except it were repentance
and faith in God.
23. And now there were seven churches in the land of Zarahemla.
And it came to pass that whosoever were desirous to take upon
them the name of Christ, or of God, they did join the churches of
God;
24. And they were called the people of God. And the Lord did
pour out his Spirit upon them, and they were blessed, and prospered in the land.

CHAPTER 26

1. NOW it came to pass that there were many of the rising generation that could not understand the words of king Benjamin, being
little children at the time he spake unto his people; and they did
not believe the tradition of their fathers.
2. They did not believe what had been said concerning the resurrection of the dead, neither did they believe concerning the coming of Christ.
3. And now because of their unbelief they could not understand
the word of God; and their hearts were hardened.
4. And they would not be baptized; neither would they join the
church. And they were a separate people as to their faith, and
remained so ever after, even in their carnal and sinful state; for
they would not call upon the Lord their God.
5. And now in the reign of Mosiah they were not half so numerous
as the people of God; but because of the dissensions among the
brethren they became more numerous.
6. For it came to pass that they did deceive many with their flattering words, who were in the church, and did cause them to commit many sins; therefore it became expedient

Mosiah 26:2–4

Faith in the Lord Jesus Christ, His Church and teachings, is the motivating factor for all correct choices. David O. McKay taught: "What you sincerely in your heart think of Christ will determine what you are, will largely determine what your acts will be." (O/C)

that those who committed sin, that were in the church, should be admonished by the church.
7. And it came to pass that they were brought before the priests, and delivered up unto the priests by the teachers; and the priests brought them before Alma, who was the high priest.
8. Now king Mosiah had given Alma the authority over the church.
9. And it came to pass that Alma did not know concerning them; but there were many witnesses against them; yea, the people stood and testified of their iniquity in abundance.
10. Now there had not any such thing happened before in the church; therefore Alma was troubled in his spirit, and he caused that they should be brought before the king.
11. And he said unto the king: Behold, here are many whom we have brought before thee, who are accused of their brethren; yea, and they have been taken in divers iniquities. And they do not repent of their iniquities; therefore we have brought them before thee, that thou mayest judge them according to their crimes.
12. But king Mosiah said unto Alma: Behold, I judge them not; therefore I deliver them into thy hands to be judged.
13. And now the spirit of Alma was again troubled; and he went and inquired of the Lord what he should do concerning this matter, for he feared that he should do wrong in the sight of God.
14. And it came to pass that after he had poured out his whole soul to God, the voice of the Lord came to him, saying:
15. Blessed art thou, Alma, and blessed are they who were baptized in the waters of Mormon. Thou art blessed because of thy exceeding faith in the words alone of my servant Abinadi.
16. And blessed are they because of their exceeding faith in the words alone which thou hast spoken unto them.
17. And blessed art thou because thou hast established a church among this people; and they shall be established, and they shall be my people.
18. Yea, blessed is this people who are willing to bear my name; for in my name shall they be called; and they are mine.
19. And because thou hast inquired of me concerning the transgressor, thou art blessed.
20. Thou art my servant; and I covenant with thee that thou shalt have eternal life; and thou shalt serve me and go forth in my name, and shalt gather together my sheep.
21. And he that will hear my voice shall be my sheep; and him shall ye receive into the church, and him will I also receive.
22. For behold, this is my church; whosoever is baptized shall be baptized unto repentance. And whomsoever ye receive shall believe in my name; and him will I freely forgive.
23. For it is I that taketh upon me the sins of the world; for it is I that hath created them; and it is I that granteth unto him that believeth

Mosiah 26:12

King Mosiah knew the people had sinned, but he also knew they had not broken the laws of the land—and, as he was not the spiritual judge or leader of the people, he wisely refused to get involved. His decision forced Alma to turn to the Lord for help.

Mosiah 26:14

In describing the process of "pouring out his whole soul," Alma demonstrates that the Lord requires great effort on our part.

Mosiah 26:20

Joseph Smith said, "When the Lord has thoroughly proved him, and finds that the man is determined to serve Him at all hazards, then the man will find his calling and his election made sure, then it will be his privilege to receive the other Comforter, which the Lord has promised the Saints. . . . [He then read John 14:12–27]. Now what is this other Comforter? It is no more nor less than the Lord Jesus Christ Himself; and this is the sum and substance of the whole matter; that when any man obtains this last Comforter, he will have the personage of Jesus Christ to attend him, or appear unto him from time to time. . . ."

Mosiah 26:20–22

These verses give us a glimpse of how the Lord feels about His church.

unto the end a place at my right hand.
24. For behold, in my name are they called; and if they know me they shall come forth, and shall have a place eternally at my right hand.
25. And it shall come to pass that when the second trump shall sound then shall they that never knew me come forth and shall stand before me.
26. And then shall they know that I am the Lord their God, that I am their Redeemer; but they would not be redeemed.
27. And then I will confess unto them that I never knew them; and they shall depart into everlasting fire prepared for the devil and his angels.
28. Therefore I say unto you, that he that will not hear my voice, the same shall ye not receive into my church, for him I will not receive at the last day.
29. Therefore I say unto you, Go; and whosoever transgresseth against me, him shall ye judge according to the sins which he has committed; and if he confess his sins before thee and me, and repenteth in the sincerity of his heart, him shall ye forgive, and I will forgive him also.
30. Yea, and as often as my people repent will I forgive them their trespasses against me.
31. And ye shall also forgive one another your trespasses; for verily I say unto you, he that forgiveth not his neighbor's trespasses when he says that he repents, the same hath brought himself under condemnation.
32. Now I say unto you, Go; and whosoever will not repent of his sins the same shall not be numbered among my people; and this shall be observed from this time forward.
33. And it came to pass when Alma had heard these words he wrote them down that he might have them, and that he might judge the people of that church according to the commandments of God.
34. And it came to pass that Alma went and judged those that had been taken in iniquity, according to the word of the Lord.
35. And whosoever repented of their sins and did confess them, them he did number among the people of the church;
36. And those that would not confess their sins and repent of their iniquity, the same were not numbered among the people of the church, and their names were blotted out.
37. And it came to pass that Alma did regulate all the affairs of the church; and they began again to have peace and to prosper exceedingly in the affairs of the church, walking circumspectly before God, receiving many, and baptizing many.
38. And now all these things did Alma and his fellow laborers do who were over the church, walking in all diligence, teaching the word of God in all things, suffering all manner of afflictions, being persecuted by all those who did not belong to the church of God.
39. And they did admonish their

Mosiah 26:29

All who have sinned offend the Lawgiver. All who acknowledge their offenses by confessing their sins and living the commandments will be forgiven of the Lord. Members of the Church who refuse to repent are subject to the discipline of the Lord's Church. The Lord revealed, ". . . [he] that repenteth not of his sins, and confesseth them not, ye shall bring before the church, and do with him as the scripture saith unto you, either by commandment or by revelation. And this ye shall do that God may be glorified—not because ye forgive not, having not compassion, but that ye may be justified in the eyes of the law, that ye may not offend him who is your lawgiver" (D&C 64:12–13).

Church disciplinary councils are councils of love. One major purpose of disciplinary councils is to help the transgressor gain forgiveness. Elder Robert L. Simpson taught, "Priesthood courts [disciplinary councils] of the Church are not courts [disciplinary councils] of retribution. They are courts [disciplinary councils] of love. Oh, that members of the Church could understand this one fact.

"The adversary places a fear in the heart of the transgressor that makes it so difficult for him to do what needs to be done; and in the words of James E. Talmage, 'As the time of repentance is procrastinated the ability to repent grows weaker; neglect of opportunity in holy things develops inability' (*Articles of Faith*, 114). This simply means that doing what needs to be done will never be easier than right now. . . . [H]e who procrastinates the day or hopes for an alternate method that might require less courage waits in vain, and in the meantime, the possibilities grow dimmer. He is playing the game as Satan would have him play it, and exaltation in the presence of God grows more remote with each passing day." (O/C)

Mosiah 26:36

The words "cut off," "cast out," or "blotted out" mean to be excommunicated.

brethren; and they were also admonished, every one by the word of God, according to his sins, or to the sins which he had committed, being commanded of God to pray without ceasing, and to give thanks in all things.

CHAPTER 27

1. AND now it came to pass that the persecutions which were inflicted on the church by the unbelievers became so great that the church began to murmur, and complain to their leaders concerning the matter; and they did complain to Alma. And Alma laid the case before their king, Mosiah. And Mosiah consulted with his priests.
2. And it came to pass that king Mosiah sent a proclamation throughout the land round about that there should not any unbeliever persecute any of those who belonged to the church of God.
3. And there was a strict command throughout all the churches that there should be no persecutions among them, that there should be an equality among all men;
4. That they should let no pride nor haughtiness disturb their peace; that every man should esteem his neighbor as himself, laboring with their own hands for their support.
5. Yea, and all their priests and teachers should labor with their own hands for their support, in all cases save it were in sickness, or in much want; and doing these things, they did abound in the grace of God.
6. And there began to be much peace again in the land; and the people began to be very numerous, and began to scatter abroad upon the face of the earth, yea, on the north and on the south, on the east and on the west, building large cities and villages in all quarters of the land.
7. And the Lord did visit them and prosper them, and they became a large and wealthy people.
8. Now the sons of Mosiah were numbered among the unbelievers; and also one of the sons of Alma was numbered among them, he being called Alma, after his father; nevertheless, he became a very wicked and an idolatrous man. And he was a man of many words, and did speak much flattery to the people; therefore he led many of the people to do after the manner of his iniquities.
9. And he became a great hinderment to the prosperity of the church of God; stealing away the hearts of the people; causing much dissension among the people; giving a chance for the enemy of God to exercise his power over them.
10. And now it came to pass that while he was going about to destroy the church of God, for he did go about secretly with the sons of Mosiah seeking to destroy the church,

Mosiah 27:8

Alma the Elder, a former member of King Noah's notorious court, had a personal understanding of the transition from a state of impiety to a state of penitent spirituality. He freely confessed his shadowed background to those who had gathered in self-imposed exile in the wilderness: "But remember the iniquity of king Noah and his priests; and I myself was caught in a snare, and did many things which were abominable in the sight of the Lord, which caused me sore repentance" (Mosiah 23:9). Then, in a remarkable foreshadowing of the life of his future son, Alma, he added: "Nevertheless, after much tribulation, the Lord did hear my cries, and did answer my prayers, and has made me an instrument in his hands in bringing so many of you to a knowledge of his truth" (Mosiah 23:10).

Alma the Younger was a member of the rising, free-spirited generation of young people at Zarahemla who were not personal witnesses to the extraordinary teachings of King Benjamin and were not aligned with the spiritual traditions of the prophet-kings (see Mosiah 26:1–4). He and his colleagues, the sons of Mosiah, were renegades toward the Church in the capital city and environs. Their injurious behavior drew many from the fountain of truth. Years later, the reformed Alma characterized his earlier behavior in rather strong terms before his son Helaman: "Yea, and I had murdered many of [God's] children, or rather led them away unto destruction; yea, and in fine so great had been my iniquities, that the very thought of coming into the presence of my God did rack my soul with inexpressible horror" (Alma 36:14).

The two Almas provide persuasive testimony that an influence of darkness can be transformed into one of overwhelming light through repentance and faith in Jesus Christ. On the other hand, the Apostle Paul pointed out the deleterious effects of setting a bad example:

"But take heed lest by any means this liberty of yours become a stumbling block to them that are weak. . . .

"And through thy knowledge shall the weak . . . perish, for whom Christ died?

"But when ye sin so against the brethren, and would their weak conscience, ye sin against Christ" (1 Cor. 8:9, 11–12). (P/A)

and to lead astray the people of the Lord, contrary to the commandments of God, or even the king—
11. And as I said unto you, as they were going about rebelling against God, behold, the angel of the Lord appeared unto them; and he descended as it were in a cloud; and he spake as it were with a voice of thunder, which caused the earth to shake upon which they stood;
12. And so great was their astonishment, that they fell to the earth, and understood not the words which he spake unto them.
13. Nevertheless he cried again, saying: Alma, arise and stand forth, for why persecutest thou the church of God? For the Lord hath said: This is my church, and I will establish it; and nothing shall overthrow it, save it is the transgression of my people.
14. And again, the angel said: Behold, the Lord hath heard the prayers of his people, and also the prayers of his servant, Alma, who is thy father; for he has prayed with much faith concerning thee that thou mightest be brought to the knowledge of the truth; therefore, for this purpose have I come to convince thee of the power and authority of God, that the prayers of his servants might be answered according to their faith.
15. And now behold, can ye dispute the power of God? For behold, doth not my voice shake the earth? And can ye not also behold me before you? And I am sent from God.
16. Now I say unto thee: Go, and remember the captivity of thy fathers in the land of Helam, and in the land of Nephi; and remember how great things he has done for them; for they were in bondage, and he has delivered them. And now I say unto thee, Alma, go thy way, and seek to destroy the church no more, that their prayers may be answered, and this even if thou wilt of thyself be cast off.
17. And now it came to pass that these were the last words which the angel spake unto Alma, and he departed.
18. And now Alma and those that were with him fell again to the earth, for great was their astonishment; for with their own eyes they had beheld an angel of the Lord; and his voice was as thunder, which shook the earth; and they knew that there was nothing save the power of God that could shake the earth and cause it to tremble as though it would part asunder.
19. And now the astonishment of Alma was so great that he became dumb, that he could not open his mouth; yea, and he became weak, even that he could not move his hands; therefore he was taken by those that were with him, and carried helpless, even until he was laid before his father.
20. And they rehearsed unto his father all that had happened unto them; and his father rejoiced, for he knew that it was the power of God.
21. And he caused that a multitude should be gathered together that they might witness what the Lord

Mosiah 27:11–17

Although angels from God have appeared to righteous people, President Wilford Woodruff indicated that God always has a purpose in sending such messages:

"One of the Apostles said to me years ago, 'Brother Woodruff, I have prayed for a long time for the Lord to send me the administration of an angel. I have had a great desire for this, but I have never had my prayers answered.' I said to him that if he were to pray a thousand years to the God of Israel for that gift, it would not be granted, unless the Lord had a motive in sending an angel to him. . .

"Now, I have always said, and I want to say it to you, that the Holy Ghost is what every Saint of God needs. It is far more important that a man should have that gift than he should have the ministration of an angel, unless it is necessary for an angel to teach him something that he has not been taught" (address given at Weber Stake Conference, Ogden, Utah, October 19, 1896, and published in *Deseret Weekly*, 53:641). (Ludlow)

Mosiah 27:14–16

The Lord has promised that if we ask in faith for that which is right, we shall receive. (3 Nephi 18:20.) However, he has not promised the manner or the time in which the prayer will be answered. When the angel appeared to Alma the younger and the four sons of Mosiah, the angel made it clear that he had not appeared to them because of their own worthiness. . . . Evidently it was primarily because of the faithful prayers of Alma the elder and the other members of the church that the angel appeared to Alma the younger and the four sons of Mosiah. (Ludlow)

Mosiah 27:16

Even though they were told of the error of their endeavors, the angel made it very clear to Alma that he was free to choose righteousness or continue to destroy his soul. (See Mosiah 27:16.) It is vital and important to emphasize this divine principle. God answers the prayers of His children who ask in faith, but He will never force them to be good. They are free to choose good or evil. He may send a bishop, home teachers, visiting teachers, a neighbor, an inspired Sunday School teacher, a stake president, a high council speaker, or He may employ a host of other methods to answer their prayers, but He will never force His will upon them. (O/C)

had done for his son, and also for those that were with him.
22. And he caused that the priests should assemble themselves together; and they began to fast, and to pray to the Lord their God that he would open the mouth of Alma, that he might speak, and also that his limbs might receive their strength—that the eyes of the people might be opened to see and know of the goodness and glory of God.
23. And it came to pass after they had fasted and prayed for the space of two days and two nights, the limbs of Alma received their strength, and he stood up and began to speak unto them, bidding them to be of good comfort:
24. For, said he, I have repented of my sins, and have been redeemed of the Lord; behold I am born of the Spirit.
25. And the Lord said unto me: Marvel not that all mankind, yea, men and women, all nations, kindreds, tongues and people, must be born again; yea, born of God, changed from their carnal and fallen state, to a state of righteousness, being redeemed of God, becoming his sons and daughters;
26. And thus they become new creatures; and unless they do this, they can in nowise inherit the kingdom of God.
27. I say unto you, unless this be the case, they must be cast off; and this I know, because I was like to be cast off.
28. Nevertheless, after wading through much tribulation, repenting nigh unto death, the Lord in mercy hath seen fit to snatch me out of an everlasting burning, and I am born of God.
29. My soul hath been redeemed from the gall of bitterness and bonds of iniquity. I was in the darkest abyss; but now I behold the marvelous light of God. My soul was racked with eternal torment; but I am snatched, and my soul is pained no more.
30. I rejected my Redeemer, and denied that which had been spoken of by our fathers; but now that they may foresee that he will come, and that he remembereth every creature of his creating, he will make himself manifest unto all.
31. Yea, every knee shall bow, and every tongue confess before him. Yea, even at the last day, when all men shall stand to be judged of him, then shall they confess that he is God; then shall they confess, who live without God in the world, that the judgment of an everlasting punishment is just upon them; and they shall quake, and tremble, and shrink beneath the glance of his all-searching eye.
32. And now it came to pass that Alma began from this time forward to teach the people, and those who were with Alma at the time the angel appeared unto them, traveling round about through all the land,publishing to all the people the things which they had heard and seen, and preaching the word of God in much tribulation, being greatly persecuted by those who were unbelievers, being smitten by many of them.

Mosiah 27:24–26

The process of being spiritually born again isn't a single episode; instead, it happens each day as we strive to obey, repent of mistakes we have made, and draw closer to the Lord, bit by bit. In describing this process, Paul said that he died "daily" (see 1 Cor. 15:31). With the companionship of the Holy Ghost, the cleansing power of the Atonement is part of our lives, and we are able to gradually put off the natural man, the old self, and take on the new self, which enables us to eventually create of ourselves a more godlike creature.

Mosiah 27:32

One may know that conversion is complete if the convert is spiritually moved by an overwhelming desire to share the good news with others, even as Alma and the sons of Mosiah were motivated to do missionary work. (P/A)

POINT OF INTEREST

The llama is a South American camelid that, according to known records, was widely used as a pack animal by the Inca and other natives of the Andes.

33. But notwithstanding all this, they did impart much consolation to the church, confirming their faith, and exhorting them with long-suffering and much travail to keep the commandments of God.
34. And four of them were the sons of Mosiah; and their names were Ammon, and Aaron, and Omner, and Himni; these were the names of the sons of Mosiah.
35. And they traveled throughout all the lands of Zarahemla, and among all the people who were under the reign of king Mosiah, zealously striving to repair all the injuries which they had done to the church, confessing all their sins, and publishing all the things which they had seen, and explaining the prophecies and the scriptures to all who desired to hear them.
36. And thus they were instruments in the hands of God in bringing many to the knowledge of the truth, yea, to the knowledge of their Redeemer.
37. And how blessed are they! For they did publish peace; they did publish good tidings of good; and they did declare unto the people that the Lord reigneth.

CHAPTER 28

1. NOW it came to pass that after the sons of Mosiah had done all these things, they took a small number with them and returned to their father, the king, and desired of him that he would grant unto them that they might, with these whom they had selected, go up to the land of Nephi that they might preach the things which they had heard, and that they might impart the word of God to their brethren, the Lamanites—
2. That perhaps they might bring them to the knowledge of the Lord their God, and convince them of the iniquity of their fathers; and that perhaps they might cure them of their hatred towards the Nephites, that they might also be brought to rejoice in the Lord their God, that they might become friendly to one another, and that there should be no more contentions in all the land which the Lord their God had given them.
3. Now they were desirous that salvation should be declared to every creature, for they could not bear that any human soul should perish; yea, even the very thoughts that any soul should endure endless torment did cause them to quake and tremble.
4. And thus did the Spirit of the Lord work upon them, for they were the very vilest of sinners. And the Lord saw fit in his infinite mercy to spare them; nevertheless they suffered much anguish of soul because of their iniquities, suffering much and fearing that they should be cast off forever.
5. And it came to pass that they did plead with their father many days that they might go up to the land of Nephi.
6. And king Mosiah went and inquired of the Lord if he should let his sons go up among the Lamanites to preach the word.

Mosiah 27:34

The order of the birth of the four sons of Mosiah is never made clear in the Book of Mormon. The listing in Mosiah 27:34 would indicate that Ammon was the first born followed by Aaron, then Omner, and Himni. Also, the fact that Ammon was the leader on their missionary journey to the Lamanites would seem to indicate that Ammon was the eldest. (See Alma, chapters 17–26.) However, when King Mosiah asked his people to select his successor, they first desired that Aaron should be their king and their ruler. (Mosiah 29:1–2.) In this single instance it appears as though Aaron may have been the eldest son. (Ludlow)

Mosiah 28:1–3

When the Saints came West, President Brigham Young declared: "We wish the brethren to understand the facts just as they are; that is, there is neither man or woman in this Church who is not on a mission. That mission will last as long as they live, and it is to do good, to promote righteousness, to teach the principles of truth, and to prevail upon themselves and everybody around them to live those principles that they may obtain eternal life. This is the mission of every Latter-day Saint" (*Journal of Discourses* 12:19). (P/A)

Mosiah 28:3

When we are truly converted, we will feel like the sons of Mosiah. We will have an overwhelming concern for the welfare of others. We will seek to serve and bless their lives (see Mosiah 18:8–9; D&C 108:7; Matt. 25:40). The question we need to answer is how much do we love God and our fellow brothers and sisters . . . for on this commandment—love—hangs all the law and the prophets (see Matt. 22:36–40). (P/A)

Mosiah 28:3–4

Many of us recall hearing President Ezra Taft Benson speak often about missionary work and say, "The Spirit is the most important matter in this glorious work." With the Spirit, missionaries cannot fail. Without the Spirit, they cannot succeed. Performing missionary motions of service alone does not change people's lives. Only the Holy Spirit can do that. (O/C)

POINT OF INTEREST

"The World Tree (or Tree of Life) is found all over Central America. [At right] is a stylized representation from the ruins of Palenque [Mexico]. The World Tree had a strong association with the Mayan kings who considered themselves personification of the Tree of Life made flesh" (S. Michael Wilcox, *Land of Promise: Images of Book of Mormon Lands* [American Fork, Utah: Covenant Communications, Inc., 2003]).

7. And the Lord said unto Mosiah: Let them go up, for many shall believe on their words, and they shall have eternal life; and I will deliver thy sons out of the hands of the Lamanites.
8. And it came to pass that Mosiah granted that they might go and do according to their request.
9. And they took their journey into the wilderness to go up to preach the word among the Lamanites; and I shall give an account of their proceedings hereafter.
10. Now king Mosiah had no one to confer the kingdom upon, for there was not any of his sons who would accept of the kingdom.
11. Therefore he took the records which were engraven on the plates of brass, and also the plates of Nephi, and all the things which he had kept and preserved according to the commandments of God, after having translated and caused to be written the records which were on the plates of gold which had been found by the people of Limhi, which were delivered to him by the hand of Limhi;
12. And this he did because of the great anxiety of his people; for they were desirous beyond measure to know concerning those people who had been destroyed.
13. And now he translated them by the means of those two stones which were fastened into the two rims of a bow.
14. Now these things were prepared from the beginning, and were handed down from generation to generation, for the purpose of interpreting languages;
15. And they have been kept and preserved by the hand of the Lord, that he should discover to every creature who should possess the land the iniquities and abominations of his people;
16. And whosoever has these things is called seer, after the manner of old times.
17. Now after Mosiah had finished translating these records, behold, it gave an account of the people who were destroyed, from the time that they were destroyed back to the building of the great tower, at the time the Lord confounded the language of the people and they were scattered abroad upon the face of all the earth, yea, and even from that time back until the creation of Adam.
18. Now this account did cause the people of Mosiah to mourn exceedingly, yea, they were filled with sorrow; nevertheless it gave them much knowledge, in the which they did rejoice.
19. And this account shall be written hereafter; for behold, it is expedient that all people should know the things which are written in this account.
20. And now, as I said unto you, that after king Mosiah had done these things, he took the plates of brass, and all the things which he had kept, and conferred them upon Alma, who was the son of Alma; yea, all the records, and also the interpreters, and conferred them upon him, and commanded him that he should keep and preserve them, and also keep a record of the people, handing them down from one generation

Mosiah 28:11–13

The "two stones" that were used by Mosiah in translating the records written on the gold plates found by the people of Limhi were evidently the Urim and Thummim. (Ludlow)

Mosiah 28:11–19

Mosiah's translation of the gold plates discovered by the people of Limhi was evidently made available to the people of Mosiah (Mosiah 28:11, 18), and Mormon promises that an account of this record "shall be written hereafter; for behold, it is expedient that all people should know the things which are written in this account" (Mosiah 28:19). Mormon's son Moroni later abridges the account contained in these records, and his abridgment appears in our present Book of Mormon as the book of Ether. (Ludlow)

to another, even as they had been handed down from the time that Lehi left Jerusalem.

CHAPTER 29

1. NOW when Mosiah had done this he sent out throughout all the land, among all the people, desiring to know their will concerning who should be their king.
2. And it came to pass that the voice of the people came, saying: We are desirous that Aaron thy son should be our king and our ruler.
3. Now Aaron had gone up to the land of Nephi, therefore the king could not confer the kingdom upon him; neither would Aaron take upon him the kingdom; neither were any of the sons of Mosiah willing to take upon them the kingdom.
4. Therefore king Mosiah sent again among the people; yea, even a written word sent he among the people. And these were the words that were written, saying:
5. Behold, O ye my people, or my brethren, for I esteem you as such, I desire that ye should consider the cause which ye are called to consider—for ye are desirous to have a king.
6. Now I declare unto you that he to whom the kingdom doth rightly belong has declined, and will not take upon him the kingdom.
7. And now if there should be another appointed in his stead, behold I fear there would rise contentions among you. And who knoweth but what my son, to whom the kingdom doth belong, should turn to be angry and draw away a part of this people after him, which would cause wars and contentions among you, which would be the cause of shedding much blood and perverting the way of the Lord, yea, and destroy the souls of many people.
8. Now I say unto you let us be wise and consider these things, for we have no right to destroy my son, neither should we have any right to destroy another if he should be appointed in his stead.
9. And if my son should turn again to his pride and vain things he would recall the things which he had said, and claim his right to the kingdom, which would cause him and also this people to commit much sin.
10. And now let us be wise and look forward to these things, and do that which will make for the peace of this people.
11. Therefore I will be your king the remainder of my days; nevertheless, let us appoint judges, to judge this people according to our law; and we will newly arrange the affairs of this people, for we will appoint wise men to be judges, that will judge this people according to the commandments of God.
12. Now it is better that a man should be judged of God than of man, for the judgments of God are always just, but the judgments of man are not always just.
13. Therefore, if it were possible that you could have just men to be your kings, who would establish the laws of God, and judge this people according to his commandments, yea, if ye could have men for your

Mosiah 29:11

In his farewell address, President George Washington talked about the ideas of the men who were founding fathers of America, and he emphasized the need for an intertwining relationship between religious principles and governmental practices: "Of all the dispositions and habits which lead to political prosperity, religion and morality are indispensable supports . . . reason and experience both forbid us to expect that national morality can prevail in exclusion of religious principle. It is substantially true that virtue or morality is a necessary spring of popular government . . ." (O/C)

Mosiah 29:11

Brigham Young said, "I like a good government, and then I like to have it wisely and justly administered. The government of heaven, if wickedly administered, would become one of the worst governments upon the face of the earth. No matter how good a government is, unless it is administered by righteous men, an evil government will be made of it."

kings who would do even as my father Benjamin did for this people—I say unto you, if this could always be the case then it would be expedient that ye should always have kings to rule over you.

14. And even I myself have labored with all the power and faculties which I have possessed, to teach you the commandments of God, and to establish peace throughout the land, that there should be no wars nor contentions, no stealing, nor plundering, nor murdering, nor any manner of iniquity;

15. And whosoever has committed iniquity, him have I punished according to the crime which he has committed, according to the law which has been given to us by our fathers.

16. Now I say unto you, that because all men are not just it is not expedient that ye should have a king or kings to rule over you.

17. For behold, how much iniquity doth one wicked king cause to be committed, yea, and what great destruction!

18. Yea, remember king Noah, his wickedness and his abominations, and also the wickedness and abominations of his people. Behold what great destruction did come upon them; and also because of their iniquities they were brought into bondage.

19. And were it not for the interposition of their all-wise Creator, and this because of their sincere repentance, they must unavoidably remain in bondage until now.

20. But behold, he did deliver them because they did humble themselves before him; and because they cried mightily unto him he did deliver them out of bondage; and thus doth the Lord work with his power in all cases among the children of men, extending the arm of mercy towards them that put their trust in him.

21. And behold, now I say unto you, ye cannot dethrone an iniquitous king save it be through much contention, and the shedding of much blood.

22. For behold, he has his friends in iniquity, and he keepeth his guards about him; and he teareth up the laws of those who have reigned in righteousness before him; and he trampleth under his feet the commandments of God;

23. And he enacteth laws, and sendeth them forth among his people, yea, laws after the manner of his own wickedness; and whosoever doth not obey his laws he causeth to be destroyed; and whosoever doth rebel against him he will send his armies against them to war, and if he can he will destroy them; and thus an unrighteous king doth pervert the ways of all righteousness.

24. And now behold I say unto you, it is not expedient that such abominations should come upon you.

25. Therefore, choose you by the voice of this people, judges, that ye may be judged according to the laws which have been given you by our fathers, which are correct, and which were given them by the hand of the Lord.

26. Now it is not common that the voice of the people desireth anything

POINT OF INTEREST

The stela at right is a part of the ruins in Copán and was first discovered by European explorers in 1834. All four sides of the statue are covered in Mayan hieroglyphs, as revealed by the first drawings of the stela by Frederick Catherwood in 1839.

Mosiah 29:25

Following that pattern today, the Constitution of the United States is the foundation upon which all laws of this country are to be based. And it was the Lord who inspired the writing of that enabling document. (See D&C 101:80. . . Those who make laws as well as those who apply and interpret laws should rely upon the giver and maker of laws, even God, for the good of the people. . . . If legislators and judges are to fulfill their vital mandate, they must be involved, even immersed, in the processes of revelation. Removing prayer and references to God from governmental interests and activity is a sure formula for failure in the enactment and administering of laws for the good of the citizens of the country. We read from latter-day scripture: "We believe that governments were instituted of God for the benefit of man; and that he holds men accountable for their acts in relation to them, both in making laws and administering them, for the good and safety of society" (D&C 134:1) (O/C)

contrary to that which is right; but it is common for the lesser part of the people to desire that which is not right; therefore this shall ye observe and make it your law—to do your business by the voice of the people.
27. And if the time comes that the voice of the people doth choose iniquity, then is the time that the judgments of God will come upon you; yea, then is the time he will visit you with great destruction even as he has hitherto visited this land.
28. And now if ye have judges, and they do not judge you according to the law which has been given, ye can cause that they may be judged of a higher judge.
29. If your higher judges do not judge righteous judgments, ye shall cause that a small number of your lower judges should be gathered together, and they shall judge your higher judges, according to the voice of the people.
30. And I command you to do these things in the fear of the Lord; and I command you to do these things, and that ye have no king; that if these people commit sins and iniquities they shall be answered upon their own heads.
31. For behold I say unto you, the sins of many people have been caused by the iniquities of their kings; therefore their iniquities are answered upon the heads of their kings.
32. And now I desire that this inequality should be no more in this land, especially among this my people; but I desire that this land be a land of liberty, and every man may enjoy his rights and privileges alike, so long as the Lord sees fit that we may live and inherit the land, yea, even as long as any of our posterity remains upon the face of the land.
33. And many more things did king Mosiah write unto them, unfolding unto them all the trials and troubles of a righteous king, yea, all the travails of soul for their people, and also all the murmurings of the people to their king; and he explained it all unto them.
34. And he told them that these things ought not to be; but that the burden should come upon all the people, that every man might bear his part.
35. And he also unfolded unto them all the disadvantages they labored under, by having an unrighteous king to rule over them;
36. Yea, all his iniquities and abominations, and all the wars, and contentions, and bloodshed, and the stealing, and the plundering, and the committing of whoredoms, and all manner of iniquities which cannot be enumerated—telling them that these things ought not to be, that they were expressly repugnant to the commandments of God.
37. And now it came to pass, after king Mosiah had sent these things forth among the people they were convinced of the truth of his words.
38. Therefore they relinquished their desires for a king, and became exceedingly anxious that every man should have an equal chance throughout all the land; yea, and every man expressed a willingness to answer for his own sins.
39. Therefore, it came to pass that they assembled themselves together in bodies throughout the land, to cast in their voices concerning who should be their judges,

Mosiah 29:26–27

We notice that the type of government that is best depends upon the level of righteousness of the people. Speaking on the forms of government utilized among the Nephites, William E. Berrett observed: "It did not seem to make much difference what the form of government was. The thing which did make a difference was how righteous the people were. When the people were righteous, any form of government worked. When they were unrighteous, every form of government failed. . . . The form of government that could fail most quickly when all of the people became unrighteous was a democracy." (O/C)

to judge them according to the law which had been given them;
and they were exceedingly rejoiced because of the liberty which
had been granted unto them.
40. And they did wax strong in love towards Mosiah; yea, they did
esteem him more than any other man; for they did not look upon
him as a tyrant who was seeking for gain, yea, for that lucre which
doth corrupt the soul; for he had not exacted riches of them, neither had he delighted in the shedding of blood; but he had established peace in the land, and he had granted unto his people that
they should be delivered from all manner of bondage; therefore
they did esteem him, yea, exceedingly, beyond measure.
41. And it came to pass that they did appoint judges to rule over
them, or to judge them according to the law; and this they did
throughout all the land.
42. And it came to pass that Alma was appointed to be the first
chief judge, he being also the high priest, his father having conferred the office upon him, and having given him the charge concerning all the affairs of the church.
43. And now it came to pass that Alma did walk in the ways of the
Lord, and he did keep his commandments, and he did judge righteous
judgments; and there was continual peace through the land.
44. And thus commenced the reign of the judges throughout all
the land of Zarahemla, among all the people who were called the
Nephites; and Alma was the first and chief judge.
45. And now it came to pass that his father died, being eighty and
two years old, having lived to fulfil the commandments of God.
46. And it came to pass that Mosiah died also, in the thirty and
third year of his reign, being sixty and three years old; making in
the whole, five hundred and nine years from the time Lehi left
Jerusalem.
47. And thus ended the reign of the kings over the people of
Nephi; and thus ended the days of Alma, who was the founder of
their church.

Mosiah 29:40

Reynolds and Sjodahl wrote that "we must go back to the days of the antediluvian patriarchs to find the peers of these three kings (the two Mosiahs and Benjamin)."

Mosiah 29:42

This change in the structure of government was considered so significant that from this point on, the Nephites recorded time from the beginning of the reign of judges instead of from the time since Lehi left Jerusalem.

POINT OF INTEREST

Agouti (below) and paca are a couple of rodent species that inhabit areas of Central America and South America. They are related to guinea pigs and look quite similar to them, but have longer legs. It's hard to believe that they could be the "sheep" referred to in the Book of Mormon, but that's what some scholars propose.

THE BOOK OF ALMA

THE SON OF ALMA

The account of Alma, who was the son of Alma the first, and Chief Judge over the people of Nephi, and also the High Priest over the Church. An account of the reign of the Judges, and the wars and contentions among the people. And also an account of a war between the Nephites and the Lamanites, according to the record of Alma, the first and chief Judge.

CHAPTER 1

1. NOW it came to pass that in the first year of the reign of the judges over the people of Nephi, from this time forward, king Mosiah having gone the way of all the earth, having warred a good warfare, walking uprightly before God, leaving none to reign in his stead; nevertheless he had established laws, and they were acknowledged by the people; therefore they were obliged to abide by the laws which he had made.

2. And it came to pass that in the first year of the reign of Alma in the judgment-seat, there was a man brought before him to be judged, a man who was large, and was noted for his much strength.

3. And he had gone about among the people, preaching to them that which he termed to be the word of God, bearing down against the church; declaring unto the people that every priest and teacher ought to become popular; and they ought not to labor with their hands, but that they ought to be supported by the people.

4. And he also testified unto the people that all mankind should be saved at the last day, and that they need not fear nor tremble, but that they might lift up their heads and rejoice; for the Lord had created all men, and had also redeemed all men; and, in the end, all men should have eternal life.

5. And it came to pass that he did teach these things so much that many did believe on his words, even so many that they began to support him and give him money.

6. And he began to be lifted up in the pride of his heart, and to wear very costly apparel, yea, and even began to establish a church after the manner of his preaching.

7. And it came to pass as he was going, to preach to those who believed on his word, he met a man who belonged to the church of God, yea, even one of their teachers; and he began to contend with him sharply, that he might lead away the people of the church; but the man withstood him, admonishing him with the words of God.

8. Now the name of the man was Gideon; and it was he who was an instrument in the hands of God in delivering the people of Limhi out of bondage.

9. Now, because Gideon withstood him with the words of God he was wroth with Gideon, and drew his sword and began to smite him. Now Gideon being stricken with many years, therefore he was not able to withstand his blows, therefore he was slain by the sword.

10. And the man who slew him was taken by the people of the church, and was brought before Alma, to be judged according to the crimes which he had committed.

11. And it came to pass that he stood before Alma and pleaded for himself with much boldness.

12. But Alma said unto him: Behold, this is the first time that priestcraft has been introduced among this people. And behold, thou art not only guilty of priestcraft, but hast endeavored to enforce it by the sword; and were

Alma 1:2–3

The motivation for teaching perverted doctrine is to gain popularity among the people, elicit economic support and riches, and attain to the honors of men. (See Alma 1:2–3, 16.) Teaching false doctrine by precept or example is a grievous sin and can be a catalyst for rebellion and committing even greater sins. In the case of Nehor, he continued to practice priestcrafts until he committed the grosser sin of murder (see Alma 1:7–15). . . .

Falsifying the Savior's gospel by precept or by example leads people away from divine truth and principles of salvation and can be tantamount to being a party to the destruction of the souls of men. President N. Eldon Tanner likened those who practice priestcraft to Satan, "who in the pre-existence wanted to save all mankind, but with one condition attached—that the honor and glory go to him, not to God. He was more concerned with credit than with results; glory and praise were the end in themselves." (O/C)

Alma 1:2–3, 12

A large and articulate figure by the name of Nehor [lured] many members of the Church away through his flattering discourse and attempting to professionalize the clergy. When confronted by Gideon, . . . Nehor responded by slaying this revered man. As a result, Alma passed a sentence of execution upon Nehor for his acts of malice and murder. . . . But the seeds of priestcraft were sown, and Amlici, of the order of Nehor, soon launched a revolution to challenge not only the Church, but the very institutions of civil liberty established by Mosiah.

Speaking about priestcraft, Elder Dallin H. Oaks said, "Priestcraft is the sin committed by the combination of a good act—such as preaching or teaching the gospel—and a bad motive. The act may be good and visible, but the sin is in the motive. On earth, the wrong motive may be known only to the actor, but in heaven it is always known to God." (P/A)

Alma 1:3–5, 16

Priesthood and priestcraft represent two polar opposites. Priesthood is the authority to act on behalf of God, using power that has been properly gained by the laying on of hands by those who are in authority to do so. Priestcraft is engaged in by those who are more interested in popularity or financial gain than in truly serving their fellow men; those who practice priestcraft do not hold the priesthood, have not been given authority by God, and do not preach the full gospel to their congregations.

Alma 1:4

It would be well for all of us to understand that when someone sets himself up as the source of doctrine that is not in harmony with revealed truth, he is practicing priestcraft. (O/C)

priestcraft to be enforced among this people it would prove their entire destruction.
13. And thou hast shed the blood of a righteous man, yea, a man who has done much good among this people; and were we to spare thee his blood would come upon us for vengeance.
14. Therefore thou art condemned to die, according to the law which has been given us by Mosiah, our last king; and it has been acknowledged by this people; therefore this people must abide by the law.
15. And it came to pass that they took him; and his name was Nehor; and they carried him upon the top of the hill Manti, and there he was caused, or rather did acknowledge, between the heavens and the earth, that what he had taught to the people was contrary to the word of God; and there he suffered an ignominious death.
16. Nevertheless, this did not put an end to the spreading of priestcraft through the land; for there were many who loved the vain things of the world, and they went forth preaching false doctrines; and this they did for the sake of riches and honor.
17. Nevertheless, they durst not lie, if it were known, for fear of the law, for liars were punished; therefore they pretended to preach according to their belief; and now the law could have no power on any man for his belief.
18. And they durst not steal, for fear of the law, for such were punished; neither durst they rob, nor murder, for he that murdered was punished unto death.
19. But it came to pass that whosoever did not belong to the church of God began to persecute those that did belong to the church of God, and had taken upon them the name of Christ.
20. Yea, they did persecute them, and afflict them with all manner of words, and this because of their humility; because they were not proud in their own eyes, and because they did impart the word of God, one with another, without money and without price.
21. Now there was a strict law among the people of the church that there should not any man, belonging to the church, arise and persecute those that did not belong to the church, and that there should be no persecution among themselves.
22. Nevertheless, there were many among them who began to be proud, and began to contend warmly with their adversaries, even unto blows; yea, they would smite one another with their fists.
23. Now this was in the second year of the reign of Alma, and it was a cause of much affliction to the church; yea, it was the cause of much trial with the church.
24. For the hearts of many were hardened, and their names were blotted out, that they were remembered no more among the people of God. And also many withdrew themselves from among them.
25. Now this was a great trial to those that did stand fast in the faith; nevertheless, they were steadfast

Alma 1:16

The motivation for teaching perverted doctrine is to gain popularity among the people, elicit economic support and riches, and attain to the honors of men. Teaching false doctrine by precept or example is a grievous sin and can be a catalyst for rebellion and committing even greater sins. (O/C)

Alma 1:22

Contention of any kind is of the devil. Sometimes members of the Church contend with others, members and nonmembers, over doctrinal interpretation and other matters. Their behavior impedes the progress of the Church and causes many to yield to sin. (O/C)

and immovable in keeping the commandments of God, and they bore
with patience the persecution which was heaped upon them.
26. And when the priests left their labor to impart the word of God
unto the people, the people also left their labors to hear the word of
God. And when the priest had imparted unto them the word of God
they all returned again diligently unto their labors; and the priest, not
esteeming himself above his hearers, for the preacher was no better
than the hearer, neither was the teacher any better than the learner;
and thus they were all equal, and they did all labor, every man according to his strength.
27. And they did impart of their substance, every man according
to that which he had, to the poor, and the needy, and the sick, and
the afflicted; and they did not wear costly apparel, yet they were
neat and comely.
28. And thus they did establish the affairs of the church; and thus
they began to have continual peace again, notwithstanding all
their persecutions.
29. And now, because of the steadiness of the church they began
to be exceedingly rich, having abundance of all things whatsoever
they stood in need—an abundance of flocks and herds, and fatlings
of every kind, and also abundance of grain, and of gold, and of silver, and of precious things, and abundance of silk and fine-twined
linen, and all manner of good homely cloth.
30. And thus, in their prosperous circumstances, they did not send
away any who were naked, or that were hungry, or that were athirst,
or that were sick, or that had not been nourished; and they did not
set their hearts upon riches; therefore they were liberal to all, both
old and young, both bond and free, both male and female, whether
out of the church or in the church, having no respect to persons as
to those who stood in need.
31. And thus they did prosper and become far more wealthy than
those who did not belong to their church.
32. For those who did not belong to their church did indulge themselves in sorceries, and in idolatry or idleness, and in babblings, and
in envyings and strife; wearing costly apparel; being lifted up in the
pride of their own eyes; persecuting, lying, thieving, robbing, committing whoredoms, and murdering, and all manner of wickedness;
nevertheless, the law was put in force upon all those who did transgress it, inasmuch as it was possible.
33. And it came to pass that by thus exercising the law upon them,
every man suffering according to that which he had done, they
became more still, and durst not commit any wickedness if it were
known; therefore, there was much peace among the people of
Nephi until the fifth year of the reign of the judges.

Alma 1:26

Alma taught that the preacher teacher is no better than the learner, for they are equal, each according to his own strength. . . . Let us never forget in the role of teaching or learning that each must labor according to his or her role in the learning process. . . . Thus both are edified, for it is done in the Spirit of truth (see D&C 50:17–22). (P/A)

Alma 1:32

We have been counseled to be law-abiding people and to sustain and obey the laws of the land in which we live. Various prophets have stated that those who do not obey the laws of the land are being disloyal to God, and President Howard W. Hunter taught that there is no conflict in simultaneously worshiping God as the supreme ruler of heaven while upholding the laws of the land.

CHAPTER 2

Alma 2

Chapter 2 describes the first major challenge to the system of judges.

1. AND it came to pass in the commencement of the fifth year of their reign there began to be a contention among the people; for a certain man, being called Amlici, he being a very cunning man, yea, a wise man as to the wisdom of the world, he being after the order of the man that slew Gideon by the sword, who was executed according to the law—

2. Now this Amlici had, by his cunning, drawn away much people after him; even so much that they began to be very powerful; and they began to endeavor to establish Amlici to be a king over the people.

3. Now this was alarming to the people of the church, and also to all those who had not been drawn away after the persuasions of Amlici; for they knew that according to their law that such things must be established by the voice of the people.

4. Therefore, if it were possible that Amlici should gain the voice of the people, he, being a wicked man, would deprive them of their rights and privileges of the church; for it was his intent to destroy the church of God.

5. And it came to pass that the people assembled themselves together throughout all the land, every man according to his mind, whether it were for or against Amlici, in separate bodies, having much dispute and wonderful contentions one with another.

6. And thus they did assemble themselves together to cast in their voices concerning the matter; and they were laid before the judges.

7. And it came to pass that the voice of the people came against Amlici, that he was not made king over the people.

8. Now this did cause much joy in the hearts of those who were against him; but Amlici did stir up those who were in his favor to anger against those who were not in his favor.

9. And it came to pass that they gathered themselves together, and did consecrate Amlici to be their king.

10. Now when Amlici was made king over them he commanded them that they should take up arms against their brethren; and this he did that he might subject them to him.

11. Now the people of Amlici were distinguished by the name of Amlici, being called Amlicites; and the remainder were called Nephites, or the people of God.

12. Therefore the people of the Nephites were aware of the intent of the Amlicites, and therefore they did prepare to meet them; yea, they did arm themselves with swords, and with cimeters, and with bows, and with arrows, and with stones, and with slings, and with all manner of weapons of war, of every kind.

13. And thus they were prepared to meet the Amlicites at the time of their coming. And there were appointed captains, and higher captains, and chief captains, according to their numbers.

14. And it came to pass that Amlici did arm his men with all manner of weapons of war of every kind; and he also appointed rulers and leaders over his people, to lead them to war against their brethren.

15. And it came to pass that the

Alma 2:1–31

Soon after the establishment of a system of elected judges among the Nephites, several revolts take place against this type of government. The first of these revolts is headed by Amlici, who, in addition to being an avowed kingman, is also a follower of the order of Nehor and thus advocates priestcraft. (Alma 2:1.) Although Amlici is not successful in his desire to obtain the kingship, he precipitates a civil war that results in the deaths of over 19,000 people. (Alma 2:19.) (Ludlow)

Alma 2:3

Amlici sought to become the king, thus promoting contention. He was defeated first by the voice of the people and in the resulting widespread conflict—despite his having secured an alliance with the Lamanite hordes. Many people lost their lives as they contended over whether to be ruled by Amlici, who sought to be their king. In death they would be judged according to the spirit which they chose to obey.

Regarding our role in choosing leaders, the Prophet Joseph Smith said, "It is our duty to concentrate all our influence to make popular that which is sound and good, and unpopular that which is unsound." (P/A)

Alma 2:6–7

The Kingdom of God can best flourish in an environment where the inviolable agency of mankind is upheld through laws and institutions of liberty. It is incumbent upon free people to take every needful action for preserving freedom of conscience, including the freedom to worship Almighty God in peace. (P/A)

POINT OF INTEREST

Witness *comes from the Old English* wit, *which means "knowledge." A witness is considered to be as one who has special knowledge.*

Testament *comes from the Latin* testis, *which means "witness."* Testament *is also related to the Latin roots* tres *and* stare, *which mean "three stand."*

Covenant *comes from the Latin* convenire, *which means "to come with" or "to agree."*

Amlicites came upon the hill Amnihu, which was east of the river Sidon, which ran by the land of Zarahemla, and there they began to make war with the Nephites.
16. Now Alma, being the chief judge and the governor of the people of Nephi, therefore he went up with his people, yea, with his captains, and chief captains, yea, at the head of his armies, against the Amlicites to battle.
17. And they began to slay the Amlicites upon the hill east of Sidon. And the Amlicites did contend with the Nephites with great strength, insomuch that many of the Nephites did fall before the Amlicites.
18. Nevertheless the Lord did strengthen the hand of the Nephites, that they slew the Amlicites with great slaughter, that they began to flee before them.
19. And it came to pass that the Nephites did pursue the Amlicites all that day, and did slay them with much slaughter, insomuch that there were slain of the Amlicites twelve thousand five hundred thirty and two souls; and there were slain of the Nephites six thousand five hundred sixty and two souls.
20. And it came to pass that when Alma could pursue the Amlicites no longer he caused that his people should pitch their tents in the valley of Gideon, the valley being called after that Gideon who was slain by the hand of Nehor with the sword; and in this valley the Nephites did pitch their tents for the night.
21. And Alma sent spies to follow the remnant of the Amlicites, that he might know of their plans and their plots, whereby he might guard himself against them, that he might preserve his people from being destroyed.
22. Now those whom he had sent out to watch the camp of the Amlicites were called Zeram, and Amnor, and Manti, and Limher; these were they who went out with their men to watch the camp of the Amlicites.
23. And it came to pass that on the morrow they returned into the camp of the Nephites in great haste, being greatly astonished, and struck with much fear, saying:
24. Behold, we followed the camp of the Amlicites, and to our great astonishment, in the land of Minon, above the land of Zarahemla, in the course of the land of Nephi, we saw a numerous host of the Lamanites; and behold, the Amlicites have joined them;
25. And they are upon our brethren in that land; and they are fleeing before them with their flocks, and their wives, and their children, towards our city; and except we make haste they obtain possession of our city, and our fathers, and our wives, and our children be slain.
26. And it came to pass that the people of Nephi took their tents, and departed out of the valley of Gideon towards their city, which was the city of Zarahemla.
27. And behold, as they were crossing the river Sidon, the Lamanites and the Amlicites, being as numerous almost, as it were, as the sands of the sea, came upon them to destroy them.
28. Nevertheless, the Nephites being strengthened by the hand of the Lord, having prayed mightily to him that he would deliver them out of the hands of their enemies, therefore the Lord did hear their cries, and did strengthen them, and the Lamanites and the Amlicites did fall before them.
29. And it came to pass that Alma fought with Amlici with the sword,

Alma 2:28

The Nephites were saved becasue they relied on the Lord—a powerful lesson for us in our day.

face to face; and they did contend mightily, one with another.
30. And it came to pass that Alma, being a man of God, being exercised with much faith, cried, saying: O Lord, have mercy and spare my life, that I may be an instrument in thy hands to save and preserve this people.
31. Now when Alma had said these words he contended again with Amlici; and he was strengthened, insomuch that he slew Amlici with the sword.
32. And he also contended with the king of the Lamanites; but the king of the Lamanites fled back from before Alma and sent his guards to contend with Alma.
33. But Alma, with his guards, contended with the guards of the king of the Lamanites until he slew and drove them back.
34. And thus he cleared the ground, or rather the bank, which was on the west of the river Sidon, throwing the bodies of the Lamanites who had been slain into the waters of Sidon, that thereby his people might have room to cross and contend with the Lamanites and the Amlicites on the west side of the river Sidon.
35. And it came to pass that when they had all crossed the river Sidon that the Lamanites and the Amlicites began to flee before them, notwithstanding they were so numerous that they could not be numbered.
36. And they fled before the Nephites towards the wilderness which was west and north, away beyond the borders of the land; and the Nephites did pursue them with their might, and did slay them.
37. Yea, they were met on every hand, and slain and driven, until they were scattered on the west, and on the north, until they had reached the wilderness, which was called Hermounts; and it was that part of the wilderness which was infested by wild and ravenous beasts.
38. And it came to pass that many died in the wilderness of their wounds, and were devoured by those beasts and also the vultures of the air; and their bones have been found, and have been heaped up on the earth.

CHAPTER 3

1. AND it came to pass that the Nephites who were not slain by the weapons of war, after having buried those who had been slain—now the number of the slain were not numbered, because of the greatness of their number—after they had finished burying their dead they all returned to their lands, and to their houses, and their wives, and their children.
2. Now many women and children had been slain with the sword, and also many of their flocks and their herds; and also many of their fields of grain were destroyed, for they were trodden down by the hosts of men.
3. And now as many of the Lamanites and the Amlicites who had been slain upon the bank of the river Sidon were cast into the waters of Sidon; and behold their bones are in the depths of the sea, and they are many.
4. And the Amlicites were distinguished from the Nephites, for they had marked themselves with red in their foreheads after the manner of the Lamanites; nevertheless they had not shorn their heads like unto the Lamanites.
5. Now the heads of the Lamanites were shorn; and they were naked,

Alma 3:1

The entire war referred to in this verse happened because one man wanted to be king (see Alma 46:9). The "greatness of their number" is difficult to grasp: more than 19,000 were killed in a single battle (see Alma 2:19), and tens of thousands were slain in just one year (see Alma 3:26).

Alma 3:4–9

The Amlicites who escaped from Alma and his armies joined with the attacking Lamanite armies. Evidently they soon felt the need of marking themselves so their new allies, the dark-skinned Lamanites, could identify them as these two groups battled against the Nephites. Thus the Amlicites "marked themselves with red in their foreheads after the manner of the Lamanites." (Alma 3:4.)

This statement has two possible interpretations: (1) the Lamanites had red skin so the Amlicites marked themselves with red, or (2) the Lamanites marked themselves with red, and the Amlicites imitated them by marking themselves with red. Regardless of which interpretation is correct, this statement may provide a clue concerning the origin of painted war faces among this people, which continued to the coming of the white man some 1600 years later. (Ludlow)

save it were skin which was girded about their loins, and also their armor, which was girded about them, and their bows, and their arrows, and their stones, and their slings, and so forth.
6. And the skins of the Lamanites were dark, according to the mark which was set upon their fathers, which was a curse upon them because of their transgression and their rebellion against their brethren, who consisted of Nephi, Jacob, and Joseph, and Sam, who were just and holy men.
7. And their brethren sought to destroy them, therefore they were cursed; and the Lord God set a mark upon them, yea, upon Laman and Lemuel, and also the sons of Ishmael, and Ishmaelitish women.
8. And this was done that their seed might be distinguished from the seed of their brethren, that thereby the Lord God might preserve his people, that they might not mix and believe in incorrect traditions which would prove their destruction.
9. And it came to pass that whosoever did mingle his seed with that of the Lamanites did bring the same curse upon his seed.
10. Therefore, whosoever suffered himself to be led away by the Lamanites was called under that head, and there was a mark set upon him.
11. And it came to pass that whosoever would not believe in the tradition of the Lamanites, but believed those records which were brought out of the land of Jerusalem, and also in the tradition of their fathers, which were correct, who believed in the commandments of God and kept them, were called the Nephites, or the people of Nephi, from that time forth—
12. And it is they who have kept the records which are true of their people, and also of the people of the Lamanites.
13. Now we will return again to the Amlicites, for they also had a mark set upon them; yea, they set the mark upon themselves, yea, even a mark of red upon their foreheads.
14. Thus the word of God is fulfilled, for these are the words which he said to Nephi: Behold, the Lamanites have I cursed, and I will set a mark on them that they and their seed may be separated from thee and thy seed, from this time henceforth and forever, except they repent of their wickedness and turn to me that I may have mercy upon them.
15. And again: I will set a mark upon him that mingleth his seed with thy brethren, that they may be cursed also.
16. And again: I will set a mark upon him that fighteth against thee and thy seed.
17. And again, I say he that departeth from thee shall no more be called thy seed; and I will bless thee, and whomsoever shall be called thy seed, henceforth and forever; and these were the promises of the Lord unto Nephi and to his seed.
18. Now the Amlicites knew not that they were fulfilling the words of God when they began to mark themselves in their foreheads; nevertheless they had come out in open rebellion against God; therefore it was expedient that the curse should fall upon them.
19. Now I would that ye should see that they brought upon themselves the curse; and even so doth every man that is cursed bring

Alma 3:8

The difficulty with intermarriage with the Lamanites was not an issue of mixing races; instead, the Lord wanted to prevent the Lamanites from introducing incorrect traditions and doctrines to other groups.

Alma 3:19

We hurt ourselves when we rebel. When we choose to follow Satan, we soon find ourselves caught in a snare of our own design.

upon himself his own condemnation.
20. Now it came to pass that not many days after the battle which was fought in the land of Zarahemla, by the Lamanites and the Amlicites, that there was another army of the Lamanites came in upon the people of Nephi, in the same place where the first army met the Amlicites.
21. And it came to pass that there was an army sent to drive them out of their land.
22. Now Alma himself being afflicted with a wound did not go up to battle at this time against the Lamanites;
23. But he sent up a numerous army against them; and they went up and slew many of the Lamanites, and drove the remainder of them out of the borders of their land.
24. And then they returned again and began to establish peace in the land, being troubled no more for a time with their enemies.
25. Now all these things were done, yea, all these wars and contentions were commenced and ended in the fifth year of the reign of the judges.
26. And in one year were thousands and tens of thousands of souls sent to the eternal world, that they might reap their rewards according to their works, whether they were good or whether they were bad, to reap eternal happiness or eternal misery, according to the spirit which they listed to obey, whether it be a good spirit or a bad one.
27. For every man receiveth wages of him whom he listeth to obey, and this according to the words of the spirit of prophecy; therefore let it be according to the truth. And thus endeth the fifth year of the reign of the judges.

CHAPTER 4

1. NOW it came to pass in the sixth year of the reign of the judges over the people of Nephi, there were no contentions nor wars in the land of Zarahemla;
2. But the people were afflicted, yea, greatly afflicted for the loss of their brethren, and also for the loss of their flocks and herds, and also for the loss of their fields of grain, which were trodden under foot and destroyed by the Lamanites.
3. And so great were their afflictions that every soul had cause to mourn; and they believed that it was the judgments of God sent upon them because of their wickedness and their abominations; therefore they were awakened to a remembrance of their duty.
4. And they began to establish the church more fully; yea, and many were baptized in the waters of Sidon and were joined to the church of God; yea, they were baptized by the hand of Alma, who had been consecrated the high priest over the people of the church, by the hand of his father Alma.
5. And it came to pass in the seventh year of the reign of the judges there were about three thousand five hundred souls that united themselves to the church of God and were baptized. And thus endeth the seventh year of the reign of the judges over the people

Alma 3:22

The wound referred to in this verse was inflicted during Alma's swordfight with Amlici.

Alma 3:27

The Lord stands ready to reward us according to our faith, works, and the desires of our hearts (see Alma 41:3). The devil, on the other hand, will never support those who follow him but will speedily bring them down to hell (see Alma 30:60). (p/A 263) We are told that "the wages of sin is death" (Romans 6:23); sin, not the devil, exacts the reward (see Alma 30:60).

Alma 4:3–4

As described in these verses, affliction often causes people to repent, turn back to the truth, and resume activity in the Church.

of Nephi; and there was continual peace in all that time.
6. And it came to pass in the eighth year of the reign of the judges, that the people of the church began to wax proud, because of their exceeding riches, and their fine silks, and their fine-twined linen, and because of their many flocks and herds, and their gold and their silver, and all manner of precious things, which they had obtained by their industry; and in all these things were they lifted up in the pride of their eyes, for they began to wear very costly apparel.
7. Now this was the cause of much affliction to Alma, yea, and to many of the people whom Alma had consecrated to be teachers, and priests, and elders over the church; yea, many of them were sorely grieved for the wickedness which they saw had begun to be among their people.
8. For they saw and beheld with great sorrow that the people of the church began to be lifted up in the pride of their eyes, and to set their hearts upon riches and upon the vain things of the world, that they began to be scornful, one towards another, and they began to persecute those that did not believe according to their own will and pleasure.
9. And thus, in this eighth year of the reign of the judges, there began to be great contentions among the people of the church; yea, there were envyings, and strife, and malice, and persecutions, and pride, even to exceed the pride of those who did not belong to the church of God.
10. And thus ended the eighth year of the reign of the judges; and the wickedness of the church was a great stumbling-block to those who did not belong to the church; and thus the church began to fail in its progress.
11. And it came to pass in the commencement of the ninth year, Alma saw the wickedness of the church, and he saw also that the example of the church began to lead those who were unbelievers on from one piece of iniquity to another, thus bringing on the destruction of the people.
12. Yea, he saw great inequality among the people, some lifting themselves up with their pride, despising others, turning their backs upon the needy and the naked and those who were hungry, and those who were athirst, and those who were sick and afflicted.
13. Now this was a great cause for lamentations among the people, while others were abasing themselves, succoring those who stood in need of their succor, such as imparting their substance to the poor and the needy, feeding the hungry, and suffering all manner of afflictions, for Christ's sake, who should come according to the spirit of prophecy;
14. Looking forward to that day, thus retaining a remission of their sins; being filled with great joy because of the resurrection of the dead, according to the will and power and deliverance of Jesus Christ from the bands of death.
15. And now it came to pass that Alma, having seen the afflictions of the humble followers of God, and

Alma 4:11

During the eight years Alma reigned as chief judge, the examples set by Church members became a determining factor for contention or peace. . . .

Contention of any kind is of the devil. Sometimes members of the Church contend with others, both members and nonmembers, over doctrinal interpretation and other matters. Their behavior impedes the progress of the Church and causes many to yield to sin. Many Nephites belonging to the Church were guilty of this sin. . . .

Elder Joseph Fielding Smith counseled members of the Church about the dangers of being improper examples to our fellowmen. He said, ". . . we are all going to be judged according to our works, every soul. I have often thought of my place and responsibility in this Church. What a dreadful thing it would be to be going forth to teach, to lead men, to guide them into something that wasn't true. . . . The Lord says if we labor all our days and save but one soul, how great will be our joy with him; on the other hand how great will be our sorrow and condemnation if through our acts we have led one soul away from this truth." (O/C)

POINT OF INTEREST

These ruins in the Petén Basin of northern Guatemala illustrate what Nephite defensive earthenworks may have looked like.

the persecutions which were heaped upon them by the remainder of his people, and seeing all their inequality, began to be very sorrowful; nevertheless the Spirit of the Lord did not fail him.
16. And he selected a wise man who was among the elders of the church, and gave him power according to the voice of the people, that he might have power to enact laws according to the laws which had been given, and to put them in force according to the wickedness and the crimes of the people.
17. Now this man's name was Nephihah, and he was appointed chief judge; and he sat in the judgment-seat to judge and to govern the people.
18. Now Alma did not grant unto him the office of being high priest over the church, but he retained the office of high priest unto himself; but he delivered the judgment-seat unto Nephihah.
19. And this he did that he himself might go forth among his people, or among the people of Nephi, that he might preach the word of God unto them, to stir them up in remembrance of their duty, and that he might pull down, by the word of God, all the pride and craftiness and all the contentions which were among his people, seeing no way that he might reclaim them save it were in bearing down in pure testimony against them.
20. And thus in the commencement of the ninth year of the reign of the judges over the people of Nephi, Alma delivered up the judgment-seat to Nephihah, and confined himself wholly to the high priesthood of the holy order of God, to the testimony of the word, according to the spirit of revelation and prophecy.

The words which Alma, the High Priest according to the holy order of God, delivered to the people in their cities and villages throughout the land.

CHAPTER 5

1. NOW it came to pass that Alma began to deliver the word of God unto the people, first in the land of Zarahemla, and from thence throughout all the land.
2. And these are the words which he spake to the people in the church which was established in the city of Zarahemla, according to his own record, saying:
3. I, Alma, having been consecrated by my father, Alma, to be a high priest over the church of God, he having power and authority from God to do these things, behold, I say unto you that he began to

Alma 4:18–19

So often individuals, communities, or entire nations allow abundance and prosperity to cloud spiritual vision and elevate pride as their primary motivator in life.

It is a matter of ongoing urgency to follow prophetic counsel in avoiding pride and hard-heartedness, which inevitably lead to the collapse of moral values and the destruction of the spiritual aspect of life. There is no lesson from the Book of Mormon that is more pervasive than the admonition to avoid pride.

Following the defeat of Amlici and his revolutionary initiatives, many members of the Church became prosperous, forgot God, and became prideful. Many became unkind and uncharitable, so much that their behavior impeded the growth of the Church. To counter this pernicious influence, Alma gave up the chief judgeship seat to preach the gospel, "bearing down in pure testimony against them" (Alma 4:19).

Speaking of this situation, President Ezra Taft Benson said, "One of Satan's greatest tools is pride: to cause a man or a woman to center so much attention on self that he or she becomes insensitive to his Creator or fellow beings. . . .

"As we cleanse the inner vessel, there will have to be changes made in our own personal lives, in our families, and in the Church. The proud do not change to improve, but defend their position by rationalizing. Repentance means change, and it takes a humble person to change. But we can do it." (P/A)

Alma 4:19

There is a specific reason why Alma chose to preach "the word" to the people in order to reclaim them. The lifestyle of the people revealed their real problem. Since their works were unrighteous and out of harmony with the Lord's ways, one can accurately and easily conclude that their faith in Christ was lacking. After all, James declared, ". . . I will shew thee my faith by my works" (James 2:18). (O/C)

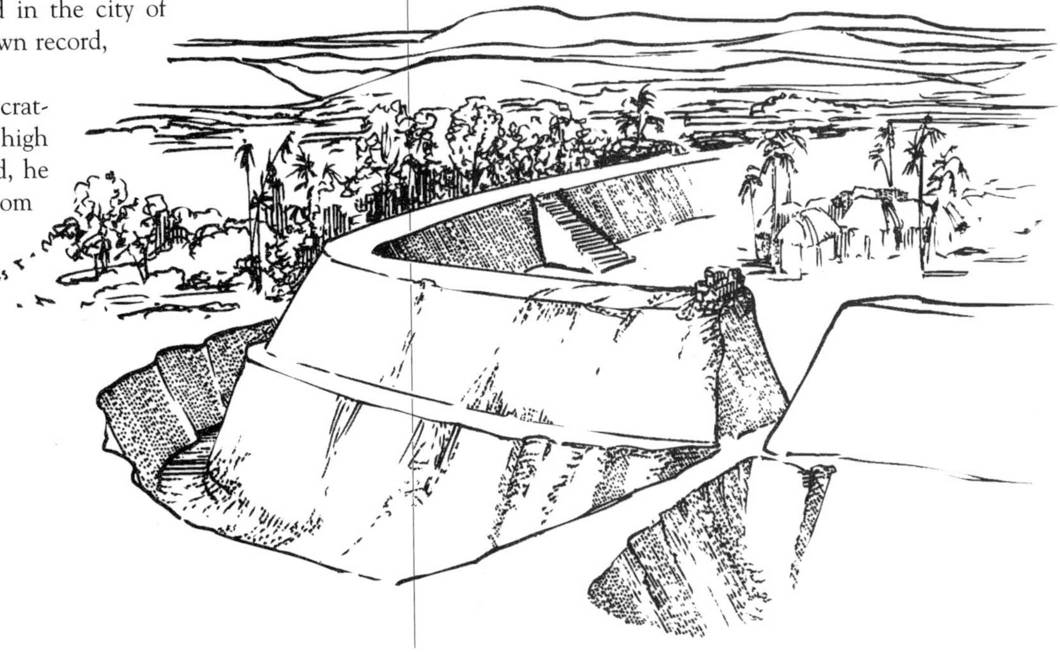

establish a church in the land which was in the borders of Nephi; yea, the land which was called the land of Mormon; yea, and he did baptize his brethren in the waters of Mormon.
4. And behold, I say unto you, they were delivered out of the hands of the people of king Noah, by the mercy and power of God.
5. And behold, after that, they were brought into bondage by the hands of the Lamanites in the wilderness; yea, I say unto you, they were in captivity, and again the Lord did deliver them out of bondage by the power of his word; and we were brought into this land, and here we began to establish the church of God throughout this land also.
6. And now behold, I say unto you, my brethren, you that belong to this church, have you sufficiently retained in remembrance the captivity of your fathers? Yea, and have you sufficiently retained in remembrance his mercy and long-suffering towards them? And moreover, have ye sufficiently retained in remembrance that he has delivered their souls from hell?
7. Behold, he changed their hearts; yea, he awakened them out of a deep sleep, and they awoke unto God. Behold, they were in the midst of darkness; nevertheless, their souls were illuminated by the light of the everlasting word; yea, they were encircled about by the bands of death, and the chains of hell, and an everlasting destruction did await them.
8. And now I ask of you, my brethren, were they destroyed? Behold, I say unto you, Nay, they were not.
9. And again I ask, were the bands of death broken, and the chains of hell which encircled them about, were they loosed? I say unto you, Yea, they were loosed, and their souls did expand, and they did sing redeeming love. And I say unto you that they are saved.
10. And now I ask of you on what conditions are they saved? Yea, what grounds had they to hope for salvation? What is the cause of their being loosed from the bands of death, yea, and also the chains of hell?
11. Behold, I can tell you—did not my father Alma believe in the words which were delivered by the mouth of Abinadi? And was he not a holy prophet? Did he not speak the words of God, and my father Alma believe them?
12. And according to his faith there was a mighty change wrought in his heart. Behold I say unto you that this is all true.
13. And behold, he preached the word unto your fathers, and a mighty change was also wrought in their hearts, and they humbled themselves and put their trust in the true and living God. And behold, they were faithful until the end; therefore they were saved.
14. And now behold, I ask of you, my brethren of the church, have ye spiritually been born of God? Have ye received his image in your countenances? Have ye experienced this mighty change in your hearts?
15. Do ye exercise faith in the

Alma 5:7

Satan uses false teachings and ideas, which encourage impure thoughts and lead to unrighteous practices, to ensnare people in a state of spiritual bondage. But all of that can be overcome and avoided by an acceptance of and adherence to the word of God. Those who grasp the iron rod, which is the word of God, can recognize and resist temptations and thus avoid satanic pitfalls of spiritual darkness. They can safely follow the path leading to the blessings of the Savior's Atonement and the ultimate reward of eternal life in the kingdom of God. (O/C)

Alma 5:13

So often individuals, communities, or entire nations allow abundance and prosperity to cloud spiritual vision and elevate pride as their primary motivator in life. It is a matter of ongoing urgency to follow prophetic counsel in avoiding pride and hard-heartedness, which inevitably lead to the collapse of moral values and the destruction of the spiritual aspect of life. There is no lesson from the Book of Mormon that is more pervasive than the admonition to avoid pride. (P/A)

Alma 5:14

Verses 14 through 59 provide an excellent "self-interview"—questions you can ask yourself as you ponder, "Do I spiritually qualify as a saint?"

Alma 5:14

Consider what has transpired in the years leading up to this singularly significant discourse by the prophet Alma. The Church survived the onslaught of two highly articulate con artists, Nehor and Amlici—the one sectarian and the other political. . . . The Church, brought to a state of humility by these events, experienced a great expansion. Peace returned to the land. The people once again prospered. But with that prosperity came the chronic malaise: pride. . . . [Alma's] speech, faithfully recorded by the prophet/historian Mormon, is one of the greatest missives in all of holy writ and stands as a stark warning to our own generation to repent and experience the mighty change of heart that alone can lead to spiritual rebirth. (P/A)

Alma 5:14, 21

The baptism of water which qualifies one for membership in the church does not assure one of the spiritual rebirth necessary to regain the presence of God. The "right" to receive the Holy Ghost is bestowed upon a person when he is confirmed a member of the Church and after he has been baptized by water. But unless a person fully repents of his sins and *actually receives* the Holy Ghost, he cannot be sanctified and be born again spiritually. (See Alma 7:14, 21; 3 Nephi 27:19–20; and John 3:5.) (Ludlow)

redemption of him who created you? Do you look forward with an eye
of faith, and view this mortal body raised in immortality, and this corruption raised in incorruption, to stand before God to be judged
according to the deeds which have been done in the mortal body?
16. I say unto you, can you imagine to yourselves that ye hear the
voice of the Lord, saying unto you, in that day: Come unto me ye
blessed, for behold, your works have been the works of righteousness upon the face of the earth?
17. Or do ye imagine to yourselves that ye can lie unto the Lord in
that day, and say—Lord, our works have been righteous works
upon the face of the earth—and that he will save you?
18. Or otherwise, can ye imagine yourselves brought before the tri-
bunal of God with your souls filled with guilt and remorse, having
a remembrance of all your guilt, yea, a perfect remembrance of all
your wickedness, yea, a remembrance that ye have set at defiance
the commandments of God?
19. I say unto you, can ye look up to God at that day with a pure
heart and clean hands? I say unto you, can you look up, having the
image of God engraven upon your countenances?
20. I say unto you, can ye think of being saved when you have
yielded yourselves to become subjects to the devil?
21. I say unto you, ye will know at that day that ye cannot be
saved; for there can no man be saved except his garments are
washed white; yea, his garments must be purified until they are
cleansed from all stain, through the blood of him of whom it has
been spoken by our fathers, who should come to redeem his people
from their sins.
22. And now I ask of you, my brethren, how will any
of you feel, if ye shall stand before the bar of God, having your garments stained with blood and all manner
of filthiness? Behold, what will these things testify
against you?
23. Behold will they not testify that ye are murderers,
yea, and also that ye are guilty of all manner of
wickedness?
24. Behold, my brethren, do ye suppose that such an one
can have a place to sit down in the kingdom of God,
with Abraham, with Isaac, and with Jacob, and also all
the holy prophets, whose garments are cleansed and are
spotless, pure and white?
25. I say unto you, Nay; except ye make our Creator a liar
from the beginning, or suppose that he is a liar from the
beginning, ye cannot suppose that such can have place in
the kingdom of heaven; but they shall be cast out for they
are the children of the kingdom of the devil.
26. And now behold, I say unto you, my brethren, if ye
have experienced a change of heart, and if ye have felt
to sing the song of redeeming love, I would ask, can ye
feel so now?

POINT OF INTEREST

This is a section of a wall in the Temple of Inscriptions at Palenque, Mexico. The three glyphs highlighted in black have been interpreted by Mayan scholars as "and it came to pass."

27. Have ye walked, keeping yourselves blameless before God? Could ye say, if ye were called to die at this time, within yourselves, that ye have been sufficiently humble? That your garments have been cleansed and made white through the blood of Christ, who will come to redeem his people from their sins?
28. Behold, are ye stripped of pride? I say unto you, if ye are not ye are not prepared to meet God. Behold ye must prepare quickly; for the kingdom of heaven is soon at hand, and such an one hath not eternal life.
29. Behold, I say, is there one among you who is not stripped of envy? I say unto you that such an one is not prepared; and I would that he should prepare quickly, for the hour is close at hand, and he knoweth not when the time shall come; for such an one is not found guiltless.
30. And again I say unto you, is there one among you that doth make a mock of his brother, or that heapeth upon him persecutions?
31. Wo unto such an one, for he is not prepared, and the time is at hand that he must repent or he cannot be saved!
32. Yea, even wo unto all ye workers of iniquity; repent, repent, for the Lord God hath spoken it!
33. Behold, he sendeth an invitation unto all men, for the arms of mercy are extended towards them, and he saith: Repent, and I will receive you.
34. Yea, he saith: Come unto me and ye shall partake of the fruit of the tree of life; yea, ye shall eat and drink of the bread and the waters of life freely;
35. Yea, come unto me and bring forth works of righteousness, and ye shall not be hewn down and cast into the fire—
36. For behold, the time is at hand that whosoever bringeth forth not good fruit, or whosoever doeth not the works of righteousness, the same have cause to wail and mourn.
37. O ye workers of iniquity; ye that are puffed up in the vain things of the world, ye that have professed to have known the ways of righteousness nevertheless have gone astray, as sheep having no shepherd, notwithstanding a shepherd hath called after you and is still calling after you, but ye will not hearken unto his voice!
38. Behold, I say unto you, that the good shepherd doth call you; yea, and in his own name he doth call you, which is the name of Christ; and if ye will not hearken unto the voice of the good shepherd, to the name by which ye are called, behold, ye are not the sheep of the good shepherd.
39. And now if ye are not the sheep of the good shepherd, of what fold are ye? Behold, I say unto you, that the devil is your shepherd, and ye are of his fold; and now,

Alma 5:28

From C. S. Lewis we read: "As long as you are proud, you cannot know God. A proud man is always looking down on things and people: and, of course, as long as you are looking down, you cannot see something that is above you" (*Mere Christianity* [New York: Macmillan, 1960], 96). (O/C)

Alma 5:29

In order to receive the spirit of revelation, we must be as little children—free not only of envy, but of malice, wrath, strife, bitter feelings, and evil speaking.

Alma 5:30

Remembering that there was a feeling sometime in the past does not mean a person still feels deeply about that matter now. It is critical for each of us to continue to be exposed to and participate in feeling-level experiences. So Alma provides . . . checklist questions for us to consider as we determine whether we are still in possession of earlier feelings. . . .

1. Have you walked, keeping yourselves blameless before God? Are you sufficiently humble? Are you still clean through the blood of Christ? In other words, are you still worthy?

2. Are you stripped of pride? Are you teachable? . . .

3. Are you stripped of envy? Are worldly things the focus of your attention and is obtaining them the object of your expenditure of energies and endeavors?

4. Do you make a mock of your brother? Do you persecute or ridicule or criticize others? Dr. Gary L. Bunker observed, "To mock is to humiliate, ridicule, insult, revile, make fun of, deride, sneer at, scorn, or hold in contempt. Teasing is a 'mild' form of mockery that sometimes occurs without malice or intent to harm, but frequently results in strained interpersonal relations and a loss of self-esteem on the part of the object of laughter. Mockery costs our brother or sister severe physical and/or psychological pain. It also jeopardizes our hope of eternal life." (P/A)

Alma 5:39

Spencer W. Kimball taught that to sin is to serve Satan. And Paul wrote that "of whom a man is overcome, of the same is he brought in bondage" (2 Peter 2:19).

who can deny this? Behold, I say unto you, whosoever denieth this
is a liar and a child of the devil.
40. For I say unto you that whatsoever is good cometh from God,
and whatsoever is evil cometh from the devil.
41. Therefore, if a man bringeth forth good works he hearkeneth
unto the voice of the good shepherd, and he doth follow him; but
whosoever bringeth forth evil works, the same becometh a child of
the devil, for he hearkeneth unto his voice, and doth follow him.
42. And whosoever doeth this must receive his wages of him;
therefore, for his wages he receiveth death, as to things pertaining
unto righteousness, being dead unto all good works.
43. And now, my brethren, I would that ye should hear me, for I
speak in the energy of my soul; for behold, I have spoken unto you
plainly that ye cannot err, or have spoken according to the commandments of God.
44. For I am called to speak after this manner, according to the
holy order of God, which is in Christ Jesus; yea, I am commanded
to stand and testify unto this people the things which have been
spoken by our fathers concerning the things which are to come.
45. And this is not all. Do ye not suppose that I know of these
things myself? Behold, I testify unto you that I do know that these
things whereof I have spoken are true. And how do ye suppose that
I know of their surety?
46. Behold, I say unto you they are made known unto me by the
Holy Spirit of God. Behold, I have fasted and prayed many days
that I might know these things of myself. And now I do know of
myself that they are true; for the Lord God hath made them manifest unto me by his Holy Spirit; and this is the spirit of revelation
which is in me.
47. And moreover, I say unto you that it has thus been revealed
unto me, that the words which have been spoken by our fathers are
true, even so according to the spirit of prophecy which is in me,
which is also by the manifestation of the Spirit of God.
48. I say unto you, that I know of myself that whatsoever I shall say
unto you, concerning that which is to come, is true; and I say unto
you, that I know that Jesus Christ shall come, yea, the Son, the Only
Begotten of the Father, full of grace, and mercy, and truth. And
behold, it is he that cometh to take away the sins of the world, yea,
the sins of every man who steadfastly believeth on his name.
49. And now I say unto you that this is the order after which I am
called, yea, to preach unto my beloved brethren, yea, and every
one that dwelleth in the land; yea, to preach unto all, both old and
young, both bond and free; yea, I say unto you the aged, and also
the middle aged, and the rising generation; yea, to cry unto them
that they must repent and be born again.
50. Yea, thus saith the Spirit: Repent, all ye ends of the earth, for
the kingdom of heaven is soon at hand; yea, the Son of God
cometh in his glory, in his might,

Alma 5:44

"The holy order of God" to which Alma is called refers to the Melchizedek priesthood.

Alma 5:45

The things of God are not known or received by the natural man, but only by a person who is truly converted and who receives repeated witnesses through the Holy Ghost. For a description of how the Spirit operates, see D&C 46.

Alma 5:46

This verse provides powerful testimony that through fasting and prayer, we can know the truths of all things.

majesty, power, and dominion. Yea, my beloved brethren, I say
unto you, that the Spirit saith: Behold the glory of the King of all
the earth; and also the King of heaven shall very soon shine forth
among all the children of men.
51. And also the Spirit saith unto me, yea, crieth unto me with a
mighty voice, saying: Go forth and say unto this people—Repent,
for except ye repent ye can in nowise inherit the kingdom of heav-
en.
52. And again I say unto you, the Spirit saith: Behold, the ax is laid
at the root of the tree; therefore every tree that bringeth not forth
good fruit shall be hewn down and cast into the fire, yea, a fire
which cannot be consumed, even an unquenchable fire. Behold,
and remember, the Holy One hath spoken it.
53. And now my beloved brethren, I say unto you, can ye withstand
these sayings; yea, can ye lay aside these things, and trample the Holy
One under your feet; yea, can ye be puffed up in the pride of your
hearts; yea, will ye still persist in the wearing of costly apparel and setting your hearts upon the vain things of the world, upon your riches?
54. Yea, will ye persist in supposing that ye are better one than
another; yea, will ye persist in the persecution of your brethren,
who humble themselves and do walk after the holy order of God,
wherewith they have been brought into this church, having been
sanctified by the Holy Spirit, and they do bring forth works which
are meet for repentance—
55. Yea, and will you persist in turning your backs upon the poor,
and the needy, and in withholding your substance from them?
56. And finally, all ye that will persist in your wickedness, I say
unto you that these are they who shall be hewn down and cast into
the fire except they speedily repent.
57. And now I say unto you, all you that are desirous to follow the
voice of the good shepherd, come ye out from the wicked, and be
ye separate, and touch not their unclean things; and behold, their
names shall be blotted out, that the names of the wicked shall not
be numbered among the names of the righteous, that the word of
God may be fulfilled, which saith: The names of the wicked shall
not be mingled with the names of my people;
58. For the names of the righteous shall be written in the book of
life, and unto them will I grant an inheritance at my right hand.
And now, my brethren, what have ye to say against this? I say unto
you, if ye speak against it, it matters not, for the word of God must
be fulfilled.
59. For what shepherd is there among you having many sheep doth
not watch over them, that the wolves enter not and devour his flock?
And behold, if a wolf enter his flock doth he not drive him out? Yea,
and at the last, if he can, he will destroy him.
60. And now I say unto you that the good shepherd doth call after
you; and if you will hearken unto his voice he will bring you into
his

Alma 5:53

To "trample the Holy One under your feet" means to cast the Lord aside and to pay no attention to His teachings (see 1 Nephi 19:7).

Alma 5:53–54

The traits listed in these verses provide a good description of those who will be cast out and hewn down by the Lord.

Alma 5:57

To have your name "blotted out" is to be excommunicated. Remember, the same priesthood power that can bind on earth and in heaven can also loose on earth and in heaven.

Alma 5:58

A "mighty change" affects much more than outward appearances. Someone who has experienced a mighty change strives continually to improve the deepest part of his or her soul, persistently addressing and correcting weaknesses, thereby drawing closer to the Lord on a daily basis.

fold, and ye are his sheep; and he commandeth you that ye suffer no ravenous wolf to enter among you, that ye may not be destroyed.
61. And now I, Alma, do command you in the language of him who hath commanded me, that ye observe to do the words which I have spoken unto you.
62. I speak by way of command unto you that belong to the church; and unto those who do not belong to the church I speak by way of invitation, saying: Come and be baptized unto repentance, that ye also may be partakers of the fruit of the tree of life.

CHAPTER 6

1. AND now it came to pass that after Alma had made an end of speaking unto the people of the church, which was established in the city of Zarahemla, he ordained priests and elders, by laying on his hands according to the order of God, to preside and watch over the church.
2. And it came to pass that whosoever did not belong to the church who repented of their sins were baptized unto repentance, and were received into the church.
3. And it also came to pass that whosoever did belong to the church that did not repent of their wickedness and humble themselves before God—I mean those who were lifted up in the pride of their hearts—the same were rejected, and their names were blotted out, that their names were not numbered among those of the righteous.
4. And thus they began to establish the order of the church in the city of Zarahemla.
5. Now I would that ye should understand that the word of God was liberal unto all, that none were deprived of the privilege of assembling themselves together to hear the word of God.
6. Nevertheless the children of God were commanded that they should gather themselves together oft, and join in fasting and mighty prayer in behalf of the welfare of the souls of those who knew not God.
7. And now it came to pass that when Alma had made these regulations he departed from them, yea, from the church which was in the city of Zarahemla, and went over upon the east of the river Sidon, into the valley of Gideon, there having been a city built, which was called the city of Gideon, which was in the valley that was called Gideon, being called after the man who was slain by the hand of Nehor with the sword.
8. And Alma went and began to declare the word of God unto the church which was established in the valley of Gideon, according to the revelation of the truth of the word which had been spoken by his fathers, and according to the spirit of prophecy which was in him, according to the testimony of Jesus Christ, the Son of God, who should come to redeem his people from their sins, and the holy order by which he was called. And thus it is written. Amen.

The words of Alma which he delivered to the people in Gideon, according to his own record. Comprising chapter 7.

Alma 6

God's house is a house of order, and maintaining order in the Church is one of the great responsibilities of presiding prophets. As is illustrated in Chapter 6, prophets must occasionally cleanse the Church and regulate its affairs through revelation.

Alma 6:1

God has ordained that prophets shall regulate the affairs of His Church and kingdom according to eternal principles. President David O. McKay verified that the Church "reveals the fact that it embodies all the strength of a strong central government and every virtue and necessary safeguard of a democracy. . . . Truly, from the standpoint of enhancing efficiency and progress, the Church has that form of government which the nations today are seeking. This is because it is patterned after the order which Christ himself established."

Everything of God is done in order (see Mosiah 4:27; D&C 28:13; 109:8; 93:43, 50; 107:78–84). Orderliness in the Church sets the tone for the Spirit. How many times have you witnessed a moment when someone is late, is ill-prepared, or does something contrary to the normally accepted practice? Sadly, the Spirit of the meeting or event may be lost. (P/A)

Alma 7

While he was in Zarahemla, Alma was forced to preach repentance to the people there. In Gideon, he is able to commend the people for their righteousness and to preach about the importance of being spiritually reborn. Because of their faith and righteousness, he is able to talk to them about Christ's coming.

CHAPTER 7

1. BEHOLD my beloved brethren, seeing that I have been permitted to come unto you, therefore I attempt to address you in my language; yea, by my own mouth, seeing that it is the first time that I have spoken unto you by the words of my mouth, I having been wholly confined to the judgment-seat, having had much business that I could not come unto you.
2. And even I could not have come now at this time were it not that the judgment-seat hath been given to another, to reign in my stead; and the Lord in much mercy hath granted that I should come unto you.
3. And behold, I have come having great hopes and much desire that I should find that ye had humbled yourselves before God, and that ye had continued in the supplicating of his grace, that I should find that ye were blameless before him, that I should find that ye were not in the awful dilemma that our brethren were in at Zarahemla.
4. But blessed be the name of God, that he hath given me to know, yea, hath given unto me the exceedingly great joy of knowing that they are established again in the way of his righteousness.
5. And I trust, according to the Spirit of God which is in me, that I shall also have joy over you; nevertheless I do not desire that my joy over you should come by the cause of so much afflictions and sorrow which I have had for the brethren at Zarahemla, for behold, my joy cometh over them after wading through much affliction and sorrow.
6. But behold, I trust that ye are not in a state of so much unbelief as were your brethren; I trust that ye are not lifted up in the pride of your hearts; yea, I trust that ye have not set your hearts upon riches and the vain things of the world; yea, I trust that you do not worship idols, but that ye do worship the true and the living God, and that ye look forward for the remission of your sins, with an everlasting faith, which is to come.
7. For behold, I say unto you there be many things to come; and behold, there is one thing which is of more importance than they all—for behold, the time is not far distant that the Redeemer liveth and cometh among his people.
8. Behold, I do not say that he will come among us at the time of his dwelling in his mortal tabernacle; for behold, the Spirit hath not said unto me that this should be the case. Now as to this thing I do not know; but this much I do know, that the Lord God hath power to do all things which are according to his word.
9. But behold, the Spirit hath said this much unto me, saying: Cry unto this people, saying—Repent ye, and prepare the way of the Lord, and walk in his paths, which are straight; for behold, the kingdom of heaven is at hand, and the Son of God cometh upon the face of the earth.
10. And behold, he shall be born of Mary, at Jerusalem which is the land of our forefathers, she being a virgin, a precious and chosen

Alma 7:6

While speaking in the city of Gideon, Alma . . . said, ". . . I trust that you do not worship idols, but that ye do worship the true and the living God" (Alma 7:6). Those who trust God do not need and should not have a substitute form or function upon which to focus. President Spencer W. Kimball spoke openly and with great insight on this subject when he said that ". . . [other Gods] would include both tangible and less tangible things, and everything which entices a person away from duty, loyalty, and love for and service to God. Idolatry is among the most serious of sins. . . ." (O/C)

Alma 7:7

Joy centers in our testimony of Jesus Christ and in the confirmation that others who are in our care and keeping are likewise motivated and inspired by their testimony of the Savior. . . .

Having set in order the affairs of the Church in the capital city of Zarahemla, Alma journeyed to the east to preach in the city of Gideon. . . . Alma's joy in Gideon was to learn that the people were indeed humble and faithful followers of Christ, whereas his joy in Zarahemla was to have seen the people snatched from the "awful dilemma" (Alma 7:3) of graceless pride and destructive hard-heartedness.

Regarding the importance of such a testimony of Christ, Elder Neal A. Maxwell said that at "the gate to heaven, Christ, the King of kings, waits for us with open arms. He awaits not only to certify us, but also to bestow a Shepherd's divine affection upon His sheep as we come Home. The reality that, if we are worthy, we should one day be so warmly received by the Lord of lords and King of kings is marvelous beyond comprehension! Yet He cannot fully receive us until we fully follow Him." (P/A)

Alma 7:10

Alma said that the Savior should be "born of Mary, at Jerusalem which is the land of our forefathers." (Alma 7:10.) Inasmuch as the Savior was evidently born at Bethlehem, not in Jerusalem, how should we interpret Alma's statement? At first glance the statement appears to be in error. However, archaeological evidences that have come forth since the Book of Mormon was published indicate that in 600 B.C. Bethlehem was probably a part of the "greater" land of Jerusalem. In this connection, it is of interest to note that the Book of Mormon refers to the *land* of Jerusalem, not the city; also, Bethlehem is only about six miles from the city of Jerusalem. (If you desire additional information on this subject, read *An Approach to the Book of Mormon*, pp. 81–82, by Hugh Nibley.) (Ludlow)

vessel, who shall be overshadowed and conceive by the power of the Holy Ghost, and bring forth a son, yea, even the Son of God.
11. And he shall go forth, suffering pains and afflictions and temptations of every kind; and this that the word might be fulfilled which saith he will take upon him the pains and the sicknesses of his people.
12. And he will take upon him death, that he may loose the bands of death which bind his people; and he will take upon him their infirmities, that his bowels may be filled with mercy, according to the flesh, that he may know according to the flesh how to succor his people according to their infirmities.
13. Now the Spirit knoweth all things; nevertheless the Son of God suffereth according to the flesh that he might take upon him the sins of his people, that he might blot out their transgressions according to the power of his deliverance; and now behold, this is the testimony which is in me.
14. Now I say unto you that ye must repent, and be born again; for the Spirit saith if ye are not born again ye cannot inherit the kingdom of heaven; therefore come and be baptized unto repentance, that ye may be washed from your sins, that ye may have faith on the Lamb of God, who taketh away the sins of the world, who is mighty to save and to cleanse from all unrighteousness.
15. Yea, I say unto you come and fear not, and lay aside every sin, which easily doth beset you, which doth bind you down to destruction, yea, come and go forth, and show unto your God that ye are willing to repent of your sins and enter into a covenant with him to keep his commandments, and witness it unto him this day by going into the waters of baptism.
16. And whosoever doeth this, and keepeth the commandments of God from thenceforth, the same will remember that I say unto him, yea, he will remember that I have said unto him, he shall have eternal life, according to the testimony of the Holy Spirit, which testifieth in me.
17. And now my beloved brethren, do you believe these things? Behold, I say unto you, yea, I know that ye believe them; and the way that I know that ye believe them is by the manifestation of the Spirit which is in me. And now because your faith is strong concerning that, yea, concerning the things which I have spoken, great is my joy.
18. For as I said unto you from the beginning, that I had much desire that ye were not in the state of dilemma like your brethren, even so I have found that my desires have been gratified.
19. For I perceive that ye are in the paths of righteousness; I perceive that ye are in the path which leads to the kingdom of God; yea, I perceive that ye are making his paths straight.
20. I perceive that it has been made known unto you, by the testimony of his word, that he cannot walk in crooked paths; neither doth he vary from that which he hath said; neither hath he a shadow of turning from the right to the left, or from that which is right to that which is wrong; therefore, his course is one eternal round.

Alma 7:11–12

We should come to understand the goodness of our Savior and His overwhelming concern for us. He not only suffered in Gethsemane, died on the cross at Calvary, opened the gates through the power of the resurrection, and provided all things for us to gain eternal life; He also lends us breath (see Mosiah 2:21). He goes before our face (see D&C 84:85–88). He lends us strength (see Alma 26:12; Mosiah 24:15) and He succors us according to our infirmities. Now, are we not filled with gratitude? Oh how we ought to show our love and appreciation by keeping His commandments and serving our fellow human beings! (P/A)

Alma 7:14

Alma indicated that a person must be "born again" in order to inherit the kingdom of heaven. (Alma 7:14.) Concerning the importance of this rebirth, Elder Bruce R. McConkie has written:

"The first birth takes place when spirits pass from their pre-existent first estate into mortality; the second birth or birth "into the kingdom of heaven" takes place when mortal men are born again and become alive to the things of the Spirit and of righteousness. The elements of water, blood, and Spirit are present in both births. (Moses 6:59–60.) The second birth begins when men are baptized in water by a legal administrator; it is completed when they actually receive the companionship of the Holy Ghost, becoming new creatures by the cleansing power of that member of the Godhead"

President David O. McKay has indicated that a real rebirth also involves a change in feeling:

"No man can sincerely resolve to apply to his daily life the teachings of Jesus of Nazareth without sensing a change in his own nature. The phrase, 'born again' has a deeper significance than many people attach to it. This *changed feeling* may be indescribable, *but it is real.* Happy the person who has truly sensed the uplifting, transforming power that comes from this nearness to the Savior, this kinship to the Living Christ. (Ludlow)

21. And he doth not dwell in unholy temples; neither can filthiness or anything which is unclean be received into the kingdom of God; therefore I say unto you the time shall come, yea, and it shall be at the last day, that he who is filthy shall remain in his filthiness.
22. And now my beloved brethren, I have said these things unto you that I might awaken you to a sense of your duty to God, that ye may walk blameless before him, that ye may walk after the holy order of God, after which ye have been received.
23. And now I would that ye should be humble, and be submissive and gentle; easy to be entreated; full of patience and long-suffering; being temperate in all things; being diligent in keeping the commandments of God at all times; asking for whatsoever things ye stand in need, both spiritual and temporal; always returning thanks unto God for whatsoever things ye do receive.
24. And see that ye have faith, hope, and charity, and then ye will always abound in good works.
25. And may the Lord bless you, and keep your garments spotless, that ye may at last be brought to sit down with Abraham, Isaac, and Jacob, and the holy prophets who have been ever since the world began, having your garments spotless even as their garments are spotless, in the kingdom of heaven to go no more out.
26. And now my beloved brethren, I have spoken these words unto you according to the Spirit which testifieth in me; and my soul doth exceedingly rejoice, because of the exceeding diligence and heed which ye have given unto my word.
27. And now, may the peace of God rest upon you, and upon your houses and lands, and upon your flocks and herds, and all that you possess, your women and your children, according to your faith and good works, from this time forth and forever. And thus I have spoken. Amen.

Alma 7:23

President George Albert Smith taught that sensitivity to sin and the consistent desire to repent of those things we do wrong is a sign that we have the constant companionship of the Holy Ghost. When we lose that companionship, our hearts become hardened and we find it difficult—if not impossible—to experience the true spirit of repentance.

CHAPTER 8

1. AND now it came to pass that Alma returned from the land of Gideon, after having taught the people of Gideon many things which cannot be written, having established the order of the church, according as he had before done in the land of Zarahemla, yea, he returned to his own house at Zarahemla to rest himself from the labors which he had performed.
2. And thus ended the ninth year of the reign of the judges over the people of Nephi.
3. And it came to pass in the commencement of the tenth year of the reign of the judges over the people of Nephi, that Alma departed from thence and took his journey over into the land of Melek, on the west of the river Sidon, on the west by the borders of the wilderness.
4. And he began to teach the people in the land of Melek according to the holy order of God, by which he had been called; and he began to teach the people throughout all the land of Melek.
5. And it came to pass that the people came to him throughout all

Alma 8

Alma was rejected in—and subsequently left—Ammonihah because wickedness among the people had led to full-scale apostasy. In stark contrast, the people in Melek were humble and accepted both Alma and the message he taught.

Alma 8:4

The "holy order of God" refers to the Melchizedek priesthood.

the borders of the land which was by the wilderness side. And they were baptized throughout all the land;
6. So that when he had finished his work at Melek he departed thence, and traveled three days' journey on the north of the land of Melek; and he came to a city which was called Ammonihah.
7. Now it was the custom of the people of Nephi to call their lands, and their cities, and their villages, yea, even all their small villages, after the name of him who first possessed them; and thus it was with the land of Ammonihah.
8. And it came to pass that when Alma had come to the city of Ammonihah he began to preach the word of God unto them.
9. Now Satan had gotten great hold upon the hearts of the people of the city of Ammonihah; therefore they would not hearken unto the words of Alma.
10. Nevertheless Alma labored much in the spirit, wrestling with God in mighty prayer, that he would pour out his Spirit upon the people who were in the city; that he would also grant that he might baptize them unto repentance.
11. Nevertheless, they hardened their hearts, saying unto him: Behold, we know that thou art Alma; and we know that thou art high priest over the church which thou hast established in many parts of the land, according to your tradition; and we are not of thy church, and we do not believe in such foolish traditions.
12. And now we know that because we are not of thy church we know that thou hast no power over us; and thou hast delivered up the judgment-seat unto Nephihah; therefore thou art not the chief judge over us.
13. Now when the people had said this, and withstood all his words, and reviled him, and spit upon him, and caused that he should be cast out of their city, he departed thence and took his journey towards the city which was called Aaron.
14. And it came to pass that while he was journeying thither, being weighed down with sorrow, wading through much tribulation and anguish of soul, because of the wickedness of the people who were in the city of Ammonihah, it came to pass while Alma was thus weighed down with sorrow, behold an angel of the Lord appeared unto him, saying:
15. Blessed art thou, Alma; therefore, lift up thy head and rejoice, for thou hast great cause to rejoice; for thou hast been faithful in keeping the commandments of God from the time which thou receivedst thy first message from him. Behold, I am he that delivered it unto you.
16. And behold, I am sent to command thee that thou return to the city of Ammonihah, and preach again unto the people of the city; yea, preach unto them. Yea, say unto them, except they repent the Lord God will destroy them.
17. For behold, they do study at this time that they may destroy the liberty of thy people, (for thus saith the Lord) which is contrary to the statutes, and judgments, and commandments which he has given unto his people.
18. Now it came to pass that after Alma had received his message from the angel of the Lord he returned speedily to the land of Ammonihah. And he entered the city by another way, yea, by the way which is on the south of the city of Ammonihah.
19. And as he entered the city he

Alma 8:8–9

After Alma had enjoyed remarkable success in his ministry in Gideon and had rested for a season at his home in Zarahemla, he continued his initiative in the city of Melek, whose inhabitants likewise welcomed him in the spirit of righteousness. When Alma went northward to the city of Ammonihah, however, he found himself in the haunts of the hard-hearted who resolutely defied his entreaties. Thus he was forced to abandon his service on their behalf, and it was only through the intervention of an angel that he "speedily" (Alma 8:18) returned to the city to deliver the declaration of the Lord that the city would be destroyed if its inhabitants did not repent.

The Prophet Joseph Smith saw some of the same things in our modern world. "I think it is high time," he wrote, "for a Christian world to awake out of sleep, and cry mightily to that God, day and night, whose anger we have justly incurred." He wrote that the condition of the world should be a stimulant "to arouse the faculties, and call forth the energies of every man, woman or child that possesses feelings of sympathy for their fellows, or that is in any degree endeared to the budding cause of our glorious Lord." (P/A)

Alma 8:15

It was the same angel who had guided Alma himself from a state of impenetrable hard-heartedness to transformational repentance in the early years of his life . . . thus Alma was surely the most experienced and understanding spokesman for the Lord on this errand. His ultimatum to the people of Ammonihah was swift, sure, and powerful, for he taught with the Spirit of the Lord. (P/A)

Alma 8:18

The fact that Alma returned "speedily" to the land of Ammonihah after receiving the message from the angel of the Lord is evidence that he possessed some of the same character traits as Nephi, who repeatedly avowed that he would go and do the things that were commanded of him. Our response should be the same when we are asked anything of the Lord or His servants.

was an hungered, and he said to a man: Will ye give to an humble servant of God something to eat?
20. And the man said unto him: I am a Nephite, and I know that thou art a holy prophet of God, for thou art the man whom an angel said in a vision: Thou shalt receive. Therefore, go with me into my house and I will impart unto thee of my food; and I know that thou wilt be a blessing unto me and my house.
21. And it came to pass that the man received him into his house; and the man was called Amulek; and he brought forth bread and meat and set before Alma.
22. And it came to pass that Alma ate bread and was filled; and he blessed Amulek and his house, and he gave thanks unto God.
23. And after he had eaten and was filled he said unto Amulek: I am Alma, and am the high priest over the church of God throughout the land.
24. And behold, I have been called to preach the word of God among all this people, according to the spirit of revelation and prophecy; and I was in this land and they would not receive me, but they cast me out and I was about to set my back towards this land forever.
25. But behold, I have been commanded that I should turn again and prophesy unto this people, yea, and to testify against them concerning their iniquities.
26. And now, Amulek, because thou hast fed me and taken me in, thou art blessed; for I was an hungered, for I had fasted many days.
27. And Alma tarried many days with Amulek before he began to preach unto the people.
28. And it came to pass that the people did wax more gross in their iniquities.
29. And the word came to Alma, saying: Go; and also say unto my servant Amulek, go forth and prophesy unto this people, saying—Repent ye, for thus saith the Lord, except ye repent I will visit this people in mine anger; yea, and I will not turn my fierce anger away.
30. And Alma went forth, and also Amulek, among the people, to declare the words of God unto them; and they were filled with the Holy Ghost.
31. And they had power given unto them, insomuch that they could not be confined in dungeons; neither was it possible that any man could slay them; nevertheless they did not exercise their power until they were bound in bands and cast into prison. Now, this was done that the Lord might show forth his power in them.
32. And it came to pass that they went forth and began to preach and to prophesy unto the people, according to the spirit and power which the Lord had given them.

The words of Alma, and also the words of Amulek, which were declared unto the people who were in the land of Ammonihah. And also they are cast into prison, and delivered by the miraculous power of God which was in them, according to the record of Alma. Comprising chapters 9 to 14 inclusive.

CHAPTER 9

Alma 8:20

For clarity in this verse, review Alma 10:7-9, which contains Amulek's account of the angel's visit to him.

Alma 8:26

Alma senses Amulek's righteousness in this situation because Amulek listened to the angel and responded by taking Alma in, feeding him, and offering him shelter. For each of us, our worthiness and righteousness is determined by the interrelationship of our motives, our thoughts, and our actions.

Alma 8:29

Like the missionary companionships of today, these two prophetic messengers of the Lord embody in dramatic fashion the law of multiple witnesses according to which our Heavenly Father always establishes His truth among men. The central theme of the message imparted by Alma and Amulek is the same as with missionaries in all dispensations, for they preached faith unto repentance and called for the people to practice righteousness. (P/A)

Alma 9

Remember that this is the second time Alma tries to preach repentance to the people of Ammonihah; they have heard his message before.

1. AND again, I, Alma, having been commanded of God that I should take Amulek and go forth and preach again unto this people, or the people who were in the city of Ammonihah, it came to pass as I began to preach unto them, they began to contend with me, saying:
2. Who art thou? Suppose ye that we shall believe the testimony of one man, although he should preach unto us that the earth should pass away?
3. Now they understood not the words which they spake; for they knew not that the earth should pass away.
4. And they said also: We will not believe thy words if thou shouldst prophesy that this great city should be destroyed in one day.
5. Now they knew not that God could do such marvelous works, for they were a hard-hearted and a stiffnecked people.
6. And they said: Who is God, that sendeth no more authority than one man among this people, to declare unto them the truth of such great and marvelous things?
7. And they stood forth to lay their hands on me; but behold, they did not. And I stood with boldness to declare unto them, yea, I did boldly testify unto them, saying:
8. Behold, O ye wicked and perverse generation, how have ye forgotten the tradition of your fathers; yea, how soon ye have forgotten the commandments of God.
9. Do ye not remember that our father, Lehi, was brought out of Jerusalem by the hand of God? Do ye not remember that they were all led by him through the wilderness?
10. And have ye forgotten so soon how many times he delivered our fathers out of the hands of their enemies, and preserved them from being destroyed, even by the hands of their own brethren?
11. Yea, and if it had not been for his matchless power, and his mercy, and his long-suffering towards us, we should unavoidably have been cut off from the face of the earth long before this period of time, and perhaps been consigned to a state of endless misery and woe.
12. Behold, now I say unto you that he command-eth you to repent; and except ye repent, ye can in nowise inherit the kingdom of God. But behold, this is not all—he has commanded you to repent, or he will utterly destroy you from off the face of the earth; yea, he will visit you in his anger, and in his fierce anger he will not turn away.
13. Behold, do ye not remember the words which he spake unto Lehi, saying that: Inasmuch as ye shall keep my commandments, ye shall prosper in the land? And again it is said that: Inasmuch as ye will not keep my commandments ye shall be cut off from the presence of the Lord.
14. Now I would that ye should remember, that inasmuch as the Lamanites have not kept the commandments of God, they have been cut off from the presence of the Lord. Now we see that the word of the Lord has been verified in this thing, and the Lamanites have been cut off from his presence, from the beginning of their transgressions in the land.
15. Nevertheless I say unto you, that it shall be more tolerable for them in the day of judgment than for you, if ye remain in your sins,

Alma 9:4

To the people of Ammonihah, the notion that their great city could be destroyed in a single day seemed a tremendous exaggeration. In reality, however, that's exactly what did happen (see Alma 16).

Alma 9:9–20

Rebellion is possible only when mankind has received divine knowledge, light, and truth. The Nephite people living in the city of Ammonihah were previously taught the saving principles of the gospel of Jesus Christ. They deliberately, voluntarily, and knowingly sinned against light and truth. . . . Mortal men who have received light and truth from God cannot sin with impunity; they bring down the wrath of God upon them. (O/C)

Alma 9:13

Lehi is quoted repeatedly throughout the Book of Mormon record to remind various people of their responsibility. For other instances, see 1 Nephi 2:20-21, 2 Nephi 1:7-9, and Alma 45:10–14, 16.

yea, and even more tolerable for them in this life than for you,
except ye repent.
16. For there are many promises which are extended to the
Lamanites; for it is because of the traditions of their fathers that
caused them to remain in their state of ignorance; therefore the
Lord will be merciful unto them and prolong their existence in the
land.
17. And at some period of time they will be brought to believe in
his word, and to know of the incorrectness of the traditions of their
fathers; and many of them will be saved, for the Lord will be merciful unto all who call on his name.
18. But behold, I say unto you that if ye persist in your wickedness
that your days shall not be prolonged in the land, for the Lamanites
shall be sent upon you; and if ye repent not they shall come in a
time when you know not, and ye shall be visited with utter destruction; and it shall be according to the fierce anger of the Lord.
19. For he will not suffer you that ye shall live in your iniquities, to
destroy his people. I say unto you, Nay; he would rather suffer that
the Lamanites might destroy all his people who are called the people of Nephi, if it were possible that they could fall into sins and
transgressions, after having had so much light and so much knowledge given unto them of the Lord their God;
20. Yea, after having been such a highly favored people of the Lord;
yea, after having been favored above every other nation, kindred,
tongue, or people; after having had all things made known unto
them, according to their desires, and their faith, and prayers, of
that which has been, and which is, and which is to come;
21. Having been visited by the Spirit of God; having conversed
with angels, and having been spoken unto by the voice of the Lord;
and having the spirit of prophecy, and the spirit of revelation, and
also many gifts, the gift of speaking with tongues, and the gift of
preaching, and the gift of the Holy Ghost, and the gift of translation;
22. Yea, and after having been delivered of God out of the land of
Jerusalem, by the hand of the Lord; having been saved from
famine, and from sickness, and all manner of diseases of every kind;
and they having waxed strong in battle, that they might not be
destroyed; having been brought out of bondage time after time,
and having been kept and preserved until now; and they have been
prospered until they are rich in all manner of things—
23. And now behold I say unto you, that if this people, who have
received so many blessings from the hand of the Lord, should transgress contrary to the light and knowledge which they do have, I say
unto you that if this be the case, that if they should fall into transgression, it would be far more tolerable for the Lamanites than for
them.
24. For behold, the promises of the Lord are extended to the
Lamanites, but they are not unto you if ye transgress; for has not
the Lord expressly

Alma 9:16

According to President Brigham Young, those who know nothing of the Lord are far better off than we are unless we live our religion.

Alma 9:20–22

In these verses, Alma specifies the ways in which the Lamanites had been favored by the Lord: all things had been made known unto them; they had been visited by the Spirit of God; they conversed with angels; they had been spoken to by the voice of the Lord; they were given the spirit of prophecy and the spirit of revelation; they were given many gifts (including the gift of the Holy Ghost); they were delivered of God out of the land of Jerusalem; they had been saved from famine, sickness, and all manner of diseases of every kind; they were brought out of bondage time after time; and they had prospered until they were rich in all manner of things. Despite being highly favored by the Lord, however, they still rejected God's word as preached by Alma.

promised and firmly decreed, that if ye will rebel against him that ye shall utterly be destroyed from off the face of the earth?
25. And now for this cause, that ye may not be destroyed, the Lord has sent his angel to visit many of his people, declaring unto them that they must go forth and cry mightily unto this people, saying: Repent ye, for the kingdom of heaven is nigh at hand;
26. And not many days hence the Son of God shall come in his glory; and his glory shall be the glory of the Only Begotten of the Father, full of grace, equity, and truth, full of patience, mercy, and long-suffering, quick to hear the cries of his people and to answer their prayers.
27. And behold, he cometh to redeem those who will be baptized unto repentance, through faith on his name.
28. Therefore, prepare ye the way of the Lord, for the time is at hand that all men shall reap a reward of their works, according to that which they have been—if they have been righteous they shall reap the salvation of their souls, according to the power and deliverance of Jesus Christ; and if they have been evil they shall reap the damnation of their souls, according to the power and captivation of the devil.
29. Now behold, this is the voice of the angel, crying unto the people.
30. And now, my beloved brethren, for ye are my brethren, and ye ought to be beloved, and ye ought to bring forth works which are meet for repentance, seeing that your hearts have been grossly hardened against the word of God, and seeing that ye are a lost and a fallen people.
31. Now it came to pass that when I, Alma, had spoken these words, behold, the people were wroth with me because I said unto them that they were a hard-hearted and a stiffnecked people.
32. And also because I said unto them that they were a lost and a fallen people they were angry with me, and sought to lay their hands upon me, that they might cast me into prison.
33. But it came to pass that the Lord did not suffer them that they should take me at that time and cast me into prison.
34. And it came to pass that Amulek went and stood forth, and began to preach unto them also. And now the words of Amulek are not all written, nevertheless a part of his words are written in this book.

CHAPTER 10

1. NOW these are the words which Amulek preached unto the people who were in the land of Ammonihah, saying:
2. I am Amulek; I am the son of Giddonah, who was the son of Ishmael, who was a descendant of Aminadi; and it was that same Aminadi who interpreted the writing which was upon the wall of the temple, which was written by the finger of God.

Alma 9:30

We should always realize that prophets have our welfare and possibility of eternal life in mind—and the greatest we can do for our personal welfare is to repent. Chastening helps us return to righteousness. Chastening is a form of God's love towards us (see D&C 95:1–2), as also with His prophets. (P/A)

Alma 9:2

This verse is the only reference known to Aminadi interpreting writing on the wall of the temple—writing that was made by the finger of God. We have no other information about this event.

Alma 10:2–3

Concerning the fact that Ishmael was also a descendant of Joseph, Elder Erastus Snow said:

"Whoever has read the Book of Mormon carefully will have learned that the remnants of the house of Joseph dwelt upon the American continent; and that Lehi learned . . . that he was of the lineage of Manasseh. . . . [that] Ishmael was of the lineage of Ephraim, and that his sons married into Lehi's family, and Lehi's sons married Ishmael's daughters, thus fulfilling the words of Jacob . . . in the 48th chapter of Genesis, which says: 'And let my name be named on them, and the name of my fathers Abraham and Isaac; and let them grow into a multitude in the midst of the land.' Thus these descendants of Manasseh and Ephraim grew together upon this American continent, with a sprinkling from the house of Judah, from Mulek descended, who left Jerusalem eleven years after Lehi. . . thus making a combination, an intermixture of Ephraim and Manasseh with the remnants of Judah . . . (*Journal of Discourses*, 23:184–85). (Ludlow)

3. And Aminadi was a descendant of Nephi, who was the son of Lehi, who came out of the land of Jerusalem, who was a descendant of Manasseh, who was the son of Joseph who was sold into Egypt by the hands of his brethren.
4. And behold, I am also a man of no small reputation among all those who know me; yea, and behold, I have many kindreds and friends, and I have also acquired much riches by the hand of my industry.
5. Nevertheless, after all this, I never have known much of the ways of the Lord, and his mysteries and marvelous power. I said I never had known much of these things; but behold, I mistake, for I have seen much of his mysteries and his marvelous power; yea, even in the preservation of the lives of this people.
6. Nevertheless, I did harden my heart, for I was called many times and I would not hear; therefore I knew concerning these things, yet I would not know; therefore I went on rebelling against God, in the wickedness of my heart, even until the fourth day of this seventh month, which is in the tenth year of the reign of the judges.
7. As I was journeying to see a very near kindred, behold an angel of the Lord appeared unto me and said: Amulek, return to thine own house, for thou shalt feed a prophet of the Lord; yea, a holy man, who is a chosen man of God; for he has fasted many days because of the sins of this people, and he is an hungered, and thou shalt receive him into thy house and feed him, and he shall bless thee and thy house; and the blessing of the Lord shall rest upon thee and thy house.
8. And it came to pass that I obeyed the voice of the angel, and returned towards my house. And as I was going thither I found the man whom the angel said unto me: Thou shalt receive into thy house—and behold it was this same man who has been speaking unto you concerning the things of God.
9. And the angel said unto me he is a holy man; wherefore I know he is a holy man because it was said by an angel of God.
10. And again, I know that the things whereof he hath testified are true; for behold I say unto you, that as the Lord liveth, even so has he sent his angel to make these things manifest unto me; and this he has done while this Alma hath dwelt at my house.
11. For behold, he hath blessed mine house, he hath blessed me, and my women, and my children, and my father and my kinsfolk; yea, even all my kindred hath he blessed, and the blessing of the Lord hath rested upon us according to the words which he spake.
12. And now, when Amulek had spoken these words the people began to be astonished, seeing there was more than one witness who testified of the things whereof they were accused, and also of the things which were to come, according to the spirit of prophecy which was in them.
13. Nevertheless, there were some among them who thought to question them, that by their cunning devices they might catch them in their words, that they might find

Alma 10:3

In further identifying himself, Amulek mentioned that his forefather Aminadi "was a descendant of Nephi, who was the son of Lehi . . . who was a descendant of Manasseh, who was the son of Joseph who was sold into Egypt. . . ." (Alma 10:3.) Earlier in the Book of Mormon it was mentioned that Lehi was a descendant of Joseph. (1 Nephi 5:14.) However, Joseph had two sons, Manasseh and Ephraim, and this is the first time the Book of Mormon indicates that Lehi was a descendant of Joseph's eldest son, Manasseh.

Some students of the Book of Mormon have wondered how descendants of Joseph were still living in Jerusalem in 600 B.C. when most members of the tribes of Ephraim and Manasseh were taken into captivity by the Assyrians about 721 B.C. A scripture in 2 Chronicles may provide a clue to this problem. This account mentions that in about 941 B.C. Asa, the king of the land, gathered together at Jerusalem all of Judah and Benjamin "and the strangers with them out of Ephraim and Manasseh." (2 Chronicles 15:9.) These "strangers. . . out of Ephraim and Manasseh" who were gathered to Jerusalem in approximately 941 B.C. may have included the forefathers of Lehi and Ishmael. (Ludlow)

Alma 10:6–7

It is interesting that Amulek specifies the exact day on which he ceased rebelling against God. We know that part of his conversion consisted of Alma coming to him and being received into his home—a reminder that the Lord often blesses people through His mortal servants.

Alma 10:12

The Lord has proclaimed that His doctrine shall be established through the testimony of multiple witnesses: "In the mouth of two or three witnesses shall every word be established" (2 Cor. 13:1; comp. Matt. 18:16; D&C 6:28; 128:3). . . .

Alma tarried many days with Amulek, blessing all members of his family (Alma 8:27; 10:11). Then . . . Amulek received his official calling as Alma's companion, a calling that would shortly prove highly effective in establishing the truth of the Lord's word in the mouth of more than one witness.

Elder Bruce R. McConkie referred to the importance of witnesses when he said, "Whenever the Lord has established a dispensation by revealing his gospel and by conferring priesthood and keys upon men, he has acted in accordance with the law of witnesses which he himself ordained. . . . Never does one man stand alone in establishing a new dispensation of revealed truth, or in carrying the burden of such a message and warning to the world. In every dispensation . . . , two or more witnesses have always joined their testimonies, thus leaving their hearers without excuse in the day of judgment should the testimony be rejected." (P/A)

witness against them, that they might deliver them to their judges that they might be judged according to the law, and that they might be slain or cast into prison, according to the crime which they could make appear or witness against them.
14. Now it was those men who sought to destroy them, who were lawyers, who were hired or appointed by the people to administer the law at their times of trials, or at the trials of the crimes of the people before the judges.
15. Now these lawyers were learned in all the arts and cunning of the people; and this was to enable them that they might be skilful in their profession.
16. And it came to pass that they began to question Amulek, that thereby they might make him cross his words, or contradict the words which he should speak.
17. Now they knew not that Amulek could know of their designs. But it came to pass as they began to question him, he perceived their thoughts, and he said unto them: O ye wicked and perverse generation, ye lawyers and hypocrites, for ye are laying the foundations of the devil; for ye are laying traps and snares to catch the holy ones of God.
18. Ye are laying plans to pervert the ways of the righteous, and to bring down the wrath of God upon your heads, even to the utter destruction of this people.
19. Yea, well did Mosiah say, who was our last king, when he was about to deliver up the kingdom, having no one to confer it upon, causing that this people should be governed by their own voices—yea, well did he say that if the time should come that the voice of this people should choose iniquity, that is, if the time should come that this people should fall into transgression, they would be ripe for destruction.
20. And now I say unto you that well doth the Lord judge of your iniquities; well doth he cry unto this people, by the voice of his angels: Repent ye, repent, for the kingdom of heaven is at hand.
21. Yea, well doth he cry, by the voice of his angels that: I will come down among my people, with equity and justice in my hands.
22. Yea, and I say unto you that if it were not for the prayers of the righteous, who are now in the land, that ye would even now be visited with utter destruction; yet it would not be by flood, as were the people in the days of Noah, but it would be by famine, and by pestilence, and the sword.
23. But it is by the prayers of the righteous that ye are spared; now therefore, if ye will cast out the righteous from among you then will not the Lord stay his hand; but in his fierce anger he will come out against you; then ye shall be smitten by famine, and by pestilence, and by the sword; and the time is soon at hand except ye repent.
24. And now it came to pass that the people were more angry with Amulek, and they cried out, saying: This man doth revile against our laws which are just, and our wise lawyers whom we have selected.
25. But Amulek stretched forth his hand, and cried the mightier unto them, saying: O ye wicked and

Alma 10:22

This verse demonstrates the power and effect that the prayers of righteous people can have on a nation. President Spencer W. Kimball said of our day that there are many, many upright and faithful people whose "prayers keep the world from destruction."

Alma 10:23

The Lord has never destroyed wicked people or removed them from mortality without giving them ample warning and an opportunity to repent. Even the faith and prayers of the righteous have been extended to the wicked in an attempt to bring them to repentance. (O/C)

perverse generation, why hath Satan got such great hold upon your hearts? Why will ye yield yourselves unto him that he may have power over you, to blind your eyes, that ye will not understand the words which are spoken, according to their truth?

26. For behold, have I testified against your law? Ye do not understand; ye say that I have spoken against your law; but I have not, but I have spoken in favor of your law, to your condemnation.

27. And now behold, I say unto you, that the foundation of the destruction of this people is beginning to be laid by the unrighteousness of your lawyers and your judges.

28. And now it came to pass that when Amulek had spoken these words the people cried out against him, saying: Now we know that this man is a child of the devil, for he hath lied unto us; for he hath spoken against our law. And now he says that he has not spoken against it.

29. And again, he has reviled against our lawyers, and our judges.

30. And it came to pass that the lawyers put it into their hearts that they should remember these things against him.

31. And there was one among them whose name was Zeezrom. Now he was the foremost to accuse Amulek and Alma, he being one of the most expert among them, having much business to do among the people.

32. Now the object of these lawyers was to get gain; and they got gain according to their employ.

CHAPTER 11

1. NOW it was in the law of Mosiah that every man who was a judge of the law, or those who were appointed to be judges, should receive wages according to the time which they labored to judge those who were brought before them to be judged.

2. Now if a man owed another, and he would not pay that which he did owe, he was complained of to the judge; and the judge executed authority, and sent forth officers that the man should be brought before him; and he judged the man according to the law and the evidences which were brought against him, and thus the man was compelled to pay that which he owed, or be stripped, or be cast out from among the people as a thief and a robber.

3. And the judge received for his wages according to his time—a senine of gold for a day, or a senum of silver, which is equal to a senine of gold; and this is according to the law which was given.

4. Now these are the names of the different pieces of their gold, and of their silver, according to their value. And the names are given by the Nephites, for they did not reckon after the manner of the Jews who were at Jerusalem; neither did they measure after the manner of the Jews; but they altered their reckoning and their measure, according to the minds and the circumstances of the people, in every generation, until the reign of the judges, they having been established by king Mosiah.

POINT OF INTEREST

"The 'weights and measures' that are used by the native people of Guatemala and El Salvador [right] follow the same pattern as outlined in the Book of Mormon" (Joseph L. Allen, *Exploring the Lands of the Book of Mormon* [Orem, Utah: S. A. Publishers, Inc., 1989]).

Alma 11:3

If a value of "1" is attributed to this unit, the monetary system of the Nephites might be summarized as follows: Leah equals 1/8; shiblum = 1/4; shiblon = 1/2; antion of gold = 1 1/2; senum of silver or senine of gold = 1; amnor of silver or seon of gold = 2; ezrom of silver or shum of gold = 4; onti of silver or limna of gold = 7. One senine of gold (or senum of silver) = wages of a judge for one day. The Nephite monetary system was based on a barley standard, with a senine of gold or a senum of silver equal to a measure of barley. (Ludlow)

5. Now the reckoning is thus—a senine of gold, a seon of gold, a shum of gold, and a limnah of gold.
6. A senum of silver, an amnor of silver, an ezrom of silver, and an onti of silver.
7. A senum of silver was equal to a senine of gold, and either for a measure of barley, and also for a measure of every kind of grain.
8. Now the amount of a seon of gold was twice the value of a senine.
9. And a shum of gold was twice the value of a seon.
10. And a limnah of gold was the value of them all.
11. And an amnor of silver was as great as two senums.
12. And an ezrom of silver was as great as four senums.
13. And an onti was as great as them all.
14. Now this is the value of the lesser numbers of their reckoning—
15. A shiblon is half of a senum; therefore, a shiblon for half a measure of barley.
16. And a shiblum is a half of a shiblon.
17. And a leah is the half of a shiblum.
18. Now this is their number, according to their reckoning.
19. Now an antion of gold is equal to three shiblons.
20. Now, it was for the sole purpose to get gain, because they received their wages according to their employ, therefore, they did stir up the people to riotings, and all manner of disturbances and wickedness, that they might have more employ, that they might get money according to the suits which were brought before them; therefore they did stir up the people against Alma and Amulek.
21. And this Zeezrom began to question Amulek, saying: Will ye answer me a few questions which I shall ask you? Now Zeezrom was a man who was expert in the devices of the devil, that he might destroy that which was good; therefore, he said unto Amulek: Will ye answer the questions which I shall put unto you?
22. And Amulek said unto him: Yea, if it be according to the Spirit of the Lord, which is in me; for I shall say nothing which is contrary to the Spirit of the Lord. And Zeezrom said unto him: Behold, here are six onties of silver, and all these will I give thee if thou wilt deny the existence of a Supreme Being.
23. Now Amulek said: O thou child of hell, why tempt ye me? Knowest thou that the righteous yieldeth to no such temptations?
24. Believest thou that there is no God? I say unto you, Nay, thou knowest that there is a God, but thou lovest that lucre more than him.
25. And now thou hast lied before God unto me. Thou saidst unto me—Behold these six onties, which are of great worth, I will give unto thee—when thou hadst it in thy heart to retain them from me; and it was only thy desire that I should deny the true and living God, that thou mightest have cause to destroy me. And now behold, for this great evil thou shalt have thy reward.
26. And Zeezrom said unto him: Thou sayest there is a true and living God?
27. And Amulek said: Yea, there is a true and living God.
28. Now Zeezrom said: Is there more than one God?

Alma 11:20

The lawyers sought to stir up the people against one another so they would sue each other; when those lawsuits were brought up, the lawyers were then able to earn a living.

Alma 11:21

All those who embark in the service of God will from time to time encounter contrary spirits who vilify divine truth and disparage the good news of the Gospel of Christ. The Lord has made it clear that the most powerful strategy to use in all such cases is teaching by the Spirit. (P/A)

Alma 11:21–22

All those who embark in the service of God will from time to time encounter contrary spirits who vilify divine truth and disparage the good news of the Gospel of Christ. The Lord has made it clear that the most powerful strategy to use in all such cases is teaching by the Spirit. . . .

The lawyers of Ammonihah were skilled in the cunning of rhetoric and the opportunism of generating diversionary reasons why people should retain their services. Among these was Zeezrom, he "being one of the most expert among them, having much business to do among the people" (Alma 10:31). . . .

Regarding this kind of situation, President Gordon B. Hinckley said, "As surely as this is the work of the Lord, there will be opposition. There will be those, perhaps not a few, who with the sophistry of beguiling words and clever design will spread doubt and seek to undermine the foundation on which this cause is established. They will have their brief day in the sun. They may have for a brief season the plaudits of the doubters and the skeptics and critics. But they will fade and be forgotten as have their kind in the past." (P/A)

29. And he answered, No.
30. Now Zeezrom said unto him again: How knowest thou these things?
31. And he said: An angel hath made them known unto me.
32. And Zeezrom said again: Who is he that shall come? Is it the Son of God?
33. And he said unto him, Yea.
34. And Zeezrom said again: Shall he save his people in their sins? And Amulek answered and said unto him: I say unto you he shall not, for it is impossible for him to deny his word.
35. Now Zeezrom said unto the people: See that ye remember these things; for he said there is but one God; yet he saith that the Son of God shall come, but he shall not save his people—as though he had authority to command God.
36. Now Amulek saith again unto him: Behold thou hast lied, for thou sayest that I spake as though I had authority to command God because I said he shall not save his people in their sins.
37. And I say unto you again that he cannot save them in their sins; for I cannot deny his word, and he hath said that no unclean thing can inherit the kingdom of heaven; therefore, how can ye be saved, except ye inherit the kingdom of heaven? Therefore, ye cannot be saved in your sins.
38. Now Zeezrom saith again unto him: Is the Son of God the very Eternal Father?
39. And Amulek said unto him: Yea, he is the very Eternal Father of heaven and of earth, and all things which in them are; he is the beginning and the end, the first and the last;
40. And he shall come into the world to redeem his people; and he shall take upon him the transgressions of those who believe on his name; and these are they that shall have eternal life, and salvation cometh to none else.
41. Therefore the wicked remain as though there had been no redemption made, except it be the loosing of the bands of death; for behold, the day cometh that all shall rise from the dead and stand before God, and be judged according to their works.
42. Now, there is a death which is called a temporal death; and the death of Christ shall loose the bands of this temporal death, that all shall be raised from this temporal death.
43. The spirit and the body shall be reunited again in its perfect form; both limb and joint shall be restored to its proper frame, even as we now are at this time; and we shall be brought to stand before God, knowing even as we know now, and have a bright recollection of all our guilt.
44. Now, this restoration shall come to all, both old and young, both bond and free, both male and female, both the wicked and the righteous; and even there shall not so much as a hair of their heads be lost; but every thing shall be restored to its perfect frame, as it is now, or in the body, and shall be

Alma 11:22

As we are told in Alma 15:16, Amulek had given up all his gold, silver, and precious things for the word of God; he had also been disowned by his family, so he did not stand to inherit any riches of any kind. With that in mind, the offer of six onties of silver—an ontie having the highest possible value—would have been a considerable temptation for the penniless Amulek.

Alma 11:32–37

Amulek taught that God cannot save people "*in* their sins." The Lord can save (or redeem) them *from* their sins after they have repented, but he cannot save them *in* their sins because they have not repented of their wickedness. (Read also Helaman 5:10–11.) (Ludlow)

Alma 11:41

In essence, Amulek is saying that the wicked are all resurrected, but they are not redeemed into the presence of God unless they repent of their sins and become spotless before him. (See also Mosiah 16:5; 3 Nephi 27:19–20.) (Ludlow)

Alma 11:41–45

The exact type of body that resurrected beings will have after the resurrection has not been made clear in the scriptures except that it will be an immortal, glorified body animated by spirit. For example, the Book of Mormon prophets clearly teach that the actual physical body will be resurrected; "both limb and joint shall be restored to its proper frame, even as we now are at this time." (Alma 11:43). Unfortunately, the teachings in the New Testament concerning a resurrected body have been misinterpreted by many Christian theologians; thus many churches teach that the actual physical body is not resurrected. Concerning the false teachings of many of the Christian churches, President Joseph Fielding Smith has said:

" After the resurrection from the dead our bodies will be spiritual bodies, but they will be bodies that are tangible, bodies that have been purified, but they will nevertheless be bodies of flesh and bones, but they will not be blood bodies, they will no longer be quickened by blood but quickened by the spirit which is eternal and they shall become immortal and shall never die." (Ludlow)

brought and be arraigned before the bar of Christ the Son, and God the Father, and the Holy Spirit, which is one Eternal God, to be judged according to their works, whether they be good or whether they be evil.
45. Now, behold, I have spoken unto you concerning the death of the mortal body, and also concerning the resurrection of the mortal body. I say unto you that this mortal body is raised to an immortal body, that is from death, even from the first death unto life, that they can die no more; their spirits uniting with their bodies, never to be divided; thus the whole becoming spiritual and immortal, that they can no more see corruption.
46. Now, when Amulek had finished these words the people began again to be astonished, and also Zeezrom began to tremble. And thus ended the words of Amulek, or this is all that I have written.

CHAPTER 12

1. NOW Alma, seeing that the words of Amulek had silenced Zeezrom, for he beheld that Amulek had caught him in his lying and deceiving to destroy him, and seeing that he began to tremble under a consciousness of his guilt, he opened his mouth and began to speak unto him, and to establish the words of Amulek, and to explain things beyond, or to unfold the scriptures beyond that which Amulek had done.
2. Now the words that Alma spake unto Zeezrom were heard by the people round about; for the multitude was great, and he spake on this wise:
3. Now Zeezrom, seeing that thou hast been taken in thy lying and craftiness, for thou hast not lied unto men only but thou hast lied unto God; for behold, he knows all thy thoughts, and thou seest that thy thoughts are made known unto us by his Spirit;
4. And thou seest that we know that thy plan was a very subtle plan, as to the subtlety of the devil, for to lie and to deceive this people that thou mightest set them against us, to revile us and to cast us out—
5. Now this was a plan of thine adversary, and he hath exercised his power in thee. Now I would that ye should remember that what I say unto thee I say unto all.
6. And behold I say unto you all that this was a snare of the adversary, which he has laid to catch this people, that he might bring you into subjection unto him, that he might encircle you about with his chains, that he might chain you down to everlasting destruction, according to the power of his captivity.
7. Now when Alma had spoken these words, Zeezrom began to tremble more exceedingly, for he was convinced more and more of the power of God; and he was also

Alma 11:44

"Restored" refers to our being restored to the condition we were in before we came to earth; at that time, we were perfect in every way. According to President Joseph F. Smith, at the time of resurrection we will have perfect bodies and perfect spirits—all things restored, without defect ("in the restoration of all things there shall come perfection"). And President Joseph Fielding Smith assures us that we will come forth in our "full vigor," not suffering the maladies that come with aging. Children will come forth as children, since they do not grow in the grave, and will attain their full stature after they are resurrected.

Alma 11:44

Every man that is born into the world will die. It matters not who he is, nor where he is, whether his birth be among the rich and the noble, or among the lowly and poor in the world, his days are numbered with the Lord. . . . I rejoice that I am born to live, to die, and to live again. . . . the spirit dies not at all; . . . it passes through no change, except the change from imprisonment in this mortal clay to freedom and to the sphere in which it acted before it came to this earth (Joseph F. Smith, *CR*, October 1899, 70).

Alma 12:3

This gift of discernment is one of the gifts of the Holy Spirit, and it is through the proper use of this gift that the evils and designs of wicked men are made known to the prophets of God. In further explanation of this principle, Ammon, one of the sons of Mosiah, said: "[God] knows all the thoughts and intents of the heart; for by his hand were they all created from the beginning" (Alma 18:32). (Ludlow)

convinced that Alma and Amulek had a knowledge of him, for he was convinced that they knew the thoughts and intents of his heart; for power was given unto them that they might know of these things according to the spirit of prophecy.
8. And Zeezrom began to inquire of them diligently, that he might know more concerning the kingdom of God. And he said unto Alma: What does this mean which Amulek hath spoken concerning the resurrection of the dead, that all shall rise from the dead, both the just and the unjust, and are brought to stand before God to be judged according to their works?
9. And now Alma began to expound these things unto him, saying: It is given unto many to know the mysteries of God; nevertheless they are laid under a strict command that they shall not impart only according to the portion of his word which he doth grant unto the children of men, according to the heed and diligence which they give unto him.
10. And therefore, he that will harden his heart, the same receiveth the lesser portion of the word; and he that will not harden his heart, to him is given the greater portion of the word, until it is given unto him to know the mysteries of God until he know them in full.
11. And they that will harden their hearts, to them is given the lesser portion of the word until they know nothing concerning his mysteries; and then they are taken captive by the devil, and led by his will down to destruction. Now this is what is meant by the chains of hell.
12. And Amulek hath spoken plainly concerning death, and being raised from this mortality to a state of immortality, and being brought before the bar of God, to be judged according to our works.
13. Then if our hearts have been hardened, yea, if we have hardened our hearts against the word, insomuch that it has not been found in us, then will our state be awful, for then we shall be condemned.
14. For our words will condemn us, yea, all our works will condemn us; we shall not be found spotless; and our thoughts will also condemn us; and in this awful state we shall not dare to look up to our God; and we would fain be glad if we could command the rocks and the mountains to fall upon us to hide us from his presence.
15. But this cannot be; we must come forth and stand before him in his glory, and in his power, and in his might, majesty, and dominion, and acknowledge to our everlasting shame that all his judgments are just; that he is just in all his works, and that he is merciful unto the children of men, and that he has all power to save every man that believeth on his name and bringeth forth fruit meet for repentance.
16. And now behold, I say unto you then cometh a death, even a second death, which is a spiritual death;

Alma 12:11

The degree to which [men] may know His truth is dependent upon how open their hearts are to receive such truth, and the heed and diligence they give to it. Thus the quality of one's heart—how receptive and soft it is, or how rejecting and hard it is—will determine how much of His word is "found in us" in the last day (Alma 12:13). And how much of His word is found in us will determine our ultimate future state of glory. (P/A)

Alma 12:11

Alma has identified a marvelous principle of the gospel. Satan uses false teachings and ideas, which encourage impure thoughts and lead to unrighteous practices, to ensnare people in a state of spiritual bondage. But all of that can be overcome and avoided by an acceptance of and adherence to the word of God. (O/C)

Alma 12:14

Alma and Benjamin both state we shall be judged of our words, our works, and our thoughts. (Alma 12:14; Mosiah 4:30.) Elsewhere in the Book of Mormon it is made clear that we shall also be judged of our responsibilities concerning the welfare of others. (Jacob 1:18–19; Mosiah 2:20–28, 36–41; Mosiah 4:19–30.) Perhaps the most difficult area of judgment for people to understand is that which deals with our thoughts. Yet the Savior very clearly taught that we shall be responsible for what we think (Matthew 5:27–28), and this truth has also been taught by other prophets (1 Chronicles 28:9; Job 42:2; Psalm 94:11; Romans 2:16).

[Joseph F. Smith said] "In reality a man cannot forget anything. He may have a lapse of memory; he may not be able to recall at the moment a thing that he knows or words that he has spoken; he may not have the power at his will to call up these events and words; but let God Almighty touch the mainspring of the memory and awaken recollection, and you will find then that you have not even forgotten a single idle word that you have spoken! I believe the word of God to be true, and, therefore, I warn the youth of Zion, as well as those who are advanced in years, to beware of saying wicked things, of speaking evil, and taking in vain the name of sacred things and sacred beings. Guard your words, that you may not offend even man, much less offend God."

The Book of Mormon clearly teaches that God knows our thoughts (Alma 18:32) and that we shall be held responsible for them. (Ludlow)

then is a time that whosoever dieth in his sins, as to a temporal death, shall also die a spiritual death; yea, he shall die as to things pertaining unto righteousness.

17. Then is the time when their torments shall be as a lake of fire and brimstone, whose flame ascendeth up forever and ever; and then is the time that they shall be chained down to an everlasting destruction, according to the power and captivity of Satan, he having subjected them according to his will.

18. Then, I say unto you, they shall be as though there had been no redemption made; for they cannot be redeemed according to God's justice; and they cannot die, seeing there is no more corruption.

19. Now it came to pass that when Alma had made an end of speaking these words, the people began to be more astonished;

20. But there was one Antionah, who was a chief ruler among them, came forth and said unto him: What is this that thou hast said, that man should rise from the dead and be changed from this mortal to an immortal state that the soul can never die?

21. What does the scripture mean, which saith that God placed cherubim and a flaming sword on the east of the garden of Eden, lest our first parents should enter and partake of the fruit of the tree of life, and live forever? And thus we see that there was no possible chance that they should live forever.

22. Now Alma said unto him: This is the thing which I was about to explain. Now we see that Adam did fall by the partaking of the forbidden fruit, according to the word of God; and thus we see, that by his fall, all mankind became a lost and fallen people.

23. And now behold, I say unto you that if it had been possible for Adam to have partaken of the fruit of the tree of life at that time, there would have been no death, and the word would have been void, making God a liar, for he said: If thou eat thou shalt surely die.

24. And we see that death comes upon mankind, yea, the death which has been spoken of by Amulek, which is the temporal death; nevertheless there was a space granted unto man in which he might repent; therefore this life became a probationary state; a time to prepare to meet God; a time to prepare for that endless state which has been spoken of by us, which is after the resurrection of the dead.

25. Now, if it had not been for the plan of redemption, which was laid from the foundation of the world, there could have been no resurrection of the dead; but there was a plan of redemption laid, which shall bring to pass the resurrection of the dead, of which has been spoken.

26. And now behold, if it were possible that our first parents could have gone forth and partaken of the tree of life they would have been forever miserable, having no preparatory state; and thus the plan

of redemption would have been frustrated, and the word of God would have been void, taking none effect.
27. But behold, it was not so; but it was appointed unto men that they must die; and after death, they must come to judgment, even that same judgment of which we have spoken, which is the end.
28. And after God had appointed that these things should come unto man, behold, then he saw that it was expedient that man should know concerning the things whereof he had appointed unto them;
29. Therefore he sent angels to converse with them, who caused men to behold of his glory.
30. And they began from that time forth to call on his name; therefore God conversed with men, and made known unto them the plan of redemption, which had been prepared from the foundation of the world; and this he made known unto them according to their faith and repentance and their holy works.
31. Wherefore, he gave commandments unto men, they having first transgressed the first commandments as to things which were temporal, and becoming as Gods, knowing good from evil, placing themselves in a state to act, or being placed in a state to act according to their wills and pleasures, whether to do evil or to do good—
32. Therefore God gave unto them commandments, after having made known unto them the plan of redemption, that they should not do evil, the penalty thereof being a second death, which was an everlasting death as to things pertaining unto righteousness; for on such the plan of redemption could have no power, for the works of justice could not be destroyed, according to the supreme goodness of God.
33. But God did call on men, in the name of his Son, (this being the plan of redemption which was laid) saying: If ye will repent, and harden not your hearts, then will I have mercy upon you, through mine Only Begotten Son;
34. Therefore, whosoever repenteth, and hardeneth not his heart, he shall have claim on mercy through mine Only Begotten Son, unto a remission of his sins; and these shall enter into my rest.
35. And whosoever will harden his heart and will do iniquity, behold, I swear in my wrath that he shall not enter into my rest.
36. And now, my brethren, behold I say unto you, that if ye will harden your hearts ye shall not enter into the rest of the Lord; therefore your iniquity provoketh him that he sendeth down his wrath upon you as in the first provocation, yea, according to his word in the last provocation as well as the first, to the everlasting destruction of your souls; therefore, according to his word, unto the last death, as well as the first.
37. And now, my brethren, seeing we know these things, and they are true, let us repent, and harden not

Alma 12:32

God must give us commandments, which are an effect of the Fall and its associated transgression.

Alma:35

According to Joseph Smith, blessings that are offered, but then rejected, are no longer blessings; they will be taken away.

our hearts, that we provoke not the Lord our God to pull down his wrath upon us in these his second commandments which he has given unto us; but let us enter into the rest of God, which is prepared according to his word.

CHAPTER 13

1. AND again, my brethren, I would cite your minds forward to the time when the Lord God gave these commandments unto his children; and I would that ye should remember that the Lord God ordained priests, after his holy order, which was after the order of his Son, to teach these things unto the people.
2. And those priests were ordained after the order of his Son, in a manner that thereby the people might know in what manner to look forward to his Son for redemption.
3. And this is the manner after which they were ordained—being called and prepared from the foundation of the world according to the foreknowledge of God, on account of their exceeding faith and good works; in the first place being left to choose good or evil; therefore they having chosen good, and exercising exceedingly great faith, are called with a holy calling, yea, with that holy calling which was prepared with, and according to, a preparatory redemption for such.
4. And thus they have been called to this holy calling on account of their faith, while others would reject the Spirit of God on account of the hardness of their hearts and blindness of their minds, while, if it had not been for this they might have had as great privilege as their brethren.
5. Or in fine, in the first place they were on the same standing with their brethren; thus this holy calling being prepared from the foundation of the world for such as would not harden their hearts, being in and through the atonement of the Only Begotten Son, who was prepared—
6. And thus being called by this holy calling, and ordained unto the high priesthood of the holy order of God, to teach his commandments unto the children of men, that they also might enter into his rest—
7. This high priesthood being after the order of his Son, which order was from the foundation of the world; or in other words, being without beginning of days or end of years, being prepared from eternity to all eternity, according to his foreknowledge of all things—
8. Now they were ordained after this manner—being called with a holy calling, and ordained with a holy ordinance, and taking upon them the high priesthood of the holy order, which calling, and ordinance,

Alma 13:3

The Prophet Joseph Smith understood and taught the principle of foreordination that took place in pre-earth life. He said: "Every man who has a calling to minister to the inhabitants of the world was ordained to that very purpose in the Grand Council of heaven before this world was." (O/C)

Alma 13:4

The Book of Mormon has preserved for our comfort and instruction many grand truths pertaining to salvation. In the experiences of Alma and Amulek as ministers among the people we see precious reminders of God's compassionate guidance and forebearance on behalf of His children. We learn that our sonship and daughtership with God is rooted in the premortal existence, where the purposes of life were unfolded for our future blessing, and callings were imparted to us on the premise of future faithfulness to covenant promises. We come to understand better through these remarkable pages that persecution is not foreign to our mortal journey, and that we can be freed of the agony of guilt and the consequences of sin by bringing ourselves into alignment with the patterns of faith and repentance upon which the plan of redemption is based. We come to appreciate more fully that the Lord's word will always be fulfilled.

We were prepared for our callings here upon the earth long before our birth. In the premortal courts of heaven we received our "first lessons in the world of spirits and were prepared to come forth in the due time of the Lord to labor in his vineyard for the salvation of the souls of men" (D&C 138:56).

Speaking of that preparation, President Spencer W. Kimball said, "Remember, in the world before we came here, faithful women were given certain assignments while faithful men were foreordained to certain priesthood tasks. While we do not now remember the particulars, this does not alter the glorious reality of what we once agreed to. We are accountable for those things which long ago were expected of us just as are those whom we sustain as prophets and Apostles." (P/A)

Alma 13:5

According to Elder Bruce R. McConkie, everyone in the pre-existence initially had an equal opportunity to progress through righteousness. And President Joseph Fielding Smith taught that we all had our free agency in the pre-existence; some were more valiant and thus earned a greater reward through the wise exercise of that free agency. Thus, while the spirits of men may have had an equal start in the pre-existence, the wise exercise of free agency enabled some to surpass others and, in the process, become more intelligent.

and high priesthood, is without beginning or end—
9. Thus they become high priests forever, after the order of the Son, the Only Begotten of the Father, who is without beginning of days or end of years, who is full of grace, equity, and truth. And thus it is. Amen.
10. Now, as I said concerning the holy order, or this high priesthood, there were many who were ordained and became high priests of God; and it was on account of their exceeding faith and repentance, and their righteousness before God, they choosing to repent and work righteousness rather than to perish;
11. Therefore they were called after this holy order, and were sanctified, and their garments were washed white through the blood of the Lamb.
12. Now they, after being sanctified by the Holy Ghost, having their garments made white, being pure and spotless before God, could not look upon sin save it were with abhorrence; and there were many, exceedingly great many, who were made pure and entered into the rest of the Lord their God.
13. And now, my brethren, I would that ye should humble yourselves before God, and bring forth fruit meet for repentance, that ye may also enter into that rest.
14. Yea, humble yourselves even as the people in the days of Melchizedek, who was also a high priest after this same order which I have spoken, who also took upon him the high priesthood forever.
15. And it was this same Melchizedek to whom Abraham paid tithes; yea, even our father Abraham paid tithes of one-tenth part of all he possessed.
16. Now these ordinances were given after this manner, that thereby the people might look forward on the Son of God, it being a type of his order, or it being his order, and this that they might look forward to him for a remission of their sins, that they might enter into the rest of the Lord.
17. Now this Melchizedek was a king over the land of Salem; and his people had waxed strong in iniquity and abomination; yea, they had all gone astray; they were full of all manner of wickedness;
18. But Melchizedek having exercised mighty faith, and received the office of the high priesthood according to the holy order of God, did preach repentance unto his people. And behold, they did repent; and Melchizedek did establish peace in the land in his days; therefore he was called the prince of peace, for he was the king of Salem; and he did reign under his father.
19. Now, there were many before him, and also there were many afterwards, but none were greater; therefore, of him they have more particularly made mention.
20. Now I need not rehearse the matter; what I have said may suffice. Behold, the scriptures are

Alma 13:9, 14–19

Melchizedek is one of the most misinterpreted persons in the Bible. He lived approximately 2000 B.C., was a contemporary of Abraham, and was one of the most righteous men who ever lived on the earth. Yet little is known about him, and the little that is said about him in the Bible has been misunderstood by most biblical scholars. For example, in the book of Hebrews we read the following concerning this great prophet:

"For this Melchisedec, king of Salem, priest of the most high God . . .

"To whom also Abraham gave a tenth part of all; first being by interpretation King of righteousness, and after that also King of Salem, which is, King of peace;

"Without father, without mother, without descent, having neither beginning of days, nor end of life; but made like unto the Son of God; abideth a priest continually" (Hebrews 7:1–3).

Some biblical scholars have interpreted these verses to mean that Melchizedek was born without a mother or a father! In other words, they believe that the words "without father, without mother, without descent, having neither beginning of days nor end of life" refer to Melchizedek. That these words do not refer to Melchizedek, but instead refer to the priesthood he held, is made clear in both the Doctrine and Covenants and the Book of Mormon (D&C 84:14, 17; Alma 13:8–9.) (Ludlow)

Alma 13:11–13

All blessings from God extended to His children come through the Melchizedek Priesthood, which is after the order of the Son of God. The purpose of the priesthood is to bless all mankind with the saving principles and ordinances of the gospel of Jesus Christ. It is through this power that God's children gain access to the saving powers of the Atonement of Jesus Christ. It is through this power that all mankind can enter into the rest of the Lord. (O/C)

Alma 13:18

The statement that Melchizedek reigned "under his father" should not necessarily be interpreted to mean that he reigned at the same time his father was king or even while his father was living. The term "under his father" evidently is a Hebrew idiom meaning that he "takes the place of his father" or "reigns in his father's stead." (For several examples of similar terminology in the Bible, see Genesis 36:33–39.) (Ludlow)

before you; if ye will wrest them it shall be to your own destruction.
21. And now it came to pass that when Alma had said these words unto them, he stretched forth his hand unto them and cried with a mighty voice, saying: Now is the time to repent, for the day of salvation draweth nigh;
22. Yea, and the voice of the Lord, by the mouth of angels, doth declare it unto all nations; yea, doth declare it, that they may have glad tidings of great joy; yea, and he doth sound these glad tidings among all his people, yea, even to them that are scattered abroad upon the face of the earth; wherefore they have come unto us.
23. And they are made known unto us in plain terms, that we may understand, that we cannot err; and this because of our being wanderers in a strange land; therefore, we are thus highly favored, for we have these glad tidings declared unto us in all parts of our vineyard.
24. For behold, angels are declaring it unto many at this time in our land; and this is for the purpose of preparing the hearts of the children of men to receive his word at the time of his coming in his glory.
25. And now we only wait to hear the joyful news declared unto us by the mouth of angels, of his coming; for the time cometh, we know not how soon. Would to God that it might be in my day; but let it be sooner or later, in it I will rejoice.
26. And it shall be made known unto just and holy men, by the mouth of angels, at the time of his coming, that the words of our fathers may be fulfilled, according to that which they have spoken concerning him, which was according to the spirit of prophecy which was in them.
27. And now, my brethren, I wish from the inmost part of my heart, yea, with great anxiety even unto pain, that ye would hearken unto my words, and cast off your sins, and not procrastinate the day of your repentance;
28. But that ye would humble yourselves before the Lord, and call on his holy name, and watch and pray continually, that ye may not be tempted above that which ye can bear, and thus be led by the Holy Spirit, becoming humble, meek, submissive, patient, full of love and all long-suffering;
29. Having faith on the Lord; having a hope that ye shall receive eternal life; having the love of God always in your hearts, that ye may be lifted up at the last day and enter into his rest.
30. And may the Lord grant unto you repentance, that ye may not bring down his wrath upon you, that ye may not be bound down by the chains of hell, that ye may not suffer the second death.
31. And Alma spake many more words unto the people, which are not written in this book.

CHAPTER 14

Alma 13:25–26

As Alma describes the feelings of those who waited to see the Savior, we are reminded of our own feelings as we anticipate the Second Coming of the Savior. "Would to God that it might be in my day" he exclaimed. But, he added, whether it be sooner or later, it will be a glorious event in which we will all rejoice.

Alma 13:27–30

In Alma's words of guidance, we find excellent advice for ourselves as we await the day of the Savior's Second Coming. In these times of wickedness, we can learn much from Alma's admonition to pray that we will not be tempted above that which we can bear.

We would be most wise to watch and pray continually, to allow ourselves to be led by the Holy Spirit, and to be characterized by humility, meekness, submissiveness, patience, love, long-suffering, faith, hope, and having the love of God continually in our hearts.

1. AND it came to pass after he had made an end of speaking unto the people many of them did believe on his words, and began to repent, and to search the scriptures.
2. But the more part of them were desirous that they might destroy Alma and Amulek; for they were angry with Alma, because of the plainness of his words unto Zeezrom; and they also said that Amulek had lied unto them, and had reviled against their law and also against their lawyers and judges.
3. And they were also angry with Alma and Amulek; and because they had testified so plainly against their wickedness, they sought to put them away privily.
4. But it came to pass that they did not; but they took them and bound them with strong cords, and took them before the chief judge of the land.
5. And the people went forth and witnessed against them—testifying that they had reviled against the law, and their lawyers and judges of the land, and also of all the people that were in the land; and also testified that there was but one God, and that he should send his Son among the people, but he should not save them; and many such things did the people testify against Alma and Amulek. Now this was done before the chief judge of the land.
6. And it came to pass that Zeezrom was astonished at the words which had been spoken; and he also knew concerning the blindness of the minds, which he had caused among the people by his lying words; and his soul began to be harrowed up under a consciousness of his own guilt; yea, he began to be encircled about by the pains of hell.
7. And it came to pass that he began to cry unto the people, saying: Behold, I am guilty, and these men are spotless before God. And he began to plead for them from that time forth; but they reviled him, saying: Art thou also possessed with the devil? And they spit upon him, and cast him out from among them, and also all those who believed in the words which had been spoken by Alma and Amulek; and they cast them out, and sent men to cast stones at them.
8. And they brought their wives and children together, and whosoever believed or had been taught to believe in the word of God they caused that they should be cast into the fire, and they also brought forth their records which contained the holy scriptures, and cast them into the fire also, that they might be burned and destroyed by fire.
9. And it came to pass that they took Alma and Amulek, and carried them forth to the place of martyrdom, that they might witness the destruction of those who were consumed by fire.
10. And when Amulek saw the pains of the women and children who were consuming in the fire, he also was pained; and he said unto Alma: How can we witness this awful scene? Therefore let us stretch forth our hands, and exercise the power of God which is in us, and save them from the flames.
11. But Alma said unto him: The Spirit constrain-eth me that I must not stretch forth mine hand; for behold the Lord receiveth them up

Alma 14:3

Brigham Young taught that the gospel is "perfectly calculated to cause division"; because it strikes at the roots of evil, it makes wicked people very uncomfortable.

Alma 14:6

Harrow is a term used to describe the process of breaking up earth that has hardened through disuse and neglect; it must be done before seeds can be planted in the earth. The same process must happen to our hearts before a mighty change can take place therein.

Alma 14:6–7

Far from shaming [Alma and Amulek] with his legal manipulations, [Zeezrom] is himself induced to take up their cause, so powerful and persuasive is their witness of the Savior and His plan of redemption. (P/A)

Alma 14:8

The righteous are not always, by virtue of their goodness, protected from harm. . . .

In commenting on why the Lord allows the righteous to suffer, Joseph Fielding McConkie and Robert Millet said, "God is not the author of evil, yet within limits and bounds he allows it to exist. This is done so that the righteous might merit the fulness of his glory and that the wicked, the workers of evil, might in like fashion merit the fulness of his wrath." . . .

There is a great principle demonstrated in trials. Recall that when Nephi was bound by his brothers he prayed for strength to burst the bands (see 1 Ne. 7:17). Likewise did Alma pray for strength; also, like Nephi, Alma and Amulek were freed according to their faith.

This is a great lesson in life: pray for strength to overcome, not necessarily for the challenges and problems to go away. Remember: in the strength of the Lord we can do all things (see Alma 26:11–12). (P/A)

Alma 14:10

It is difficult for mortals—who see events only through eyes that are restricted by time—to see things in their proper relationship so far as the eternities are concerned. Thus, because we as mortals have only limited vision it is understandable why we sometimes desire or wish for things in this life that would not be for our best welfare in the eternities to come. For example, if we had unlimited power and followed our mortal feelings, we would probably never suffer pain, or disease, or even death. But would this be the best thing for us from an eternal perspective? (Ludlow)

unto himself, in glory; and he doth suffer that they may do this thing, or that the people may do this thing unto them, according to the hardness of their hearts, that the judgments which he shall exercise upon them in his wrath may be just; and the blood of the innocent shall stand as a witness against them, yea, and cry mightily against them at the last day.
12. Now Amulek said unto Alma: Behold, perhaps they will burn us also.
13. And Alma said: Be it according to the will of the Lord. But, behold, our work is not finished; therefore they burn us not.
14. Now it came to pass that when the bodies of those who had been cast into the fire were consumed, and also the records which were cast in with them, the chief judge of the land came and stood before Alma and Amulek, as they were bound; and he smote them with his hand upon their cheeks, and said unto them: After what ye have seen, will ye preach again unto this people, that they shall be cast into a lake of fire and brimstone?
15. Behold, ye see that ye had not power to save those who had been cast into the fire; neither has God saved them because they were of thy faith. And the judge smote them again upon their cheeks, and asked: What say ye for yourselves?
16. Now this judge was after the order and faith of Nehor, who slew Gideon.
17. And it came to pass that Alma and Amulek answered him nothing; and he smote them again, and delivered them to the officers to be cast into prison.
18. And when they had been cast into prison three days, there came many lawyers, and judges, and priests, and teachers, who were of the profession of Nehor; and they came in unto the prison to see them, and they questioned them about many words; but they answered them nothing.
19. And it came to pass that the judge stood before them, and said: Why do ye not answer the words of this people? Know ye not that I have power to deliver you up unto the flames? And he commanded them to speak; but they answered nothing.
20. And it came to pass that they departed and went their ways, but came again on the morrow; and the judge also smote them again on their cheeks. And many came forth also, and smote them, saying: Will ye stand again and judge this people, and condemn our law? If ye have such great power why do ye not deliver yourselves?
21. And many such things did they say unto them, gnashing their teeth upon them, and spitting upon them, and saying: How shall we look when we are damned?
22. And many such things, yea, all manner of such things did they say unto them; and thus they did mock them for many days. And they did withhold food from them that they might hunger, and water that they might thirst; and they also did take from them their clothes that they were naked; and thus they were bound with strong cords, and confined in prison.
23. And it came to pass after they had thus suffered for many days, (and it was on the twelfth day, in the tenth month, in the tenth year of the reign of the judges over the

Alma 14:11

It appears only natural that Amulek should plead with Alma to exercise the power of the priesthood and save the righteous people from being burned to death. However, Alma, through the impressions of the Spirit, was able to see things through the eyes of eternity . . .

Concerning the fact that we should live righteous lives and then leave the final judgment to God as to what should be done with our lives, President Spencer W. Kimball has said:

"Now, we find many people critical when a righteous person is killed, a young father or mother is taken from a family, or when violent deaths occur. Some become bitter when oft-repeated prayers seem unanswered. Some lose faith and turn sour when solemn administrations by holy men seem to be ignored and no restoration seems to come from repeated prayer circles. But if all the sick were healed, if all the righteous were protected and the wicked destroyed, the whole program of the Father would be annulled and the basic principle of the Gospel, free agency, would be ended.

"If pain and sorrow and total punishment immediately followed the doing of evil, no soul would repeat a misdeed. If joy and peace and rewards were instantaneously given the doer of good, there could be no evil—all would do good and not because of the rightness of doing good. There would be no test of strength, no development of character, no growth of powers, no free agency. . . ." (Ludlow)

people of Nephi) that the chief judge over the land of Ammonihah and many of their teachers and their lawyers went in unto the prison where Alma and Amulek were bound with cords.
24. And the chief judge stood before them, and smote them again, and said unto them: If ye have the power of God deliver yourselves from these bands, and then we will believe that the Lord will destroy this people according to your words.
25. And it came to pass that they all went forth and smote them, saying the same words, even until the last; and when the last had spoken unto them the power of God was upon Alma and Amulek, and they rose and stood upon their feet.
26. And Alma cried, saying: How long shall we suffer these great afflictions, O Lord? O Lord, give us strength according to our faith which is in Christ, even unto deliverance. And they broke the cords with which they were bound; and when the people saw this, they began to flee, for the fear of destruction had come upon them.
27. And it came to pass that so great was their fear that they fell to the earth, and did not obtain the outer door of the prison; and the earth shook mightily, and the walls of the prison were rent in twain, so that they fell to the earth; and the chief judge, and the lawyers, and priests, and teachers, who smote upon Alma and Amulek, were slain by the fall thereof.
28. And Alma and Amulek came forth out of the prison, and they were not hurt; for the Lord had granted unto them power, according to their faith which was in Christ. And they straightway came forth out of the prison; and they were loosed from their bands; and the prison had fallen to the earth, and every soul within the walls thereof, save it were Alma and Amulek, was slain; and they straightway came forth into the city.
29. Now the people having heard a great noise came running together by multitudes to know the cause of it; and when they saw Alma and Amulek coming forth out of the prison, and the walls thereof had fallen to the earth, they were struck with great fear, and fled from the presence of Alma and Amulek even as a goat fleeth with her young from two lions; and thus they did flee from the presence of Alma and Amulek.

CHAPTER 15

1. AND it came to pass that Alma and Amulek were commanded to depart out of that city; and they departed, and came out even into the land of Sidom; and behold, there they found all the people who had departed out of the land of Ammonihah, who had been cast out and stoned, because they believed in the words of Alma.
2. And they related unto them all that had happened unto their wives and children, and also concerning themselves, and of their power of deliverance.
3. And also Zeezrom lay sick at Sidom, with a burning fever, which was caused by the great tribulations

Alma 14:24–26

The harvest of the season of preaching by Alma and Amulek in the city of Ammonihah was only modest, for the more part of the people refused to believe in the words they had heard, instead reviling against the men of God and condemning the circle of believers to a fiery martyrdom. The Spirit constrained Alma from intervening to stop this persecution of the innocent, "for behold the Lord receiveth them up unto himself, in glory; and he doth suffer that the people may do this thing unto them, according to the hardness of their hearts, that the judgments which he shall exercise upon them in his wrath may be just" (Alma 14:11). After many days of silent suffering and abuse in prison, Alma and Amulek were empowered by the Spirit, "according to their faith which was in Christ" (Alma 14:28), to invoke judgment upon the Nehorian priests of the city, and the prison was destroyed by an earthquake, killing many and allowing the two prophets of God to emerge unscathed. As the prophet/abridger Mormon aptly described it, the people of the city fled in panic, "even as a goat fleeth with her young from two lions" (Alma 14:29).

In speaking of this kind of opposition and persecution, President Harold B. Lee said, "To be persecuted for righteousness sake in a great cause where truth and virtue and honor are at stake is god-like. Always there have been martyrs to every great cause. . . . persecution seems to be so universal against those engaged in a righteous cause that the Master warns us, 'Woe unto you when all men shall speak well of you! For so did their fathers to the false prophets' (Luke 6:26)." (P/A)

Alma 15:3

Pioneering medical research has demonstrated the powerful effect that the mind and the spirit have on the body. Zeezrom suffered tremendous physical torment until he was able to achieve peace of mind.

Alma 15:3–4, 12

The Spirit can transform the travail of guilt in an anguished soul into the joy of redemption through penitence and obedience.

Regarding those who temporarily fall away in sin, Elder Orson F. Whitney said, "Though some of the sheep may wander, the eye of the Shepherd is upon them and sooner or later they will feel the tentacles of Divine Providence reaching out after them, and drawing them back to the fold. Either in this life or in the life to come, they will return. . . . [T]hey will suffer for their sins; and may tread a thorny path, but if it leads them at last, like the penitent prodigal, to a loving and forgiving Father's heart and home, the painful experience will not have been in vain." (P/A)

of his mind on account of his wickedness, for he supposed that Alma
and Amulek were no more; and he supposed that they had been slain
because of his iniquity. And this great sin, and his many other sins, did
harrow up his mind until it did become exceedingly sore, having no
deliverance; therefore he began to be scorched with a burning heat.
4. Now, when he heard that Alma and Amulek were in the land of
Sidom, his heart began to take courage; and he sent a message
immediately unto them, desiring them to come unto him.
5. And it came to pass that they went immediately, obeying the message which he had sent unto them; and they went in unto the house
unto Zeezrom; and they found him upon his bed, sick, being very low
with a burning fever; and his mind also was exceedingly sore because
of his iniquities; and when he saw them he stretched forth his hand,
and besought them that they would heal him.
6. And it came to pass that Alma said unto him, taking him by the
hand: Believest thou in the power of Christ unto salvation?
7. And he answered and said: Yea, I believe all the words that thou
hast taught.
8. And Alma said: If thou believest in the redemption of Christ
thou canst be healed.
9. And he said: Yea, I believe according to thy words.
10. And then Alma cried unto the Lord, saying: O Lord our God,
have mercy on this man, and heal him according to his faith which
is in Christ.
11. And when Alma had said these words, Zeezrom leaped upon
his feet, and began to walk; and this was done to the great astonishment of all the people; and the knowledge of this went forth
throughout all the land of Sidom.
12. And Alma baptized Zeezrom unto the Lord; and he began from
that time forth to preach unto the people.
13. And Alma established a church in the land of Sidom, and consecrated priests and teachers in the land, to baptize unto the Lord
whosoever were desirous to be baptized.
14. And it came to pass that they were many; for they did flock in
from all the region round about Sidom, and were baptized.
15. But as to the people that were in the land of Ammonihah, they
yet remained a hard-hearted and a stiffnecked people; and they
repented not of their sins, ascribing all the power of Alma and
Amulek to the devil; for they were of the profession of Nehor, and did
not believe in the repentance of their sins.
16. And it came to pass that Alma and Amulek, Amulek having
forsaken all his gold, and silver, and his precious things, which
were in the land of Ammonihah, for the word of God, he being
rejected by those who were once his friends and also by his father
and his kindred;
17. Therefore, after Alma having established the church at Sidom,
seeing a great check, yea, seeing that the people were checked as
to the pride of their hearts, and began to humble themselves before
God, and began to assemble themselves together at their sanctuaries to worship God before the altar, watching and praying continually, that they might be delivered from Satan, and from death,
and from destruction—

Alma 15:3–11

These verses are a powerful example of how vital spiritual well-being is to physical health. Until he was able to achieve peace of mind and spiritual "wellness," Zeezrom was not able to achieve the physical well-being he so desired.

Alma 15:16

As we learn in this verse, Amulek had been very rich and very popular among the people; he sacrificed not only his riches, but his social status in order to embrace the truth. His is a great example of what we must be prepared to sacrifice and what we may be called upon to give up as we commit ourselves to the gospel.

18. Now as I said, Alma having seen all these things, therefore he took Amulek and came over to the land of Zarahemla, and took him to his own house, and did administer unto him in his tribulations, and strengthened him in the Lord.
19. And thus ended the tenth year of the reign of the judges over the people of Nephi.

CHAPTER 16

1. AND it came to pass in the eleventh year of the reign of the judges over the people of Nephi, on the fifth day of the second month, there having been much peace in the land of Zarahemla, there having been no wars nor contentions for a certain number of years, even until the fifth day of the second month in the eleventh year, there was a cry of war heard throughout the land.
2. For behold, the armies of the Lamanites had come in upon the wilderness side, into the borders of the land, even into the city of Ammonihah, and began to slay the people and destroy the city.
3. And now it came to pass, before the Nephites could raise a sufficient army to drive them out of the land, they had destroyed the people who were in the city of Ammonihah, and also some around the borders of Noah, and taken others captive into the wilderness.
4. Now it came to pass that the Nephites were desirous to obtain those who had been carried away captive into the wilderness.
5. Therefore, he that had been appointed chief captain over the armies of the Nephites, (and his name was Zoram, and he had two sons, Lehi and Aha)—now Zoram and his two sons, knowing that Alma was high priest over the church, and having heard that he had the spirit of prophecy, therefore they went unto him and desired of him to know whither the Lord would that they should go into the wilderness in search of their brethren, who had been taken captive by the Lamanites.
6. And it came to pass that Alma inquired of the Lord concerning the matter. And Alma returned and said unto them: Behold, the Lamanites will cross the river Sidon in the south wilderness, away up beyond the borders of the land of Manti. And behold there shall ye meet them, on the east of the river Sidon, and there the Lord will deliver unto thee thy brethren who have been taken captive by the Lamanites.
7. And it came to pass that Zoram and his sons crossed over the river Sidon, with their armies, and marched away beyond the borders of Manti into the south wilderness, which was on the east side of the river Sidon.
8. And they came upon the armies of the Lamanites, and the Lamanites were scattered and driven into the wilderness; and they took their brethren who had been taken captive by the Lamanites, and there was not one soul of them had been lost that were taken captive. And they were brought by their brethren to possess their own lands.
9. And thus ended the eleventh year of the judges, the Lamanites having been driven out of the land, and the people of Ammonihah were destroyed; yea, every living soul

Alma 16:2

Prophecy, accurately termed "history reversed," cannot be refuted. If woe is prophesied contingent upon repentance, woe will come in the absence of repentance. (P/A)

Alma 16:2–3

The destruction of Ammonihah was a direct fulfillment of prophecy; see Alma 9:4. Despite the power of Alma's preaching to the people, they rejected the truth, and Satan had hold of their hearts (see Alma 8:9).

Alma 16:5

The commanding general, Zoram, is only mentioned twice in the Book of Mormon; he is not the same Zoram who founded the Lamanites, nor is he the Zoram who, as Laban's servant, joined Lehi's family in the wilderness. The fact that Zoram, as a military man, submitted to ecclesiastical authority shows that he was a righteous man.

Alma 16:9

Brigham Young said, "Let one go forth who is careful to prove logically all he says by numerous quotations from the revelations, and let another travel with him who can say, by the power of the Holy Ghost, Thus saith the Lord, and tell what the people should believe . . . though he may not be capable of producing a single logical argument, though he may tremble under a sense of his weakness, cleaving to the Lord for strength, as such men generally do, you will invariably find that the man who testifies by the power of the Holy Ghost will convince and gather many more of the honest and upright than will the merely logical reasoner." (P/A)

of the Ammonihahites was destroyed, and also their great city, which
they said God could not destroy, because of its greatness.
10. But behold, in one day it was left desolate; and the carcases
were mangled by dogs and wild beasts of the wilderness.
11. Nevertheless, after many days their dead bodies were heaped up
upon the face of the earth, and they were covered with a shallow covering. And now so great was the scent thereof that the people did not
go in to possess the land of Ammonihah for many years. And it was
called Desolation of Nehors; for they were of the profession of Nehor,
who were slain; and their lands remained desolate.
12. And the Lamanites did not come again to war against the
Nephites until the fourteenth year of the reign of the judges over
the people of Nephi. And thus for three years did the people of
Nephi have continual peace in all the land.
13. And Alma and Amulek went forth preaching repentance to
the people in their temples, and in their sanctuaries, and also in
their synagogues, which were built after the manner of the Jews.
14. And as many as would hear their words, unto them they did
impart the word of God, without any respect of persons, continually.
15. And thus did Alma and Amulek go forth, and also many more
who had been chosen for the work, to preach the word throughout
all the land. And the establishment of the church became general
throughout the land, in all the region round about, among all the
people of the Nephites.
16. And there was no inequality among them; the Lord did pour
out his Spirit on all the face of the land to prepare the minds of the
children of men, or to prepare their hearts to receive the word
which should be taught among them at the time of his coming—
17. That they might not be hardened against the word, that they
might not be unbelieving, and go on to destruction, but that they
might receive the word with joy, and as a branch be grafted into
the true vine, that they might enter into the rest of the Lord their
God.
18. Now those priests who did go forth among the people did preach
against all lyings, and deceivings, and envyings, and strifes, and malice, and revilings, and stealing, robbing, plundering, murdering, committing adultery, and all manner of lasciviousness, crying that these
things ought not so to be—
19. Holding forth things which must shortly come; yea, holding
forth the coming of the Son of God, his sufferings and death, and
also the resurrection of the dead.
20. And many of the people did inquire concerning the place
where the Son of God should come; and they were taught that he
would appear unto them after his resurrection; and this the people
did hear with great joy and gladness.
21. And now after the church had been established throughout all
the land—having got the victory over

Alma 16:10

Prophecy, accurately termed "history reversed," cannot be refuted. If woe is prophesied contingent upon repentance, woe will come in the absence of repentance.

President John Taylor spoke about fulfilling of prophecy when he said, "This nation and other nations will be overthrown . . . for the prophecies will be fulfilled. . . ."

Alma's prophecy of the destruction of the city of Ammonihah was utterly fulfilled. The prophets have declared throughout time: repent or perish. If not destroyed in mortality, then we will pay for our sins in the hereafter (see D&C 19:15–19). Where do we stand in regard to our own personal repentance? Where does our country stand as to its reverence toward God? (P/A)

Alma 16:16

We learn from modern scripture the following: "Nevertheless, in your temporal things you shall be equal, and this not grudgingly, otherwise the abundance of the manifestations of the Spirit shall be withheld" (D&C 70:14). (P/A)

Alma 16:17

The "rest" of the Lord has several different meanings: 1) Physical rest is a blessing, and sleep is more peaceful for the righteous who have peace of mind. 2) The Sabbath is a day of rest, a time set aside to glorify God. 3) Spiritual rest—also known as peace—comes from the Lord (as an example, consider Joseph Smith's calm as he went to his martyrdom). 4) Ultimate rest, overcoming physical and spiritual death, is gained by entering the presence of the Lord, but true saints can enter it in this life as well. To enter the rest of the Lord in this life, wrote Elder Bruce R. McConkie, we must know and love God, have faith in His purpose and plan, know we are right, not spend our effort searching for something else, and not be disturbed by people who are trying to deceive us.

the devil, and the word of God being preached in its purity in all the land, and the Lord pouring out his blessings upon the people—thus ended the fourteenth year of the reign of the judges over the people of Nephi.

An account of the sons of Mosiah, who rejected their rights to the kingdom for the word of God, and went up to the land of Nephi to preach to the Lamanites; their sufferings and deliverance—according to the record of Alma. Comprising chapters 17 to 26 inclusive.

CHAPTER 17

1. AND now it came to pass that as Alma was journeying from the land of Gideon southward, away to the land of Manti, behold, to his astonishment, he met with the sons of Mosiah journeying towards the land of Zarahemla.
2. Now these sons of Mosiah were with Alma at the time the angel first appeared unto him; therefore Alma did rejoice exceedingly to see his brethren; and what added more to his joy, they were still his brethren in the Lord; yea, and they had waxed strong in the knowledge of the truth; for they were men of a sound understanding and they had searched the scriptures diligently, that they might know the word of God.
3. But this is not all; they had given themselves to much prayer, and fasting; therefore they had the spirit of prophecy, and the spirit of revelation, and when they taught, they taught with power and authority of God.
4. And they had been teaching the word of God for the space of fourteen years among the Lamanites, having had much success in bringing many to the knowledge of the truth; yea, by the power of their words many were brought before the altar of God, to call on his name and confess their sins before him.
5. Now these are the circumstances which attended them in their journeyings, for they had many afflictions; they did suffer much, both in body and in mind, such as hunger, thirst and fatigue, and also much labor in the spirit.
6. Now these were their journeyings: Having taken leave of their father, Mosiah, in the first year of the judges; having refused the kingdom which their father was desirous to confer upon them, and also this was the minds of the people;
7. Nevertheless they departed out of the land of Zarahemla, and took their swords, and their spears, and their bows, and their arrows, and their slings; and this they did that they might provide food for themselves while in the wilderness.
8. And thus they departed into the wilderness with their numbers which they had selected, to go up to the land of Nephi, to preach the word of God unto the Lamanites.
9. And it came to pass that they journeyed many days in the wilderness, and they fasted much and prayed much that the Lord would grant unto them a portion of his

Alma 17:2

This verse, along with verses 3 and 9, give us important information on how to retain our spirituality after repenting of very serious sins. We learn that the Sons of Mosiah searched the scriptures diligently. Knowing that we need to do the same in order to maintain our spirituality, we need to ask ourselves how we can balance our spiritual life with our everyday duties.

Alma 17:3

Missionary work is a "labour of love" (Heb. 6:10) anchored in a Christlike attitude of service toward those we teach. . . .

In missionary work, people must know you care before they will listen to your teachings. The old saying is true: "People don't care how much you know until they know how much you care." . . .

If we are willing, the Lord will provide the opportunity and give us the strength—as well as the words—to bless people's lives. Elder Maxwell taught this beautiful principle: "God does not begin by asking us about our ability, but only about our availability, and if we then prove our dependability, he will increase our capability!" (P/A)

Alma 17:4

The sons of Mosiah demonstrated the attitude and behavior of truly converted souls. They were dedicated missionaries for the Lord Jesus Christ. They teach with the power and authority of God. They are led by the Spirit in all that they do. . . .

Dedication, scripture study, fasting, and prayer serve as the gateway for gaining the spirit of prophecy and revelation, and thereby teaching with the power and authority of God. . . .

In regard to missionary work, President Gordon B. Hinckley said, "I believe . . . with all my heart that the field is white ready to harvest. . . . I think the answer to an increased number of converts does not lie particularly in our methods—effective as those methods are. . . .

"I think every member of the Church has the capacity to teach the gospel to nonmembers. . . . We need an awareness, an everyday awareness of the great power that we have to do this thing.

"Let us prepare ourselves more diligently for the great assignment which God has laid upon us to carry this work to the children of the earth wherever we may be permitted to go." . . .

The reward is to have the Spirit of prophecy and revelation so that you will teach with the power and authority of God. Missionaries who are willing to work hard, being exactly, immediately, and courageously obedient, will always enjoy the Spirit on their missions and have greater success in working with the people. (P/A)

Spirit to go with them, and abide with them, that they might be an instrument in the hands of God to bring, if it were possible, their brethren, the Lamanites, to the knowledge of the truth, to the knowledge of the baseness of the traditions of their fathers, which were not correct.
10. And it came to pass that the Lord did visit them with his Spirit, and said unto them: Be comforted. And they were comforted.
11. And the Lord said unto them also: Go forth among the Lamanites, thy brethren, and establish my word; yet ye shall be patient in long-suffering and afflictions, that ye may show forth good examples unto them in me, and I will make an instrument of thee in my hands unto the salvation of many souls.
12. And it came to pass that the hearts of the sons of Mosiah, and also those who were with them, took courage to go forth unto the Lamanites to declare unto them the word of God.
13. And it came to pass when they had arrived in the borders of the land of the Lamanites, that they separated themselves and departed one from another, trusting in the Lord that they should meet again at the close of their harvest; for they supposed that great was the work which they had undertaken.
14. And assuredly it was great, for they had undertaken to preach the word of God to a wild and a hardened and a ferocious people; a people who delighted in murdering the Nephites, and robbing and plundering them; and their hearts were set upon riches, or upon gold and silver, and precious stones; yet they sought to obtain these things by murdering and plundering, that they might not labor for them with their own hands.
15. Thus they were a very indolent people, many of whom did worship idols, and the curse of God had fallen upon them because of the traditions of their fathers; notwithstanding the promises of the Lord were extended unto them on the conditions of repentance.
16. Therefore, this was the cause for which the sons of Mosiah had undertaken the work, that perhaps they might bring them unto repentance; that perhaps they might bring them to know of the plan of redemption.
17. Therefore they separated themselves one from another, and went forth among them, every man alone, according to the word and power of God which was given unto him.
18. Now Ammon being the chief among them, or rather he did administer unto them, and he departed from them, after having blessed them according to their several stations, having imparted the word of God unto them, or administered unto them before his departure; and thus they took their several journeys throughout the land.
19. And Ammon went to the land of Ishmael, the land being called after the sons of Ishmael, who also became Lamanites.
20. And as Ammon entered the land of Ishmael, the Lamanites took him and bound him, as was their custom to bind all the Nephites who fell into their hands, and carry them before the king; and thus it was left to the pleasure of the king to slay them, or to retain them in captivity, or to cast them into prison, or to

Alma 17:3–5

The Sons of Mosiah enjoyed prophecy and revelation because they searched the scriptures, prayed and fasted often, and served the Lord even under the most trying of circumstances. They gave up power—their rights to rule the kingdom—and wealth in order to serve the Lord. We might ask ourselves what we could do to develop that kind of dedication.

Alma 17:9

From the lives and experiences of the missionaries to the Lamanites, we learn of some of the elements that assist people in obtaining the power of God in His service. . . .

Much prayer and fasting are required (see Alma 17:3, 9). President Gordon B. Hinckley has said, "Prayer unlocks the powers of heaven in our behalf. Prayer is the great gift which our Eternal Father has given us by which we may approach Him and speak with Him in the name of the Lord Jesus Christ." (O/C)

Alma 17:14

The Sons of Mosiah went to the Lamanites because the Lord commanded them to. This verse gives a detailed description of the condition of the Lamanites at that time—undoubtedly a difficult task for the sons of Mosiah. The Lord had begun to prepare the Lamanites for the preaching of the gospel; through earlier contact with the Nephites, the Lamanites had learned the Nephite language (see Mosiah 24:1-7). For added insight into the condition of the Lamanites, see Jarom 6, 2 Nephi 5:24, and Enos 1:20.

Alma 17:17

Knowing the attitudes of the Lamanites as described in verse 14, consider how much courage it required for each of the Sons of Mosiah to split up and go forth among the Lamanites alone. Part of that courage came from the declaration of the Lord in verse 11: that they would each be an instrument of the Lord unto the salvation of many souls.

Alma 17:18

Alma 17:2–3 gives the basic formula for preparing to serve as a successful missionary.

1. Be "in the Lord" by following our Savior and keeping His commandments.
2. Wax strong in the knowledge of the truth.
3. Be of a sound understanding.
4. Search the scriptures diligently to know the word of God.
5. Pray and fast.

Regarding this preparation, President Gordon B. Hinckley said, "Our young people have an obligation to prepare themselves for missionary service . . . Live for the opportunity when you may go out as a servant of the Lord and an ambassador of eternal truth to the people of the world." (P/A)

cast them out of his land, according to his will and pleasure.

21. And thus Ammon was carried before the king who was over the land of Ishmael; and his name was Lamoni; and he was a descendant of Ishmael.

22. And the king inquired of Ammon if it were his desire to dwell in the land among the Lamanites, or among his people.

23. And Ammon said unto him: Yea, I desire to dwell among this people for a time; yea, and perhaps until the day I die.

24. And it came to pass that king Lamoni was much pleased with Ammon, and caused that his bands should be loosed; and he would that Ammon should take one of his daughters to wife.

25. But Ammon said unto him: Nay, but I will be thy servant. Therefore Ammon became a servant to king Lamoni. And it came to pass that he was set among other servants to watch the flocks of Lamoni, according to the custom of the Lamanites.

26. And after he had been in the service of the king three days, as he was with the Lamanitish servants going forth with their flocks to the place of water, which was called the water of Sebus, and all the Lamanites drive their flocks hither, that they may have water—

27. Therefore, as Ammon and the servants of the king were driving forth their flocks to this place of water, behold, a certain number of the Lamanites, who had been with their flocks to water, stood and scattered the flocks of Ammon and the servants of the king, and they scattered them insomuch that they fled many ways.

28. Now the servants of the king began to murmur, saying: Now the king will slay us, as he has our brethren because their flocks were scattered by the wickedness of these men. And they began to weep exceedingly, saying: Behold, our flocks are scattered already.

29. Now they wept because of the fear of being slain. Now when Ammon saw this his heart was swollen within him with joy; for, said he, I will show forth my power unto these my fellow-servants, or the power which is in me, in restoring these flocks unto the king, that I may win the hearts of these my fellow-servants, that I may lead them to believe in my words.

30. And now, these were the thoughts of Ammon, when he saw the afflictions of those whom he termed to be his brethren.

31. And it came to pass that he flattered them by his words, saying: My brethren, be of good cheer and let us go in search of the flocks, and we will gather them together and bring them back unto the place of water; and thus we will preserve the flocks unto the king and he will not slay us.

32. And it came to pass that they went in search of the flocks, and they did follow Ammon, and they rushed forth with much swiftness and did head the flocks of the king, and did gather them together again to the place of water.

33. And those men again stood to scatter their flocks; but Ammon said unto his brethren: Encircle the flocks round about that they flee not; and I go and contend with these men who do scatter our flocks.

34. Therefore, they did as Ammon commanded them, and he went forth and stood to contend with those who stood by the waters of Sebus; and they were in number not a few.

35. Therefore they did not fear Ammon, for they supposed that one of their men could slay him according to their pleasure, for they knew not that the Lord had promised Mosiah that he would deliver

Alma 17:25

This verse provides a great lesson for us in how to reach someone's heart: spiritually prepare, then serve the person with love. We must truly love any person we want to teach or to change—and we must demonstrate that sincere love before we call a personal to repentance. We must seek the help of the Lord in touching the hearts of those we want to teach, and avoid teaching them prematurely—before we or they are ready.

Alma 17:25

The famous incident in which Ammon displays his amazing strength in protecting the king's flocks from poachers serves as the tipping point for his missionary debut. Thereafter he is able to win over the confidence of King Lamoni and guide him over the threshold of honest curiosity and into the realm of spiritual enlightenment. . . .

Ammon is then able to enlarge the circle of conversion to include the queen and "many that did believe in their words. . . . And thus the work of the Lord did commence among the Lamanites; thus the Lord did begin to pour out his Spirit upon them; and we see that his arm is extended to all people who will repent and believe on his name" (Alma 19:35–36).

Speaking of the importance of the Spirit in missionary work, President Ezra Taft Benson said, "[On my first mission] I learned through experience that I could not convince another soul to come unto Christ. I learned that one cannot convert another by just quoting scripture. Conversion comes when another is touched by the Spirit of the Lord. . . . I learned that a missionary is only a vessel through whom the Lord can transmit His Spirit. To acquire that Spirit, a missionary must humble himself in prayer and ask our Heavenly Father to use him to touch the hearts of investigators." (P/A)

POINT OF INTEREST

At right are examples of ancient Mesoamerican weapons, which might have been like those used by the Nephites.

his sons out of their hands; neither did they know anything concerning the Lord; therefore they delighted in the destruction of
their brethren; and for this cause they stood to scatter the flocks of
the king.
36. But Ammon stood forth and began to cast stones at them with
his sling; yea, with mighty power he did sling stones amongst
them; and thus he slew a certain number of them insomuch that
they began to be astonished at his power; nevertheless they were
angry because of the slain of their brethren, and they were determined that he should fall; therefore, seeing that they could not hit
him with their stones, they came forth with clubs to slay him.
37. But behold, every man that lifted his club to smite Ammon, he
smote off their arms with his sword; for he did withstand their
blows by smiting their arms with the edge of his sword, insomuch
that they began to be astonished, and began to flee before him; yea,
and they were not few in number; and he caused them to flee by
the strength of his arm.
38. Now six of them had fallen by the sling, but he slew none save
it were their leader with his sword; and he smote off as many of
their arms as were lifted against him, and they were not a few.
39. And when he had driven them afar off, he returned and they
watered their flocks and returned them to the pasture of the king,
and then went in unto the king, bearing the arms which had been
smitten off by the sword of Ammon, of those who sought to slay
him; and they were carried in unto the king for a testimony of the
things which they had done.

CHAPTER 18

1. AND it came to pass that king Lamoni caused that his servants
should stand forth and testify to all the things which they had seen
concerning the matter.
2. And when they had all testified to the things which they had
seen, and he had learned of the faithfulness of Ammon in preserving his flocks, and also of his great power in contending against those
who sought to slay him, he was astonished exceedingly, and said:
Surely, this is more than a man. Behold, is not this the Great Spirit
who doth send such great punishments upon this people, because of
their murders?
3. And they answered the king, and said: Whether he be the Great
Spirit or a man, we know not; but this much we do know, that he
cannot be slain by the enemies of the king; neither can they scatter the king's flocks when he is with us, because of his expertness
and great strength; therefore, we know that he is a friend to the
king. And now, O king, we do not believe that a man has such
great power, for we know he cannot be slain.
4. And now, when the king heard these words, he said unto them:
Now I know that it is the Great Spirit; and he has come down at
this time to preserve your lives, that I might not slay you as I did
your brethren. Now this is the Great Spirit of whom our fathers
have spoken.
5. Now this was the tradition of Lamoni, which he had received
from

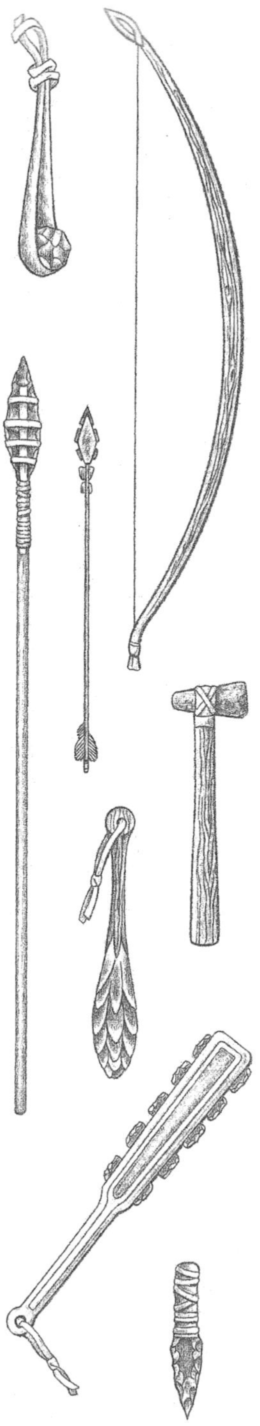

Alma 18:5

The tradition referred to here is evidence that the Lamanites had retained a fragment of the truth. The thing that impressed Lamoni most about Ammon was that Ammon reflected the Spirit of the Lord; we need that same confidence and quality as we teach the gospel.

his father, that there was a Great Spirit. Notwithstanding they believed in a Great Spirit they supposed that whatsoever they did was right; nevertheless, Lamoni began to fear exceedingly, with fear lest he had done wrong in slaying his servants;

6. For he had slain many of them because their brethren had scattered their flocks at the place of water; and thus, because they had had their flocks scattered they were slain.

7. Now it was the practice of these Lamanites to stand by the waters of Sebus to scatter the flocks of the people, that thereby they might drive away many that were scattered unto their own land, it being a practice of plunder among them.

8. And it came to pass that king Lamoni inquired of his servants, saying: Where is this man that has such great power?

9. And they said unto him: Behold, he is feeding thy horses. Now the king had commanded his servants, previous to the time of the watering of their flocks, that they should prepare his horses and chariots, and conduct him forth to the land of Nephi; for there had been a great feast appointed at the land of Nephi, by the father of Lamoni, who was king over all the land.

10. Now when king Lamoni heard that Ammon was preparing his horses and his chariots he was more astonished, because of the faithfulness of Ammon, saying: Surely there has not been any servant among all my servants that has been so faithful as this man; for even he doth remember all my commandments to execute them.

11. Now I surely know that this is the Great Spirit, and I would desire him that he come in unto me, but I durst not.

12. And it came to pass that when Ammon had made ready the horses and the chariots for the king and his servants, he went in unto the king, and he saw that the countenance of the king was changed; therefore he was about to return out of his presence.

13. And one of the king's servants said unto him, Rabbanah, which is, being interpreted, powerful or great king, considering their kings to be powerful; and thus he said unto him: Rabbanah, the king desireth thee to stay.

14. Therefore Ammon turned himself unto the king, and said unto him: What wilt thou that I should do for thee, O king? And the king answered him not for the space of an hour, according to their time, for he knew not what he should say unto him.

15. And it came to pass that Ammon said unto him again: What desirest thou of me? But the king answered him not.

16. And it came to pass that Ammon, being filled with the Spirit of God, therefore he perceived the thoughts of the king. And he said unto him: Is it because thou hast heard that I defended thy servants and thy flocks, and slew seven of their brethren with the sling and with the sword, and smote off the arms of others, in order to defend thy flocks and thy servants; behold, is it this that causeth thy marvelings?

17. I say unto you, what is it, that thy marvelings are so great? Behold, I am a man, and am thy servant; therefore, whatsoever thou desirest which is right, that will I do.

18. Now when the king had heard

Alma 18:8–9

By doing exactly what he had been asked to do, Ammon was building a relationship of trust with the king and his people. He also possessed the proper motivation for missionary work—which is, according to President David O. McKay, the love of people and the desire to bring them joy and peace. Our spirituality is demonstrated by how we live and the way we treat those with whom we interact.

Alma 18:10

In missionary work, people must know you care before they will listen to your teachings. The old saying is true: "People don't care how much you know until they know how much you care." This was exemplified in the letters new converts wrote me. I would ask them to tell me of their conversion. They'd reply, "I felt the love of the missionaries so much I had to listen to what they were teaching . . . while listening I felt the Spirit and I knew the gospel was true and I wanted to be baptized." (P/A)

Alma 18:13

The Lamanite word "Rabbanah," meaning "powerful or great king," is strikingly similar to other Semitic words having essentially the same meaning. For example, the New Testament word *rabboni* clearly refers to one who is a leader (John 20:16). Also the word *rabbi*, which is used frequently by Jewish people, designates "one who teaches or leads." That the spoken language of both the Nephites and the Lamanites is derived from the Hebrew is made quite clear in several places in the Book of Mormon. In fact, even as late as the fourth century A.D. one Book of Mormon prophet said, ". . . if our plates had been sufficiently large we should have written in Hebrew" (Mormon 9:33). (Ludlow)

these words, he marveled again, for he beheld that Ammon could discern his thoughts; but notwithstanding this, king Lamoni did open his mouth, and said unto him: Who art thou? Art thou that Great Spirit, who knows all things?
19. Ammon answered and said unto him: I am not.
20. And the king said: How knowest thou the thoughts of my heart? Thou mayest speak boldly, and tell me concerning these things; and also tell me by what power ye slew and smote off the arms of my brethren that scattered my flocks—
21. And now, if thou wilt tell me concerning these things, whatsoever thou desirest I will give unto thee; and if it were needed, I would guard thee with my armies; but I know that thou art more powerful than all they; nevertheless, whatsoever thou desirest of me I will grant it unto thee.
22. Now Ammon being wise, yet harmless, he said unto Lamoni: Wilt thou hearken unto my words, if I tell thee by what power I do these things? And this is the thing that I desire of thee.
23. And the king answered him, and said: Yea, I will believe all thy words. And thus he was caught with guile.
24. And Ammon began to speak unto him with boldness, and said unto him: Believest thou that there is a God?
25. And he answered, and said unto him: I do not know what that meaneth.
26. And then Ammon said: Believest thou that there is a Great Spirit?
27. And he said, Yea.
28. And Ammon said: This is God. And Ammon said unto him again: Believest thou that this Great Spirit, who is God, created all things which are in heaven and in the earth?
29. And he said: Yea, I believe that he created all things which are in the earth; but I do not know the heavens.
30. And Ammon said unto him: The heavens is a place where God dwells and all his holy angels.
31. And king Lamoni said: Is it above the earth?
32. And Ammon said: Yea, and he looketh down upon all the children of men; and he knows all the thoughts and intents of the heart; for by his hand were they all created from the beginning.
33. And king Lamoni said: I believe all these things which thou hast spoken. Art thou sent from God?
34. Ammon said unto him: I am a man; and man in the beginning was created after the image of God, and I am called by his Holy Spirit to teach these things unto this people, that they may be brought to a knowledge of that which is just and true;
35. And a portion of that Spirit dwelleth in me, which giveth me knowledge, and also power according to my faith and desires which are in God.
36. Now when Ammon had said these words, he began at the creation of the world, and also the creation of Adam, and told him all the things concerning the fall of man, and rehearsed and laid before him the records and the holy scriptures of the people, which had been spoken by the prophets, even down to the time that their father, Lehi, left Jerusalem.
37. And he also rehearsed unto

Alma 18:23

While president of the Central States Mission [Elder Alvin R. Dyer] conducted a mission-wide research poll among all of the converts of the mission, asking them to declare when they first knew that the gospel was true. Several thousand participated in the project. Elder Dyer learned that 82% of the converts knew the gospel was true *the first time they heard the missionaries bear witness of it*. Thus in most cases the transforming witness came not after a period of experience with the Church but *immediately* upon hearing the message for the first time as the missionaries spoke with the power of the Spirit. Elder Dyer testified that this phenomenon was a substantiation of the Savior's statement: "My sheep hear my voice, and I know them, and they follow me" (John 10:27). (P/A)

Alma 18:23

Although the word *guile* is frequently used to mean "deceitful cunning" or "treachery," it can also denote the use of strategy. It is evidently used in the latter sense in Alma 18:23; in other words, Ammon *planned* or *used strategy* in arranging the questions he asked King Lamoni. (Ludlow)

Alma 18:35

By ourselves, we do not have sufficient strength or power to endure all of our trials and adversities, or to resist all of the tempting appeals of the devil, or to faithfully press onward under the defeating pressures of disappointment or discouragement. Likewise, we do not have the power to perform the required tasks inherent in Church service calls extended to us to help build the Lord's Kingdom, or strengthen our children in our own homes. But the Holy Spirit can add power to our spiritual reservoir, sustain us, and cause us to be equal to each of our challenges. (O/C)

them (for it was unto the king and to his servants) all the journeyings of their fathers in the wilderness, and all their sufferings with
hunger and thirst, and their travail, and so forth.
38. And he also rehearsed unto them concerning the rebellions of
Laman and Lemuel, and the sons of Ishmael, yea, all their rebellions did he relate unto them; and he expounded unto them all the
records and scriptures from the time that Lehi left Jerusalem down
to the present time.
39. But this is not all; for he expounded unto them the plan of
redemption, which was prepared from the foundation of the world;
and he also made known unto them concerning the coming of
Christ, and all the works of the Lord did he make known unto
them.
40. And it came to pass that after he had said all these things, and
expounded them to the king, that the king believed all his words.
41. And he began to cry unto the Lord, saying: O Lord, have
mercy; according to thy abundant mercy which thou hast had
upon the people of Nephi, have upon me, and my people.
42. And now, when he had said this, he fell unto the earth, as if he
were dead.
43. And it came to pass that his servants took him and carried him
in unto his wife, and laid him upon a bed; and he lay as if he were
dead for the space of two days and two nights; and his wife, and his
sons, and his daughters mourned over him, after the manner of the
Lamanites, greatly lamenting his loss.

CHAPTER 19

1. AND it came to pass that after two days and two nights they were
about to take his body and lay it in a sepulchre, which they had
made for the purpose of burying their dead.
2. Now the queen having heard of the fame of Ammon, therefore
she sent and desired that he should come in unto her.
3. And it came to pass that Ammon did as he was commanded, and
went in unto the queen, and desired to know what she would that
he should do.
4. And she said unto him: The servants of my husband have made
it known unto me that thou art a prophet of a holy God, and that
thou hast power to do many mighty works in his name;
5. Therefore, if this is the case, I would that ye should go in and see
my husband, for he has been laid upon his bed for the space of two
days and two nights; and some say that he is not dead, but others
say that he is dead and that he stinketh, and that he ought to be
placed in the sepulchre; but as for myself, to me he doth not stink.
6. Now, this was what Ammon desired, for he knew that king
Lamoni was under the power of God; he knew that the dark veil of
unbelief was being cast away from his mind, and the light which
did light up his mind, which was the light of the glory of God,
which was a marvelous light of his goodness—yea, this light had
infused such joy into his soul, the cloud of darkness having been
dispelled, and that the light of everlasting life was lit up in

Alma 18:39

When Ammon taught King Lamoni and when Aaron taught King Lamoni's father, they began their instruction from the scriptures. They taught the reality of the existence of God. Unless people have a conviction there is a God, they will be unable to grasp or understand His ways or His teachings. Spencer W. Kimball said:

"Perhaps the most important thing I can say about Jesus Christ, more important than all else I have said, is that he lives. He really does embody all those virtues and attributes the scriptures tell us of. If we can come to know that, we then know the central reality about man and the universe. If we don't accept that truth and that reality, then we will not have the fixed principles or the transcendent truths by which to live out our lives in happiness and in service." (O/C)

Alma 19

If for no other reason, Abish, the Lamanitish woman, is distinguished because her actual name appears in the Book of Mormon. She is one of only three women in the entire Nephite-Lamanite-Mulekite-Jaredite records to have her name in the Book of Mormon. The other two are Sariah, the wife of Lehi (1 Nephi 2:5), and Isabel, the harlot (Alma 39:3).

The brief account of the conversion of Abish is not clear. The statement that Abish had been converted "unto the Lord for many years, on account of a remarkable vision of her father" (Alma 19:16) may have two possible interpretations. One interpretation is that Abish herself had this vision and in her vision she saw her father. Another possible interpretation is that the vision was actually had by the father of Abish. Regardless of which interpretation is correct, this conversion of Abish plays an important role in converting large numbers of Lamanites. (Ludlow)

his soul, yea, he knew that this had overcome his natural frame, and he was carried away in God—
7. Therefore, what the queen desired of him was his only desire. Therefore, he went in to see the king according as the queen had desired him; and he saw the king, and he knew that he was not dead.
8. And he said unto the queen: He is not dead, but he sleepeth in God, and on the morrow he shall rise again; therefore bury him not.
9. And Ammon said unto her: Believest thou this? And she said unto him: I have had no witness save thy word, and the word of our servants; nevertheless I believe that it shall be according as thou hast said.
10. And Ammon said unto her: Blessed art thou because of thy exceeding faith; I say unto thee, woman, there has not been such great faith among all the people of the Nephites.
11. And it came to pass that she watched over the bed of her husband, from that time even until that time on the morrow which Ammon had appointed that he should rise.
12. And it came to pass that he arose, according to the words of Ammon; and as he arose, he stretched forth his hand unto the woman, and said: Blessed be the name of God, and blessed art thou.
13. For as sure as thou livest, behold, I have seen my Redeemer; and he shall come forth, and be born of a woman, and he shall redeem all mankind who believe on his name. Now, when he had said these words, his heart was swollen within him, and he sunk again with joy; and the queen also sunk down, being overpowered by the Spirit.
14. Now Ammon seeing the Spirit of the Lord poured out according to his prayers upon the Lamanites, his brethren, who had been the cause of so much mourning among the Nephites, or among all the people of God because of their iniquities and their traditions, he fell upon his knees, and began to pour out his soul in prayer and thanksgiving to God for what he had done for his brethren; and he was also overpowered with joy; and thus they all three had sunk to the earth.
15. Now, when the servants of the king had seen that they had fallen, they also began to cry unto God, for the fear of the Lord had come upon them also, for it was they who had stood before the king and testified unto him concerning the great power of Ammon.
16. And it came to pass that they did call on the name of the Lord, in their might, even until they had all fallen to the earth, save it were one of the Lamanitish women, whose name was Abish, she having been converted unto the Lord for many years, on account of a remarkable vision of her father—
17. Thus, having been converted to the Lord, and never having made it known, therefore, when she saw that all the servants of Lamoni had fallen to the earth, and also her mistress, the queen, and the king, and Ammon lay prostrate upon the earth, she knew that it was the power of God; and supposing that this opportunity, by making known unto the people what had happened among them, that by beholding this scene it would cause them to believe in the power of God, therefore she ran forth from house to house, making it known unto the people.
18. And they began to assemble themselves together unto the house

Alma 19:14

No one can be converted to the Lord unless he knows the Lord. We can't really know anyone unless we spend time together and talk with each other. Otherwise, we only know *about* the person. Prayer is the means our Heavenly Father has provided by which we can communicate with Him. We are taught and encouraged to seek His guidance, wisdom, and counsel in order to know His will concerning us. The more we talk with Him, the stronger our relationship with Him becomes. (O/C)

Alma 19:16

Abish is one of only three women named in the Book of Mormon. The other two are Sariah, Lehi's wife (see 1 Nephi 2:5), and Isabel, the harlot (see Alma 39:3). Through her faithfulness, Abish was instrumental in converting hundreds of Lamanites.

of the king. And there came a multitude, and to their astonishment they beheld the king, and the queen, and their servants prostrate upon the earth, and they all lay there as though they were dead; and they also saw Ammon, and behold, he was a Nephite.

19. And now the people began to murmur among themselves; some saying that it was a great evil that had come upon them, or upon the king and his house, because he had suffered that the Nephite should remain in the land.

20. But others rebuked them, saying: The king hath brought this evil upon his house, because he slew his servants who had had their flocks scattered at the waters of Sebus.

21. And they were also rebuked by those men who had stood at the waters of Sebus and scattered the flocks which belonged to the king, for they were angry with Ammon because of the number which he had slain of their brethren at the waters of Sebus, while defending the flocks of the king.

22. Now, one of them, whose brother had been slain with the sword of Ammon, being exceedingly angry with Ammon, drew his sword and went forth that he might let it fall upon Ammon, to slay him; and as he lifted the sword to smite him, behold, he fell dead.

23. Now we see that Ammon could not be slain, for the Lord had said unto Mosiah, his father: I will spare him, and it shall be unto him according to thy faith—therefore, Mosiah trusted him unto the Lord.

24. And it came to pass that when the multitude beheld that the man had fallen dead, who lifted the sword to slay Ammon, fear came upon them all, and they durst not put forth their hands to touch him or any of those who had fallen; and they began to marvel again among themselves what could be the cause of this great power, or what all these things could mean.

25. And it came to pass that there were many among them who said that Ammon was the Great Spirit, and others said he was sent by the Great Spirit;

26. But others rebuked them all, saying that he was a monster, who had been sent from the Nephites to torment them.

27. And there were some who said that Ammon was sent by the Great Spirit to afflict them because of their iniquities; and that it was the Great Spirit that had always attended the Nephites, who had ever delivered them out of their hands; and they said that it was this Great Spirit who had destroyed so many of their brethren, the Lamanites.

28. And thus the contention began to be exceedingly sharp among them. And while they were thus contending, the woman servant who had caused the multitude to be gathered together came, and when she saw the contention which was among the multitude she was exceedingly sorrowful, even unto tears.

29. And it came to pass that she went and took the queen by the hand, that perhaps she might raise her from the ground; and as soon as she touched her hand she arose and stood upon her feet, and cried with a loud voice, saying: O blessed Jesus, who has saved me from an awful hell! O blessed God, have mercy on this people!

30. And when she had said this, she clasped her hands, being filled with joy, speaking many words which were not understood; and when she had done this, she took the king,

Lamoni, by the hand, and behold he arose and stood upon his feet.
31. And he, immediately, seeing the contention among his people, went forth and began to rebuke them, and to teach them the words which he had heard from the mouth of Ammon; and as many as heard his words believed, and were converted unto the Lord.
32. But there were many among them who would not hear his words; therefore they went their way.
33. And it came to pass that when Ammon arose he also administered unto them, and also did all the servants of Lamoni; and they did all declare unto the people the selfsame thing—that their hearts had been changed; that they had no more desire to do evil.
34. And behold, many did declare unto the people that they had seen angels and had conversed with them; and thus they had told them things of God, and of his righteousness.
35. And it came to pass that there were many that did believe in their words; and as many as did believe were baptized; and they became a righteous people, and they did establish a church among them.
36. And thus the work of the Lord did commence among the Lamanites; thus the Lord did begin to pour out his Spirit upon them; and we see that his arm is extended to all people who will repent and believe on his name.

CHAPTER 20

1. AND it came to pass that when they had established a church in that land, that king Lamoni desired that Ammon should go with him to the land of Nephi, that he might show him unto his father.
2. And the voice of the Lord came to Ammon saying: Thou shalt not go up to the land of Nephi, for behold, the king will seek thy life; but thou shalt go to the land of Middoni; for behold, thy brother Aaron, and also Muloki and Ammah are in prison.
3. Now it came to pass that when Ammon had heard this, he said unto Lamoni: Behold, my brother and brethren are in prison at Middoni, and I go that I may deliver them.
4. Now Lamoni said unto Ammon: I know, in the strength of the Lord thou canst do all things. But behold, I will go with thee to the land of Middoni; for the king of the land of Middoni, whose name is Antiomno, is a friend unto me; therefore I go to the land of Middoni, that I may flatter the king of the land, and he will cast thy brethren out of prison. Now Lamoni said unto him: Who told thee that thy brethren were in prison?
5. And Ammon said unto him: No one hath told me, save it be God; and he said unto me—Go and deliver thy brethren, for they are in prison in the land of Middoni.
6. Now when Lamoni had heard this he caused that his servants should make ready his horses and his chariots.
7. And he said unto Ammon: Come, I will go with thee down to the land of Middoni, and there I will plead with the king that he will cast thy brethren out of prison.
8. And it came to pass that as Ammon and Lamoni were journeying

Alma 19:33

This verse provides a clear definition of conversion—a mighty change of heart that results in no more desire to do evil.

Alma 20:2–3

The Book of Mormon does not specifically state how many missionary companions accompanied the four sons of Mosiah on their long-term mission (about fourteen years!—see Mosiah 28:1, 8–9; Alma 17:6; Alma 16:21); yet the record clearly indicates there were additional missionaries (Mosiah 28:1; Alma 22:35), and at least two of them, Muloki and Ammah, are mentioned by name (Alma 20:2–3). (Ludlow)

POINT OF INTEREST

A portion of a Zapotec manuscript.

thither, they met the father of Lamoni, who was king over all the land.
9. And behold, the father of Lamoni said unto him: Why did ye not come to the feast on that great day when I made a feast unto my sons, and unto my people?
10. And he also said: Whither art thou going with this Nephite, who is one of the children of a liar?
11. And it came to pass that Lamoni rehearsed unto him whither he was going, for he feared to offend him.
12. And he also told him all the cause of his tarrying in his own kingdom, that he did not go unto his father to the feast which he had prepared.
13. And now when Lamoni had rehearsed unto him all these things, behold, to his astonishment, his father was angry with him, and said: Lamoni, thou art going to deliver these Nephites, who are sons of a liar. Behold, he robbed our fathers; and now his children are also come amongst us that they may, by their cunning and their lyings, deceive us, that they again may rob us of our property.
14. Now the father of Lamoni commanded him that he should slay Ammon with the sword. And he also commanded him that he should not go to the land of Middoni, but that he should return with him to the land of Ishmael.
15. But Lamoni said unto him: I will not slay Ammon, neither will I return to the land of Ishmael, but I go to the land of Middoni that I may release the brethren of Ammon, for I know that they are just men and holy prophets of the true God.
16. Now when his father had heard these words, he was angry with him, and he drew his sword that he might smite him to the earth.
17. But Ammon stood forth and said unto him: Behold, thou shalt not slay thy son; nevertheless, it were better that he should fall than thee, for behold, he has repented of his sins; but if thou shouldst fall at this time, in thine anger, thy soul could not be saved.
18. And again, it is expedient that thou shouldst forbear; for if thou shouldst slay thy son, he being an innocent man, his blood would cry from the ground to the Lord his God, for vengeance to come upon thee; and perhaps thou wouldst lose thy soul.
19. Now when Ammon had said these words unto him, he answered him, saying: I know that if I should slay my son, that I should shed innocent blood; for it is thou that hast sought to destroy him.
20. And he stretched forth his hand to slay Ammon. But Ammon withstood his blows, and also smote his arm that he could not use it.
21. Now when the king saw that Ammon could slay him, he began to plead with Ammon that he would spare his life.
22. But Ammon raised his sword, and said unto him: Behold, I will smite thee except thou wilt grant unto me that my brethren may be cast out of prison.
23. Now the king, fearing he should lose his life, said: If thou wilt spare me I will grant unto thee whatsoever thou wilt ask, even to half of the kingdom.
24. Now when Ammon saw that he had wrought upon the old king according to his desire, he said unto him: If thou wilt grant that my brethren may be cast out of prison, and also that Lamoni may retain his kingdom, and that ye be not displeased with him, but grant that he may do according to his own desires in whatsoever thing he thinketh,

Alma 20:17–24

In these verses, Ammon creates a powerful teaching moment by the way he reacts in a crisis.

then will I spare thee; otherwise I will smite thee to the earth.
25. Now when Ammon had said these words, the king began to rejoice because of his life.
26. And when he saw that Ammon had no desire to destroy him, and when he also saw the great love he had for his son Lamoni, he was astonished exceedingly, and said: Because this is all that thou hast desired, that I would release thy brethren, and suffer that my son Lamoni should retain his kingdom, behold, I will grant unto you that my son may retain his kingdom from this time and forever; and I will govern him no more—
27. And I will also grant unto thee that thy brethren may be cast out of prison, and thou and thy brethren may come unto me, in my kingdom; for I shall greatly desire to see thee. For the king was greatly astonished at the words which he had spoken, and also at the words which had been spoken by his son Lamoni, therefore he was desirous to learn them.
28. And it came to pass that Ammon and Lamoni proceeded on their journey towards the land of Middoni. And Lamoni found favor in the eyes of the king of the land; therefore the brethren of Ammon were brought forth out of prison.
29. And when Ammon did meet them he was exceedingly sorrowful, for behold they were naked, and their skins were worn exceedingly because of being bound with strong cords. And they also had suffered hunger, thirst, and all kinds of afflictions; nevertheless they were patient in all their sufferings.
30. And, as it happened, it was their lot to have fallen into the hands of a more hardened and a more stiffnecked people; therefore they would not hearken unto their words, and they had cast them out, and had smitten them, and had driven them from house to house, and from place to place, even until they had arrived in the land of Middoni; and there they were taken and cast into prison, and bound with strong cords, and kept in prison for many days, and were delivered by Lamoni and Ammon.

An account of the preaching of Aaron, and Muloki, and their brethren, to the Lamanites. Comprising chapters 21 to 26 inclusive.

CHAPTER 21

1. NOW when Ammon and his brethren separated themselves in the borders of the land of the Lamanites, behold Aaron took his journey towards the land which was called by the Lamanites, Jerusalem, calling it after the land of their fathers' nativity; and it was away joining the borders of Mormon.
2. Now the Lamanites and the Amalekites and the people of Amulon had built a great city, which was called Jerusalem.
3. Now the Lamanites of themselves were sufficiently hardened, but the Amalekites and the Amulonites were still harder; therefore they did cause the Lamanites that they should harden their hearts, that they should wax strong in wickedness and their abominations.
4. And it came to pass that Aaron came to the city of Jerusalem, and

Alma 21:2

The Amalekites are mentioned for the first time in Alma 21:2; the exact source of their name is never made clear in the Book of Mormon. The Amulonites mentioned here are the descendants and the followers of Amulon, the wicked priest of King Noah. (Mosiah 23:31–35; Mosiah 24:3–4) Both of these groups of people believed in the "order of the Nehors" (Alma 21:4; read also Alma 1:2–6, 15–16), and they were so hardened in wickedness that only one Amalekite and no Amulonites were converted by the four sons of Mosiah and their companions (Alma 23:14). (Ludlow)

first began to preach to the Amalekites. And he began to preach to them in their synagogues, for they had built synagogues after the order of the Nehors; for many of the Amalekites and the Amulonites were after the order of the Nehors.
5. Therefore, as Aaron entered into one of their synagogues to
preach unto the people, and as he was speaking unto them, behold there arose an Amalekite and began to contend with him, saying: What is that thou hast testified? Hast thou seen an angel? Why do not angels appear unto us? Behold are not this people as good as thy people?
6. Thou also sayest, except we repent we shall perish. How know-
est thou the thought and intent of our hearts? How knowest thou that we have cause to repent? How knowest thou that we are not a righteous people? Behold, we have built sanctuaries, and we do assemble ourselves together to worship God. We do believe that God will save all men.
7. Now Aaron said unto him: Believest thou that the Son of God
shall come to redeem mankind from their sins?
8. And the man said unto him: We do not believe that thou know-
est any such thing. We do not believe in these foolish traditions. We do not believe that thou knowest of things to come, neither do we believe that thy fathers and also that our fathers did know concerning the things which they spake, of that which is to come.
9. Now Aaron began to open the scriptures unto them concerning
the coming of Christ, and also concerning the resurrection of the dead, and that there could be no redemption for mankind save it were through the death and sufferings of Christ, and the atonement of his blood.
10. And it came to pass as he began to expound these things unto
them they were angry with him, and began to mock him; and they would not hear the words which he spake.
11. Therefore, when he saw that they would not hear his words, he
departed out of their synagogue, and came over to a village which was called Ani-Anti, and there he found Muloki preaching the word unto them; and also Ammah and his brethren. And they contended with many about the word.
12. And it came to pass that they saw that the people would hard-
en their hearts, therefore they departed and came over into the land of Middoni. And they did preach the word unto many, and few believed on the words which they taught.
13. Nevertheless, Aaron and a certain number of his brethren were
taken and cast into prison, and the remainder of them fled out of the land of Middoni unto the regions round about.
14. And those who were cast into prison suffered many things, and
they were delivered by the hand of Lamoni and Ammon, and they were fed and clothed.
15. And they went forth again to declare the word, and thus they
were delivered for the first time out of prison; and thus they had suffered.
16. And they went forth whithersoever they were led by the Spirit
of the Lord, preaching the word of God in every synagogue of the Amalekites, or in every assembly of the Lamanites where they could be admitted.
17. And it came to pass that the

Alma 21:4

The order of the Nehors began with an anti-Christ named Nehor (see Alma 1:1–16). The order of Nehors had a core of three major beliefs: 1) Simply meeting together constituted worship. 2) God would save all men, regardless of their beliefs or behaviors. 3) No man could know of things to come, so no one could know that Christ existed or would come to earth. In fact, they denied Christ. The teachings of the Nehors hardened the hearts of the people of Ammonihah so much that the ruins of Ammonihah were called the "Desolation of Nehors" (see Alma 16:11).

Lord began to bless them, insomuch that they brought many to the knowledge of the truth; yea, they did convince many of their sins, and of the traditions of their fathers, which were not correct.
18. And it came to pass that Ammon and Lamoni returned from the land of Middoni to the land of Ishmael, which was the land of their inheritance.
19. And king Lamoni would not suffer that Ammon should serve him, or be his servant.
20. But he caused that there should be synagogues built in the land of Ishmael; and he caused that his people, or the people who were under his reign, should assemble themselves together.
21. And he did rejoice over them, and he did teach them many things. And he did also declare unto them that they were a people who were under him, and that they were a free people, that they were free from the oppressions of the king, his father; for that his father had granted unto him that he might reign over the people who were in the land of Ishmael, and in all the land round about.
22. And he also declared unto them that they might have the liberty of worshiping the Lord their God according to their desires, in whatsoever place they were in, if it were in the land which was under the reign of king Lamoni.
23. And Ammon did preach unto the people of king Lamoni; and it came to pass that he did teach them all things concerning things pertaining to righteousness. And he did exhort them daily, with all diligence; and they gave heed unto his word, and they were zealous for keeping the commandments of God.

CHAPTER 22

1. Now, as Ammon was thus teaching the people of Lamoni continually, we will return to the account of Aaron and his brethren; for after he departed from the land of Middoni he was led by the Spirit to the land of Nephi, even to the house of the king which was over all the land save it were the land of Ishmael; and he was the father of Lamoni.
2. And it came to pass that he went in unto him into the king's palace, with his brethren, and bowed himself before the king, and said unto him: Behold, O king, we are the brethren of Ammon, whom thou hast delivered out of prison.
3. And now, O king, if thou wilt spare our lives, we will be thy servants. And the king said unto them: Arise, for I will grant unto you your lives, and I will not suffer that ye shall be my servants; but I will insist that ye shall administer unto me; for I have been somewhat troubled in mind because of the generosity and the greatness of the words of thy brother Ammon; and I desire to know the cause why he has not come up out of Middoni with thee.
4. And Aaron said unto the king: Behold, the Spirit of the Lord has called him another way; he has gone to the land of Ishmael, to teach the people of Lamoni.
5. Now the king said unto them: What is this that ye have said concerning the Spirit of the Lord?

Alma 21:21

This verse describes one of the purposes of government: to allow for the free exercise of religious worship.

Alma 21:23

We can learn about the Lord by listening to those who truly serve Him, just as the people of king Lamoni learned about the Lord by listening to Ammon as he taught them the principles of righteousness.

Alma 21:23

He who repents of sin must forsake sin, meaning he no longer dwells in sin, neither in thought or deed. Instead he is obedient to the principles and laws of the gospel. The Lord declared, ". . . he that repents *and does the commandments* of the Lord shall be forgiven; And he that repents not, from him shall be taken even the light which he has received . . ." (D&C 1:32–33, emphasis added). (O/C)

Alma 22:1–4

The creation, the fall of Adam, and the plan of redemption through Christ are the fundamental principles that should be taught by every missionary. These verses describe some of the most powerful principles of missionary work: being led by the Spirit (verse 1), respecting the position of those we teach (verse 2), being committed to service (verse 3), and being honest and straightforward. Giving ourselves over to the Lord is an important component not only of missionary work, but of everyday life—our payment for the privilege of exaltation is "the heart and a willing mind" (see D&C 64:34).

Behold, this is the thing which doth trouble me.
6. And also, what is this that Ammon said—If ye will repent ye shall be saved, and if ye will not repent, ye shall be cast off at the last day?
7. And Aaron answered him and said unto him: Believest thou that there is a God? And the king said: I know that the Amalekites say that there is a God, and I have granted unto them that they should build sanctuaries, that they may assemble themselves together to worship him. And if now thou sayest there is a God, behold I will believe.
8. And now when Aaron heard this, his heart began to rejoice, and he said: Behold, assuredly as thou livest, O king, there is a God.
9. And the king said: Is God that Great Spirit that brought our fathers out of the land of Jerusalem?
10. And Aaron said unto him: Yea, he is that Great Spirit, and he created all things both in heaven and in earth. Believest thou this?
11. And he said: Yea, I believe that the Great Spirit created all things, and I desire that ye should tell me concerning all these things, and I will believe thy words.
12. And it came to pass that when Aaron saw that the king would believe his words, he began from the creation of Adam, reading the scriptures unto the king—how God created man after his own image, and that God gave him commandments, and that because of transgression, man had fallen.
13. And Aaron did expound unto him the scriptures from the creation of Adam, laying the fall of man before him, and their carnal state and also the plan of redemption, which was prepared from the foundation of the world, through Christ, for all whosoever would believe on his name.
14. And since man had fallen he could not merit anything of himself; but the sufferings and death of Christ atone for their sins, through faith and repentance, and so forth; and that he breaketh the bands of death, that the grave shall have no victory, and that the sting of death should be swallowed up in the hopes of glory; and Aaron did expound all these things unto the king.
15. And it came to pass that after Aaron had expounded these things unto him, the king said: What shall I do that I may have this eternal life of which thou hast spoken? Yea, what shall I do that I may be born of God, having this wicked spirit rooted out of my breast, and receive his Spirit, that I may be filled with joy, that I may not be cast off at the last day? Behold, said he, I will give up all that I possess, yea, I will forsake my kingdom, that I may receive this great joy.
16. But Aaron said unto him: If thou desirest this thing, if thou wilt bow down before God, yea, if thou wilt repent of all thy sins, and will bow down before God, and call on his name in faith, believing that ye shall receive, then shalt thou receive the hope which thou desirest.
17. And it came to pass that when Aaron had said these words, the king did bow down before the Lord, upon his knees; yea, even he did

Alma 22:8

The God to whom Aaron refers in this verse is Jesus Christ, the god of the Old Testament.

Alma 22:9–10

At the time Aaron was teaching the king, Jesus had not yet been born into mortality—and was, therefore, still a spirit being.

Alma 22:15–16

In his plaintive declaration of what he was willing to give up, the king gives insight into the level of his desire. But instead of giving up all the material things we possess, we see in verse 16 that our requirement for eternal life is much different: we must bow down before God in humility, truly repent of our sins, and call upon His name in faith, believing that we will inherit eternal life.

prostrate himself upon the earth, and cried mightily, saying:
18. O God, Aaron hath told me that there is a God; and if there is a God, and if thou art God, wilt thou make thyself known unto me, and I will give away all my sins to know thee, and that I may be raised from the dead, and be saved at the last day. And now when the king had said these words, he was struck as if he were dead.
19. And it came to pass that his servants ran and told the queen all that had happened unto the king. And she came in unto the king; and when she saw him lay as if he were dead, and also Aaron and his brethren standing as though they had been the cause of his fall, she was angry with them, and commanded that her servants, or the servants of the king, should take them and slay them.
20. Now the servants had seen the cause of the king's fall, therefore they durst not lay their hands on Aaron and his brethren; and they pled with the queen saying: Why commandest thou that we should slay these men, when behold one of them is mightier than us all? Therefore we shall fall before them.
21. Now when the queen saw the fear of the servants she also began to fear exceedingly, lest there should some evil come upon her. And she commanded her servants that they should go and call the people, that they might slay Aaron and his brethren.
22. Now when Aaron saw the determination of the queen, he, also knowing the hardness of the hearts of the people, feared lest that a multitude should assemble themselves together, and there should be a great contention and a disturbance among them; therefore he put forth his hand and raised the king from the earth, and said unto him: Stand. And he stood upon his feet, receiving his strength.
23. Now this was done in the presence of the queen and many of the servants. And when they saw it they greatly marveled, and began to fear. And the king stood forth, and began to minister unto them. And he did minister unto them, insomuch that his whole household were converted unto the Lord.
24. Now there was a multitude gathered together because of the commandment of the queen, and there began to be great murmurings among them because of Aaron and his brethren.
25. But the king stood forth among them and administered unto them. And they were pacified towards Aaron and those who were with him.
26. And it came to pass that when the king saw that the people were pacified, he caused that Aaron and his brethren should stand forth in the midst of the multitude, and that they should preach the word unto them.
27. And it came to pass that the king sent a proclamation throughout all the land, amongst all his people who were in all his land, who were in all the regions round about, which was bordering even to the sea, on the east and on the west, and which was divided from the land of Zarahemla by a narrow strip of wilderness, which ran from the sea east even to the sea west, and round about on the borders of the seashore, and the borders of the wilderness which was on the north by the land of Zarahemla, through the borders of Manti, by the head of the river Sidon, running from the east towards the west—and thus were the Lamanites and the Nephites divided.

Alma 22:18

When a person accepts and knows the life style and standards the Lord teaches and expects of us, he has a desire to put his life in harmony with the teachings of the Savior. If anything is out of order or ever has been, he seeks to be forgiven and cleansed of the effects of sin. He is willing to pay any price for an eternal inheritance in the Kingdom of God. (O/C)

Alma 22:18

The king of the Lamanites promised the Lord, "I will give away all my sins to know thee." (Alma 22:18.) As is evident in his subsequent life, the king was promising the Lord that he would repent of all of his sins, forsake them, and start keeping the commandments of God. Some students of the Book of Mormon have wondered concerning the miraculous and almost instantaneous conversions of King Lamoni (Alma 18:40–43 and 19:1–36) and the king of the Lamanites (Alma 22:15–23). However, it is possible for people to be immediately converted to the gospel if they are sincere in wanting to repent of their sins and in learning the truth. Concerning how long it takes a person to repent, Heber C. Kimball said:

"On the day of Pentecost, when Peter proclaimed the Gospel, about 3,000 souls were added to the Church that day. How long did it take them to repent? No longer than they were willing to believe, and put away their sins, with a determination to forsake them, and not sin again" (*Journal of Discourses*, 1:36). (Ludlow)

Alma 22:22–26

These verses show the pattern of conversion that occurred as a result of Aaron's teachings. First the king was converted, and then the members of the king's household. Finally, generally all people in the kingdom were converted to the truthfulness of what Aaron preached.

28. Now, the more idle part of the Lamanites lived in the wilderness, and dwelt in tents; and they were spread through the wilderness on the west, in the land of Nephi; yea, and also on the west of the land of Zarahemla, in the borders by the seashore, and on the west in the land of Nephi, in the place of their fathers' first inheritance, and thus bordering along by the seashore.
29. And also there were many Lamanites on the east by the seashore, whither the Nephites had driven them. And thus the Nephites were nearly surrounded by the Lamanites; nevertheless the Nephites had taken possession of all the northern parts of the land bordering on the wilderness, at the head of the river Sidon, from the east to the west, round about on the wilderness side; on the north, even until they came to the land which they called Bountiful.
30. And it bordered upon the land which they called Desolation, it being so far northward that it came into the land which had been peopled and been destroyed, of whose bones we have spoken, which was discovered by the people of Zarahemla, it being the place of their first landing.
31. And they came from there up into the south wilderness. Thus the land on the northward was called Desolation, and the land on the southward was called Bountiful, it being the wilderness which is filled with all manner of wild animals of every kind, a part of which had come from the land northward for food.
32. And now, it was only the distance of a day and a half's journey for a Nephite, on the line Bountiful and the land Desolation, from the east to the west sea; and thus the land of Nephi and the land of Zarahemla were nearly surrounded by water, there being a small neck of land between the land northward and the land southward.
33. And it came to pass that the Nephites had inhabited the land Bountiful, even from the east unto the west sea, and thus the Nephites in their wisdom, with their guards and their armies, had hemmed in the Lamanites on the south, that thereby they should have no more possession on the north, that they might not overrun the land northward.
34. Therefore the Lamanites could have no more possessions only in the land of Nephi, and the wilderness round about. Now this was wisdom in the Nephites—as the Lamanites were an enemy to them, they would not suffer their afflictions on every hand, and also that they might have a country whither they might flee, according to their desires.
35. And now I, after having said this, return again to the account of Ammon and Aaron, Omner and Himni, and their brethren.

CHAPTER 23

1. BEHOLD, now it came to pass that the king of the Lamanites sent a proclamation among all his people, that they should not lay their hands on Ammon, or Aaron, or Omner, or Himni, nor either of their brethren who should go forth preaching the word of God, in whatsoever place

Alma 22:28–33

According to President George Q. Cannon, the Book of Mormon is not a geography primer. Its purpose is to teach spiritual truths, not geographical truths. President Cannon taught that we are not meant to be able to tie the Nephite cities described in the Book of Mormon to current geographies—and attempts to do so tend to confuse instead of enlighten. As we read these physical and geographical descriptions, we can appreciate the distances and the geographical challenges faced by the people of the Book of Mormon, but our focus should be on the spiritual truths contained in its passages.

they should be, in any part of their land.

2. Yea, he sent a decree among them, that they should not lay their hands on them to bind them, or to cast them into prison; neither should they spit upon them, nor smite them, nor cast them out of their synagogues, nor scourge them; neither should they cast stones at them, but that they should have free access to their houses, and also their temples, and their sanctuaries.

3. And thus they might go forth and preach the word according to their desires, for the king had been converted unto the Lord, and all his household; therefore he sent his proclamation throughout the land unto his people, that the word of God might have no obstruction, but that it might go forth throughout all the land, that his people might be convinced concerning the wicked traditions of their fathers, and that they might be convinced that they were all brethren, and that they ought not to murder, nor to plunder, nor to steal, nor to commit adultery, nor to commit any manner of wickedness.

4. And now it came to pass that when the king had sent forth this proclamation, that Aaron and his brethren went forth from city to city, and from one house of worship to another, establishing churches, and consecrating priests and teachers throughout the land among the Lamanites, to preach and to teach the word of God among them; and thus they began to have great success.

5. And thousands were brought to the knowledge of the Lord, yea, thousands were brought to believe in the traditions of the Nephites; and they were taught the records and prophecies which were handed down even to the present time.

6. And as sure as the Lord liveth, so sure as many as believed, or as many as were brought to the knowledge of the truth, through the preaching of Ammon and his brethren, according to the spirit of revelation and of prophecy, and the power of God working miracles in them—yea, I say unto you, as the Lord liveth, as many of the Lamanites as believed in their preaching, and were converted unto the Lord, never did fall away.

7. For they became a righteous people; they did lay down the weapons of their rebellion, that they did not fight against God any more, neither against any of their brethren.

8. Now, these are they who were converted unto the Lord:

9. The people of the Lamanites who were in the land of Ishmael;

10. And also of the people of the Lamanites who were in the land of Middoni;

11. And also of the people of the Lamanites who were in the city of Nephi;

12. And also of the people of the Lamanites who were in the land of Shilom, and who were in the land of Shemlon, and in the city of Lemuel, and in the city of Shimnilom.

13. And these are the names of the cities of the Lamanites which were converted unto the Lord; and these are they that laid down the weapons of their rebellion, yea, all their weapons of war; and they were all Lamanites.

14. And the Amalekites were not

Alma 23:5–6

Conversion to the Lord is a transforming experience, resulting in inner peace and a commitment to follow the commandments. . . . As a result of the adoption of a policy of religious freedom by the reigning king of the realm, many thousands of Lamanites in seven cities were converted through the efforts of the sons of Mosiah.

In defining conversion, Elder Richard G. Scott said, "Stated simply, true conversion is the fruit of faith, repentance, and consistent obedience. . . . True conversion will strengthen your capacity to do what you know you should do, when you should do it, regardless of the circumstances." (P/A)

Alma 23:6

For some Church members, conversion remains an unfulfilled destiny. They may have even had a testimony sometime in the distant past, but they let it decay into a nonexistent state. Or they may have a testimony still, but have concluded they have reached their self-determined pinnacle of spirituality. What they have not done is press on through the cleansing from sin process into the refreshing results of peace provided by the redeeming blood of the Savior. Nor have they continued in righteous obedience. They have presumed that their testimony provided sufficient contentment for them.

President Harold B. Lee taught that conversion is much more when he said, "To become converted, according to the scriptures, meant having a change of heart and the moral character of a person turned from the controlled power of sin into a righteous life. It meant to 'wait patiently on the Lord' until one's prayers can be answered and until his heart, as Cyprian, a defender of the faith in the Apostolic Period, testified, 'Into my heart purified of all sin, there entered a light which came from on high, and then suddenly and in a marvelous manner, I saw certainty succeed doubt.'" (O/C)

Alma 23:6

Whereas authority is conferred, we must personally seek to obtain spiritual power from the heavens. Those who are guided by the Spirit have a power beyond themselves, and are able to be a means by which the Lord can extend His blessings to His children. (O/C)

Alma 23:8–12

These verses demonstrate that the people of the Lamanites who had been taught and who had accepted the gospel were blessed both spiritually and physically. This same thing is true of any nation that opens its doors to the gospel and whose people embrace the truth and covenant to obey the commandments.

converted, save only one; neither were any of the Amulonites; but they did harden their hearts, and also the hearts of the Lamanites in that part of the land wheresoever they dwelt, yea, and all their villages and all their cities.
15. Therefore, we have named all the cities of the Lamanites in which they did repent and come to the knowledge of the truth, and were converted.
16. And now it came to pass that the king and those who were converted were desirous that they might have a name, that thereby they might be distinguished from their brethren; therefore the king consulted with Aaron and many of their priests, concerning the name that they should take upon them, that they might be distinguished.
17. And it came to pass that they called their names Anti-Nephi-Lehies; and they were called by this name and were no more called Lamanites.
18. And they began to be a very industrious people; yea, and they were friendly with the Nephites; therefore, they did open a correspondence with them, and the curse of God did no more follow them.

Alma 23:15

In other cases, the Lord has directed His people to go to war. Examples include the Nephites who fought for their liberty (see Alma 43-62) and the Israelites in the Land of Promise (see Joshua 1:1-9). Essentially, once people become a Zion people, they go to war only when directed to do so by inspiration.

Alma 23:17–18

The Lamanites converted by the four sons of Mosiah and their missionary companions took upon themselves the name of "Anti-Nephi-Lehies." (Alma 23:17; Alma 24:1–5.) The "Nephi-Lehi" part of the title probably had reference to the lands of Nephi and Lehi (or the people then living in those lands) rather than to the descendants of Nephi or Lehi.

However, Dr. Hugh Nibley has found "a Semitic and common Indo-European root corresponding to anti that means 'in the face of' or 'facing,' as of one facing a mirror, and by extension either 'one who opposes' or 'one who imitates.'" Thus the term "Anti-Nephi-Lehies" might refer to those who imitate the teachings of the descendants of Nephi and Lehi. (Ludlow)

CHAPTER 24

1. AND it came to pass that the Amalekites and the Amulonites and the Lamanites who were in the land of Amulon, and also in the land of Helam, and who were in the land of Jerusalem, and in fine, in all the land round about, who had not been converted and had not taken upon them the name of Anti-Nephi-Lehi, were stirred up by the Amalekites and by the Amulonites to anger against their brethren.
2. And their hatred became exceedingly sore against them, even insomuch that they began to rebel against their king, insomuch that they would not that he should be their king; therefore, they took up arms against the people of Anti-Nephi-Lehi.
3. Now the king conferred the kingdom upon his son, and he called his name Anti-Nephi-Lehi.
4. And the king died in that selfsame year that the Lamanites began to make preparations for war against the people of God.
5. Now when Ammon and his brethren and all those who had come up with him saw the preparations of the Lamanites to destroy their brethren, they came forth to the land of Midian, and there Ammon met all his brethren; and from thence they came to the land of Ishmael that they might hold a council with Lamoni and also with his brother Anti-Nephi-Lehi, what they should do to defend themselves against the Lamanites.
6. Now there was not one soul among all the people who had been converted unto the Lord that would take up arms against their brethren; nay, they would not even make any preparations for war; yea, and also their king commanded them that they should not.
7. Now, these are the words which he said unto the people concerning the matter: I thank my God, my beloved people, that our great God has in goodness sent these our brethren, the Nephites, unto us to

Alma 24:6

In other cases, the Lord has drected His people to go to war. Examples include the Nephites, who fought for their liberty (see Alma 43–62), and the Israelites in the land of Promise (see Joshua 1:1–19). Essentially, once people become a Zion people, they go to war only when directed to do so by inspiration.

preach unto us, and to convince us of the traditions of our wicked fathers.
8. And behold, I thank my great God that he has given us a portion of his Spirit to soften our hearts, that we have opened a correspondence with these brethren, the Nephites.
9. And behold, I also thank my God, that by opening this correspondence we have been convinced of our sins, and of the many murders which we have committed.
10. And I also thank my God, yea, my great God, that he hath granted unto us that we might repent of these things, and also that he hath forgiven us of those our many sins and murders which we have committed, and taken away the guilt from our hearts, through the merits of his Son.
11. And now behold, my brethren, since it has been all that we could do, (as we were the most lost of all mankind) to repent of all our sins and the many murders which we have committed, and to get God to take them away from our hearts, for it was all we could do to repent sufficiently before God that he would take away our stain—
12. Now, my best beloved brethren, since God hath taken away our stains, and our swords have become bright, then let us stain our swords no more with the blood of our brethren.
13. Behold, I say unto you, Nay, let us retain our swords that they be not stained with the blood of our brethren; for perhaps, if we should stain our swords again they can no more be washed bright through the blood of the Son of our great God, which shall be shed for the atonement of our sins.
14. And the great God has had mercy on us, and made these things known unto us that we might not perish; yea, and he has made these things known unto us beforehand, because he loveth our souls as well as he loveth our children; therefore, in his mercy he doth visit us by his angels, that the plan of salvation might be made known unto us as well as unto future generations.
15. Oh, how merciful is our God! And now behold, since it has been as much as we could do to get our stains taken away from us, and our swords are made bright, let us hide them away that they may be kept bright, as a testimony to our God at the last day, or at the day that we shall be brought to stand before him to be judged, that we have not stained our swords in the blood of our brethren since he imparted his word unto us and has made us clean thereby.
16. And now, my brethren, if our brethren seek to destroy us, behold, we will hide away our swords, yea, even we will bury them deep in the earth, that they may be kept bright, as a testimony that we have never used them, at the last day; and if our brethren destroy us, behold, we shall go to our God and shall be saved.
17. And now it came to pass that when the king had made an end of these sayings, and all the people were assembled together, they took their swords, and all the weapons which were used for the shedding of man's blood, and they did bury them up deep in the earth.
18. And this they did, it being in their view a testimony to God, and also to men, that they never would use weapons again for the shedding of man's blood; and this they did, vouching and covenanting with God, that rather than shed the

Alma 24:10

King Lamoni expresses his gratitude to God for the opportunity to repent. Guilt had been taken away through the Savior, Jesus Christ. . . . We should never forget the blessing of the principle of repentance. This is a gift from God through our Savior, Jesus Christ. When we repent, we bring joy to the Lord (see D&C 18:13). (P/A)

Alma 24:10–11

In calling his people "the most lost of all mankind," King Lamoni demonstrates a critical principle for us to remember: even the "most lost" can be saved through repentance. Other than the sin of denying the Holy Ghost, no sin is so awful that the sinner cannot partake of the Atonement of Jesus Christ, go through the process of repentance, and enjoy the glorious peace of forgiveness.

Alma 24:16–17

It is entirely possible that this interesting incident could have served as the source of the "bury-the-hatchet" tradition of showing peace, which was a common practice among some of the tribes of American Indians when Columbus and other white men came to their lands. (Ludlow)

Alma 24:17–18

"By this ye may know if a man repenteth of his sins—behold, he will confess them and forsake them" (D&C 58:43). As with the converted Lamanites who entered into a covenant of peace—eschewing the murderous practices they had hitherto embraced—all followers of Christ should repent of their sinful ways and forever abandon those practices that are contrary to the teachings of the Savior. (P/A)

blood of their brethren they would give up their own lives; and rather than take away from a brother they would give unto him; and rather than spend their days in idleness they would labor abundantly with their hands.
19. And thus we see that, when these Lamanites were brought to believe and to know the truth, they were firm, and would suffer even unto death rather than commit sin; and thus we see that they buried their weapons of peace, or they buried the weapons of war, for peace.
20. And it came to pass that their brethren, the Lamanites, made preparations for war, and came up to the land of Nephi for the purpose of destroying the king, and to place another in his stead, and also of destroying the people of Anti-Nephi-Lehi out of the land.
21. Now when the people saw that they were coming against them they went out to meet them, and prostrated themselves before them to the earth, and began to call on the name of the Lord; and thus they were in this attitude when the Lamanites began to fall upon them, and began to slay them with the sword.
22. And thus without meeting any resistance, they did slay a thousand and five of them; and we know that they are blessed, for they have gone to dwell with their God.
23. Now when the Lamanites saw that their brethren would not flee from the sword, neither would they turn aside to the right hand or to the left, but that they would lie down and perish, and praised God even in the very act of perishing under the sword—
24. Now when the Lamanites saw this they did forbear from slaying them; and there were many whose hearts had swollen in them for those of their brethren who had fallen under the sword, for they repented of the things which they had done.
25. And it came to pass that they threw down their weapons of war, and they would not take them again, for they were stung for the murders which they had committed; and they came down even as their brethren, relying upon the mercies of those whose arms were lifted to slay them.
26. And it came to pass that the people of God were joined that day by more than the number who had been slain; and those who had been slain were righteous people, therefore we have no reason to doubt but what they were saved.
27. And there was not a wicked man slain among them; but there were more than a thousand brought to the knowledge of the truth; thus we see that the Lord worketh in many ways to the salvation of his people.
28. Now the greatest number of those of the Lamanites who slew so many of their brethren were Amalekites and Amulonites, the greatest number of whom were after the order of the Nehors.
29. Now, among those who joined the people of the Lord, there were none who were Amalekites or Amulonites, or who were of the order of Nehor, but they were actual descendants of Laman and Lemuel.
30. And thus we can plainly discern, that after a people have been once enlightened by the Spirit of God, and have had great knowledge of things pertaining to righteousness, and then have fallen away into

Alma 24:19

. . . we must remember that we don't change any faster than we make and keep commitments. The Lord calls them covenants. Our exaltation is determined by how well we have kept our . . . covenants. And when we keep those covenants, the promises and blessings are ours. . . . When covenants are deepened because our commitment is strong, our lives are different. If in your lives you find yourselves vacillating, look deep into your souls and check your level of commitment to your covenants. And when your level of commitment to your covenants has deepened to where you feel that it is life eternal to keep them, you will be a missionary for life. You will help many souls come unto Christ. . . . Our blessings here and hereafter are dependent upon keeping the covenants we make with God. . . . (P/A)

Alma 24:19

Mormon wrote his abridgment of the large plates of Nephi on "plates of ore" that he had made with his own hands. He does not mention the technique used in writing the language characters on the metal plates (etching, embossing, etc.), but students have sometimes wondered how Mormon could correct something he had already written. Alma 24:19 might give us some clue to this matter. Concerning the converted Lamanites, Mormon had written that "they buried their weapons of peace." Then, evidently realizing that he had not intended exactly what he had written, he added "or they buried the weapons of war, for peace." Other examples of similar changes in the Book of Mormon are found in Mosiah 7:8, Alma 50:32, Helaman 3:33, and 3 Nephi 16:4. (Ludlow)

Alma 24:29

The Prophet Joseph Smith shared the principle of leaving neutral ground, after being enlightened with divine light and truth. . . . "Before you joined this Church you stood on neutral ground. When the gospel was preached, good and evil were set before you. You could choose either or neither. There were two opposite masters inviting you to serve them. When you joined this Church you enlisted to serve God. When you did that you left the neutral ground, and you never can get back on to it. Should you forsake the Master you enlisted to serve, it will be by the instigation of the evil one, and you will follow his dictation and be his servant." (O/C)

sin and transgression, they become more hardened, and thus their state becomes worse than though they had never known these things.

CHAPTER 25

1. AND behold, now it came to pass that those Lamanites were more angry because they had slain their brethren; therefore they swore vengeance upon the Nephites; and they did no more attempt to slay the people of Anti-Nephi-Lehi at that time.
2. But they took their armies and went over into the borders of the land of Zarahemla, and fell upon the people who were in the land of Ammonihah and destroyed them.
3. And after that, they had many battles with the Nephites, in the which they were driven and slain.
4. And among the Lamanites who were slain were almost all the seed of Amulon and his brethren, who were the priests of Noah, and they were slain by the hands of the Nephites;
5. And the remainder, having fled into the east wilderness, and having usurped the power and authority over the Lamanites, caused that many of the Lamanites should perish by fire because of their belief—
6. For many of them, after having suffered much loss and so many afflictions, began to be stirred up in remembrance of the words which Aaron and his brethren had preached to them in their land; therefore they began to disbelieve the traditions of their fathers, and to believe in the Lord, and that he gave great power unto the Nephites; and thus there were many of them converted in the wilderness.
7. And it came to pass that those rulers who were the remnant of the children of Amulon caused that they should be put to death, yea, all those that believed in these things.
8. Now this martyrdom caused that many of their brethren should be stirred up to anger; and there began to be contention in the wilderness; and the Lamanites began to hunt the seed of Amulon and his brethren and began to slay them; and they fled into the east wilderness.
9. And behold they are hunted at this day by the Lamanites. Thus the words of Abinadi were brought to pass, which he said concerning the seed of the priests who caused that he should suffer death by fire.
10. For he said unto them: What ye shall do unto me shall be a type of things to come.
11. And now Abinadi was the first that suffered death by fire because of his belief in God; now this is what he meant, that many should suffer death by fire, according as he had suffered.
12. And he said unto the priests of Noah that their seed should cause many to be put to death, in the like manner as he was, and that they should be scattered abroad and slain, even as a sheep having no shepherd is driven and slain by wild beasts; and now behold, these words were verified, for they were driven by the Lamanites, and they were hunted, and they were smitten.
13. And it came to pass that when

Alma 25:4

Slaying almost all the seed of Amulon—who were the wicked priests of Noah—was a direct fulfillment of the prophecy of Abinadi upon the wicked priests of Noah (see Mosiah 17:15-20).

Alma 25:9–11

Regarding the slaying of the wicked priests of Noah, some have claimed that such was no more than a natural consequence—certainly not the fulfillment of prophecy. Such a claim is a powerful example of how Satan blinds us to the truth.

the Lamanites saw that they could not overpower the Nephites they returned again to their own land; and many of them came over to dwell in the land of Ishmael and the land of Nephi, and did join themselves to the people of God, who were the people of Anti-Nephi-Lehi.

14. And they did also bury their weapons of war, according as their brethren had, and they began to be a righteous people; and they did walk in the ways of the Lord, and did observe to keep his commandments and his statutes.

15. Yea, and they did keep the law of Moses; for it was expedient that they should keep the law of Moses as yet, for it was not all fulfilled. But notwithstanding the law of Moses, they did look forward to the coming of Christ, considering that the law of Moses was a type of his coming, and believing that they must keep those outward performances until the time that he should be revealed unto them.

16. Now they did not suppose that salvation came by the law of Moses; but the law of Moses did serve to strengthen their faith in Christ; and thus they did retain a hope through faith, unto eternal salvation, relying upon the spirit of prophecy, which spake of those things to come.

17. And now behold, Ammon, and Aaron, and Omner, and Himni, and their brethren did rejoice exceedingly, for the success which they had had among the Lamanites, seeing that the Lord had granted unto them according to their prayers, and that he had also verified his word unto them in every particular.

CHAPTER 26

1. AND now, these are the words of Ammon to his brethren, which say thus: My brothers and my brethren, behold I say unto you, how great reason have we to rejoice; for could we have supposed when we started from the land of Zarahemla that God would have granted unto us such great blessings?

2. And now, I ask, what great blessings has he bestowed upon us? Can ye tell?

3. Behold, I answer for you; for our brethren, the Lamanites, were in darkness, yea, even in the darkest abyss, but behold, how many of them are brought to behold the marvelous light of God! And this is the blessing which hath been bestowed upon us, that we have been made instruments in the hands of God to bring about this great work.

4. Behold, thousands of them do rejoice, and have been brought into the fold of God.

5. Behold, the field was ripe, and blessed are ye, for ye did thrust in the sickle, and did reap with your might, yea, all the day long did ye labor; and behold the number of your sheaves! And they shall be

Alma 25:14

The converted Lamanites faithfully kept the Law of Moses because they were commanded to do so—even though they believed a greater law would come with Jesus Christ. There are many evidences throughout this section of the Book of Mormon that they were blessed as a result of their obedience.

Alma 25:15

A "type"—used to describe the Law of Moses in this verse—means a representation. In other words, the Law of Moses was a representation of what the Savior would bring.

Alma 25:17

The greatest lesson we can take away from this section of the Book of Mormon is that the Lord always keeps His promises. He had promised Ammon, Aaron, Omner, Himni, and their brethren that He would deliver them from the Lamanites who did not convert to the truth—and He did exactly as He promised.

Alma 26:2–3

According to Elder Bruce R. McConkie, those who accept the gospel and begin living according to its principles move from darkness into light—much as what is described here. The "marvelous light of God" referred to in this verse is the gospel of Christ (see 2 Corinthians 4:4-6).

Alma 26:5

The word *sheaves* in this verse refers to converts who are brought into the Church.

gathered into the garners, that they are not wasted.
6. Yea, they shall not be beaten down by the storm at the last day; yea, neither shall they be harrowed up by the whirlwinds; but when the storm cometh they shall be gathered together in their place, that the storm cannot penetrate to them; yea, neither shall they be driven with fierce winds whithersoever the enemy listeth to carry them.
7. But behold, they are in the hands of the Lord of the harvest, and they are his; and he will raise them up at the last day.
8. Blessed be the name of our God; let us sing to his praise, yea, let us give thanks to his holy name, for he doth work righteousness forever.
9. For if we had not come up out of the land of Zarahemla, these our dearly beloved brethren, who have so dearly beloved us, would still have been racked with hatred against us, yea, and they would also have been strangers to God.
10. And it came to pass that when Ammon had said these words, his brother Aaron rebuked him, saying: Ammon, I fear that thy joy doth carry thee away unto boasting.
11. But Ammon said unto him: I do not boast in my own strength, nor in my own wisdom; but behold, my joy is full, yea, my heart is brim with joy, and I will rejoice in my God.
12. Yea, I know that I am nothing; as to my strength I am weak; therefore I will not boast of myself, but I will boast of my God, for in his strength I can do all things; yea, behold, many mighty miracles we have wrought in this land, for which we will praise his name forever.
13. Behold, how many thousands of our brethren has he loosed from the pains of hell; and they are brought to sing redeeming love, and this because of the power of his word which is in us, therefore have we not great reason to rejoice?
14. Yea, we have reason to praise him forever, for he is the Most High God, and has loosed our brethren from the chains of hell.
15. Yea, they were encircled about with everlasting darkness and destruction; but behold, he has brought them into his everlasting light, yea, into everlasting salvation; and they are encircled about with the matchless bounty of his love; yea, and we have been instruments in his hands of doing this great and marvelous work.
16. Therefore, let us glory, yea, we will glory in the Lord; yea, we will rejoice, for our joy is full; yea, we will praise our God forever. Behold, who can glory too much in the Lord? Yea, who can say too much of his great power, and of his mercy, and of his long-suffering towards the children of men? Behold, I say unto you, I cannot say the smallest part which I feel.
17. Who could have supposed that our God would have been so merciful as to have snatched us from our awful, sinful, and polluted state?
18. Behold, we went forth even in

Alma 26:6

This verse details those blessings that will be given to those who accept the gospel and remain faithful. These promises have special application for us in our day as we face the disasters and tribulations that will precede the Savior's Second Coming.

Alma 26:11–14

In answering Aaron's charges that he might be boasting, Ammon takes no glory for himself; instead, he credits the Lord completely with the success of their missionary labors. It is critical for us to remember that the Lord is not dependent on us—we are dependent on the Lord. He can do all things; in contrast, we can do nothing without Him. A great example of this principle is what happened to Oliver Cowdery: he thought the Church would fall without him. Instead, he fell when he left the Church.

Alma 26:12

Brigham Young once said that he would rather hear five words spoken with the power of the Spirit than an entire sermon spoken without it.

Alma 26:14–15

As every missionary who has ever taught an investigator probably knows, we are able to teach and convince—but only the power of God, or the Spirit, can truly convert.

wrath, with mighty threatenings to destroy his church.
19. Oh then, why did he not consign us to an awful destruction,
yea, why did he not let the sword of his justice fall upon us, and
doom us to eternal despair?
20. Oh, my soul, almost as it were, fleeth at the thought. Behold,
he did not exercise his justice upon us, but in his great mercy hath
brought us over that everlasting gulf of death and misery, even to
the salvation of our souls.
21. And now behold, my brethren, what natural man is there that
knoweth these things? I say unto you, there is none that knoweth
these things, save it be the penitent.
22. Yea, he that repenteth and exerciseth faith, and bringeth forth
good works, and prayeth continually without ceasing—unto such
it is given to know the mysteries of God; yea, unto such it shall be
given to reveal things which never have been revealed; yea, and it
shall be given unto such to bring thousands of souls to repentance,
even as it has been given unto us to bring these our brethren to
repentance.
23. Now do ye remember, my brethren, that we said unto our
brethren in the land of Zarahemla, we go up to the land of Nephi,
to preach unto our brethren, the Lamanites, and they laughed us
to scorn?
24. For they said unto us: Do ye suppose that ye can bring the
Lamanites to the knowledge of the truth? Do ye suppose that ye can
convince the Lamanites of the incorrectness of the traditions of their
fathers, as stiffnecked a people as they are; whose hearts delight in the
shedding of blood; whose days have been spent in the grossest iniquity; whose ways have been the ways of a transgressor from the beginning? Now my brethren, ye remember that this was their language.
25. And moreover they did say: Let us take up arms against them,
that we destroy them and their iniquity out of the land, lest they
overrun us and destroy us.
26. But behold, my beloved brethren, we came into the wilderness
not with the intent to destroy our brethren, but with the intent
that perhaps we might save some few of their souls.
27. Now when our hearts were depressed, and we were about to
turn back, behold, the Lord comforted us, and said: Go amongst
thy brethren, the Lamanites, and bear with patience thine afflictions, and I will give unto you success.
28. And now behold, we have come, and been forth amongst
them; and we have been patient in our sufferings, and we have suffered every privation; yea, we have traveled from house to house,
relying upon the mercies of the world—not upon the mercies of
the world alone but upon the mercies of God.
29. And we have entered into their houses and taught them, and
we have taught them in their streets; yea, and we have taught them
upon their hills; and we have also entered into their temples and
their synagogues and taught them; and we have been cast out, and
mocked, and spit upon, and smote upon our

Alma 26:21–22

The truths of the gospel are plain and simple to understand to those who have the Spirit. As President Joseph Fielding Smith taught, the best scholars in the world may not be able to comprehend simple gospel truths because their spirits are not in tune. Verse 22 outlines the things we need to do to have great understanding and to accomplish mighty works.

Alma 26:27

Great satisfaction comes from investing our talents in full measure to the building up of the kingdom of God. . . .

Mormon preserves for us the intimate and confessional expressions of Alma as he describes the rich feelings of being a committed missionary servant of the Lord. Alma had a great desire to preach the gospel to the whole world, and thus allows himself for a moment to wish for extramortal powers to reach the many: "O that I were an angel" (Alma 29:1). But then he repents of his zeal and glories in being just a mortal (albeit one of great prophetic gifts!) and confirms his gratitude before the Lord just to be able to do his job to the best of his ability. Missionary work was his joy and glory, and he also felt joy in the success of others.

Elder Henry B. Eyring said, "Pray for the chance to encounter people who sense there could be something better in their lives. Pray to know what you should do to help them. Your prayers will be answered. You will meet people prepared by the Lord." (P/A)

cheeks; and we have been stoned, and taken and bound with strong cords, and cast into prison; and through the power and wisdom of God we have been delivered again.
30. And we have suffered all manner of afflictions, and all this, that perhaps we might be the means of saving some soul; and we supposed that our joy would be full if perhaps we could be the means of saving some.
31. Now behold, we can look forth and see the fruits of our labors; and are they few? I say unto you, Nay, they are many; yea, and we can witness of their sincerity, because of their love towards their brethren and also towards us.
32. For behold, they had rather sacrifice their lives than even to take the life of their enemy; and they have buried their weapons of war deep in the earth, because of their love towards their brethren.
33. And now behold I say unto you, has there been so great love in all the land? Behold, I say unto you, Nay, there has not, even among the Nephites.
34. For behold, they would take up arms against their brethren; they would not suffer themselves to be slain. But behold how many of these have laid down their lives; and we know that they have gone to their God, because of their love and of their hatred to sin.
35. Now have we not reason to rejoice? Yea, I say unto you, there never were men that had so great reason to rejoice as we, since the world began; yea, and my joy is carried away, even unto boasting in my God; for he has all power, all wisdom, and all understanding; he comprehendeth all things, and he is a merciful Being, even unto salvation, to those who will repent and believe on his name.
36. Now if this is boasting, even so will I boast; for this is my life and my light, my joy and my salvation, and my redemption from everlasting wo. Yea, blessed is the name of my God, who has been mindful of this people, who are a branch of the tree of Israel, and has been lost from its body in a strange land; yea, I say, blessed be the name of my God, who has been mindful of us, wanderers in a strange land.
37. Now my brethren, we see that God is mindful of every people, whatsoever land they may be in; yea, he numbereth his people, and his bowels of mercy are over all the earth. Now this is my joy, and my great thanksgiving; yea, and I will give thanks unto my God forever. Amen.

CHAPTER 27

1. NOW it came to pass that when those Lamanites who had gone to war against the Nephites had found, after their many struggles to destroy them, that it was in vain to seek their destruction, they returned again to the land of Nephi.
2. And it came to pass that the Amalekites, because of their loss, were exceedingly angry. And when they saw that they could not seek revenge from the Nephites, they began to stir up the people in anger

Alma 26:30

In an expressive outpouring of emotion, Ammon recounted before his brethren the trials and blessings of their missionary labors and rejoiced in the triumphs of conversion presided over by "the Lord of the harvest" (Alma 26:7). Aaron suspected that Ammon was carried away "unto boasting" (Alma 26:10), but Ammon assured him that he was fully aware of his nothingness, and only wished to glorify God, "for in his strength I can do all things" (Alma 26:12).

President Ezra Taft Benson said, "The Lord has said that no one can assist with this work unless he is humble and full of love. . . . But humility does not mean weakness. It does not mean timidity; it does not mean fear. A man can be humble and also fearless.

A man can be humble and also courageous. Humility is the recognition of our dependence upon a higher power, a constant need for the Lord's support in His work. . . ." (P/A)

Alma 26:35

This verse details some of the characteristics of God and is one of many sources we can look to for an idea of what God is like. Joseph Smith taught that the thing that sets us apart from the beasts is our ability to know God. He also taught that if we do not comprehend the character of God, we can never comprehend ourselves.

Alma 26:37

Orson F. Whitney . . . beautifully expressed the love and concern our Heavenly Father has for all His children.

"All down the ages men bearing the authority of the Holy Priesthood—patriarchs, prophets, apostles and others, have officiated in the name of the Lord, doing the things that he required of them; and outside the pale of their activities other good and great men, not bearing the priesthood, but possessing profundity of thought, great wisdom, and a desire to uplift their fellows, have been sent by the Almighty into many nations, to give them, not the fulness of the gospel, but that portion of truth that they were able to receive and wisely use. Such men as Confucius, the Chinese philosopher; Zoroaster, the Persian sage; Guatama, or Buddha, of the Hindus; Socrates and Plato, of the Greeks; these all had some of the light that is universally diffused. . . .They were servants of the Lord in a lesser sense, and were sent to those . . . nations to give them the measure of truth that a wise Providence had allotted to them.

"And not only teachers—not poets and philosophers alone; but inventors, discoverers, warriors, statesmen, rulers, et al. These also have been used from the beginning to help along the Lord's word—mighty auxiliaries in the hands of an Almighty God, carrying out his purposes, consciously or unconsciously." (O/C)

against their brethren, the people of Anti-Nephi-Lehi; therefore they began again to destroy them.
3. Now this people again refused to take their arms, and they suffered themselves to be slain according to the desires of their enemies.
4. Now when Ammon and his brethren saw this work of destruction among those whom they so dearly beloved, and among those who had so dearly beloved them—for they were treated as though they were angels sent from God to save them from everlasting destruction—therefore, when Ammon and his brethren saw this great work of destruction, they were moved with compassion, and they said unto the king:
5. Let us gather together this people of the Lord, and let us go down to the land of Zarahemla to our brethren the Nephites, and flee out of the hands of our enemies, that we be not destroyed.
6. But the king said unto them: Behold, the Nephites will destroy us, because of the many murders and sins we have committed against them.
7. And Ammon said: I will go and inquire of the Lord, and if he say unto us, go down unto our brethren, will ye go?
8. And the king said unto him: Yea, if the Lord saith unto us go, we will go down unto our brethren, and we will be their slaves until we repair unto them the many murders and sins which we have committed against them.
9. But Ammon said unto him: It is against the law of our brethren, which was established by my father, that there should be any slaves among them; therefore let us go down and rely upon the mercies of our brethren.
10. But the king said unto him: Inquire of the Lord, and if he saith unto us go, we will go; otherwise we will perish in the land.
11. And it came to pass that Ammon went and inquired of the Lord, and the Lord said unto him:
12. Get this people out of this land, that they perish not; for Satan has great hold on the hearts of the Amalekites, who do stir up the Lamanites to anger against their brethren to slay them; therefore get thee out of this land; and blessed are this people in this generation, for I will preserve them.
13. And now it came to pass that Ammon went and told the king all the words which the Lord had said unto him.
14. And they gathered together all their people, yea, all the people of the Lord, and did gather together all their flocks and herds, and departed out of the land, and came into the wilderness which divided the land of Nephi from the land of Zarahemla, and came over near the borders of the land.
15. And it came to pass that Ammon said unto them: Behold, I and my brethren will go forth into the land of Zarahemla, and ye shall remain here until we return; and we will try the hearts of our brethren, whether they will that ye shall come into their land.
16. And it came to pass that as Ammon was going forth into the land, that he and his brethren met Alma, over in the place of which has been spoken; and behold, this was a joyful meeting.
17. Now the joy of Ammon was so great even that he was full; yea, he was swallowed up in the joy of his God, even to the exhausting of his strength; and he fell again to the earth.

Alma 27:4–5

Ammon exhibited a true missionary spirit because, as is shown in these verses, he was concerned with both the spiritual and temporal well-being of those he converted. This is demonstrated by his desire to help the converts relocate to the land of Zarahemla, where they would be welcomed by the Nephites.

Alma 27:7–8

When Ammon's plan to relocate the converts to the land of Zarahemla was met with resistance from the king, he offered to take the matter to the Lord—a concept that the king felt comfortable with. This reaction on Ammon's part demonstrates how important it is for us to take matters of concern to our Heavenly Father in prayer and to accept and do His will once it is revealed to us.

Alma 27:16

The "joyful meeting" referred to in this verse was first described in Alma 17:1–2.

18. Now was not this exceeding joy? Behold, this is joy which none receiveth save it be the truly penitent and humble seeker of happiness.
19. Now the joy of Alma in meeting his brethren was truly great, and also the joy of Aaron, of Omner, and Himni; but behold their joy was not that to exceed their strength.
20. And now it came to pass that Alma conducted his brethren back to the land of Zarahemla; even to his own house. And they went and told the chief judge all the things that had happened unto them in the land of Nephi, among their brethren, the Lamanites.
21. And it came to pass that the chief judge sent a proclamation throughout all the land, desiring the voice of the people concerning the admitting their brethren, who were the people of Anti-Nephi-Lehi.
22. And it came to pass that the voice of the people came, saying: Behold, we will give up the land of Jershon, which is on the east by the sea, which joins the land Bountiful, which is on the south of the land Bountiful; and this land Jershon is the land which we will give unto our brethren for an inheritance.
23. And behold, we will set our armies between the land Jershon and the land Nephi, that we may protect our brethren in the land Jershon; and this we do for our brethren, on account of their fear to take up arms against their brethren lest they should commit sin; and this their great fear came because of their sore repentance which they had, on account of their many murders and their awful wickedness.
24. And now behold, this will we do unto our brethren, that they may inherit the land Jershon; and we will guard them from their enemies with our armies, on condition that they will give us a portion of their substance to assist us that we may maintain our armies.
25. Now, it came to pass that when Ammon had heard this, he returned to the people of Anti-Nephi-Lehi, and also Alma with him, into the wilderness, where they had pitched their tents, and made known unto them all these things. And Alma also related unto them his conversion, with Ammon and Aaron, and his brethren.
26. And it came to pass that it did cause great joy among them. And they went down into the land of Jershon, and took possession of the land of Jershon; and they were called by the Nephites the people of Ammon; therefore they were distinguished by that name ever after.
27. And they were among the people of Nephi, and also numbered among the people who were of the church of God. And they were also distinguished for their zeal towards God, and also towards men; for they were perfectly honest and upright in all things; and they were firm in the faith of Christ, even unto the end.
28. And they did look upon shedding the blood of their brethren with the greatest abhorrence; and they never could be prevailed upon to take up arms against their brethren; and they never did look upon death with any degree of terror, for their hope and views of Christ and the resurrection; therefore, death was swallowed up to them by the victory of Christ over it.
29. Therefore, they would suffer

Alma 27:22

This verse indicates that the people of Anti-Nephi-Lehi expressed willingness to give up the land of Jershon. Jershon is a Hebrew word for "land of the expelled" or "land of the strangers."

Alma 27:26–28

These verses demonstrate the power of true conversion. The characteristics in these verses describe the converted Lamanites—who were once described as a wild, hardened, ferocious people who delighted in robbing and plundering. As a converted people, we see them described as being distinguished for their zeal toward God and toward men, perfectly honest and upright in all things, firm in the faith of Christ. Once described as a people who delighted in murdering, these converted Lamanites are described as people who looked upon the shedding of the blood of their brethren with "the greatest abhorrence," people who "never could be prevailed upon to take up arms against their brethren." This is the power that true conversion has over the soul!

death in the most aggravating and distressing manner which could be inflicted by their brethren, before they would take the sword or cimeter to smite them.

30. And thus they were a zealous and beloved people, a highly favored people of the Lord.

CHAPTER 28

1. AND now it came to pass that after the people of Ammon were established in the land of Jershon, and a church also established in the land of Jershon, and the armies of the Nephites were set round about the land of Jershon, yea, in all the borders round about the land of Zarahemla; behold the armies of the Lamanites had followed their brethren into the wilderness.

2. And thus there was a tremendous battle; yea, even such an one as never had been known among all the people in the land from the time Lehi left Jerusalem; yea, and tens of thousands of the Lamanites were slain and scattered abroad.

3. Yea, and also there was a tremendous slaughter among the people of Nephi; nevertheless, the Lamanites were driven and scattered, and the people of Nephi returned again to their land.

4. And now this was a time that there was a great mourning and lamentation heard throughout all the land, among all the people of Nephi—

5. Yea, the cry of widows mourning for their husbands, and also of fathers mourning for their sons, and the daughter for the brother, yea, the brother for the father; and thus the cry of mourning was heard among all of them, mourning for their kindred who had been slain.

6. And now surely this was a sorrowful day; yea, a time of solemnity, and a time of much fasting and prayer.

7. And thus endeth the fifteenth year of the reign of the judges over the people of Nephi;

8. And this is the account of Ammon and his brethren, their journeyings in the land of Nephi, their sufferings in the land, their sorrows, and their afflictions, and their incomprehensible joy, and the reception and safety of the brethren in the land of Jershon. And now may the Lord, the Redeemer of all men, bless their souls forever.

9. And this is the account of the wars and contentions among the Nephites, and also the wars between the Nephites and the Lamanites; and the fifteenth year of the reign of the judges is ended.

10. And from the first year to the fifteenth has brought to pass the destruction of many thousand lives; yea, it has brought to pass an awful scene of bloodshed.

11. And the bodies of many thousands are laid low in the earth, while the bodies of many thousands are moldering in heaps upon the face of the earth; yea, and many thousands are mourning for the loss of their kindred, because they have reason to fear, according to the promises of the Lord, that they are consigned to a state of endless wo.

12. While many thousands of others truly mourn for the loss of their kindred, yet they rejoice and exult in the hope, and even know, according to the promises of the Lord, that

Alma 28:2

In commenting on this and other descriptions of the great battles of the Book of Mormon, the Prophet Joseph Smith was prompted to reflect on the blessings of the Resurrection: "The expectation of seeing my friends in the morning of the resurrection cheers my soul and makes me bear up against the evils of life. It is like their taking a long journey, and on their return we meet them with increased joy."

POINT OF INTEREST

Because scholars did not know of any Hebrew root of the name Alma, it was for years considered to be a feminine form of a Latin root that meant "to nurture." Scholars have since found that Alma does appear in Hebrew documents from A.D. 130, or the Bar Kochba period. In that period, we find the masculine name spelled 'Im' (Alma).

they are raised to dwell at the right hand of God, in a state of never-ending happiness.

13. And thus we see how great the inequality of man is because of sin and transgression, and the power of the devil, which comes by the cunning plans which he hath devised to ensnare the hearts of men.

14. And thus we see the great call of diligence of men to labor in the vineyards of the Lord; and thus we see the great reason of sorrow, and also of rejoicing—sorrow because of death and destruction among men, and joy because of the light of Christ unto life.

CHAPTER 29

1. O THAT I were an angel, and could have the wish of mine heart, that I might go forth and speak with the trump of God, with a voice to shake the earth, and cry repentance unto every people!

2. Yea, I would declare unto every soul, as with the voice of thunder, repentance and the plan of redemption, that they should repent and come unto our God, that there might not be more sorrow upon all the face of the earth.

3. But behold, I am a man, and do sin in my wish; for I ought to be content with the things which the Lord hath allotted unto me.

4. I ought not to harrow up in my desires, the firm decree of a just God, for I know that he granteth unto men according to their desire, whether it be unto death or unto life; yea, I know that he allotteth unto men, yea, decreeth unto them decrees which are unalterable, according to their wills, whether they be unto salvation or unto destruction.

5. Yea, and I know that good and evil have come before all men; he that knoweth not good from evil is blameless; but he that knoweth good and evil, to him it is given according to his desires, whether he desireth good or evil, life or death, joy or remorse of conscience.

6. Now, seeing that I know these things, why should I desire more than to perform the work to which I have been called?

7. Why should I desire that I were an angel, that I could speak unto all the ends of the earth?

8. For behold, the Lord doth grant unto all nations, of their own nation and tongue, to teach his word, yea, in wisdom, all that he seeth fit that they should have; therefore we see that the Lord doth counsel in wisdom, according to that which is just and true.

9. I know that which the Lord hath commanded me, and I glory in it. I do not glory of myself, but I glory in that which the Lord hath commanded me; yea, and this is my glory, that perhaps I may be an instrument in the hands of God to bring some soul to repentance; and this is my joy.

10. And behold, when I see many of my brethren truly penitent, and coming to the Lord their God, then is my soul filled with joy; then do I remember what the Lord has done

Alma 28:14

Alma and the sons of Mosiah stand as beacons of light to show us the blessings of missionary work. They were truly instruments in the hands of God. They were ready to be used, they had a strong desire to serve, they were clean and pure, they knew their purpose, and they trusted in the Lord. They worked with all their heart, might, mind, and strength. They thrust in their sickles, and many souls were saved. We too can be instruments in the hands of God. . . . In everything we do, every day of our lives, we should ask the question, "Whom can I bless? How can I serve?" (P/A)

Alma 29:4–5

It should be understood that God is a just God. He has given His children moral agency. They can choose good or evil and are free to choose eternal life or spiritual death. They are totally free to exercise their wills according to the desires of their hearts. Once choices have been made, wills and desires expressed to the satisfaction of the individual, God will grant unto them the desires of their hearts. . . .

One of the great blessings of being obedient to God is that our desires are schooled in things pertaining to righteousness. Joseph F. Smith declared that God's ways of educating our desires are the most perfect. (O/C)

Alma 29:8

Sometimes it is difficult to understand why some groups of people are given so much more knowledge than other groups, especially when one remembers we are all children of our Heavenly Father and thus are spiritual knowledge and those opportunities which we have. Thus, simply because one group of people has less knowledge or understanding than another does not mean they are less worthy or righteous . . . We should not presume to judge why God deals with nations the way that he does, but should acknowledge that this is all done in the wisdom and justice of God. (Ludlow)

for me, yea, even that he hath heard my prayer; yea, then do I remember his merciful arm which he extended towards me.
11. Yea, and I also remember the captivity of my fathers; for I surely do know that the Lord did deliver them out of bondage, and by this did establish his church; yea, the Lord God, the God of Abraham, the God of Isaac, and the God of Jacob, did deliver them out of bondage.
12. Yea, I have always remembered the captivity of my fathers; and that same God who delivered them out of the hands of the Egyptians did deliver them out of bondage.
13. Yea, and that same God did establish his church among them; yea, and that same God hath called me by a holy calling, to preach the word unto this people, and hath given me much success, in the which my joy is full.
14. But I do not joy in my own success alone, but my joy is more full because of the success of my brethren, who have been up to the land of Nephi.
15. Behold, they have labored exceedingly, and have brought forth much fruit; and how great shall be their reward!
16. Now, when I think of the success of these my brethren my soul is carried away, even to the separation of it from the body, as it were, so great is my joy.
17. And now may God grant unto these, my brethren, that they may sit down in the kingdom of God; yea, and also all those who are the fruit of their labors that they may go no more out, but that they may praise him forever. And may God grant that it may be done according to my words, even as I have spoken. Amen.

CHAPTER 30

1. BEHOLD, now it came to pass that after the people of Ammon were established in the land of Jershon, yea, and also after the Lamanites were driven out of the land, and their dead were buried by the people of the land—
2. Now their dead were not numbered because of the greatness of their numbers; neither were the dead of the Nephites numbered—but it came to pass after they had buried their dead, and also after the days of fasting, and mourning, and prayer, (and it was in the sixteenth year of the reign of the judges over the people of Nephi) there began to be continual peace throughout all the land.
3. Yea, and the people did observe to keep the commandments of the Lord; and they were strict in observing the ordinances of God, according to the law of Moses; for they were taught to keep the law of Moses until it should be fulfilled.
4. And thus the people did have no disturbance in all the sixteenth year of the reign of the judges over the people of Nephi.
5. And it came to pass that in the commencement of the seventeenth year of the reign of the judges, there was continual peace.
6. But it came to pass in the latter end of the seventeenth year, there came a man into the land of Zarahemla,

Alma 30:2

Excessive mourning over the loss of a loved one can indicate spiritual instability; proper mourning is demonstrated in Job 1:21. According to Elder Bruce R. McConkie, mourning is bad only when the mourner refuses to find comfort and solace in the gospel.

Alma 30:6

The definition of an anti-Christ is someone who denies Christ (see 1 John 4:2-3). It is the content of this person's message—that there is no Christ—that makes him an anti-Christ, not his character or his behavior. President Ezra Taft Benson said, "The Book of Mormon exposes the enemies of Christ. It confounds false doctrine and lays down contention. It fortifies the humble followers of Christ against the evil designs, strategies, and doctrines in our day. The type of apostates in the Book of Mormon are similar to the type we have today. God, with His infinite foreknowledge, so molded the Book of Mormon that we might see the error and know how to combat false educational, political, religious, and philosophical concepts of our time."

Alma 30:6–59

The teachings of the anti-Christs in the Book of Mormon are essentially the same, although Korihor adds a few teachings to those proposed by Nehor. . . In essence, Korihor denies the existence of God, the need for a Savior, the power of the priesthood, and the power of prophecy. He apparently accepts only those things which he can perceive through the five physical senses. (Ludlow)

and he was Anti-Christ, for he began to preach unto the people against the prophecies which had been spoken by the prophets, concerning the coming of Christ.
7. Now there was no law against a man's belief; for it was strictly contrary to the commands of God that there should be a law which should bring men on to unequal grounds.
8. For thus saith the scripture: Choose ye this day, whom ye will serve.
9. Now if a man desired to serve God, it was his privilege; or rather, if he believed in God it was his privilege to serve him; but if he did not believe in him there was no law to punish him.
10. But if he murdered he was punished unto death; and if he robbed he was also punished; and if he stole he was also punished; and if he committed adultery he was also punished; yea, for all this wickedness they were punished.
11. For there was a law that men should be judged according to their crimes. Nevertheless, there was no law against a man's belief; therefore, a man was punished only for the crimes which he had done; therefore all men were on equal grounds.
12. And this Anti-Christ, whose name was Korihor, (and the law could have no hold upon him) began to preach unto the people that there should be no Christ. And after this manner did he preach, saying:
13. O ye that are bound down under a foolish and a vain hope, why do ye yoke yourselves with such foolish things? Why do ye look for a Christ? For no man can know of anything which is to come.
14. Behold, these things which ye call prophecies, which ye say are handed down by holy prophets, behold, they are foolish traditions of your fathers.
15. How do ye know of their surety? Behold, ye cannot know of things which ye do not see; therefore ye cannot know that there shall be a Christ.
16. Ye look forward and say that ye see a remission of your sins. But behold, it is the effect of a frenzied mind; and this derangement of your minds comes because of the traditions of your fathers, which lead you away into a belief of things which are not so.
17. And many more such things did he say unto them, telling them that there could be no atonement made for the sins of men, but every man fared in this life according to the management of the creature; therefore every man prospered according to his genius, and that every man conquered according to his strength; and whatsoever a man did was no crime.
18. And thus he did preach unto them, leading away the hearts of many, causing them to lift up their heads in their wickedness, yea, leading away many women, and also men, to commit whoredoms—telling them that when a man was dead, that was the end thereof.
19. Now this man went over to the land of Jershon also, to preach these things among the people of Ammon, who were once the people of the Lamanites.
20. But behold they were more wise than many of the Nephites; for they took him, and bound him, and carried him before Ammon, who was a high priest over that people.

Alma 30:12–13

Korihor exemplifies all of the false teachings of the devil in the form of misguided philosophies and sophistries of man. Anything that takes us away from our Savior is anti-Christ, whether it is found in magazines, newspapers, books, movies, television, videos, the Internet, or in sinister and alluring relationships. Anti-Christ temptations abound everywhere, for the devil is busy. The Lord has instructed us to fortify ourselves with the armor of Christ to withstand the temptations and every form of anti-Christian teaching. By studying the inspired strategies of Alma for vanquishing the onslaught of pernicious minds such as that of Korihor, we can learn how to take a stand for truth in the world and deflect "all the fiery darts of the wicked" (D&C 27:17). (P/A)

Alma 30:16

Some professionals maintain that you can only determine acceptability of teachings on the basis of behavioral observation or through the physical senses, such as sight, sound, touch, etc. . . . If something is not within the boundaries of known law or evidence, it is considered to be ". . . the effect of a frenzied [or deranged] mind.". . . Generally speaking, those who suggest this as the sole method of acquiring knowledge have not experienced the process of learning by the Spirit. (O/C)

Alma 30:16

Once again, Korihor taught something he knew nothing about. Since he had failed to respond to the directing power of the Light of Christ, and perhaps had never admitted to being sinful, he never would have known the refreshing peace of personally receiving a remission of sins. Only when one comes to the Savior with a broken heart and contrite spirit, pleading for mercy through the atoning blood of Christ, is there a conviction of the Atonement born of experience. Korihor had missed it all. (O/C)

Alma 30:17

A commonly taught concept is that human life is an evolutionary result of accidental occurrence and chance development during a very lengthy time of reproduction, mutation, and death of the species. Korihor taught about the "management of the creature" and prosperity according to the genius and strength of man. . . . Such theories contradict the scriptural accounts of the earth's creation and the Fall of man, thus eliminating the role of Christ and His Atonement. (O/C)

21. And it came to pass that he caused that he should be carried out of the land. And he came over into the land of Gideon, and began to preach unto them also; and here he did not have much success, for he was taken and bound and carried before the high priest, and also the chief judge over the land.

22. And it came to pass that the high priest said unto him: Why do ye go about perverting the ways of the Lord? Why do ye teach this people that there shall be no Christ, to interrupt their rejoicings? Why do ye speak against all the prophecies of the holy prophets?

23. Now the high priest's name was Giddonah. And Korihor said unto him: Because I do not teach the foolish traditions of your fathers, and because I do not teach this people to bind themselves down under the foolish ordinances and performances which are laid down by ancient priests, to usurp power and authority over them, to keep them in ignorance, that they may not lift up their heads, but be brought down according to thy words.

24. Ye say that this people is a free people. Behold, I say they are in bondage. Ye say that those ancient prophecies are true. Behold, I say that ye do not know that they are true.

25. Ye say that this people is a guilty and a fallen people, because of the transgression of a parent. Behold, I say that a child is not guilty because of its parents.

26. And ye also say that Christ shall come. But behold, I say that ye do not know that there shall be a Christ. And ye say also that he shall be slain for the sins of the world—

27. And thus ye lead away this people after the foolish traditions of your fathers, and according to your own desires; and ye keep them down, even as it were in bondage, that ye may glut yourselves with the labors of their hands, that they durst not look up with boldness, and that they durst not enjoy their rights and privileges.

28. Yea, they durst not make use of that which is their own lest they should offend their priests, who do yoke them according to their desires, and have brought them to believe, by their traditions and their dreams and their whims and their visions and their pretended mysteries, that they should, if they did not do according to their words, offend some unknown being, who they say is God—a being who never has been seen or known, who never was nor ever will be.

29. Now when the high priest and the chief judge saw the hardness of his heart, yea, when they saw that he would revile even against God, they would not make any reply to his words; but they caused that he should be bound; and they delivered him up into the hands of the officers, and sent him to the land of Zarahemla, that he might be brought before Alma, and the chief judge who was governor over all the land.

30. And it came to pass that when he was brought before Alma and the chief judge, he did go on in the same manner as he did in the land of Gideon; yea, he went on to blaspheme.

31. And he did rise up in great swelling words before Alma, and did revile against the priests and teachers, accusing them of leading away the people after the silly traditions of their fathers, for the sake of glutting on the labors of the people.

32. Now Alma said unto him: Thou knowest that we do not glut ourselves upon the labors of this people; for behold I have labored even from

Alma 30:22

Since all prophets testify of Christ (see Jacob 7:11), an anti-Christ must eliminate people's confidence in the prophets' teachings. Because Korihor did not believe in prophets, and had never personally known of things to come, he dismissed the possibility that any man could know the future. He had ignored statements like that of the prophet Amos, who said, "Surely the Lord God will do nothing, but he revealeth his secret unto his servants the prophets" (Amos 3:7). (O/C)

Alma 30:25

This man either did not understand the Fall of Adam and Eve and its results, or he deliberately attempted to present a mistaken perspective of the event. His conclusion portrayed an erroneous concept that was clearly in conflict with truth. His actual purpose for presenting this twisted line of reasoning was to eliminate the doctrine of the Fall of man. After all, if there was no Fall of man, there would be no need for a Redeemer. This is always the position of an anti-Christ, and it is a prime example of the doctrine of Lucifer. (O/C)

Alma 30:26–28

Just because Korihor had never seen or known God, he concluded no one else ever had or ever would. What he either did not know or was not willing to admit was that untold numbers of people had borne witness, based on their own experience, that God lives. In addition, he did not realize that to know God requires a spiritual connection and experience, and he was not spiritually capable of receiving such a witness. The Apostle Paul taught that "no man can say that Jesus is the Lord, but by the Holy Ghost" (1 Cor. 12:3). Without the Holy Ghost, no one—including Korihor—could know of the living reality of Christ. (O/C)

Alma 30:29–30

When the people resisted Korihor and his teachings, they "caused that he should be bound; and they delivered him up into the hands of the officers." (Alma 30:29.) The officers before whom Korihor was taken included Alma (who was the religious leader) and Nephihah ("the chief judge who was governor over all the land"—Alma 30:29). The fact that Korihor was brought before Alma would seem to indicate that Korihor was or had been a member of the church. (Ludlow)

POINT OF INTEREST

Mayan writing uses a system of dots and bars to represent dates. Each bar represents five, each dot represents one. The glyphs at right come from the top of an altar at Palenque, Mexico, and demonstrate how often date glyphs appear in Mayan writing.

the commencement of the reign of the judges until now, with mine
own hands for my support, notwithstanding my many travels round
about the land to declare the word of God unto my people.
33. And notwithstanding the many labors which I have performed
in the church, I have never received so much as even one senine
for my labor; neither has any of my brethren, save it were in the
judgment-seat; and then we have received only according to law
for our time.
34. And now, if we do not receive anything for our labors in the
church, what doth it profit us to labor in the church save it were to
declare the truth, that we may have rejoicings in the joy of our
brethren?
35. Then why sayest thou that we preach unto this people to get
gain, when thou, of thyself, knowest that we receive no gain? And
now, believest thou that we deceive this people, that causes such
joy in their hearts?
36. And Korihor answered him, Yea.
37. And then Alma said unto him: Believest thou that there is a
God?
38. And he answered, Nay.
39. Now Alma said unto him: Will ye deny again that there is a
God, and also deny the Christ? For behold, I say unto you, I know
there is a God, and also that Christ shall come.
40. And now what evidence have ye that there is no God, or that
Christ cometh not? I say unto you that ye have none, save it be
your word only.
41. But, behold, I have all things as a testimony that these things
are true; and ye also have all things as a testimony unto you that
they are true; and will ye deny them? Believest thou that these
things are true?
42. Behold, I know that thou believest, but thou art possessed with
a lying spirit, and ye have put off the Spirit of God that it may have
no place in you; but the devil has power over you, and
he doth carry you about, working devices that he may
destroy the children of God.
43. And now Korihor said unto Alma: If thou wilt
show me a sign, that I may be convinced that there is a
God, yea, show unto me that he hath power, and then
will I be convinced of the truth of thy words.
44. But Alma said unto him: Thou hast had signs
enough; will ye tempt your God? Will ye say, Show
unto me a sign, when ye have the testimony of all these
thy brethren, and also all the holy prophets? The scriptures are laid before thee, yea, and all things denote
there is a God; yea, even the earth, and all things that
are upon the face of it, yea, and its motion, yea, and
also all the planets which move in their regular form do
witness that there is a Supreme Creator.
45. And yet do ye go about, leading away the hearts of
this people, testifying unto them there is no God? And
yet will ye deny against all these witnesses? And he
said: Yea, I will deny, except ye shall show me a sign.
46. And now it came to pass that Alma said unto him:
Behold, I am grieved because of the hardness of your
heart, yea, that ye will still resist the spirit of the truth,
that thy soul may be destroyed.
47. But behold, it is better that thy

Alma 30:40

The story is told of a college student whose professor claimed there is no God. The student asked the instructor what documentation he had for his conclusion. The professor had to admit he had none. The student replied, "Then it is just your opinion." (O/C)

Alma 30:44

Marion G. Romney testified of the . . . evidence of the existence of God:

"Dr. Thomas J. Parmley . . . has eloquently written: 'The moon and stars in the night sky, one hundred million suns with their attendant planets, space, oceans, earth and nature, the flight of a bird, the wonder of a flower, the intricate design and unbelievable coordination of the human body, all of these and countless other creations proclaim the handiwork of God.'"

The Lord gave his own personal witness that the orderliness of the universe is probative evidence of his existence, in these words:

"The earth rolls upon her wings, and the sun giveth his light by day, and the moon giveth her light by night, and the stars also give their light, as they roll upon their wings in their glory, in the midst of the power of God.

"Behold, all these are kingdoms, and any man who hath seen any or the least of these hath seen God moving in his majesty and power." (D&C 88:45, 47). (O/C)

soul should be lost than that thou shouldst be the means of bringing many souls down to destruction, by thy lying and by thy flattering words; therefore if thou shalt deny again, behold God shall smite thee, that thou shalt become dumb, that thou shalt never open thy mouth any more, that thou shalt not deceive this people any more.
48. Now Korihor said unto him: I do not deny the existence of a God, but I do not believe that there is a God; and I say also, that ye do not know that there is a God; and except ye show me a sign, I will not believe.
49. Now Alma said unto him: This will I give unto thee for a sign, that thou shalt be struck dumb, according to my words; and I say, that in the name of God, ye shall be struck dumb, that ye shall no more have utterance.
50. Now when Alma had said these words, Korihor was struck dumb, that he could not have utterance, according to the words of Alma.
51. And now when the chief judge saw this, he put forth his hand and wrote unto Korihor, saying: Art thou convinced of the power of God? In whom did ye desire that Alma should show forth his sign? Would ye that he should afflict others, to show unto thee a sign? Behold, he has showed unto you a sign; and now will ye dispute more?
52. And Korihor put forth his hand and wrote, saying: I know that I am dumb, for I cannot speak; and I know that nothing save it were the power of God could bring this upon me; yea, and I always knew that there was a God.
53. But behold, the devil hath deceived me; for he appeared unto me in the form of an angel, and said unto me: Go and reclaim this people, for they have all gone astray after an unknown God. And he said unto me: There is no God; yea, and he taught me that which I should say. And I have taught his words; and I taught them because they were pleasing unto the carnal mind; and I taught them, even until I had much success, insomuch that I verily believed that they were true; and for this cause I withstood the truth, even until I have brought this great curse upon me.
54. Now when he had said this, he besought that Alma should pray unto God, that the curse might be taken from him.
55. But Alma said unto him: If this curse should be taken from thee thou wouldst again lead away the hearts of this people; therefore, it shall be unto thee even as the Lord will.
56. And it came to pass that the curse was not taken off of Korihor; but he was cast out, and went about from house to house begging for his food.
57. Now the knowledge of what had happened unto Korihor was immediately published throughout all the land; yea, the proclamation was sent forth by the chief judge to all the people in the land, declaring unto those who had believed in the words of Korihor that they must speedily repent, lest the same judgments would come unto them.
58. And it came to pass that they were all convinced of the wickedness of Korihor; therefore they were all converted again unto the Lord; and this put an end to the iniquity after the manner of Korihor. And Korihor did go about from house to house, begging food for his support.
59. And it came to pass that as he went forth among the people, yea, among a people who had separated themselves from the Nephites and called themselves Zoramites, being

Alma 30:48

Joseph Smith taught that "nothing is a greater injury to the children of men than to be under the influence of a false spirit when they think they have the Spirit of God."

Alma 30:53

Satan can appear as an angel; other instances in the scriptures where this has occurred or is discussed include D&C 128:20, 2 Corinthians 11:14, and 2 Nephi 9:9. Joseph Smith verified that Satan can appear as an angel, and said that it requires the priesthood and the discerning of spirits to detect when an angel is evil.

Alma 30:53

Anti-Christs (like Korihor) taught deluded doctrines such as these: that there should be no Christ, hope is in vain, there can be no prophecy, righteous traditions are foolishness, you cannot know things that you cannot see, there could be no Atonement, everyone fares according to his own strength, whatever one does is not a crime, and when one dies that is the end of his or her existence. . . .

Through inspiration and sound reasoning we can recognize anti-Christs for what they are: servants of the devil, seeking to make us miserable like unto the devil. They seek to destroy our faith in Christ by placing doubt in our hearts. Let us quickly discern conflict between man's teachings and God's teachings, thereby cleaving to the word of God from our living prophets and the scriptures. . . .

By following the promptings of the Spirit, we can stand strong against the revilings of those who seek to discredit the truths of the Gospel of Jesus Christ. . . . Elder John A. Widtsoe said, "The existence of God is made evident to man because, first, all men have an inner consciousness of a higher power; second, nature is orderly, betokening the operation of an intelligent master mind; third, every experience is the effect of a cause, itself an effect of a higher cause, leading to a great first cause—God; fourth, men have received personal revelations of God; and fifth, every man by prayer may know that God lives. It is doubtful if the truth of any other fact of human experience is or can be so well attested." (P/A)

Alma 30:53

The "carnal mind" in this verse refers to the sensual and worldly desires we are subjected to in mortality.

led by a man whose name was Zoram—and as he went forth amongst them, behold, he was run upon and trodden down, even until he was dead.
60. And thus we see the end of him who perverteth the ways of the Lord; and thus we see that the devil will not support his children at the last day, but doth speedily drag them down to hell.

CHAPTER 31

1. NOW it came to pass that after the end of Korihor, Alma having received tidings that the Zoramites were perverting the ways of the Lord, and that Zoram, who was their leader, was leading the hearts of the people to bow down to dumb idols, his heart again began to sicken because of the iniquity of the people.
2. For it was the cause of great sorrow to Alma to know of iniquity among his people; therefore his heart was exceedingly sorrowful because of the separation of the Zoramites from the Nephites.
3. Now the Zoramites had gathered themselves together in a land which they called Antionum, which was east of the land of Zarahemla, which lay nearly bordering upon the seashore, which was south of the land of Jershon, which also bordered upon the wilderness south, which wilderness was full of the Lamanites.
4. Now the Nephites greatly feared that the Zoramites would enter into a correspondence with the Lamanites, and that it would be the means of great loss on the part of the Nephites.
5. And now, as the preaching of the word had a great tendency to lead the people to do that which was just—yea, it had had more powerful effect upon the minds of the people than the sword, or anything else, which had happened unto them—therefore Alma thought it was expedient that they should try the virtue of the word of God.
6. Therefore he took Ammon, and Aaron, and Omner; and Himni he did leave in the church in Zarahemla; but the former three he took with him, and also Amulek and Zeezrom, who were at Melek; and he also took two of his sons.
7. Now the eldest of his sons he took not with him, and his name was Helaman; but the names of those whom he took with him were Shiblon and Corianton; and these are the names of those who went with him among the Zoramites, to preach unto them the word.
8. Now the Zoramites were dissenters from the Nephites; therefore they had had the word of God preached unto them.
9. But they had fallen into great errors, for they would not observe to keep the commandments of God,

Alma 30:59–60

The brief mention in verse 59 of Zoram being trampled and killed is an example of what is described in Mormon 4:5: "It is by the wicked that the wicked are punished." We know that the Zoramites were wicked people (see Alma 31:8-9), who were led by a wicked man. For those who are tempted to follow the adversary, the words in verse 60 are particularly applicable—while the Lord always supports His children, Satan does not support his. They are dragged to hell and left alone, something that is forever true.

Alma 31:4

Alma was afraid that by opening up correspondence with the Lamanites, the Zoramites would incite the Lamanites to war. That is exactly what happened.

Alma 31:5

Knowing that any success in their mission depended upon the help and assistance of the Lord, Alma prayed for the work of the missionaries. He didn't pray for himself or the missionaries personally, but rather for success in their work in the ministry. His prayerful desire was not to bring the people back to the Church only, but rather to bring them back to the Lord. (See Alma 31:34.) (O/C)

Alma 31:5

When Alma received word of these religious diversions, he determined, as a true priesthood leader would, to undertake a mission to them in an effort to reclaim them and bring them back into the fold of God. After arriving in their land. . . . He settled on a proven process of conversion which he had used successfully before. He knew that "the preaching of the word had a great tendency to lead the people to do that which was just." (O/C)

Alma 31:5

Teaching the word of the Lord is the greatest tool at our disposal for retention as well as conversion. (See Alma 31:5.) (O/C)

Alma 31:6

A priesthood leader needs to be apprised of needs, then be involved personally and labor for the souls of his people. (See Alma 31:6.) (O/C)

Alma 31:8

It is better to strengthen people so they stay close to the Church and family than to bring them back after they stray. Church and family membership is fragile. A continuing relationship depends upon a consistent extension of love, responsible involvement, and ongoing spiritual nourishment. We all need to focus on enduring to the end. (O/C)

and his statutes, according to the law of Moses.
10. Neither would they observe the performances of the church, to continue in prayer and supplication to God daily, that they might not enter into temptation.
11. Yea, in fine, they did pervert the ways of the Lord in very many instances; therefore, for this cause, Alma and his brethren went into the land to preach the word unto them.
12. Now, when they had come into the land, behold, to their astonishment they found that the Zoramites had built synagogues, and that they did gather themselves together on one day of the week, which day they did call the day of the Lord; and they did worship after a manner which Alma and his brethren had never beheld;
13. For they had a place built up in the center of their synagogue, a place for standing, which was high above the head; and the top thereof would only admit one person.
14. Therefore, whosoever desired to worship must go forth and stand upon the top thereof, and stretch forth his hands towards heaven, and cry with a loud voice, saying:
15. Holy, holy God; we believe that thou art God, and we believe that thou art holy, and that thou wast a spirit, and that thou art a spirit, and that thou wilt be a spirit forever.
16. Holy God, we believe that thou hast separated us from our brethren; and we do not believe in the tradition of our brethren, which was handed down to them by the childishness of their fathers; but we believe that thou hast elected us to be thy holy children; and also thou hast made it known unto us that there shall be no Christ.
17. But thou art the same yesterday, today, and forever; and thou hast elected us that we shall be saved, whilst all around us are elected to be cast by thy wrath down to hell; for the which holiness, O God, we thank thee; and we also thank thee that thou hast elected us, that we may not be led away after the foolish traditions of our brethren, which doth bind them down to a belief of Christ, which doth lead their hearts to wander far from thee, our God.
18. And again we thank thee, O God, that we are a chosen and a holy people. Amen.
19. Now it came to pass that after Alma and his brethren and his sons had heard these prayers, they were astonished beyond all measure.
20. For behold, every man did go forth and offer up these same prayers.
21. Now the place was called by them Rameumptom, which, being interpreted, is the holy stand.
22. Now, from this stand they did offer up, every man, the selfsame prayer unto God, thanking their God that they were chosen of him, and that he did not lead them away after the tradition of their brethren, and that their hearts were not stolen away to believe in things to come, which they knew nothing about.
23. Now, after the people had all offered up thanks after this manner, they returned to their homes, never speaking of their God again until they had assembled themselves together again to the holy stand, to offer up thanks after their manner.
24. Now when Alma saw this his heart was grieved; for he saw that they were a wicked and a perverse people; yea, he saw that their hearts were set upon gold, and upon silver, and upon all manner of fine goods.

Alma 31:13–18, 26–35

Several places in the scriptures the prophets have warned us to avoid "vain repetition" in our prayers and have encouraged us to pray according to our needs and sincere feelings. This chapter contains classic examples both of what we should not do and what we should do when praying. The example of a wrong prayer is the memorized, rote prayer of the apostate Zoramites. (Alma 31:15–18.) The example of an effective prayer is the humble and sincere petition of Alma (Alma 31:26–35). (Ludlow)

Alma 31:15–18

Notice how many elements of apostasy are indicated in the set prayer of the apostate Zoramites: (1) They believe God is a spirit only (verse 15). (2) They do not believe in the divinity of Jesus Christ (verse 16). (3) They do not accept the teachings of the prophets because the "tradition" of their brethren "was handed down to them by the childishness of their fathers"; nevertheless, they readily accepted some of the false teachings or "traditions" which had been passed down by other people (verse 16). (4) They believe in "double predestination"—i.e., God has "elected" them to be saved, but he has elected everyone else to be cast down to hell (verses 17 and 18). Also, note other common practices of religious groups in a state of apostasy: the repetition of memorized prayers in worship, and the relegation of religion to a "Sunday" activity (verses 22 and 23). (Ludlow)

Alma 31:21

The name of the holy stand of the apostate Zoramites, upon which they stood when they offered their weekly prayer, was the "Rameumptom." Although this name may look strange in English, it has appropriate Semitic roots recognizable to students of Semitic languages. The preface "ram" is frequently used to indicate a high place. For example, later in the Book of Mormon we read of the hill Ramah. Also, in modern Israel are the town of Ramallah (located in the tops of the Judean hills just north of Jerusalem) and Rameem (which literally means "the heights" and is located on the top of the hills near the Lebanese border). (Ludlow)

25. Yea, and he also saw that their hearts were lifted up unto great boasting, in their pride.
26. And he lifted up his voice to heaven, and cried, saying: O, how long, O Lord, wilt thou suffer that thy servants shall dwell here below in the flesh, to behold such gross wickedness among the children of men?
27. Behold, O God, they cry unto thee, and yet their hearts are swallowed up in their pride. Behold, O God, they cry unto thee with their mouths, while they are puffed up, even to greatness, with the vain things of the world.
28. Behold, O my God, their costly apparel, and their ringlets, and their bracelets, and their ornaments of gold, and all their precious things which they are ornamented with; and behold, their hearts are set upon them, and yet they cry unto thee and say—We thank thee, O God, for we are a chosen people unto thee, while others shall perish.
29. Yea, and they say that thou hast made it known unto them that there shall be no Christ.
30. O Lord God, how long wilt thou suffer that such wickedness and infidelity shall be among this people? O Lord, wilt thou give me strength, that I may bear with mine infirmities. For I am infirm, and such wickedness among this people doth pain my soul.
31. O Lord, my heart is exceedingly sorrowful; wilt thou comfort my soul in Christ. O Lord, wilt thou grant unto me that I may have strength, that I may suffer with patience these afflictions which shall come upon me, because of the iniquity of this people.
32. O Lord, wilt thou comfort my soul, and give unto me success, and also my fellow laborers who are with me—yea, Ammon, and Aaron, and Omner, and also Amulek and Zeezrom, and also my two sons—yea, even all these wilt thou comfort, O Lord. Yea, wilt thou comfort their souls in Christ.
33. Wilt thou grant unto them that they may have strength, that they may bear their afflictions which shall come upon them because of the iniquities of this people.
34. O Lord, wilt thou grant unto us that we may have success in bringing them again unto thee in Christ.
35. Behold, O Lord, their souls are precious, and many of them are our brethren; therefore, give unto us, O Lord, power and wisdom that we may bring these, our brethren, again unto thee.
36. Now it came to pass that when Alma had said these words, that he clapped his hands upon all them who were with him. And behold, as he clapped his hands upon them, they were filled with the Holy Spirit.
37. And after that they did separate themselves one from another, taking no thought for themselves what they should eat, or what they should drink, or what they should put on.
38. And the Lord provided for them that they should hunger not, neither should they thirst; yea, and he also gave them strength, that they should suffer no manner of afflictions, save it were swallowed up in the joy of Christ. Now this was according to the prayer of Alma; and this because he prayed in faith.

Alma 31:27–28

The type of pride described in these verses is the reason why people often invent their own forms of worship.

Alma 31:30–35

These tender verses illustrate the prayer of a prophet for his people.

Alma 31:35

Brigham Young said, “Only a few men on the earth understand the charity that fills the bosom of our Savior. We should have charity; we should do all we can to reclaim the lost sons and daughters of Adam and Eve, and bring them back to be saved in the presence of our Father and God. If we do this, our charity will extend to the utmost extent that it is designed for the charity of God to extend in the midst of this people.”

CHAPTER 32

1. AND it came to pass that they did go forth, and began to preach the word of God unto the people, entering into their synagogues, and into their houses; yea, and even they did preach the word in their streets.
2. And it came to pass that after much labor among them, they began to have success among the poor class of people; for behold, they were cast out of the synagogues because of the coarseness of their apparel—
3. Therefore they were not permitted to enter into their synagogues to worship God, being esteemed as filthiness; therefore they were poor; yea, they were esteemed by their brethren as dross; therefore they were poor as to things of the world; and also they were poor in heart.
4. Now, as Alma was teaching and speaking unto the people upon the hill Onidah, there came a great multitude unto him, who were those of whom we have been speaking, of whom were poor in heart, because of their poverty as to the things of the world.
5. And they came unto Alma; and the one who was the foremost among them said unto him: Behold, what shall these my brethren do, for they are despised of all men because of their poverty, yea, and more especially by our priests; for they have cast us out of our synagogues which we have labored abundantly to build with our own hands; and they have cast us out because of our exceeding poverty; and we have no place to worship our God; and behold, what shall we do?
6. And now when Alma heard this, he turned him about, his face immediately towards him, and he beheld with great joy; for he beheld that their afflictions had truly humbled them, and that they were in a preparation to hear the word.
7. Therefore he did say no more to the other multitude; but he stretched forth his hand, and cried unto those whom he beheld, who were truly penitent, and said unto them:
8. I behold that ye are lowly in heart; and if so, blessed are ye.
9. Behold thy brother hath said, What shall we do?—for we are cast out of our synagogues, that we cannot worship our God.
10. Behold I say unto you, do ye suppose that ye cannot worship God save it be in your synagogues only?
11. And moreover, I would ask, do ye suppose that ye must not worship God only once in a week?
12. I say unto you, it is well that ye are cast out of your synagogues, that ye may be humble, and that ye may learn wisdom; for it is necessary that ye should learn wisdom; for it is because that ye are cast out, that ye are despised of your brethren because of your exceeding poverty, that ye are brought to a lowliness of heart; for ye are necessarily brought to be humble.

Alma 32

Salvation comes to mankind through the grace of God. "For God so loved the world, that he gave his only begotten Son" (John 3:16). The Son of God, even Jesus Christ, is the only ". . . name given whereby man can be saved" (D&C 18:23). (O/C)

Alma 32

This is Alma's great discourse on faith. We can all enter the laboratory of faith and, by applying proper principles, gain spiritual evidence of the truth. President Heber J. Grant described faith as a gift of God given to those who serve him. Elder Bruce R. McConkie said that we grow in faith, going step by step from a lower degree to a higher degree. The people Alma is preaching to in this section of the Book of Mormon were at that "lower degree"—they were the poorest among the Zoramites, who had only false doctrine. For that reason, Alma did not try to give them the entire doctrine of faith all at once.

Alma 32:12–14

Whenever people do not humble themselves before God or even think of God except in times of dire need or danger, they are being "compelled to be humble" through the seriousness of the circumstance. Such people are more blessed than those who never think of God, but how much better it would be for them if they were humble and prayerful before God at all times—in prosperity as well as in poverty, in health as well as sickness. (Ludlow)

13. And now, because ye are compelled to be humble blessed are ye; for a man sometimes, if he is compelled to be humble, seeketh repentance; and now surely, whosoever repenteth shall find mercy; and he that findeth mercy and endureth to the end the same shall be saved.
14. And now, as I said unto you, that because ye were compelled to be humble ye were blessed, do ye not suppose that they are more blessed who truly humble themselves because of the word?
15. Yea, he that truly humbleth himself, and repenteth of his sins, and endureth to the end, the same shall be blessed—yea, much more blessed than they who are compelled to be humble because of their exceeding poverty.
16. Therefore, blessed are they who humble themselves without being compelled to be humble; or rather, in other words, blessed is he that believeth in the word of God, and is baptized without stubbornness of heart, yea, without being brought to know the word, or even compelled to know, before they will believe.
17. Yea, there are many who do say: If thou wilt show unto us a sign from heaven, then we shall know of a surety; then we shall believe.
18. Now I ask, is this faith? Behold, I say unto you, Nay; for if a man knoweth a thing he hath no cause to believe, for he knoweth it.
19. And now, how much more cursed is he that knoweth the will of God and doeth it not, than he that only believeth, or only hath cause to believe, and falleth into transgression?
20. Now of this thing ye must judge. Behold, I say unto you, that it is on the one hand even as it is on the other; and it shall be unto every man according to his work.
21. And now as I said concerning faith—faith is not to have a perfect knowledge of things; therefore if ye have faith ye hope for things which are not seen, which are true.
22. And now, behold, I say unto you, and I would that ye should remember, that God is merciful unto all who believe on his name; therefore he desireth, in the first place, that ye should believe, yea, even on his word.
23. And now, he imparteth his word by angels unto men, yea, not only men but women also. Now this is not all; little children do have words given unto them many times, which confound the wise and the learned.
24. And now, my beloved brethren, as ye have desired to know of me what ye shall do because ye are afflicted and cast out—now I do not desire that ye should suppose that I mean to judge you only according to that which is true—
25. For I do not mean that ye all of you have been compelled to humble yourselves; for I verily believe that there are some among you who would humble themselves, let them be in whatsoever circumstances they might.
26. Now, as I said concerning faith—that it was not a perfect knowledge—even so it is with my words. Ye cannot know of their surety at first, unto perfection, any more than faith is a perfect knowledge.
27. But behold, if ye will awake and arouse your faculties, even to an experiment upon my words, and

Alma 32:16

Humility is the beginning of change and growth in one's life. . . . When we understand our dependence upon God, we will be humble. (P/A)

Alma 32:17–43

The terms faith and belief are sometimes regarded as synonyms; nevertheless each of them has a specific meaning in our language, although in earlier usage there was little distinction between them, and therefore the words are used interchangeably in many scriptural passages. Belief, in one of its accepted senses, may consist in a merely intellectual assent, while faith implies such confidence and conviction as will impel to action. . . . Belief is in a sense passive, an agreement or acceptance only; faith is active and positive, embracing such reliance and confidence as will lead to works. Faith in Christ comprises belief in Him, combined with trust in Him. One cannot have faith without belief; yet he may believe and still lack faith. Faith is vivified, vitalized, living belief. . . . ? Knowledge is to wisdom what belief is to faith, one an abstract principle, the other a living application. Not possession merely, but the proper use of knowledge constitutes wisdom. (James E. Talmage, *Articles of Faith.*)

Alma 32:27

As the prophets of the Lord spread the word of God among the people, it attracts those whose hearts are accepting and humble. This process of gathering was likened by the Savior to the action of fishing: "Again, the kingdom of heaven is like unto a net, that was cast into the sea, and gathered of every kind: Which, when it was full, they drew to shore, and sat down, and gathered the good into vessels, but cast the bad away" (Matt. 13:47–48). . . .

We have the opportunity to respond to the word of God with gratitude and humility, planting it within our hearts, where it can grow through nourishment and charity. Elder Neal A. Maxwell said, "To supply what is lacking in our faith we must first make room for its conscious development—in our souls and in our schedules. . . . In the process of building faith, wrote Alma, we must 'experiment on the word' of the Master, giving 'place' sufficient to experiment upon each essential 'thing' the gospel requires of us. Out of such cumulative experience comes the real, cumulative evidence."

The capacity to learn and grow is dependent on one's humility. Humility is the beginning of change and growth in one's life. . . . When we understand our dependence on God, we will be humble. . . . Humility brings with it many blessings and traits: submissiveness, the state of being easily entreated, a broken heart and contrite spirit, a willingness to change and to be teachable. This makes it possible for the seed or the word of God to be planted in our hearts. So begins the great experiment of faith. (P/A)

exercise a particle of faith, yea, even if ye can no more than desire
to believe, let this desire work in you, even until ye believe in a
manner that ye can give place for a portion of my words.
28. Now, we will compare the word unto a seed. Now, if ye give
place, that a seed may be planted in your heart, behold, if it be a
true seed, or a good seed, if ye do not cast it out by your unbelief,
that ye will resist the Spirit of the Lord, behold, it will begin to
swell within your breasts; and when you feel these swelling
motions, ye will begin to say within yourselves—It must needs be
that this is a good seed, or that the word is good, for it beginneth
to enlarge my soul; yea, it beginneth to enlighten my understanding, yea, it beginneth to be delicious to me.
29. Now behold, would not this increase your faith? I say unto you,
Yea; nevertheless it hath not grown up to a perfect knowledge.
30. But behold, as the seed swelleth, and sprouteth, and beginneth
to grow, then you must needs say that the seed is good; for behold
it swelleth, and sprouteth, and beginneth to grow. And now,
behold, will not this strengthen your faith? Yea, it will strengthen
your faith: for ye will say I know that this is a good seed; for behold
it sprouteth and beginneth to grow.
31. And now, behold, are ye sure that this is a good seed? I say unto
you, Yea; for every seed bringeth forth unto its own likeness.
32. Therefore, if a seed groweth it is good, but if it groweth not,
behold it is not good, therefore it is cast away.
33. And now, behold, because ye have tried the experiment, and
planted the seed, and it swelleth and sprouteth, and beginneth to
grow, ye must needs know that the seed is good.
34. And now, behold, is your knowledge perfect? Yea, your knowledge is perfect in that thing, and your faith is dormant; and this
because ye know, for ye know that the word hath swelled your souls,
and ye also know that it hath sprouted up, that your understanding
doth begin to be enlightened, and your mind doth begin to expand.
35. O then, is not this real? I say unto you, Yea, because it is light;
and whatsoever is light, is good, because it is discernible, therefore
ye must know that it is good; and now behold, after ye have tasted
this light is your knowledge perfect?
36. Behold I say unto you, Nay; neither must ye lay aside your
faith, for ye have only exercised your faith to plant the seed that ye
might try the experiment to know if the seed was good.
37. And behold, as the tree beginneth to grow, ye will say: Let us
nourish it with great care, that it may get root, that it may grow up,
and bring forth fruit unto us. And now behold, if ye nourish it with
much care it will get root, and grow up, and bring forth fruit.
38. But if ye neglect the tree, and take no thought for its nourishment, behold it will not get any root; and when the heat of the sun
cometh and scorcheth it, because it hath no root it withers away,
and ye pluck it up and cast it out.
39. Now, this is not because the seed was not good, neither is it
because the fruit thereof would not be desirable; but it is because
your ground is barren, and ye will not nourish the tree, therefore ye
cannot have the fruit thereof.

Alma 32:28

One of the missions of the Holy Ghost is to bear witness of gospel truth, the pure word of God. When a sincere, humble child of God begins to conform his life to the word of God (plants the seed in his heart), he will receive a witness of the Holy Spirit (the swelling in his breast). His understanding is enlightened, and the word of God becomes very desirable unto him. (O/C)

Alma 32:34–35

[Alma's] masterful discourse . . . enlarges on this theme by comparing the operation of faith with the germination of a seed within the soul. By careful observation of the unfolding of the seed (the vitality of the word of God as it opens up within the penitent and humble heart), the seeker after truth can know of the seed's goodness. He or she can then exercise ongoing faith by nourishing the seed with diligence and patience until it can take root and develop into a tree of life, bearing supernal blessings of spiritual fruit for the faithful. (P/A)

Alma 32:37–43

Faith is a gift from God to man. When an individual conforms his life to the word of God, he receives a witness from the Holy Ghost. When this occurs, faith in Jesus Christ, the Son of God, is born. As the individual continues to live by every word that proceedeth forth from the mouth of God, he continues to receive the witness of the Holy Ghost, and his faith in Jesus Christ increases continually. Alma compares this spiritual growth to the growth of a tree, which if nourished with much care will bring forth fruit that is most precious and sweet above all that is sweet, springing up to eternal life. (O/C)

Alma 32:39

Humility is the spiritual seedbed of the soul where the word of God is planted. (O/C)

40. And thus, if ye will not nourish the word, looking forward with an eye of faith to the fruit thereof, ye can never pluck of the fruit of the tree of life.
41. But if ye will nourish the word, yea, nourish the tree as it beginneth to grow, by your faith with great diligence, and with patience, looking forward to the fruit thereof, it shall take root; and behold it shall be a tree springing up unto everlasting life.
42. And because of your diligence and your faith and your patience with the word in nourishing it, that it may take root in you, behold, by and by ye shall pluck the fruit thereof, which is most precious, which is sweet above all that is sweet, and which is white above all that is white, yea, and pure above all that is pure; and ye shall feast upon this fruit even until ye are filled, that ye hunger not, neither shall ye thirst.
43. Then, my brethren, ye shall reap the rewards of your faith, and your diligence, and patience, and long-suffering, waiting for the tree to bring forth fruit unto you.

CHAPTER 33

1. NOW after Alma had spoken these words, they sent forth unto him desiring to know whether they should believe in one God, that they might obtain this fruit of which he had spoken, or how they should plant the seed, or the word of which he had spoken, which he said must be planted in their hearts; or in what manner they should begin to exercise their faith.
2. And Alma said unto them: Behold, ye have said that ye could not worship your God because ye are cast out of your synagogues. But behold, I say unto you, if ye suppose that ye cannot worship God, ye do greatly err, and ye ought to search the scriptures; if ye suppose that they have taught you this, ye do not understand them.
3. Do ye remember to have read what Zenos, the prophet of old, has said concerning prayer or worship?
4. For he said: Thou art merciful, O God, for thou hast heard my prayer, even when I was in the wilderness; yea, thou wast merciful when I prayed concerning those who were mine enemies, and thou didst turn them to me.
5. Yea, O God, and thou wast merciful unto me when I did cry unto thee in my field; when I did cry unto thee in my prayer, and thou didst hear me.
6. And again, O God, when I did turn to my house thou didst hear me in my prayer.
7. And when I did turn unto my closet, O Lord, and prayed unto thee, thou didst hear me.
8. Yea, thou art merciful unto thy children when they cry unto thee, to be heard of thee and not of men, and thou wilt hear them.
9. Yea, O God, thou hast been merciful unto me, and heard my cries in the midst of thy congregations.

Alma 32:40

We see contrasting patterns in the lives of people. Sometimes people obtain a testimony, then fail to nourish it, and their feelings toward God's plan of salvation diminish and die. (See Alma 32:40.) Others maintain their determination to study and learn, pray, and listen that they might continue to grow stronger spiritually and be strengthened in their faith. Some people retire from their religion by avoiding calls to church service, feeling they have done enough, and it is time for someone else to take the responsibility. Yet others are found serving and giving of themselves and sharing their talents well into their older ages, as long as health conditions permit. Their convictions are evident in their responses to duty and opportunity. Through the duration of our mortal lives, we need to be diligent in our discipleship and constant in our continued growth. (O/C)

Alma 32:41–43

As we heed and nourish the word of God, given to mankind through Jesus Christ, the seed grows into a tree containing precious fruit. The tree is symbolic of Jesus Christ, and the fruit thereof is symbolic of the sweetness of the Savior's grace, sacrifice, and Atonement for all of Father's children. Thus, the Savior becomes the center of our lives. We become converted to Him by developing faith in His word, repenting of our sins, receiving the witness of the Holy Ghost, and receiving the Savior's atoning sacrifice, symbolized by partaking of the fruit of the tree—fruit that is sweet above all else, fruit that fills our souls with exceedingly great joy and divine peace. (O/C)

Alma 33:3–11

We worship our Heavenly Father through prayer. These are our private and sacred moments with God, to be heard of Him and not man. This communion—built upon love, trust, respect, and reverence—is explained by the words of Alma as he quotes from the prophet Zenos. He tells how his prayers are heard in the wilderness, in his fields, in his home, in his closet, and in congregations—and how they are answered through the goodness and mercy of God because of His Beloved Son, Jesus Christ. The power of prayer is the key for knowing God and our Savior and drawing on the powers of heaven. (P/A)

Alma 33:3–17

The prophets Zenos and Zenock are mentioned several times in the Book of Mormon, and each time they are mentioned we learn something new about these remarkable prophets. In 1 Nephi 19:10–17 we read of the strong and clear witness of these prophets concerning the divine mission of Jesus Christ, and here in Alma 33:17 we learn that at least one of these prophets, Zenock, sealed his testimony with his life, for the people of his day "stoned him to death." (Ludlow)

10. Yea, and thou hast also heard me when I have been cast out
and have been despised by mine enemies; yea, thou didst hear my
cries, and wast angry with mine enemies, and thou didst visit them
in thine anger with speedy destruction.
11. And thou didst hear me because of mine afflictions and my sincerity; and it is because of thy Son that thou hast been thus merciful unto me, therefore I will cry unto thee in all mine afflictions, for
in thee is my joy; for thou hast turned thy judgments away from me,
because of thy Son.
12. And now Alma said unto them: Do ye believe those scriptures
which have been written by them of old?
13. Behold, if ye do, ye must believe what Zenos said; for, behold
he said: Thou hast turned away thy judgments because of thy Son.
14. Now behold, my brethren, I would ask if ye have read the scriptures? If ye have, how can ye disbelieve on the Son of God?
15. For it is not written that Zenos alone spake of these things, but
Zenock also spake of these things—
16. For behold, he said: Thou art angry, O Lord, with this people,
because they will not understand thy mercies which thou hast
bestowed upon them because of thy Son.
17. And now, my brethren, ye see that a second prophet of old has
testified of the Son of God, and because the people would not
understand his words they stoned him to death.
18. But behold, this is not all; these are not the only ones who have
spoken concerning the Son of God.
19. Behold, he was spoken of by Moses; yea, and behold a type was
raised up in the wilderness, that whosoever would look upon it
might live. And many did look and live.
20. But few understood the meaning of those things, and this because
of the hardness of their hearts. But there were many who were so
hardened that they would not look, therefore they perished. Now the
reason they would not look is because they did not believe that it
would heal them.
21. O my brethren, if ye could be healed by merely casting about
your eyes that ye might be healed, would ye not behold quickly, or
would ye rather harden your hearts in unbelief, and be slothful,
that ye would not cast about your eyes, that ye might perish?
22. If so, wo shall come upon you; but if not so, then cast about your
eyes and begin to believe in the Son of God, that he will come to
redeem his people, and that he shall suffer and die to atone for their
sins; and that he shall rise again from the dead, which shall bring to
pass the resurrection, that all men shall stand before him, to be judged
at the last and judgment day, according to their works.
23. And now, my brethren, I desire that ye shall plant this word in your
hearts, and as it beginneth to swell even so nourish it by your faith.
And behold, it will become a tree, springing up in you unto ever-last-
ing

Alma 33:21

"Casting about your eyes" in this verse is a metaphor, helping us understand that we must always look to the Savior.

Alma 33:22–23

Verse 22 powerfully describes a belief in Christ, words that apply to us equally in our day. In verse 23, "this word" refers to Christ and His Atonement—what Alma defines as "the seed."

POINT OF INTEREST

The "jot" (the equivalent of the Greek iota*) is the tenth letter of the Hebrew alphabet and is similar to the English apostrophe in shape and size. "Tittle" refers to the small flourish of a Hebrew letter.*

life. And then may God grant unto you that your burdens may be light, through the joy of his Son. And even all this can ye do if ye will. Amen.

CHAPTER 34

1. AND now it came to pass that after Alma had spoken these
words unto them he sat down upon the ground, and Amulek arose
and began to teach them, saying:
2. My brethren, I think that it is impossible that ye should be ignorant of the things which have been spoken concerning the coming
of Christ, who is taught by us to be the Son of God; yea, I know that
these things were taught unto you bountifully before your dissension from among us.
3. And as ye have desired of my beloved brother that he should
make known unto you what ye should do, because of your afflictions; and he hath spoken somewhat unto you to prepare your
minds; yea, and he hath exhorted you unto faith and to patience—
4. Yea, even that ye would have so much faith as even to plant the
word in your hearts, that ye may try the experiment of its goodness.
5. And we have beheld that the great question which is in your
minds is whether the word be in the Son of God, or whether there
shall be no Christ.
6. And ye also beheld that my brother has proved unto you, in
many instances, that the word is in Christ unto salvation.
7. My brother has called upon the words of Zenos, that redemption
cometh through the Son of God, and also upon the words of
Zenock; and also he has appealed unto Moses, to prove that these
things are true.
8. And now, behold, I will testify unto you of myself that these
things are true. Behold, I say unto you, that I do know that Christ
shall come among the children of men, to take upon him the transgressions of his people, and that he shall atone for the sins of the
world; for the Lord God hath spoken it.
9. For it is expedient that an atonement should be made; for
according to the great plan of the Eternal God there must be an
atonement made, or else all mankind must unavoidably perish;
yea, all are hardened; yea, all are fallen and are lost, and must perish except it be through the atonement which it is expedient
should be made.
10. For it is expedient that there should be a great and last sacrifice; yea, not a sacrifice of man, neither of beast, neither of any
manner of fowl; for it shall not be a human sacrifice; but it must be
an infinite and eternal sacrifice.

Alma 34

Chapter 34 consists of Amulek's testimony about the plan of God; in bearing testimony immediately following Alma, he is fulfilling the principle of two or three witnesses (see Deuteronomy 17:6). Amulek's testimony covers 12 points: (1) Atonement will be made for the sins of man (v. 8). (2) The sacrifice of Christ will be infinite and eternal (v. 10). (3) We are responsible for our own sins, and cannot atone for the sins of others (v. 11). (4) Christ's sacrifice will fulfill the Law of Moses (v. 13). (5) Christ's sacrifice brings about mercy (v. 15). (6) Those who exercise faith and repentance are encircled in the arms of mercy; those who won't will be subject to the demands of justice (v. 16). (7) Men can call upon God at all times and in all places, both for themselves and for others (vv. 18–27). (8) We must repent now (v. 31). (9) If we don't prepare for eternity now, darkness will overcome us (v. 33). (10) Our spirit rises with us in the resurrection (v. 34). (11) If we procrastinate our repentance until we die, we have subjected ourselves to the devil (v. 35). (12) Amulek tells how to inherit eternal life (vv. 38–40).

Alma 34:10

The great and last sacrifice of Christ ended the sacrifice of beasts; the sinner must now offer the sacrifice of his own life. Christ was able to make an eternal and infinite sacrifice because as the Son of God, He is eternal and infinite (see D&C 20:17).

Alma 34:10, 14

Amulek's understanding of the depth of the Savior's Atonement is marvelous to read. His words are some of the most sacred ever recorded in Holy Writ. . . .

The redemption of mankind had to be infinite and eternal. Man cannot save himself from his lost and fallen state. Only a God, who is infinite and eternal, can rescue fallen man.

Elder Bruce R. McConkie taught, "Man cannot resurrect himself; man cannot save himself; human power cannot save another; human power cannot atone for the sins of another. The work of redemption must be infinite and eternal; it must be done by an infinite being; God himself must atone for the sins of the world." (O/C)

11. Now there is not any man that can sacrifice his own blood which will atone for the sins of another. Now, if a man murdereth, behold will our law, which is just, take the life of his brother? I say unto you, Nay.
12. But the law requireth the life of him who hath murdered; therefore there can be nothing which is short of an infinite atonement which will suffice for the sins of the world.
13. Therefore, it is expedient that there should be a great and last sacrifice, and then shall there be, or it is expedient there should be, a stop to the shedding of blood; then shall the law of Moses be fulfilled; yea, it shall be all fulfilled, every jot and tittle, and none shall have passed away.
14. And behold, this is the whole meaning of the law, every whit pointing to that great and last sacrifice; and that great and last sacrifice will be the Son of God, yea, infinite and eternal.
15. And thus he shall bring salvation to all those who shall believe on his name; this being the intent of this last sacrifice, to bring about the bowels of mercy, which overpowereth justice, and bringeth about means unto men that they may have faith unto repentance.
16. And thus mercy can satisfy the demands of justice, and encircles them in the arms of safety, while he that exercises no faith unto repentance is exposed to the whole law of the demands of justice; therefore only unto him that has faith unto repentance is brought about the great and eternal plan of redemption.
17. Therefore may God grant unto you, my brethren, that ye may begin to exercise your faith unto repentance, that ye begin to call upon his holy name, that he would have mercy upon you;
18. Yea, cry unto him for mercy; for he is mighty to save.
19. Yea, humble yourselves, and continue in prayer unto him.
20. Cry unto him when ye are in your fields, yea, over all your flocks.
21. Cry unto him in your houses, yea, over all your household, both morning, mid-day, and evening.
22. Yea, cry unto him against the power of your enemies.
23. Yea, cry unto him against the devil, who is an enemy to all righteousness.
24. Cry unto him over the crops of your fields, that ye may prosper in them.
25. Cry over the flocks of your fields, that they may increase.
26. But this is not all; ye must pour out your souls in your closets, and your secret places, and in your wilderness.
27. Yea, and when you do not cry unto the Lord, let your hearts be full, drawn out in prayer unto him continually for your welfare, and also for the welfare of those who are around you.

Alma 34:12, 14

According to Elder Bruce R. McConkie, an "infinite atonement" covers all men, the earth itself, and all forms of life on the earth. Covering all other worlds and beings that God created, the Atonement reaches out "into the endless expanses of eternity."

Alma 34:21–34

It is the infinite Atonement of Christ that "brings about means unto men that they may have faith unto repentance" (Alma 34:15). . . .

As Alma completed his moving and inspiring discourse on faith in Christ, Amulek stood to blend his testimony with that of his missionary companion. He testified of Christ, defining the infinite Atonement of the Redeemer as the essential empowering act that ignites and sustains faith, infuses hope with eternal meaning and substance, and generates the reality that the great plan of redemption can be brought about "immediately" for the penitent, humble, and obedient (see Alma 34:31). . . .

President Spencer W. Kimball said, "Note Amulek's words, especially those forceful statements involving timing. . . . Even if we leave aside the many scriptures which bear similar testimony, reading and prayerfully meditating upon this one [Alma 34:21–34] brings an awe-inspiring conviction of the need to repent—now!"

Throughout the Book of Mormon there is emphasis on the goodness of God and the invitation to come unto Christ. To do this one must exercise faith unto repentance. All the prophets have preached the doctrine of repentance, from Father Adam to our present day, and the message will never change. . . .

All have sinned. All need to repent. There are sins of commission and omission. What do we need to stop doing and what do we need to start doing?

Repentance is not so much an event as it is a process. True, there is the event of baptism, with guilt being swept away, and knowing one's forgiveness in regard to a particular sin in time—but there is also a continuing process of becoming better. We are not yet in a state of perfection, hence we are in the state of becoming through repentance. If we understand this, we acknowledge our unworthiness and dependence upon God, repenting earnestly and often. Repentance brings about sanctification and justification through our Savior, Jesus Christ, by the power of the Holy Ghost. We can progress. We can become "just." Those who are just will be made perfect "through Jesus" (D&C 76:69). (P/A)

Alma 34:27

This verse describes the act of having our hearts full, drawn out in prayer continually. As taught in 1 Thessalonians 5:17, it is possible to "pray without ceasing" if our hearts are always full and drawn out toward our Heavenly Father.

28. And now behold, my beloved brethren, I say unto you, do not suppose that this is all; for after ye have done all these things, if ye turn away the needy, and the naked, and visit not the sick and afflicted, and impart of your substance, if ye have, to those who stand in need—I say unto you, if ye do not any of these things behold, your prayer is vain, and availeth you nothing, and ye are as hypocrites who do deny the faith.
29. Therefore, if ye do not remember to be charitable, ye are as dross, which the refiners do cast out, (it being of no worth) and is trodden under foot of men.
30. And now, my brethren, I would that, after ye have received so many witnesses, seeing that the holy scriptures testify of these things, ye come forth and bring fruit unto repentance.
31. Yea, I would that ye would come forth and harden not your hearts any longer; for behold, now is the time and the day of your salvation; and therefore, if ye will repent and harden not your hearts, immediately shall the great plan of redemption be brought about unto you.
32. For behold, this life is the time for men to prepare to meet God; yea, behold the day of this life is the day for men to perform their labors.
33. And now, as I said unto you before, as ye have had so many witnesses, therefore, I beseech of you that ye do not procrastinate the day of your repentance until the end; for after this day of life, which is given us to prepare for eternity, behold, if we do not improve our time while in this life, then cometh the night of darkness wherein there can be no labor performed.
34. Ye cannot say, when ye are brought to that awful crisis, that I will repent, that I will return to my God. Nay, ye cannot say this; for that same spirit which doth possess your bodies at the time that ye go out of this life, that same spirit will have power to possess your body in that eternal world.
35. For behold, if ye have procrastinated the day of your repentance even until death, behold, ye have become subjected to the spirit of the devil, and he doth seal you his; therefore, the Spirit of the Lord hath withdrawn from you, and hath no place in you, and the devil hath all power over you; and this is the final state of the wicked.
36. And this I know, because the Lord hath said he dwelleth not in unholy temples, but in the hearts of the righteous doth he dwell; yea, and he has also said that the righteous shall sit down in his kingdom, to go no more out; but their garments should be made white through the blood of the Lamb.
37. And now, my beloved brethren, I desire that ye should remember

Alma 34:31–32

Someone once said that the greatest question to be asked of all mankind is, Am I prepared to meet my God? This thought—the thought of coming into the presence of our Father in Heaven and giving an account of our years lived in mortality—is sobering. The words of Amulek should awaken in all of us the urgency to increase our faith in Christ unto repentance, to come unto Him and partake of His atoning sacrifice. (O/C)

Alma 34:32–35

We should not conclude from these statements by Amulek that it is impossible for a person to repent once he has left this earth life. Other scriptures indicate that repentance may be obtained under certain conditions beyond the veil of mortality. For example, Peter mentions that after the crucifixion of Jesus Christ, the Savior "preached unto the spirits" of those who had died during the days of Noah (1 Peter 3:18–20) so that they "might be judged according to men in the flesh, but live according to God in the spirit" (1 Peter 4:6). However, we do not know the full conditions of repentance in the post-earthly spirit world, and, as Brother Talmage has stated, ". . . to suppose that the soul who has wilfully rejected the opportunity of repentance in this life will find it easy to repent there is contrary to reason. To procrastinate the day of repentance is to deliberately place ourselves in the power of the adversary" (*Articles of Faith*, 115). (Ludlow)

Alma 34:33

Amulek warns us not to procrastinate the day of our repentance, because if we do not improve our time while in this life, "then cometh the night of darkness wherein there can be no labor performed." (Alma 34:33.) The "night of darkness" referred to by Amulek is that period of a person's existence when he loses the *will* to repent. Thus when a person loses the desire to repent or decides he is not going to repent, then his "night of darkness" has come whether it is in this life or in the life to come. (Ludlow)

Alma 34:34

All men and women who are worthy to be called Latter-day Saints should live hour by hour in such a way that if they should be called suddenly from this life into the next they would be prepared. The preparation should be such that we should not fear to be called away suddenly into the spirit life. It is our privilege to so live as to have the spirit of light and intelligence to that extent that we shall feel satisfied that all will be well if we should be called away at any hour (Lorenzo Snow, CR, Oct. 1899, 2). (Ludlow)

these things, and that ye should work out your salvation with fear before God, and that ye should no more deny the coming of Christ;

38. That ye contend no more against the Holy Ghost, but that ye receive it, and take upon you the name of Christ; that ye humble yourselves even to the dust, and worship God, in whatsoever place ye may be in, in spirit and in truth; and that ye live in thanksgiving daily, for the many mercies and blessings which he doth bestow upon you.

39. Yea, and I also exhort you, my brethren, that ye be watchful unto prayer continually, that ye may not be led away by the temptations of the devil, that he may not overpower you, that ye may not become his subjects at the last day; for behold, he rewardeth you no good thing.

40. And now my beloved brethren, I would exhort you to have patience, and that ye bear with all manner of afflictions; that ye do not revile against those who do cast you out because of your exceeding poverty, lest ye become sinners like unto them;

41. But that ye have patience, and bear with those afflictions, with a firm hope that ye shall one day rest from all your afflictions.

CHAPTER 35

1. NOW it came to pass that after Amulek had made an end of these words, they withdrew themselves from the multitude and came over into the land of Jershon.

2. Yea, and the rest of the brethren, after they had preached the word unto the Zoramites, also came over into the land of Jershon.

3. And it came to pass that after the more popular part of the Zoramites had consulted together concerning the words which had been preached unto them, they were angry because of the word, for it did destroy their craft; therefore they would not hearken unto the words.

4. And they sent and gathered together throughout all the land all the people, and consulted with them concerning the words which had been spoken.

5. Now their rulers and their priests and their teachers did not let the people know concerning their desires; therefore they found out privily the minds of all the people.

6. And it came to pass that after they had found out the minds of all the people, those who were in favor of the words which had been spoken by Alma and his brethren were cast out of the land; and they were many; and they came over also into the land of Jershon.

7. And it came to pass that Alma and his brethren did minister unto them.

8. Now the people of the Zoramites were angry with the people of Ammon who were in Jershon, and the chief ruler of the Zoramites, being a very wicked man, sent over unto the people of Ammon desiring them that they should cast out of their land all those who came over from them into their land.

9. And he breathed out many

POINT OF INTEREST

The Temple of the Warriors at Chichén Itzá includes rows of carved columns depicting warriors.

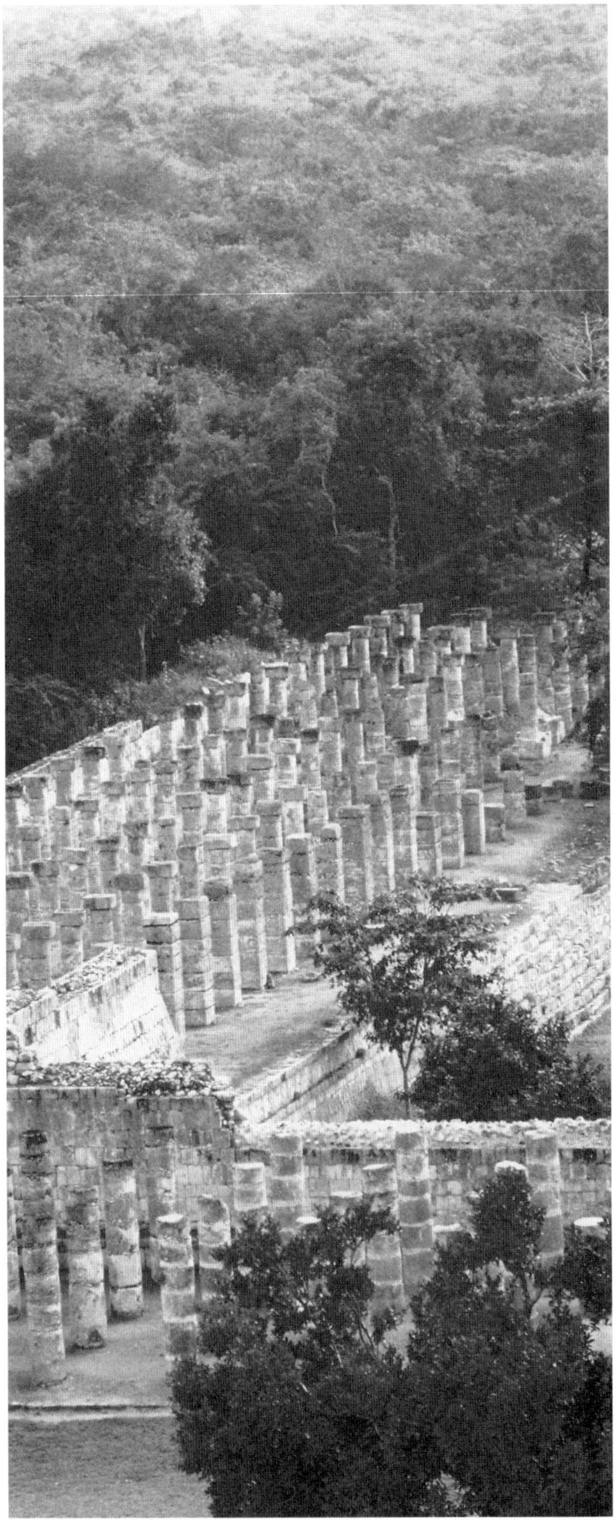

threatenings against them. And now the people of Ammon did not fear their words; therefore they did not cast them out, but they did receive all the poor of the Zoramites that came over unto them; and they did nourish them, and did clothe them, and did give unto them lands for their inheritance; and they did administer unto them according to their wants.

10. Now this did stir up the Zoramites to anger against the people of Ammon, and they began to mix with the Lamanites and to stir them up also to anger against them.

11. And thus the Zoramites and the Lamanites began to make preparations for war against the people of Ammon, and also against the Nephites.

12. And thus ended the seventeenth year of the reign of the judges over the people of Nephi.

13. And the people of Ammon departed out of the land of Jershon, and came over into the land of Melek, and gave place in the land of Jershon for the armies of the Nephites, that they might contend with the armies of the Lamanites and the armies of the Zoramites; and thus commenced a war betwixt the Lamanites and the Nephites, in the eighteenth year of the reign of the judges; and an account shall be given of their wars hereafter.

14. And Alma, and Ammon, and their brethren, and also the two sons of Alma returned to the land of Zarahemla, after having been instruments in the hands of God of bringing many of the Zoramites to repentance; and as many as were brought to repentance were driven out of their land; but they have lands for their inheritance in the land of Jershon, and they have taken up arms to defend themselves, and their wives, and children, and their lands.

15. Now Alma, being grieved for the iniquity of his people, yea for the wars, and the bloodsheds, and the contentions which were among them; and having been to declare the word, or sent to declare the word, among all the people in every city; and seeing that the hearts of the people began to wax hard, and that they began to be offended because of the strictness of the word, his heart was exceedingly sorrowful.

16. Therefore, he caused that his sons should be gathered together, that he might give unto them every one his charge, separately, concerning the things pertaining unto righteousness. And we have an account of his commandments, which he gave unto them according to his own record.

The commandments of Alma to his son, Helaman. Comprising chapters 36 and 37.

CHAPTER 36

1. MY son, give ear to my words; for I swear unto you, that inasmuch as ye shall keep the commandments of God ye shall prosper in the land.

2. I would that ye should do as I have done, in remembering the captivity of our fathers; for they were in bondage, and none could

Alma 36

This and the next six chapters have been inserted into the account before the final forty-four chapters of Alma, which are the accounts of war. The counsel Alma gives his sons also applies to us in our day. In these chapters, Alma is like a guide who protects us from the spiritual beasts that have the potential to mutilate us spiritually.

Alma 36:1

The Book of Mormon is one of the Lord's greatest tools for teaching parents how to counsel their children in righteousness. From the loving concern of Lehi and Sariah for their children at the outset of the chronicle to the intimate partnership of Mormon and his son Moroni at the end there is a continuous flow of inspiring examples of parent-child relationships. Consider the elder Alma's anxiety and ultimate joy in his son Alma. Consider further the latter's splendid legacy of instruction for his sons recorded in these current chapters. (P/A)

Alma 36:2

In this verse, Alma alludes to the importance of example; living the way we teach is what makes our testimony powerful (see D&C 65). This verse is also a reminder that we can learn important lessons from the lives of our parents, grandparents, and others we have been privileged to observe.

Alma 36:1, 30

Considering all the subjects about which Alma desired to counsel his sons, it is of great interest that he chose to speak first about keeping the commandments. Furthermore, he referred to this topic many times in the discussion. Without question, our happiness and eternal life depend on keeping the commandments—indeed, this is part of our baptismal covenants (see Mosiah 18:8–10). (O/C)

deliver them except it was the God of Abraham, and the God of Isaac, and the God of Jacob; and he surely did deliver them in their afflictions.
3. And now, O my son Helaman, behold, thou art in thy youth, and therefore, I beseech of thee that thou wilt hear my words and learn of me; for I do know that whosoever shall put their trust in God shall be supported in their trials, and their troubles, and their afflictions, and shall be lifted up at the last day.
4. And I would not that ye think that I know of myself—not of the temporal but of the spiritual, not of the carnal mind but of God.
5. Now, behold, I say unto you, if I had not been born of God I should not have known these things; but God has, by the mouth of his holy angel, made these things known unto me, not of any worthiness of myself;
6. For I went about with the sons of Mosiah, seeking to destroy the church of God; but behold, God sent his holy angel to stop us by the way.
7. And behold, he spake unto us, as it were the voice of thunder, and the whole earth did tremble beneath our feet; and we all fell to the earth, for the fear of the Lord came upon us.
8. But behold, the voice said unto me: Arise. And I arose and stood up, and beheld the angel.
9. And he said unto me: If thou wilt of thyself be destroyed, seek no more to destroy the church of God.
10. And it came to pass that I fell to the earth; and it was for the space of three days and three nights that I could not open my mouth, neither had I the use of my limbs.
11. And the angel spake more things unto me, which were heard by my brethren, but I did not hear them; for when I heard the words—If thou wilt be destroyed of thyself, seek no more to destroy the church of God—I was struck with such great fear and amazement lest perhaps I should be destroyed, that I fell to the earth and I did hear no more.
12. But I was racked with eternal torment, for my soul was harrowed up to the greatest degree and racked with all my sins.
13. Yea, I did remember all my sins and iniquities, for which I was tormented with the pains of hell; yea, I saw that I had rebelled against my God, and that I had not kept his holy commandments.
14. Yea, and I had murdered many of his children, or rather led them away unto destruction; yea, and in fine so great had been myiniquities, that the very thought of coming into the presence of my God did rack my soul with inexpressible horror.
15. Oh, thought I, that I could be banished and become extinct both soul and body, that I might not be brought to stand in the presence of my God, to be judged of my deeds.
16. And now, for three days and for three nights was I racked, even with the pains of a damned soul.
17. And it came to pass that as I was thus racked with torment, while I

Alma 36:3

We note that the prophet did not make promises *in case* we have trials, but rather *when* we do. We need not wonder why the Lord doesn't prevent our troubles from occurring, or whether He actually *causes* our trials and tribulations. While we bring many afflictions upon ourselves by committing sin, most afflictions are simply hazards of mortality and cannot be avoided. Saints who wonder why the Lord doesn't protect His people from suffering must realize that the Lord's purpose is to prepare people for problems instead of preventing those problems. In other words, we would have the Lord remove our burdens; instead He increases our capacity to carry them. (O/C)

Alma 36:5

In the Lord's scheme of family organization, the father has an inherent duty or responsibility, as well as a right or privilege, to counsel his children. This pattern exists in the heavens as well, where Heavenly Father extends His counsel when He sees the need, choosing the appropriate time and circumstances to do so. (O/C)

Alma 36:6–10

Some readers of the Book of Mormon have claimed there is a discrepancy in the accounts of the conversion of Alma as recorded in Mosiah 27:23 and Alma 36:10. It is true that one account mentions "two days and two nights" and the other says "three days and three nights," but there is no apparent discrepancy because they are not referring to exactly the same thing. In the account in the book of Mosiah the time element clearly refers to the period of fasting by the priests; no exact length of time is indicated for Alma's unconscious state. Note the major details of the account: After Alma was confronted by an angel and realized the enormity of his sins, he fell to the earth almost as if dead. Then he was carried to his father in this helpless condition. The father of Alma then called in the priests of the church and "*after they had fasted and prayed for the space of two days and two nights*, the limbs of Alma received their strength, and he stood up." (Mosiah 27:22–23. Italics added.) In the account in the book of Alma, however, the term "three days and three nights" clearly refers to the *total time* Alma could not open his mouth nor use his limbs. (Alma 36:10.) (Ludlow)

Alma 36:14

In recounting his sinful past to his son Helaman, Alma said that he had "murdered" many people, and then he adds, "or rather led them away unto destruction." . . . As Alma mentions later to his son Corianton, the murder of a human physical body is a grave sin. However, an even more serious sin is to murder the spiritual life of a person or, in other words, to purposely lead one away from the saving principles of the gospel. Concerning such people Alma says: ". . . whosoever murdereth against the light and knowledge of God, it is not easy for him to obtain forgiveness." (Alma 39:6.)

was harrowed up by the memory of my many sins, behold, I remembered also to have heard my father prophesy unto the people concerning the coming of one Jesus Christ, a Son of God, to atone for
the sins of the world.
18. Now, as my mind caught hold upon this thought, I cried within my heart: O Jesus, thou Son of God, have mercy on me, who am
in the gall of bitterness, and am encircled about by the everlasting
chains of death.
19. And now, behold, when I thought this, I could remember my
pains no more; yea, I was harrowed up by the memory of my sins
no more.
20. And oh, what joy, and what marvelous light I did behold; yea,
my soul was filled with joy as exceeding as was my pain!
21. Yea, I say unto you, my son, that there could be nothing so
exquisite and so bitter as were my pains. Yea, and again I say unto
you, my son, that on the other hand, there can be nothing so
exquisite and sweet as was my joy.
22. Yea, methought I saw, even as our father Lehi saw, God sitting
upon his throne, surrounded with numberless concourses of angels,
in the attitude of singing and praising their God; yea, and my soul
did long to be there.
23. But behold, my limbs did receive their strength again, and I
stood upon my feet, and did manifest unto the people that I had
been born of God.
24. Yea, and from that time even until now, I have labored without ceasing, that I might bring souls unto repentance; that I might
bring them to taste of the exceeding joy of which I did taste; that
they might also be born of God, and be filled with the Holy Ghost.
25. Yea, and now behold, O my son, the Lord doth give me exceedingly great joy in the fruit of my labors;
26. For because of the word which he has imparted unto me, behold,
many have been born of God, and have tasted as I have tasted, and
have seen eye to eye as I have seen; therefore they do know of these
things of which I have spoken,
as I do know; and the knowledge which I have is of God.
27. And I have been supported under trials and troubles of
every kind, yea, and in all
manner of afflictions; yea,
God has delivered me from
prison, and from bonds, and
from death; yea, and I do put
my trust in him, and he will
still deliver me.
28. And I know that he will
raise me up at the last day, to
dwell with him in glory; yea,
and I will praise him forever,
for he has brought our fathers
out of Egypt, and he has swallowed up the Egyptians in the
Red Sea; and he led them by
his power into the promised
land; yea, and he has delivered them out of

Alma 36:17–21

What Alma provides here is a wonderful description of the process that leads from the exquisite pain of sin to the exquisite joy of forgiveness. As President Marion G. Romney taught, all men must follow these steps to cry unto the Lord in sincere repentance; until we do, we cannot be reborn and will not experience the wonderful relief described by Alma.

Alma 36:24

The labors Alma describes in this verse provide powerful evidence that a person has truly repented and been born again.

Alma 36:27–28

As Alma describes the process of being lifted up by God, we are reminded of an important principle we should consistently apply in our own lives: once our spiritual progression has brought us to stand on higher ground, we are able to lift others up—but we can't lift others until we ourselves are standing on higher ground.

POINT OF INTEREST

A codex is a common type of Mesoamerican record (see below for an example of a codex). Codices typically consist of written pages made from tree bark or animal skins and are flattened, then structured to be folded in a manner similar to that of modern road maps.

bondage and captivity from time to time.
29. Yea, and he has also brought our fathers out of the land of
Jerusalem; and he has also, by his everlasting power, delivered
them out of bondage and captivity, from time to time even down
to the present day; and I have always retained in remembrance
their captivity; yea, and ye also ought to retain in remembrance, as
I have done, their captivity.
30. But behold, my son, this is not all; for ye ought to know as I do
know, that inasmuch as ye shall keep the commandments of God
ye shall prosper in the land; and ye ought to know also, that inasmuch as ye will not keep the commandments of God ye shall be
cut off from his presence. Now this is according to his word.

CHAPTER 37

1. AND now, my son Helaman, I command you that ye take the
records which have been entrusted with me;
2. And I also command you that ye keep a record of this people,
according as I have done, upon the plates of Nephi, and keep all
these things sacred which I have kept, even as I have kept them;
for it is for a wise purpose that they are kept.
3. And these plates of brass, which contain these engravings,
which have the records of the holy scriptures upon them, which
have the genealogy of our forefathers, even from the beginning—
4. Behold, it has been prophesied by our fathers, that they should
be kept and handed down from one generation to another, and be
kept and preserved by the hand of the Lord until they should go
forth unto every nation, kindred, tongue, and people, that they
shall know of the mysteries contained thereon.
5. And now behold, if they are kept they must retain their brightness; yea, and they will retain their brightness; yea, and also shall
all the plates which do contain that which is holy writ.
6. Now ye may suppose that this is foolishness in me; but behold I
say unto you, that by small and simple things are great things
brought to pass; and small means in many instances doth confound
the wise.
7. And the Lord God doth work by means to bring about his great
and eternal purposes; and by very small means the Lord doth confound the wise and bringeth about the salvation of many souls.
8. And now, it has hitherto been wisdom in God that these things
should be preserved; for behold, they have enlarged the memory of this people, yea, and convinced many of the error of
their ways, and brought them to the knowledge of

Alma 36:29

This verse is one more example, of many, in which Alma always gives the credit for his success to the Lord. It is a potent reminder to all of us that we need to acknowledge the Lord in all our dealings.

Alma 36:30

Too often we fail as parents in actually teaching our children the word of God. We do so many wonderful things, but we leave it to seminary and Church auxiliaries to teach the precious word of God to our children. We are responsible to teach our children. (P/A)

POINT OF INTEREST

Below is a "rolled out" representation of a roller seal uncovered at the site of Tlatilco, just west of Mexico City. The writing appears to date to between 700 and 400 B.C. When one scholar compared the characters to those from the Charles Anthon manuscript, he concluded that only a few of the characters were not *shared by the two sources* (see John L. Sorenson, *Images of Ancient America: Visualizing Book of Mormon Life* [Provo, Utah: FARMS, 1998]).

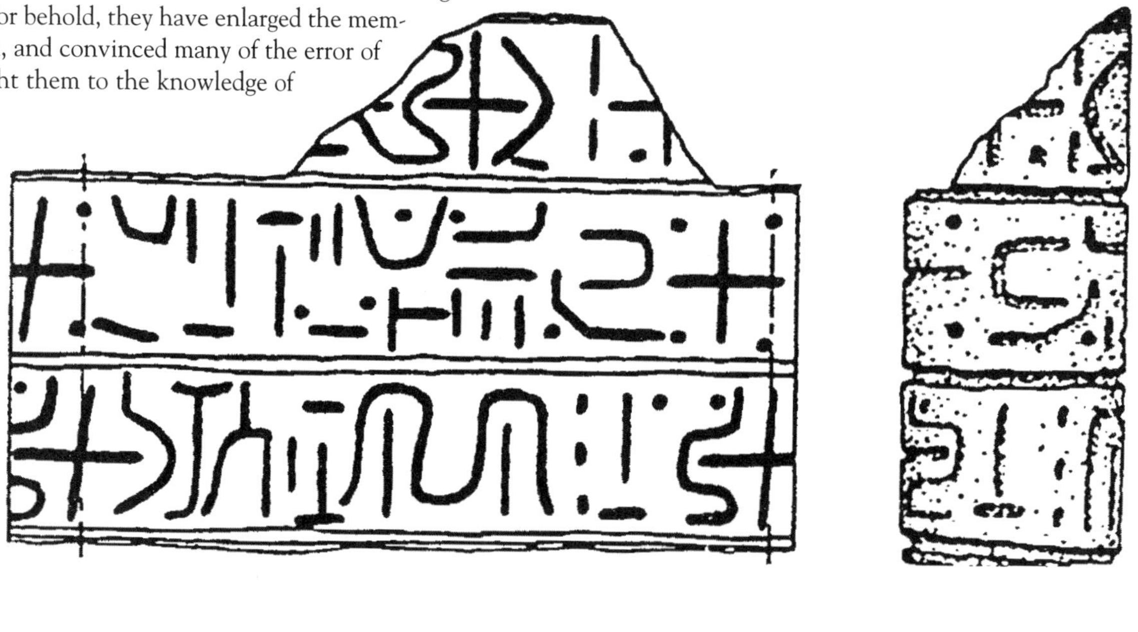

their God unto the salvation of their souls.
9. Yea, I say unto you, were it not for these things that these records do contain, which are on these plates, Ammon and his brethren could not have convinced so many thousands of the Lamanites of the incorrect tradition of their fathers; yea, these records and their words brought them unto repentance; that is, they brought them to the knowledge of the Lord their God, and to rejoice in Jesus Christ their Redeemer.
10. And who knoweth but what they will be the means of bringing many thousands of them, yea, and also many thousands of our stiffnecked brethren, the Nephites, who are now hardening their hearts in sin and iniquities, to the knowledge of their Redeemer?
11. Now these mysteries are not yet fully made known unto me; therefore I shall forbear.
12. And it may suffice if I only say they are preserved for a wise purpose, which purpose is known unto God; for he doth counsel in wisdom over all his works, and his paths are straight, and his course is one eternal round.
13. O remember, remember, my son Helaman, how strict are the commandments of God. And he said: If ye will keep my commandments ye shall prosper in the land—but if ye keep not his commandments ye shall be cut off from his presence.
14. And now remember, my son, that God has entrusted you with these things, which are sacred, which he has kept sacred, and also which he will keep and preserve for a wise purpose in him, that he may show forth his power unto future generations.
15. And now behold, I tell you by the spirit of prophecy, that if ye transgress the commandments of God, behold, these things which are sacred shall be taken away from you by the power of God, and ye shall be delivered up unto Satan, that he may sift you as chaff before the wind.
16. But if ye keep the commandments of God, and do with these things which are sacred according to that which the Lord doth command you, (for you must appeal unto the Lord for all things whatsoever ye must do with them) behold, no power of earth or hell can take them from you, for God is powerful to the fulfilling of all his words.
17. For he will fulfil all his promises which he shall make unto you, for he has fulfilled his promises which he has made unto our fathers.
18. For he promised unto them that he would preserve these things for a wise purpose in him, that he might show forth his power unto future generations.
19. And now behold, one purpose hath he fulfilled, even to the restoration of many thousands of the Lamanites to the knowledge of the truth; and he hath shown forth his power in them, and he will also still show forth his power in them unto future generations; therefore they shall be preserved.
20. Therefore I command you, my son Helaman, that ye be diligent in fulfilling all my words, and that ye be diligent in keeping the commandments of God as they are written.
21. And now, I will speak unto

you concerning those twenty-four plates, that ye keep them, that the mysteries and the works of darkness, and their secret works, or the secret works of those people who have been destroyed, may be made manifest unto this people; yea, all their murders, and robbings, and their plunderings, and all their wickedness and abominations, may be made manifest unto this people; yea, and that ye preserve these interpreters.
22. For behold, the Lord saw that his people began to work in darkness, yea, work secret murders and abominations; therefore the Lord said, if they did not repent they should be destroyed from off the face of the earth.
23. And the Lord said: I will prepare unto my servant Gazelem, a stone, which shall shine forth in darkness unto light, that I may discover unto my people who serve me, that I may discover unto them the works of their brethren, yea, their secret works, their works of darkness, and their wickedness and abominations.
24. And now, my son, these interpreters were prepared that the word of God might be fulfilled, which he spake, saying:
25. I will bring forth out of darkness unto light all their secret works and their abominations; and except they repent I will destroy them from off the face of the earth; and I will bring to light all their secrets and abominations, unto every nation that shall hereafter possess the land.
26. And now, my son, we see that they did not repent; therefore they have been destroyed, and thus far the word of God has been fulfilled; yea, their secret abominations have been brought out of darkness and made known unto us.
27. And now, my son, I command you that ye retain all their oaths, and their covenants, and their agreements in their secret abominations; yea, and all their signs and their wonders ye shall keep from this people, that they know them not, lest peradventure they should fall into darkness also and be destroyed.
28. For behold, there is a curse upon all this land, that destruction shall come upon all those workers of darkness, according to the power of God, when they are fully ripe; therefore I desire that this people might not be destroyed.
29. Therefore ye shall keep these secret plans of their oaths and their covenants from this people, and only their wickedness and their murders and their abominations shall ye make known unto them; and ye shall teach them to abhor such wickedness and abominations and murders; and ye shall also teach them that these people were destroyed on account of their wickedness and abominations and their murders.
30. For behold, they murdered all the prophets of the Lord who came among them to declare unto them concerning their iniquities; and the blood of those whom they murdered did cry unto the Lord their God for vengeance upon those who were their murderers; and thus the judgments of God did come upon these workers of darkness and secret combinations.
31. Yea, and cursed be the land forever and ever unto those workers of

Alma 37:21

The twenty-four plates referred to in this verse are the plates of gold found by the people of King Limhi. Prepared by the prophet Ether, they contain the history of the Jaredites and comprise the book of Ether in the Book of Mormon.

Alma 37:23

Two interesting words that appear for the first time in the book of Alma are *Gazelem* (Alma 37:23) and *Liahona* (Alma 37:38). Possible meanings of these two words are given by Reynolds and Sjodahl as follows:

"*Gazelem* is a name given to a servant of God. The word appears to have its roots in Gaz—a stone, and Aleim, a name of God as a revelator, or the interposer in the affairs of men. If this suggestion is correct, its roots admirably agree with its apparent meaning—a seer.

"*Liahona.* This interesting word is Hebrew with an Egyptian ending. . . . *L* is a Hebrew preposition meaning 'to,' and sometimes used to express the possessive case. *Iah* is a Hebrew abbreviated form of 'Jehovah,' common in Hebrew names. *On* is the Hebrew name of the Egyptian 'City of the Sun.' . . . *L-iah-on* means, therefore, literally, 'To God is Light'; or, 'of God is Light.' That is to say, God gives light, as does the Sun. The final *a* reminds us that the Egyptian form of the Hebrew name *On* is *Annu*, and that seems to be the form Lehi used." (Ludlow)

Alma 37:23

Alma specifically instructed Helaman not to record the secret oaths, agreements, and covenants of the secret combinations; he did not want us in our day to be able to read those accounts and learn how to use the evil oaths and covenants (see Helaman 6:25-26).

darkness and secret combinations, even unto destruction, except they repent before they are fully ripe.
32. And now, my son, remember the words which I have spoken unto you; trust not those secret plans unto this people, but teach them an everlasting hatred against sin and iniquity.
33. Preach unto them repentance, and faith on the Lord Jesus Christ; teach them to humble themselves and to be meek and lowly in heart; teach them to withstand every temptation of the devil, with their faith on the Lord Jesus Christ.
34. Teach them to never be weary of good works, but to be meek and lowly in heart; for such shall find rest to their souls.
35. O, remember, my son, and learn wisdom in thy youth; yea, learn in thy youth to keep the commandments of God.
36. Yea, and cry unto God for all thy support; yea, let all thy doings be unto the Lord, and whithersoever thou goest let it be in the Lord; yea, let all thy thoughts be directed unto the Lord; yea, let the affections of thy heart be placed upon the Lord forever.
37. Counsel with the Lord in all thy doings, and he will direct thee for good; yea, when thou liest down at night lie down unto the Lord, that he may watch over you in your sleep; and when thou risest in the morning let thy heart be full of thanks unto God; and if ye do these things, ye shall be lifted up at the last day.
38. And now, my son, I have somewhat to say concerning the thing which our fathers call a ball, or director—or our fathers called it Liahona, which is, being interpreted, a compass; and the Lord prepared it.
39. And behold, there cannot any man work after the manner of so curious a workmanship. And behold, it was prepared to show unto our fathers the course which they should travel in the wilderness.
40. And it did work for them according to their faith in God; therefore, if they had faith to believe that God could cause that those spindles should point the way they should go, behold, it was done; therefore they had this miracle, and also many other miracles wrought by the power of God, day by day.
41. Nevertheless, because those miracles were worked by small means it did show unto them marvelous works. They were slothful, and forgot to exercise their faith and diligence and then those marvelous works ceased, and they did not progress in their journey;
42. Therefore, they tarried in the wilderness, or did not travel a direct course, and were afflicted with hunger and thirst, because of their transgressions.
43. And now, my son, I would that ye should understand that these things are not without a shadow; for as our fathers were slothful to give heed to this compass (now these things were temporal) they

Alma 37:33–37

The points given as part of Alma's advice to Helaman serve as a pattern for modern living and as an effective and righteous pattern for a parent's advice to a child. Some of the most important parts of that advice are to pray continually and to keep our hearts centered on the Savior. In addition, Heavenly Father should be the first thing on our minds in the morning and the last thing on our minds at night.

Alma 37:35–37

The word *wisdom* in the Book of Mormon is used to denote the wise or effective use of knowledge; it not only concerns the acquisition of knowledge, but also the right use of knowledge. . . . (Ludlow)

Alma 37:37

Members of the Church and other God-fearing people often ask, Can a man have a career in the military service and still be in good standing with the Lord? The Book of Mormon gives several examples of righteous men who served in the military most of their lives and stood approved of the Lord. One such example is Captain Moroni . . .

As a practical army leader, Moroni followed the best military procedures he knew, sending spies to watch the enemy. In addition, he did something almost unheard of in our age of so-called enlightenment. He sent men to inquire of the Lord's living prophet, to learn what the Lord would have him do as military commander. Of course, this was the key to Moroni's success, and we will also be successful in our righteous endeavors if we will "counsel with the Lord in all [our] doings." (O/C)

Alma 37:41–43

We know that Lehi and his family were given the Liahona as a guide—but we also know it was up to them to live appropriately and exercise sufficient faith, or the Liahona would not guide them. The compass would be useful. Accordingly, we must exercise sufficient faith and be obedient to the commandments and our covenants if we expect to be guided. According to President Harold B. Lee, even if we were called in the pre-existence to do a great work on earth, we can lose our birthright and squander our blessings if we are not obedient. And just because we are members of the Church, we do not automatically gain favor with the Lord; we need to learn while young to keep the commandments of God, and then endure to the end if we hope to gain favor with the Lord and inherit eternal life.

did not prosper; even so it is with things which are spiritual.
44. For behold, it is as easy to give heed to the word of Christ,
which will point to you a straight course to eternal bliss, as it was
for our fathers to give heed to this compass, which would point
unto them a straight course to the promised land.
45. And now I say, is there not a type in this thing? For just as surely as this director did bring our fathers, by following its course, to
the promised land, shall the words of Christ, if we follow their
course, carry us beyond this vale of sorrow into a far better land of
promise.
46. O my son, do not let us be slothful because of the easiness of
the way; for so was it with our fathers; for so was it prepared for
them, that if they would look they might live; even so it is with us.
The way is prepared, and if we will look we may live forever.
47. And now, my son, see that ye take care of these sacred things,
yea, see that ye look to God and live. Go unto this people and
declare the word, and be sober. My son, farewell.

The commandments of Alma to his son, Shiblon.

CHAPTER 38

1. MY son, give ear to my words, for I say unto you, even as I said
unto Helaman, that inasmuch as ye shall keep the commandments
of God ye shall prosper in the land; and inasmuch as ye will not
keep the commandments of God ye shall be cut off from his presence.
2. And now, my son, I trust that I shall have great joy in you,
because of your steadiness and your faithfulness unto God; for as
you have commenced in your youth to look to the Lord your God,
even so I hope that you will continue in keeping his commandments; for blessed is he that endureth to the end.
3. I say unto you, my son, that I have had great joy in thee already,
because of thy faithfulness and thy diligence, and thy patience and
thy long-suffering among the people of the Zoramites.
4. For I know that thou wast in bonds; yea, and I also know that
thou wast stoned for the word's sake; and thou didst bear all these
things with patience because the Lord was with thee; and now
thou knowest that the Lord did deliver thee.
5. And now my son, Shiblon, I would that ye should remember, that
as much as ye shall put your trust in God even so much ye shall be
delivered out of your trials, and your troubles, and your afflictions,
and ye shall be lifted up at the last day.
6. Now, my son, I would not that ye

Alma 38:2

An important aspect of parental instruction is to recognize the good in young people and to encourage, energize, and motivate them to attain their divine potential. (P/A)

Alma 38:2–3

An important aspect of parental instruction is to recognize the good in young people and to encourage, energize, and motivate them to attain their divine potential. . . .

Alma bestowed his fatherly blessing and counsel on his son Shiblon. He praises him and encourages him to continue in his faithfulness. He outlines positive character traits, as well as their bounds.

President Ezra Taft Benson said, "Praise your children more than you correct them. Praise them for even their smallest achievement. Encourage your children to come to you for counsel with their problems and questions by listening to them every day. Discuss with them such important matters as dating, sex, and other matters affecting their growth and development, and do it early enough so they will not obtain information from questionable sources." (P/A)

should think that I know these things of myself, but it is the Spirit of God which is in me which maketh these things known unto me; for if I had not been born of God I should not have known these things.
7. But behold, the Lord in his great mercy sent his angel to declare unto me that I must stop the work of destruction among his people; yea, and I have seen an angel face to face, and he spake with me, and his voice was as thunder, and it shook the whole earth.
8. And it came to pass that I was three days and three nights in the most bitter pain and anguish of soul; and never, until I did cry out unto the Lord Jesus Christ for mercy, did I receive a remission of my sins. But behold, I did cry unto him and I did find peace to my soul.
9. And now, my son, I have told you this that ye may learn wisdom, that ye may learn of me that there is no other way or means whereby man can be saved, only in and through Christ. Behold, he is the life and the light of the world. Behold, he is the word of truth and righteousness.
10. And now, as ye have begun to teach the word even so I would that ye should continue to teach; and I would that ye would be diligent and temperate in all things.
11. See that ye are not lifted up unto pride; yea, see that ye do not boast in your own wisdom, nor of your much strength.
12. Use boldness, but not overbearance; and also see that ye bridle all your passions, that ye may be filled with love; see that ye refrain from idleness.
13. Do not pray as the Zoramites do, for ye have seen that they pray to be heard of men, and to be praised for their wisdom.
14. Do not say: O God, I thank thee that we are better than our brethren; but rather say: O Lord, forgive my unworthiness, and remember my brethren in mercy—yea, acknowledge your unworthiness before God at all times.
15. And may the Lord bless your soul, and receive you at the last day into his kingdom, to sit down in peace. Now go, my son, and teach the word unto this people. Be sober. My son, farewell.

The commandments of Alma to his son, Corianton. Comprising chapters 39 to 42 inclusive.

CHAPTER 39

1. AND now, my son, I have somewhat more to say unto thee than what I said unto thy brother; for behold, have ye not observed the steadiness of thy brother, his faithfulness, and his diligence in keeping the commandments of God? Behold, has he not set a good example for thee?
2. For thou didst not give so much heed unto my words as did thy brother, among the people of the Zoramites. Now this is what I have against thee; thou didst go on unto

Alma 38:9–14

Although Alma's counsel to his son Shiblon occupies only one brief chapter in the Book of Mormon, yet it is filled with good advice for young people of all times and places. Among other things, Alma counsels Shiblon (and, indirectly, all of us): (1) to "learn wisdom . . . that there is no other way or means whereby man can be saved, only in and through Christ"; (2) to teach the word of God; (3) to "be diligent and temperate in all things"; (4) to be humble—not to boast of wisdom or strength; (5) to "use boldness, but not overbearance"; (6) to bridle the passions; (7) to refrain from idleness; (8) to pray with sincerity of heart and not "to be heard of men"; (9) to acknowledge unworthiness before God and to ask him for forgiveness of sin. (Ludlow)

Alma 39:1–6

Concerning murder, the authorities of the Church have published the following brief statement:

"It is in the same category as the rebellion of Satan and his hosts and therefore it would not be surprising if the penalties to be imposed upon a murderer were to be of similar character as the penalties meted out to those spirits which were cast out of heaven with Satan."

The teaching of the Church is equally strong on the sin of unchastity or adultery. . . . (Ludlow)

Alma 39:2

How does one counsel a son (or daughter) who chooses to travel on byways rather than highways, who lapses into unrighteous behavior and misses the mark when it comes to understanding the plain and precious truths of the gospel? Alma's handling of this delicate situation in the case of his son Corianton is a model of both exactitude and compassion. He introduces the dialogue with this charitable understatement: "For thou didst not give so much heed unto my words as did thy brother" (Alma 39:2). He then teaches his son concerning righteousness, death, the spirit world, the resurrection, and the God-bestowed freedom that mortals have to choose the right. (P/A)

Alma 39:3

When Corianton abandoned his post to seek after the harlot Isabel, he followed the example of Lucifer, who abandoned his holy calling for self-satisfaction and self-aggrandizement. Corianton yielded to the temptations of the evil one, yielding up his own power to the powers of darkness. One of the great lessons of life is that we must safeguard ourselves from becoming subject to the power of the devil. We can do this by remaining true to our covenants with the Savior Jesus Christ. To be entrusted by the Lord and to be true to that trust is one of the most sacred experiences of mortality. (O/C)

boasting in thy strength and thy wisdom.
3. And this is not all, my son. Thou didst do that which was grievous unto me; for thou didst forsake the ministry, and did go over into the land of Siron among the borders of the Lamanites, after the harlot Isabel.
4. Yea, she did steal away the hearts of many; but this was no excuse for thee, my son. Thou shouldst have tended to the ministry wherewith thou wast entrusted.
5. Know ye not, my son, that these things are an abomination in the sight of the Lord; yea, most abominable above all sins save it be the shedding of innocent blood or denying the Holy Ghost?
6. For behold, if ye deny the Holy Ghost when it once has had place in you, and ye know that ye deny it, behold, this is a sin which is unpardonable; yea, and whosoever murdereth against the light and knowledge of God, it is not easy for him to obtain forgiveness; yea, I say unto you, my son, that it is not easy for him to obtain a forgiveness.
7. And now, my son, I would to God that ye had not been guilty of so great a crime. I would not dwell upon your crimes, to harrow up your soul, if it were not for your good.
8. But behold, ye cannot hide your crimes from God; and except ye repent they will stand as a testimony against you at the last day.
9. Now my son, I would that ye should repent and forsake your sins, and go no more after the lusts of your eyes, but cross yourself in all these things; for except ye do this ye can in nowise inherit the kingdom of God. Oh, remember, and take it upon you, and cross yourself in these things.
10. And I command you to take it upon you to counsel with your elder brothers in your undertakings; for behold, thou art in thy youth, and ye stand in need to be nourished by your brothers. And give heed to their counsel.
11. Suffer not yourself to be led away by any vain or foolish thing; suffer not the devil to lead away your heart again after those wicked harlots. Behold, O my son, how great iniquity ye brought upon the Zoramites; for when they saw your conduct they would not believe in my words.
12. And now the Spirit of the Lord doth say unto me: Command thy children to do good, lest they lead away the hearts of many people to destruction; therefore I command you, my son, in the fear of God, that ye refrain from your iniquities;
13. That ye turn to the Lord with all your mind, might, and strength; that ye lead away the hearts of no more to do wickedly; but rather return unto them, and acknowledge your faults and that wrong which ye have done.
14. Seek not after riches nor the vain things of this world; for behold, you cannot carry them with you.

Alma 39:4–7

The most serious of these sins is to deny the Holy Ghost and become a son of perdition. . . .

This is an *unpardonable* sin because it cannot be paid for (or pardoned) either by the sinner himself or through the atonement of Jesus Christ. . . .

The word *pardon* as used in the scriptures means to be sanctified, to be clean, to reach a point where a broken law has no further claim upon the sinner. Thus the most serious sin is *unpardonable* because the law will always have a claim upon the sinner, and the sinner will always remain unclean; he cannot ever regain the presence of God, for "no unclean thing can enter into his kingdom." (3 Nephi 27:19.) All unpardonable sins are of necessity also unforgivable.

The word *forgiveness* as used in the scriptures indicates one is "given something before." Thus when a person repents of a sin, Jesus Christ, through his atonement, pays for (or atones for) part of the broken law *before* the person makes *full* payment. Thus he is "fore-given" that part of the penalty paid for by Jesus Christ. Forgiveness is possible only upon repentance; thus those who refuse to repent "remain as though there had been no redemption made, except it be the loosing of the bands of death." (Alma 11:41; read also D&C 19:15–20.) (Ludlow)

Alma 39:9

The question is sometimes asked concerning the meaning of the expression "cross yourself in all these things." Some people evidently read into this statement something that is not intended; they think it pertains to the practice of physically drawing a cross as it is done by members of some Christian churches.

The meaning of the expression "cross yourself" is clarified in other scriptures. For example, 3 Nephi 12:30 says: "For it is better that ye should deny yourselves of these things, wherein ye will take up your cross, than that ye should be cast into hell." In Matthew 16:24 the Savior says, "If any man will come after me, let him deny himself, and take up his cross, and follow me." Both of these scriptures indicate that to "cross yourself" means to deny yourself. In the Inspired Version of the New Testament the Savior makes it absolutely clear that this is the meaning of the term: "And now for a man to take up his cross, is to deny himself all ungodliness, and every worldly lust, and keep my commandments." (Matthew 16:26.) (Ludlow)

15. And now, my son, I would say somewhat unto you concerning the coming of Christ. Behold, I say unto you, that it is he that surely shall come to take away the sins of the world; yea, he cometh to declare glad tidings of salvation unto his people.
16. And now, my son, this was the ministry unto which ye were called, to declare these glad tidings unto this people to prepare their minds; or rather that salvation might come unto them, that they may prepare the minds of their children to hear the word at the time of his coming.
17. And now I will ease your mind somewhat on this subject. Behold, you marvel why these things should be known so long beforehand. Behold, I say unto you, is not a soul at this time as precious unto God as a soul will be at the time of his coming?
18. Is it not as necessary that the plan of redemption should be made known unto this people as well as unto their children?
19. Is it not as easy at this time for the Lord to send his angel to declare these glad tidings unto us as unto our children, or as after the time of his coming?

CHAPTER 40

1. NOW my son, here is somewhat more I would say unto thee; for I perceive that thy mind is worried concerning the resurrection of the dead.
2. Behold, I say unto you, that there is no resurrection—or, I would say, in other words, that this mortal does not put on immortality, this corruption does not put on incorruption—until after the coming of Christ.
3. Behold, he bringeth to pass the resurrection of the dead. But behold, my son, the resurrection is not yet. Now, I unfold unto you a mystery; nevertheless, there are many mysteries which are kept, that no one knoweth them save God himself. But I show unto you one thing which I have inquired diligently of God that I might know—that is concerning the resurrection.
4. Behold, there is a time appointed that all shall come forth from the dead. Now when this time cometh no one knows; but God knoweth the time which is appointed.
5. Now, whether there shall be one time, or a second time, or a third time, that men shall come forth from the dead, it mattereth not; for God knoweth all these things; and it sufficeth me to know that this is the case—that there is a time appointed that all shall rise from the dead.
6. Now there must needs be a space betwixt the time of death and the time of the resurrection.
7. And now I would inquire what becometh of the souls of men from this time of death to the time appointed for the resurrection?
8. Now whether there is more than one time appointed for men to rise it mattereth not; for all do not die at once, and this mattereth not; all is

Alma 39:15

When Alma exhorted his sons to live righteously, he did so in the context of his own grievous past. He taught repentance with authority, because he himself was an authority on repentance: "Yea, I say unto you, my son, that there could be nothing so exquisite and so bitter as were my pains. Yea, and again I say unto you, my son, that on the other hand, there can be nothing so exquisite and sweet as was my joy" (Alma 36:21). What a powerful testimony of the effects of repentance and the application of the principles of the Atonement! (P/A)

Alma 40:1

Alma, having chastened Corianton, seeks to help him understand precious doctrines that can help him reform. Alma realized that his son's mind was troubled as to the doctrines that give specific hope for the future as well as accountability for the present. The devil teaches the opposite of accountability and hope (see 2 Ne. 28:7–8; Alma 30:18). When we see that people believe the misguided philosophy of "Eat, drink, and be merry, for tomorrow we die—and that is the end of our existence," it is easier to understand their behavior, though we grieve over the resulting negative consequences that must surely befall them. Such was the case of Corianton. The good news was that Corianton listened to his father, and his life was apparently turned around for the better. (P/A)

Alma 40:4–5

People [who] say, "Eat, drink, and be merry, for tomorrow we die" (2 Nephi 28:7) . . . mistakenly conclud[e] that they can sinfully satisfy their lustful desires without suffering any consequences. In essence, they deny God's laws of justice. Alma asserted that, contrary to the mistaken notions of some, all people who die will eventually come forth from the dead and experience a resurrection of their physical body. (See Alma 40:4–5.) (O/C)

as one day with God, and time only is measured unto men.
9. Therefore, there is a time appointed unto men that they shall rise from the dead; and there is a space between the time of death and the resurrection. And now, concerning this space of time, what becometh of the souls of men is the thing which I have inquired diligently of the Lord to know; and this is the thing of which I do know.
10. And when the time cometh when all shall rise, then shall they know that God knoweth all the times which are appointed unto man.
11. Now, concerning the state of the soul between death and the resurrection—Behold, it has been made known unto me by an angel, that the spirits of all men, as soon as they are departed from this mortal body, yea, the spirits of all men, whether they be good or evil, are taken home to that God who gave them life.
12. And then shall it come to pass, that the spirits of those who are righteous are received into a state of happiness, which is called paradise, a state of rest, a state of peace, where they shall rest from all their troubles and from all care, and sorrow.
13. And then shall it come to pass, that the spirits of the wicked, yea, who are evil—for behold, they have no part nor portion of the Spirit of the Lord; for behold, they chose evil works rather than good; therefore the spirit of the devil did enter into them, and take possession of their house—and these shall be cast out into outer darkness; there shall be weeping, and wailing, and gnashing of teeth, and this because of their own iniquity, being led captive by the will of the devil.
14. Now this is the state of the souls of the wicked, yea, in darkness, and a state of awful, fearful looking for the fiery indignation of the wrath of God upon them; thus they remain in this state, as well as the righteous in paradise, until the time of their resurrection.
15. Now, there are some that have understood that this state of happiness and this state of misery of the soul, before the resurrection, was a first resurrection. Yea, I admit it may be termed a resurrection, the raising of the spirit or the soul and their consignation to happiness or misery, according to the words which have been spoken.
16. And behold, again it hath been spoken, that there is a first resurrection, a resurrection of all those who have been, or who are, or who shall be, down to the resurrection of Christ from the dead.
17. Now, we do not suppose that this first resurrection, which is spoken of in this manner, can be the resurrection of the souls and their consignation to happiness or misery. Ye cannot suppose that this is what it meaneth.
18. Behold, I say unto you, Nay; but it meaneth the reuniting of the

Alma 40:11

Brigham Young said, "Many wonder where people go after death. In other words, where is the world of spirits? It is right here. . . . It is incorporated within this celestial system. Can you see it with your natural eyes? No. Can you see spirits in this room? No. Suppose the Lord should touch your eyes that you might see, could you then see the spirits? Yes, as plainly as you now see bodies, as did the servant of Elijah. If the Lord would permit it, and it was his will that it should be done, you could see the spirits that have departed from this world, as plainly as you now see bodies with your natural eyes."

Alma 40:11–14

The scriptures teach us the answers to the grand queries of life: Where do we come from? Where do we go after death? What is our ultimate destiny? Alma's counsel to his son Corianton lifts us to a fuller understanding of the future stages of human life along the way to perfection.

Elder Bruce R. McConkie explained, "There are two distinct senses in which the expression *spirit prison* is used:

"1. Since disembodied spirits cannot gain a fulness of joy until their resurrection (D&C 93:33–34), they consider their habitation in the spirit world as one of imprisonment, and so the whole spirit world (including both paradise and hell) is a *spirit prison*. . . .

"2. In a more particular sense, however, the *spirit prison* is hell, that portion of the spirit world where the wicked dwell. (Moses 7:37–39.)" (P/A)

Alma 40:14–26

Alma makes it very clear that the wicked will have no part in the first resurrection; the wicked, no matter when they lived, will have to wait until the final resurrection. The term "first resurrection" is used in the scriptures as a synonym for "the resurrection of the just." Thus, if one comes forth the first opportunity he has to be resurrected after he dies, he comes forth in the morning of *his* first resurrection. (Ludlow)

Alma 40:15

When our spirits leave these bodies, will they be happy? Not perfectly so. Why? Because the spirit is absent from the body; it cannot be perfectly happy while a part of the man is lying in the earth. How can the happiness be complete when only a part of the redemption is accomplished? You cannot be perfectly happy until you get a new house. You . . . will be at ease in paradise; but still you will be looking for a house where your spirit can enter, and act as you did in former times, only more perfectly, having superior powers (Orson Pratt, *Journal of Discourses*, 1:289–90). (Ludlow)

soul with the body, of those from the days of Adam down to the resurrection of Christ.
19. Now, whether the souls and the bodies of those of whom has been spoken shall all be reunited at once, the wicked as well as the righteous, I do not say; let it suffice, that I say that they all come forth; or in other words, their resurrection cometh to pass before the resurrection of those who die after the resurrection of Christ.
20. Now, my son, I do not say that their resurrection cometh at the resurrection of Christ; but behold, I give it as my opinion, that the souls and the bodies are reunited, of the righteous, at the resurrection of Christ, and his ascension into heaven.
21. But whether it be at his resurrection or after, I do not say; but this much I say, that there is a space between death and the resurrection of the body, and a state of the soul in happiness or in misery until the time which is appointed of God that the dead shall come forth, and be reunited, both soul and body, and be brought to stand before God, and be judged according to their works.
22. Yea, this bringeth about the restoration of those things of which has been spoken by the mouths of the prophets.
23. The soul shall be restored to the body, and the body to the soul; yea, and every limb and joint shall be restored to its body; yea, even a hair of the head shall not be lost; but all things shall be restored to their proper and perfect frame.
24. And now, my son, this is the restoration of which has been spoken by the mouths of the prophets—
25. And then shall the righteous shine forth in the kingdom of God.
26. But behold, an awful death cometh upon the wicked; for they die as to things pertaining to things of righteousness; for they are unclean, and no unclean thing can inherit the kingdom of God; but they are cast out, and consigned to partake of the fruits of their labors or their works, which have been evil; and they drink the dregs of a bitter cup.

CHAPTER 41

1. AND now, my son, I have somewhat to say concerning the restoration of which has been spoken; for behold, some have wrested the scriptures, and have gone far astray because of this thing. And I perceive that thy mind has been worried also concerning this thing. But behold, I will explain it unto thee.
2. I say unto thee, my son, that the plan of restoration is requisite with the justice of God; for it is requisite that all things should be restored to their proper order. Behold, it is requisite and just, according to the power and resurrection of Christ,

Alma 40:18

Bruce R. McConkie taught that two events of transcendent importance make possible the resurrection: 1. *The fall of Adam;* and 2. *The redemptive sacrifice of the Son of God.* Adam's fall brought temporal or natural death into the world; that is, as a result of Adam's fall mortality was introduced, and mortality is the forerunner of death. Christ's redeeming sacrifice ransomed men from the effects of Adam's fall in that mortality is replaced by immortality, or in other words in that the dead come forth in the resurrection. (P/A)

Alma 40:23

The prophets of the Book of Mormon definitely teach that all mankind will be resurrected from the dead. . . . The prophets of this dispensation have also taught that the actual, physical body will be resurrected and, through the law of restoration, will essentially become perfect. The Prophet Joseph Smith taught the following concerning the resurrected body:

As concerning the resurrection, I will merely say that all men will come from the grave as they lie down, whether old or young; there will not be "added unto their stature one cubit," neither taken from it; all will be raised by the power of God, having spirit in their bodies, and not blood. Children will be enthroned in the presence of God and the Lamb with bodies of the same stature that they had on earth, having been redeemed by the blood of the Lamb; they will there enjoy the fulness of that light, glory and intelligence, which is prepared in the celestial kingdom. "Blessed are the dead who die in the Lord, for they rest from their labors and their works do follow them" (Revelation 14:13) (HC, 4:555–56). (Ludlow)

Alma 41:1, 2

[At the time of resurrection], the spirit is restored to the body in which it will dwell for eternity, a condition referred to as immortality. This is the universal blessing the Savior provided for all mankind as part of His Atonement.

As part of the resurrection process, . . . "all things shall be restored to their proper and perfect frame" (Alma 40:23). When bodies have physical or mental impairments in mortality, they will be whole and complete in the immortal life to come. Joseph F. Smith explained:

"[T]hese same mortal bodies as they are now, bearing the marks just as much as Christ's body bore the marks that were upon him. They will come forth from their graves, but they will be immediately immortalized, restored to their perfect frame, limb and joint, and the poor, unfortunate creature who has lost a leg or an arm or a finger will have it restored to its proper frame, every joint to its place, and every part to its part, and it will be made perfect, for that is the law of restoration that God has instituted by which His own purpose cannot fail, by which His own designs concerning His children must be consummated." (O/C)

that the soul of man should be restored to its body, and that every part of the body should be restored to itself.
3. And it is requisite with the justice of God that men should be judged according to their works; and if their works were good in this life, and the desires of their hearts were good, that they should also, at the last day, be restored unto that which is good.
4. And if their works are evil they shall be restored unto them for evil. Therefore, all things shall be restored to their proper order, every thing to its natural frame—mortality raised to immortality, corruption to incorruption—raised to endless happiness to inherit the kingdom of God, or to endless misery to inherit the kingdom of the devil, the one on one hand, the other on the other—
5. The one raised to happiness according to his desires of happiness, or good according to his desires of good; and the other to evil according to his desires of evil; for as he has desired to do evil all the day long even so shall he have his reward of evil when the night cometh.
6. And so it is on the other hand. If he hath repented of his sins, and desired righteousness until the end of his days, even so he shall be rewarded unto righteousness.
7. These are they that are redeemed of the Lord; yea, these are they that are taken out, that are delivered from that endless night of darkness; and thus they stand or fall; for behold, they are their own judges, whether to do good or do evil.
8. Now, the decrees of God are unalterable; therefore, the way is prepared that whosoever will may walk therein and be saved.
9. And now behold, my son, do not risk one more offense against your God upon those points of doctrine, which ye have hitherto risked to commit sin.
10. Do not suppose, because it has been spoken concerning restoration, that ye shall be restored from sin to happiness. Behold, I say unto you, wickedness never was happiness.
11. And now, my son, all men that are in a state of nature, or I would say, in a carnal state, are in the gall of bitterness and in the bonds of iniquity; they are without God in the world, and they have gone contrary to the nature of God; therefore, they are in a state contrary to the nature of happiness.
12. And now behold, is the meaning of the word restoration to take a thing of a natural state and place it in an unnatural state, or to place it in a state opposite to its nature?
13. O, my son, this is not the case; but the meaning of the word restoration is to bring back again evil for evil, or carnal for carnal, or devilish for devilish—good for that which is good; righteous for that which is righteous; just for that which is just; merciful for that which is merciful.

Alma 41:3–5

"Whatever principle of intelligence we attain unto in this life, it will rise with us in the resurrection" (D&C 130:18). This is how the Prophet Joseph Smith expressed an important dimension of the doctrine of restoration: "There is no discontinuity in one's spiritual makeup in the transition from this world to the next. Goodness translates to goodness, evil to evil. If we align ourselves in this life with that which is evil, then this same disposition will continue with us into the next sphere of existence."

If an individual chooses not to repent, he must suffer for his own sins. The consequences of sin are often serious. Through dishonesty, we may lose our business or occupation; through immoral acts, we may lose our family and Church membership, as well as our sacred covenants. Some may avoid making payment for sin in mortal life, but in the next world, they will be required to pay the spiritual price of suffering before they can be resurrected. (O/C)

Alma 41:12–13

As individuals, what we ultimately become is determined by what we do and what we desire. We cannot live one type of life and then expect to be raised in immortality as a different type of person. In the next life, the righteous would certainly not want to find themselves different from what they were in this life. Neither is the reverse true. The wicked cannot expect to inherit the nature and blessings of righteousness in the next world when such nature is foreign to them and their lifestyle here. We do not change when we die. (O/C)

Alma 42:12–13

In these verses, we note the division of the spirit world into two different environments, designed to accommodate the same four classes of people that will ultimately be resurrected. Alma identifies the two divisions as follows:

A. Paradise

This is the home of the righteous. And who are they? The righteous are the faithful, covenant-keeping members of the Lord's Church, who will be heirs of the celestial kingdom in the first resurrection. (See D&C 76:64.)

B. Spirit Prison

This condition or place comprises two separate divisions of people:

1. Honorable people who lived terrestrial lives. (See D&C 76:71–75.) . . . Either these persons did not receive the opportunity to hear the gospel in mortality, or they rejected it there. Those in spirit prison will have adequate opportunity to hear the gospel, but they may choose to remain without celestial law, thus giving up any claims to celestial glory. However, these spirits will still have part in the first resurrection. (See D&C 45:54.)

2. Wicked people who lived telestial lives, as well as those who became sons of perdition. (O/C)

14. Therefore, my son, see that you are merciful unto your brethren; deal justly, judge righteously, and do good continually; and if ye do all these things then shall ye receive your reward; yea, ye shall have mercy restored unto you again; ye shall have justice restored unto you again; ye shall have a righteous judgment restored unto you again; and ye shall have good rewarded unto you again.
15. For that which ye do send out shall return unto you again, and be restored; therefore, the word restoration more fully condemneth the sinner, and justifieth him not at all.

CHAPTER 42

1. AND now, my son, I perceive there is somewhat more which doth worry your mind, which ye cannot understand—which is concerning the justice of God in the punishment of the sinner; for ye do try to suppose that it is injustice that the sinner should be consigned to a state of misery.
2. Now behold, my son, I will explain this thing unto thee. For behold, after the Lord God sent our first parents forth from the garden of Eden, to till the ground, from whence they were taken—yea, he drew out the man, and he placed at the east end of the garden of Eden, cherubim, and a flaming sword which turned every way, to keep the tree of life—
3. Now, we see that the man had become as God, knowing good and evil; and lest he should put forth his hand, and take also of the tree of life, and eat and live forever, the Lord God placed cherubim and the flaming sword, that he should not partake of the fruit—
4. And thus we see, that there was a time granted unto man to repent, yea, a probationary time, a time to repent and serve God.
5. For behold, if Adam had put forth his hand immediately, and partaken of the tree of life, he would have lived forever, according to the word of God, having no space for repentance; yea, and also the word of God would have been void, and the great plan of salvation would have been frustrated.
6. But behold, it was appointed unto man to die—therefore, as they were cut off from the tree of life they should be cut off from the face of the earth—and man became lost forever, yea, they became fallen man.
7. And now, ye see by this that our first parents were cut off both temporally and spiritually from the presence of the Lord; and thus we see they became subjects to follow after their own will.
8. Now behold, it was not expedient

Alma 41:14

Hope lends optimism to life. It helps us carry on when we are downhearted and discouraged. It helps us repent. Hope is the doctrine that is expressly connected to faith and charity. We cannot live without hope. If hope is gone, sin lies at the door. When we realize that there is life after death and that our reward is directly connected to our actions here on earth, we look to God and seek to keep His commandments. Our hope must extend beyond this life, or we would be "of all men most miserable" (1 Cor. 15:19). (P/A)

POINT OF INTEREST

This Aztec speech urging a young man to prepare for adulthood has a similar tone to Alma's admonition to his son Corianton in Alma 39:

Even though you may long for women,
hold back, hold back with your heart
until you are a grown man,
strong and robust.
Look at the maguey plant.
If it is opened before it has grown
and its liquid is taken out,
it has no substance.
It does not produce liquid; it is useless.
Before it is opened
to withdraw its water,
it should be allowed to grow and attain full size.
Then its sweet water is removed
all in good time.

This is how you must act:
before you know woman
you must grow and be a complete man.
And then you will be ready for marriage;
you will beget children of good stature,
healthy, agile, and comely.

(John L. Sorenson, *Images of Ancient America: Visualizing Book of Mormon Life* [Provo, Utah: FARMS, 1998].)

that man should be reclaimed from this temporal death, for that would destroy the great plan of happiness.
9. Therefore, as the soul could never die, and the fall had brought upon all mankind a spiritual death as well as a temporal, that is, they were cut off from the presence of the Lord, it was expedient that mankind should be reclaimed from this spiritual death.
10. Therefore, as they had become carnal, sensual, and devilish, by nature, this probationary state became a state for them to prepare; it became a preparatory state.
11. And now remember, my son, if it were not for the plan of redemption, (laying it aside) as soon as they were dead their souls were miserable, being cut off from the presence of the Lord.
12. And now, there was no means to reclaim men from this fallen state, which man had brought upon himself because of his own disobedience;
13. Therefore, according to justice, the plan of redemption could not be brought about, only on conditions of repentance of men in this probationary state, yea, this preparatory state; for except it were for these conditions, mercy could not take effect except it should destroy the work of justice. Now the work of justice could not be destroyed; if so, God would cease to be God.
14. And thus we see that all mankind were fallen, and they were in the grasp of justice; yea, the justice of God, which consigned them forever to be cut off from his presence.
15. And now, the plan of mercy could not be brought about except an atonement should be made; therefore God himself atoneth for the sins of the world, to bring about the plan of mercy, to appease the demands of justice, that God might be a perfect, just God, and a merciful God also.
16. Now, repentance could not come unto men except there were a punishment, which also was eternal as the life of the soul should be, affixed opposite to the plan of happiness, which was as eternal also as the life of the soul.
17. Now, how could a man repent except he should sin? How could he sin if there was no law? How could there be a law save there was a punishment?
18. Now, there was a punishment affixed, and a just law given, which brought remorse of conscience unto man.
19. Now, if there was no law given—if a man murdered he should die—would he be afraid he would die if he should murder?
20. And also, if there was no law given against sin men would not be afraid to sin.
21. And if there was no law given, if men sinned what could justice do, or mercy either, for they would have no claim upon the creature?
22. But there is a law given, and a

Alma 42:13–15, 23

In a masterful process of divine balance, the fulcrum being the Atonement of Jesus Christ, justice and mercy are eternally harmonized for "the truly penitent" (Alma 42:24). It is through the balancing grace of our Lord that we are saved, "after all we can do" (2 Ne. 25:23). . . .

Alma continued his counsel to Corianton by teaching him the great doctrines of justice and mercy and how they relate one to another. Alma instructed his son that it is through the Atonement of Christ that mercy is empowered on behalf of the obedient (see Alma 42:15). He counseled his son: "Do not endeavor to excuse yourself in the least point because of your sins, by denying the justice of God; but do you let the justice of God, and his mercy, and his long-suffering have full sway in your heart; and let it bring you down to the dust in humility" (Alma 42:30). . . .

Our Heavenly Father and Savior, Jesus Christ, mete out justice. They have made the laws upon which it operates. Mercy is ours to claim in repentance through the power of the Atonement. We must be willing to accept the goodness of God. Guilt can and will be swept away through repentance—we can and will be forgiven. Remember that guilt unto repentance is of the Lord but guilt beyond repentance is of the devil. (P/A)

Alma 42:22

Inasmuch as every law has both a punishment and a blessing affixed to it, punishments (or miseries) are the natural result of disobedience to the law, whereas blessings are the natural results of obedience. Thus, when a person transgresses a law (or sins) and suffering or punishment results, he brings upon himself the suffering and the "law inflicteth the punishment." (Read Helaman 14:30–31.) It is foolish to blame God for our suffering, for if all men were 100 percent righteous there would be no suffering. The following analogy might help to illustrate this point: If you counsel a person not to touch a hot stove or he will be burned, and he then disregards your counsel, touches the hot stove, and is burned, what caused him to be burned—you or the stove? Likewise, if the Lord commands you not to do a certain thing or you will suffer, and you then disregard the counsel of the Lord, commit the sin, and then suffer, who caused your suffering—the Lord, or your willful disobedience of divine law? (Ludlow)

punishment affixed, and a repentance granted; which repentance, mercy claimeth; otherwise, justice claimeth the creature and executeth the law, and the law inflicteth the punishment; if not so, the works of justice would be destroyed, and God would cease to be God.
23. But God ceaseth not to be God, and mercy claimeth the penitent, and mercy cometh because of the atonement; and the atonement bringeth to pass the resurrection of the dead; and the resurrection of the dead bringeth back men into the presence of God; and thus they are restored into his presence, to be judged according to their works, according to the law and justice.
24. For behold, justice exerciseth all his demands, and also mercy claimeth all which is her own; and thus, none but the truly penitent are saved.
25. What, do ye suppose that mercy can rob justice? I say unto you, Nay; not one whit. If so, God would cease to be God.
26. And thus God bringeth about his great and eternal purposes, which were prepared from the foundation of the world. And thus cometh about the salvation and the redemption of men, and also their destruction and misery.
27. Therefore, O my son, whosoever will come may come and partake of the waters of life freely; and whosoever will not come the same is not compelled to come; but in the last day it shall be restored unto him according to his deeds.
28. If he has desired to do evil, and has not repented in his days, behold, evil shall be done unto him, according to the restoration of God.
29. And now, my son, I desire that ye should let these things trouble you no more, and only let your sins trouble you, with that trouble which shall bring you down unto repentance.
30. O my son, I desire that ye should deny the justice of God no more. Do not endeavor to excuse yourself in the least point because of your sins, by denying the justice of God; but do you let the justice of God, and his mercy, and his long-suffering have full sway in your heart; and let it bring you down to the dust in humility.
31. And now, O my son, ye are called of God to preach the word unto this people. And now, my son, go thy way, declare the word with truth and soberness, that thou mayest bring souls unto repentance, that the great plan of mercy may have claim upon them. And may God grant unto you even according to my words. Amen.

CHAPTER 43

Alma Chapters 43–62

One of the most difficult aspects of the reading of this part of the book of Alma is to keep in mind the battlefronts, cities, and leaders involved in each war. . . .

It is well to keep in mind that you are not reading about the battles in chronological order. Many of the battles on the eastern front that you read about first actually occurred after some of the major battles on the western front. For example, the "decoy method" of capturing cities was employed by Helaman and Antipus in their attempt to recapture the city of Antiparah on the western front (Alma 56:20, 27–57) before it was used successfully by Moroni and Teancum in recapturing the city of Mulek on the eastern front (Alma 52:19–26). (Ludlow)

1. AND now it came to pass that the sons of Alma did go forth among the people, to declare the word unto them. And Alma, also, himself, could not rest, and he also went forth.
2. Now we shall say no more concerning their preaching, except that they preached the word, and the truth, according to the spirit of prophecy and revelation; and they preached after the holy order of God by which they were called.
3. And now I return to an account of the wars between the Nephites and the Lamanites, in the eighteenth year of the reign of the judges.
4. For behold, it came to pass that the Zoramites became Lamanites; therefore, in the commencement of the eighteenth year the people of the Nephites saw that the Lamanites were coming upon them; therefore they made preparations for war; yea, they gathered together their armies in the land of Jershon.
5. And it came to pass that the Lamanites came with their thousands; and they came into the land of Antionum, which is the land of the Zoramites; and a man by the name of Zerahemnah was their leader.
6. And now, as the Amalekites were of a more wicked and murderous disposition than the Lamanites were, in and of themselves, therefore, Zerahemnah appointed chief captains over the Lamanites, and they were all Amalekites and Zoramites.
7. Now this he did that he might preserve their hatred towards the Nephites, that he might bring them into subjection to the accomplishment of his designs.
8. For behold, his designs were to stir up the Lamanites to anger against the Nephites; this he did that he might usurp great power over them, and also that he might gain power over the Nephites by bringing them into bondage.
9. And now the design of the Nephites was to support their lands, and their houses, and their wives, and their children, that they might preserve them from the hands of their enemies; and also that they mightpreserve their rights and their privileges, yea, and also their liberty, that they might worship God according to their desires.
10. For they knew that if they should fall into the hands of the Lamanites, that whosoever should worship God in spirit and in truth, the true and the living God, the Lamanites would destroy.
11. Yea, and they also knew the extreme hatred of the Lamanites towards their brethren, who were the people of Anti-Nephi-Lehi, who were called the people of Ammon—and they would not take up arms, yea, they had entered into a covenant and they would not break it—therefore, if they should fall into the hands of the Lamanites they would be destroyed.
12. And the Nephites would not suffer that they should be destroyed; therefore they gave them lands for their inheritance.

Alma 43:1

Why did Mormon choose to abridge so much of the Nephites' history at war? Perhaps this is because the Lord knew that many good people in our day would struggle to maintain their freedom from evil forces, and He wanted them to learn from the Nephites' experiences. A major lesson that surfaces many times is that when men put their trust in Jesus Christ and live His commandments, they will be preserved, their freedom will be maintained, and the Lord will destroy their enemies. (O/C)

Alma 43:6–7

Many who apostatize from a true cause become the most bitter enemies of righteousness. The Nephite record contains abundant evidence that the devil works most effectively through apostates who have abandoned the truth. . . . The Prophet Joseph Smith taught: "When you joined this Church you enlisted to serve God. When you did that you left the neutral ground, and you never can get back on to it. Should you forsake the Master you enlisted to serve it will be by the instigation of the evil one, and you will follow his dictations and be his servant." (O/C)

Alma 43:6–7

Like all hardened apostates, the contenders against the faith cannot leave the Church alone, for their leader is now the devil himself. (P/A)

Alma 43:9

The same law pertaining to war given to the Nephites, is also given to us in this dispensation. Satan uses war as a tool to enslave mankind. The Lord's way is peace. However, when all efforts have failed in pursuing peace and denouncing war, the Lord justifies us in defending our families, country, and religion. (O/C)

13. And the people of Ammon did give unto the Nephites a large portion of their substance to support their armies; and thus the Nephites were compelled, alone, to withstand against the Lamanites, who were a compound of Laman and Lemuel, and the sons of Ishmael, and all those who had dissented from the Nephites, who were Amalekites and Zoramites, and the descendants of the priests of Noah.
14. Now those descendants were as numerous, nearly, as were the Nephites; and thus the Nephites were obliged to contend with their brethren, even unto bloodshed.
15. And it came to pass as the armies of the Lamanites had gathered together in the land of Antionum, behold, the armies of the Nephites were prepared to meet them in the land of Jershon.
16. Now, the leader of the Nephites, or the man who had been appointed to be the chief captain over the Nephites—now the chief captain took the command of all the armies of the Nephites—and his name was Moroni;
17. And Moroni took all the command, and the government of their wars. And he was only twenty and five years old when he was appointed chief captain over the armies of the Nephites.
18. And it came to pass that he met the Lamanites in the borders of Jershon, and his people were armed with swords, and with cimeters, and all manner of weapons of war.
19. And when the armies of the Lamanites saw that the people of Nephi, or that Moroni, had prepared his people with breastplates and with arm-shields, yea, and also shields to defend their heads, and also they were dressed with thick clothing—
20. Now the army of Zerahemnah was not prepared with any such thing; they had only their swords and their cimeters, their bows and their arrows, their stones and their slings; and they were naked, save it were a skin which was girded about their loins; yea, all were naked, save it were the Zoramites and the Amalekites;
21. But they were not armed with breastplates, nor shields—therefore, they were exceedingly afraid of the armies of the Nephites because of their armor, notwithstanding their number being so much greater than the Nephites.
22. Behold, now it came to pass that they durst not come against the Nephites in the borders of Jershon; therefore they departed out of the land of Antionum into the wilderness, and took their journey round about in the wilderness, away by the head of the river Sidon, that they might come into the land of Manti and take possession of the land; for they did not suppose that the armies of Moroni would know whither they had gone.
23. But it came to pass, as soon as they had departed into the wilderness Moroni sent spies into the wilderness to watch their camp; and Moroni, also, knowing of the prophecies of Alma, sent certain men unto him, desiring him that he should inquire of the Lord whither the armies of the Nephites should go to defend themselves against the Lamanites.
24. And it came to pass that the word of the Lord came unto Alma, and Alma informed the messengers of Moroni, that the armies of the

Alma 43:17–19

Notice the new and surprising military strategy and techniques used by Moroni in these military campaigns. Moroni prepared his people with breastplates, arm-shields, thick clothing, and shields to protect their heads. (Alma 43:19.) He also fortified the Nephite cities by having the people cast up "heaps of earth round about all the cities . . . And upon the top of these ridges of earth he caused that there should be timbers . . . built up to the height of a man. . . . And he caused that upon these works of timbers there should be a frame of pickets built . . . and they were strong and high. And he caused towers to be erected that overlooked those works of pickets, and he caused places of security to be built upon those towers." (Alma 50:1–4.) In actual battle, Moroni often used decoy and encircling tactics to confuse and defeat the enemy. (Alma 43:27–35.)

Moroni may have obtained some of his new ideas on warfare from Mosiah's translation of the twenty-four gold plates of Ether, which contained an account of the wars and contentions of the people of Jared. (See Alma 37:23–29.) If so, this may have given him an advantage over the Lamanites, because they did not have access to this record. (Ludlow)

Alma 43:23–24

Members of the Church and other God-fearing people often ask, Can a man have a career in the military service and still be in good standing with the Lord? The Book of Mormon gives several examples of righteous men who served in the military most of their lives and stood approved of the Lord. One such example is Captain Moroni, who exercised great faith and relied totally upon the Lord Jesus Christ. . . . As a practical army leader, Moroni followed the best military procedures he knew.. . . In addition, he did something almost unheard of in our age of so-called enlightenment. He sent men to inquire of the Lord's living prophet, to learn what the Lord would have him do as military commander. Of course, this was the key to Moroni's success, and we will also be successful in our righteous endeavors if we will "counsel with the Lord in all [our] doings" (Alma 37:37). (O/C)

Lamanites were marching round about in the wilderness, that they might come over into the land of Manti, that they might commence an attack upon the weaker part of the people. And those messengers went and delivered the message unto Moroni.
25. Now Moroni, leaving a part of his army in the land of Jershon, lest by any means a part of the Lamanites should come into the land and take possession of the city, took the remaining part of his army and marched over into the land of Manti.
26. And he caused that all the people in that quarter of the land should gather themselves together to battle against the Lamanites, to defend their lands and their country, their rights and their liberties; therefore they were prepared against the time of the coming of the Lamanites.
27. And it came to pass that Moroni caused that his army should be secreted in the valley which was near the bank of the river Sidon, which was on the west of the river Sidon in the wilderness.
28. And Moroni placed spies round about, that he might know when the camp of the Lamanites should come.
29. And now, as Moroni knew the intention of the Lamanites, that it was their intention to destroy their brethren, or to subject them and bring them into bondage that they might establish a kingdom unto themselves over all the land;
30. And he also knowing that it was the only desire of the Nephites to preserve their lands, and their liberty, and their church, therefore he thought it no sin that he should defend them by stratagem; therefore, he found by his spies which course the Lamanites were to take.
31. Therefore, he divided his army and brought a part over into the valley, and concealed them on the east, and on the south of the hill Riplah;
32. And the remainder he concealed in the west valley, on the west of the river Sidon, and so down into the borders of the land Manti.
33. And thus having placed his army according to his desire, he was prepared to meet them.
34. And it came to pass that the Lamanites came up on the north of the hill, where a part of the army of Moroni was concealed.
35. And as the Lamanites had passed the hill Riplah, and came into the valley, and began to cross the river Sidon, the army which was concealed on the south of the hill, which was led by a man whose name was Lehi, and he led his army forth and encircled the Lamanites about on the east in their rear.
36. And it came to pass that the Lamanites, when they saw the Nephites coming upon them in their rear, turned them about and began to contend with the army of Lehi.
37. And the work of death commenced on both sides, but it was more dreadful on the part of the Lamanites, for their nakedness was exposed to the heavy blows of the Nephites with their swords and their cimeters, which brought death almost at every stroke.
38. While on the other hand, there was now and then a man fell among the Nephites, by their swords and the loss of blood, they being shielded from the more vital parts of the body, or the more vital parts of the body being shielded from the strokes of the Lamanites, by their breastplates, and their armshields, and their head-plates; and thus the Nephites did carry on the work of death among the Lamanites.

Alma 43:27–35

Moroni may have obtained some of his new ideas on warfare from Mosiah's translation of the twenty-four gold plates of Ether, which contained an account of the wars and contentions of the people of Jared. (See Alma 37:23–29.) If so, this may have given him an advantage over the Lamanites, because they did not have access to this record.

39. And it came to pass that the Lamanites became frightened, because of the great destruction among them, even until they began to flee towards the river Sidon.
40. And they were pursued by Lehi and his men; and they were driven by Lehi into the waters of Sidon, and they crossed the waters of Sidon. And Lehi retained his armies upon the bank of the river Sidon that they should not cross.
41. And it came to pass that Moroni and his army met the Lamanites in the valley, on the other side of the river Sidon, and began to fall upon them and to slay them.
42. And the Lamanites did flee again before them, towards the land of Manti; and they were met again by the armies of Moroni.
43. Now in this case the Lamanites did fight exceedingly; yea, never had the Lamanites been known to fight with such exceedingly great strength and courage, no, not even from the beginning.
44. And they were inspired by the Zoramites and the Amalekites, who were their chief captains and leaders, and by Zerahemnah, who was their chief captain, or their chief leader and commander; yea, they did fight like dragons, and many of the Nephites were slain by their hands, yea, for they did smite in two many of their headplates, and they did pierce many of their breastplates, and they did smite off many of their arms; and thus the Lamanites did smite in their fierce anger.
45. Nevertheless, the Nephites were inspired by a better cause, for they were not fighting for monarchy nor power but they were fighting for their homes and their liberties, their wives and their children, and their all, yea, for their rites of worship and their church.
46. And they were doing that which they felt was the duty which they owed to their God; for the Lord had said unto them, and also unto their fathers, that: Inasmuch as ye are not guilty of the first offense, neither the second, ye shall not suffer yourselves to be slain by the hands of your enemies.
47. And again, the Lord has said that: Ye shall defend your families even unto bloodshed. Therefore for this cause were the Nephites contending with the Lamanites, to defend themselves, and their families, and their lands, their country, and their rights, and their religion.
48. And it came to pass that when the men of Moroni saw the fierceness and the anger of the Lamanites, they were about to shrink and flee from them. And Moroni, perceiving their intent, sent forth and inspired their hearts with these thoughts—yea, the thoughts of their lands, their liberty, yea, their freedom from bondage.
49. And it came to pass that they turned upon the Lamanites, and they cried with one voice unto the Lord their God, for their liberty and their freedom from bondage.
50. And they began to stand against the Lamanites with power; and in that selfsame hour that they cried unto the Lord for their freedom, the Lamanites began to flee before them; and they fled even to the waters of Sidon.
51. Now, the Lamanites were more numerous, yea, by more than double the number of the Nephites; nevertheless, they were driven insomuch

Alma 43:45–46

There was war in heaven and it continues today. It was—and is—a war over the souls of mankind. In a portion of that conflict, the Lamanites and apostate Nephites combined to war against the Nephites. When people ripen in iniquity the result is always war. Those who are attacked have the right to defend themselves. The wars we see in the Book of Mormon and in the world today are a reflection of life as it unfolds in larger perspective. Life itself is a battle. We are at war individually with the wicked one—even the devil. We must defend ourselves. In the war with Satan and his servants, we must come off conqueror (see D&C 10:5). Those who are righteous and keep the commandments are blessed of the Lord and preserved. Moroni was such a man. . . .

"For it must needs be, that there is an opposition in all things," Father Lehi proclaimed (2 Ne. 2:11). "But woe to that man by whom the offense cometh!" (Matt. 18:7). One perennial manifestation of this is the constant clash among humankind of the force of materialism and unrighteous dominion on the one hand and the force of liberty and justice for all on the other. In the end, freedom and the dignity of humankind as the offspring of Deity will prevail, but not without constant vigilance in upholding the standards of the gospel with courage and faithfulness. (P/A)

Alma 43:45–47

Although the Nephites were commanded by the Lord not to begin a war, they were also counseled by him: "Inasmuch as ye are not guilty of the first offense, neither the second, ye shall not suffer yourselves to be slain by the hands of your enemies." (Alma 43:46.) The Lord further instructed the Nephites: "Ye shall defend your families even unto bloodshed." (Alma 43:47.) Thus the Nephites felt justified in resisting the invasion of the Lamanites, so long as the Nephites were fighting for their lives, their homes, and their liberty. (Ludlow)

that they were gathered together in one body in the valley, upon the bank by the river Sidon.
52. Therefore the armies of Moroni encircled them about, yea, even on both sides of the river, for behold, on the east were the men of Lehi.
53. Therefore when Zerahemnah saw the men of Lehi on the east of the river Sidon, and the armies of Moroni on the west of the river Sidon, that they were encircled about by the Nephites, they were struck with terror.
54. Now Moroni, when he saw their terror, commanded his men that they should stop shedding their blood.

CHAPTER 44

1. AND it came to pass that they did stop and withdrew a pace from them. And Moroni said unto Zerahemnah: Behold, Zerahemnah, that we do not desire to be men of blood. Ye know that ye are in our hands, yet we do not desire to slay you.
2. Behold, we have not come out to battle against you that we might shed your blood for power; neither do we desire to bring any one to the yoke of bondage. But this is the very cause for which ye have come against us; yea, and ye are angry with us because of our religion.
3. But now, ye behold that the Lord is with us; and ye behold that he has delivered you into our hands. And now I would that ye should understand that this is done unto us because of our religion and our faith in Christ. And now ye see that ye cannot destroy this our faith.
4. Now ye see that this is the true faith of God; yea, ye see that God will support, and keep, and preserve us, so long as we are faithful unto him, and unto our faith, and our religion; and never will the Lord suffer that we shall be destroyed except we should fall into transgression and deny our faith.
5. And now, Zerahemnah, I command you, in the name of that all-powerful God, who has strengthened our arms that we have gained power over you, by our faith, by our religion, and by our rites of worship, and by our church, and by the sacred support which we owe to our wives and our children, by that liberty which binds us to our lands and our country; yea, and also by the maintenance of the sacred word of God, to which we owe all our happiness; and by all that is most dear unto us—
6. Yea, and this is not all; I command you by all the desires which ye have for life, that ye deliver up your weapons of war unto us, and we will seek not your blood, but we will spare your lives, if ye will go your way and come not again to war against us.
7. And now, if ye do not this, behold, ye are in our hands, and I will command my men that they shall fall upon you, and inflict the wounds of death in your bodies, that ye may become extinct; and then we will see who shall have power over this people; yea, we will see who shall be brought into bondage.
8. And now it came to pass that when Zerahemnah had heard these sayings he came forth and delivered up his sword and his cimeter, and his bow into the hands of Moroni, and said unto him: Behold, here are

Alma 44:5

The prophet-chronicler Mormon here shifts his attention from the ecclesiastical ministry of Alma and his sons among the people to focus on the lessons that flow from a different arena: the consuming conflict between the invading Lamanites (led by apostate Nephite commanders) and the forces of Captain Moroni. This conflagration was the collision of two diametrically opposite forces: power-hungry pride and opportunism on the one hand and the cause of liberty for church and family on the other. The Lamanites, under king Zerahemnah, sought to bring the Nephites into bondage. Moroni, the great captain of the armies, led the Nephites to victory on the basis of several factors: they were better prepared, their desires were pure, they were "inspired by a better cause" (Alma 43:45), they were not guilty of the first offense nor the second (see Alma 43:46), and they had a strong faith in Jesus Christ (Alma 44:5).

Abraham Lincoln said, "This love of liberty which God has planted in us constitutes the bulwark of our liberty and independence. It is not our frowning battlements, our bristling seacoasts, our army, and our navy. Our defense is in the spirit which prizes liberty as the heritage of all men, in all lands, everywhere. Destroy this spirit, and we have planted the seeds of despotism at our very doors." (P/A)

our weapons of war; we will deliver them up unto you, but we will not suffer ourselves to take an oath unto you, which we know that we shall break, and also our children; but take our weapons of war, and suffer that we may depart into the wilderness; otherwise we will retain our swords, and we will perish or conquer.

9. Behold, we are not of your faith; we do not believe that it is God that has delivered us into your hands; but we believe that it is your cunning that has preserved you from our swords. Behold, it is your breastplates and your shields that have preserved you.

10. And now when Zerahemnah had made an end of speaking these words, Moroni returned the sword and the weapons of war, which he had received, unto Zerahemnah, saying: Behold, we will end the conflict.

11. Now I cannot recall the words which I have spoken, therefore as the Lord liveth, ye shall not depart except ye depart with an oath that ye will not return again against us to war. Now as ye are in our hands we will spill your blood upon the ground, or ye shall submit to the conditions which I have proposed.

12. And now when Moroni had said these words, Zerahemnah retained his sword, and he was angry with Moroni, and he rushed forward that he might slay Moroni; but as he raised his sword, behold, one of Moroni's soldiers smote it even to the earth, and it broke by the hilt; and he also smote Zerahemnah that he took off his scalp and it fell to the earth. And Zerahemnah withdrew from before them into the midst of his soldiers.

13. And it came to pass that the soldier who stood by, who smote off the scalp of Zerahemnah, took up the scalp from off the ground by the hair, and laid it upon the point of his sword, and stretched it forth unto them, saying unto them with a loud voice:

14. Even as this scalp has fallen to the earth, which is the scalp of your chief, so shall ye fall to the earth except ye will deliver up your weapons of war and depart with a covenant of peace.

15. Now there were many, when they heard these words and saw the scalp which was upon the sword, that were struck with fear; and many came forth and threw down their weapons of war at the feet of Moroni, and entered into a covenant of peace. And as many as entered into a covenant they suffered to depart into the wilderness.

16. Now it came to pass that Zerahemnah was exceedingly wroth, and he did stir up the remainder of his soldiers to anger, to contend more powerfully against the Nephites.

17. And now Moroni was angry, because of the stubbornness of the Lamanites; therefore he commanded his people that they should fall upon them and slay them. And it came to pass that they began to slay them; yea, and the Lamanites did contend with their swords and their might.

18. But behold, their naked skins and their bare heads were exposed to the sharp swords of the Nephites; yea, behold they were pierced and smitten, yea, and did fall exceedingly fast before the swords of the Nephites; and they began to be swept down, even as the soldier of Moroni had prophesied.

19. Now Zerahemnah, when he saw that they were all about to be destroyed, cried mightily unto Moroni, promising that he would covenant and also his people with them, if they would spare the remainder of their lives, that they

Alma 44:12–14

The question might be raised as to whether or not the "scalping" of the Lamanite leader, Zerahemnah, might have led to the scalping tradition of the American Indian. (Alma 44:12–14.) However, recent evidence would seem to indicate the American Indian did not have a scalping tradition until *after* the coming of the white man—that is, until the seventeenth century A.D. Apparently it was the white man who started the scalping custom, when some of the early colonists offered money for the scalps or hair of dead Indians. In order to get even with the evil white men who killed Indians just for their scalps (in much the same way as they would kill a buffalo for its hide), the Indians started to kill and scalp the whites in return. (Ludlow)

never would come to war again against them.
20. And it came to pass that Moroni caused that the work of death should cease again among the people. And he took the weapons of war from the Lamanites; and after they had entered into a covenant with him of peace they were suffered to depart into the wilderness.
21. Now the number of their dead was not numbered because of the greatness of the number; yea, the number of their dead was exceedingly great, both on the Nephites and on the Lamanites.
22. And it came to pass that they did cast their dead into the waters of Sidon, and they have gone forth and are buried in the depths of the sea.
23. And the armies of the Nephites, or of Moroni, returned and came to their houses and their lands.
24. And thus ended the eighteenth year of the reign of the judges over the people of Nephi. And thus ended the record of Alma, which was written upon the plates of Nephi.

The account of the people of Nephi, and their wars and dissensions, in the days of Helaman, according to the record of Helaman, which he kept in his days. Comprising chapters 45 to 62 inclusive.

CHAPTER 45

1. BEHOLD, now it came to pass that the people of Nephi were exceedingly rejoiced, because the Lord had again delivered them out of the hands of their enemies; therefore they gave thanks unto the Lord their God; yea, and they did fast much and pray much, and they did worship God with exceedingly great joy.
2. And it came to pass in the nineteenth year of the reign of the judges over the people of Nephi, that Alma came unto his son Helaman and said unto him: Believest thou the words which I spake unto thee concerning those records which have been kept?
3. And Helaman said unto him: Yea, I believe.
4. And Alma said again: Believest thou in Jesus Christ, who shall come?
5. And he said: Yea, I believe all the words which thou hast spoken.
6. And Alma said unto him again: Will ye keep my commandments?
7. And he said: Yea, I will keep thy commandments with all my heart.
8. Then Alma said unto him: Blessed art thou; and the Lord shall prosper thee in this land.
9. But behold, I have somewhat to prophesy unto thee; but what I prophesy unto thee ye shall not make known; yea, what I prophesy unto thee shall not be made known, even until the prophecy is fulfilled; therefore write the words which I shall say.
10. And these are the words: Behold, I perceive that this very people, the Nephites, according to the spirit of revelation which is in me, in four hundred years from the time that Jesus Christ shall manifest himself unto them, shall dwindle in unbelief.
11. Yea, and then shall they see wars and pestilences, yea, famines and bloodshed, even until the

people of Nephi shall become extinct—

12. Yea, and this because they shall dwindle in unbelief and fall into the works of darkness, and lasciviousness, and all manner of iniquities; yea, I say unto you, that because they shall sin against so great light and knowledge, yea, I say unto you, that from that day, even the fourth generation shall not all pass away before this great iniquity shall come.

13. And when that great day cometh, behold, the time very soon cometh that those who are now, or the seed of those who are now numbered among the people of Nephi, shall no more be numbered among the people of Nephi.

14. But whosoever remaineth, and is not destroyed in that great and dreadful day, shall be numbered among the Lamanites, and shall become like unto them, all, save it be a few who shall be called the disciples of the Lord; and them shall the Lamanites pursue even until they shall become extinct. And now, because of iniquity, this prophecy shall be fulfilled.

15. And now it came to pass that after Alma had said these things to Helaman, he blessed him, and also his other sons; and he also blessed the earth for the righteous' sake.

16. And he said: Thus saith the Lord God—Cursed shall be the land, yea, this land, unto every nation, kindred, tongue, and people, unto destruction, which do wickedly, when they are fully ripe; and as I have said so shall it be; for this is the cursing and the blessing of God upon the land, for the Lord cannot look upon sin with the least degree of allowance.

17. And now, when Alma had said these words he blessed the church, yea, all those who should stand fast in the faith from that time henceforth.

18. And when Alma had done this he departed out of the land of Zarahemla, as if to go into the land of Melek. And it came to pass that he was never heard of more; as to his death or burial we know not of.

19. Behold, this we know, that he was a righteous man; and the saying went abroad in the church that he was taken up by the Spirit, or buried by the hand of the Lord, even as Moses. But behold, the scriptures saith the Lord took Moses unto himself; and we suppose that he has also received Alma in the spirit, unto himself; therefore, for this cause we know nothing concerning his death and burial.

20. And now it came to pass in the commencement of the nineteenth year of the reign of the judges over the people of Nephi, that Helaman went forth among the people to declare the word unto them.

21. For behold, because of their wars with the Lamanites and the many little dissensions and disturbances which had been among the people, it became expedient that the word of God should be declared among them, yea, and that a regulation should be made throughout the church.

22. Therefore, Helaman and his brethren went forth to establish the church again in all the land, yea, in every city throughout all the land which was possessed by the people

POINT OF INTEREST

Tikal is the largest of the ancient Mayan cities and is located in Guatemala. The Temple of the Jaguar, left, is the largest of the site's structures.

of Nephi. And it came to pass that they did appoint priests and teachers throughout all the land, over all the churches.
23. And now it came to pass that after Helaman and his brethren had appointed priests and teachers over the churches that there arose a dissension among them, and they would not give heed to the words of Helaman and his brethren;
24. But they grew proud, being lifted up in their hearts, because of their exceedingly great riches; therefore they grew rich in their own eyes, and would not give heed to their words, to walk uprightly before God.

CHAPTER 46

1. AND it came to pass that as many as would not hearken to the words of Helaman and his brethren were gathered together against their brethren.
2. And now behold, they were exceedingly wroth, insomuch that they were determined to slay them.
3. Now the leader of those who were wroth against their brethren was a large and a strong man; and his name was Amalickiah.
4. And Amalickiah was desirous to be a king; and those people who were wroth were also desirous that he should be their king; and they were the greater part of them the lower judges of the land, and they were seeking for power.
5. And they had been led by the flatteries of Amalickiah, that if they would support him and establish him to be their king that he would make them rulers over the people.
6. Thus they were led away by Amalickiah to dissensions, notwithstanding the preaching of Helaman and his brethren, yea, notwithstanding their exceedingly great care over the church, for they were high priests over the church.
7. And there were many in the church who believed in the flattering words of Amalickiah, therefore they dissented even from the church; and thus were the affairs of the people of Nephi exceedingly precarious and dangerous, notwithstanding their great victory which they had had over the Lamanites, and their great rejoicings which they had had because of their deliverance by the hand of the Lord.
8. Thus we see how quick the children of men do forget the Lord their God, yea, how quick to do iniquity, and to be led away by the evil one.
9. Yea, and we also see the great wickedness one very wicked man can cause to take place among the children of men.
10. Yea, we see that Amalickiah, because he was a man of cunning device and a man of many flattering words, that he led away the hearts of many people to do wickedly; yea, and to seek to destroy the church of God, and to destroy the foundation of liberty which

Alma 46:5–7

Mormon reminds us in the midst of his account: "Yea, and we also see the great wickedness one very wicked man can cause to take place among the children of men" (Alma 5:9).

We of the twentieth century are well aware of the truth of this statement, for we have lived through the horrendous consequences of tyrannical dominance imposed by evil men upon countless millions of human beings. But tyranny is not indomitable. The light of the gospel, illuminating the hearts and motivations of devoted sons and daughters of God, can cause tyranny to dissipate beneath the inexorable onward force of God's plan. (P/A)

Alma 46:10

Liberty in the pursuit of God's agenda "to bring to pass the immortality and eternal life of man" (Moses 1:39) is a cause that supersedes all mortal priorities and worldly interests. The security and well-being of our families, an environment of liberty in which the kingdom of God can flourish, and the right to practice our inalienable rights of conscience—all these are invaluable assets worth preserving and fighting for in order that spiritual progress can continue unimpeded.

President Ezra Taft Benson said that "the war in heaven over free agency is now being waged here on earth. . . .

"Moroni raised a title of liberty and wrote upon it these words: 'In memory of our God, our religion, and freedom, and our peace, our wives, and our children.' Why didn't he write upon it 'Just live your religion; there's no need to concern yourselves about your freedom, your peace, your wives, or your children'? The reason he didn't do this was because all these things were a part of his religion, as they are of our religion today. . . .

"[O]ur stand for freedom is a most basic part of our religion; this stand helped get us to this earth, and our reaction to freedom in this life will have eternal consequences. Man has many duties, but he has no excuse that can compensate for his loss of liberty."

We see repeatedly the problem of forgetting our God and thus making ourselves more vulnerable to the evil one. We need an individual title of liberty, a mission statement of what we believe. . . . Take the time to write down your values and standards for your life. Look to the scriptures and counsel from prophets. Reflect upon these and your personal goals, and merge them together into a comprehensive statement so you will have a plan to follow our Savior and enjoy the blessings of exaltation. (P/A)

God had granted unto them, or which blessing God had sent upon the face of the land for the righteous' sake.
11. And now it came to pass that when Moroni, who was the chief commander of the armies of the Nephites, had heard of these dissensions, he was angry with Amalickiah.
12. And it came to pass that he rent his coat; and he took a piece thereof, and wrote upon it—In memory of our God, our religion, and freedom, and our peace, our wives, and our children—and he fastened it upon the end of a pole.
13. And he fastened on his head-plate, and his breastplate, and his shields, and girded on his armor about his loins; and he took the pole, which had on the end thereof his rent coat, (and he called it the title of liberty) and he bowed himself to the earth, and he prayed mightily unto his God for the blessings of liberty to rest upon his brethren, so long as there should a band of Christians remain to possess the land—
14. For thus were all the true believers of Christ, who belonged to the church of God, called by those who did not belong to the church.
15. And those who did belong to the church were faithful; yea, all those who were true believers in Christ took upon them, gladly, the name of Christ, or Christians as they were called, because of their belief in Christ who should come.
16. And therefore, at this time, Moroni prayed that the cause of the Christians, and the freedom of the land might be favored.
17. And it came to pass that when he had poured out his soul to God, he named all the land which was south of the land Desolation, yea, and in fine, all the land, both on the north and on the south—A chosen land, and the land of liberty.
18. And he said: Surely God shall not suffer that we, who are despised because we take upon us the name of Christ, shall be trodden down and destroyed, until we bring it upon us by our own transgressions.
19. And when Moroni had said these words, he went forth among the people, waving the rent part of his garment in the air, that all might see the writing which he had written upon the rent part, and crying with a loud voice, saying:
20. Behold, whosoever will maintain this title upon the land, let them come forth in the strength of the Lord, and enter into a covenant that they will maintain their rights, and their religion, that the Lord God may bless them.
21. And it came to pass that when Moroni had proclaimed these words, behold, the people came running together with their armor girded about their loins, rending their garments in token, or as a covenant, that they would not forsake the Lord their God; or, in other words, if they should transgress the commandments of God, or fall into transgression, and be ashamed to take upon them the name of Christ, the Lord should rend them even as they had rent their garments.

Alma 46:12–13

We see repeatedly the problem of forgetting our God and thus making ourselves more vulnerable to the evil one. We need an individual title of liberty, a mission statement of what we believe. We then need to set goals for carrying out our mission statement. Think of Abraham Lincoln's personal creed:

"I believe in God, the Almighty Ruler of nations, our great and good merciful Maker, our Father in heaven, who notes the fall of a sparrow and numbers the hairs on our heads. I recognize the sublime truth announced in the Holy Scriptures and proved by all history that those nations are blessed whose God is the Lord. I believe that the will of God prevails. Without him, all human reliance is vain. With that assistance I cannot fall. I have a solemn vow registered in heaven to finish the work I am in, in full view of my responsibility to God, with malice toward none; with charity for all; with firmness in the right, as God gives me to see the right." (P/A)

Alma 46:12–24

One of the most fascinating stories in the entire Book of Mormon is the account of Moroni and the Title of Liberty, which he used to rally the Nephites in defense of their lands and liberty. This story is filled with types, shadows, and idiomatic expressions foreign to most of us in the modern world, but they were not strange to the ancient eastern mind, as is indicated in the following quotation from Dr. Hugh Nibley:

". . . One of the most remarkable aspects of the story is the manner in which Moroni sought to stir up patriotic fervor by appealing to ancient and traditional devices. He connected the whole business of the rent garment with the story of the tribal ancestors Jacob and Joseph, and suggested that '. . . those who have dissented from us . . .' were the very '. . . remnant of the seed of Joseph . . .' to which the dying Jacob prophetically referred. [Alma 46:27.] It was not merely a resemblance or a type, but the very event foreseen by the patriarch of old. . . .

". . . aside from the great symbolic force of the tale, there can be no doubt that the story told by Moroni as one familiar to all the people actually was one that circulated among the Jews in ancient times. . . . It was totally unknown to the world in which Joseph Smith lived.

". . . This is an acid test that no forgery could pass; it not only opens a window on a world we dreamed not of, but it brings to our unsuspecting and uninitiated minds a first glimmering suspicion of the true scope and vastness of a book nobody knows." (Ludlow)

22. Now this was the covenant which they made, and they cast their garments at the feet of Moroni, saying: We covenant with our God, that we shall be destroyed, even as our brethren in the land northward, if we shall fall into transgression; yea, he may cast us at the feet of our enemies, even as we have cast our garments at thy feet to be trodden under foot, if we shall fall into transgression.
23. Moroni said unto them: Behold, we are a remnant of the seed of Jacob; yea, we are a remnant of the seed of Joseph, whose coat was rent by his brethren into many pieces; yea, and now behold, let us remember to keep the commandments of God, or our garments shall be rent by our brethren, and we be cast into prison, or be sold, or be slain.
24. Yea, let us preserve our liberty as a remnant of Joseph; yea, let us remember the words of Jacob, before his death, for behold, he saw that a part of the remnant of the coat of Joseph was preserved and had not decayed. And he said—Even as this remnant of garment of my son hath been preserved, so shall a remnant of the seed of my son be preserved by the hand of God, and be taken unto himself, while the remainder of the seed of Joseph shall perish, even as the remnant of his garment.
25. Now behold, this giveth my soul sorrow; nevertheless, my soul hath joy in my son, because of that part of his seed which shall be taken unto God.
26. Now behold, this was the language of Jacob.
27. And now who knoweth but what the remnant of the seed of Joseph, which shall perish as his garment, are those who have dissented from us? Yea, and even it shall be ourselves if we do not stand fast in the faith of Christ.
28. And now it came to pass that when Moroni had said these words he went forth, and also sent forth in all the parts of the land where there were dissensions, and gathered together all the people who were desirous to maintain their liberty, to stand against Amalickiah and those who had dissented, who were called Amalickiahites.
29. And it came to pass that when Amalickiah saw that the people of Moroni were more numerous than the Amalickiahites—and he also saw that his people were doubtful concerning the justice of the cause in which they had undertaken—therefore, fearing that he should not gain the point, he took those of his people who would and departed into the land of Nephi.
30. Now Moroni thought it was not expedient that the Lamanites should have any more strength; therefore he thought to cut off the people of Amalickiah, or to take them and bring them back, and put Amalickiah to death; yea, for he knew that he would stir up the Lamanites to anger against them, and cause them to come to battle against them; and this he knew that Amalickiah would do that he might obtain his purposes.
31. Therefore Moroni thought it was expedient that he should take his armies, who had gathered themselves together, and armed themselves, and entered into a covenant to keep the peace—and it came to pass that he took his army and marched out with his tents into the wilderness, to cut off the course of Amalickiah in the wilderness.
32. And it came to pass that he did

Alma 46:23–27

The Book of Mormon provides the biblical scholar with additional information on the famed "coat of many colors" which was given to Joseph by his father, Jacob. The Bible does not mention what happened to Joseph's coat after it was smeared with blood by Joseph's brothers and taken to Jacob, but according to the Book of Mormon, the coat was preserved, and, miraculously, part of the coat never decayed. . . . (Ludlow)

according to his desires, and marched forth into the wilderness,
and headed the armies of Amalickiah.
33. And it came to pass that Amalickiah fled with a small number
of his men, and the remainder were delivered up into the hands of
Moroni and were taken back into the land of Zarahemla.
34. Now, Moroni being a man who was appointed by the chief
judges and the voice of the people, therefore he had power according to his will with the armies of the Nephites, to establish and to
exercise authority over them.
35. And it came to pass that whomsoever of the Amalickiahites
that would not enter into a covenant to support the cause of freedom, that they might maintain a free government, he caused to be
put to death; and there were but few who denied the covenant of
freedom.
36. And it came to pass also, that he caused the title of liberty to
be hoisted upon every tower which was in all the land, which was
possessed by the Nephites; and thus Moroni planted the standard
of liberty among the Nephites.
37. And they began to have peace again in the land; and thus they
did maintain peace in the land until nearly the end of the nineteenth year of the reign of the judges.
38. And Helaman and the high priests did also maintain order in
the church; yea, even for the space of four years did they have
much peace and rejoicing in the church.
39. And it came to pass that there were many who died, firmly
believing that their souls were redeemed by the Lord Jesus Christ;
thus they went out of the world rejoicing.
40. And there were some who died with fevers, which at some seasons of the year were very frequent in the land—but not so much
so with fevers, because of the excellent qualities of the many plants
and roots which God had prepared to remove the cause of diseases,
to which men were subject by the nature of the climate—
41. But there were many who died with old age; and those who
died in the faith of Christ are happy in him, as we must needs suppose.

CHAPTER 47

1. NOW we will return in our record to Amalickiah and those who
had fled with him into the wilderness; for, behold, he had taken
those who went with him, and went up in the land of Nephi among
the Lamanites, and did stir up the Lamanites to anger against the
people of Nephi, insomuch that the king of the Lamanites sent a
proclamation throughout all his land, among all his people, that
they should gather themselves together again to go to battle against
the Nephites.
2. And it came to pass that when the proclamation had gone forth
among them they were exceedingly afraid; yea, they feared to dis-
please the king, and they also feared to go to battle against the
Nephites lest they should lose their lives. And it came to pass that
they would not, or the more part of them would not, obey the commandments of the king.
3. And now it came to pass that the

Alma 46:35

This is one of the only times in history when prisoners of war were freed while the war still raged simply because they were willing to take an oath.

Alma 46:40

Very little information is provided in the Book of Mormon concerning the climate where the Nephites and Lamanites lived. However, some scholars have assumed that the reference to fevers that occurred at certain seasons of the year in the land of Zarahemla might indicate this particular land was in a tropical or semitropical area. However, as noted by the historian, the effects of these fevers were not too serious "because of the excellent qualities of the many plants and roots which God had prepared to remove the cause of diseases" (Alma 46:40).

Alma 47

This chapter is a powerful demonstration of why we should not place our trust in men: there is no way for us to know their thoughts, their desires, their motives, and the intents of their hearts. It also shows that the Nephite dissenters are much more wicked and ferocious than the Lamanites—something that still holds true in our day when we see that apostates from the Church tend to be much more vitriolic than people who have never been members of the Church.

king was wroth because of their disobedience; therefore he gave
Amalickiah the command of that part of his army which was obedient unto his commands, and commanded him that he should go
forth and compel them to arms.
4. Now behold, this was the desire of Amalickiah; for he being a
very subtle man to do evil therefore he laid the plan in his heart to
dethrone the king of the Lamanites.
5. And now he had got the command of those parts of the
Lamanites who were in favor of the king; and he sought to gain
favor of those who were not obedient; therefore he went forward to
the place which was called Onidah, for thither had all the
Lamanites fled; for they discovered the army coming, and, supposing that they were coming to destroy them, therefore they fled to
Onidah, to the place of arms.
6. And they had appointed a man to be a king and a leader over
them, being fixed in their minds with a determined resolution that
they would not be subjected to go against the Nephites.
7. And it came to pass that they had gathered themselves together
upon the top of the mount which was called Antipas, in preparation
to battle.
8. Now it was not Amalickiah's intention to give them battle
according to the commandments of the king; but behold, it was his
intention to gain favor with the armies of the Lamanites, that he
might place himself at their head and dethrone the king and take
possession of the kingdom.
9. And behold, it came to pass that he caused his army to pitch
their tents in the valley which was near the mount Antipas.
10. And it came to pass that when it was night he sent a secret
embassy into the mount Antipas, desiring that the leader of those
who were upon the mount, whose name was Lehonti, that he
should come down to the foot of the mount, for he desired to speak
with him.
11. And it came to pass that when Lehonti received the message he
durst not go down to the foot of the mount. And it came to pass that
Amalickiah sent again the second time, desiring him to come down.
And it came to pass that Lehonti would not; and he sent again the
third time.
12. And it came to pass that when Amalickiah found that he could
not get Lehonti to come down off from the mount, he went up into
the mount, nearly to Lehonti's camp; and he sent again the fourth
time his message unto Lehonti, desiring that he would come down,
and that he would bring his guards with him.
13. And it came to pass that when Lehonti had come down with his
guards to Amalickiah, that Amalickiah desired him to come down
with his army in the night-time, and surround those men in their
camps over whom the king had given him command, and that he
would deliver them up into Lehonti's hands, if he would make him
(Amalickiah) a second leader over the whole army.
14. And it came to pass that Lehonti came down with his men and
surrounded the men of Amalickiah, so that before they awoke at
the dawn of day they were surrounded by the armies of Lehonti.
15. And it came to pass that when they saw that they were surrounded, they plead with Amalickiah that he would suffer them to
fall in with their brethren, that they might not be destroyed. Now
this was the very thing which Amalickiah desired.
16. And it came to pass that he delivered his men, contrary to the
commands of the king. Now this was the thing that Amalickiah

Alma 47:10

These verses describe how apostasy is spread. First, the apostate gains a little power. Next, we see that the apostate always has a detailed plan for spreading the apostasy. The apostate then finds a "pawn"—such as Lehonti in these verses—he can use in executing his detailed plan. Finally, the apostate seduces the pawn with promises in order to sway the pawn over to his beliefs.

POINT OF INTEREST

Reign of the Judges

91–83 B.C.	*Alma; retires to preach the gospel*
83–68 B.C.	*Nephihah*
68–52 B.C.	*Pahoran I*
52 B.C.	*Pahoran II; murdered in office*
52–51 B.C.	*Pacumeni; killed by Lamanites*
51–50 B.C.	*Judgment seat is vacant due to war*
50–39 B.C.	*Helaman*
39–30 B.C.	*Nephi; retires to preach the gospel*
30–26 B.C.	*Cezoram; murdered in office*
26 B.C.	*Son of Cezoram; murdered in office*
26–23 B.C.	*Seezoram; murdered in office*
23 B.C.–A.D. 1	*Unknown*
A.D. 1–30	*Lachoneus I*
A.D. 30	*Lachoneus II; murdered in office*
	Government collapses

desired, that he might accomplish his designs in dethroning the king.
17. Now it was the custom among the Lamanites, if their chief leader was killed, to appoint the second leader to be their chief leader.
18. And it came to pass that Amalickiah caused that one of his servants should administer poison by degrees to Lehonti, that he died.
19. Now, when Lehonti was dead, the Lamanites appointed Amalickiah to be their leader and their chief commander.
20. And it came to pass that Amalickiah marched with his armies (for he had gained his desires) to the land of Nephi, to the city of Nephi, which was the chief city.
21. And the king came out to meet him with his guards, for he supposed that Amalickiah had fulfilled his commands, and that Amalickiah had gathered together so great an army to go against the Nephites to battle.
22. But behold, as the king came out to meet him Amalickiah caused that his servants should go forth to meet the king. And they went and bowed themselves before the king, as if to reverence him because of his greatness.
23. And it came to pass that the king put forth his hand to raise them, as was the custom with the Lamanites, as a token of peace, which custom they had taken from the Nephites.
24. And it came to pass that when he had raised the first from the ground, behold he stabbed the king to the heart; and he fell to the earth.
25. Now the servants of the king fled; and the servants of Amalickiah raised a cry, saying:
26. Behold, the servants of the king have stabbed him to the heart, and he has fallen and they have fled; behold, come and see.
27. And it came to pass that Amalickiah commanded that his armies should march forth and see what had happened to the king; and when they had come to the spot, and found the king lying in his gore, Amalickiah pretended to be wroth, and said: Whosoever loved the king, let him go forth, and pursue his servants that they may be slain.
28. And it came to pass that all they who loved the king, when they heard these words, came forth and pursued after the servants of the king.
29. Now when the servants of the king saw an army pursuing after them, they were frightened again, and fled into the wilderness, and came over into the land of Zarahemla and joined the people of Ammon.
30. And the army which pursued after them returned, having pursued after them in vain; and thus Amalickiah, by his fraud, gained the hearts of the people.
31. And it came to pass on the morrow he entered the city Nephi with his armies, and took possession of the city.
32. And now it came to pass that the queen, when she had heard that the king was slain—for Amalickiah had sent an embassy to the queen informing her that the king had been slain by his servants, that he had pursued them with his army, but it was in vain, and they had made their escape—
33. Therefore, when the queen had received this message she sent unto Amalickiah, desiring him that he would spare the people of the city; and she also desired him that he should come in unto her; and she also desired him that he should bring witnesses with him to testify concerning the death of the king.
34. And it came to pass that Amalickiah took the same servant that slew the king, and all them who

were with him, and went in unto the queen, unto the place where she sat; and they all testified unto her that the king was slain by his own servants; and they said also: They have fled; does not this testify against them? And thus they satisfied the queen concerning the death of the king.
35. And it came to pass that Amalickiah sought the favor of the queen, and took her unto him to wife; and thus by his fraud, and by the assistance of his cunning servants, he obtained the kingdom; yea, he was acknowledged king throughout all the land, among all the people of the Lamanites, who were composed of the Lamanites and the Lemuelites and the Ishmaelites, and all the dissenters of the Nephites, from the reign of Nephi down to the present time.
36. Now these dissenters, having the same instruction and the same information of the Nephites, yea, having been instructed in the same knowledge of the Lord, nevertheless, it is strange to relate, not long after their dissensions they became more hardened and impenitent, and more wild, wicked and ferocious than the Lamanites—drinking in with the traditions of the Lamanites; giving way to indolence, and all manner of lasciviousness; yea, entirely forgetting the Lord their God.

CHAPTER 48

1. AND now it came to pass that, as soon as Amalickiah had obtained the kingdom he began to inspire the hearts of the Lamanites against the people of Nephi; yea, he did appoint men to speak unto the Lamanites from their towers, against the Nephites.
2. And thus he did inspire their hearts against the Nephites, insomuch that in the latter end of the nineteenth year of the reign of the judges, he having accomplished his designs thus far, yea, having been made king over the Lamanites, he sought also to reign over all the land, yea, and all the people who were in the land, the Nephites as well as the Lamanites.
3. Therefore he had accomplished his design, for he had hardened the hearts of the Lamanites and blinded their minds, and stirred them up to anger, insomuch that he had gathered together a numerous host to go to battle against the Nephites.
4. For he was determined, because of the greatness of the number of his people, to overpower the Nephites and to bring them into bondage.
5. And thus he did appoint chief captains of the Zoramites, they being the most acquainted with the strength of the Nephites, and their places of resort, and the weakest parts of their cities; therefore he appointed them to be chief captains over his armies.
6. And it came to pass that they took their camp, and moved forth toward the land of Zarahemla in the wilderness.
7. Now it came to pass that while Amalickiah had thus been obtaining power by fraud and deceit, Moroni, on the other hand, had been preparing

Alma 47:36

Joseph Smith. . . . said, that the very step of apostasy commenced with losing confidence in the leaders of this Church . . . , and that whenever you discerned that spirit, you might know that it would lead the possessor of it on the road to apostasy. If then you have got this spirit in your hearts, or in your families, and if brethren and sisters, husbands and wives are contending and quarreling one with another, I say, there is the spirit of apostasy, . . . Then let us banish all strife and contention; let no children contend against their parents, nor wives against their husbands, nor any one against the authorities which God has established. . . . (Heber C. Kimball, *Journal of Discourses*, 3:270). (O/C)

Alma 47:36

This verse describes aptly what happens to apostates who continue in their apostasy: they become hardened and impenitent; they become more wild, wicked, and ferocious than those who have never embraced the truth; they give way to laziness and all kinds of sins; and, finally, they entirely forget the Lord their God.

the minds of the people to be faithful unto the Lord their God.
8. Yea, he had been strengthening the armies of the Nephites, and
erecting small forts, or places of resort; throwing up banks of earth
round about to enclose his armies, and also building walls of stone
to encircle them about, round about their cities and the borders of
their lands; yea, all round about the land.
9. And in their weakest fortifications he did place the greater number of men; and thus he did fortify and strengthen the land which
was possessed by the Nephites.
10. And thus he was preparing to support their liberty, their lands,
their wives, and their children, and their peace, and that they
might live unto the Lord their God, and that they might maintain
that which was called by their enemies the cause of Christians.
11. And Moroni was a strong and a mighty man; he was a man of a perfect understanding; yea, a man that did not delight in bloodshed; a man
whose soul did joy in the liberty and the freedom of his country, and his
brethren from bondage and slavery;
12. Yea, a man whose heart did swell with thanksgiving to his God,
for the many privileges and blessings which he bestowed upon his
people; a man who did labor exceedingly for the welfare and safety
of his people.
13. Yea, and he was a man who was firm in the faith of Christ, and
he had sworn with an oath to defend his people, his rights, and his
country, and his religion, even to the loss of his blood.
14. Now the Nephites were taught to defend themselves against
their enemies, even to the shedding of blood if it were necessary;
yea, and they were also taught never to give an offense, yea, and
never to raise the sword except it were against an enemy, except
it were to preserve their lives.
15. And this was their faith, that by so doing God would prosper
them in the land, or in other words, if they were faithful in keeping
the commandments of God that he would prosper them in the land;
yea, warn them to flee, or to prepare for war, according to their danger;
16. And also, that God would make it known unto them whither
they should go to defend themselves against their enemies, and by so
doing, the Lord would deliver them; and this was the faith of
Moroni, and his heart did glory in it; not in the shedding of blood
but in doing good, in preserving his people, yea, in keeping the commandments of God, yea, and resisting iniquity.
17. Yea, verily, verily I say unto you, if all men had been, and were,
and ever would be, like unto Moroni, behold, the very powers of hell
would have been shaken forever; yea, the devil would never have
power over the hearts of the children of men.
18. Behold, he was a man like unto Ammon, the son of Mosiah,
yea, and even the other sons of Mosiah, yea, and also Alma and his
sons, for they were all men of God.
19. Now behold, Helaman and his brethren were no less servicea-
ble unto the people than was Moroni; for they did preach the word
of God, and they did baptize unto repentance

Alma 48:10

According to Elder Anthony W. Ivins, the Lord will give victory to armies who are fighting for the principles listed in this verse—those who are fighting for their liberty, their lands, their wives, their children, their peace, and their right to worship God.

Alma 48:11–13

These verses provide a description of the characteristics of Moroni. This warrior is considered great because he:

- Sought for and heeded the words of the Lord through His prophets
- Was concerned for those under his command
- Made sure those under his command were completely prepared for battle
- Was firm in the right but willing to forgive
- Was patriotic
- Was prayerful
- Provided a standard of righteousness that others could follow
- Was a man of God

As a result of Moroni's leadership and example, the Nephites believed that if they were faithful and righteous, God would deliver them from their enemies.

Alma 48:17

This is a powerful statement regarding Moroni's righteousness. What can we learn from studying about Moroni, and how can we apply those principles in our own lives?

all men whosoever would hearken unto their words.
20. And thus they went forth, and the people did humble themselves because of their words, insomuch that they were highly favored of the Lord, and thus they were free from wars and contentions among themselves, yea, even for the space of four years.
21. But, as I have said, in the latter end of the nineteenth year, yea, notwithstanding their peace amongst themselves, they were compelled reluctantly to contend with their brethren, the Lamanites.
22. Yea, and in fine, their wars never did cease for the space of many years with the Lamanites, notwithstanding their much reluctance.
23. Now, they were sorry to take up arms against the Lamanites, because they did not delight in the shedding of blood; yea, and this was not all—they were sorry to be the means of sending so many of their brethren out of this world into an eternal world, unprepared to meet their God.
24. Nevertheless, they could not suffer to lay down their lives, that their wives and their children should be massacred by the barbarous cruelty of those who were once their brethren, yea, and had dissented from their church, and had left them and had gone to destroy them by joining the Lamanites.
25. Yea, they could not bear that their brethren should rejoice over the blood of the Nephites, so long as there were any who should keep the commandments of God, for the promise of the Lord was, if they should keep his commandments they should prosper in the land.

CHAPTER 49

1. AND now it came to pass in the eleventh month of the nineteenth year, on the tenth day of the month, the armies of the Lamanites were seen approaching towards the land of Ammonihah.
2. And behold, the city had been rebuilt, and Moroni had stationed an army by the borders of the city, and they had cast up dirt around about to shield them from the arrows and the stones of the Lamanites; for behold, they fought with stones and with arrows.
3. Behold, I said that the city of Ammonihah had been rebuilt. I say unto you, yea, that it was in part rebuilt; and because the Lamanites had destroyed it once because of the iniquity of the people, they supposed that it would again become an easy prey for them.
4. But behold, how great was their disappointment; for behold, the Nephites had dug up a ridge of earth round about them, which was so high that the Lamanites could not cast their stones and their arrows at them that they might take effect, neither could they come upon them save it was by their place of entrance.
5. Now at this time the chief captains of the Lamanites were astonished exceedingly, because of the wisdom of the Nephites in preparing their places of security.
6. Now the leaders of the Lamanites

Alma 49

We know that it took great effort to engrave metal plates with the reformed Egyptian characters used to create the records. We also know that Mormon, as an abridger of the records, saw our day in vision. Knowing both of those things, we should ponder what Mormon read in the accounts of these wars that he wanted us to have in our day—causing him to leave them in the abridgement—and what he saw in our day that makes these accounts so critical for us. Instead of mentally "dismissing" these chapters as dreary war accounts, we should pray for the inspiration to know why they have been left for us to study.

had supposed, because of the greatness of their numbers, yea, they supposed that they should be privileged to come upon them as they had hitherto done; yea, and they had also prepared themselves with shields, and with breastplates; and they had also prepared themselves with garments of skins, yea, very thick garments to cover their nakedness.
7. And being thus prepared they supposed that they should easily overpower and subject their brethren to the yoke of bondage, or slay and massacre them according to their pleasure.
8. But behold, to their uttermost astonishment, they were prepared for them, in a manner which never had been known among the children of Lehi. Now they were prepared for the Lamanites, to battle after the manner of the instructions of Moroni.
9. And it came to pass that the Lamanites, or the Amalickiahites, were exceedingly astonished at their manner of preparation for war.
10. Now, if king Amalickiah had come down out of the land of Nephi, at the head of his army, perhaps he would have caused the Lamanites to have attacked the Nephites at the city of Ammonihah; for behold, he did care not for the blood of his people.
11. But behold, Amalickiah did not come down himself to battle. And behold, his chief captains durst not attack the Nephites at the city of Ammonihah, for Moroni had altered the management of affairs among the Nephites, insomuch that the Lamanites were disappointed in their places of retreat and they could not come upon them.
12. Therefore they retreated into the wilderness, and took their camp and marched towards the land of Noah, supposing that to be the next best place for them to come against the Nephites.
13. For they knew not that Moroni had fortified, or had built forts of security, for every city in all the land round about; therefore, they marched forward to the land of Noah with a firm determination; yea, their chief captains came forward and took an oath that they would destroy the people of that city.
14. But behold, to their astonishment, the city of Noah, which had hitherto been a weak place, had now, by the means of Moroni, become strong, yea, even to exceed the strength of the city Ammonihah.
15. And now, behold, this was wisdom in Moroni; for he had supposed that they would be frightened at the city Ammonihah; and as the city of Noah had hitherto been the weakest part of the land, therefore they would march thither to battle; and thus it was according to his desires.
16. And behold, Moroni had appointed Lehi to be chief captain over the men of that city; and it was that same Lehi who fought with the Lamanites in the valley on the east of the river Sidon.
17. And now behold it came to pass, that when the Lamanites had found that Lehi commanded the city they were again disappointed, for they feared Lehi exceedingly; nevertheless their chief captains had sworn with an oath to attack the city; therefore, they brought up their armies.
18. Now behold, the Lamanites could not get into their forts of security by any other way save by the entrance, because of the highness of the bank which had been thrown up, and the depth of the

ditch which had been dug round about, save it were by the entrance.
19. And thus were the Nephites prepared to destroy all such as should attempt to climb up to enter the fort by any other way, by casting over stones and arrows at them.
20. Thus they were prepared, yea, a body of their strongest men, with their swords and their slings, to smite down all who should attempt to come into their place of security by the place of entrance; and thus were they prepared to defend themselves against the Lamanites.
21. And it came to pass that the captains of the Lamanites brought up their armies before the place of entrance, and began to contend with the Nephites, to get into their place of security; but behold, they were driven back from time to time, insomuch that they were slain with an immense slaughter.
22. Now when they found that they could not obtain power over the Nephites by the pass, they began to dig down their banks of earth that they might obtain a pass to their armies, that they might have an equal chance to fight; but behold, in these attempts they were swept off by the stones and arrows which were thrown at them; and instead of filling up their ditches by pulling down the banks of earth, they were filled up in a measure with their dead and wounded bodies.
23. Thus the Nephites had all power over their enemies; and thus the Lamanites did attempt to destroy the Nephites until their chief captains were all slain; yea, and more than a thousand of the Lamanites were slain; while, on the other hand, there was not a single soul of the Nephites which was slain.
24. There were about fifty who were wounded, who had been exposed to the arrows of the Lamanites through the pass, but they were shielded by their shields, and their breastplates, and their head-plates, insomuch that their wounds were upon their legs, many of which were very severe.
25. And it came to pass, that when the Lamanites saw that their chief captains were all slain they fled into the wilderness. And it came to pass that they returned to the land of Nephi, to inform their king, Amalickiah, who was a Nephite by birth, concerning their great loss.
26. And it came to pass that he was exceedingly angry with his people, because he had not obtained his desire over the Nephites; he had not subjected them to the yoke of bondage.
27. Yea, he was exceedingly wroth, and he did curse God, and also Moroni, swearing with an oath that he would drink his blood; and this because Moroni had kept the commandments of God in preparing for the safety of his people.
28. And it came to pass, that on the other hand, the people of Nephi did thank the Lord their God, because of his matchless power in delivering them from the hands of their enemies.
29. And thus ended the nineteenth year of the reign of the judges over the people of Nephi.
30. Yea, and there was continual peace among them, and exceedingly great prosperity in the church because of their heed and diligence which they gave unto the word of God, which was declared unto them by Helaman, and Shiblon, and Corianton, and Ammon and his brethren, yea, and by all those who had been ordained by the holy order of God, being baptized unto repentance, and sent forth to preach among the people.

Alma 49:27

Mormon reminds us in the midst of his account: "Yea, and we also see the great wickedness one very wicked man can cause to take place among the children of men" (Alma 5:9). We of the [twenty-first] century are well aware of the truth of this statement, for we have lived through the horrendous consequences of tyrannical dominance imposed by evil men upon countless millions of human beings. But tyranny is not indomitable. The light of the gospel, illuminating the hearts and motivations of devoted sons and daughters of God, can cause tyranny to dissipate beneath the inexorable onward force of God's plan.

In a telling comparison, Mormon shows the contrast between the vile and fraudulent Amalickiah and the inspiring and noble Moroni—portraits of suffocating darkness versus dazzling light cast against the canvas of epic events. The apostate Nephites, those who had dissented from the Church, now joined forces with the Lamanites. They are more hardened and wicked than even the Lamanites. Amalickiah conspires to become the king over all the Lamanites. He incites them to battle against the Nephites to bring about his wicked agenda. Like all hardened apostates, the contenders against the faith can not leave the Church alone, for their leader is now the devil himself.

Joseph Smith warned, "When a man begins to be an enemy to this work, . . . He gets the spirit of the devil—the same spirit that they had who crucified the Lord of life—the same spirit that sins against the Holy Ghost. You cannot save such persons; you cannot bring them to repentance; they make open war, like the devil, and awful is the consequence." (P/A)

CHAPTER 50

1. AND now it came to pass that Moroni did not stop making preparations for war, or to defend his people against the Lamanites; for he caused that his armies should commence in the commencement of the twentieth year of the reign of the judges, that they should commence in digging up heaps of earth round about all the cities, throughout all the land which was possessed by the Nephites.

2. And upon the top of these ridges of earth he caused that there should be timbers, yea, works of timbers built up to the height of a man, round about the cities.

3. And he caused that upon those works of timbers there should be a frame of pickets built upon the timbers round about; and they were strong and high.

4. And he caused towers to be erected that overlooked those works of pickets, and he caused places of security to be built upon those towers, that the stones and the arrows of the Lamanites could not hurt them.

5. And they were prepared that they could cast stones from the top thereof, according to their pleasure and their strength, and slay him who should attempt to approach near the walls of the city.

6. Thus Moroni did prepare strongholds against the coming of their enemies, round about every city in all the land.

7. And it came to pass that Moroni caused that his armies should go forth into the east wilderness; yea, and they went forth and drove all the Lamanites who were in the east wilderness into their own lands, which were south of the land of Zarahemla.

8. And the land of Nephi did run in a straight course from the east sea to the west.

9. And it came to pass that when Moroni had driven all the Lamanites out of the east wilderness, which was north of the lands of their own possessions, he caused that the inhabitants who were in the land of Zarahemla and in the land round about should go forth into the east wilderness, even to the borders by the seashore, and possess the land.

10. And he also placed armies on the south, in the borders of their possessions, and caused them to erect fortifications that they might secure their armies and their people from the hands of their enemies.

11. And thus he cut off all the strongholds of the Lamanites in the east wilderness, yea, and also on the west, fortifying the line between the Nephites and the Lamanites, between the land of Zarahemla and the land of Nephi, from the west sea, running by the head of the river Sidon—the Nephites possessing all the land northward, yea, even all the land which was northward of the land Bountiful, according to their pleasure.

12. Thus Moroni, with his armies, which did increase daily because of the assurance of protection which his works did bring forth unto them, did seek to cut off the strength and the power of the Lamanites from off the lands of their possessions, that they should have no power upon the lands of their possession.

13. And it came to pass that the Nephites began the foundation of a

Alma 50–58

In these "war chapters," Mormon included historical material containing many insights applicable to the present day, when conflict and turmoil exist in many areas of the world. Like his son Moroni, the prophet Mormon must have seen our day and realized we would need principles and examples to follow as we confront our own circumstances. (See Morm. 8:35.) (O/C)

Alma 50:1

There is a war going on for the souls of all mankind. We must never let up in our righteous preparations and resistance of evil. (P/A)

Alma 50:1–4

We are told that Moroni never stopped making preparations for war, and never stopped preparing to defend his people. He dug up heaps of earth, built up walls of timbers, topped the timbers with a frame of pickets, built towers to overlook the pickets, and built places of security on the towers. His methods were secure, and he implemented them in every city. Perhaps we should ask ourselves: How do I fortify my life against the forces of evil that threaten me?

POINT OF INTEREST

This mask is part of the engravings at the Temple of the Sun in Palenque, Mexico.

city, and they called the name of the city Moroni; and it was by the east sea; and it was on the south by the line of the possessions of the Lamanites.
14. And they also began a foundation for a city between the city of Moroni and the city of Aaron, joining the borders of Aaron and Moroni; and they called the name of the city, or the land, Nephihah.
15. And they also began in that same year to build many cities on the north, one in a particular manner which they called Lehi, which was in the north by the borders of the seashore.
16. And thus ended the twentieth year.
17. And in these prosperous circumstances were the people of Nephi in the commencement of the twenty and first year of the reign of the judges over the people of Nephi.
18. And they did prosper exceedingly, and they became exceedingly rich; yea, and they did multiply and wax strong in the land.
19. And thus we see how merciful and just are all the dealings of the Lord, to the fulfilling of all his words unto the children of men; yea, we can behold that his words are verified, even at this time, which he spake unto Lehi, saying:
20. Blessed art thou and thy children; and they shall be blessed, inasmuch as they shall keep my commandments they shall prosper in the land. But remember, inasmuch as they will not keep my commandments they shall be cut off from the presence of the Lord.
21. And we see that these promises have been verified to the people of Nephi; for it has been their quarrelings and their contentions, yea, their murderings, and their plunderings, their idolatry, their whoredoms, and their abominations, which were among themselves, which brought upon them their wars and their destructions.
22. And those who were faithful in keeping the commandments of the Lord were delivered at all times, whilst thousands of their wicked brethren have been consigned to bondage, or to perish by the sword, or to dwindle in unbelief, and mingle with the Lamanites.
23. But behold there never was a happier time among the people of Nephi, since the days of Nephi, than in the days of Moroni, yea, even at this time, in the twenty and first year of the reign of the judges.
24. And it came to pass that the twenty and second year of the reign of the judges also ended in peace; yea, and also the twenty and third year.
25. And it came to pass that in the commencement of the twenty and fourth year of the reign of the judges, there would also have been peace among the people of Nephi had it not been for a contention which took place among them concerning the land of Lehi, and the land of Morianton, which joined upon the borders of Lehi; both of which were on the borders by the seashore.
26. For behold, the people who possessed the land of Morianton did claim a part of the land of Lehi; therefore there began to be a warm contention between them, insomuch that the people of Morianton took up arms against their brethren, and they were determined by the sword to slay them.
27. But behold, the people who possessed the land of Lehi fled to the camp of Moroni, and appealed unto

Alma 50:21

Our country is rampant with moral breakdown, violence, and lawlessness. Examples are abundant: pornography thrust upon involuntary viewers; theft of personal identity for purposes of fraud; financial dishonesty and deception; removal of and restrictions against religious objects and activity; violent behavior towards others by physical beatings, shootings, rape and even murder; terrorist activities; whoredoms; and a host of other evils. The prophet Mormon observed that such abominations bring about "wars and destructions." . . . In this cause-and-effect situation, whenever someone unrighteously imposes his or her will upon others, innocent citizens lose their personal liberties and become victims of destructive decisions. (O/C)

him for assistance; for behold they were not in the wrong.
28. And it came to pass that when the people of Morianton, who were led by a man whose name was Morianton, found that the people of Lehi had fled to the camp of Moroni, they were exceedingly fearful lest the army of Moroni should come upon them and destroy them.
29. Therefore, Morianton put it into their hearts that they should flee to the land which was northward, which was covered with large bodies of water, and take possession of the land which was northward.
30. And behold, they would have carried this plan into effect, (which would have been a cause to have been lamented) but behold, Morianton being a man of much passion, therefore he was angry with one of his maid servants, and he fell upon her and beat her much.
31. And it came to pass that she fled, and came over to the camp of Moroni, and told Moroni all things concerning the matter, and also concerning their intentions to flee into the land northward.
32. Now behold, the people who were in the land Bountiful, or rather Moroni, feared that they would hearken to the words of Morianton and unite with his people, and thus he would obtain possession of those parts of the land, which would lay a foundation for serious consequences among the people of Nephi, yea, which consequences would lead to the overthrow of their liberty.
33. Therefore Moroni sent an army, with their camp, to head the people of Morianton, to stop their flight into the land northward.
34. And it came to pass that they did not head them until they had come to the borders of the land Desolation; and there they did head them, by the narrow pass which led by the sea into the land northward, yea, by the sea, on the west and on the east.
35. And it came to pass that the army which was sent by Moroni, which was led by a man whose name was Teancum, did meet the people of Morianton; and so stubborn were the people of Morianton, (being inspired by his wickedness and his flattering words) that a battle commenced between them, in the which Teancum did slay Morianton and defeat his army, and took them prisoners, and returned to the camp of Moroni. And thus ended the twenty and fourth year of the reign of the judges over the people of Nephi.
36. And thus were the people of Morianton brought back. And upon their covenanting to keep the peace they were restored to the land of Morianton, and a union took place between them and the people of Lehi; and they were also restored to their lands.
37. And it came to pass that in the same year that the people of Nephi had peace restored unto them, that Nephihah, the second chief judge, died, having filled the judgment-seat with perfect uprightness before God.
38. Nevertheless, he had refused Alma to take possession of those records and those things which were esteemed by Alma and his fathers to be most sacred; therefore Alma had conferred them upon his son, Helaman.
39. Behold, it came to pass that the son of Nephihah was appointed to fill the judgment-seat, in the stead of his father; yea, he was appointed

Alma 50:36

In a move that is highly unusual in the history of civilization, Moroni had his prisoners of war restored to their own lands as long as they agreed to simply make a covenant not to fight again.

chief judge and governor over the people, with an oath and sacred ordinance to judge righteously, and to keep the peace and the freedom of the people, and to grant unto them their sacred privileges to worship the Lord their God, yea, to support and maintain the cause of God all his days, and to bring the wicked to justice according to their crime.
40. Now behold, his name was Pahoran. And Pahoran did fill the seat of his father, and did commence his reign in the end of the twenty and fourth year, over the people of Nephi.

CHAPTER 51

1. AND now it came to pass in the commencement of the twenty and fifth year of the reign of the judges over the people of Nephi, they having established peace between the people of Lehi and the people of Morianton concerning their lands, and having commenced the twenty and fifth year in peace;
2. Nevertheless, they did not long maintain an entire peace in the land, for there began to be a contention among the people concerning the chief judge Pahoran; for behold, there were a part of the people who desired that a few particular points of the law should be altered.
3. But behold, Pahoran would not alter nor suffer the law to be altered; therefore, he did not hearken to those who had sent in their voices with their petitions concerning the altering of the law.
4. Therefore, those who were desirous that the law should be altered were angry with him, and desired that he should no longer be chief judge over the land; therefore there arose a warm dispute concerning the matter, but not unto bloodshed.
5. And it came to pass that those who were desirous that Pahoran should be dethroned from the judgment-seat were called king-men, for they were desirous that the law should be altered in a manner to overthrow the free government and to establish a king over the land.
6. And those who were desirous that Pahoran should remain chief judge over the land took upon them the name of freemen; and thus was the division among them, for the freemen had sworn or covenanted to maintain their rights and the privileges of their religion by a free government.
7. And it came to pass that this matter of their contention was settled by the voice of the people. And it came to pass that the voice of the people came in favor of the freemen, and Pahoran retained the judgment-seat, which caused much rejoicing among the brethren of Pahoran and also many of the people of liberty, who also put the king-men to silence, that they durst not oppose but were obliged to maintain the cause of freedom.
8. Now those who were in favor of kings were those of high birth, and they sought to be kings; and they were supported by those who sought power and authority over the people.

9. But behold, this was a critical time for such contentions to be among the people of Nephi; for behold, Amalickiah had again stirred up the hearts of the people of the Lamanites against the people of the Nephites, and he was gathering together soldiers from all parts of his land, and arming them, and preparing for war with all diligence; for he had sworn to drink the blood of Moroni.

10. But behold, we shall see that his promise which he made was rash; nevertheless, he did prepare himself and his armies to come to battle against the Nephites.

11. Now his armies were not so great as they had hitherto been, because of the many thousands who had been slain by the hand of the Nephites; but notwithstanding their great loss, Amalickiah had gathered together a wonderfully great army, insomuch that he feared not to come down to the land of Zarahemla.

12. Yea, even Amalickiah did himself come down, at the head of the Lamanites. And it was in the twenty and fifth year of the reign of the judges; and it was at the same time that they had begun to settle the affairs of their contentions concerning the chief judge, Pahoran.

13. And it came to pass that when the men who were called king-men had heard that the Lamanites were coming down to battle against them, they were glad in their hearts; and they refused to take up arms, for they were so wroth with the chief judge, and also with the people of liberty, that they would not take up arms to defend their country.

14. And it came to pass that when Moroni saw this, and also saw that the Lamanites were coming into the borders of the land, he was exceedingly wroth because of the stubbornness of those people whom he had labored with so much diligence to preserve; yea, he was exceedingly wroth; his soul was filled with anger against them.

15. And it came to pass that he sent a petition, with the voice of the people, unto the governor of the land, desiring that he should read it, and give him (Moroni) power to compel those dissenters to defend their country or to put them to death.

16. For it was his first care to put an end to such contentions and dissensions among the people; for behold, this had been hitherto a cause of all their destruction. And it came to pass that it was granted according to the voice of the people.

17. And it came to pass that Moroni commanded that his army should go against those king-men, to pull down their pride and their nobility and level them with the earth, or they should take up arms and support the cause of liberty.

18. And it came to pass that the armies did march forth against them; and they did pull down their pride and their nobility, insomuch that as they did lift their weapons of war to fight against the men of Moroni they were hewn down and leveled to the earth.

19. And it came to pass that there were four thousand of those dissenters who were hewn down by the sword; and those of their leaders who were not slain in battle were taken and cast into prison, for there was no time for their trials at this period.

20. And the remainder of those dissenters, rather than be smitten down to the earth by the sword, yielded to the standard of liberty, and were compelled to hoist the title of liberty upon their towers, and in their cities, and to take up arms in defence of their country.

Alma 51:9

The relentless Lamanites and Amalickiahites continue their campaign against the Nephites. Moroni and the Nephites had prepared well for war. Because of their fidelity to the principles of righteousness, they prosper for a time, largely because Moroni's defensive strategy proved so effective. However, internal strife and wickedness brought about through the insurrection of the king-men weaken the Nephites, and they lose many cities to the enemy. (P/A)

Alma 51:15

Where there is internal division, the body politic cannot stand with enduring strength. Victory over the forces of evil requires unity of the faith and diligence in keeping the commandments of God. (P/A)

Alma 51:20

Rampant in our land are incidents of moral breakdown, violence and lawlessness. Examples are abundant: Thrusting of pornographic views upon involuntary viewers; theft of personal identity for purposes of fraud; financial dishonesty and deception; removal of and restrictions against religious objects and activity; violent behavior towards others through physical beatings, shootings, rape, and even murder; terrorist activities; whoredoms; and a host of other evils. The prophet Mormon observed that such abominations bring about ". . . wars and destructions" (Alma 50:21). This is a cause-and-effect situation. Whenever someone imposes his will upon others unrighteously, personal liberty is lost and innocent citizens become victims of destructive decisions.

From the scriptures we are reminded that the laws of the Lord should be the laws of the land, as they were in Nephite days. (See Mosiah 29:25.) When laws have divine endorsement, they should be our standard of behavior and we should know that efforts to avoid an observance of righteous laws are steps along the path leading to tyranny and a loss of individual freedom.

Reminiscent of the righteous determination of Chief Captain Moroni are the words of Elder Mark E. Petersen: ". . . this is God's land. He raised it up specially as he has raised up no other nation. He has given us our flag. So far as I am concerned the flag of the United States is the flag of Almighty God. Old Glory to me stands for everything that the gospel of Christ stands for, because Old Glory was raised up because there was to be a restoration of the gospel. I cannot separate my flag and my religion. I would fight for my flag as I would fight for my religion." (O/C)

21. And thus Moroni put an end to those king-men, that there were not any known by the appellation of king-men; and thus he put an end to the stubbornness and the pride of those people who professed the blood of nobility; but they were brought down to humble themselves like unto their brethren, and to fight valiantly for their freedom from bondage.
22. Behold, it came to pass that while Moroni was thus breaking down the wars and contentions among his own people, and subjecting them to peace and civilization, and making regulations to prepare for war against the Lamanites, behold, the Lamanites had come into the land of Moroni, which was in the borders by the seashore.
23. And it came to pass that the Nephites were not sufficiently strong in the city of Moroni; therefore Amalickiah did drive them, slaying many. And it came to pass that Amalickiah took possession of the city, yea, possession of all their fortifications.
24. And those who fled out of the city of Moroni came to the city of Nephihah; and also the people of the city of Lehi gathered themselves together, and made preparations and were ready to receive the Lamanites to battle.
25. But it came to pass that Amalickiah would not suffer the Lamanites to go against the city of Nephihah to battle, but kept them down by the seashore, leaving men in every city to maintain and defend it.
26. And thus he went on, taking possession of many cities, the city of Nephihah, and the city of Lehi, and the city of Morianton, and the city of Omner, and the city of Gid, and the city of Mulek, all of which were on the east borders by the seashore.
27. And thus had the Lamanites obtained, by the cunning of Amalickiah, so many cities, by their numberless hosts, all of which were strongly fortified after the manner of the fortifications of Moroni; all of which afforded strongholds for the Lamanites.
28. And it came to pass that they marched to the borders of the land Bountiful, driving the Nephites before them and slaying many.
29. But it came to pass that they were met by Teancum, who had slain Morianton and had headed his people in his flight.
30. And it came to pass that he headed Amalickiah also, as he was marching forth with his numerous army that he might take possession of the land Bountiful, and also the land northward.
31. But behold he met with a disappointment by being repulsed by Teancum and his men, for they were great warriors; for every man of Teancum did exceed the Lamanites in their strength and in their skill of war, insomuch that they did gain advantage over the Lamanites.
32. And it came to pass that they did harass them, insomuch that they did slay them even until it was dark. And it came to pass that Teancum and his men did pitch their tents in the borders of the land Bountiful; and Amalickiah did pitch his tents in the borders on the beach by the seashore, and after this manner were they driven.
33. And it came to pass that when the night had come, Teancum and his servant stole forth and went out by night, and went into the camp of Amalickiah; and behold, sleep

Alma 51:26

Although the historian of this part of the record mentions in Alma 51:25 that the Lamanites decided not "to go against the city of Nephihah to battle," in the next verse the historian records that the Lamanites went on "taking possession of many cities, the city of Nephihah, and the city of Lehi . . . ," etc. Although it is not clear whether or not the historian intended to include the city of Nephihah in this list, it is evident that the city is captured later by the Lamanites. (See Alma 59:7–9.) (Ludlow)

had overpowered them because of their much fatigue, which was
caused by the labors and heat of the day.
34. And it came to pass that Teancum stole privily into the tent of
the king, and put a javelin to his heart; and he did cause the death
of the king immediately that he did not awake his servants.
35. And he returned again privily to his own camp, and behold, his
men were asleep, and he awoke them and told them all the things that
he had done.
36. And he caused that his armies should stand in readiness, lest
the Lamanites had awakened and should come upon them.
37. And thus endeth the twenty and fifth year of the reign of the
judges over the people of Nephi; and thus endeth the days of
Amalickiah.

CHAPTER 52

1. AND now, it came to pass in the twenty and sixth year of the
reign of the judges over the people of Nephi, behold, when the
Lamanites awoke on the first morning of the first month, behold,
they found Amalickiah was dead in his own tent; and they also saw
that Teancum was ready to give them battle on that day.
2. And now, when the Lamanites saw this they were affrighted; and
they abandoned their design in marching into the land northward,
and retreated with all their army into the city of Mulek, and sought
protection in their fortifications.
3. And it came to pass that the brother of Amalickiah was appointed king over the people; and his name was Ammoron; thus king
Ammoron, the brother of king Amalickiah, was appointed to reign
in his stead.
4. And it came to pass that he did command that his people should
maintain those cities, which they had taken by the shedding of blood;
for they had not taken any cities save they had lost much blood.
5. And now, Teancum saw that the Lamanites were determined to
maintain those cities which they had taken, and those parts of the
land which they had obtained possession of; and also seeing the
enormity of their number, Teancum thought it was not expedient
that he should attempt to attack them in their forts.
6. But he kept his men round about, as if making preparations for
war; yea, and truly he was preparing to defend himself against them,
by casting up walls round about and preparing places of resort.
7. And it came to pass that he kept thus preparing for war until
Moroni had sent a large number of men to strengthen his army.
8. And Moroni also sent orders unto him that he should retain all
the prisoners who fell into his hands; for as the Lamanites had
taken many prisoners, that he should retain all the prisoners of the
Lamanites as a ransom for those whom the Lamanites had taken.
9. And he also sent orders unto him that he should fortify the land
Bountiful, and secure the narrow pass which led into the land
northward, lest the Lamanites should obtain that point and should
have power to harass them on every side.

Alma 52

Throughout the description of his battles, it is clear that even though he was a great warrior, Moroni was always reluctant to take up and sword—and equally quick to lay it down. He knew that even when his armies were victorious, thousands died in battle. His attitude resembles that of the Savior, who said, "All they that take the sword shall perish with the sword" (Matthew 26:52).

10. And Moroni also sent unto him, desiring him that he would be
faithful in maintaining that quarter of the land, and that he would
seek every opportunity to scourge the Lamanites in that quarter, as
much as was in his power, that perhaps he might take again by
stratagem or some other way those cities which had been taken out
of their hands; and that he also would fortify and strengthen the
cities round about, which had not fallen into the hands of the
Lamanites.
11. And he also said unto him, I would come unto you, but behold,
the Lamanites are upon us in the borders of the land by the west sea;
and behold, I go against them, therefore I cannot come unto you.
12. Now, the king (Ammoron) had departed out of the land of
Zarahemla, and had made known unto the queen concerning the
death of his brother, and had gathered together a large number of
men, and had marched forth against the Nephites on the borders
by the west sea.
13. And thus he was endeavoring to harass the Nephites, and to draw
away a part of their forces to that part of the land, while he had commanded those whom he had left to possess the cities which he had
taken, that they should also harass the Nephites on the borders by the
east sea, and should take possession of their lands as much as it was
in their power, according to the power of their armies.
14. And thus were the Nephites in those dangerous circumstances
in the ending of the twenty and sixth year of the reign of the judges
over the people of Nephi.
15. But behold, it came to pass in the twenty and seventh year of
the reign of the judges, that Teancum, by the command of
Moroni—who had established armies to protect the south and the
west borders of the land, and had begun his march towards the land
Bountiful, that he might assist Teancum with his men in retaking
the cities which they had lost—
16. And it came to pass that Teancum had received orders to make
an attack upon the city of Mulek, and retake it if it were possible.
17. And it came to pass that Teancum made preparations to make
an attack upon the city of Mulek, and march forth with his army
against the Lamanites; but he saw that it was impossible that he
could overpower them while they were in their fortifications;
therefore he abandoned his designs and returned again to the city
Bountiful, to wait for the coming of Moroni, that he might receive
strength to his army.
18. And it came to pass that Moroni did arrive with his army at the
land of Bountiful, in the latter end of the twenty and seventh year
of the reign of the judges over the people of Nephi.
19. And in the commencement of the twenty and eighth year,
Moroni and Teancum and many of the chief captains held a council of war—what they should do to cause the Lamanites to come
out against them to battle; or that they might by some means flatter them out of their strongholds, that they might gain advantage
over them and take again the city of Mulek.
20. And it came to pass they sent embassies to the army of the
Lamanites, which protected the city of Mulek, to their leader,
whose name was Jacob, desiring him that he would come out with
his armies to meet them upon the plains between the two cities.
But behold, Jacob, who was a Zoramite, would not come out with
his army to meet them upon the plains.
21. And it came to pass that Moroni, having no hopes of meeting
them upon fair grounds, therefore, he resolved upon a plan that he
might

POINT OF INTEREST

Record Keepers of the Small Plates

Nephi I
Jacob, brother of Nephi
Enos, son of Jacob
Jarom, son of Enos
Omni, son of Jarom
Amaron, son of Omni
Chemish, brother of Amaron
Abinadom, son of Chemish
Amaleki, son of Abinadom

Record Keepers of the Large Plates

Nephi I
Succession of kings named Nephi
Mosiah
Benjamin, son of Mosiah
Mosiah, son of Benjamin
Alma II, son of Alma I
Helaman I, son of Alma II
Shiblon, son of Alma II
Helaman II, son of Helaman I
Nephi II, son of Helaman II
Nephi III, son of Nephi II
Nephi IV, son of Nephi III
Amos I, son of Nephi IV
Amos II, son of Amos I
Ammaron, brother of Amos II
Mormon II, son of Mormon I
Moroni, son of Mormon II

decoy the Lamanites out of their strongholds.
22. Therefore he caused that Teancum should take a small number of men and march down near the seashore; and Moroni and his army, by night, marched in the wilderness, on the west of the city Mulek; and thus, on the morrow, when the guards of the Lamanites had discovered Teancum, they ran and told it unto Jacob, their leader.
23. And it came to pass that the armies of the Lamanites did march forth against Teancum, supposing by their numbers to overpower Teancum because of the smallness of his numbers. And as Teancum saw the armies of the Lamanites coming out against him he began to retreat down by the seashore, northward.
24. And it came to pass that when the Lamanites saw that he began to flee, they took courage and pursued them with vigor. And while Teancum was thus leading away the Lamanites who were pursuing them in vain, behold, Moroni commanded that a part of his army who were with him should march forth into the city, and take possession of it.
25. And thus they did, and slew all those who had been left to protect the city, yea, all those who would not yield up their weapons of war.
26. And thus Moroni had obtained possession of the city Mulek with a part of his army, while he marched with the remainder to meet the Lamanites when they should return from the pursuit of Teancum.
27. And it came to pass that the Lamanites did pursue Teancum until they came near the city Bountiful, and then they were met by Lehi and a small army, which had been left to protect the city Bountiful.
28. And now behold, when the chief captains of the Lamanites had beheld Lehi with his army coming against them, they fled in much confusion, lest perhaps they should not obtain the city Mulek before Lehi should overtake them; for they were wearied because of their march, and the men of Lehi were fresh.
29. Now the Lamanites did not know that Moroni had been in their rear with his army; and all they feared was Lehi and his men.
30. Now Lehi was not desirous to overtake them till they should meet Moroni and his army.
31. And it came to pass that before the Lamanites had retreated far they were surrounded by the Nephites, by the men of Moroni on one hand, and the men of Lehi on the other, all of whom were fresh and full of strength; but the Lamanites were wearied because of their long march.
32. And Moroni commanded his men that they should fall upon them until they had given up their weapons of war.
33. And it came to pass that Jacob, being their leader, being also a Zoramite, and having an unconquerable spirit, he led the Lamanites forth to battle with exceeding fury against Moroni.
34. Moroni being in their course of march, therefore Jacob was determined to slay them and cut his way through to the city of Mulek. But behold, Moroni and his men were more powerful; therefore they did not give way before the Lamanites.
35. And it came to pass that they fought on both hands with exceeding fury; and there were many slain on both sides; yea, and Moroni was wounded and Jacob was killed.
36. And Lehi pressed upon their rear with such fury with his strong men, that the Lamanites in the rear delivered up their weapons of war; and the remainder of them, being much confused, knew not whither to go or to strike.
37. Now Moroni seeing their confusion,

Alma 52:25

Even though it is sometimes justified, war is always the result of sin and disobedience on someone's part. Whenever there is war, Satan laughs—and the Lord weeps (see Moses 7:26, 28).

Alma 52:32–33

Based on all we know of Moroni, he would have directed his armies to spare those who surrendered. Unfortunately, they continued to fight with fury against Moroni and his army. That fury is described in verses 33–36.

he said unto them: If ye will bring forth your weapons of war and
deliver them up, behold we will forbear shedding your blood.
38. And it came to pass that when the Lamanites had heard these
words, their chief captains, all those who were not slain, came
forth and threw down their weapons of war at the feet of Moroni,
and also commanded their men that they should do the same.
39. But behold, there were many that would not; and those who
would not deliver up their swords were taken and bound, and their
weapons of war were taken from them, and they were compelled to
march with their brethren forth into the land Bountiful.
40. And now the number of prisoners who were taken exceeded
more than the number of those who had been slain, yea, more than
those who had been slain on both sides.

CHAPTER 53

1. AND it came to pass that they did set guards over the prisoners
of the Lamanites, and did compel them to go forth and bury their
dead, yea, and also the dead of the Nephites who were slain; and
Moroni placed men over them to guard them while they should
perform their labors.
2. And Moroni went to the city of Mulek with Lehi, and took command of the city and gave it unto Lehi. Now behold, this Lehi was
a man who had been with Moroni in the more part of all his battles; and he was a man like unto Moroni, and they rejoiced in each
other's safety; yea, they were beloved by each other, and also
beloved by all the people of Nephi.
3. And it came to pass that after the Lamanites had finished burying their dead and also the dead of the Nephites, they were
marched back into the land Bountiful; and Teancum, by the orders
of Moroni, caused that they should commence laboring in digging
a ditch round about the land, or the city, Bountiful.
4. And he caused that they should build a breastwork of timbers
upon the inner bank of the ditch; and they cast up dirt out of the
ditch against the breastwork of timbers; and thus they did cause the
Lamanites to labor until they had encircled the city of Bountiful
round about with a strong wall of timbers and earth, to an exceeding height.
5. And this city became an exceeding stronghold ever after; and in this
city they did guard the prisoners of the Lamanites; yea, even within a
wall which they had caused them to build with their own hands. Now
Moroni was compelled to cause the Lamanites to labor, because it was
easy to guard them while at their labor; and he desired all his forces
when he should make an attack upon the Lamanites.
6. And it came to pass that Moroni had thus gained a victory over
one of the greatest of the armies of the Lamanites, and had obtained
possession of the city of Mulek, which was one of the strongest holds
of the Lamanites in the land of Nephi; and thus he had also built a
stronghold to retain his prisoners.
7. And it came to pass that he did no more attempt a battle with
the Lamanites in that year, but he did employ his men in preparing for war, yea, and in making fortifications to guard against the
Lamanites, yea, and also delivering their women and their children
from famine and

Alma 53:6

The reference to the city of Mulek as "one of the strongest holds of the Lamanites in the land of Nephi" is puzzling because the city of Mulek is evidently located in the greater land of Zarahemla. (See Alma 51:26.)

Here are three possible explanations of this puzzle: (1) Perhaps this land is being called "the land of Nephi" by the Lamanites because they now possess it as they also possess the land of Nephi in the south. (2) The Nephites could have a "land of Nephi" in the north, although such a land has not been mentioned before and is not mentioned later. (3) The phrase "in the land of Nephi" might be used to identify those particular Lamanites mentioned in the verse and to differentiate them from Lamanites living in other parts of the country. (Ludlow)

affliction, and providing food for their armies.
8. And now it came to pass that the armies of the Lamanites, on the west sea, south, while in the absence of Moroni on account of some intrigue amongst the Nephites, which caused dissension amongst them, had gained some ground over the Nephites, yea insomuch that they had obtained possession of a number of their cities in that part of the land.
9. And thus because of iniquity amongst themselves, yea, because of dissensions and intrigue among themselves they were placed in the most dangerous circumstances.
10. And now behold, I have somewhat to say concerning the people of Ammon, who in the beginning, were Lamanites; but by Ammon and his brethren, or rather by the power and word of God, they had been converted unto the Lord; and they had been brought down into the land of Zarahemla, and had ever since been protected by the Nephites.
11. And because of their oath they had been kept from taking up arms against their brethren; for they had taken an oath that they never would shed blood more; and according to their oath they would have perished; yea, they would have suffered themselves to have fallen into the hands of their brethren, had it not been for the pity and the exceeding love which Ammon and his brethren had had for them.
12. And for this cause they were brought down into the land of Zarahemla; and they ever had been protected by the Nephites.
13. But it came to pass that when they saw the danger, and the many afflictions and tribulations which the Nephites bore for them, they were moved with compassion and were desirous to take up arms in the defence of their country.
14. But behold, as they were about to take their weapons of war, they were overpowered by the persuasions of Helaman and his brethren, for they were about to break the oath which they had made.
15. And Helaman feared lest by so doing they should lose their souls; therefore all those who had entered into this covenant were compelled to behold their brethren wade through their afflictions, in their dangerous circumstances at this time.
16. But behold, it came to pass they had many sons, who had not entered into a covenant that they would not take their weapons of war to defend themselves against their enemies; therefore they did assemble themselves together at this time, as many as were able to take up arms, and they called themselves Nephites.
17. And they entered into a covenant to fight for the liberty of the Nephites, yea, to protect the land unto the laying down of their lives; yea, even they covenanted that they never would give up their liberty, but they would fight in all cases to protect the Nephites and themselves from bondage.
18. Now behold, there were two thousand of those young men, who entered into this covenant and took their weapons of war to defend their country.
19. And now behold, as they never had hitherto been a disadvantage to the Nephites, they became now at this period of time also a great support; for they took their weapons of war, and they would that Helaman should be their leader.
20. And they were all young men,

Alma 53:8

When the Nephites first landed in the promised land, they gave names to some of the seas and lands around them. At that time the sea to the west of their landing place was evidently called the "west sea." Later, Nephi left this land, took his followers, and went northward where they settled in the land of Nephi. The descendants of Nephi and his group lived there for several hundred years. Then Mosiah, under the inspiration of the Lord, led a group of Nephites even farther north to the land of Zarahemla. The major group of the Nephites is now located in the land of Zarahemla, far north of the original landing place. Thus, the original "west sea" is actually far to the south of where they are now living, and they refer to "the west sea, south" (Alma 53:8). (Ludlow)

Alma 53:11

The bonds between Heavenly Father and His children are always sealed and confirmed by covenants. Zion is a covenant society. Honor and dignity attend the covenant promises made in the name of Christ and perpetuated through obedience and integrity. There is no greater legacy than an uninterrupted chain of honored covenants that illuminate the lives of God's people; there is no greater hope in life than the hope of covenants fulfilled and the bestowal of blessings from on high in answer to covenant valor. (P/A)

Alma 53:11–17

Joseph Smith said, "And may God enable us to perform our vows and covenants with each other, in all fidelity and righteousness before Him, that our influence may be felt among the nations of the earth, in mighty power, even to rend the kingdoms of darkness asunder, and triumph over priestcraft and spiritual wickedness in high places, and break in pieces all kingdoms that are opposed to the kingdom of Christ, and spread the light and truth of the everlasting Gospel from the rivers to the ends of the earth."

and they were exceedingly valiant for courage, and also for strength and activity; but behold, this was not all—they were men who were true at all times in whatsoever thing they were entrusted.
21. Yea, they were men of truth and soberness, for they had been taught to keep the commandments of God and to walk uprightly before him.
22. And now it came to pass that Helaman did march at the head of his two thousand stripling soldiers, to the support of the people in the borders of the land on the south by the west sea.
23. And thus ended the twenty and eighth year of the reign of the judges over the people of Nephi.

CHAPTER 54

1. AND now it came to pass in the commencement of the twenty and ninth year of the judges, that Ammoron sent unto Moroni desiring that he would exchange prisoners.
2. And it came to pass that Moroni felt to rejoice exceedingly at this request, for he desired the provisions which were imparted for the support of the Lamanite prisoners for the support of his own people; and he also desired his own people for the strengthening of his army.
3. Now the Lamanites had taken many women and children, and there was not a woman nor a child among all the prisoners of Moroni, or the prisoners whom Moroni had taken; therefore Moroni resolved upon a stratagem to obtain as many prisoners of the Nephites from the Lamanites as it were possible.
4. Therefore he wrote an epistle, and sent it by the servant of Ammoron, the same who had brought an epistle to Moroni. Now these are the words which he wrote unto Ammoron, saying:
5. Behold, Ammoron, I have written unto you somewhat concerning this war which ye have waged against my people, or rather which thy brother hath waged against them, and which ye are still determined to carry on after his death.
6. Behold, I would tell you somewhat concerning the justice of God, and the sword of his almighty wrath, which doth hang over you except ye repent and withdraw your armies into your own lands, or the land of your possessions, which is the land of Nephi.
7. Yea, I would tell you these things if ye were capable of hearkening unto them; yea, I would tell you concerning that awful hell that awaits to receive such murderers as thou and thy brother have been, except ye repent and withdraw your murderous purposes, and return with your armies to your own lands.
8. But as ye have once rejected these things, and have fought against the people of the Lord, even so I may expect you will do it again.
9. And now behold, we are prepared to receive you; yea, and except you withdraw your purposes, behold, ye will pull down the wrath of that God whom you have rejected upon you, even to your utter destruction.
10. But, as the Lord liveth, our armies shall come upon you except ye withdraw, and ye shall soon be visited with death, for we will retain our cities and our lands; yea,

Alma 53:21

Central to the eternal plan of happiness is the family. The crowning blessing of our mortal experience is the assurance from our Father in Heaven that our families can be eternal. The fulness of salvation is the exaltation of the family; this is the purpose of mortality. This is the purpose of temples. The divine desire of our loving Father in Heaven is that we experience successful parenthood and have joy in our posterity.

The first entry Nephi recorded in his record was the principle of divinely approved parenthood. He records: "I, Nephi, having been born of goodly parents, therefore I was taught . . ." (1 Ne. 1:1).

Commenting on this divine principle, President Spencer W. Kimball taught, "We do not go beyond the first verse in the Book of Mormon, the book the Prophet Joseph Smith said was the keystone of our religion, before we learn the correct principle of parenthood: 'I, Nephi, having been born of goodly parents, therefore I was taught . . . '

"It is the divine role of parents to teach the truths of the gospel to their children. . . ."

Wise are the Latter-day Saint parents who understand this divine principle of parenthood, who understand that the fulness of salvation is the exaltation of their families. Wise are the Latter-day Saint parents who have so ordered their lives that the teaching of the gospel of Jesus Christ to their children is the central function in their homes. They have eternal perspective. (O/C)

Alma 54

Chapters 54–61 contain word-for-word quotes of the epistles that were exchanged between Ammoron and Moroni as they negotiated for the exchange of prisoners of war. Considering again the difficulty involved in engraving on the plates and the fact that Mormon saw our day in vision, it is curious that he devoted so much space in the record for long sections of quoted material.

and we will maintain our religion and the cause of our God.
11. But behold, it supposeth me that I talk to you concerning these things in vain; or it supposeth me that thou art a child of hell; therefore I will close my epistle by telling you that I will not exchange prisoners, save it be on conditions that ye will deliver up a man and his wife and his children, for one prisoner; if this be the case that ye will do it, I will exchange.
12. And behold, if you do not this, I will come against you with my armies; yea, even I will arm my women and my children, and I will come against you, and I will follow you even into your own land, which is the land of our first inheritance; yea, and it shall be blood for blood, yea, life for life; and I will give you battle even until you are destroyed from off the face of the earth.
13. Behold, I am in my anger, and also my people; ye have sought to murder us, and we have only sought to defend ourselves. But behold, if ye seek to destroy us more we will seek to destroy you; yea, and we will seek our land, the land of our first inheritance.
14. Now I close my epistle. I am Moroni; I am a leader of the people of the Nephites.
15. Now it came to pass that Ammoron, when he had received this epistle, was angry; and he wrote another epistle unto Moroni, and these are the words which he wrote, saying:
16. I am Ammoron, the king of the Lamanites; I am the brother of Amalickiah whom ye have murdered. Behold, I will avenge his blood upon you, yea, and I will come upon you with my armies for I fear not your threatenings.
17. For behold, your fathers did wrong their brethren, insomuch that they did rob them of their right to the government when it rightly belonged unto them.
18. And now behold, if ye will lay down your arms, and subject yourselves to be governed by those to whom the government doth rightly belong, then will I cause that my people shall lay down their weapons and shall be at war no more.
19. Behold, ye have breathed out many threatenings against me and my people; but behold, we fear not your threatenings.
20. Nevertheless, I will grant to exchange prisoners according to your request, gladly, that I may preserve my food for my men of war; and we will wage a war which shall be eternal, either to the subjecting the Nephites to our authority or to their eternal extinction.
21. And as concerning that God whom ye say we have rejected, behold, we know not such a being; neither do ye; but if it so be that there is such a being, we know not but that he hath made us as well as you.
22. And if it so be that there is a devil and a hell, behold will he not send you there to dwell with my brother whom ye have murdered, whom ye have hinted that he hath gone to such a place? But behold these things matter not.
23. I am Ammoron, and a descendant of Zoram, whom your fathers pressed and brought out of Jerusalem.
24. And behold now, I am a bold Lamanite; behold, this war hath been waged to avenge their wrongs, and to maintain and to obtain their rights to the government; and I close my epistle to Moroni.

CHAPTER 55

Alma 54:13

According to President Harold B. Lee, those who kill during acts of war are not accountable for murder as long as they are following their leader's command to fight.

Alma 54:24

Ammoron agreed to exchange prisoners, but he refused to put down his arms and end the war; clearly, he was seeking vengeance. He wanted the Nephites to be under Lamanite rule, and the only way he could see that happening was to continue fighting until his armies had subdued the Nephite armies.

1. Now it came to pass that when Moroni had received this epistle he was more angry, because he knew that Ammoron had a perfect knowledge of his fraud; yea, he knew that Ammoron knew that it was not a just cause that had caused him to wage a war against the people of Nephi.
2. And he said: Behold, I will not exchange prisoners with Ammoron save he will withdraw his purpose, as I have stated in my epistle; for I will not grant unto him that he shall have any more power than what he hath got.
3. Behold, I know the place where the Lamanites do guard my people whom they have taken prisoners; and as Ammoron would not grant unto me mine epistle, behold, I will give unto him according to my words; yea, I will seek death among them until they shall sue for peace.
4. And now it came to pass that when Moroni had said these words, he caused that a search should be made among his men, that perhaps he might find a man who was a descendant of Laman among them.
5. And it came to pass that they found one, whose name was Laman; and he was one of the servants of the king who was murdered by Amalickiah.
6. Now Moroni caused that Laman and a small number of his men should go forth unto the guards who were over the Nephites.
7. Now the Nephites were guarded in the city of Gid; therefore Moroni appointed Laman and caused that a small number of men should go with him.
8. And when it was evening Laman went to the guards who were over the Nephites, and behold, they saw him coming and they hailed him; but he saith unto them: Fear not; behold, I am a Lamanite. Behold, we have escaped from the Nephites, and they sleep; and behold we have taken of their wine and brought with us.
9. Now when the Lamanites heard these words they received him with joy; and they said unto him: Give us of your wine, that we may drink; we are glad that ye have thus taken wine with you for we are weary.
10. But Laman said unto them: Let us keep of our wine till we go against the Nephites to battle. But this saying only made them more desirous to drink of the wine;
11. For, said they: We are weary, therefore let us take of the wine, and by and by we shall receive wine for our rations, which will strengthen us to go against the Nephites.
12. And Laman said unto them: You may do according to your desires.
13. And it came to pass that they did take of the wine freely; and it was pleasant to their taste, therefore they took of it more freely; and it was strong, having been prepared in its strength.
14. And it came to pass they did drink and were merry, and by and by they were all drunken.
15. And now when Laman and his men saw that they were all drunken, and were in a deep sleep, they returned to Moroni and told him all the things that had happened.
16. And now this was according to the design of Moroni. And Moroni had prepared his men with weapons of war; and he went to the city Gid, while the Lamanites were in a deep sleep and drunken, and cast in weapons of war unto the prisoners, insomuch that they were all armed;
17. Yea, even to their women, and all those of their children, as many as were able to use a weapon of war,

when Moroni had armed all those prisoners; and all those things were done in a profound silence.
18. But had they awakened the Lamanites, behold they were drunken and the Nephites could have slain them.
19. But behold, this was not the desire of Moroni; he did not delight in murder or bloodshed, but he delighted in the saving of his people from destruction; and for this cause he might not bring upon him injustice, he would not fall upon the Lamanites and destroy them in their drunkenness.
20. But he had obtained his desires; for he had armed those prisoners of the Nephites who were within the wall of the city, and had given them power to gain possession of those parts which were within the walls.
21. And then he caused the men who were with him to withdraw a pace from them, and surround the armies of the Lamanites.
22. Now behold this was done in the night-time, so that when the Lamanites awoke in the morning they beheld that they were surrounded by the Nephites without, and that their prisoners were armed within.
23. And thus they saw that the Nephites had power over them; and in these circumstances they found that it was not expedient that they should fight with the Nephites; therefore their chief captains demanded their weapons of war, and they brought them forth and cast them at the feet of the Nephites, pleading for mercy.
24. Now behold, this was the desire of Moroni. He took them prisoners of war, and took possession of the city, and caused that all the prisoners should be liberated, who were Nephites; and they did join the army of Moroni, and were a great strength to his army.
25. And it came to pass that he did cause the Lamanites, whom he had taken prisoners, that they should commence a labor in strengthening the fortifications round about the city Gid.
26. And it came to pass that when he had fortified the city Gid, according to his desires, he caused that his prisoners should be taken to the city Bountiful; and he also guarded that city with an exceedingly strong force.
27. And it came to pass that they did, notwithstanding all the intrigues of the Lamanites, keep and protect all the prisoners whom they had taken, and also maintain all the ground and the advantage which they had retaken.
28. And it came to pass that the Nephites began again to be victorious, and to reclaim their rights and their privileges.
29. Many times did the Lamanites attempt to encircle them about by night, but in these attempts they did lose many prisoners.
30. And many times did they attempt to administer of their wine to the Nephites, that they might destroy them with poison or with drunkenness.
31. But behold, the Nephites were not slow to remember the Lord their God in this their time of affliction. They could not be taken in their snares; yea, they would not partake of their wine, save they had first given to some of the Lamanite prisoners.
32. And they were thus cautious that no poison should be administered among them; for if their wine would poison a Lamanite it would also poison a Nephite; and thus they did try all their liquors.
33. And now it came to pass that it was expedient for Moroni to make preparations to attack the city Morianton; for behold, the Lamanites

had, by their labors, fortified the city Morianton until it had become an exceeding stronghold.
34. And they were continually bringing new forces into that city, and also new supplies of provisions.
35. And thus ended the twenty and ninth year of the reign of the judges over the people of Nephi.

CHAPTER 56

1. AND now it came to pass in the commencement of the thirtieth year of the reign of the judges, on the second day in the first month, Moroni received an epistle from Helaman, stating the affairs of the people in that quarter of the land.
2. And these are the words which he wrote, saying: My dearly beloved brother, Moroni, as well in the Lord as in the tribulations of our warfare; behold, my beloved brother, I have somewhat to tell you concerning our warfare in this part of the land.
3. Behold, two thousand of the sons of those men whom Ammon brought down out of the land of Nephi—now ye have known that these were descendants of Laman, who was the eldest son of our father Lehi;
4. Now I need not rehearse unto you concerning their traditions or their unbelief, for thou knowest concerning all these things—
5. Therefore it sufficeth me that I tell you that two thousand of these young men have taken their weapons of war, and would that I should be their leader; and we have come forth to defend our country.
6. And now ye also know concerning the covenant which their fathers made, that they would not take up their weapons of war against their brethren to shed blood.
7. But in the twenty and sixth year, when they saw our afflictions and our tribulations for them, they were about to break the covenant which they had made and take up their weapons of war in our defence.
8. But I would not suffer them that they should break this covenant which they had made, supposing that God would strengthen us, insomuch that we should not suffer more because of the fulfilling the oath which they had taken.
9. But behold, here is one thing in which we may have great joy. For behold, in the twenty and sixth year, I, Helaman, did march at the head of these two thousand young men to the city of Judea, to assist Antipus, whom ye had appointed a leader over the people of that part of the land.
10. And I did join my two thousand sons, (for they are worthy to be called sons) to the army of Antipus, in which strength Antipus did rejoice exceedingly; for behold, his army had been reduced by the Lamanites because their forces had slain a vast number of our men, for which cause we have to mourn.
11. Nevertheless, we may console ourselves in this point, that they have died in the cause of their country and of their God, yea, and they are happy.
12. And the Lamanites had also retained many prisoners, all of whom are chief captains, for none other have they spared alive. And we suppose that they are now at this

Alma 56:10–11

As we suffer the loss of loved ones, our faith must look beyond the grave. As President Harold B. Lee taught, divine providence will bring all things into proper perspective in due time. That knowledge, exercised with faith, can give us hope and calm our fears.

time in the land of Nephi; it is so if they are not slain.
13. And now these are the cities of which the Lamanites have obtained possession by the shedding of the blood of so many of our valiant men;
14. The land of Manti, or the city of Manti, and the city of Zeezrom, and the city of Cumeni, and the city of Antiparah.
15. And these are the cities which they possessed when I arrived at the city of Judea; and I found Antipus and his men toiling with their might to fortify the city.
16. Yea, and they were depressed in body as well as in spirit, for they had fought valiantly by day and toiled by night to maintain their cities; and thus they had suffered great afflictions of every kind.
17. And now they were determined to conquer in this place or die; therefore you may well suppose that this little force which I brought with me, yea, those sons of mine, gave them great hopes and much joy.
18. And now it came to pass that when the Lamanites saw that Antipus had received a greater strength to his army, they were compelled by the orders of Ammoron to not come against the city of Judea, or against us, to battle.
19. And thus were we favored of the Lord; for had they come upon us in this our weakness they might have perhaps destroyed our little army; but thus were we preserved.
20. They were commanded by Ammoron to maintain those cities which they had taken. And thus ended the twenty and sixth year. And in the commencement of the twenty and seventh year we had prepared our city and ourselves for defence.
21. Now we were desirous that the Lamanites should come upon us; for we were not desirous to make an attack upon them in their strongholds.
22. And it came to pass that we kept spies out round about, to watch the movements of the Lamanites, that they might not pass us by night nor by day to make an attack upon our other cities which were on the northward.
23. For we knew in those cities they were not sufficiently strong to meet them; therefore we were desirous, if they should pass by us, to fall upon them in their rear, and thus bring them up in the rear at the same time they were met in the front. We supposed that we could overpower them; but behold, we were disappointed in this our desire.
24. They durst not pass by us with their whole army, neither durst they with a part, lest they should not be sufficiently strong and they should fall.
25. Neither durst they march down against the city of Zarahemla; neither durst they cross the head of Sidon, over to the city of Nephihah.
26. And thus, with their forces, they were determined to maintain those cities which they had taken.
27. And now it came to pass in the second month of this year, there was brought unto us many provisions from the fathers of those my two thousand sons.
28. And also there were sent two thousand men unto us from the land of Zarahemla. And thus we were prepared with ten thousand men, and provisions for them, and also for their wives and their children.
29. And the Lamanites, thus seeing our forces increase daily, and provisions arrive for our support, they began to be fearful, and began to sally forth, if it were possible to put an end to our receiving provisions and strength.
30. Now when we saw that the Lamanites began to grow uneasy on this wise, we were desirous to bring a stratagem into effect upon them; therefore Antipus ordered that I should march forth with my

little sons to a neighboring city, as if we were carrying provisions to a neighboring city.
31. And we were to march near the city of Antiparah, as if we were going to the city beyond, in the borders by the seashore.
32. And it came to pass that we did march forth, as if with our provisions, to go to that city.
33. And it came to pass that Antipus did march forth with a part of his army, leaving the remainder to maintain the city. But he did not march forth until I had gone forth with my little army, and came near the city Antiparah.
34. And now, in the city Antiparah were stationed the strongest army of the Lamanites; yea, the most numerous.
35. And it came to pass that when they had been informed by their spies, they came forth with their army and marched against us.
36. And it came to pass that we did flee before them, northward. And thus we did lead away the most powerful army of the Lamanites;
37. Yea, even to a considerable distance, insomuch that when they saw the army of Antipus pursuing them, with their might, they did not turn to the right nor to the left, but pursued their march in a straight course after us; and, as we suppose, it was their intent to slay us before Antipus should overtake them, and this that they might not be surrounded by our people.
38. And now Antipus, beholding our danger, did speed the march of his army. But behold, it was night; therefore they did not overtake us, neither did Antipus overtake them; therefore we did camp for the night.
39. And it came to pass that before the dawn of the morning, behold, the Lamanites were pursuing us. Now we were not sufficiently strong to contend with them; yea, I would not suffer that my little sons should fall into their hands; therefore we did continue our march, and we took our march into the wilderness.
40. Now they durst not turn to the right nor to the left lest they should be surrounded; neither would I turn to the right nor to the left lest they should overtake me, and we could not stand against them, but be slain, and they would make their escape; and thus we did flee all that day into the wilderness, even until it was dark.
41. And it came to pass that again, when the light of the morning came we saw the Lamanites upon us, and we did flee before them.
42. But it came to pass that they did not pursue us far before they halted; and it was in the morning of the third day of the seventh month.
43. And now, whether they were overtaken by Antipus we knew not, but I said unto my men: Behold, we know not but they have halted for the purpose that we should come against them, that they might catch us in their snare;
44. Therefore what say ye, my sons, will ye go against them to battle?
45. And now I say unto you, my beloved brother Moroni, that never had I seen so great courage, nay, not amongst all the Nephites.
46. For as I had ever called them my sons (for they were all of them very young) even so they said unto me: Father, behold our God is with us, and he will not suffer that we should fall; then let us go forth; we would not slay our brethren if they would let us alone; therefore let us go, lest they should overpower the army of Antipus.
47. Now they never had fought, yet they did not fear death; and they did think more upon the liberty of their fathers than they did upon their lives; yea, they had

Alma 56:46–48; 57:25–26

. . . This story is frequently told to illustrate the importance of correct teaching in the home and the blessings that come from honoring parents. These young men told Helaman that "they had been taught by their mothers, that if they did not doubt, God would deliver them." Then they added: "We do not doubt our mothers knew it" (Alma 56:47–48). (Ludlow)

Alma 56:47

I wonder sometimes as I see mothers leaving their children to the care of somebody else, seeking the social privileges of life, how many of them have read the story of the 2,060 sons of Helaman. I want to say to the mothers of this Church, if they will do their duty, they hold in their hands a power for righteousness and an uplift for a race of people not yet born, that will have something more to do than we have yet done, and it will take giants all their time to do it. So, I say, along with love, along with tenderness, along with charity and kindness to your associates, teach your daughters that are soon to become the mothers of men, what a power is placed in their keeping, and how they may exercise it to bless the world. (George Albert Smith, *Millennial Star,* 95:173.)

been taught by their mothers, that if they did not doubt, God would deliver them.
48. And they rehearsed unto me the words of their mothers, saying: We do not doubt our mothers knew it.
49. And it came to pass that I did return with my two thousand against these Lamanites who had pursued us. And now behold, the armies of Antipus had overtaken them, and a terrible battle had commenced.
50. The army of Antipus being weary, because of their long march in so short a space of time, were about to fall into the hands of the Lamanites; and had I not returned with my two thousand they would have obtained their purpose.
51. For Antipus had fallen by the sword, and many of his leaders, because of their weariness, which was occasioned by the speed of their march—therefore the men of Antipus, being confused because of the fall of their leaders, began to give way before the Lamanites.
52. And it came to pass that the Lamanites took courage, and began to pursue them; and thus were the Lamanites pursuing them with great vigor when Helaman came upon their rear with his two thousand, and began to slay them exceedingly, insomuch that the whole army of the Lamanites halted and turned upon Helaman.
53. Now when the people of Antipus saw that the Lamanites had turned them about, they gathered together their men and came again upon the rear of the Lamanites.
54. And now it came to pass that we, the people of Nephi, the people of Antipus, and I with my two thousand, did surround the Lamanites, and did slay them; yea, insomuch that they were compelled to deliver up their weapons of war and also themselves as prisoners of war.
55. And now it came to pass that when they had surrendered themselves up unto us, behold, I numbered those young men who had fought with me, fearing lest there were many of them slain.
56. But behold, to my great joy, there had not one soul of them fallen to the earth; yea, and they had fought as if with the strength of God; yea, never were men known to have fought with such miraculous strength; and with such mighty power did they fall upon the Lamanites, that they did frighten them; and for this cause did the Lamanites deliver themselves up as prisoners of war.
57. And as we had no place for our prisoners, that we could guard them to keep them from the armies of the Lamanites, therefore we sent them to the land of Zarahemla, and a part of those men who were not slain of Antipus, with them; and the remainder I took and joined them to my stripling Ammonites, and took our march back to the city of Judea.

CHAPTER 57

1. AND now it came to pass that I received an epistle from Ammoron, the king, stating that if I would deliver up those prisoners of war whom we had taken that he would deliver up the city of Antiparah unto us.
2. But I sent an epistle unto the king, that we were sure our forces were sufficient to take the city of

Alma 56:47–48

The story of the stripling warriors, the sons of Helaman, is legendary in the Church. These young men, full of faith, having been taught by their mothers, were courageous and indomitable in battle. They would lay down their lives for the higher cause if necessary—but the Lord did preserve them. They became the rallying cry and energy that enabled Moroni and his generals to redeem the land eventually from the scourge of invading Lamanites and the cancerous influence of internal rebellion. We may be a strength to church and country if we similarly honor our covenants in faith.

President Marion G. Romney said, "Latter-day Saints are instructed by the Lord to bring up their children 'in light and truth' (D&C 93:40). . . . When children reach maturity they usually reflect in their lives what their parents taught them. This is illustrated in the tribute paid to their mothers by the 2,000 young men referred to in the Book of Mormon as the sons of Helaman. . . .

"Without a knowledge of the word of God, these noble mothers never could have built into their sons such an abiding conviction that 'if they did not doubt, God would deliver them'; and neither could they have inspired in their sons an unshakable faith that their mothers knew what they were talking about." (P/A)

Antiparah by our force; and by delivering up the prisoners for that city we should suppose ourselves unwise, and that we would only deliver up our prisoners on exchange.
3. And Ammoron refused mine epistle, for he would not exchange prisoners; therefore we began to make preparations to go against the city of Antiparah.
4. But the people of Antiparah did leave the city, and fled to their other cities, which they had possession of, to fortify them; and thus the city of Antiparah fell into our hands.
5. And thus ended the twenty and eighth year of the reign of the judges.
6. And it came to pass that in the commencement of the twenty and ninth year, we received a supply of provisions, and also an addition to our army, from the land of Zarahemla, and from the land round about, to the number of six thousand men, besides sixty of the sons of the Ammonites who had come to join their brethren, my little band of two thousand. And now behold, we were strong, yea, and we had also plenty of provisions brought unto us.
7. And it came to pass that it was our desire to wage a battle with the army which was placed to protect the city Cumeni.
8. And now behold, I will show unto you that we soon accomplished our desire; yea, with our strong force, or with a part of our strong force, we did surround, by night, the city Cumeni, a little before they were to receive a supply of provisions.
9. And it came to pass that we did camp round about the city for many nights; but we did sleep upon our swords, and keep guards, that the Lamanites could not come upon us by night and slay us, which they attempted many times; but as many times as they attempted this their blood was spilt.
10. At length their provisions did arrive, and they were about to enter the city by night. And we, instead of being Lamanites, were Nephites; therefore, we did take them and their provisions.
11. And notwithstanding the Lamanites being cut off from their support after this manner, they were still determined to maintain the city; therefore it became expedient that we should take those provisions and send them to Judea, and our prisoners to the land of Zarahemla.
12. And it came to pass that not many days had passed away before the Lamanites began to lose all hopes of succor; therefore they yielded up the city unto our hands; and thus we had accomplished our designs in obtaining the city Cumeni.
13. But it came to pass that our prisoners were so numerous that, notwithstanding the enormity of our numbers, we were obliged to employ all our force to keep them, or to put them to death.
14. For behold, they would break out in great numbers, and would fight with stones, and with clubs, or whatsoever thing they could get into their hands, insomuch that we did slay upwards of two thousand of them after they had surrendered themselves prisoners of war.
15. Therefore it became expedient for us, that we should put an end to their lives, or guard them, sword in hand, down to the land of Zarahemla; and also our provisions were not any more than sufficient for our own people, notwithstanding that which we had taken from the Lamanites.
16. And now, in those critical circumstances, it became a very serious matter to determine concerning these prisoners of war; nevertheless, we did resolve to send them down to the land of Zarahemla; therefore we selected a part of our men, and gave them charge over our prisoners to go down to the land of Zarahemla.

17. But it came to pass that on the morrow they did return. And now behold, we did not inquire of them concerning the prisoners; for behold, the Lamanites were upon us, and they returned in season to save us from falling into their hands. For behold, Ammoron had sent to their support a new supply of provisions and also a numerous army of men.
18. And it came to pass that those men whom we sent with the prisoners did arrive in season to check them, as they were about to overpower us.
19. But behold, my little band of two thousand and sixty fought most desperately; yea, they were firm before the Lamanites, and did administer death unto all those who opposed them.
20. And as the remainder of our army were about to give way before the Lamanites, behold, those two thousand and sixty were firm and undaunted.
21. Yea, and they did obey and observe to perform every word of command with exactness; yea, and even according to their faith it was done unto them; and I did remember the words which they said unto me that their mothers had taught them.
22. And now behold, it was these my sons, and those men who had been selected to convey the prisoners, to whom we owe this great victory; for it was they who did beat the Lamanites; therefore they were driven back to the city of Manti.
23. And we retained our city Cumeni, and were not all destroyed by the sword; nevertheless, we had suffered great loss.
24. And it came to pass that after the Lamanites had fled, I immediately gave orders that my men who had been wounded should be taken from among the dead, and caused that their wounds should be dressed.
25. And it came to pass that there were two hundred, out of my two thousand and sixty, who had fainted because of the loss of blood; nevertheless, according to the goodness of God, and to our great astonishment, and also the joy of our whole army, there was not one soul of them who did perish; yea, and neither was there one soul among them who had not received many wounds.
26. And now, their preservation was astonishing to our whole army, yea, that they should be spared while there was a thousand of our brethren who were slain. And we do justly ascribe it to the miraculous power of God, because of their exceeding faith in that which they had been taught to believe—that there was a just God, and whosoever did not doubt, that they should be preserved by his marvelous power.
27. Now this was the faith of these of whom I have spoken; they are young, and their minds are firm, and they do put their trust in God continually.
28. And now it came to pass that after we had thus taken care of our wounded men, and had buried our dead and also the dead of the Lamanites, who were many, behold, we did inquire of Gid concerning the prisoners whom they had started to go down to the land of Zarahemla with.
29. Now Gid was the chief captain over the band who was appointed to guard them down to the land.
30. And now, these are the words which Gid said unto me: Behold, we did start to go down to the land of Zarahemla with our prisoners. And it came to pass that we did meet the spies of our armies, who

Alma 57:21

As with the stripling warriors, the only safety we can have comes from obeying with exactness.

POINT OF INTEREST

This design was copied from Uxmal, a Yucatan ruin.

had been sent out to watch the camp of the Lamanites.
31. And they cried unto us, saying—Behold, the armies of the Lamanites are marching towards the city of Cumeni; and behold, they will fall upon them, yea, and will destroy our people.
32. And it came to pass that our prisoners did hear their cries, which caused them to take courage; and they did rise up in rebellion against us.
33. And it came to pass because of their rebellion we did cause that our swords should come upon them. And it came to pass that they did in a body run upon our swords, in the which, the greater number of them were slain; and the remainder of them broke through and fled from us.
34. And behold, when they had fled and we could not overtake them, we took our march with speed towards the city Cumeni; and behold, we did arrive in time that we might assist our brethren in preserving the city.
35. And behold, we are again delivered out of the hands of our enemies. And blessed is the name of our God; for behold, it is he that has delivered us; yea, that has done this great thing for us.
36. Now it came to pass that when I, Helaman, had heard these words of Gid, I was filled with exceeding joy because of the goodness of God in preserving us, that we might not all perish; yea, and I trust that the souls of them who have been slain have entered into the rest of their God.

CHAPTER 58

1. AND behold, now it came to pass that our next object was to obtain the city of Manti; but behold, there was no way that we could lead them out of the city by our small bands. For behold, they remembered that which we had hitherto done; therefore we could not decoy them away from their strongholds.
2. And they were so much more numerous than was our army that we durst not go forth and attack them in their strongholds.
3. Yea, and it became expedient that we should employ our men to the maintaining those parts of the land which we had regained of our possessions; therefore it became expedient that we should wait, that we might receive more strength from the land of Zarahemla and also a new supply of provisions.
4. And it came to pass that I thus did send an embassy to the governor of our land, to acquaint him concerning the affairs of our people. And it came to pass that we did wait to receive provisions and strength from the land of Zarahemla.
5. But behold, this did profit us but little; for the Lamanites were also receiving great strength from day to day, and also many provisions; and thus were our circumstances at this period of time.
6. And the Lamanites were sallying forth against us from time to time, resolving by stratagem to destroy us; nevertheless we could not come to battle with them, because of their retreats and their strongholds.
7. And it came to pass that we did wait in these difficult circumstances for the space of many months, even until we were about to perish for the want of food.
8. But it came to pass that we did receive food, which was guarded to us by an army of two thousand men to our assistance; and this is all the assistance which we did receive, to defend ourselves and our country

Alma 58

This chapter illustrates the importance of being prepared as a nation—and demonstrates that the intangible defenses are the most important.

from falling into the hands of our enemies, yea, to contend with an enemy which was innumerable.
9. And now the cause of these our embarrassments, or the cause why they did not send more strength unto us, we knew not; therefore we were grieved and also filled with fear, lest by any means the judgments of God should come upon our land, to our overthrow and utter destruction.
10. Therefore we did pour out our souls in prayer to God, that he would strengthen us and deliver us out of the hands of our enemies, yea, and also give us strength that we might retain our cities, and our lands, and our possessions, for the support of our people.
11. Yea, and it came to pass that the Lord our God did visit us with assurances that he would deliver us; yea, insomuch that he did speak peace to our souls, and did grant unto us great faith, and did cause us that we should hope for our deliverance in him.
12. And we did take courage with our small force which we had received, and were fixed with a determination to conquer our enemies, and to maintain our lands, and our possessions, and our wives, and our children, and the cause of our liberty.
13. And thus we did go forth with all our might against the Lamanites, who were in the city of Manti; and we did pitch our tents by the wilderness side, which was near to the city.
14. And it came to pass that on the morrow, that when the Lamanites saw that we were in the borders by the wilderness which was near the city, that they sent out their spies round about us that they might discover the number and the strength of our army.
15. And it came to pass that when they saw that we were not strong, according to our numbers, and fearing that we should cut them off from their support except they should come out to battle against us and kill us, and also supposing that they could easily destroy us with their numerous hosts, therefore they began to make preparations to come out against us to battle.
16. And when we saw that they were making preparations to come out against us, behold, I caused that Gid, with a small number of men, should secrete himself in the wilderness, and also that Teomner and a small number of men should secrete themselves also in the wilderness.
17. Now Gid and his men were on the right and the others on the left; and when they had thus secreted themselves, behold, I remained, with the remainder of my army, in that same place where we had first pitched our tents against the time that the Lamanites should come out to battle.
18. And it came to pass that the Lamanites did come out with their numerous army against us. And when they had come and were about to fall upon us with the sword, I caused that my men, those who were with me, should retreat into the wilderness.
19. And it came to pass that the Lamanites did follow after us with great speed, for they were exceedingly desirous to overtake us that they might slay us; therefore they did follow us into the wilderness; and we did pass by in the midst of Gid and Teomner, insomuch that they were not discovered by the Lamanites.
20. And it came to pass that when the Lamanites had passed by, or when the army had passed by, Gid and Teomner did rise up from their secret places, and did cut off the spies of the Lamanites that they should not return to the city.

Alma 58:10–11

Joseph Smith said, "And may God enable us to perform our vows and covenants with each other, in all fidelity and righteousness before Him, that our influence may be felt among the nations of the earth, in mighty power, even to rend the kingdoms of darkness asunder, and triumph over priestcraft and spiritual wickedness in high places, and break in pieces all kingdoms that are opposed to the kingdom of Christ, and spread the light and truth of the everlasting Gospel from the rivers to the ends of the earth."

21. And it came to pass that when they had cut them off, they ran to the city and fell upon the guards who were left to guard the city, insomuch that they did destroy them and did take possession of the city.
22. Now this was done because the Lamanites did suffer their whole army, save a few guards only, to be led away into the wilderness.
23. And it came to pass that Gid and Teomner by this means had obtained possession of their strongholds. And it came to pass that we took our course, after having traveled much in the wilderness towards the land of Zarahemla.
24. And when the Lamanites saw that they were marching towards the land of Zarahemla, they were exceedingly afraid, lest there was a plan laid to lead them on to destruction; therefore they began to retreat into the wilderness again, yea, even back by the same way which they had come.
25. And behold, it was night and they did pitch their tents, for the chief captains of the Lamanites had supposed that the Nephites were weary because of their march; and supposing that they had driven their whole army therefore they took no thought concerning the city of Manti.
26. Now it came to pass that when it was night, I caused that my men should not sleep, but that they should march forward by another way towards the land of Manti.
27. And because of this our march in the night-time, behold, on the morrow we were beyond the Lamanites, insomuch that we did arrive before them at the city of Manti.
28. And thus it came to pass, that by this stratagem we did take possession of the city of Manti without the shedding of blood.
29. And it came to pass that when the armies of the Lamanites did arrive near the city, and saw that we were prepared to meet them, they were astonished exceedingly and struck with great fear, insomuch that they did flee into the wilderness.
30. Yea, and it came to pass that the armies of the Lamanites did flee out of all this quarter of the land. But behold, they have carried with them many women and children out of the land.
31. And those cities which had been taken by the Lamanites, all of them are at this period of time in our possession; and our fathers and our women and our children are returning to their homes, all save it be those who have been taken prisoners and carried off by the Lamanites.
32. But behold, our armies are small to maintain so great a number of cities and so great possessions.
33. But behold, we trust in our God who has given us victory over those lands, insomuch that we have obtained those cities and those lands, which were our own.
34. Now we do not know the cause that the government does not grant us more strength; neither do those men who came up unto us know why we have not received greater strength.
35. Behold, we do not know but what ye are unsuccessful, and ye have drawn away the forces into that quarter of the land; if so, we do not desire to murmur.
36. And if it is not so, behold, we fear that there is some faction in the government, that they do not send more men to our assistance; for we know that they are more numerous than that which they have sent.
37. But, behold, it mattereth not—we trust God will deliver us, notwithstanding the weakness of our

armies, yea, and deliver us out of the hands of our enemies.
38. Behold, this is the twenty and ninth year, in the latter end, and we are in the possession of our lands; and the Lamanites have fled to the land of Nephi.
39. And those sons of the people of Ammon, of whom I have so highly spoken, are with me in the city of Manti; and the Lord has supported them, yea, and kept them from falling by the sword, insomuch that even one soul has not been slain.
40. But behold, they have received many wounds; nevertheless they stand fast in that liberty wherewith God has made them free; and they are strict to remember the Lord their God from day to day; yea, they do observe to keep his statutes, and his judgments, and his commandments continually; and their faith is strong in the prophecies concerning that which is to come.
41. And now, my beloved brother, Moroni, may the Lord our God, who has redeemed us and made us free, keep you continually in his presence; yea, and may he favor this people, even that ye may have success in obtaining the possession of all that which the Lamanites have taken from us, which was for our support. And now, behold, I close mine epistle. I am Helaman, the son of Alma.

CHAPTER 59

1. NOW it came to pass in the thirtieth year of the reign of the judges over the people of Nephi, after Moroni had received and had read Helaman's epistle, he was exceedingly rejoiced because of the welfare, yea, the exceeding success which Helaman had had, in obtaining those lands which were lost.
2. Yea, and he did make it known unto all his people, in all the land round about in that part where he was, that they might rejoice also.
3. And it came to pass that he immediately sent an epistle to Pahoran, desiring that he should cause men to be gathered together to strengthen Helaman, or the armies of Helaman, insomuch that he might with ease maintain that part of the land which he had been so miraculously prospered in regaining.
4. And it came to pass when Moroni had sent this epistle to the land of Zarahemla, he began again to lay a plan that he might obtain the remainder of those possessions and cities which the Lamanites had taken from them.
5. And it came to pass that while Moroni was thus making preparations to go against the Lamanites to battle, behold, the people of Nephihah, who were gathered together from the city of Moroni and the city of Lehi and the city of Morianton, were attacked by the Lamanites.
6. Yea, even those who had been compelled to flee from the land of Manti, and from the land round about, had come over and joined the Lamanites in this part of the land.
7. And thus being exceedingly numerous, yea, and receiving strength from day to day, by the command of Ammoron they came forth against the people of Nephihah, and they did begin to slay them with an exceedingly great slaughter.
8. And their armies were so numerous that the remainder of the people of Nephihah were obliged to flee before them; and they came even and joined the army of Moroni.

Alma 58:40

People with integrity keep their pledges, fulfill their promises, and accomplish the work they have agreed to do. They also stand firm in their convictions, unwavering in the defense of their position. When we make a covenant with the Lord, we promise to fulfill His expectations and be worthy of His blessings. The Lord commands us to be firm and undaunted, and to obey His commandments with exactness. (P/A)

9. And now as Moroni had supposed that there should be men sent
to the city of Nephihah, to the assistance of the people to maintain that city, and knowing that it was easier to keep the city from
falling into the hands of the Lamanites than to retake it from
them, he supposed that they would easily maintain that city.
10. Therefore he retained all his force to maintain those places
which he had recovered.
11. And now, when Moroni saw that the city of Nephihah was lost
he was exceedingly sorrowful, and began to doubt, because of the
wickedness of the people, whether they should not fall into the
hands of their brethren.
12. Now this was the case with all his chief captains. They doubted and marveled also because of the wickedness of the people, and
this because of the success of the Lamanites over them.
13. And it came to pass that Moroni was angry with the government, because of their indifference concerning the freedom of their
country.

Alma 59:13

Righteous motives are the basis for true loyalty. It is a truism that we are what we are no matter where we are. Moroni was a great patriot; his motives were pure and totally loyal to his God and country. (O/C)

CHAPTER 60

1. AND it came to pass that he wrote again to the governor of the
land, who was Pahoran, and these are the words which he wrote,
saying: Behold, I direct mine epistle to Pahoran, in the city of
Zarahemla, who is the chief judge and the governor over the land,
and also to all those who have been chosen by this people to govern and manage the affairs of this war.
2. For behold, I have somewhat to say unto them by the way of condemnation; for behold, ye yourselves know that ye have been appointed to gather together men, and arm them with swords, and with cimeters, and all manner of weapons of war of every kind, and send forth
against the Lamanites, in whatsoever parts they should come into our
land.
3. And now behold, I say unto you that myself, and also my men,
and also Helaman and his men, have suffered exceedingly great
sufferings; yea, even hunger, thirst, and fatigue, and all manner of
afflictions of every kind.
4. But behold, were this all we had suffered we would not murmur
nor complain.
5. But behold, great has been the slaughter among our people; yea,
thousands have fallen by the sword, while it might have otherwise
been if ye had rendered unto our armies sufficient strength and succor for them. Yea, great has been your neglect towards us.
6. And now behold, we desire to know the cause of this exceedingly great neglect; yea, we desire to know the cause of your
thoughtless state.
7. Can you think to sit upon your thrones in a state of thoughtless
stupor, while your enemies are spreading the work of death around
you? Yea, while they are murdering thousands of your brethren—
8. Yea, even they who have looked up to you for protection, yea,
have placed you in a situation that ye might have succored them,
yea, ye might have sent armies unto them, to have strengthened
them, and have saved thousands of them from falling by the sword.

Alma 60:1–5

These verses demonstrate how Moroni dealt with his anger toward the government for their seeming indifference toward the freedom of the country: he wrote again to the governor of the land—Pahoran—and told him three things:

1. The armies, including Moroni and Helaman, were suffering tremendously from hunger, thirst, and fatigue, as well as "afflictions of every kind."
2. Thousands of their people had fallen by the sword in a great slaughter.
3. The slaughter that had killed thousands could have been prevented if Pahoran had responded to requests for food, supplies, and reinforcements.

In writing the epistle to Pahoran, Moroni assumed that Pahoran was indifferent to the plight of the armies who had fought so valiantly to protect the country and who were struggling without the supplies and reinforcements they needed.

9. But behold, this is not all—ye have withheld your provisions from them, insomuch that many have fought and bled out their lives because of their great desires which they had for the welfare of this people; yea, and this they have done when they were about to perish with hunger, because of your exceedingly great neglect towards them.
10. And now, my beloved brethren—for ye ought to be beloved; yea, and ye ought to have stirred yourselves more diligently for the welfare and the freedom of this people; but behold, ye have neglected them insomuch that the blood of thousands shall come upon your heads for vengeance; yea, for known unto God were all their cries, and all their sufferings—
11. Behold, could ye suppose that ye could sit upon your thrones, and because of the exceeding goodness of God ye could do nothing and he would deliver you? Behold, if ye have supposed this ye have supposed in vain.
12. Do ye suppose that, because so many of your brethren have been killed it is because of their wickedness? I say unto you, if ye have supposed this ye have supposed in vain; for I say unto you, there are many who have fallen by the sword; and behold it is to your condemnation;
13. For the Lord suffereth the righteous to be slain that his justice and judgment may come upon the wicked; therefore ye need not suppose that the righteous are lost because they are slain; but behold, they do enter into the rest of the Lord their God.
14. And now behold, I say unto you, I fear exceedingly that the judgments of God will come upon this people, because of their exceeding slothfulness, yea, even the slothfulness of our government, and their exceedingly great neglect towards their brethren, yea, towards those who have been slain.
15. For were it not for the wickedness which first commenced at our head, we could have withstood our enemies that they could have gained no power over us.
16. Yea, had it not been for the war which broke out among ourselves; yea, were it not for these king-men, who caused so much bloodshed among ourselves; yea, at the time we were contending among ourselves, if we had united our strength as we hitherto have done; yea, had it not been for the desire of power and authority which those king-men had over us; had they been true to the cause of our freedom, and united with us, and gone forth against our enemies, instead of taking up their swords against us, which was the cause of so much bloodshed among ourselves; yea, if we had gone forth against them in the strength of the Lord, we should have dispersed our enemies, for it would have been done, according to the fulfilling of his word.
17. But behold, now the Lamanites are coming upon us, taking possession of our lands, and they are murdering our people with the sword, yea, our women and our children, and also carrying them away captive, causing them that they should suffer all manner of afflictions, and this because of the great wickedness of those who are seeking for power and authority, yea, even those king-men.
18. But why should I say much concerning this matter? For we know not but what ye yourselves are seeking for authority. We know not but what ye are also traitors to your country.

Alma 60:10

The sin of omission is a serious sin as is the sin of commission. Possessing divine truth, then failing to act upon its principles in a righteous manner before God is a most serious sin. (O/C)

Alma 60:14

The sin of omission is a serious sin, as is the sin of commission. Possessing divine truth and failing to act upon true principles in a righteous manner before God is a most serious sin. Chief Captain Moroni wrote:

"And now behold, I say unto you, I fear exceedingly that the judgments of God will come upon this people, because of their exceeding slothfulness, yea, even the slothfulness of our government, and their exceedingly great neglect towards their brethren, yea, towards those who have been slain. . . .

"Yea, will ye sit in idleness while ye are surrounded with thousands of those, yea, and tens of thousands, who do also sit in idleness, while there are thousands round about in the borders of the land who are falling by the sword, yea, wounded and bleeding?" (Alma 60:14, 22.)

Commenting on the sin of omission, President Spencer W. Kimball said, ". . . God has created 'things to act and things to be acted upon' (2 Ne. 2:14), and man is in the former category. He does not fill the measure of his creation unless he acts, and that in righteousness. 'Therefore to him that knoweth to do good and doeth it not,' warned James, 'to him it is sin' (Jas. 4:17). . . .

"The covenants we make with God involve promises to do, not merely to refrain from doing, to work righteousness as well as to avoid evil." (O/C)

Alma 60:16

As demonstrated here, there is an important lesson for our time: civil dispute robs a nation of the strength and resources to right external enemies.

19. Or is it that ye have neglected us because ye are in the heart of
our country and ye are surrounded by security, that ye do not cause
food to be sent unto us, and also men to strengthen our armies?
20. Have ye forgotten the commandments of the Lord your God?
Yea, have ye forgotten the captivity of our fathers? Have ye forgotten the many times we have been delivered out of the hands of
our enemies?
21. Or do ye suppose that the Lord will still deliver us, while we sit
upon our thrones and do not make use of the means which the
Lord has provided for us?
22. Yea, will ye sit in idleness while ye are surrounded with thousands of those, yea, and tens of thousands, who do also sit in idleness, while there are thousands round about in the borders of the
land who are falling by the sword, yea, wounded and bleeding?
23. Do ye suppose that God will look upon you as guiltless while ye
sit still and behold these things? Behold I say unto you, Nay. Now
I would that ye should remember that God has said that the inward
vessel shall be cleansed first, and then shall the outer vessel be
cleansed also.
24. And now, except ye do repent of that which ye have done, and
begin to be up and doing, and send forth food and men unto us,
and also unto Helaman, that he may support those parts of our
country which he has regained, and that we may also recover the
remainder of our possessions in these parts, behold it will be expedient that we contend no more with the Lamanites until we have
first cleansed our inward vessel, yea, even the great head of our
government.
25. And except ye grant mine epistle, and come out and show unto
me a true spirit of freedom, and strive to strengthen and fortify our
armies, and grant unto them food for their support, behold I will
leave a part of my freemen to maintain this part of our land, and I
will leave the strength and the blessings of God upon them, that
none other power can operate against them—
26. And this because of their exceeding faith, and their patience in
their tribulations—
27. And I will come unto you, and if there be any among you that
has a desire for freedom, yea, if there be even a spark of freedom
remaining, behold I will stir up insurrections among you, even
until those who have desires to usurp power and authority shall
become extinct.
28. Yea, behold I do not fear your power nor your authority, but it
is my God whom I fear; and it is according to his commandments
that I do take my sword to defend the cause of my country, and it is
because of your iniquity that we have suffered so much loss.
29. Behold it is time, yea, the time is now at hand, that except ye do
bestir yourselves in the defence of your country and your little ones,
the sword of justice doth hang over you; yea, and it shall fall upon you
and visit you even to your utter destruction.
30. Behold, I wait for assistance from you; and, except ye do
administer unto our relief, behold, I come unto you, even in the
land of Zarahemla, and smite you with the sword, insomuch that
ye can have no more power to impede the progress of this people
in the cause of our freedom.
31. For behold, the Lord will not suffer that ye shall live and wax
strong in your iniquities to destroy his righteous people.
32. Behold, can you suppose that the Lord will spare you and come

Alma 60:21–23

The Lord expects us to work. In fact He has made it a commandment. (See Ex. 20:9.) We are to use the means the Lord has provided for us to enhance our surroundings for good. We are to do all we can to protect ourselves from evil. . . .

Failing to do nothing for ourselves or to use the means that God has provided for us is addressed by Charles Steizle:

"What must I do to be damned? Nothing. That's all. You're damned—condemned—if you just sit still. That is the law of this physical world.

"If you sit still long enough, you'll never get up again. If you never lift your arm, you'll soon be unable to raise it at all. If you remain in darkness and never use your eyes, you'll soon become blind.

"It is the law in the mental world. If you never exercise your brain—never read, study, nor talk to anyone, never permit anyone to talk to you, your mind will become blank—maybe you'll become insane.

"The most horrible punishment that could be inflicted upon you is not twenty years of hard labor, but twenty years of solitary confinement.

"It's the law in the spiritual world. Simply shut your heart to all truth, and after a while you won't be able to believe anything—that is the severest penalty for not accepting truth.

"The process of disintegration and death begins when a man shuts himself out from the forces that make for life. The body and mind and spirit are kept alive through constant constructive use" (*Utah Labor News*, December 12, 1937). (O/C)

out in judgment against the Lamanites, when it is the tradition of their fathers that has caused their hatred, yea, and it has been redoubled by those who have dissented from us, while your iniquity is for the cause of your love of glory and the vain things of the world?
33. Ye know that ye do transgress the laws of God, and ye do know that ye do trample them under your feet. Behold, the Lord saith unto me: If those whom ye have appointed your governors do not repent of their sins and iniquities, ye shall go up to battle against them.
34. And now behold, I, Moroni, am constrained, according to the covenant which I have made to keep the commandments of my God; therefore I would that ye should adhere to the word of God, and send speedily unto me of your provisions and of your men, and also to Helaman.
35. And behold, if ye will not do this I come unto you speedily; for behold, God will not suffer that we should perish with hunger; therefore he will give unto us of your food, even if it must be by the sword. Now see that ye fulfil the word of God.
36. Behold, I am Moroni, your chief captain. I seek not for power, but to pull it down. I seek not for honor of the world, but for the glory of my God, and the freedom and welfare of my country. And thus I close mine epistle.

CHAPTER 61

1. BEHOLD, now it came to pass that soon after Moroni had sent his epistle unto the chief governor, he received an epistle from Pahoran, the chief governor. And these are the words which he received:
2. I, Pahoran, who am the chief governor of this land, do send these words unto Moroni, the chief captain over the army. Behold, I say unto you, Moroni, that I do not joy in your great afflictions, yea, it grieves my soul.
3. But behold, there are those who do joy in your afflictions, yea, insomuch that they have risen up in rebellion against me, and also those of my people who are freemen, yea, and those who have risen up are exceedingly numerous.
4. And it is those who have sought to take away the judgment-seat from me that have been the cause of this great iniquity; for they have used great flattery, and they have led away the hearts of many people, which will be the cause of sore affliction among us; they have withheld our provisions, and have daunted our freemen that they have not come unto you.
5. And behold, they have driven me out before them, and I have fled to the land of Gideon, with as many men as it were possible that I could get.
6. And behold, I have sent a proclamation throughout this part of the land; and behold, they are flocking to us daily, to their arms, in the defence of their country and their freedom, and to avenge our wrongs.
7. And they have come unto us, insomuch that those who have risen up in rebellion against us are set at defiance, yea, insomuch that they do fear us and durst not come out against us to battle.

Alma 60:36

It's important to remember that Moroni was a faithful man of God. The anger we read in his epistles to the government was expressed solely in the desire to maintain liberty.

Alma 61

This chapter is a classic in scriptural literature and a primer in how to prevent the breakdown of communication as Pahoran explains Moroni's misunderstanding.

Alma 61:2

In all great campaigns to advance the cause of liberty and righteousness, leaders motivated by nobility of purpose and grandness of heart overcome misunderstanding and dissension through openness, charity, meekness, and a willingness to follow the guidance of the Almighty. Inspired unity brings strength; keeping an eye single to the glory of God—rather than succumbing to egocentric interests—fosters fellowship in building the kingdom of God. (P/A)

8. They have got possession of the land, or the city, of Zarahemla; they have appointed a king over them, and he hath written unto the king of the Lamanites, in the which he hath joined an alliance with him; in the which alliance he hath agreed to maintain the city of Zarahemla, which maintenance he supposeth will enable the Lamanites to conquer the remainder of the land, and he shall be placed king over this people when they shall be conquered under the Lamanites.
9. And now, in your epistle you have censured me, but it mattereth not; I am not angry, but do rejoice in the greatness of your heart. I, Pahoran, do not seek for power, save only to retain my judgment-seat that I may preserve the rights and the liberty of my people. My soul standeth fast in that liberty in the which God hath made us free.
10. And now, behold, we will resist wickedness even unto bloodshed. We would not shed the blood of the Lamanites if they would stay in their own land.
11. We would not shed the blood of our brethren if they would not rise up in rebellion and take the sword against us.
12. We would subject ourselves to the yoke of bondage if it were requisite with the justice of God, or if he should command us so to do.
13. But behold he doth not command us that we shall subject ourselves to our enemies, but that we should put our trust in him, and he will deliver us.
14. Therefore, my beloved brother, Moroni, let us resist evil, and whatsoever evil we cannot resist with our words, yea, such as rebellions and dissensions, let us resist them with our swords, that we may retain our freedom, that we may rejoice in the great privilege of our church, and in the cause of our Redeemer and our God.
15. Therefore, come unto me speedily with a few of your men, and leave the remainder in the charge of Lehi and Teancum; give unto them power to conduct the war in that part of the land, according to the Spirit of God, which is also the spirit of freedom which is in them.
16. Behold I have sent a few provisions unto them, that they may not perish until ye can come unto me.
17. Gather together whatsoever force ye can upon your march hither, and we will go speedily against those dissenters, in the strength of our God according to the faith which is in us.
18. And we will take possession of the city of Zarahemla, that we may obtain more food to send forth unto Lehi and Teancum; yea, we will go forth against them in the strength of the Lord, and we will put an end to this great iniquity.
19. And now, Moroni, I do joy in receiving your epistle, for I was somewhat worried concerning what we should do, whether it should be just in us to go against our brethren.
20. But ye have said, except they repent the Lord hath commanded you that ye should go against them.
21. See that ye strengthen Lehi and Teancum in the Lord; tell them to fear not, for God will deliver them, yea, and also all those who stand fast in that liberty wherewith God hath made them free. And now I close mine epistle to my beloved brother, Moroni.

Alma 61:9

"Charity Never Faileth." Just as charity transformed the situation with Moroni and Pahoran into one of amity and cooperation, it is well to remember that the doctrine and principle of charity may defuse many contentious situations. (P/A)

Alma 61:9

"Oh, the comfort, the inexpressible comfort of feeling safe with a person having neither to weigh thoughts and measure words, but to pour them out just as they are—chaff and grain together—knowing that a faithful hand will take and sift them, keep what is worth keeping and then with the breath of kindness blow the rest away" (Anonymous). This wonderful principle was a part of Pahoran's character. He was accused by a sincere, honest man of serious misbehavior. It is obvious to Pahoran that Moroni did not understand all the circumstances and trials facing Pahoran. Yet under these circumstances the Chief Governor responded to these charges manfully; his motives were pure because they were founded upon the gospel of Jesus Christ. (O/C)

CHAPTER 62

1. AND now it came to pass that when Moroni had received this epistle his heart did take courage, and was filled with exceedingly great joy because of the faithfulness of Pahoran, that he was not also a traitor to the freedom and cause of his country.
2. But he did also mourn exceedingly because of the iniquity of those who had driven Pahoran from the judgment-seat, yea, in fine because of those who had rebelled against their country and also their God.
3. And it came to pass that Moroni took a small number of men, according to the desire of Pahoran, and gave Lehi and Teancum command over the remainder of his army, and took his march towards the land of Gideon.
4. And he did raise the standard of liberty in whatsoever place he did enter, and gained what-soever force he could in all his march towards the land of Gideon.
5. And it came to pass that thousands did flock unto his standard, and did take up their swords in the defence of their freedom, that they might not come into bondage.
6. And thus, when Moroni had gathered together whatsoever men he could in all his march, he came to the land of Gideon; and uniting his forces with those of Pahoran they became exceedingly strong, even stronger than the men of Pachus, who was the king of those dissenters who had driven the freemen out of the land of Zarahemla and had taken possession of the land.
7. And it came to pass that Moroni and Pahoran went down with their armies into the land of Zarahemla, and went forth against the city, and did meet the men of Pachus, insomuch that they did come to battle.
8. And behold, Pachus was slain and his men were taken prisoners, and Pahoran was restored to his judgment-seat.
9. And the men of Pachus received their trial, according to the law, and also those king-men who had been taken and cast into prison; and they were executed according to the law; yea, those men of Pachus and those king-men, whosoever would not take up arms in the defence of their country, but would fight against it, were put to death.
10. And thus it became expedient that this law should be strictly observed for the safety of their country; yea, and whosoever was found denying their freedom was speedily executed according to the law.
11. And thus ended the thirtieth year of the reign of the judges over the people of Nephi; Moroni and Pahoran having restored peace to the land of Zarahemla, among their own people, having inflicted death upon all those who were not true to the cause of freedom.
12. And it came to pass in the commencement of the thirty and first year of the reign of the judges over the people of Nephi, Moroni immediately caused that provisions should be sent, and also an army of six thousand men should be sent unto Helaman, to assist him in preserving that part of the land.
13. And he also caused that an

Alma 62:1

With supplies dangerously low and troop strength being rapidly depleted, Moroni found himself in a crisis of survival. Helaman, too, was finding that his margin of safety was dissipating, even though the stripling warriors had provided, for a time, the edge of victory. Why had reinforcements not come from the government in Zarahemla, Helaman asks in his report to Moroni. Moroni had his suspicions, since the Lord had informed him through the Spirit: "If those whom ye have appointed your governors do not repent of their sins and iniquities, ye shall go up to battle against them" (Alma 60:33).

In an urgent and candidly direct epistle to Pahoran, governor of the land, Moroni demanded immediate support for the armies, lest he return to the capital and compel action through military intervention. Pahoran responded with the startling news that an internal insurrection had deposed the administration and called on Moroni for recourse against the king-men traitors. The tragic developments in Zarahemla constituted an altogether sad commentary on the consequences of iniquity in high places. Through bold and brilliant maneuvers, Moroni and Pahoran were able to restore the government and ultimately rid the land of enemy influence.

We can learn a lifetime of boldness from Moroni's appeal to Pahoran for redress, just as we can learn a lifetime of nobility and pure-heartedness from Pahoran's charitable response.

Elder Neal A. Maxwell said, "There was an exchange of correspondence between Moroni, the chief captain of the armies, and Pahoran, who was chief judge and governor of the land in a time of great turmoil. (Alma 60–61.) Anxious Moroni did not have all the facts, as is evident in his biting complaint to Pahoran. Pahoran's meek reply is a lesson to us all, as it certainly must have been to Moroni. . . . Where individuals have said too much with too little data, meekness plays a very crucial, correcting role in what follows." (P/A)

Alma 62:9

Those who were put to death were executed on charges of treason. In this case, the treason consisted of fighting against God.

army of six thousand men, with a sufficient quantity of food, should be sent to the armies of Lehi and Teancum. And it came to pass that this was done to fortify the land against the Lamanites.
14. And it came to pass that Moroni and Pahoran, leaving a large body of men in the land of Zarahemla, took their march with a large body of men towards the land of Nephihah, being determined to overthrow the Lamanites in that city.
15. And it came to pass that as they were marching towards the land, they took a large body of men of the Lamanites, and slew many of them, and took their provisions and their weapons of war.
16. And it came to pass after they had taken them, they caused them to enter into a covenant that they would no more take up their weapons of war against the Nephites.
17. And when they had entered into this covenant they sent them to dwell with the people of Ammon, and they were in number about four thousand who had not been slain.
18. And it came to pass that when they had sent them away they pursued their march towards the land of Nephihah. And it came to pass that when they had come to the city of Nephihah, they did pitch their tents in the plains of Nephihah, which is near the city of Nephihah.
19. Now Moroni was desirous that the Lamanites should come out to battle against them, upon the plains; but the Lamanites, knowing of their exceedingly great courage, and beholding the greatness of their numbers, therefore they durst not come out against them; therefore they did not come to battle in that day.
20. And when the night came, Moroni went forth in the darkness of the night, and came upon the top of the wall to spy out in what part of the city the Lamanites did camp with their army.
21. And it came to pass that they were on the east, by the entrance; and they were all asleep. And now Moroni returned to his army, and caused that they should prepare in haste strong cords and ladders, to be let down from the top of the wall into the inner part of the wall.
22. And it came to pass that Moroni caused that his men should march forth and come upon the top of the wall, and let themselves down into that part of the city, yea, even on the west, where the Lamanites did not camp with their armies.
23. And it came to pass that they were all let down into the city by night, by the means of their strong cords and their ladders; thus when the morning came they were all within the walls of the city.
24. And now, when the Lamanites awoke and saw that the armies of Moroni were within the walls, they were affrighted exceedingly, insomuch that they did flee out by the pass.
25. And now when Moroni saw that they were fleeing before him, he did cause that his men should march forth against them, and slew many, and surrounded many others, and took them prisoners; and the remainder of them fled into the land of Moroni, which was in the borders by the seashore.
26. Thus had Moroni and Pahoran obtained the possession of the city of Nephihah without the loss of one soul; and there were many of the Lamanites who were slain.
27. Now it came to pass that many of the Lamanites that were prisoners were desirous to join the people of Ammon and become a free people.
28. And it came to pass that as many as were desirous, unto them it was granted according to their desires.
29. Therefore, all the prisoners of

POINT OF INTEREST

The Temple of Kukulcan (the Mayan name for Quetzalcoatl), often referred to as El Castillo *(the castle), is the dominating feature of Chichén Itzá. On the spring and fall equinox, at the rising and setting of the sun, the corner of the structure casts a shadow in the shape of a plumed serpent.*

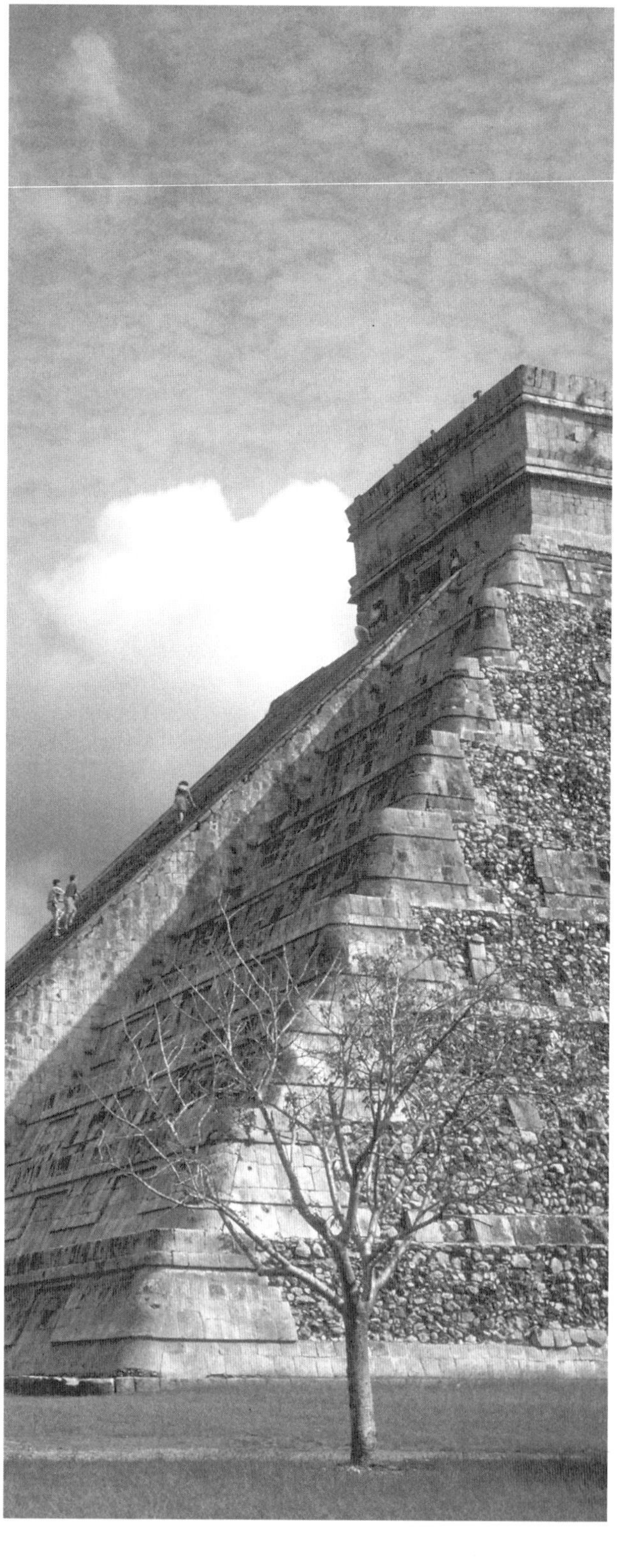

the Lamanites did join the people of Ammon, and did begin to labor exceedingly, tilling the ground, raising all manner of grain, and flocks and herds of every kind; and thus were the Nephites relieved from a great burden; yea, insomuch that they were relieved from all the prisoners of the Lamanites.
30. Now it came to pass that Moroni, after he had obtained possession of the city of Nephihah, having taken many prisoners, which did reduce the armies of the Lamanites exceedingly, and having regained many of the Nephites who had been taken prisoners, which did strengthen the army of Moroni exceedingly; therefore Moroni went forth from the land of Nephihah to the land of Lehi.
31. And it came to pass that when the Lamanites saw that Moroni was coming against them, they were again frightened and fled before the army of Moroni.
32. And it came to pass that Moroni and his army did pursue them from city to city, until they were met by Lehi and Teancum; and the Lamanites fled from Lehi and Teancum, even down upon the borders by the seashore, until they came to the land of Moroni.
33. And the armies of the Lamanites were all gathered together, insomuch that they were all in one body in the land of Moroni. Now Ammoron, the king of the Lamanites, was also with them.
34. And it came to pass that Moroni and Lehi and Teancum did encamp with their armies round about in the borders of the land of Moroni, insomuch that the Lamanites were encircled about in the borders by the wilderness on the south, and in the borders by the wilderness on the east.
35. And thus they did encamp for the night. For behold, the Nephites and the Lamanites also were weary because of the greatness of the march; therefore they did not resolve upon any stratagem in the night-time, save it were Teancum; for he was exceedingly angry with Ammoron, insomuch that he considered that Ammoron, and Amalickiah his brother, had been the cause of this great and lasting war between them and the Lamanites, which had been the cause of so much war and bloodshed, yea, and so much famine.
36. And it came to pass that Teancum in his anger did go forth into the camp of the Lamanites, and did let himself down over the walls of the city. And he went forth with a cord, from place to place, insomuch that he did find the king; and he did cast a javelin at him, which did pierce him near the heart. But behold, the king did awaken his servants before he died, insomuch that they did pursue Teancum, and slew him.
37. Now it came to pass that when Lehi and Moroni knew that Teancum was dead they were exceedingly sorrowful; for behold, he had been a man who had fought valiantly for his country, yea, a true friend to liberty; and he had suffered very many exceedingly sore afflictions. But behold, he was dead, and had gone the way of all the earth.
38. Now it came to pass that Moroni marched forth on the morrow, and came upon the Lamanites, insomuch that they did slay them with a great slaughter; and they did drive them out of the land; and they did flee, even that they did not return at that time against the Nephites.
39. And thus ended the thirty and first year of the reign of the judges over the people of Nephi; and thus they had had wars, and bloodsheds, and famine, and affliction, for the space of many years.
40. And there had been murders,

and contentions, and dissensions, and all manner of iniquity among the people of Nephi; nevertheless for the righteous' sake, yea, because of the prayers of the righteous, they were spared.
41. But behold, because of the exceedingly great length of the war between the Nephites and the Lamanites many had become hardened, because of the exceedingly great length of the war; and many were softened because of their afflictions, insomuch that they did humble themselves before God, even in the depth of humility.
42. And it came to pass that after Moroni had fortified those parts of the land which were most exposed to the Lamanites, until they were sufficiently strong, he returned to the city of Zarahemla; and also Helaman returned to the place of his inheritance; and there was once more peace established among the people of Nephi.
43. And Moroni yielded up the command of his armies into the hands of his son, whose name was Moronihah; and he retired to his own house that he might spend the remainder of his days in peace.
44. And Pahoran did return to his judgment-seat; and Helaman did take upon him again to preach unto the people the word of God; for because of so many wars and contentions it had become expedient that a regulation should be made again in the church.
45. Therefore, Helaman and his brethren went forth, and did declare the word of God with much power unto the convincing of many people of their wickedness, which did cause them to repent of their sins and to be baptized unto the Lord their God.
46. And it came to pass that they did establish again the church of God, throughout all the land.
47. Yea, and regulations were made concerning the law. And their judges, and their chief judges were chosen.
48. And the people of Nephi began to prosper again in the land, and began to multiply and to wax exceedingly strong again in the land. And they began to grow exceedingly rich.
49. But notwithstanding their riches, or their strength, or their prosperity, they were not lifted up in the pride of their eyes; neither were they slow to remember the Lord their God; but they did humble themselves exceedingly before him.
50. Yea, they did remember how great things the Lord had done for them, that he had delivered them from death, and from bonds, and from prisons, and from all manner of afflictions, and he had delivered them out of the hands of their enemies.
51. And they did pray unto the Lord their God continually, insomuch that the Lord did bless them, according to his word, so that they did wax strong and prosper in the land.
52. And it came to pass that all these things were done. And Helaman died, in the thirty and fifth year of the reign of the judges over the people of Nephi.

CHAPTER 63

Alma 62:41

It has been truthfully remarked on many occasions that a man did not know himself or know his fellows until he or they embraced the Gospel in its fulness and purity. Then whatever good or evil qualities or dispositions he or they might have would be brought to the surface, and their true character would be known. A man, under the influence of the Gospel, either becomes a very faithful, true man, or a very unfaithful, bad man. He cannot, while professing to be a believer in the truth and connected with the Church stand still. He must inevitably progress or go backward, and the signs of his progress or of his retrogression have been made so familiar to the people by long experience that they have not the least difficulty in discerning his true condition.

There are certain rules with which experience has made the people familiar, that cannot be persistently violated without retrogression and apostasy following. They are as familiar as 'household words' to all the members of the Church who have had any experience.

Experience has proved that the indulgence in whoredom, adultery and lust is fatal to faith in the Gospel. This practice is so antagonistic to the spirit of the Gospel that the two cannot co-exist in the same individual.

Experience has also proved that opposing or speaking against the Priesthood, or the authority which God has placed in His Church to govern it, is inevitably followed, sooner or later, by a loss of faith and by complete apostasy.

These are two rules, or they may be termed laws, which, during the experience of nearly forty years, have never been known to be violated without apostasy following, unless, indeed the transgressor of them repented humbly and sincerely and succeeded in obtaining forgiveness (George Q. Cannon, *Gospel Truth*, Vol. 2, 263). (O/C)

Alma 62:41

War and trouble bring varying responses among societies. People who have access to the saving principles of the gospel of Jesus Christ respond to troubling times based upon the degree of their conversion to Jesus Christ. Conversion to the Savior brings peace, divine guidance, and inspiration from the Holy Ghost. The following verse illustrates two different responses of the Nephite people following many years of war and distress. (O/C)

1. AND it came to pass in the commencement of the thirty and
sixth year of the reign of the judges over the people of Nephi, that
Shiblon took possession of those sacred things which had been
delivered unto Helaman by Alma.
2. And he was a just man, and he did walk uprightly before God;
and he did observe to do good continually, to keep the commandments of the Lord his God; and also did his brother.
3. And it came to pass that Moroni died also. And thus ended the
thirty and sixth year of the reign of the judges.
4. And it came to pass that in the thirty and seventh year of the
reign of the judges, there was a large company of men, even to the
amount of five thousand and four hundred men, with their wives and
their children, departed out of the land of Zarahemla into the land
which was northward.
5. And it came to pass that Hagoth, he being an exceedingly curious
man, therefore he went forth and built him an exceedingly large ship,
on the borders of the land Bountiful, by the land Desolation, and
launched it forth into the west sea, by the narrow neck which led into
the land northward.
6. And behold, there were many of the Nephites who did enter
therein and did sail forth with much provisions, and also many
women and children; and they took their course northward. And
thus ended the thirty and seventh year.
7. And in the thirty and eighth year, this man built other ships.
And the first ship did also return, and many more people did enter
into it; and they also took much provisions, and set out again to
the land northward.
8. And it came to pass that they were never heard of more. And we
suppose that they were drowned in the depths of the sea. And it
came to pass that one other ship also did sail forth; and whither she
did go we know not.
9. And it came to pass that in this year there were many people
who went forth into the land northward. And thus ended the thirty and eighth year.
10. And it came to pass in the thirty and ninth year of the reign of
the judges, Shiblon died also, and Corianton had gone forth to the
land northward in a ship, to carry forth provisions unto the people
who had gone forth into that land.
11. Therefore it became expedient for Shiblon to confer those
sacred things, before his death, upon the son of Helaman, who was
called Helaman, being called after the name of his father.
12. Now behold, all those engravings which were in the possession
of Helaman were written and sent forth among the children of
men throughout all the land, save it were those parts which had
been commanded by Alma should not go forth.
13. Nevertheless, these things were to be kept sacred, and handed
down from one generation to another; therefore, in this year, they
had been conferred upon Helaman, before the death of Shiblon.
14. And it came to pass also in this year that there were some dissenters who had gone forth unto the

Alma 63:5

According to Matthew Cowley, these colonists were probably the forefathers of the people now inhabiting the South Pacific. This verse describes two separate migrations—one by land and one by sea.

Alma 63:10–12

By tradition, the sacred plates should have been given to Shiblon's brother; instead, since he was gone, they went to Shiblon's nephew, Helaman. We know from these verses that copies of the plates were made and distributed—something that was highly unusual.

Lamanites; and they were stirred up again to anger against the Nephites.
15. And also in this same year they came down with a numerous army to war against the people of Moronihah, or against the army of Moronihah, in the which they were beaten and driven back again to their own lands, suffering great loss.
16. And thus ended the thirty and ninth year of the reign of the judges over the people of Nephi.
17. And thus ended the account of Alma, and Helaman his son, and also Shiblon, who was his son.

THE BOOK OF HELAMAN

CHAPTER 1

1. AND now behold, it came to pass in the commencement of the fortieth year of the reignof the judges over the people of Nephi, there began to be a serious difficulty among the people of the Nephites.
2. For behold, Pahoran had died, and gone the way of all the earth; therefore there began to be a serious contention concerning who should have the judgment-seat among the brethren, who were the sons of Pahoran.
3. Now these are their names who did contend for the judgment-seat, who did also cause the people to contend: Pahoran, Paanchi, and Pacumeni.
4. Now these are not all the sons of Pahoran (for he had many), but these are they who did contend for the judgment-seat; therefore, they did cause three divisions among the people.
5. Nevertheless, it came to pass that Pahoran was appointed by the voice of the people to be chief judge and a governor over the people of Nephi.
6. And it came to pass that Pacumeni, when he saw that he could not obtain the judgment-seat, he did unite with the voice of the people.
7. But behold, Paanchi, and that part of the people that were desirous that he should be their governor, was exceedingly wroth; therefore,

POINT OF INTEREST

This cut-away sketch is of a tomb at the Kaminaljuyu archaeological site in Guatemala, dating from the first century B.C. The luxury of burial offerings found within indicates that royalty was interred here. The "sepulchre, which [the Lamanites] had made for the purpose of burying their dead" (Alma 19:1, 5), may have looked like this.

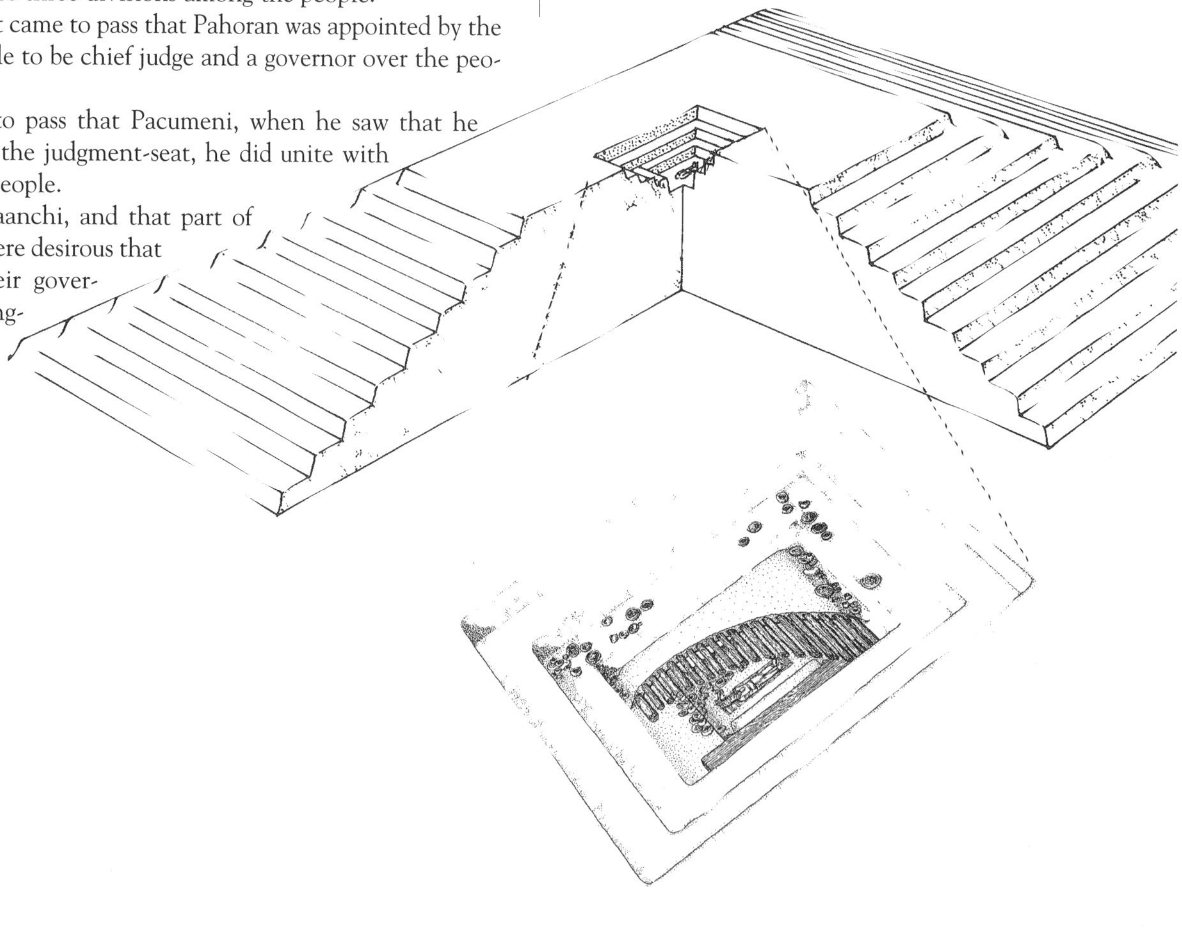

he was about to flatter away those people to rise up in rebellion against their brethren.
8. And it came to pass as he was about to do this, behold, he was taken, and was tried according to the voice of the people, and condemned unto death; for he had raised up in rebellion and sought to destroy the liberty of the people.
9. Now when those people who were desirous that he should be their governor saw that he was condemned unto death, therefore they were angry, and behold, they sent forth one Kishkumen, even to the judgment-seat of Pahoran, and murdered Pahoran as he sat upon the judgment-seat.
10. And he was pursued by the servants of Pahoran; but behold, so speedy was the flight of Kishkumen that no man could overtake him.
11. And he went unto those that sent him, and they all entered into a covenant, yea, swearing by their everlasting Maker, that they would tell no man that Kishkumen had murdered Pahoran.
12. Therefore, Kishkumen was not known among the people of Nephi, for he was in disguise at the time that he murdered Pahoran. And Kishkumen and his band, who had covenanted with him, did mingle themselves among the people, in a manner that they all could not be found; but as many as were found were condemned unto death.
13. And now behold, Pacumeni was appointed, according to the voice of the people, to be a chief judge and a governor over the people, to reign in the stead of his brother Pahoran; and it was according to his right. And all this was done in the fortieth year of the reign of the judges; and it had an end.
14. And it came to pass in the forty and first year of the reign of the judges, that the Lamanites had gathered together an innumerable army of men, and armed them with swords, and with cimeters and with bows, and with arrows, and with head-plates, and with breastplates, and with all manner of shields of every kind.
15. And they came down again that they might pitch battle against the Nephites. And they were led by a man whose name was Coriantumr; and he was a descendant of Zarahemla; and he was a dissenter from among the Nephites; and he was a large and a mighty man.
16. Therefore, the king of the Lamanites, whose name was Tubaloth, who was the son of Ammoron, supposing that Coriantumr, being a mighty man, could stand against the Nephites, with his strength and also with his great wisdom, insomuch that by sending him forth he should gain power over the Nephites—
17. Therefore he did stir them up to anger, and he did gather together his armies, and he did appoint Coriantumr to be their leader, and did cause that they should march down to the land of Zarahemla to battle against the Nephites.
18. And it came to pass that because of so much contention and so much difficulty in the government, that they had not kept sufficient guards in the land of Zarahemla; for they had supposed that the Lamanites durst not come into the heart of their lands to attack that great city Zarahemla.
19. But it came to pass that Coriantumr did march forth at the head of his numerous host, and came upon the inhabitants of the city, and their march was with such exceedingly great speed that there

Helaman 1:8

Though the record does not specify, it is likely that Paanchi was executed.

Helaman 1:11

The "covenant" spoken of in this verse refers to the religious oath made by members of the secret combination; today, as then, those who circumvent the law will resort to violence in order to gain power. The origin of these murderous oaths can be traced back to Cain.

Helaman 1:16

Coriantumr was chosen in part because of tradition: it was the common custom to choose Nephite dissenters to be leaders in the Lamanite armies (see verse 15), since they had great hatred toward the Nephites. The Lamanites hoped to leverage that hatred into ferocious and victorious battles.

Helaman 1:18

The difficulties in the government and the significant contention over the judgment seat put the Lamanites at a decided advantage over the Nephites, who had stationed troops only around the borders in the land of Zarahemla—not a wise battle strategy.

was no time for the Nephites to gather together their armies.
20. Therefore Coriantumr did cut down the watch by the entrance
of the city, and did march forth with his whole army into the city,
and they did slay every one who did oppose them, insomuch that
they did take possession of the whole city.
21. And it came to pass that Pacumeni, who was the chief judge,
did flee before Coriantumr, even to the walls of the city. And it
came to pass that Coriantumr did smite him against the wall, insomuch that he died. And thus ended the days of Pacumeni.
22. And now when Coriantumr saw that he was in possession of
the city of Zarahemla, and saw that the Nephites had fled before
them, and were slain, and were taken, and were cast into prison,
and that he had obtained the possession of the strongest hold in all
the land, his heart took courage insomuch that he was about to go
forth against all the land.
23. And now he did not tarry in the land of Zarahemla, but he did
march forth with a large army, even towards the city of Bountiful;
for it was his determination to go forth and cut his way through
with the sword, that he might obtain the north parts of the land.
24. And, supposing that their greatest strength was in the center of
the land, therefore he did march forth, giving them no time to
assemble themselves together save it were in small bodies; and in
this manner they did fall upon them and cut them down to the
earth.
25. But behold, this march of Coriantumr through the center of the
land gave Moronihah great advantage over them, notwithstanding
the greatness of the number of the Nephites who were slain.
26. For behold, Moronihah had supposed that the Lamanites durst
not come into the center of the land, but that they would attack
the cities round about in the borders as they had hitherto done;
therefore Moronihah had caused that their strong armies should
maintain those parts round about by the borders.
27. But behold, the Lamanites were not frightened according to his
desire, but they had come into the center of the land, and had
taken the capital city which was the city of Zarahemla, and were
marching through the most capital parts of the land, slaying the
people with a great slaughter, both men, women, and children, taking possession of many cities and of many strongholds.
28. But when Moronihah had discovered this, he immediately sent
forth Lehi with an army round about to head them before they
should come to the land Bountiful.
29. And thus he did; and he did head them before they came to the
land Bountiful, and gave unto them battle, insomuch that they
began to retreat back towards the land of Zarahemla.
30. And it came to pass that Moronihah did head them in their
retreat, and did give unto them battle, insomuch that it became an
exceedingly bloody battle; yea, many were slain, and among the number who were slain Coriantumr was also found.
31. And now, behold, the Lamanites could not retreat either way,
neither on the north, nor on the south, nor on the east, nor on the
west, for they were surrounded on every hand by the Nephites.
32. And thus had Coriantumr plunged the Lamanites into the midst
of the Nephites, insomuch that they were in the power of the
Nephites, and he himself was slain, and the Lamanites did yield
themselves into the hands of the Nephites.

Helaman 1:31

The Nephite strategy at this point was interesting and effective: after the Nephites saw that Coriantumr's armies were focusing their attacks at the centers of the Nephite lands, the Nephite armies worked to surround the Lamanite armies by building up strongholds along the borders. As a result, the Lamanite armies drove into the center of the land, then found themselves surrounded by Nephites—and, as a result, unable to escape.

33. And it came to pass that Moronihah took possession of the city of Zarahemla again, and caused that the Lamanites who had been taken prisoners should depart out of the land in peace.
34. And thus ended the forty and first year of the reign of the judges.

CHAPTER 2

1. AND it came to pass in the forty and second year of the reign of the judges, after Moronihah had established again peace between the Nephites and the Lamanites, behold there was no one to fill the judgment-seat; therefore there began to be a contention again among the people concerning who should fill the judgment-seat.
2. And it came to pass that Helaman, who was the son of Helaman, was appointed to fill the judgment-seat, by the voice of the people.
3. But behold, Kishkumen, who had murdered Pahoran, did lay wait to destroy Helaman also; and he was upheld by his band, who had entered into a covenant that no one should know his wickedness.
4. For there was one Gadianton, who was exceedingly expert in many words, and also in his craft, to carry on the secret work of murder and of robbery; therefore he became the leader of the band of Kishkumen.
5. Therefore he did flatter them, and also Kishkumen, that if they would place him in the judgment-seat he would grant unto those who belonged to his band that they should be placed in power and authority among the people; therefore Kishkumen sought to destroy Helaman.
6. And it came to pass as he went forth towards the judgment-seat to destroy Helaman, behold one of the servants of Helaman, having been out by night, and having obtained, through disguise, a knowledge of those plans which had been laid by this band to destroy Helaman—
7. And it came to pass that he met Kishkumen, and he gave unto him a sign; therefore Kishkumen made known unto him the object of his desire, desiring that he would conduct him to the judgment-seat that he might murder Helaman.
8. And when the servant of Helaman had known all the heart of Kishkumen, and how that it was his object to murder, and also that it was the object of all those who belonged to his band to murder, and to rob, and to gain power, (and this was their secret plan, and their combination) the servant of Helaman said unto Kishkumen: Let us go forth unto the judgment-seat.
9. Now this did please Kishkumen exceedingly, for he did suppose that he should accomplish his design; but behold, the servant of Helaman, as they were going forth unto the judgment-seat, did stab Kishkumen even to the heart, that he fell dead without a groan. And he ran and told Helaman all the things which he had seen, and heard, and done.
10. And it came to pass that Helaman did send forth to take this band of robbers and secret murderers, that they might be executed according to the law.
11. But behold, when Gadianton had found that Kishkumen did not return he feared lest that he should be destroyed; therefore he caused that his band should follow him. And they took their flight out of

Helaman 1:33

In this verse we see that Moronihah continued the policy established by Moroni: prisoners of war were allowed to return to their own lands in peace.

Helaman 2:11

When Kishkumen did not return, Gadianton began to fear that his band of robbers would be discovered and destroyed. In a sense of fear and panic, he commanded the robbers to follow him into the wilderness, where they could stay hidden and hopefully escape detection. They are not heard from again for several years.

the land, by a secret way, into the wilderness; and thus when Helaman sent forth to take them they could nowhere be found.
12. And more of this Gadianton shall be spoken hereafter. And thus ended the forty and second year of the reign of the judges over the people of Nephi.
13. And behold, in the end of this book ye shall see that this Gadianton did prove the overthrow, yea, almost the entire destruction of the people of Nephi.
14. Behold I do not mean the end of the book of Helaman, but I mean the end of the book of Nephi, from which I have taken all the account which I have written.

CHAPTER 3

1. AND now it came to pass in the forty and third year of the reign of the judges, there was no contention among the people of Nephi save it were a little pride which was in the church, which did cause some little dissensions among the people, which affairs were settled in the ending of the forty and third year.
2. And there was no contention among the people in the forty and fourth year; neither was there much contention in the forty and fifth year.
3. And it came to pass in the forty and sixth, yea, there was much contention and many dissensions; in the which there were an exceedingly great many who departed out of the land of Zarahemla, and went forth unto the land northward to inherit the land.
4. And they did travel to an exceedingly great distance, insomuch that they came to large bodies of water and many rivers.
5. Yea, and even they did spread forth into all parts of the land, into whatever parts it had not been rendered desolate and without timber, because of the many inhabitants who had before inherited the land.
6. And now no part of the land was desolate, save it were for timber; but because of the greatness of the destruction of the people who had before inhabited the land it was called desolate.
7. And there being but little timber upon the face of the land, nevertheless the people who went forth became exceedingly expert in the working of cement; therefore they did build houses of cement, in the which they did dwell.
8. And it came to pass that they did multiply and spread, and did go forth from the land southward to the land northward, and did spread insomuch that they began to cover the face of the whole earth, from the sea south to the sea north, from the sea west to the sea east.
9. And the people who were in the land northward did dwell in tents, and in houses of cement, and they did suffer whatsoever tree should spring up upon the face of the land that it should grow up, that in time they might have timber to build their houses, yea, their cities, and their temples, and their synagogues, and their sanctuaries, and all manner of their buildings.
10. And it came to pass as timber was exceedingly scarce in the land northward, they did send forth much by the way of shipping.

Helaman 3:3

According to Joseph Smith, "the land northward" refers to North America.

Helaman 3:9

Some use the mention of cement in this verse to argue against the authenticity of the Book of Mormon as an ancient record, claiming that cement was not available to people on the American continent before the time of Christ. Modern archaeology has lent credence to this verse, however. In Guatemala, archaeologists have unearthed 2,000-year-old cement tombs and burial vaults. And at a site near Mexico City, scientists have found the ruins of cement houses as well as a 210-foot cement monument.

11. And thus they did enable the people in the land northward that they might build many cities, both of wood and of cement.
12. And it came to pass that there were many of the people of Ammon, who were Lamanites by birth, did also go forth into this land.
13. And now there are many records kept of the proceedings of this people, by many of this people, which are particular and very large, concerning them.
14. But behold, a hundredth part of the proceedings of this people, yea, the account of the Lamanites and of the Nephites, and their wars, and contentions, and dissensions, and their preaching, and their prophecies, and their shipping and their building of ships, and their building of temples, and of synagogues and their sanctuaries, and their righteousness, and their wickedness, and their murders, and their robbings, and their plundering, and all manner of abominations and whoredoms, cannot be contained in this work.
15. But behold, there are many books and many records of every kind, and they have been kept chiefly by the Nephites.
16. And they have been handed down from one generation to another by the Nephites, even until they have fallen into transgression and have been murdered, plundered, and hunted, and driven forth, and slain, and scattered upon the face of the earth, and mixed with the Lamanites until they are no more called the Nephites, becoming wicked, and wild, and ferocious, yea, even becoming Lamanites.
17. And now I return again to mine account; therefore, what I have spoken had passed after there had been great contentions, and disturbances, and wars, and dissensions, among the people of Nephi.
18. The forty and sixth year of the reign of the judges ended;
19. And it came to pass that there was still great contention in the land, yea, even in the forty and seventh year, and also in the forty and eighth year.
20. Nevertheless Helaman did fill the judgment-seat with justice and equity; yea, he did observe to keep the statutes, and the judgments, and the commandments of God; and he did do that which was right in the sight of God continually; and he did walk after the ways of his father, insomuch that he did prosper in the land.
21. And it came to pass that he had two sons. He gave unto the eldest the name of Nephi, and unto the youngest, the name of Lehi. And they began to grow up unto the Lord.
22. And it came to pass that the wars and contentions began to cease, in a small degree, among the people of the Nephites, in the latter end of the forty and eighth year of the reign of the judges over the people of Nephi.
23. And it came to pass in the forty and ninth year of the reign of the judges, there was continual peace established in the land, all save it were the secret combinations which Gadianton the robber had established in the more settled parts of the land, which at that time were not known unto those who were at the head of government; therefore they were not destroyed out of the land.
24. And it came to pass that in this same year there was exceedingly great prosperity in the church, insomuch that there were thousands who did join themselves unto the

Helaman 3:16

In the days of Helaman, the word *Lamanite* was being used to refer to the wicked people who had joined with the blood descendants of Laman and his early followers. Thus the wicked who joined with the Lamanites were "no more called the Nephites, becoming wicked, and wild, and ferocious, yea, even becoming Lamanites." (Helaman 3:16.)

It is quite evident that some of the Lamanites converted by Nephi and Lehi in the prison were really apostate Nephites, for Aminadab said that they had had the gospel preached unto them by "Alma, and Amulek, and Zeezrom." (Helaman 5:41.) So far as the Book of Mormon relates, the only missionary venture engaged in by these three men together was to the apostate Zoramites who were then living in the land of Antionum. (Alma 31:3–6.) (Ludlow)

church and were baptized unto repentance.
25. And so great was the prosperity of the church, and so many the blessings which were poured out upon the people, that even the high priests and the teachers were themselves astonished beyond measure.
26. And it came to pass that the work of the Lord did prosper unto the baptizing and uniting to the church of God, many souls, yea, even tens of thousands.
27. Thus we may see that the Lord is merciful unto all who will, in the sincerity of their hearts, call upon his holy name.
28. Yea, thus we see that the gate of heaven is open unto all, even to those who will believe on the name of Jesus Christ, who is the Son of God.
29. Yea, we see that whosoever will may lay hold upon the word of God, which is quick and powerful, which shall divide asunder all the cunning and the snares and the wiles of the devil, and lead the man of Christ in a strait and narrow course across that everlasting gulf of misery which is prepared to engulf the wicked—
30. And land their souls, yea, their immortal souls, at the right hand of God in the kingdom of heaven, to sit down with Abraham, and Isaac, and with Jacob, and with all our holy fathers, to go no more out.
31. And in this year there was continual rejoicing in the land of Zarahemla, and in all the regions round about, even in all the land which was possessed by the Nephites.
32. And it came to pass that there was peace and exceedingly great joy in the remainder of the forty and ninth year; yea, and also there was continual peace and great joy in the fiftieth year of the reign of the judges.
33. And in the fifty and first year of the reign of the judges there was peace also, save it were the pride which began to enter into the church—not into the church of God, but into the hearts of the people who professed to belong to the church of God—
34. And they were lifted up in pride, even to the persecution of many of their brethren. Now this was a great evil, which did cause the more humble part of the people to suffer great persecutions, and to wade through much affliction.
35. Nevertheless they did fast and pray oft, and did wax stronger and stronger in their humility, and firmer and firmer in the faith of Christ, unto the filling their souls with joy and consolation, yea, even to the purifying and the sanctification of their hearts, which sanctification cometh because of their yielding their hearts unto God.
36. And it came to pass that the fifty and second year ended in peace also, save it were the exceedingly great pride which had gotten into the hearts of the people; and it was because of their exceedingly great riches and their prosperity in the land; and it did grow upon them from day to day.
37. And it came to pass in the fifty and third year of the reign of the judges, Helaman died, and his eldest son Nephi began to reign in his stead. And it came to pass that he did fill the judgment-seat with justice and equity; yea, he did keep

Helaman 3:27–32

The period of peace under Helaman the Younger was marked by "continual rejoicing in the land" (verse 31) and "peace and exceedingly great joy" (verse 32). We learn three great lessons from this period of peace, demonstrating three things that are accomplished through the word of God:

1. The word of God divides and breaks up the cunning, snares, and wiles of the devil.
2. The word of God leads righteous people in a strait and narrow course across the gulf of misery that is designed to ensnare the wicked.
3. Once the righteous have been led across the gulf of misery without becoming engulfed, the word of God lands them at the right hand of God, where they will remain eternally, enjoying the blessings of Abraham, Isaac, and Jacob.

Helaman 3:36

Sanctification is the process by which fallen man becomes pure and holy, and eventually becomes free from sin. The Holy Ghost is the major catalyst in the sanctification process; how much the process purifies us depends on the level of our obedience.

Helaman 3:35

The harvest of good fruit is bounteous when the weeds of pride are eradicated.

Beware of the seeds of pride concealed below the surface, waiting to germinate. . . .

Pride, the universal sin, was the downfall of the Jaredite and Nephite nations. It is our problem, too, as individuals. During the period of time where Helaman the Second was guiding the people, a great many responded in righteousness to the teachings of the gospel, and the Church prospered spiritually; nevertheless, many struggled to one degree or another with pride. This commentary would not be complete without a portion of the masterful discourse on pride by President Ezra Taft Benson:

"Pride is a damning sin in the true sense of that word. It limits or stops progression. . . . Pride adversely affects all our relationships—our relationship with God and His servants, between husband and wife, parent and child, employer and employee, teacher and student, and all mankind. Our degree of pride determines how we treat our God and our brothers and sisters. Christ wants to lift us to where He is. Do we desire to do the same for others?" (P/A)

Helaman 3:36

The people in the land of Zarahemla continued to struggle with pride as a result of "their exceedingly great riches and their prosperity in the land." Even those who have been blessed with wealth can choose to be humble; that choice involves, among other things, raising others above us, serving others, attending and worshiping in the temple, and submitting our will to that of the Father.

the commandments of God, and did walk in the ways of his father.

CHAPTER 4

1. AND it came to pass in the fifty and fourth year there were many dissensions in the church, and there was also a contention among the people, insomuch that there was much bloodshed.
2. And the rebellious part were slain and driven out of the land, and they did go unto the king of the Lamanites.
3. And it came to pass that they did endeavor to stir up the Lamanites to war against the Nephites; but behold, the Lamanites were exceedingly afraid, insomuch that they would not hearken to the words of those dissenters.
4. But it came to pass in the fifty and sixth year of the reign of the judges, there were dissenters who went up from the Nephites unto the Lamanites; and they succeeded with those others in stirring them up to anger against the Nephites; and they were all that year preparing for war.
5. And in the fifty and seventh year they did come down against the Nephites to battle, and they did commence the work of death; yea, insomuch that in the fifty and eighth year of the reign of the judges they succeeded in obtaining possession of the land of Zarahemla; yea, and also all the lands, even unto the land which was near the land Bountiful.
6. And the Nephites and the armies of Moronihah were driven even into the land of Bountiful;
7. And there they did fortify against the Lamanites, from the west sea, even unto the east; it being a day's journey for a Nephite, on the line which they had fortified and stationed their armies to defend their north country.
8. And thus those dissenters of the Nephites, with the help of a numerous army of the Lamanites, had obtained all the possession of the Nephites which was in the land southward. And all this was done in the fifty and eighth and ninth years of the reign of the judges.
9. And it came to pass in the sixtieth year of the reign of the judges, Moronihah did succeed with his armies in obtaining many parts of the land; yea, they regained many cities which had fallen into the hands of the Lamanites.
10. And it came to pass in the sixty and first year of the reign of the judges they succeeded in regaining even the half of all their possessions.
11. Now this great loss of the Nephites, and the great slaughter which was among them, would not have happened had it not been for their wickedness and their abomination which was among them; yea, and it was among those also who professed to belong to the church of God.
12. And it was because of the pride of their hearts, because of their exceeding riches, yea, it was because of their oppression to the poor, withholding their food from the hungry, withholding their clothing from the naked, and smiting their humble brethren upon the cheek, making a mock of that which was sacred, denying the spirit of prophecy and of revelation, murdering, plundering, lying, stealing,

Helaman 4:4

According to Elder Bruce R. McConkie, dissension is a tool Satan uses to hinder spiritual growth.

Helaman 4:10

It is important to understand that the Nephites regained what possessions they did only after they humbled themselves and repented of their wrongdoings.

Helaman 4:11

As alluded to in this verse, there were members of the Church who were among the wicked Nephites.

Helaman 4:11–13

Although the Book of Mormon lists several causes of war (wickedness, greed, personal ambition, selfishness, etc.), one of the most frequently listed causes is pride. Perhaps it should be obvious how pride could lead to war, because pride causes a person to feel he is better than others. Therefore, when a person or a nation is lifted up in "the pride of their hearts" they feel others should not have the same rights and privileges they have; thus they are willing to fight either to prevent other people from getting these rights or to gain other privileges for themselves. (Ludlow)

Helaman 4:12

This verse lists specific wicked practices that lead to the defeat of the Nephites: developing pride as a result of exceeding riches; oppressing of the poor; withholding food from the hungry; withholding clothing from the naked; making mockery of that which was sacred; denying the spirit of prophecy and revelation; murdering, plundering, lying, stealing, and committing adultery; and rising up in great contentions.

committing adultery, rising up in great contentions, and deserting away into the land of Nephi, among the Lamanites—
13. And because of this their great wickedness, and their boastings in their own strength, they were left in their own strength; therefore they did not prosper, but were afflicted and smitten, and driven before the Lamanites, until they had lost possession of almost all their lands.
14. But behold, Moronihah did preach many things unto the people because of their iniquity, and also Nephi and Lehi, who were the sons of Helaman, did preach many things unto the people, yea, and did prophesy many things unto them concerning their iniquities, and what should come unto them if they did not repent of their sins.
15. And it came to pass that they did repent, and inasmuch as they did repent they did begin to prosper.
16. For when Moronihah saw that they did repent he did venture to lead them forth from place to place, and from city to city, even until they had regained the one-half of their property and the one-half of all their lands.
17. And thus ended the sixty and first year of the reign of the judges.
18. And it came to pass in the sixty and second year of the reign of the judges, that Moronihah could obtain no more possessions over the Lamanites.
19. Therefore they did abandon their design to obtain the remainder of their lands, for so numerous were the Lamanites that it became impossible for the Nephites to obtain more power over them; therefore Moronihah did employ all his armies in maintaining those parts which he had taken.
20. And it came to pass, because of the greatness of the number of the Lamanites the Nephites were in great fear, lest they should be overpowered, and trodden down, and slain, and destroyed.
21. Yea, they began to remember the prophecies of Alma, and also the words of Mosiah; and they saw that they had been a stiffnecked people, and that they had set at naught the commandments of God.
22. And that they had altered and trampled under their feet the laws of Mosiah, or that which the Lord commanded him to give unto the people; and they saw that their laws had become corrupted, and that they had become a wicked people, insomuch that they were wicked even like unto the Lamanites.
23. And because of their iniquity the church had begun to dwindle; and they began to disbelieve in the spirit of prophecy and in the spirit of revelation; and the judgments of God did stare them in the face.
24. And they saw that they had become weak, like unto their brethren, the Lamanites, and that the Spirit of the Lord did no more preserve them; yea, it had withdrawn from them because the Spirit of the Lord doth not dwell in unholy temples—
25. Therefore the Lord did cease to preserve them by his miraculous and matchless power, for they had fallen into a state of unbelief and awful wickedness; and they saw that the Lamanites were exceedingly more numerous than they, and except they should cleave unto the Lord their God they must unavoidably perish.
26. For behold, they saw that the strength of the Lamanites was as

Helaman 4:13

When covenant people are righteous, faithful, and obedient in keeping the covenants they have made with the Lord, even the most mighty empires cannot overthrow them. Examples of this principle were available to the people in the land of Zarahemla as part of the Old Testament records they had—specific examples include Moses fighting Pharoah's army and taking the Israelites across the Red Sea (see Exodus 14) and the battle of Assyria at Jerusalem (see 2 Kings 19). As the Nephites sadly discovered, those who abandon their covenants and revel in their wickedness are left to their own devices—and, no longer offered protection by the Lord, are afflicted, smitten, and defeated.

great as their strength, even man for man. And thus had they fallen into this great transgression; yea, thus had they become weak, because of their transgression, in the space of not many years.

CHAPTER 5

1. AND it came to pass that in this same year, behold, Nephi delivered up the judgment-seat to a man whose name was Cezoram.
2. For as their laws and their governments were established by the voice of the people, and they who chose evil were more numerous than they who chose good, therefore they were ripening for destruction, for the laws had become corrupted.
3. Yea, and this was not all; they were a stiffnecked people, insomuch that they could not be governed by the law nor justice, save it were to their destruction.
4. And it came to pass that Nephi had become weary because of their iniquity; and he yielded up the judgment-seat, and took it upon him to preach the word of God all the remainder of his days, and his brother Lehi also, all the remainder of his days;
5. For they remembered the words which their father Helaman spake unto them. And these are the words which he spake:
6. Behold, my sons, I desire that ye should remember to keep the commandments of God; and I would that ye should declare unto the people these words. Behold, I have given unto you the names of our first parents who came out of the land of Jerusalem; and this I have done that when you remember your names ye may remember them; and when ye remember them ye may remember their works; and when ye remember their works ye may know how that it is said, and also written, that they were good.
7. Therefore, my sons, I would that ye should do that which is good, that it may be said of you, and also written, even as it has been said and written of them.
8. And now my sons, behold I have somewhat more to desire of you, which desire is, that ye may not do these things that ye may boast, but that ye may do these things to lay up for yourselves a treasure in heaven, yea, which is eternal, and which fadeth not away; yea, that ye may have that precious gift of eternal life, which we have reason to suppose hath been given to our fathers.
9. O remember, remember, my sons, the words which king Benjamin spake unto his people; yea, remember that there is no other way nor means whereby man can be saved, only through the atoning blood of Jesus Christ, who shall come, yea, remember that he cometh to redeem the world.

Helaman 5:2

This verse demonstrates the importance of choosing laws that reflect the principles of truth and righteousness. Brigham Young taught that any nation or government that "gives no heed to the principles of truth and religion will be utterly wasted away and destroyed."

Helaman 5:4

The iniquity of the people "wearied" Nephi because he realized that unless the hearts of men changed, the nation could not be saved. At this point, he undoubtedly felt that the only way he could assure his nation safety and peace was to help his people go through that mighty change of heart—and so he chose to fight for his people from the judgment seat instead of in a military arena.

Helaman 5:5–14; 11:7, 34

In addressing a group of religious educators, President Spencer W. Kimball said that *remember* is the most important word in the English language.

Helaman 5:5–14; 11:7, 34

Brigham Young said, "If you love the truth you can remember it."

10. And remember also the words which Amulek spake unto Zeezrom, in the city of Ammonihah; for he said unto him that the Lord surely should come to redeem his people, but that he should not come to redeem them in their sins, but to redeem them from their sins.

11. And he hath power given unto him from the Father to redeem them from their sins because of repentance; therefore he hath sent his angels to declare the tidings of the conditions of repentance, which bringeth unto the power of the Redeemer, unto the salvation of their souls.

12. And now, my sons, remember, remember that it is upon the rock of our Redeemer, who is Christ, the Son of God, that ye must build your foundation; that when the devil shall send forth his mighty winds, yea, his shafts in the whirlwind, yea, when all his hail and his mighty storm shall beat upon you, it shall have no power over you to drag you down to the gulf of misery and endless wo, because of the rock upon which ye are built, which is a sure foundation, a foundation whereon if men build they cannot fall.

13. And it came to pass that these were the words which Helaman taught to his sons; yea, he did teach them many things which are not written, and also many things which are written.

14. And they did remember his words; and therefore they went forth, keeping the commandments of God, to teach the word of God among all the people of Nephi, beginning at the city Bountiful;

15. And from thenceforth to the city of Gid; and from the city of Gid to the city of Mulek;

16. And even from one city to another, until they had gone forth among all the people of Nephi who were in the land southward; and from thence into the land of Zarahemla, among the Lamanites.

17. And it came to pass that they did preach with great power, insomuch that they did confound many of those dissenters who had gone over from the Nephites, insomuch that they came forth and did confess their sins and were baptized unto repentance, and immediately returned to the Nephites to endeavor to repair unto them the wrongs which they had done.

18. And it came to pass that Nephi and Lehi did preach unto the Lamanites with such great power and authority, for they had power and authority given unto them that they might speak, and they also had what they should speak given unto them—

19. Therefore they did speak unto the great astonishment of the Lamanites, to the convincing them, insomuch that there were eight thousand of the Lamanites who were in the land of Zarahemla and round about baptized unto repentance, and were convinced of the wickedness of the traditions of their fathers.

20. And it came to pass that Nephi and Lehi did proceed from thence to go to the land of Nephi.

21. And it came to pass that they were taken by an army of the Lamanites and cast into prison; yea, even in that same prison in which Ammon and his brethren were cast by the servants of Limhi.

Helaman 5:12

People are in need of powers beyond their own that will provide them with anchors and spiritual forms of firmness to which they can cling. Drifting without direction develops desperation. All of us must determine for ourselves what foundation we will choose on which to build and structure our lives. Thankfully, we are free to decide the degree to which our personal interests, gifts, talents, and opportunities will be used to determine the focus of our lives. Unfortunately, we sometimes develop tunnel vision and lose our perspective. Some people, without the clear views of the Spirit, mistakenly seek satisfaction by building temporal or temporary structures only.

Some build their life on foundations of educational attainments, positions of prestige, worldly wealth, athletics, physical skills, or talents. There is nothing inherently wrong with choosing many of life's opportunities as a focus of our lives. But by themselves, they simply are not sufficient. (O/C)

Helaman 5:12

Through the wise and experienced perspective of the prophet-historian Mormon, we here encounter a panoramic vista of vast opposing forces: the inexorable forward thrust of divine power, as contrasted to the halting, corrupting, all-too-enticing and often irrepressible force of pride. There is no doubt about the final outcome, for "the works, and the designs, and the purposes of God cannot be frustrated, neither can they come to naught" (D&C 3:1). But what painful lessons we mortals have to learn before we can proclaim defeat over the seeds of pride and rebellion constantly germinating within our souls. "And thus we may see" is Mormon's frequent editorial signature statement introducing his readers to the obvious truth that only faith, repentance, and compliance with all of the Lord's commandments can make us as little children, eradicating pride from our lives and preparing us to receive the blessings of the Spirit. . . .

Helaman's wonderful teachings as recalled by his sons, Lehi and Nephi, teach us the power of the doctrine of remembering. In the contrasting portraits of pride and humility, rebellion and alignment with God's will, iniquity and righteousness, we see clearly in these pages the lessons we are to remember. . . .

President Gordon B. Hinckley reminded us, "Like the polar star in the heavens, regardless of what the future holds, there stands the Redeemer of the world, the Son of God, certain and sure as the anchor of our immortal lives. He is the rock of our salvation, our strength, our comfort, the very focus of our faith. In sunshine and in shadow we look to Him, and He is there to assure and smile upon us. He is the central focus of our worship." (P/A)

22. And after they had been cast into prison many days without food, behold, they went forth into the prison to take them that they might slay them.
23. And it came to pass that Nephi and Lehi were encircled about as if by fire, even insomuch that they durst not lay their hands upon them for fear lest they should be burned. Nevertheless, Nephi and Lehi were not burned; and they were as standing in the midst of fire and were not burned.
24. And when they saw that they were encircled about with a pillar of fire, and that it burned them not, their hearts did take courage.
25. For they saw that the Lamanites durst not lay their hands upon them; neither durst they come near unto them, but stood as if they were struck dumb with amazement.
26. And it came to pass that Nephi and Lehi did stand forth and began to speak unto them, saying: Fear not, for behold, it is God that has shown unto you this marvelous thing, in the which is shown unto you that ye cannot lay your hands on us to slay us.
27. And behold, when they had said these words, the earth shook exceedingly, and the walls of the prison did shake as if they were about to tumble to the earth; but behold, they did not fall. And behold, they that were in the prison were Lamanites and Nephites who were dissenters.
28. And it came to pass that they were overshadowed with a cloud of darkness, and an awful solemn fear came upon them.
29. And it came to pass that there came a voice as if it were above the cloud of darkness, saying: Repent ye, repent ye, and seek no more to destroy my servants whom I have sent unto you to declare good tidings.
30. And it came to pass when they heard this voice, and beheld that it was not a voice of thunder, neither was it a voice of a great tumultuous noise, but behold, it was a still voice of perfect mildness, as if it had been a whisper, and it did pierce even to the very soul—
31. And notwithstanding the mildness of the voice, behold the earth shook exceedingly, and the walls of the prison trembled again, as if it were about to tumble to the earth; and behold the cloud of darkness, which had overshadowed them, did not disperse—
32. And behold the voice came again, saying: Repent ye, repent ye, for the kingdom of heaven is at hand; and seek no more to destroy my servants. And it came to pass that the earth shook again, and the walls trembled.
33. And also again the third time the voice came, and did speak unto them marvelous words which cannot be uttered by man; and the walls did tremble again, and the earth shook as if it were about to divide asunder.
34. And it came to pass that the Lamanites could not flee because of the cloud of darkness which did overshadow them; yea, and also they were immovable because of the fear which did come upon them.
35. Now there was one among them who was a Nephite by birth, who had once belonged to the church of God but had dissented from them.
36. And it came to pass that he turned him about, and behold, he saw through the cloud of darkness the faces of Nephi and Lehi; and behold, they did shine exceedingly,

Helaman 5:23–24

It's an interesting exercise to compare these verses to other events recorded in the scriptures:

• Compare verse 23 to Shadrach and his companions (see Daniel 3:19-27)

• Compare verse 27 to the walls falling around Alma and Amulek (see Alma 14:27, 28)

• Compare verse 29 to the account in 3 Nephi 9:1–22

• Compare verse 31 again to the walls falling around Alma and Amulek

• Compare verse 33 to the conditions among the Nephites just prior to Christ's appearance on the American continent (see 3 Nephi 10: 3–7)

• Compare verse 34 to the conditions among the Nephites when Christ was crucified in Jerusalem (see 3 Nephi 8:20–23)

Helaman 5:30

. . . We hear the following comments describing the voice of Lucifer, or in other words, the voice of wickedness:

". . . treasure up wisdom in your bosoms, lest the wickedness of men reveal these things unto you by their wickedness, in a manner which shall speak in your ears with a voice louder than that which shall shake the earth. . . " (D&C 38:30).

"And now, when Moses had said these words, Satan cried with a loud voice, and ranted upon the earth. . . .

"And it came to pass that Satan cried with a *loud voice*, with weeping, and wailing, and gnashing of teeth. . . " (Moses 1:19, 22, emphasis added).

Lucifer's voice of wickedness is both loud and harsh and lacks the mildness and softness of a heavenly voice. Elder Boyd K. Packer taught that "the Spirit does not get our attention by shouting or shaking us with a heavy hand. Rather it whispers. It caresses so gently that if we are preoccupied we may not feel it at all." (O/C)

Helaman 5:35–36

The "one among them" referred to in verse 35 is Aminadab—who, as the following verse signifies, was the first to notice that Nephi and Lehi were talking to angels, and who subsequently bore powerful testimony.

even as the faces of angels. And he beheld that they did lift their eyes to heaven; and they were in the attitude as if talking or lifting their voices to some being whom they beheld.
37. And it came to pass that this man did cry unto the multitude, that they might turn and look. And behold, there was power given unto them that they did turn and look; and they did behold the faces of Nephi and Lehi.
38. And they said unto the man: Behold, what do all these things mean, and who is it with whom these men do converse?
39. Now the man's name was Aminadab. And Aminadab said unto them: They do converse with the angels of God.
40. And it came to pass that the Lamanites said unto him: What shall we do, that this cloud of darkness may be removed from overshadowing us?
41. And Aminadab said unto them: You must repent, and cry unto the voice, even until ye shall have faith in Christ, who was taught unto you by Alma, and Amulek, and Zeezrom; and when ye shall do this, the cloud of darkness shall be removed from overshadowing you.
42. And it came to pass that they all did begin to cry unto the voice of him who had shaken the earth; yea, they did cry even until the cloud of darkness was dispersed.
43. And it came to pass that when they cast their eyes about, and saw that the cloud of darkness was dispersed from overshadowing them, behold, they saw that they were encircled about, yea every soul, by a pillar of fire.
44. And Nephi and Lehi were in the midst of them; yea, they were encircled about; yea, they were as if in the midst of a flaming fire, yet it did harm them not, neither did it take hold upon the walls of the prison; and they were filled with that joy which is unspeakable and full of glory.
45. And behold, the Holy Spirit of God did come down from heaven, and did enter into their hearts, and they were filled as if with fire, and they could speak forth marvelous words.
46. And it came to pass that there came a voice unto them, yea, a pleasant voice, as if it were a whisper, saying:
47. Peace, peace be unto you, because of your faith in my Well Beloved, who was from the foundation of the world.
48. And now, when they heard this they cast up their eyes as if to behold from whence the voice came; and behold, they saw the heavens open; and angels came down out of heaven and ministered unto them.
49. And there were about three hundred souls who saw and heard these things; and they were bidden to go forth and marvel not, neither should they doubt.
50. And it came to pass that they did go forth, and did minister unto the people, declaring throughout all the regions round about all the things which they had heard and seen, insomuch that the more part of the Lamanites were convinced of them, because of the greatness of the evidences which they had received.
51. And as many as were convinced did lay down their weapons of war, and also their hatred and the tradition of their fathers.
52. And it came to pass that they did yield up unto the Nephites the lands of their possession.

Helaman 5:41

The Book of Mormon does not expressly give the identity of the people who are in the prison at the time of the miraculous manifestation mentioned in Helaman 5. However, a clue as to who these people were is given by Aminadab when he said unto them, "You must repent, and cry unto the voice, even until ye shall have faith in Christ, who was taught unto you by Alma, and Amulek, and Zeezrom." (Helaman 5:41.) The only time Alma and Amulek and Zeezrom were on a missionary trip together was to the apostate Zoramites who were then living in the land of Antionum. (See Alma 31:1–8.) The Zoramites later fled from this area and joined with the Lamanites in the greater land of Nephi, and from this statement by Aminadab we learn they have now occupied the land of Lehi-Nephi, which had just been deserted by Limhi and his people.

Again, the Book of Mormon proves to be a very complex book but also a wonderfully consistent one. (Ludlow)

Helaman 5:49

These 300 people became the bulwark of the converted Lamanites to whom Samuel would preach.

Helaman 5:50–51

Throughout the history of the Church we have been warned against war and all the things that come with it—injury, death, degradation, cruelty, destruction, and suffering. Though we eschew those things, there are times when war is necessary: to protect our lives, our homes, our religion, and our families. There are many throughout the world who are striving for peace through summits, councils, and governmental efforts of various kinds. We know, however, that the only way to gain true peace is by following the example and the teachings of Jesus Christ, who is the Prince of Peace.

CHAPTER 6

1. AND it came to pass that when the sixty and second year of the reign of the judges had ended, all these things had happened and the Lamanites had become, the more part of them, a righteous people, insomuch that their righteousness did exceed that of the Nephites, because of their firmness and their steadiness in the faith.
2. For behold, there were many of the Nephites who had become hardened and impenitent and grossly wicked, insomuch that they did reject the word of God and all the preaching and prophesying which did come among them.
3. Nevertheless, the people of the church did have great joy because of the conversion of the Lamanites, yea, because of the church of God, which had been established among them. And they did fellowship one with another and did rejoice one with another, and did have great joy.
4. And it came to pass that many of the Lamanites did come down into the land of Zarahemla, and did declare unto the people of the Nephites the manner of their conversion, and did exhort them to faith and repentance.
5. Yea, and many did preach with exceedingly great power and authority, unto the bringing down many of them into the depths of humility, to be the humble followers of God and the Lamb.
6. And it came to pass that many of the Lamanites did go into the land northward; and also Nephi and Lehi went into the land northward, to preach unto the people. And thus ended the sixty and third year.
7. And behold, there was peace in all the land, insomuch that the Nephites did go into whatsoever part of the land they would, whether among the Nephites or the Lamanites.
8. And it came to pass that the Lamanites did also go whithersoever they would, whether it were among the Lamanites or among the Nephites; and thus they did have free intercourse one with another, to buy and to sell, and to get gain, according to their desire.
9. And it came to pass that they became exceedingly rich, both the Lamanites and the Nephites; and they did have an exceeding plenty of gold, and of silver, and of all manner of precious metals, both in the land south and in the land north.
10. Now the land south was called Lehi and the land north was called Mulek, which was after the son of Zedekiah; for the Lord did bring Mulek into the land north, and Lehi into the land south.
11. And behold, there was all manner of gold in both these lands, and of silver, and of precious ore of every kind; and there were also curious workmen, who did work all kinds of ore and did refine it; and thus they did become rich.
12. They did raise grain in abundance, both in the north and in the south; and they did flourish exceedingly, both in the north and in the

Helaman 6:7–8

When we learn "to be the humble followers of God and the Lamb" (Hel. 6:5), the Lord blesses us with peace of heart and "the fulness of the earth" (D&C 59:16). Righteousness brings both spiritual prosperity and temporal blessings, though not always in immediate conjunction.

As a result of the extraordinary ministry of Lehi and Nephi among the Lamanites, even in the strongholds of the land of Nephi to the south, "the more part of the Lamanites were convinced of them [the miraculous events attending the missionary campaign], because of the greatness of the evidences which they had received" (Hel. 5:50). This efflorescence of peace and righteousness among the Lamanites resulted in a widespread reformation of the spiritual life of the people: "And they did fellowship one with another, and did rejoice one with another, and did have great joy" (Hel. 6:3). The prosperity of reformed thought and practice extended to the commercial life of the entire land, including the land to the south, called Lehi, and the land to the north, called Mulek after the immigrant son of Zedekiah (Hel. 6:10). There was a tremendous upsurge in the wealth and well-being of the people because they remembered the covenants of the Lord.

Regarding peace of heart, President Spencer W. Kimball said, "Peace is the fruit of righteousness. It cannot be bought with money, and cannot be traded nor bartered. It must be earned. The wealthy often spend much of their gains in a bid for peace, only to find that it is not for sale. But the poorest as well as the richest may have it in abundance if the total price is paid. Those who abide the laws and live the Christ-like life may have peace and other kindred blessings, principal among which are exaltation and eternal life." (P/A)

Helaman 6:10; 8:21

Zedekiah was the king of Judah at the time Lehi and his colony fled from Jerusalem. (1 Nephi 1:4.) A few years later when the Babylonians besieged Jerusalem, they "slew the sons of Zedekiah before his eyes." (2 Kings 25:7.) Most people have assumed all of the sons of Zedekiah were killed at that time; however, the Book of Mormon records that the sons of Zedekiah were slain "all except it were Mulek." (Helaman 8:21.) (Ludlow)

south. And they did multiply and wax exceedingly strong in the
land. And they did raise many flocks and herds, yea, many fatlings.
13. Behold their women did toil and spin, and did make all manner of cloth, of fine-twined linen and cloth of every kind, to clothe
their nakedness. And thus the sixty and fourth year did pass away
in peace.
14. And in the sixty and fifth year they did also have great joy and
peace, yea, much preaching and many prophecies concerning that
which was to come. And thus passed away the sixty and fifth year.
15. And it came to pass that in the sixty and sixth year of the reign
of the judges, behold, Cezoram was murdered by an unknown hand
as he sat upon the judgment-seat. And it came to pass that in the
same year, that his son, who had been appointed by the people in his
stead, was also murdered. And thus ended the sixty and sixth year.
16. And in the commencement of the sixty and seventh year the
people began to grow exceedingly wicked again.
17. For behold, the Lord had blessed them so long with the riches
of the world that they had not been stirred up to anger, to wars, nor
to bloodshed; therefore they began to set their hearts upon their
riches; yea, they began to seek to get gain that they might be lifted up one above another; therefore they began to commit secret
murders, and to rob and to plunder, that they might get gain.
18. And now behold, those murderers and plunderers were a band
who had been formed by Kishkumen and Gadianton. And now it
had come to pass that there were many, even among the Nephites,
of Gadianton's band. But behold, they were more numerous among
the more wicked part of the Lamanites. And they were called
Gadianton's robbers and murderers.
19. And it was they who did murder the chief judge Cezoram, and
his son, while in the judgment-seat; and behold, they were not
found.
20. And now it came to pass that when the Lamanites found that
there were robbers among them they were exceedingly sorrowful;
and they did use every means in their power to destroy them off the
face of the earth.
21. But behold, Satan did stir up the hearts of the more part of the
Nephites, insomuch that they did unite with those bands of robbers,
and did enter into their covenants and their oaths, that they would
protect and preserve one another in whatsoever difficult circumstances they should be placed, that they should not suffer for their
murders, and their plunderings, and their stealings.
22. And it came to pass that they did have their signs, yea, their
secret signs, and their secret words; and this that they might distinguish a brother who had entered into the covenant, that whatsoever wickedness his brother should do he should not be injured
by his brother, nor by those who did belong to his band, who had
taken this covenant.
23. And thus they might murder, and plunder, and steal, and commit whoredoms and all manner of wickedness, contrary to the laws
of their country and also the laws of their God.
24. And whosoever of those who belonged to their band should
reveal unto the world of their wickedness and their abominations,
should be

Helaman 6:16–17

In these brief verses are described the cycle of pride that is so prevalent throughout the Book of Mormon—a cycle against we must guard in our day.

Helaman 6:21–24

These verses give us important insight into how the secret combinations of the Book of Mormon worked—insight that can help us identify those organizations in our day.

- Satan stirred up the hearts of people against those who were righteous and law-abiding.
- Members of secret combinations made covenants and oaths to preserve and protect each other, no matter how difficult the circumstances in which they might find themselves.
- Members of secret combinations identified themselves to other members with secret signs and secret passwords.
- Those involved with the secret combination were able to violate the laws of the land by stealing, plundering, murdering, committing whoredoms, and generally doing anything else they desired against righteousness.
- Any member of the secret combination who revealed to outsiders what they were doing was tried—not by the courts of the land, but by the leaders and other members of the secret combination. This threat alone was generally enough to ensure loyalty and silence.

tried, not according to the laws of their country, but according to the laws of their wickedness, which had been given by Gadianton and Kishkumen.
25. Now behold, it is these secret oaths and covenants which Alma commanded his son should not go forth unto the world, lest they should be a means of bringing down the people unto destruction.
26. Now behold, those secret oaths and covenants did not come forth unto Gadianton from the records which were delivered unto Helaman; but behold, they were put into the heart of Gadianton by that same being who did entice our first parents to partake of the forbidden fruit—
27. Yea, that same being who did plot with Cain, that if he would murder his brother Abel it should not be known unto the world. And he did plot with Cain and his followers from that time forth.
28. And also it is that same being who put it into the hearts of the people to build a tower sufficiently high that they might get to heaven. And it was that same being who led on the people who came from that tower into this land; who spread the works of darkness and abominations over all the face of the land, until he dragged the people down to an entire destruction, and to an everlasting hell.
29. Yea, it is that same being who put it into the heart of Gadianton to still carry on the work of darkness, and of secret murder; and he has brought it forth from the beginning of man even down to this time.
30. And behold, it is he who is the author of all sin. And behold, he doth carry on his works of darkness and secret murder, and doth hand down their plots, and their oaths, and their covenants, and their plans of awful wickedness, from generation to generation according as he can get hold upon the hearts of the children of men.
31. And now behold, he had got great hold upon the hearts of the Nephites; yea, insomuch that they had become exceedingly wicked; yea, the more part of them had turned out of the way of righteousness, and did trample under their feet the commandments of God, and did turn unto their own ways, and did build up unto themselves idols of their gold and their silver.
32. And it came to pass that all these iniquities did come unto them in the space of not many years, insomuch that a more part of it had come unto them in the sixty and seventh year of the reign of the judges over the people of Nephi.
33. And they did grow in their iniquities in the sixty and eighth year also, to the great sorrow and lamentation of the righteous.
34. And thus we see that the Nephites did begin to dwindle in unbelief, and grow in wickedness and abominations, while the Lamanites began to grow exceedingly in the knowledge of their God; yea, they did begin to keep his statutes and commandments, and to walk in truth and uprightness before him.
35. And thus we see that the Spirit of the Lord began to withdraw from the Nephites, because of the wickedness and the hardness of their hearts.
36. And thus we see that the Lord began to pour out his Spirit upon the Lamanites, because of their easiness

Helaman 6:25–30

In his farewell instructions to his son Helaman, Alma warns him to withhold from the Nephites those references from Jaredite history pertaining to "all their oaths, and their covenants, and their agreements in their secret abominations; yea . . . ye shall keep these secret plans of their oaths and their covenants from this people." (Alma 37:27, 29.) But in Helaman 6, which covers a period about fifty years later than Alma's instructions to his son, it is obvious that the Nephites (especially the Gadianton Robbers) are in possession of these secret oaths and covenants. The historian hastens to inform us, however, that these "secret oaths and covenants did not come forth unto Gadianton from the records which were delivered unto Helaman; but behold, they were put into the heart of Gadianton by that same being who did entice our first parents to partake of the forbidden fruit." (Helaman 6:26.) In subsequent verses the historian makes it clear that these secret oaths and covenants came from the devil, "he who is the author of all sin." (Helaman 6:30.) (Ludlow)

and willingness to believe in his words.
37. And it came to pass that the Lamanites did hunt the band of
robbers of Gadianton; and they did preach the word of God among
the more wicked part of them, insomuch that this band of robbers
was utterly destroyed from among the Lamanites.
38. And it came to pass on the other hand, that the Nephites did
build them up and support them, beginning at the more wicked
part of them, until they had overspread all the land of the
Nephites, and had seduced the more part of the righteous until
they had come down to believe in their works and partake of their
spoils, and to join with them in their secret murders and combinations.
39. And thus they did obtain the sole management of the government, insomuch that they did trample under their feet and smite
and rend and turn their backs upon the poor and the meek, and the
humble followers of God.
40. And thus we see that they were in an awful state, and ripening
for an everlasting destruction.
41. And it came to pass that thus ended the sixty and eighth year
of the reign of the judges over the people of Nephi.

THE PROPHECY OF NEPHI, THE SON OF HELAMAN—*God threatens the people of Nephi that he will visit them in his anger, to their utter destruction except they repent of their wickedness. God smiteth the people of Nephi with pestilence; they repent and turn unto him. Samuel, a Lamanite, prophesies unto the Nephites. Comprising chapters 7 to 16 inclusive.*

CHAPTER 7

1. BEHOLD, now it came to pass in the sixty and ninth year of the
reign of the judges over the people of the Nephites, that Nephi,
the son of Helaman, returned to the land of Zarahemla from the
land northward.
2. For he had been forth among the people who were in the land
northward and did preach the word of God unto them, and did
prophesy many things unto them;
3. And they did reject all his words, insomuch that he could not
stay among them, but returned again unto the land of his nativity.
4. And seeing the people in a state of such awful wickedness, and
those Gadianton robbers filling the judgment-seats—having
usurped the power and authority of the land; laying aside the commandments of God, and not in the least aright before him; doing
no justice unto the children of men;
5. Condemning the righteous because of their righteousness; let-
ting the guilty and the wicked go unpunished because of their
money; and moreover to be held in office at the head of government, to rule and do according to their wills, that they might get
gain and glory of the world, and, moreover, that they might the
more easily commit adultery, and steal, and kill, and do according
to their own wills—
6. Now this great iniquity had come upon the Nephites, in the
space of not many years; and when Nephi saw it, his heart was
swollen with sorrow within his breast; and he did exclaim in the
agony of his soul:

POINT OF INTEREST

Stela 11, from Kaminaljuyu, Guatemala, shows a standing ruler with a world tree growing in his headdress.

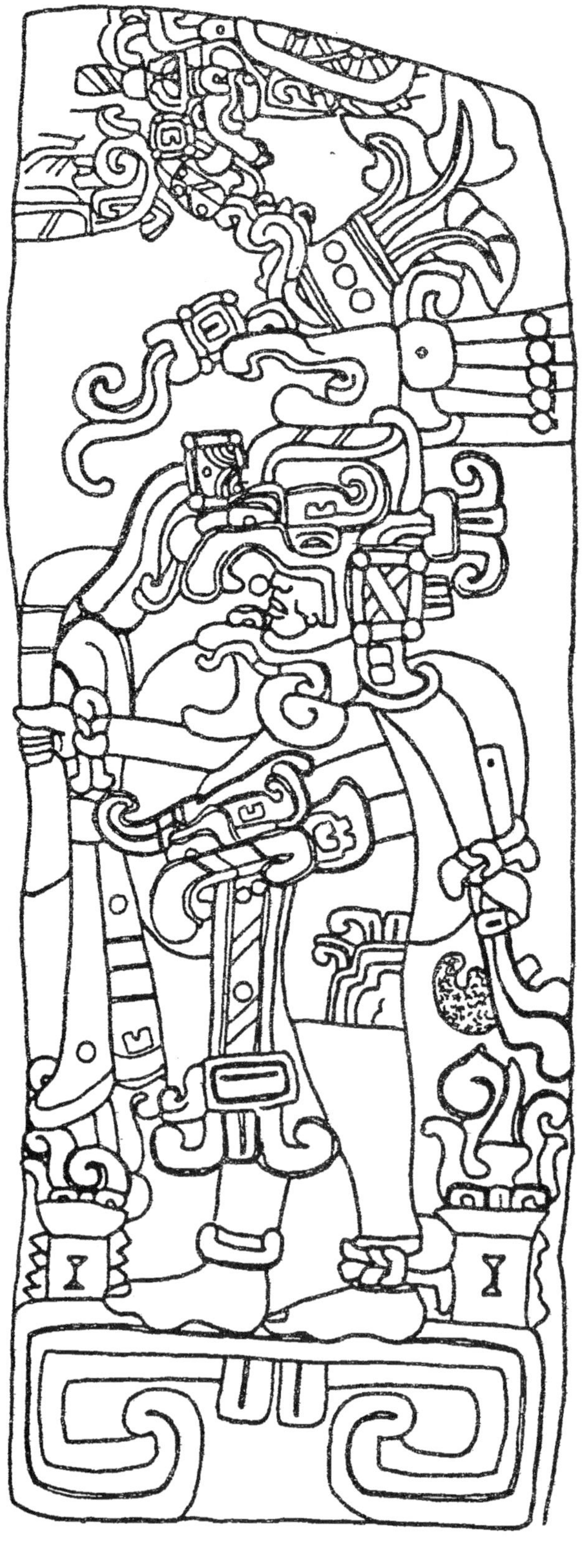

7. Oh, that I could have had my days in the days when my father Nephi first came out of the land of Jerusalem, that I could have joyed with him in the promised land; then were his people easy to be entreated, firm to keep the commandments of God, and slow to be led to do iniquity; and they were quick to hearken unto the words of the Lord—
8. Yea, if my days could have been in those days, then would my soul have had joy in the righteousness of my brethren.
9. But behold, I am consigned that these are my days, and that my soul shall be filled with sorrow because of this the wickedness of my brethren.
10. And behold, now it came to pass that it was upon a tower, which was in the garden of Nephi, which was by the highway which led to the chief market, which was in the city of Zarahemla; therefore, Nephi had bowed himself upon the tower which was in his garden, which tower was also near unto the garden gate by which led the highway.
11. And it came to pass that there were certain men passing by and saw Nephi as he was pouring out his soul unto God upon the tower; and they ran and told the people what they had seen, and the people came together in multitudes that they might know the cause of so great mourning for the wickedness of the people.
12. And now, when Nephi arose he beheld the multitudes of people who had gathered together.
13. And it came to pass that he opened his mouth and said unto them: Behold, why have ye gathered yourselves together? That I may tell you of your iniquities?
14. Yea, because I have got upon my tower that I might pour out my soul unto my God, because of the exceeding sorrow of my heart, which is because of your iniquities!
15. And because of my mourning and lamentation ye have gathered yourselves together, and do marvel; yea, and ye have great need to marvel; yea, ye ought to marvel because ye are given away that the devil has got so great hold upon your hearts.
16. Yea, how could you have given away to the enticing of him who is seeking to hurl away your souls down to everlasting misery and endless wo?
17. O repent ye, repent ye! Why will ye die? Turn ye, turn ye unto the Lord your God. Why has he forsaken you?
18. It is because you have hardened your hearts; yea, ye will not hearken unto the voice of the good shepherd; yea, ye have provoked him to anger against you.
19. And behold, instead of gathering you, except ye will repent, behold, he shall scatter you forth that ye shall become meat for dogs and wild beasts.
20. O, how could you have forgotten your God in the very day that he had delivered you?
21. But behold, it is to get gain, to be praised of men, yea, and that ye might get gold and silver. And ye have set your hearts upon the riches and the vain things of this world, for the which ye do murder, and plunder, and steal, and bear false witness against your neighbor, and do all manner of iniquity.
22. And for this cause wo shall come unto you except ye shall repent.

Helaman 7:7

The prophet Nephi (the son of Helaman) apparently believes in the sayings that "the grass is always greener on the other side of the fence" and "the good old days are best."

. . . However, students of the Book of Mormon probably remember that all things were not perfect during this early time period. This was the time of bitter hatred between the Lamanites and Nephites when they finally broke away from each other. In fact, Jacob (the brother of Nephi, who had grown up during this period) expressed his feelings concerning this same period as follows: ". . . we being a lonesome and a solemn people, wanderers, cast out from Jerusalem, born in tribulation, in a wilderness, and hated of our brethren, which caused wars and contentions; wherefore, we did mourn out our days." (Jacob 7:26.) (Ludlow)

Helaman 7:17

Repent and *turn* come from the same Hebrew word—shûwb—which means to "go back home" or to "turn away."

For if ye will not repent, behold, this great city, and also all those great cities which are round about, which are in the land of our possession, shall be taken away that ye shall have no place in them; for behold, the Lord will not grant unto you strength, as he has hitherto done, to withstand against your enemies.
23. For behold, thus saith the Lord: I will not show unto the wicked of my strength, to one more than the other, save it be unto those who repent of their sins, and hearken unto my words. Now therefore, I would that ye should behold, my brethren, that it shall be better for the Lamanites than for you except ye shall repent.
24. For behold, they are more righteous than you, for they have not sinned against that great knowledge which ye have received; therefore the Lord will be merciful unto them; yea, he will lengthen out their days and increase their seed, even when thou shalt be utterly destroyed except thou shalt repent.
25. Yea, wo be unto you because of that great abomination which has come among you; and ye have united yourselves unto it, yea, to that secret band which was established by Gadianton!
26. Yea, wo shall come unto you because of that pride which ye have suffered to enter your hearts, which has lifted you up beyond that which is good because of your exceedingly great riches!
27. Yea, wo be unto you because of your wickedness and abominations!
28. And except ye repent ye shall perish; yea, even your lands shall be taken from you, and ye shall be destroyed from off the face of the earth.
29. Behold now, I do not say that these things shall be, of myself, because it is not of myself that I know these things; but behold, I know that these things are true because the Lord God has made them known unto me, therefore I testify that they shall be.

CHAPTER 8

1. AND now it came to pass that when Nephi had said these words, behold, there were men who were judges, who also belonged to the secret band of Gadianton, and they were angry, and they cried out against him, saying unto the people: Why do ye not seize upon this man and bring him forth, that he may be condemned according to the crime which he has done?
2. Why seest thou this man, and hearest him revile against this people and against our law?
3. For behold, Nephi had spoken unto them concerning the corruptness of their law; yea, many things did Nephi speak which cannot be written; and nothing did he speak which was contrary to the commandments of God.
4. And those judges were angry with him because he spake plainly unto them concerning their secret works of darkness; nevertheless, they durst not lay their own hands upon him, for they feared the people lest they should cry out against them.
5. Therefore they did cry unto the people, saying: Why do you suffer this man to revile against us? For behold he doth condemn all this

Helaman 7:24

Brigham Young taught that those who have less knowledge are not as accountable as those who have greater knowledge. Thus, as specified in this verse, the Lord will be more merciful to those who, through no fault of their own, do not have the greater knowledge.

people, even unto destruction; yea, and also that these our great cities shall be taken from us, that we shall have no place in them.
6. And now we know that this is impossible, for behold, we are powerful, and our cities great, therefore our enemies can have no power over us.
7. And it came to pass that thus they did stir up the people to anger against Nephi, and raised contentions among them; for there were some who did cry out: Let this man alone, for he is a good man, and those things which he saith will surely come to pass except we repent;
8. Yea, behold, all the judgments will come upon us which he has testified unto us; for we know that he has testified aright unto us concerning our iniquities. And behold they are many, and he knoweth as well all things which shall befall us as he knoweth of our iniquities;
9. Yea, and behold, if he had not been a prophet he could not have testified concerning those things.
10. And it came to pass that those people who sought to destroy Nephi were compelled because of their fear, that they did not lay their hands on him; therefore he began again to speak unto them, seeing that he had gained favor in the eyes of some, insomuch that the remainder of them did fear.
11. Therefore he was constrained to speak more unto them saying: Behold, my brethren, have ye not read that God gave power unto one man, even Moses, to smite upon the waters of the Red Sea, and they parted hither and thither, insomuch that the Israelites, who were our fathers, came through upon dry ground, and the waters closed upon the armies of the Egyptians and swallowed them up?
12. And now behold, if God gave unto this man such power, then why should ye dispute among yourselves, and say that he hath given unto me no power whereby I may know concerning the judgments that shall come upon you except ye repent?
13. But, behold, ye not only deny my words, but ye also deny all the words which have been spoken by our fathers, and also the words which were spoken by this man, Moses, who had such great power given unto him, yea, the words which he hath spoken concerning the coming of the Messiah.
14. Yea, did he not bear record that the Son of God should come? And as he lifted up the brazen serpent in the wilderness, even so shall he be lifted up who should come.
15. And as many as should look upon that serpent should live, even so as many as should look upon the Son of God with faith, having a contrite spirit, might live, even unto that life which is eternal.
16. And now behold, Moses did not only testify of these things, but also all the holy prophets, from his days even to the days of Abraham.
17. Yea, and behold, Abraham saw of his coming, and was filled with gladness and did rejoice.
18. Yea, and behold I say unto you, that Abraham not only knew of these things, but there were many before the days of Abraham who were called by the order of God;

Helaman 8:11–13

The greatest prophet to grace this earth was Jesus Christ. He walked among the Jews, yet most of them failed to recognize their Messiah, their prophet. The Savior said: ". . . A prophet is not without honor, save in his own country, and in his own house" (Matt. 13:57). Then we see additional evidence of the Jews' rejection of the Savior. "Your father Abraham rejoiced to see my day: and he saw it, and was glad. Then said the Jews unto him, Thou are not yet fifty years old, and hast thou seen Abraham? Jesus said unto them, Verily, verily, I say unto you, Before Abraham was, I am. Then took they up stones to cast at him . . ." (John 8:56–59).

Many people honor dead prophets, but few recognize and honor living prophets. One reason so many of Heavenly Father's children will go to the telestial kingdom is their failure to recognize and heed the words of living prophets. (See D&C 76:98–101.) Many Nephites failed to recognize the Lord's living prophet Nephi. (O/C)

Helaman 8:13

This verse provides interesting and critical perspective to those of us who are in a position to sustain and obey our living prophet: when we reject the living prophet by failing to heed his words, we also reject all the prophets of God who came before him.

Helaman 8:13–15

The Savior . . . indicated that the "brazen serpent lifted up by Moses" was a type (shadow, or example) of his own crucifixion when he said: "And as Moses lifted up the serpent in the wilderness, even so must the Son of man be lifted up: That whosoever believeth in him should not perish, but have eternal life." (John 3:14–15.)

Some scholars of the Book of Mormon have wondered if this story of the serpent as given in the book of Helaman did not account for the "serpent motif" in the art and architecture of some of the American Indian cultures. Also, it is of interest to note that one of the names given by some of the American Indians to the great white God who appeared out of the eastern sky was the name of *Quetzalcoatl*, which literally means the bird-serpent, or the serpent of precious plumage. (Ludlow)

yea, even after the order of his Son; and this that it should be shown
unto the people, a great many thousand years before his coming, that
even redemption should come unto them.
19. And now I would that ye should know, that even since the days
of Abraham there have been many prophets that have testified
these things; yea, behold, the prophet Zenos did testify boldly; for
the which he was slain.
20. And behold, also Zenock, and also Ezias, and also Isaiah, and
Jeremiah, (Jeremiah being that same prophet who testified of the
destruction of Jerusalem) and now we know that Jerusalem was
destroyed according to the words of Jeremiah. O then why not the
Son of God come, according to his prophecy?
21. And now will you dispute that Jerusalem was destroyed? Will
ye say that the sons of Zedekiah were not slain, all except it were
Mulek? Yea, and do ye not behold that the seed of Zedekiah are
with us, and they were driven out of the land of Jerusalem? But
behold, this is not all—
22. Our father Lehi was driven out of Jerusalem because he testified of these things. Nephi also testified of these things, and also
almost all of our fathers, even down to this time; yea, they have
testified of the coming of Christ, and have looked forward, and
have rejoiced in his day which is to come.
23. And behold, he is God, and he is with them, and he did manifest himself unto them, that they were redeemed by him; and they
gave unto him glory, because of that which is to come.
24. And now, seeing ye know these things and cannot deny them
except ye shall lie, therefore in this ye have sinned, for ye have
rejected all these things, notwithstanding so many evidences
which ye have received; yea, even ye have received all things, both
things in heaven, and all things which are in the earth, as a witness that they are true.
25. But behold, ye have rejected the truth, and rebelled against
your holy God; and even at this time, instead of laying up for yourselves treasures in heaven, where nothing doth corrupt, and where
nothing can come which is unclean, ye are heaping up for yourselves wrath against the day of judg-
ment.
26. Yea, even at this time ye are
ripening, because of your murders
and your fornication and wickedness, for everlasting destruction;
yea, and except ye repent it will
come unto you soon.
27. Yea, behold it is now even at
your doors; yea, go ye in unto the
judgment-seat, and search; and
behold, your judge is murdered, and
he lieth in his blood; and he hath
been murdered by his brother, who
seeketh to sit in the judgment-seat.
28. And behold, they both belong
to your secret band, whose author is
Gadianton and the evil one who
seeketh to destroy the souls of men.

Helaman 8:19–20

Four ancient prophets whose writings do not appear in our present Bible are mentioned in the Book of Mormon. These four prophets and the Book of Mormon references to them are as follows: (1) Zenos, who is mentioned 12 times in the Book of Mormon; . . . (2) Zenock, who is mentioned five times in the Book of Mormon . . . ; (3) Neum, who is mentioned once in the Book of Mormon; 4) Ezias, who is mentioned once in the Book of Mormon, in Helaman 8:20. The reference in Helaman 8:19–20 to three of these prophets seems to indicate they lived sometime between the "days of Abraham" and the time of Isaiah. (Ludlow)

Helaman 8:21

Mulek was the son of Zedekiah, the king of Judah, who was spared at the time of the Babylonian captivity and who later came to the Americas. The descendants of Mulek were included among the people of Zarahemla, and later they were numbered among the Nephites. Thus, among the combined Nephite-Lamanite-Mulekite peoples are represented at least three of the twelve tribes of ancient Israel: (1) the tribe of Manasseh, represented by the descendants of Lehi; (2) the tribe of Ephraim, represented by the descendants of Ishmael; (3) the tribe of Judah, represented by the descendants of Mulek. (For further information concerning the lineage of Lehi, Ishmael, and Mulek, see the material listed after Helaman 6:10 and after Alma 10:3.) (Ludlow)

CHAPTER 9

1. BEHOLD, now it came to pass that when Nephi had spoken these words, certain men who were among them ran to the judgment-seat; yea, even there were five who went, and they said among themselves, as they went:

2. Behold, now we will know of a surety whether this man be a prophet and God hath commanded him to prophesy such marvelous things unto us. Behold, we do not believe that he hath; yea, we do not believe that he is a prophet; nevertheless, if this thing which he has said concerning the chief judge be true, that he be dead, then will we believe that the other words which he has spoken are true.

3. And it came to pass that they ran in their might, and came in unto the judgment-seat; and behold, the chief judge had fallen to the earth, and did lie in his blood.

4. And now behold, when they saw this they were astonished exceedingly, insomuch that they fell to the earth; for they had not believed the words which Nephi had spoken concerning the chief judge.

5. But now, when they saw they believed, and fear came upon them lest all the judgments which Nephi had spoken should come upon the people; therefore they did quake, and had fallen to the earth.

6. Now, immediately when the judge had been murdered—he being stabbed by his brother by a garb of secrecy, and he fled, and the servants ran and told the people, raising the cry of murder among them;

7. And behold the people did gather themselves together unto the place of the judgment-seat—and behold, to their astonishment they saw those five men who had fallen to the earth.

8. And now behold, the people knew nothing concerning the multitude who had gathered together at the garden of Nephi; therefore they said among themselves: These men are they who have murdered the judge, and God has smitten them that they could not flee from us.

9. And it came to pass that they laid hold on them, and bound them and cast them into prison. And there was a proclamation sent abroad that the judge was slain, and that the murderers had been taken and were cast into prison.

10. And it came to pass that on the morrow the people did assemble themselves together to mourn and to fast, at the burial of the great chief judge who had been slain.

11. And thus also those judges who were at the garden of Nephi, and heard his words, were also gathered together at the burial.

12. And it came to pass that they inquired among the people, saying: Where are the five who were sent to inquire concerning the chief judge whether he was dead? And they answered and said: Concerning this five whom ye say ye have sent, we know not; but there are five who are the murderers, whom we have cast into prison.

13. And it came to pass that the judges desired that they should be brought; and they were brought, and behold they were the five who were sent; and behold the judges inquired of them to know, concerning the matter, and they told them all that they had done, saying:

14. We ran and came to the place of the judgment-seat, and when we saw all things even as Nephi had testified, we were astonished insomuch

POINT OF INTEREST

Machu Picchu, or "Old Peak," is an Incan city on a mountain ridge above the Urubamba Valley in Peru. It was brought back to international attention by archaeologist Hiram Bingham in 1911, who made the first scientific confirmation of the site. Machu Picchu is probably the most familiar symbol of the Incan Empire and is often referred to as the "lost city of the Incas."

that we fell to the earth; and when we were recovered from our
astonishment, behold they cast us into prison.
15. Now, as for the murder of this man, we know not who has done
it; and only this much we know, we ran and came according as ye
desired, and behold he was dead, according to the words of Nephi.
16. And now it came to pass that the judges did expound the matter unto the people, and did cry out against Nephi, saying: Behold,
we know that this Nephi must have agreed with some one to slay
the judge, and then he might declare it unto us, that he might convert us unto his faith, that he might raise himself to be a great man,
chosen of God, and a prophet.
17. And now behold, we will detect this man, and he shall confess
his fault and make known unto us the true murderer of this judge.
18. And it came to pass that the five were liberated on the day of
the burial. Nevertheless, they did rebuke the judges in the words
which they had spoken against Nephi, and did contend with them
one by one, insomuch that they did confound them.
19. Nevertheless, they caused that Nephi should be taken and
bound and brought before the multitude, and they began to question him in divers ways that they might cross him, that they might
accuse him to death—
20. Saying unto him: Thou art confederate; who is this man that
hath done this murder? Now tell us, and acknowledge thy fault;
saying, Behold here is money; and also we will grant unto thee thy
life if thou wilt tell us, and acknowledge the agreement which thou
hast made with him.
21. But Nephi said unto them: O ye fools, ye uncircumcised of
heart, ye blind, and ye stiffnecked people, do ye know how long the
Lord your God will suffer you that ye shall go on in this your way
of sin?
22. O ye ought to begin to howl and mourn, because of the great
destruction which at this time doth await you, except ye shall
repent.
23. Behold ye say that I have agreed with a man that he should
murder Seezoram, our chief judge. But behold, I say unto you, that
this is because I have testified unto you that ye might know concerning this thing; yea, even for a witness unto you, that I did
know of the wickedness and abominations which are among you.
24. And because I have done this, ye say that I have agreed with a
man that he should do this thing; yea, because I showed unto you
this sign ye are angry with me, and seek to destroy my life.
25. And now behold, I will show unto you another sign, and see if
ye will in this thing seek to destroy me.
26. Behold I say unto you: Go to the house of Seantum, who is the
brother of Seezoram, and say unto him—
27. Has Nephi, the pretended prophet, who doth prophesy so
much evil concerning this people, agreed with thee, in the which
ye have murdered Seezoram, who is your brother?
28. And behold, he shall say unto you, Nay.
29. And ye shall say unto him: Have ye murdered your brother?
30. And he shall stand with fear, and wist not what to say. And
behold, he shall deny unto you; and he shall make as if he were
astonished; nevertheless, he shall declare unto you that he is innocent.
31. But behold, ye shall examine

him, and ye shall find blood upon the skirts of his cloak.
32. And when ye have seen this, ye shall say: From whence cometh this blood? Do we not know that it is the blood of your brother?
33. And then shall he tremble, and shall look pale, even as if death had come upon him.
34. And then shall ye say: Because of this fear and this paleness which has come upon your face, behold, we know that thou art guilty.
35. And then shall greater fear come upon him; and then shall he confess unto you, and deny no more that he has done this murder.
36. And then shall he say unto you, that I, Nephi, know nothing concerning the matter save it were given unto me by the power of God. And then shall ye know that I am an honest man, and that I am sent unto you from God.
37. And it came to pass that they went and did, even according as Nephi had said unto them. And behold, the words which he had said were true; for according to the words he did deny; and also according to the words he did confess.
38. And he was brought to prove that he himself was the very murderer, insomuch that the five were set at liberty, and also was Nephi.
39. And there were some of the Nephites who believed on the words of Nephi; and there were some also, who believed because of the testimony of the five, for they had been converted while they were in prison.
40. And now there were some among the people, who said that Nephi was a prophet.
41. And there were others who said: Behold, he is a god, for except he was a god he could not know of all things. For behold, he has told us the thoughts of our hearts, and also has told us things; and even he has brought unto our knowledge the true murderer of our chief judge.

CHAPTER 10

1. AND it came to pass that there arose a division among the people, insomuch that they divided hither and thither and went their ways, leaving Nephi alone, as he was standing in the midst of them.
2. And it came to pass that Nephi went his way towards his own house, pondering upon the things which the Lord had shown unto him.
3. And it came to pass as he was thus pondering—being much cast down because of the wickedness of the people of the Nephites, their secret works of darkness, and their murderings, and their plunderings, and all manner of iniquities—and it came to pass as he was thus pondering in his heart, behold, a voice came unto him saying:
4. Blessed art thou, Nephi, for those things which thou hast done; for I have beheld how thou hast with unwearyingness declared the word, which I have given unto thee, unto this people. And thou hast not feared them, and hast not sought thine own life, but hast sought my will, and to keep my commandments.
5. And now, because thou hast done this with such unwearyingness, behold, I will bless thee forever; and I will make thee mighty in word and in deed, in faith and in works; yea, even that all things shall be done

Helaman 10:1–4
One on God's side is a majority (Geoffrey C. Ward, Kenneth Burns, and Richard Burns, *The Civil War* [New York: Vintage, 1994], 399).

unto thee according to thy word, for thou shalt not ask that which is contrary to my will.
6. Behold, thou art Nephi, and I am God. Behold, I declare it unto thee in the presence of mine angels, that ye shall have power over this people, and shall smite the earth with famine, and with pestilence, and destruction, according to the wickedness of this people.
7. Behold, I give unto you power, that whatsoever ye shall seal on earth shall be sealed in heaven; and whatsoever ye shall loose on earth shall be loosed in heaven; and thus shall ye have power among this people.
8. And thus, if ye shall say unto this temple it shall be rent in twain, it shall be done.
9. And if ye shall say unto this mountain, Be thou cast down and become smooth, it shall be done.
10. And behold, if ye shall say that God shall smite this people, it shall come to pass.
11. And now behold, I command you, that ye shall go and declare unto this people, that thus saith the Lord God, who is the Almighty: Except ye repent ye shall be smitten, even unto destruction.
12. And behold, now it came to pass that when the Lord had spoken these words unto Nephi, he did stop and did not go unto his own house, but did return unto the multitudes who were scattered about upon the face of the land, and began to declare unto them the word of the Lord which had been spoken unto him, concerning their destruction if they did not repent.
13. Now behold, notwithstanding that great miracle which Nephi had done in telling them concerning the death of the chief judge, they did harden their hearts and did not hearken unto the words of the Lord.
14. Therefore Nephi did declare unto them the word of the Lord, saying: Except ye repent, thus saith the Lord, ye shall be smitten even unto destruction.
15. And it came to pass that when Nephi had declared unto them the word, behold, they did still harden their hearts and would not hearken unto his words; therefore they did revile against him, and did seek to lay their hands upon him that they might cast him into prison.
16. But behold, the power of God was with him, and they could not take him to cast him into prison, for he was taken by the Spirit and conveyed away out of the midst of them.
17. And it came to pass that thus he did go forth in the Spirit, from multitude to multitude, declaring the word of God, even until he had declared it unto them all, or sent it forth among all the people.
18. And it came to pass that they would not hearken unto his words; and there began to be contentions, insomuch that they were divided against themselves and began to slay one another with the sword.
19. And thus ended the seventy and first year of the reign of the judges over the people of Nephi.

CHAPTER 11

Helaman 10:6–9

Because of the righteousness and great faith of Nephi, the Lord promised him: "Behold, I give unto you power, that whatsoever ye shall seal on earth shall be sealed in heaven; and whatsoever ye shall loose on earth shall be loosed in heaven; and thus shall ye have power among this people." (Helaman 10:7.) This is the same sealing power of the priesthood that was later promised by the Savior to Peter on the eastern continent: "And I will give unto thee the keys of the kingdom of heaven: and whatsoever thou shalt bind on earth shall be bound in heaven: and whatsoever thou shalt loose on earth shall be loosed in heaven." (Matthew 16:19.) This sealing power can be used not only to seal things on earth so they will be sealed in heaven (such as priesthood ordinances, marriages, etc.), but also actually to "seal the heavens" so it cannot rain. This power was used by Nephi during the drought mentioned in Helaman 11:4–17. (Ludlow)

Helaman 10:16–17

The term "in the Spirit," which is used to indicate how Nephi taught the people, evidently means that Nephi went forth "by the power of the Spirit." It does *not* mean Nephi's body was separated from his spirit; rather it probably means he was protected in his missionary work by the power of the Spirit. (Ludlow)

1. AND now it came to pass in the seventy and second year of the reign of the judges that the contentions did increase, insomuch that there were wars throughout all the land among all the people of Nephi.
2. And it was this secret band of robbers who did carry on this work of destruction and wickedness. And this war did last all that year; and in the seventy and third year it did also last.
3. And it came to pass that in this year Nephi did cry unto the Lord, saying:
4. O Lord, do not suffer that this people shall be destroyed by the sword; but O Lord, rather let there be a famine in the land, to stir them up in remembrance of the Lord their God, and perhaps they will repent and turn unto thee.
5. And so it was done, according to the words of Nephi. And there was a great famine upon the land, among all the people of Nephi. And thus in the seventy and fourth year the famine did continue, and the work of destruction did cease by the sword but became sore by famine.
6. And this work of destruction did also continue in the seventy and fifth year. For the earth was smitten that it was dry, and did not yield forth grain in the season of grain; and the whole earth was smitten, even among the Lamanites as well as among the Nephites, so that they were smitten that they did perish by thousands in the more wicked parts of the land.
7. And it came to pass that the people saw that they were about to perish by famine, and they began to remember the Lord their God; and they began to remember the words of Nephi.
8. And the people began to plead with their chief judges and their leaders, that they would say unto Nephi: Behold, we know that thou art a man of God, and therefore cry unto the Lord our God that he turn away from us this famine, lest all the words which thou hast spoken concerning our destruction be fulfilled.
9. And it came to pass that the judges did say unto Nephi, according to the words which had been desired. And it came to pass that when Nephi saw that the people had repented and did humble themselves in sackcloth, he cried again unto the Lord, saying:
10. O Lord, behold this people repenteth; and they have swept away the band of Gadianton from amongst them insomuch that they have become extinct, and they have concealed their secret plans in the earth.
11. Now, O Lord, because of this their humility wilt thou turn away thine anger, and let thine anger be appeased in the destruction of those wicked men whom thou hast already destroyed.
12. O Lord, wilt thou turn away thine anger, yea, thy fierce anger, and cause that this famine may cease in this land.
13. O Lord, wilt thou hearken unto me, and cause that it may be done according to my words, and send forth rain upon the face of the earth, that she may bring forth her fruit, and her grain in the season of grain.
14. O Lord, thou didst hearken unto my words when I said, Let there be a famine, that the pestilence of the sword might cease; and I know that thou wilt, even at this time, hearken unto my words, for thou saidst that: If this people repent I will spare them.
15. Yea, O Lord, and thou seest that they have repented, because of the famine and the pestilence and

Helaman 11:4

As the leader of his people, Nephi requested that the Lord cause a famine to afflict the people. Why would a leader request that affliction be poured out upon his people? Nephi knew that the only way the people would be driven to repentance would be through such an affliction—and his greatest desire was to see his people repent and return to righteousness.

destruction which has come unto them.
16. And now, O Lord, wilt thou turn away thine anger, and try again if they will serve thee? And if so, O Lord, thou canst bless them according to thy words which thou hast said.
17. And it came to pass that in the seventy and sixth year the Lord did turn away his anger from the people, and caused that rain should fall upon the earth, insomuch that it did bring forth her fruit in the season of her fruit. And it came to pass that it did bring forth her grain in the season of her grain.
18. And behold, the people did rejoice and glorify God, and the whole face of the land was filled with rejoicing; and they did no more seek to destroy Nephi, but they did esteem him as a great prophet, and a man of God, having great power and authority given unto him from God.
19. And behold, Lehi, his brother, was not a whit behind him as to things pertaining to righteousness.
20. And thus it did come to pass that the people of Nephi began to prosper again in the land, and began to build up their waste places, and began to multiply and spread, even until they did cover the whole face of the land, both on the northward and on the southward, from the sea west to the sea east.
21. And it came to pass that the seventy and sixth year did end in peace. And the seventy and seventh year began in peace; and the church did spread throughout the face of all the land; and the more part of the people, both the Nephites and the Lamanites, did belong to the church; and they did have exceedingly great peace in the land; and thus ended the seventy and seventh year.
22. And also they had peace in the seventy and eighth year, save it were a few contentions concerning the points of doctrine which had been laid down by the prophets.
23. And in the seventy and ninth year there began to be much strife. But it came to pass that Nephi and Lehi, and many of their brethren who knew concerning the true points of doctrine, having many revelations daily, therefore they did preach unto the people, insomuch that they did put an end to their strife in that same year.
24. And it came to pass that in the eightieth year of the reign of the judges over the people of Nephi, there were a certain number of the dissenters from the people of Nephi, who had some years before gone over unto the Lamanites, and taken upon themselves the name of Lamanites, and also a certain number who were real descendants of the Lamanites, being stirred up to anger by them, or by those dissenters, therefore they commenced a war with their brethren.
25. And they did commit murder and plunder; and then they would retreat back into the mountains, and into the wilderness and secret places, hiding themselves that they could not be discovered, receiving daily an addition to their numbers, inasmuch as there were dissenters that went forth unto them.
26. And thus in time, yea, even in the space of not many years, they became an exceedingly great band of robbers; and they did search out all the secret plans of Gadianton; and thus they became robbers of Gadianton.
27. Now behold, these robbers did make great havoc, yea, even great destruction among the people of Nephi, and also among the people of the Lamanites.

Helaman 11:23

Many who read verse 23 might wonder how they themselves can qualify to receive "many revelations daily," as did Nephi, Lehi, and their brethren. Elder Bruce R. McConkie taught that the way to qualify for such revelation begins with reading the scriptures daily and doing all we can to place ourselves in tune with the Lord. Once we become immersed in the scriptures and in tune with the Lord, He will open our mind and let new truths flood in—allowing us the privilege of learning added things in the spirit of revelation.

28. And it came to pass that it was expedient that there should be a stop put to this work of destruction; therefore they sent an army of strong men into the wilderness and upon the mountains to search out this band of robbers, and to destroy them.
29. But behold, it came to pass that in that same year they were driven back even into their own lands. And thus ended the eightieth year of the reign of the judges over the people of Nephi.
30. And it came to pass in the commencement of the eighty and first year they did go forth again against this band of robbers, and did destroy many; and they were also visited with much destruction.
31. And they were again obliged to return out of the wilderness and out of the mountains unto their own lands, because of the exceeding greatness of the numbers of those robbers who infested the mountains and the wilderness.
32. And it came to pass that thus ended this year. And the robbers did still increase and wax strong, insomuch that they did defy the whole armies of the Nephites, and also of the Lamanites; and they did cause great fear to come unto the people upon all the face of the land.
33. Yea, for they did visit many parts of the land, and did do great destruction unto them; yea, did kill many, and did carry away others captive into the wilderness, yea, and more especially their women and their children.
34. Now this great evil, which came unto the people because of their iniquity, did stir them up again in remembrance of the Lord their God.
35. And thus ended the eighty and first year of the reign of the judges.
36. And in the eighty and second year they began again to forget the Lord their God. And in the eighty and third year they began to wax strong in iniquity. And in the eighty and fourth year they did not mend their ways.
37. And it came to pass in the eighty and fifth year they did wax stronger and stronger in their pride, and in their wickedness; and thus they were ripening again for destruction.
38. And thus ended the eighty and fifth year.

CHAPTER 12

1. AND thus we can behold how false, and also the unsteadiness of the hearts of the children of men; yea, we can see that the Lord in his great infinite goodness doth bless and prosper those who put their trust in him.
2. Yea, and we may see at the very time when he doth prosper his people, yea, in the increase of their fields, their flocks and their herds, and in gold, and in silver, and in all manner of precious things of every kind and art; sparing their lives, and delivering them out of the hands of their enemies; softening the hearts of their enemies that they should not declare wars against them; yea, and in fine, doing all things for the welfare and happiness of his people; yea, then is the time that they do harden their hearts, and do forget the Lord their God, and do trample under their feet the

Helaman 11:37

Pride is a repeated theme in the Book of Mormon and a sin we need to zealously guard against. President Ezra Taft Benson described the characteristics of pride as:

- Being extremely competitive with our fellow man
- Pitting our will against the will of God
- Wishing God would agree with our point of view
- Being more afraid of man's judgment than of God's judgment

Helaman 12

In *The Decline and Fall of the Roman Empire* (New York: Harper Brothers Publishers, 1851), celebrated British historian Edward Gibbons attributed the fall of the empire to the following factors:

1. The undermining of the home, which is the basic unit of society.
2. Increasingly higher taxes, with public money being used to provide food and entertainment for the public.
3. A delirious craze for pleasure, with sporting contests becoming increasingly more violent.
4. The building of huge arsenals of weapons, when the real enemy was the decadence of the people.
5. The decay of religion, with people losing touch with the spiritual side of life.

Many historians have made the case that great civilizations are never conquered by their enemies until they have been conquered from within. This sobering list of factors that led to the fall of one of the world's greatest empires should cause us to take a serious look at our own society with an effort to make necessary course corrections while we can.

Helaman 12:2–3

The Nephites exhibited a trait common to so many of us from time to time: we forget the goodness of God and fail to honor our covenants with full devotion. In this we offend God most grievously (see D&C 59:21). . . .

After a brief resurgence of spirituality, the people again began to fall prey to the culture and practices. The people continued on with their misguided decline in the process of "ripening again for destruction" (Hel. 11:37). It is at this point that Mormon, weary perhaps at the distressing cycle of pride that manifests itself repeatedly in the chronicle of the people, gave vent to the anguish of his soul. . . . The great prophet-historian expressed in poetic cadence his unmitigated distress over the hard-heartedness of the people after so many witnesses had been proffered them and so many blessings bestowed. Even the dust of the earth moves under God's command, he pointed out—but mankind, in its iniquity, refuses to move according to the patterns of truth. That is the reason the plan of repentance was initiated: "for this cause, that men might be saved, hath repentance been declared. Therefore, blessed are they who will repent and hearken unto the voice of the Lord their God; for these are they that shall be saved" (Hel. 12:22–23).

Holy One—yea, and this because of their ease, and their exceedingly great prosperity.
3. And thus we see that except the Lord doth chasten his people with many afflictions, yea, except he doth visit them with death and with terror, and with famine and with all manner of pestilence, they will not remember him.
4. O how foolish, and how vain, and how evil, and devilish, and how quick to do iniquity, and how slow to do good, are the children of men; yea, how quick to hearken unto the words of the evil one, and to set their hearts upon the vain things of the world!
5. Yea, how quick to be lifted up in pride; yea, how quick to boast, and do all manner of that which is iniquity; and how slow are they to remember the Lord their God, and to give ear unto his counsels, yea, how slow to walk in wisdom's paths!
6. Behold, they do not desire that the Lord their God, who hath created them, should rule and reign over them; notwithstanding his great goodness and his mercy towards them, they do set at naught his counsels, and they will not that he should be their guide.
7. O how great is the nothingness of the children of men; yea, even they are less than the dust of the earth.
8. For behold, the dust of the earth moveth hither and thither, to the dividing asunder, at the command of our great and everlasting God.
9. Yea, behold at his voice do the hills and the mountains tremble and quake.
10. And by the power of his voice they are broken up, and become smooth, yea, even like unto a valley.
11. Yea, by the power of his voice doth the whole earth shake;
12. Yea, by the power of his voice, do the foundations rock, even to the very center.
13. Yea, and if he say unto the earth—Move—it is moved.
14. Yea, if he say unto the earth—Thou shalt go back, that it lengthen out the day for many hours—it is done;
15. And thus, according to his word the earth goeth back, and it appeareth unto man that the sun standeth still; yea, and behold, this is so; for surely it is the earth that moveth and not the sun.
16. And behold, also, if he say unto the waters of the great deep—Be thou dried up—it is done.
17. Behold, if he say unto this mountain—Be thou raised up, and come over and fall upon that city, that it be buried up—behold it is done.
18. And behold, if a man hide up a treasure in the earth, and the Lord shall say—Let it be accursed, because of the iniquity of him who hath hid it up—behold, it shall be accursed.
19. And if the Lord shall say—Be thou accursed, that no man shall find thee from this time henceforth and forever—behold, no man getteth it henceforth and forever.

President Harold B. Lee said, "It is frightening to observe that in places where there is the greater prosperity, there is the unmistakable evidence that, like the peoples of other dispensations, when they prosper they forget God. They are seemingly rich in things that money can buy, but they are devoid of most of the precious things money cannot buy." (P/A)

Helaman 12:2–8

This statement should not be interpreted that Mormon believes men are worth even less than the dust of the earth. Rather Mormon is saying that men sometimes appear to be less wise than the dust of the earth. When the Lord tells the dust of the earth to move, it obeys, whereas when the Lord tells men to do something, they frequently do not obey. (Ludlow)

20. And behold, if the Lord shall say unto a man—Because of thine iniquities, thou shalt be accursed forever—it shall be done.
21. And if the Lord shall say—Because of thine iniquities thou shalt be cut off from my presence—he will cause that it shall be so.
22. And wo unto him to whom he shall say this, for it shall be unto him that will do iniquity, and he cannot be saved; therefore, for this cause, that men might be saved, hath repentance been declared.
23. Therefore, blessed are they who will repent and hearken unto the voice of the Lord their God; for these are they that shall be saved.
24. And may God grant, in his great fulness, that men might be brought unto repentance and good works, that they might be restored unto grace for grace, according to their works.
25. And I would that all men might be saved. But we read that in the great and last day there are some who shall be cast out, yea, who shall be cast off from the presence of the Lord;
26. Yea, who shall be consigned to a state of endless misery, fulfilling the words which say: They that have done good shall have everlasting life; and they that have done evil shall have everlasting damnation. And thus it is. Amen.

The prophecy of Samuel, the Lamanite, to the Nephites. Comprising chapters 13 to 15 inclusive.

CHAPTER 13

1. AND now it came to pass in the eighty and sixth year, the Nephites did still remain in wickedness, yea, in great wickedness, while the Lamanites did observe strictly to keep the commandments of God, according to the law of Moses.
2. And it came to pass that in this year there was one Samuel, a Lamanite, came into the land of Zarahemla, and began to preach unto the people. And it came to pass that he did preach, many days, repentance unto the people, and they did cast him out, and he was about to return to his own land.
3. But behold, the voice of the Lord came unto him, that he should return again, and prophesy unto the people whatsoever things should come into his heart.
4. And it came to pass that they would not suffer that he should enter into the city; therefore he went and got upon the wall thereof, and stretched forth his hand and cried with a loud voice, and prophesied unto the people whatsoever things the Lord put into his heart.
5. And he said unto them: Behold, I, Samuel, a Lamanite, do speak the words of the Lord which he doth put into my heart; and behold he hath put it into my heart to say unto this people that the sword of justice hangeth over this people; and four hundred years pass not away save the sword of justice falleth upon this people.
6. Yea, heavy destruction awaiteth

Helaman 13–16

. . . [H]is entire sermon was given under the influence of the Lord, and it contains the following remarkable prophecies in rather detailed form:

The eventual destruction of the Nephites . . .

The destruction of the city of Zarahemla . . .

The birth of the Savior . . .

The death of the Savior . . .

The treasures of the people shall become slippery . . .

Samuel's final warning to the Nephites was that the Lord would "utterly destroy them" unless they repented of their sins. (Helaman 15:17.) Some of the people heeded this warning by Samuel, and they sought out Nephi, confessed their sins, and desired to be baptized. (Helaman 16:1.) Others, however, did not believe the words of Samuel; they became angry at him and tried to kill him. (Helaman 16:2, 6–8.). (Ludlow)

Helaman 13:6

The Lord has predicted wars and rumors of wars (see D&C 45:26) in the latter days. President Ezra Taft Benson taught that the only way to stay the destructive forces of war and calamity was true repentance.

this people, and it surely cometh unto this people, and nothing can save this people save it be repentance and faith on the Lord Jesus Christ, who surely shall come into the world, and shall suffer many things and shall be slain for his people.
7. And behold, an angel of the Lord hath declared it unto me, and he did bring glad tidings to my soul. And behold, I was sent unto you to declare it unto you also, that ye might have glad tidings; but behold ye would not receive me.
8. Therefore, thus saith the Lord: Because of the hardness of the hearts of the people of the Nephites, except they repent I will take away my word from them, and I will withdraw my Spirit from them, and I will suffer them no longer, and I will turn the hearts of their brethren against them.
9. And four hundred years shall not pass away before I will cause that they shall be smitten; yea, I will visit them with the sword and with famine and with pestilence.
10. Yea, I will visit them in my fierce anger, and there shall be those of the fourth generation who shall live, of your enemies, to behold your utter destruction; and this shall surely come except ye repent, saith the Lord; and those of the fourth generation shall visit your destruction.
11. But if ye will repent and return unto the Lord your God I will turn away mine anger, saith the Lord; yea, thus saith the Lord, blessed are they who will repent and turn unto me, but wo unto him that repenteth not.
12. Yea, wo unto this great city of Zarahemla; for behold, it is because of those who are righteous that it is saved; yea, wo unto this great city, for I perceive, saith the Lord, that there are many, yea, even the more part of this great city, that will harden their hearts against me, saith the Lord.
13. But blessed are they who will repent, for them will I spare. But behold, if it were not for the righteous who are in this great city, behold, I would cause that fire should come down out of heaven and destroy it.
14. But behold, it is for the righteous' sake that it is spared. But behold, the time cometh, saith the Lord, that when ye shall cast out the righteous from among you, then shall ye be ripe for destruction; yea, wo be unto this great city, because of the wickedness and abominations which are in her.
15. Yea, and wo be unto the city of Gideon, for the wickedness and abominations which are in her.
16. Yea, and wo be unto all the cities which are in the land round about, which are possessed by the Nephites, because of the wickedness and abominations which are in them.
17. And behold, a curse shall come upon the land, saith the Lord of Hosts, because of the peoples' sake who are upon the land, yea, because of their wickedness and their abominations.
18. And it shall come to pass, saith the Lord of Hosts, yea, our great and true God, that whoso shall hide up treasures in the earth shall find them again no more, because of the great curse of the land, save he be a righteous man and shall hide it up unto the Lord.
19. For I will, saith the Lord, that they shall hide up their treasures

Helaman 13:8; 4:24; 6:35

The Prophet Joseph Smith appeared to Brigham Young following Joseph's death and instructed his successor as follows: "Tell the people to be humble and faithful, and be sure to keep the Spirit of the Lord and it will lead them right. . . . They can tell the Spirit of the Lord from all other spirits; it will whisper peace and joy to their souls; it will take malice, hatred, strife and all evil from their hearts; and their whole desire will be to do good . . ." (Brigham Young, *Journal History*, 23 Feb. 1847).

Helaman 13:8; 4:24; 6:35

The gift of the Holy Ghost is one of the primary things that distinguish The Church of Jesus Christ of Latter-day Saints from other churches; without it, this Church would be the same as all the other churches on the earth today. The gift of the Holy Ghost is as important to our souls as food and water are to our physical bodies—without it, the soul loses the capacity to thrive, just as the body will die without nourishment.

Helaman 13:13

Many times, the wicked were spared terrible destruction because God considered the few righteous who were among the wicked. Even Sodom and Gomorrah would have been spared if there had been even ten righteous among them (see Genesis 18:23–33).

unto me; and cursed be they who hide not up their treasures unto
me; for none hideth up their treasures unto me save it be the righteous; and he that hideth not up his treasures unto me, cursed is he,
and also the treasure, and none shall redeem it because of the curse
of the land.
20. And the day shall come that they shall hide up their treasures,
because they have set their hearts upon riches; and because they
have set their hearts upon their riches, and will hide up their treasures when they shall flee before their enemies; because they will
not hide them up unto me, cursed be they and also their treasures;
and in that day shall they be smitten, saith the Lord.
21. Behold ye, the people of this great city, and hearken unto my
words; yea, hearken unto the words which the Lord saith; for
behold, he saith that ye are cursed because of your riches, and also
are your riches cursed because ye have set your hearts upon them,
and have not hearkened unto the words of him who gave them
unto you.
22. Ye do not remember the Lord your God in the things with
which he hath blessed you, but ye do always remember your riches, not to thank the Lord your God for them; yea, your hearts are
not drawn out unto the Lord, but they do swell with great pride,
unto boasting, and unto great swelling, envyings, strifes, malice,
persecutions, and murders, and all manner of iniquities.
23. For this cause hath the Lord God caused that a curse should
come upon the land, and also upon your riches, and this because of
your iniquities.
24. Yea, wo unto this people, because of this time which has
arrived, that ye do cast out the prophets, and do mock them, and
cast stones at them, and do slay them, and do all manner of iniquity unto them, even as they did of old time.
25. And now when ye talk, ye say: If our days had been in the days
of our fathers of old, we would not have slain the prophets; we
would not have stoned them, and cast them out.
26. Behold ye are worse than they; for as the Lord liveth, if a
prophet come among you and declareth unto you the word of the
Lord, which testifieth of your sins and iniquities, ye are angry with
him, and cast him out and seek all manner of ways to destroy him;
yea, you will say that he is a false prophet, and that he is a sinner,
and of the devil, because he testifieth that your deeds are evil.
27. But behold, if a man shall come among you and shall say: Do
this, and there is no iniquity; do that and ye shall not suffer; yea,
he will say: Walk after the pride of your own hearts; yea, walk after
the pride of your eyes, and do whatsoever your heart desireth—and
if a man shall come among you and say this, ye will receive him,
and say that he is a prophet.
28. Yea, ye will lift him up, and ye will give unto him of your substance; ye will give unto him of your gold, and of your silver, and
ye will clothe him with costly apparel; and because he speaketh
flattering words unto you, and he saith that all is

Helaman 13:25–26

According to President Harold B. Lee, the only safety we have as members of the Church is to follow the living prophet as though his words came straight from the mouth of the Lord.

well, then ye will not find fault with him.
29. O ye wicked and ye perverse generation; ye hardened and ye
stiffnecked people, how long will ye suppose that the Lord will suffer you? Yea, how long will ye suffer yourselves to be led by foolish
and blind guides? Yea, how long will ye choose darkness rather
than light?
30. Yea, behold, the anger of the Lord is already kindled against
you; behold, he hath cursed the land because of your iniquity.
31. And behold, the time cometh that he curseth your riches, that
they become slippery, that ye cannot hold them; and in the days of
your poverty ye cannot retain them.
32. And in the days of your poverty ye shall cry unto the Lord; and
in vain shall ye cry, for your desolation is already come upon you,
and your destruction is made sure; and then shall ye weep and howl
in that day, saith the Lord of Hosts. And then shall ye lament, and
say:
33. O that I had repented, and had not killed the prophets, and
stoned them, and cast them out. Yea, in that day ye shall say: O
that we had remembered the Lord our God in the day that he gave
us our riches, and then they would not have become slippery that
we should lose them; for behold, our riches are gone from us.
34. Behold, we lay a tool here and on the morrow it is gone; and
behold, our swords are taken from us in the day we have sought
them for battle.
35. Yea, we have hid up our treasures and they have slipped away
from us, because of the curse of the land.
36. O that we had repented in the day that the word of the Lord
came unto us; for behold the land is cursed, and all things are
become slippery, and we cannot hold them.
37. Behold, we are surrounded by demons, yea, we are encircled
about by the angels of him who hath sought to destroy our souls.
Behold, our iniquities are great. O Lord, canst thou not turn away
thine anger from us? And this shall be your language in those days.
38. But behold, your days of probation are past; ye have procrastinated the day of your salvation until it is everlastingly too late, and
your destruction is made sure; yea, for ye have sought all the days of
your lives for that which ye could not obtain; and ye have sought for
happiness in doing iniquity, which thing is contrary to the nature of
that righteousness which is in our great and Eternal Head.
39. O ye people of the land, that ye would hear my words! And I
pray that the anger of the Lord be turned away from you, and that
ye would repent and be saved.

CHAPTER 14

1. AND now it came to pass that Samuel, the Lamanite, did prophesy a great many more things which cannot be written.
2. And behold, he said unto them: Behold, I give unto you a sign;
for five years more cometh, and behold, then cometh the Son of
God to

Helaman 13:29

It seems to be an easy decision for mankind to decide whom to follow, since we know the ultimate destiny attached to our choice of the leader of each cause. It is difficult to imagine that anyone would knowingly choose to follow Satan. But the problem isn't just a choice of whom we choose to follow. The real challenge for us is to discover the true identity of those who encourage and persuade us. One reason it is so difficult is that we don't personally see or deal directly with Satan. He is a master of camouflage, desiring that he be not discovered as being the author of his work. He has legions of agents who also hide in sinful shadows while helping him in the battle for our soul. We have to recognize the evil inherent in the enticements of his representatives before we will reject him and his ways.

We don't deal directly with the Savior, either. Our contact is with those who represent Him, but they declare that relationship openly. The Savior's name is clearly displayed upon that which is of Him and those who represent Him. His work is done in the light. If we respond positively to His authorized representatives, His Spirit, and especially the words of His prophets, we will receive a witness through the Holy Spirit that verifies the truthfulness of His words. We will be safe while we pursue the well-marked path to salvation. But if we ignore or reject the Lord's agents, we will, by default, be choosing to travel the obscure trail leading to Lucifer's kingdom of evil. (O/C)

Helaman 13:37

The Prophet Joseph Smith taught, "When those have come into this world and received tabernacles, then died and again have risen and received glorified bodies, they will have an ascendency over the spirits who have received no bodies, or kept not their first estate, like the devil. The punishment of the devil was that he should not have a habitation like men. The devil's retaliation is, he comes into this world, binds up men's bodies, and occupies them himself."

Helaman 13:37

I have come to the conclusion that if our eyes were open to see the spirit world around us, we should feel differently [about evil influences] than we do; we would not be so unguarded and careless and so indifferent whether we had the spirit and power of God with us or not; but we would be continually watchful and prayerful to our Heavenly Father for His Holy Spirit and His holy angels to be around about us to strengthen us to overcome every evil influence (George Q. Cannon, *Gospel Truths*, 1:82).

redeem all those who shall believe on his name.
3. And behold, this will I give unto you for a sign at the time of his
coming; for behold, there shall be great lights in heaven, insomuch
that in the night before he cometh there shall be no darkness, insomuch that it shall appear unto man as if it was day.
4. Therefore, there shall be one day and a night and a day, as if it
were one day and there were no night; and this shall be unto you
for a sign; for ye shall know of the rising of the sun and also of its
setting; therefore they shall know of a surety that there shall be two
days and a night; nevertheless the night shall not be darkened; and
it shall be the night before he is born.
5. And behold, there shall a new star arise, such an one as ye never
have beheld; and this also shall be a sign unto you.
6. And behold this is not all, there shall be many signs and wonders in heaven.
7. And it shall come to pass that ye shall all be amazed, and wonder, insomuch that ye shall fall to the earth.
8. And it shall come to pass that whosoever shall believe on the
Son of God, the same shall have everlasting life.
9. And behold, thus hath the Lord commanded me, by his angel,
that I should come and tell this thing unto you; yea, he hath commanded that I should prophesy these things unto you; yea, he hath
said unto me: Cry unto this people, repent and prepare the way of
the Lord.
10. And now, because I am a Lamanite, and have spoken unto you
the words which the Lord hath commanded me, and because it was
hard against you, ye are angry with me and do seek to destroy me,
and have cast me out from among you.
11. And ye shall hear my words, for, for this intent have I come up
upon the walls of this city, that ye might hear and know of the
judgments of God which do await you because of your iniquities,
and also that ye might know the conditions of repentance;
12. And also that ye might know of the coming of Jesus Christ, the
Son of God, the Father of heaven and of earth, the Creator of all
things from the beginning; and that ye might know of the signs of
his coming, to the intent that ye might believe on his name.
13. And if ye believe on his name ye will repent of all your sins,
that thereby ye may have a remission of them through his merits.
14. And behold, again, another sign I give unto you, yea, a sign of
his death.
15. For behold, he surely must die that salvation may come; yea, it
behooveth him and becometh expedient that he dieth, to bring to
pass the resurrection of the dead, that thereby men may be brought
into the presence of the Lord.
16. Yea, behold, this death bringeth to pass the resurrection, and
redeemeth all mankind from the first death—that spiritual death;
for all mankind, by the fall of Adam being cut off from the presence of

Helaman 14:2–7

Helaman 14 is one of the most specific prophecies in all of scripture. Consider how each of these prophecies was specifically fulfilled by reading first the prophecy regarding Christ's birth, contained in the verse in Helaman, and by then reading the fulfillment of that prophecy:

- Verse 2 → 3 Nephi 1:13
- Verse 3 → 3 Nephi 1:15
- Verse 5 → 3 Nephi 1:21
- Verse 6 → 3 Nephi 2:1
- Verse 7 → 3 Nephi 1:16–17

Helaman 14:12

Recognizing signs of His imminent arrival serves as a reminder of the actuality of his soon-to-be presence among us and our ongoing need to be sufficiently prepared for that indescribable opportunity. President Ezra Taft Benson taught that preparation prevents destruction and provides preservation: ". . . in the Book of Mormon we find a pattern for preparing for the Second Coming. A major portion of the book centers on the few decades just prior to Christ's coming to America. By careful study of that time period, we can determine why some were destroyed in the terrible judgments that preceded His coming and what brought others to stand at the temple in the land of Bountiful and thrust their hands into the wounds of His hands and feet." (O/C)

Helaman 14:12

Latter-day Saints generally identify with righteous Nephites. It's easy to think of ourselves as the righteous people today, but that isn't going to help us become or continue to be what we should be. Prophetic warnings . . . are continuing to be heard from latter-day prophets concerning the Lord's Second Coming with its accompanying destruction of the wicked. We need to be prepared to receive Him. President Gordon B. Hinckley spoke of many of the catastrophes of the past and then said, "Just as there have been calamities in the past, we expect more in the future. What do we do? We can so live that we can call upon the Lord for His protection and guidance. This is a first priority. We cannot expect His help if we are unwilling to keep His commandments." (O/C)

Helaman 14:15–17

The Book of Mormon mentions two major types of spiritual death. The term "first spiritual death" refers to the original transgression of Adam and Eve when they were cast out of the Garden of Eden and to the condition which comes upon a person when he commits his first sin. Jesus Christ atoned for the first spiritual death of Adam and Eve, and each individual person can be redeemed from his "first spiritual death" upon the conditions of repentance. However, the "second spiritual death" is much more serious. . . . This second spiritual death refers essentially to the state or condition of those who become sons of perdition. (Ludlow)

the Lord, are considered as dead, both as to things temporal and to
things spiritual.
17. But behold, the resurrection of Christ redeemeth mankind,
yea, even all mankind, and bringeth them back into the presence
of the Lord.
18. Yea, and it bringeth to pass the condition of repentance, that
whosoever repenteth the same is not hewn down and cast into the
fire; but whosoever repenteth not is hewn down and cast into the
fire; and there cometh upon them again a spiritual death, yea, a
second death, for they are cut off again as to things pertaining to
righteousness.
19. Therefore repent ye, repent ye, lest by knowing these things
and not doing them ye shall suffer yourselves to come under condemnation, and ye are brought down unto this second death.
20. But behold, as I said unto you concerning another sign, a sign
of his death, behold, in that day that he shall suffer death the sun
shall be darkened and refuse to give his light unto you; and also the
moon and the stars; and there shall be no light upon the face of
this land, even from the time that he shall suffer death, for the
space of three days, to the time that he shall rise again from the
dead.
21. Yea, at the time that he shall yield up the ghost there shall be
thunderings and lightnings for the space of many hours, and the
earth shall shake and tremble; and the rocks which are upon the
face of this earth, which are both above the earth and beneath,
which ye know at this time are solid, or the more part of it is one
solid mass, shall be broken up;
22. Yea, they shall be rent in twain, and shall ever after be found
in seams and in cracks, and in broken fragments upon the face of
the whole earth, yea, both above the earth and beneath.
23. And behold, there shall be great tempests, and there shall be
many mountains laid low, like unto a valley, and there shall be
many places which are now called valleys which shall become
mountains, whose height is great.
24. And many highways shall be broken up, and many cities shall
become desolate.
25. And many graves shall be opened, and shall yield up many of
their dead; and many saints shall appear unto many.
26. And behold, thus hath the angel spoken unto me; for he said
unto me that there should be thunderings and lightnings for the
space of many hours.
27. And he said unto me that while the thunder and the lightning
lasted, and the tempest, that these things should be, and that darkness should cover the face of the whole earth for the space of three
days.
28. And the angel said unto me that many shall see greater things
than these, to the intent that they might believe that these signs
and these wonders should come to pass upon all the face of this
land, to the intent that there should be no cause for unbelief
among the children of men—
29. And this to the intent that whosoever will believe might be
saved,

Helaman 14:18

The fire referred to in this verse is not actual fire; according to President Joseph Fielding Smith, it represents the torment that will be suffered by the wicked.

Helaman 14:20–25

Again we see the very specific prophecies contained in Helaman 14, this time regarding Christ's death. Read the verse in Helaman and then the corresponding fulfillment of each prophecy:

- Verse 20 → 3 Nephi 8:19–23
- Verse 21 → 3 Nephi 8:6–7
- Verse 22 → 3 Nephi 8:12, 17–18
- Verse 23 → 3 Nephi 8:5–6
- Verse 24 → 3 Nephi 8:8–11, 13
- Verse 25 → 3 Nephi 23:9–14

and that whosoever will not believe, a righteous judgment might come upon them; and also if they are condemned they bring upon themselves their own condemnation.
30. And now remember, remember, my brethren, that whosoever perisheth, perisheth unto himself; and whosoever doeth iniquity, doeth it unto himself; for behold, ye are free; ye are permitted to act for yourselves; for behold, God hath given unto you a knowledge and he hath made you free.
31. He hath given unto you that ye might know good from evil, and he hath given unto you that ye might choose life or death; and ye can do good and be restored unto that which is good, or have that which is good restored unto you; or ye can do evil, and have that which is evil restored unto you.

CHAPTER 15

1. AND now, my beloved brethren, behold, I declare unto you that except ye shall repent your houses shall be left unto you desolate.
2. Yea, except ye repent, your women shall have great cause to mourn in the day that they shall give suck; for ye shall attempt to flee and there shall be no place for refuge; yea, and wo unto them which are with child, for they shall be heavy and cannot flee; therefore, they shall be trodden down and shall be left to perish.
3. Yea, wo unto this people who are called the people of Nephi except they shall repent, when they shall see all these signs and wonders which shall be showed unto them; for behold, they have been a chosen people of the Lord; yea, the people of Nephi hath he loved, and also hath he chastened them; yea, in the days of their iniquities hath he chastened them because he loveth them.
4. But behold my brethren, the Lamanites hath he hated because their deeds have been evil continually, and this because of the iniquity of the tradition of their fathers. But behold, salvation hath come unto them through the preaching of the Nephites; and for this intent hath the Lord prolonged their days.
5. And I would that ye should behold that the more part of them are in the path of their duty, and they do walk circumspectly before God, and they do observe to keep his commandments and his statutes and his judgments according to the law of Moses.
6. Yea, I say unto you, that the more part of them are doing this, and they are striving with unwearied diligence that they may bring the remainder of their brethren to the knowledge of the truth; therefore there are many who do add to their numbers daily.
7. And behold, ye do know of yourselves, for ye have witnessed it, that as many of them as are brought to the knowledge of the truth, and to know of the wicked and abominable traditions of their fathers, and are led to believe the holy scriptures, yea, the prophecies of the holy prophets, which are written, which

Helaman 14:30–31

Samuel the Lamanite warns us that when we disobey God we cannot use the excuse that we were forced to commit sin. . . .

This gift of free agency is one of the greatest gifts ever given to man by God. It is true that without free agency man could not be condemned in the justice of God, but it is also true that without it man could not be blessed for keeping the laws. President David O. McKay has explained the value and importance of free agency as follows:

"Man's free agency is an eternal principle of progress, and any form of government that curtails or inhibits its free exercise is wrong. Satan's plan in the beginning was one of coercion, and it was rejected because he sought to destroy the agency of man which God had given him. . . .

"With free agency, however, there comes responsibility. If man is to be rewarded for righteousness and punished for evil, then common justice demands that he be given the power of independent action. A knowledge of good and evil is essential to man's progress on earth. If he were coerced to do right at all times or helplessly enticed to commit sin, he would merit neither a blessing for the first nor punishment for the second. Man's responsibility is correspondingly operative with his free agency. Actions in harmony with divine law and the laws of nature will bring happiness, and those in opposition to divine truth, misery. Man is responsible not only for every deed, but also for every idle word and thought." (Ludlow)

Helaman 15:5–7

At this point, the majority of the Lamanites had become righteous and were engaged in converting their brethren. In verse 7, it is clear that the Nephites have seen the changes in the Lamanites. President Spencer W. Kimball proclaimed that the day of the Lamanite is here—a brighter day has dawned for the Lamanites, and we are the nursing parents who are helping them as they gather into the folds of the Church.

leadeth them to faith on the Lord, and unto repentance, which
faith and repentance bringeth a change of heart unto them—
8. Therefore, as many as have come to this, ye know of yourselves
are firm and steadfast in the faith, and in the thing wherewith they
have been made free.
9. And ye know also that they have buried their weapons of war, and
they fear to take them up lest by any means they should sin; yea, ye
can see that they fear to sin—for behold they will suffer themselves
that they be trodden down and slain by their enemies, and will not
lift their swords against them, and this because of their faith in
Christ.
10. And now, because of their steadfastness when they do believe
in that thing which they do believe, for because of their firmness
when they are once enlightened, behold, the Lord shall bless them
and prolong their days, notwithstanding their iniquity—
11. Yea, even if they should dwindle in unbelief the Lord shall prolong their days, until the time shall come which hath been spoken
of by our fathers, and also by the prophet Zenos, and many other
prophets, concerning the restoration of our brethren, the
Lamanites, again to the knowledge of the truth—
12. Yea, I say unto you, that in the latter times the promises of the
Lord have been extended to our brethren, the Lamanites; and
notwithstanding the many afflictions which they shall have, and
notwithstanding they shall be driven to and fro upon the face of
the earth, and be hunted, and shall be smitten and scattered
abroad, having no place for refuge, the Lord shall be merciful unto
them.
13. And this is according to the prophecy, that they shall again be
brought to the true knowledge, which is knowledge of their
Redeemer, and their great and true shepherd, and be numbered
among his sheep.
14. Therefore I say unto you, it shall be better for them than for
you except ye repent.
15. For behold, had the mighty works been shown unto them
which have been shown unto you, yea, unto them who have dwindled in unbelief because of the traditions of their fathers, ye can see
of yourselves that they never would again have dwindled in unbelief.
16. Therefore, saith the Lord: I will not utterly destroy them, but I
will cause that in the day of my wisdom they shall return again
unto me, saith the Lord.
17. And now behold, saith the Lord, concerning the people of the
Nephites: If they will not repent, and observe to do my will, I will
utterly destroy them, saith the Lord, because of their unbelief
notwithstanding the many mighty works which I have done among
them; and as surely as the Lord liveth shall these things be, saith the
Lord.

CHAPTER 16

1. AND now, it came to pass that there were many who heard the words of Samuel, the Lamanite, which he spake upon the walls of the city. And as many as believed on his word went forth and sought for Nephi; and when they had come forth and found him they confessed unto him their sins and denied not, desiring that they might be baptized unto the Lord.
2. But as many as there were who did not believe in the words of Samuel were angry with him; and they cast stones at him upon the wall, and also many shot arrows at him as he stood upon the wall; but the Spirit of the Lord was with him, insomuch that they could not hit him with their stones neither with their arrows.
3. Now when they saw that they could not hit him, there were many more who did believe on his words, insomuch that they went away unto Nephi to be baptized.
4. For behold, Nephi was baptizing, and prophesying, and preaching, crying repentance unto the people, showing signs and wonders, working miracles among the people, that they might know that the Christ must shortly come—
5. Telling them of things which must shortly come, that they might know and remember at the time of their coming that they had been made known unto them beforehand, to the intent that they might believe; therefore as many as believed on the words of Samuel went forth unto him to be baptized, for they came repenting and confessing their sins.
6. But the more part of them did not believe in the words of Samuel; therefore when they saw that they could not hit him with their stones and their arrows, they cried unto their captains, saying: Take this fellow and bind him, for behold he hath a devil; and because of the power of the devil which is in him we cannot hit him with our stones and our arrows; therefore take him and bind him, and away with him.
7. And as they went forth to lay their hands on him, behold, he did cast himself down from the wall, and did flee out of their lands, yea, even unto his own country, and began to preach and to prophesy among his own people.
8. And behold, he was never heard of more among the Nephites; and thus were the affairs of the people.
9. And thus ended the eighty and sixth year of the reign of the judges over the people of Nephi.
10. And thus ended also the eighty and seventh year of the reign of the judges, the more part of the people remaining in their pride and wickedness, and the lesser part walking more circumspectly before God.
11. And these were the conditions also, in the eighty and eighth year of the reign of the judges.
12. And there was but little alteration in the affairs of the people, save it were the people began to be more hardened in iniquity, and do more and more of that which was contrary to the commandments of God, in the eighty and ninth year of the reign of the judges.
13. But it came to pass in the ninetieth year of the reign of the judges, there were great signs given unto the people, and wonders; and the words of the prophets began to be fulfilled.
14. And angels did appear unto men, wise men, and did declare unto them glad tidings of great joy; thus in this year the scriptures began to be fulfilled.
15. Nevertheless, the people began to harden their hearts, all save it were the most believing part of them, both of the Nephites and also of the

Lamanites, and began to depend upon their own strength and upon their own wisdom, saying:
16. Some things they may have guessed right, among so many; but behold, we know that all these great and marvelous works cannot come to pass, of which has been spoken.
17. And they began to reason and to contend among themselves, saying:
18. That it is not reasonable that such a being as a Christ shall come; if so, and he be the Son of God, the Father of heaven and of earth, as it has been spoken, why will he not show himself unto us as well as unto them who shall be at Jerusalem?
19. Yea, why will he not show himself in this land as well as in the land of Jerusalem?
20. But behold, we know that this is a wicked tradition, which has been handed down unto us by our fathers, to cause us that we should believe in some great and marvelous thing which should come to pass, but not among us, but in a land which is far distant, a land which we know not; therefore they can keep us in ignorance, for we cannot witness with our own eyes that they are true.
21. And they will, by the cunning and the mysterious arts of the evil one, work some great mystery which we cannot understand, which will keep us down to be servants to their words, and also servants unto them, for we depend upon them to teach us the word; and thus will they keep us in ignorance if we will yield ourselves unto them, all the days of our lives.
22. And many more things did the people imagine up in their hearts, which were foolish and vain; and they were much disturbed, for Satan did stir them up to do iniquity continually; yea, he did go about spreading rumors and contentions upon all the face of the land, that he might harden the hearts of the people against that which was good and against that which should come.
23. And notwithstanding the signs and the wonders which were wrought among the people of the Lord, and the many miracles which they did, Satan did get great hold upon the hearts of the people upon all the face of the land.
24. And thus ended the ninetieth year of the reign of the judges over the people of Nephi.
25. And thus ended the book of Helaman, according to the record of Helaman and his sons.

Helaman 16:21

Satan's purposes are always and forever directly opposed to the purposes of the Lord. President Marion G. Romney taught that Satan is completely evil and always seeks to destroy man; he is irrevocably committed to countering and overcoming the influence of the Spirit of Christ on man. In this and the following verses, Satan tries to convince the people that the signs they had seen were meaningless.

THIRD NEPHI
THE BOOK OF NEPHI

THE SON OF NEPHI, WHO WAS THE SON OF HELAMAN

CHAPTER 1

3 Nephi

The Book of 3 Nephi discusses many signs and wonders. We are reminded that signs flow from faith and are a product of faith—the chief purpose of signs is not to produce faith, but to reward it. We are in trouble if we rely on signs to build our faith. It is common in scripture to see even the most marvelous signs rationalized away by those who lack faith—and we can fall into the same trap if we are relying on signs to increase our faith.

1. NOW it came to pass that the ninety and first year had passed away and it was six hundred years from the time that Lehi left Jerusalem; and it was in the year that Lachoneus was the chief judge and the governor over the land.
2. And Nephi, the son of Helaman, had departed out of the land of Zarahemla, giving charge unto his son Nephi, who was his eldest son, concerning the plates of brass, and all the records which had been kept, and all those things which had been kept sacred from the departure of Lehi out of Jerusalem.
3. Then he departed out of the land, and whither he went, no man knoweth; and his son Nephi did keep the records in his stead, yea, the record of this people.
4. And it came to pass that in the commencement of the ninety and second year, behold, the prophecies of the prophets began to be fulfilled more fully; for there began to be greater signs and greater miracles wrought among the people.
5. But there were some who began to say that the time was past for the words to be fulfilled, which were spoken by Samuel, the Lamanite.
6. And they began to rejoice over their brethren, saying: Behold the time is past, and the words of Samuel are not fulfilled; therefore, your joy and your faith concerning this thing hath been vain.
7. And it came to pass that they did make a great uproar throughout the land; and the people who believed began to be very sorrowful, lest by any means those things which had been spoken might not come to pass.
8. But behold, they did watch steadfastly for that day and that night and that day which should be as one day as if there were no night, that they might know that their faith had not been vain.
9. Now it came to pass that there was a day set apart by the unbelievers, that all those who believed in those traditions should be put to death except the sign should come to pass, which had been given by Samuel the prophet.
10. Now it came to pass that when Nephi, the son of Nephi, saw this wickedness of his people, his heart was exceedingly sorrowful.
11. And it came to pass that he went out and bowed himself down upon the earth, and cried mightily to his God in behalf of his people, yea, those who were about to be destroyed because of their faith in the tradition of their fathers.
12. And it came to pass that he cried mightily unto the Lord all that day; and behold, the voice of the Lord came unto him, saying:
13. Lift up your head and be of good cheer; for behold, the time is at hand, and on this night shall the sign be given, and on the morrow come I into the world, to show unto the world that I will fulfill all that which I have caused to be spoken by the mouth of my holy prophets.
14. Behold, I come unto my own, to fulfill all things which I have made known unto the children of men from the foundation of the

3 Nephi 1:2–3

The disappearance of Nephi the son of Helaman is somewhat similar to the disappearance seventy-three years earlier of his great-great-grandfather, Alma the younger. The Book of Mormon provides no further information concerning what became of these two great prophets. (Ludlow)

3 Nephi 1:12–14

The day before the Savior was born on the eastern continent, he spoke to the prophet Nephi . . . This prebirth statement of the Savior again indicates something concerning the nature and power of pre-earthly beings. Also, the Savior's statement that he was to do the will "of the Father *because of me*" evidently refers to his status as the first born spiritual child of our Heavenly Father. His statement that he is coming into the world to "fulfill all things" and to do the will "of the Son *because of my flesh*" evidently refers to his coming mission on earth as the Savior and Redeemer of the world. (Ludlow)

world, and to do the will, both of the Father and of the Son—of
the Father because of me, and of the Son because of my flesh. And
behold, the time is at hand, and this night shall the sign be given.
15. And it came to pass that the words which came unto Nephi
were fulfilled, according as they had been spoken; for behold, at the
going down of the sun there was no darkness; and the people began
to be astonished because there was no darkness when the night
came.
16. And there were many, who had not believed the words of the
prophets, who fell to the earth and became as if they were dead, for
they knew that the great plan of destruction which they had laid
for those who believed in the words of the prophets had been frustrated; for the sign which had been given was already at hand.
17. And they began to know that the Son of God must shortly
appear; yea, in fine, all the people upon the face of the whole earth
from the west to the east, both in the land north and in the land
south, were so exceedingly astonished that they fell to the earth.
18. For they knew that the prophets had testified of these things for
many years, and that the sign which had been given was already at
hand; and they began to fear because of their iniquity and their
unbelief.
19. And it came to pass that there was no darkness in all that
night, but it was as light as though it was mid-day. And it came to
pass that the sun did rise in the morning again, according to its
proper order; and they knew that it was the day that the Lord
should be born, because of the sign which had been given.
20. And it had come to pass, yea, all things, every whit, according
to the words of the prophets.
21. And it came to pass also that a new star did appear, according
to the word.
22. And it came to pass that from this time forth there began to be
lyings sent forth among the people, by Satan, to harden their
hearts, to the intent that they might not believe in those signs and
wonders which they had seen; but notwithstanding these lyings
and deceivings the more part of the people did believe, and were
converted unto the Lord.
23. And it came to pass that Nephi went forth among the people,
and also many others, baptizing unto repentance, in the which
there was a great remission of sins. And thus the people began
again to have peace in the land.
24. And there were no contentions, save it were a few that began
to preach, endeavoring to prove by the scriptures that it was no
more expedient to observe the law of Moses. Now in this thing
they did err, having not understood the scriptures.
25. But it came to pass that they soon became converted, and were
convinced of the error which they were in, for it was made known
unto them that the law was not yet fulfilled, and that it must be fulfilled in every whit; yea, the word came unto them that it must be
fulfilled; yea, that one jot or tittle should not pass away till it
should all be fulfilled; therefore in this same year were they brought
to a knowledge of their error and did confess their faults.
26. And thus the ninety and second

3 Nephi 1:22

Imagine the joy of seeing the prophesied sign of the Lord Jesus Christ's birth. And yet some would still not believe, though they'd seen the signs of His birth. . . .

Faith, not signs, brings true change. Change occurs within the heart and is not due to external signs. We should not seek signs to believe, for they will follow those with faith (see D&C 63:7–12). President Joseph F. Smith cautioned, "Show me Latter-day Saints who have to feed upon miracles, signs and visions in order to keep them steadfast in the Church, and I will show you members of the Church who are not in good standing before God, and who are walking in slippery paths. It is not by marvelous manifestations unto us that we shall be established in the truth, but it is by humility and faithful obedience to the commandments and laws of God." . . . As President Kimball's title teaches us, faith *precedes* the miracle. Faith adds meaning to the miracle. (P/A)

3 Nephi 1:24–25

About five hundred years before the birth of the Savior, Nephi the son of Lehi had prophesied that at the coming of the Christ the law of Moses "shall be fulfilled." (2 Nephi 25:24.) Thus at the sign of the birth of Christ, some of the descendants of Nephi claimed "it was no more expedient to observe the law of Moses" because according to their interpretation of the scriptures the law of Moses had been fulfilled. (3 Nephi 1:24.) However, it was made known unto them "that the law was not yet fulfilled, and that it must be fulfilled in every whit." (3 Nephi 1:25.)

Later, during the three days between his crucifixion and resurrection, the Savior spoke to the righteous Nephites living on the American continent and said "in me is the law of Moses fulfilled." (3 Nephi 9:17.) Still later the resurrected Savior appeared to the Nephites and taught, ". . . verily I say unto you, one jot nor one tittle hath not passed away from the law, but in me it hath all been fulfilled." (3 Nephi 12:18.) Evidently the law of Moses was fulfilled by the Savior at the time of his crucifixion and resurrection. (Ludlow)

year did pass away, bringing glad tidings unto the people because of the signs which did come to pass, according to the words of the prophecy of all the holy prophets.
27. And it came to pass that the ninety and third year did also pass away in peace, save it were for the Gadianton robbers, who dwelt upon the mountains, who did infest the land; for so strong were their holds and their secret places that the people could not overpower them; therefore they did commit many murders, and did do much slaughter among the people.
28. And it came to pass that in the ninety and fourth year they began to increase in great degree, because there were many dissenters of the Nephites who did flee unto them, which did cause much sorrow unto those Nephites who did remain in the land.
29. And there was also a cause of much sorrow among the Lamanites; for behold, they had many children who did grow up and began to wax strong in years, that they became for themselves, and were led away by some who were Zoramites, by their lyings and their flattering words, to join those Gadianton robbers.
30. And thus were the Lamanites afflicted also, and began to decrease as to their faith and righteousness, because of the wickedness of the rising generation.

CHAPTER 2

1. AND it came to pass that thus passed away the ninety and fifth year also, and the people began to forget those signs and wonders which they had heard, and began to be less and less astonished at a sign or a wonder from heaven, insomuch that they began to be hard in their hearts, and blind in their minds, and began to disbelieve all which they had heard and seen—
2. Imagining up some vain thing in their hearts, that it was wrought by men and by the power of the devil, to lead away and deceive the hearts of the people; and thus did Satan get possession of the hearts of the people again, insomuch that he did blind their eyes and lead them away to believe that the doctrine of Christ was a foolish and a vain thing.
3. And it came to pass that the people began to wax strong in wickedness and abominations; and they did not believe that there should be any more signs or wonders given; and Satan did go about, leading away the hearts of the people, tempting them and causing them that they should do great wickedness in the land.
4. And thus did pass away the ninety and sixth year; and also the ninety and seventh year; and also the ninety and eighth year; and also the ninety and ninth year;
5. And also an hundred years had passed away since the days of Mosiah, who was king over the people of the Nephites.
6. And six hundred and nine years had passed away since Lehi left Jerusalem.
7. And nine years had passed away from the time when the sign was given, which was spoken of by the prophets, that Christ should come into the world.
8. Now the Nephites began to reckon their time from this period

3 Nephi 2:5–8

The Nephites used three systems of reckoning time:

(1) The first method was to determine the number of years since father Lehi left Jerusalem; this system was used from 600 B.C. to 92 B.C. (Mosiah 29:44–47; Alma 1:1.)

(2) The second method was to calculate the number of years from the beginning of the reign of the judges; this system was used for about 100 years, from 91 B.C. to A.D. 9. (3 Nephi 2:5–7.)

(3) The last method was to "reckon their time from this period when the sign was given, or from the coming of Christ" (3 Nephi 2:7–8); this system was used for the remainder of their record. (Ludlow)

when the sign was given, or from the coming of Christ; therefore,
nine years had passed away.
9. And Nephi, who was the father of Nephi, who had the charge
of the records, did not return to the land of Zarahemla, and could
nowhere be found in all the land.
10. And it came to pass that the people did still remain in wickedness, notwithstanding the much preaching and prophesying which
was sent among them; and thus passed away the tenth year also;
and the eleventh year also passed away in iniquity.
11. And it came to pass in the thirteenth year there began to be
wars and contentions throughout all the land; for the Gadianton
robbers had become so numerous, and did slay so many of the people, and did lay waste so many cities, and did spread so much death
and carnage throughout the land, that it became expedient that all
the people, both the Nephites and the Lamanites, should take up
arms against them.
12. Therefore, all the Lamanites who had become converted unto
the Lord did unite with their brethren, the Nephites, and were
compelled, for the safety of their lives and their women and their
children, to take up arms against those Gadianton robbers, yea,
and also to maintain their rights, and the privileges of their church
and of their worship, and their freedom and their liberty.
13. And it came to pass that before this thirteenth year had passed
away the Nephites were threatened with utter destruction because
of this war, which had become exceedingly sore.
14. And it came to pass that those Lamanites who had united with
the Nephites were numbered among the Nephites;
15. And their curse was taken from them, and their skin became
white like unto the Nephites;
16. And their young men and their daughters became exceedingly
fair, and they were numbered among the Nephites, and were called
Nephites. And thus ended the thirteenth year.
17. And it came to pass in the commencement of the fourteenth
year, the war between the robbers and the people of Nephi did continue and did become exceedingly sore; nevertheless, the people of
Nephi did gain some advantage of the robbers, insomuch that they
did drive them back out of their lands into the mountains and into
their secret places.
18. And thus ended the fourteenth year. And in the fifteenth year
they did come forth against the people of Nephi; and because of
the wickedness of the people of Nephi, and their many contentions and dissensions, the Gadianton robbers did gain many
advantages over them.
19. And thus ended the fifteenth year, and thus were the people in
a state of many afflictions; and the sword of destruction did hang
over them, insomuch that they were about to be smitten down by
it, and this because of their iniquity.

CHAPTER 3

1. AND now it came to pass that in the sixteenth year from the coming of Christ, Lachoneus, the governor of the land, received an epistle from

3 Nephi 2:11–12

After disappearing and seeking safety in the wilderness for several years, the Gadianton robbers appear again among the people. With the return of the band of robbers, the converted followers of Christ had to unite for their own safety.

3 Nephi 2:12, 14–16

Dark skin is no longer considered the sign of a "curse." The actual curse, according to President Joseph Fielding Smith, was withdrawal of the Spirit of the Lord from those who were disobedient.

POINT OF INTEREST

Uxmal, pronounced "Oosh-mahl," is usually assumed to be an archaic Mayan phrase meaning "built three times." If the interpretation is accurate, it could explain why these ruins are in so much better shape than those of equal age in other areas. Uxmal is found in modern-day Yucatán, Mexico.

the leader and the governor of this band of robbers; and these were
the words which were written, saying:
2. Lachoneus, most noble and chief governor of the land, behold,
I write this epistle unto you, and do give unto you exceedingly
great praise because of your firmness, and also the firmness of your
people, in maintaining that which ye suppose to be your right and
liberty; yea, ye do stand well, as if ye were supported by the hand
of a god, in the defence of your liberty, and your property, and your
country, or that which ye do call so.
3. And it seemeth a pity unto me, most noble Lachoneus, that ye
should be so foolish and vain as to suppose that ye can stand
against so many brave men who are at my command, who do now
at this time stand in their arms, and do await with great anxiety for
the word—Go down upon the Nephites and destroy them.
4. And I, knowing of their unconquerable spirit, having proved
them in the field of battle, and knowing of their everlasting hatred
towards you because of the many wrongs which ye have done unto
them, therefore if they should come down against you they would
visit you with utter destruction.
5. Therefore I have written this epistle, sealing it with mine own
hand, feeling for your welfare, because of your firmness in that
which ye believe to be right, and your noble spirit in the field of
battle.
6. Therefore I write unto you, desiring that ye would yield up unto
this my people, your cities, your lands, and your possessions, rather
than that they should visit you with the sword and that destruction
should come upon you.
7. Or in other words, yield yourselves up unto us, and unite with us
and become acquainted with our secret works, and become our
brethren that ye may be like unto us—not our slaves, but our
brethren and partners of all our substance.
8. And behold, I swear unto you, if ye will do this, with an oath, ye
shall not be destroyed; but if ye will not do this, I swear unto you
with an oath, that on the morrow month I will command that my
armies shall come down against you, and they shall not stay their
hand and shall spare not, but shall slay you, and shall let fall the
sword upon you even until ye shall become extinct.
9. And behold, I am Giddianhi; and I am the governor of this the
secret society of Gadianton; which society and the works thereof I
know to be good; and they are of ancient date and they have been
handed down unto us.
10. And I write this epistle unto you, Lachoneus, and I hope that ye
will deliver up your lands and your possessions, without the shedding
of blood, that this my people may recover their rights and government, who have dissented away from you because of your wickedness
in retaining from them their rights of government, and except ye do
this, I will avenge their wrongs. I am Giddianhi.
11. And now it came to pass when Lachoneus received this epistle
he was exceedingly astonished, because of the boldness of
Giddianhi demanding the possession of the land of the Nephites,
and also of threatening the people and avenging the wrongs of
those that had received no wrong, save it were they had wronged
themselves by dissenting away unto those wicked and abominable
robbers.
12. Now behold, this Lachoneus,

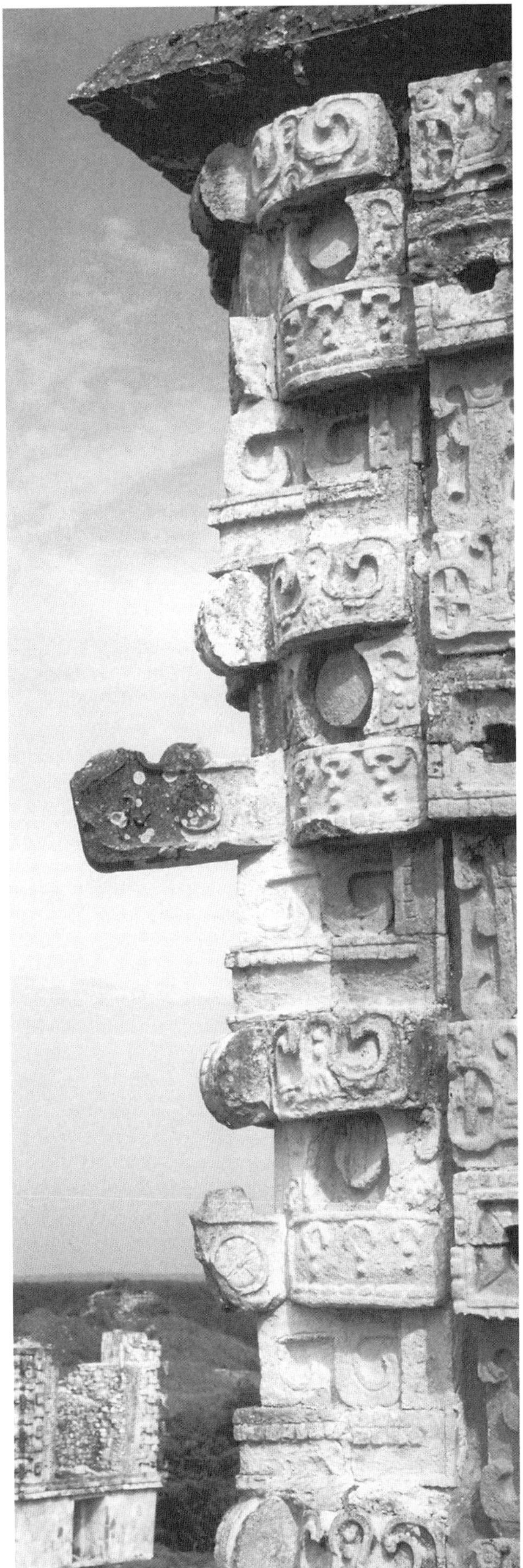

the governor, was a just man, and could not be frightened by the demands and the threatenings of a robber; therefore he did not hearken to the epistle of Giddianhi, the governor of the robbers, but he did cause that his people should cry unto the Lord for strength against the time that the robbers should come down against them.
13. Yea, he sent a proclamation among all the people, that they should gather together their women, and their children, their flocks and their herds, and all their substance, save it were their land, unto one place.
14. And he caused that fortifications should be built round about them, and the strength thereof should be exceedingly great. And he caused that armies, both of the Nephites and of the Lamanites, or of all them who were numbered among the Nephites, should be placed as guards round about to watch them, and to guard them from the robbers day and night.
15. Yea, he said unto them: As the Lord liveth, except ye repent of all your iniquities, and cry unto the Lord, ye will in no wise be delivered out of the hands of those Gadianton robbers.
16. And so great and marvelous were the words and prophecies of Lachoneus that they did cause fear to come upon all the people; and they did exert themselves in their might to do according to the words of Lachoneus.
17. And it came to pass that Lachoneus did appoint chief captains over all the armies of the Nephites, to command them at the time that the robbers should come down out of the wilderness against them.
18. Now the chiefest among all the chief captains and the great commander of all the armies of the Nephites was appointed, and his name was Gidgiddoni.
19. Now it was the custom among all the Nephites to appoint for their chief captains, (save it were in their times of wickedness) some one that had the spirit of revelation and also prophecy; therefore, this Gidgiddoni was a great prophet among them, as also was the chief judge.
20. Now the people said unto Gidgiddoni: Pray unto the Lord, and let us go up upon the mountains and into the wilderness, that we may fall upon the robbers and destroy them in their own lands.
21. But Gidgiddoni saith unto them: The Lord forbid; for if we should go up against them the Lord would deliver us into their hands; therefore we will prepare ourselves in the center of our lands, and we will gather all our armies together, and we will not go against them, but we will wait till they shall come against us; therefore as the Lord liveth, if we do this he will deliver them into our hands.
22. And it came to pass in the seventeenth year, in the latter end of the year, the proclamation of Lachoneus had gone forth throughout all the face of the land, and they had taken their horses, and their chariots, and their cattle, and all their flocks, and their herds, and their grain, and all their substance, and did march forth by thousands and by tens of thousands, until they had all gone forth to the place which had been appointed that they should gather themselves together, to defend themselves against their enemies.
23. And the land which was appointed

3 Nephi 3:12, 19

The description of Lachoneus as "a just man" is an important key to the deliverance of the Nephites. They were delivered as a result of their own righteousness and the righteousness and courage of their leaders.

3 Nephi 3:20–21

This counsel of the Lord not to wage offensive war has apparently been given to people of all dispensations, as is indicated in this statement in the Doctrine and Covenants (Section 98:32–38):

This principle is also the teaching of the Church at this time, as is indicated in the following statement by President George Q. Cannon:

"We must proclaim peace; do all in our power to appease the wrath of our enemies; make any sacrifice that honorable people can to avert war, with all its horrors, entailing as it does dreadful consequences so numerous that they cannot be mentioned. It is our duty, I say, as a nation. The influence of the Latter-day Saints should be used in this direction. We should seek to quell these feelings of anxiety to fight and to shed blood. Our influence should go forth like oil poured upon the troubled waters, quieting the waves of discontent and wrath that are aroused by this fearful spirit. . . .

"To us as Latter-day Saints these principles are of the utmost importance. I do not want to see our young men get filled with the spirit of war and be eager for the conflict. God forbid that such a spirit should prevail in our land, or that we should contribute in any manner to the propagation of a spirit of that kind! But one may say, 'Is it not our duty to defend our country and our flag? Is it not our duty to maintain the institutions which the Lord has given to us?' Certainly it is. And it is no part of cowardice to take the plan that the Lord has pointed out. No man need be afraid that the Lord or any just man will look upon him as a coward (CR, Apr. 1898, 86–87). (Ludlow)

3 Nephi 3:20–21

We as Latter-day Saints . . . [should not] manifest a bloodthirsty disposition. We should be a peaceful people, seeking peace, and endeavoring to escape all the horrors of war, and to avert them from the nations of the earth . . . (George Q. Cannon, *CR*, Apr. 1898, 85).

was the land of Zarahemla, and the land which was between the land Zarahemla and the land Bountiful, yea, to the line which was between the land Bountiful and the land Desolation.
24. And there were a great many thousand people who were called Nephites, who did gather themselves together in this land. Now Lachoneus did cause that they should gather themselves together in the land southward, because of the great curse which was upon the land northward.
25. And they did fortify themselves against their enemies; and they did dwell in one land, and in one body, and they did fear the words which had been spoken by Lachoneus, insomuch that they did repent of all their sins; and they did put up their prayers unto the Lord their God, that he would deliver them in the time that their enemies should come down against them tobattle.
26. And they were exceedingly sorrowful because of their enemies. And Gidgiddoni did cause that they should make weapons of war of every kind, and they should be strong with armor, and with shields, and with bucklers, after the manner of his instruction.

CHAPTER 4

1. AND it came to pass that in the latter end of the eighteenth year those armies of robbers had prepared for battle, and began to come down and to sally forth from the hills, and out of the mountains, and the wilderness, and their strongholds, and their secret places, and began to take possession of the lands, both which were in the land south and which were in the land north, and began to take possession of all the lands which had been deserted by the Nephites, and the cities which had been left desolate.
2. But behold, there were no wild beasts nor game in those lands which had been deserted by the Nephites, and there was no game for the robbers save it were in the wilderness.
3. And the robbers could not exist save it were in the wilderness, for the want of food; for the Nephites had left their lands desolate, and had gathered their flocks and their herds and all their substance, and they were in one body.
4. Therefore, there was no chance for the robbers to plunder and to obtain food, save it were to come up in open battle against the Nephites; and the Nephites being in one body, and having so great a number, and having reserved for themselves provisions, and horses and cattle, and flocks of every kind, that they might subsist for the space of seven years, in the which time they did hope to destroy the robbers from off the face of the land; and thus the eighteenth year did pass away.
5. And it came to pass that in the nineteenth year Giddianhi found that it was expedient that he should go up to battle against the Nephites, for there was no way that they could subsist save it were to plunder and rob and murder.
6. And they durst not spread themselves upon the face of the land insomuch that they could raise grain, lest the Nephites should come upon

3 Nephi 4:3–4

The main strategy of the people in these verses was to gather to the center of their lands and force the robbers to come to them—all the while leaving the areas they had abandoned desolate of crops and livestock. In essence, they starved out the robbers.

them and slay them; therefore Giddianhi gave commandment unto his armies that in this year they should go up to battle against the Nephites.
7. And it came to pass that they did come up to battle; and it was in the sixth month; and behold, great and terrible was the day that they did come up to battle; and they were girded about after the manner of robbers; and they had a lamb-skin about their loins, and they were dyed in blood, and their heads were shorn, and they had headplates upon them; and great and terrible was the appearance of the armies of Giddianhi, because of their armor, and because of their being dyed in blood.
8. And it came to pass that the armies of the Nephites, when they saw the appearance of the army of Giddianhi, had all fallen to the earth, and did lift their cries to the Lord their God, that he would spare them and deliver them out of the hands of their enemies.
9. And it came to pass that when the armies of Giddianhi saw this they began to shout with a loud voice, because of their joy, for they had supposed that the Nephites had fallen with fear because of the terror of their armies.
10. But in this thing they were disappointed, for the Nephites did not fear them; but they did fear their God and did supplicate him for protection; therefore, when the armies of Giddianhi did rush upon them they were prepared to meet them; yea, in the strength of the Lord they did receive them.
11. And the battle commenced in this the sixth month; and great and terrible was the battle thereof, yea, great and terrible was the slaughter thereof, insomuch that there never was known so great a slaughter among all the people of Lehi since he left Jerusalem.
12. And notwithstanding the threatenings and the oaths which Giddianhi had made, behold, the Nephites did beat them, insomuch that they did fall back from before them.
13. And it came to pass that Gidgiddoni commanded that his armies should pursue them as far as the borders of the wilderness, and that they should not spare any that should fall into their hands by the way; and thus they did pursue them and did slay them, to the borders of the wilderness, even until they had fulfilled the commandment of Gidgiddoni.
14. And it came to pass that Giddianhi, who had stood and fought with boldness, was pursued as he fled; and being weary because of his much fighting he was overtaken and slain. And thus was the end of Giddianhi the robber.
15. And it came to pass that the armies of the Nephites did return again to their place of security. And it came to pass that this nineteenth year did pass away, and the robbers did not come again to battle; neither did they come again in the twentieth year.
16. And in the twenty and first year they did not come up to battle, but they came up on all sides to lay siege round about the people of Nephi; for they did suppose that if they should cut off the people of Nephi from their lands, and should hem them in on every side, and if they should cut them off from all their outward privileges, that they could cause them to yield themselves up according to their wishes.
17. Now they had appointed unto themselves another leader, whose name was Zemnarihah; therefore it was Zemnarihah that did cause that this siege should take place.
18. But behold, this was an advantage to the Nephites; for it was impossible for the robbers to lay

siege sufficiently long to have any effect upon the Nephites,
because of their much provision which they had laid up in store,
19. And because of the scantiness of provisions among the robbers—for behold, they had nothing save it were meat for their sub-
sistence, which meat they did obtain in the wilderness;
20. And it came to pass that the wild game became scarce in the
wilderness insomuch that the robbers were about to perish with
hunger.
21. And the Nephites were continually marching out by day and
by night, and falling upon their armies, and cutting them off by
thousands and by tens of thousands.
22. And thus it became the desire of the people of Zemnarihah to
withdraw from their design, because of the great destruction which
came upon them by night and by day.
23. And it came to pass that Zemnarihah did give command unto
his people that they should withdraw themselves from the siege,
and march into the furthermost parts of the land northward.
24. And now, Gidgiddoni being aware of their design, and knowing of their weakness because of the want of food, and the great
slaughter which had been made among them, therefore he did send
out his armies in the night-time, and did cut off the way of their
retreat, and did place his armies in the way of their retreat.
25. And this did they do in the night-time, and got on their march
beyond the robbers, so that on the morrow, when the robbers
began their march, they were met by the armies of the Nephites
both in their front and in their rear.
26. And the robbers who were on the south were also cut off in their
places of retreat. And all these things were done by command of
Gidgiddoni.
27. And there were many thousands who did yield themselves up
prisoners unto the Nephites, and the remainder of them were slain.
28. And their leader, Zemnarihah, was taken and hanged upon a
tree, yea, even upon the top thereof until he was dead. And when
they had hanged him until he was dead they did fell the tree to the
earth, and did cry with a loud voice, saying:
29. May the Lord preserve his people in righteousness and in holiness of heart, that they may cause to be felled to the earth all who
shall seek to slay them because of power and secret combinations,
even as this man hath been felled to the earth.
30. And they did rejoice and cry again with one voice, saying: May
the God of Abraham, and the God of Isaac, and the God of Jacob,
protect this people in righteousness, so long as they shall call on
the name of their God for protection.
31. And it came to pass that they did break forth, all as one, in
singing, and praising their God for the great thing which he had
done for them, in preserving them from falling into the hands of
their enemies.
32. Yea, they did cry: Hosanna to the Most High God. And they
did cry: Blessed be the name of the Lord God Almighty, the Most
High God.
33. And their hearts were swollen with joy, unto the gushing out
of many tears, because of the great goodness of God in delivering
them out of the hands of their enemies; and they knew it was
because of their repentance and their humility that they had been
delivered from an everlasting destruction.

POINT OF INTEREST

Stela F, left, is on the the north side of the ruins at Quiriguá, Guatemala, which is on the border between Guatemala and Belize.

CHAPTER 5

1. AND now behold, there was not a living soul among all the people of the Nephites who did doubt in the least the words of all the holy prophets who had spoken; for they knew that it must needs be that they must be fulfilled.
2. And they knew that it must be expedient that Christ had come, because of the many signs which had been given, according to the words of the prophets; and because of the things which had come to pass already they knew that it must needs be that all things should come to pass according to that which had been spoken.
3. Therefore they did forsake all their sins, and their abominations, and their whoredoms, and did serve God with all diligence day and night.
4. And now it came to pass that when they had taken all the robbers prisoners, insomuch that none did escape who were not slain, they did cast their prisoners into prison, and did cause the word of God to be preached unto them; and as many as would repent of their sins and enter into a covenant that they would murder no more were set at liberty.
5. But as many as there were who did not enter into a covenant, and who did still continue to have those secret murders in their hearts, yea, as many as were found breathing out threatenings against their brethren were condemned and punished according to the law.
6. And thus they did put an end to all those wicked, and secret, and abominable combinations, in the which there was so much wickedness, and so many murders committed.
7. And thus had the twenty and second year passed away, and the twenty and third year also, and the twenty and fourth, and the twenty and fifth; and thus had twenty and five years passed away.
8. And there had many things transpired which, in the eyes of some, would be great and marvelous; nevertheless, they cannot all be written in this book; yea, this book cannot contain even a hundredth part of what was done among so many people in the space of twenty and five years;
9. But behold there are records which do contain all the proceedings of this people; and a shorter but true account was given by Nephi.
10. Therefore I have made my record of these things according to the record of Nephi, which was engraven on the plates which were called the plates of Nephi.
11. And behold, I do make the record on plates which I have made with mine own hands.
12. And behold, I am called Mormon, being called after the land of Mormon, the land in which Alma did establish the church among the people, yea, the first church which was established among them after their transgression.
13. Behold, I am a disciple of Jesus Christ, the Son of God. I have been called of him to declare his word among his people, that they might have everlasting life.
14. And it hath become expedient that I, according to the will of God, that the prayers of those who have

3 Nephi 5:4–5

Again, we see a philosophy that was undoubtedly influenced by the style of Captain Moroni. After they had taken the robbers prisoner, they preached the gospel to them; all those who were converted and who covenanted to no longer murder were set free. Only those who continued to threaten to murder the Nephites were condemned and punished according to the law.

3 Nephi 5:8–12

When Mormon abridged the material from the large plates of Nephi over to his own plates, he said he did not write "even a hundredth part" of that which was written in their records, including the large plates. Thus, apparently our present Book of Mormon consists of only about one percent of the original Nephite record. (Ludlow)

gone hence, who were the holy ones, should be fulfilled according to their faith, should make a record of these things which have been done—
15. Yea, a small record of that which hath taken place from the time that Lehi left Jerusalem, even down until the present time.
16. Therefore I do make my record from the accounts which have been given by those who were before me, until the commencement of my day;
17. And then I do make a record of the things which I have seen with mine own eyes.
18. And I know the record which I make to be a just and a true record; nevertheless there are many things which, according to our language, we are not able to write.
19. And now I make an end of my saying, which is of myself, and proceed to give my account of the things which have been before me.
20. I am Mormon, and a pure descendant of Lehi. I have reason to bless my God and my Savior Jesus Christ, that he brought our fathers out of the land of Jerusalem, (and no one knew it save it were himself and those whom he brought out of that land) and that he hath given me and my people so much knowledge unto the salvation of our souls.
21. Surely he hath blessed the house of Jacob, and hath been merciful unto the seed of Joseph.
22. And insomuch as the children of Lehi have kept his commandments he hath blessed them and prospered them according to his word.
23. Yea, and surely shall he again bring a remnant of the seed of Joseph to the knowledge of the Lord their God.
24. And as surely as the Lord liveth, will he gather in from the four quarters of the earth all the remnant of the seed of Jacob, who are scattered abroad upon all the face of the earth.
25. And as he hath covenanted with all the house of Jacob, even so shall the covenant wherewith he hath covenanted with the house of Jacob be fulfilled in his own due time, unto the restoring all the house of Jacob unto the knowledge of the covenant that he hath covenanted with them.
26. And then shall they know their Redeemer, who is Jesus Christ, the Son of God; and then shall they be gathered in from the four quarters of the earth unto their own lands, from whence they have been dispersed; yea, as the Lord liveth so shall it be. Amen.

CHAPTER 6

1. AND now it came to pass that the people of the Nephites did all return to their own lands in the twenty and sixth year, every man, with his family, his flocks and his herds, his horses and his cattle, and all

3 Nephi 5:24, 26

[P]ertaining to the blessing of gathering, we quote the prophet Joseph Smith as to the Lord's main purpose in gathering His people:

"What was the object of gathering the Jews, or the people of God in any age of the world?

"The main object was to build unto the Lord a house whereby He could reveal unto His people the ordinances of His house and the glories of His kingdom, and teach the people the ways of salvation; for there are certain ordinances and principles that, when they are taught and practiced, must be done in a place or house built for that purpose.

"It is for the same purpose that God gathers together His people in the last days, to build unto the Lord a house to prepare them for the ordinances and endowments, washings and anointings, etc.

"If a man gets a fullness of the priesthood of God, he has to get it in the same way that Jesus Christ obtained it, and that was by keeping all the commandments and obeying all the ordinances of the house of the Lord" (*History of the Church*, Vol. 5, 423–424). (O/C)

things whatsoever did belong unto them.

2. And it came to pass that they had not eaten up all their provisions; therefore they did take with them all that they had not devoured, of all their grain of every kind, and their gold, and their silver, and all their precious things, and they did return to their own lands and their possessions, both on the north and on the south, both on the land northward and on the land southward.

3. And they granted unto those robbers who had entered into a covenant to keep the peace of the land, who were desirous to remain Lamanites, lands, according to their numbers, that they might have, with their labors, wherewith to subsist upon; and thus they did establish peace in all the land.

4. And they began again to prosper and to wax great; and the twenty and sixth and seventh years passed away, and there was great order in the land; and they had formed their laws according to equity and justice.

5. And now there was nothing in all the land to hinder the people from prospering continually, except they should fall into transgression.

6. And now it was Gidgiddoni, and the judge, Lachoneus, and those who had been appointed leaders, who had established this great peace in the land.

7. And it came to pass that there were many cities built anew, and there were many old cities repaired.

8. And there were many highways cast up, and many roads made, which led from city to city, and from land to land, and from place to place.

9. And thus passed away the twenty and eighth year, and the people had continual peace.

10. But it came to pass in the twenty and ninth year there began to be some disputings among the people; and some were lifted up unto pride and boastings because of their exceedingly great riches, yea, even unto great persecutions;

11. For there were many merchants in the land, and also many lawyers, and many officers.

12. And the people began to be distinguished by ranks, according to their riches and their chances for learning, yea, some were ignorant because of their poverty, and others did receive great learning because of their riches.

13. Some were lifted up in pride, and others were exceedingly humble; some did return railing for railing, while others would receive railing and persecution and all manner of afflictions, and would not turn and revile again, but were humble and penitent before God.

14. And thus there became a great inequality in all the land, insomuch that the church began to be broken up; yea, insomuch that in the thirtieth year the church was broken up in all the land save it were among a few of the Lamanites who were converted unto the true faith; and they would not depart from it, for they were firm, and steadfast, and immovable, willing with all diligence to keep the commandments of the Lord.

15. Now the cause of this iniquity of the people was this—Satan had great power, unto the stirring up of the people to do all manner of iniquity, and to the puffing them up

3 Nephi 6:10–15

Despite the miraculous signs given at the birth of Christ, within thirty years many members of the church had apostatized. Apparently the beginning cause of this apostasy was the pride of the people. . . . Apparently pride is the first slope down on the "roller coaster" so far as both apostasy and war are concerned. When people start to believe they are better than others, then they start ridiculing and persecuting other people, and apostasy and war are the inevitable results. (Ludlow)

3 Nephi 6:10–16

Pride gets no pleasure out of possessing something, but possessing more of it than the next man. . . . It is the comparison that makes you proud: the pleasure of being above the rest. Once the element of competition has gone, pride has gone (C. S. Lewis, *Mere Christianity* [New York: Macmillan, 1960], 109–110).

3 Nephi 6:10–16

Thomas Jefferson said, "Material abundance without character is the surest way to destruction."

3 Nephi 6:15

Pride, as it clouds spiritual vision and filters out the promptings of the Lord, leads to inevitable destruction. Penitent humility and obedience to divine commandments are the only sure antidotes to pride.

After the great victory over the forces of evil, the Nephites returned to their own places of residence throughout the land and enjoyed an abundance of prosperity. That is when they came face to face with their nemesis: "And now there was nothing in all the land to hinder the people from prospering continually, except they should fall into transgression" (3 Ne. 6:5). On the slippery slope of wealth and pride they quickly lapsed into forgetfulness and neglect of their covenant obligations. . . . Save for a few righteous and stalwart Lamanites, the people degraded into gross inequality and began to sin willfully against the light of the gospel. Prophets arose and were rejected. Civil justice collapsed through the spread of secret and murderous combinations, and the government dissolved into tribal compacts. . . .

With great power, Nephi, who had daily interaction with angels (see 3 Ne. 7:18), commanded the people to repent, and performed astounding miracles among them. However, there were relatively few who were willing to be reclaimed from their iniquity on the eve of the great geophysical dislocations that were to attend the death and resurrection of the Lord.

Elder Jeffrey R. Holland said, "That kind of faithfulness brought prosperity so great that 'nothing in all the land [could] hinder the people from prospering continually, except they should fall into transgression.' But fall into transgression they did, as a result of those two challenges that were forever the destruction of Nephite righteousness—pride and riches." (P/A)

with pride, tempting them to seek for power, and authority, and riches, and the vain things of the world.
16. And thus Satan did lead away the hearts of the people to do all manner of iniquity; therefore they had enjoyed peace but a few years.
17. And thus, in the commencement of the thirtieth year—the people having been delivered up for the space of a long time to be carried about by the temptations of the devil whithersoever he desired to carry them, and to do whatsoever iniquity he desired they should—and thus in the commencement of this, the thirtieth year, they were in a state of awful wickedness.
18. Now they did not sin ignorantly, for they knew the will of God concerning them, for it had been taught unto them; therefore they did wilfully rebel against God.
19. And now it was in the days of Lachoneus, the son of Lachoneus, for Lachoneus did fill the seat of his father and did govern the people that year.
20. And there began to be men inspired from heaven and sent forth, standing among the people in all the land, preaching and testifying boldly of the sins and iniquities of the people, and testifying unto them concerning the redemption which the Lord would make for his people, or in other words, the resurrection of Christ; and they did testify boldly of his death and sufferings.
21. Now there were many of the people who were exceedingly angry because of those who testified of these things; and those who were angry were chiefly the chief judges, and they who had been high priests and lawyers; yea, all those who were lawyers were angry with those who testified of these things.
22. Now there was no lawyer nor judge nor high priest that could have power to condemn any one to death save their condemnation was signed by the governor of the land.
23. Now there were many of those who testified of the things pertaining to Christ who testified boldly, who were taken and put to death secretly by the judges, that the knowledge of their death came not unto the governor of the land until after their death.
24. Now behold, this was contrary to the laws of the land, that any man should be put to death except they had power from the governor of the land—
25. Therefore a complaint came up unto the land of Zarahemla, to the governor of the land, against these judges who had condemned the prophets of the Lord unto death, not according to the law.
26. Now it came to pass that they were taken and brought up before the judge, to be judged of the crime which they had done, according to the law which had been given by the people.
27. Now it came to pass that those judges had many friends and kindreds; and the remainder, yea, even almost all the lawyers and the high priests, did gather themselves together, and unite with the kindreds of those judges who were to be tried according to the law.
28. And they did enter into a covenant one with another, yea, even into that covenant which was given by them of old, which covenant was given and administered by the devil, to combine against all righteousness.

29. Therefore they did combine against the people of the Lord, and enter into a covenant to destroy them, and to deliver those who were guilty of murder from the grasp of justice, which was about to be administered according to the law.
30. And they did set at defiance the law and the rights of their country; and they did covenant one with another to destroy the governor, and to establish a king over the land, that the land should no more be at liberty but should be subject unto kings.

CHAPTER 7

1. NOW behold, I will show unto you that they did not establish a king over the land; but in this same year, yea, the thirtieth year, they did destroy upon the judgment-seat, yea, did murder the chief judge of the land.
2. And the people were divided one against another; and they did separate one from another into tribes, every man according to his family and his kindred and friends; and thus they did destroy the government of the land.
3. And every tribe did appoint a chief or a leader over them; and thus they became tribes and leaders of tribes.
4. Now behold, there was no man among them save he had much family and many kindreds and friends; therefore their tribes became exceedingly great.
5. Now all this was done, and there were no wars as yet among them; and all this iniquity had come upon the people because they did yield themselves unto the power of Satan.
6. And the regulations of the government were destroyed, because of the secret combination of the friends and kindreds of those who murdered the prophets.
7. And they did cause a great contention in the land, insomuch that the more righteous part of the people had nearly all become wicked; yea, there were but few righteous men among them.
8. And thus six years had not passed away since the more part of the people had turned from their righteousness, like the dog to his vomit, or like the sow to her wallowing in the mire.
9. Now this secret combination, which had brought so great iniquity upon the people, did gather themselves together, and did place at their head a man whom they did call Jacob;
10. And they did call him their king; therefore he became a king over this wicked band; and he was one of the chiefest who had given his voice against the prophets who testified of Jesus.
11. And it came to pass that they were not so strong in number as the tribes of the people, who were united together save it were their leaders did establish their laws, every one according to his tribe; nevertheless they were enemies; notwithstanding they were not a righteous people, yet they were united in the hatred of those who had entered into a covenant to destroy the government.
12. Therefore, Jacob seeing that their enemies were more numerous than they, he being the king of the band, therefore he commanded his

3 Nephi 7:2

In our day, prophets have warned us about the presence of secret combinations (see Ether 8:22–25) and the impending disruption of our constitutional government. On July 19, 1840, the Prophet Joseph Smith declared: "Even this Nation will be on the very verge of crumbling to pieces and tumbling to the ground and when the constitution is upon the brink of ruin this people will be the Staff upon which the Nation shall lean and they shall bear the constitution away from the very verge of destruction." (O/C)

3 Nephi 7:2–3

The strong family ties indicated here are reminiscent of the emphasis of the early Hebrews on the family. After the appearance of the resurrected Jesus Christ to these people, they again have a strong central government for over three hundred years. However, after that time, the government begins to disintegrate and by the close of the Book of Mormon almost complete anarchy exists. Apparently after A.D. 400 the people divide into tribes again, for this is the system of government they had when the white man came almost 1,000 years later. (Ludlow)

people that they should take their flight into the northernmost part of the land, and there build up unto themselves a kingdom, until they were joined by dissenters, (for he flattered them that there would be many dissenters) and they become sufficiently strong to contend with the tribes of the people; and they did so.
13. And so speedy was their march that it could not be impeded until they had gone forth out of the reach of the people. And thus ended the thirtieth year; and thus were the affairs of the people of Nephi.
14. And it came to pass in the thirty and first year that they were divided into tribes, every man according to his family, kindred and friends; nevertheless they had come to an agreement that they would not go to war one with another; but they were not united as to their laws, and their manner of government, for they were established according to the minds of those who were their chiefs and their leaders. But they did establish very strict laws that one tribe should not trespass against another, insomuch that in some degree they had peace in the land; nevertheless, their hearts were turned from the Lord their God, and they did stone the prophets and did cast them out from among them.
15. And it came to pass that Nephi—having been visited by angels and also the voice of the Lord, therefore having seen angels, and being eye-witness, and having had power given unto him that he might know concerning the ministry of Christ, and also being eye-witness to their quick return from righteousness unto their wickedness and abominations;
16. Therefore, being grieved for the hardness of their hearts and the blindness of their minds—went forth among them in that same year, and began to testify, boldly, repentance and remission of sins through faith on the Lord Jesus Christ.
17. And he did minister many things unto them; and all of them cannot be written, and a part of them would not suffice, therefore they are not written in this book. And Nephi did minister with power and with great authority.
18. And it came to pass that they were angry with him, even because he had greater power than they, for it were not possible that they could disbelieve his words, for so great was his faith on the Lord Jesus Christ that angels did minister unto him daily.
19. And in the name of Jesus did he cast out devils and unclean spirits; and even his brother did he raise from the dead, after he had been stoned and suffered death by the people.
20. And the people saw it, and did witness of it, and were angry with him because of his power; and he did also do many more miracles, in the sight of the people, in the name of Jesus.
21. And it came to pass that the thirty and first year did pass away, and there were but few who were converted unto the Lord; but as many as were converted did truly signify unto the people that they had been visited by the power and Spirit of God, which was in Jesus Christ, in whom they believed.
22. And as many as had devils cast out from them, and were healed of their sicknesses and their infirmities, did truly manifest unto the

3 Nephi 7:18

Brigham Young said, "The Lord is here with us, not in person, but his angels are around us, and he takes cognizance of every act of the children of men, as individuals and as nations. He is here ready by his agents, the angels, . . . to bring most perfect and absolute deliverance unto all who put their trust in him, when they are ready to receive it. . . . What is the difference between Saints of God and an angel of God? One is clothed upon with mortality, the other has passed through mortality and has received the celestial glory of our Heavenly Father, and is free from the contaminating influences of sin that we have to contend with. . . . When the Lord commands those invisible beings, shall I say, those who have had their resurrection? yes, millions and millions more than the inhabitants of this earth, they can fight your battles."

people that they had been wrought upon by the Spirit of God, and had been healed; and they did show forth signs also and did do some miracles among the people.
23. Thus passed away the thirty and second year also. And Nephi did cry unto the people in the commencement of the thirty and third year; and he did preach unto them repentance and remission of sins.
24. Now I would have you to remember also, that there were none who were brought unto repentance who were not baptized with water.
25. Therefore, there were ordained of Nephi, men unto this ministry, that all such as should come unto them should be baptized with water, and this as a witness and a testimony before God, and unto the people, that they had repented and received a remission of their sins.
26. And there were many in the commencement of this year that were baptized unto repentance; and thus the more part of the year did pass away.

CHAPTER 8

1. AND now it came to pass that according to our record, and we know our record to be true, for behold, it was a just man who did keep the record—for he truly did many miracles in the name of Jesus; and there was not any man who could do a miracle in the name of Jesus save he were cleansed every whit from his iniquity—
2. And now it came to pass, if there was no mistake made by this man in the reckoning of our time, the thirty and third year had passed away;
3. And the people began to look with great earnestness for the sign which had been given by the prophet Samuel, the Lamanite, yea, for the time that there should be darkness for the space of three days over the face of the land.
4. And there began to be great doubtings and disputations among the people, notwithstanding so many signs had been given.
5. And it came to pass in the thirty and fourth year, in the first month, on the fourth day of the month, there arose a great storm, such an one as never had been known in all the land.
6. And there was also a great and terrible tempest; and there was terrible thunder, insomuch that it did shake the whole earth as if it was about to divide asunder.
7. And there were exceedingly sharp lightnings, such as never had been known in all the land.
8. And the city of Zarahemla did take fire.
9. And the city of Moroni did sink into the depths of the sea, and the inhabitants thereof were drowned.
10. And the earth was carried up upon the city of Moronihah that in the place of the city there became a great mountain.

3 Nephi 8:5

The New Testament account of the crucifixion of Christ would seem to indicate that the Savior was crucified the very week he became thirty-three years of age. The Book of Mormon not only substantiates this account, but also provides us with an exact date of the crucifixion. . . . Although we are not certain when the first month of the Nephite calendar would occur, if the Nephites were using the same calendar system as the Hebrews, the first month would be in the spring of the year sometime between about the middle of March and the middle of April. (Ludlow)

11. And there was a great and terrible destruction in the land southward.
12. But behold, there was a more great and terrible destruction in the land northward; for behold, the whole face of the land was changed, because of the tempest and the whirlwinds, and the thunderings and the lightnings, and the exceedingly great quaking of the whole earth;
13. And the highways were broken up, and the level roads were spoiled, and many smooth places became rough.
14. And many great and notable cities were sunk, and many were burned, and many were shaken till the buildings thereof had fallen to the earth, and the inhabitants thereof were slain, and the places were left desolate.
15. And there were some cities which remained; but the damage thereof was exceedingly great, and there were many in them who were slain.
16. And there were some who were carried away in the whirlwind; and whither they went no man knoweth, save they know that they were carried away.
17. And thus the face of the whole earth became deformed, because of the tempests, and the thunderings, and the lightnings, and the quaking of the earth.
18. And behold, the rocks were rent in twain; they were broken up upon the face of the whole earth, insomuch that they were found in broken fragments, and in seams and in cracks, upon all the face of the land.
19. And it came to pass that when the thunderings, and the lightnings, and the storm, and the tempest, and the quakings of the earth did cease—for behold, they did last for about the space of three hours; and it was said by some that the time was greater; nevertheless, all these great and terrible things were done in about the space of three hours—and then behold, there was darkness upon the face of the land.
20. And it came to pass that there was thick darkness upon all the face of the land, insomuch that the inhabitants thereof who had not fallen could feel the vapor of darkness;
21. And there could be no light, because of the darkness, neither candles, neither torches; neither could there be fire kindled with their fine and exceedingly dry wood, so that there could not be any light at all;
22. And there was not any light seen, neither fire, nor glimmer, neither the sun, nor the moon, nor the stars, for so great were the mists of darkness which were upon the face of the land.
23. And it came to pass that it did last for the space of three days that there was no light seen; and there was great mourning and howling and weeping among all the people continually; yea, great were the groanings of the people, because of the darkness and the great destruction which had come upon them.
24. And in one place they were heard to cry, saying: O that we had repented before this great and terrible day, and then would our brethren have been spared, and they would not have been burned in that great city Zarahemla.
25. And in another place they were heard to cry and mourn, saying: O that we had repented before this great and terrible day, and had not killed and stoned the prophets, and cast them out; then would our

3 Nephi 8:19

Why was there darkness on all the face of the land? Christ, the Light of the World, had been extinguished from this sphere, and could not return until His resurrection.

mothers and our fair daughters, and our children have been spared, and not have been buried up in that great city Moronihah. And thus were the howlings of the people great and terrible.

CHAPTER 9

1. AND it came to pass that there was a voice heard among all the inhabitants of the earth, upon all the face of this land, crying:
2. Wo, wo, wo unto this people; wo unto the inhabitants of the whole earth except they shall repent; for the devil laugheth, and his angels rejoice, because of the slain of the fair sons and daughters of my people; and it is because of their iniquity and abominations that they are fallen!
3. Behold, that great city Zarahemla have I burned with fire, and the inhabitants thereof.
4. And behold, that great city Moroni have I caused to be sunk in the depths of the sea, and the inhabitants thereof to be drowned.
5. And behold, that great city Moronihah have I covered with earth, and the inhabitants thereof, to hide their iniquities and their abominations from before my face, that the blood of the prophets and the saints shall not come any more unto me against them.
6. And behold, the city of Gilgal have I caused to be sunk, and the inhabitants thereof to be buried up in the depths of the earth;
7. Yea, and the city of Onihah and the inhabitants thereof, and the city of Mocum and the inhabitants thereof, and the city of Jerusalem and the inhabitants thereof; and waters have I caused to come up in the stead thereof, to hide their wickedness and abominations from before my face, that the blood of the prophets and the saints shall not come up any more unto me against them.
8. And behold, the city of Gadiandi, and the city of Gadiomnah, and the city of Jacob, and the city of Gimgimno, all these have I caused to be sunk, and made hills and valleys in the places thereof; and the inhabitants thereof have I buried up in the depths of the earth, to hide their wickedness and abominations from before my face, that the blood of the prophets and the saints should not come up any more unto me against them.
9. And behold, that great city Jacobugath, which was inhabited by the people of king Jacob, have I caused to be burned with fire because of their sins and their wickedness, which was above all the wickedness of the whole earth, because of their secret murders and combinations; for it was they that did destroy the peace of my people and the government of the land; therefore I did cause them to be burned, to destroy them from before my face, that the blood of the prophets and the saints should not come up unto me any more against them.

3 Nephi 9—10

From our understanding of the reasons for the cataclysmic destructions that took place at the crucifixion of the Savior, we can see the law of justice in operation in both of its dimensions. First of all, it was the means of **condemnation and destruction of the wicked**. Book of Mormon readers readily see that connection. But secondly, and maybe not so apparent, is that it was also an outward manifestation of the Savior's intense suffering in His act of **redemption for the righteous**, in order that they might be saved from physical as well as spiritual destructive forces and thus blessed for their righteousness. (O/C)

10. And behold, the city of Laman, and the city of Josh, and the city of Gad, and the city of Kishkumen, have I caused to be burned with fire, and the inhabitants thereof, because of their wickedness in casting out the prophets, and stoning those whom I did send to declare unto them concerning their wickedness and their abominations.

11. And because they did cast them all out, that there were none righteous among them, I did send down fire and destroy them, that their wickedness and abominations might be hid from before my face, that the blood of the prophets and the saints whom I sent among them might not cry unto me from the ground against them.

12. And many great destructions have I caused to come upon this land, and upon this people, because of their wickedness and their abominations.

13. O all ye that are spared because ye were more righteous than they, will ye not now return unto me, and repent of your sins, and be converted, that I may heal you?

14. Yea, verily I say unto you, if ye will come unto me ye shall have eternal life. Behold, mine arm of mercy is extended towards you, and whosoever will come, him will I receive; and blessed are those who come unto me.

15. Behold, I am Jesus Christ the Son of God. I created the heavens and the earth, and all things that in them are. I was with the Father from the beginning. I am in the Father, and the Father in me; and in me hath the Father glorified his name.

16. I came unto my own, and my own received me not. And the scriptures concerning my coming are fulfilled.

17. And as many as have received me, to them have I given to become the sons of God; and even so will I to as many as shall believe on my name, for behold, by me redemption cometh, and in me is the law of Moses fulfilled.

18. I am the light and the life of the world. I am Alpha and Omega, the beginning and the end.

19. And ye shall offer up unto me no more the shedding of blood; yea, your sacrifices and your burnt offerings shall be done away, for I will accept none of your sacrifices and your burnt offerings.

20. And ye shall offer for a sacrifice unto me a broken heart and a contrite spirit. And whoso cometh unto me with a broken heart and a contrite spirit, him will I baptize with fire and with the Holy Ghost, even as the Lamanites, because of their faith in me at the time of their conversion, were baptized with fire and with the Holy Ghost, and they knew it not.

21. Behold, I have come unto the world to bring redemption unto the world, to save the world from sin.

POINT OF INTEREST

The Nunnery Quadrangle (a nickname given to it by the Spanish from the time when it served as a governor's palace) is the finest of Uxmal's several quadrangles of long buildings in Yucatán, Mexico.

3 Nephi 9:17

The Savior's statement in this scripture is quite similar to a statement he made to the Brother of Jared over 2,000 years earlier as a pre-earthly spirit: "In me shall all mankind have light, and that eternally, even they who shall believe on my name; and they shall become my sons and my daughters" (Ether 3:14). (Ludlow)

3 Nephi 9:19–20

While it was yet dark following the great destructions upon the land and prior to His appearance to the people, the Lord spoke from the heavens. One of the subjects He addressed was the need for the people to change the manner in which they were to obey the Lord's law of sacrifice. [He then gave the instruction found in 3 Ne. 9:19-20.]

President J. Reuben Clark explained the concept associated with this dramatic change in keeping the law of sacrifice:

"It is difficult for us today to realize the tremendous revolution involved in altering the ritualism of the Law of Moses into the humble and lowly concept of worship, not with the sacrificial blood of animals, but with this broken heart and contrite spirit of the worshiper.

". . . under the new covenant that came in with Christ, the sinner must offer the sacrifice out of his own life, not by offering the blood of some other creature; he must give up his sins, he must repent, he himself must make the sacrifice, and that sacrifice was calculated to reach out into the life of the sinner in the future so that he would become a better and changed man." . . .

This change represents a transition in emphasis from the physical to the spiritual and a change from a vicarious sacrifice to a personal one. The principle involved is that one can only come unto Christ by removing barriers between the individual and the Savior. (O/C)

22. Therefore, whoso repenteth and cometh unto me as a little child, him will I receive, for of such is the kingdom of God. Behold, for such I have laid down my life, and have taken it up again; therefore repent, and come unto me ye ends of the earth, and be saved.

CHAPTER 10

1. AND now behold, it came to pass that all the people of the land did hear these sayings, and did witness of it. And after these sayings there was silence in the land for the space of many hours;
2. For so great was the astonishment of the people that they did cease lamenting and howling for the loss of their kindred which had been slain; therefore there was silence in all the land for the space of many hours.
3. And it came to pass that there came a voice again unto the people, and all the people did hear, and did witness of it, saying:
4. O ye people of these great cities which have fallen, who are descendants of Jacob, yea, who are of the house of Israel, how oft have I gathered you as a hen gathereth her chickens under her wings, and have nourished you.
5. And again, how oft would I have gathered you as a hen gathereth her chickens under her wings, yea, O ye people of the house of Israel, who have fallen; yea, O ye people of the house of Israel, ye that dwell at Jerusalem, as ye that have fallen; yea, how oft would I have gathered you as a hen gathereth her chickens, and ye would not.
6. O ye house of Israel whom I have spared, how oft will I gather you as a hen gathereth her chickens under her wings, if ye will repent and return unto me with full purpose of heart.
7. But if not, O house of Israel, the places of your dwellings shall become desolate until the time of the fulfilling of the covenant to your fathers.
8. And now it came to pass that after the people had heard these words, behold, they began to weep and howl again because of the loss of their kindred and friends.
9. And it came to pass that thus did the three days pass away. And it was in the morning, and the darkness dispersed from off the face of the land, and the earth did cease to tremble, and the rocks did cease to rend, and the dreadful groanings did cease, and all the tumultuous noises did pass away.
10. And the earth did cleave together again, that it stood; and the mourning, and the weeping, and the wailing of the people who were spared alive did cease; and their mourning was turned into joy, and their lamentations into the praise and thanksgiving unto the Lord Jesus Christ, their Redeemer.
11. And thus far were the scriptures fulfilled which had been spoken by the prophets.
12. And it was the more righteous part of the people who were saved, and it was they who received the

3 Nephi 10:4

The comparison of the Savior to a hen is an interesting one. A hen cares for her chicks and would sacrifice her life for them; whenever danger threatens, she gathers them under her wings for protection. The Lord loves His people and gave His life for them; He seeks to gather them so He can nourish and protect them. Sadly, some reject His efforts—and, like helpless chicks who are separated from their mother, are left to suffer the ravages of destruction as a result.

3 Nephi 10:12–13

This verse provides a description of those who were spared from destruction. When Karl G. Maeser was leading a group of missionaries through the Alps, he said that prophets are like the poles stuck in the glacier to mark the safe path. Just as hikers through the treacherous Alps, if we step off the path they mark for us, we are lost.

prophets and stoned them not; and it was they who had not shed the blood of the saints, who were spared—

13. And they were spared and were not sunk and buried up in the earth; and they were not drowned in the depths of the sea; and they were not burned by fire, neither were they fallen upon and crushed to death; and they were not carried away in the whirlwind; neither were they overpowered by the vapor of smoke and of darkness.

14. And now, whoso readeth, let him understand; he that hath the scriptures, let him search them, and see and behold if all these deaths and destructions by fire, and by smoke, and by tempests, and by whirlwinds, and by the opening of the earth to receive them, and all these things are not unto the fulfilling of the prophecies of many of the holy prophets.

15. Behold, I say unto you, Yea, many have testified of these things at the coming of Christ, and were slain because they testified of these things.

16. Yea, the prophet Zenos did testify of these things, and also Zenock spake concerning these things, because they testified particularly concerning us, who are the remnant of their seed.

17. Behold, our father Jacob also testified concerning a remnant of the seed of Joseph. And behold, are not we a remnant of the seed of Joseph? And these things which testify of us, are they not written upon the plates of brass which our father Lehi brought out of Jerusalem?

18. And it came to pass that in the ending of the thirty and fourth year, behold, I will show unto you that the people of Nephi who were spared, and also those who had been called Lamanites, who had been spared, did have great favors shown unto them, and great blessings poured out upon their heads, insomuch that soon after the ascension of Christ into heaven he did truly manifest himself unto them—

19. Showing his body unto them, and ministering unto them; and an account of his ministry shall be given hereafter. Therefore for this time I make an end of my sayings.

Jesus Christ did show himself unto the people of Nephi, as the multitude were gathered together in the land Bountiful, and did minister unto them; and on this wise did he show himself unto them. Comprising chapters 11 to 26 inclusive.

CHAPTER 11

1. AND now it came to pass that there were a great multitude gathered together, of the people of Nephi, round about the temple which was in the land Bountiful; and they were marveling and wondering one with another, and were showing one to another the great and marvelous change which had taken place.

2. And they were also conversing about this Jesus Christ, of whom the sign had been given concerning his death.

3 Nephi 10:14

Many who heard the prophets believed that the prophets were wrong and out of touch. When the destruction began—essentially, when it was too late—it became immediately obvious to even the doubters how right the prophets had been. At that point, the opportunity for preparation and salvation was gone. The destructions in our day will be just as terrible; for examples, see D&C 29:14–21; D&C 43:19–25; D&C 45:39–42; D&C 88:87–91; and D&C 133:4–49.

3 Nephi 11

The people assembled themselves to ponder the extraordinary events they had experienced. Thrice they heard a small but piercing voice from the heavens, and upon the third occasion they were finally able to understand the thrilling message. God the Father, Elohim, introduced His Beloved Son, the Savior and Redeemer of the World, the Lord Jesus Christ. Christ descended from heaven in full view of the people, identified Himself as the living Christ, and began teaching the doctrine of the kingdom. His message was one of covenant: His will was that the people should exercise faith in Him, repent of their sins, and be baptized in water and through the Holy Ghost as a sacred covenant of obedience and righteousness.

Elder Jeffrey R. Holland said, "To the Nephites gathered at the temple, He would say, 'Behold, I am Jesus Christ, . . . the light and the life of the world; and I have drunk out of that bitter cup which the father hath given me, and . . . I have suffered the will of the Father in all things from the beginning' (3 Nephi 11:10–11). That is His own introduction of Himself, the declaration He feels best tells us who He is." (P/A)

3. And it came to pass that while they were thus conversing one with another, they heard a voice as if it came out of heaven; and they cast their eyes round about, for they understood not the voice which they heard; and it was not a harsh voice, neither was it a loud voice; nevertheless, and notwithstanding it being a small voice it did pierce them that did hear to the center, insomuch that there was no part of their frame that it did not cause to quake; yea, it did pierce them to the very soul, and did cause their hearts to burn.
4. And it came to pass that again they heard the voice, and they understood it not.
5. And again the third time they did hear the voice, and did open their ears to hear it; and their eyes were towards the sound thereof; and they did look steadfastly towards heaven, from whence the sound came.
6. And behold, the third time they did understand the voice which they heard; and it said unto them:
7. Behold my Beloved Son, in whom I am well pleased, in whom I have glorified my name—hear ye him.
8. And it came to pass, as they understood they cast their eyes up again towards heaven; and behold, they saw a Man descending out of heaven; and he was clothed in a white robe; and he came down and stood in the midst of them; and the eyes of the whole multitude were turned upon him, and they durst not open their mouths, even one to another, and wist not what it meant, for they thought it was an angel that had appeared unto them.
9. And it came to pass that he stretched forth his hand and spake unto the people, saying:
10. Behold, I am Jesus Christ, whom the prophets testified shall come into the world.
11. And behold, I am the light and the life of the world; and I have drunk out of that bitter cup which the Father hath given me, and have glorified the Father in taking upon me the sins of the world, in the which I have suffered the will of the Father in all things from the beginning.
12. And it came to pass that when Jesus had spoken these words the whole multitude fell to the earth; for they remembered that it had been prophesied among them that Christ should show himself unto them after his ascension into heaven.
13. And it came to pass that the Lord spake unto them saying:
14. Arise and come forth unto me, that ye may thrust your hands into my side, and also that ye may feel the prints of the nails in my hands and in my feet, that ye may know that I am the God of Israel, and the God of the whole earth, and have been slain for the sins of the world.
15. And it came to pass that the multitude went forth, and thrust their hands into his side, and did feel the prints of the nails in his hands and in his feet; and this they

3 Nephi 11:11

Jesus Christ is the light and the life of the world. The light of Christ enlighteneth our eyes, quickeneth our understanding, fills the immensity of space, is in all things, giveth life to all things, governs all things and is the power of God (see D&C 88:11–13). Without the light of Christ, all things would cease to exist. Is it any wonder that all mankind will bow the knee and acknowledge that Jesus is the Christ, the God of this world? (See Mosiah 27:31.)

The plan of redemption is of the Father. He chose His Son Jesus Christ to be the redeemer of His children. (See Moses 4:1–3) The resurrected Savior said:

". . . I have drunk out of that bitter cup which the Father hath given me, and have glorified the Father in taking upon me the sins of the world, in the which I have suffered the will of the Father in all things from the beginning" (3 Ne. 11:11).

Speaking to King Noah and his wicked priests, the prophet Abinadi testified that God the Father gained the victory over death through the power He gave His Son Jesus Christ:

"And thus God breaketh the bands of death, having gained the victory over death; *giving the Son power to make intercession for the children of men*" (Mosiah 15:8, emphasis added).

Thus the Savior's Atonement was an act of His being proxy for two parties, namely, His father and His Father's children.

We wonder what it would have been like to have the same experience the Nephites had. We wonder what it would be like to hear His own voice, to hear His own words, to see His glory, to touch His glorified body, and to receive His personal witness of Himself. We wonder what we would give to have this same experience. This wonderment is recorded in the anticipated treasures of our minds; for we are promised that if we keep His commandments, we may be in His presence and partake of His glory (see D&C 93:1). (O/C)

did do, going forth one by one until they had all gone forth, and did
see with their eyes and did feel with their hands, and did know of a
surety and did bear record, that it was he, of whom it was written by
the prophets, that should come.
16. And when they had all gone forth and had witnessed for themselves, they did cry out with one accord, saying:
17. Hosanna! Blessed be the name of the Most High God! And
they did fall down at the feet of Jesus, and did worship him.
18. And it came to pass that he spake unto Nephi (for Nephi was
among the multitude) and he commanded him that he should
come forth.
19. And Nephi arose and went forth, and bowed himself before the
Lord and did kiss his feet.
20. And the Lord commanded him that he should arise. And he
arose and stood before him.
21. And the Lord said unto him: I give unto you power that ye
shall baptize this people when I am again ascended into heaven.
22. And again the Lord called others, and said unto them likewise;
and he gave unto them power to baptize. And he said unto them:
On this wise shall ye baptize; and there shall be no disputations
among you.
23. Verily I say unto you, that whoso repenteth of his sins through
your words, and desireth to be baptized in my name, on this wise
shall ye baptize them—Behold, ye shall go down and stand in the
water, and in my name shall ye baptize them.
24. And now behold, these are the words which ye shall say, calling them by name, saying:
25. Having authority given me of Jesus Christ, I baptize you in the
name of the Father, and of the Son, and of the Holy Ghost. Amen.
26. And then shall ye immerse them in the water, and come forth
again out of the water.
27. And after this manner shall ye baptize in my name; for behold,
verily I say unto you, that the Father, and the Son, and the Holy
Ghost are one; and I am in the Father, and the Father in me, and
the Father and I are one.
28. And according as I have commanded you thus shall ye baptize.
And there shall be no disputations among you, as there have hitherto been; neither shall there be disputations among you concerning the points of my doctrine, as there have hitherto been.
29. For verily, verily I say unto you, he that hath the spirit of contention is not of me, but is of the devil, who is the father of contention, and he stirreth up the hearts of men to contend with
anger, one with another.
30. Behold, this is not my doctrine, to stir up the hearts of men
with anger, one against another; but this

3 Nephi 11:16–21

The word *Hosanna* is a transliteration of a Hebrew word of supplication which means in essence "Oh, grant salvation." Evidently the people were asking the Savior to teach them the way to salvation; thus it is not surprising that he immediately teaches them the basic principles and ordinances of the gospel. (Ludlow)

3 Nephi 11:21–34

. . . Some students have raised the question as to why the words of the baptismal prayer in the Book of Mormon differ slightly from the prayer listed in the Doctrine and Covenants. In this dispensation the Lord has counseled us to use these words in baptizing a person, after calling the candidate by name: "Having been commissioned of Jesus Christ, I baptize you in the name of the Father, and of the Son, and of the Holy Ghost. Amen." (D&C 20:73.) The only difference in the two prayers is the introductory statement. In the Book of Mormon the disciples were counseled to say "having authority given me of Jesus Christ," whereas in this dispensation we are told to say "having been commissioned of Jesus Christ."

One possible explanation for this difference may be associated with the problem of translation. For example, it is not always possible to translate exact words into other languages; thus, the baptismal prayer is not exactly the same in all languages. Another possibility for explaining this difference is that the disciples in the Book of Mormon received their authority *directly* from Jesus Christ; therefore, they rightfully could say "having authority given me of Jesus Christ." However, in this dispensation priesthood bearers have been given the power to baptize from John the Baptist, who was commissioned by Jesus Christ to come to earth and restore this authority. Therefore, in this dispensation we use the words "having been commissioned of Jesus Christ." (Ludlow)

3 Nephi 11:27, 32

The complete oneness of the Father, the Son, and the Holy Ghost was expressed by President George Q. Cannon:

"Now, can you conceive of a oneness more close, more complete than the oneness that exists between the Father and the Son? It is impossible for the human mind to get the faintest idea of any difference of opinion or expression or action between the Father and the Son. We worship them as one God—not three Gods, not two Gods but as one God. The Father and the Son are the two personages of the Deity, with the Holy Ghost as their ministering Spirit or agent. We worship them as one. We do not separate them in our thought and in our feelings." (George Q. Cannon, *Gospel Truth*, Vol. 1, 205). (O/C)

is my doctrine, that such things should be done away.
31. Behold, verily, verily, I say unto you, I will declare unto you my doctrine.
32. And this is my doctrine, and it is the doctrine which the Father hath given unto me; and I bear record of the Father, and the Father beareth record of me, and the Holy Ghost beareth record of the Father and me; and I bear record that the Father commandeth all men, everywhere, to repent and believe in me.
33. And whoso believeth in me, and is baptized, the same shall be saved; and they are they who shall inherit the kingdom of God.
34. And whoso believeth not in me, and is not baptized, shall be damned.
35. Verily, verily, I say unto you, that this is my doctrine, and I bear record of it from the Father; and whoso believeth in me believeth in the Father also; and unto him will the Father bear record of me, for he will visit him with fire and with the Holy Ghost.
36. And thus will the Father bear record of me, and the Holy Ghost will bear record unto him of the Father and me; for the Father, and I, and the Holy Ghost are one.
37. And again I say unto you, ye must repent, and become as a little child, and be baptized in my name, or ye can in nowise receive these things.
38. And again I say unto you, ye must repent, and be baptized in my name, and become as a little child, or ye can in nowise inherit the kingdom of God.
39. Verily, verily, I say unto you, that this is my doctrine, and whoso buildeth upon this buildeth upon my rock, and the gates of hell shall not prevail against them.
40. And whoso shall declare more or less than this, and establish it for my doctrine, the same cometh of evil, and is not built upon my rock; but he buildeth upon a sandy foundation, and the gates of hell stand open to receive such when the floods come and the winds beat upon them.
41. Therefore, go forth unto this people, and declare the words which I have spoken, unto the ends of the earth.

CHAPTER 12

1. AND it came to pass that when Jesus had spoken these words unto Nephi, and to those who had been called, (now the number of them who had been called, and received power and authority to baptize, was twelve) and behold, he stretched forth his hand unto the multitude,

3 Nephi 12

It is noted that the first five beatitudes portray men coming unto the Savior, entering into His rest and partaking of His peace. They are in a blessed and happy condition. They are new creatures in Christ, they walk in newness of life, they have been born again. They now live the commandments. They are *doing* good as well as *being* good. They are bringing to pass much righteousness. The remaining Beatitudes portray these new creatures in Christ, those who are born again, being instruments for righteousness. (O/C)

and cried unto them, saying: Blessed are ye if ye shall give heed unto the words of these twelve whom I have chosen from among you to minister unto you, and to be your servants; and unto them I have given power that they may baptize you with water; and after that ye are baptized with water, behold, I will baptize you with fire and with the Holy Ghost; therefore blessed are ye if ye shall believe in me and be baptized, after that ye have seen me and know that I am.
2. And again, more blessed are they who shall believe in your words because that ye shall testify that ye have seen me, and that ye know that I am. Yea, blessed are they who shall believe in your words, and come down into the depths of humility and be baptized, for they shall be visited with fire and with the Holy Ghost, and shall receive a remission of their sins.
3. Yea, blessed are the poor in spirit who come unto me, for theirs is the kingdom of heaven.
4. And again, blessed are all they that mourn, for they shall be comforted.
5. And blessed are the meek, for they shall inherit the earth.
6. And blessed are all they who do hunger and thirst after righteousness, for they shall be filled with the Holy Ghost.
7. And blessed are the merciful, for they shall obtain mercy.
8. And blessed are all the pure in heart, for they shall see God.
9. And blessed are all the peacemakers, for they shall be called the children of God.
10. And blessed are all they who are persecuted for my name's sake, for theirs is the kingdom of heaven.
11. And blessed are ye when men shall revile you and persecute, and shall say all manner of evil against you falsely, for my sake;
12. For ye shall have great joy and be exceedingly glad, for great shall be your reward in heaven; for so persecuted they the prophets who were before you.
13. Verily, verily, I say unto you, I give unto you to be the salt of the earth; but if the salt shall lose its savor wherewith shall the earth be salted? The salt shall be thenceforth good for nothing, but to be cast out and to be trodden under foot of men.
14. Verily, verily, I say unto you, I give unto you to be the light of this people. A city that is set on a hill cannot be hid.
15. Behold, do men light a candle and put it under a bushel? Nay, but on a candlestick, and it giveth light to all that are in the house;
16. Therefore let your light so shine before this people, that they may see your good works and glorify your Father who is in heaven.
17. Think not that I am come to destroy the law or the prophets.

3 Nephi 12

The Lord Jesus Christ, the Savior of the world, delivered the higher law to the people at the temple. This is the law of celestial living. This is the law which, when kept, leads to eternal life. It is the pattern of the life for the disciples of the Lord Jesus Christ—the law that will make us free. When we learn to love His law it will become our way of living, and we will become even as He is.

The Savior teaches the doctrine of happiness through the magnificent beatitudes. The word "blessed" refers to "enjoying spiritual happiness and the favor of God; enjoying heavenly felicity" (*An American Dictionary of the English Language*, Noah Webster, 1828).

President Harold B. Lee said, "In His Sermon on the Mount the Master has given us somewhat of a revelation of His own character, which was perfect, or what might be said to be 'an autobiography, every syllable of which He had written down in deeds,' and in so doing has given us a blueprint for our own lives." (P/A)

3 Nephi 12:1–2

Before delivering the Sermon on the Mount on the eastern continent and his similar sermon to the Nephites, the Savior stated that what he was about to say pertained to those who were willing to believe in his words, "come down into the depths of humility and be baptized" so that they could "be visited with fire and with the Holy Ghost," and could "receive a remission of their sins." (3 Nephi 12:2. See also Matthew 5:3–4 of the Inspired Version.)

Unfortunately, this introductory statement does not appear in either the King James or the Catholic version of the Bible. Thus most Christians have a misconception as to the meaning of the Sermon on the Mount. They assume that this sermon was meant either for the whole world or for only the chosen disciples. However, the Book of Mormon and the Inspired Version of the Bible indicate that the major parts of this sermon were intended for all those who were willing to accept Christ and keep his commandments. (Ludlow)

3 Nephi 12:3–11

The Beatitudes in the Book of Mormon are listed in the same order as those in the New Testament. However, some significant differences of wording should be noted:

1. Each Beatitude in the Book of Mormon begins with a conjunction that relates it to the previous Beatitude and helps to relate all of the Beatitudes to the introductory statement of the Savior.

2. The Beatitude that reads in the New Testament "Blessed are the poor in spirit: for theirs is the kingdom of heaven" is clarified in the Book of Mormon: "*Yea*, blessed are the poor in spirit *who come unto me*, for theirs is the kingdom of heaven." (3 Nephi 12:3. Italics added.) The word *yea* and the clause "who come unto me" relate this Beatitude to the conditional introductory statement of the Savior.

3. The Beatitude that reads in the New Testament "Blessed are they which do hunger and thirst after righteousness: for they shall be filled" is clarified in the Book of Mormon as follows: "*And* blessed are *all* they who do hunger and thirst after righteousness, for they shall be filled *with the Holy Ghost*." (3 Nephi 12:6. Italics added.)

4. The Beatitude in the New Testament that reads "Blessed are they which are persecuted for righteousness' sake: for theirs is the kingdom of heaven" has been clarified in the Book of Mormon: "*And* blessed are *all* they who are persecuted for *my name's sake*, for theirs is the kingdom of heaven." (3 Nephi 12:10. Italics added.) (Ludlow)

3 Nephi 12:5

He was the meekest of elders, a humble farm boy called as a servant of the Lord among a distant people. His speech was homey, his social skills basic, his only polish the weather-tanned skin of a man of the soil. But when he opened his mouth to bear fervent testimony of the truth of the gospel and the sacredness of the Book of Mormon, there was something special there, something that resonated with simple grandeur. He spoke the words that were in his heart as conveyed by the Holy Spirit. We, his missionary colleagues, noticed the radiance shining from his frontier countenance and learned from him. So did the families he taught.

The lesson is simple: It is not the learning of the world or cultural sophistication that changes hearts; rather, it is the word of God, spoken by His humble servants, and confirmed by the Spirit, that touches lives and opens the soul for gospel illumination. "And blessed are the meek, for they shall inherit the earth" was the promise of the Savior to his listeners in Jerusalem (see Matt. 5:5) as well as in America (see 3 Ne. 12:5). This young elder, by now of patriarchal age, is doubtless just the type of person who shall indeed inherit the earth.

President Gordon B. Hinckley said, "The Lord has said that the meek shall inherit the earth. (Matthew 5:5.) I cannot escape the interpretation that meekness implies a spirit of gratitude as opposed to an attitude of self-sufficiency, an acknowledgment of a greater power beyond oneself, a recognition of God, and an acceptance of His commandments. This is the beginning of wisdom. Walk with gratitude before Him who is the giver of life and every good gift." (P/A)

3 Nephi 12:13

Being part of the fold of Christ brings great blessings but also great responsibilities to glorify God through righteous living.

The Savior, having outlined the blessings awaiting those who follow in His footsteps, now explained that His disciples were to be "the salt of the earth" and "the light of this people" (3 Ne. 12:13, 14). With that opportunity and privilege comes great responsibility, for participating in the Abrahamic covenant entails becoming servants of the Most High who carry the gospel message to the world.

President Joseph F. Smith said, "Christ, teaching his disciples, called attention to the importance of their position and place in the world. Though poor and despised of men, yet he told them they were the salt of the earth, the light of the world.

"Then he encouraged them to effort and achievement by showing them that their exalted position would avail them little, unless they made proper use of their high callings. These conditions and instructions apply admirably to the Latter-day Saints, who are indeed the salt of the earth, and in whom is vested the gospel light of the world; who, as the apostle said of the Former-day Saints, are a chosen generation, a royal priesthood, an holy nation, a peculiar people; that they should show forth the praises of him who called them out of darkness into his marvelous light."

As members of the Church, we are reminded by the Lord to honor our covenants. We are the salt of the earth, and if we lose our savor, we are good for nothing. The Lord also indicates that we are to be a light unto the world and to do good works that we might glorify our Heavenly Father.

We, as disciples of Christ, are duty-bound because we have made covenants with the Lord. "When men are called unto mine everlasting gospel, and covenant with an everlasting covenant, they are accounted as the salt of the earth and the savor of men; They are called to be the savor of men; therefore, if that salt of the earth lose its savor, behold, it is thenceforth good for nothing only to be cast out and trodden under the feet of men" (D&C 101:39–40). We, as salt of the earth, as Elder McConkie indicates, "ha[ve] power, in other words, to be the seasoning, savoring, preserving influence in the world, the influence which would bring peace and blessings to all others." (P/A)

3 Nephi 12:14

As defined by the Lord, the "light to the world" is the everlasting covenant, or, in other words, the fulness of the gospel of Jesus Christ as revealed through His church (D&C 45:9, 28). Isaiah wrote of a "standard" that was to be set up to the people of this world (Isa. 49:22; 1 Ne. 21:22). Elder Marion G. Romney identified the Church as that standard of which Isaiah spoke. (P/A)

POINT OF INTEREST

Each of the Twelve Tribes is described allegorically in Genesis 49, and symbols for the tribes have been derived from these descriptions, as well as from other biblical passages. The emblems are arranged in a number of different ways, depending on your source. These are clockwise, according to a bar mitzvah medal.

1) *Simeon is a tower. "And the tribes of Israel were gathered together" (Deut. 33:5).*
2) *Levi is the ephod or breastplate of the high priest. "They shall teach Jacob thy judgments, and Israel thy law" (Deut. 33:10).*
3) *"Judah is a lion's whelp [young]" (Gen. 49:9).*
4) *Zebulun is a ship. "Zebulun shall dwell at the haven of the sea; and he shall be for an haven of ships" (Gen. 49:13).*
5) *"Issachar is a strong ass couching down between two burdens" (Gen. 49:14).*
6) *Dan is the scales of justice. "Dan shall judge his people" (Gen. 49:16).*
7) *Gad is a tent. "He shall overcome at the last" (Gen. 49:19).*
8) *"Naftali is a hind [deer] let loose" (Gen. 49:21).*
9) *Benjamin is a wolf. "In the morning he shall devour the prey" (Gen. 49:27).*
10) *Asher is an olive tree. "Out of Asher his bread shall be fat" (Gen. 49:20).*
11) *Joseph is a sheaf of wheat. "Blessed of the Lord be his land" (Deut. 33:13).*
12) *Reuben is the sun. "Thou art . . . the excellency of dignity, and the excellency of power" (Gen. 49:3).*

I am not come to destroy but to fulfil;
18. For verily I say unto you, one jot nor one tittle hath not passed away from the law, but in me it hath all been fulfilled.
19. And behold, I have given you the law and the commandments of my Father, that ye shall believe in me, and that ye shall repent of your sins, and come unto me with a broken heart and a contrite spirit. Behold, ye have the commandments before you, and the law is fulfilled.
20. Therefore come unto me and be ye saved; for verily I say unto you, that except ye shall keep my commandments, which I have commanded you at this time, ye shall in no case enter into the kingdom of heaven.
21. Ye have heard that it hath been said by them of old time, and it is also written before you, that thou shalt not kill, and whosoever shall kill shall be in danger of the judgment of God;
22. But I say unto you, that whosoever is angry with his brother shall be in danger of his judgment. And whosoever shall say to his brother, Raca, shall be in danger of the council; and whosoever shall say, Thou fool, shall be in danger of hell fire.
23. Therefore, if ye shall come unto me, or shall desire to come unto me, and rememberest that thy brother hath aught against thee—
24. Go thy way unto thy brother, and first be reconciled to thy brother, and then come unto me with full purpose of heart, and I will receive you.
25. Agree with thine adversary quickly while thou art in the way with him, lest at any time he shall get thee, and thou shalt be cast into prison.
26. Verily, verily, I say unto thee, thou shalt by no means come out thence until thou hast paid the uttermost senine. And while ye are in prison can ye pay even one senine? Verily, verily, I say unto you, Nay.
27. Behold, it is written by them of old time, that thou shalt not commit adultery;
28. But I say unto you, that whosoever looketh on a woman, to lust after her, hath committed adultery already in his heart.
29. Behold, I give unto you a commandment, that ye suffer none of these things to enter into your heart;
30. For it is better that ye should deny yourselves of these things, wherein ye will take up your cross, than that ye should be cast into hell.
31. It hath been written, that whosoever shall put away his wife, let him give her a writing of divorcement.
32. Verily, verily, I say unto you, that whosoever shall put away his wife, saving for the cause of fornication, causeth her to commit adultery; and whoso shall marry her who is divorced committeth adultery.
33. And again it is written, thou shalt not forswear thyself, but

3 Nephi 12:22

In the New Testament the Savior counseled his followers: ". . . whosoever is angry with his brother without a cause shall be in danger of the judgment: and whosoever shall say to his brother, Raca, shall be in danger of the council." (Matthew 5:22.) The Savior's teachings on this subject in the Book of Mormon are the same except the phrase "without a cause" is deleted. The word *raca* is used in both accounts, however, and students often wonder what this word means. In the original Semite tongue *raca* means *vain* or *empty*. Thus, the Savior is telling us not to call other people by such derogatory titles. (Ludlow)

3 Nephi 12:31–32

Divorce was definitely discouraged by Jesus Christ. . . . It should be remembered that the "putting away of a wife" referred to by Jesus was not equal to a legal divorce. As James E. Talmage has indicated, "Jesus announced no specific or binding rule as to legal divorces; the putting away of a wife, as contemplated under the Mosaic custom, involved no judicial investigation or action by an established court." (*Jesus the Christ*, 474.)

These same ideas on marriage and divorce are included in the Savior's statement in the Book of Mormon. Divorce (or permanent separation) is not good; but if a couple decides to separate permanently, they should follow the legal procedures. This requirement is equally applicable to the man or the woman, for if a man "puts away his wife" but does not give her a legal divorce, he causes both her and any subsequent husband she might marry to commit adultery. (3 Nephi 12:31–32; compare Matthew 5:31–32; 19:3–9; Luke 16:18.) In this regard, it is well to remember that the word *divorce* as used by the Savior in 3 Nephi 12:32 is not a legal term; it simply implies a separation or "putting away." The legal term used by the Savior is "writing of divorcement." (3 Nephi 12:31.) (Ludlow)

shalt perform unto the Lord thine oaths;
34. But verily, verily, I say unto you, swear not at all; neither by heaven, for it is God's throne;
35. Nor by the earth, for it is his footstool;
36. Neither shalt thou swear by thy head, because thou canst not make one hair black or white;
37. But let your communication be Yea, yea; Nay, nay; for whatsoever cometh of more than these is evil.
38. And behold, it is written, an eye for an eye, and a tooth for a tooth;
39. But I say unto you, that ye shall not resist evil, but whosoever shall smite thee on thy right cheek, turn to him the other also;
40. And if any man will sue thee at the law and take away thy coat, let him have thy cloak also;
41. And whosoever shall compel thee to go a mile, go with him twain.
42. Give to him that asketh thee, and from him that would borrow of thee turn thou not away.
43. And behold it is written also, that thou shalt love thy neighbor and hate thine enemy;
44. But behold I say unto you, love your enemies, bless them that curse you, do good to them that hate you, and pray for them who despitefully use you and persecute you;
45. That ye may be the children of your Father who is in heaven; for he maketh his sun to rise on the evil and on the good.
46. Therefore those things which were of old time, which were under the law, in me are all fulfilled.
47. Old things are done away, and all things have become new.
48. Therefore I would that ye should be perfect even as I, or your Father who is in heaven is perfect.

CHAPTER 13

1. VERILY, verily, I say that I would that ye should do alms unto the poor; but take heed that ye do not your alms before men to be seen of them; otherwise ye have no reward of your Father who is in heaven.
2. Therefore, when ye shall do your alms do not sound a trumpet before you, as will hypocrites do in the synagogues and in the streets, that they may have glory of men. Verily I say unto you, they have their reward.
3. But when thou doest alms let not thy left hand know what thy right hand doeth;
4. That thine alms may be in secret; and thy Father who seeth in secret, himself shall reward thee openly.
5. And when thou prayest thou shalt not do as the hypocrites, for

3 Nephi 12:48

In closing a major part of the Sermon on the Mount on the eastern continent, the Savior said: "Be ye therefore perfect, even as your Father which is in heaven is perfect." (Matthew 5:48.) To the Nephites, the Savior makes a significant addition: "Therefore I would that ye should be perfect even as I, or your Father who is in heaven is perfect." (3 Nephi 12:48.) When the Savior delivered this sermon on the eastern continent, he was just beginning his ministry; he had not yet brought about the atonement in the Garden of Gethsemane nor had he been resurrected from the dead. Thus, at that time he was not perfect in every sense. However, when he appeared to the Nephites as a glorified, resurrected God of glory, then he could rightfully counsel them to be perfect "even as I." (Ludlow)

3 Nephi 12:48

"The command *Be ye perfect* is not idealistic gas. Nor is it a command to do the impossible. He [Christ] is going to make us creatures that can obey that command. He said (in the Bible) that we were 'Gods' and He is going to make good His words. If we let Him—for we can prevent Him, if we choose—He will make the feeblest and filthiest of us into a god or goddess, a dazzling, radiant, immortal creature, pulsating all through with such energy and joy and wisdom and love as we cannot now imagine, a bright stainless mirror which reflects back to God perfectly (though, of course, on a smaller scale) His own boundless power and delight and goodness. The process will be long and in parts very painful; but that is what we are in for. Nothing less. He meant what He said" (C. S. Lewis, *Mere Christianity* [New York: Macmillan, 1960], 172).

they love to pray, standing in the synagogues and in the corners of the streets, that they may be seen of men. Verily I say unto you, they have their reward.
6. But thou, when thou prayest, enter into thy closet, and when thou hast shut thy door, pray to thy Father who is in secret; and thy Father, who seeth in secret, shall reward thee openly.
7. But when ye pray, use not vain repetitions, as the heathen, for they think that they shall be heard for their much speaking.
8. Be not ye therefore like unto them, for your Father knoweth what things ye have need of before ye ask him.
9. After this manner therefore pray ye: Our Father who art in heaven, hallowed be thy name.
10. Thy will be done on earth as it is in heaven.
11. And forgive us our debts, as we forgive our debtors.
12. And lead us not into temptation, but deliver us from evil.
13. For thine is the kingdom, and the power, and the glory, forever. Amen.
14. For, if ye forgive men their trespasses your heavenly Father will also forgive you;
15. But if ye forgive not men their trespasses neither will your Father forgive your trespasses.
16. Moreover, when ye fast be not as the hypocrites, of a sad countenance, for they disfigure their faces that they may appear unto men to fast. Verily I say unto you, they have their reward.
17. But thou, when thou fastest, anoint thy head, and wash thy face;
18. That thou appear not unto men to fast, but unto thy Father, who is in secret; and thy Father, who seeth in secret, shall reward thee openly.
19. Lay not up for yourselves treasures upon earth, where moth and rust doth corrupt, and thieves break through and steal;
20. But lay up for yourselves treasures in heaven, where neither moth nor rust doth corrupt, and where thieves do not break through nor steal.
21. For where your treasure is, there will your heart be also.
22. The light of the body is the eye; if, therefore, thine eye be single, thy whole body shall be full of light.
23. But if thine eye be evil, thy whole body shall be full of darkness. If, therefore, the light that is in thee be darkness, how great is that darkness!
24. No man can serve two masters; for either he will hate the one and love the other, or else he will hold to the one and despise the other. Ye cannot serve God and Mammon.
25. And now it came to pass that when Jesus had spoken these words he looked upon the twelve whom he had chosen, and said unto them: Remember the words which I have spoken. For behold, ye are they whom I have chosen to minister unto this people. Therefore I say unto you, take no thought for your

3 Nephi 13:9–13

Some Latter-day Saints have raised the question as to why the clause "Lead us not into temptation" appears in the Book of Mormon account whereas the Prophet Joseph Smith apparently later changed this in his inspired revision of the Bible to read "And suffer us not to be led into temptation." The following statement is a possible answer to this question:

"Few of the present generation can comprehend the attitude of the Protestant Christian world to the Bible at the time the Book of Mormon was published. Every word in it was regarded as sacred and the word of God. The people worshipped the book rather than the Author. Such was the condition of the minds of those to whom the latter-day gospel was carried. Therefore, not to put fresh obstacles in the way of the honest, or further hurt their susceptibilities, the Lord, in his divine wisdom and loving kindness, permitted those portions of the Bible that were incorporated in the Book of Mormon to appear in the identical language to which the people were accustomed. It was only when a change was absolutely necessary that he permitted it. If this supposition be correct, then in no case would this precaution have to be observed more strictly than in the utterances of the Redeemer himself, as, for instance, in the Lord's prayer. . . .

"Another thing that must be remembered: it was not until considerably later in the history of the Prophet Joseph Smith, that it was shown to him that the more correct translation of this portion of the prayer would be, 'Suffer us not to be led into temptation.'" (Ludlow)

POINT OF INTEREST

The Pyramid of the Moon is one of the pyramids at Teotihuacán, northeast of Mexico City. The name Teotihuacán *was given by the Aztec centuries after the city's fall. The term has been interpreted by some to mean "birthplace of the gods." The city's original name is unknown, but it appears in hieroglyphic texts from the Mayan region as* puh, *or "Place of Reeds."*

3 Nephi 13:14–15

At the end of the Lord's Prayer, the Savior reminds the Nephites that if they are to pray sincerely "forgive us our debts, as we forgive our debtors" (3 Nephi 13:11), they must be willing to forgive others: "For, if ye forgive men their trespasses your heavenly Father will also forgive you; but if ye forgive not men their trespasses neither will your Father forgive your trespasses." (3 Nephi 3:14–15.)

. . . President Spencer W. Kimball has explained what it means to forgive others:

"Remember that we must forgive even if our offender did not repent and ask forgiveness. . . .

"It frequently happens that offenses are committed when the offender is not aware of it. Something he has said or done is misconstrued or misunderstood. The offended one treasures in his heart the offense, adding to it such other things as might give fuel to the fire and justify his conclusions. Perhaps this is one of the reasons why the Lord requires that the offended one should make the overtures toward peace. . . .

"No bitterness of past frictions can be held in memory if we forgive with all our hearts." (Ludlow)

3 Nephi 13:25–26

The way the Sermon on the Mount appears in the present King James Version would indicate that the entire sermon was given either to the whole world or to the Savior's chosen disciples only, depending on the interpretation placed upon Matthew 5:1–2. However, the Book of Mormon indicates that although most of the sermon was intended for the multitude, at least a portion of it was intended only for the chosen leaders. In the New Testament there is no break between the teachings "Ye cannot serve God and mammon" and "Therefore I say unto you, Take no thought for your life," etc. (Matthew 6:24–25.) However, in the Book of Mormon the Savior pauses between these two statements, turns from the multitude, and speaks only to "the twelve whom he had chosen." (3 Nephi 13:25.) The next ten verses are directed only to these chosen leaders. (Ludlow)

3 Nephi 13:19–24, 33

Brigham Young said, "They who love and serve God with all their hearts rejoice evermore. . . . But they who try to serve God and still cling to the spirit of the world, have got on two yokes—the yoke of Jesus and the yoke of the devil. . . . They will have a warfare inside and outside, and the labor will be very galling, for they are directly in opposition one to the other. Cast off the yoke of the enemy, and put on the yoke of Christ, and you will say that his yoke is easy and his burden is light. This I know by experience" (*Journal of Discourses*, 16:123).

life, what ye shall eat, or what ye shall drink; nor yet for your body, what ye shall put on. Is not the life more than meat, and the body than raiment?
26. Behold the fowls of the air, for they sow not, neither do the reap nor gather into barns; yet your heavenly Father feedeth them Are ye not much better than they?
27. Which of you by taking thought can add one cubit unto his stature?
28. And why take ye thought for raiment? Consider the lilies of the field how they grow; they toil not, neither do they spin;
29. And yet I say unto you, that even Solomon, in all his glory, was not arrayed like one of these.
30. Wherefore, if God so clothe the grass of the field, which today is, and tomorrow is cast into the oven, even so will he clothe you, if ye are not of little faith.
31. Therefore take no thought, saying, What shall we eat? or, What shall we drink? or, Wherewithal shall we be clothed?
32. For your heavenly Father knoweth that ye have need of all these things.
33. But seek ye first the kingdom of God and his righteousness, and all these things shall be added unto you.
34. Take therefore no thought for the morrow, for the morrow shall take thought for the things of itself. Sufficient is the day unto the evil thereof.

CHAPTER 14

1. AND now it came to pass that when Jesus had spoken these words he turned again to the multitude, and did open his mouth unto them again, saying: Verily, verily, I say unto you, Judge not, that ye be not judged.
2. For with what judgment ye judge, ye shall be judged; and with what measure ye mete, it shall be measured to you again.
3. And why beholdest thou the mote that is in thy brother's eye, but considerest not the beam that is in thine own eye?
4. Or how wilt thou say to thy brother: Let me pull the mote out of thine eye—and behold, a beam is in thine own eye?
5. Thou hypocrite, first cast the beam out of thine own eye; and then shalt thou see clearly to cast the mote out of thy brother's eye.
6. Give not that which is holy unto the dogs, neither cast ye your pearls before swine, lest they trample them under their feet, and turn again and rend you.
7. Ask, and it shall be given unto you; seek, and ye shall find; knock, and it shall be opened unto you.
8. For every one that asketh, receiveth; and he that seeketh, findeth; and to him that knocketh, it shall be opened.
9. Or what man is there of you, who, if his son ask bread, will give him a stone?
10. Or if he ask a fish, will he give him a serpent?
11. If ye then, being evil, know how to give good gifts unto your children, how much more shall your Father who is in heaven give good things to them that ask him?
12. Therefore, all things whatsoever ye would that men should do to you, do ye even so to them, for this is the law and the prophets.

3 Nephi 13:34

Brigham Young said, "The men and women who desire to obtain seats in the Celestial Kingdom will find that they must battle with the enemy of all righteousness every day" (*Journal of Discourses*, 11:14).

POINT OF INTEREST

The plumed serpent is sculpted at the base of the stairs of El Castillo at Chichén Itzá. The Mayan name Chichén Itzá *means "at the mouth of the well of the Itzá." The site is also referred to as* Uucyabnal, *meaning "seven great rulers."*

13. Enter ye in at the strait gate; for wide is the gate, and broad is the way, which leadeth to destruction, and many there be who go in thereat;
14. Because strait is the gate, and narrow is the way, which leadeth unto life, and few there be that find it.
15. Beware of false prophets, who come to you in sheep's clothing, but inwardly they are ravening wolves.
16. Ye shall know them by their fruits. Do men gather grapes of thorns, or figs of thistles?
17. Even so every good tree bringeth forth good fruit; but a corrupt tree bringeth forth evil fruit.
18. A good tree cannot bring forth evil fruit, neither a corrupt tree bring forth good fruit.
19. Every tree that bringeth not forth good fruit is hewn down, and cast into the fire.
20. Wherefore, by their fruits ye shall know them.
21. Not every one that saith unto me, Lord, Lord, shall enter into the kingdom of heaven; but he that doeth the will of my Father who is in heaven.
22. Many will say to me in that day: Lord, Lord, have we not prophesied in thy name, and in thy name have cast out devils, and in thy name done many wonderful works?
23. And then will I profess unto them: I never knew you; depart from me, ye that work iniquity.
24. Therefore, whoso heareth these sayings of mine and doeth them, I will liken him unto a wise man, who built his house upon a rock—
25. And the rain descended, and the floods came, and the winds blew, and beat upon that house; and it fell not, for it was founded upon a rock.
26. And every one that heareth these sayings of mine and doeth them not shall be likened unto a foolish man, who built his house upon the sand—
27. And the rain descended, and the floods came, and the winds blew, and beat upon that house; and it fell, and great was the fall of it.

CHAPTER 15

1. AND now it came to pass that when Jesus had ended these sayings he cast his eyes round about on the multitude, and said unto them: Behold, ye have heard the things which I taught before I ascended to my Father; therefore, whoso remembereth these sayings of mine and doeth them, him will I raise up at the last day.
2. And it came to pass that when Jesus had said these words he perceived that there were some among them who marveled, and wondered what he would concerning the law

3 Nephi 14:24–27

There are no gallery Christians in the true church of Jesus Christ. We are to *do* good, not just *be* good. We are to bring to pass much righteousness. It seems fitting that the Savior concluded His discourse to the Nephites by teaching the principle of being doers of His word.

President Howard W. Hunter said, "The value of participating in church services . . . is realized when the word heard becomes the word in action. If anyone considers himself to be a devout worshiper without carrying over into his daily living the truths he has heard, his worship is as useless as a glance in a mirror, which is straightway forgotten.

"This same principle is true as it affects other relationships. Friendships cannot endure if they are based on the sands of selfishness. Marriages do not endure when they have no ground except in physical attraction, and do not have the foundation of a deeper love and loyalty. The same principle is true of the individual's relationship to the Church. Traditions are not enough; dogmatic orthodoxies are not enough; formal creeds are not enough. It is not sufficient to say 'Lord, Lord.' Such beliefs have their foundations in sand." (O/C)

POINT OF INTEREST

A stone box from Mesoamerica

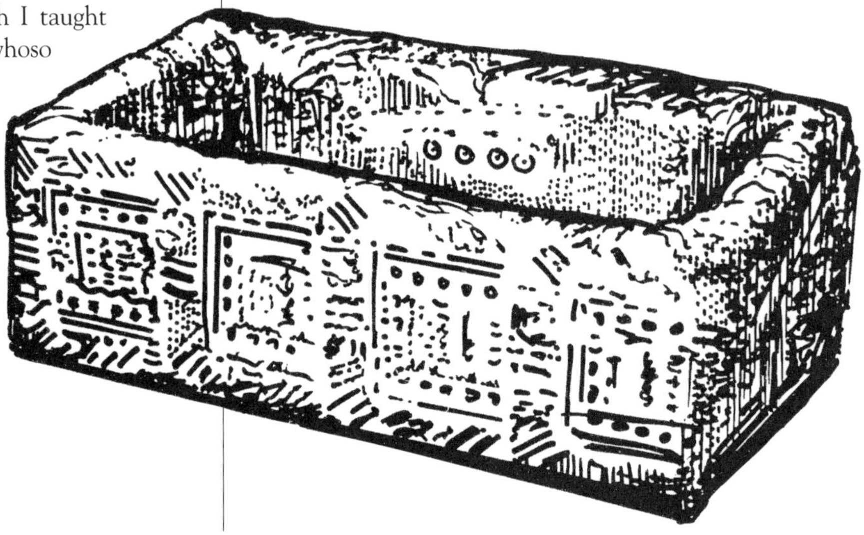

of Moses; for they understood not the saying that old things had passed away, and that all things had become new.
3. And he said unto them: Marvel not that I said unto you that old things had passed away, and that all things had become new.
4. Behold, I say unto you that the law is fulfilled that was given unto Moses.
5. Behold, I am he that gave the law, and I am he who covenanted with my people Israel; therefore, the law in me is fulfilled, for I have come to fulfil the law; therefore it hath an end.
6. Behold, I do not destroy the prophets, for as many as have not been fulfilled in me, verily I say unto you, shall all be fulfilled.
7. And because I said unto you that old things have passed away, I do not destroy that which hath been spoken concerning things which are to come.
8. For behold, the covenant which I have made with my people is not all fulfilled; but the law which was given unto Moses hath an end in me.
9. Behold, I am the law, and the light. Look unto me, and endure to the end, and ye shall live; for unto him that endureth to the end will I give eternal life.
10. Behold, I have given unto you the commandments; therefore keep my commandments. And this is the law and the prophets, for they truly testified of me.
11. And now it came to pass that when Jesus had spoken these words, he said unto those twelve whom he had chosen:
12. Ye are my disciples; and ye are a light unto this people, who are a remnant of the house of Joseph.
13. And behold, this is the land of your inheritance; and the Father hath given it unto you.
14. And not at any time hath the Father given me commandment that I should tell it unto your brethren at Jerusalem.
15. Neither at any time hath the Father given me commandment that I should tell unto them concerning the other tribes of the house of Israel, whom the Father hath led away out of the land.
16. This much did the Father command me, that I should tell unto them:
17. That other sheep I have which are not of this fold; them also I must bring, and they shall hear my voice; and there shall be one fold, and one shepherd.
18. And now, because of stiffneckedness and unbelief they understood not my word; therefore I was commanded to say no more of the Father concerning this thing unto them.
19. But, verily, I say unto you that the Father hath commanded me, and I tell it unto you, that ye were separated from among them because of their iniquity; therefore it

3 Nephi 15:4–8

Jesus identifies himself as the God who gave the law to Moses on the Mount of Sinai: "Behold, I am he that gave the law." (3 Nephi 15:5.) (Ludlow)

3 Nephi 15:9

The gospel is structured to help us progress to ever higher levels of spirituality in ever more perfect compliance with the patterns of heaven. The law of Moses was a schoolmaster that was intended to help the people look forward to Christ. . . .

The Lord had already announced a new and illuminating doctrine to the people during the three-day period of profound darkness: "And ye shall offer up unto me no more the shedding of blood; yea, your sacrifices and your burnt offerings shall be done away, for I will accept none of your sacrifices and your burnt offerings. And ye shall offer for a sacrifice unto me a broken heart and a contrite spirit. And whoso cometh unto me with a broken heart and a contrite spirit, him will I baptize with fire and with the Holy Ghost" (3 Ne. 9:19–20).

. . . [C]ontinuing His sermon at the temple in Bountiful, the Lord expounded on this remarkable new form of sacrifice by unfolding to the people the transition from the old patterns of external ordinances under the law of Moses to the new patterns of devotion and spirituality characteristic of the higher law. He made it clear that the law of Moses was fulfilled in Him. . . .

Elder Jeffrey R. Holland said, "Thus it is crucial to understand that the law of Moses was overlaid upon, and thereby included, many basic parts of the gospel of Jesus Christ, which had existed before it. It was never intended to be something apart or separated from, and certainly not something antagonistic to, the gospel of Jesus Christ. It was more elementary than the full gospel—thus its schoolmaster's role in bringing people to the gospel—but its purpose was never to have been different from the higher law. Both were to bring people to Christ."

The law of Moses was a preparatory gospel. It was a schoolmaster to help people not only look forward to Christ, but prepare for Christ. In life there are many preparatory experiences that prepare us for greater blessings. It is line upon line, precept upon precept, here a little and there a little—such is the process of growth. (P/A)

3 Nephi 15:11–24

During his earthly ministry, the Savior taught the people on the eastern continent as follows: "And other sheep I have, which are not of this fold: them also I must bring, and they shall hear my voice; and there shall be one fold, and one shepherd." (John 10:16.) In teaching the Nephite disciples, the resurrected Jesus Christ relates this teaching on the eastern continent; then he said concerning the Nephites, ". . . ye are they of whom I said: Other sheep I have which are not of this fold." (3 Nephi 15:21.) Thus the appearance of the resurrected Christ to the Nephites at least partially fulfilled his promise that his "other sheep" should hear his voice. (Ludlow)

is because of their iniquity that they know not of you.

20. And verily, I say unto you again that the other tribes hath the Father separated from them; and it is because of their iniquity that they know not of them.

21. And verily I say unto you, that ye are they of whom I said: Other sheep I have which are not of this fold; them also I must bring, and they shall hear my voice; and there shall be one fold, and one shepherd.

22. And they understood me not, for they supposed it had been the Gentiles; for they understood not that the Gentiles should be converted through their preaching.

23. And they understood me not that I said they shall hear my voice; and they understood me not that the Gentiles should not at any time hear my voice—that I should not manifest myself unto them save it were by the Holy Ghost.

24. But behold, ye have both heard my voice, and seen me; and ye are my sheep, and ye are numbered among those whom the Father hath given me.

CHAPTER 16

1. AND verily, verily, I say unto you that I have other sheep, which are not of this land, neither of the land of Jerusalem, neither in any parts of that land round about whither I have been to minister.

2. For they of whom I speak are they who have not as yet heard my voice; neither have I at any time manifested myself unto them.

3. But I have received a commandment of the Father that I shall go unto them, and that they shall hear my voice, and shall be numbered among my sheep, that there may be one fold and one shepherd; therefore I go to show myself unto them.

4. And I command you that ye shall write these sayings after I am gone, that if it so be that my people at Jerusalem, they who have seen me and been with me in my ministry, do not ask the Father in my name, that they may receive a knowledge of you by the Holy Ghost, and also of the other tribes whom they know not of, that these sayings which ye shall write shall be kept and shall be manifested unto the Gentiles, that through the fulness of the Gentiles, the remnant of their seed, who shall be scattered forth upon the face of the earth because of their unbelief, may be brought in, or may be brought to a knowledge of me, their Redeemer.

5. And then will I gather them in from the four quarters of the earth; and then will I fulfill the covenant which the Father hath made unto all the people of the house of Israel.

6. And blessed are the Gentiles, because of their belief in me, in and of the Holy Ghost, which witnesses

3 Nephi 16:4–5

When the risen Lord visited the remnants of Israel in America, He gave them divine standards for righteous living and the power and authority to minister in all things for the salvation of His children within the covenant framework of Zion. Moreover, He granted a higher perspective of how they fit into the grand design for the future gathering of Israel from the four quarters of the earth in fulfillment of sacred promises to their forefathers, Abraham, Isaac, and Jacob. Just as He had caused them to be gathered to the temple for instruction, in like manner would the Father, through the Son, gather His children from their long dispersal over time back to holy places of refuge and enlightenment as part of the gospel plan of redemption. The Savior's instruction to the ancient American Saints about the gathering—including His interpretive citation of the Old Testament prophets, especially Isaiah—is a magnificent reaffirmation for us today of the covenant patterns of Zion that would emerge as part of the restoration of all things leading up to the Second Coming.

According to the dynamics of the grand covenant enterprise, the Lord scatters and gathers His people for the ultimate blessing of mankind. The scattering process may serve to protect (as with Lehi's emigrating colony), correct (because of iniquity or wickedness), or connect (as with the modern-day dispersal of missionaries throughout the world to spread the gospel message among the honest-at-heart). The gathering process is much the same: to protect the Saints by bringing them to holy places of refuge within the stakes of Zion where houses of

POINT OF INTEREST

This tenth-century figure represents a ruler who took on the name Quetzalcoatl. *Such a practice has sometimes caused confusion as to whether an account or image is of a ruler who took on the name or the actual god figure.*

unto them of me and of the Father.
7. Behold, because of their belief in me, saith the Father, and
because of the unbelief of you, O house of Israel, in the latter day
shall the truth come unto the Gentiles, that the fulness of these
things shall be made known unto them.
8. But wo, saith the Father, unto the unbelieving of the Gentiles—
for notwithstanding they have come forth upon the face of this
land, and have scattered my people who are of the house of Israel;
and my people who are of the house of Israel have been cast out
from among them, and have been trodden under feet by them;
9. And because of the mercies of the Father unto the Gentiles, and
also the judgments of the Father upon my people who are of the
house of Israel, verily, verily, I say unto you, that after all this, and
I have caused my people who are of the house of Israel to be smitten, and to be afflicted, and to be slain, and to be cast out from
among them, and to become hated by them, and to become a hiss
and a byword among them—
10. And thus commandeth the Father that I should say unto you:
At that day when the Gentiles shall sin against my gospel, and
shall reject the fulness of my gospel, and shall be lifted up in the
pride of their hearts above all nations, and above all the people of
the whole earth, and shall be filled with all manner of lyings, and
of deceits, and of mischiefs, and all manner of hypocrisy, and murders, and priestcrafts, and whoredoms, and of secret abominations;
and if they shall do all those things, and shall reject the fulness of
my gospel, behold, saith the Father, I will bring the fulness of my
gospel from among them.
11. And then will I remember my covenant which I have made
unto my people, O house of Israel, and I will bring my gospel unto
them.
12. And I will show unto thee, O house of Israel, that the Gentiles
shall not have power over you; but I will remember my covenant
unto you, O house of Israel, and ye shall come unto the knowledge
of the fulness of my gospel.
13. But if the Gentiles will repent and return unto me, saith the
Father, behold they shall be numbered among my people, O house
of Israel.
14. And I will not suffer my people, who are of the house of Israel,
to go through among them, and tread them down, saith the Father.
15. But if they will not turn unto me, and hearken unto my voice,
I will suffer them, yea, I will suffer my people, O house of Israel,
that they shall go through among them, and shall tread them
down, and they shall be as salt that hath lost its savor, which is
thenceforth good for nothing but to be cast out, and to be trodden
under foot of my people, O house of Israel.
16. Verily, verily, I say unto you, thus hath the Father commanded

the Lord abound (sacred temples, as well as chapels and righteous homes), to correct the Saints in an ongoing way through inspired instruction by the prophets of God, and to connect the Saints one with another and with the Holy Spirit. . . .

President Brigham Young said, "We are to build up and establish Zion, gather the House of Israel, and redeem the nations of the earth. This people have this work to do, whether we live to see it or not. This is all in our hands. . . .

"It is obligatory upon us to see that the House of Israel have the Gospel preached to them; to do all that is in our power to gather them to the land of their fathers, and to gather up the fulness of the Gentiles before the Gospel can go with success to the Jews. . . .

"We are now gathering the children of Abraham who have come through the loins of Joseph and his sons, more especially through Ephraim, whose children are mixed among all the nations of the earth."

The gathering of Israel proceeds at multiple levels in full spiritual vigor. While tens of thousands of stalwart missionaries seek to gather the remnants of Israel from around the world, families of the Church—"the children of the prophets" and "the children of the covenant" as Christ characterized them (3 Ne. 20:25, 26)—gather together continually. . . .

Through missionary work, temple work, worship services, and family activities (especially family home evening and family reunions), we can participate in the gathering of Zion foretold by prophets in every age and confirmed by the risen Lord: "And I will remember the covenant which I have made with my people; and I have covenanted with them that I would gather them together in mine own due time" (3 Ne. 20:29). (P/A)

3 Nephi 16:10–16

At one time, Jews were considered to be the literal descendants of Jacob and his twelve sons, and Gentiles, as the word is actually translated, were considered to the "the other people." That is the concept that Lehi, Mulek, and others who came to western hemisphere would have understood, so it's natural that the Book of Mormon would repeatedly refer to "Jew and Gentile" as though they were two very different divisions of people. Eventually, the terms started being used in an enlarged scope, and the term Israel replaced "Jew." At that point, "Israel" was used to designate those who covenanted to accept the true religion; the Gentiles were those who did not. The terms were also eventually used to designate divisions of land.

me—that I should give unto this people this land for their inheritance.
17. And then the words of the prophet Isaiah shall be fulfilled, which say:
18. Thy watchmen shall lift up the voice; with the voice together shall they sing, for they shall see eye to eye when the Lord shall bring again Zion.
19. Break forth into joy, sing together, ye waste places of Jerusalem; for the Lord hath comforted his people, he hath redeemed Jerusalem.
20. The Lord hath made bare his holy arm in the eyes of all the nations; and all the ends of the earth shall see the salvation of God.

CHAPTER 17

1. BEHOLD, now it came to pass that when Jesus had spoken these words he looked round about again on the multitude, and he said unto them: Behold, my time is at hand.
2. I perceive that ye are weak, that ye cannot understand all my words which I am commanded of the Father to speak unto you at this time.
3. Therefore, go ye unto your homes, and ponder upon the things which I have said, and ask of the Father, in my name, that ye may understand, and prepare your minds for the morrow, and I come unto you again.
4. But now I go unto the Father, and also to show myself unto the lost tribes of Israel, for they are not lost unto the Father, for he knoweth whither he hath taken them.
5. And it came to pass that when Jesus had thus spoken, he cast his eyes round about again on the multitude, and beheld they were in tears, and did look steadfastly upon him as if they would ask him to tarry a little longer with them.
6. And he said unto them: Behold, my bowels are filled with compassion towards you.
7. Have ye any that are sick among you? Bring them hither. Have ye any that are lame, or blind, or halt, or maimed, or leprous, or that are withered, or that are deaf, or that are afflicted in any manner? Bring them hither and I will heal them, for I have compassion upon you; my bowels are filled with mercy.
8. For I perceive that ye desire that I should show unto you what I have done unto your brethren at Jerusalem, for I see that your faith is sufficient that I should heal you.
9. And it came to pass that when he had thus spoken, all the multitude, with one accord, did go forth with their sick and their afflicted, and their lame, and with their blind, and with their dumb, and with all them that were afflicted in any manner; and he did heal them every one as they were brought forth unto him.

3 Nephi 17:3

Spiritual blessings flow to those whose hearts and minds are open, who search diligently, and who are sincerely prayerful in their quest to know the truth and become worthy, obedient children of God. . . .

Jesus directed the people to go to their homes, where they were to ponder the things they had seen and heard and pray sincerely that they might understand His teachings. In this manner, they prepared themselves for the following day when He should return. Thus He gave a memorable lesson concerning the vital importance of pondering about, and praying concerning, the principles of righteousness.

Elder Bruce R. McConkie said, "Faith is thus born of scriptural study. Those who study, ponder, and pray about the scriptures, seeking to understand their deep and hidden meanings, receive from time to time great outpourings of light and knowledge from the Holy Spirit. . . .

"However talented men may be in administrative matters; however eloquent they may be in expressing their views; however learned they may be in worldly things—they will be denied the sweet whisperings of the Spirit that might have been theirs unless they pay the price of studying, pondering, and praying about the scriptures."

The Savior then tarried long enough [with the Nephites] to bless their infirm and their little children. Miracles took place and angels ministered to the little children encircled by fire. The people were blessed with unforgettable images to take with them to their homes as the basis for pondering and praying. (P/A)

3 Nephi 17:4

Earlier in the Book of Mormon (2 Nephi 29:11–14), the Lord promises that in the mouths of three great scriptural witnesses the divinity of Christ would be established. It is of interest to note that evidently the resurrected Jesus Christ appeared to all of the peoples who were to write these great scriptural witnesses. He appeared as a resurrected being to the Jews, from whom we get the Bible; he appeared as a resurrected being to the Nephites, from whom we get the Book of Mormon; and he promises here that he is going to appear as a resurrected being to the lost tribes of Israel, from whom shall come the third great scriptural witness. (Ludlow)

10. And they did all, both they who had been healed and they who were whole, bow down at his feet, and did worship him; and as many as could come for the multitude did kiss his feet, insomuch that they did bathe his feet with their tears.
11. And it came to pass that he commanded that their little children should be brought.
12. So they brought their little children and set them down upon the ground round about him, and Jesus stood in the midst; and the multitude gave way till they had all been brought unto him.
13. And it came to pass that when they had all been brought, and Jesus stood in the midst, he commanded the multitude that they should kneel down upon the ground.
14. And it came to pass that when they had knelt upon the ground, Jesus groaned within himself, and said: Father, I am troubled because of the wickedness of the people of the house of Israel.
15. And when he had said these words, he himself also knelt upon the earth; and behold he prayed unto the Father, and the things which he prayed cannot be written, and the multitude did bear record who heard him.
16. And after this manner do they bear record: The eye hath never seen, neither hath the ear heard, before, so great and marvelous things as we saw and heard Jesus speak unto the Father;
17. And no tongue can speak, neither can there be written by any man, neither can the hearts of men conceive so great and marvelous things as we both saw and heard Jesus speak; and no one can conceive of the joy which filled our souls at the time we heard him pray for us unto the Father.
18. And it came to pass that when Jesus had made an end of praying unto the Father, he arose; but so great was the joy of the multitude that they were overcome.
19. And it came to pass that Jesus spake unto them, and bade them arise.
20. And they arose from the earth, and he said unto them: Blessed are ye because of your faith. And now behold, my joy is full.
21. And when he had said these words, he wept, and the multitude bare record of it, and he took their little children, one by one, and blessed them, and prayed unto the Father for them.
22. And when he had done this he wept again;
23. And he spake unto the multitude, and said unto them: Behold your little ones.
24. And as they looked to behold they cast their eyes towards heaven, and they saw the heavens open, and they saw angels descending out of heaven as it were in the midst of fire; and they came down and encircled those little ones about, and they were encircled about with fire; and the angels did minister unto them.
25. And the multitude did see and hear and bear record; and they know that their record is true for they all of them did see and hear, every man for himself; and they were in number about two thousand and five hundred souls; and they did consist of men, women, and children.

3 Nephi 17:14–15

Although the Savior undoubtedly frequently prayed while he was on the earth, only a few of his prayers are listed in the scriptures. One account of his praying is in 3 Nephi 17:14–25, and the witnesses of this prayer testified: "The eye hath never seen, neither hath the ear heard, before, so great and marvelous things as we saw and heard Jesus speak unto the Father; And no tongue can speak, neither can there be written by any man, neither can the hearts of men conceive so great and marvelous things as we both saw and heard Jesus speak; and no one can conceive of the joy which filled our souls at the time we heard him pray for us unto the Father." (3 Nephi 17:16–17.) Perhaps this description helps explain why we do not have more accounts in the scriptures of the prayers of the Savior; even for the righteous Nephites the experience was so overpowering that "they were overcome." (3 Nephi 17:18.) (Ludlow)

3 Nephi 17:20

The Lord loves us. He wants us to be happy and partake of the blessings of eternal life. His joy is for us to grow and become even as He is. He wants us to understand the doctrines, principles, and covenants that will help us return to the presence of our Heavenly Father. This is why He takes time to commission others to teach us the same. We must do certain things through our own agency in order to partake of the blessings of His gospel teachings. If we draw on the powers of heaven through our prayers, we will be protected and blessed in all that we do.

Elder Stephen L Richards said, "I do not look upon the Savior of the world as a man of gloom, nor do I regard the Gospel he gave to the world as one of despair, or one which is intended to kill the joy in humanity. . . .

"'Men are that they might have joy.' It is as natural to long for joy as it is to live, and it would be a perversion of the fundamental philosophy of things if religion were to be interpreted as an imposition upon life, to take out its joy and its gladness." (P/A)

CHAPTER 18

1. AND it came to pass that Jesus commanded his disciples that they should bring forth some bread and wine unto him.
2. And while they were gone for bread and wine, he commanded the multitude that they should sit themselves down upon the earth.
3. And when the disciples had come with bread and wine, he took of the bread and brake and blessed it; and he gave unto the disciples and commanded that they should eat.
4. And when they had eaten and were filled, he commanded that they should give unto the multitude.
5. And when the multitude had eaten and were filled, he said unto the disciples: Behold there shall one be ordained among you, and to him will I give power that he shall break bread and bless it and give it unto the people of my church, unto all those who shall believe and be baptized in my name.
6. And this shall ye always observe to do, even as I have done, even as I have broken bread and blessed it and given it unto you.
7. And this shall ye do in remembrance of my body, which I have shown unto you. And it shall be a testimony unto the Father that ye do always remember me. And if ye do always remember me ye shall have my Spirit to be with you.
8. And it came to pass that when he said these words, he commanded his disciples that they should take of the wine of the cup and drink of it, and that they should also give unto the multitude that they might drink of it.
9. And it came to pass that they did so, and did drink of it and were filled; and they gave unto the multitude, and they did drink, and they were filled.
10. And when the disciples had done this, Jesus said unto them: Blessed are ye for this thing which ye have done, for this is fulfilling my commandments, and this doth witness unto the Father that ye are willing to do that which I have commanded you.
11. And this shall ye always do to those who repent and are baptized in my name; and ye shall do it in remembrance of my blood, which I have shed for you, that ye may witness unto the Father that ye do always remember me. And if ye do always remember me ye shall have my Spirit to be with you.
12. And I give unto you a commandment that ye shall do these things. And if ye shall always do these things blessed are ye, for ye are built upon my rock.
13. But whoso among you shall do more or less than these are not built upon my rock, but are built upon a sandy foundation; and when the rain descends, and the floods come, and the winds blow, and beat upon them, they shall fall, and the gates of hell are ready open to receive them.
14. Therefore blessed are ye if ye shall keep my commandments, which the Father hath commanded me that I should give unto you.

3 Nephi 18:1–2

The Book of Mormon account of the sacrament of the Lord's Supper greatly clarifies the four accounts given in the New Testament. (See Matthew 26:26–29; Mark 14:22–25; Luke 22:19–20; and 1 Corinthians 11:24–27.) Also, the account in the Book of Mormon (3 Nephi 18:1–12) would indicate that the Catholic doctrine of real presence (or transubstantiation) is not true. . . .

The Book of Mormon . . . indicates that when we partake of the emblems of the sacrament we should do so *in remembrance* of the body and the blood of Jesus Christ; we are not partaking of the actual flesh and blood of the Savior. Also, the Lord has said:

"Listen to the voice of Jesus Christ, your Lord, your God, and your Redeemer, whose word is quick and powerful. For, behold, I say unto you, that it mattereth not what ye shall eat or what ye shall drink when ye partake of the sacrament, if it so be that ye do it with an eye single to my glory—remembering unto the Father my body which was laid down for you, and my blood which was shed for the remission of your sins." (D&C 27:1–2.)

The Book of Mormon also clarifies the following points concerning the sacrament:

> It should be administered to only by those who have the proper authority.
>
> It should be given to those people who are members of the Church.
>
> It is a remembrance ordinance of the atonement of Jesus Christ.
>
> It is a covenant ordinance, and those who partake of it promise that they will keep all the commandments of God. It should be partaken of often by members of the Church.
>
> It should not be partaken of by one who is unworthy. (Ludlow)

3 Nephi 18:2–3

As He did in Jerusalem, Jesus also instituted the sacrament among the Nephites to be a part of their worship experience. . . .He directed that the people should partake in remembrance of His body and blood. His flesh and blood are tokens of His Atonement and sacrifice in our behalf. As we partake of the sacrament we should think of His willing suffering for us. By doing so frequently, we become increasingly aware of the blessings He bestows upon us through His redemption and reaffirm our determination to live lives worthy of His blessings.

Elder Melvin J. Ballard shared his thoughts and testimony concerning the value of participating in the sacrament service: "I have always looked upon this blessed privilege [partaking of the sacrament] as the means of spiritual growth, and there is none other quite so fruitful in the achievement of that end as the partaking, worthily, of the sacrament of the Lord's supper." (O/C)

15. Verily, verily, I say unto you, ye must watch and pray always, lest ye be tempted by the devil, and ye be led away captive by him.
16. And as I have prayed among you even so shall ye pray in my church, among my people who do repent and are baptized in my name. Behold I am the light; I have set an example for you.
17. And it came to pass that when Jesus had spoken these words unto his disciples, he turned again unto the multitude and said unto them:
18. Behold, verily, verily, I say unto you, ye must watch and pray always lest ye enter into temptation; for Satan desireth to have you, that he may sift you as wheat.
19. Therefore ye must always pray unto the Father in my name;
20. And whatsoever ye shall ask the Father in my name, which is right, believing that ye shall receive, behold it shall be given unto you.
21. Pray in your families unto the Father, always in my name, that your wives and your children may be blessed.
22. And behold, ye shall meet together oft; and ye shall not forbid any man from coming unto you when ye shall meet together, but suffer them that they may come unto you and forbid them not;
23. But ye shall pray for them, and shall not cast them out; and if it so be that they come unto you oft ye shall pray for them unto the Father, in my name.
24. Therefore, hold up your light that it may shine unto the world. Behold I am the light which ye shall hold up—that which ye have seen me do. Behold ye see that I have prayed unto the Father, and ye all have witnessed.
25. And ye see that I have commanded that none of you should go away, but rather have commanded that ye should come unto me, that ye might feel and see; even so shall ye do unto the world; and whosoever breaketh this commandment suffereth himself to be led into temptation.
26. And now it came to pass that when Jesus had spoken these words, he turned his eyes again upon the disciples whom he had chosen, and said unto them:
27. Behold verily, verily, I say unto you, I give unto you another commandment, and then I must go unto my Father that I may fulfil other commandments which he hath given me.
28. And now behold, this is the commandment which I give unto you, that ye shall not suffer any one knowingly to partake of my flesh and blood unworthily, when ye shall minister it;
29. For whoso eateth and drinketh my flesh and blood unworthily eateth and drinketh damnation to his soul; therefore if ye know that a man is unworthy to eat and drink of my flesh and blood ye shall forbid him.
30. Nevertheless, ye shall not cast him out from among you, but ye

3 Nephi 18:15, 18

Prayer is intimate communication with God, the channel for inspiration, the most direct means for expressing gratitude, the posture and essence of humility, the witness of a broken heart, the voice of a contrite spirit, the start and the finish of the quest for forgiveness. All of these things and many more characterize the nobility and the sacredness of prayer to our Heavenly Father. . . . Prayer is the soul of gospel living.

The Lord has counseled us to pray lest we be tempted beyond that which we can withstand (see Alma 13:27–28; 3 Ne. 18:15, 18). Elder J. Golden Kimball reminded us, "Remember this always: Temptation somewhere in the life of all finds us, as this life is a testing time. Therefore, watch and pray and ask God to leave us not in temptation and deliver us from evil. . . ." (P/A)

3 Nephi 18:15–25

The best recorded sermon on prayer given by the Savior is found in the Book of Mormon, 3 Nephi 18. In eleven brief verses the Savior gives the following counsel and reasons for praying: We should pray because he has set the example (verse 16); we should pray lest we should enter into temptation (verse 18); we should pray so that we will not be led away captive by the devil (verse 15); we should pray "unto the Father" in the name of Jesus Christ (verse 19); we should pray for things which are right for us (verse 20); we should pray in faith (verse 20); we should pray with our families so that our wives and children may be blessed (verse 21); we should meet together and pray often (verse 22); we should pray for others to meet with us (verse 23); we should pray as an example for others (verse 24). (Ludlow)

3 Nephi 18:20

How do we know what is right and expedient for us to ask? The Lord said, "Ask the Father in my name, in faith believing that you shall receive, and you shall have the Holy Ghost, which manifesteth *all things which are expedient* unto the children of men" (D&C 18:18, emphasis added). (O/C)

3 Nephi 18:28–29

Concerning the evil of partaking of the sacrament unworthily, President David O. McKay has said: "To partake of the sacrament unworthily is to take a step toward spiritual death. No man can be dishonest within himself without deadening the susceptibility of his spirit. Sin can stun the conscience as a blow on the head can stun the physical senses. He who promises one thing and deliberately fails to keep his word, adds sin to sin. On natural principles such a man 'eats and drinks condemnation to his soul.' " (Ludlow)

shall minister unto him and shall pray for him unto the Father, in my name; and if it so be that he repenteth and is baptized in my name, then shall ye receive him, and shall minister unto him of my flesh and blood.
31. But if he repent not he shall not be numbered among my people, that he may not destroy my people, for behold I know my sheep, and they are numbered.
32. Nevertheless, ye shall not cast him out of your synagogues, or your places of worship, for unto such shall ye continue to minister; for ye know not but what they will return and repent, and come unto me with full purpose of heart, and I shall heal them; and ye shall be the means of bringing salvation unto them.
33. Therefore, keep these sayings which I have commanded you that ye come not under condemnation; for wo unto him whom the Father condemneth.
34. And I give you these commandments because of the disputations which have been among you. And blessed are ye if ye have no disputations among you.
35. And now I go unto the Father, because it is expedient that I should go unto the Father for your sakes.
36. And it came to pass that when Jesus had made an end of these sayings, he touched with his hand the disciples whom he had chosen, one by one, even until he had touched them all, and spake unto them as he touched them.
37. And the multitude heard not the words which he spake, therefore they did not bear record; but the disciples bare record that he gave them power to give the Holy Ghost. And I will show unto you hereafter that this record is true.
38. And it came to pass that when Jesus had touched them all, there came a cloud and overshadowed the multitude that they could not see Jesus.
39. And while they were overshadowed he departed from them, and ascended into heaven. And the disciples saw and did bear record that he ascended again into heaven.

CHAPTER 19

1. AND now it came to pass that when Jesus had ascended into heaven, the multitude did disperse, and every man did take his wife and his children and did return to his own home.
2. And it was noised abroad among the people immediately, before it was yet dark, that the multitude had seen Jesus, and that he had ministered unto them, and that he would also show himself on the morrow unto the multitude.
3. Yea, and even all the night it was noised abroad concerning Jesus; and insomuch did they send forth unto the people that there were many, yea, an exceedingly great number, did labor exceedingly all that night, that they might be on the morrow in the place where Jesus should show himself unto the multitude.

3 Nephi 18:32

President David O. McKay described a phenomenon of which we should be aware:

"Every man and every person who lives in this world wields an influence, whether for good or for evil. It is not what he says alone; it is not alone what he does. It is what he is. Every man, every person radiates what he or she really is. . . .

"As individuals, we must think nobler thoughts. We must not encourage vile thoughts or low aspirations. We shall radiate them if we do. If we think noble thoughts; if we encourage and cherish noble aspirations, there will be that radiation when we meet people, especially when we associate with them."

What we radiate to the Lord reflects our hopes and desires, our weaknesses and failings, our determination to serve the Lord or our unwillingness to do so, our love and admiration for loved ones or our disdain for certain others, and we convey our true feelings of respect and reverence for Him. We realize we cannot hide our inappropriate interests and desires. He knows what we really are. So for us to truly worship Him, we must possess a freedom from sin and a genuine level of love and gratitude for Him and for all that He has done for us. (O/C)

3 Nephi 18:36–39

Evidently the pronoun *I* in this quotation refers to the historian Mormon when he promises "I will show unto you hereafter that this record is true"; that is, Mormon is going to show later in his record that the Savior did give the disciples the power to bestow the Holy Ghost. Some persons might question whether or not Mormon does indicate this later in his record. However, it is of interest to note that as soon as Moroni starts writing, he gives us the exact wording of the prayer of the Savior on this occasion. (See Moroni 2.) (Ludlow)

3 Nephi 19:4, 11–13

Concerning the baptism of the Nephites at this particular time, President Joseph Fielding Smith has written: "When Christ appeared to the Nephites on this continent, he commanded them to be baptized, although they had been baptized previously for the remission of their sins. . . . The Savior commanded Nephi and the people to be baptized again, *because he had organized anew the Church under the gospel. Before that it had been organized under the law.* For the same reason Joseph Smith and those who had been baptized prior to April 6, 1830, were again baptized on the day of the organization of the Church." (Ludlow)

4. And it came to pass that on the morrow, when the multitude was gathered together, behold, Nephi and his brother whom he had raised from the dead, whose name was Timothy, and also his son, whose name was Jonas, and also Mathoni, and Mathonihah, his brother, and Kumen, and Kumenonhi, and Jeremiah, and Shemnon, and Jonas, and Zedekiah, and Isaiah—now these were the names of the disciples whom Jesus had chosen—and it came to pass that they went forth and stood in the midst of the multitude.
5. And behold, the multitude was so great that they did cause that they should be separated into twelve bodies.
6. And the twelve did teach the multitude; and behold, they did cause that the multitude should kneel down upon the face of the earth, and should pray unto the Father in the name of Jesus.
7. And the disciples did pray unto the Father also in the name of Jesus. And it came to pass that they arose and ministered unto the people.
8. And when they had ministered those same words which Jesus had spoken—nothing varying from the words which Jesus had spoken—behold, they knelt again and prayed to the Father in the name of Jesus.
9. And they did pray for that which they most desired; and they desired that the Holy Ghost should be given unto them.
10. And when they had thus prayed they went down unto the water's edge, and the multitude followed them.
11. And it came to pass that Nephi went down into the water and was baptized.
12. And he came up out of the water and began to baptize. And he baptized all those whom Jesus had chosen.
13. And it came to pass when they were all baptized and had come up out of the water, the Holy Ghost did fall upon them, and they were filled with the Holy Ghost and with fire.
14. And behold, they were encircled about as if it were by fire; and it came down from heaven, and the multitude did witness it, and did bear record; and angels did come down out of heaven and did minister unto them.
15. And it came to pass that while the angels were ministering unto the disciples, behold, Jesus came and stood in the midst and ministered unto them.
16. And it came to pass that he spake unto the multitude, and commanded them that they should kneel down again upon the earth, and also that his disciples should kneel down upon the earth.
17. And it came to pass that when they had all knelt down upon the earth, he commanded his disciples that they should pray.
18. And behold, they began to pray; and they did pray unto Jesus, calling him their Lord and their God.
19. And it came to pass that Jesus departed out of the midst of them, and went a little way off from them and bowed himself to the earth, and he said:
20. Father, I thank thee that thou hast given the Holy Ghost unto these whom I have chosen; and it is because of their belief in me that I have chosen them out of the world.
21. Father, I pray thee that thou wilt give the Holy Ghost unto all them that shall believe in their words.

3 Nephi 19:20–23

With the exception of the Lord's Prayer, which he gave to us as an example, the scriptures contain very few personal prayers of the Savior. However, a notable exception to this is 3 Nephi 19:20–23, which contains the exact words of a personal prayer given by the Savior. This prayer is a classic example for several reasons. First, the prayer is very personal. This brief prayer of only four verses contains forty personal pronouns used by the Savior. Also, the prayer contains the thanks of the Savior to our Heavenly Father (verse 20) and a petition to the Father for a future blessing (verse 21). Another interesting feature of this prayer is that the Savior explains to the Father why the Nephites are praying directly to him rather than to the Father: ". . . they pray unto me because I am with them." (3 Nephi 19:22.) Elsewhere the Savior clearly taught that we should pray unto the Father in the name of the Savior. (See 3 Nephi 18:20. (Ludlow)

22. Father, thou hast given them the Holy Ghost because they believe in me; and thou seest that they believe in me because thou hearest them, and they pray unto me; and they pray unto me because I am with them.
23. And now Father, I pray unto thee for them, and also for all those who shall believe on their words, that they may believe in me, that I may be in them as thou, Father, art in me, that we may be one.
24. And it came to pass that when Jesus had thus prayed unto the Father, he came unto his disciples, and behold, they did still continue, without ceasing, to pray unto him; and they did not multiply many words, for it was given unto them what they should pray, and they were filled with desire.
25. And it came to pass that Jesus blessed them as they did pray unto him; and his countenance did smile upon them, and the light of his countenance did shine upon them, and behold they were as white as the countenance and also the garments of Jesus; and behold the whiteness thereof did exceed all the whiteness, yea, even there could be nothing upon earth so white as the whiteness thereof.
26. And Jesus said unto them: Pray on; nevertheless they did not cease to pray.
27. And he turned from them again, and went a little way off and bowed himself to the earth; and he prayed again unto the Father, saying:
28. Father, I thank thee that thou hast purified those whom I have chosen, because of their faith, and I pray for them, and also for them who shall believe on their words, that they may be purified in me, through faith on their words, even as they are purified in me.
29. Father, I pray not for the world, but for those whom thou hast given me out of the world, because of their faith, that they may be purified in me, that I may be in them as thou, Father, art in me, that we may be one, that I may be glorified in them.
30. And when Jesus had spoken these words he came again unto his disciples; and behold they did pray steadfastly, without ceasing, unto him; and he did smile upon them again; and behold they were white, even as Jesus.
31. And it came to pass that he went again a little way off and prayed unto the Father;
32. And tongue cannot speak the words which he prayed, neither can be written by man the words which he prayed.
33. And the multitude did hear and do bear record; and their hearts were open and they did understand in their hearts the words which he prayed.
34. Nevertheless, so great and marvelous were the words which he prayed that they cannot be written, neither can they be uttered by man.
35. And it came to pass that when Jesus had made an end of praying he came again to the disciples, and said unto them: So great faith have I never seen among all the Jews; wherefore I could not show unto them so great miracles, because of their unbelief.

3 Nephi 19:31–34

The Savior . . . demonstrated pointedly the manner of prayer: "And as I have prayed among you even so shall ye pray in my church, among my people who do repent and are baptized in my name. Behold I am the light; I have set an example for you" (3 Ne. 18:16). The people were told to pray in their families—always in the Savior's name. Following His departure, the disciples prayed for what they desired most: the Holy Ghost (see 3 Ne. 19:9).

Elder Jeffrey R. Holland said, "I can hardly imagine what it might be like to have heard the Savior pray in that setting, but I cannot even comprehend what is meant when they say that 'no tongue can speak, neither can there be written by any man, neither can the hearts of men conceive' what they saw the Savior pray. It's one thing to hear such a prayer. It's surely something altogether more to see one. . . . [T]his is the great, consummate, concluding example the Savior sets for those people that day, the culminating jewel, the crowning, post-sacramental counsel given to the Twelve and all others who would take up the cross and follow him—they must pray always."

The Lord instructs us to pray in His name. We are to ask (as directed by the Spirit) the things that are right (see D&C 88:64–65), doing so with faith that it shall be given us. We are instructed to pray in our families that all might be blessed.

We should always remember that our Savior, Jesus Christ, is our advocate. We pray in His name. We can only come to the Father in and through the Lord, Jesus Christ (see John 14:6). Let us seek in our prayers for wisdom and strength to do the will of the Father (see Hel. 10:5). (P/A)

36. Verily I say unto you, there are none of them that have seen so great things as ye have seen; neither have they heard so great things as ye have heard.

CHAPTER 20

1. AND it came to pass that he commanded the multitude that they should cease to pray, and also his disciples. And he commanded them that they should not cease to pray in their hearts.
2. And he commanded them that they should arise and stand up upon their feet. And they arose up and stood upon their feet.
3. And it came to pass that he brake bread again and blessed it, and gave to the disciples to eat.
4. And when they had eaten he commanded them that they should break bread, and give unto the multitude.
5. And when they had given unto the multitude he also gave them wine to drink, and commanded them that they should give unto the multitude.
6. Now, there had been no bread, neither wine, brought by the disciples, neither by the multitude;
7. But he truly gave unto them bread to eat, and also wine to drink.
8. And he said unto them: He that eateth this bread eateth of my body to his soul; and he that drinketh of this wine drinketh of my blood to his soul; and his soul shall never hunger nor thirst, but shall be filled.
9. Now, when the multitude had all eaten and drunk, behold, they were filled with the Spirit; and they did cry out with one voice, and gave glory to Jesus, whom they both saw and heard.
10. And it came to pass that when they had all given glory unto Jesus, he said unto them: Behold now I finish the commandment which the Father hath commanded me concerning this people, who are a remnant of the house of Israel.
11. Ye remember that I spake unto you, and said that when the words of Isaiah should be fulfilled—behold they are written, ye have them before you, therefore search them—
12. And verily, verily, I say unto you, that when they shall be fulfilled then is the fulfilling of the covenant which the Father hath made unto his people, O house of Israel.
13. And then shall the remnants, which shall be scattered abroad upon the face of the earth, be gathered in from the east and from the west, and from the south and from the north; and they shall be brought to the knowledge of the Lord their God, who hath redeemed them.
14. And the Father hath commanded me that I should give unto you this land, for your inheritance.
15. And I say unto you, that if the Gentiles do not repent after the

3 Nephi 20:6–7

A miracle has been defined as the use of natural law in a way that is not fully understood. In this sense the term *miracle* could be used to describe electricity, for no scientist professes to understand all the laws upon which electricity is based. Certainly the Savior's providing bread and wine for the sacrament could be termed a miracle. The Savior did not circumvent natural law; rather, he used the law in a way we do not fully understand. Many people can make bread by taking wheat and adding other ingredients such as yeast and sugar; this process also requires the presence of the ingredients plus heat and time. However, Jesus Christ, the Creator of the heavens and the earth, was able to apply these natural laws almost instantaneously. That is, although there was no bread present, he was able to reach out his hands, gather the elements, and break bread that could be used in the sacrament. (Ludlow)

3 Nephi 20:13

Joseph Smith said, "One of the most important points in the faith of the Church of the Latter-day Saints, through the fullness of the everlasting Gospel, is the gathering of Israel (of whom the Lamanites constitute a part)—that happy time when Jacob shall go up to the house of the Lord, to worship Him in spirit and in truth, to live in holiness; when the Lord will restore His judges as at first, and His counselors as at the beginning; when every man may sit under his own vine and fig tree, and there will be none to molest or make afraid; when He will turn to them a pure language, and the earth will be filled with sacred knowledge, as the waters cover the great deep; when it shall no longer be said, the Lord lives that brought up the children of Israel out of the land of Egypt, but the Lord lives that brought up the children of Israel from the land of the north, and from all the lands whither He has driven them. That day is one, all important to all men" (*HC*, 2:357).

blessing which they shall receive, after they have scattered my people—
16. Then shall ye, who are a remnant of the house of Jacob, go forth among them; and ye shall be in the midst of them who shall be many; and ye shall be among them as a lion among the beasts of the forest, and as a young lion among the flocks of sheep, who, if he goeth through both treadeth down and teareth in pieces, and none can deliver.
17. Thy hand shall be lifted up upon thine adversaries, and all thine enemies shall be cut off.
18. And I will gather my people together as a man gathereth his sheaves into the floor.
19. For I will make my people with whom the Father hath covenanted, yea, I will make thy horn iron, and I will make thy hoofs brass. And thou shalt beat in pieces many people; and I will consecrate their gain unto the Lord, and their substance unto the Lord of the whole earth. And behold, I am he who doeth it.
20. And it shall come to pass, saith the Father, that the sword of my justice shall hang over them at that day; and except they repent it shall fall upon them, saith the Father, yea, even upon all the nations of the Gentiles.
21. And it shall come to pass that I will establish my people, O house of Israel.
22. And behold, this people will I establish in this land, unto the fulfilling of the covenant which I made with your father Jacob; and it shall be a New Jerusalem. And the powers of heaven shall be in the midst of this people; yea, even I will be in the midst of you.
23. Behold, I am he of whom Moses spake, saying: A prophet shall the Lord your God raise up unto you of your brethren, like unto me; him shall ye hear in all things whatsoever he shall say unto you. And it shall come to pass that every soul who will not hear that prophet shall be cut off from among the people.
24. Verily I say unto you, yea, and all the prophets from Samuel and those that follow after, as many as have spoken, have testified of me.
25. And behold, ye are the children of the prophets; and ye are of the house of Israel; and ye are of the covenant which the Father made with your fathers, saying unto Abraham: And in thy seed shall all the kindreds of the earth be blessed.
26. The Father having raised me up unto you first, and sent me to bless you in turning away every one of you from his iniquities; and this because ye are the children of the covenant—
27. And after that ye were blessed then fulfilleth the Father the covenant which he made with Abraham, saying: In thy seed shall all the kindreds of the earth be blessed—unto the pouring out of the Holy

3 Nephi 20:27–28

[I]n 1830, they were still calling the United States "that great and foolish American experiment." Europe didn't even give us the status of a nation. . . . Chicago was known as little Ft. Dearborn, way out on the western frontier, with sixty-five inhabitants, most of them military men who slept with their rifles within reach for fear the savage Indians would scalp them in their sleep. We had only three miles of steam railway. We were so poor as a nation that the president and his cabinet had to borrow on their personal finances to pay the cost of government in the year of 1830. . . . [It was not until] 1917 before we stepped into first place as [the wealthiest] nation of the earth. The statement that this was "a land and choice above all other lands" sounded fantastic in 1830. Today we know it is absolutely true (Jack West, as quoted in Ross W. Warner, *Fulfillment of Book of Mormon Prophecies* [Salt Lake City: Hawkes Publishing, 1975], 87–88).

Ghost through me upon the Gentiles, which blessing upon the Gentiles shall make them mighty above all, unto the scattering of my people, O house of Israel.
28. And they shall be a scourge unto the people of this land. Nevertheless, when they shall have received the fulness of my gospel, then if they shall harden their hearts against me I will return their iniquities upon their own heads, saith the Father.
29. And I will remember the covenant which I have made with my people; and I have covenanted with them that I would gather them together in mine own due time, that I would give unto them again the land of their fathers for their inheritance, which is the land of Jerusalem, which is the promised land unto them forever, saith the Father.
30. And it shall come to pass that the time cometh, when the fulness of my gospel shall be preached unto them;
31. And they shall believe in me, that I am Jesus Christ, the Son of God, and shall pray unto the Father in my name.
32. Then shall their watchmen lift up their voice, and with the voice together shall they sing; for they shall see eye to eye.
33. Then will the Father gather them together again, and give unto them Jerusalem for the land of their inheritance.
34. Then shall they break forth into joy—Sing together, ye waste places of Jerusalem; for the Father hath comforted his people, he hath redeemed Jerusalem.
35. The Father hath made bare his holy arm in the eyes of all the nations; and all the ends of the earth shall see the salvation of the Father; and the Father and I are one.
36. And then shall be brought to pass that which is written: Awake, awake again, and put on thy strength, O Zion; put on thy beautiful garments, O Jerusalem, the holy city, for henceforth there shall no more come into thee the uncircumcised and the unclean.
37. Shake thyself from the dust; arise, sit down, O Jerusalem; loose thyself from the bands of thy neck, O captive daughter of Zion.
38. For thus saith the Lord: Ye have sold yourselves for naught, and ye shall be redeemed without money.
39. Verily, verily, I say unto you, that my people shall know my name; yea, in that day they shall know that I am he that doth speak.
40. And then shall they say: How beautiful upon the mountains are the feet of him that bringeth good tidings unto them, that publisheth peace; that bringeth good tidings unto them of good, that publisheth salvation; that saith unto Zion: Thy God reigneth!
41. And then shall a cry go forth: Depart ye, depart ye, go ye out from thence, touch not that which is unclean; go ye out of the midst of her; be ye clean that bear the vessels of the Lord.

POINT OF INTEREST

Elder Bruce R. McConkie reminded us that our eternal salvation might depend on our ability to understand the writings of Isaiah as fully and truly as Nephi understood them. He then suggested ten ways to better understand Isaiah:

1. *Gain a broad understanding of the plan of salvation and of how God deals with His children on earth.*
2. *Learn where the house of Israel is in the overall eternal scheme.*
3. *Understand the major doctrines Isaiah wrote about.*
4. *Study the writings of Isaiah in the Book of Mormon.*
5. *Read what latter-day prophets have revealed about the writings of Isaiah.*
6. *Read how Isaiah is interpreted in the New Testament.*
7. *Study Isaiah in the context provided by the Old Testament.*
8. *Learn what type of prophesying was used by the Jews in Isaiah's day.*
9. *Strive for the spirit of prophecy through fasting, prayer, and righteous living.*
10. *Study diligently and conscientiously.*

42. For ye shall not go out with haste nor go by flight; for the Lord will go before you, and the God of Israel shall be your rearward.
43. Behold, my servant shall deal prudently; he shall be exalted and extolled and be very high.
44. As many were astonished at thee—his visage was so marred, more than any man, and his form more than the sons of men—
45. So shall he sprinkle many nations; the kings shall shut their mouths at him, for that which had not been told them shall they see; and that which they had not heard shall they consider.
46. Verily, verily, I say unto you, all these things shall surely come, even as the Father hath commanded me. Then shall this covenant which the Father hath covenanted with his people be fulfilled; and then shall Jerusalem be inhabited again with my people, and it shall be the land of their inheritance.

CHAPTER 21

1. AND verily I say unto you, I give unto you a sign, that ye may know the time when these things shall be about to take place—that I shall gather in, from their long dispersion, my people, O house of Israel, and shall establish again among them my Zion;
2. And behold, this is the thing which I will give unto you for a sign—for verily I say unto you that when these things which I declare unto you, and which I shall declare unto you hereafter of myself, and by the power of the Holy Ghost which shall be given unto you of the Father, shall be made known unto the Gentiles that they may know concerning this people who are a remnant of the house of Jacob, and concerning this my people who shall be scattered by them;
3. Verily, verily, I say unto you, when these things shall be made known unto them of the Father, and shall come forth of the Father, from them unto you;
4. For it is wisdom in the Father that they should be established in this land, and be set up as a free people by the power of the Father, that these things might come forth from them unto a remnant of your seed, that the covenant of the Father may be fulfilled which he hath covenanted with his people, O house of Israel;
5. Therefore, when these works and the works which shall be wrought among you hereafter shall come forth from the Gentiles, unto your seed which shall dwindle in unbelief because of iniquity;
6. For thus it behooveth the Father that it should come forth from the Gentiles, that he may show forth his power unto the Gentiles, for this cause that the Gentiles, if they will not harden their hearts, that they may repent and come unto me and

3 Nephi 21:1–7, 9, 12, 22–29

This statement by the Savior is one of the most significant statements in all scripture concerning the gathering of Israel in the last days. It is of particular significance because (1) it is given by the resurrected Jesus Christ himself, (2) he clearly indicates that these aspects of the gathering are to take place in the last days, and (3) the gathering of Israel includes much more than the gathering of the Jewish people to the land of Israel.

Elder LeGrand Richards has pointed out the major concepts that are included in these brief verses:

"In considering the above declaration, it should be remembered that the Book of Mormon was published and given to the world in 1830, the year the Church was organized, when Joseph Smith was only twenty-four years old. And yet this statement covers all the essential points with respect to the gathering of latter-day Israel, to wit:

"1. That the New Jerusalem would be established in the land of America.

"2. That the church of Jesus Christ would be established in the land of America.

"3. That the church would be established among the gentiles. . . .

"4. That at the time that his church would be established among the gentiles in America, it would be a sign that the time had arrived.

"That the accomplishment of these things shall precede the second coming of the Christ

"That at that time, the Lord would set his hand to gather his people from among all nations:

"These declarations of the Savior confirm the statements of the prophets already referred to, to the effect that Israel would be sifted among all nations." (Ludlow)

3 Nephi 21:4

The Lord revealed to Joseph Smith, His prophet, that He established the constitution of America for the purpose of protecting the moral agency given to man. The Lord revealed: "Therefore, it is not right that any man should be in bondage one to another. And for this purpose have I established the Constitution of this land, by the hands of wise men whom I raised up unto this very purpose, and redeemed the land by the shedding of blood" (D&C 101:79–80). (O/C)

3 Nephi 21:22–26

The "New Jerusalem" of the last days will be built on the American continent by (1) "the remnant of Jacob," (2) the Gentiles who "shall come into the covenant and be numbered among . . . the remnant of Jacob," and (3) "as many of the house of Israel as shall come." (3 Nephi 21:22–25. Read also 3 Nephi 20:22; Ether 13:1–12.) After quoting extensively from chapters 20 and 21 of 3 Nephi, President Marion G. Romney explained the role of the "remnant of Jacob" in building the New Jerusalem:

From these declarations by Jesus, it is certain that the believing, repentant, righteous, faithful Indians shall be among "the remnant of Jacob" who are to build the New

be baptized in my name and know of the true points of my doctrine, that they may be numbered among my people, O house of Israel;
7. And when these things come to pass that thy seed shall begin to know these things—it shall be a sign unto them, that they may know that the work of the Father hath already commenced unto the fulfilling of the covenant which he hath made unto the people who are of the house of Israel.
8. And when that day shall come, it shall come to pass that kings shall shut their mouths; for that which had not been told them shall they see; and that which they had not heard shall they consider.
9. For in that day, for my sake shall the Father work a work, which shall be a great and a marvelous work among them; and there shall be among them those who will not believe it, although a man shall declare it unto them.
10. But behold, the life of my servant shall be in my hand; therefore they shall not hurt him, although he shall be marred because of them. Yet I will heal him, for I will show unto them that my wisdom is greater than the cunning of the devil.
11. Therefore it shall come to pass that whosoever will not believe in my words, who am Jesus Christ, which the Father shall cause him to bring forth unto the Gentiles, and shall give unto him power that he shall bring them forth unto the Gentiles, (it shall be done even as Moses said) they shall be cut off from among my people who are of the covenant.
12. And my people who are a remnant of Jacob shall be among the Gentiles, yea, in the midst of them as a lion among the beasts of the forest, as a young lion among the flocks of sheep, who, if he go through both treadeth down and teareth in pieces, and none can deliver.
13. Their hand shall be lifted up upon their adversaries, and all their enemies shall be cut off.
14. Yea, wo be unto the Gentiles except they repent; for it shall come to pass in that day, saith the Father, that I will cut off thy horses out of the midst of thee, and I will destroy thy chariots;
15. And I will cut off the cities of thy land, and throw down all thy strongholds;
16. And I will cut off witchcrafts out of thy land, and thou shalt have no more soothsayers;
17. Thy graven images I will also cut off, and thy standing images out of the midst of thee, and thou shalt no more worship the works of thy hands;
18. And I will pluck up thy groves out of the midst of thee; so will I destroy thy cities.
19. And it shall come to pass that all lyings, and deceivings, and envyings, and strifes, and priestcrafts, and whoredoms, shall be done away.
20. For it shall come to pass, saith the Father, that at that day whosoever will not repent and come unto my Beloved Son, them will I

Jerusalem to which the Savior will come.

As early as 1831 the Lord assured the Prophet Joseph that "before the great day of" his coming should arrive "Jacob shall flourish in the wilderness, and the Lamanites shall blossom as the rose" (D&C 49:24). (Ludlow)

POINT OF INTEREST

Colossal heads such as this one are characteristic of the Olmec, a people who lived in the tropical lowlands of south-central Mexico, roughly in what are the modern-day states of Veracruz and Tabasco, Mexico.

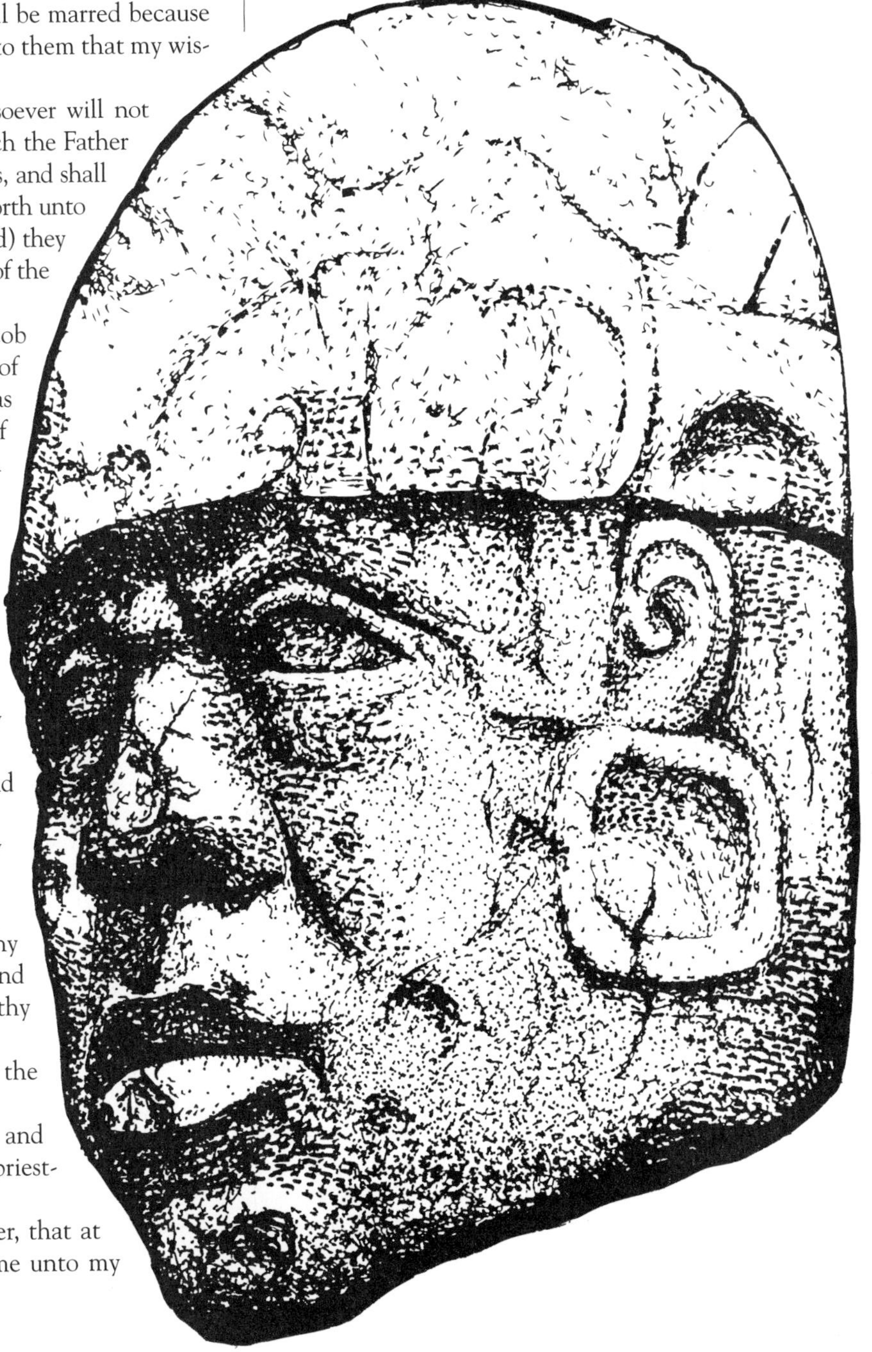

cut off from among my people, O house of Israel;
21. And I will execute vengeance and fury upon them, even as upon the heathen, such as they have not heard.
22. But if they will repent and hearken unto my words, and harden not their hearts, I will establish my church among them, and they shall come in unto the covenant and be numbered among this the remnant of Jacob, unto whom I have given this land for their inheritance;
23. And they shall assist my people, the remnant of Jacob, and also as many of the house of Israel as shall come, that they may build a city, which shall be called the New Jerusalem.
24. And then shall they assist my people that they may be gathered in, who are scattered upon all the face of the land, in unto the New Jerusalem.
25. And then shall the power of heaven come down among them; and I also will be in the midst.
26. And then shall the work of the Father commence at that day, even when this gospel shall be preached among the remnant of this people. Verily I say unto you, at that day shall the work of the Father commence among all the dispersed of my people, yea, even the tribes which have been lost, which the Father hath led away out of Jerusalem.
27. Yea, the work shall commence among all the dispersed of my people, with the Father to prepare the way whereby they may come unto me, that they may call on the Father in my name.
28. Yea, and then shall the work commence, with the Father among all nations in preparing the way whereby his people may be gathered home to the land of their inheritance.
29. And they shall go out from all nations; and they shall not go out in haste, nor go by flight, for I will go before them, saith the Father, and I will be their rearward.

CHAPTER 22

1. AND then shall that which is written come to pass: Sing, O barren, thou that didst not bear; break forth into singing, and cry aloud, thou that didst not travail with child; for more are the children of the desolate than the children of the married wife, saith the Lord.
2. Enlarge the place of thy tent, and let them stretch forth the curtains of thy habitations; spare not, lengthen thy cords and strengthen thy stakes;
3. For thou shalt break forth on the right hand and on the left, and thy seed shall inherit the Gentiles and make the desolate cities to be inhabited.

3 Nephi 21:24

It has been established by revelation that the New Jerusalem will be established in Jackson County, Missouri.

3 Nephi 21:28–29

The Savior's true church has been restored among the Gentile people who are citizens of a free Gentile nation. Members of the Savior's true church are taking the Book of Mormon, which contains the fulness of the gospel of Jesus Christ, to the descendents of the Lamanites. Many have come to know the true points of doctrine and are worshiping the Father in the name of Jesus Christ.

The Savior [spoke to the Nephites] of other happenings and reviewed again some of the events to take place when His covenant is beginning to be fulfilled. [One of those events is that the] gospel will be preached to the Lamanites and among the lost tribes of Israel (see 3 Ne. 21:26–27).

The covenant the Lord made with the house of Israel is now beginning to be fulfilled. It is marvelous to behold. The honest in heart, who treasure divine truths, bear testimony of the Living Christ. The events that are unfolding witness to the world of His reality and the truth of His word recorded in Holy Writ. (O/C)

3 Nephi 22:7

One of the grand themes of the Book of Mormon is the "great mercies" and "everlasting kindness" of the Lord in watching over and lifting up Israel (see 3 Ne. 22:7–8). Emanating from the account of the Lord's dealings with His people over the millennia there is always the promise of the ultimate gathering together of the House of Israel in the latter days and the establishment of an enduring theocratic society of Zion with the Lord Himself as the Lawgiver and Head. . . .

President Ezra Taft Benson said, "In the scriptures there are set forth three phases of the gathering of Israel. One, the gathering of Israel to the land of Zion, which is America, this land. That is under way and has been under way since the Church was established and our missions abroad were inaugurated. Then two, the return of the lost tribes, the ten lost tribes, from the land of the north (see D&C 133). And the third phase is the reestablishment of the Jews in Palestine as one of the events to precede the second coming of the Master."

And Elder David B. Haight said, "What a privilege and a blessing to be a small part of this great work! With that heritage, however, comes a great responsibility. The Lord needs messengers to match His message. He needs those who are able to wield the mighty and eternal influence that He has placed in their hands. . . ."

The Lord quotes Isaiah (He having given Isaiah these words in the first place) and teaches the concept of establishing the kingdom, comparing it to a large tent. The tent is literally held up and strengthened by the individual stakes. These stakes are units of the kingdom throughout the earth.

4. Fear not, for thou shalt not be ashamed; neither be thou confounded, for thou shalt not be put to shame; for thou shalt forget the shame of thy youth, and shalt not remember the reproach of thy youth, and shalt not remember the reproach of thy widowhood any more.
5. For thy maker, thy husband, the Lord of Hosts is his name; and thy Redeemer, the Holy One of Israel—the God of the whole earth shall he be called.
6. For the Lord hath called thee as a woman forsaken and grieved in spirit, and a wife of youth, when thou wast refused, saith thy God.
7. For a small moment have I forsaken thee, but with great mercies will I gather thee.
8. In a little wrath I hid my face from thee for a moment, but with everlasting kindness will I have mercy on thee, saith the Lord thy Redeemer.
9. For this, the waters of Noah unto me, for as I have sworn that the waters of Noah should no more go over the earth, so have I sworn that I would not be wroth with thee.
10. For the mountains shall depart and the hills be removed, but my kindness shall not depart from thee, neither shall the covenant of my peace be removed, saith the Lord that hath mercy on thee.
11. O thou afflicted, tossed with tempest, and not comforted! Behold, I will lay thy stones with fair colors, and lay thy foundations with sapphires.
12. And I will make thy windows of agates, and thy gates of carbuncles, and all thy borders of pleasant stones.
13. And all thy children shall be taught of the Lord; and great shall be the peace of thy children.
14. In righteousness shalt thou be established; thou shalt be far from oppression for thou shalt not fear, and from terror for it shall not come near thee.
15. Behold, they shall surely gather together against thee, not by me; whosoever shall gather together against thee shall fall for thy sake.
16. Behold, I have created the smith that bloweth the coals in the fire, and that bringeth forth an instrument for his work; and I have created the waster to destroy.
17. No weapon that is formed against thee shall prosper; and every tongue that shall revile against thee in judgment thou shalt condemn. This is the heritage of the servants of the Lord, and their righteousness is of me, saith the Lord.

CHAPTER 23

1. AND now, behold, I say unto you, that ye ought to search these things. Yea, a commandment I give unto you that ye search these things diligently; for great are the words of Isaiah.
2. For surely he spake as touching all things concerning my people which are of the house of Israel;

Each stake in the Church is part of the kingdom of God. As members of the Church grow in righteousness and numbers, the tent (the kingdom of God on earth) is enlarged and made stronger. Our duty is to prepare the people and gather the righteous into the Lord's fold that they might partake of eternal life. (P/A)

3 Nephi 22:15–17

An additional prophecy by Isaiah (and repeated here by the Savior) concerns the gathering of the house of Israel in the last days. . . . Some biblical scholars have assumed that the prophecies in Isaiah were fulfilled before the coming of Jesus Christ. However, the fact that the Savior quotes these prophecies from Isaiah 54 and relates them to the events of the last days would indicate they pertain to the dispensation of the fulness of times. (Ludlow)

3 Nephi 22:17

Joseph Smith said, "No unhallowed hand can stop the work from progressing; persecutions may rage, mobs may combine, armies may assemble, calumny may defame, but the truth of God will go forth boldly, nobly, and independent, till it has penetrated every clime, swept every country, and sounded in every ear, till the purposes of God shall be accomplished, and the Great Jehovah shall say the work is done." (*HC*, 4:540.)

3 Nephi 23:1–5

The Lord testified of the greatness of the words of Isaiah—"For surely he spake as touching all things concerning my people which are of the house of Israel" (3 Ne. 23:2)—and encouraged the people to search the words of the prophets as the source of truth unto salvation. It is instructive that the Lord demonstrates for the people the actions He calls for, for He expounds the scriptures unto them, even "all things" (3 Ne. 26:1) from the beginning until the consummation of His work. What greater instruction concerning the word of God can one have than from the Word Himself (see Luke 24:27, 32)?

Nephi wrote of Isaiah's prophecies, "I know that they shall be of great worth unto them *in the last days; for in that day* shall they understand them; wherefore, for their good I have written them" (2 Ne. 25:8; italics added). His brother Jacob wrote, "And now, behold, I would speak unto you concerning things which are, and *which are to come:* wherefore, I will read you the words of Isaiah" (2 Ne. 6:4; italics added).

Elder Bruce R. McConkie said, "Much of what Isaiah . . . has to say is yet to be fulfilled. . . . [H]e is in fact the prophet of the restoration, the mighty seer of Jacob's seed who foresaw our day."

The Lord commands the people to search these things (the words of Isaiah), for Isaiah's words are great. When we come to understand Isaiah, we will truly understand the role of the house of Israel. (P/A)

therefore it must needs be that he must speak also to the Gentiles.
3. And all things that he spake have been and shall be, even
according to the words which he spake.
4. Therefore give heed to my words; write the things which I have
told you; and according to the time and the will of the Father they
shall go forth unto the Gentiles.
5. And whosoever will hearken unto my words and repenteth and
is baptized, the same shall be saved. Search the prophets, for many
there be that testify of these things.
6. And now it came to pass that when Jesus had said these words
he said unto them again, after he had expounded all the scriptures
unto them which they had received, he said unto them: Behold,
other scriptures I would that ye should write, that ye have not.
7. And it came to pass that he said unto Nephi: Bring forth the
record which ye have kept.
8. And when Nephi had brought forth the records, and laid them
before him, he cast his eyes upon them and said:
9. Verily I say unto you, I commanded my servant Samuel, the
Lamanite, that he should testify unto this people, that at the day
that the Father should glorify his name in me that there were many
saints who should arise from the dead, and should appear unto
many, and should minister unto them. And he said unto them:
Was it not so?
10. And his disciples answered him and said: Yea, Lord, Samuel did
prophesy according to thy words, and they were all fulfilled.
11. And Jesus said unto them: How be it that ye have not written this
thing, that many saints did arise and appear unto many and did minister unto them?
12. And it came to pass that Nephi remembered that this thing
had not been written.
13. And it came to pass that Jesus commanded that it should be
written; therefore it was written according as he commanded.
14. And now it came to pass that when Jesus had expounded all the
scriptures in one, which they had written, he commanded them that
they should teach the things which he had expounded unto them.

CHAPTER 24

1. AND it came to pass that he commanded them that they should
write the words which the Father had given unto Malachi, which
he should tell unto them. And it came to pass that after they were
written he expounded them. And these are the words which he did
tell unto them, saying: Thus said the Father unto Malachi—
Behold, I will send my messenger, and he shall prepare the way
before me, and the Lord whom ye seek shall suddenly come to his
temple, even the messenger of the covenant, whom ye delight in;
behold, he shall come, saith the Lord of Hosts.
2. But who may abide the day of his coming, and who shall stand
when he appeareth? For he is like

3 Nephi 24–25

Malachi, the last writer in our present Old Testament, lived approximately 400 B.C. Since his writings were not included on the brass plates of Laban, the Savior gave the words of Malachi to the Nephites. . . . (Ludlow)

a refiner's fire, and like fuller's soap.
3. And he shall sit as a refiner and purifier of silver; and he shall purify the sons of Levi, and purge them as gold and silver, that they may offer unto the Lord an offering in righteousness.
4. Then shall the offering of Judah and Jerusalem be pleasant unto the Lord, as in the days of old, and as in former years.
5. And I will come near to you to judgment; and I will be a swift witness against the sorcerers, and against the adulterers, and against false swearers, and against those that oppress the hireling in his wages, the widow and the fatherless, and that turn aside the stranger, and fear not me, saith the Lord of Hosts.
6. For I am the Lord, I change not; therefore ye sons of Jacob are not consumed.
7. Even from the days of your fathers ye are gone away from mine ordinances, and have not kept them. Return unto me and I will return unto you, saith the Lord of Hosts. But ye say: Wherein shall we return?
8. Will a man rob God? Yet ye have robbed me. But ye say: Wherein have we robbed thee? In tithes and offerings.
9. Ye are cursed with a curse, for ye have robbed me, even this whole nation.
10. Bring ye all the tithes into the storehouse, that there may be meat in my house; and prove me now herewith, saith the Lord of Hosts, if I will not open you the windows of heaven, and pour you out a blessing that there shall not be room enough to receive it.
11. And I will rebuke the devourer for your sakes, and he shall not destroy the fruits of your ground; neither shall your vine cast her fruit before the time in the fields, saith the Lord of Hosts.
12. And all nations shall call you blessed, for ye shall be a delightsome land, saith the Lord of Hosts.
13. Your words have been stout against me, saith the Lord. Yet ye say: What have we spoken against thee?
14. Ye have said: It is vain to serve God, and what doth it profit that we have kept his ordinances and that we have walked mournfully before the Lord of Hosts?
15. And now we call the proud happy; yea, they that work wickedness are set up; yea, they that tempt God are even delivered.
16. Then they that feared the Lord spake often one to another, and the Lord hearkened and heard; and a book of remembrance was written before him for them that feared the Lord, and that thought upon his name.
17. And they shall be mine, saith the Lord of Hosts, in that day when I make up my jewels; and I will

3 Nephi 24:3

In order to fulfill the restoration of all things, the temple that will be built in the City of Zion (New Jerusalem, which will be located in Jackson County, Missouri) will actually consist of twelve buildings. Some of those will likely be provided for the ordinances of the Aaronic priesthood, where the descendants of Levi will make their offering in righteousness, as has been prophesied. Also as part of the restoration of all things, President Joseph Fielding Smith taught that animal sacrifices and other blood sacrifices will briefly be made at these temples; after that, the sacrifices will be of some other kind.

3 Nephi 24:10

It is difficult to imagine how much scripture would need to be written to record all that Jesus taught [the Nephites]. Mormon indicated not even a hundredth part of it is included in the writings we have received. . . . So there is much we do not have. . . .

President Joseph Fielding Smith confirmed the existence of additional scriptural records that contain the vision of the brother of Jared and the teachings of Jesus to the Nephites, and then commented on the reason we have not yet received them:

"Now the Lord has placed us on probation as members of the Church. He has given us the Book of Mormon, which is the lesser part, to build up our faith through our obedience to the counsels which it contains, and when we ourselves, members of the Church, are willing to keep the commandments as they have been given to us and show our faith as the Nephites did for a short period of time, then the Lord is ready to bring forth the other record and give it to us, but we are not ready now to receive it. Why? Because we have not lived up to the requirements in this probationary state in the reading of the record which had been given to us and in following its counsels." (O/C)

spare them as a man spareth his own son that serveth him.
18. Then shall ye return and discern between the righteous and the wicked, between him that serveth God and him that serveth him not.

CHAPTER 25

1. FOR behold, the day cometh that shall burn as an oven; and all the proud, yea, and all that do wickedly, shall be stubble; and the day that cometh shall burn them up, saith the Lord of Hosts, that it shall leave them neither root nor branch.
2. But unto you that fear my name, shall the Son of Righteousness arise with healing in his wings; and ye shall go forth and grow up as calves in the stall.
3. And ye shall tread down the wicked; for they shall be ashes under the soles of your feet in the day that I shall do this, saith the Lord of Hosts.
4. Remember ye the law of Moses, my servant, which I commanded unto him in Horeb for all Israel, with the statutes and judgments.
5. Behold, I will send you Elijah the prophet before the coming of the great and dreadful day of the Lord;
6. And he shall turn the heart of the fathers to the children, and the heart of the children to their fathers, lest I come and smite the earth with a curse.

CHAPTER 26

1. AND now it came to pass that when Jesus had told these things he expounded them unto the multitude; and he did expound all things unto them, both great and small.
2. And he saith: These scriptures, which ye had not with you, the Father commanded that I should give unto you; for it was wisdom in him that they should be given unto future generations.
3. And he did expound all things, even from the beginning until the time that he should come in his glory—yea, even all things which should come upon the face of the earth, even until the elements should melt with fervent heat, and the earth should be wrapt together as a scroll, and the heavens and the earth should pass away;
4. And even unto the great and last day, when all people, and all kindreds, and all nations and tongues shall stand before God, to be

3 Nephi 25:5–6

. . . Many biblical scholars have assumed that the prophesied "second coming of Elijah" took place during the lifetime of the Savior when Elijah appeared on the Mount of Transfiguration. (See Mark 9:4.) However, the fact that the Savior quoted this prophecy to the Nephites after his resurrection would indicate the fulfillment was still in the future. Also, a careful wording of this scripture indicates that the prophesied coming of Elijah pertained not to the first coming of the Savior, but to his second coming; Malachi said that Elijah the prophet should be sent before the coming of "*the great and dreadful day* of the Lord." The first coming of the Savior was a great day, but it was not dreadful; however, the second coming of the Savior will be both a great day (for the righteous) and a dreadful day (for the wicked).

Final proof that this prophecy pertains to the last days is found in the statement by Joseph Smith that on September 21, 1823, the angel Moroni quoted this prophecy and said it was about to be fulfilled. (See Joseph Smith 2:36–40.) Most Latter-day Saints believe this prophecy was fulfilled on April 3, 1836, when Elijah appeared in the Kirtland Temple and restored the sealing powers of the priesthood. . . . (Ludlow)

3 Nephi 26:1–3

There are some who become impatient with the Lord, thinking He should be revealing more than He is. President Harold B. Lee suggested that we have already received from the Lord more than we are able to fully take in.

judged of their works, whether they be good or whether they be evil—
5. If they be good, to the resurrection of everlasting life; and if they
be evil, to the resurrection of damnation; being on a parallel, the
one on the one hand and the other on the other hand, according
to the mercy, and the justice, and the holiness which is in Christ,
who was before the world began.
6. And now there cannot be written in this book even a hundredth
part of the things which Jesus did truly teach unto the people;
7. But behold the plates of Nephi do contain the more part of the
things which he taught the people.
8. And these things have I written, which are a lesser part of the
things which he taught the people; and I have written them to the
intent that they may be brought again unto this people, from the
Gentiles, according to the words which Jesus hath spoken.
9. And when they shall have received this, which is expedient that
they should have first, to try their faith, and if it shall so be that
they shall believe these things then shall the greater things be
made manifest unto them.
10. And if it so be that they will not believe these things, then
shall the greater things be withheld from them, unto their condemnation.
11. Behold, I was about to write them, all which were engraven
upon the plates of Nephi, but the Lord forbade it, saying: I will try
the faith of my people.
12. Therefore I, Mormon, do write the things which have been
commanded me of the Lord. And now I, Mormon, make an end of
my sayings, and proceed to write the things which have been commanded me.
13. Therefore, I would that ye should behold that the Lord truly
did teach the people, for the space of three days; and after that
he did show himself unto them oft, and did break bread
oft, and bless it, and give it unto them.
14. And it came to pass that he did teach and minister unto the children of the multitude of whom hath
been spoken, and he did loose their tongues, and they did
speak unto their fathers great and marvelous things, even
greater than he had revealed unto the people; and he loosed
their tongues that they could utter.
15. And it came to pass that after he had ascended into heav-
en—the second time that he showed himself unto them, and
had gone unto the Father, after having healed all their sick, and
their lame, and opened the eyes of their blind and unstopped
the ears of the deaf, and even had done all manner of cures
among them, and raised a man from the dead, and had
shown forth his power unto them, and had ascended unto
the Father—
16. Behold, it came to pass on the morrow that the multitude gathered themselves together, and they both saw and
heard these children; yea, even babes did open their mouths

POINT OF INTEREST

This four-horned incense burner dates to the Monte Alban period I, 500–100 B.C., and is similar to the types of urns used in Jerusalem during the same time period.

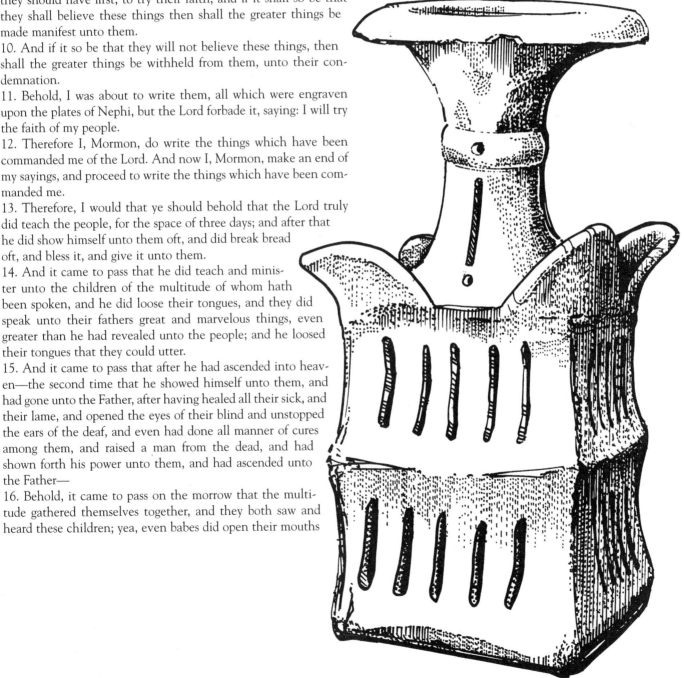

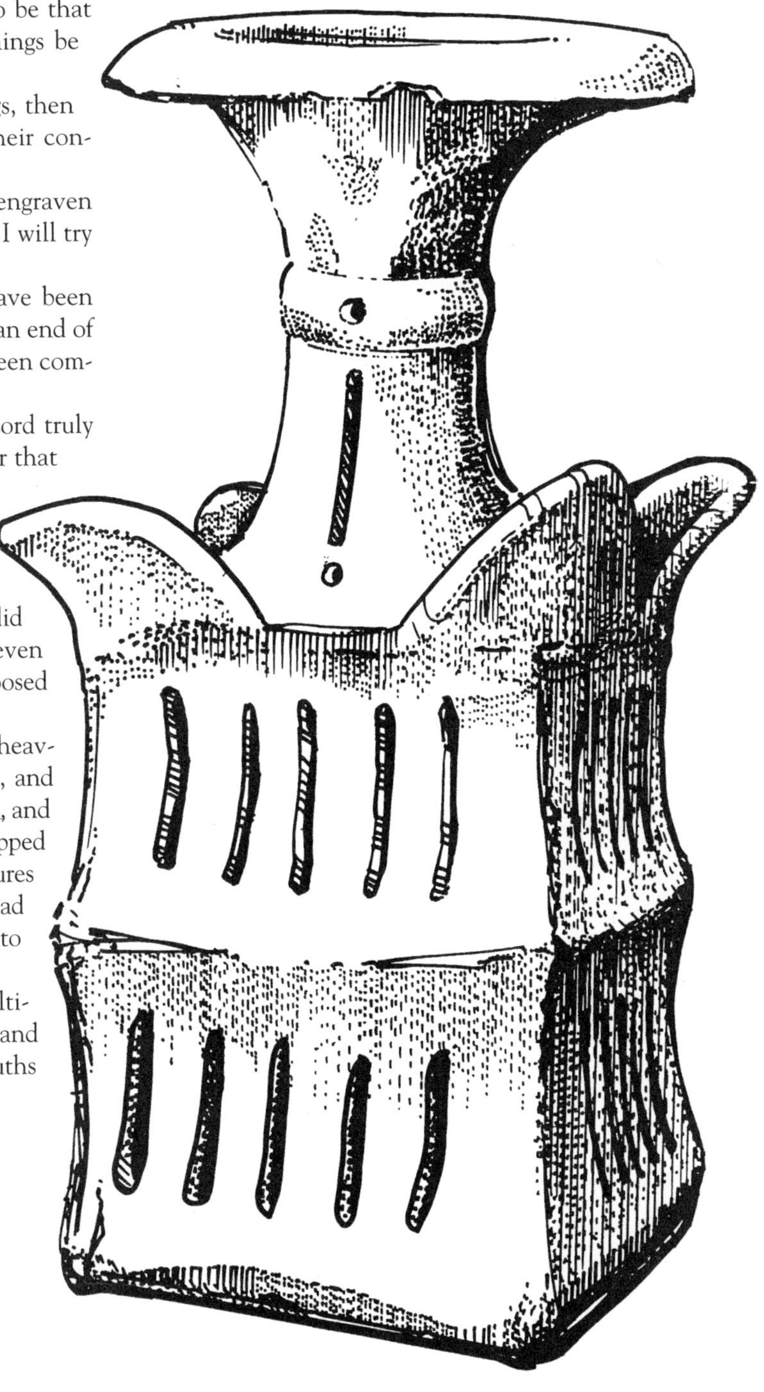

and utter marvelous things; and the things which they did utter were forbidden that there should not any man write them.
17. And it came to pass that the disciples whom Jesus had chosen began from that time forth to baptize and to teach as many as did come unto them; and as many as were baptized in the name of Jesus were filled with the Holy Ghost.
18. And many of them saw and heard unspeakable things, which are not lawful to be written.
19. And they taught, and did minister one to another; and they had all things common among them, every man dealing justly, one with another.
20. And it came to pass that they did do all things even as Jesus had commanded them.
21. And they who were baptized in the name of Jesus were called the church of Christ.

CHAPTER 27

1. AND it came to pass that as the disciples of Jesus were journeying and were preaching the things which they had both heard and seen, and were baptizing in the name of Jesus, it came to pass that the disciples were gathered together and were united in mighty prayer and fasting.
2. And Jesus again showed himself unto them, for they were praying unto the Father in his name; and Jesus came and stood in the midst of them, and said unto them: What will ye that I shall give unto you?
3. And they said unto him: Lord, we will that thou wouldst tell us the name whereby we shall call this church; for there are disputations among the people concerning this matter.
4. And the Lord said unto them: Verily, verily, I say unto you, why is it that the people should murmur and dispute because of this thing?
5. Have they not read the scriptures, which say ye must take upon you the name of Christ, which is my name? For by this name shall ye be called at the last day;
6. And whoso taketh upon him my name, and endureth to the end, the same shall be saved at the last day.
7. Therefore, whatsoever ye shall do, ye shall do it in my name; therefore ye shall call the church in my name; and ye shall call upon the Father in my name that he will bless the church for my sake.
8. And how be it my church save it be called in my name? For if a church be called in Moses' name then it be Moses' church; or if it be called in the name of a man then it be the church of a man; but if it be called in my name then it is my church, if it so be that they are built upon my gospel.
9. Verily I say unto you, that ye are built upon my gospel; therefore ye shall call whatsoever things ye do call, in my name; therefore if ye call upon the Father, for the church, if it be in my name the Father will hear you;
10. And if it so be that the church

3 Nephi 26:21 and 27:1–8

In answer to a question among the disciples as to what the name of the church should be, the Savior said that the church should be called after his name if it is established by him, and if it is built upon his gospel. (3 Nephi 27:8.) The Savior also reminds his disciples of the scripture that says, ". . . ye must take upon you the name of Christ." (3 Nephi 27:5.) Thus the name of the true church is The Church of Jesus Christ. However, to differentiate the true church of Christ on the earth now from the church established during the meridian of time, the Savior has directed that in this dispensation the name of his church should be The Church of Jesus Christ of Latter-day Saints. (D&C 115:4.) (Ludlow)

3 Nephi 27:3–9

At the time the Church was restored, there was not another church on the face of the earth that bore the name of the Savior. The name of this Church was not decided by committee, by research, by popular opinion, or by ballot; it was given to the Prophet Joseph Smith by the Lord Himself, who wanted His Church to bear His name: The Church of Jesus Christ of Latter-day Saints.

is built upon my gospel then will the Father show forth his own works in it.
11. But if it be not built upon my gospel, and is built upon the works of men, or upon the works of the devil, verily I say unto you they have joy in their works for a season, and by and by the end cometh, and they are hewn down and cast into the fire, from whence there is no return.
12. For their works do follow them, for it is because of their works that they are hewn down; therefore remember the things that I have told you.
13. Behold I have given unto you my gospel, and this is the gospel which I have given unto you—that I came into the world to do the will of my Father, because my Father sent me.
14. And my Father sent me that I might be lifted up upon the cross; and after that I had been lifted up upon the cross, that I might draw all men unto me, that as I have been lifted up by men even so should men be lifted up by the Father, to stand before me, to be judged of their works, whether they be good or whether they be evil—
15. And for this cause have I been lifted up; therefore, according to the power of the Father I will draw all men unto me, that they may be judged according to their works.
16. And it shall come to pass, that whoso repenteth and is baptized in my name shall be filled; and if he endureth to the end, behold, him will I hold guiltless before my Father at that day when I shall stand to judge the world.
17. And he that endureth not unto the end, the same is he that is also hewn down and cast into the fire, from whence they can no more return, because of the justice of the Father.
18. And this is the word which he hath given unto the children of men. And for this cause he fulfilleth the words which he hath given, and he lieth not, but fulfilleth all his words.
19. And no unclean thing can enter into his kingdom; therefore nothing entereth into his rest save it be those who have washed their garments in my blood, because of their faith, and the repentance of all their sins, and their faithfulness unto the end.
20. Now this is the commandment: Repent, all ye ends of the earth, and come unto me and be baptized in my name, that ye may be sanctified by the reception of the Holy Ghost, that ye may stand spotless before me at the last day.
21. Verily, verily, I say unto you, this is my gospel; and ye know the things that ye must do in my church; for the works which ye have seen me do that shall ye also do; for that which ye have seen me do even that shall ye do;

3 Nephi 27:13–18

In explaining his gospel to the Nephites of about A.D. 34, the resurrected Jesus Christ also explained why it was necessary for him to come here upon this earth and atone for sin and provide for the resurrection. Concerning this dual contribution of the Savior and Redeemer of mankind, B. H. Roberts has written:

". . . The penalty of the law then, transgressed by Adam, must be executed, or else an adequate atonement must be made for man's transgression. This the work of the Christ. He makes the atonement. He comes to earth and assumes responsibility for this transgression of law, and gathers up into his own soul all the suffering due to the transgression of the law by Adam. All the suffering due to individual transgression of law—the direct consequences of the original transgression—from Adam to the end of the world.

"The burden of us all is laid upon him. He will bear our griefs and carry our sorrows. He will be wounded for our transgressions, and be bruised for our iniquities. The chastisement of our peace will be upon him; on him is laid the iniquity of us all; by his stripes shall we be healed. That is to say, having gathered into himself all the suffering and sorrows due to all the sinning that shall be in the world, he is able to dictate the terms upon which man may lay hold of mercy—by which mercy may heal his wounds—and these terms he names in the conditions of the gospel, the acceptance of which brings complete redemption. The Christ brings to pass the resurrection of the dead. The spirit and the body are eternally reunited; the temporal death—one of the effects of Adam's transgression—is overcome. There is no more physical death; the 'soul'—the eternally united spirit and body are now to be immortal as spirit alone before was immortal. The man so immortal is brought back into the presence of God, and if he has accepted the terms of the gospel by which he is redeemed from the effects of his own, as well as from Adam's transgression, his spiritual death is ended, and henceforth he may be spiritually immortal as well as physically immortal—eternally with God in an atmosphere of righteousness—the spiritual death is overcome.

"Such I make out to be the Book of Mormon doctrine of the atonement, and the redemption of man through the gospel." (Ludlow)

3 Nephi 27:13–21

One of the conditions to be met by the true church is that it should be based upon the gospel of Christ. After explaining this point to his disciples, the Savior then reviews the gospel of Jesus Christ. One of the high points of all scripture is found in 3 Nephi 27:13-21 wherein the Savior outlines the essential doctrines of the gospel and explains their importance. He then summarizes the gospel in one brief statement: "Now this is the commandment: Repent, all ye ends of the earth, and come unto me and be baptized in my name, that ye may be sanctified by the reception of the Holy Ghost, that ye may stand spotless before me at the last day. Verily, verily, I say unto you, this is my gospel . . ." (3 Nephi 27:20-21.)

Thus a major purpose of the gospel is to provide those principles and ordinances which enable us to become sanctified and worthy to live again in the presence of our Heavenly Father. Concerning the importance of the atonement of Jesus Christ and the gospel plan of salvation, President Marion G. Romney has said:

"I cannot here discuss with you in detail what the atonement of the Savior means to us. But without it, no man or woman would ever be resurrected. . . . And so all the world, believers and nonbelievers, are indebted to the Redeemer for their certain resurrection, because the resurrection will be as wide as was the fall, which brought death to every man.

"There is another phase of the atonement which makes me love the Savior even more, and fills my soul with gratitude beyond expression. It is that in addition to atoning for Adam's transgression, thereby bringing about the resurrection, the Savior by his suffering paid the debt for my personal sins. He paid the debt for your personal sins and for the personal sins of every living soul that ever dwelt upon the earth or that ever will dwell in mortality upon the earth. But this he did conditionally. The benefits of this suffering for our individual transgressions will not come to us unconditionally in the same sense that the resurrection will come regardless of what we do. If we partake of the blessings of the atonement as far as our individual transgressions are concerned, we must obey the law. . . .

"We cannot of ourselves, no matter how we may try, rid ourselves of the stain which is upon us as a result of our own transgressions. That stain must be washed away by the blood of the Redeemer, and he has set up the way by which that stain may be removed. That way is the gospel of Jesus Christ. The gospel requires us to believe in the Redeemer, accept his atonement, repent of our sins, be baptized by immersion for the remission of our sins, receive the gift of the Holy Ghost by the laying on of hands, and continue faithfully to observe, or do the best we can to observe, the principles of the gospel all the days of our lives." (Ludlow)

POINT OF INTEREST

This Mayan glyph from the engravings at Palenque, Mexico, has been interpreted to mean "and it came to pass."

3 Nephi 27:19–20

In the Doctrine and Covenants, section 20, verses 8–10, the Lord has said that the Book of Mormon contains "the fulness of the gospel of Jesus Christ to the Gentiles and to the Jews also." Many people have raised the question as to how the Book of Mormon could actually contain the fulness of the gospel when it doesn't even refer to such important ordinances as the temple endowment and marriage for eternity. Concerning this question, Joseph Fielding Smith has written:

"First of all, let us consider what the Lord means by 'a fulness of the gospel.' He did not mean to convey the impression that every truth belonging to exaltation in the kingdom of God had been delivered to the Nephites and was recorded in the Book of Mormon, to be delivered to Gentiles and Jews in this dispensation. Neither would this statement imply that every truth belonging to the celestial kingdom and exaltation therein was to be found within the covers of the Book of Mormon. There are many truths belonging to the exaltation that have not been revealed, nor will they be revealed to man while he is in mortality. We must concede it to be a fact that there are many things related to the exaltation which cannot be received now and do not concern mortal men. These truths were not given to the Nephites; neither can they be given to us in this present day, for they do not in any way apply to the needs of the mortal condition, nor could we comprehend them while we are in mortality. These things belong to the kingdom of God and will be revealed to those who attain to the celestial exaltation.

". . . The fulness of the gospel then, as expressed in the Doctrine and Covenants, has reference to the principles of salvation by which we attain unto this glory. Therefore the Lord has revealed in the Book of Mormon all that is needful to direct people who are willing to hearken to its precepts, to a fulness of the blessings of the kingdom of God. The Book of Mormon then, does contain all the truths which are essential for Gentiles and Jews or any other people, to prepare them for this glorious exaltation in the celestial kingdom of God. . . ." (Ludlow)

3 Nephi 27:20

The sanctification spoken of in this verse is a complete cleansing, which can only be possible because of the Savior's Atonement. Because He offered Himself to pay the price for our sins, we are able to become clean through repentance. But there is another aspect of sanctification: we are cleansed of the effects of sin by the Holy Ghost, who has the power to purge sin from our souls.

3 Nephi 27:20

President Lorenzo Snow said, "Take it individually or take it collectively, we have suffered and we shall have to suffer again; and why? Because the Lord requires it at our hands for our sanctification" (*Journal of Discourses*, 5:323).

22. Therefore, if ye do these things blessed are ye, for ye shall be lifted up at the last day.
23. Write the things which ye have seen and heard, save it be those which are forbidden.
24. Write the works of this people, which shall be, even as hath been written, of that which hath been.
25. For behold, out of the books which have been written, and which shall be written, shall this people be judged, for by them shall their works be known unto men.
26. And behold, all things are written by the Father; therefore out of the books which shall be written shall the world be judged.
27. And know ye that ye shall be judges of this people, according to the judgment which I shall give unto you, which shall be just. Therefore, what manner of men ought ye to be? Verily I say unto you, even as I am.
28. And now I go unto the Father. And verily I say unto you, whatsoever things ye shall ask the Father in my name shall be given unto you.
29. Therefore, ask, and ye shall receive; knock, and it shall be opened unto you; for he that asketh, receiveth; and unto him that knocketh, it shall be opened.
30. And now, behold, my joy is great, even unto fulness, because of you, and also this generation; yea, and even the Father rejoiceth, and also all the holy angels, because of you and this generation; for none of them are lost.
31. Behold, I would that ye should understand; for I mean them who are now alive of this generation; and none of them are lost; and in them I have fulness of joy.
32. But behold, it sorroweth me because of the fourth generation from this generation, for they are led away captive by him even as was the son of perdition; for they will sell me for silver and for gold, and for that which moth doth corrupt and which thieves can break through and steal. And in that day will I visit them, even in turning their works upon their own heads.
33. And it came to pass that when Jesus had ended these sayings he said unto his disciples: Enter ye in at the strait gate; for strait is the gate, and narrow is the way that leads to life, and few there be that find it; but wide is the gate, and broad the way which leads to death, and many there be that travel therein, until the night cometh, wherein no man can work.

CHAPTER 28

1. AND it came to pass when Jesus had said these words, he spake unto his disciples, one by one, saying unto them: What is it that ye desire of

3 Nephi 28

In a little while you will find another prophecy will be fulfilled, and that is the prophecy that Jesus made to the three Nephites who, having power over death, are still living upon this continent. He spoke to them of a time when they would perform a great and mighty work among the Gentiles; and that has not yet been fulfilled, but it will be. You will find that many districts where the Elders of Israel cannot reach will be penetrated by these men who have power over death. . . . My testimony is that these men are going abroad in the nations of the earth before the face of your sons, and they are preparing the hearts of the children of men to receive the Gospel. They are administering to those who are heirs of salvation, and preparing their hearts to receive the truth, just as the farmer prepares the soil to receive the seed. The Lord has promised that He would send His angels before the face of His servants, and He does so (John W. Taylor, *CR*, Oct. 1902, 75).

3 Nephi 28

While in every instance the Nephite twelve are spoken of as disciples, the fact remains that they had been endowed with divine authority to be special witnesses for Christ among their own people. Therefore, they were virtually apostles to the Nephite race, although their jurisdiction was . . . eventually to be subject to the authority and jurisdiction of Peter and the twelve chosen in Palestine. According to the definition prevailing in the world an apostle is a witness for Christ, or one who evangelizes a certain nation or people. "A zealous advocate of a doctrine or cause." Therefore the Nephite twelve became apostles, as special witnesses, just as did Joseph Smith and Oliver Cowdery in the Dispensation of the Fulness of Times. . . . (Ludlow)

me, after that I am gone to the Father?
2. And they all spake, save it were three, saying: We desire that after we have lived unto the age of man, that our ministry, wherein thou hast called us, may have an end, that we may speedily come unto thee in thy kingdom.
3. And he said unto them: Blessed are ye because ye desired this thing of me; therefore, after that ye are seventy and two years old ye shall come unto me in my kingdom; and with me ye shall find rest.
4. And when he had spoken unto them, he turned himself unto the three, and said unto them: What will ye that I should do unto you, when I am gone unto the Father?
5. And they sorrowed in their hearts, for they durst not speak unto him the thing which they desired.
6. And he said unto them: Behold, I know your thoughts, and ye have desired the thing which John, my beloved, who was with me in my ministry, before that I was lifted up by the Jews, desired of me.
7. Therefore, more blessed are ye, for ye shall never taste of death; but ye shall live to behold all the doings of the Father unto the children of men, even until all things shall be fulfilled according to the will of the Father, when I shall come in my glory with the powers of heaven.
8. And ye shall never endure the pains of death; but when I shall come in my glory ye shall be changed in the twinkling of an eye from mortality to immortality; and then shall ye be blessed in the kingdom of my Father.
9. And again, ye shall not have pain while ye shall dwell in the flesh, neither sorrow save it be for the sins of the world; and all this will I do because of the thing which ye have desired of me, for ye have desired that ye might bring the souls of men unto me, while the world shall stand.
10. And for this cause ye shall have fulness of joy; and ye shall sit down in the kingdom of my Father; yea, your joy shall be full, even as the Father hath given me fulness of joy; and ye shall be even as I am, and I am even as the Father; and the Father and I are one;
11. And the Holy Ghost beareth record of the Father and me; and the Father giveth the Holy Ghost unto the children of men, because of me.
12. And it came to pass that when Jesus had spoken these words, he touched every one of them with his finger save it were the three who were to tarry, and then he departed.
13. And behold, the heavens were opened, and they were caught up into heaven, and saw and heard unspeakable things.
14. And it was forbidden them that they should utter; neither was it given unto them power that they could utter the things which they saw and heard;
15. And whether they were in the body or out of the body, they could not tell; for it did seem unto them like a transfiguration of them, that

3 Nephi 28:1–8, 13–17, 37–40

One of the beliefs of the Latter-day Saints that help to make them a "peculiar people" in the eyes of others is that concerning translated beings; that is, Latter-day Saints believe there are people now living on the earth whose physical bodies have been changed or "translated" into another order or state of existence. Although this doctrine is almost unique with Latter-day Saints, it should not be so, for it is clearly taught in the New Testament. After his resurrection, Jesus Christ appeared to some of his disciples at the sea of Tiberias. He counseled his disciples and commanded Peter to "feed my sheep." Then Peter asked the Master concerning the future mission of John the Beloved. The account of the conversation is written in the book of John as follows:

"Peter . . . saith to Jesus, Lord, and what shall this man do?

"Jesus saith unto him, If I will that he tarry till I come, what is that to thee? follow thou me.

"Then went this saying abroad among the brethren, that that disciple should not die: yet Jesus said not unto him, He shall not die; but, If I will that he tarry till I come, what is that to thee?" (John 21:21–23.) . . .

The Savior gave the three Nephite disciples in the Book of Mormon the same promise he had given earlier to John. . . .

Joseph Fielding Smith has written the following concerning the present mortal condition of John the Beloved and the three Nephite disciples: ". . . translated beings are still mortal and will have to pass through the experience of death . . . although this will be instantaneous. . . . Translated beings have not passed through death; that is, they have not had the separation of the spirit and the body."

And finally, the Prophet Joseph Smith has indicated that translated beings have future missions to perform: "Translated bodies cannot enter into rest until they have undergone a change equivalent to death. Translated bodies are designed for future missions" (*HC*, 4:425). (Ludlow)

3 Nephi 28:13–15, 36–40

Those who were translated before the Savior was resurrected were resurrected with Him (see D&C 133:55). All those who have since been translated will be resurrected at the Second Coming of the Savior, when they will receive immortal glory; until then, they will continue to live as mortals. All who are translated will eventually experience a type of instant death and resurrection. They will not experience a "death" until they are ready to be changed to an immortal glory through resurrection.

they were changed from this body of flesh into an immortal state,
that they could behold the things of God.
16. But it came to pass that they did again minister upon the face
of the earth; nevertheless they did not minister of the things which
they had heard and seen, because of the commandment which was
given them in heaven.
17. And now, whether they were mortal or immortal, from the day
of their transfiguration, I know not;
18. But this much I know, according to the record which hath been
given—they did go forth upon the face of the land, and did minister
unto all the people, uniting as many to the church as would believe
in their preaching; baptizing them, and as many as were baptized did
receive the Holy Ghost.
19. And they were cast into prison by them who did not belong to
the church. And the prisons could not hold them, for they were
rent in twain.
20. And they were cast down into the earth; but they did smite the
earth with the word of God, insomuch that by his power they were
delivered out of the depths of the earth; and therefore they could
not dig pits sufficient to hold them.
21. And thrice they were cast into a furnace and received no harm.
22. And twice were they cast into a den of wild beasts; and behold
they did play with the beasts as a child with a suckling lamb, and
received no harm.
23. And it came to pass that thus they did go forth among all the
people of Nephi, and did preach the gospel of Christ unto all people upon the face of the land; and they were converted unto the
Lord, and were united unto the church of Christ, and thus the people of that generation were blessed, according to the word of Jesus.
24. And now I, Mormon, make an end of speaking concerning
these things for a time.
25. Behold, I was about to write the names of those who were
never to taste of death, but the Lord forbade; therefore I write
them not, for they are hid from the world.
26. But behold, I have seen them, and they have ministered unto
me.
27. And behold they will be among the Gentiles, and the Gentiles
shall know them not.
28. They will also be among the Jews, and the Jews shall know
them not.
29. And it shall come to pass, when the Lord seeth fit in his wisdom that they shall minister unto all the scattered tribes of Israel,
and unto all nations, kindreds, tongues and people, and shall bring
out of them unto Jesus many souls, that their desire may be fulfilled, and also because of the convincing power of God which is in
them.
30. And they are as the angels of God, and if they shall pray unto
the Father in the name of Jesus they can show themselves unto
whatsoever man it seemeth them good.
31. Therefore, great and marvelous works shall be wrought by
them, before the great and coming day when all people must surely stand before the judgment-seat of Christ;
32. Yea even among the Gentiles shall there be a great and marvelous work wrought by them, before that judgment day.
33. And if ye had all the scriptures which give an account of all the

POINT OF INTEREST

The plumed-serpent figure of Kukulcan is sometimes mistaken for Quetzalcoatl.

marvelous works of Christ, ye would, according to the words of Christ, know that these things must surely come.
34. And wo be unto him that will not hearken unto the words of Jesus, and also to them whom he hath chosen and sent among them; for whoso receiveth not the words of Jesus and the words of those whom he hath sent receiveth not him; and therefore he will not receive them at the last day;
35. And it would be better for them if they had not been born. For do ye suppose that ye can get rid of the justice of an offended God, who hath been trampled under feet of men, that thereby salvation might come?
36. And now behold, as I spake concerning those whom the Lord hath chosen, yea, even three who were caught up into the heavens, that I knew not whether they were cleansed from mortality to immortality—
37. But behold, since I wrote, I have inquired of the Lord, and he hath made it manifest unto me that there must needs be a change wrought upon their bodies, or else it needs be that they must taste of death;
38. Therefore, that they might not taste of death there was a change wrought upon their bodies, that they might not suffer pain nor sorrow save it were for the sins of the world.
39. Now this change was not equal to that which shall take place at the last day; but there was a change wrought upon them, insomuch that Satan could have no power over them, that he could not tempt them; and they were sanctified in the flesh, that they were holy, and that the powers of the earth could not hold them.
40. And in this state they were to remain until the judgment day of Christ; and at that day they were to receive a greater change, and to be received into the kingdom of the Father to go no more out, but to dwell with God eternally in the heavens.

CHAPTER 29

1. AND now behold, I say unto you that when the Lord shall see fit, in his wisdom, that these sayings shall come unto the Gentiles according to his word, then ye may know that the covenant which the Father hath made with the children of Israel, concerning their restoration to the lands of their inheritance, is already beginning to be fulfilled.
2. And ye may know that the words of the Lord, which have been spoken by the holy prophets, shall all be fulfilled; and ye need not say that the Lord delays his coming unto the children of Israel.
3. And ye need not imagine in your hearts that the words which have been spoken are vain, for behold, the Lord will remember his covenant which he hath made unto his people of the house of Israel.
4. And when ye shall see these sayings coming forth among you, then ye need not any longer spurn at the doings of the Lord, for the sword of his justice is in his right hand;

3 Nephi 28:37–40

Prior to His ascension into heaven the Savior asked His disciples: ". . . What is it that ye desire of me, after that I am gone to the Father?" (3 Ne. 28:1). All but three of His disciples desired to enter His heavenly kingdom after they completed their mortal mission (see 3 Ne. 28:2–3). Three of His disciples desired to stay on earth and continue their ministry until the Savior would come in His glory. Their desires were granted (see 3 Ne. 28:6–12). Pertaining to the three Nephite disciples who tarried, we learn from Mormon's writings that many of the limitations of mortality were removed from them (see 3 Ne. 28:19–22). Mormon learned their physical bodies underwent a change. He recorded [the information found in 3 Ne. 28:37–40].

Our understanding is limited as to why the Lord has translated beings upon the earth. President Harold B. Lee said, "I have always wondered what the purpose was that there should be in the earth translated beings. . . . I remember a few years ago, one of the brethren in a general conference made a statement like this that caused quite a flurry among the brethren. He said, 'That gospel plan he gave, and when he gave it, he said it would never be taken away until the end of the world. It is my faith that the Gospel plan has always been here, that his priesthood has always been here on the earth, and that it will continue to be so until the end comes.' . . .

"After that sermon was delivered, I walked over to the Church Office Building with President Joseph Fielding Smith and we were discussing this discourse. He said this: 'I believe that God has never for one moment of time since the creation, abandoned the earth to Satan without having someone holding the priesthood to check him.' To me that was the answer as to why translated beings have been here on the earth always among men and will be until the coming of the Savior." (O/C)

and behold, at that day, if ye shall spurn at his doings he will cause
that it shall soon overtake you.
5. Wo unto him that spurneth at the doings of the Lord; yea, wo
unto him that shall deny the Christ and his works!
6. Yea, wo unto him that shall deny the revelations of the Lord,
and that shall say the Lord no longer worketh by revelation, or by
prophecy, or by gifts, or by tongues, or by healings, or by the power
of the Holy Ghost!
7. Yea, and wo unto him that shall say at that day, to get gain, that
there can be no miracle wrought by Jesus Christ; for he that doeth
this shall become like unto the son of perdition, for whom there was
no mercy, according to the word of Christ!
8. Yea, and ye need not any longer hiss, nor spurn, nor make game
of the Jews, nor any of the remnant of the house of Israel; for
behold, the Lord remembereth his covenant unto them, and he
will do unto them according to that which he hath sworn.
9. Therefore ye need not suppose that ye can turn the right hand
of the Lord unto the left, that he may not execute judgment unto
the fulfilling of the covenant which he hath made unto the house
of Israel.

CHAPTER 30

1. HEARKEN, O ye Gentiles, and hear the words of Jesus Christ, the
Son of the living God, which he hath commanded me that I
should speak concerning you, for, behold he commandeth me that
I should write, saying:
2. Turn, all ye Gentiles, from your wicked ways; and repent of your
evil doings, of your lyings and deceivings, and of your whoredoms,
and of your secret abominations, and your idolatries, and of your
murders, and your priestcrafts, and your envyings, and your strifes,
and from all your wickedness and abominations, and come unto
me, and be baptized in my name, that ye may receive a remission
of your sins, and be filled with the Holy Ghost, that ye may be
numbered with my people who are of the house of Israel.

POINT OF INTEREST

This cylindrical stamp was found in Piedras Negras, Veracruz, and has a serpent (coatl) motif.

FOURTH NEPHI
THE BOOK OF NEPHI

WHO IS THE SON OF NEPHI—ONE OF THE DISCIPLES OF JESUS CHRIST

An account of the people of Nephi, according to his record.

1. AND it came to pass that the thirty and fourth year passed away, and also the thirty and fifth, and behold the disciples of Jesus had formed a church of Christ in all the lands round about. And as many as did come unto them, and did truly repent of their sins, were baptized in the name of Jesus; and they did also receive the Holy Ghost.
2. And it came to pass in the thirty and sixth year, the people were all converted unto the Lord, upon all the face of the land, both Nephites and Lamanites, and there were no contentions and disputations among them, and every man did deal justly one with another.
3. And they had all things common among them; therefore there were not rich and poor, bond and free, but they were all made free, and partakers of the heavenly gift.
4. And it came to pass that the thirty and seventh year passed away also, and there still continued to be peace in the land.
5. And there were great and marvelous works wrought by the disciples of Jesus, insomuch that they did heal the sick, and raise the dead, and cause the lame to walk, and the blind to receive their sight, and the deaf to hear; and all manner of miracles did they work among the children of men; and in nothing did they work miracles save it were in the name of Jesus.
6. And thus did the thirty and eighth year pass away, and also the thirty and ninth, and forty and first, and the forty and second, yea, even until forty and nine years had passed away, and also the fifty and first, and the fifty and second; yea, and even until fifty and nine years had passed away.
7. And the Lord did prosper them exceedingly in the land; yea, insomuch that they did build cities again where there had been cities burned.
8. Yea, even that great city Zarahemla did they cause to be built again.
9. But there were many cities which had been sunk, and waters came up in the stead thereof; therefore these cities could not be renewed.
10. And now, behold, it came to pass that the people of Nephi did wax strong, and did multiply exceedingly fast, and became an exceedingly fair and delightsome people.

4 Nephi 1:3

The Prophet Joseph Smith himself established that the United Order was not a communal system (see *HC*, 3:28). One of the main tenets of the Order was the concept of private ownership of property; each man owned his stewardship, and was able to treat his property as his own. In commenting on the various tenets of the United Order, President J. Reuben Clark said that the Church never has been, and never will be, a communal society.

4 Nephi 1:9–21, 47

Several instances could be cited to indicate that many of the Nephites lived to a rather old age. For example, Jacob, the son of Lehi, was born during the eight-year trek from Jerusalem to Bountiful—that is, between 600 B.C. and 592 B.C. Jacob's son Enos died sometime after 420 B.C. (Enos 25.) Thus the lives of Jacob and his son Enos covered at least 172 years. Other examples can be taken from the book of Fourth Nephi. . . .

The life expectancy of the people was quite long during this period; the first historian kept the record for 77 years, the second for 84 years, and the third for 112 years! Of course, their age when they obtained the record would have to be added to the figures listed above to determine their age at the time of death. (Ludlow)

11. And they were married, and given in marriage, and were blessed according to the multitude of the promises which the Lord had made unto them.
12. And they did not walk any more after the performances and ordinances of the law of Moses; but they did walk after the commandments which they had received from their Lord and their God, continuing in fasting and prayer, and in meeting together oft both to pray and to hear the word of the Lord.
13. And it came to pass that there was no contention among all the people, in all the land; but there were mighty miracles wrought among the disciples of Jesus.
14. And it came to pass that the seventy and first year passed away, and also the seventy and second year, yea, and in fine, till the seventy and ninth year had passed away; yea, even an hundred years had passed away, and the disciples of Jesus, whom he had chosen, had all gone to the paradise of God, save it were the three who should tarry; and there were other disciples ordained in their stead; and also many of that generation had passed away.
15. And it came to pass that there was no contention in the land, because of the love of God which did dwell in the hearts of the people.
16. And there were no envyings, nor strifes, nor tumults, nor whoredoms, nor lyings, nor murders, nor any manner of lasciviousness; and surely there could not be a happier people among all the people who had been created by the hand of God.
17. There were no robbers, nor murderers, neither were there Lamanites, nor any manner of -ites; but they were in one, the children of Christ, and heirs to the kingdom of God.
18. And how blessed were they! For the Lord did bless them in all their doings; yea, even they were blessed and prospered until an hundred and ten years had passed away; and the first generation from Christ had passed away, and there was no contention in all the land.
19. And it came to pass that Nephi, he that kept this last record, (and he kept it upon the plates of Nephi) died, and his son Amos kept it in his stead; and he kept it upon the plates of Nephi also.
20. And he kept it eighty and four years, and there was still peace in the land, save it were a small part of the people who had revolted from the church and taken upon them the name of Lamanites; therefore there began to be Lamanites again in the land.
21. And it came to pass that Amos died also, (and it was an hundred and ninety and four years from the coming of Christ) and his son Amos kept the record in his stead; and he also kept it upon the plates of Nephi; and it was also written in the book of Nephi, which is this book.
22. And it came to pass that two hundred years had passed away; and the second generation had all passed away save it were a few.
23. And now I, Mormon, would that ye should know that the people had multiplied, insomuch that they were spread upon all the face of the land,

4 Nephi 1:14

As the original twelve Nephite disciples chosen by the Savior passed away, new disciples were chosen to take their place. This practice evidently continued as long as the Nephites were righteous enough to have a church organization amongst them. The three Nephite disciples who were promised by the Savior that they should live on the earth until his second coming (3 Nephi 28:4–8) apparently continued to work with the people for several hundred years; both Mormon and Moroni were ministered to by them (Mormon 8:11). (Ludlow)

4 Nephi 1:15–16

Love is an intangible quality that cannot be bestowed by or upon others. It can only be developed individually by doing that which results in love. The Lord gave us a great clue as to how that can be done. He said, "A new commandment I give unto you, That ye love one another; *as I have loved you*, that ye also love one another" (John 13:34, emphasis added). . . . As we search the record of His mortal life, we find nothing He ever did was for himself. Always He was giving, serving, caring, sacrificing, and providing for others. And the result was a love unprecedented in the history of this world.

When people live and do as He did, they also find an increasing love for those whom they serve and for whom they give and sacrifice. It is true with husbands and wives, parents, missionaries, friends, and others. These people are selfless, do not take advantage of others, are honest, kind, and patient. They have a love like unto God's love. They are at peace with one another. . . .

President David O. McKay described the internal strengths that precipitate external manifestations of our love of God:

". . . the testimony of the gospel is an anchor to the soul in the midst of confusion and strife. Knowledge of God and his laws means stability, means contentment, means peace, and with that a heart full of love reaching out to our fellow men, offering the same blessings, the same privileges. Love will beget tolerance and kindness.

". . . all members [of the Church] are striving to establish the kingdom of God. Let us hold to that fact as the anchor of our soul and then breathe forth charity and love to those who may not see just as we do." (O/C)

4 Nephi 1:17, 20, 38–39

At this point, the term *Lamanite* was used not to identify a descendant of Laman or Lemuel, but to identify a person who had rebelled against the Church. Some of these people undoubtedly were direct descendants of Laman and Lemuel, but many were not.

and that they had become exceedingly rich, because of their prosperity in Christ.
24. And now, in this two hundred and first year there began to be among them those who were lifted up in pride, such as the wearing of costly apparel, and all manner of fine pearls, and of the fine things of the world.
25. And from that time forth they did have their goods and their substance no more common among them.
26. And they began to be divided into classes; and they began to build up churches unto themselves to get gain, and began to deny the true church of Christ.
27. And it came to pass that when two hundred and ten years had passed away there were many churches in the land; yea, there were many churches which professed to know the Christ, and yet they did deny the more parts of his gospel, insomuch that they did receive all manner of wickedness, and did administer that which was sacred unto him to whom it had been forbidden because of unworthiness.
28. And this church did multiply exceedingly because of iniquity, and because of the power of Satan who did get hold upon their hearts.
29. And again, there was another church which denied the Christ; and they did persecute the true church of Christ, because of their humility and their belief in Christ; and they did despise them because of the many miracles which were wrought among them.
30. Therefore they did exercise power and authority over the disciples of Jesus who did tarry with them, and they did cast them into prison; but by the power of the word of God, which was in them, the prisons were rent in twain, and they went forth doing mighty miracles among them.
31. Nevertheless, and notwithstanding all these miracles, the people did harden their hearts, and did seek to kill them, even as the Jews at Jerusalem sought to kill Jesus, according to his word.
32. And they did cast them into furnaces of fire, and they came forth receiving no harm.
33. And they also cast them into dens of wild beasts, and they did play with the wild beasts even as a child with a lamb; and they did come forth from among them, receiving no harm.
34. Nevertheless, the people did harden their hearts, for they were led by many priests and false prophets to build up many churches, and to do all manner of iniquity. And they did smite upon the people of Jesus; but the people of Jesus did not smite again. And thus they did dwindle in unbelief and wickedness, from year to year, even until two hundred and thirty years had passed away.
35. And now it came to pass in this year, yea, in the two hundred and thirty and first year, there was a great division among the people.
36. And it came to pass that in this year there arose a people who were called the Nephites, and they were true believers in Christ; and among them there were those who were called by the Lamanites—Jacobites, and Josephites, and Zoramites;
37. Therefore the true believers in Christ, and the true worshipers of

4 Nephi 1:20, 36–39

[T]he Lamanites of the last two hundred years of Book of Mormon history are descendants of those who revolted against the true church of Christ between about A.D. 194 and 231. (Ludlow)

4 Nephi 1:26–29

Elder Spencer W. Kimball expressed his feelings as he saw certain symptoms of these same lowering levels of dedication and diligence in our day. He must surely also have been echoing those feelings of the Savior who knew of the deteriorating conditions among the Nephites: "It is a disappointment sometimes, however, to find some who are not willing to trust the Lord—to trust in his promise when he says, 'Prove me and see.' I often wonder why men cannot trust their Lord. He has promised his children every blessing contingent upon their faithfulness, but fickle man places his trust in 'the arm of flesh' and sets about to make his own way unaided by him who could do so much." (O/C)

Christ, (among whom were the three disciples of Jesus who should tarry) were called Nephites, and Jacobites, and Josephites, and Zoramites.
38. And it came to pass that they who rejected the gospel were called Lamanites, and Lemuelites, and Ishmaelites; and they did not dwindle in unbelief, but they did wilfully rebel against the gospel of Christ; and they did teach their children that they should not believe, even as their fathers, from the beginning, did dwindle.
39. And it was because of the wickedness and abomination of their fathers, even as it was in the beginning. And they were taught to hate the children of God, even as the Lamanites were taught to hate the children of Nephi from the beginning.
40. And it came to pass that two hundred and forty and four years had passed away, and thus were the affairs of the people. And the more wicked part of the people did wax strong, and became exceedingly more numerous than were the people of God.
41. And they did still continue to build up churches unto themselves, and adorn them with all manner of precious things. And thus did two hundred and fifty years pass away, and also two hundred and sixty years.
42. And it came to pass that the wicked part of the people began again to build up the secret oaths and combinations of Gadianton.
43. And also the people who were called the people of Nephi began to be proud in their hearts, because of their exceeding riches, and become vain like unto their brethren, the Lamanites.
44. And from this time the disciples began to sorrow for the sins of the world.
45. And it came to pass that when three hundred years had passed away, both the people of Nephi and the Lamanites had become exceedingly wicked one like unto another.
46. And it came to pass that the robbers of Gadianton did spread over all the face of the land; and there were none that were righteous save it were the disciples of Jesus. And gold and silver did they lay up in store in abundance, and did traffic in all manner of traffic.
47. And it came to pass that after three hundred and five years had passed away, (and the people did still remain in wickedness) Amos died; and his brother, Ammaron, did keep the record inhis stead.
48. And it came to pass that when three hundred and twenty years had passed away, Ammaron, being constrained by the Holy Ghost, did hide up the records which were sacred—yea, even all the sacred records which had been handed down from generation to generation, which were sacred—even until the three hundred and twentieth year from the coming of Christ.
49. And he did hide them up unto the Lord, that they might come again unto the remnant of the house of Jacob, according to the prophecies and the promises of the Lord. And thus is the end of the record of Ammaron.

4 Nephi 1:38

Without the gospel and Church of Jesus Christ, there can never be a conversion to Christ, which was the beginning basis upon which the two-hundred-year period of peace was founded. Since peace is not now universally available to all of us, perhaps now is a time for some questions of self-introspection to help us in our quest for personal peace:

1. Do I know the gospel and do I know it is true?
2. Am I faithful in my Church responsibilities and opportunities?
3. Am I converted to my Savior?
4. Am I a recipient of the love of God? Do I have a deep love for Him? Do I have love for others, as He does?
5. Do I live a life of unity with the Lord, and thus with others who do also?

Many will be able to answer these questions in the affirmative and are already reaping the promises of the Savior, who said:

"But learn that he who doeth the works of righteousness shall receive his reward, even *peace in this world,* and eternal life in the world to come" (D&C 59:23, emphasis added).

Elder Jeffrey R. Holland spoke of many challenging barriers we need to overcome to obtain the peace we seek and desire:

"The search for peace is one of the ultimate quests of the human soul. We all have highs and lows, but such times come and they usually always go. . . . But there are times in all of our lives when deep sorrow or suffering or fear or loneliness makes us cry out for the peace which only God Himself can bring.

"Christ and His angels and His prophets forever labor to buoy up our spirits, steady our nerves, calm our hearts, send us forth with renewed strength and resolute hope. They wish all to know that . . . Christ has overcome the world. Through His suffering and His obedience He has earned and rightly bears the crown of 'Prince of Peace.'

"In that spirit we declare to all the world that for real and abiding peace to come, we must strive to be more like that exemplary Son of God. . . . He has overcome the world, and if we will take upon us His name and 'walk in His paths' and keep our covenants with Him, we shall, ere long, have peace. Such a reward is not only possible; it is certain." (O/C)

THE BOOK OF MORMON

CHAPTER 1

1. AND now I, Mormon, make a record of the things which I have both seen and heard, and call it the Book of Mormon.
2. And about the time that Ammaron hid up the records unto the Lord, he came unto me, (I being about ten years of age, and I began to be learned somewhat after the manner of the learning of my people) and Ammaron said unto me: I perceive that thou art a sober child, and art quick to observe;
3. Therefore, when ye are about twenty and four years old I would that ye should remember the things that ye have observed concerning this people; and when ye are of that age go to the land Antum, unto a hill which shall be called Shim; and there have I deposited unto the Lord all the sacred engravings concerning this people.
4. And behold, ye shall take the plates of Nephi unto yourself, and the remainder shall ye leave in the place where they are; and ye shall engrave on the plates of Nephi all the things that ye have observed concerning this people.
5. And I, Mormon, being a descendant of Nephi, (and my father's name was Mormon) I remembered the things which Ammaron commanded me.
6. And it came to pass that I, being eleven years old, was carried by my father into the land southward, even to the land of Zarahemla.
7. The whole face of the land had become covered with buildings, and the people were as numerous almost, as it were the sand of the sea.
8. And it came to pass in this year there began to be a war between the Nephites, who consisted of the Nephites and the Jacobites and the Josephites and the Zoramites; and this war was between the Nephites, and the Lamanites and the Lemuelites and the Ishmaelites.
9. Now the Lamanites and the Lemuelites and the Ishmaelites were called Lamanites, and the two parties were Nephites and Lamanites.
10. And it came to pass that the war began to be among them in the borders of Zarahemla, by the waters of Sidon.
11. And it came to pass that the Nephites had gathered together a great number of men, even to exceed the number of thirty thousand. And it came to pass that they did have in this same year a number of battles, in which the Nephites did beat the Lamanites and did slay many of them.
12. And it came to pass that the Lamanites withdrew their design, and there was peace settled in the land; and peace did remain for the space of about four years, that there was no bloodshed.
13. But wickedness did prevail upon the face of the whole land, insomuch that the Lord did take away his beloved disciples, and the work of miracles and of healing did cease because of the iniquity of the people.
14. And there were no gifts from

Mormon 1:1–7

Mormon has an interesting and remarkable history. At age 15, like Samuel at Shiloh, he received a personal visitation from the Lord. And at age 16 he was launched upon what so far as I can find was the greatest military career in history, stretching as it did over a period of 58 years. (Mormon 1:15, 2:16.) . . .

. . . No one had to push Mormon, neither were his abilities confined to one field. He was a prophet, general, author, historian, and almost the last survivor of a great civilization. . . . If you think it an inspiration that a 16 year old boy could win the leadership of a great national army what would you think of a man between the ages of 65 and 74 who was still the best man among his entire people for this top position of leadership, and in those days the general marched at the head and not in the rear of his troops. (Mormon 6:11) It is one thing to shoot a guided missile at an enemy a thousand miles away, but it is quite another thing to meet the enemy face to face, and with a sword or a battle axe, take on all comers, old and young, on any basis they might choose to elect; and still be in there fighting at age 74. No weakling or coward survives a test like that. His leadership and great skill in battle must have been an inspiration to those fortunate companions in arms who were privileged to fight at his side. . . . (Ludlow)

Mormon 1:14–17

The most essential element in any of our teaching is the power of the Holy Ghost. Without it, true learning and conversion do not occur.

the Lord, and the Holy Ghost did not come upon any, because of their wickedness and unbelief.
15. And I, being fifteen years of age and being somewhat of a sober mind, therefore I was visited of the Lord, and tasted and knew of the goodness of Jesus.
16. And I did endeavor to preach unto this people, but my mouth was shut, and I was forbidden that I should preach unto them; for behold they had wilfully rebelled against their God; and the beloved disciples were taken away out of the land, because of their iniquity.
17. But I did remain among them, but I was forbidden to preach unto them, because of the hardness of their hearts; and because of the hardness of their hearts the land was cursed for their sake.
18. And these Gadianton robbers, who were among the Lamanites, did infest the land, insomuch that the inhabitants thereof began to hide up their treasures in the earth; and they became slippery, because the Lord had cursed the land, that they could not hold them, nor retain them again.
19. And it came to pass that there were sorceries, and witchcrafts, and magics; and the power of the evil one was wrought upon all the face of the land, even unto the fulfilling of all the words of Abinadi, and also Samuel the Lamanite.

CHAPTER 2

1. AND it came to pass in that same year there began to be a war again between the Nephites and the Lamanites. And notwithstanding I being young, was large in stature; therefore the people of Nephi appointed me that I should be their leader, or the leader of their armies.
2. Therefore it came to pass that in my sixteenth year I did go forth at the head of an army of the Nephites, against the Lamanites; therefore three hundred and twenty and six years had passed away.
3. And it came to pass that in the three hundred and twenty and seventh year the Lamanites did come upon us with exceedingly great power, insomuch that they did frighten my armies; therefore they would not fight, and they began to retreat towards the north countries.
4. And it came to pass that we did come to the city of Angola, and we did take possession of the city, and make preparations to defend ourselves against the Lamanites. And it came to pass that we did fortify the city with our might; but notwithstanding all our fortifications the Lamanites did come upon us and did drive us out of the city.
5. And they did also drive us forth out of the land of David.
6. And we marched forth and came to the land of Joshua, which was in the borders west by the seashore.
7. And it came to pass that we did gather in our people as fast as it were

POINT OF INTEREST

A Mayan image.

possible, that we might get them together in one body.
8. But behold, the land was filled with robbers and with Lamanites;
and notwithstanding the great destruction which hung over my
people, they did not repent of their evil doings; therefore there was
blood and carnage spread throughout all the face of the land, both
on the part of the Nephites and also on the part of the Lamanites;
and it was one complete revolution throughout all the face of the
land.
9. And now, the Lamanites had a king, and his name was Aaron; and
he came against us with an army of forty and four thousand. And
behold, I withstood him with forty and two thousand. And it came
to pass that I beat him with my army that he fled before me. And
behold, all this was done, and three hundred and thirty years had
passed away.
10. And it came to pass that the Nephites began to repent of their iniquity, and began to cry even as had been prophesied by Samuel the
prophet; for behold no man could keep that which was his own, for the
thieves, and the robbers, and the murderers, and the magic art, and the
witchcraft which was in the land.
11. Thus there began to be a mourning and a lamentation in all the
land because of these things, and more especially among the people
of Nephi.
12. And it came to pass that when I, Mormon, saw their lamentation and their mourning and their sorrow before the Lord, my heart
did begin to rejoice within me, knowing the mercies and the long-
suffering of the Lord, therefore supposing that he would be merciful unto them that they would again become a righteous people.
13. But behold this my joy was vain, for their sorrowing was not
unto repentance, because of the goodness of God; but it was rather
the sorrowing of the damned, because the Lord would not always
suffer them to take happiness in sin.
14. And they did not come unto Jesus with broken hearts and contrite spirits, but they did curse God, and wish to die. Nevertheless
they would struggle with the sword for their lives.
15. And it came to pass that my sorrow did return unto me again,
and I saw that the day of grace was passed with them, both temporally and spiritually; for I saw thousands of them hewn down in
open rebellion against their God, and heaped up as dung upon the
face of the land. And thus three hundred and forty and four years
had passed away.
16. And it came to pass that in the three hundred and forty and fifth
year the Nephites did begin to flee before the Lamanites; and they
were pursued until they came even to the land of Jashon, before it
was possible to stop them in their retreat.
17. And now, the city of Jashon was near the land where Ammaron
had deposited the records unto the Lord, that they might not be
destroyed. And behold I had gone according to the word of
Ammaron, and taken the plates of Nephi, and did make a record
according to the words of Ammaron.
18. And upon the plates of Nephi I

Mormon 2:13

True repentance involves proper sorrow for sin—a sorrow over having offended God and having risked spiritual death, or being cut off from Him. Any other kind of sorrow is of the world and does not lead to true repentance.

Mormon 2:17–18

When Ammaron turned the responsibility of the records over to Mormon, he indicated that Mormon should "engrave on the plates of Nephi all the things that [he] had observed concerning his people." (Morm. 1:4.) Thus Mormon's major record of the events of his day was written on the large plates of Nephi. However, later in his life he was commanded by the Lord to make a separate set of plates, the plates of Mormon. He then abridged onto his own plates all of the writings from the large plates of Nephi, including his own writings. . . . Earlier in his writings, Mormon indicated he did not write on the plates of Mormon even one hundredth part of the things that were written on the large plates of Nephi. (See 3 Ne. 26:6–8.) (Ludlow)

did make a full account of all the wickedness and abominations; but upon these plates I did forbear to make a full account of their wickedness and abominations, for behold, a continual scene of wickedness and abominations has been before mine eyes ever since I have been sufficient to behold the ways of man.

19. And wo is me because of their wickedness; for my heart has been filled with sorrow because of their wickedness, all my days; nevertheless, I know that I shall be lifted up at the last day.

20. And it came to pass that in this year the people of Nephi again were hunted and driven. And it came to pass that we were driven forth until we had come northward to the land which was called Shem.

21. And it came to pass that we did fortify the city of Shem, and we did gather in our people as much as it were possible, that perhaps we might save them from destruction.

22. And it came to pass in the three hundred and forty and sixth year they began to come upon us again.

23. And it came to pass that I did speak unto my people, and did urge them with great energy, that they would stand boldly before the Lamanites and fight for their wives, and their children, and their houses, and their homes.

24. And my words did arouse them somewhat to vigor, insomuch that they did not flee from before the Lamanites, but did stand with boldness against them.

25. And it came to pass that we did contend with an army of thirty thousand against an army of fifty thousand. And it came to pass that we did stand before them with such firmness that they did flee from before us.

26. And it came to pass that when they had fled we did pursue them with our armies, and did meet them again, and did beat them; nevertheless the strength of the Lord was not with us; yea, we were left to ourselves, that the Spirit of the Lord did not abide in us; therefore we had become weak like unto our brethren.

27. And my heart did sorrow because of this the great calamity of my people, because of their wickedness and their abominations. But behold, we did go forth against the Lamanites and the robbers of Gadianton, until we had again taken possession of the lands of our inheritance.

28. And the three hundred and forty and ninth year had passed away. And in the three hundred and fiftieth year we made a treaty with the Lamanites and the robbers of Gadianton, in which we did get the lands of our inheritance divided.

29. And the Lamanites did give unto us the land northward, yea, even to the narrow passage which led into the land southward. And we did give unto the Lamanites all the land southward.

CHAPTER 3

1. AND it came to pass that the Lamanites did not come to battle again until ten years more had passed away. And behold, I had employed my people, the Nephites, in preparing their lands and their arms against the time of battle.

2. And it came to pass that the Lord did say unto me: Cry unto this

Mormon 2:19

In this verse, in which Mormon shares his knowledge that he will be lifted up at the last day, we learn that his calling and election was made sure. Others who have received this blessing include Enos (see Enos 1:27), Alma (see Mosiah 26:20), and the Three Nephites (see 3 Ne. 28:3).

people—Repent ye, and come unto me, and be ye baptized, and
build up again my church, and ye shall be spared.
3. And I did cry unto this people, but it was in vain; and they did
not realize that it was the Lord that had spared them, and granted
unto them a chance for repentance. And behold they did harden
their hearts against the Lord their God.
4. And it came to pass that after this tenth year had passed away,
making, in the whole, three hundred and sixty years from the coming of Christ, the king of the Lamanites sent an epistle unto me,
which gave unto me to know that they were preparing to come
again to battle against us.
5. And it came to pass that I did cause my people that they should
gather themselves together at the land Desolation, to a city which
was in the borders, by the narrow pass which led into the land
southward.
6. And there we did place our armies, that we might stop the armies
of the Lamanites, that they might not get possession of any of our
lands; therefore we did fortify against them with all our force.
7. And it came to pass that in the three hundred and sixty and first
year the Lamanites did come down to the city of Desolation to battle against us; and it came to pass that in that year we did beat
them, insomuch that they did return to their own lands again.
8. And in the three hundred and sixty and second year they did
come down again to battle. And we did beat them again, and did
slay a great number of them, and their dead were cast into the sea.
9. And now, because of this great thing which my people, the
Nephites, had done, they began to boast in their own strength, and
began to swear before the heavens that they would avenge themselves of the blood of their brethren who had been slain by their
enemies.
10. And they did swear by the heavens, and also by the throne of
God, that they would go up to battle against their enemies, and
would cut them off from the face of the land.
11. And it came to pass that I, Mormon, did utterly refuse from this
time forth to be a commander and a leader of this people, because
of their wickedness and abomination.
12. Behold, I had led them, notwithstanding their wickedness I had
led them many times to battle, and had loved them, according to
the love of God which was in me, with all my heart; and my soul
had been poured out in prayer unto my God all the day long for
them; nevertheless, it was without faith, because of the hardness of
their hearts.
13. And thrice have I delivered them out of the hands of their enemies, and they have repented not of their sins.
14. And when they had sworn by all that had been forbidden them
by our Lord and Savior Jesus Christ, that they would go up unto
their enemies to battle, and avenge themselves of the blood of
their brethren, behold the voice of the Lord came unto me, saying:
15. Vengeance is mine, and I will

POINT OF INTEREST

This Mayan image of the god of war is from the engravings at Palenque, Mexico.

Mormon 3:10, 14, 16

The people of the Land of Promise—the Americas—have a unique promise that is in force as long as we are righteous. That promise is that the Lord will either prevent our enemies from coming upon us, or He will fight our battles for us. If we forget God and languish in wickedness, that promise is no longer in force.

Mormon 3:12

Mormon admits that the Nephites went into battle without the sanction of the Lord. This type of participation in war led to the eventual destruction of an entire nation. Though Mormon loved his people and had strived with them through countless situations, he refused to follow them in wickedness.

Mormon 3:15

Vengeance is not the same as self-defense, and the differences are important. While the Lord does permit us to fight in defense of our liberty, our homes and families, and our freedom of religious worship, He does not justify our participation in an offensive war. It is God, not us, who is authorized to deal out retribution to men. Charles Penrose taught that there is a huge difference between going to war for blood, conquest, or to gain territory or power and going to war to defend ourselves in the spirit of justice, righteousness, and equity. It is essential that we rely on the Spirit in all matters of war.

repay; and because this people repented not after I had delivered
them, behold, they shall be cut off from the face of the earth.
16. And it came to pass that I utterly refused to go up against mine
enemies; and I did even as the Lord had commanded me; and I did
stand as an idle witness to manifest unto the world the things which I
saw and heard, according to the manifestations of the Spirit which
had testified of things to come.
17. Therefore I write unto you, Gentiles, and also unto you, house
of Israel, when the work shall commence, that ye shall be about to
prepare to return to the land of your inheritance;
18. Yea, behold, I write unto all the ends of the earth; yea, unto
you, twelve tribes of Israel, who shall be judged according to your
works by the twelve whom Jesus chose to be his disciples in the
land of Jerusalem.
19. And I write also unto the remnant of this people, who shall
also be judged by the twelve whom Jesus chose in this land; and
they shall be judged by the other twelve whom Jesus chose in the
land of Jerusalem.
20. And these things doth the Spirit manifest unto me; therefore I
write unto you all. And for this cause I write unto you, that ye may
know that ye must all stand before the judgment-seat of Christ, yea,
every soul who belongs to the whole human family of Adam; and ye
must stand to be judged of your works, whether they be good or evil;
21. And also that ye may believe the gospel of Jesus Christ, which
ye shall have among you; and also that the Jews, the covenant people of the Lord, shall have other witness besides him whom they
saw and heard, that Jesus, whom they slew, was the very Christ and
the very God.
22. And I would that I could persuade all ye ends of the earth to
repent and prepare to stand before the judgment-seat of Christ.

CHAPTER 4

1. AND now it came to pass that in the three hundred and sixty and
third year the Nephites did go up with
their armies to battle against the
Lamanites, out of the land Desolation.
2. And it came to pass that the armies of
the Nephites were driven back again to the
land of Desolation. And while they were yet
weary, a fresh army of the Lamanites did come
upon them; and they had a sore battle, insomuch that the Lamanites did take possession
of the city Desolation, and did slay many of
the Nephites, and did take many prisoners.
3. And the remainder did flee and join the
inhabitants of the city Teancum. Now the
city Teancum lay in the borders by the
seashore; and it was also near the city
Desolation.
4. And it was because the armies of the
Nephites went up unto the Lamanites that
they began to be

Mormon 3:16

When the people are ensconced with prideful self-satisfaction in iniquity and evil, they are "as a vessel is tossed about upon the waves, without sail or anchor, or without anything wherewith to steer her" (Morm. 5:18). Only through faith in Jesus Christ, through humility and obedience, and through honoring the covenant promises can a people emerge from the mortal vale in a state of spiritual liberty and joy, having stayed on the course toward the destination of the heavenly home.

Mormon proceeded to compile his final record. . . . Mayhem and chaos had been no strangers to him, "for behold, a continual scene of wickedness and abominations has been before mine eyes ever since I have been sufficient to behold the ways of man" (Morm. 2:18). Yet in his exemplary mission as prophet, general, priesthood leader, historian, and father, this remarkable figure on the landscape of God's earthly footstool stands as an example of courage, faithfulness, hope, and unbounded charity—even toward a benighted people whose "day of grace was passed" (Morm. 2:15).

Elder Bruce R. McConkie said, "Truly, wrath and vengeance are bedfellows. When the Lord pours out his wrath without measure, the wicked suffer the vengeance of a just God in exactly the same proportion. It is their

POINT OF INTEREST

These images are from a Mextec-Zapotec codex.

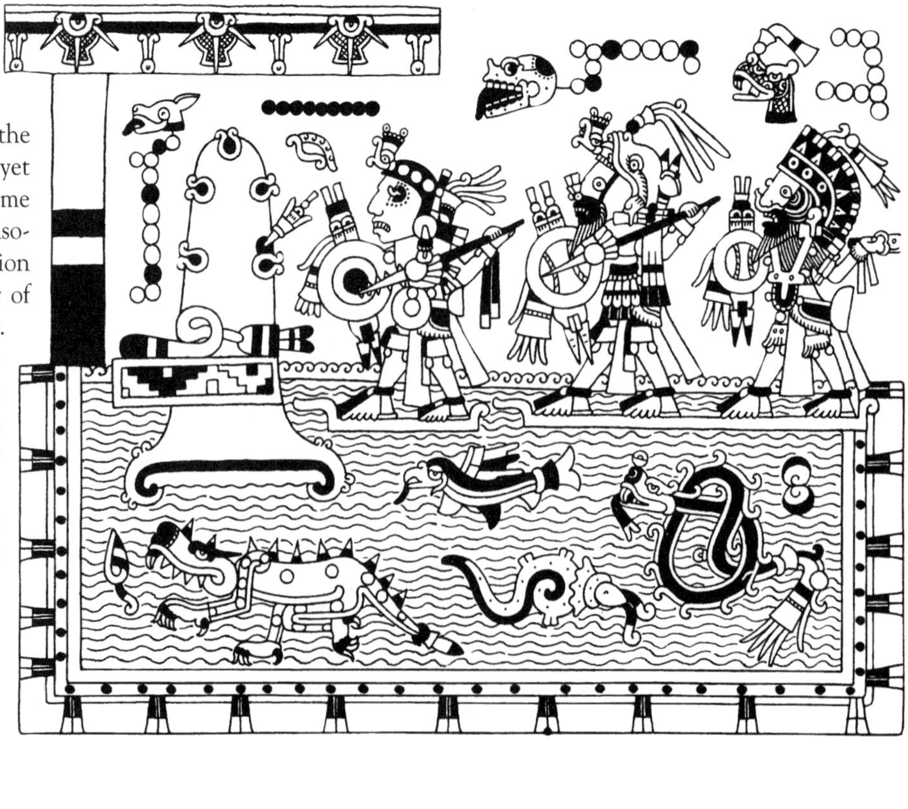

smitten; for were it not for that, the Lamanites could have had no
power over them.
5. But, behold, the judgments of God will overtake the wicked; and
it is by the wicked that the wicked are punished; for it is the wicked
that stir up the hearts of the children of men unto bloodshed.
6. And it came to pass that the Lamanites did make preparations to
come against the city Teancum.
7. And it came to pass in the three hundred and sixty and fourth
year the Lamanites did come against the city Teancum, that they
might take possession of the city Teancum also.
8. And it came to pass that they were repulsed and driven back by
the Nephites. And when the Nephites saw that they had driven
the Lamanites they did again boast of their own strength; and they
went forth in their own might, and took possession again of the
city Desolation.
9. And now all these things had been done, and there had been
thousands slain on both sides, both the Nephites and the
Lamanites.
10. And it came to pass that the three hundred and sixty and sixth
year had passed away, and the Lamanites came again upon the
Nephites to battle; and yet the Nephites repented not of the evil
they had done, but persisted in their wickedness continually.
11. And it is impossible for the tongue to describe, or for man to
write a perfect description of the horrible scene of the blood and
carnage which was among the people, both of the Nephites and of
the Lamanites; and every heart was hardened, so that they delighted in the shedding of blood continually.
12. And there never had been so great wickedness among all the
children of Lehi, nor even among all the house of Israel, according
to the words of the Lord, as was among this people.
13. And it came to pass that the Lamanites did take possession of
the city Desolation, and this because their number did exceed the
number of the Nephites.
14. And they did also march forward against the city Teancum, and
did drive the inhabitants forth out of her, and did take many prisoners both women and children, and did offer them up as sacrifices
unto their idol gods.
15. And it came to pass that in the three hundred and sixty and
seventh year, the Nephites being angry because the Lamanites had
sacrificed their women and their children, that they did go against
the Lamanites with exceedingly great anger, insomuch that they
did beat again the Lamanites, and drive them out of their lands.
16. And the Lamanites did not come again against the Nephites
until the three hundred and seventy and fifth year.
17. And in this year they did come down against the Nephites with
all their powers; and they were not numbered because of the greatness of their number.
18. And from this time forth did the Nephites gain no power over
the Lamanites, but began to be swept off by them even as a dew
before the sun.
19. And it came to pass that the Lamanites did come down against
the city Desolation; and there was an exceedingly sore battle
fought in the land Desolation, in the which they did beat the
Nephites.

day of reckoning; they are given measure for measure as their deeds warrant; it is a day of retribution and avengement. It is 'the day when the Lord shall come to recompense unto every man according to his work, and measure to every man according to the measure which he has measured to his fellow man' (D&C 1:10)." (P/A)

Mormon 3:18–19

These verses refer to the twelve that the Savior has appointed to be judges; as Elder Bruce R. McConkie taught, there will be an entire hierarchy of judges who will work under the Savior's direction to judge the righteous. However, the Savior is the only one who can and will judge the wicked and issue the decrees of punishment for them.

Mormon 4:5

How are the wicked punished? The Lord withdraws and leaves the people to themselves. At that point, the wicked punish—and eventually destroy—each other.

Mormon 4:10–12

Once the Nephite soldiers started to wage offensive war they soon became so bloodthirsty they were concerned only with the taking of human life. Thus both the Nephites and Lamanites became obsessed with the desire to kill. . . .

The leaders of this dispensation have . . . warned against the dangers of starting an offensive war. President Charles W. Penrose has said:

"Now if a nation essays to go forth against another nation for the purpose of conquest, to gain territory, to grasp something that does not belong to that nation, then the nation thus assailed has the right to resist even to the shedding of blood, as it was in this land in the war for independence. But we have to be careful as to what spirit we are guided by. . . .

"There is a very great difference between arising to go forth for conquest, for blood, for plunder, to gain territory and power in the earth, and in fighting to defend our own possessions in the spirit of justice and righteousness and equity, and standing up like men for those things that we have a right to contend for." (Ludlow)

20. And they fled again from before them, and they came to the city Boaz; and there they did stand against the Lamanites with exceeding boldness, insomuch that the Lamanites did not beat them until they had come again the second time.
21. And when they had come the second time, the Nephites were driven and slaughtered with an exceedingly great slaughter; their women and their children were again sacrificed unto idols.
22. And it came to pass that the Nephites did again flee from before them, taking all the inhabitants with them, both in towns and villages.
23. And now I, Mormon, seeing that the Lamanites were about to overthrow the land, therefore I did go to the hill Shim, and did take up all the records which Ammaron had hid up unto the Lord.

CHAPTER 5

1. AND it came to pass that I did go forth among the Nephites, and did repent of the oath which I had made that I would no more assist them; and they gave me command again of their armies, for they looked upon me as though I could deliver them from their afflictions.
2. But behold, I was without hope, for I knew the judgments of the Lord which should come upon them; for they repented not of their iniquities, but did struggle for their lives without calling upon that Being who created them.
3. And it came to pass that the Lamanites did come against us as we had fled to the city of Jordan; but behold, they were driven back that they did not take the city at that time.
4. And it came to pass that they came against us again, and we did maintain the city. And there were also other cities which were maintained by Nephites, which strongholds did cut them off that they could not get into the country which lay before us, to destroy the inhabitants of our land.
5. And it came to pass that whatsoever lands we had passed by, and the inhabitants thereof were not gathered in, were destroyed by the Lamanites, and their towns, and villages, and cities were burned with fire; and thus three hundred and seventy and nine years passed away.
6. And it came to pass that in the three hundred and eightieth year the Lamanites did come again against us to battle, and we did stand against them boldly; but it was all in vain, for so great were their numbers that they did tread the people of the Nephites under their feet.
7. And it came to pass that we did again take to flight, and those whose flight was swifter than the Lamanites' did escape, and those whose flight did not exceed the Lamanites' were swept down and destroyed.
8. And now behold, I, Mormon, do not desire to harrow up the souls of men in casting before them such an awful scene of blood and carnage as was laid before mine eyes; but I, knowing that these things must surely be made known, and that all things which are hid must be revealed upon the house-tops—
9. And also that a knowledge of these things must come unto the remnant of these people, and also

Mormon 5:1–2

In referring to these verses, Hugh Nibley said that "in this crucible of wickedness the true greatness of Mormon shines like a star." In these verses, Mormon provides the powerful example to us that no matter how bad things get, we must never stop trying to improve the circumstances and we should never give up on those we love.

unto the Gentiles, who the Lord hath said should scatter this people, and this people should be counted as naught among them—therefore I write a small abridgment, daring not to give a full account of the things which I have seen, because of the commandment which I have received, and also that ye might not have too great sorrow because of the wickedness of this people.

10. And now behold, this I speak unto their seed, and also to the Gentiles who have care for the house of Israel, that realize and know from whence their blessings come.

11. For I know that such will sorrow for the calamity of the house of Israel; yea, they will sorrow for the destruction of this people; they will sorrow that this people had not repented that they might have been clasped in the arms of Jesus.

12. Now these things are written unto the remnant of the house of Jacob; and they are written after this manner, because it is known of God that wickedness will not bring them forth unto them; and they are to be hid up unto the Lord that they may come forth in his own due time.

13. And this is the commandment which I have received; and behold, they shall come forth according to the commandment of the Lord, when he shall see fit, in his wisdom.

14. And behold, they shall go unto the unbelieving of the Jews; and for this intent shall they go—that they may be persuaded that Jesus is the Christ, the Son of the living God; that the Father may bring about, through his most Beloved, his great and eternal purpose, in restoring the Jews, or all the house of Israel, to the land of their inheritance, which the Lord their God hath given them, unto the fulfilling of his covenant;

15. And also that the seed of this people may more fully believe his gospel, which shall go forth unto them from the Gentiles; for this people shall be scattered, and shall become a dark, a filthy, and a loathsome people, beyond the description of that which ever hath been amongst us, yea, even that which hath been among the Lamanites, and this because of their unbelief and idolatry.

16. For behold, the Spirit of the Lord hath already ceased to strive with their fathers; and they are without Christ and God in the world; and they are driven about as chaff before the wind.

17. They were once a delightsome people, and they had Christ for their shepherd; yea, they were led even by God the Father.

18. But now, behold, they are led about by Satan, even as chaff is driven before the wind, or as a vessel is tossed about upon the waves, without sail or anchor, or without anything wherewith to steer her; and even as she is, so are they.

19. And behold, the Lord hath reserved their blessings, which they

Mormon 5:12–14

Lehi offers up patriarchal exhortations to his family circle. He pleads with Laman and Lemuel to remember the goodness of God, repent and keep the commandments, put on the armor of righteousness, and rebel no more against their brother Nephi. He reminds them pointedly that only righteous behavior will preserve liberty in the land for those who occupy it. . . .

The Prophet Joseph Smith said that "if parents fail to do this and the children go astray and turn from the truth, then the Lord has said the sin shall be upon the heads of the parents. The loss of the children will be charged to the parents and they will be responsible for their apostasy and darkness. . . . I do not believe that it would be possible for me to be admitted into exaltation and glory in the Kingdom of God, if through my neglect of duty my children should become the children of darkness in this regard. . . . I will endeavor with all the power I possess to have them as true and faithful to this gospel as it is possible for me to be; because, without all of them in the Kingdom of God I would feel that my household was not perfect." (P/A)

Mormon 5:17–19

According to Hugh Nibley, at this point the Nephite nation was broken up into tribes, each following its own tribal laws. Those who refused to pull up stakes were, one by one, completely wiped out by the Lamanites—similar to what happened to the Barbarians in the Old World.

might have received in the land, for the Gentiles who shall possess the land.

20. But behold, it shall come to pass that they shall be driven and scattered by the Gentiles; and after they have been driven and scattered by the Gentiles, behold, then will the Lord remember the covenant which he made unto Abraham and unto all the house of Israel.

21. And also the Lord will remember the prayers of the righteous, which have been put up unto him for them.

22. And then, O ye Gentiles, how can ye stand before the power of God, except ye shall repent and turn from your evil ways?

23. Know ye not that ye are in the hands of God? Know ye not that he hath all power, and at his great command the earth shall be rolled together as a scroll?

24. Therefore, repent ye, and humble yourselves before him, lest he shall come out in justice against you—lest a remnant of the seed of Jacob shall go forth among you as a lion, and tear you in pieces, and there is none to deliver.

CHAPTER 6

1. AND now I finish my record concerning the destruction of my people, the Nephites. And it came to pass that we did march forth before the Lamanites.

2. And I, Mormon, wrote an epistle unto the king of the Lamanites, and desired of him that he would grant unto us that we might gather together our people unto the land of Cumorah, by a hill which was called Cumorah, and there we could give them battle.

3. And it came to pass that the king of the Lamanites did grant unto me the thing which I desired.

4. And it came to pass that we did march forth to the land of Cumorah, and we did pitch our tents around about the hill Cumorah; and it was in a land of many waters, rivers, and fountains; and here we had hope to gain advantage over the Lamanites.

5. And when three hundred and eighty and four years had passed away, we had gathered in all the remainder of our people unto the land Cumorah.

6. And it came to pass that when we had gathered in all our people in one to the land Cumorah, behold I, Mormon, began to be old; and knowing it to be the last struggle of my people, and having been commanded of the Lord that I should not suffer the records which had been handed down by our fathers, which were sacred, to fall into the hands of the Lamanites, (for the Lamanites would destroy them) therefore I made this record out of the plates of Nephi, and hid up in the hill Cumorah all the records which had been entrusted to me by the hand of the Lord, save it were these few plates which I gave unto my son Moroni.

7. And it came to pass that my people, with their wives and their children, did now behold the armies of the Lamanites marching towards
them; and with that awful fear of death which fills the breasts of all the
wicked, did they await to receive them.
8. And it came to pass that they came to battle against us, and
every soul was filled with terror because of the greatness of their
numbers.
9. And it came to pass that they did fall upon my people with the
sword, and with the bow, and with the arrow, and with the ax, and
with all manner of weapons of war.
10. And it came to pass that my men were hewn down, yea, even my
ten thousand who were with me, and I fell wounded in the midst; and
they passed by me that they did not put an end to my life.
11. And when they had gone through and hewn down all my people save it were twenty and four of us, (among whom was my son
Moroni) and we having survived the dead of our people, did behold
on the morrow, when the Lamanites had returned unto their camps,
from the top of the hill Cumorah, the ten thousand of my people
who were hewn down, being led in the front by me.
12. And we also beheld the ten thousand of my people who were
led by my son Moroni.
13. And behold, the ten thousand of Gidgiddonah had fallen, and
he also in the midst.
14. And Lamah had fallen with his ten thousand; and Gilgal had
fallen with his ten thousand; and Limhah had fallen with his ten
thousand; and Jeneum had fallen with his ten thousand; and
Cumenihah, and Moronihah, and Antionum, and Shiblom, and
Shem, and Josh, had fallen with their ten thousand each.
15. And it came to pass that there were ten more who did fall by
the sword, with their ten thousand each; yea, even all my people,
save it were those twenty and four who were with me, and also a
few who had escaped into the south countries, and a few who had
deserted over unto the Lamanites, had fallen; and their flesh, and
bones, and blood lay upon the face of the earth, being left by the
hands of those who slew them to molder upon the land, and to
crumble and to return to their mother earth.
16. And my soul was rent with anguish, because of the slain of my
people, and I cried:
17. O ye fair ones, how could ye have departed from the ways of
the Lord! O ye fair ones, how could ye have rejected that Jesus,
who stood with open arms to receive you!
18. Behold, if ye had not done this, ye would not have fallen. But
behold, ye are fallen, and I mourn your loss.
19. O ye fair sons and daughters, ye fathers and mothers, ye husbands and wives, ye fair ones, how is it that ye could have fallen!
20. But behold, ye are gone, and my sorrows cannot bring your
return.
21. And the day soon cometh that your mortal must put on immortality, and these bodies which are now moldering in corruption
must soon become incorruptible bodies; and then ye must stand
before the judgment-seat of Christ, to be judged according to your
works and if it so be that ye are righteous, then are ye blessed with
your fathers who have gone before you.
22. O that ye had repented before this great destruction had come
upon you. But behold, ye are gone,

Mormon 6:15

The sacred records reach one of the final Nephite chroniclers, Mormon. He, like all the prophets before him, writes with the intent to persuade people to come unto Christ. In this case, he is constrained, by commandment, to show us the chaos and calumny that characterize the final state of a people "without Christ and God in the world" (Morm. 5:16)—to the end that we might all realize the awful consequences of iniquity. In their wickedness, the Nephites are eventually destroyed in the great battles with the Lamanites. However, in the midst of this bleak landscape, we may see the stalwart valor and love of Mormon and his son Moroni. . . .

President Spencer W. Kimball said, "How his heart must have pained and his whole being ached. . . . Then as he saw both armies at Cumorah, in their last bloody struggles, too late to reform, too hardened to repent, too stubborn to change, observing with terror their destroyers marching to the final battlefield where their bodies, too numerous to ever be buried, would rot in the sun: . . . .

"There was little else that the wounded general could do now but to weep and to write and to prophesy and warn."

The Book of Mormon is a welcome voice from the past—the sacred record of truth preserved by the Lord as a compass for our day and age. It is a beacon of hope amidst the gloom of iniquity that all too frequently characterizes worldly conditions. The Lord has preserved His sacred record that all might be persuaded to come unto Christ. The Lord will not allow us to have happiness in wickedness. Faith, repentance, and obedience are the requisite gateways to the peace and joy that come as blessings from the Lord. (P/A)

and the Father, yea, the Eternal Father of heaven, knoweth your state; and he doeth with you according to his justice and mercy.

CHAPTER 7

1. AND now, behold, I would speak somewhat unto the remnant of this people who are spared, if it so be that God may give unto them my words, that they may know of the things of their fathers; yea, I speak unto you, ye remnant of the house of Israel; and these are the words which I speak:
2. Know ye that ye are of the house of Israel.
3. Know ye that ye must come unto repentance, or ye cannot be saved.
4. Know ye that ye must lay down your weapons of war, and delight no more in the shedding of blood, and take them not again, save it be that God shall command you.
5. Know ye that ye must come to the knowledge of your fathers, and repent of all your sins and iniquities, and believe in Jesus Christ, that he is the Son of God, and that he was slain by the Jews, and by the power of the Father he hath risen again, whereby he hath gained the victory over the grave; and also in him is the sting of death swallowed up.
6. And he bringeth to pass the resurrection of the dead, whereby man must be raised to stand before his judgment-seat.
7. And he hath brought to pass the redemption of the world, whereby he that is found guiltless before him at the judgment day hath it given unto him to dwell in the presence of God in his kingdom, to sing ceaseless praises with the choirs above, unto the Father, and unto the Son, and unto the Holy Ghost, which are one God, in a state of happiness which hath no end.
8. Therefore repent, and be baptized in the name of Jesus, and lay hold upon the gospel of Christ, which shall be set before you, not only in this record but also in the record which shall come unto the Gentiles from the Jews, which record shall come from the Gentiles unto you.
9. For behold, this is written for the intent that ye may believe that; and if ye believe that ye will believe this also; and if ye believe this ye will know concerning your fathers, and also the marvelous works which were wrought by the power of God among them.
10. And ye will also know that ye are a remnant of the seed of Jacob; therefore ye are numbered among the people of the first covenant; and if it so be that ye believe in Christ, and are baptized, first with water, then with fire and with the Holy Ghost, following the example of

Mormon 7:1–2

The Lamanites of today are the literal descendants of great Book of Mormon leaders. See Abraham 2:8–11 for a description of the blessings for these descendants as well as the attendant responsibilities.

Mormon 7:4–5

These verses provide important instruction to the Lamanites—instructions that contain eternal principles applicable to us in our day.

Mormon 7:5–8

Mormon offers up his final witness of the truth of the gospel and calls for all to repent and come unto Christ. His son Moroni then announces that his father has been killed in battle, leaving him alone to uphold the sacred trust of preserving the record. Their joint declarations encapsulate the essence of the gospel of Jesus Christ, constituting a prophetic summary of the covenant promises and a profoundly moving exhortation for all their modern readers to receive the message of truth and prepare for the Day of Judgment through faith and righteous obedience.

President George Albert Smith said, "It is the gospel of Jesus Christ that we bear. It is the desire to save the souls of the children of men that burns in our hearts. It is not that we may build ourselves up and become a mighty people financially; it is not that we may have our names glorified in the earth for our accomplishments; but it is that the sons and daughters of God, wherever they may be, may hear this gospel, which is the power of God unto salvation to all those who believe and obey its precepts." (P/A)

Mormon 7:9

As we see in this verse, the Bible and Book of Mormon reinforce each other. As Brigham Young taught, if one is true, then they are both true.

our Savior, according to that which he hath commanded us, it shall be well with you in the day of judgment. Amen.

CHAPTER 8

1. BEHOLD I, Moroni, do finish the record of my father, Mormon. Behold, I have but few things to write, which things I have been commanded by my father.
2. And now it came to pass that after the great and tremendous battle at Cumorah, behold, the Nephites who had escaped into the country southward were hunted by the Lamanites, until they were all destroyed.
3. And my father also was killed by them, and I even remain alone to write the sad tale of the destruction of my people. But behold, they are gone, and I fulfil the commandment of my father. And whether they will slay me, I know not.
4. Therefore I will write and hide up the records in the earth; and whither I go it mattereth not.
5. Behold, my father hath made this record, and he hath written the intent thereof. And behold, I would write it also if I had room upon the plates, but I have not; and ore I have none, for I am alone. My father hath been slain in battle, and all my kinsfolk, and I have not friends nor whither to go; and how long the Lord will suffer that I may live I know not.
6. Behold, four hundred years have passed away since the coming of our Lord and Savior.
7. And behold, the Lamanites have hunted my people, the Nephites, down from city to city and from place to place, even until they are no more; and great has been their fall; yea, great and marvelous is the destruction of my people, the Nephites.
8. And behold, it is the hand of the Lord which hath done it. And behold also, the Lamanites are at war one with another; and the whole face of this land is one continual round of murder and bloodshed; and no one knoweth the end of the war.
9. And now, behold, I say no more concerning them, for there are none save it be the Lamanites and robbers that do exist upon the face of the land.
10. And there are none that do know the true God save it be the disciples of Jesus, who did tarry in the land until the wickedness of the people was so great that the Lord would not suffer them to remain with the people; and whether they be upon the face of the land no man knoweth.
11. But behold, my father and I have seen them, and they have ministered unto us.
12. And whoso receiveth this record, and shall not condemn it because of the imperfections which are in it, the same shall know of greater things than these. Behold, I am Moroni; and were it possible, I would make all things known unto you.

Mormon 8

Moroni actually offers three distinct witnesses in the pages of the Book of Mormon. In order, they are:

1. The concluding chapters (8 and 9) of his father's book (Mormon)
2. The comments he interjected into the Book of Ether
3. His own book, the concluding dialogue of the Book of Mormon, in which he urges readers to exercise faith and sincerity of heart in seeking a testimony of its truthfulness

Mormon 8:2–5

Concerning whether or not all of the Nephites were destroyed, Hugh Nibley has written the following:

"Are there not many Latter-day Saints who will insist that every American of pre-Columbian descent must be a Lamanite because, forsooth, there were once Nephites and Lamanites, and the Nephites were destroyed? Yet the Book of Mormon itself makes such an interpretation impossible. The Nephites were destroyed, we are told, but . . . what does the Book of Mormon mean by 'destroyed'? The word is to be taken, as are so many other key words in the book, in its primary and original sense: 'to unbuild; to separate violently into its constituent parts; to break up the structure.' To destroy is to wreck the structure, not to annihilate the parts. . . .

"Only once in the Book of Mormon do we read of a case of annihilation, when we are specifically told that 'every living soul of the Ammonihahites was destroyed' (Alma 16:9), where not only the social structure but each individual is undone. In other instances the Lord promises that he will not utterly destroy the descendants of Lehi's youngest son, Joseph (2 Ne. 3:3), or of Lemuel (id., 4:9), and even Nephi is told that God 'will not suffer that the Gentiles will utterly destroy the mixture of thy seed which are among thy brethren' (1 Ne. 13:30), even though the promises and fulfillment were that the Nephites should be 'destroyed' (Ether 8:21), and even though Moroni can say: 'there is none, save it be Lamanites' (Ether 4:3)."

Also, it is of interest to note that the Lord has referred to Nephites in this dispensation. (See D&C 3:16–19.) (Ludlow)

13. Behold, I make an end of speaking concerning this people. I am the son of Mormon, and my father was a descendant of Nephi.
14. And I am the same who hideth up this record unto the Lord; the plates thereof are of no worth, because of the commandment of the Lord. For he truly saith that no one shall have them to get gain; but the record thereof is of great worth; and whoso shall bring it to light, him will the Lord bless.
15. For none can have power to bring it to light save it be given him of God; for God wills that it shall be done with an eye single to his glory, or the welfare of the ancient and long dispersed covenant people of the Lord.
16. And blessed be he that shall bring this thing to light; for it shall be brought out of darkness unto light, according to the word of God; yea, it shall be brought out of the earth, and it shall shine forth out of darkness, and come unto the knowledge of the people; and it shall be done by the power of God.
17. And if there be faults they be the faults of a man. But behold, we know no fault; nevertheless God knoweth all things; therefore, he that condemneth, let him be aware lest he shall be in danger of hell fire.
18. And he that saith: Show unto me, or ye shall be smitten—let him beware lest he commandeth that which is forbidden of the Lord.
19. For behold, the same that judgeth rashly shall be judged rashly again; for according to his works shall his wages be; therefore, he that smiteth shall be smitten again, of the Lord.
20. Behold what the scripture says—man shall not smite, neither shall he judge; for judgment is mine, saith the Lord, and vengeance is mine also, and I will repay.
21. And he that shall breathe out wrath and strifes against the work of the Lord, and against the covenant people of the Lord who are the house of Israel, and shall say: We will destroy the work of the Lord, and the Lord will not remember his covenant which he hath made unto the house of Israel—the same is in danger to be hewn down and cast into the fire;
22. For the eternal purposes of the Lord shall roll on, until all his promises shall be fulfilled.
23. Search the prophecies of Isaiah. Behold, I cannot write them. Yea, behold I say unto you, that those saints who have gone before me, who have possessed this land, shall cry, yea, even from the dust will they cry unto the Lord; and as the Lord liveth he will remember the covenant which he hath made with them.
24. And he knoweth their prayers, that they were in behalf of their brethren. And he knoweth their faith, for in his name could they remove mountains; and in his name could they cause the earth to shake; and by the power of his word did they cause prisons to tumble to the earth; yea, even the fiery furnace could not harm them, neither wild

beasts nor poisonous serpents, because of the power of his word.
25. And behold, their prayers were also in behalf of him that the
Lord should suffer to bring these things forth.
26. And no one need say they shall not come, for they surely shall,
for the Lord hath spoken it; for out of the earth shall they come,
by the hand of the Lord, and none can stay it; and it shall come in
a day when it shall be said that miracles are done away; and it shall
come even as if one should speak from the dead.
27. And it shall come in a day when the blood of saints shall cry
unto the Lord, because of secret combinations and the works of
darkness.
28. Yea, it shall come in a day when the power of God shall be
denied, and churches become defiled and be lifted up in the pride
of their hearts; yea, even in a day when leaders of churches and
teachers shall rise in the pride of their hearts, even to the envying
of them who belong to their churches.
29. Yea, it shall come in a day when there shall be heard of fires,
and tempests, and vapors of smoke in foreign lands;
30. And there shall also be heard of wars, rumors of wars, and
earthquakes in divers places.
31. Yea, it shall come in a day when there shall be great pollutions
upon the face of the earth; there shall be murders, and robbing, and
lying, and deceivings, and whoredoms, and all manner of abominations; when there shall be many who will say, Do this, or do that,
and it mattereth not, for the Lord will uphold such at the last day.
But wo unto such, for they are in the gall of bitterness and in the
bonds of iniquity.
32. Yea, it shall come in a day when there shall be churches built
up that shall say: Come unto me, and for your money you shall be
forgiven of your sins.
33. O ye wicked and perverse and stiffnecked people, why have ye
built up churches unto yourselves to get gain? Why have ye trans-
figured the holy word of God, that ye might bring damnation upon
your souls? Behold, look ye unto the revelations of God; for
behold, the time cometh at that day when all these things must be
fulfilled.
34. Behold, the Lord hath shown unto me great and marvelous
things concerning that which must shortly come, at that day when
these things shall come forth among you.
35. Behold, I speak unto you as if ye were present, and yet ye are
not. But behold, Jesus Christ hath shown you unto me, and I know
your doing.
36. And I know that ye do walk in the pride of your hearts; and
there are none save a few only who do not lift themselves up in the
pride of their hearts, unto the wearing of very fine apparel, unto
envying,

Mormon 8:26–36

In these verses, Moroni goes to great lengths to describe the conditions that would exist in the world at the time the Book of Mormon would come forth. Those same conditions—false prophets, false religions, false philosophies, and great deceptions that will fool all but the very elect—still exist in our day. This is the day when Satan has been unleashed in all his power, and we as covenant people need to guard zealously against being deceived ourselves.

Mormon 8:31–32

". . . there shall be great pollutions upon the face of the earth; there shall be murders, and robbing, and lying, and deceivings, and whoredoms, and all manner of abominations. . ." (Morm. 8:31). Pollution in our day is not just unclean air or water. It is more clearly seen in the form of polluted thoughts, language, entertainment, and behavior. President Spencer W. Kimball warned of these unacceptable levels of filth in our society:

"We hope that our parents and leaders will not tolerate pornography. It is really garbage, but today is peddled as normal and satisfactory food. . . . How low can humans plunge! We pray with our Lord that we may be kept from being in the world. It is sad that decent people are thrown into a filthy area of mental and spiritual pollution. We call upon all of our people to do all in their power to offset this ugly revolution." (O/C)

and strifes, and malice, and persecutions, and all manner of iniquities; and your churches, yea, even every one, have become polluted because of the pride of your hearts.
37. For behold, ye do love money, and your substance, and your fine apparel, and the adorning of your churches, more than ye love the poor and the needy, the sick and the afflicted.
38. O ye pollutions, ye hypocrites, ye teachers, who sell yourselves for that which will canker, why have ye polluted the holy church of God? Why are ye ashamed to take upon you the name of Christ? Why do ye not think that greater is the value of an endless happiness than that misery which never dies—because of the praise of the world?
39. Why do ye adorn yourselves with that which hath no life, and yet suffer the hungry, and the needy, and the naked, and the sick and the afflicted to pass by you, and notice them not?
40. Yea, why do ye build up your secret abominations to get gain, and cause that widows should mourn before the Lord, and also orphans to mourn before the Lord, and also the blood of their fathers and their husbands to cry unto the Lord from the ground, for vengeance upon your heads?
41. Behold, the sword of vengeance hangeth over you; and the time soon cometh that he avengeth the blood of the saints upon you, for he will not suffer their cries any longer.

CHAPTER 9

1. AND now, I speak also concerning those who do not believe in Christ.
2. Behold, will ye believe in the day of your visitation—behold, when the Lord shall come, yea, even that great day when the earth shall be rolled together as a scroll, and the elements shall melt with fervent heat, yea, in that great day when ye shall be brought to stand before the Lamb of God—then will ye say that there is no God?
3. Then will ye longer deny the Christ, or can ye behold the Lamb of God? Do ye suppose that ye shall dwell with him under a consciousness of your guilt? Do ye suppose that ye could be happy to dwell with that holy Being, when your souls are racked with a consciousness of guilt that ye have ever abused his laws?
4. Behold, I say unto you that ye would be more miserable to dwell with a holy and just God, under a consciousness of your filthiness before him, than ye would to dwell with the damned souls in hell.
5. For behold, when ye shall be brought to see your nakedness before God, and also the glory of God, and the holiness of Jesus Christ, it will kindle a flame of unquenchable fire upon you.
6. O then ye unbelieving, turn ye unto the Lord; cry mightily unto the Father in the name of Jesus, that perhaps ye may be found spotless,

pure, fair, and white, having been cleansed by the blood of the
Lamb, at that great and last day.
7. And again I speak unto you who deny the revelations of God,
and say that they are done away, that there are no revelations, nor
prophecies, nor gifts, nor healing, nor speaking with tongues, and
the interpretation of tongues;
8. Behold I say unto you, he that denieth these things knoweth not
the gospel of Christ; yea, he has not read the scriptures; if so, he
does not understand them.
9. For do we not read that God is the same yesterday, today, and
forever, and in him there is no variableness neither shadow of
changing?
10. And now, if ye have imagined up unto yourselves a god who doth
vary, and in whom there is shadow of changing, then have ye imagined up unto yourselves a god who is not a God of miracles.
11. But behold, I will show unto you a God of miracles, even the
God of Abraham, and the God of Isaac, and the God of Jacob; and
it is that same God who created the heavens and the earth, and all
things that in them are.
12. Behold, he created Adam, and by Adam came
the fall of man. And because of the fall of man
came Jesus Christ, even the Father and the Son;
and because of Jesus Christ came the redemption
of man.
13. And because of the redemption of man, which
came by Jesus Christ, they are brought back into
the presence of the Lord; yea, this is wherein all
men are redeemed, because the death of Christ
bringeth to pass the resurrection, which bringeth
to pass a redemption from an endless sleep, from
which sleep all men shall be awakened by the
power of God when the trump shall sound; and
they shall come forth, both small and great, and all
shall stand before his bar, being redeemed and
loosed from this eternal band of death, which
death is a temporal death.
14. And then cometh the judgment of the Holy
One upon them; and then cometh the time that
he that is filthy shall be filthy still; and he that is
righteous shall be righteous still; he that is happy
shall be happy still; and he that is unhappy shall
be unhappy still.
15. And now, O all ye that have imagined up unto
yourselves a god who can do no miracles, I would
ask of you, have all these things passed, of which I
have spoken? Has the end come yet? Behold I say
unto you, Nay; and God has not ceased to be a
God of miracles.
16. Behold, are not the things that God hath
wrought marvelous in our eyes? Yea, and who can
comprehend the marvelous works of God?
17. Who shall say that it was not a miracle that by
his word the heaven and the earth should be; and
by the power of his word man was created of the
dust of the earth; and by the power of his word
have miracles been wrought?

POINT OF INTEREST

Ollantaytambo, Peru, is just northwest of Cuzco and is best known for its ruins and as the only major site where the Incas defeated the Spaniards in battle.

18. And who shall say that Jesus Christ did not do many mighty miracles? And there were many mighty miracles wrought by the hands of the apostles.
19. And if there were miracles wrought then, why has God ceased to be a God of miracles and yet be an unchangeable Being? And behold, I say unto you he changeth not; if so he would cease to be God; and he ceaseth not to be God, and is a God of miracles.
20. And the reason why he ceaseth to do miracles among the children of men is because that they dwindle in unbelief, and depart from the right way, and know not the God in whom they should trust.
21. Behold, I say unto you that whoso believeth in Christ, doubting nothing, whatsoever he shall ask the Father in the name of Christ it shall be granted him; and this promise is unto all, even unto the ends of the earth.
22. For behold, thus said Jesus Christ, the Son of God, unto his disciples who should tarry, yea, and also to all his disciples, in the hearing of the multitude: Go ye into all the world, and preach the gospel to every creature;
23. And he that believeth and is baptized shall be saved, but he that believeth not shall be damned;
24. And these signs shall follow them that believe—in my name shall they cast out devils; they shall speak with new tongues; they shall take up serpents; and if they drink any deadly thing it shall not hurt them; they shall lay hands on the sick and they shall recover;
25. And whosoever shall believe in my name, doubting nothing, unto him will I confirm all my words, even unto the ends of the earth.
26. And now, behold, who can stand against the works of the Lord? Who can deny his sayings? Who will rise up against the almighty power of the Lord? Who will despise the works of the Lord? Who will despise the children of Christ? Behold, all ye who are despisers of the works of the Lord, for ye shall wonder and perish.
27. O then despise not, and wonder not, but hearken unto the words of the Lord, and ask the Father in the name of Jesus for what things soever ye shall stand in need. Doubt not, but be believing, and begin as in times of old, and come unto the Lord with all your heart, and work out your own salvation with fear and trembling before him.
28. Be wise in the days of your probation; strip yourselves of all uncleanness; ask not, that ye may consume it on your lusts, but ask with a firmness unshaken, that ye will yield to no temptation, but that ye will serve the true and living God.
29. See that ye are not baptized unworthily; see that ye partake not of the sacrament of Christ unworthily; but see that ye do all

Mormon 9:21–23

President Ezra Taft Benson said, "God the Father and his beloved Son did appear to Joseph Smith. This was the greatest event that has transpired in the world since the resurrection of the Master. This is our message and our warning to the world. It is a world message from a world organization—The Church of Jesus Christ of Latter-day Saints. These warnings of the prophets, ancient and modern, shall in very deed be fulfilled. The Lord is 'angry with the wicked.' He is 'holding his Spirit from the inhabitants of the earth.' The one hope for this wicked world is to accept and live the gospel, to keep the commandments, to heed the warnings of the prophets, ancient and modern."

Mormon and Moroni exhort us to repent, believe in Christ, be baptized, and prepare ourselves for the imminent return of the great Lawgiver and Judge of mankind in His glory. They graphically describe the conditions of wickedness that will prevail at the time of the coming forth of the Book of Mormon. This mighty word of Christ, preserved by the hand of God and brought forth miraculously in a day when miracles had ceased because the people "dwindle in unbelief, and depart from the right way, and know not the God in whom they should trust" (Morm. 9:20), confirms the truth of the Bible and proves that God is the same yesterday, today, and forever.

The unchanging God of miracles has brought forth a latter-day miracle, even the restoration of the gospel and the Book of Mormon, which supports the Bible and invites all mankind to repent, believe in Christ, and prepare for the Day of Judgment. (P/A)

Mormon 9:27–31

These verses contain Moroni's counsel to latter-day readers of the Book of Mormon.

things in worthiness, and do it in the name of Jesus Christ, the Son of the living God; and if ye do this, and endure to the end, ye will in nowise be cast out.
30. Behold, I speak unto you as though I spake from the dead; for I know that ye shall have my words.
31. Condemn me not because of mine imperfection, neither my father, because of his imperfection, neither them who have written before him; but rather give thanks unto God that he hath made manifest unto you our imperfections, that ye may learn to be more wise than we have been.
32. And now, behold, we have written this record according to our knowledge, in the characters which are called among us the reformed Egyptian, being handed down and altered by us, according to our manner of speech.
33. And if our plates had been sufficiently large we should have written in Hebrew; but the Hebrew hath been altered by us also; and if we could have written in Hebrew, behold, ye would have had no imperfection in our record.
34. But the Lord knoweth the things which we have written, and also that none other people knoweth our language; and because that none other people knoweth our language, therefore he hath prepared means for the interpretation thereof.
35. And these things are written that we may rid our garments of the blood of our brethren, who have dwindled in unbelief.
36. And behold, these things which we have desired concerning our brethren, yea, even their restoration to the knowledge of Christ, are according to the prayers of all the saints who have dwelt in the land.
37. And may the Lord Jesus Christ grant that their prayers may be answered according to their faith; and may God the Father remember the covenant which he hath made with the house of Israel; and may he bless them forever, through faith on the name of Jesus Christ. Amen.

THE BOOK OF ETHER

The record of the Jaredites, taken from the twenty-four plates found by the people of Limhi in the days of king Mosiah.

CHAPTER 1

1. AND now I, Moroni, proceed to give an account of those ancient inhabitants who were destroyed by the hand of the Lord upon the face of this north country.
2. And I take mine account from the twenty and four plates which

Mormon 9:33

At this point, the Nephites were still speaking some form of Hebrew. (Ludlow)

Mormon 9:36

In 1845, the First Presidency issued a proclamation concerning the restoration of the Lamanites to a knowledge of Christ. The righteous Lamanites will be crowned with power and authority that will never end. Their hearts will expand with knowledge as wide as eternity, and their minds will comprehend the vast creations of God. These righteous Lamanites will behold their Redeemer.

Ether 1:1–2

It is not made absolutely clear in the Book of Mormon whether Moroni made his abridgment of the record of Ether from Mosiah's earlier translation (see Mosiah 28:1–20) or whether Moroni took his account directly from the plates of Ether—in which case he would have needed to translate the record as well as abridge it. Sidney B. Sperry has suggested the following concerning this question:

From Ether 1:2 one naturally assumes that Moroni made his abridgment directly from the plates themselves. If he did so, we are driven to the conclusion that it was necessary for him to find his way into the hill Cumorah, where his father had hidden them. Inasmuch as the language of the plates was that of the Jaredite people, it would have been incumbent upon Moroni to translate them by means of the holy "interpreters" or Urim and Thummim before he could abridge them. This would have been a tremendous task, because Moroni says (Ether 15:33) that he had not written the hundredth part of the record, and as it is we have fifteen chapters or about thirty-one and one-half printed pages in our current edition. It seems much more reasonable—for the writer at least—to believe that Moroni abridged the translation of the Book of Ether which had been made many hundreds of years before by king Mosiah. (Mosiah 28:1–20.) This translation would also have been available to Moroni in the hill. (Ludlow)

were found by the people of Limhi, which is called the Book of Ether.
3. And as I suppose that the first part of this record, which speaks concerning the creation of the world, and also of Adam, and an account from that time even to the great tower, and whatsoever things transpired among the children of men until that time, is had among the Jews—
4. Therefore I do not write those things which transpired from the days of Adam until that time; but they are had upon the plates; and whoso findeth them, the same will have power that he may get the full account.
5. But behold, I give not the full account, but a part of the account I give, from the tower down until they were destroyed.
6. And on this wise do I give the account. He that wrote this record was Ether, and he was a descendant of Coriantor.
7. Coriantor was the son of Moron.
8. And Moron was the son of Ethem.
9. And Ethem was the son of Ahah.
10. And Ahah was the son of Seth.
11. And Seth was the son of Shiblon.
12. And Shiblon was the son of Com.
13. And Com was the son of Coriantum.
14. And Coriantum was the son of Amnigaddah.
15. And Amnigaddah was the son of Aaron.
16. And Aaron was a descendant of Heth, who was the son of Hearthom.
17. And Hearthom was the son of Lib.
18. And Lib was the son of Kish.
19. And Kish was the son of Corom.
20. And Corom was the son of Levi.
21. And Levi was the son of Kim.
22. And Kim was the son of Morianton.
23. And Morianton was a descendant of Riplakish.
24. And Riplakish was the son of Shez.
25. And Shez was the son of Heth.
26. And Heth was the son of Com.
27. And Com was the son of Coriantum.
28. And Coriantum was the son of Emer.
29. And Emer was the son of Omer.
30. And Omer was the son of Shule.
31. And Shule was the son of Kib.
32. And Kib was the son of Orihah, who was the son of Jared;
33. Which Jared came forth with his brother and their families, with some others and their families, from the great tower, at the time the Lord confounded the language of the people, and swore in his wrath that they should be scattered upon all the face of the earth; and according to the word of the Lord the people were scattered.
34. And the brother of Jared being a large and mighty man, and a man highly favored of the Lord, Jared, his brother, said unto him: Cry unto the Lord, that he will not confound us that we may not understand our words.
35. And it came to pass that the brother of Jared did cry unto the Lord, and the Lord had compassion upon Jared; therefore he did not confound the language of Jared; and Jared and his brother were not confounded.
36. Then Jared said unto his brother: Cry again unto the Lord, and it may be that he will turn away his anger from them who are our friends, that he confound not their language.
37. And it came to pass that the brother of Jared did cry unto the Lord, and the Lord had compassion

Ether 1:6–33

It is not clear from the record whether or not the genealogies listed in Ether 1:6–33 are complete. Thirty names are listed, but in three instances the word *descendant* is used in place of the word *son*, which might indicate a gap of several generations. It may be that the original word could be translated as both son and descendant; thus, the translator would have to know the exact sense in which the word was originally used. (Ludlow)

Ether 1:33–37

The key word in the verses that pertain directly to the problem (Ether 1:34–37) is *confound.* What does it mean when the record states that the Lord "did not confound the language of Jared"? Does it mean the same as saying that the Lord did not *change* the language of Jared? If so, Jared and his people apparently spoke and wrote the language of Adam, because so far as we know there was only one language before the "great tower" of Babel. . . . Joseph Fielding Smith indicates he believes Jared and his people did speak and write the Adamic language even after they arrived in the promised land. . . . (Ludlow)

Ether 1:34

It is not clear why the name of the brother of Jared does not appear in the Book of Mormon. However, the following are possible reasons: (1) He may have omitted his name out of modesty (John the Beloved did essentially this same thing in the Gospel of John, which he wrote). (2) The book of Ether is clearly a family record of Jared, not of the brother of Jared; Ether . . . was a descendant of Jared and might naturally have emphasized the achievements of his direct ancestor rather than the brother of his ancestor. (3) Moroni may have omitted the name in his abridgment because of difficulty in translating (or transliterating) the name into the Nephite language.

Although the actual name of the brother of Jared is not mentioned in the scriptures . . . his name was revealed to the Prophet Joseph Smith after the translation of the Book of Mormon:

"While residing in Kirtland Elder Reynolds Cahoon had a son born to him. One day when President Joseph Smith was passing his door he called the Prophet in and asked him to bless and name the baby. Joseph did so and gave the boy the name of Mahonri Moriancumer. When he had finished the blessing he laid the child on the bed, and turning to Elder Cahoon he said, the name I have given your son is the name of the brother of Jared; the Lord has just shown (or revealed) it to me. . . . This was the first time the name of the brother of Jared was known in the Church in this dispensation."

In connection with this name, it is interesting to note that the major encampment of the Jaredites on the shore of "that great sea which divideth the lands" was called "Moriancumer." (Ether 2:13.) (Ludlow)

upon their friends and their families also, that they were not confounded.
38. And it came to pass that Jared spake again unto his brother,
saying: Go and inquire of the Lord whether he will drive us out of
the land, and if he will drive us out of the land, cry unto him
whither we shall go. And who knoweth but the Lord will carry us
forth into a land which is choice above all the earth? And if it so
be, let us be faithful unto the Lord, that we may receive it for our
inheritance.
39. And it came to pass that the brother of Jared did cry unto the
Lord according to that which had been spoken by the mouth of
Jared.
40. And it came to pass that the Lord did hear the brother of Jared,
and had compassion upon him, and said unto him:
41. Go to and gather together thy flocks, both male and female, of
every kind; and also of the seed of the earth of every kind; and thy
families; and also Jared thy brother and his family; and also thy
friends and their families, and the friends of Jared and their families.
42. And when thou hast done this thou shalt go at the head of
them down into the valley which is northward. And there will I
meet thee, and I will go before thee into a land which is choice
above all the lands of the earth.
43. And there will I bless thee and thy seed, and raise up unto me
of thy seed, and of the seed of thy brother, and they who shall go
with thee, a great nation. And there shall be none greater than the
nation which I will raise up unto me of thy seed, upon all the face
of the earth. And thus I will do unto thee because this long time
ye have cried unto me.

CHAPTER 2

1. AND it came to pass that Jared and his brother, and their families, and also the friends of Jared and his brother and their families,
went down into the valley which was northward, (and the name of
the valley was Nimrod, being called after the mighty hunter) with
their flocks which they had gathered together, male and female, of
every kind.
2. And they did also lay snares and catch fowls of the air; and they
did also prepare a vessel, in which they did carry with them the fish
of the waters.
3. And they did also carry with them deseret, which, by interpretation, is a honey bee; and thus they did carry with them swarms of
bees, and all manner of that which was upon the face of the land,
seeds of every kind.
4. And it came to pass that when they had come down into the valley
of Nimrod the Lord came down and talked with the brother of Jared;
and he was in a cloud, and the brother of Jared saw him not.
5. And it came to pass that the Lord commanded them that they
should go forth into the wilderness, yea,

Ether 2:12

President Joseph Fielding Smith . . . indicated that the people in America must keep the commandments if they are to be protected:

"These passages of scripture from the Book of Mormon are true (Ether 2:7–12); this nation is not exempt, and the people, if they continue to pursue the course of evil and ungodliness that they are now treading, shall eventually be punished. If they continue to disregard the warning voice of the Lord, deny their Redeemer, turn from his gospel unto fables and false theories, and rebel against all that he has through his servants in this day declared for the salvation of man; and if they increase in the practice of iniquity, I want to say to you, that if they do these things, *the judgments of the Lord will come upon this land, and this nation will not be saved*; we will not be spared from war, from famine, from pestilence and finally from destruction, as a nation.

"Therefore, I call upon the people, not only Latter-day Saints, but to all throughout the whole land to repent of their sins and to accept the Lord Jesus Christ, who is our Redeemer and the God of this land. Turn from your evil ways, repent of your sins and receive the fulness of the gospel through the waters of baptism and obedience, that the judgments which shall be poured out upon the ungodly may pass you by." (Ludlow)

into that quarter where there never had man been. And it came to pass that the Lord did go before them, and did talk with them as he stood in a cloud, and gave directions whither they should travel.

6. And it came to pass that they did travel in the wilderness, and did build barges, in which they did cross many waters, being directed continually by the hand of the Lord.

7. And the Lord would not suffer that they should stop beyond the sea in the wilderness, but he would that they should come forth even unto the land of promise, which was choice above all other lands, which the Lord God had preserved for a righteous people.

8. And he had sworn in his wrath unto the brother of Jared, that whoso should possess this land of promise, from that time henceforth and forever, should serve him, the true and only God, or they should be swept off when the fulness of his wrath should come upon them.

9. And now, we can behold the decrees of God concerning this land, that it is a land of promise; and whatsoever nation shall possess it shall serve God, or they shall be swept off when the fulness of his wrath shall come upon them. And the fulness of his wrath cometh upon them when they are ripened in iniquity.

10. For behold, this is a land which is choice above all other lands; wherefore he that doth possess it shall serve God or shall be swept off; for it is the everlasting decree of God. And it is not until the fulness of iniquity among the children of the land, that they are swept off.

11. And this cometh unto you, O ye Gentiles, that ye may know the decrees of God—that ye may repent, and not continue in your iniquities until the fulness come, that ye may not bring down the fulness of the wrath of God upon you as the inhabitants of the land have hitherto done.

12. Behold, this is a choice land, and whatsoever nation shall possess it shall be free from bondage, and from captivity, and from all other nations under heaven, if they will but serve the God of the land, who is Jesus Christ, who hath been manifested by the things which we have written.

13. And now I proceed with my record; for behold, it came to pass that the Lord did bring Jared and his brethren forth even to that great sea which divideth the lands. And as they came to the sea they pitched their tents; and they called the name of the place Moriancumer; and they dwelt in tents, and dwelt in tents upon the seashore for the space of four years.

14. And it came to pass at the end of four years that the Lord came again unto the brother of Jared, and stood in a cloud and talked with him. And for the space of three hours did the Lord talk with the brother of Jared, and chastened him because he remembered not to call upon the name of the Lord.

15. And the brother of Jared repented of the evil which he had done, and did call upon the name of the Lord for his brethren who were with him. And the Lord said unto him: I will forgive thee and thy brethren of their sins; but thou shalt not sin

Ether 2:19–20

In providing a solution for the difficulty of obtaining air, the Lord informed Jared: "Behold, thou shall make a hole in the top *thereof* and also in the bottom *thereof;* and when thou shalt suffer for air, thou shalt unstop the hole *thereof*, and receive air. And if it so be that the water come in upon thee, behold, ye shall stop the hole *thereof*, that ye may not perish in the flood." (Page 542 of the first edition. Italics added.) This quotation is taken from the first edition of the Book of Mormon because the four *thereofs* underlined above appear in the early editions, but for some unexplainable reasons were deleted from the 1920 edition and all subsequent editions (perhaps the revising committee thought they were superfluous). A careful reading of this verse in the first edition seems to indicate that the terms "in the top" and "in the bottom" do not refer to the barge itself. Rather, they refer to the top and bottom of something else such as a chamber or cylinder (designated here as "thereof") which could be used to admit air.

Dr. Hugh Nibley has explained the possible significance of the "thereofs" and the possibility of an air chamber as follows:

"An exacting editor by removing those very significant '*thereof's*' has made it appear that when Jared wanted air he was to open the top window of the boat and admit fresh air from the outside. But that is *not* what the original edition of the Book of Mormon says. For one thing, the ships had no windows communicating with the outside—'ye cannot have windows . . .' (2:23); each ship had an airtight door (2:17), and that was all. Air was received not by opening and closing doors and windows, but by unplugging air holes ('thou shalt *unstop* the *hole* thereof, and receive air . . .'), this being done *only* when the ship was not on the surface—'when thou shalt *suffer* for air' i.e., when they were not able to open the hatches, the ships being submerged."

. . . It is entirely feasible that such an air chamber could have been constructed in each boat. Some of the advantages of such an air chamber have been suggested by A. L. Zobell, Sr., as follows:

"A tube is built from the bottom to the top of the barge, housing in both holes completely. Now we have a funnel right through the boat. Water can come into the tube as high as the water line of the vessel.

"The model of the barge we have built has a stop hole both in front and in back of the tube. . . . These stop holes can easily be opened or closed as needed.

"The purpose of the bottom hole is at least two-fold: First, it acted as a stabilizer to keep the barge at an even keel; second, it could be used to get rid of refuse." (Ludlow)

any more, for ye shall remember that my Spirit will not always strive with man; wherefore, if ye will sin until ye are fully ripe ye shall be cut off from the presence of the Lord. And these are my thoughts upon the land which I shall give you for your inheritance; for it shall be a land choice above all other lands.

16. And the Lord said: Go to work and build, after the manner of barges which ye have hitherto built. And it came to pass that the brother of Jared did go to work, and also his brethren, and built barges after the manner which they had built, according to the instructions of the Lord. And they were small, and they were light upon the water, even like unto the lightness of a fowl upon the water.

17. And they were built after a manner that they were exceedingly tight, even that they would hold water like unto a dish; and the bottom thereof was tight like unto a dish; and the sides thereof were tight like unto a dish; and the ends thereof were peaked; and the top thereof was tight like unto a dish; and the length thereof was the length of a tree; and the door thereof, when it was shut, was tight like unto a dish.

18. And it came to pass that the brother of Jared cried unto the Lord, saying: O Lord, I have performed the work which thou hast commanded me, and I have made the barges according as thou hast directed me.

19. And behold, O Lord, in them there is no light; whither shall we steer? And also we shall perish, for in them we cannot breathe, save it is the air which is in them; therefore we shall perish.

20. And the Lord said unto the brother of Jared: Behold, thou shalt make a hole in the top, and also in the bottom; and when thou shalt suffer for air thou shalt unstop the hole and receive air. And if it be so that the water come in upon thee, behold, ye shall stop the hole, that ye may not perish in the flood.

21. And it came to pass that the brother of Jared did so, according as the Lord had commanded.

22. And he cried again unto the Lord saying: O Lord, behold I have done even as thou hast commanded me; and I have prepared the vessels for my people, and behold there is no light in them. Behold, O Lord, wilt thou suffer that we shall cross this great water in darkness?

23. And the Lord said unto the brother of Jared: What will ye that I should do that ye may have light in your vessels? For behold, ye cannot have windows, for they will be dashed in pieces; neither shall ye take fire with you, for ye shall not go by the light of fire.

24. For behold, ye shall be as a whale in the midst of the sea; for the mountain waves shall dash upon you. Nevertheless, I will bring you up again out of the depths of the sea; for the winds have gone forth out of my mouth, and also the rains and the floods have I sent forth.

25. And behold, I prepare you against these things; for ye cannot cross this great deep save I prepare you against the waves of the sea, and the winds which have gone forth, and the floods which shall come. Therefore what will ye that I should prepare for you that ye may have light when ye are swallowed up in the depths of the sea?

POINT OF INTEREST

Deshret *is the formal name for the red crown of Lower Egypt (left), which had a coil on its face that closely resembles the antennae of the bee (right), another symbol of Lower Egypt. Both images are taken directly from hieroglyphics.*

CHAPTER 3

1. AND it came to pass that the brother of Jared, (now the number of the vessels which had been prepared was eight) went forth unto the mount, which they called the mount Shelem, because of its exceeding height, and did molten out of a rock sixteen small stones; and they were white and clear, even as transparent glass; and he did carry them in his hands upon the top of the mount, and cried again unto the Lord, saying:
2. O Lord, thou hast said that we must be encompassed about by the floods. Now behold, O Lord, and do not be angry with thy servant because of his weakness before thee; for we know that thou art holy and dwellest in the heavens, and that we are unworthy before thee; because of the fall our natures have become evil continually; nevertheless, O Lord, thou hast given us a commandment that we must call upon thee, that from thee we may receive according to our desires.
3. Behold, O Lord, thou hast smitten us because of our iniquity, and hast driven us forth, and for these many years we have been in the wilderness; nevertheless, thou hast been merciful unto us. O Lord, look upon me in pity, and turn away thine anger from this thy people, and suffer not that they shall go forth across this raging deep in darkness; but behold these things which I have molten out of the rock.
4. And I know, O Lord, that thou hast all power, and can do whatsoever thou wilt for the benefit of man; therefore touch these stones, O Lord, with thy finger, and prepare them that they may shine forth in darkness; and they shall shine forth unto us in the vessels which we have prepared, that we may have light while we shall cross the sea.
5. Behold, O Lord, thou canst do this. We know that thou art able to show forth great power, which looks small unto the understanding of men.
6. And it came to pass that when the brother of Jared had said these words, behold, the Lord stretched forth his hand and touched the stones one by one with his finger. And the veil was taken from off the eyes of the brother of Jared, and he saw the finger of the Lord; and it was as the finger of a man, like unto flesh and blood; and the brother of Jared fell down before the Lord, for he was struck with fear.
7. And the Lord saw that the brother of Jared had fallen to the earth; and the Lord said unto him: Arise, why hast thou fallen?
8. And he saith unto the Lord: I saw the finger of the Lord, and I feared lest he should smite me; for I knew not that the Lord had flesh and blood.
9. And the Lord said unto him: Because of thy faith thou hast seen that I shall take upon me flesh and blood; and never has man come before me with such exceeding faith as thou hast; for were it not so ye

Ether 3:5–16

One of the spiritual highlights of the entire Book of Mormon is the appearance of the pre-earthly Jesus Christ to the brother of Jared. The conversation of the Savior with the brother of Jared sheds tremendous light on the pre-earthly role of Jesus Christ as well as the later role he is to play as the Savior and Redeemer of the world. It is significant to note, for example, that even in the pre-earthly existence Jesus Christ referred to himself as both the Father and the Son. Even before his birth on the earth the Savior indicates how all members of the human race can become his sons and daughters.

Another significant part of the Savior's statement is the reference to his pre-earthly spirit body. He says to the brother of Jared: "Seest thou that ye are created after mine own image? Yea, even all men are created in the beginning after mine own image." (Ether 3:15.) This statement seems to indicate that in the scripture that says "God created man in his own image" (Genesis 1:27), the word *God* refers not to Elohim but to Jesus Christ, and the word *image* refers not to the physical resurrected body of Elohim but to the pre-earthly spiritual body of Jesus Christ. (Ludlow)

could not have seen my finger. Sawest thou more than this?
10. And he answered: Nay; Lord, show thyself unto me.
11. And the Lord said unto him: Believest thou the words which I shall speak?
12. And he answered: Yea, Lord, I know that thou speakest the truth, for thou art a God of truth, and canst not lie.
13. And when he had said these words, behold, the Lord showed himself unto him, and said: Because thou knowest these things ye are redeemed from the fall; therefore ye are brought back into my presence; therefore I show myself unto you.
14. Behold, I am he who was prepared from the foundation of the world to redeem my people. Behold, I am Jesus Christ. I am the Father and the Son. In me shall all mankind have life, and that eternally, even they who shall believe on my name; and they shall become my sons and my daughters.
15. And never have I showed myself unto man whom I have created, for never has man believed in me as thou hast. Seest thou that ye are created after mine own image? Yea, even all men were created in the beginning after mine own image.
16. Behold, this body, which ye now behold, is the body of my spirit; and man have I created after the body of my spirit; and even as I appear unto thee to be in the spirit will I appear unto my people in the flesh.
17. And now, as I, Moroni, said I could not make a full account of these things which are written, therefore it sufficeth me to say that Jesus showed himself unto this man in the spirit, even after the manner and in the likeness of the same body even as he showed himself unto the Nephites.
18. And he ministered unto him even as he ministered unto the Nephites; and all this, that this man might know that he was God, because of the many great works which the Lord had showed unto him.
19. And because of the knowledge of this man he could not be kept from beholding within the veil; and he saw the finger of Jesus, which, when he saw, he fell with fear; for he knew that it was the finger of the Lord; and he had faith no longer, for he knew, nothing doubting.
20. Wherefore, having this perfect knowledge of God, he could not be kept from within the veil; therefore he saw Jesus; and he did minister unto him.
21. And it came to pass that the Lord said unto the brother of Jared: Behold, thou shalt not suffer these things which ye have seen and heard to go forth unto the world, until the time cometh that I shall glorify my name in the flesh; wherefore, ye shall treasure up the things which ye have seen and heard, and show it to no man.

Ether 3:15

In Ether 3:15 the pre-earthly Jesus Christ told the brother of Jared: "And never have I showed myself unto man whom I have created, for never has man believed in me as thou hast." This statement introduces something of a problem inasmuch as we read in Moses 7:4 that the Lord talked with Enoch "even as a man talketh one with another, face to face"—and Enoch lived on the earth *before* the time of the brother of Jared! Also, in the Doctrine and Covenants 107:54 it states that the "Lord appeared" unto Adam and his descendants. . . .

Concerning the possible contradiction between Ether 3:15 and Moses 7:4, Joseph Fielding Smith has written:

"There is no contradiction. When Adam was in the Garden of Eden and before the Fall, he was in the presence of God the Father. He walked with God, for he was free from sin and in possession of an eternal body that could have endured forever. When he and Eve partook of the forbidden fruit, they were cast out of the presence of the Father and became subject to death, or mortal. From that time forth Jesus Christ became the Advocate and Mediator between the Father and mankind. This fall brought the first, or spiritual death, as well as mortality on Adam. Now there are several references in the Old Testament which declare that the Lord appeared to Enoch and talked with him. . . .

"It is true that the Savior appeared to the prophets before the flood, but it is evident that he did not reveal himself in the fulness as he did to the Brother of Jared. Talking 'face to face,' as stated in this revelation, does not mean that the Lord did not appear in a cloud; or, that his body was partially hidden from the view of the prophet. All of this could occur and yet the Lord still be partially, if not completely, hidden from the prophet's view. The great difference rests in this, which the conversation of the Lord with the Brother of Jared clearly indicates: The Savior was conversing with the Brother of Jared in person. . . .

"It is a reasonable conclusion for us to reach, and fully in accordance with the facts, that the Lord had never before revealed himself so completely and in such a manner. We may truly believe that very few of the ancient prophets at any time actually beheld the full person of the Lord. (Ludlow)

22. And behold, when ye shall come unto me, ye shall write them and shall seal them up, that no one can interpret them; for ye shall write them in a language that they cannot be read.
23. And behold, these two stones will I give unto thee, and ye shall seal them up also with the things which ye shall write.
24. For behold, the language which ye shall write I have confounded; wherefore I will cause in my own due time that these stones shall magnify to the eyes of men these things which ye shall write.
25. And when the Lord had said these words, he showed unto the brother of Jared all the inhabitants of the earth which had been, and also all that would be; and he withheld them not from his sight, even unto the ends of the earth.
26. For he had said unto him in times before, that if he would believe in him that he could show unto him all things—it should be shown unto him; therefore the Lord could not withhold anything from him, for he knew that the Lord could show him all things.
27. And the Lord said unto him: Write these things and seal them up; and I will show them in mine own due time unto the children of men.
28. And it came to pass that the Lord commanded him that he should seal up the two stones which he had received, and show them not, until the Lord should show them unto the children of men.

CHAPTER 4

1. AND the Lord commanded the brother of Jared to go down out of the mount from the presence of the Lord, and write the things which he had seen; and they were forbidden to come unto the children of men until after that he should be lifted up upon the cross; and for this cause did king Mosiah keep them, that they should not come unto the world until after Christ should show himself unto his people.
2. And after Christ truly had showed himself unto his people he commanded that they should be made manifest.
3. And now, after that, they have all dwindled in unbelief; and there is none save it be the Lamanites, and they have rejected the gospel of Christ; therefore I am commanded that I should hide them up again in the earth.
4. Behold, I have written upon these plates the very things which the brother of Jared saw; and there never were greater things made manifest than those which were made manifest unto the brother of Jared.
5. Wherefore the Lord hath commanded me to write them; and I have written them. And he commanded

Ether 3:20

The brother of Jared, while pleading with the Lord to give them light for the journey across the sea, beholds the finger of the Lord as He touches the stones to illuminate them. The perception of the divine presence causes the beholder to fall down in fear: "And he saith unto the Lord: I saw the finger of the Lord, and I feared lest he should smite me; for I knew not that the Lord had flesh and blood" (Ether 3:8). The Lord confirms that He would take upon Himself flesh and blood during His mortal ministry, commends the brother of Jared for his great faith, and proceeds to show Himself fully, bearing witness of His atoning mission.

"Wherefore, having this perfect knowledge of God, he could not be kept from within the veil; therefore he saw Jesus; and he did minister unto him" (Ether 3:20).

Elder Bruce R. McConkie said, "And as with the prophets and seers of ancient and modern times, so with all the saints who will obey the same laws, all shall see the Lord, for God is no respecter of persons. 'Verily, thus saith the Lord,' he decrees: 'It shall come to pass that every soul who forsaketh his sins and cometh unto me, and calleth on my name, and obeyeth my voice, and keepeth my commandments, shall see my face and know that I am' (D&C 93:1)." (P/A)

Ether 4:4

When the Prophet Joseph Smith received Mormon's plates, he was forbidden to translate the sealed portion, which contained the prophecies of the brother of Jared. Elder Joseph Fielding Smith explained that: "Joseph Smith was forbidden to break the seals of the portion of the plates which contain the prophecies of the brother of Jared because the hearts of the people were not susceptible to the divine truth which the record contained." (O/C)

Ether 4:4–5; 5:1

Moroni wrote his account of the vision of the brother of Jared on the plates of Mormon, but he was commanded by the Lord to "seal up" this account. (Ether 4:4–5.) Joseph Smith was commanded not to translate this sealed portion. It is not absolutely clear what portion of the plates of Mormon was sealed. Joseph Smith simply said: "The volume was something near six inches in thickness, a part of which was sealed" (*HC*, 4:537). (Ludlow)

me that I should seal them up; and he also hath commanded that
I should seal up the interpretation thereof; wherefore I have sealed
up the interpreters, according to the commandment of the Lord.
6. For the Lord said unto me: They shall not go forth unto the
Gentiles until the day that they shall repent of their iniquity, and
become clean before the Lord.
7. And in that day that they shall exercise faith in me, saith the
Lord, even as the brother of Jared did, that they may become sanctified in me, then will I manifest unto them the things which the
brother of Jared saw, even to the unfolding unto them all my revelations, saith Jesus Christ, the Son of God, the Father of the heavens and of the earth, and all things that in them are.
8. And he that will contend against the word of the Lord, let him
be accursed; and he that shall deny these things, let him be
accursed; for unto them will I show no greater things, saith Jesus
Christ; for I am he who speaketh.
9. And at my command the heavens are opened and are shut; and
at my word the earth shall shake; and at my command the inhabitants thereof shall pass away, even so as by fire.
10. And he that believeth not my words believeth not my disciples; and if it so be that I do not speak, judge ye; for ye shall know
that it is I that speaketh, at the last day.
11. But he that believeth these things which I have spoken, him will
I visit with the manifestations of my Spirit, and he shall know and
bear record. For because of my Spirit he shall know that these things
are true; for it persuadeth men to do good.
12. And whatsoever thing persuadeth men to do good is of me; for
good cometh of none save it be of me. I am the same that leadeth
men to all good; he that will not believe my words will not believe
me—that I am; and he that will not believe me will not believe the
Father who sent me. For behold, I am the Father, I am the light,
and the life, and the truth of the world.
13. Come unto me, O ye Gentiles, and I will show unto you the
greater things, the knowledge which is hid up because of unbelief.
14. Come unto me, O ye house of Israel, and it shall be made manifest unto you how great things the Father hath laid up for you,
from the foundation of the world; and it hath not come unto you,
because of unbelief.
15. Behold, when ye shall rend that veil of unbelief which doth
cause you to remain in your awful state of wickedness, and hardness of heart, and blindness of mind, then shall the great and marvelous things which have been hid up from the foundation of the
world from you—yea, when ye shall call upon the Father in my
name, with a broken heart and a contrite spirit, then shall ye know
that the Father hath

Ether 4:4–8

. . . The Lord has indicated that the contents of the vision of the brother of Jared should not be revealed in a day when the people are wicked. Thus Moroni was commanded to write the account of the vision, but he was also commanded to "seal up the interpretation thereof . . .

It is not clear in the Book of Mormon exactly when the sealed record is to be revealed. However, some of the prior conditions that must exist are enumerated. For example, the Lord said that before the record is revealed the people must exercise faith in him "even as the brother of Jared did." (Ether 4:7.) Also, the Savior indicated that the people must "become sanctified" in him. (Ether 4:7.) Only then will the sealed portion of the records be revealed. (Ludlow)

POINT OF INTEREST

"In the course of the work of translation, we ascertained that three special witnesses were to be provided by the Lord, to whom He would grant that they should see the plates from which this work (the Book of Mormon) should be translated. . . . Almost immediately after we had made this discovery, it occurred to Oliver Cowdery, David Whitmer and . . . Martin Harris . . . that they would have me inquire of the Lord to know if they might not obtain of him the privilege to be these three special witnesses" (Joseph Smith, *HC,* 1:52–53).

remembered the covenant which he made unto your fathers, O house of Israel.
16. And then shall my revelations which I have caused to be written by my servant John be unfolded in the eyes of all the people. Remember, when ye see these things, ye shall know that the time is at hand that they shall be made manifest in very deed.
17. Therefore, when ye shall receive this record ye may know that the work of the Father has commenced upon all the face of the land.
18. Therefore, repent all ye ends of the earth, and come unto me, and believe in my gospel, and be baptized in my name; for he that believeth and is baptized shall be saved; but he that believeth not shall be damned; and signs shall follow them that believe in my name.
19. And blessed is he that is found faithful unto my name at the last day, for he shall be lifted up to dwell in the kingdom prepared for him from the foundation of the world. And behold it is I that hath spoken it. Amen.

CHAPTER 5

1. AND now I, Moroni, have written the words which were commanded me, according to my memory; and I have told you the things which I have sealed up; therefore touch them not in order that ye may translate; for that thing is forbidden you, except by and by it shall be wisdom in God.
2. And behold, ye may be privileged that ye may show the plates unto those who shall assist to bring forth this work;
3. And unto three shall they be shown by the power of God; wherefore they shall know of a surety that these things are true.
4. And in the mouth of three witnesses shall these things be established; and the testimony of three, and this work, in the which shall be shown forth the power of God and also his word, of which the Father, and the Son, and the Holy Ghost bear record—and all this shall stand as a testimony against the world at the last day.
5. And if it so be that they repent and come unto the Father in the name of Jesus, they shall be received into the kingdom of God.
6. And now, if I have no authority for these things, judge ye; for ye shall know that I have authority when ye shall see me, and we shall stand before God at the last day. Amen.

CHAPTER 6

1. AND now I, Moroni, proceed to give the record of Jared and his brother.
2. For it came to pass after the Lord had prepared the stones which the brother of Jared had carried up into the mount, the brother of Jared

Ether 4:16

The Brother of Jared and Nephi (the son of Lehi) both had foreknowledge of the book of Revelation found in our current New Testament. The sealed portion of the Book of Mormon describe some things that will give us a much better understanding of John's revelation.

came down out of the mount, and he did put forth the stones into
the vessels which were prepared, one in each end thereof; and
behold, they did give light unto the vessels.
3. And thus the Lord caused stones to shine in darkness, to give
light unto men, women, and children, that they might not cross
the great waters in darkness.
4. And it came to pass that when they had prepared all manner of
food, that thereby they might subsist upon the water, and also food
for their flocks and herds, and whatsoever beast or animal or fowl
that they should carry with them—and it came to pass that when
they had done all these things they got aboard of their vessels or
barges, and set forth into the sea, commending themselves unto
the Lord their God.
5. And it came to pass that the Lord God caused that there should
be a furious wind blow upon the face of the waters, towards the
promised land; and thus they were tossed upon the waves of the sea
before the wind.
6. And it came to pass that they were many times buried in the
depths of the sea, because of the mountain waves which broke
upon them, and also the great and terrible tempests which were
caused by the fierceness of the wind.
7. And it came to pass that when they were buried in the deep
there was no water that could hurt them, their vessels being tight
like unto a dish, and also they were tight like unto the ark of Noah;
therefore when they were encompassed about by many waters they
did cry unto the Lord, and he did bring them forth again upon the
top of the waters.
8. And it came to pass that the wind did never cease to blow
towards the promised land while they were upon the waters; and
thus they were driven forth before the wind.
9. And they did sing praises unto the Lord; yea, the brother of Jared
did sing praises unto the Lord, and he did thank and praise the
Lord all the day long; and when the night came, they did not cease
to praise the Lord.
10. And thus they were driven forth; and no monster of the sea
could break them, neither whale that could mar them; and they
did have light continually, whether it was above the water or under
the water.
11. And thus they were driven forth, three hundred and forty and
four days upon the water.
12. And they did land upon the shore of the promised land. And
when they had set their feet upon the shores of the promised land
they bowed themselves down upon the face of the land, and did
humble themselves before the Lord, and did shed tears of joy before
the Lord, because of the multitude of his tender mercies over them.
13. And it came to pass that they went forth upon the face of the
land, and began to till the earth.
14. And Jared had four sons; and they were called Jacom, and
Gilgah, and Mahah, and Orihah.
15. And the brother of Jared also begat sons and daughters.
16. And the friends of Jared and his brother were in number about
twenty and two souls; and they also begat sons and daughters
before they came to the promised land; and therefore they began
to be many.
17. And they were taught to walk

Ether 6:5–8

The winds, which "did never cease to blow" seemed like a hardship, but they were actually blowing the Jaredites to the promised land; without the winds, they would have bobbed around aimlessly in the sea forever, unable to steer themselves in the direction they should go. What seemed like adversity was actually the Lord delivering the people to the promised land.

Ether 6:9, 12

The Jaredites here set the example for us of never forgetting to thank the Lord for His goodness and tender mercies to us—even in times when we feel that we are crushed by affliction. Even in those times, as we look for it, we can see the work of His hand in guiding, directing, and protecting us.

humbly before the Lord; and they were also taught from on high.
18. And it came to pass that they began to spread upon the face of the land, and to multiply and to till the earth; and they did wax strong in the land.
19. And the brother of Jared began to be old, and saw that he must soon go down to the grave; wherefore he said unto Jared: Let us gather together our people that we may number them, that we may know of them what they will desire of us before we go down to our graves.
20. And accordingly the people were gathered together. Now the number of the sons and the daughters of the brother of Jared were twenty and two souls; and the number of sons and daughters of Jared were twelve, he having four sons.
21. And it came to pass that they did number their people; and after that they had numbered them, they did desire of them the things which they would that they should do before they went down to their graves.
22. And it came to pass that the people desired of them that they should anoint one of their sons to be a king over them.
23. And now behold, this was grievous unto them. And the brother of Jared said unto them: Surely this thing leadeth into captivity.
24. But Jared said unto his brother: Suffer them that they may have a king. And therefore he said unto them: Choose ye out from among our sons a king, even whom ye will.
25. And it came to pass that they chose even the firstborn of the brother of Jared; and his name was Pagag. And it came to pass that he refused and would not be their king. And the people would that his father should constrain him, but his father would not; and he commanded them that they should constrain no man to be their king.
26. And it came to pass that they chose all the brothers of Pagag, and they would not.
27. And it came to pass that neither would the sons of Jared, even all save it were one; and Orihah was anointed to be king over the people.
28. And he began to reign, and the people began to prosper; and they became exceedingly rich.
29. And it came to pass that Jared died, and his brother also.
30. And it came to pass that Orihah did walk humbly before the Lord, and did remember how great things the Lord had done for his father, and also taught his people how great things the Lord had done for their fathers.

CHAPTER 7

1. AND it came to pass that Orihah did execute judgment upon the land in righteousness all his days, whose days were exceedingly many.
2. And he begat sons and daughters; yea, he begat thirty and one, among whom were twenty and three sons.
3. And it came to pass that he also begat Kib in his old age. And it came to pass that Kib reigned in his stead; and Kib begat Corihor.
4. And when Corihor was thirty and two years old he rebelled against his father, and went over and dwelt in the land of Nehor; and he begat sons and daughters, and they became exceedingly fair; wherefore Corihor drew away many people after him.
5. And when he had gathered together an army he came up unto the

Ether 6:22–23

At this point, the Brother of Jared knows that when people begin to worship a king, they forget to worship the Lord. The Brother of Jared's prophecy in verse 23 was fulfilled when Corihor took Kib (his father, the king) captive, and when Noah took Shule captive. Shule's son, King Omer, was in captivity for fully half his days (see Ether 8:4).

land of Moron where the king dwelt, and took him captive, which
brought to pass the saying of the brother of Jared that they would
be brought into captivity.
6. Now the land of Moron, where the king dwelt, was near the land
which is called Desolation by the Nephites.
7. And it came to pass that Kib dwelt in captivity, and his people
under Corihor his son, until he became exceedingly old; nevertheless Kib begat Shule in his old age, while he was yet in captivity.
8. And it came to pass that Shule was angry with his brother; and
Shule waxed strong, and became mighty as to the strength of a
man; and he was also mighty in judgment.
9. Wherefore, he came to the hill Ephraim, and he did molten out
of the hill, and made swords out of steel for those whom he had
drawn away with him; and after he had armed them with swords he
returned to the city Nehor, and gave battle unto his brother
Corihor, by which means he obtained the kingdom and restored it
unto his father Kib.
10. And now because of the thing which Shule had done, his
father bestowed upon him the kingdom; therefore he began to
reign in the stead of his father.
11. And it came to pass that he did execute judgment in righteousness; and he did spread his kingdom upon all the face of the
land, for the people had become exceedingly numerous.
12. And it came to pass that Shule also begat many sons and
daughters.
13. And Corihor repented of the many evils which he had done;
wherefore Shule gave him power in his kingdom.
14. And it came to pass that Corihor had many sons and daughters. And among the sons of Corihor there was one whose name
was Noah.
15. And it came to pass that Noah rebelled against Shule, the king,
and also his father Corihor, and drew away Cohor his brother, and
also all his brethren and many of the people.
16. And he gave battle unto Shule the king, in which he did
obtain the land of their first inheritance; and he became a king
over that part of the land.
17. And it came to pass that he gave battle again unto Shule, the
king; and he took Shule, the king, and carried him away captive
into Moron.
18. And it came to pass as he was about to put him to death, the sons
of Shule crept into the house of Noah by night and slew him, and
broke down the door of the prison and brought out their father, and
placed him upon his throne in his own kingdom.
19. Wherefore, the son of Noah did build up his kingdom in his
stead; nevertheless they did not gain power any more over Shule
the king, and the people who were under the reign of Shule the
king did prosper exceedingly and wax great.
20. And the country was divided; and there were two kingdoms,
the kingdom of Shule, and the kingdom of Cohor, the son of Noah.
21. And Cohor, the son of Noah, caused that his people should give
battle unto Shule, in which Shule did beat them and did slay Cohor.
22. And now Cohor had a son who was called Nimrod; and
Nimrod gave up the kingdom of Cohor unto Shule, and he did
gain favor in the eyes of Shule; wherefore Shule did bestow great
favors upon him, and he did do in the kingdom of Shule according
to his desires.
23. And also in the reign of Shule there came prophets among the
people, who were sent from the Lord, prophesying that the wickedness and idolatry of the people was bringing a curse upon the land,
and they should be destroyed if they did not repent.

Ether 7:6

Moroni, the abridger of the Jaredite record and the last historian of the Nephites, is in an ideal position to indicate some of the geographical relationships between the lands of the Jaredites and the lands of the Nephites. Unfortunately, Moroni does not give us very much information concerning this matter. However, he does indicate that the "land of Moron" of the Jaredites "was near the land which is called Desolation by the Nephites." (Ether 7:6.) Inasmuch as the land of Moron was the capital land of the Jaredites and the Nephite land of Desolation was north of the narrow neck of land, it is assumed that the major portion of the Jaredite civilization lived north of the narrow neck of land. (Ludlow)

POINT OF INTEREST

"Genealogy was crucial to the holders of power and leadership in ancient Mesoamerican societies. It served to validate elite rights. Oral transmission and recitation of genealogy was frequently sufficient in pre-Spanish times. For some of the nobility, . . . stone monuments or entries in painted books reported and supported specific relationships. . . . The European invaders wanted documentary proof of noble ancestry before they would allow some Amerindian rulers to continue their right to impose tribute payments on their subjects. A variety of visual forms for documenting nobility sprang up in the sixteenth century under Spanish literary influence to meet the conquistadors' demand. So while the presentation formats may have come from Spanish mentors, the factual information and the general sense of the importance of descent records were older" (John L. Sorenson, *Images of Ancient America: Visualizing Book of Mormon Life* [Provo, Utah: FARMS, 1998]).

24. And it came to pass that the people did revile against the prophets, and did mock them. And it came to pass that king Shule did execute judgment against all those who did revile against the prophets.
25. And he did execute a law throughout all the land, which gave power unto the prophets that they should go whithersoever they would; and by this cause the people were brought unto repentance.
26. And because the people did repent of their iniquities and idolatries the Lord did spare them, and they began to prosper again in the land. And it came to pass that Shule begat sons and daughters in his old age.
27. And there were no more wars in the days of Shule; and he remembered the great things that the Lord had done for his fathers in bringing them across the great deep into the promised land; wherefore he did execute judgment in righteousness all his days.

CHAPTER 8

1. AND it came to pass that he begat Omer, and Omer reigned in his stead. And Omer begat Jared; and Jared begat sons and daughters.
2. And Jared rebelled against his father, and came and dwelt in the land of Heth. And it came to pass that he did flatter many people, because of his cunning words, until he had gained the half of the kingdom.
3. And when he had gained the half of the kingdom he gave battle unto his father, and he did carry away his father into captivity, and did make him serve in captivity;
4. And now, in the days of the reigns of Omer he was in captivity the half of his days. And it came to pass that he begat sons and daughters among whom were Esrom and Coriantumr;
5. And they were exceedingly angry because of the doings of Jared their brother, insomuch that they did raise an army and gave battle unto Jared. And it came to pass that they did give battle unto him by night.
6. And it came to pass that when they had slain the army of Jared they were about to slay him also; and he plead with them that they would not slay him, and he would give up the kingdom unto his father. And it came to pass that they did grant unto him his life.
7. And now Jared became exceedingly sorrowful because of the loss of the kingdom, for he had set his heart upon the kingdom and upon the glory of the world.
8. Now the daughter of Jared being exceedingly expert, and seeing the sorrows of her father, thought to devise a plan whereby she could redeem the kingdom unto her father.
9. Now the daughter of Jared was exceedingly fair. And it came to pass that she did talk with her father, and said unto him: Whereby hath my father so much sorrow? Hath he not read the record which our fathers brought across the great deep? Behold, is there not an account concerning them of old, that they by their secret plans did obtain kingdoms and great glory?
10. And now, therefore, let my father send for Akish, the son of

Ether 8

Moroni paused in his rapid summary of Jaredite history to give a detailed description of how secret combinations were instituted among these people. This description is critical to our understanding because the secret combinations caused the complete downfall of the entire Jaredite and Nephite civilizations. Unless we repent and learn to defeat these types of organizations, the same thing will happen to us (see verses 23–25).

Ether 8:9

It is possible that these records contained accounts of the earliest secret combinations (see Moses 5:29–33 and 47–55).

Kimnor; and behold, I am fair, and I will dance before him, and I will please him, that he will desire me to wife; wherefore if he shall desire of thee that ye shall give unto him me to wife, then shall ye say: I will give her if ye will bring unto me the head of my father, the king.
11. And now Omer was a friend to Akish; wherefore, when Jared had sent for Akish, the daughter of Jared danced before him that she pleased him, insomuch that he desired her to wife. And it came to pass that he said unto Jared: Give her unto me to wife.
12. And Jared said unto him: I will give her unto you, if ye will bring unto me the head of my father, the king.
13. And it came to pass that Akish gathered in unto the house of Jared all his kinsfolk, and said unto them: Will ye swear unto me that ye will be faithful unto me in the thing which I shall desire of you?
14. And it came to pass that they all sware unto him, by the God of heaven, and also by the heavens, and also by the earth, and by their heads, that whoso should vary from the assistance which Akish desired should lose his head; and whoso should divulge whatsoever thing Akish made known unto them, the same should lose his life.
15. And it came to pass that thus they did agree with Akish. And Akish did administer unto them the oaths which were given by them of old who also sought power, which had been handed down even from Cain, who was a murderer from the beginning.
16. And they were kept up by the power of the devil to administer these oaths unto the people, to keep them in darkness, to help such as sought power to gain power, and to murder, and to plunder, and to lie, and to commit all manner of wickedness and whoredoms.
17. And it was the daughter of Jared who put it into his heart to search up these things of old; and Jared put it into the heart of Akish; wherefore, Akish administered it unto his kindred and friends, leading them away by fair promises to do whatsoever thing he desired.
18. And it came to pass that they formed a secret combination, even as they of old; which combination is most abominable and wicked above all, in the sight of God;
19. For the Lord worketh not in secret combinations, neither doth he will that man should shed blood, but in all things hath forbidden it, from the beginning of man.
20. And now I, Moroni, do not write the manner of their oaths and combinations, for it hath been made known unto me that they are had among all people, and they are had among the Lamanites.
21. And they have caused the destruction of this people of whom I am now speaking, and also the destruction of the people of Nephi.
22. And whatsoever nation shall uphold such secret combinations, to get power and gain, until they shall spread over the nation, behold, they shall be destroyed; for the Lord will not suffer that the blood of his saints, which shall be shed by them, shall always cry unto him from the ground for vengeance upon them and yet he avenge them not.
23. Wherefore, O ye Gentiles, it is wisdom in God that these things should be shown unto you, that thereby ye may repent of your sins, and suffer not that these murderous combinations shall get above you,

which are built up to get power and gain—and the work, yea, even
the work of destruction come upon you, yea, even the sword of the
justice of the Eternal God shall fall upon you, to your overthrow
and destruction if ye shall suffer these things to be.
24. Wherefore, the Lord commandeth you, when ye shall see these
things come among you that ye shall awake to a sense of your awful
situation, because of this secret combination which shall be among
you; or wo be unto it, because of the blood of them who have been
slain; for they cry from the dust for vengeance upon it, and also
upon those who built it up.
25. For it cometh to pass that whoso buildeth it up seeketh to overthrow the freedom of all lands, nations, and countries; and it
bringeth to pass the destruction of all people, for it is built up by
the devil, who is the father of all lies; even that same liar who
beguiled our first parents, yea, even that same liar who hath caused
man to commit murder from the beginning; who hath hardened
the hearts of men that they have murdered the prophets, and
stoned them, and cast them out from the beginning.
26. Wherefore, I, Moroni, am commanded to write these things
that evil may be done away, and that the time may come that
Satan may have no power upon the hearts of the children of men,
but that they may be persuaded to do good continually, that they
may come unto the fountain of all righteousness and be saved.

CHAPTER 9

1. AND now I, Moroni, proceed with my record. Therefore, behold,
it came to pass that because of the secret combinations of Akish
and his friends, behold, they did overthrow the kingdom of Omer.
2. Nevertheless, the Lord was merciful unto Omer, and also to his
sons and to his daughters who did not seek his destruction.
3. And the Lord warned Omer in a dream that he should depart
out of the land; wherefore Omer departed out of the land
with his family, and traveled many days, and came over
and passed by the hill of Shim, and came over by the
place where the Nephites were destroyed, and from
thence eastward, and came to a place which was
called Ablom, by the seashore, and there he
pitched his tent, and also his sons and his daughters, and all his household, save it were Jared
and his family.
4. And it came to pass that Jared was anointed
king over the people, by the hand of wickedness; and he gave unto Akish his daughter to
wife.
5. And it came to pass that Akish sought the life
of his father-in-law; and he applied unto those
whom he had sworn by the oath of the ancients,
and they obtained the head of his father-in-law, as
he sat upon his throne, giving audience to his people.
6. For so great had been the spreading of this wicked
and secret society that it had corrupted the hearts of all
the people; therefore Jared was murdered upon his
throne, and Akish reigned in his stead.

Ether 8:24

President Ezra Taft Benson said that this is a warning to us in our day about secret conspiracies to overthrow the freedom of the people; we stand in danger of losing our liberties—and, once lost, only blood will bring them back. We must be especially alert, he said, to godlessness in government, our schools, our unions, and the military. We must make absolutely certain that the only covenants we make are with the Lord. According to President J. Reuben Clark, if the conspiracies come, there will be many vacant places among those who direct both the Church and the government.

POINT OF INTEREST

Cycle of Prosperity and Destruction *(Ether 9)*

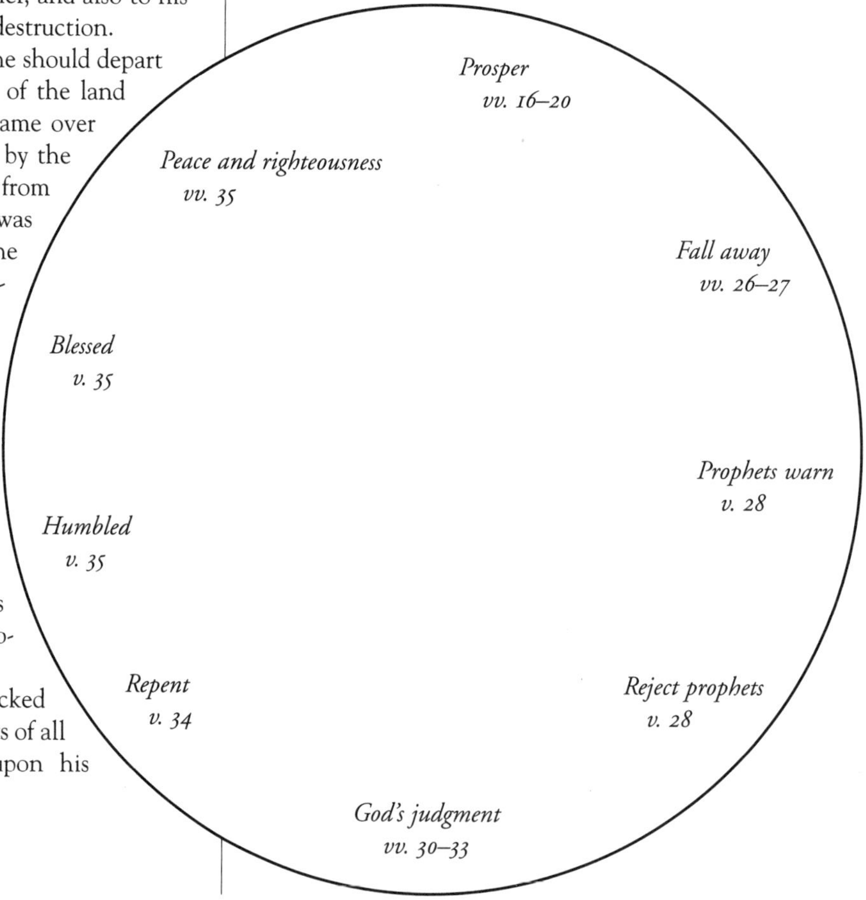

7. And it came to pass that Akish began to be jealous of his son, therefore he shut him up in prison, and kept him upon little or no food until he had suffered death.
8. And now the brother of him that suffered death, (and his name was Nimrah) was angry with his father because of that which his father had done unto his brother.
9. And it came to pass that Nimrah gathered together a small number of men, and fled out of the land, and came over and dwelt with Omer.
10. And it came to pass that Akish begat other sons, and they won the hearts of the people, notwithstanding they had sworn unto him to do all manner of iniquity according to that which he desired.
11. Now the people of Akish were desirous for gain, even as Akish was desirous for power; wherefore, the sons of Akish did offer them money, by which means they drew away the more part of the people after them.
12. And there began to be a war between the sons of Akish and Akish, which lasted for the space of many years, yea, unto the destruction of nearly all the people of the kingdom, yea, even all, save it were thirty souls, and they who fled with the house of Omer.
13. Wherefore, Omer was restored again to the land of his inheritance.
14. And it came to pass that Omer began to be old; nevertheless, in his old age he begat Emer; and he anointed Emer to be king to reign in his stead.
15. And after that he had anointed Emer to be king he saw peace in the land for the space of two years, and he died, having seen exceedingly many days, which were full of sorrow. And it came to pass that Emer did reign in his stead, and did fill the steps of his father.
16. And the Lord began again to take the curse from off the land, and the house of Emer did prosper exceedingly under the reign of Emer; and in the space of sixty and two years they had become exceedingly strong, insomuch that they became exceedingly rich—
17. Having all manner of fruit, and of grain, and of silks, and of fine linen, and of gold, and of silver, and of precious things;
18. And also all manner of cattle, of oxen, and cows, and of sheep, and of swine, and of goats, and also many other kinds of animals which were useful for the food of man.
19. And they also had horses, and asses, and there were elephants and cureloms and cumoms; all of which were useful unto man, and more especially the elephants and cureloms and cumoms.
20. And thus the Lord did pour out his blessings upon this land, which was choice above all other lands; and he commanded that whoso should possess the land should possess it unto the Lord, or they should be destroyed when they were ripened in iniquity; for upon such, saith the Lord: I will pour out the fulness of my wrath.
21. And Emer did execute judgment in righteousness all his days, and he begat many sons and daughters; and he begat Coriantum, and he anointed Coriantum to reign in his stead.
22. And after he had anointed Coriantum to reign in his stead he lived four years, and he saw peace in the land; yea, and he even saw the Son of Righteousness, and did rejoice and glory in his day; and he died in peace.
23. And it came to pass that Coriantum did walk in the steps of his father, and did build many mighty cities, and did administer that which was good unto his people in all his

Ether 9:15–25

The Jaredite nation lived peacefully in wealth and prosperity for more than 225 years. Their accomplishment was possible only because of their righteousness. Toward the end of this period, we see the beginning of the cycle of pride that is so pervasive throughout the Book of Mormon; in the case of the Jaredites, the pride cycle allowed the secret combinations to take hold, which eventually destroyed the entire Jaredite civilization.

Ether 9:19

We read in verse 19 of cureloms and cumoms. These animals were unknown either to the Nephites or to us (probably both), according to Hugh Nibley, so their names could not be translated. Nibley also said that elephants became extinct in Asia sometime between 1500 and 500 B.C., and the only mention of them is in Ether.

days. And it came to pass that he had no children even until he
was exceedingly old.
24. And it came to pass that his wife died, being an hundred and
two years old. And it came to pass that Coriantum took to wife, in
his old age, a young maid, and begat sons and daughters; wherefore
he lived until he was an hundred and forty and two years old.
25. And it came to pass that he begat Com, and Com reigned in
his stead; and he reigned forty and nine years, and he begat Heth;
and he also begat other sons and daughters.
26. And the people had spread again over all the face of the land,
and there began again to be an exceedingly great wickedness upon
the face of the land, and Heth began to embrace the secret plans
again of old, to destroy his father.
27. And it came to pass that he did dethrone his father, for he slew
him with his own sword; and he did reign in his stead.
28. And there came prophets in the land again, crying repentance
unto them—that they must prepare the way of the Lord or there
should come a curse upon the face of the land; yea, even there
should be a great famine, in which they should be destroyed if they
did not repent.
29. But the people believed not the words of the prophets, but they
cast them out; and some of them they cast into pits and left them to
perish. And it came to pass that they did all these things according
to the commandment of the king, Heth.
30. And it came to pass that there began to be a great dearth upon
the land, and the inhabitants began to be destroyed exceedingly
fast because of the dearth, for there was no rain upon the face of
the earth.
31. And there came forth poisonous serpents also upon the face of
the land, and did poison many people. And it came to pass that
their flocks began to flee before the poisonous serpents, towards the
land southward, which was called by the Nephites Zarahemla.
32. And it came to pass that there were many of them which did perish by the way; nevertheless, there were some which fled into the land
southward.
33. And it came to pass that the Lord did cause the serpents that
they should pursue them no more, but that they should hedge up the
way that the people could not pass, that whoso should attempt to
pass might fall by the poisonous serpents.
34. And it came to pass that the people did follow the course of the
beasts, and did devour the carcasses of them which fell by the way,
until they had devoured them all. Now when the people saw that
they must perish they began to repent of their iniquities and cry
unto the Lord.
35. And it came to pass that when they had humbled themselves sufficiently before the Lord he did send rain upon the face of the earth;
and the people began to revive again, and there began to be fruit in
the north countries, and in all the countries round about. And the
Lord did show forth his power unto them in preserving them from
famine.

CHAPTER 10

1. AND it came to pass that Shez, who was a descendant of Heth—
for

Ether 9:26–35

These verses describe the general pattern that occurs following prosperity, a central theme of the Book of Mormon:

- The people become wicked (v. 26)
- Prophets preach repentance to the people (v. 28)
- The people reject the prophets and their teachings (v. 29)
- The Lord sends judgments upon the people (vv. 30–33)
- The people are humbled as a result of the judgments of the Lord, and they repent of their wickedness (v. 34)
- The Lord blesses the people again with prosperity (v. 35)
- The cycle begins all over again

Heth had perished by the famine, and all his household save it
were Shez—wherefore, Shez began to build up again a broken people.
2. And it came to pass that Shez did remember the destruction of
his fathers, and he did build up a righteous kingdom; for he remembered what the Lord had done in bringing Jared and his brother
across the deep; and he did walk in the ways of the Lord; and he
begat sons and daughters.
3. And his eldest son, whose name was Shez, did rebel against him;
nevertheless, Shez was smitten by the hand of a robber, because of
his exceeding riches, which brought peace again unto his father.
4. And it came to pass that his father did build up many cities upon
the face of the land, and the people began again to spread over all
the face of the land. And Shez did live to an exceedingly old age;
and he begat Riplakish. And he died, and Riplakish reigned in his
stead.
5. And it came to pass that Riplakish did not do that which was
right in the sight of the Lord, for he did have many wives and concubines, and did lay that upon men's shoulders which was grievous
to be borne; yea, he did tax them with heavy taxes; and with the
taxes he did build many spacious buildings.
6. And he did erect him an exceedingly beautiful throne; and he
did build many prisons, and whoso would not be subject unto taxes
he did cast into prison; and whoso was not able to pay taxes he did
cast into prison; and he did cause that they should labor continually for their support; and whoso refused to labor he did cause to be
put to death.
7. Wherefore he did obtain all his fine work, yea, even his fine gold
he did cause to be refined in prison, and all manner of fine workmanship he did cause to be wrought in prison. And it came to pass
that he did afflict the people with his whoredoms and abominations.
8. And when he had reigned for the space of forty and two years
the people did rise up in rebellion against him; and there began to
be war again in the land, insomuch that Riplakish was killed, and
his descendants were driven out of the land.
9. And it came to pass after the space of many years, Morianton,
(he being a descendant of Riplakish) gathered together an army of
outcasts, and went forth and gave battle unto the people; and he
gained power over many cities; and the war became exceedingly
sore, and did last for the space of many years; and he did gain power
over all the land, and did establish himself king over all the land.
10. And after that he had established himself king he did ease the
burden of the people, by which he did gain favor in the eyes of the
people, and they did anoint him to be their king.
11. And he did do justice unto the people, but not unto himself
because of his many whoredoms; wherefore he was cut off from the
presence of the Lord.
12. And it came to pass that Morianton built up many cities, and
the people became exceedingly rich under his reign, both in buildings, and in gold and silver, and in raising grain, and in flocks, and
herds, and such things which had been restored unto them.
13. And Morianton did live to an exceedingly great age, and then
he begat Kim; and Kim did reign in the stead of his father; and he
did reign eight years, and his father died. And it came to pass that
Kim did not reign in righteousness,

Ether 10:5–8

These verses demonstrate the similarities between Riplakish and King Noah. Both Riplakish and King Noah:

- Were very immoral (see Mosiah 11:2); even if the Lord allowed the Jaredites to have plural wives (see Ether 14:2), this privilege was clearly abused by Riplakish
- Levied heavy taxes on the people (see Mosiah 11:3)
- Built spacious buildings (see Mosiah 11:8)
- Glutted themselves on the work of others (see Mosiah 11:6)
- Were killed by their own people (see Mosiah 19:20)

POINT OF INTEREST

How history repeats itself . . .

Riplakish (Ether 10)	Characteristics	Noah (Mosiah 11)
v. 5	*very immoral*	*v. 2*
v. 5	*taxed heavily*	*v. 3*
v. 6	*built spacious buildings*	*v. 8*
v. 7	*lived off others' work*	*v. 6*
v. 8	*killed by own people*	*Mosiah 19:20*

wherefore he was not favored of the Lord.
14. And his brother did rise up in rebellion against him, by which
he did bring him into captivity; and he did remain in captivity all
his days; and he begat sons and daughters in captivity, and in his
old age he begat Levi; and he died.
15. And it came to pass that Levi did serve in captivity after the
death of his father, for the space of forty and two years. And he did
make war against the king of the land, by which he did obtain unto
himself the kingdom.
16. And after he had obtained unto himself the kingdom he did
that which was right in the sight of the Lord; and the people did
prosper in the land; and he did live to a good old age, and begat
sons and daughters; and he also begat Corom, whom he anointed
king in his stead.
17. And it came to pass that Corom did that which was good in the
sight of the Lord all his days; and he begat many sons and daughters; and after he had seen many days he did pass away, even like
unto the rest of the earth; and Kish reigned in his stead.
18. And it came to pass that Kish passed away also, and Lib reigned
in his stead.
19. And it came to pass that Lib also did that which was good in
the sight of the Lord. And in the days of Lib the poisonous serpents
were destroyed. Wherefore they did go into the land southward, to
hunt food for the people of the land, for the land was covered with
animals of the forest. And Lib also himself became a great hunter.
20. And they built a great city by the narrow neck of land, by the
place where the sea divides the land.
21. And they did preserve the land southward for a wilderness, to
get game. And the whole face of the land northward was covered
with inhabitants.
22. And they were exceedingly industrious, and they did buy and
sell and traffic one with another, that they might get gain.
23. And they did work in all manner of ore, and they did make
gold, and silver, and iron, and brass, and all manner of metals; and
they did dig it out of the earth; wherefore, they did cast up mighty
heaps of earth to get ore, of gold, and of silver, and of iron, and of
copper. And they did work all manner of fine work.
24. And they did have silks, and fine-twined linen; and they did work
all manner of cloth, that they might clothe themselves from their
nakedness.
25. And they did make all manner of tools to till the earth, both
to plow and to sow, to reap and to hoe, and also to thrash.
26. And they did make all manner of tools with which they did
work their beasts.
27. And they did make all manner of weapons of war. And they did
work all manner of work of exceedingly curious workmanship.
28. And never could be a people more blessed than were they, and
more prospered by the hand of the Lord. And they were in a land
that was choice above all lands, for the Lord had spoken it.
29. And it came to pass that Lib did live many years, and begat
sons and daughters; and he also begat Hearthom.

Ether 10:22–27

These verses are indicative of a high state of civilization, demonstrating that the Jaredites were an extremely refined people. Those signs include:

- Exceeding industry
- Trade with one another
- Metal work, including gold, silver, iron, copper, and brass, among others
- Beautiful clothing fashioned of silk, fine-twined linen, and all manner of cloth
- The ability to make all manner of agricultural tools to assist in hoeing, plowing, sowing, reaping, and thrashing
- The ability to make all kinds of tools to assist with their livestock
- The ability to make all kinds of weapons of war
- Their ability to make things of fine workmanship (the word curious means "fine")

30. And it came to pass that Hearthom reigned in the stead of his father. And when Hearthom had reigned twenty and four years, behold, the kingdom was taken away from him. And he served many years in captivity, yea, even all the remainder of his days.

31. And he begat Heth, and Heth lived in captivity all his days. And Heth begat Aaron, and Aaron dwelt in captivity all his days; and he begat Amnigaddah, and Amnigaddah also dwelt in captivity all his days; and he begat Coriantum, and Coriantum dwelt in captivity all his days; and he begat Com.

32. And it came to pass that Com drew away the half of the kingdom. And he reigned over the half of the kingdom forty and two years; and he went to battle against the king, Amgid, and they fought for the space of many years, during which time Com gained power over Amgid, and obtained power over the remainder of the kingdom.

33. And in the days of Com there began to be robbers in the land; and they adopted the old plans, and administered oaths after the manner of the ancients, and sought again to destroy the kingdom.

34. Now Com did fight against them much; nevertheless, he did not prevail against them.

CHAPTER 11

1. AND there came also in the days of Com many prophets, and prophesied of the destruction of that great people except they should repent, and turn unto the Lord, and forsake their murders and wickedness.

2. And it came to pass that the prophets were rejected by the people, and they fled unto Com for protection, for the people sought to destroy them.

3. And they prophesied unto Com many things; and he was blessed in all the remainder of his days.

4. And he lived to a good old age, and begat Shiblom; and Shiblom reigned in his stead. And the brother of Shiblom rebelled against him, and there began to be an exceedingly great war in all the land.

5. And it came to pass that the brother of Shiblom caused that all the prophets who prophesied of the destruction of the people should be put to death;

6. And there was great calamity in all the land, for they had testified that a great curse should come upon the land, and also upon the people, and that there should be a great destruction among them, such an one as never had been upon the face of the earth, and their bones should become as heaps of earth upon the face of the land except they should repent of their wickedness.

7. And they hearkened not unto the voice of the Lord, because of their wicked combinations; wherefore, there began to be wars and contentions in all the land, and also many famines and pestilences, insomuch that there was a great destruction, such an one as never had been known upon the face of the earth; and all this came to pass in the days of Shiblom.

8. And the people began to repent of their iniquity; and inasmuch as they did the Lord did have mercy on them.

9. And it came to pass that Shiblom was slain, and Seth was brought into captivity, and did dwell in captivity all his days.

10. And it came to pass that Ahah,

Ether 11

Chapter 11 describes the final decline of the Jaredites into apostasy. Even though laws had been made to protect the prophets (see verse 2), all the prophets who foretold the destruction of the Jaredite civilization were put to death (see verse 5). There was great calamity throughout the land (see verse 6)—a land that had once been the greatest of all the civilizations (see Ether 1:43, which says there was "none greater" than the Jaredite nation).

his son, did obtain the kingdom; and he did reign over the people all his days. And he did do all manner of iniquity in his days, by which he did cause the shedding of much blood; and few were his days.

11. And Ethem, being a descendant of Ahah, did obtain the kingdom; and he also did do that which was wicked in his days.

12. And it came to pass that in the days of Ethem there came many prophets, and prophesied again unto the people; yea, they did prophesy that the Lord would utterly destroy them from off the face of the earth except they repented of their iniquities.

13. And it came to pass that the people hardened their hearts, and would not hearken unto their words; and the prophets mourned and withdrew from among the people.

14. And it came to pass that Ethem did execute judgment in wickedness all his days; and he begat Moron. And it came to pass that Moron did reign in his stead; and Moron did that which was wicked before the Lord.

15. And it came to pass that there arose a rebellion among the people, because of that secret combination which was built up to get power and gain; and there arose a mighty man among them in iniquity, and gave battle unto Moron, in which he did overthrow the half of the kingdom; and he did maintain the half of the kingdom for many years.

16. And it came to pass that Moron did overthrow him, and did obtain the kingdom again.

17. And it came to pass that there arose another mighty man; and he was a descendant of the brother of Jared.

18. And it came to pass that he did overthrow Moron and obtain the kingdom; wherefore, Moron dwelt in captivity all the remainder of his days; and he begat Coriantor.

19. And it came to pass that Coriantor dwelt in captivity all his days.

20. And in the days of Coriantor there also came many prophets, and prophesied of great and marvelous things, and cried repentance unto the people, and except they should repent the Lord God would execute judgment against them to their utter destruction;

21. And that the Lord God would send or bring forth another people to possess the land, by his power, after the manner by which he brought their fathers.

22. And they did reject all the words of the prophets, because of their secret society and wicked abominations.

23. And it came to pass that Coriantor begat Ether, and he died, having dwelt in captivity all his days.

CHAPTER 12

1. AND it came to pass that the days of Ether were in the days of Coriantumr; and Coriantumr was king over all the land.

2. And Ether was a prophet of the Lord; wherefore Ether came forth

Ether 12

This chapter is a great discourse on faith, hope, and charity. Faith, according to President Spencer W. Kimball, involves planting for an eternal harvest; we must have faith in the Lord, not in the arm of flesh. Hope allows us to exercise faith in the face of tribulations. And charity is the pure love of Christ; according to Elder Gene R. Cook, all men have the love of Christ—but charity is a gift that must be bestowed upon us.

in the days of Coriantumr, and began to prophesy unto the people, for he could not be restrained because of the Spirit of the Lord which was in him.
3. For he did cry from the morning, even until the going down of the sun, exhorting the people to believe in God unto repentance lest they should be destroyed, saying unto them that by faith all things are fulfilled—
4. Wherefore, whoso believeth in God might with surety hope for a better world, yea, even a place at the right hand of God, which hope cometh of faith, maketh an anchor to the souls of men, which would make them sure and steadfast, always abounding in good works, being led to glorify God.
5. And it came to pass that Ether did prophesy great and marvelous things unto the people, which they did not believe, because they saw them not.
6. And now, I, Moroni, would speak somewhat concerning these things; I would show unto the world that faith is things which are hoped for and not seen; wherefore, dispute not because ye see not, for ye receive no witness until after the trial of your faith.
7. For it was by faith that Christ showed himself unto our fathers, after he had risen from the dead; and he showed not himself unto them until after they had faith in him; wherefore, it must needs be that some had faith in him, for he showed himself not unto the world.
8. But because of the faith of men he has shown himself unto the world, and glorified the name of the Father, and prepared a way that thereby others might be partakers of the heavenly gift, that they might hope for those things which they have not seen.
9. Wherefore, ye may also have hope, and be partakers of the gift, if ye will but have faith.
10. Behold it was by faith that they of old were called after the holy order of God.
11. Wherefore, by faith was the law of Moses given. But in the gift of his Son hath God prepared a more excellent way; and it is by faith that it hath been fulfilled.
12. For if there be no faith among the children of men God can do no miracle among them; wherefore, he showed not himself until after their faith.
13. Behold, it was the faith of Alma and Amulek that caused the prison to tumble to the earth.
14. Behold, it was the faith of Nephi and Lehi that wrought the change upon the Lamanites, that they were baptized with fire and with the Holy Ghost.
15. Behold, it was the faith of Ammon and his brethren which wrought so great a miracle among the Lamanites.
16. Yea, and even all they who

Ether 12:3–4

Joseph Smith said, "It is only necessary for us to say that the whole visible creation, as it now exists, is the effect of faith. . . . So, then, faith is truly the first principle in the science of Theology, and, when understood, leads the mind back to the beginning, and carries it forward to the end; or, in other words, from eternity to eternity . . ." *(Lectures on Faith)*.

Ether 12:16

As Ether declared: "by faith all things are fulfilled" (Ether 12:3). Faith is "an anchor to the souls of men," making them "sure and steadfast, always abounding in good works, being led to glorify God" (Ether 12:4). . . .

In making his abridgement of the 24 plates of gold, Moroni comes across the prophecies of Ether, who "could not be restrained because of the Spirit of the Lord which was in him" (Ether 12:2). Ether's inspired discourse on faith stimulates Moroni to provide his own commentary on this subject, declaring that "faith is things which are hoped for and not seen" (Ether 12:6; cf. Alma 32:21; Heb. 11:1). Moroni's exposition on the importance and power of faith in doing all things is among the most glorious statements on this subject in holy writ, for he saw Jesus and testified that He "hath talked with me face to face" (Ether 12:39).

President Gordon B. Hinckley said, "As we reflect on those who have gone before us, and as we consider our present labors for the good of ourselves and others, would that we all might say each day, 'I am doing my work faithfully and in good faith.'

"Let us look again to the power of faith in ourselves, faith in our associates, and faith in God our Eternal Father. Let us prayerfully implement such faith in our lives." (P/A)

wrought miracles wrought them by faith, even those who were before Christ and also those who were after.
17. And it was by faith that the three disciples obtained a promise that they should not taste of death; and they obtained not the promise until after their faith.
18. And neither at any time hath any wrought miracles until after their faith; wherefore they first believed in the Son of God.
19. And there were many whose faith was so exceedingly strong, even before Christ came, who could not be kept from within the veil, but truly saw with their eyes the things which they had beheld with an eye of faith, and they were glad.
20. And behold, we have seen in this record that one of these was the brother of Jared; for so great was his faith in God, that when God put forth his finger he could not hide it from the sight of the brother of Jared, because of his word which he had spoken unto him, which word he had obtained by faith.
21. And after the brother of Jared had beheld the finger of the Lord, because of the promise which the brother of Jared had obtained by faith, the Lord could not withhold anything from his sight; wherefore he showed him all things, for he could no longer be kept without the veil.
22. And it is by faith that my fathers have obtained the promise that these things should come unto their brethren through the Gentiles; therefore the Lord hath commanded me, yea, even Jesus Christ.
23. And I said unto him: Lord, the Gentiles will mock at these things, because of our weakness in writing; for Lord thou hast made us mighty in word by faith, but thou hast not made us mighty in writing; for thou hast made all this people that they could speak much, because of the Holy Ghost which thou hast given them;
24. And thou hast made us that we could write but little, because of the awkwardness of our hands. Behold, thou hast not made us mighty in writing like unto the brother of Jared, for thou madest him that the things which he wrote were mighty even as thou art, unto the overpowering of man to read them.
25. Thou hast also made our words powerful and great, even that we cannot write them; wherefore, when we write we behold our weakness, and stumble because of the placing of our words; and I fear lest the Gentiles shall mock at our words.
26. And when I had said this, the Lord spake unto me, saying: Fools mock, but they shall mourn; and my grace is sufficient for the meek, that they shall take no advantage of your weakness;
27. And if men come unto me I will show unto them their weakness. I give unto men weakness that they may be humble; and my grace is sufficient for all men that humble themselves before me; for if they humble themselves before me, and have faith in me, then will I make weak things become strong unto them.

Ether 12:19

The Brother of Jared is one of many in the scriptures whose faith allowed him to see within the veil.

Ether 12:26–27

. . . Even though we might have weaknesses, if we have faith in the Lord as he indicated, then our weaknesses may be turned into strengths. (Ludlow)

Ether 12:27–28

Faith in the Lord Jesus Christ is a simple act of humility. Humility is the seed bed of our souls in which faith in the Lord Jesus Christ is planted. If this spiritual soil is fertile and receives the warmth of the divine spirit, it will give life to this infant faith. There is no room for arrogance or conceit in our approach to embracing gospel truths. (O/C)

Ether 12:27

Some have mistakenly believed that the Lord gave us weaknesses. He did not. We inherited the weakness that come as part of being mortals who are in a fallen state, and who are susceptible to weaknesses—individual character flaws—that may beset us as a result of our being in this fallen state. We did not have those character flaws as spirits in our pre-mortal state. Identifying the weaknesses that do develop, and working to overcome them, is the way we eventually become like the Savior.

28. Behold, I will show unto the Gentiles their weakness, and I will show unto them that faith, hope and charity bringeth unto me—the fountain of all righteousness.
29. And I, Moroni, having heard these words, was comforted, and said: O Lord, thy righteous will be done, for I know that thou workest unto the children of men according to their faith;
30. For the brother of Jared said unto the mountain Zerin, Remove—and it was removed. And if he had not had faith it would not have moved; wherefore thou workest after men have faith.
31. For thus didst thou manifest thyself unto thy disciples; for after they had faith, and did speak in thy name, thou didst show thyself unto them in great power.
32. And I also remember that thou hast said that thou hast prepared a house for man, yea, even among the mansions of thy Father, in which man might have a more excellent hope; wherefore man must hope, or he cannot receive an inheritance in the place which thou hast prepared.
33. And again, I remember that thou hast said that thou hast loved the world, even unto the laying down of thy life for the world, that thou mightest take it again to prepare a place for the children of men.
34. And now I know that this love which thou hast had for the children of men is charity; wherefore, except men shall have charity they cannot inherit that place which thou hast prepared in the mansions of thy Father.
35. Wherefore, I know by this thing which thou hast said, that if the Gentiles have not charity, because of our weakness, that thou wilt prove them, and take away their talent, yea, even that which they have received, and give unto them who shall have more abundantly.
36. And it came to pass that I prayed unto the Lord that he would give unto the Gentiles grace, that they might have charity.
37. And it came to pass that the Lord said unto me: If they have not charity it mattereth not unto thee, thou hast been faithful; wherefore, thy garments shall be made clean. And because thou hast seen thy weakness thou shalt be made strong, even unto the sitting down in the place which I have prepared in the mansions of my Father.
38. And now I, Moroni, bid farewell unto the Gentiles, yea, and also unto my brethren whom I love, until we shall meet before the judgment-seat of Christ, where all men shall know that my garments are not spotted with your blood.
39. And then shall ye know that I have seen Jesus, and that he hath talked with me face to face, and that he told me in plain humility, even as a man telleth another in mine own language, concerning these things;
40. And only a few have I written, because of my weakness in writing.
41. And now, I would commend you to seek this Jesus of whom the

Ether 12:38–39

One major purpose for the coming forth of the Book of Mormon is to witness of the divinity of Jesus Christ. It therefore seems fitting and proper that many of the writers in this book should be personal witnesses of the Savior. Most of our present Book of Mormon was written by four men: Nephi, Jacob, Mormon, and Moroni, and all four of these men personally saw the Savior and visited with him. . . . (Ludlow)

prophets and apostles have written, that the grace of God the Father, and also the Lord Jesus Christ, and the Holy Ghost, which beareth record of them, may be and abide in you forever. Amen.

CHAPTER 13

1. AND now I, Moroni, proceed to finish my record concerning the destruction of the people of whom I have been writing.
2. For behold, they rejected all the words of Ether; for he truly told them of all things, from the beginning of man; and that after the waters had receded from off the face of this land it became a choice land above all other lands, a chosen land of the Lord; wherefore the Lord would have that all men should serve him who dwell upon the face thereof;
3. And that it was the place of the New Jerusalem, which should come down out of heaven, and the holy sanctuary of the Lord.
4. Behold, Ether saw the days of Christ, and he spake concerning a New Jerusalem upon this land.
5. And he spake also concerning the house of Israel, and the Jerusalem from whence Lehi should come—after it should be destroyed it should be built up again, a holy city unto the Lord; wherefore, it could not be a new Jerusalem for it had been in a time of old; but it should be built up again, and become a holy city of the Lord; and it should be built unto the house of Israel.
6. And that a New Jerusalem should be built up upon this land, unto the remnant of the seed of Joseph, for which things there has been a type.
7. For as Joseph brought his father down into the land of Egypt, even so he died there; wherefore, the Lord brought a remnant of the seed of Joseph out of the land of Jerusalem, that he might be merciful unto the seed of Joseph that they should perish not, even as he was merciful unto the father of Joseph that he should perish not.
8. Wherefore, the remnant of the house of Joseph shall be built upon this land; and it shall be a land of their inheritance; and they shall build up a holy city unto the Lord, like unto the Jerusalem of old; and they shall no more be confounded, until the end come when the earth shall pass away.
9. And there shall be a new heaven and a new earth; and they shall be like unto the old save the old have passed away, and all things have become new.
10. And then cometh the New Jerusalem; and blessed are they who dwell therein, for it is they whose garments are white through the blood of the Lamb; and they are they who are numbered among the remnant of the seed of Joseph, who were of the house of Israel.
11. And then also cometh the Jerusalem of old; and the inhabitants thereof, blessed are they, for

Ether 13:2–11

In the day of regeneration, when all things are made new, there will be three great cities that will be holy. One will be the Jerusalem of old which shall be rebuilt according to the prophecy of Ezekiel. One will be the city of Zion, or of Enoch, which was taken from the earth when Enoch was translated and which will be restored; and the city Zion, or New Jerusalem, which is to be built by the seed of Joseph on this the American continent. . . .

After the close of the millennial reign we are informed that Satan, who was bound during the millennium, shall be loosed and go forth to deceive the nations. Then will come the end. The earth will die and be purified and receive its resurrection. During this cleansing period the City Zion, or New Jerusalem, will be taken from the earth; and when the earth is prepared for the celestial glory, the city will come down according to the prediction in the Book of Revelation. (Ludlow)

Ether 13:4–5

Joseph Smith said, "Now many will feel disposed to say, that this New Jerusalem spoken of, is the Jerusalem that was built by the Jews on the eastern continent. But you will see, from Revelation 21:2, there was a New Jerusalem coming down from God out of heaven, adorned as a bride for her husband; that after this, the Revelator was caught away in the Spirit, to a great and high mountain, and saw the great and holy city descending out of heaven from God. Now there are two cities spoken of here. As everything cannot be had in so narrow a compass as a letter, I shall say with brevity, that there is a New Jerusalem to be established on this continent, and also Jerusalem shall be rebuilt on the eastern continent." [See Ether 13:1–12] (*HC*, 2:262). (P/A)

they have been washed in the blood of the Lamb; and they are they who were scattered and gathered in from the four quarters of the earth, and from the north countries, and are partakers of the fulfilling of the covenant which God made with their father, Abraham.
12. And when these things come, bringeth to pass the scripture which saith, there are they who were first, who shall be last; and there are they who were last, who shall be first.
13. And I was about to write more, but I am forbidden; but great and marvelous were the prophecies of Ether; but they esteemed him as naught, and cast him out; and he hid himself in the cavity of a rock by day, and by night he went forth viewing the things which should come upon the people.
14. And as he dwelt in the cavity of a rock he made the remainder of this record, viewing the destructions which came upon the people, by night.
15. And it came to pass that in that same year in which he was cast out from among the people there began to be a great war among the people, for there were many who rose up, who were mighty men, and sought to destroy Coriantumr by their secret plans of wickedness, of which hath been spoken.
16. And now Coriantumr, having studied, himself, in all the arts of war and all the cunning of the world, wherefore he gave battle unto them who sought to destroy him.
17. But he repented not, neither his fair sons nor daughters; neither the fair sons and daughters of Cohor; neither the fair sons and daughters of Corihor; and in fine, there were none of the fair sons and daughters upon the face of the whole earth who repented of their sins.
18. Wherefore, it came to pass that in the first year that Ether dwelt in the cavity of a rock, there were many people who were slain by the sword of those secret combinations, fighting against Coriantumr that they might obtain the kingdom.
19. And it came to pass that the sons of Coriantumr fought much and bled much.
20. And in the second year the word of the Lord came to Ether, that he should go and prophesy unto Coriantumr that, if he would repent, and all his household, the Lord would give unto him his kingdom and spare the people—
21. Otherwise they should be destroyed, and all his household save it were himself. And he should only live to see the fulfilling of the prophecies which had been spoken concerning another people receiving the land for their inheritance; and Coriantumr should receive a burial by them; and every soul should be destroyed save it were Coriantumr.
22. And it came to pass that Coriantumr repented not, neither his household, neither the people; and the wars ceased not; and they sought to kill Ether, but he fled from before them and hid again in the cavity of the rock.
23. And it came to pass that there arose up Shared, and he also gave battle unto Coriantumr; and he did beat him, insomuch that in the third year he did bring him into captivity.
24. And the sons of Coriantumr, in the fourth year, did beat Shared, and did obtain the kingdom again unto their father.
25. Now there began to be a war

Ether 13:20–21

This prophecy of Ether to Coriantumr is fulfilled in Ether 15:1–3, Ether 15:26–32, and Omni 1:20–22.

upon all the face of the land, every man with his band fighting for that which he desired.
26. And there were robbers, and in fine, all manner of wickedness upon all the face of the land.
27. And it came to pass that Coriantumr was exceedingly angry with Shared, and he went against him with his armies to battle; and they did meet in great anger, and they did meet in the valley of Gilgal; and the battle became exceedingly sore.
28. And it came to pass that Shared fought against him for the space of three days. And it came to pass that Coriantumr beat him, and did pursue him until he came to the plains of Heshlon.
29. And it came to pass that Shared gave him battle again upon the plains; and behold, he did beat Coriantumr, and drove him back again to the valley of Gilgal.
30. And Coriantumr gave Shared battle again in the valley of Gilgal, in which he beat Shared and slew him.
31. And Shared wounded Coriantumr in his thigh, that he did not go to battle again for the space of two years, in which time all the people upon the face of the land were shedding blood, and there was none to restrain them.

CHAPTER 14

1. AND now there began to be a great curse upon all the land because of the iniquity of the people, in which, if a man should lay his tool or his sword upon his shelf, or upon the place whither he would keep it, behold, upon the morrow, he could not find it, so great was the curse upon the land.
2. Wherefore every man did cleave unto that which was his own, with his hands, and would not borrow neither would he lend; and every man kept the hilt of his sword in his right hand, in the defence of his property and his own life and of his wives and children.
3. And now, after the space of two years, and after the death of Shared, behold, there arose the brother of Shared and he gave battle unto Coriantumr, in which Coriantumr did beat him and did pursue him to the wilderness of Akish.
4. And it came to pass that the brother of Shared did give battle unto him in the wilderness of Akish; and the battle became exceedingly sore, and many thousands fell by the sword.
5. And it came to pass that Coriantumr did lay siege to the wilderness; and the brother of Shared did march forth out of the wilderness by night, and slew a part of the army of Coriantumr, as they were drunken.
6. And he came forth to the land of Moron, and placed himself upon the throne of Coriantumr.
7. And it came to pass that Coriantumr dwelt with his army in the wilderness for the space of two years, in which he did receive great strength to his army.
8. Now the brother of Shared, whose name was Gilead, also received great strength to his army, because of secret combinations.
9. And it came to pass that his high priest murdered him as he sat upon his throne.
10. And it came to pass that one of the secret combinations murdered him in a secret pass, and obtained unto himself the kingdom; and his name was Lib; and Lib was a man of great stature, more than any other man among all the people.
11. And it came to pass that in the first year of Lib, Coriantumr came up unto the land of Moron, and gave battle unto Lib.

12. And it came to pass that he fought with Lib, in which Lib did smite upon his arm that he was wounded; nevertheless, the army of Coriantumr did press forward upon Lib, that he fled to the borders upon the seashore.
13. And it came to pass that Coriantumr pursued him; and Lib gave battle unto him upon the seashore.
14. And it came to pass that Lib did smite the army of Coriantumr, that they fled again to the wilderness of Akish.
15. And it came to pass that Lib did pursue him until he came to the plains of Agosh. And Coriantumr had taken all the people with him as he fled before Lib in that quarter of the land whither he fled.
16. And when he had come to the plains of Agosh he gave battle unto Lib, and he smote upon him until he died; nevertheless, the brother of Lib did come against Coriantumr in the stead thereof, and the battle became exceedingly sore, in the which Coriantumr fled again before the army of the brother of Lib.
17. Now the name of the brother of Lib was called Shiz. And it came to pass that Shiz pursued after Coriantumr, and he did overthrow many cities, and he did slay both women and children, and he did burn the cities.
18. And there went a fear of Shiz throughout all the land; yea, a cry went forth throughout the land—Who can stand before the army of Shiz? Behold, he sweepeth the earth before him!
19. And it came to pass that the people began to flock together in armies, throughout all the face of the land.
20. And they were divided; and a part of them fled to the army of Shiz, and a part of them fled to the army of Coriantumr.
21. And so great and lasting had been the war, and so long had been the scene of bloodshed and carnage, that the whole face of the land was covered with the bodies of the dead.
22. And so swift and speedy was the war that there was none left to bury the dead, but they did march forth from the shedding of blood to the shedding of blood, leaving the bodies of both men, women, and children strewed upon the face of the land, to become a prey to the worms of the flesh.
23. And the scent thereof went forth upon the face of the land, even upon all the face of the land; wherefore the people became troubled by day and by night, because of the scent thereof.
24. Nevertheless, Shiz did not cease to pursue Coriantumr; for he had sworn to avenge himself upon Coriantumr of the blood of his brother, who had been slain, and the word of the Lord which came to Ether that Coriantumr should not fall by the sword.
25. And thus we see that the Lord did visit them in the fulness of his wrath, and their wickedness and abominations had prepared a way for their everlasting destruction.
26. And it came to pass that Shiz did pursue Coriantumr eastward, even to the borders by the seashore, and there he gave battle unto Shiz for the space of three days.
27. And so terrible was the destruction among the armies of Shiz that the people began to be frightened, and began to flee before the armies of Coriantumr; and they fled to the land of Corihor, and swept off the inhabitants before them, all them that would not join them.
28. And they pitched their tents in the valley of Corihor; and Coriantumr pitched his tents in the valley of Shurr. Now the valley of Shurr was near the hill Comnor; wherefore,

Ether 14:22–23

According to Hugh Nibley, the Book of Ether is one of many instances in which kings were kept in prison for many years, but were not killed. As long as the king was alive, the war could continue; as soon as the king was dead, the war was over and his side was declared the loser, regardless of the strength of his surviving forces.

There were several circumstances, taught Nibley, that were peculiar to Asiatic warfare:

- Every war was a strictly personal contest between kings, so battle had to continue until one of the kings failed.
- The king must be the very last person to fall; the entire army existed for the sole purpose of defending the king.
- As in chess, the king does not die—the game (or war, in this case) ends when the king cannot escape.

Coriantumr did gather his armies together upon the hill Comnor, and did sound a trumpet unto the armies of Shiz to invite them forth to battle.

29. And it came to pass that they came forth, but were driven again; and they came the second time, and they were driven again the second time. And it came to pass that they came again the third time, and the battle became exceedingly sore.

30. And it came to pass that Shiz smote upon Coriantumr that he gave him many deep wounds; and Coriantumr, having lost his blood, fainted, and was carried away as though he were dead.

31. Now the loss of men, women and children on both sides was so great that Shiz commanded his people that they should not pursue the armies of Coriantumr; wherefore, they returned to their camp.

CHAPTER 15

1. AND it came to pass when Coriantumr had recovered of his wounds, he began to remember the words which Ether had spoken unto him.

2. He saw that there had been slain by the sword already nearly two millions of his people, and he began to sorrow in his heart; yea, there had been slain two millions of mighty men, and also their wives and their children.

3. He began to repent of the evil which he had done; he began to remember the words which had been spoken by the mouth of all the prophets, and he saw them that they were fulfilled thus far, every whit; and his soul mourned and refused to be comforted.

4. And it came to pass that he wrote an epistle unto Shiz, desiring him that he would spare the people, and he would give up the kingdom for the sake of the lives of the people.

5. And it came to pass that when Shiz had received his epistle he wrote an epistle unto Coriantumr, that if he would give himself up, that he might slay him with his own sword, that he would spare the lives of the people.

6. And it came to pass that the people repented not of their iniquity; and the people of Coriantumr were stirred up to anger against the people of Shiz; and the people of Shiz were stirred up to anger against the people of Coriantumr; wherefore, the people of Shiz did give battle unto the people of Coriantumr.

7. And when Coriantumr saw that he was about to fall he fled again before the people of Shiz.

8. And it came to pass that he came to the waters of Ripliancum, which, by interpretation, is large, or to exceed all; wherefore, when they came to these waters they pitched their tents; and Shiz also pitched his tents near unto them; and therefore on the morrow they did come to battle.

9. And it came to pass that they fought an exceedingly sore battle, in which Coriantumr was wounded again, and he fainted with the loss of blood.

10. And it came to pass that the armies of Coriantumr did press upon the armies of Shiz that they beat them, that they caused them to flee before them; and they did flee southward, and did pitch their tents in a place which was called Ogath.

11. And it came to pass that the army of Coriantumr did pitch their tents by the hill Ramah; and it was that same hill where my father Mormon did hide up the records unto the Lord, which were sacred.

Ether 15:11

The hill Ramah was one of the major hills in the lands of the Jaredites. Later when the Nephites moved into this area, they evidently called this same hill by the name of Cumorah. Moroni says that the hill Ramah "was that same hill where my father Mormon did hide up the records unto the Lord, which were sacred." (Ether 15:11.) In Mormon 6:6 this hill is identified as the hill Cumorah. (Ludlow)

12. And it came to pass that they did gather together all the people upon all the face of the land, who had not been slain, save it was Ether.
13. And it came to pass that Ether did behold all the doings of the people; and he beheld that the people who were for Coriantumr were gathered together to the army of Coriantumr; and the people who were for Shiz were gathered together to the army of Shiz.
14. Wherefore, they were for the space of four years gathering together the people, that they might get all who were upon the face of the land, and that they might receive all the strength which it was possible that they could receive.
15. And it came to pass that when they were all gathered together, every one to the army which he would, with their wives and their children—both men women and children being armed with weapons of war, having shields, and breastplates, and head-plates, and being clothed after the manner of war—they did march forth one against another to battle; and they fought all that day, and conquered not.
16. And it came to pass that when it was night they were weary, and retired to their camps; and after they had retired to their camps they took up a howling and a lamentation for the loss of the slain of their people; and so great were their cries, their howlings and lamentations, that they did rend the air exceedingly.
17. And it came to pass that on the morrow they did go again to battle, and great and terrible was that day; nevertheless, they conquered not, and when the night came again they did rend the air with their cries, and their howlings, and their mournings, for the loss of the slain of their people.
18. And it came to pass that Coriantumr wrote again an epistle unto Shiz, desiring that he would not come again to battle, but that he would take the kingdom, and spare the lives of the people.
19. But behold, the Spirit of the Lord had ceased striving with them, and Satan had full power over the hearts of the people; for they were given up unto the hardness of their hearts, and the blindness of their minds that they might be destroyed; wherefore they went again to battle.
20. And it came to pass that they fought all that day, and when the night came they slept upon their swords.
21. And on the morrow they fought even until the night came.
22. And when the night came they were drunken with anger, even as a man who is drunken with wine; and they slept again upon their swords.
23. And on the morrow they fought again; and when the night came they had all fallen by the sword save it were fifty and two of the people of Coriantumr, and sixty and nine of the people of Shiz.
24. And it came to pass that they slept upon their swords that night, and on the morrow they fought again, and they contended in their might with their swords and with their shields, all that day.
25. And when the night came there were thirty and two of the people of Shiz, and twenty and seven of the people of Coriantumr.
26. And it came to pass that they ate and slept, and prepared for death on the morrow. And they were large and mighty men as to the strength of men.
27. And it came to pass that they fought for the space of three hours, and they fainted with the loss of blood.
28. And it came to pass that when the men of Coriantumr had received

Ether 15:15, 19

In this battle, we are told in verse 15, even women and children are armed and sent into battle. The only situation in which this horrible situation can exist is clarified in verse 19—the spirit of the Lord had ceased striving with the people, and Satan had full power over their hearts. Hugh Nibley wrote, "Let no one think the final chapter of Ether is at all fanciful or overdrawn. Wars of extermination are a standard institution in the history of Asia."

Ether 15:29–30

Many people have raised questions concerning the plausibility of Coriantumr and Shiz being the last survivors of the great Jaredite armies numbering millions of men. Hugh Nibley has written the following concerning this problem:

"The insane wars of the Jaredite chiefs ended in the complete annihilation of both sides, with the kings the last to go. The same thing had almost happened earlier in the days of Akish, when a civil war between him and his sons reduced the population to thirty. (Ether 9:12) This all seems improbable to us, but two circumstances peculiar to Asiatic warfare explain why the phenomenon is by no means without parallel: (1) Since every war is strictly a personal contest between kings, the battle *must* continue until one of the kings falls or is taken. (2) And yet things are so arranged that the king must be very *last* to fall, the whole army existing for the sole purpose of defending his person. . . ." (Ludlow)

sufficient strength that they could walk, they were about to flee for their lives; but behold, Shiz arose, and also his men, and he swore in his wrath that he would slay Coriantumr or he would perish by the sword.
29. Wherefore, he did pursue them, and on the morrow he did overtake them; and they fought again with the sword. And it came to pass that when they had all fallen by the sword, save it were Coriantumr and Shiz, behold Shiz had fainted with the loss of blood.
30. And it came to pass that when Coriantumr had leaned upon his sword, that he rested a little, he smote off the head of Shiz.
31. And it came to pass that after he had smitten off the head of Shiz, that Shiz raised up on his hands and fell; and after that he had struggled for breath, he died.
32. And it came to pass that Coriantumr fell to the earth, and became as if he had no life.
33. And the Lord spake unto Ether, and said unto him: Go forth. And he went forth, and beheld that the words of the Lord had all been fulfilled; and he finished his record; (and the hundredth part I have not written) and he hid them in a manner that the people of Limhi did find them.
34. Now the last words which are written by Ether are these: Whether the Lord will that I be translated, or that I suffer the will of the Lord in the flesh, it mattereth not, if it so be that I am saved in the kingdom of God. Amen.

THE BOOK OF MORONI

CHAPTER 1

1. NOW I, Moroni, after having made an end of abridging the account of the people of Jared, I had supposed not to have written more, but I have not as yet perished; and I make not myself known to the Lamanites lest they should destroy me.
2. For behold, their wars are exceedingly fierce among themselves; and because of their hatred they put to death every Nephite that will not deny the Christ.
3. And I, Moroni, will not deny the Christ; wherefore, I wander whithersoever I can for the safety of mine own life.
4. Wherefore, I write a few more things, contrary to that which I had supposed; for I had supposed not to have written any more; but I write a few more things, that perhaps they may be of worth unto my brethren, the Lamanites, in some future day, according to the will of the Lord.

CHAPTER 2

Moroni 1:1

We know [Moroni] had access to a Nephite library, where he might have spent considerable time reading, writing, or maybe just living and hiding away from his enemies. President Brigham Young related an experience in the life of Joseph Smith and Oliver Cowdery:

Oliver Cowdery went with the Prophet Joseph when he deposited these plates. Joseph did not translate all of the plates; there was a portion of them sealed, which you can learn from the Book of Doctrine and Covenants. When Joseph got the plates, the angel instructed him to carry them back to the hill Cumorah, which he did. Oliver says that when Joseph and Oliver went there, the hill opened, and they walked into a cave, in which there was a large and spacious room. He says he did not think, at the time, whether they had the light of the sun or artificial light; but that it was just as light as day. They laid the plates on a table; it was a large table that stood in the room. Under this table there was a pile of plates as much as two feet high, and there were altogether in the room more plates than probably many wagon loads; they were piled up in the corners and along the walls . . . (*Journal of Discourses*, 19:38). (O/C)

Moroni 2:1–3

In 3 Nephi 18:39, Mormon tells of the departure of the resurrected Jesus Christ from his chosen twelve disciples at the end of his first visit to them. Before departing, the Savior "touched with his hand the disciples whom he had chosen, . . . even until he had touched them all, and spake unto them as he touched them. . . . the disciples bear record that he gave them power to give the Holy Ghost. And I will show unto you hereafter that this record is true." (3 Nephi 18:36–37.) Here in chapter 2 of his own book, consisting primarily of a series of small "appendices," Moroni includes the exact words of the Savior in this prayer. In speaking to his disciples, the Savior said: ". . . in my name shall ye give it [the Holy Ghost], for thus do mine apostles." (Moroni 2:2.) This is the only time the word *apostles* is used in the Book of Mormon in such a way that it might refer to the twelve Nephite disciples. (Ludlow)

1. THE words of Christ, which he spake unto his disciples, the twelve whom he had chosen, as he laid his hands upon them—
2. And he called them by name, saying: Ye shall call on the Father in my name, in mighty prayer; and after ye have done this ye shall have power that to him upon whom ye shall lay your hands, ye shall give the Holy Ghost; and in my name shall ye give it, for thus do mine apostles.
3. Now Christ spake these words unto them at the time of his first appearing; and the multitude heard it not, but the disciples heard it; and on as many as they laid their hands, fell the Holy Ghost.

CHAPTER 3

1. THE manner which the disciples, who were called the elders of the church, ordained priests and teachers—
2. After they had prayed unto the Father in the name of Christ, they laid their hands upon them, and said:
3. In the name of Jesus Christ I ordain you to be a priest, (or, if he be a teacher) I ordain you to be a teacher, to preach repentance and remission of sins through Jesus Christ, by the endurance of faith on his name to the end. Amen.
4. And after this manner did they ordain priests and teachers, according to the gifts and callings of God unto men; and they ordained them by the power of the Holy Ghost, which was in them.

CHAPTER 4

1. THE manner of their elders and priests administering the flesh and blood of Christ unto the church; and they administered it according to the commandments of Christ; wherefore we know the manner to be true; and the elder or priest did minister it—
2. And they did kneel down with the church, and pray to the Father in the name of Christ, saying:
3. O God, the Eternal Father, we ask thee in the name of thy Son, Jesus Christ, to bless and sanctify this bread to the souls of all those who partake of it; that they may eat in remembrance of the body of thy Son, and witness unto thee, O God, the Eternal Father, that they are willing to take upon them the name of thy Son, and always remember him, and keep his commandments which he hath given them, that they may always have his Spirit to be with them. Amen.

CHAPTER 5

1. THE manner of administering the wine—Behold, they took the cup, and said:
2. O God, the Eternal Father, we

Moroni 4:1–3

Elder Delbert L. Stapley has indicated the importance of keeping the covenants we make with the Lord when we partake of the sacramental emblems:

"Now my brothers and sisters—there are only three prayers that the Lord has revealed to the Church, and two of them have to do with the ordinance of the sacrament, the blessing of the bread and the blessing of the water. These prayers are found in the fourth and fifth chapters of Moroni in the Book of Mormon and also in the 20th Section of the Doctrine and Covenants. . . . First, we partake of the sacrament in remembrance of the broken body and spilled blood of Christ. Then we witness unto the Father, and I think we should take note of that, first, that we will take upon us the name of his Son. . . .

"If we take upon us the name of Christ, even as we pledge to do—when we partake of the emblems of his body and blood, we agree to keep all the commandments until the end of our days.

"Second, we witness or pledge that we will always remember him. As President McKay said, 'Always remember him in the home, in business, in society,'"and I would assume wherever else we might be.

"Third, we pledge to keep the commandments which he has given unto us, and last, we have a promise that if we do these things, and it is assumed that we do so worthily, that we shall always have his spirit to be with us. . . .

"In partaking of the sacramental emblems, we should always call to mind Christ's suffering and sacrifice, the death upon the cross, with faithful obedience to his appointed mission. . . .

"We know that no one but a God could suffer or go through what Christ experienced to redeem men from the effects of the fall. His sacrifice was an infinite sacrifice and that sacrifice was required of a God to satisfy broken law. . . .

"Another important purpose of the sacrament is to renew and keep in force the covenants and obligations which we have entered into with our God. . . ." (Ludlow)

ask thee, in the name of thy Son, Jesus Christ, to bless and sanctify this wine to the souls of all those who drink of it, that they may do it in remembrance of the blood of thy Son, which was shed for them; that they may witness unto thee, O God, the Eternal Father, that they do always remember him, that they may have his Spirit to be with them. Amen.

CHAPTER 6

1. AND now I speak concerning baptism. Behold, elders, priests, and teachers were baptized; and they were not baptized save they brought forth fruit meet that they were worthy of it.
2. Neither did they receive any unto baptism save they came forth with a broken heart and a contrite spirit, and witnessed unto the church that they truly repented of all their sins.
3. And none were received unto baptism save they took upon them the name of Christ, having a determination to serve him to the end.
4. And after they had been received unto baptism, and were wrought upon and cleansed by the power of the Holy Ghost, they were numbered among the people of the church of Christ; and their names were taken, that they might be remembered and nourished by the good word of God, to keep them in the right way, to keep them continually watchful unto prayer, relying alone upon the merits of Christ, who was the author and the finisher of their faith.
5. And the church did meet together oft, to fast and to pray, and to speak one with another concerning the welfare of their souls.
6. And they did meet together oft to partake of bread and wine, in remembrance of the Lord Jesus.
7. And they were strict to observe that there should be no iniquity among them; and whoso was found to commit iniquity, and three witnesses of the church did condemn them before the elders, and if they repented not, and confessed not, their names were blotted out, and they were not numbered among the people of Christ.
8. But as oft as they repented and sought forgiveness, with real intent, they were forgiven.
9. And their meetings were conducted by the church after the manner of the workings of the Spirit, and by the power of the Holy Ghost; for as the power of the Holy Ghost led them whether to preach, or to exhort, or to pray, or to supplicate, or to sing, even so it was done.

CHAPTER 7

1. AND now I, Moroni, write a few of the words of my father Mormon, which he spake concerning faith, hope, and charity; for after this manner did he speak unto the people, as he taught them in the synagogue which they had built for the place of worship.
2. And now I, Mormon, speak unto you, my beloved brethren; and it is by the grace of God the Father, and our Lord Jesus Christ, and his holy will, because of the gift of his calling unto me, that I am permitted to speak unto you at this time.
3. Wherefore, I would speak unto you that are of the church, that are the peaceable followers of Christ, and that have obtained a sufficient hope by which ye can enter into the rest of the Lord, from this time henceforth until ye shall rest with him in heaven.
4. And now my brethren, I judge these things of you because of your peaceable walk with the children of men.
5. For I remember the word of God which saith by their works ye shall know them; for if their works be good, then they are good also.
6. For behold, God hath said a man being evil cannot do that which is good; for if he offereth a gift, or prayeth unto God, except he shall do it with real intent it profiteth him nothing.
7. For behold, it is not counted unto him for righteousness.
8. For behold, if a man being evil giveth a gift, he doeth it grudgingly; wherefore it is counted unto him the same as if he had retained the gift; wherefore he is counted evil before God.
9. And likewise also is it counted evil unto a man, if he shall pray and not with real intent of heart; yea, and it profiteth him nothing, for God receiveth none such.
10. Wherefore, a man being evil cannot do that which is good; neither will he give a good gift.
11. For behold, a bitter fountain cannot bring forth good water; neither can a good fountain bring forth bitter water; wherefore, a man being a servant of the devil cannot follow Christ; and if he follow Christ he cannot be a servant of the devil.
12. Wherefore, all things which are good cometh of God; and that which is evil cometh of the devil; for the devil is an enemy unto God, and fighteth against him continually, and inviteth and enticeth

Moroni 7–9

Consider the eclipsing circumstances in which Moroni is writing at this time. His father's epistle to him about conditions in the land establishes the framework: the people "have lost their love, one towards another; and they thirst after blood and revenge continually" (Moro. 9:5). "And they have become strong in their perversion; and they are alike brutal, sparing none, neither old nor young; and they delight in everything save that which is good; and the suffering of our women and our children upon all the face of this land doth exceed everything; yea, tongue cannot tell, neither can it be written" (Moro. 9:19). Not knowing from one moment to the next whether he is to be murdered through the fomenting hatred and all-consuming anger of the people surrounding him, Moroni writes (through the words of his father) of things dear to the "peaceable followers of Christ" (Moro. 7:3), of love, and of discerning that which is good "in the light of Christ." Not knowing from whence his next meal might come, he writes of the nourishment that comes to the people from receiving "the word of Christ" (Moro. 7:31). The contrasts are poignant and compelling: anger and love, darkness and light, evil and goodness, degrading hopelessness and edifying hope. (P/A)

to sin, and to do that which is evil continually.
13. But behold, that which is of God inviteth and enticeth to do
good continually; wherefore, every thing which inviteth and
enticeth to do good, and to love God, and to serve him, is inspired
of God.
14. Wherefore, take heed, my beloved brethren, that ye do not
judge that which is evil to be of God, or that which is good and of
God to be of the devil.
15. For behold, my brethren, it is given unto you to judge, that ye
may know good from evil; and the way to judge is as plain, that ye
may know with a perfect knowledge, as the daylight is from the
dark night.
16. For behold, the Spirit of Christ is given to every man, that he
may know good from evil; wherefore, I show unto you the way to
judge; for every thing which inviteth to do good, and to persuade
to believe in Christ, is sent forth by the power and gift of Christ;
wherefore ye may know with a perfect knowledge it is of God.
17. But whatsoever thing persuadeth men to do evil, and believe
not in Christ, and deny him, and serve not God, then ye may know
with a perfect knowledge it is of the devil; for after this manner
doth the devil work, for he persuadeth no man to do good, no, not
one; neither do his angels; neither do they who subject themselves
unto him.
18. And now, my brethren, seeing that ye know the light by which
ye may judge, which light is the light of Christ, see that ye do not
judge wrongfully; for with that same judgment which ye judge ye
shall also be judged.
19. Wherefore, I beseech of you, brethren, that ye should search
diligently in the light of Christ that ye may know good from evil;
and if ye will lay hold upon every good thing, and condemn it not,
ye certainly will be a child of Christ.
20. And now, my brethren, how is it possible that ye can lay hold
upon every good thing?
21. And now I come to that faith, of which I said I would speak;
and I will tell you the way whereby ye may lay hold on every good
thing.
22. For behold, God knowing all things, being from everlasting to
everlasting, behold, he sent angels to minister unto the children of
men, to make manifest concerning the coming of Christ; and in
Christ there should come every good thing.
23. And God also declared unto prophets, by his own mouth, that
Christ should come.
24. And behold, there were divers ways that he did manifest things
unto the children of men, which were good; and all things which
are good cometh of Christ; otherwise men were fallen, and there
could no good thing come unto them.

Moroni 7:15–17

The "Spirit of Christ," which Mormon tells us "is given to every man, that he may know good from evil" (Moroni 7:16), is not the same as the Holy Ghost. The difference between the Spirit of Christ and the Holy Ghost has been explained by Joseph F. Smith as follows:

"The question is often asked, is there any difference between the Spirit of the Lord and the Holy Ghost? . . . The Holy Ghost is a personage in the Godhead, and is not that which lighteth every man that comes into the world. It is the Spirit of God which proceeds through Christ to the world, that enlightens every man that comes into the world, and that strives with the children of men, and will continue to strive with them, until it brings them to a knowledge of the truth and the possession of the greater light and testimony of the Holy Ghost."

If a person is obedient to the commandments of God, however, it is possible for the Holy Ghost also to be with him as a "comforter within." This idea has been expressed as follows by President Wilford Woodruff:

"The Holy Ghost . . . is different from the common Spirit of God, which we are told lighteth every man that cometh into the world. The Holy Ghost is only given to men through their obedience to the Gospel of Christ; and every man who receives that Spirit has a comforter within—a leader to dictate and guide him. This Spirit reveals, day by day, to every man who has faith, those things which are for his benefit. As Job said, 'There is a spirit in man and the inspiration of the Almighty giveth it understanding.' It is this inspiration of God to His children in every age of the world that is one of the necessary gifts to sustain man and enable him to walk by faith, and to go forth and obey all the dictations and commandments and revelations which God gives to His children to guide and direct them in life." (Ludlow)

25. Wherefore, by the ministering of angels, and by every word which proceeded forth out of the mouth of God, men began to exercise faith in Christ; and thus by faith, they did lay hold upon every good thing; and thus it was until the coming of Christ.
26. And after that he came men also were saved by faith in his name; and by faith, they become the sons of God. And as surely as Christ liveth he spake these words unto our fathers, saying: Whatsoever thing ye shall ask the Father in my name, which is good, in faith believing that ye shall receive, behold, it shall be done unto you.
27. Wherefore, my beloved brethren, have miracles ceased because Christ hath ascended into heaven, and hath sat down on the right hand of God, to claim of the Father his rights of mercy which he hath upon the children of men?
28. For he hath answered the ends of the law, and he claimeth all those who have faith in him; and they who have faith in him will cleave unto every good thing; wherefore he advocateth the cause of the children of men; and he dwelleth eternally in the heavens.
29. And because he hath done this, my beloved brethren, have miracles ceased? Behold I say unto you, Nay; neither have angels ceased to minister unto the children of men.
30. For behold, they are subject unto him, to minister according to the word of his command, showing themselves unto them of strong faith and a firm mind in every form of godliness.
31. And the office of their ministry is to call men unto repentance, and to fulfill and to do the work of the covenants of the Father, which he hath made unto the children of men, to prepare the way among the children of men, by declaring the word of Christ unto the chosen vessels of the Lord, that they may bear testimony of him.
32. And by so doing, the Lord God prepareth the way that the residue of men may have faith in Christ, that the Holy Ghost may have place in their hearts, according to the power thereof; and after this manner bringeth to pass the Father, the covenants which he hath made unto the children of men.
33. And Christ hath said: If ye will have faith in me ye shall have power to do whatsoever thing is expedient in me.
34. And he hath said: Repent all ye ends of the earth, and come unto me, and be baptized in my name, and have faith in me, that ye may be saved.
35. And now, my beloved brethren, if this be the case that these things are true which I have spoken unto you, and God will show unto you, with power and great glory at the last day, that they are true, and if they are true has the day of miracles ceased?
36. Or have angels ceased to appear unto the children of men? Or has he withheld the power of the Holy Ghost from them? Or will he, so

long as time shall last, or the earth shall stand, or there shall be one man upon the face thereof to be saved?
37. Behold I say unto you, Nay; for it is by faith that miracles are wrought; and it is by faith that angels appear and minister unto men; wherefore, if these things have ceased wo be unto the children of men, for it is because of unbelief, and all is vain.
38. For no man can be saved, according to the words of Christ, save they shall have faith in his name; wherefore, if these things have ceased, then has faith ceased also; and awful is the state of man, for they are as though there had been no redemption made.
39. But behold, my beloved brethren, I judge better things of you, for I judge that ye have faith in Christ because of your meekness; for if ye have not faith in him then ye are not fit to be numbered among the people of his church.
40. And again, my beloved brethren, I would speak unto you concerning hope. How is it that ye can attain unto faith, save ye shall have hope?
41. And what is it that ye shall hope for? Behold I say unto you that ye shall have hope through the atonement of Christ and the power of his resurrection, to be raised unto life eternal, and this because of your faith in him according to the promise.
42. Wherefore, if a man have faith he must needs have hope; for without faith there cannot be any hope.
43. And again, behold I say unto you that he cannot have faith and hope, save he shall be meek, and lowly of heart.
44. If so, his faith and hope is vain, for none is acceptable before God, save the meek and lowly in heart; and if a man be meek and lowly in heart, and confesses by the power of the Holy Ghost that Jesus is the Christ, he must needs have charity; for if he have not charity he is nothing; wherefore he must needs have charity.
45. And charity suffereth long, and is kind, and envieth not, and is not puffed up, seeketh not her own, is not easily provoked, thinketh no evil, and rejoiceth not in iniquity but rejoiceth in the truth, beareth all things, believeth all things, hopeth all things, endureth all things.
46. Wherefore, my beloved brethren, if ye have not charity, ye are nothing, for charity never faileth. Wherefore, cleave unto charity, which is the greatest of all, for all things must fail—
47. But charity is the pure love of Christ, and it endureth forever; and whoso is found possessed of it at the last day, it shall be well with him.
48. Wherefore, my beloved brethren, pray unto the Father with all the energy of heart, that ye may be filled with this love, which he hath bestowed upon all who are true followers of his Son, Jesus Christ; that ye may become the sons of God; that when he shall appear we

Moroni 7:41

People who have hope in Christ are not exempt from physical suffering and the onset of disease or death, either for themselves or for loved ones. But their hope provides immeasurable comfort based on the same conviction expressed by Job: ". . . I know that my redeemer liveth, and that he shall stand at the latter day upon the earth: And though after my skin worms destroy this body, yet in my flesh shall I see God: Whom I shall see for myself, and mine eyes shall behold, and not another; though my reins be consumed within me" (Job 19:25–27). (O/C)

Moroni 7:44–48

Some students of the Book of Mormon have asked the question how the teachings of Mormon on faith, hope, and charity (found in Moroni 7) could be so similar to the teachings of Paul on this same subject (1 Corinthians 13:4–8). Although the Book of Mormon does not provide the exact answer to this question, at least two possibilities exist: (1) The statement on faith, hope, and charity may not have been original with either Mormon or Paul; it may have been contained in an ancient record available to both of them, or it may have been included in the teachings of the Savior that are not recorded either in the New Testament or in the Book of Mormon. (2) All revelation is received through the power of the Holy Ghost, and the Holy Ghost may have revealed this idea in essentially the same way to both Mormon and Paul. (Ludlow)

shall be like him, for we shall see him as he is; that we may have this hope; that we may be purified even as he is pure. Amen.

CHAPTER 8

1. AN epistle of my father Mormon, written to me, Moroni; and it was written unto me soon after my calling to the ministry. And on this wise did he write unto me, saying:
2. My beloved son, Moroni, I rejoice exceedingly that your Lord Jesus Christ hath been mindful of you, and hath called you to his ministry, and to his holy work.
3. I am mindful of you always in my prayers, continually praying unto God the Father in the name of his Holy Child, Jesus, that he, through his infinite goodness and grace, will keep you through the endurance of faith on his name to the end.
4. And now, my son, I speak unto you concerning that which grieveth me exceedingly; for it grieveth me that there should disputations rise among you.
5. For, if I have learned the truth, there have been disputations among you concerning the baptism of your little children.
6. And now, my son, I desire that ye should labor diligently, that this gross error should be removed from among you; for, for this intent I have written this epistle.
7. For immediately after I had learned these things of you I inquired of the Lord concerning the matter. And the word of the Lord came to me by the power of the Holy Ghost, saying:
8. Listen to the words of Christ, your Redeemer, your Lord and your God. Behold, I came into the world not to call the righteous but sinners to repentance; the whole need no physician, but they that are sick; wherefore, little children are whole, for they are not capable of committing sin; wherefore the curse of Adam is taken from them in me, that it hath no power over them; and the law of circumcision is done away in me.
9. And after this manner did the Holy Ghost manifest the word of God unto me; wherefore, my beloved son, I know that it is solemn mockery before God, that ye should baptize little children.
10. Behold I say unto you that this thing shall ye teach—repentance and baptism unto those who are accountable and capable of committing sin; yea, teach parents that they must repent and be baptized, and humble themselves as their little children, and they shall all be saved with their little children.
11. And their little children need no repentance, neither baptism. Behold, baptism is unto repentance to the fulfilling the commandments unto the remission of sins.
12. But little children are alive in Christ, even from the foundation of the world; if not so, God is a partial

Moroni 8:5

Joseph Smith said, "The doctrine of baptizing children, or sprinkling them, or they must welter in hell, is a doctrine not true, not supported in Holy Writ, and is not consistent with the character of God. All children are redeemed by the blood of Jesus Christ, and the moment that children leave this world, they are taken to the bosom of Abraham" (*HC*, 4:5).

Moroni 8:5–24

Baptism is perhaps the most basic ordinance in Christianity, and the question of the baptism of infants is certainly one of the most fundamental questions related to this ordinance. The largest Christian church in the world today, as well as many other churches, teaches that because of the original sin of Adam and Eve no person can enter heaven without baptism. Thus these churches deny that Jesus Christ atoned for original sin, and they say that little infants and others who die without baptism cannot be saved in heaven.

The Book of Mormon definitely teaches that Jesus Christ did atone for the original transgression of Adam and Eve, and little children do not need to be baptized until they arrive at the age of accountability and are responsible for their own acts. . . .

Mormon also indicates why he is so definite and strong in his teachings on this subject: "I speak it boldly; God hath commanded me." (Ludlow)

Moroni 8:11–12

Joseph Smith said, "'Do you believe in the baptism of infants?' asks the Presbyterian. No. 'Why?' Because it is nowhere written in the Bible. Circumcision is not baptism, neither was baptism instituted in the place of circumcision. Baptism is for remission of sins. Children have no sins. Jesus blessed them and said, 'Do what you have seen me do.' Children are all made alive in Christ, and those of riper years through faith and repentance."

God, and also a changeable God, and a respecter to persons; for how many little children have died without baptism!
13. Wherefore, if little children could not be saved without baptism, these must have gone to an endless hell.
14. Behold I say unto you, that he that supposeth that little children need baptism is in the gall of bitterness and in the bonds of iniquity, for he hath neither faith, hope, nor charity; wherefore, should he be cut off while in the thought, he must go down to hell.
15. For awful is the wickedness to suppose that God saveth one child because of baptism, and the other must perish because he hath no baptism.
16. Wo be unto them that shall pervert the ways of the Lord after this manner, for they shall perish except they repent. Behold, I speak with boldness, having authority from God; and I fear not what man can do; for perfect love casteth out all fear.
17. And I am filled with charity, which is everlasting love; wherefore, all children are alike unto me; wherefore, I love little children with a perfect love; and they are all alike and partakers of salvation.
18. For I know that God is not a partial God, neither a changeable being; but he is unchangeable from all eternity to all eternity.
19. Little children cannot repent; wherefore, it is awful wickedness to deny the pure mercies of God unto them, for they are all alive in him because of his mercy.
20. And he that saith that little children need baptism denieth the mercies of Christ, and setteth at naught the atonement of him and the power of his redemption.
21. Wo unto such, for they are in danger of death, hell, and an endless torment. I speak it boldly; God hath commanded me. Listen unto them and give heed, or they stand against you at the judgment-seat of Christ.
22. For behold that all little children are alive in Christ, and also all they that are without the law. For the power of redemption cometh on all them that have no law; wherefore, he that is not condemned, or he that is under no condemnation, cannot repent; and unto such baptism availeth nothing—
23. But it is mockery before God, denying the mercies of Christ, and the power of his Holy Spirit, and putting trust in dead works.
24. Behold, my son, this thing ought not to be; for repentance is unto them that are under condemnation and under the curse of a broken law.
25. And the first fruits of repentance is baptism; and baptism cometh by faith unto the fulfilling the commandments; and the fulfilling the commandments bringeth remission of sins;
26. And the remission of sins bringeth meekness, and lowliness of heart; and because of meekness and lowliness of heart cometh the visitation

Moroni 8:22

We know by revelation that those who are mentally handicapped will be regarded by the Lord the same as little children who die before the age of accountability: incapable of distinguishing between right and wrong, they will be redeemed without baptism and will inherit the celestial kingdom—where their full mental faculties will be restored.

Moroni 8:25–26

All that man can do is to perform the physical act of baptism which, when performed by one having authority, binds the recipient in a covenant with God, a witness that he will keep God's commandments. But this baptism, in and of itself is valueless if the commandments are not kept and the baptism of the Holy Ghost does not follow. (Ludlow)

of the Holy Ghost, which Comforter filleth with hope and perfect love, which love endureth by diligence unto prayer, until the end shall come, when all the saints shall dwell with God.
27. Behold, my son, I will write unto you again if I go not out soon against the Lamanites. Behold, the pride of this nation, or the people of the Nephites, hath proven their destruction except they should repent.
28. Pray for them, my son, that repentance may come unto them. But behold, I fear lest the Spirit hath ceased striving with them; and in this part of the land they are also seeking to put down all power and authority which cometh from God; and they are denying the Holy Ghost.
29. And after rejecting so great a knowledge, my son, they must perish soon, unto the fulfilling of the prophecies which were spoken by the prophets, as well as the words of our Savior himself.
30. Farewell, my son, until I shall write unto you, or shall meet you again. Amen.

CHAPTER 9

1. My beloved son, I write unto you again that ye may know that I am yet alive; but I write somewhat of that which is grievous.
2. For behold, I have had a sore battle with the Lamanites, in which we did not conquer; and Archeantus has fallen by the sword, and also Luram and Emron; yea, and we have lost a great number of our choice men.
3. And now behold, my son, I fear lest the Lamanites shall destroy this people; for they do not repent, and Satan stirreth them up continually to anger one with another.
4. Behold, I am laboring with them continually; and when I speak the word of God with sharpness they tremble and anger against me; and when I use no sharpness they harden their hearts against it; wherefore, I fear lest the Spirit of the Lord hath ceased striving with them.
5. For so exceedingly do they anger that it seemeth me that they have no fear of death; and they have lost their love, one towards another; and they thirst after blood and revenge continually.
6. And now, my beloved son, notwithstanding their hardness, let us labor diligently; for if we should cease to labor, we should be brought under condemnation; for we have a labor to perform whilst in this tabernacle of clay, that we may conquer the enemy of all righteousness, and rest our souls in the kingdom of God.
7. And now I write somewhat concerning the sufferings of this people.

Moroni 8:27–28

Joseph Smith said, "I prophesy, in the name of the Lord God of Israel, anguish and wrath and tribulation and the withdrawing of the Spirit of God from the earth await this generation, until they are visited with utter desolation."

POINT OF INTEREST

The Micmac nation is indigenous to the northeastern Canadian provinces. This image represents their traditional mobile housing, an example of how the Lamanites eventually broke into familial tribes that were usually nomadic in nature.

For according to the knowledge which I have received from Amoron, behold, the Lamanites have many prisoners, which they took from the tower of Sherrizah; and there were men, women, and children.

8. And the husbands and fathers of those women and children they have slain; and they feed the women upon the flesh of their husbands, and the children upon the flesh of their fathers; and no water, save a little, do they give unto them.

9. And notwithstanding this great abomination of the Lamanites, it doth not exceed that of our people in Moriantum. For behold, many of the daughters of the Lamanites have they taken prisoners; and after depriving them of that which was most dear and precious above all things, which is chastity and virtue—

10. And after they had done this thing, they did murder them in a most cruel manner, torturing their bodies even unto death; and after they have done this, they devour their flesh like unto wild beasts, because of the hardness of their hearts; and they do it for a token of bravery.

11. O my beloved son, how can a people like this, that are without civilization—

12. (And only a few years have passed away, and they were a civil and a delightsome people)

13. But O my son, how can a people like this, whose delight is in so much abomination—

14. How can we expect that God will stay his hand in judgment against us?

15. Behold, my heart cries: Wo unto this people. Come out in judgment, O God, and hide their sins, and wickedness, and abominations from before thy face!

16. And again, my son, there are many widows and their daughters who remain in Sherrizah; and that part of the provisions which the Lamanites did not carry away, behold, the army of Zenephi has carried away, and left them to wander whithersoever they can for food; and many old women do faint by the way and die.

17. And the army which is with me is weak; and the armies of the Lamanites are betwixt Sherrizah and me; and as many as have fled to the army of Aaron have fallen victims to their awful brutality.

18. O the depravity of my people! They are without order and without mercy. Behold, I am but a man, and I have but the strength of a man, and I cannot any longer enforce my commands.

19. And they have become strong in their perversion; and they are alike brutal, sparing none, neither old nor young; and they delight in everything save that which is good; and the suffering of our women and our children upon all the face of this land doth exceed everything; yea, tongue cannot tell, neither can it be written.

20. And now, my son, I dwell no longer upon this horrible scene. Behold, thou knowest the wickedness of this people; thou knowest that they are without principle, and past feeling; and their wickedness doth exceed that of the Lamanites.

21. Behold, my son, I cannot recommend them unto God lest he should smite me.

22. But behold, my son, I recommend thee unto God, and I trust in Christ that thou wilt be saved; and I pray unto God that he will spare thy life, to witness the return of his

people unto him, or their utter destruction; for I know that they
must perish except they repent and return unto him.
23. And if they perish it will be like unto the Jaredites, because of
the wilfulness of their hearts, seeking for blood and revenge.
24. And if it so be that they perish, we know that many of our
brethren have deserted over unto the Lamanites, and many more
will also desert over unto them; wherefore, write somewhat a few
things, if thou art spared and I shall perish and not see thee; but I
trust that I may see thee soon; for I have sacred records that I
would deliver up unto thee.
25. My son, be faithful in Christ; and may not the things which I
have written grieve thee, to weigh thee down unto death; but may
Christ lift thee up, and may his sufferings and death, and the showing his body unto our fathers, and his mercy and long-suffering, and
the hope of his glory and of eternal life, rest in your mind forever.
26. And may the grace of God the Father, whose throne is high in
the heavens, and our Lord Jesus Christ, who sitteth on the right
hand of his power, until all things shall become subject unto him,
be, and abide with you forever. Amen.

CHAPTER 10

1. Now I, Moroni, write somewhat as seemeth me good; and I write
unto my brethren, the Lamanites; and I would that they should know
that more than four hundred and twenty years have passed away since
the sign was given of the coming of Christ.
2. And I seal up these records, after I have spoken a few words by
way of exhortation unto you.
3. Behold, I would exhort you that when ye shall read these things,
if it be wisdom in God that ye should read them, that ye would
remember how merciful the Lord hath been unto the children of
men, from the creation of Adam even down unto the time that ye
shall receive these things, and ponder it in your hearts.
4. And when ye shall receive these things, I would exhort you that
ye would ask God, the Eternal Father, in the name of Christ, if these
things are not true; and if ye shall ask with a sincere heart, with real
intent, having faith in Christ, he will manifest the truth of it unto
you, by the power of the Holy Ghost.
5. And by the power of the Holy Ghost ye may know the truth of
all things.
6. And whatsoever thing is good is

Moroni 10:3–5

Joseph Smith said, "Search the scriptures . . . and ask your Heavenly Father, in the name of His Son Jesus Christ, to manifest the truth unto you, and if you do it with an eye single to His glory nothing doubting, He will answer you by the power of His Holy Spirit. You will then know for yourselves and not for another. You will not then be dependent on man for the knowledge of God; nor will there be any room for speculation."

Moroni 10:4–5

God has made it very clear in his scriptures that he is a God of law. Among other statements he has said: "There is a law, irrevocably decreed in heaven before the foundations of this world, upon which all blessings are predicated—And when we obtain any blessing from God, it is by obedience to that law upon which it is predicated." (D&C 130:20–21.)

The blessing of a testimony of the truthfulness of the Book of Mormon is thus based on law. According to Moroni, the following steps fulfill the law by which one can gain a testimony of the Book of Mormon: (1) read the book and "ponder it in your hearts" (Moroni 10:3), and (2) "ask God, the Eternal Father, in the name of Christ, if these things are not true; and if ye shall ask with a sincere heart, with real intent, having faith in Christ, he will manifest the truth of it unto you, by the power of the Holy Ghost. And by the power of the Holy Ghost ye may know the truth of all things" (Moroni 10:4–5). (Ludlow)

just and true; wherefore, nothing that is good denieth the Christ,
but acknowledgeth that he is.
7. And ye may know that he is, by the power of the Holy Ghost;
wherefore I would exhort you that ye deny not the power of God; for
he worketh by power, according to the faith of the children of men,
the same today and tomorrow, and forever.
8. And again, I exhort you, my brethren, that ye deny not the gifts
of God, for they are many; and they come from the same God.
And there are different ways that these gifts are administered; but
it is the same God who worketh all in all; and they are given by
the manifestations of the Spirit of God unto men, to profit them.
9. For behold, to one is given by the Spirit of God, that he may
teach the word of wisdom;
10. And to another, that he may teach the word of knowledge by
the same Spirit;
11. And to another, exceedingly great faith; and to another, the
gifts of healing by the same Spirit;
12. And again, to another, that he may work mighty miracles;
13. And again, to another, that he may prophesy concerning all
things;
14. And again, to another, the beholding of angels and ministering
spirits;
15. And again, to another, all kinds of tongues;
16. And again, to another, the interpretation of languages and of
divers kinds of tongues.
17. And all these gifts come by the Spirit of Christ; and they come
unto every man severally, according as he will.
18. And I would exhort you, my beloved brethren, that ye remember that every good gift cometh of Christ.
19. And I would exhort you, my beloved brethren, that ye remember that he is the same yesterday, today, and forever, and that all
these gifts of which I have spoken, which are spiritual, never will
be done away, even as long as the world shall stand, only according to the unbelief of the children of men.
20. Wherefore, there must be faith; and if there must be faith there
must also be hope; and if there must be hope there must also be
charity.
21. And except ye have charity ye can in nowise be saved in the
kingdom of God; neither can ye be saved in the kingdom of God if
ye have not faith; neither can ye if ye have no hope.
22. And if ye have no hope ye must needs be in despair; and despair
cometh because of iniquity.
23. And Christ truly said unto our fathers: If ye have faith ye can
do all things which are expedient unto me.
24. And now I speak unto all the ends of the earth—that if the day
cometh that the power and gifts of God shall be done away among
you, it shall be because of unbelief.
25. And wo be unto the children of men if this be the case; for
there shall be none that doeth good among you, no not one. For if
there

Moroni 10:8–18

In the concluding chapter of his record, Moroni exhorted the future readers to accept the gifts of God. Elder Bruce R. McConkie has indicated the importance of the gifts of the Spirit:

"By the grace of God—following devotion, faith, and obedience on man's part—certain special spiritual blessings called *gifts of the Spirit* are bestowed upon men. Their receipt is always predicated upon obedience to law, but because they are freely available to all the obedient, they are called gifts. They are signs and miracles reserved for the faithful and for none else. . . .

"Their purpose is to enlighten, encourage, and edify the faithful so that they will inherit peace in this life and be guided toward eternal life in the world to come. Their presence is proof of the divinity of the Lord's work; where they are not found, there the Church and kingdom of God is not. . . . In the fullest sense, they are infinite in number and endless in their manifestations." (Ludlow)

Moroni 10:9–17

Some people have been bothered by the similarity between the two scriptures listed above inasmuch as the reference in the New Testament was written on the eastern continent in the first century A.D. and the reference in the Book of Mormon was written several hundred years later and without any known access to the New Testament account. Several plausible explanations of this similarity could be given; however, the following possibility seems to be most reasonable: The Savior could have given a great sermon on the manifestations or gifts of the Spirit on both the eastern and western continents. Thus both Paul and Moroni would have been acquainted with the teachings of this sermon, just as they were both acquainted with the teachings of the Sermon on the Mount. Neither the New Testament nor the Book of Mormon claims to contain all the teachings of Jesus Christ. In fact, the Book of Mormon specifically states the "more part" of the teachings of the resurrected Christ were not included on the plates of Mormon (3 Nephi 26:6–11), and John indicates that not all of the teachings of the Savior were contained in the New Testament (John 21:25).

Two other possible explanations of this similarity are as follows: (1) These teachings on the gifts of the Spirit could have been recorded by a prophet in Old Testament times, and thus could have been available to Moroni through the brass plates of Laban and to Paul through one of the manuscripts that has not been included in our Old Testament; (2) the truths of the gospel are revealed to man through the power of the Holy Ghost, and the teachings concerning the gifts of the Spirit could have been revealed to both Moroni and Paul in essentially the same order. (Ludlow)

be one among you that doeth good, he shall work by the power and gifts of God.
26. And wo unto them who shall do these things away and die, for they die in their sins, and they cannot be saved in the kingdom of God; and I speak it according to the words of Christ; and I lie not.
27. And I exhort you to remember these things; for the time speedily cometh that ye shall know that I lie not, for ye shall see me at the bar of God; and the Lord God will say unto you: Did I not declare my words unto you, which were written by this man, like as one crying from the dead, yea, even as one speaking out of the dust?
28. I declare these things unto the fulfilling of the prophecies. And behold, they shall proceed forth out of the mouth of the everlasting God; and his word shall hiss forth from generation to generation.
29. And God shall show unto you, that that which I have written is true.
30. And again I would exhort you that ye would come unto Christ, and lay hold upon every good gift, and touch not the evil gift, nor the unclean thing.
31. And awake, and arise from the dust, O Jerusalem; yea, and put on thy beautiful garments, O daughter of Zion; and strengthen thy stakes and enlarge thy borders forever, that thou mayest no more be confounded, that the covenants of the Eternal Father which he hath made unto thee, O house of Israel, may be fulfilled.
32. Yea, come unto Christ, and be perfected in him, and deny yourselves of all ungodliness; and if ye shall deny yourselves of all ungodliness, and love God with all your might, mind and strength, then is his grace sufficient for you, that by his grace ye may be perfect in Christ; and if by the grace of God ye are perfect in Christ, ye can in nowise deny the power of God.
33. And again, if ye by the grace of God are perfect in Christ, and deny not his power, then are ye sanctified in Christ by the grace of God, through the shedding of the blood of Christ, which is in the covenant of the Father unto the remission of your sins, that ye become holy, without spot.
34. And now I bid unto all, farewell. I soon go to rest in the paradise of God, until my spirit and body shall again reunite, and I am brought forth triumphant through the air, to meet you before the pleasing bar of the great Jehovah, the Eternal Judge of both quick and dead. Amen.

THE END

Moroni 10:33

All the children of God who have graced this earth will look back on their mortal experience and take inventory as to the motives of their hearts and the object of their desires. Happy is the man or woman who receives the gospel of Jesus Christ, repents of his or her sins, pursues the path of perfection in Christ, and through the grace and power of God becomes ". . . holy, without spot." (O/C)

In the final pages of the Book of Mormon, we are presented with a banquet of spiritual nourishment: how to search for happiness in the light of Christ; how to foster faith, hope, and charity in our lives; how to become like little children (who in their innocence are saved through the Atonement); how to know the truth of all things through the Spirit; and how to come unto Christ and be perfected in Him.

This wisdom is the essence of the gospel of Jesus Christ in a succinct and illuminating summary of truth. What more can be said? The goodness of God is showered down upon His children through this glorious book. We can become perfected in and through our Savior, Jesus Christ, by virtue of the grace of God. How we ought to thank our Heavenly Father and our Savior for the words of eternal life that so many have suffered and sacrificed to bring to us, enabling us to live by "every word that proceedeth out of the mouth of God" (Matt. 4:4; Moro. 7:25; D&C 84:44; 98:11). The long sequence of prophets of the Book of Mormon: Mormon (the magnificent abridger), the beloved Prophet Joseph Smith, who translated the records by the gift and power of God; and all the rest who have made this record possible—these are the valiant servants of God who have assisted in the restoration of the gospel in its fulness through the grace and mercy of the Lord. This work can be an instrument of salvation as we live the gospel of Jesus Christ and seek to share its message with others. (P/A)

Notes

Notes

Notes

NOTES

NOTES